The ITALIANS
of Lackawanna, NY
Steelworkers, Merchants and Gardeners

by John Andreozzi

CABIN SIX BOOKS

SHOREVIEW, MINNESOTA

ISBN: 0-9728945-2-7

Cover and book design by Linda Andreozzi.

**To order more copies of this book
or for more discussion on** *The Italians of Lackawanna***, contact:**

CABIN SIX BOOKS
P. O. BOX 130664
ROSEVILLE, MN 55113-0006

1-888-652-2529

About the cover.

Front cover: The top of the front cover is a 1917 view of the north end of the Lackawanna Steel Company. Photo source, Larry Platz. Middle right, the town of Falvaterra, Lazio, taken by the author in 1993. Lower right is the 1928 passport photo of Giuseppina Ferrelli with sons Aldo on the left and Cesidio on the right. Photo source: the Collection of Josephine Ferrelli. Lower left shows steel being tapped from an open hearth furnace. Photo source: the Bethlehem Steel Company's "Lackawanna Plant" booklet 309-A, 1952.

Back cover: The upper right photo of the author was taken at his home, in 2009, by his wife Linda. Middle upper photo of friends and neighbors Giovanna Viglietta-Fanone, left, and Giulia Violanti-Fiore, both immigrants from Lazio. Photo source: Rose Fiore-Pacholczak. Left upper, Michele Grasso, circa 1926, working his Ingham Avenue garden. From the Collection of Tony Grasso. Left middle, South Buffalo Railway switch engine, late 1930s, from the Collection of Frank Chiodo. Lower left is the badge of the Lake Erie Cooperative Mutual Aid Society, provided by the Lake Erie Italian Club.

In memory of my parents,
Adeline B. Covelli and Phillip N. Andreozzi—
an immigrant and a child of an immigrant.
Their two generations endured the most difficult years of
the Italian experience in America.

CONTENTS

PREFACE

Sociologist C. Wright Mills wrote that it is crucial for an individual to recognize the connection between huge events, such as World War II, and his or her personal biography. One of my most compelling reasons for writing this book is that the story of the immigration of 5.5 million Italians to the United States, as well as the story of Lackawanna and its Italian community, are integral parts of my family and personal history. The informal lessons I learned as a youth on the outskirts of Lackawanna led me to look to sociology to answer the mixture of fascinating, confusing, and challenging things I encountered there.

My parents and grandparents spent much of their lives in Lackawanna's First Ward. My father, Phillip Andreozzi, was born in Lackawanna in 1917. His father and step-father were both immigrants from Falvaterra, Lazio, and his mother, Jenny Limongiello, was born in "the Hooks," the Italian tenement district on Buffalo's waterfront. Her parents were immigrants from San Fele, Basilicata. My mother, Adeline Covelli, was nine years old when she and her family immigrated from Marano Principato, Calabria to Buffalo in 1927, and a few months later to Lackawanna. Since my mother was fairly young when she arrived in Lackawanna, and grandma Andreozzi was born in this country, I figure I am, roughly speaking, a third-generation Italian American, that is, the grandchild of immigrants. I grew up on just off Abbott Road, where the boundaries of Lackawanna, West Seneca, Orchard Park, and Hamburg intersect—our family home was in West Seneca township.

The stories told by my parents and other relatives, about life in Italy and Lackawanna's Bethlehem Park neighborhood really interested me by the time I was in my late teens. They carried on traditions, such as frequent visits with relatives, planting large vegetable gardens, and making wine, pasta (then known as "macaroni"), and Easter bread. At family gatherings, my parents, aunts, and uncles all spoke in Italian, out of respect for the three grandparents who were much more fluent in Italian than English. At home, my father and mother spoke in Italian to keep private matters from us five kids; regrettably, I learned only a few expressions in the language. As I child, I assumed that everyone's parents or grandparents were born in the Old Country, be it Italy, Poland, or wherever. At age ten I was surprised to hear the grandfather of my Irish American friend speaking perfect English.

Virtually all the families in our neighborhood had roots in southern or eastern Europe, especially Poland and Italy, or in Ireland or Germany. Most of the men worked at Bethlehem Steel, other local factories, or at the grain elevators in Buffalo. It was a working-class area, populated mainly by Roman Catholic and Eastern Orthodox families. My father and uncles spoke often about the steel plant, where most of them spent their entire working lives— 42 years, in my father's case. I felt fortunate that we lived three miles east of the plant, well out of range of the ore dust and soot that permeated the air surrounding the plant. Many neighbors of my parents' generation had grown up in the ethnic neighborhoods of Lackawanna or Buffalo.

As a boy, I saw my parents smile and glow with pride when Italian American entertainers and athletes appeared on television. I recall singers Julius LaRosa, Frank Sinatra, Frankie Laine, Perry Como, Dean Martin, and Tony Bennett—my mother always boasted that he was Calabrese. They admired comedians Jimmy Durante, Kay Ballard, and Imogene Coca, and athletes, including boxers Carmen Basilio and Rocky Marciano and football stars Joe Bellino and Franco Harris. But my parents were often infuriated by the constant media reports on Italian gangsters in western New York, such as Stefano Magaddino, and the *Untouchables* television series. As a young man, I often wondered if the only occupations that won fame for Italians were those in entertainment and organized crime. Many first- and second-generation Polish Americans, Italian Americans, and other white ethnics retained a strong cultural pride and reacted defensively to the many jokes and stereotypes directed at them. Their dignity and social honor were important, and I later came to understand how they were wounded by the bigotry, poverty, and lack of opportunities they endured prior to World War II.

We often drove to Lackawanna's First Ward to visit relatives in Bethlehem Park. When we pulled up to the Andreozzi house on Jackson Avenue my parents exchanged greetings in English and Italian with many old friends. On the trip there and back, my father pointed out specific mills in the steel plant, towers and service centers of the South Buffalo Railway, the site of the former Old Village, and the house off Ingham Avenue where he was born. I gradually came to learn that blacks, Latinos, and Arabs were usually confined to housing in the northern part of Lackawanna's First Ward, where the ore dust and soot were heaviest. The railroad tracks separating that ward from the eastern part of the city represented the racial dividing line. I knew as a child that people of color were not welcome if they crossed this line, and was told that whites weren't welcome if they went over the Ridge Road bridge into the First Ward.

My informal education continued in my late teens and early 20s when I met a few people who actively voiced their dislike of Italians. I also discovered that not everyone in western New York came from a working-class background, and that some people looked down on those of us with blue-collar roots in the Lackawanna area. During my work with a federal poverty program in the 1960s I learned a great deal not only about poverty but also about urban politics and race relations. During this time it seemed to me that working class white ethnics were branded by the media as having a monopoly on racist sentiments. After wrestling with this idea I concluded that it was another unfair stereotype of Italians and other blue collar workers.

In college I studied sociology to get a better understanding of race, religion, nationality, poverty, and politics. After graduating from the University of Buffalo (SUNYAB), I worked as a teacher in the inner-city schools of Hartford, Connecticut, then for a year at Lackawanna High School, which at the time was torn by racial strife. I again returned to the study of sociology, doing research for my master's thesis on Milwaukee's Italian community. Interviewing many Italians in Milwaukee and, later, in Cumberland, Wisconsin, helped my understanding of Italian American history and assimilation. Researching the similarities and differences in the assimilation of European ethnic groups as compared with African Americans and other people of color was another eye-opener for me.

Later my attention shifted to my own roots and how the various issues covered in my college work—ethnicity, social class, assimilation, bigotry—had been present in western New York during my childhood and adolescence. In the late 1960s, I started recording family stories and gathering information from my relatives for a family history. In 1976, I began interviewing other Italian Americans in Lackawanna about their roots in Italy and what brought their families to the Steel City. Based on these interviews and other data I wrote an article about the city's Italian colony and prepared a slide show and photo display. In 1994, I decided to write this book, which has taken 16 years to complete. The process has reaffirmed what my work as a therapist in a mental health clinic has taught me—that it is crucial for every individual to know his or her personal story and how that story fits into the world of six billion other human beings. Exploring one's individual history, in all its complexity and diverse aspects, is a key contributor to good mental health. Discovering your family roots and

ethnic history is an vital element of this journey which can truly be enlightening.

As I did my research for this book, it became apparent that much of Italian American history, as well as the histories of many other ethnic groups in Lackawanna and the United States, has been ignored in textbooks and popular folklore, or seriously distorted and stereotyped. A quest for the truth about the Italian American experience and how it fit into the overall history of immigrants, minorities, and working-class people in America became the driving force behind my research. Like my parents, I had become upset by the stereotype equating Italians with organized crime. I wanted a more accurate portrayal of Italian American history in general and, specifically, to set the record straight about the Italian community in Lackawanna.

My research was also inspired by my visits to Italy—a solo trip in 1980 and accompanied by my sister Jeanette in 1993. Although we were unable to locate any relatives in Basilicata, those in Lazio and Calabria provided a warm and wonderful reception. Our *parenti* (relatives) in Italy told many stories about our family history, providing new information and insights. Simply being in Italy gave me a fuller knowledge and understanding of Italian culture, and, most important, renewed connections with relatives that were interrupted by immigration almost a century ago.

I have not lived in the Lackawanna area since 1972. School and jobs first drew me away from western New York, then the collapse of the area's industrial base, beginning in the 1970s and finalized 10 years later, cancelled the possibility of returning and finding a job in my field. Buffalo and Lackawanna had become rustbelt cities. I have lived in the Midwest for more than 35 years, enjoying regular trips to visit my relatives in western New York. Doing the research on Lackawanna has helped me to better understand the painful transitions made by hundreds of Italian American families, including my own. This book represents my symbolic and permanent homecoming.

Acknowledgements

Many people assisted in the preparation of this book. Among the most enjoyable aspects of the research were my interviews with 346 individuals, which ranged from brief telephone discussions to many hours of in-depth meetings. Most of those interviewed were first- and second-generation Italian Americans with roots in Lackawanna, but some were members of other ethnic groups—Polish, Irish, Croatian, Serbian, French, Yemeni, African American, and Puerto Rican—as well as friends of my family and relatives of the Andreozzi, Covelli, Ceccarelli, Lemoncello, and Vittorini branches of the extended family.

Valuable comments were offered by readers of specific sections of the book. Those in academia include Michael

Fritsch, SUNY at Buffalo; Jim McDonnell, State University College at Buffalo; Michael LaSorte, SUNY at Brockport; Donna Gabaccia, director, Immigration History Research Center, University of Minnesota; Joel Wurl, former curator, Immigration History Research Center, University of Minnesota; Douglas Hartmann, University of Minnesota; Peter Rachleff, Macalester College; Peter Belmonte; Nancy Sauro; and Gigi Lambrecht. Coworkers Don Nevins, Geoff Garwick, Dee Hiatt, and Kara Witt, as well as friends Pat Ronken and Pat Means also assisted as readers. Special thanks to my good friend Harry Palmer, who read through a number of the chapters.

The collections of many libraries and archives in western New York and throughout the country supplied invaluable documents and photographs for this book. The staff of the Lackawanna Library has been of tremendous assistance. The library's current director, Jennifer Hoffman, and the past director, Sal Bordonaro, afforded me ready access to the library's many collections. Especially useful was the project, spearheaded by Sal Bordonaro, to microfilm the library's newspaper collection. This extraordinary series of Lackawanna newspapers, dating back to 1913, is a gold mine of material for research. The Steel Plant Museum, located within the library and run by volunteers, has been another great source of documents and artifacts regarding the local steel industry. In particular, the museum's guiding spirit, Mike Malyak, has provided a wealth of insights, data, and leads to other resources.

The Lackawanna City Clerk's office provided access to past Common Council proceedings and other documents, as did the office of the West Seneca Town Clerk. The offices of the Lackawanna Public Schools and the West Seneca Public Schools were also helpful in this regard, as was the Blasdell Library. Members of the Lackawanna Historical Association and the West Seneca Historical Society made available a number of useful records. The staff of the Grosvenor Room at the downtown branch of the Buffalo & Erie County Public Library provided much assistance, as did the workers in the research library at the Buffalo & Erie County Historical Society. Bill Seiner, the society's former director, provided helpful leads to other resources. Joe Streamer guided me through the excellent collection at the Hamburg Historical Society.

The records at the Presbytery in Buffalo, the Committee on Archives and History of the Western New York conference of the United Methodist Church, the Roman Catholic parishes of St. Agnes in Buffalo, and Our Mother of Good Counsel in Blasdell, along with the Catholic Center of Buffalo, and Canisuis College, were all very helpful. I am greatly indebted to the members of St. Anthony's parish in Lackawanna for their assistance, and especially to office manager Luz Rivera and former pastors Rev. Peter Drilling and Rev. David Glassmire.

Among the many other institutions providing information and photographs were the Center For Urban Policy Studies and the University Archives of the State University of New York at Buffalo, the Special Collections of the Butler Library at the State University College at Buffalo, the Buffalo News Library, the Canisius College Library, the Baker Museum in Fredonia, New York, the Hagley Museum and Library in Wilmington, Delaware, and Swiss Labor Institute.

The officers and members of the Lake Erie Italian Club, Lake Erie Women's Auxiliary, Galanti Athletic Association, New Beginnings Italian Club, and Roland Wildcats gave much of their time to talk with me and share written records and photographs. Researchers Phillip C. Andreozzi, Bernie Montanari, Mike Malyak, Joan Christiano, Ward Bray, Jeff Mondo, and Ned Schimminger spent many hours procuring documents at western New York archives. Photographer Paul Pasquarello captured a number of the images used in this book. A number of people helped edit the book, and I am especially indebted to Mindy Keskinan, Jennifer Monan, and Pam Christian for their insightful work. Patty Murtaugh was a great help with layout and graphic production.

My family played a large part in the writing of this book. My parents, the late Phillip and Adeline Andreozzi, proofread every chapter and shared stories and insights about growing up in Lackawanna's First Ward. My father knew every track and spur of the South Buffalo Railway and which mills they served, while my mother could eloquently describe the daily life in a small Calabrese town in the 1920s and translate Italian documents into English. My godparents, Gene Covelli and the late Josie Andreozzi, shared their gifts for storytelling and relaying family history. I have received much support from my siblings—Roz, Jeanette, Phil Jr., and Mike—who helped out in a variety of ways throughout the many phases of my project. Finally, thanks and appreciation go to my wife Linda, who tolerated my many hours dedicated to writing this book, provided invaluable computer know-how, designed and laid out the entire book, and published this title through her Cabin Six Books, gently encouraging me throughout the entire process.

A Note on Terms and Abbreviations Used

Little Italy: the term used to designate Italian neighborhoods in many cities (though the author rarely heard it used in Lackawanna); employed in this book as an easy way to indicate neighborhoods with a concentration of Italians.

Old Country—a term widely used in Lackawanna to refer to the country from which an immigrant came.

[sic]—used in a quote to indicate that the grammatical mistake is in the original document

?—information is uncertain

Photo Captions

circa—means about, as in "circa 1917;" the exact date on which the photo was taken is unknown.

[Unk]—used in a photo caption to indicate the identity of a person is unknown.

_?_—used in a photo caption to indicate that a person's first name is unknown.

Generational Status

1st generation—the immigrant

1.5 generation—immigrant less than 10 years of age at time of emigration

2nd generation—American-born child of the immigrant

3rd generation—grandchild of the immigrant

4th generation—great-grandchild of the immigrant

5th generation—great-great-grandchild of the immigrant

Italian Words and Phrases

- Translations of Italian words and phrases are usually provided in parentheses following the first use of the word; as in *paesano* (a person from the same hometown)

- Words in italics are those that are not commonly used in the English language of the United States; for example *paesano*.

- For uniformity, the Italian names for the 20 regions of Italy will be used, for example: Sicilia, not Sicily; Sardegna, not Sardinia; Toscana, not Tuscany.

- Italians in America often speak Italian and do not pronounce the ending vowel of words. This is indicated by use an apostrophe (') at the end of the word, as in *conserv'* for *conserva*.

- In Italian, the ending of nouns and adjectives depends on the gender of the person or the word, as in: *contadino* (a male farmer). For example:
  - (a) *festa*: a religious festival
    feste: several religious festivals
  - (b) Marchegiano—a man from the region of Marche
    Marchegiani—several men, or several men and women, from Marche
    Marchegiana—a woman from Marche
    Marchegiane—several women from Marche

- *Americani* or *Mericani*: terms used by Italian immigrants in the United States to refer to any person who was not Italian, and by Italians in Italy to designate immigrants who returned to Italy after spending time in the United States.

- People from certain regions in Italy are sometimes referred to using the name of a large city in that region; as in:
  - (a) Napolitani: residents of the city of Napoli (Naples) in the region of Campania
  - (b) Romani: residents of the city of Roma (Rome) in the region of Lazio. In Lackawanna this term was anglicized with the letter i (the Italian plural) replaced by the letter s (the English plural). What resulted was a word pronounced as in Italian but with an s at the end: ROW - mons.

- *Il Duce*: the leader; specifically this referred to Benito Mussolini.

INTRODUCTION

A CITY OF IMMIGRANTS AND MINORITIES IS BORN

During the July 4th holiday in 1899 Walter Scranton, president of the Lackawanna Iron and Steel Company of Scranton, Pennsylvania, was wined and dined by some of the most powerful entrepreneurs in Buffalo, New York. Led by attorney John Milburn (an immigrant from England), the Western New York electric power and railroad magnates convinced Scranton that they had the solution to his problems of a dwindling coal supply and a growing steelworkers union in Pennsylvania.

By moving his steel plant to the Buffalo area Walter Scranton was told he would realize many benefits. The close proximity to Niagara Falls meant inexpensive electric power. There would be easy access to railroad and shipping lines from the newly discovered Mesabi iron ore mines in Minnesota and a plant site out of the jurisdiction of Buffalo—where property taxes would be nonexistent. Lastly, Scranton was promised a large and comparatively docile force of immigrant laborers. By the following year, 1900, Scranton's friends in Buffalo had purchased 1,000 acres of land, to which the City of Buffalo and New York State added, free of charge, another 325 acres.[1]

The site for the new steel plant was a stretch of Lake Erie shoreland in the township of West Seneca, just south of Buffalo. Inland the terrain was low and swampy for about three-quarters of a mile, where it then rose to form gently rolling hills. At this point there ran a vast strip of railroad tracks that headed northward into Buffalo. Known as the Limestone Hill district, the area was sparsely inhabited and, other than the institutions and cemetery of the Catholic Diocese, consisted mostly of farmland. In 1900, with the construction of the huge plant of the Lackawanna Steel Company, there was a rapid expansion of population, and in 1909 Limestone Hill became the City of Lackawanna. The quiet beaches along Lake Erie and the swamp adjacent to it were soon transformed into steel mills, railroads, and a town bustling with land speculators, immigrants, and boarding houses.

Some 200 workers, mostly European immigrants, began clearing the land by the end of 1900. Soon work focused on constructing mills, offices, and a canal for lake freighters, and the need for an expanded work force drew immigrants from throughout the northeastern United States. The steel plant became the largest of its kind in the world, and the population of Limestone Hill, which was also known as the steel plant district, rapidly grew, especially in the area between the plant and the maze of railroad tracks. This section became the First Ward of Lackawanna, and up until at least 1925, over half of the city's population resided there.[2]

By 1920, the city's population had grown to 17,918, as immigrants and migrants from other parts of the United States flocked to the jobs offered in the mills of the Lackawanna Steel Company. An astounding 83% of the inhabitants were immigrants and their children, that is, "foreign stock," one of the highest such percentages of any American city. Lackawanna

< 1904. A South Buffalo Railway (SBR) engine heads south across Smokes Creek. Hamburg Turnpike is to the left and Lake Erie is off to the right. This whole area, called Stoney Point, was covered with trees until 1900 when the Lackawanna Steel Company hired workman, including many Italians, to clear the land. The tree trunks were then used to make ties on which the SBR tracks were laid. This part of the plant grounds was not developed until later years. Photo source: Paul Pietrak

1

FIGURE I.1

Population of Lackawanna and its Italian Community

			Italians					
Year	City Total:	Total[a]	Immigrants		2nd Generation		3rd Generation	
1892[b]	?	10	10	100%	—	—	—	—
1900[b]	1,833	23	11	48%	12	52%	—	—
1905[b]	11,034	288	238	83%	50	17%	—	—
1910	14,549	551	375	68%	176	32%	—	—
1915	15,737	766	437	57%	329	43%	—	—
1920	17,918	1,215	586	48%	629	52%	—	—
1925	20,196	1,336	626	47%	701	53%	—	—
1930	23,948	1,902	752	40%	1,072	58%	78	4%
1940	24,058	NA[c]	775					
1950	27,658	NA	658					
1960	29,564	2085						
1970	28,657	1921						
1980	22,701	3291[d]						
1990	20,585	3752[d]	173					
2000	19,064	3,231[d]						
2007	17,707[e]	NA						

[a] Included are young people living in the Our Lady of Victory institutions.

[b] Limestone Hill or steel plant district of West Seneca.

[c] NA = data not available.

[d] These figures include all persons of total or partial Italian ancestry.

[e] Estimate by Bureau of the Census, 2007.

Sources: New York State Census, 1905, 1915, 1925; United States Census, 1900–2000

was indeed an immigrant town, and in 1930 fifty-seven percent of the population was composed of immigrants from southern and eastern Europe and their children. In that year Polish Americans alone accounted for over one-third of the city's residents. During the early 20th century, Italians were the 3rd or 4th largest ethnic group in the city (see Figure I-2). The city's population climb was abated by the strict immigration laws of the early 1920s and the Great Depression of the 1930s. During the past century, individuals representing dozens of ethnic groups have lived in the Steel City, including immigrants from Africa, the Middle East, the Caribbean, Canada, Mexico, Central and South America, Asia, and the Pacific Islands, as well as Native Americans and African Americans (see Figure I-2). Indeed, the city's name, in the Algonquian language of Native Americans, means "where the two rivers meet," a reference to the Scranton Pennsylvania area. As early as 1917 the *Lackawanna Journal* claimed that children with roots in 77 countries were attending First Ward schools and eventually people from 92 ethnic groups settled in the city.[3]

Lackawanna's population again expanded in the early 1940s as war production boomed at the steel plant, which had been purchased by Bethlehem Steel in 1922. The post-war economic prosperity lead to the expansion of the production capacity at the plant, and population growth followed on the increased job opportunities. Many blacks, Latinos, and Arabs migrated to the city, adding to its ethnic diversity. The number of residents in the Steel City, as the city was nicknamed, peaked in 1960 at 29,564, and five years later the Bethlehem plant had its largest workforce, employing 21,500 people from throughout western New York. However, production at the aging Lackawanna plant was soon reduced and transferred to newer Bethlehem facilities, and in 1983 most of the mills were permanently shut down. By 2000 over a third of Lackawannans had departed and the trend continues. The city, with help from the State of New York, has brought in a number of small industries, but like its larger neighbor to the north, Buffalo, it is still reeling from the loss of its industrial base.[4]

Immigrants and the American Reception

The Italian experience in Lackawanna is one thread of the city's diverse ethnic mosaic. It is important to recognize that a fundamental theme of American history has been the movement of people—immigrants arriving from other countries and the internal migration of population groups. Prior to the 1880s, the vast majority of voluntary immigrants arriving in America had roots in northwestern Europe. Coming mainly from Great Britain, these immigrants shaped the WASP—white, Anglo-Saxon, protestant—society. They were the majority of the colonists who fought in the Revolutionary War and freed themselves of British colonialism. As the founding fathers, they put in place the English language, a democratic form of government, Judeo-Christian religious beliefs, the capitalist economic system, and other beliefs and customs that compose American culture. Up until the 1960s, the WASP descendent of the founding fathers was considered the essence of the ideal American.

The arrival of large numbers of immigrants from Ireland and Germany in the mid–1800s added Catholics to America's ethnic mix, and was not welcomed by nativists (i.e. people who thought they were the only true Americans and viewed immigrants as a threat). Even more upsetting to many WASPs were the emigrants from southeast Europe during the period 1880 to 1924, most of whom were Roman Catholic, Eastern Orthodox, or Jewish. Of the approximately 5,500,000 Italian who immigrated to the United States, 4,000,000 arrived during this period. Among these "new immigrants," Italians were the largest group, and eastern European Jews next in size. WASP capitalists had succeeded in keeping the gates of mass migration open for over four decades to supply cheap labor for their factories and railroads, but they could no longer stave off the reaction of nativists who felt America was being degraded by the arrival of millions of Italians, Jews, and Slavs. The nativists finally stemmed the tide of immigration with a series of laws that began with the literacy test in 1917 and culminated in the national origins and quota act of 1924. Americans always expected immigrants to quickly assimilate and disown their native cultures, and this Anglo-conformity movement was energetically renewed during the 1920s. The assimilation experience of immigrants and minorities has involved eight processes that will be examined in this study.[5]

The Italian Experience in Lackawanna

Four years after the start of construction the Lackawanna Steel Company, the world's largest steel plant, was producing steel on the shores of Lake Erie. A plant superintendent "stated that his company is entirely dependent upon the immigrant labor supply to fill certain positions, and if the immigrants had not been available in 1901 the company could not have commenced operations." Among the thousands of immigrants who travelled there in search of jobs were ex-farmers from Italy, who initially used their pick and shovel skills to clear the land and construct the mills, and then to work in the steel plant's Yard Department. Other Italians who had worked in foundries and steel plants elsewhere in the United States found their way to Lackawanna. They utilized a chain of relatives and *paesani* (people from the same town) to guide them from country to country, and, within the United States, from one town to another, and to provide housing and information about jobs.[6]

The Italian experience in the Lackawanna was unique in several ways. Working in a steel plant in the early years of the twentieth century was unusual for Italian immigrants, only 3.5 % of all Italian workers in America did so. The regional makeup of the Italian colony has been different from many other settlements. Natives of Sicily and Campania compose almost half of all Italian immigrants who came to America, and in the Buffalo area the majority of Italians have their roots in Sicily or Basilicata. In Lackawanna, however, over half of the Italian immigrants came from Lazio and Abruzzo (see Figure 1.19, page 51). Many Italian migrants settled in large cities, such as Buffalo and New York City, and these Little Italies have been the subject of a great body of studies. Research on Italian colonies in small industrial cities is less common, and it is hoped that this study will be a useful addition to the literature on this aspect of Italian American life.[7]

Lackawanna's Italian population has been relatively small, yet influential, as it represented the third largest ethnic group in the city by 1930. A total of 3,070 Italian immigrants lived in the city at one time or another and the largest number at any one time was 752 in 1930. Because of the small size of the Italian community, the movement of immigrants into and out of the city has been more easy to track and quantify. The statistics demonstrate the tremendous mobility of Italian immigrants as they travelled to a variety of locations within the United States, some of them after first stopping in other countries.[8]

As Italians in Lackawanna endured the pressures to assimilate, they encountered prejudice and discrimination, and immigration laws that labelled southeast Europeans as "inferior." The group struggled through the stages of assimilation during the 1920s and 1930s and emerged from World War II as part of mainstream society and no longer a minority group. In the second half of the twentieth century a significant number of Italians eventually attained a prosperity that had never been available in Italy. Italians throughout the United States have risen to some of the highest positions in our society, and those in Lackawanna became skilled blue collar workers who in the last 40 years have been able to move to the suburban areas in the eastern section of the city. They were now secure in their acceptance by society and their identity as Americans. Yet many also maintained their ethnic traditions and organizations, some of which continue to this day.

The experience of Italian immigrants and their descendents in Lackawanna's crucible of steel and ethnicity represents an important chapter in the city's history, as well as one episode in the emigration of over five million people from Italy to the United States. In his 1932 study of Lackawanna men on relief during the Depression, Donald Adams Clarke, offered a poignant, and stereotyped, description of the city and it's ethnic mix.

> Just south of the city of Buffalo, and merging into the city's urban fringe, is sprawled one of those ugly blotches that civilization in an industrial era has sprewed up. It is a drab and dirt-depressed satellite of its larger neighbor to the north. But beneath the caked surface of grime that greets the casual passer is a community rich in human interest, vivid in local colour. Black and white, Poles, Croats, Magyars, Arabs, Irishmen, Somalilanders, and the representatives of some three dozen more peoples live in close proximity. Roman Catholics, Greek Catholics, Russian Orthodox and Moslems pass in the streets. Men with fierce eye and long curling mustaches, the descendants of the horsemen who swept the plains of Europe with Attila, the Hun, fifteen hundred years ago, men with kinky black hair and brown skins whose racial memory retains the steamy jungle, little men with lighter skins and blacker eyes that first opened on white robed figures and burning sands—all have come to the shadow of the cross and under the pall of the mill. Here is Lackawanna, the Cosmopolis of Steel.

This book tells the story of one of the city's ethnic groups and offers a general background on Lackawanna's fascinating history and ethnic tapestry.[9]

Following this introduction, the Italian hometowns and customs of peasants who emigrated to the U.S. will be explored in Chapter I. Their journey to the United States and the chain migration process they utilized are described in Chapter 2. The overall history of Lackawanna's Italians is the subject of Chapter 3, which gives a framework of the major events and themes from 1900 to 2009. This sets the ground for Chapter 4, the most theoretical of the book, which presents eight processes or stages of assimilation of the major ethnic groups—racial, religious, and nationality—into American society, and then applies this format to the Lackawanna's Italian experience. It discusses aspects of America's biracial (white/ non white) social hierarchy as seen in Lackawanna, as well as the stereotype of organized crime that still haunts Italians in the United States. The following seven chapters provide detailed examinations of Italian community life: Chapter 5 describes temporary housing in shanties and the establishment of four Italian neighborhoods—lower Ingham Avenue, the Old Village, Roland Avenue, and Bethlehem Park. In their ethnic enclaves the former agriculturalists from the Mediterranean spoke their native language, made wine and planted gardens in their yards and on vacant lots throughout the city and in nearby Woodlawn.

The religious life of Steel City Italians, described in Chaper 6, centered on St. Anthony's church and the celebration of patron saints, and later on the acceptance of American Catholic values. Chapter 7 looks at work in the steel mills and on the railroads, and how Italians gradually moved from unskilled to skilled jobs; going from Yard Department jobs to those in the mills, and from railroad trackmen to engine crewmen. Chapter 8 describes how supposedly "docile" immigrant groups united to make a strong showing in the 1919 steel strike, and how 20 years later first and second generation Italians joined ranks with other steelworkers in a victorious strike that unionized the Lackawanna plant and led to full unionization of America's steel industry. The unions had an important role in assimilating Italians into Lackawanna's working class, and opening up opportunities for advancement and better wages. Chapter 9 focuses on the many Italian families who operated groceries and other small businesses, some floundering and some flourishing, and how this assisted in the development of a small class of professionals.

The formation of 76 Italian American organizations is described in Chapter 10, and the gradual shift in their goals and membership is analyzed. Chapter 11 offers an overview of the city's rough and tumble ethnic politics and traces the advance of Italians in this arena. The original power brokers, the Irish, and then the numerous Poles, were often able to split the Italian vote, but Italians eventually became an important political force in a city where the votes of every family were courted. The Afterword summarizes the transitions made by Lackawanna's Italians, identifies some themes, and comments on preserving ethnic traditions.

Figure I.2

ETHNIC GROUPS IN LACKAWANNA: 1900–2009

NORTH AMERICA:
American Indian:
1. Seneca
2. Mohawk

Canada:
3. English & other
4. French
5. Mexico

CENTRAL AMERICA:
6. El Salvador
7. Guatemala
8. Nicaragua
9. Costa Rica
10. Other Latino (Hispanic)

WEST INDIES:
11. Cuba
12. Puerto Rico
13. Dominican Republic
14. Jamaica
15. St. Thomas
16. Other West Indian:
    (Fortune Island)

SOUTH AMERICA:
17. Argentina
18. Brazil
19. Chile
20. Columbia
21. Paraguay
22. Peru

EUROPE:
23. Albania
24. Austria
25. Belgium
26. Bulgaria
Former Czechoslovakia:
27. Czech
28. Slovakia

29. Denmark
30. England
31. Finland
32. France
33. Germany
34. Greece
35. Gypsies
36. Holland
37. Hungary
38. Ireland
39. Italy
40. Jewish (European)
41. Latvia
42. Lithuania
43. Northern Ireland
44. Norway
45. Poland
46. Portugal
47. Prussia
48. Rumania
49. Scotland
Former Soviet Union:
50. Russia
51. Armenia
52. Ruthenian: (Carpatho-Rusyn)
53. Ukraine
54. Spain
55. Sweden
56. Switzerland
57. Wales
Former Yugoslavia:
58. Croatia
59. Dalmatia
60. Macedonia
61. Montenegro
62. Serbia
63. Slovenia

AFRICA:
64. African American
65. Morocco
66. Senegal
67. Egypt
68. Sudan
69. Somalia
70. Ethiopia
71. East Africa

NEAR EAST:
72. Saudi Arabia
73. Palestine
74. Syria
75. Jordan
76. Lebanon
77. Turkey
78. Yemen
79. Persia (Iran)
80. Afghanistan

ASIA:
81. China
82. India
83. Japan
84. Korea
85. Vietnam

PACIFIC:
86. Australia
87. New Guinea
88. Philippines
89. Guam
90. Hawaii
91. Samoa
92. East Indies

Sources: U. S. Census, 1900-2000; N.Y. Census, 1905-1925; records of St. Anthony's Church; interviews, newspaper articles, and naturalization papers.

FIGURE I.3

Largest Ethnic Groups in Lackawanna: 1910–1930

Year	Group	Total	Foreign Born	US-Born, Foreign or Mixed Parentage
1910	Austrian (mostly Polish)[a]	5,534	4,105	1,429
	Russian (many Polish)[a]	1,556	1,276	280
	Irish	1,104	340	764
	German (many Polish)[a]	1,060	420	640
	Italian	551[b]	375	176
	Hungarian	246	193	53
	Negro	197	NA	NA
	Canadian (other than French)	195	151	44
1920	Polish	NA	3,170	NA
	Hungarian	NA	1,282	NA
	Italian	1,215	586	629
	Negro	NA	269	
	Russian	NA	262	NA
	Austrian	NA	256	NA
	Ireland	NA	233	NA
	Spain	NA	166	NA
1930	Polish	8,129	2,575	5,554
	Negro	2,051	NA	NA
	Italian	1,824	752	1,072
	Yugoslavia[c]	1,672	1,007	665
	Irish	1,026	196	830
	Hungary	760	354	406
	Germany	698	174	52
	Canadian (other than French)	509	288	221

[a] Between 1795 and 1918 Poland was divided up between Austria, Germany, and Russia.

[b] This count differs from that of the total of 538 in the 1910 U.S. Census Summary.

[c] The nation of Yugoslavia, formed after World War I, included six distinct ethnic groups: Serbian, Croatian, Slovenian, Dalmatian, Montenegran, Macedonian, as well as 3 religions: Roman Catholic, Eastern Orthodox, and Muslim.

Sources: U. S. Census, 1910, 1920, 1930

Aerial view looking south at the steel plant in the late 1920s. In the foreground is the ship canal; to the left are blast furnaces (the silo-shaped towers). The long building with 10 smokestacks is No. 2 Open Hearth. Hamburg Turnpike cuts diagonally across the top of the photo. Between it and Ingham Avenue (upper right) is vacant land created when the swamp was filled in, In the upper center is the soccer field along Dona Street, the long row houses of the Old Village, and the Bethlehem Park housing development. Photo source: Jerry Soltis

CHAPTER 1

ITALIAN ROOTS

A series of major events were significant in the lives of Italians during the first five decades of the twentieth century. These, in conjunction with conditions in the United States and other receiving countries, influenced the stream of emigrants leaving Italy.

Approximately 5.5 million Italians immigrated to the United States between 1820 and 2000. Understanding the experience of these immigrants and their descendants requires looking at the institutions, beliefs, and practices in their native towns in Italy. This chapter offers sketches of Italian towns and the culture and lifestyles typical of the immigrants who came to Lackawanna. Knowing this background information helps put into perspective the migration of Italians to an industrial American city and their adjustments to a new culture. As the immigrants established roots in the Steel City, they attempted to create some semblance of the town life they had known in Italy. Information from interviews with immigrants to Lackawanna helps provide a description of town life in six regions of Italy in the early twentieth century (see Figures 1.2, 1.4).

Town Life in Six Regions

Lackawanna's Italians have roots in 17 of the 20 regions of Italy. They came from 191 towns, more than 40% of which are in the regions of Lazio and Abruzzo. In each of the two regions, the majority of towns are concentrated in a single province (see Figure 1-14). The province of Frosinone in Lazio claims 26 of the towns, while Aquila province in Abruzzo is the location for another 24 towns. Similar clusters are seen in Calabria and Marche. The categorization of towns by province and region is based on current regional and provincial boundaries, a number of which have changed during the past nine decades.[1]

< View of Morolo in 1958. It is located in Frosinone province, south of Rome. Photo source: Iole Schiavi-Murray

Social Class, Home Life, and Livelihoods

Many southern Italian towns, such as Falvaterra and Bagnoli Irpino, consist of tightly clustered buildings situated on the slopes of or atop mountains. Some lie along the steep banks of rivers or ravines, as in the case of Pettorano sul Gizio. (Interestingly, *Pettorano* means "chest of the frog," and *sul Gizio* means "on the Gizio" River.) Others are similar to Marano Principato, which is located on gradually sloping land at the base of a mountain. Clusters of individual homes and row houses are scattered across open land, and in the center is the main street, where the church, stores, and municipal buildings are found. A study of Calabria found that this latter type of town is typical at altitudes less than 1,900 feet above sea level, while those in higher elevations are usually of the tightly clustered variety.[2]

The cities and towns of Italy have long and often colorful histories. Bagnoli Irpino has roots going back to 800 AD, and Falvaterra was founded in Roman times. The city of Fano, located on the Adriatic Sea, was a resort town for the Romans of antiquity. It is surrounded by a moat and a wall with three gates, each named for a Roman leader. Italian towns were affected by migration long before the mass population movements of the late nineteenth and early twentieth centuries. In the 1500s, Italian artisans, mostly weavers, potters, and glassmakers, could be found throughout Europe. Emigrants from Pettorano sul Gizio say that the town was founded in approximately 1200 and that Scottish royalty settled there. A century later, in Giuliano di Roma, a colony of Jews lived in a district called Giudea, which is recalled today in street names such as Giudaea. The many DeSantis families in Giuliano, according to Lelio DeSantis, are the descendants of several families who migrated from France in the 1700s.[3]

Figure 1.1
A BOY LEARNS OF SOCIAL CLASS IN CAMPANIA

In Quadrelle, Campania, Andrea Nappi's skill as a gardener did not escape the notice of the wealthy Mayor Pagano, who sometimes summoned Nappi to tend his walled garden. Antonio "Tony" Grasso accompanied his Grandfather Nappi and later wrote that he learned something about social class when he beheld "what mysterious things were concealed behind those foreboding walls." While Andrea trimmed trees and vines, Antonio wandered through the garden. He recalls:

I gawked at the nude statues on both sides of the walk every so many feet. … I was awed and bewildered. Never in all my boyhood days had I seen anything like it before. I never imagined that in a poor village like ours an individual possessed all this treasure. In our village there wasn't a statue in a public square, or in the square facing the church. … I went back to the statue that caught my interest. It was a man at a tipsy angle, with a huge cup that seemed to be spilling its contents. In my adult life I came to find out that this was Bacchus, the god of wine and patron of drunkards. Further along there were statues of satyrs, each a human form with a tail and horns … I made a beeline to the splashing sound of the waters. This part was unknown to me, yet, drawing closer, I could see from a short distance through the lacey overhang of the trees a monstrous face. Made of stone and cemented into the high wall, it continuously spouted a stream of water into a large basin. … The cool shimmering pool was dotted with a few aquatic plants, and a large partly submerged tree trunk. As I looked down into the pool goldfish were languidly swimming by. I was overwhelmed, utterly enchanted.

Never had I seen or believed that this bit of heaven ever existed in our poor sun baked village.

Antonio knew of another dark and secret spot in Quadrelle that offered a lesson in the hierarchy of social class. With his grandmother and aunt, he often visited his mother's grave at the cemetery just outside of town. The sign over the gate reads: "Oh friend! Oh passerby! Pause for a moment and reflect. That what you are, we were. And what we are, you will be." Maria Nappi's tomb, which was on the fourth or fifth tier above the mausoleum floor, was inscribed with the words: "Michele Grasso gave up his beloved mate Nappi, Maria Carmina 23 years old. Died January 11, 1907. Grieving tearfully the loss. Peace." Nearby a flight of stairs led to a "dank, subterranean, cavernous room" that contained "a great pile of human skulls piled behind an iron spiked fence," Antonio recalled; these were the remains of countless villagers whose families could not afford the tombs in the upper room.

Sources: Tony Grasso, "Grandfather's Little Helper," unpublished, 1983, pp. 4-5; "Oh! Friend, Oh! Passerby," unpublished, undated, pp. 1-3.

Lazio, also known as Latium, the region in which Rome is situated, was the southernmost part of the Papal States prior to the unification of Italy between 1861 and 1870. Natives of Falvaterra report that it was just within the southern border of the Papal States. The towns in the southern part of Frosinone Province, such as Giuliano, Morolo, and Falvaterra, were the hometowns of many who immigrated to Lackawanna. Originally this area was called *Ciociaria*, and its inhabitants *Ciociari*. The name is based on the distinctive mule-skin sandal, the *cioce*, worn by natives of antiquity. It had an upturned toepiece and leather straps that were wrapped around the lower leg.[4]

A century ago, the towns in southern Italy, according to historian Franc Sturino, had a social class structure topped by large-scale landowners and professionals—such as doctors, lawyers, priests, teachers, and pharmacists—typically from those land-owning families. The *galantuomini*, or gentlemen, of this upper class were addressed using the title Don (sir), and the women using *Donna* (lady), but often they were referred to as *pezzi grossi* (big shots) by people lower in the pecking order. In the middle class, the upper level included government functionaries, clerks, and merchants. On the lower level were artisans and craftsmen, such as barbers, tailors, and shoemakers. At the bottom was the peasant class, the largest grouping, which had several subdivisions. The contadino (farmer) and his family worked land that he owned or rented from others as a sharecropper. Below this group were the landless farm laborers, the poorest of the poor: the braccianti (agricultural laborers), who were employed with some regularity throughout the year, and the giornalieri (day laborers), who worked sporadically. The only other group that one might have encountered in southern Italy would have been the Gypsies, who served as livestock traders. They were generally seen as outcasts to be mistrusted, if not despised, and were not a part of town life. For example, in Giuliano di Roma, Rosa Sperduti, who owned a sizable amount of land, allowed Gypsies to live on her land because she feared reprisal. When a neighboring

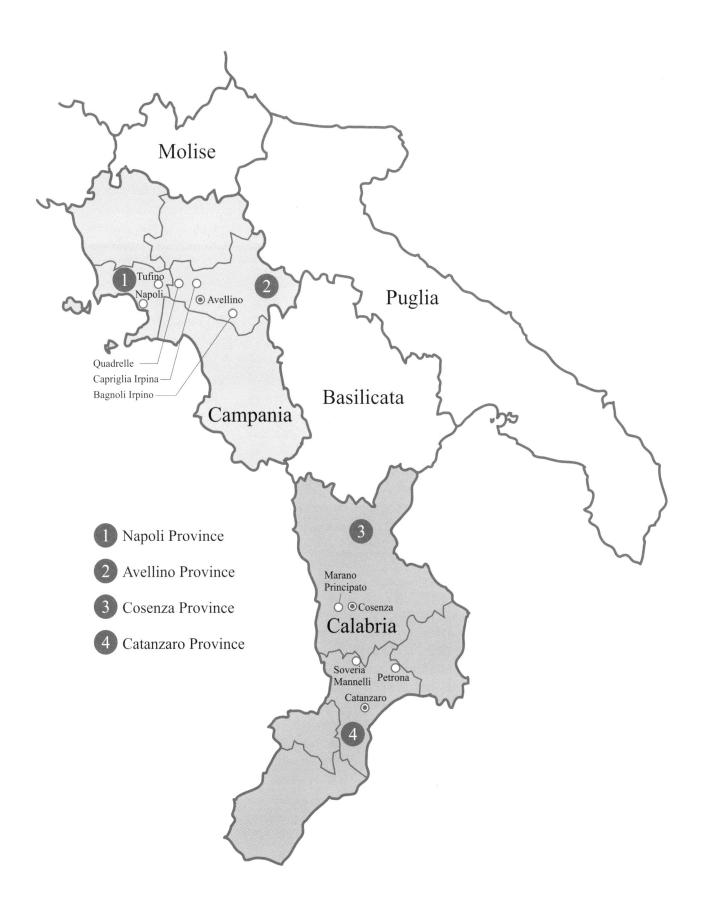

Molise

Campania

Puglia

Basilicata

Calabria

1 Napoli Province

2 Avellino Province

3 Cosenza Province

4 Catanzaro Province

Tufino
Napoli
Avellino
Quadrelle
Capriglia Irpina
Bagnoli Irpino

Marano
Principato
Cosenza

Soveria
Mannelli
Petrona
Catanzaro

Figure 1.2. Map of Southern Italian mainland and selected towns and provinces in Campania and Calabria.

Figure 1.3

IMMIGRATION AND CLIMBING THE SOCIAL LADDER

Giovanni Battista and Crocifissa DeSantis were originally from Castro dei Volsci and moved to nearby Pofi with their children. The family was better off than those of the many farmers in Pofi. Not only did DeSantis and his eight siblings share the large house in Castro that was left by their father, but who also owned a nine-room farm house just outside Pofi. The DeSantis family had about 40 acres of land that they and hired laborers (*giornalieri*) worked, and two barns, one of which housed cows, horses, sheep, pigs, and chickens. DeSantis also owned a horse and a two-wheel wagon that helped in another enterprise. He bought stands of trees, had them chopped down and cut up, and then carted the wood to a paper mill near Ceprano. His sons joined in; Giustino was working with his dad on the wood wagon by the age of 12. The carting went on year-round, and when the DeSantis weren't hauling wood, they delivered sand and coal to businessmen, or subcontracted these tasks.

After his military discharge in 1920, Giustino DeSantis got married, and he and his wife were given a room in the DeSantis house. Giustino returned to the carting business, joining his father and his brother Domenico, and purchased 40 acres of land to add to the family's acreage. However, he soon grew discouraged because his father kept most of the profits from the family business. Because of this, and his desire to see the United States, Giustino emigrated from Pofi.

Nicola Campoli, too, emigrated after trying but failing to better his social status. Born into a poor peasant family in 1883, he was the youngest of four. The family could afford school only for the eldest child, and the other three remained illiterate. Nicola, according to his son, Rocco, "was a prison guard for a while, but he flunked the periodic marksmanship test." He then worked as a farmer with his father. Nicola met Arcangela Maiuri in Ceprano, where her family had a silk farm. They married, settled in Ceprano, and soon had two children, Giuseppina and Rocco. Nicola went to the United States in 1914 to get settled and then sent for Arcangela and the children in 1920.

Onorato Luigi Scarsella of Ceccano, who went by Luigi, followed a series of middle-class vocations on two continents. Not only could he read and write, as a young man he also sang opera with a group that traveled a regular circuit. In 1902, he was performing in Ceccano when he spotted an attractive 16-year-old girl in the audience. He made sure that he was introduced to Colomba Maria Germani, then started to call on her. However, her parents disapproved of Luigi because he was in show business. He soon changed professions and opened his own shoemaking shop. As a shoemaker, he also acted as a dentist, perhaps because he had tools such as pliers that could be used in dental work. Even after Scarsella and his brother Pietro emigrated to New Jersey and set up a shoe shop, he continued to court Colomba. They were married in 1908, and after a number of stays in the United States and Italy, the family eventually settled in Lackawanna.

Sources: Interviews with Giustino DeSantis, July 9, 1985; Rocco Campoli, July 5, 1995; and Anna Scarsella-Antes, December 26, 1995.

---

family had earlier refused their request, the Gypsies reportedly cut off the ear of one of the family's children.[5]

At the top of the pyramid of towns in the province of Frosinone were the few rich families with large land holdings. In Giuliano, the Narducci, Felici, and some Anticoli families were among this small elite. The Narducci family patriarch, a doctor, lived away from town, most likely in Rome. Two of his sons, one a doctor and the other a lawyer, lived in town and oversaw the family's holdings. During the 1920s, an automobile was a symbol of wealth, and in nearby Settefrati, the doctor made house calls using his car, one of only two vehicles in that town.[6]

Giustino DeSantis recalls the powerful Ciletti family in the town of Pofi. Michele Ciletti was the town mayor; Publeo, the secretary at the town hall; Edoardo, a teacher; and Carlo, the owner of a clothing store. While the DeSantis family prospered through its large land holdings and lumber and carting businesses, it did not enjoy the wealth and social

prominence of the Cilettis. In Falvaterra, the Pompeii family was powerful via its large land holdings, and Aristide Pompeii owned the flour mill on the Sacco River. Social class was apparent to everyone, even children. As a girl growing up in Morolo, Iole Schiavi observed that the house across the street was owned by rich people who had their own nursery. "They had beautiful shoes, and made goat skin sandals," she recalls. Schiavi and some of her cousins often had no footwear at all. In Marano Principato, Calabria, the few families with power and prestige included the Molinaro clan. The Molinaro family members held four key positions in the social structure of the town: priest, doctor, pharmacist, and lawyer. The Molinaro family had a large mansion and the chapel of Sant' Antonio was on the grounds of its estate.[7]

Life in these towns was static and unchanging, and for the most part, this also held true for the rigid class system. The few occasions for some upward social mobility only became more significant with the mass emigration to the western

Figure 1.4. Map of South central Italy towns and provinces in Molise, Abruzzo, Lazio, and Marche.

hemisphere. Some emigrants from Lazio to Lackawanna were part of the middle class; others aspired to it. In Giuliano, Armando Torella, the son of a farmer, had already moved up the social ladder, but he recalls that his vocation, that of shoemaker, "was number 99; I had to handle shoes and whatever was on the bottom: *merda* (shit)."[8]

Social class also defined the type of home each family lived in, and the homes of middle-class and upper-class families were larger and offered more amenities than those of the less well off, including peasants. The typical home of farming families was made of stone and usually had two to four rooms. In many homes, part of the ground floor served as a storage room and a barn for livestock; the living quarters were on the upper level. Most homes had cramped quarters.

In Settefrati the home of Domenico and Elisabetta Ventre had a kitchen and food-storage room with a dirt floor on the first level, and two bedrooms upstairs. Lighting was provided by kerosene lamps, and the toilet was outside the house. An outdoor stairway led to the bedrooms upstairs, one of which was occupied by Domenico's brother Filippo and his family, who were also farmers.

As families grew larger, some peasants were able to expand their abodes. In Giuliano, when Arcangelo and Luisa Petricca's offspring grew to eight, they added a second story and increased the number of rooms from two to four. Giovanni and Maria Lampazzi had only three rooms for their family of seven. A number of extended families lived in row houses—long buildings divided into units by vertical walls. In Giuliano,

Alessandro and Giulia Guglielmi and their five children were fortunate to have a unit in a row house that included five or six rooms.[9]

In 1903, teenager Gaetano DelMonaco left Pettorano, Abruzzo, to join *paesani* in Boston. After returning to Italy and serving in the army in World War I, he had trouble procuring travel papers and decided that he would do best by staying with his family in Italy and farming the land left to him by his father. He married, established a household just outside Pettorano, and farmed about 22 acres. The couple and their seven children lived in a two-story stone house with an attached barn that sheltered livestock. In Marano Principato, the extended Covelli family had a row house that was continually expanded (see Figure 1-5). By 1920, the two-and-a-half-story structure had six units, and the stone-and-mortar walls were one-foot thick. Across the path was a small, two-unit row house, and each unit was connected to the larger building by a second floor room that arched over the path. The first floor of each section was used for storage and curing food, the second as a

large bedroom, and the third, with its fireplace, as the kitchen. A small opening in the roof served as a chimney. The last unit in the big building had an open area used as a corral that was straddled by the second and third floor. A detached unit was occupied by Sanumele Covelli ("G" in Figure 1.5). A large outdoor oven, some 12 feet in diameter, was used by all families in the row house to bake bread and other foods. Heated stones placed in the conical oven, or *furnu*, provided hours of concentrated heat. The communal outhouse accommodated two persons at a time, and waste fell directly into a pit that extended out from the structure and sloped upward. Sewage was later pulled out with long hoes from under the outhouse into the open pit to dry and then be used as fertilizer.[10]

The Tristani family in Pettorano was on the lower-middle rung of the social ladder, as it owned a large vineyard, an olive grove, and a three-story house. The structure had a unique feature; in a room attached to the kitchen, grapes were stomped in a large built-in tub, and the juice flowed down a drain hole to the basement, where there were wine barrels large enough to hold a person.

Some peasants never owned their homes. Luigi and Domenica Violanti and their eight children lived in a rented house in Giuliano. The seventh child, Giuseppe, described the home as one large room that measured 15 feet by 40 feet. A fireplace served as a stove and furnace, and near it were a table, benches, and several chairs. In front of the fireplace, hanging from the ceiling, were smoked sausages, *prosciutto*, and bacon. Sometime between 1905 and 1912, Domenica Violanti died, and the couple's four oldest children emigrated to America. Thereafter, Luigi and his three sons shared a large bed, and daughter Giulia slept in a smaller bed.[11]

On the outskirts of Fano, Marche, wealthy merchants owned four farms that they rented out to laborers. Vincenzo and Ermina Campanelli and two related families rented one of the farms. Their son Alfredo remembered the building that housed the families was a two-story, brick and stucco structure with walls three feet thick. Each of the eight rooms had a fireplace, and tunnels under the building were used to store wine. There was a barn in which the owners kept a variety of livestock, including two horses to pull a wagon. At age 12, Alfredo went to live with an aunt whose family rented a farm 10 miles away. This farm was one of 60 area farms owned by a Duke Barbarini, who lived in Rome and owned land throughout Italy.[12]

In addition to owning or renting homes in the towns, some families had small structures or huts near farmlands or in the mountain groves. The family of Antonio and Giulia Torella had a home in Giuliano and a plot of land in the mountains, where Antonio's father lived year-round in the *pagliaro* (straw hut) they had constructed. Giovanni Lampazzi and his brothers shared two huts, or *carpane*, one at the top of the mountain, and the other at the foot. The *carpana*, a one-room shed with stone walls and a roof made of wood and straw, was larger and more sturdy than the *pagliaro*. The upper *carpana* was used at harvest time, and the lower one in the summer. In Quadrelle, Campania, Andrea Nappi used a thatched hut at his garden plot to store tools and pails. The family of Filiberto Covelli had a plot of land on the mountain above Marano Principato. Here, the family had an A-frame *pagliaro* that could shelter six or seven people during the annual fall harvest of chestnuts.[13]

Food: The food consumed by Italian peasants in their often modest homes was basic and did not offer a great deal of variety. Because her husband was in America, Nazzarena Schiavi and her daughter Iole, living in Morolo, ate meat only on holidays. Ricotta cheese was the mainstay of their diet, and a common meal was bread dough and cheese wrapped in fig leaves and cooked over coals. In a process that was later repeated in Lackawanna, tomato paste was made by spreading crushed tomatoes on large boards, which were then placed in the sun to allow the substance to dry out. This *conserva* was then stored in crocks and covered with oil. Iole's status as the

The carpana shown here is a substantial hut with stone walls and a roof of wood and straw.
Illustration by Patricia Murtaugh

eldest of Lorenzo Schiavi's grandchildren did bring welcome help, as he and other adults lavished her with attention. On his frequent visits, Lorenzo brought presents, sometimes including a chicken, which Nazzarena prepared for dinner.[14]

Rosina Covelli and her four children in Marano Principato survived only because her husband, Filiberto, regularly sent money from the United States. They were basically vegetarians

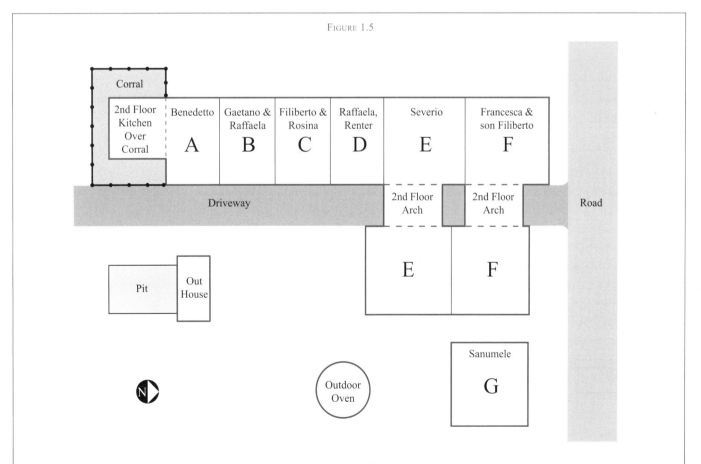

FIGURE 1.5

The Covelli rowhouse in Marano Principato, Calabria, circa 1927. The walls, made of stone, were one-foot thick. All residents were members of the extended Covelli family; only their first names are indicated here. Illustration by Patricia Murtaugh

because meat, and sometimes even pasta, was in short supply. Rosina often prepared *minestra*, a stew of cabbage, potatoes, chickpeas, beans, escarole; and dandelion greens. If she had pasta or meat, these were also added. *Pasta-fasuli*, beans and noodles in a tomato broth, was a dish eaten in Marano Principato and throughout Italy by frugal *contadini*. Many peasants in Calabria and other regions of the south during the early 1920s could not afford to buy the ingredients for ravioli, manicotti, or lasagna. Ironically, it was only in America that the Covelli family could afford to prepare these delicacies.[15]

Chores: Daily chores were performed in elemental settings, utilizing natural resources. Women in Marano Principato used smooth rocks in the Passodellanoce River as laundry washboards. They bleached clothes by sprinkling white fireplace ashes on them and adding boiling water. The clothes were then rinsed in the river and hung to dry and bleach in the sun. Heavier clothes were draped over blackberry branches or raspberry bushes, while lighter-weight garments were hung on clotheslines. The women in Morolo washed their clothes in *la trolla,* a section of a stream channeled through a large, rectangular trough made of stone.[16]

Nazzarena Schiavi obtained water from a fountain on the upper level of Morolo. A pipeline from the mountains brought cold, fresh water to Marano Principato, all year. The water emptied into a series of cisterns and the fountain *Micantonio*, a square, sunken structure with concrete steps. Women and girls came here to gather their water, carrying it in a *cuccome*, a bucket with a hinged cover that the women balanced on their head as they journeyed between the fountain and their homes. Only in 1938 did the town acquire running water and electricity.[17]

Most inhabitants of towns from which Lackawanna immigrants came were farmers. Italian farm life in the early twentieth century was very different from that in America, where abundant, fertile land allowed for large plots and isolated farm homes. In Italy, tillable land was in short supply, and malarial swamps were a danger in the lowlands. Therefore, most peasants lived in compact villages and made daily treks to their land, which often consisted of small, scattered plots, sometimes in the mountains. Italian farms were tiny by American standards, and their farmers more accurately described as gardeners.

The *contadini* raised a variety of crops: wheat, corn, squash, potatoes, fava beans, tomatoes, sweet and hot peppers, eggplant, escarole and other greens, cabbage, and chickpeas. Those who were more fortunate had grape vineyards or some trees including: olive, chestnut, filbert, walnut, plum, apple, cherry, and fig. Because the farm plots and tree groves were usually quite distant from the towns, it was common for men to rise at 3:00 or 4:00 a.m. to begin the trek to the countryside. In Quadrelle, Antonio

Grasso watched his grandfather Andrea Nappi and other men quietly walk to their plots well before dawn. Each carried a hoe, and tied to the tool was a handkerchief that held food and a bottle of wine for nourishment during the long workday.[18]

Giovanni Lampazzi and his three brothers helped each other work their individual plots in a style of family cooperative farming that was common among the Giulianesi. Alessandro Guglielmi, being the only son among five offspring of a farmer, was fortunate to own several scattered plots of land that he cultivated. When he went to America in 1920, his wife, Giulia, rented the land to relatives. Landless farmers often rented land from absentee owners. Luigi Violanti cultivated several plots he rented near Giuliano, paying the landlord with one-third to one-half his crop of wheat and corn. Arcangelo Petricca owned a small plot of land on which olive trees grew, and he planted vegetables there. In an interesting arrangement, he had a farm laborer tend his plot while he, his wife, and children worked as laborers for an elderly priest who owned a large tract of land.[19]

Many farmers had small plots on the slopes of Monte Chiuzzo, on the outskirts of Giuliano. Antonio Torella had two plots there, on each of which he constructed a *carpana*. The upper parcel was a chestnut grove, and he stored and prepared the chestnuts in the *carpana*. Torella cleared the lower parcel of brush and rocks, then terraced the land with walls, called *filon'*, fashioned from the rocks. He cultivated olive and fig trees and a grape vineyard, and also tended sheep, goats, cows, and pigs at this site. The livestock were kept in the second *carpana*, where Torella made ricotta cheese in the summer. Landless farm laborers, *giornalieri*, had a more tenuous existence. In Quadrelle, during the years just prior to World War I, those who worked the fields of others received about 40 cents for laboring from sunrise to sunset. In Marano Principato, *giornalieri* were allowed by those owning land to gather grain, chestnuts, apples, and walnuts that had been missed in the original harvests.[20]

Water for irrigation was essential, and the topography of Italy, with its steep hills and mountains in close proximity to the sea, meant that water quickly flowed away and had to be carefully managed. A variety of techniques were used to accomplish this. A pipe brought fresh, cool water from the hills to the gardens of Andrea Nappi and other *contadini* on the outskirts of Quadrelle. In Pettorano, the three irrigation canals that diverted water from the Gizio River were a boon for the farmers. However, actually gathering the water could be challenging. Helping out on the family farm, Concezio Novelli carried water to the field hands while his aunt carted a basket of food on her head. "I found out that the Gizio had a swift current when I tried to fill a wooden cask," he explained.[21]

Marano Principato had a more complex irrigation system. A ditch tapped into the Passodellanoce River in the mountain above the town and eventually merged with a narrow road. At specified nighttime hours, water was allowed to flow down the ditch and road. Each family was allowed to divert water into its field for an hour, directing it into the furrows. A town official turned off the flow of water at 7:00 a.m. Families carefully monitored the process to make sure each received a full hour of water. While an honor system was in place, occasional fistfights erupted when one family felt it had been cheated by another. As the Passodellanoce River ran through Marano Principato, it was a tiny stream in the summer but swelled into a torrent during the rainy season in the spring. Giuseppe Belmonte and the mule on which he rode were swept to their deaths by the torrent of the swollen river in the nineteenth century.[22]

The culmination of the work of *contadini* came at harvest time, when the families used age-old methods to gather and thresh wheat. In Settefrati, Lazio, the Ventre family cut the wheat, gathered it into small bundles, then tied several of these together to make a *fascio*. The *fasci* were loaded onto the family's donkey and transported back to the house. Young Tomasso Ventre was not tall enough to place the *fasci* on the donkey himself, so he laid one *fascio* on the ground and stood on it, then held another bundle on top of the donkey's back while his mother tied it in place. At threshing time, the Ventres and other families spread the wheat over a flat area of ground covered with huge stones, and cows dragged a stone over the grain to crack it. Following behind with scoops of mesh, adults and children tossed the leavings in the air, letting the chafe blow away. A local mill ground the wheat kernels into flour. Towns located on rivers had water-powered mills. There were three flour mills on the Gizio River in Pettorano. After farmers in Falvaterra cut the wheat, they hauled it down the hill to a water-powered mill on the Sacco River, where two large stones were turned on a stone base to grind the wheat. When the water level was low, a mule was used to power the grindstones.[23]

Andrea Nappi, known to his friends as *scarpelegge* (light-footed), raised wheat on a terraced hillside plot overlooking Quadrelle. His grandson, Antonio Grasso, observed as Nappi harvested his stand of wheat:

> When it was ripe, Grandpa cut it into small bundles with a hand scythe, tied them, then set them in the full sun until they were good and dry. He then laid a big bedsheet on the level ground, spreading the untied bundles evenly on the sheet … (and) with a flayer tied to a pole, pounded the wheat stalks on the bedsheet until the grain was released. Andrea then set up two seven foot poles with a crossbar and hung a sheet that trailed along the

This stone-lined section of a stream in Morolo, Lazio, was used to wash laundry, circa 1958. It was called la trolla. Photo source: Iole Schiavi-Murray

Another view of la trolla *in Morolo. It emptied into a reservoir formed by a dam, and a waterway led to water wheels at nearby mills.* Photo source: Iole Schiavi-Murray

Porto Romana *(the Roman Gate), Morolo, Lazio, in 1958. This area of Frosinone Province was called Ciociaria in ancient times.* Photo source: Iole Schiavi-Murray

View of Pettorano sul Gizio, circa 1920. The number of people from this town in Abruzzo who immigrated to Lackawanna is second only to that of Giuliano di Roma. Photo source: Collection of Josephine Ferrelli

Maria Cellini, seated, with children Nazzarena and Domenico, Morolo, Lazio, circa 1918. Nazzarena later married Giovanni Schiavi, and the couple migrated to Lackawanna. Photo source: Iole Schiavi-Murray

one on the ground. This bedsheet was a barrier set against the prevailing winds. With a wooden shovel Grandpa threw the threshed grain against the wind toward the … bedsheet; it fell as clean as a whistle on the bedsheet on the ground—a system used since Biblical times.

The harvest was crucial to the subsistence farmers. Michele Petrucci, a *contadino* in Rotelle, Molise, used grain as barter, even paying his taxes, which were based on the size of his crop, with part of the harvest. Just outside of Fano, the Campanelli family, who rented their home and livestock from their landlord, paid rent by giving the owner half their crop and the livestock.[24]

Many *contadini* participated in two other types of activities: harvesting chestnuts and raising silkworms. Chestnuts were a very important part of the food economy in towns where chestnut groves were plentiful in nearby hills and mountains. Immigrants told of a variety of methods for harvesting this valuable food. On the mountain outside Giuliano, the family of Antonio Torella gathered chestnuts, buried them in the dirt floor of their *carpana* to preserve them, and later dug them up to be roasted or boiled and eaten. In Marano Principato, many peasants had stands of chestnut trees on the slopes of Mount Cucuzza. Children helped gather the fallen pods and open them to get the fruit. The flour from these sweet chestnuts was used to make bread and deep-fried dumplings called *pittuliddi*. In other communes, harvesting chestnuts was a larger scale operation.[25]

In Bagnoli Irpino, workers gathered the chestnuts then sorted them by size. The larger ones were sold to people from Naples and other cities. The smaller ones were usually purchased by two businessmen, whose workers prepared them in a building where the fruit was piled two to three feet high on flat racks near the ceiling. The drying procedure took 10 or 12 days, during which the chestnuts were turned over and occasionally stirred. Next came the shelling process, in which chestnuts were placed in narrow, sock-like sacks that were eight to 10 feet long. Two men, one on each end, then beat the sacks against a log. The chestnuts were then placed in a contraption that consisted of a fan with a wire mesh bin underneath. As the fan was turned by hand, the shells were propelled out and the chestnut pulp settled into the bin. Some farmers ground the chestnuts to feed to their livestock, while others stored them for family consumption in the winter. In Petrona, local businessmen hired women and girls to gather the chestnuts. They hauled the chestnuts to a long wooden shed, where the nuts were piled on wooden racks and smoked until they were dried. The process took three or four days, during which the women camped nearby. After the women loaded the chestnuts into burlap sacks, two workmen hit each sack against wooden planks to remove the shells, then the women reloaded the

View of Giuliano di Roma in 1995. This town sent more immigrants to Lackawanna than any other in Italy.
Photo source: Joe and Rose Guglielmi

chestnuts into clean sacks and carried them to a mill to be ground into flour.[26]

Throughout Italy, many families added to their income by raising silkworms. This was generally considered women's and children's work. On the outskirts of Fano, Alfredo Campanelli recalls one room in the house filled with four-by-five-foot wooden trays stacked on racks. These held the eggs that, if kept warm, would hatch into silkworms. As a boy, Campanelli chopped up mulberry leaves to feed them and changed the paper in each tray every three days. He tied branches together in a vertical position, and the worms attached to these to spin their cocoons. He recalled, "During a 40 day period the worms hibernate four times, each time for three or four days. Cocoons appear at the very end as the worms turn yellow."

Following a similar routine, Raffaela Covelli, assisted by her niece Adelina, raised silkworms in the third-floor attic of her home, in Marano Principato. They chopped up leaves of the white-berry mulberry tree for young worms and the red-berry variety for more mature worms. When the silkworms died, Raffaela and Adelina removed the fuzz-like balls of raw silk from the *cucuddi* (cocoons) and placed them in bags to be taken to vendors in Cosenza. In Fano, Campanelli's family sold the hardened cocoons to a nearby silk factory.[27]

Peasants in southern Italy had other types of jobs that either were the main source of income or supplemented the family income. After Giovanni Piccirilli gathered his own crop, he worked as a farm laborer, harvesting the crops of the large landholders in Falvaterra. Paolo Andreozzi and two of his sons supplemented their family income by working at the flour mill on the Sacco River. Michele Grasso, born in 1875 in Tufino, east of Naples, learned the techniques for pruning grapevines from his father. As a young farm laborer, Grasso traveled to towns in Campania and Puglia, where farmers with small

vineyards hired him to prune their grapevines during the dormant season.[28]

Some families straddled class and occupational boundaries by combining farming with business ventures. Luigi and Rosa Maturani first lived in Giuliano, then moved to a farm outside of town. There, Luigi worked with his father, Giovanni Battista, raising horses for sale to teamsters. One of the teamsters who purchased horses from the Maturanis was Biagio DeSantis, who, like his father before him, was a transporter of goods, primarily foodstuffs, from Ceccano and Frosinone to merchants in Giuliano. DeSantis owned a small parcel of land where his two horses grazed. With Biagio in America during the 1930s, his eldest child, Lelio, quit school after fifth grade and worked with a cousin who transported wine to local merchants.[29]

Forests and stands of trees provided seasonal work for some Italian farmers. The commune of Bagnoli Irpino owned the heavily wooded hills around it and allowed companies to purchase the wood and cut down trees for lumber and to make charcoal. A privately owned contraption similar to a chairlift was used to bring the lumber and charcoal down from the steep hills, and most of it was transported by railroad to buyers. In Calabria, the lumber camps in the Sila Mountains offered seasonal work that was often pursued by landless farm laborers. After crops were harvested, farmers in Marano Principato and neighboring towns in the Rende area made use of the chestnut trees—not only to gather chestnuts but also to produce charcoal. They then sold these commodities in the larger towns, such as Rende.[30]

Peasants living near wooded areas often produced charcoal. In Pettorano, charcoal making provided seasonal work for the peasants, occupations for the middle class, and a source of wealth for the upper class. The charcoal makers, or *carbonari*, traveled to forests, where they felled trees and stacked the

Rosa Sperduti and one of her two daughters in Giuliano di Roma. They and two of the Rosa's sons remained in Italy, while Rosa's husband Luigi and other four sons went to America. Photo source: Collection of Yolanda Sperduti-Tobias

wood. They covered the pile with branches, then with mud and dirt. What emerged was a dome some six feet high, with a hole in the top and the bottom. A fire lit in the bottom of the dome burned for weeks. The resulting charcoal was then removed with forked sticks and, after cooling, hauled by mule, and later by truck, to customers who paid by the ton. From October through March, gangs of *carbonari* from Pettorano dispersed throughout Italy to do their work. They sometimes traveled into northern Italy or as far south as Calabria. A stint might last up to eight months, but a typical job lasted four to six weeks. Some workers took their families along with them. The carbonari lived in wooden huts they built themselves.

The middle-class workers included the charcoal companies' buyers, who purchased the forest plots. Innocenzo D'Alessandro was not only a buyer for a charcoal company; he also ran the store where employees purchased provisions for their work in the field and was one of the foremen sent out with the laborer crews. The contractor provided food—in the form of beans, flour, and potatoes—but subtracted money from each worker's pay to cover the expense. Carmine DelMonaco recalls that

some men used up virtually all their pay on food. The laborers were paid each month or at the end of the contract. D'Alessandro's crews worked in Lazio, in the woods between Anzio and Cisterna. The charcoal company was owned by Alessandro Zanella, who reportedly became a millionaire from this enterprise. Another contractor, Cristoforo D'Alessio, was one of the contractors who purchased stands of trees from various communes. He usually hired three or four nephews as his crew and reportedly made a good living at this. His daughter Giovanna married Giovanni D'Alessandro, the son of another contractor. D'Alessandro spent some time in America, and his four sons all settled permanently in Lackawanna.[31]

Just outside of the city of Fano, there was a small brick factory that provided jobs for a handful of male and female workers. Near Marano Principato, three textile factories, two in Marano Marchesato and one in Montalto, employed a total of 160 workers in 1911. In Sulmona, Abruzzo, a confetti factory and a factory that made *torrone* candy employed people in nearby towns. Some residents of Giuliano di Roma worked in a munitions factory located 10 miles from town. Such factories were not plentiful in southern Italy but there were occasional jobs in road and railroad construction. In another attempt to earn livelihoods, many peasant families raised sheep. Umele Covelli, a resident of Marano Principato, was a *pecoraro*, or shepherd, who took his sheep to the mountains in summer and lived there in a *pagliaro*. He carried an axe, which he used to chop wood, fight off wolves, and dispatch snakes. He was always accompanied by a dog. In the winter, the sheep were taken to the mountains each morning and returned each evening to the safety of the corral attached to the Covelli row house.

Adults utilized other opportunities to earn money or produce goods needed by their families. Women and older girls in Marano Principato, Rende, and surrounding towns spun wool and flax and sold them to weavers, and made clothing for their own families. From the residue of olive-oil production, they made soap. They produced syrup from figs that was used as sugar. Some peasants in small towns made and sold craftwork; in Petrona, the elderly Pasquale Colosimo wove baskets.[32]

Migrating, or moving in search of work, was a common experience. Many Giulianesi traveled to Rome and Milan for seasonal work, and some went as far as Romania. After military service in World War I, Michele Petrucci could not find a job in his hometown of Rotelle, but an army officer found him work at Castellamare, a town near Pescara, Abruzzo. With his wife and son, Petrucci moved there and did both railroad and gardening work, a job combination that he and many other Italian immigrants repeated in the United States.[33]

Every occupation practiced by the *contadini* had its hazards. In San Pio Delle Camere, Antonio Paolini made a living by

Luigi Sperduti and four of his sons moved to Lackawanna. Luigi went back to Giuliano di Roma after one year to be with his wife Rosa and their other four children. The four Lackawanna sons—Giuseppe, Angelo, Domenico, and Armando—settled there permanently.
Photo source: Collection of Yolanda Sperduti-Tobias

Margherita and Nicola Germani lived in Ceccano, Lazio. Their daughter Colomba married Luigi Scarsella, and the couple immigrated to Lackawanna in the 1920s.
Photo source: Anne Scarsella-Antes

transporting people to Aquila in his wagon drawn by two horses. Tragically, he died after being kicked by one of the horses. Malaria was a scourge for workers in southern Italy. *Contadini* in Giuliano did seasonal work planting corn in the Pontine marshes some 20 miles away. Many caught malaria and some, such as Giovanni Lampazzi, mentioned below, died of it. In about 1895, Michele Grasso was pruning grapevines on a farm in a swampy area of Puglia when he contracted malaria. The pharmacist who provided him medicine told Grasso to expect a relapse around age 50. The prophecy came true years later in Lackawanna when Grasso developed leukemia and died.[34]

Children: In addition to tending to silkworms, children supported their families by helping with many household and farm chores. Girls and boys helped gather chestnuts and firewood in the mountains. In Petrona, Michelina Colosimo was age five when she joined her mother harvesting chestnuts. She gathered firewood and learned to balance a small bundle on her head as she imitated her mother and other women. This wood was used to heat the house in winter. Further north, in Marano Principato, Angelina and Gelsomina Caira not only helped their parents garden and pick chestnuts in the hills but also made trips to sell farm produce. Each girl balanced a basket of vegetables on her head for the two-hour walk to Cosenza, where they sold their goods to vendors who ran fruit and vegetable stands. Children's labor became even more crucial if the head of the family had migrated to other parts of Italy or Europe for seasonal work, or was off in America. Concezio Novelli spent his childhood in Pettorano while his father was in America. Following his mother's, death he lived with an aunt and uncle, helping them with farm chores. He often visited his grandmother's house, where he read books aloud to her. And, he adds, "I held the wool while Grandma spun it."[35]

While Domenico Ventre was working in France and England, his wife Elisabetta and three sons in Settefrati cultivated wheat and vegetables on one plot. At a second location, the family had a small corral, sheltered by a lean-to roof, which was home to a cow and several pigs. The children did much of the work of looking after the livestock, a practice reported by many other immigrants. Near Fano, teenager Alfredo Campanelli helped tend to the cows, bulls, horses, pigs, sheep, and turkeys housed in a small barn. The DelMonaco family in Pettorano owned a horse, a mule, four cows, and 100 sheep and goats. The children and young men took the sheep and goats to the mountains to graze. In nearby Cocullo, Concetta Marinelli helped tend the family's sheep in the mountains—a difficult job for a child without a hut for shelter. Despite the hard work of adults and children, the small farm plots often could not support the families, especially as children became adults and started their own families. In fact, the lack of economic viability of family farms led many to leave Italy for destinations overseas.[36]

Social Institutions

Throughout southern Italy, several institutions gave shape and continuity to local culture. First, of course, came the family, followed by the Catholic Church. Schools, organizations, and recreation traditions also strengthened community identity. These traditions would live on, in varying forms, in immigrant culture in America. The following sketches help provide a greater understanding of immigrants' experience before they left Italy, underscoring the themes of continuity and change that migrants grappled with in Lackawanna.

Family: The southern Italian family of the early twentieth century usually consisted of parents and their unmarried children. While there were regional and social class variations, sociologists have identified some common family traits. The tightly knit Italian family was a patriarchy in which the father, and sometimes the grandfather, was the leader and final authority, depending who was the oldest and strongest male. The wife and mother, however, had a strong influence in important decisions, and the home was her domain. "Italian women have always been exclusively responsible for the children; attending to their children's religious education; preparing their children for marriage; articulating social relations with friends, kin, and townsmen; and, above all, preventing the ever-present animus between father and children from erupting into violence." The family was father led but mother centered. Careful not to publicly undermine her husband's image as the authority figure, the mother stood humbly by his side as he announced decisions. Prior to such pronouncements, however, she often influenced him in private discussion on the best approach to a given issue.

Sora, Lazio, mid-1930s. The newly engaged Iolanda Fanone and Vincenzo Gemmiti meet with Iolanda's family. From left are: Mario Fanone (brother), Iolanda Fanone, Vincenzo Gemmiti, Giovanna Fanone (mother), and Filippo Fanone (grandfather). Photo source: Phil Fanone

Thus, the patriarchy was public and known, while the matriarchy was private and hidden.

The peasant family in Italy was an economic unit that busied all members 10 years of age or older in tilling small plots of land, tending to livestock, and doing similar chores. The wealth produced was viewed as belonging to the whole family. The nuclear family—the parents and their children—was often the economic unit, but there were strong social connections with the closest blood relatives and more limited ties with distant relatives that sometimes broadened into mutual aid and uniting

Sora, Lazio, mid-1930s. Celebration of the engagement of Iolanda Fanone and Vincenzo Gemmiti. The new couple is standing in the center behind the musicians. Mario Fanone, who later immigrated to Lackawanna, is the accordion player. Photo source: Phil Fanone

against outsiders. At times, the parents or a married sibling of one spouse might live with the family, but the typical small house didn't allow this to be a frequent practice. Family solidarity, be it an emphasis on the nuclear or more extended blood ties, was the basic glue that held southern Italian society together.[37]

Religion: In the early twentieth century, the Catholicism of Italy was distinct from that of other European countries. In fact, the religious practices of southern Italians differed from those of northern Italians. The religious culture north of Rome more closely resembled that of the rest of Europe, while that south of Rome "preserved in modified form many of the elements found associated with ancient Greek, Roman, and Mohammedan beliefs.... The worship of objects, such as statues and sacred relics, and the attribution of specific powers and qualities to individual saints reflected the earlier religions."[38]

Unlike in the United States, the Church in Italy was for many years considered a government-sponsored institution. Kings and princes gave large sums to found and support local churches. However, after the unification of Italy in 1870, the new central government took possession of most Church properties and gradually cut back on its financial support. During the period of change over the following decades, some municipal governments supported local churches, while wealthy families did so in other areas. The Church retained part of its preunification wealth and helped supplement the incomes of priests and parishes that had limited income. The peasants, however, gave meager donations, usually on special occasions, such as marriages and baptisms. Collections at Sunday Mass were low.

Prior to national unification, a local priest could provide some financial support to the poor, and the Church provided other services, such as hospitals and charitable institutions, that directly aided the peasants. But after 1870, "the Church became impoverished and ceased to be the feeder of the poor." The priest not only lost power and prestige in the eyes of the peasants, but further alienated them by seeking greater donations. Parishioners in Pettorano believed that "the Vatican supported poor churches," recalls Giuseppina Ferrelli. "Some men said, 'Why doesn't the priest go to work?'" Feeling undercut by the new Italian government, the Church had its priests tell parishioners not to vote in elections. This further antagonized the peasants, who felt that clerics should not intrude in political matters.[39]

Peasants in southern Italy have traditionally displayed mixed attitudes toward the Church and its priests, as described by Rudolph Vecoli:

The Church they had known as an oppressive landlord allied with their historic exploiters, the signori (upper class, especially landlords) ... Celibate and dressed in women's garb, the priest was a sexual anomaly in a

Falvaterra, Lazio, in 1993. It is one of many towns in Frosinone Province that sent immigrants to Lackawanna. Photo source: the author

society that prized virility as the highest male attribute.... Yet in the carrying out of their priestly functions, the clergy were respected and even feared.

Often, because priests were from an upper-class background, peasants used the cleric as a scapegoat upon whom to vent their anger toward the *signori*.[40]

Participation in religious activities usually was based on gender and age. Church attendance was important for women and children. As a child in Morolo, for example, Iole Schiavi went to church each morning with her grandmother. The older females in the family provided most of the religious education to the youth, as the Church offered instruction only prior to confirmation. However, in southern Italy, few young men went to Mass regularly, and a only a small number of men, mostly middle-aged and elderly, were seen in church, although Masses were given at 3:00 or 4:00 a.m. on Sunday to accommodate farmers who set out for their fields before daybreak. During the early 1940s in Pettorano, Gaetano Iannarelli noticed that he and the other altar boys were some of the few males present at Mass. Among the men in attendance were both the devout and the less serious. At Annunziata Church in Marano Principato, a male sextant played the organ and sang wonderfully, according to Adelina Covelli, whose brother Leopoldo sometimes pumped the organ while the sextant played. She recalled that some brazen young men stood along the walls and threw pieces of paper or orange skins at the women sitting in pews—anticlerical attitudes that would be echoed in Lackawanna.[41]

Sora, Lazio. The Napoli bridge over the Liri River.
Photo source: Phil Fanone

In some churches, peasants brought their own chairs. In others, seats could be rented, and still others offered free seating. During the 1920s, Giuseppina Ferrelli attended Chiesa Madre, the mother church among the nine churches in and near Pettorano, where some of the parishioners rented bench space by paying the sacristan two or three cents per week. Other families owned chairs with kneelers on the back, which were chained to the walls when not in use. People with less money sat on the steps along the wall beneath the stations of the cross. At the church of Annunziata in Marano Principato, pew space was rented; otherwise, one had to stand during services. Nearby, the Sant'Antonio chapel had two or three crude pews, which people paid for the right to occupy. Most farmers brought their own chairs, put their names on them, and left them in the chapel. Sant'Antonio's was situated on the land of the wealthy Molinaro family, whose members sat in privacy in a special room adjacent to the altar. Alfredo Campanelli's family attended the church of San Filippo e Giacoma near Fano, where parishioners enjoyed the luxury of free seating.[42]

Early Christians set up the churches of Santa Nicola and Santa Di Meo in the catacombs under Giuliano di Roma 2000 years ago. Giuliano has five above-ground churches, including Santa Maria Maggiore, the central church in town. The church of San Biagio, built around the year 1000, shortly after the saint's image appeared to one of the townspeople, honors the protector of the throat and the patron saint of Giuliano. The seven churches in Pettorano include Chiesa Madre, San Benigno, San Rocco, San Nicolo, San Giovanni, Sant'Antonio Abate, and Madonna della Libera. Three priests based at Chiesa Madre served at least nine of the churches in the vicinity, including San Sebastiano and Santa Margherita.[43]

Christmas and Easter were special times for southern Italians, and even reluctant males were likely to show up at Mass. Tomasso Ventre remembers that the mortars used during the *feste* in Settefrati were also fired at Christmas. On Palm Sunday in Marano Principato, olive branches decorated with oranges, flowers, and confetti were carried into church and blessed by the priest. In Pettorano, a similar ceremony involved olive branches adorned with ribbons. Throughout southern Italy, Easter bread represented another type of offering. Loaves of sweet bread shaped as dolls and other figures had hard-boiled eggs inserted at one end. According to sociologist Phyllis Williams, "The egg here had the same traditional reference to life and awakening life processes as it does in Greek mythology and in the case of Easter eggs in this country."[44]

The religious practices of southern Italians focused on the worship of saints and the various manifestations of the Madonna. Leonard Covello, an American educator who emigrated from Basilicata, describes this aspect of Italian life:

> Since the southern Italian divinities had significance primarily as protectors and as possessors of occult powers and furthermore, since the long list of Madonnas and saints represent a variety of personalities, specific powers were attributed to each of them.… The saints were not necessarily benevolent creatures. They had to be propitiated by gifts and promises. If a promise was not kept the saints could be vengeful, even malicious.
>
> But likewise, they [the saints] were endowed with human nature, and therefore finicky, given to hesitation, and would not infrequently show bad faith. The peasant in such cases would intimidate or even curse the saint.

Each saint or Madonna had attributes; St. Vito made dogs unable to bite, and Santa Barbara protected people against lightning. The powers of a specific saint, however, might change from one locale to another. In Basilicata, San Rocco protected sheep from anthrax, while in Lazio, he looked after sick men. The southern Italians, intense devotion to the Madonna was driven more by her miraculous powers than her role as the mother of Jesus. The strong cult of the Madonna amazed Irish Catholic priests and Protestant missionaries who proselytized in America's Little Italys. This devotion to the Madonna was reflected in gifts from *Americani*, townspeople who returned from stays in the United States. In 1954, a man named Cicchetti returned to Falvaterra and had a large statue of the Madonna erected on the mountain overlooking the town. This is referred to by locals as Madonna di Cicchetti.[45]

The highest expression of religious devotion was the *festa*, the annual festival in honor of a local saint. *Feste* were usually the domain of men, as many towns had one or more male religious societies that made arrangements for the festivals. In some cases, men went through town prior to the celebration collecting donations to cover the expenses incurred. The typical *festa* was a one- to three-day event on the weekend. It included a High Mass, celebrated in the main church, followed by a procession in which the statue of the saint being honored was placed on a wooden vada and carried by four to 10 men through the streets of the town. The procession was led by the priest and town officials and accompanied by a band playing music, with some townspeople following behind. Along the path of the march, banners and bright cloth adorned the walls and balconies of houses. Flowers were thrown from street level and the balconies. People lined the streets, and many either laid gifts at the feet of the saint or pinned them to the saint's vestments. The offerings included food, money, jewelry, and an occasional bride's wedding dress. Phyllis Williams noted another type of offering: "The personal clothing of sick persons was also brought on these occasions and laid at the foot of the statue; when the garments were again worn, [it was believed that] the virtue of the saint flowed into the body of the supplicant and restored health." Following the procession there was entertainment, dancing, and fireworks at night. Booths sold fruit, sweets, and beverages as well as crafts and clothing. These *feste* are still held in many towns.[46]

Sora, Lazio, 1952. Mario and Maria Fanone and their son Phil praying to the Madonna. The altar was left at each home for one day. Each afternoon, the priest led a procession that took the altar to a different home.
Photo source: Phil Fanone

Immigrants to Lackawanna in the early twentieth century have vivid memories of the *feste* as these events were usually the most important social events in their towns. In Petrona, the feast of St. Lucy was held in June. As a young girl, Michelina Colosimo was awestruck by the statue of Santa Lucia: "She was beautiful, and she was only 16 years old … I admired her so much." During the procession, Michelina watched some townspeople throw fragrant rose petals from balconies while others fashioned strings of rose petals and placed them on the statue. She loved the cookies and lemon marmalade her mother bought for her at the celebration's food booths.[47]

Augusta Lampazzi recalled the gaiety of the San Biagio celebration in Giuliano on the last Sunday of August. People carried candles in the procession, and the entertainment included donkey races and men climbing greased poles to grab prizes dangling from the top. Giulio Maturani, who was her neighbor in both Italy and Lackawanna, was very good at making his way up the greased pole. Ennio Guglielmi enjoyed playing trombone in the church band that marched in the processions playing music. Giuseppe Violanti remembered that, while some people sold food at booths, others donated cookies and *ciammele*, a sweet bread. During a return visit to the area, Violanti was honored to be one of six men asked to carry the statue of San Giuseppe. Some 70 years later, he remembered the date of the event—March 19, 1926—with much pride.[48]

At the *festa* of the Madonna dell'Assunta in Morolo, young Iola Schiavi looked forward to seeing the craftworks being sold and to tasting the watermelon and other fruits at the food booths. The Ventre family went to the mountains near Settefrati in August for the festival of Madonna di Cannetto, one of the well-known Black Madonnas of southern Italy. Tomasso Ventre and other children loved the loud noise produced by the crude fireworks, which were created by stuffing metal tubes with powder and a fuse. Giustino DeSantis reported that a unique aspect of the two- and three-day *feste* in Pofi was the bingo games. In the town of San Pio delle Camere, named for its patron saint, Flora Paolini recalls that two men from the religious society visited each family and collected money prior to the feast day in July. Emigrants in America also sent donations. Paolini was impressed by the red and white garments that adorned the statue of San Pio.[49]

In Bagnoli Irpino, six *feste* were held yearly, five of which lasted one day and included a local band and a carnival. The exception was the feast of the Immaculate Conception, a two-day celebration in June for which a special band was brought in from outside the area, a platform was erected for dancing, and fireworks were set off at nightfall. The whole town was decorated with banners and lights. In addition to including a statue of the Virgin Mary, the procession included a float

San Rocco is the patron saint of Sora, Lazio, and is a popular saint throughout southern Italy. Source: Phil Fanone

Funeral procession in Ceccano, Lazio, circa 1968. Photo source: Phil Fanone

carrying children dressed as angels and virgin brides. The northern Italians in Fano were less elaborate. At the *festa* in honor of San Paternianno, the only donations the Marchegiani offered were coins in a basket that was passed around.[50]

Certain *feste* have unique features that underscore the attributes or powers of the saints. On San Giuseppe day in Giuliano, many townspeople set up altars in their homes. The tradition is to invite poor people to one's home to partake of food and beverages laid out on the altar or a table nearby. Typically displayed are meatless foods, such as artichokes, pasta with fish sauce, *manestra*, bread, and eels and other fish. People visit each other's homes to admire these displays. On the *festa* of San Rocco in August, people honor the legend that dogs stole scraps of bread to take to San Rocco as he lay dying of cancer in the woods. In remembrance of this story, the Giulianesi make small loaves of bread to celebrate the event.[51]

People in Pettorano, according to Guy Iannarelli, believe that the festival in honor of Santa Margherita represents an attempt to preserve the town's water supply. There is a fountain located near Santa Margherita Church, and it is said that the nearby city of Sulmona draws its water from the same source.

Pettorano's townspeople thought that "the Sulmonesi would take the statue unless the Pettoranesi honored her." The *feste* for Sant' Antonio and San Sebastiano are held in January, sometimes in competition with each other. "People collected wood," states Iannarelli, "and started fires to keep San Sebastiano warm; he was only in a loin cloth." For the feast of the Corpus Domini in May, altars are erected at each of the eight archways in Pettorano. Silk and fine blankets are used to cover the altars, which are then adorned with candles and flowers. People hang their best blankets and silk from their windows or on ropes along the road. When the procession bearing the sacrament passes by, roses are strewn on the ground. Another annual celebration in Pettorano and other towns is the *carnevale*, held in February. Townspeople wear costumes and masks, ride around on horses and mules, make fun of each other, and speak of individual foibles without mentioning names. In Cocullo, townspeople honor San Domenico, the patron saint of teeth and the prevention of rabies. During the procession, the statue of the saint is adorned with defanged snakes, which are repeatedly placed back on the statue and vada as they crawl off. Priests bless the peasants' livestock as part of the religious rite. Some of the specific attributes of other popular southern Italian saints are: San Rocco, protector against illness; Santa Lucia, guardian of eyesight; and Sant'Anna, protector against the pain and dangers of childbirth. In Marano Principato, residents have held an annual festa in honor of Annunziata since the earthquake of 1906. They believe that her divine interaction limited the earthquake's ill effects to just two deaths and a few damaged homes. In Ceccano, young Vincenzo Scarsella became very sick after swimming (his mother believed it was because he had eaten a cucumber with the skin on), and the doctor said he would die. His mother Colomba promised to crawl on her hands and knees to Our Lady of Mount Carmel if she would allow him to recover. The boy did recover, the mother crawled on her hands and knees in thanks, and from then on, she always said a special prayer to the saint.[52]

As the highlight of social and recreational activities in small towns, *feste* provided entertainment and a chance for young people from neighboring towns to meet and court.

Antonio Carnevale of Pico met his future wife at the *festa* of Santa Croce (Holy Cross) in Pastena, a town nine miles away. He later walked there to visit her, and once asked his mother to accompany him so that she could meet the woman he wanted to marry. Responding that she was too busy for such a journey, she advised Antonio to take along a pair of pants with a hole in them. Antonio's sweetheart mended the pants, and, according to his grandson Santino, when he arrived home and "returned the pants in good shape, his mother said 'marry her!'"[53]

In addition to southern Italian belief in the magical powers of patron saints, there were their superstitions regarding the *mal'occhio*, or evil eye. Phyllis Williams wrote of southern Italian immigrants in the 1930s:

> They were incapable of looking upon misfortune as something precipitated by natural causation, as due to lack of foresight, error, or the entrance into the situation of forces over which they had no control. Rather did they think in terms of specific human causation and

FIGURE 1.6

A FESTA IN QUADRELLE, CAMPANIA

The patron saint of Quadrelle is San Giovanni Battista (St. John the Baptist), and it is for him that the town's church is named. The July celebration in honor of this saint is the highlight of the year's religious and social events. In preparation for the mass and festival, the statue of St. John is moved from its pedestal in the church and placed on a wooden platform, or vada, that is decorated with bunting and religious artifacts.

On the day of the feast, a High Mass is offered by several priests as the band and a fireworks expert with six mortars wait just outside the church. When the priest finishes saying the Eucharistic prayer, he raises the Host into the air. On one such day, Antonio Grasso watched as a man stationed in the doorway of the church signaled that the elevation of the Host was occurring. At that point, the "mortars go off in a deafening roar and the band strikes up the music. It's something beautiful and impressive to behold, and sets the festive mood for the

feast and the day long celebration."

The procession begins as men grip the poles and hoist the platform bearing the statue of St. John to their shoulders and carry it into the street as the band plays. The band then falls in behind the statue, followed by the clergy, the mayor, other town dignitaries, and, finally, the townspeople. Some of the people in the procession walk barefooted on the cobblestone streets to do penance for past sins or in anticipation of future favors from the patron saint. During one festival, Grasso watched as the procession "slowly swayed from side to side in and down the narrow streets; at times it seemed as if they brushed the sides of the buildings. Onlookers jammed the balconies, windows, and doorways with rosaries in their hands; praying, kissing the crucifix, and crossing themselves as the statue of the saint neared. On each corner of a side street the procession stopped, thus giving the men carrying the heavy statue some time to rest. The men rested the platform

on forked poles, while other men with baskets mingled in the crowd seeking donations." During this break, a group of the faithful sang religious hymns.

The religious procession slowly made its way to an open area where a bandstand and booths had been set up. "The stand was festooned with bunting and Chinese lanterns, giving the occasion an Oriental flavor. … The band played popular songs and, now and then, a small scale of opera that thrilled the crowd. … The parents with children went from booth to booth to buy all sorts of sweets, especially *torrone* nougat candy and other delicious sweets the vendors offered. … The band stopped playing as the fireworks lit up the night sky, and then the cascading fireworks lit up the whole place as they came downward. The wheels whirling round and round were going off at the end of the bridge." The thunderous roar from a series of mortars marked the close of the festival.

Source: Tony Grasso. "The Saint Feast Day," unpublished, 1983, pp. 1-3.

Madonna di Canneto is the patron saint of Settefrati, Lazio. Photo source: Phil Fanone

FIGURE 1.7

Southern Italian Saints and Their Powers

Sant'Anna	Helps pregnant women
San Pantaleone	Helps pick winning lottery numbers
San Simone	Blinds or injures one's enemies
Santa Francesca di Paola	Makes bread rise well
San Nicola	Provides a suitable husband for one's daughter
Santa Bologna	Cures toothaches
San Filippo Nero	Fulfills one's wishes
Our Lady of Mt. Carmel	Fulfills one's wish
Santa Oliva	Instills humility

Sources: Leonard Covello, The Social Background of the Italo-American School: A Study of the Southern Italian Family Mores and Their Effect on the School Situation in Italy and America, 1967, pp. 122–123; interview with Lucia Caracci-Cullens, November, 2008.

attributed mishaps to the influence of an ever-present menace, the power of envy.

… The South Italian thought of the evil eye as a power inborn in certain men and women, who by a mere glance could cause physical injury, business reverses, sickness, and even death.

Peasants countered such perceived evil by wearing amulets, pieces of jewelry in the shape of a horn, a tooth, a fish, or a hand with the first and little finger extended. Children were thought to be especially vulnerable to the *mal'occhio*. Parents placed open scissors near their infants' beds to cut the gaze of one possessing "the eyes," and pinned red ribbons on the underwear of older children. Anyone complimenting a child's good health or attributes had to add the phrase "God bless you" or be immediately suspected of invoking a curse. When it was thought that the *mal'occhio* may have been placed on a family member, a *mago* (wizard) or *strega* (witch) was called in. This man or woman often placed drops of oil in a cup of water to discern if a curse was present, and, if so, used a series of ritual prayers, incantations, and anointing with oil to remove it. These rituals could be passed on to another healer only at Easter and Christmas.[54]

Lackawanna immigrants report that many people in their hometowns believed in the power of the evil eye. The most common occurrence was an envious person causing another to have a headache. People also believed that harmful spirits were present at night. In Pettorano, some people believed that certain *streghe* (witches) sucked blood out of babies and that one infant died from this. Another young child was reported to have felt the presence of a *strega* in the house. A neighbor of Concezio Novelli had the power to remove the *mal'occhio*, and she taught him how to perform this ritual. She instructed him to repeat certain secret prayers each Christmas and Easter so as to maintain his curative powers.[55]

Organizations: Following the unification of Italy, many mutual-aid societies were founded throughout the country. By 1895, there were 6,587 organizations with 994,183 members, most of them in northern Italy. A large number of these groups were in cities, and many were composed of middle-class artisans and tradespeople. Of the 191 towns that provided immigrants to Lackawanna, 85 had organizations in 1895. With the exception of Fano, each of these towns sent only a few immigrants to the Steel City. Excluding a few select cities—such as Rome, Naples, and Fano—there were 104 organizations, with a total membership of 9,811, in the towns of southern Italy and Marche from which Lackawanna immigrants migrated. Of the 21 towns that sent the highest numbers of people to Lackawanna, 10 of them held a total of 15 organizations, and the city of Fano was home to eight additional groups. Benefits provided by the groups included loans plus aid to families of deceased members, the elderly, the injured and unemployed, widows and orphans, women with infants, and members' school children. Membership bases for the groups were church dioceses, veterans organizations, and various occupation groups, including sailors, bricklayers, and gardeners. With a population of 12,000 in 1911, Ceccano was one of the larger towns sending immigrants to Lackawanna and apparently was home to many craftsmen. Two of the three organizations there in 1885 had a combined membership of 62 artisans.[56]

Several factors worked against the functioning of mutual-aid societies, as illustrated by events in Calabria. Before the outbreak of World War I, the city of Cosenza was home base for a Catholic league that attempted to set up rural banks for the *contadini* and to get better agricultural contracts for them in the Rende area. "This effort," writes historian Franc Sturino, "was strongly opposed by the local landlords, who, supported by the state police, reportedly put an end to the organizing campaign within a few months." *Carabinieri*, federal police, broke up a meeting of peasants and arrested the leaders. Sturino notes, "Such state action, along with the use of intimidation by the landlords, was a major factor in the failure of the league. The less than enthusiastic response of the peasants themselves to the organizing campaign of the agricultural union also retarded the prospects for success." The mass emigration from southern Italy also caused the number of societies to dwindle. An Italian government survey in 1912 listed only 54 mutual-aid groups in 42 of the towns from which the Lackawanna immigrants came. This may explain why the immigrants

FIGURE 1.8

Patron Saints of Specific Towns

Giuliano di Roma	San Biagio
Castro dei Volsci	Santa Oliva
Pofi	Santa Maria
Sora	San Rocco
Pettorano sul Gizio	San Benigno and Santa Margherita
San Pio delle Camere	San Pio
Cocullo, Casale	San Domenico
Quadrelle	San Giovanni Battista
Marano Principato	Annunziata

Sources: Interviews with Augusta Lampazzi-Anticoli, December 26, 1995; Lucy Caracci-Cullins, March 22, 1989; Guy Iannarelli, April 7, 1994; Adeline Covelli-Andreozzi, August 23, 1970; Flora Paolini-Olivieri, July 13, 1994; Giustino DeSantis, July 9, 1985; Phil Fanone, November 28, 2008. Tony Grasso, "The Saint Feast Day," 1983, p. 1.

interviewed for this study—all of whom were born after 1900, and many of whom had emigrated as children—remembered only a handful of organizations. Limited experience with organizational life, distrust of formal institutions, fear of government in general, and tremendous emphasis on family all hampered the efforts of peasants to organize and maintain societies in both Italy and Lackawanna. However, many immigrants did have some knowledge about associations in their hometowns, if only that they existed and had goals of mutual benefit.[57]

Rev. Dante Gemmiti leading a procession in honor of Madonna di Canneto, 1968. A native of Sora, Lazio, he visited relatives in Lackawanna in that same year.
Photo source: Phil Fanone

Chapel in Pedace, Calabria. Many small towns have a chapel in addition to the main church.
Photo source: Mary Leonetti

FIGURE 1-9

A MIRACLE IN GIULIANO DI ROMA

As a youngster growing up in Giuliano, Armando Torella heard the story of the founding of the church of the Madonna della Speranza (Our Lady of Hope). In 1500, an artist created a fresco shrine to the Madonna. Two hundred and fifty years later, a woman paused during her work in the fields to pray at the shrine. She heard a very gentle voice say, "Go to the priest and tell him that I wish to be visited here." The woman did so, but the priest doubted her story and did not go to the shrine. The next day, the voice repeated the original message to the woman, adding, "Remind Pietro Antonio Bonelli of the promise he made to the Madonna." Hearing this, the priest spoke to Bonelli, who confirmed that he had made a secret vow to build a chapel in honor of the Madonna, who had rescued him from a man intent on killing him. With the vow made public, work began on the chapel, which was completed in seven years. In later years, a statue and arch were erected at this site.

Source: Interview with Armando Torella, December 23, 1986.

An agricultural cooperative organized on the outskirts of Fano following World War I focused on purchasing tools, seeds, and other basic items for its members. Alfredo Campanelli recalls that the members and officers were all farmers and farm laborers. Fano was also home to separate church societies for young men and young women. In many towns, a men's group sponsored the *festa* honoring the town's patron saint. Luigi Violanti was in the Holy Name Society at the Santa Maria Maggiore church in Giuliano. A fellow townsman, Armando Torella, recalls a religious group known as *Compagnie di Morte*, whose members dressed in black and marched in religious processions, sometimes singing. During the 1920s and 1930s, there was only one society in Bagnoli Irpino, a church fraternity for the Immaculate Conception. There were a number of organizations in Pofi, mostly religious societies, none of which offered sickness or death benefits. Giustino DeSantis joined the Madonna del Carmine Society in Ceprano, a religious organization that charged dues equivalent to one dollar per month, a hefty sum in those days. After attending mass, the society's members joined the priest for *biscotti* (cookies) and liqueur. Membership in this "expensive" club was a clear indicator that DeSantis and his family were doing well in the carting business. The Garibaldini Society, which existed in Giuliano prior to World War I, prepared young men for the armed services by teaching them how to use firearms. This type of group was replaced during the reign of Mussolini by Fascist youth groups, which are described below.[58]

FIGURE 1.10

Religious Festivals Held in Southern Italian Towns in the Early Twentieth Century

LAZIO

Giuliano	San Biagio, L'Assunta (the Assumption), San Rocco, Madonna della Speranza, San Giuseppe, San Antonio, Sacro Cuore (the Sacred Heart)
Pofi	Santa Maria, Sant'Antonio, San Rocco, San Pietro.
Falvaterra	Sant'Antonio Abate, San Paolo delle Croce, Corpus Domani, San Rocco, Madonna L'Assunta, San Sosio
Sora	San Rocco

ABRUZZO

Pettorano	Corpus Domini, Sant' Antonio, San Sebastiano, San Benigno, San Margherita

CAMPANIA

Bagnoli Irpino	San Domenico, San Giuseppe, Immaculate Conception, All Saints, San Lorenzo, San Rocco

CALABRIA

Marano Principato	Annunziata, Madonna Del Carmine
Petrona	Santa Lucia, Madonna D'Ancona

Sources: Interviews with Armando Torella, December 23, 1986; Giustino DeSantis, July 9, 1985; Alberto Andreozzi, September 7, 1980; Guy Iannarelli, April 7, 1994; Mario Infante, July 7, 1995; Adeline Covelli-Andreozzi, August 23, 1970; Michelina Colosimo-Bevilacqua, October 17, 1996.

Several immigrants from Giuliano tell of a tragedy involving the Financial Bank of Rome, which had a branch in the Catholic Workers Bank in Giuliano. According to Ezio Millanti, the Vatican secretly owned the bank, which folded in 1929. The bank, Romolo Petricca reports, was founded by priests who defrauded the peasants of their savings by declaring bankruptcy. "The priest and some others ran off with the money," said Ennio Guglielmi. The money that his father Alessandro had regularly sent to this bank from Lackawanna was gone. "My father lost 54,000 lire; my mother had to write and tell him this," recalls Guglielmi.[59]

Education: The quality of education in southern Italy, even after the Risorgimento, was poor and contributed to a very high rate of illiteracy. There were relatively few schools in the Mezzogiorno; the central government provided limited funds for secondary education, and elementary education was placed under the control of local officials. The schools that did exist were often inadequate and a long walk for children living in rural hamlets. To make things even more difficult, many rich landowners were against education for the peasants. They believed that ignorant farmers were more submissive, and municipal officials usually reflected this attitude. A Calabrian mayor stated, "The illiterate contadini are docile, the truly dangerous individuals are the semi-literate who believe themselves to be something extraordinary because they can read and write." Educators were unable or unwilling to enforce compulsory attendance laws, which called for children to be in school until age nine, and, after 1904, to age twelve. In addition, southern peasants often kept their children out of school. They needed the youngsters to help them with the crops, especially at planting time. The school year was based on the climate of northern Italy, where spring came as much as one month later than in the south. Lastly, the *contadino* saw schooling as valuable only if it "provided the means to better one's economic condition, or for breaking through the caste system," and he knew there was little chance of his son becoming a professional. For the peasant, education meant teaching children cultural and moral values, something that was done by the family elders via folklore.[60]

It was not until the Mussolini era that education was more adequately financed by the central government and took on a strong political dimension. In 1929, the Lateran Treaty ended the struggle between the central government and the Church, and the late 1920s marked the beginning of a more rigorous enforcement of compulsory attendance laws. In Morolo, Iole Schiavi, who was named for a teacher her father had admired when he was a student, went to kindergarten and nursery school, where girls wore black smocks and boys dressed in black uniforms. At the public school, teachers often spoke in praise of Mussolini. Later, Iole was taught by nuns at a Catholic school, where every night in May and October, the students said the rosary in honor of the Madonna.[61]

Settefrati had a one-room schoolhouse, which Antonio Ventre eagerly attended. He was more into studying than his younger brother, Tomasso (called Tom in Lackawanna), who recalled, "I usually played hooky from school. I looked for bird nests and observed birds hatching and flying." Alfredo Campanelli went to a one-room public school just outside of Fano. Children went to one of the school's three shifts, each lasting two hours, with the first beginning at 8:00 a.m.

Campanelli started school at age seven and completed grades one through three. His school career ended when he fought with a teacher and refused to return to classes. Flora Paolini completed third grade at the school in San Pio delle Camere; most of her brothers attained a fourth-grade education there. One of them, Luca, was fortunate enough to attend electrical school in Aquila for a period—a feat made possible by the money his father earned in America.[62]

Giovanna Nappi of Quadrelle was illiterate and knew well the frustrations and indignities of being unable to read or write. Determined that her grandson, Tony Grasso, would attend public school, she was convinced that learning the alphabet prior to that time would be a great help to him. She promptly enrolled her grandson in a summer class taught by a priest in

FIGURE 1.11

THE PILGRIMAGE TO MONTEVERGINE

Every September, residents of Quadrelle and other towns in Campania went on a pilgrimage to nearby Montevergine to honor the Madonna of that name. As a young boy, Antonio Grasso once accompanied his grandfather and other men to this shrine, which stands near the summit of the mountain, 4,800 feet above sea level. As the group walked along, they encountered other pilgrims, including a large group from Mugnano that was singing religious hymns in praise of the Madonna of Montevergine. During the long climb up the mountain, they passed monks in white robes who staffed four aid stations for pilgrims with swollen feet or twisted ankles. Arriving at the Sanctuary of the Blessed Mother of Montevergine, the party descended into the area in front of the Abbey. "The square in front of the church, [which] was cut out from the side of the mountain, was called *Piazzale dei Tigli* [Lime Tree Square]. It was dotted by booths selling a large variety of food and sweets, except meat. The whole plaza was filled with the faithful from Calabria, Abruzzo, and other regions of Italy, but the majority were from Naples and the towns of Campania."

At 11:30 a.m. the pilgrims gathered at the foot of a huge staircase that circled up to the sanctuary. Some of the more devout pilgrims climbed the stairs on their knees, pausing to pray on each step, "their prayers directed skyward to the Blessed Mother to intercede on behalf of a sick child left back home, or anyone in the family who needed divine help." A High Mass was offered at noon.

Source: Tony Grasso. "Impressions of a Young Pilgrim," unpublished, 1982, pp. 4-5.

nearby Sirignano. The classroom was on the ground floor of a large building that faced the town square. "On one wall," Tony recalled, "was a shabby blackboard that had a chunk broken off one corner. The man was about 40 years old, of medium height, [with] a long ascetic face; stamped on it were years of hardship and self denial." The priest specialized in both pulling ears and pinching boys who misbehaved, as Tony learned when he dozed off one sleepy summer day. However, he faithfully attended all two months of the summer tutoring classes so as not to disappoint his grandmother. And the basic knowledge he gained helped him in elementary school.[63]

In the Cosenza district of Calabria, 85% of the inhabitants age six or older were illiterate in 1881. Literacy increased so that by 1911, the illiteracy rate fell to 55% of school-age males and 74% of females. Marano Principato, located in this district, had its school in a basement for a period of time, but ran two small schools during the 1920s. Grades one, two, and three were taught by Donna ("Lady") Richetta in a room at the home of Serafino Savaglio, a well-off townsperson. Children usually started school at age five or six. Fourth grade and up were taught by Professor Cribari in one room on the other end of town. Students in grades one through three had a four-hour school day, divided into two shifts: 8:00 a.m. to noon and 1:00 to 5:00 p.m. Donna Richetta's pupils sat on open-back benches and automatically stood when she approached the building. The teacher's three children also attended her class. Adelina Covelli recalls that Donna Richetta used a stick or her bare hand to administer corporal punishment. The curriculum included reading, writing, arithmetic, and drawing. An official weekly newspaper was utilized to teach the Calabrese children to read and speak proper Italian.[64]

Leopoldo Covelli, Adelina's elder brother, attended the school taught by Professor Cribari. The Italian government sought to ensure that at least one child in each family could read and write—especially the boys, who at age 18 were required to enter the military for an 18-month stint. The only young men exempted from military service were sons of widows or sole male offspring, who were needed to help the family maintain its farm. The Mussolini government broke a long-standing tradition by demanding that girls, too, be sent to public school. Some southern Italian peasants displeased with the new mandate, reasoned that "girls weren't going into the army, so why send them to school?"[65]

Concert band in Pedace, circa 1920. Armando Leonetti is in the first row of seated boys, second from the right. The band won a gold medal.
Photo source: Mary Leonetti

The members of this Italian Army band included Vincenzo Ferrelli (circled) in the top row, who immigrated to Lackawanna in 1922.
Photo source: Collection of Josephine Ferrelli

Vocational schooling was usually accomplished via an informal apprenticeship system. Concezio Novelli attended elementary school and added to his knowledge by reading the newspapers posted in Pettorano's town square. After completing the fifth grade, he began, at age 11, to learn a trade. Novelli worked with an artisan who painted flowers or the likeness of marble on walls and ceilings. After mixing paints for this artist for sometime, Novelli wondered about his wages. "The man didn't pay me. When I asked him about it he said my 'pay' was learning the trade." However, it was soon evident that Novelli had artistic talent, and people approached him to paint designs on plates and other objects.[66]

During the 1910s, Giuseppe Violanti wasn't able to go to school because he had to help his siblings with farm chores. But as a teenager who realized the importance of being literate, he paid a lady in Giuliano 40 cents a month for daily instruction in reading and writing. He did this over the course of two winters when the demands of family farming were less intense. Simply by being literate, Violanti achieved a higher level of education than many of his *paesani*.[67]

Recreation: In Italian villages recreation was simple and often tied in with farm work or religious festivals. Entertainment was sometimes part of the work rituals of Italian peasants and included people of all ages. At a fall festival in Settefrati, corn was piled up and husked by farmers. "They would sing songs, have food and drink—the kids loved this," recalls Tom Ventre. "At night, they built a fire. There was a sense of community among the 12 adults and eight kids. Each night, they worked on one family's produce."[68]

Adult recreation took place at the *feste*, at family activities, and when chatting with neighbors. Most towns had a small *cantina* where men drank wine, played cards, and conversed. Men also played *morra,* and some cantinas even featured bocce courts. Not only did Serafino Savaglio, the well-to-do resident of Marano Principato, rent out a room for school in his house, he also ran a *cantina* there. On Sundays, men gathered to relax, and some got drunk and engaged in fistfights, and there was the occasional urination on nearby rose bushes. Despite being the scene of such rowdy behavior, the Savaglio home had the distinction of being the only one in Marano Principato with an indoor toilet.[69]

Between attending school and doing farm chores, children managed to have some fun. Ennio Guglielmi, born in 1920, played soccer and bocce, as well as a game called a *massetta,* as a boy in Giuliano. This game, called "nip" by boys in Lackawanna, involved hitting a small stick that was pointed at both ends with another stick. One team of boys would try to hit the stick farther than the other team. Tony Grasso and his friends in Quadrelle pitched buttons—they didn't have

marbles—and played bocce on a long section of concrete that straddled the narrow river running through town. When the boys wanted more excitement, they slid down the embankment to the creek bed and divided into two groups of five or six each. One team went under the bridge into the darkness, and the other remained out in the open. With about 25 feet separating them, the two teams hurled stones at each other. Obviously, the boys under the bridge could hide in the darkness, while those out in the sunlight scurried for cover. In the spring, Grasso and his buddies sneaked into garden plots and raided the cherry trees.[70]

Grasso remembers only one snowfall during the 10 years he lived in Quadrelle. On that occasion, several inches covered the ground. He and a few friends frolicked in the snow-covered creek bed, throwing snowballs as they moved along. On the rare occasion of hail in Marano Principato, the four Covelli children gathered a bucket of snow, topped it with honey or jam, and feasted on this "delicious treat."[7]

Events Affecting Emigration from Italy

A series of major events were significant in the lives of Italians during the first five decades of the twentieth century. These, in conjunction with conditions in the United States and other receiving countries, influenced the stream of emigrants leaving Italy. Poverty was a constant that pushed Italians to leave their homeland throughout the period from 1880 to 1960. Crop failures and tariff battles between countries often had a devastating effect on southern Italian peasants. Immigrants in Lackawanna described natural disasters, the reign of Mussolini, and two world wars as events that shaped their lives and influenced both their departure from and return to Italy.[72]

Earthquakes

Italy has long been vulnerable to floods, volcanos, and, especially, earthquakes. In Calabria, for example, major earthquakes occurred in 1638, 1854, 1870, 1894, 1905, 1907, and 1908. These natural disasters were one factor in causing emigration. One of Gelsomina Caira's most vivid memories occurred when she was four years old in her hometown of Marano Principato. In the middle of the night on September 8, 1905, an earthquake shook the region. Gelsomina awoke to the terrifying sight of a corner of the house opening up and then closing. "Everyone was scared, and we slept outside on haystacks for a couple of days." The earthquake leveled about a third of the homes in Marano Principato, but fortunately, only two people were killed. The government constructed small wooden sheds to temporarily house the homeless victims of the disaster.[73]

When an earthquake struck near the town of Bagnoli Irpino during the 1920s, Domenica Infante quickly got her children out of the house. "We slept outside in a straw hut for two nights," recalls her son Mario. A devastating earthquake struck Abruzzo in 1915. In the hamlet of Casale, 12-year-old Concetta Marinelli was buried in the wreckage of her family's house. It took rescuers four hours to find her. As done during earlier earthquakes, government workers constructed large wooden barracks to house the victims. The spartan quarters had no water, heating units, or fireplaces. Concetta remembers them as being very cold. The "temporary" housing turned out to be long term; all nine members of the Marinelli family remained there for nine years. One effect of the earthquakes was an outpouring of money sent to stricken towns by *paesani* in the United States and other countries. Some immigrants quickly returned to their hometowns where earthquakes had occurred. Cesidio Ferrelli, had been a railroad laborer in Montana for two years when he read of the earthquake that had struck Abruzzo in 1915; he soon returned to his hometown of Pettorano.[74]

Wars, 1880–1918

Wars and compulsory military service were a part of life for all young men. Italy launched several ill-fated invasions of eastern Africa in the 1880s and 1890s. Victorious in their invasion of Libya in 1911, the Italians fought for the next 30 years in an attempt to suppress Arab revolts. Many Lackawanna immigrants spoke of how the First World War intruded harshly in their lives in May 1915, when Italy entered the struggle as an ally of England, France, and Russia. In Lazio, Giustino DeSantis and his older brother Paolo were drafted into the military. Giustino saw combat in the mountains near Bassano, in northeast Italy, and was wounded by artillery fire. Paolo was killed in action. Costantino Novelli served in the Italian Army, as did his brother, who met his death in the conflict. Michele Petrucci served in the military, was taken prisoner, held in Austria, and did not return home until 1920. For many peasants, a leading factor in the decision to emigrate was that of sparing the young men in the family mandatory military service.[75]

All Italian citizens abroad were called upon to serve the motherland in World War I, and thousands living in the United States did so. Among them was Luigi Scarsella, who departed the shoe shop he and his brother had established in New Jersey. He served in a medical unit, often pulling teeth as he had done as a shoemaker. Filiberto Covelli made one of his return trips from the United States to Italy in 1914 and was drafted into the Italian Army. He served on the Trieste front, in northeast Italy, as a mule driver—hauling supplies and performing such tasks as shoeing the animals. He rode on one of the mules in

a supply column and complained that the heavy metal helmet he wore caused his neck to ache. Some northern Italians mocked and tormented the southern Italian soldiers, who in turn heckled the northerners. When Covelli first arrived in northern Italy, a woman noticed that he didn't brush his teeth and recommended, against all common sense, that he try cleaning his teeth with bits of coal dust. He did so, and his gums bled for many days. In the cold, wet trenches, he contracted pyorrhea and eventually lost all his teeth.[76]

During his two years as a combat soldier in the frontline trenches, Domenico Vittorini witnessed the horrors of war. His unit was on a monthly rotation: 30 days in the trenches, then 30 days in a rear area. Having survived a poison—gas attack, he and his comrades were crossing a field littered with the dead and dying when they witnessed the grotesque sight of gas emitting from the mouths of corpses turned over by medics. Gaetano Paolini also witnessed scenes of death and destruction that severely affected him. He told his daughter Flora, that after the war, the Italian government feared unemployed veterans might rebel. The Italian authorities convinced the British government to help pay the passage of veterans who desired to emigrate. Paolini was among the men who took advantage of this deal and received a free ticket to the United States.[77]

Celestino Nigro served in the Italian Army prior to leaving Accadia, Puglia, in 1905 for Lackawanna.
Photo source: Collection of Nick Vertalino

The Fascist Regime of Mussolini

Italians endured the Fascist regime of Benito Mussolini from 1922 until 1943, during which *Il Duce* took the country into the invasion of Ethiopia in 1935-36 and then into World War II. The strident nationalism and military buildup of the Fascists led to laws restricting emigration from Italy and an expanded call for young people to serve the regime. The government organized youngsters into militaristic groups. Small children, ages six through eight, were part of the Balilla, teens aged 14 to 16 were members of the Avonguardista, and those in their late teens were part of the Giovane Fascista. In Giuliano, Ennio Guglielmi and all other youth had to join these groups, which were organized through the schools. Special meetings were held on Saturdays, when the children had rifle drills and marching practice. As a member of the Avonguardista, Ezio Millanti remembers having to attend youth rallies. "If you didn't join, the teachers and other officials would make fun of you," he states. In Settefrati, Antonio and Tomasso Ventre joined the other students in singing *Facetta Nera* ("Little Blackface"), a nationalistic song praising the formation of Italian colonies in Africa.[78]

Finding the Fascist regime oppressive, Italians returning to Italy from Lackawanna curtailed their visits or plans to permanently remain in their hometowns. Giuseppe Violanti emigrated from Giuliano in 1919 and returned there seven years later. He married Vincenzina Maturani, and the new couple lived with her family for four months. Violanti worked in his father-in-law's cantina and had "a good time" doing so. He did, however, notice some new developments that were disturbing: "In 1926, there were the Fascists; I didn't like them. They spied on people, wanted to know what people were talking about." However, he also noted that "a lot of people liked the Fascists because they created jobs for other Blackshirts." Violanti was happy to return to Lackawanna, and his wife joined him the following year.[79]

On one of his return trips to Ceccano in the mid-1920s, Luigi Scarsella was approached by Fascists who pressured him to join their ranks. Scarsella refused with some trepidation, but the Blackshirts did not retaliate. In Fano, the Fascists disbanded church societies organized for young men and women. According to Alfredo Campanelli, the carabinieri seized the flags and other possessions of the societies. When Lavinio Montanari, an outspoken anti-Fascist, returned to Fano for a visit, he was detained by the authorities. In Pettorano, Franco Tortis had a confrontation with several members of the Fascist party who were removing stones from his wall. "He warned them to stop, they said 'No,' and he threw a hatchet at them," recalls Concezio Novelli, Tortis's nephew. Tortis was arrested and taken to the jail in Sulmona. His wife Ascenza

Ermengildo Vincenzo Rosati of Lenola, Lazio, served in the Italian Army from 1911 to 1912, when Italy fought Turkey for control of Libya. He had traveled to the U.S. earlier, and in 1914 again left to settle in Lackawanna.
Photo source: Collection of Fred Rosati

and Novelli, unaware of this, went to the Pettorano jail and were saddened not to find Tortis there. But he was soon released from Sulmona and made his way home.[80]

The Fascist regime caused much harm and little good for Italian peasants. It perhaps helped southern Italian farmers by continuing the earlier work of draining swamps, and it did stress education and literacy. But its 21-year reign had vast negative consequences, as outlined by sociologist Joseph Lopreato. The Mussolini government urged peasants to focus solely on cultivating wheat, which does not grow well in southern Italy. The Fascists, who typically represented the interests of landowners, "hastened to wreck the various peasant organizations and to undo the concessions that had been granted the peasantry in the wake of World War I." The strict limits the regime placed on both emigration overseas and migration within Italy cut off one of the principle means of employment for many southerners.[81]

The poverty of many Italians was made worse by the Great Depression of the 1930s. Antonio Millanti discovered this when he returned to Giuliano di Roma from America in 1931. After buying three acres of land he soon learned that a full year of farming in Italy would bring money equal to what he could earn in only two months in the United States. He then returned to Lackawanna. But most peasants were not so fortunate. The increasing poverty in southern Italy caused thousands of them to move to the large cities.[82]

Figure 1.12

THREE FAMILIES WHO MADE REPEATED TRIPS TO AND FROM ITALY

Scarsellas

It was common for lone Italian men to go back and forth between various towns in America and their hometowns in Italy, and some family units followed a similar pattern. An actor and shoemaker by trade, Luigi Scarsella was a native of Ceccano, Lazio. He and his brother Pietro migrated to the American resort town of Newton, New Jersey, in about 1907 and established a shoe shop. Luigi soon returned to Ceccano, married Colomba Maria Germani, and resumed his shoe trade there while Pietro tended to their shop in America. In 1911, following the birth of two children, the Scarsellas moved to Newton, where Luigi rejoined Pietro in their shoe business. A year later, after Colomba gave birth to their third child, she told her husband she did not like being separated from her large extended family in Ceccano. So the Scarsellas traveled back to Italy, where two more children were born. Luigi returned alone to the United States in 1914, this time venturing to Germantown, Pennsylvania, where *paesani* lined him up with work in a steel mill. When Italy entered World War I the following year, he responded to the call to arms. Serving as a medic in a hospital kept him away from the front lines and enabled him to regularly visit his family in Ceccano. Between 1916 and 1919, Colomba gave birth to four more children, three of whom died as infants.

Luigi sailed from Naples in 1919, returning to Newton to work as a shoemaker. He visited Ceccano in 1924 after learning that his 11-year-old daughter Giulia had died. Luigi was then contacted by *paesani* in south Buffalo who told him of job openings in the steel plant. When he departed Ceccano, he took along 14-year-old Ugo, and the father and son lodged with the Tiberio family in the Italian district off Germania Street. Soon they moved in with the Christiano family in Lackawanna's Bethlehem Park to be closer to the steel plant. In 1928, Luigi journeyed to Ceccano, made arrangements for 16-year-old Remo to emigrate, and quickly returned to the United States. Remo emigrated a few months later and, like Ugo before him, immediately went to work in the steel plant. Luigi took his last return trip to Italy the next year, following the birth of his daughter Marianna. He made all the arrangements for Colomba and the four remaining children to immigrate to the United States. Upon his return to Lackawanna, Luigi rented a large apartment on Lehigh Avenue. When Colomba and the four children—Odile, Vincenzo, Umberta, and Marianna—arrived in New York City in October, Luigi met them and accompanied them on the train to Lackawanna. After 22 years of journeying between the two countries, and among four different towns within the United States, the Scarsella family was finally united in its permanent home.

Infantes

Three generations of a family from Bagnoli Irpino, Campania, moved back and forth between Italy and America, alternating between farming and working in steel mills. Antonio and Rosaria Infante left Italy in about 1889, immigrating to Niles, an industrial town in northeast Ohio. Rosaria gave birth to Domenico in 1890 and Aniello in 1892. When she passed away, Antonio returned to Italy with the two boys. In Bagnoli Irpino, Antonio remarried and returned to his original occupation, farming. His family again ventured to Niles, then to nearby Farrell, Pennsylvania, where Antonio worked in the steel mills. The family grew to include five more children, whom Antonio took back to Italy for periodic stays. After a while, the older boys, Domenico and Aniello, joined their father in the mills and formed their own families. Their sister Maddalena married a *paesano*, Lorenzo Basile.

Antonio eventually grew weary of work in the steel mills. Having witnessed many men being injured on the job, he feared his sons would suffer that fate. He decided it was time to move to a small town and take up farming, a much safer occupation. With his wife and four young sons, Antonio moved to Keyport, New Jersey, and started truck farming. Meanwhile, Aniello and his wife, Domenica, endured tragic circumstances of their own in Ohio. Their first child died of whooping cough, and the second, Antonio, born in 1918, contracted polio. A doctor told Aniello and Domenica that their son "needed the ocean and sand on the coast of Italy" to overcome the disease. The family returned to Bagnoli Irpino, where Aniello purchased land and began farming. Domenica gave birth to Mario in 1921 and Maria the following year. Aniello soon became bored with rural life in Italy and longed to return to the United States.

Around this time, he heard from his sister Maddalena, who had moved to Lackawanna with her husband and her father-in-law, Giuseppe Basile. In 1922, Aniello traveled alone to Lackawanna to join the Basiles and was soon working alongside them, and other *paesani*, at the Rogers Brown sintering plant. He made several return trips to Italy, including one that led to the birth of a daughter, Concetta, in 1926. Three years later, he traveled back to Bagnoli Irpino, this time remaining for seven years, farming his land and fathering another son. In 1936, Aniello made his final voyage to the United States. Upon arriving in Lackawanna, he went to work in the scrapyard of No. 2 Open Hearth at Bethlehem Steel. Two years later, he sent for 17-year-old Mario, who soon would be subject to conscription into the Italian Army. After sailing from Naples with friends, Mario was met in New York City by an uncle who drove him to Keyport. He went to school and worked on the farm established by his grandfather, as there were no jobs available in Lackawanna. When his father finally sent for him, Mario went to work as a laborer in the Yard Department. Eventually, Aniello's wife and other children joined them in Lackawanna.

Corvignos

Another family from Campania who returned to Italy from Lackawanna saw several of its members eventually go back to the Steel City. Alberto and Luisella Corvigno, natives of Capriglia Irpino, arrived in the Steel City around 1905. Following the births of three children in Lackawanna, the Corvigno family returned to Italy where Alberto resumed farming. In 1923, one of the children, Carmine, returned to Lackawanna at age 17 to live with his godmother, Adele Panzetta. He married Anna Melillo and settled permanently in the city. Back in Italy, his sister and brother-in-law, Nunzia and Orlando D'Alessandro, sought to improve the family's situation through higher education. In 1952, they sent their oldest son, Alberto, to study at a seminary, but he did not care to return after the first year. Orlando had told his son, "I don't want you to farm." A relative visiting from New Jersey provided another option, telling Alberto, "You can come to America." This idea appealed to everyone, and the decision was made that the parents and all five children would emigrate to the town where Nunzia was born. In 1953, Nunzia and two of her sons, Carmine and Vincenzo, migrated to Lackawanna, followed the next year by Orlando, Alberto, Addolorata, and Carmellina. When she received word that her mother, Luisella, wanted to join them in Lackawanna, Nunzia sent money for the steamship ticket. Tragically, Luisella died a week before her planned departure.

Sources: Interviews with Anne Scarsella-Antes, December 26, 1995; Mario Infante, July 7, 1995; and Alfredo D'Alessandro, July 10, 1995.

Sam Cardinale in the uniform of the Balilla *youth group founded by the Fascist regime of Benito Mussolini. The boy and his mother and siblings returned to Italy for three years during the Depression.*
Photo source: Collection of Sam Cardinale

A cooperative store in Giuliano was available for groceries during this period, but many people simply did not have the money for purchases. Gardens then proved to be crucial. "My family had a farm," states Ennio Guglielmi, who emigrated from Italy after World War II. "We would always have food to eat." Lavinio Montanari returned to Fano in 1930, almost two decades after he had migrated to Lackawanna. His plan was to stay for three months, set up a home near that of his parents in Italy, then return to the United States and accompany his wife and two children back to Fano. After one month, however, he had a change of heart and set sail for America. The poor conditions in Italy, and factors such as lack of central air and hot water in the homes, as well as the Fascist regime's shabby treatment of the Italian people, made Bethlehem Park in Lackawanna look pretty good by comparison. "My mother and us kids," recalls Dewey Montanari, "were relieved when my father changed his mind." The American and Italian governments limited emigration to the United States between the early 1920s and late 1930s. With the outbreak of World War II in 1939, emigration was virtually impossible.[83]

World War II

Most of the emigrants from Italy to the United States left prior to 1925 and experienced the Second World War from an American perspective. However, there was a significant emigration from Italy following the war, and these migrants had a personal knowledge of the fighting in Europe. Italy entered the war as an ally of Germany in 1940, and when their Axis partner, Japan, attacked Pearl Harbor the following year, both Italy and Germany also declared war on the United States. Southern Italy was a battleground from the time of the Allied landings in Sicily (July 1943) until the liberation of Rome (June 1944). The war then raged in northern Italy until the conflict in Europe finally ended in May 1945. Post – World War II immigrants to Lackawanna have many recollections of those tragic and dangerous war years.

Ennio Guglielmi, a native of Giuliano, was drafted into the Italian Army in April 1940. He spent time repairing railroads in northwestern Italy, saw combat in France, and was later sent to the Soviet Union, where 200,000 Italian troops fought alongside the Germans. Guglielmi was there from 1941 to 1943, much of that time in Ukraine, where he repaired railroads, built bridges, and saw lots of combat. After Italy surrendered to the Allies in September 1943, German troops occupied most of the country. Guglielmi made his way back to Giuliano, but when German soldiers started abducting men for forced labor, he and some companions fled into the mountains. They returned in the spring of 1944 following the liberation of Giuliano by American and Free French troops.[84]

During World War II, teenager Egino DeSantis worked in a munitions factory 10 miles from Giuliano. Along with his mother Maria and sister Palmira, he tended a small garden, and the family used money sent by his father and uncles in America to ensure their survival. His older brother Lelio was drafted into the Italian Army and stationed near Trieste in northeast Italy. Giuliano was bombed several times by the Allies; one bomb knocked down the steeple of Madonna L'Esperanza Church, killing four people. The DeSantis family lived with relatives outside Giuliano to be safe from bombing raids. As the Allied armies approached in 1944, the Germans fled. "As they left, they looted," recalls Lelio DeSantis. "Then the Allied soldiers looted!" Egino described the arrival of the Allied troops and the actions his family took: "The Moroccans came through the outskirts of town and raped women. We spent two nights in a cave, and then the women hid in the attic. The Americans then escorted them into town."[85]

The war directly touched the lives of the people in Pico, which was in the path of the Allied advance. Santino Carnevale remembers this period as a time of "big lice, poverty, and no food." Carnevale and his sister lived with their grandmother, Maria Colello. Four or five German soldiers were also quartered in her home. "They were friendly, except for the SS division," Carnevale recalls. "But the Moroccans were feared." Moroccans and Algerians, whose countries were French colonies at the time, composed a large segment of the Free French divisions and were led by the French. "They did lots of raping," said Carnevale. "Italians complained to the officers; the presence of officers prevented my aunts from being raped." As naive 12-year-olds, Carnevale and a friend approached a Moroccan guard at a storehouse and begged for chocolate. "The soldier said 'Take me to your sister first.' So I did," Carnevale continues, "but she wasn't home, and I got no chocolate."

The Italians in Pico scattered throughout the countryside to escape the fighting and then the degradations inflicted by the Moroccan soldiers. Many homes were damaged, and the Colello house was used as a first-aid station. When the displaced residents returned to Pico, they found devastation. "Houses were looted, everything was broke up, the trees were shot up," recalls Carnevale. By the summer of 1944, the war had passed through and the front was north of Rome, much to the relief of those living in Latina and Frosinone provinces. Records show that Moroccan and Algerian soldiers of the Free French divisions were accused of raping 50 females in Lenola and 75 in Ceccano. In Frosinone province alone, there were reports of 700 such incidents. A total of 5,000 alleged rapes, murders, and other crimes were recorded by Italian authorities. Vengeful Italians killed several of the offending soldiers, and the French responded by executing 15 North African soldiers and sentencing 54 to prison terms. After the war, the women of Castro dei Volsci persuaded the men to erect a statue of La Mamma Ciociaria, which depicts the true-life story of a mother being shot while protecting her daughters from Moroccan soldiers.[86]

Castro dei Volsci is located between Pico and Giuliano. As a young man living in the town during World War II, Angelo DeGiuli learned of the dangers of war. Much of the hazard came from American aircraft that strafed and bombed anything and anyone that appeared to be German. DeGiuli watched as shrapnel from bombs dropped on fleeing Germans killed chickens, cows, and other livestock kept in open areas. In one incident, DeGiuli and a friend were riding horses. "We were on grey horses and must have looked like Germans. The American planes bombed and strafed, but we hid in some rocky coves and crags." Another encounter,

FIGURE 1.13
WORLD WAR II IN ITALY

September 23, 1943, Acerno. World War II devastated Italy. During the Allied landings at Salerno, the roof of this church was shattered by bombs. An American infantryman seems to stand in reverence before the altar.
Photo source: National Archives

The Allied advance up the Italian peninsula in 1943 and 1944 was hard on the Italian people, and the inhabitants of Pettorano sul Gizio were no exception. "The government demanded people's rings and animals," recalls Carmine DelMonaco. When Italy surrendered to the Allies in September of 1943, the Germans immediately sent soldiers to occupy areas in the line of advance of the Allied armies.

By October, German troops entered Pettorano and took over a number of homes to use as barracks, including those of two members of the DelMonaco family. The displaced family members went outside of town to live in the farmhouse of DelMonaco's grandmother.

On November 23, 1943, the Germans forced all Pettorano inhabitants to leave as the British front line advanced toward town. Some people who had money traveled to nearby cities to rent apartments, but most Pettoranesi fled into the hills and lived in caves or large huts. Gaetano Iannarelli's family and others lived in huts measuring 18 to 20 feet in diameter, with beds to accommodate six people. An indoor fireplace provided heat, and an outdoor, cone-shaped oven was used for cooking. The townspeople were allowed to move back home after two or three weeks, when it became apparent that the front would not near the town. Many families had their young women stay with relatives on rural farms, where they would be safe from molestation by German troops.

That winter, the Germans moved their tanks and trucks into Pettorano at night, dispersing them throughout the olive groves. Carmine DelMonaco observed as German soldiers took sheets and other white linen from the residents, along with branches from ancient olive trees, to camouflage their vehicles. "When we went to get back some of our possessions, they shot at us," recalls DelMonaco. After the Allied landings at Anzio in January of 1944, the SS (storm trooper) tank division moved off toward Rome. The SS troops had been very rough with the Italian civilians, but the regular infantry units were usually not harsh and fraternized with the Italians. Gaetano Iannarelli observed that the German commander disciplined soldiers who were drunk or bothered women.

There were, however, isolated tragic incidents and acts of brutality. Carmine DelMonaco states that the Germans gave rewards to Italians who informed on others, and killed the families of anyone who helped Allied soldiers. When Donato Suffoletta's wife was in the process of giving birth, a

(continued)

drunken German soldier came into the home and pointed his rifle at the relatives tending her. He gestured as if to shoot the people, sputtering "ta-ta-ta-ta-ta" to mimic the sound of his weapon firing. His pronouncement of the word "kaput" thoroughly frightened the family.

Giovanni D'Alessandro was in his early 60s in 1943, having defied a prediction that his asthma would take his life during the late 1920s. When the Germans took over many houses in Pettorano, causing the men to flee into the woods, D'Alessandro and a niece went to see what was going on. They encountered some German soldiers, who accused the girl of being a spy and told D'Alessandro to turn around. They then fired their rifles, leading him to conclude they had executed her. He later discovered they had shot into the air, but the effect was devastating to D'Alessandro, who suffered from nervous twitches for the remaining 20 years of his life.

German soldiers in Pettorano were constantly taking possession of farmers' livestock, causing the farmers to move their animals to outlying farms or into the hills under the cover of darkness. The German SS outfits also regularly abducted men and made them do forced labor. One night, Carmine DelMonaco and one of his relatives took family livestock out to their grandmother's house for safekeeping. They were warned by a cousin not to return to Pettorano, because the Germans were looking for laborers. DelMonaco, 16 years old at the time, decided to chance it and head for home. "I heard footsteps and thought it was Filippo. I called out his name, but it was a German. He pulled a pistol, put it to my head, and took me and a younger boy to another village. The German told the smaller kid, Pasqualino, to leave. I was trembling, wondering what would happen. In this village were 54

By early 1944 the Allies had advanced north from Salerno into southern Frosinone Province in Lazio. The town of Cassino and the abbey on the mountain overlooking it were destroyed in fierce fighting with Germans entrenched in the mountains. Photo source: National Archives

other men, including my brother-in-law." Worried that the Germans would discover their untended livestock, the men were crowded into a building with two German sentinels posted at the door. "One [guard] would escort men to the bathroom—with a rifle at their head," DelMonaco recalls. The building was so cramped that the men could not lie down to sleep. "Men cried and leaned against each other to sleep. At night, one guy escaped by going up the chimney, but the others were afraid because the Germans would shoot Italians for breaking any rules. That night, [in a rare gesture of kindness] the Germans brought two loaves of bread and a little marmalade [to their prisoners]"

The following morning, about 200 women in tears gathered outside as a German truck arrived for the Italian men. "The Germans brought two pails of coffee to the barracks; one guy was left to guard us. I decided that I had to run away or die. I jumped out the door and hugged my mother. I started to work through the

crowd, Ma said, "Don't, they'll shoot you.'" After he emerged from the group of women, DelMonaco "ran three kilometers to the foot of the mountain, then bounded up the mountain to the top. Up there, I found my brother-in-law's family in a shanty made of branches." DelMonaco sent a message to his mother to have the family's sheep sent up to him. After this was done, he remained on the mountain, tending the animals, from December 1943 through January 1944.

The Germans took the other men to the front lines to dig trenches and build ammunition bunkers. The Italian laborers were then forced to load ordnance into these bunkers. They were also made to carry food supplies over the mountains to German soldiers at the front. Some of the men ran off, causing the Germans to raid Pettorano and neighboring towns twice a week to obtain more laborers. DelMonaco remembers the men finally returning home after four months of backbreaking labor.

Gaetano Iannarelli, a teenager during the war, saw Germans take resident's livestock, confiscate food, and commandeer laborers, forcing them to shovel snow off railroad tracks. During late 1943 and early 1944, at a German garrison situated in Introdacqua, Ilio DiPaolo saw the Germans take livestock and food from the farmers. Even worse, they made men and teenagers such as DiPaolo carry supplies some 18 miles to Roccarazza, near the front lines. The men had to cross over mountains, walking through deep snow. They traveled at night to avoid being detected by American airplanes, especially at the bridge over the Gizio River at Pettorano.

Despite the challenges and hardships, the Italians organized various types of resistance to the German occupiers. In Sulmonia, near Pettorano, a camp held 20,000 American and English prisoners of war. When the Germans began moving into this area in late 1943 (after Italy had surrendered to the Allies), the Italian officials allowed all of the camp's prisoners to escape. The Pettoranesi resisted the Germans by hiding livestock, escaping from forced-labor crews, and assisting British paratroopers dropped into the area. Townspeople hid the men in the mountains, and families helped to feed them. When SS soldiers mined bridges and other structures, Italians removed the explosives—in particular, from a huge railroad bridge in town—as elderly women acted as lookouts. The Germans did succeed in blowing up several road bridges, however.

By the end of June 1944, the German Army had left Pettorano. Fortunately, these units had horses and wagons for

The Allies liberated Roma in June 1944, and in April 1945 were well into northern Italy. Here, men of the 370th Infantry Regiment move through Prato, Toscana. Between July 1943, when the Allies landed in Sicilia, and the end of the war in Europe in May 1945, Italy was a battleground, and the Italian people suffered terribly. Photo source: National Archives

transport, and did not need to abduct men for forced labor. Townspeople assumed that the American Army would then arrive, but after five days, the mayor asked for volunteers to travel the 17 kilometers to the American lines at Castel di Sangro to get desperately needed food. Carmine DelMonaco was one of 36 men and teens who made the journey with mules and horses, carefully walking around minefields. They encountered an American officer who spoke Italian and

offered to pay each man 500 lire to transport food to Pettorano and take three Americans and seven carabinieri to area towns. DelMonaco was one of 10 men who transported the latter group, making their way to Sulmona, Pettorano, and other towns in between. He watched proudly as the American flag was raised at each location.

Sources: Interviews with Carmine DelMonaco, December 26, 1994; Guy Iannarelli, April 7, 1994; Jimmy D'Alessandro, April 9, 1985; Ilio DiPaolo, December 29, 1994. Some of the Allied soldiers who escaped were taken in by Italian farmers, but, sadly, many others perished in the mountains during the extremely cold winter of 1943–1944.

this one involving a German soldier, could have been tragic. DeGiuli and a friend saw the German stealing chickens that belonged to the friend's family. The friend, outraged, threw a stone that hit the soldier's helmet. The German drew his pistol and fired at the two young Italians as they fled, but to no effect.[87]

Overall, World War II was a disaster for the Italian people. In the south, ground combat took place between July 1943 and June 1944; in the north, the Allied and German armies fought until May 1945. The Allied air forces attacked targets throughout the country for more than two years. By the end of the war, southern Italy was "in a state of total economic and political chaos." Once again, Italy could not offer southern peasants sufficient options for economic survival. So they began, again, to migrate overseas, continuing the mass emigration that had begun in the late 19th century.[88]

Americani, Money from Abroad, and Those Left Waiting

Throughout the period from 1880 to 1960, Italian families awaited the chance to be reunited with fathers, husbands, and other relatives in the United States. For some, the reunification came quickly, but for others, years and decades passed before remaining family members were able to cross the ocean to America. During the intervening time, wives, children, and other relatives depended on the money sent back to Italy from those abroad as well as the assistance of relatives who'd returned to live in Italy—called *Americani*—with their earnings from the United States. These two sources of assistance were crucial, especially for the women and children awaiting the chance to emigrate. The American earnings also allowed some families to improve their social and economic status in Italy.

Giovanni Lampazzi made several trips to America before permanently returning to Giuliano, as did many lone male immigrants. In 1916, when Lampazzi went to the newly drained Pontine Marshes to plant corn, he caught malaria and died, leaving his wife Maria a widow with five young children. One of the daughters, Augusta, remembers that relatives in America sent money, enabling the family to continue working the land. The children were in charge of feeding the horse, chickens, and pigs. Disaster struck again in 1922, when Maria passed away. An uncle, Arcangelo Lampazzi, who had recently returned from America, sent the youngest child to an orphanage in Naples and supervised the remaining four. "We stayed at home," recalls Augusta, "and went to aunts' and uncles' homes most of the day and for dinners." Five years later, Augusta married an older *Americano*, Alfredo Anticoli, and left Giuliano for Lackawanna.[89]

Cantalupo nel Sannio, Molise, circa 1925. Pasqualina Monaco with granddaughter Iolanda Monaco. In 1929, Iolanda and her mother Annamaria traveled to Lackawanna to join their father/husband Antonio.
Photo source: Yolanda Monaco-Bracci

When Giovanni Violanti returned to Giuliano from the United States for a visit in 1908, he gave his father, Luigi, enough money to buy the house the family had always rented, thus fulfilling a long-held family dream. Unfortunately, Giovanni was subsequently drafted into the Italian Army and served for the next two years. Adding to his predicament, the military paid only two cents a day compared to daily wages of $1 to $1.50 that Giovanni had earned at the Lackawanna Steel Company.[90]

For the Schiavi family in Morolo, money earned in America not only helped returned immigrants to better their situation in Italy, it also strengthened the established migration chain. Lorenzo Schiavi owned a small house in town and had a modest plot of land in the valley below. In total, he made 20 trips to the United States, the last several to Lackawanna, where some of his townspeople had settled earlier. He did railroad work near Hornell, New York, then opened a small grocery that catered to railroad workers. In 1922, Schiavi returned permanently to Italy, purchasing a house nestled on a hillside

The Covelli family in Marano Principato, Calabria, circa 1925. Filiberto, the family head, went back and forth between Italy and the U.S. starting in 1899. His photo (at right) was superimposed on one of his wife Rosina and their children: Gilda upper left, Adelina, lower left, Leopoldo, upper center, and Florindo (Gene), lower center. Photo source: Collection of Phillip and Adeline Andreozzi

For other families, the reunification process covered many years. In 1901, Antonio Carnevale immigrated to the United States around the time that his wife gave birth to Antonino in Pico. Twenty years later, Antonino followed his father to America, Going first to Pittsfield, Massachusetts, and then to Seattle, Washington, before arriving in Lackawanna in 1926. On one of his return trips, he married Ausilia Ruscetta, who gave birth to Ena in 1930 and Santino in 1932. When Ausilia died shortly after giving birth to her son, various women in Pico took turns wet-nursing the infant. Finally, her mother, Maria Colello, took in and raised both Santino and Ena. For the next 15 years, Antonio, who married his second wife in Lackawanna, sent money to support his mother-in-law and two children. Eugenio Colello, Santino Carnevale's godfather, followed a similar pattern.

Prior to World War I he migrated to Alaska, where he mined for gold, swallowing the small nuggets to prevent theft. Later, he went to California, finally settling in Lackawanna. His wife Giuseppina and their daughter Maria Civita joined him during the 1920s, but a son remained in Pico. Colello continued to send money to his son and other relatives until the end of World War II.[92]

Late in the nineteenth century, most inhabitants of Pettorano, including Pietro Iannarelli, were farmers. Iannarelli made

in Morolo and farmland in the valley further south, where he had another house constructed. He had become well-to-do by local standards, and his example induced others, including his son, Giovanni, to seek their fortune in the United States. In 1921, Giovanni Schiavi married Nazzarena Cellini and soon after traveled alone to the United States. He made several trips back to Morolo, resulting in the birth of Iole in 1922. He regularly mailed money to his family. He wrote of the cold weather, working on Christmas Day in 1927, and having only beans for dinner. Finally, in 1928, Nazzarena and Iole sailed for the United States and were reunited with Giovanni in Lackawanna. Three of Nazzarena's four brothers also left for the United States and, like her husband, settled in western New York.[91]

at least one trip to the United States, and lived for a period during the 1890s in Buffalo. Pietro's son Domenico also made trips back and forth to the United States, finally bringing his three sons to join him in Lackawanna. When he eventually returned to Italy to stay in 1950, he doubled his land holdings to some 50 acres. The Iannarelli family farmed some of the scattered sites, and Domenico hired laborers for the remaining plots.[93]

In his study of social class in a Calabrian town, Joseph Lopreato concluded that immigrants who returned to Italy from the United States were the "most significant agents of social change in the history of the village." Another observer concluded that this phenomenon was not generally true of returnees, and that some came back only after failing to achieve their goals in America. Some immigrants who returned whether temporarily or permanently, had the money and ideas to help improve their families economic situation and better their social status. In the towns from which most of Lackawanna's Italian immigrants came, there was at least a handful of returnees and their families for which this certainly holds true.[94]

When the southern Italian men left for the United States, the women and children survived as best they could while waiting, often for many years, to be sent their tickets to America. Carmine Colosimo, his father, brother, and several cousins departed Petrona, Calabria, in 1911 for the United States. He left his wife Maria, who stayed with her father, Pasquale Grande. Maria soon gave birth to a daughter, Michelina. It was nine years before the family would be reunited. As Michelina grew beyond the toddler stage, she helped her mother gather wood and chestnuts. After her first outing, Michelina collected enough chestnuts that her mother told her, "With the money you earned, I'm gonna make you 'the dress' "—meaning the red dress and skirt traditionally made for girls in Petrona at the age of six or seven. Maria indeed made her the dress, and Michelina was very proud, recalling 80 years later, "I earned my own little dress." For years, families like the Colosimos endured the frustration of waiting for mail from the menfolk in America, as Michelina describes here:

> Sometimes I used to sit by my mother on our steps, and the mailman would come. And he never brought me a letter from my father. I used to say, "Where's my letter from my father?" And he felt so bad. He [probably] said: "I hate to pass that house—that little girl sitting outside, waiting for mail." So one day, I said "I'll fix him up." I got about four or five little stones, and I said: "When he comes over, I'll hit him with a stone." You know, I was mad at him because he'd bring no letters.[95]

Some 40 miles to the northwest of the Colosimos' town, in the *mandimento* (county) of Rende, there were four phases of emigration traced by historian Franc Storino: "a pioneer phase between 1876 and 1881; a growth period between 1882 and 1903; a period of mass emigration from 1904 to the First World War; and a span of heavier settler migration between the war and 1929." The experience of the Covelli family in Marano Principato, one of the towns within Rende *mandimento*, touches on three of these phases. The extended Covelli family had constructed a long row house, and with each new generation, another unit was added. Leopoldo and Teresina Covelli, residents in the row house, were fortunate enough to own a mule and several small plots of land. In 1898, however, with four children to feed, Covelli decided to join the large migration of Calabresi going to Chicago. The next year, he sent for his eldest son, Filiberto, and they were later joined by the other two sons in Kenosha, Wisconsin. During his frequent visits back to Marano Principato, Filiberto Covelli married Rosina Ruffolo and fathered four children. On one small plot of land owned by her father-in-law, Rosina and her children cultivated vegetables; on a second one, in the mountains, they harvested chestnuts and gathered brush to fuel their kitchen fire. When Covelli returned to America in 1920, he joined *paesani* in Buffalo and procured work at the Lackawanna Steel Company. The plan was for his wife and their four children to join him there, and Rosina was preparing to do so when she suddenly died in 1925. Covelli sent money from Buffalo to the relatives who subsequently cared for his children, ages five to 16. The children eagerly awaited the return of their father, which happened over a year later. A virtual stranger to his two youngest offspring, Covelli became reacquainted with his children. He sent Leopoldo, who was about to turn 18, to America to avoid the Italian military draft and maintain the American citizenship conferred by Covelli's naturalization in 1914. He married Gelsomina Caira, and the couple and the three younger children left Marano Principato in 1927, joining young Leopoldo in Buffalo, then moving to Lackawanna within a few months. This was the last of Filiberto Covelli's many voyages that had started 28 years earlier.[96]

Tony Grasso, a gifted storyteller, who came to the United States with his family in 1913, wrote over 50 stories about life in Italy and in Lackawanna's Little Italy. Those remembrances begin with his father, Michele Grasso, whose work trimming grapevines regularly took him to nearby Quadrelle, where he met Maria Nappi and married her in 1898. During the next seven years, Maria gave birth to three sons, but only Antonio survived infancy. In 1907, Maria died of pneumonia. With Michele in America, Antonio was taken in by his maternal grandparents, Andrea and Giovanna Nappi. Michele Grasso came back to Italy in 1908, married Rosina Monduori, then returned to America. Antonio went to live with his stepmother, but after one day he ran across the street and back to his grandparents' home, remaining there for five years until he immigrated to America with Rosina and his half-brother.[97]

The millions of Italian immigrants who came to the United States include those destined to settle in Lackawanna. The decision to leave Italy was the first major step in this journey, which involved psychological and social changes as well as a long ocean voyage. The migrants were about to discover many "new worlds" as they traveled to a foreign land with a strange culture. For many, it was the first time they had left their town or province, ridden on trains, experienced large cities, seen steamships, or viewed the ocean. Their treks to the new world in the United States is the subject of the next chapter.

Figure 1.14

191 HOMETOWNS OF LACKAWANNA ITALIANS, BY REGION AND PROVINCE

ABRUZZO (43)

Aquila

1. Alfedena
2. Aquila
3. Bugnara
4. Cansano
5. Capestrano
6. Caporciano
7. Casale
8. Castelnuovo di San Pio
9. Celano
10. Cocullo
11. Forme
12. Introdacqua
13. Molina Aterno
14. Pescina
15. Pettorano sul Gizio
16. Prata d'Ansidonia
17. Pratola Peligna
18. Ripa
19. San Benedetto dei Marsi
20. San Pio delle Camere
21. Scoppito
22. Sulmona
23. Tussio
24. Villalago

Chieti

25. Chieti
26. Civitaluparella
27. Furci
28. Palmoli
29. Pretoro
30. Tufillo
31. Vasto

Pescara

32. Abbotteggio
33. Civitello Casanova
34. Manoppello
35. Penne
36. Pianella
37. Popoli
38. Roccamorice

Teramo

39. San Valentino in
    Abruzzo Citeriore
40. Civitello del Fronto
41. Forcella
42. Giulianove
43. Roseto degli Abruzzi

BASILICATA (5)

Matera

44. Matera
45. Pisticci

Potenza

46. San Fele
47. Spinoso
48. Tolve

CALABRIA (27)

Catanzaro

49. Cortale
50. Filadelfia
51. Nicastro
52. Petrona
53. Soveria Mannelli

Cosenza

54. Bianchi
55. Casale Basso
56. Cellara
57. Cerisano
58. Colosimi
59. Cosenza
60. Guardia Piedmontese
61. Lattarico
62. Marano Marchesato
63. Marano Principato
64. Montalto
65. Pedace
66. Rovito
67. San Giorgio
68. San Sosti
69. Santa Lucia
70. Trearie

Reggio

71. Africo

72. Mammola
73. Stignano

Vibo Valento

74. Nardodipace
75. Simbario

CAMPANIA (32)

Avellino

76. Avellino
77. Bagnoli Irpino
78. Capriglia Irpina
79. Grottolella
80. Quadrelle
81. Roccabascerana
82. Sant'Andrea di Conza
83. Savignano
84. Summonte
85. Teora

Benevento

86. Airola
87. Arpaise
88. Baselice
89. Castelfranco in Miscano
90. Colle Sannita
91. Molinara
92. Pannarano

Caserta

93. Caserta
94. Roccaromana

Napoli

95. Agerola
96. Boscoreale
97. Flocco
98. Gragnano
99. Napoli
100. Poggiomarino
101. Tufino

Salerno

102. Acquavella
103. Casavellina
104. Castelnuovo di Conza
105. Postiglione
106. Scafati
107. San Mauro Cilento

(continued)

EMILIA – ROMAGNA (2)

Ravenna
  108. Bagnacavallo
  109. Faenza

FRIULI–VENEZIA GIULIA (1)

Udine
  110. Varmo

LAZIO (37)

Frosinone
  111. Arce
  112. Castro dei Volsci
  113. Ceccano e Ponte
  114. Ceprano
  115. Falvaterra
  116. Frosinone
  117. Fumone
  118. Giuliano di Roma
  119. Madonna del Piano
  120. Morolo
  121. Patrica
  122. Pico
  123. Pico Farnese
  124. Piglio
  125. Pofi
  126. Pontecorvo
  127. Ripi
  128. San Giovanni Incarico
  129. Settefratte
  130. Sgurgola
  131. Sora
  132. Terelle
  133. Trivigliano
  134. Vallecorsa
  135. Veroli
  136. Villa Santo Stefano

Latina
  137. Bassiano
  138. Fondi
  139. Latina
  140. Lenola
  141. Piperno [Privernum]
  142. Ponza

Roma
  143. Capranica
  144. Roma
  145. Segni

Viterbo
  146. Sutri
  147. Vetralla

LOMBARDIA (1)

Milano
  148. Milano

MARCHE (10)

Ancona
  149. Ancona
  150. Senigallia

Pesaro E Urbino
  151. Bellocchi
  152. Cartoceto
  153. Cerasa
  154. Cuccurano
  155. Fano
  156. Montemaggiore al Metauro
  157. Monteporzio
  158. Pesaro

MOLISE (6)

Campobasso
  159. Campobasso
  160. Casal Ciprano
  161. Rotello
  162. Santa Croce di Magliano

Isernia
  163. Cantalupo del Sannio
  164. Vastogirardi

PUGLIA (12)

Bari
  165. Alberobello
  166. Bari
  167. Gioia del Colle
  168. Giovinazzo
  169. Locorotundo
  170. San Michelle in Monte

Laureto
  171. Triggiano

Foggia
  172. Accadia
  173. Accadia Saldutto
  174. Apricena
  175. Delicaro
  176. Foggia

SICILIA (12)

Agrigento
  177. Bivona
  178. Licata
  179. Racalmuto

Caltanisetta
  180. Serradifalco
  181. Vallelunga

Messina
  182. Francavilla di Sicilia
  183. Novara di Sicilia

Siracusa
  184. Floridia

Palermo
  185. Palermo
  186. Poggio Pratameno
  187. Roccapolumba
  188. Valledolmo

TOSCANA (2)

Lucca
  189. Lucca

Pisa
  190. Marti

UMBRIA (1)

Terni
  191. Narni

Figure 1.15. Map showing hometowns and provinces in northern and central Italy.

Figure 1.16. Map showing hometowns and provinces in Marche, Lazio, Abruzzo and Molise

Figure 1.17. Map showing hometowns and provinces in Campania, Basilicata, Puglia and Calabria

Figure 1.18. Map showing hometowns and provinces in Sicilia

Figure 1.19. Map of modern Italy and its 20 regions.

Luisa Cardinale

Issued. In witness whereof the seal of the Department of State is impressed hereon.

OCT 10 1932

52

CHAPTER 2

THE ITALIAN IMMIGRATION

According to the Italian government, more than 26 million Italians—a number equal to the entire population of Italy in 1861—migrated to other countries between 1876 and 1980. As with the other Italian immigrants who came to the United States, those destined to settle in Lackawanna were about to discover many "new worlds" as they traveled to a foreign land with a strange culture.

Rosina Grasso, with her son Giovanni and stepson Antonio, left Quadrelle, Campania, to join her husband in the United States. "The day of departure, May 24, 1913, had arrived," recalled Antonio "Tony" Grasso, who was nine years old at the time.

> I was awakened by grandma for breakfast. I dressed in a light green suit with short knee-high pants. The minutes were ticking away. Presently, my stepmother came over with my brother Giovanni and her family. We started our journey, walking up the street that had been my playground. At the corner, *Occhipalle's* (Balleye's) coach was waiting. He helped my stepmother in with Giovanni, while grandma was hugging me and didn't want to let me go. She was crying, and the tears streaked down her sad face as she kissed me for the last time. I imprinted on her wet face my last grateful kiss for all that she had done for me on this side of heaven, kissed grandpa and Aunt Annunziata through a curtain of tears, and stepped into the coach next to Giovanni. I gave a last look to my dear loved ones and the street of my boyhood as the driver tugged on the reins and the coach started to roll. They stood on the corner, a sad, desolate group, a silent tableau of despair—a haunting picture that has always abided with me.

This scene was repeated countless times throughout Italy.[1]

Italians, writes historian Donna Gabaccia, have been "among the most migratory of peoples on earth." Migration

< *In 1923, Luisa Cardinale and her daughter Mary joined their husband/father Giuseppe in Lackawanna, where Ercolino, Margaret, and Sam were born. Luisa and the children returned to Italy in 1929 due to the Depression, and came back to Lackawanna in 1932.*
Photo source: Collection of Sam Cardinale

from the Italian peninsula began in the Middle Ages, long before the creation of the nation of Italy. The number of emigrants from the country grew to approximately two million between 1790 and 1870. Among the 26 million persons who left Italy between 1876 and 1980, three out of every four were males, and half of them eventually returned to Italy. Between 1876 and 1925, the majority traveled across the Atlantic Ocean to the Americas, but since then, other European countries have been the prime destinations. A century ago, Northern Italians, who comprised 40% of the country's emigrants, often went to South America, while those from south of Rome favored destinations in North America. According to Italian government estimates, some 5.7 million Italians immigrated to the United States between 1876 and 1980 (see Figure 2.1).[2]

The U.S. government started keeping statistics on immigration in 1820. Its records reveal that between 1820 and 2000, the United States absorbed more than 66 million immigrants. The 5,435,830 Italian immigrants represent the third-largest group, following Germans and Mexicans. The influx of new immigrants from southeast Europe began in the 1880s and included arrivals from Italy, Austria-Hungary, Russia, Romania, and Greece. Italians constituted the largest group among these immigrants. In view of the differences between Italian and American officials' statistics and the difficulty of tracking the many immigrants who went back and forth between the two countries, the figure 5.5 million is at best a functional approximation of the number of Italian immigrants who came to the United States.[3]

Italians' immigration to the United States went through definite upswings and downswings. The most intense migration took place between 1900 and 1914, when approximately three

Tony Grasso on Second Street in the Old Village, early 1920s. He moved there with his parents and siblings just after the great steel strike. Photo source: Collection of Tony Grasso

million Italians entered the United States. "No other immigrant group arrived in such numbers in so few years," writes one historian. But the flow of immigrants then went through dramatic twists. It was drastically reduced when World War I erupted in August 1914. Returning to its high level in 1919, it then was severely curtailed by restrictive American immigration laws of 1921 and 1924. While over 1,000,000 Italians arrived in America between 1911 and 1920, only 455,000 did in the following decade, mostly prior to 1925. Between 1931 and 1940 the number fell to 68,000. During the decade 1941 to 1950, 58,000 immigrants from Italy arrived in this country, almost all of them after 1945. The postwar upsurge in immigration brought 400,000 Italians to the United States between 1951 and 1970 (see Figure 2.2). In addition, during the period from 1945 to 1975, some nine million southerners migrated to northern Italian cities.[4]

From Italian Towns to Lackawanna

The early-twentieth-century emigration from 191 Italian towns to Lackawanna can be traced using census data from the 20 towns (data was unavailable for the 21st town) providing the greatest number of immigrants (see Figure 2.3). The Italian census tallies the citizens "present" and those "not present"—those temporarily living elsewhere in Italy or in a foreign country—at the time of each town's count. The data from 1901 to 1931 on residents not present gives an indication of how many people emigrated. Sixteen of the 20 towns had the highest percentage of residents not present during the period 1902 to 1921, which overlaps with the peak period of Italian immigration to the United States. San Pio delle Camere had the highest percentages of residents not present, one-fifth in 1911 and one-third in 1921, and Settefrati ran a close second. Overall, 14 of the towns had an increase of population by 1931. This was a result of Italian policies initiated in the 1920s restricting the ability of citizens to leave that country and American laws restricting the numbers of southeast Europeans who could enter. The increase in residents also suggests a high rate of immigrants returning to Italy from overseas.[5]

Giuliano di Roma, Lazio, and Pettorano sul Gizio, Abruzzo, sent the greatest numbers of immigrants to Lackawanna, and additional census data on these towns are provided in figure 2.4. The high number of residents not present in Giuliano in 1911 suggests that most townspeople who departed did so between 1902 and 1910, which led to the dip in population by 1921. Smaller spikes in residents not present in 1931 and 1936 underline the emigration of Giulianesi during the 1920s and early 1930s, when a number of immigrants arrived in Lackawanna. Of the eight other towns in southern Lazio that sent many immigrants to Lackawanna, only Falvaterra and Lenola had a similar decrease in population by 1931. Between 1936 and 1981, Giuliano lost 29% of its population, mostly in the post-World War II migration to other European countries, the Americas, and large cities in Italy.[6]

Pettorano sul Gizio's notable migration of residents by the 1860s peaked by 1881, they resumed between the 1890s and 1931. There was a more modest departure rate during the 1930s and another small peak in migration in the years just after World War II. Overall, between 1901 and 1981, Pettorano lost almost

FIGURE 2.1

Leading Destinations of Italian Immigrants: 1876 – 1980 (from Italian Government Statistics)

United States	5.7 million
France	4.4 million
Switzerland	4 million
Argentina	3 million
Germany	2.5 million
Brazil	1.5 million

Source: Gianfausto Rosoli, "The Global Picture of the Italian Diaspora to the Americas," in Lydio Tomasi, Piero Gastaldo, and Thomas Row, eds. *The Columbus People: Perspectives in Italian Immigration to the America*s, 1994, p. 309.

FIGURE 2.2 Italian Immigrants Arriving in the United States: 1820 – 2000 (from U.S. Government Statistics)	
1820	30
1821 – 1830	409
1831 – 1840	2,253
1841 – 1850	1,870
1851 – 1860	9,231
1861 – 1870	11,725
1871 – 1880	55,759
1881 – 1890	307,309
1891 – 1900	651,893
1901 – 1910	2,045,877
1911 – 1920	1,109,524
1921 – 1930	455,315
1931 – 1940	68,028
1941 – 1950	57,661
1951 – 1960	185,491
1961 – 1970	214,111
1971 – 1980	129,368
1981 – 1990	67,254
1991 – 2000	62,722
Total 1820 – 2000	**5,435,830**

Source: *Statistical Yearbook of the Immigration and Naturalization Program*: 2000, pp.19-21.

Loreto Luzi in Giuliano di Roma, 1946. He arrived in Lackawanna by 1909, then returned to Italy in 1915 to serve in the military. After World War I, he again came to Lackawanna, went on to Connecticut and permanently settled in Italy in 1946. Photo source: Lillian Colafranceschi-Bracci

three-quarters of its residents due to migration (see figures 2.3 and 2.4). Looking at all 20 towns in Figure 2-3, six gained in population and 14 suffered population declines between 1901 and 1981. The towns that had increases were the larger ones, such as Ceccano and Fano, and those on important rail and highway routes, such as Ceprano and Soveria Mannelli. The gains in population reflect the movement of peasants from rural areas to larger towns, the constant migration to other countries in Europe and the Americas, and the wave of immigration to Australia after World War II. Falvaterra lost over half of its residents, many of whom moved to Rome but kept small villas in the town. In 1981, the town had 880 permanent residents, but each summer another 1,000 people, mostly former residents, vacationed in their villas.[7]

The migration of millions of Italians to other countries in Europe and overseas was ultimately based on a combination of factors. Among these were poverty, overpopulation, crop diseases, lack of arable land, the military draft, wars, the rise of a Fascist government, and the desire to join relatives and townspeople abroad. New Italian and American immigration laws of the 1920s also affected the process by placing huge barriers to migration. Finally, personal reasons for emigration— dissatisfaction with family economics, conflict with parents or stepparents, the search for adventure, and a chance to start life anew—increased as a result of the social and political changes. All of these factors were involved in the migration of Italians from 191 southern towns to Lackawanna.[8]

The flow of emigrants rarely began in the poorest areas, since migration required money. Once the emigration by middle-income southern Italians was under way, migration chains were forged and steamship fares became cheaper, making it feasible for even the least well-off to leave. Those highest on the social ladder sometimes chose to migrate after many of their less well-off *paesani* had departed.[9]

Immigrants who settled in Lackawanna shared stories about their decisions to leave Italy. In Giuliano, Biagio Maturani and his four brothers farmed their father's plot, but the paucity of land led Biagio and one of his brothers to emigrate to Niagara Falls. Once he'd gotten settled, Biagio sent his wife Giuseppina money to buy steamship tickets and sail with their three children to the United States. According to her daughter Maria, Giuseppina "bought an olive orchard instead of tickets. My father was mad; he didn't write for a year. Then he sent her tickets to come to the U.S. She left the olives to Maria (her sister)." Giuseppina and her three children sailed from Naples in 1926.[10]

Gaetano Paolini, of San Pio delle Camere, migrated to Buffalo at age 16 in 1897 to join his older brothers, Lorenzo and Michele, who were working at a facility handling iron ore. The three men saved up $2,000, which Gaetano wanted to use to buy land in the rapidly developing area around the Lackawanna Steel Company plant in West Seneca. But this plan was vetoed by Michele, the oldest of the five Paolini

FIGURE 2.3

Towns That Sent the Most Immigrants to Lackawanna:
[Total Residents and % Not Present (NP)*], 1901 – 1931

REGION Town	1901 Total	NP	1911 Total	NP	1921 Total	NP	1931 Total	NP	
LAZIO									
Castro dei Volsci	5,071	1%	5,329	9%	5,459	7%	5,722	1%	+
Ceccano	9,996	1	12,204	7	12,970	5	14,533	3	+
Ceprano	6,201	3	7,030	8	7,283	7	7,736	2	+
Falvaterra	1,307	3	1,230	10	1,003	3	943	5	-
Giuliano di Roma	2,692	1	3,174	15	2,838	2	3,123	6	+
Lenola	3,171	5	3,147	8	3,193	12	3,038	3	-
Morolo	3,463	0	3,934	10	4,189	13	3,642	4	+
Pico	3,461	5	3,734	14	4,002	19	3,686	3	+
Settefrati	2,495	2	3,016	19	3,247	30	2,604	9	+
ABRUZZO									
Pettorano sul Gizio	5,161	13	5,189	10	4,406	12	4,037	5	-
San Pio delle Camere	1,615	9	1,902	21	2,104	33	1,411	4	-
San Valentino	2,615	7	3,063	6	3,122	8	3,328	5	+
CAMPANIA									
Bagnoli Irpino	3,906	21	4,328	18	4,024	24	3,400	3	-
Capriglia Irpina	1,885	0	2,059	5	1,980	3	2,090	0	+
MARCHE									
Cuccurano			(No data available)						
Fano	24,848	1	27,067	1	28,806	1	30,878	1	+
CALABRIA									
Marano Principato	1,631	11	1,671	16	1,613	16	1,490	6	-
Soveria Mannelli	2,828	1	3,966	17	4,101	15	4,937	1	+3
MOLISE									
Santa Croce di Magliano	5,425	11	5,187	10	4,315	6	5,593	3	+
Cantalupo del Sannio	3,244	3	3,338	4	4,008	7	3,552	1	-
PUGLIA									
Accadia	4,780	8	5,527	17	5,154	16	5,289	3	+

* Not present refers to residents temporarily staying in other Italian towns or foreign countries.
Source: Instituto Centrale di Statistica. *Popolazione Residente e Presente dai Comuni: Censimenti dal 1861 al 1981*, Roma, 1985, pp. 228-29, 244-49, 250-51, 254-55, 258-59, 262-63, 270-71, 278-79, 294-95, 300-01.

brothers and the one who "called the shots." The three brothers returned to San Pio in 1905 and used their earnings to build a two-story, 25-room row house that provided homes for all five brothers and their families. In 1906, Gaetano Paolini married Clementina Casilio, and as their family grew to include 10 children, Gaetano had a 10-room house constructed. While his four brothers remained in Italy, Gaetano had other plans. After serving in the Italian Army in World War I, he departed Italy in 1920 for Buffalo, where he had relatives. After working a variety of jobs, he purchased a farmhouse and barn on 125 acres of land in Springville, in southern Erie County. Gaetano had returned to the occupation he knew in Italy, but as a *galantuomino* (gentleman) rather than a *contadino* (farmer). In Italy, only members of the upper class could afford a large plot such as his. In San Pio, Clementina and the children assisted with the agricultural chores of the extended family. Gaetano sent for his son Luigi in 1925, just before he turned 18. Having endured the horrors of military service in World War I, Gaetano was not anxious to have his eldest son drafted. Clementina and the remaining children made the journey to Springville by 1927. Three years later, their daughter Flora married another emigrant from Abruzzo, Pasquale Olivieri, and they took up residence in Lackawanna.[11]

Rosa Anticoli in Giuliano di Roma. A widow, she joined her two sons in the United States and later settled in Bethlehem Park. Photo source: Collection of Augusta Anticoli

FIGURE 2.4

Residents of Giuliano di Roma and Pettorano sul Gizio
(Both Present and Non-present*), 1936 – 1981

Town	Year	Total Population	Residents Present	Residents Not Present*	% Not Present*
GIULIANO DI ROMA					
	1936	3,021	2,898	123	4%
	1951	2,843	2,696	147	5%
	1961	2,403	2,334	131	5%
	1971	2,026	1,945	81	4%
	1981	2,136	2,109	27	1%
PETTORANO SUL GIZIO					
	1936	3,975	3,710	265	7%
	1951	3,673	3,336	337	9%
	1961	2,500	2,287	213	9%
	1971	1,593	1,534	59	4%
	1981	1,438	1,408	30	2%

*"Not Present" refers to residents temporarily staying in other parts of Italy or foreign countries.
Source: Instituto Centrale di Statistica. *Popolazione Residente e Presente dai Comuni: Censimenti dal 1861 al 1981*, Roma, 1985, pp.246-47, 250-51.

Antonetta Nigro joined her husband Celestino in Lackawanna by 1908, several years after he had arrived from their hometown of Accadia, Puglia.
Photo source: Collection of Nick Vertalino

In Marche, teenager Alfredo Campanelli lived and worked on the nearby tenant farms of two aunts, sending his wages home. In 1918, he returned home during the flu epidemic to help feed livestock, as so many relatives were ill. Two years later, a cousin in Lackawanna sent for him, and he soon was working in the steel plant. He sent money to his parents, who eventually bought a 40-acre farm in his name. Returning to Italy in 1934, Alfredo decided he didn't want to be a farmer. He married Berta Ambrosini, and they returned to Lackawanna. Berta's father and two uncles had immigrated to the United States 30 years earlier, and with the money they earned, returned to Fano and expanded the family farm to 250 acres.[12]

Michele Petrucci, weary of trying to farm in Molise, moved his family to Abruzzo so he could both farm and do seasonal railroad work. He wanted to take his family to America but couldn't do so without a sponsor. If unable to find one, he planned to migrate first to Canada or Argentina, then make his way to the United States. Finally, his half-brother Giuseppe Lopesi agreed to sponsor Petrucci and sent money for his passage to Clyde, New York. Giuseppe, who had changed his name to Joe Lopez, ran a potato farm there and also did railroad work. When Michele arrived in 1921, he did farm, construction, and railroad work. The following year, he sent for his family, and they moved to Lackawanna in 1931.[13]

The decision to reunite families separated by thousands of miles of ocean and years of time was an important one to the southern Italians, and was treated as such in their small towns. After nine years in the United States, Carmine Colosimo finally wrote his wife Maria in Petrona and made arrangements for her and their daughter Michelina to join him in America. By this time Michelina, was in second grade at school.

> When we got our papers that we had to come to America, oh my God! When I went to school, I told my teacher; I says: 'I'm going l'America.' When they heard … everybody gathered around me, like I was the queen of England or something. And this little girl said: 'I just come back from l'America.' And she said, 'Oooh, wait till you go over there… there's something that's real cold.'

The girl was talking about ice cream, which was not available in Petrona at that time. In 1920, Maria, Michelina, and another relative left Calabria and were bound for West Virginia to reunite with Carmine and get their first taste of ice cream. Michelina's father felt like a total stranger to her—a discovery that as we shall see later, had a profound effect on their relationship.[14]

The Voyage to the United States

The towns that sent emigrants to Lackawanna had earlier sent southern Italians to various regions in Italy, other countries in Europe, and several continents overseas. Michele Grasso traveled throughout southern Italy to practice his trade of trimming grapevines. Charcoal makers from Pettorano ranged far outside of Abruzzo to carry out their seasonal work. From San Pio delle Camere, peasants migrated to perform vineyard work in nearby Chieti Province, as well as to Switzerland and France. Residents of Giuliano di Roma did seasonal work in Rome and Milan, including planting corn in the Pontine Marsh, only 21 miles away. Others, such as Natale Masocco, went to Terracina, on the coast, to break rocks by hand from June through October. Some Giulianesi

Angelina and Carmine Spagnolo were immigrants from Capriglia Irpina in Campania.
Photo source: Collection of Audrey Spagnolo-Sungenor

Buffalo, circa 1895. Gaetano and Domenico Tristani were two of the early immigrants from Pettorano sul Gizio to arrive in the Buffalo area. This photo was taken at Bliss Studio on Main Street. Photo source: Guy Iannarelli

went to Romania for temporary work, while others settled permanently in Buenos Aires, Argentina.[15]

Many of the Italians who traveled overseas did return. Augusta Anticoli said that men returned to Giuliano from the United States because they didn't want to move their families to the tough American environment. Ezio Millanti estimates that 60% of emigrants from Giuliano di Roma returned there. Evangelisto Ceccarelli, a native of Falvaterra, noted that most of his townspeople who migrated to America returned. He himself lived in the United States for 30 years, mostly in Follansbee, West Virginia, before returning to Lazio. As many came home, others departed, following the migration chain of their predecessors. The flow of departing and returning emigrants waxed and waned. Italy continued to offer significant numbers of emigrants to all corners of the world into the 1970s.[16]

Once the decision to migrate was made, many Italians looked to local agents to assist in arranging papers and purchasing steamship tickets. Arcangelo Colafranceschi, a resident of the provincial capitol of Frosinone, procured tickets

for emigrants departing Giuliano di Roma and other towns in *Ciociaria*. Early in the twentieth century, Umberto Fraschetti of Ceprano, as an agent of a steamship company, charged a fee for arranging tickets, passports, etc. He escorted emigrants to Naples and other ports but never himself traveled to the United States. Sosio DeAngelis, an emigrant from Falvaterra, facilitated the emigration of *paesani* by sending money from the United States. In Morolo, Nazzarena Schiavi depended on a *cumpadi* (a trusted friend linked to the family through the godparent relationship) who worked at the post office to arrange travel papers for her and her daughter. On one steamship passenger list, Filiberto Covelli and other natives of Marano Principato indicated Francesco Principe as the cousin they were going to join in Chicago. Actually, Principe was a native of Montalto, a nearby town, who had established a saloon and hotel on Chicago's west side and acted as a *padrone*, lining up jobs and making travel arrangements. When Andrea Ceccarelli arrived in New York City from Falvaterra in 1913, "there were *padroni* waiting for Italian immigrants; for $10 they got you

Figure 2.5

PATTERNS OF MIGRATION FROM ITALIAN TOWNS TO LACKAWANNA

It is interesting to observe that of the 191 Italian towns sending immigrants to Lackawanna, the vast majority of them sent only one to four immigrants. Of the 3,070 immigrants who were in Lackawanna at one time or another, hometowns for 1,744 of them have been identified. A summary of the numbers follows;

Number of Immigrants	Number of Towns
1	69
2	32
3	18
4	17
5 – 9	22
10 – 14	9
15 – 19	3
20 – 29	9
30 – 39	2
40 – 49	2
50 – 59	2
60 – 69	1
70 – 79	2
118	1
137	1
252	1

Total: 191

These numbers suggest that for all but a few towns, Lackawanna was not a major link in their immigration chains. Also, since so many immigrants remained only a short time in the city, it may be that they could not tolerate work in the steel plant. There is no evidence indicating that any of the men had experience in steelmaking in Europe. However, a significant number of males who gained experience in foundries and small steel plants elsewhere in the United States intentionally migrated to Lackawanna to get jobs at the steel plant. Others were drawn to the Steel City by the availability of jobs on the mainline railroads that passed through the city, and the roundhouses [locomotive repair shops] of the New York Central Railroad and South Buffalo Railway.

For the 21 Italian towns that provided the highest number of immigrants, Lackawanna was an important point on their chain-migration routes.

Town	Number of Immigrants
San Pio delle Camere, Abruzzo	20
San Valentino, Abruzzo	20
Cuccurano, Marche	21
Marano Principato, Calabria	22
Morolo, Lazio	22
Settefrati, Lazio	24
Capriglia Irpina, Campania	27
Ceccano, Lazio	28
Falvaterra, Lazio	29
Ceprano, Lazio	33
Lenola, Lazio	36
Soveria Mannelli, Calabria	40
Accadia, Puglia	41
Santa Croce di Magliano, Molise	50
Castro dei Volsci, Lazio	58
Bagnoli Irpino, Campania	62
Pico, Lazio	76
Cantalupo del Sannio, Molise	77
Fano, Marche	118
Pettorano sul Gizio, Abruzzo	137
Giuliano di Roma, Lazio	252

All but four of these towns also sent immigrants to Buffalo and several other towns in western New York. Among the

170 other towns from which emigrants came to the Steel City, 69 also had natives living in Buffalo. Larger American cities had many Italian towns represented in their "Little Italys"; immigrants from at least 515 Italian towns lived in Buffalo and from 689 towns in nearby Rochester. Lackawanna's proximity to the Italian colonies in Buffalo and nearby towns may have meant that males looking for seasonal work in western New York simply "spilled over" into Lackawanna's steel plant and railroads as they went from one location to another.

As time went on, immigrants in Buffalo who worked at the steel plant moved to Lackawanna to be closer to their jobs, and, conversely, steelworkers moved from Lackawanna to Buffalo and other nearby towns to find more comfortable living space or to be closer to relatives.

Sources: *Buffalo Daily Courier*, 3/5/1888; *Buffalo Courier*, 5/6/1907; *Buffalo Morning Express*, 5/24/1891; Virginia Yans-McLaughlin, *Family and Community: Italian Immigrants in Buffalo*, 1880–1930, 1971, p. 112; *Corriere Italiano*, 12/1/1906; 6/15/1907.

The immigrant station at Ellis Island in New York City's harbor went into service in 1892 and processed 12 million immigrants by the time it closed in 1954. Photo source: Public domain

When a ship arrived in New York Harbor, it was boarded by staff from Ellis Island, who examined first- and second-class passengers. Most were released to go ashore, but all third-class passengers had to go to Ellis Island. In the great hall there, men were separated from women and children, and both groups lined up to go through a series of checkpoints. Inspectors questioned them about occupation, literacy, and destination. The immigrants were then inspected for any signs of disease, mental illness, or criminality. Many were forced to return to their homelands because they did not pass inspection.
Photo source: Public domain

a job." Some of these labor agents were fair, while others were unscrupulous. As Italians gained experience with overseas migration, they informed relatives and *paesani* how to make travel and job arrangements without the involvement of *padroni*.[17]

This chapter began with the departure from Quadrelle of Rosina Grasso and her two sons by carriage in 1913, and we now return to their journey. As their horse and buggy made the long trek to Naples, the Grassos were jostled about, but they were able to take catnaps until they encountered increased road traffic on the outskirts of Naples. Arriving at the waterfront, Rosina located the ticket agent who a month earlier had informed her of the particulars of the ocean voyage, explaining that it would take him some time to handle all the details. "When he heard that the tickets were already paid for, his jaws tightened, his face clouded, and a blank look came to his eyes," writes Tony Grasso. "He visioned the small fee (usually added to his original one when he bought tickets for unsuspecting or illiterate emigrants) had slipped from his fingers." At boarding time, the agent attached a sticker to the family's suitcase and led them up the gangplank of the steamship *Lazio*. When they were aboard, writes Tony Grasso, the agent, the "pompous, conniving braggart ... said to my stepmother 'goodbye,' sped down the gangplank and was gone"—upset because he couldn't collect the extra fee.[18]

The Grassos descended into the bowels of the steamer to one of the steerage compartments. "There was row upon row of cots in this cavernous compartment," recalled Tony, "which served as sleeping quarters for women. I protested to the officer that I preferred to sleep with the men, but he replied I was too young. I was assigned a cot next to my stepmother. On the other side slept a young woman from a town a little way from ours, who was coming to the states to be married. The only light that came into this large cavern was from round portholes running along the side of the ship."[19]

As they shipped out of Naples, Grasso walked to the stern of the ship and stared at its churning wake. "Looking at the fading shoreline, only the giant smoking cone of Vesuvius was visible. ... Many thoughts were revolving in my mind, but uppermost was: 'What is grandma doing at this hour not having me around?' ... The land (my homeland) was shrinking in the distance." At noon, Antonio and his new companions lined up with the other passengers, each equipped with a metal dish and cup, along with a fork and spoon. They walked single file through a cafeteria, where attendants ladled out portions of food and beverage. After passing through the Strait of Gibraltar, Tony Grasso and his companions noted the more turbulent

Nazzarena Schiavi and her children Michele (infant) and Iole in Morolo, Lazio. Tragically, Michele died in Italy, and in 1929, Nazzarena and Iole journeyed to Lackawanna to be reunited with the family head, Giovanni.
Photo source: Iole Schiavi-Murray

waters of the Atlantic Ocean. The lad wondered, with some misgivings, what his new life would be like in America. Grasso put off descending into his sleeping quarters as long as possible; the steerage area had become "a stinking hellhole" for him. One morning, land was finally spotted, and passengers crowded along the railing to scan the horizon. Grasso was unable to squeeze through to get a view as he listened to people saying, "Guarda la"—look there. When he finally got through he recalled looking "at the promised land with a heavy heart, thinking what it was to be like. I knew what I had left behind, but was baffled and confused about the new land."[20]

As the *Lazio* docked at the Battery, on the southern end of Manhattan, Grasso got his first glimpse of urban America —high-rise buildings, streets teeming with people, and all types of horse-drawn and gasoline-powered vehicles. The first- and second-class passengers soon disembarked from the

vessel, while those in steerage were required to wait on board one more day. Grasso spent most of that day on deck. He observed vendors in small boats coming alongside the *Lazio* to peddle fruits, soft drinks, and beer. Passengers lowered baskets on ropes to send the vendors money and retrieve purchases. Having never seen them before, Grasso was mesmerized by bananas. He felt sad that he had no money to purchase the colorful fruits and beverages.[21]

The next day, the *Lazio's* passengers boarded a ferryboat that headed out into the harbor, soon passing a giant statue. "A seasoned passenger who had passed this way before said, 'La Statua della Liberta.'" Grasso continues, "My young mind couldn't grasp the purpose of putting such a massive statue on a jutting piece of land with water lapping all around, so far away from the mainland and human habitation." He then saw another island, one with a huge building and four towers with domes, that had a more forboding appearance. The ferry docked at Ellis Island, and the steerage passengers disembarked. "I became apprehensive that they were going to lock us up for an indefinite length of time, while dad waited in vain for our arrival. We entered a huge hall in this mammoth building, and the breadth and height of the enormous gathering place instilled awe and fear in my heart." Grasso saw that the width of the hall was crossed by dozens of wooden benches with high, straight backs. After officials checked to see that Rosina's papers were in order, the Grassos sat in an empty row just behind those that were already occupied. "Recalling that day, one of dread and anxiety for a young boy, it seemed to me it was a stockyard of human beings to be looked over." Several hours later, the Grassos were called "to face a man sitting on a stool behind a high desk looking down on us." In Italian, he posed a number of questions to Rosina. His helper then pinned a card bearing the number "5" on the coat of the mother and two sons. The three then climbed to the second floor on a grand staircase and were given physical examinations by doctors. Tony Grasso recalls that this was the worst hurdle, for the officials could detain people or send them back to Europe depending on the results of these exams. A doctor used a device resembling a shoe hook to lift Tony's eyelid and inspect his eye. He, Rosina, and Giovanni passed the exams, and were sent back downstairs, where they paid five lire (about $5 at that time) for a box containing several sandwiches, a piece of cake, and some fruit—including two of those intriguing bananas.[22]

Late that afternoon, the ferry took them back to Manhattan, where they were guided to a huge railroad station "with a big concourse, high, ornate ceilings, and chandeliers. It took some time before they verified our papers and destination. By this time, it was getting dark, and every building was lit, and the city looked like a fairyland." In accordance with the tags on their coats, railroad personnel led the Grassos to track number five. Tony was amazed by the number of tracks, steam engines, and railroad cars. The train carried the three members of the Grasso family to Wellsville, New York, where they connected with another train that finally arrived at Galeton, Pennsylvania. Michele Grasso met and transported his family to their destination, the small town of Gaffney.[23]

Early Italian Arrivals in Lackawanna

Many Italian immigrants who came to West Seneca's steel plant district were not recent arrivals in this country. They had first lived in other towns throughout the United States, then moved to western New York. Angelo Morinello came to the U.S. in 1882. After bringing his family to Buffalo, he moved them to the Limestone Hill section of West Seneca, just east of the railroad tracks, in 1900. The Morinellos were the first Italian family to settle in this area. Other than 19 of the orphans in the Our Lady of Victory institutions, the Morinellos were the only Italian residents in the steel-plant district that year. This sparsely settled rural area in the town of West Seneca became the site of the world's largest steel plant. It was incorporated as the city of Lackawanna in 1909.[24]

The Morinellos were the vanguard of more than 3,000 Italian immigrants who eventually arrived in the city. Within a year or so, another extended family of businesspeople moved to West Seneca's Limestone Hill section. Luca Tarquinio and his family, along with his daughter and son-in-law Tony Mauriello, set up a hotel/boarding house near the steel plant. The family of Calogero and Sara Fadale came to Ingham Avenue in 1904, where a small number of Italians had settled, and set up a grocery store as they had done earlier in Buffalo. Small clusters of Italians gathered around the Tarquinio-Mauriello hotel on Gates Street, the Fadale store on lower Ingham Avenue, the Morinello rooming house, store, and tavern on Roland Avenue, as well as along Smokes Creek in the Old Village row houses, and the shanty town on the plant grounds (see Figure 2.16). By 1905, more Italian immigrants had arrived, many of whom had also previously lived in other areas of the United States before settling in the steel-plant district of West Seneca.[25]

The Italian immigrants utilized a *paesani* network to share information, lodging, and job referrals as they moved from one Italian settlement to another (see "chain migration" on page 66). While some individuals and families settled permanently, many more, especially lone males, moved between Italian enclaves in western New York and other states where their *paesani* were located. Some men and a few families traveled back and forth between the United States and Italy.

So, Lackawanna's Italian population was a very fluid one. This constant movement of people continued through the 1930s. The migration chains linking Lackawanna with towns in southern Italy and throughout the United States continued to function into the 1960s.

Italians comprised about four percent of the multiethnic workforce drawn to the steel-plant district during the period from 1905 to 1915. They were an early and significant presence in the area, even though many of them remained in the city for only a short time. Approximately 3,070 Italian immigrants have resided in Lackawanna at some point in time, the earliest arrivals staying just long enough to work temporarily on construction or outdoor maintenance jobs.

One reason for the constant turnover was the immigrants' initial lack of experience in the iron and steel industry. Italians in Buffalo and elsewhere were drawn to outdoor construction and railroad work that required the same pick-and-shovel skills they had practiced in Italian agriculture. Some who arrived

Caterina and Angelo Morinello with their children Rose and Frank in Buffalo, circa 1891. The Morinellos were the only Italian family listed in the 1900 U.S. Census as residing in the Limestone Hill section of West Seneca, N.Y. Photo source: Collection of Frank Morinello Jr.

Figure 2.6

SIX JOURNEYS TO AMERICA

For most Lackawanna immigrants, the trip to America began with the journey from their small town to a city on a railroad line or a main road, and then, to Naples, or one of the other leading Italian ports of departure: Palermo in Sicily, Genoa in Liguria, or Trieste in Friuli-Venezia Giulia. They left their towns on a mule, in a horse-drawn buggy, motorized taxi, or bus, or on foot, some catching a train from the nearest city to Naples. Once their steamship reached an American port, they proceeded to their destination by railroad or automobile. In both Italy and the United States, they often ran a gauntlet of immigration officials, panhandlers, and labor agents. Their acculturation into a new society began with their dockside experiences in Italy, on the steamship voyage across the ocean, and on the train or automobile rides from New York City to their initial destination. During these phases of transport, they encountered new people, strange foods, city life, and foreign customs. Following are memories of six immigrant families' journeys:

The Petrucci Family

Angelina Petrucci made a trip to Rome in 1922 to procure immigration papers. It had been a year since her husband Michele left for America. She and her son Luigi then rode on the mail buggy from their hometown of Rotello to a nearby town, from which they took a train to Naples. Luigi, who was seven years old at the time, recalls that "in Naples, panhandlers tried to take advantage. The officials checked for lice; they made everyone take a shower. I took a shower with my ma and a bunch of women." At Ellis Island in New York Harbor, the immigrants again stood in lines to be examined. They waited three days for Michele to arrive. During that time, Luigi,

who had drunk only goat's milk in Italy, was given dry crackers and cow's milk for breakfast—the first time he had tasted either of these foods. Michele finally arrived, and the family proceeded to Clyde, New York. Ten years later, the Petruccis moved to their final homestead in Lackawanna.

The Maturani Family

Giuseppina Maturani and her three children—Pasquale, Edimondi, and Maria—left Giuliano in October 1926 to be reunited with the family head, Biagio, in Niagara Falls, New York. After they departed Naples, the voyage became difficult for two of the children. Pasquale got seasick and was sent to the ship's infirmary. Maria, who had been vaccinated by the doctor in Giuliano, developed a swollen, infected arm. "I was sick on the boat," recalls Maria. Guiseppina tried to cheer up her daughter by giving her chocolate, but "a nun took it and scolded my mother. She said it would make my fever worse. When my mother went to a different room to visit Pat [Pasquale], I was afraid and didn't want her to leave." When the ship arrived in New York Harbor, all passengers were quarantined aboard it for three days. Five-year-old Maria recalls being told that there was an election being held at the time. Apparently, city authorities wanted to make sure that ward politicians didn't march immigrants from dockside right into the voting booths.

When Giuseppina's brother Agusto DeSantis, who had been sent to meet the travelers, learned what had occurred he rented a small boat and came alongside the ocean liner, waving his hat until he got the attention of his sister and her children. Maria remembers that when they finally disembarked and went to Ellis Island, they all wore tags indicating their

destination. Agusto took them to a restaurant and bought fruit baskets. "We kids didn't like the bananas," recounts Maria. The five Italians then boarded a train bound for Niagara Falls.

The Ventre Family

Seventeen-year-old Ausilio Ventre left Settefrati in 1927 to join his father, Domenico, in the United States. Two years later, his mother Elisabetta and his two younger brothers Antonio and Tomasso made the journey. Elisabetta hired one of the two men in town who had a car to drive them to Naples. There, according to Tomasso, "the heads of all passengers were shaved to prevent lice." They departed in October on the Conte di Savoia. "I hung over the rail on the boat and watched the dolphins jump. My mother was afraid that I would fall in." When they landed at Ellis Island, Domenico and a friend met them and drove them to Lackawanna.

The Schiavi Family

In 1928, Nazzarena Schiavi and her daughter Iole got on a bus in Morolo and made the 50-mile trip to Rome, where they boarded a train for Naples. At the seaport, Iole made the first of many new discoveries. "The boat looked huge, and scary," said Iole, who was seven years old at the time of emigration. She and her mother were fortunate to have a second-class cabin. "I was afraid to move off the steps at nighttime," recalls Iole, "while waiting for mom. I was afraid of getting lost or falling into the water. There was a big storm—tables and chairs fell, and people ran." Upon arrival in New York City, they were met by Francesco Schiavi, an uncle of Nazzarena. He accompanied them on the train ride to Buffalo, then on to Lackawanna.

Concezio Novelli

In 1935, at the age of 13, Concezio Novelli went to America to join a father he had never seen. A car transported the youth and several other people from Pettorano to Naples. His traveling companion was a man who had been going back and forth between Italy and West Virginia. They lodged at a hotel in Naples and spent much time in long lines of people waiting to be checked over by American immigration officials. "I cried because I was worried about my unhealed leg injury. But an American woman said in Italian, 'Don't worry, it will be alright.' " Throughout the 10-day voyage on the *SS Conte di Savoia*, Concezio ventured from the cabin he shared with his companion to see movies and to draw and sketch. "I was drawing an apple when an American boy kicked it away. I thought the parents would discipline the boy, but they told him, 'Don't do that!' I felt no one cared, Americans don't have any discipline." Another Americanism that Concezio encountered on the ship and was unimpressed by: "The older guy bought me an ice-cream sucker; I didn't like it."

As the *Conte di Savoia* arrived in New York, Concezio saw "a beautiful, huge moon over Manhattan." In the city, he said, "The skyscrapers were fascinating; I had never seen these before." While his companion headed for West Virginia, Concezio traveled alone by train to Buffalo. He had a picture of his father that he had received in the mail prior to his voyage. When Concezio arrived at the station in Buffalo, he spotted his dad, Constantino, and his stepmother and stepsisters. They went to Lackawanna, where they ate a huge meal. Soon, Concezio began

calling himself John as he undertook the challenge of adjusting to life in a foreign country.

The Covelli Family

In December 1927, a cab transported Filiberto and Gelsomina Covelli and their three younger children the five miles from Marano Principato to Cosenza, from which they took a train to Naples. There, the family lodged in a hotel for three or four days as they stood in endless lines to fill out forms and undergo physical examinations. After 1924, American public-health officials were stationed at foreign ports to give medical inspections. Some immigration officials drew two pencils through the hair of prospective emigrants to check for lice, while others looked for physical defects. Two of the Covelli children, Florindo and Adelina, did have lice, and the inspectors combed their hair with vinegar and metal brushes to remove them.

For Florindo Covelli, emigration proved to be a great adventure that momentarily distracted him from the constant sense of sadness over the death of his mother two years earlier. In Naples, he and his sisters discovered better and tastier foods served in greater quantities than back home. The family took frequent walks in Naples, the first large city the children had visited for any length of time. One drawback in Naples, and later on the ship, was difficulty comprehending the other Italian dialects. "I couldn't understand a goddamn word they said," recalls Florindo, adding that other Italians in turn could not decipher his Calabrese dialect.

With savings accumulated from long years of work in America, Filiberto, who had traveled in steerage on earlier trips, was able to afford second-class accommodations on the *SS President Wilson*. The family had a cabin with four bunks—Adelina and Florindo shared one bunk, while their older sister Gilda and the two adults each had their own. The third-class quarters smelled of oil, the family noted in their tour of the ship. The vessel opened up a whole new world to Gelsomina, who had taken infrequent trips to Cosenza, and the three children, who had never been outside of their hometown. There were moving pictures, and even a maid who cleaned their cabin. Having never seen a black person before, Adelina was surprised by the sight of a black man playing the piano and singing "O Sole Mio."

In addition to watching silent movies, the awestruck Covelli children observed shuffleboard games, a dance hall, and a huge dining room where each long table had its own waiter. Adelina overheard a conversation between an unmarried couple in the dance hall. In his northern Italian dialect, the man asked his female companion if she had a needle and thread to sew a rip in one of his gloves. Adelina thought to herself, "he had his nerve; he must be stingy!" She was equally horrified when she saw a woman sitting on a man's lap. Such things were unheard of in southern Italian farming towns.

The *President Wilson* stopped in Spain, just east of Gibraltar, where hucksters came alongside in little boats and Filiberto purchased a sack of oranges. While everyone else in the family became seasick, Filiberto, the veteran sea traveler, snacked on *casu* (a Calabrese cheese), prosciutto, and sausage—food thought to discourage vomiting. Most of the passengers were Italian and all were friendly as they spoke to each other in their various regional dialects. Adelina overheard someone talking about going to Pennsylvania. As the ship sailed into New York Harbor, she

(continued)

remembers the American coastline, the Statue of Liberty, barges in the harbor, and the noise of many boats' horns.

Upon reaching land, the family spent a short time going through customs at a dockside building. They then proceeded to Grand Central Station, where they boarded a train bound for Buffalo. Florindo was impressed by the American trains, finding them cleaner, more modern, and more comfortable than those in Italy. Arriving at Buffalo's Central Terminal in the early morning hours, the family took a cab to their destination. Buffalo appeared as a dirty and dingy city with few trees, but there was snow—something rarely seen in southern Italy. The Covellis arrived at the East Side apartment of Fiore and Rosa Covelli. Leopoldo, the eldest Covelli child, had lived in the couple's attic since his arrival earlier in the year. Filiberto and Gelsomina and the younger children stayed in the crowded apartment for four months before moving to Lackawanna.

Sources: Interviews with Louie Petrucci, December 27, 1984; Marie Maturani-Federici, September 19, 1995; Tom Ventre, September 23, 1994; Iole Schiavi-Murray, October 18, 1996; John Novelli, April 18, 1995; Adeline Covelli-Andreozzi, April 22 and July 10, 1981; and Gene Covelli, July 22, 1990. Francesco Schiavi was one of four brothers of Lorenzo Schiavi who had returned to Italy in 1922. All the brothers did railroad work in Lackawanna and nearby towns, settling in Elmira, New York, by the late 1920s. By 1927, when the Covellis arrived in New York, the practice of requiring third-class (steerage) passengers to be processed at Ellis Island had virtually ceased.

after the construction of the Lackawanna Steel Company plant tried their hand at steelmaking simply because the jobs were available. The huge complex must have been overwhelming to them at first, but the Yard Department called for much work outside of the mills, including railroad track maintenance and other basic laborer tasks that Italian peasants could handle. At first, only a few Italians took jobs directly in the mills, eventually learning the skills of steelmaking. Other immigrants first gained experience in industrial work at small foundries and steel plants in other locales, then came to Lackawanna's mills, confident in their newly acquired knowledge of industrial tools and techniques. Italian immigrants in western New York tended to migrate from job to job, with Lackawanna's steel plant being one of several stops in a seasonal rotation.

Like all Southern European immigrants to America, the Italians had to contend with a new culture and language, a climate with tremendous extremes of weather, and the daunting task of adapting to an urban, industrial environment in which they were seen as foreigners. They drew on their experiences and customs in Italy to adapt to their challenging lives in America. In both countries, the Italians distrusted formal institutions and relied on relatives for assistance. They learned to depend on their extended family and *paesani* to form immigration chains that served as support networks. They took in boarders and arranged for females to work only in contexts where their honor was protected, such as serving boarders, minding the family store (with other family members always nearby), or joining Italian family units to harvest crops on farms. The strength of the Italian family helped create economic stability, with children working in family businesses and doing chores, such as maintaining gardens. In America, as they had in Italy, the men migrated from one seasonal job to another to make ends meet, doing unskilled laborer tasks. Former Italian farmers did outdoor construction and railroad jobs, as well as yard work within huge steel plants. Their frugality and dedication to sending most of their earnings to support their kin in Italy speak to the strong sense of family loyalty that helped the immigrants survive here.

Italian Immigration to West Seneca, Lackawanna

The Italian influx into West Seneca's steel-plant district commenced in 1900, coinciding with the onset of the period of the heaviest Italian migration to the United States. The family and village connections in the old country played a key role for many immigrants who came to Lackawanna, establishing what John and Leatrice MacDonald call "chain migration." As suggested previously, Italian immigrants, rather than relying on impersonal networks, linked resources with friends, relatives, and other townspeople to carry out their migration to the new land. Chain migration involves three distinct stages. The first occurred mostly during the years 1880 to 1914, when immigrants were usually lone male travelers, called sojourners. Once established, sojourners helped other men from their hometowns make the move to America. This second stage, called serial migration, involved one villager summoning a friend or relative from Italy, with each new arrival then sending to Italy for another man to join him. The third stage, family reunification, involved the migration of wives, and family members to reunite with the male breadwinners. All three stages of chain migration can be observed in the development of the Italian community in Lackawanna. Some of the stories told so far display features of these stages, but it is useful to lay out this pattern even more clearly as it relates to the Steel City.[26]

FIGURE 2.7

FIRST IMPRESSIONS OF LACKAWANNA: 1900 – 1936

Giuseppina Ferrelli with sons Aldo, left, and Cesidio, right; passport photo, 1928. She did not like Lackawanna at first, and told her husband Vincenzo that she missed the clear blue sky in Pettorano sul Gizio.
Photo source: collection of Josephine Ferrelli

The great majority of Italians who came to Lackawanna were from small towns in rural Italy. Some of the men first migrated to other urban and industrial centers in Europe and America before coming to the Steel City, and most got at least a glimpse of New York City or other large Eastern cities when they landed in the United States. For many Italians, however, their first view of the huge steel center and surrounding homes in Lackawanna was quite an experience, spawning a variety of reactions. There was another type of discovery awaiting some of the younger immigrants, many of whom encountered their fathers for the first time between the ages of five and 15, when their families were reunited in America. Their first impressions of the United States overlapped with their emotional first encounters with long-lost dads.

After Rosina Grasso and her sons were united with her husband in Pennsylvania, the family moved to Ohio. The eldest son, Tony, was sent to Medina, New York, to live with relatives and work in their candy store. In late 1916, he rejoined his family, which then lived in Lackawanna's New Village. "When I arrived, I saw that ore dust covered the whole place. There was a bad smell, an acrid odor. I thought Lackawanna was a terrible place to live. The ore dust would make people sick." Looking at the steel plant, he thought: "It's dirty, not like the candy store. I'll have to go to work there."

Antonio DiMillo, according to his son Tony, "said, 'Bella America'; he loved America, he was never hungry here." Antonio DePaula often scowled when talking about Italy, referring to his homeland as "la terra brusciata" (the burned land), and telling his children, "There was nothing there but poverty." Giuseppe Violanti arrived in Lackawanna from Giuliano in December 1919. "It was no worse than Italy," he recalls. "In the Old Village, there was no electricity; we had kerosene lamps, and no hot water. I was surprised to see how steel was made—all the tracks, engines, steel production—but I knew it [the steel plant] would provide work."

Romolo Petricca was 16 when he and several friends left Giuliano in 1920. After their ship arrived in New York Harbor, recalls Romolo, "We took a barge to Ellis Island; everyone had a ticket pinned to his chest." The other young men set out for various destinations while Romolo traveled alone by train to Buffalo, and from there to the Steel City, where his uncle and brother were boarding with the DeCarolis family. "In Buffalo, I showed the address to a cop who called a cab. The Italian cabbie wanted $5, but Anna DeCarolis gave him a dollar." This teen's first encounters in America were with a helpful policeman and a taxi driver who attempted to gouge a fellow Italian immigrant for cab fare.

Domenico Cellini was 17 years old in 1920 when he arrived in Lackawanna from Morolo. The steel plant struck him as being "dirty and dangerous, but eventually it provided work—jobs." Upon his arrival, he moved in with his brother Michele, who was boarding with an Italian family on First Street. Upon first glimpse of the Old Village and its series of 800- to 900-foot row houses, he was aghast. "It was too big—all one house, all the same." In April 1928, Florindo "Gene" Covelli had a similar reaction. Four months after arriving from Calabria, the eight-year-old and his family moved from Buffalo to Lackawanna's Old Village. He was familiar with row houses—the Covelli row house in Marano Principato was perhaps 90 feet in length. When he saw the Old Village, however, he couldn't imagine so many families being housed in one building a block long. "We were going to live in one house," he recalled thinking, "all those families in one house!"

(continued)

Children conceived in Italy during one of their migrant fathers' return trips typically had little or no contact with their dads, who were back in America before they were born. With their first meeting, such fathers and children were virtual strangers to one another. For a number of immigrant Italian children, their first strong impression of the United States revolved around getting used to the unknown man who was their father. This was often a difficult and trying period for both the children and adults involved.

In 1929, Annamaria Monaco and her six-year-old daughter Iolanda left Cantalupo for Naples. They sailed on the steamship *Biancomano*, arrived in New York in July, and went on to Buffalo to be reunited with Antonio, the family head. Within a few months, the family moved to Ingham Avenue in Lackawanna. "When I arrived, I was afraid of my father," recalls the daughter, whose name was Americanized to Yolanda. "I had never seen him before. He was mad because I wouldn't go to him!"

When nine-year-old Michelina Colosimo arrived in the United States, her first impressions of this country were formed on the train journey to West Virginia and her first few months in that state. After they got off the train in Fairmont, Michelina's mother Maria spotted a group of relatives. "My mother said to me, 'There's your father.'" Many cousins and other relatives had joined Carmine to greet the newcomers. Michelina approached her father. "When I got to him, he looked at me and said, 'Now you're in good hands.' I said to myself, 'I don't know, who is this guy?' I was a stranger, … I couldn't make myself feel comfortable. All I knew [in terms of men] was my grandfather in Italy."

To welcome the girl, relatives bought her some traditional American treats. "My cousin went into a little store, and he comes out with a big bunch of gum, Juicy Fruit gum, and handed it to me. I didn't know what it was." One of her relatives told Michelina: " 'That's something you put in your mouth and chew.' " Michelina did so, but she didn't like it. She did, however, think back to the train ride, where she noticed a woman who was always chewing. "My mother said, 'How come she eats all the time?' " Now Michelina understood why the American woman on the train was constantly chewing.

An uncle then purchased an ice-cream cone for Michelina, but she didn't care for that either. Another uncle bought her a bottle of Coca-Cola. "You know, I liked that Coca-Cola; I drank it all. He said: 'Would you want another bottle?' 'Si, si' " responded Michelina. "He said, 'If you want another bottle, you gotta go buy it yourself. There's a little store there, and here's a nickel; you go buy yourself another bottle of it.' So I went in. The boy behind the counter must have been 17 years old. I said 'Coca-Cola,' that's all. And I put the five cents on the counter. Ah, it was a riot!"

Michelina did not like the food in America—neither that served at restaurants nor the dishes prepared at home by her mother. The fact that the food just didn't taste right to her probably had a lot to do with her difficulty in adjusting to the presence of her newly found father—the man who had rarely written letters to his wife and child in Italy. On their first day in West Virginia, Carmine took the three new arrivals from Fairmont to Beachwood, where they dined at an Italian restaurant. "They had pork chops and mashed potatoes. I didn't eat any; I didn't like anything." At home, Michelina did not eat any of the food prepared by her mother. On the voyage from

Italy, Maria had brought a big bag of *taradde*, which were chewy, semisweet Calabrian donuts. This is all Michelina would eat. Carmine said to his daughter, "'Wait. When those go, what are you going to eat?' I said, 'I don't know.' " This continued for several months. "My father used to get so mad. He used to put my food on the table right by me, and I pushed it over." After three months, the *taradde* ran out, and Michelina had no choice but to eat the food her mother prepared. Seeking other ways to challenge her father's authority, the tenacious girl escalated her rebellion in the way she addressed her father. "I didn't like to call him 'dad.' I used to call my father 'hey.' He said, 'Don't call me hey; I'm your father.' " Eventually, Michelina made peace with her dad. Carmine helped the process with occasional gifts, such as the dress made of georgette that he bought for Michelina just after she arrived from Italy. "It took me a long time to get used to it [the georgette material], but it looked real nice."

Maria Maturani was an infant when her father left for America, so five years later when she, her brothers, and their mother Giuseppina journeyed from Italy and were escorted from New York to Niagara Falls by a relative, he was a complete stranger to her. When they arrived at the Falls Street station, Biagio Maturani boarded the train and immediately embraced his wife. Maria turned to her brother Pasquale and said, " 'Look, this man is kissing mom.' Patsy said, 'That's dad!' The train then went to the North End station and we got off. We went to my Uncle Rocco's house; there were many Giulianesi there." Indeed, a major benefit of being a later arrival was the presence of *paesani* and relatives who provided warm welcomes and helped the new immigrants get acclimated to America.

Giuseppina Ferrelli left Abruzzo in 1928 with her two small sons to join her husband Vincenzo in Lackawanna. Vincenzo and a friend met them in New York City, and the five of them rode back to Lackawanna. Giuseppina was not impressed with her new surroundings in the Steel City. "It was dirty, there were fumes and smoke, it was noisy. I saw people [ethnic groups] I had never seen." Shortly after their arrival, Vincenzo rented a unit in the Old Village that according to his wife was "dirty and had bugs." Giuseppina, upset with her husband for bringing the family to Lackawanna, asked him, "How could you bring me to a place like this?" She was very angry with him. "I told my husband that I wanted to go back to Italy." They may have been poor in Italy, she admitted, but the Pettorano sky was blue and clear, and the air was not full of soot and ore dust. Three months later, however, they moved to one of the new homes in Bethlehem Park, and Giuseppina began her adjustment to life in Lackawanna. She remained in that home long after her husband's death, living there independently until 2005. She then moved into a nursing home, where she died at the age of 106 the following year.

Iole Schiavi was seven years old when she and her mother arrived in Lackawanna in December 1928. "It was very cold in New York City and Buffalo; I wanted to go back to Italy. Mom bought me gloves in New York City." Relatives took Iole and her mother, Nazzarena, to Lehigh Avenue, where Iole's father Giovanni and an uncle lived. "There was much snow in Lackawanna. I thought Lackawanna was the ugliest place I'd ever seen—the cold, the snow, the house was ugly. No

trees or beautiful houses. It was not as nice as Italy." On top of that, Iole learned that her father had been hospitalized and was recovering from a serious work injury. Her first day in America proved to be a very difficult ordeal for her.

After serving in the Italian Army, Armando Torella left Giuliano in 1932 when his father, who had been in the United States since 1910, sent for him. Torella traveled with Giuseppe DeSantis to Naples, where they boarded the steamship *Saturnia* and sailed to New York. DeSantis went to Montgomery, New York, to work in a coal mine while Torella went to Lackawanna, where his father Antonio was boarding with the Sperduti family in Bethlehem Park. One of the first things to strike him was the number of Giulianesi living in the Steel City. "During the 1930s, there were 34 Giulianesi families in Bethlehem Park, mostly on Elm Street and Pine Street." Another native of Giuliano, Ezio Millanti, had never seen a large factory until he arrived in Lackawanna in November 1935. What most struck him was the snow. "It stood on the ground all winter. There was no sun; it was gloomy." Millanti, however, was glad to have work and appreciated the opportunities that were available in Lackawanna.

Concezio "John" Novelli arrived in the Steel City in 1935. "I didn't like the smell and dirtiness of Lackawanna—the sulphur, dust, and iron ore. There were potholes in the road, and ore dust covered everything. This depressed me; I wanted to go back to Italy." Not only did the 13-year-old have to adjust to an industrial city where he didn't speak the language, but he also had to get reacquainted with

Santo Bonitatibus, another immigrant from Pettorano sul Gizio, first immigrated to Pennsylvania, then to Lackawanna in 1923. His wife and children joined him 13 years later.
Photo source: Lake Erie Italian Club

his father, whom he hadn't seen for nine years. And get to know his stepmother and several half-sisters whom he had never met before.

Donata Bonitatibus and her two children joined their husband and father, Santo, in Lackawanna in 1936. One of the children, four-year-old Pasquale (later known as Pat), soon saw and heard things in America that he had not encountered in Italy. Their first home was a ground-floor apartment in a large building on Odell Street. "There was a cathouse in the front of the building; the walls were cardboard, and there were rats and bugs. The house was on stilts, and there was a trapdoor—without the door—in my bedroom. This was covered by a trunk." In warmer weather, he moved the trunk and had a direct view of the small swamp under the building. "I watched the ducks on the water in spring." After a while, the family moved to better accommodations in Bethlehem Park.

Sources: Interviews with Tony Grasso, December 26, 1989; Anthony DiMillo, October 17, 1996; Caroline DePaula-Silveroli, October 13, 1996; Joe Violanti, April 5, 1994; Romolo Petricca, March 27, 1986; Domenico Cellini, April 14, 1998; Gene Covelli, July 22, 1990; Yolanda Monaco-Bracci, July 9, 1996; Michelina Colosimo-Bevilacqua, October 17, 1996; Maria Maturani-Federici, September 19, 1995; Josephine Ferrelli, March 29, 1996; Iole Schiavi-Murray, October 16, 1996; Armando Torella, December 23, 1986; John Novelli, April 18, 1995; and Pat Bonitatibus, July 6, 1995.

Sojourners and Serial Migration

By the first decade of the twentieth century, when Italians began to arrive in the steel-plant district of West Seneca, the practices of labor agents, known as *padroni*, had been limited by law. Plus, after two decades of migration, the immigrants themselves were better able to organize their own resources and chains of communication, and were less likely to utilize *padroni*.

The experience of the first Italian family to settle in this area, Angelo and Caterina Morinello and their two children, provides examples of two stages of chain migration. After serving in the Italian Army, Angelo Morinello traveled to the United States in 1882 or 1883. He worked on Northern Pacific Railroad track gangs in several states, which was typical of the lone male immigrant of the sojourner stage. In 1887, Morinello initiated the family reunification stage when he returned to Italy to accompany Caterina and Francesco to the United States. After a brief stay in New York City, the family moved to the Buffalo waterfront neighborhood called "the Hooks," where Rosa was born and Morinello established a fruit stand and a store. The family's move to the steel plant district in West Seneca came when, according to the *Lackawanna Leader*, there was "a real estate boom" and "Morinello took advantage of this opportunity to 'get in on the ground floor,' as he would tell his friends." During 1902 and 03, Morinello purchased five lots along Front Street and Roland Avenue, building a three-story rooming house and general store (see Figure 5.13, p. 263). Soon *paesani* of the Morinellos were moving to Roland Avenue, where a small Italian community was taking shape. Angelo Morinello was notable as a leader of the community. Two of his sisters also came to western New York.[27]

Other Italians were sojourners and serial migrants, including those among the 200 workers, mostly European immigrants, hired to clear the land for the new Lackawanna Steel Company plant. This workforce grew as construction of the mills and railroad tracks progressed, with the men earning $1.50 per day. By 1902, there were 150 Italian laborers employed at the site. Many of them lived at the southern edge of the plant grounds, on the north bank of Smokes Creek. They had constructed a hut village from driftwood and boards, and a contractor had erected a large tent to serve as a dormitory. While short-lived, this primitive Italian shantytown no doubt included both sojourners and serial migrants. The fact that some of the laborers were related or had the same surnames, and that many hailed from five regions of Italy, suggests that they were serial migrants advised of the jobs by *paesani*.[28]

Just south of Smokes Creek, across from the shantytown, was an old farmhouse with two barns that in 1901 became a boarding house run by Angelo and Maria Sperduto. This was the culmination of a 10-year journey for Angelo Sperduto. He was a 23-year-old sojourner who in 1891, emigrated from Teora, Campania, to

1903. Standing are Angelo and Maria Antonia Sperduto, Sitting are Maria Giuseppa Milano, holding her son Joe, and Gaetano Milano, holding Nick Sperduto. Angelo and Maria Giuseppa were brother and sister. The Milanos followed the Sperdutos to West Seneca in 1901.
Photo source: Collection of Joe Milano

Newark, New Jersey, a major settlement for natives of Avellino and Salerno provinces. A few years later, his wife Maria joined him, and by 1896, the couple was living in Scranton, Pennsylvania. Back in Teora, Maria Giuseppa, Angelo's sister, married Gaetano Milano, and in 1900, the couple migrated to Newark to join relatives. Whereas many Italian males came alone, the Milanos were among those rare Italian families in 1900 who made the move to the New World as a family unit. When Angelo Sperduto notified them that there was work available in Scranton, Gaetano and Maria Giuseppa traveled there, settling in a shantytown in nearby Dunmore, the site of a large Italian colony. Gaetano worked at the mines as a slate picker, removing stone from the coal as it passed on conveyor belts.[29]

Although Angelo Sperduto did not work in the steel mills, he saw opportunities related to the construction of the new plant of the Lackawanna Steel Company. Sperduto wasted no time in migrating with his wife Maria and son Nicholas to West Seneca in 1901. Moving into the old farm building near Smokes Creek and west of the Hamburg Turnpike (see Figure 2.16), the Sperdutos are said to have had up to 24 Italian boarders. Maria washed their clothes in the waters of the creek.

FIGURE 2.8

ITALIANS THROUGHOUT WESTERN NEW YORK

About 70% of Italian immigrants to the United States settled in the Northeast—especially New York, where New York City was the main port of arrival. Of America's nearly half-million Italian immigrants in 1900, more than 183,000 lived in New York state, the majority in the New York City area. Some 10,000 Italian immigrants had, however, ventured out to smaller hub cities, such as Buffalo, Rochester, and Syracuse. Italians began arriving in Buffalo, the state's second largest city, in the 1840s. As the city grew over the next 50 years, it offered jobs in commercial fruit distribution, outdoor construction, and streetcar-line maintenance. In 1902, Giovanni Banchetti, the Italian consular agent, reported that 13,800 Italians lived in Buffalo, plus another 8,000 in nearby towns. Spread throughout western New York, the Italian immigrants settled in towns stretching from Rochester on the east, west to Niagara Falls, then south to Buffalo and Fredonia (see Figure 2.13).

Consular agent Banchetti also noted in 1902 that many Buffalo-area Italians found jobs on the railroads: 150 worked on the Erie Railroad, 510 on the Lehigh Valley, and 300 on the Lake Shore and Michigan Southern. The New York Central Railroad estimated that at the turn of the twentieth century one-fourth of its 11,000 laborers were Italian. In 1900, some Italian railroad laborers resided in Batavia and Warsaw, while others lived in railroad cars in Gainesville. In Buffalo, an Italian settlement was established in the Lovejoy district, close to the east-side rail yards where the men worked. Others clustered in nearby towns, such as Hamburg,

where 13 Italian railroad laborers boarded together.

While most Italian immigrants in western New York during the early 1900s were involved in railroad work, the rest engaged in a variety of other occupations. In Genesee County, LeRoy was home to Italian quarrymen and bean pickers. Many in Orleans County settled near the stone quarries in which they worked, some 500 in Murray alone. Italian residents of Geneseo in Livingston County worked at a bran factory, and in nearby Retsof and York, Italians labored in the salt mines. While constructing and maintaining railroad tracks along the shore of Lake Erie, some immigrants spotted available land and founded farming colonies in Fredonia, Silver Creek, Dunkirk, and Falconer in Chautauqua County. A settlement of 400 Sicilian families established farms in Mount Morris. Others established vineyards and vegetable farms near Brant, Farnham, and North Collins in southern Erie County. Lewiston and Lockport in Niagara County had small settlements of Italian day laborers, while their fellow ethnics in Niagara Falls helped build the power plant.

In 1905, some 30 day laborers, many working as brickyard laborers, lived in three boarding houses in the township of Orchard Park. That same year, the New York State Census found 82 Italian day laborers boarding together in the nearby village of Blasdell but gave no indication of the nature of their work. Over the following two decades, Italians found other types of vocations. The population of Newstead in 1920 included 72 Italian men who labored in a gypsum mine and

at a stone crushing plant. Along Abbott Road, just south of Lackawanna in Orchard Park township, several Italians took up truck farming prior to World War I. In the 1920s, they were joined by 20 others who were laborers on the railroads and at local industries.

Italian immigrants continued to migrate throughout western New York. Assisted by *paesani*, who provided information and a place to stay, some found railroad jobs and other work. Others alternated seasonal jobs, shifting from railroad labor to farm labor. Some workers who maintained mainline track beds settled in Angola, where they also found jobs in a tile factory and a bicycle shop. Railroad labor camps were a common sight. In 1915, while most Italians in North Collins were engaged in farming, an encampment of 42 railroad laborers, probably living in boxcars, was also present. That year, the eastern section of West Seneca was home to 59 Italian railroad workers, five of them track gang foremen.

A few western New York Italians worked in the iron and steel industry during the first decade of the twentieth century—60 in a foundry in Tonawanda, 45 in small iron and steel plants in Lancaster, and others at Vanadium Steel in Niagara Falls. Italians living in the Germania Street neighborhood of South Buffalo worked at New York State Steel, which later became Republic Steel. It was along the shores of Lake Erie in West Seneca, however, that Italians were concentrated in a huge steelmaking complex.

Sources: Bureau of the Census. 1900 Census, Volume 1: Population, pp. 773, 817; Giovanni Banchetti. "Gl'Italiani in Alcuni Distretti dello Stato di Nuova York," Bollettino dell'Emigrazione, No. 5, 1902, pp. 19-21; Virginia Yans-McLaughlin, *Family and Community, Italian Immigrants in Buffalo, 1880-1930*, 1971, pp. 37-39; Michael A. LaSorte, "Italians in Upstate New York, 1900: A Census Analysis," unpublished paper, 1979; and interviews. The section of the township of Orchard Park was then the town of East Hamburg

FIGURE 2.9

THE THREE ODDI BROTHERS FROM PETTORANO

Benigno and Pietro Oddi left Pettorano sul Gizio, Abruzzo, in 1892 for the United States, sent by their father to join *paesani* working in the mines of Colorado. Perhaps the twofold goal was to help Pietro avoid the military draft and ensure that Benigno, who had served in the army, would not be called up again. The two brothers disliked working underground and left the mines for railroad work in Pennsylvania. It is unclear if they remained together, but in 1896, Pietro was living among *paesani* in Bradford or Lewis Run. Some of the money that the two men sent back to Italy was used to buy an army commission for their brother Raffaele.

Although some sojourners had wives in Italy, Benigno and Pietro Oddi were single when they left. That changed in 1900, when they returned to Pettorano sul Gizio and married sisters in a double wedding arranged by their mother. Benigno married Giselda Monaco and Pietro, her sister Enrichietta. Within a year, each woman gave birth, but tragically, Benigno and Giselda's daughter Carmela died as an infant. The two brothers returned to the United States in May 1901, and went to Bradford. Pietro was in West Seneca by 1902, working on a crew building the Old Village and rooming at Sperduto's boarding house. The following year, he sent for Enrichietta

Benigno and Giselda Oddi, with children James and Annie, circa 1910. The couple soon had two more children, Dominic and Margaret. Benigno Oddi and his brother Pietro were two of the first Italians to become foremen at the Lackawanna Steel Company. Photo source: Margaret Oddy-Guastaferro

and their child, Giacontina. In 1904, the family, which now included son Nunzio, moved into the newly completed Old Village. Pietro had been promoted to foreman in the Yard Department.

Benigno, who had returned to Italy, rejoined his brother in West Seneca in 1903. His wife Gesella Oddi joined him by 1907. Raffaele immigrated to Buffalo and was living on Seneca Street in Buffalo

by 1904. He married Ermina Carfagna, the daughter of a prominent Italian American doctor, and by 1910, the couple was residing in Lackawanna. That year, all three Oddi brothers and their families lived in the Old Village, and the brothers were foremen at the steel plant. Their children later Americanized the family name to Oddy.[24]

Sources: Passenger ship list, *SS Belgravia*, May 4, 1901, Ellis Island Records website; interviews with Nunze Oddy, April 12, 1982, Margaret Oddy-Guastaferro, July 5, 1996.

They then sent word to Gaetano Milano in Scranton that Lackawanna Steel was hiring construction workers. The Milanos soon arrived in West Seneca, boarding with the Sperdutos, and Gaetano was hired by the contractor erecting No. 1 Open Hearth. For its foundation, thousands of wooden piles were driven into the swampy land, then workers sawed off the tops. The men were paid $2.25 per day. Both Gaetano Milano and Angelo Sperduto apparently decided West Seneca would be their permanent home. In 1907, Angelo sent to Italy for his parents, Nicola and Filomena Sperduto.[30]

Antonio Grossi (his son later changed the name to Grosso) also settled in the steel-plant district after first living elsewhere in the United States. He and two traveling companions, Antonio Carnevale and Giovanni Martino, had arrived in New York City in 1899, part of the serial migration of males from Pico, Lazio. Grossi and Carnevale remained in the city for a year, living on Mulberry Street and working on a garbage barge for a daily wage of 90 cents. Contacted by *paesani* in West Seneca in about 1902, Grossi and Carnevale set out for the better-paying construction jobs at the steel-plant site. Getting off the train in Blasdell, they followed the conductor's directions, walking north along the tracks to Smokes Creek, then going west to Sperduto's boarding house.[31]

The U.S. Immigration Commission noted that many Italians employed during the construction of the Lackawanna Steel plant left the area after the major mills had been erected and become operational in 1903 and 1904. Many of the men in the shantytown were Siciliani, Toscani, and Veneziani, and few people from these regions settled in Lackawanna in the early years of the century. Thousands of other European immigrants soon took their place, attracted by jobs offered at the huge steel plant. Many had simply followed the Lackawanna Steel plant from Scranton, Pennsylvania, to its new home. Most were Irish, some were Poles, and a few, such as the Sperduto and Milano families, were Italian. Brothers Benigno and Pietro Oddi, natives of Pettorano, Abruzzo, had spent time in Bradford, Pennsylvania, then moved to West Seneca. Pietro arrived by 1902 and lived at the Sperduto boarding home. Benigno came in 1903, and another Oddi brother, Raffaele, made his appearance several years later (see Figure 2.9).[32]

Another cluster of Italians was forming around the hotel established in 1902 by Luca Tarquinio and his son-in-law, Antonio Mauriello, on Gates Avenue. Their Albergo Italiano (Italian Hotel) offered "all the comforts needed by Italians working in the steel plant," according to an ad in *Corriere Italiano*. By June 1903, the hotel hosted about 80 individuals and several families. When 19-year-old Eugenio Colello left Pico in 1903, he arrived in New York City, then traveled straight to West Seneca to join his brother Gaetano on Gates Avenue.[33]

The steel plant drew Italian immigrants from all over the United States. The Italian men and women coming to the steel-plant district between 1900 and 1910 had arrived in the United States an average of four years earlier. Over 60% of the immigrants came to Lackawanna within one to five years of their arrival in the United States; the others, between six and 21 years after crossing the ocean. About one of every seven male immigrants and one of every eight females arrived in the area the same year as their arrival in the United States, so it is presumed they came directly to West Seneca's steel-plant district.[34]

Typical of the sojourner and serial-migration phases of immigration, four of every five Italians arriving in Lackawanna between 1900 and 1910 were males. One of the lone male sojourners was Giuseppe Ottariona, who joined six other Italians boarding with an Austrian family on Gates Avenue. Another was Antonio Pagliei, who was one of the 10 Italian day laborers living at the boarding house operated by Guglielmo and Lizzie Grotto on Ingham Avenue. Michele Nigro, on the other hand, came to the Old Village from Italy to board with

Luigi and Celestino Nigro, an example of serial migration, in which a newcomer is assisted by earlier arrivals. The migration of several females to Lackawanna seemed to touch on both serial immigration and family reunification, the third stage of chain migration. Likewise, Luisa D'Alessandro came directly to Lackawanna, where she joined her sister and brother-in-law, Clementina and Ruta Pellegrino. Attilia Rico journeyed to the Old Village from Abruzzo to live with her sister and brother-in-law, Teresa and Salvatore DiTommaso.[35]

Many Italians living in the steel-plant sector of West Seneca in 1905 soon departed the area, just as the construction laborers had done a year or two earlier. Of the 220 Italian males who arrived in Lackawanna between 1900 and 1905, over 70% departed within a year. Only 28 were still residents after 1930 (see Figure 2-11). This high departure rate diminished in the 1920s, when it fell to 50% but was still very significant. The Italian immigrant turnover in West Seneca-Lackawanna during the first three decades of the century was consistent with the general trend among Italians to move around throughout western New York. During this period, only a small core of Italians remained in the city. Of the 801 immigrant men who arrived between 1900 and 1915, only 174 were living in the city after 1930. These men and their families were the initial core group that provided much of the leadership and direction for the Lackawanna Italian colony (see Chapter 3). Most male immigrants came for a short period and then left. The comparatively steady work in the steel plant provided a source of jobs that, while unfamiliar or unattractive to many Italian peasants, filled a gap for those who would be migrating to other settlements in western New York or to more distant towns in America, as well as back and forth to Italy.[36]

Lackawanna was basically a one-industry town, so when the mills were slow the Italians went looking for work elsewhere as they had previously done in southern Italy. In her study of Buffalo's Italians, Virginia Yans-McLaughlin notes this pattern:

> Once in Buffalo, Italians usually worked in outdoor jobs which also left them underemployed. Many compensated for the seasonal unemployment just as they had in Italy; they took any available day laborer's job in the city or drifted around the Niagara Frontier region seeking work as construction, railroad, or agricultural laborers. Thus, their Old World patterns enabled these immigrants to deal effectively with underemployment: exploring alternatives, accepting shifts in jobs, and even moving from one town to another in order to obtain work.

Many Italian immigrants and their families moved from Lackawanna to other towns in western New York as well as to more distant locations. A number of them simply moved a

Arcangelo Cervoni, an immigrant from Ceprano in Lazio, first lived in Canandaigua, New York, before establishing a home on Holbrook Street.
Photo source: Lake Erie Italian Club

few miles to Buffalo, Blasdell, or Hamburg and commuted to work at the steel plant. This allowed them to escape the ore dust, soot, swamps, and crowded conditions of Lackawanna's First Ward. Umberto Giannotti, who moved to Blasdell by 1911, was followed by the families of Angelo Croce, and Emidio, Donato, and Giuseppe Iacobucci over the next 16 years. Some families moved away, then came back to the city. Pasquale and Teresa Ciccarelli came to the United States in the early 1890s and moved with their two children to the steel-plant district of West Seneca in 1903. Living near Germania Street in South Buffalo in 1910, the family again took up residence in Lackawanna by 1917 and in the early 1920s reestablished a home in South Buffalo.[37]

As mentioned earlier, some Italian immigrants to the United States returned to their homeland, doing so at a higher rate than most other immigrant groups. Between 1900 and 1914, 1.5 million went back to Italy. Among southern Italians arriving in the United States between 1908 and 1917, the return rate was most pronounced: for every 100 *meridianali* (southerners) arriving, 56 departed. A study of the Italian community in Utica, New York, found that despite its growing size, about half the Italians listed in the 1905 city directory were not listed in the 1910 edition. A similar rate of turnover took place between 1910 and 1915. In Lackawanna, the rate of out-migration was even higher; two-thirds of the Italian

male immigrants arriving between 1911 and 1915 departed within five years. The Italian community in Retsof, northeast of Lackawanna, had even a higher rate yet, with a 75% turnover of workers in just one year. Virtually none of the 150 Italians present in the town in 1900 were listed in the 1910 U.S. Census.[38]

Serial and Delayed Migration: 1911 – 1930

Lackawanna was incorporated as a city in July 1909 and in the following years, the Italian population grew in proportion to the city's overall population. From 1911 to 1920, more than 1,000 immigrants fed the rapid expansion of the Italian enclaves on Ingham Avenue, Roland Avenue, and in the Old Village (see Figure 2.15). Many arrived in the city prior to the outbreak of World War I in 1914, and another group migrated from various American cities in search of defense jobs in 1917 and 1918. Males continued to dominate the Italian migration to Lackawanna, comprising about three of every four immigrants between 1900 and 1930. Those arriving between 1911 and 1930 had longer stays in the United States prior to living in Lackawanna: the men averaged about seven years, the women six. And Italians were still migrating to other American cities or returning to Italy. Only 21% of the male Italian immigrants arriving in the city between 1911 and 1920 were residents after 1930. Of those arriving between 1921 and 1930, only 38% were still residing in the city by 1935. Sojourners (lone males) continued to find their way to Lackawanna. Lazio native Matteo Iorio arrived in 1910 from Pittsburgh. Luigi Scarnecchia emigrated from Abruzzo in 1906; six years later, he was working in Albion, and by 1918 he had taken up residence on Ingham

---

FIGURE 2.10

Italian Immigrants Arriving in Lackawanna by Specified Decade and Gender

Decade	Total Immigrants	Males No. (%)	Females No. (%)
1900 – 1910	637	519 (81)	118 (19)
1911 – 1920	1,054	830 (79)	224 (21)
1921 – 1930	679	475 (70)	204 (30)
1931 – 1940	150	110 (73)	40 (27)
1941 – 1950	69	32 (46)	37 (54)
1951 – 1960	56	34 (61)	22 (39)
1961 – 1970	26	15 (58)	11 (42)
1971 – 1999	2	2 (100)	— —
Date unknown	397	133 (34)	264 (66)
Grand Totals	**3,070**	**2,150 (70%)**	**920 (30%)**

Avenue. The process of serial migration was more noticeable during the decade from 1910 to 1919. Pietro Carnevale came directly to Lackawanna in 1910 to join *paesani*, as did Domenico Iacobucci, who arrived in the same year from Abruzzo. Giuseppe Baldassari left Marche in 1919 to join his uncle, Cassiano Baldassari, who had earlier migrated to Lackawanna.[39]

Increasingly, the trend became for immigrants to reunite with family members in Lackawanna or to marry and establish families there. This can be seen in the increased number of immigrants who arrived in Lackawanna in the same year they came to America. While this was rare among Italian males, the rate for women was 13% in 1900 to '10, and after a decrease in the next decade, it climbed to 18% in 1921 to '30. This indicates that Italian men frequently migrated throughout the United States during the First World War, then decided to remain in the United States. Starting in 1919, they began to return to Italy and marry, to finalize arrangements to bring their wives and children to America, or to send for their wives or fiancees in Italy. During the 1920s, wives and children were increasingly coming directly to Lackawanna. Other women came from settlements throughout the United States to either marry or be reunited with their husbands.[40]

Maria DiMillio joined her husband Antonio in Lackawanna in 1913, and Graziella Giansante was reunited with her husband Domenico in 1919. Some immigrants, after bringing their families together in America, continued to migrate to seek better jobs or more favorable living situations. In 1907, Sabato Conte migrated from Grottolella, Campania, to Pittsburgh, where his wife and children joined him. The family moved to Lackawanna's Old Village by 1917. Emilio Miniri, who migrated to the United States from Lazio in 1910, was joined by his wife Emilia by 1914. They lived in Halberton and then Fancher, New York, where Miniri worked in a quarry before the couple moved to Lackawanna in 1919.[41]

Even before World War I, more Italian immigrants had decided to remain in the United States permanently, a situation that was noticeable after 1910. Among the male immigrants coming to Lackawanna from 1911 to 1915, about one-fourth became permanent residents. The advent of World War I in August 1914 and the resulting decrease in transatlantic travel were significant factors in this process. But the decision to remain in the United States permanently didn't mean that an immigrant immediately settled in one location. While more immigrants were settling in the Steel City, a significant number continued to move around. About 60% of male Italian immigrants living in Lackawanna in 1915 were also present in January 1920. The city trailed Utica, however, where 75% of the Italians present in 1915 were still there in 1919.[42]

Some 345 Italian men came to Lackawanna in 1917 and '18 for defense jobs, but approximately 240 of them left the city after the war ended. Many other Italian men left Lackawanna temporarily in 1919 and 1920 to return to Italy to visit their relatives, find wives, or establish families before returning to the United States. Others departed from the city during the four months of the violent and divisive steel strike of 1919. During the strike some went to other towns; Michele Grasso took his family to Buffalo, and along with many others had not yet returned to Lackawanna when the census takers made their rounds in January 1920.[43]

The city's Italian population then stabilized as the immigration laws of 1921 and 1924 set stringent limits on the number of southern and eastern Europeans who could enter the United States. Over one-third of the Italian male immigrants arriving in Lackawanna between 1921 and 1925 were present in the city after 1930. *Paesani* continued to send out the word

FIGURE 2.11

Length of Residence in Lackawanna: Italian Male Immigrants Arriving in City, 1900 – 1930

Year Arrived in City	Total No.	Residing in Lackawanna for Specified Number of Years							
		1	2-5	6-10	11-15	16-20	21-25	26-30	post 1930 or 1935*
1900-05	222	71%	4%	2%	2%	5%	2%	1%	13%
1906-10	297	68	4	6	1	1	0	—	20
1911-15	298	50	14	8	3	1	—	—	24
1916-20	532	64	11	4	2	—	—	—	19
1921-25	237	51	10	1	—	—	—	—	38
1926-30	238	50	10	2	—	—	—	—	38*
Total:	**1,824**								

*For 1926-30 arrivals, the right-hand column figure is post-1935.

that jobs were available in the steel plant, drawing 220 men to the city between 1926 and 1930. Two out of every five of these men were still residing in the Steel City after 1935. While the majority of Italian immigrants arriving in Lackawanna during the 1920s were males, the number of females had increased to 30% of the total. This indicates the continuing trend of men who had arrived earlier to form families or reunite with their families and settle in Lackawanna.

Migrations: 1931 – 1945 and Post–World War II

The Great Depression slowed the flow of arrivals in Lackawanna—from both Italy and other American cities. Between 1930 and 1940, the total population of the city grew by only 110, to 24,058. During the Depression, Lackawanna may have suffered less than other industrial towns because the steel plant continued to operate, though at a reduced level. The town nevertheless felt the effects of the economic downturn. New workers arrived from towns in Ohio and Pennsylvania, where smaller steel mills had folded. Some were hired at the old Seneca Steel plant in Blasdell, which Bethlehem Steel purchased in 1932; others signed on at the new Strip Mill that opened in 1936. Many people no doubt came to Lackawanna then left during that time, so the actual number of incoming migrants was probably more than several hundred. Other plants—such as Donner Hanna Furnace, Buffalo Brake Beam, and the new Spring Perch plant, which moved to Lackawanna in 1932, hired workers, too. Approximately 150 Italian immigrants, one-fourth of them women, settled in Lackawanna between 1931 and 1940. Additional migrants arrived from other parts of the United States during World War II as defense contracts created the demand for more workers.[44]

The postwar period saw Italy devastated by war and the Italian population struggling to survive. Many Italians in small towns moved to nearby cities to escape poverty, while others immigrated abroad to seek opportunity. Those living in Frosinone Province began moving to nearby Rome in the 1920s, a migration that increased over the five following decades. Giuliano's population decreased by one-third between 1931 and 1971, with the emigration to other countries accelerating between 1951 and 1961 (see Figure 2.4). Italy continued to provide one of the largest streams of immigrants to the United States in the post–World War II decades, sending 400,000 people between 1951 and 1970. Many had relatives and *paesani* in America and were simply following the chain-migration routes established earlier in the century—but with several notable differences. Travel speed and comfort had increased as steamships improved and airplanes became available for transatlantic travel. But with restrictive immigration

Giuseppe Cardinale, better known as Josie, left Fondi, Lazio, at age 16 for Colorado. A friend later wrote him about jobs on the South Buffalo Railway, and in 1907, Cardinale began a 48-year career on the railway.
Photo source: Collection of Sam Cardinale

laws in force until 1968, Italians often had to first migrate to other countries in North or South America before coming to the United States. At the same time, new immigrants had the advantage of American relatives who were long-term residents, citizens, and financially secure, as compared to their struggling cousins in war-ravaged Italy. Italian Americans could provide housing, job contacts, and reassurance to authorities that the immigrants would not become wards of the state. Not insignificantly, prejudice against Italians had dropped considerably by 1945.[45]

Lackawanna, with its relatively small Italian population, drew approximately 115 emigrants from Italy between 1946 and 2000. Many of these had been separated from family members for 10 or 20 years and came from provinces already represented in Lackawanna, especially Frosinone in Lazio and Aquila in Abruzzo. Some traveled directly to Lackawanna, while others, like earlier immigrants, followed the chain of *paesani* settlements in the United States that eventually brought them to the Steel City.

Teenagers Ena and Santino Carnevale continued to live with their grandmother in Pico until 1946, when their father sent money for their passage to the United States. They sailed from Naples in December—Ena in second-class, Santino in third. The ship carried mostly war brides and a few other children. At dockside in New York, "all the women met their men, but we two kids couldn't find our dad." Santino continues, "A port worker took our hands and walked down the pier yelling 'Carnevale' until my dad appeared."[46]

In 1948, 14-year-old Gaetano Iannarelli left Pettorano sul Gizio with two traveling companions, a mother and her son. In New York, they parted ways, the mother and son going to Boston, Iannarelli journeying to Lackawanna to board with his father Domenico and brothers on Holland Avenue. This was really his first contact with his father, since Gaetano was only a year old when Domenico left Abruzzo. But it would be a brief reunion. By 1950, after almost 30 years in America, Domenico decided to return to Italy to join his wife and daughter. Gaetano, who had taken the name Guy, remarked, "I only knew my father for two years." He and his two older brothers remained in the United States. Guy visited Pettorano in 1957 and married Delia Suffoletta. He returned to Lackawanna, and she joined him the following year.[47]

Natives of Bagnoli Irpino, Campania, had immigrated to the Steel City early in the century and were followed by *paesani* after World War II. Domenico Russo and Raffaele Patrone arrived in Lackawanna in the early 1950s. Raffaele Vivolo first traveled from Bagnoli Irpino to Venezuela in the late 1950s, worked there seven years, then migrated to Germany, where relatives helped him procure construction jobs. In 1967, he moved to his final home in Lackawanna, where his wife Rosalina soon joined him.[48]

During these postwar years, others struggled to survive in Italy and to start their own families before emigrating. Following the war, Lelio DeSantis was a construction laborer based in a town 20 miles from his hometown of Giuliano. "I lived in Pontecorvo and went to Giuliano on weekends. I did this for five years." In 1950, he went on a vacation to Rome, where he visited a cousin working with the FAO [Food and Agricultural Organization], a United Nations group. Through his cousin, Lelio got a job with FAO and became involved in setting up field offices for engineers. He married Faustina Fabi that same year, and for the next six years they lived in Rome, where two children were born. Deciding to join Lelio's father and brother Egino in Lackawanna, they sailed for America in 1956. Lelio's mother and sister soon followed.[49]

Carlo Savaglio left Marano Principato in 1951. A friend of the family accompanied the 16-year-old Savaglio on the train ride from Cosenza to Naples. There, he boarded the *Conte Biancomano*, where he had a first-class cabin. His father Mariano had been in the United States for 13 years and had regularly mailed money to his wife and son in Italy, including the funds for Carlo's steamship ticket. "I was seasick for all 12 days," recalls Savaglio. His father and Gino Monaco greeted Carlo at dockside. "They drove down to New York in my father's 1942 Nash, and he drove us back in eight hours," states Savaglio. Apparently, Mariano wanted to waste no time getting his son to his new home in America.[50]

In 1956, 21-year-old Cesare Cardi faced a dilemma. He realized that if he went into the Italian Army, he would not be allowed to immigrate to the United States later, as American laws prohibited this. He did, however, qualify for refugee status because his family's house in Lenola had been destroyed by American bombs during World War II. Cardi had been working in Munich, Germany, and there he arranged the necessary emigration papers. In 1957, Cardi came to the United States in a manner unknown to earlier emigrants from Italy—he flew. Arriving in New York City, he joined relatives and started work in a men's pants shop. The next year, he moved to Hartford, Connecticut, where he and a cousin opened a tailor shop, but this venture failed. During a visit, Louise Cardinale, an aunt who lived in Lackawanna, said to Cardi; "Come to Lackawanna. You can earn $96 a week in the plant." So in 1959, Cardi made the trip to Lackawanna, moved in with the Cardinale family, and with a cousin's assistance, found a job in the Strip Mill. Two years later, he opened a tailor shop. His parents and sister flew to the United States to join him, and by 1964, the whole family was working in Cardi's tailor shop.[51]

Post–World War II immigrants, like those who migrated decades earlier, had vivid, lasting first impressions of Lackawanna. Elio Liberta arrived in western New York in 1947. He had expected to see "clean and nice houses, but the houses on Ingham Avenue looked like shacks. And there was the smoke and ore dust." That same year, Egino "Gene" DeSantis arrived in Lackawanna to join his father. What struck him was America's wealth. "In Italy, we had little. In Lackawanna, I saw bicycles just lying around. In 1948, my Uncle Faust [DeSantis] bought a new car and gave me his 1935 Ford." In postwar Italy, Gene didn't know many Italians who had a car, let alone any who could afford to give a used car away. Gene also made a sad discovery in the United States—bigotry. "When I first came here, I was called names." During his tour of duty in the Army, in 1952 and 1953, he was often referred to as a "dago."[52]

Gene DeSantis's older brother Lelio arrived in Lackawanna in 1956 with his wife and two children. He had a difficult time learning English and was glad that many people in Bethlehem Park spoke Italian. "At first I cried; I wanted to go back to Italy. I didn't like my laborer's job, the constant layoffs, and signing up for unemployment." But he eventually found a good job and adjusted to the new country. Santino "Sandy" Carnevale arrived in the United States in January 1947. "After one week I wanted to return to Italy. It was a very cold winter, I missed my grandparents, and the food was different, especially the bread. And I had never had butter before."[53]

Cleo Gabrielle came to Lackawanna to marry her fiance, Ezio Millanti in 1947. Prior to emigrating from Giuliano, she had a good impression of America because of the money her father sent back to Italy and the news she heard from other relatives in the United States. "I arrived in the summer and liked the house, the appliances, the conveniences. Bethlehem Park was like a small Italian town; there were many *paesani* there." There were negative aspects, too. "The language and the weather were hard; it was too cold. The steel plant made too much noise, especially at night."[54]

In 1954, Ennio Guglielmi arrived in Niagara Falls, New York, where he lived with his sister and her husband. He got a job at the Vanadium Steel Corporation, but when the plant closed six months later, he moved in with his brother Giuseppe in Lackawanna. "I didn't like living in the basement in my brother's house; it was depressing. Lackawanna had bad air. I had some doubts; I wanted to go back to Italy. I knew my sister Maria; I hardly knew my brother Giuseppe. I liked Niagara Falls; it was better than Lackawanna—not as dirty."[55]

Carlo Savaglio has two vivid memories of his arrival in Lackawanna in September 1951: "Lackawanna looked like a coal mine, and I couldn't speak English." Living with his father Mariano on Dona Street, the teenage Carlo went to the Bethlehem Park School and was placed in the kindergarten class. "I lasted six months and then quit!" Mariano was a good friend of Russell Mesi, a co-owner of the Lackawanna Laundry, who lined up a full-time job for Carlo. As he worked alongside 30 other employees, most of whom were African American or Italian, Carlo practiced his English. At night, he and his father made ice cream. They took turns on afternoon and evening shifts driving Mariano's horse and wagon throughout the streets of Lackawanna and South Buffalo selling ice cream to hundreds of eager children. This experience proved most helpful of all in developing Carlo's ability to communicate in English.[56]

Cesare Cardi lived in New York City for the year following his immigration in 1957. "I was disappointed with New York. I saw drunks on the streets, dirty streets, and empty bottles near the airport. It wasn't like the movies of New York. But I did like Staten Island." Two years later, Cardi arrived in the Steel City. "Lackawanna was amazing; chimneys, smoke, a train inside the steel plant. This was a new experience for me. I was impressed." Cardi's parents and sister Elide came to Lackawanna, but Elide returned to Italy after one year. "She missed the leisurely lifestyle in Italy," explained her brother.[57]

Family and *Paesani* Migration Routes

As we have seen, many Lackawanna Italians first resided elsewhere in America, following migration chains that included many different settlements (see figures 2.26, 2.27, and 2.28). Immigrants moved several times within the United States to accomplish specific goals, of which job security and safe working conditions were most crucial. They also wanted to be with family and *paesani*, enjoying the support of familiar faces and speaking their local dialect. The principal means of exchanging information on jobs was through the informal *paesani* communication network: word of mouth, letters, visits to other towns in America, and return trips to Italy. Families who received the migrants helped their relatives and townspeople by sharing money, housing, and emotional support, and arranging marriages.

From other New York Towns to Lackawanna

Many an Italian immigrant moved to the Steel City from neighboring Buffalo, which, by 1930 was home to 19,471 Italian natives and 31,890 of their American-born children. During the first half of the twentieth century, a number of them worked in Lackawanna and decided to move closer to their jobs, while others wanted to escape tenements and big-city problems. Available documents and interviews indicate that at least 200 adult immigrants, both male and female, migrated from Buffalo to Lackawanna. A number of American-born Italians, also moved from Buffalo, usually following marriages to Lackawanna residents.[58]

Buffalo had six large Italian neighborhoods in the early decades of the twentieth century (see Figures 2.18 and 2.19). The lower West Side and Near East Side were each served by major streetcar and, later, bus lines going south. Thus, in the early decades of the last century, many residents commuted to Lackawanna's mills. Once jobs there were secure and more housing became available, a number of them moved to the Steel City.

Between 1900 and 1910, some Buffalonians walked to the mills to save the nickel or dime fares, creating an even stronger incentive to move to Lackawanna. Saverio Morgante, later known as Sam Morgan, was one of these. Morgan first settled among other natives of Santacroce, Molise, in Buffalo's East Lovejoy district in 1903 and walked to his job at Lackawanna's Buffalo Brake Beam. Within five years, he moved to Ingham Avenue, thereby shortening his daily walk from four or five miles to four or five blocks.[59]

Francesco Falcone, like his wife Carmela, had emigrated from Campania as a child. The couple married in Buffalo and lived for many years on Buffalo's Near East Side before moving to Lackawanna in 1910. Falcone probably was a *paesano* of Angelo Morinello, as were Biagio and Fonsina Vertalino. The

Angelamaria Giorgio and her husband Antonio, immigrants from San Fele, Basilicata, moved their bakery from Buffalo to Lackawanna's Ingham Avenue in 1908. They changed the family name to George.
Photo source: Collection of Louis Petrucci

Vertalinos also married in Buffalo and settled on the Near East Side, where their two oldest children were born. Biagio Vertalino, a laborer on the streetcar line running on Electric Avenue in Lackawanna, moved his family to Lackawanna in about 1912 to join the Morinellos and other *paesani* from the province of Salerno. The eldest Vertalino child, Nick, recalls that the family lived on Milnor Avenue for about a year, then returned to Buffalo. In 1913, the Vertalinos again migrated to Lackawanna, this time for good.[60]

The Hooks, on the lower West Side, was one of Buffalo's first and most densely populated Italian settlements. Antonio and Angelamaria Giorgio, natives of San Fele, Basilicata, operated a bakery there with the help of their children; they eventually changed their surname to George. Moving to Lackawanna in 1908, the family reestablished its bakery on Ingham Avenue. There were several clusters of men from Giuliano di Roma in the Hooks by 1905. Four immigrants lived at 89 Canal Street, and nearby was a boarding house where Achille and Biagio Colafranceschi and Arcangelo Gabrielle resided. From these and other boarding houses, a number of the Giulianesi moved to Lackawanna. The family

of Bruno and Rosamaria Falbo reversed the process, moving from Roland Avenue to 13 State Street in the Hooks, where many other Calabresi lived. After a brief stay, the Falbos grew disillusioned with big-city life and returned to the relative calm of Roland Avenue.[61]

In 1907, ads in *Corriere Italiano* promised readers that small payments made it easy to purchase homes next to the newly built New York Steel Company plant in South Buffalo. This tract in the Germania Street neighborhood was only a mile-and-a-half north of Ridge Road, the main thoroughfare in the Steel City. Italians from many regions were drawn to the area, and in 1909, an Italian Catholic church was established. Among the many natives of Lazio who settled there was Gaetano Masocco, who left Giuliano di Roma in 1913 and traveled straight to Germania Street to join his *paesani*. He returned to Italy, married, then moved back to South Buffalo and resumed work on a railroad-track gang. His wife Maria and their two children joined him in 1934; five years later, they were residents of Bethlehem Park in Lackawanna.[62]

A number of Italians used Buffalo as a temporary weigh station between trips to other U.S. locales or Italy, or to await relatives coming from Italy. During these sojourns, an immigrant needed to learn of work opportunities and the most convenient locales in which to live. In about 1905, Giovanni Violanti migrated from Giuliano to Buffalo to join a cousin. After working on a road-building crew, he heard from a *paesano*, Biagio Catuzza, about available railroad jobs. The two men migrated to Sayre, Pennsylvania, and worked on the Lehigh Valley Railroad. Each married the other's sister, and both couples traveled to Lackawanna in 1918, where Violanti and Catuzza procured jobs in the Yard Department. Violanti's father and siblings then migrated to the Steel City.[63]

In addition to Buffalo, at least 37 other cities or towns in the Empire State provided Italian migrants to Lackawanna, most of them in upstate New York (see Figures 2.14, 2.15, 2.20). A large Italian community emerged on the north side of Niagara Falls, many of whose male residents worked in the Yard Department of Vanadium Steel Corporation. A number of families from Giuliano lived along Garden Avenue, including many members of the Maturani and DeSantis extended families, who also had relatives in Lackawanna. Giulianesi moved back and forth between the two cities. Biagio Maturani migrated to Niagara Falls, where in 1926 he was joined by his wife Giuseppina DeSantis and their children. Maturani's godson, Alberto Federici, came to live with the family, then moved to Lackawanna, where a relative had lined up a job for him on the South Buffalo Railway. In 1940, Federici married Biagio's daughter, Maria, and they purchased a home in Bethlehem Park.[64]

Before settling in Lackawanna, Molise native Michele Petrucci lived in upstate New York, where he labored on the railroad and on his half-brother's potato farm in Clyde. Petrucci's family joined him in 1922, but with the Depression, his job options dwindled. Bethlehem Steel, still had jobs, so in 1932 relatives sent for him. Petrucci and his 17-year-old son Luigi arrived in Lackawanna and were soon working in the Yard Department at Bethlehem Steel.[65]

Many Italians living in Olean, New York, worked on the railroads. One of them, Eugenio Galanti, had immigrated from Baselice, Campania, to New York City in 1906, then joined relatives in Olean. Six years later, *paesani* in Lackawanna, the Giovinettis, sent for him. Galanti began work as a Yard Department laborer and took up residence in the Old Village. The Giovinettis introduced him to a cousin, Filomena Paolozzi, and arranged their marriage in 1914.[66]

Migrants from other States

A significant migration took place from Pennsylvania to western New York's industrial centers, the most dramatic being the relocation of the Lackawanna Iron and Steel Company and many of its workers from Scranton to West

Seneca in 1900. The migration from Pennsylvania towns continued for many years. Some of the Italian migrants were following a series of railroad jobs that led to more stability and better pay in larger rail centers, such as Buffalo and Lackawanna. More than 100 Italians migrated to Lackawanna from 42 towns, many of them in northern and western Pennsylvania counties (see Figure 2.17).[67]

Many of the Italian immigrants who ended up in Lackawanna were escaping from the hazards of their mining jobs. They had not adjusted to working underground; mine work was dangerous, with many fatalities from cave-ins and explosions. Plus, company towns could be very oppressive, economically and otherwise. Strikes and labor unrest often led to considerable violence and severe poverty. Mines frequently shut down, causing family dislocation. Italian coal miners did not want their working-age sons to enter this dangerous occupation, or their younger children to perform the excruciating work of sorting coal from slate.

Bruno Falbo was a shepherd in Soveria Mannelli, Calabria. In 1901, at age 14, he traveled alone to the United States to join his uncle in Punxsutawney, Pennsylvania. He worked alongside his uncle in the mines but eventually grew discouraged with this type of labor. Hearing that the New York Central Railroad was hiring in western New York, Falbo traveled to West Seneca, where he did railroad work for a while. Returning to Italy in 1905, he spent four years in the military, then married Rosamaria Chiodo. By 1909, he was back in the United States, first working as a miner near Pittsburgh, then traveling to the newly chartered city of Lackawanna to work at the New York Central roundhouse. Falbo's wife and child arrived from Italy, and the family boarded with Francesco and Maddalena Sirianni, *paesani* who had earlier arrived from Pennsylvania.[68]

Santo DePasquale and his four siblings were the children of grape growers in Roccamorice, Abruzzo. In 1891, at age 19, Santo migrated to Boston, then moved on to Pottsville in eastern Pennsylvania. His three brothers joined him there by 1900, and they all labored in the coal mines. Each of the four men sent to Italy for his wife. Donato moved with his family to Lackawanna by 1918. Santo worked in the mines near Pottsville for more than 25 years and suffered from black-lung disease. His wife Assunta bore 13 of their 15 children in Pennsylvania, and the eldest, Anthony, was working as a slate picker by age 14. Santo was concerned that his sons would work in the coal mines if the family remained in Pottsville. He did not want them to experience the dangers of cave-ins and explosions, or the dread of black-lung disease. So when he received word from Donato in Lackawanna that "the steel mill was going full blast," he decided it was time to relocate. Santo

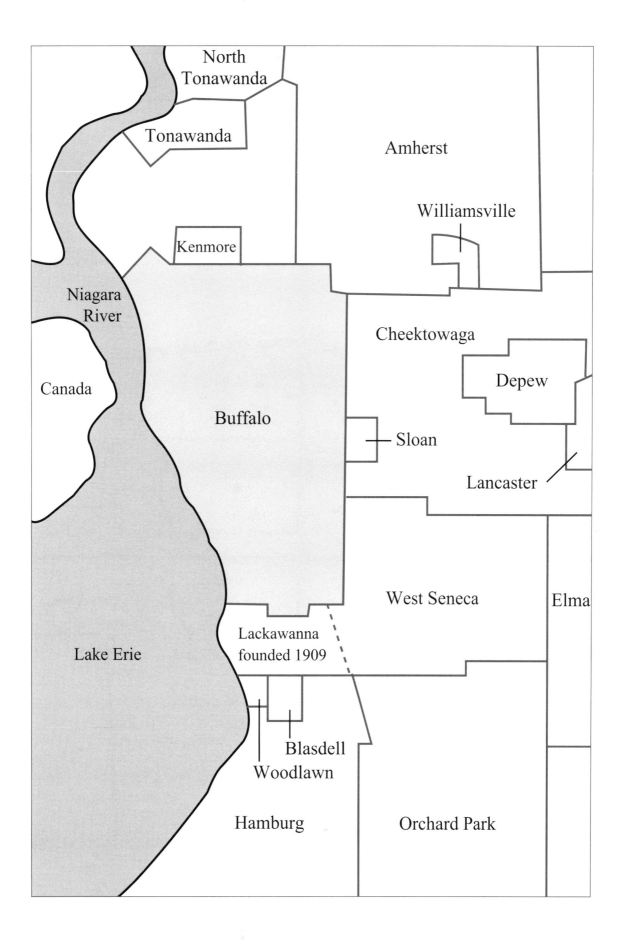

Figure 2.13. Map showing Buffalo and surrounding towns.

Figure 2.14. Map of Western New York showing towns and counties. Towns that were the first settlements for Lackawanna Italian immigrants are designated with an asterisk(*).

Canada

Lake Ontario

Vermont

Rochester

Wayne

Monroe

Clyde

Herkimer

Brandreth

Oneida

Utica

Little
Falls

Syracuse

Ontario

Onondaga

Canandaigua

Massachusett

Broome

Endicott

Pennsylvania

Connecticut

Fort
Montgomery

Orange

Westchester

New Jersey

Suffolk

Yonkers

Lindenhurst

Manhattan

New York

New Brighton
Staten Island

Richmond

Figure 2.15. Map of East and central New York state showing towns and counties where immigrants first settled before coming to Lackawanna.

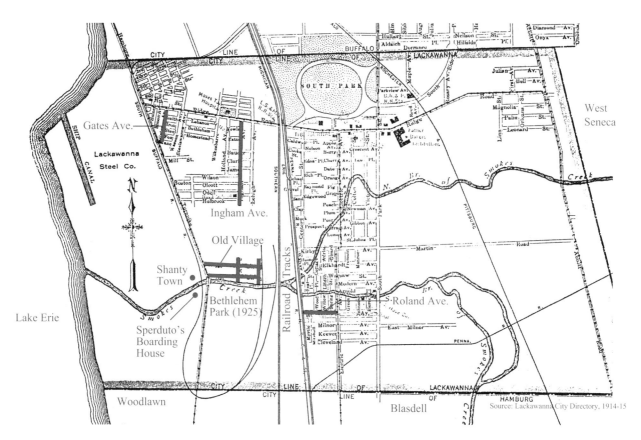

Figure 2.16. Map of Lackawanna 1900-1914. Illustration source: *Lackawanna City Directory*, 1914-15

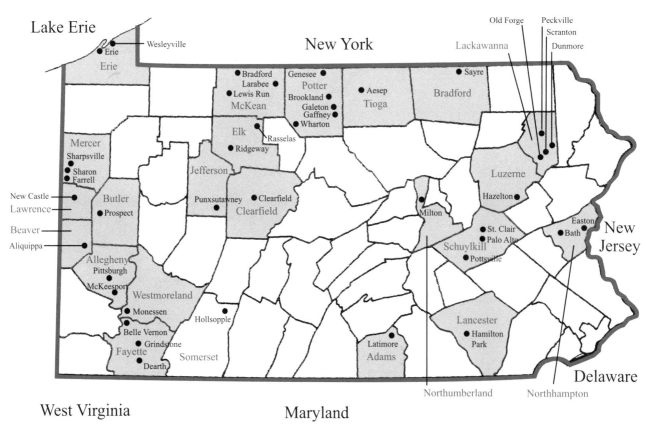

Figure 2.17. Map of Pennsylvania showing towns and counties where immigrants lived prior to moving to Lackawanna.

1 Pine Hill
2 East Ferry St.
3 East Lovejoy
4 Near East Side
5 West Side
5A Hooks
6 Germania St.

Figure 2.18. Map of Buffalo showing Italian neighborhoods in 1927. Illustration source: Buffalo and Erie County Public Library, Forman-Bassett Company, Cleveland, circa 1929-30.

Falbo from the mines. Many Italians did outdoor railroad and construction work in Pennsylvania. Railroad jobs first brought Italians to small towns and remote areas where new lines or spurs were being constructed, or where existing lines needed repair and maintenance. To advance in a railroad career often meant moving closer to the larger towns where roundhouses and repair shops were located, or to industrialized urban areas served by many rail lines. Alfonso Yoviene (he changed his name from Iovieno) was born in Agerola, Campania, where he worked as a shepherd in the mountains near Pompeii. After marrying Giuseppina Acanfora of nearby Boscoreale, he immigrated to Pennsylvania in 1896 and worked as a section foreman for the Buffalo and Susquehanna Railroad. Giuseppina and the couple's daughter Maria joined him within a year, and the family's residence changed as Alfonso's job took them to Galeton, Genesee, Bradford, and Brookland. Yoviene's supervisor, an Irishman based in Arcade, New York, appreciated the Italian's ability to quickly clear train wrecks. He called Yoviene to work in Sardinia, New York, and the family moved there in 1904. The Yovienes returned to Italy for a while but were back in the

and Assunta and their children arrived in Lackawanna in 1920; brother Salvatore and his family soon followed. Donato and Salvatore worked at Lackawanna Steel, while Santo established a pool hall on Ingham Avenue. Their brother Angelo returned to Italy from Pennsylvania and remained there for the duration of his life.[69]

Farmers, day laborers, and shepherds from Italy rarely had experience with mining prior to their arrival in the United States. There was a notable trend for Italians to do outdoor work, a preference that beckoned immigrants such as Bruno

United States in 1907. Alfonso Yoviene's railroad career in Sardinia ended in 1915 when the Buffalo and Susquehanna Railroad folded. His son-in-law, John Verel, then lined him up with a job with the South Buffalo Railway in Lackawanna.[70]

Railroad work brought Luigi Maturani from Giuliano to Sayre, Pennsylvania, a hub for the Lehigh Valley Railroad. Arriving in 1904, he joined two of his brothers already working there, then in 1923 followed other Giulianesi to Lackawanna. When Luigi's son Giulio came to Lackawanna in 1932, there was no work available for him, so he was sent to Sayre where relatives lined him up with a job on a railroad-track gang. He returned to the Steel City when his father wrote that there were openings at Bethlehem Steel.[71]

West Virginia, like Pennsylvania, offered immigrants mining and railroad jobs. Camillo and Anna Capasso left Casal Ciprano, Molise, in 1912, making their way to Morgantown, where Camillo labored in the mines. The family moved to Lackawanna in the mid-1920s, and Camillo became a steelworker. Pietro Mastrobattista followed a similar course. He departed from Lenola, Lazio, in 1906, did railroad work in West Virginia, and moved to the Steel City in 1925. Italian immigrants had jobs that were dangerous and sometimes led to tragedy. Vincenzo and Rosina Ginnetti and their eldest son left Abruzzo in 1903. After a brief stay in Virginia, they moved to Thurmond, West Virginia, where Vincenzo worked in a coal mine. In 1905, he was killed in an explosion. Luckily, relatives provided assistance to his widow and children. Salvatore and Adelina Ginnetti sent for Rosina and her three children to live with them in Lackawanna's Old Village. Two years later, Rosina married Cesidio D'Amore, a *paesano* from Pettorano sul Gizio.[72]

The Journey of One Extended Family from Calabria

Some Italians lived in several other U.S. states or locales and made intricate and prolonged journeys before settling in Lackawanna. This was the case for one Calabrese family that eventually settled in the Steel City. "We were a bunch of Gypsies," said Michelina Colosimo, recalling her extended family's frequent moves through America's mining regions—moves that finally took them to Lackawanna. Their story reflects that of many immigrants whose labor built the nation's iron and steel industry in the early 1900s.[73]

Michelina's mother and aunt were both married to miners. Her aunt Rosina had arrived from Petrona, Calabria, in 1914, with her husband Domenico Caligiuri, who found work in an iron mine in Hibbing, Minnesota. Soon a family of four, the Caligiuris moved briefly to St. Paul but by 1918 were back in Hibbing, where Domenico died of pneumonia. Rosina thereafter married his cousin, Luigi Caligiuri, who had also made his

FIGURE 2.21

States of First Settlement by Lackawanna Italian Immigrants (by U.S. region)

Northeast
  New York*
  Pennsylvania
  Massachusetts
  Rhode Island
  Connecticut
  Maine
  New Jersey

Midwest
  Ohio
  Indiana
  Illinois
  Michigan
  Wisconsin
  Minnesota
  North Dakota

Mountain
  Montana
  Wyoming
  Colorado
  Idaho

West
  California
  Nevada
  Washington
  Alaska

South
  West Virginia
  Virginia
  Maryland
  Florida
  Louisiana

*Outside of Lackawanna

way to Hibbing by way of railroad jobs throughout the upper Midwest. Probably eager for a break from the hazards of mining, Rosina again found a home in St. Paul with her new family.

Meanwhile, Rosina's sister Maria had been waiting in Italy. In 1920, Maria Colosimo, her daughter Michelina, and her uncle Francesco Grande, left for America. They traveled from Petrona to Catanzaro, the two adults walking, and Michelina riding on a small donkey. From that city, they took a train to Naples, where they embarked on the *SS Pesaro*. Maria and Michelina and three other women shared a second-class cabin furnished with two pairs of bunk beds; Maria and Michelina had to share a single bed. Francesco was in another cabin with several men. Michelina's first impression of the cabin was not encouraging. "When I seen that little cabin, it was dark, you know, and I said, 'I wanna go back to Italy, I don't wanna go, I wanna stay here.'" But the ship's dining room was another story, as the girl from a poor town in rural Calabria quickly discovered. "Well, I'll tell you the truth, it was the most beautiful thing you ever seen. … It was beautiful, [and] the food was good." Michelina was impressed by the fact that she was assigned her own seat at a large dining table, a seat that was hers throughout the voyage. Her mother was rarely at the dining table, as she was seasick for most of the voyage and stayed in the cabin. So Michelina, under the watchful eyes of the women who shared her cabin, took in the view. "All I seen, all those

17 days, was water and sky." Once they landed in New York, Francesco, who had made earlier trips to America, guided them to the railroad station for the journey to Fairmont, West Virginia. Finally, after nine long years, Maria rejoined her husband Carmine Colosimo, who had been employed all that time in an open-pit coal mine in nearby Beachwood, West Virginia.[74]

Back in St. Paul, Rosina Caligiuri was so overjoyed that her sister had at last come to America, she immediately planned her own family's move to Beachwood. She arrived by train with Luigi and their three children. After the long journey, she was stunned when the conductor called out, "Beachwood." Michelina recalled the family lore: Her aunt looked out at a cluster of houses by the tracks on the riverfront and protested, "It can't be that we gotta get off here!"—surely thinking, "It's a dump!"[75]

To make matters worse, the two families' houses were separated by the river. Carmine made a crude, flimsy raft to ferry family members across for visits. It held two people, and Michelina remembers that Carmine rowed while she bailed water. "You know," she reminisced, "I never realized that I could drown there, or I would never have went. That didn't go through your mind when you're so little, you don't think those things."[76]

Luigi Caligiuri probably thought he had seen the last of any mine work when he left northern Minnesota, settled in St. Paul, and became a factory laborer. But in West Virginia, and later in Pennsylvania, the only work available to him and his *paesani* was in the mines. He occasionally lamented: "I worked in a factory, now they put me underground!" The mines in Pennsylvania, unlike the open pits in West Virginia, were deep tunnels. Michelina recalled her uncle describing the elevator down to the Dearth, Pennsylvania, mine shaft, which descended "so fast that he dropped his lunch bucket." She also heard him say of landing at the bottom of the mine: "Where did I come to!"[77]

The Colosimos and Caligiuris moved to Rivesville, West Virginia, in 1922. It was a larger town, with two movie theaters, much to the children's delight. But the next year they again relocated, this time to Dearth, four miles outside Uniontown. Luigi Caligiuri and Carmine Colosimo worked for the Frick Mining Company, which often reassigned them to new or expanded mines. The Caligiuris relocated to Belle Vernon, Pennsylvania, then further north to Prospect. The Colosimos were back in Rivesville by 1927. For the most part, the families lived in Dearth, or nearby towns such as Grindstone, and settled there by 1929. Many Calabresi and Abruzzesi resided in Dearth, and Uniontown had an Italian settlement and an import store. The Caligiuris and Colosimos were joined by other relatives and *paesani* from Petrona, such as Carmine's sister Saveria and her husband Tomasso Marchio. As much as possible, these families stayed together throughout their many moves.[78]

Concetta Marinelli in Casale, Abruzzo, 1922. In 1928, she married Dominic Risio, who had earlier migrated to Lackawanna, and the couple returned to Lackawanna.
Photo source: Lucy Risio-Pietrocarlo

Joe Caligiuri recalls family life in the coal-mining communities of southwestern Pennsylvania. "These were towns of 400 to 500 people. The miners were mostly Italians, and some Poles. We rented company housing. People bought everything at this company store: shoes, clothes, groceries. … They cut off [your] food if you overdrew your account—bought more than your [pay]check would pay for." The company sold coal for heating the homes, deducting $3 per ton used from each worker's paycheck. To lessen this expense, Joe and other young children climbed the steep hills of mine refuse to glean pieces of coal from the slate and ashes. His older brother Louis and other teenagers gathered coal from abandoned mines, but this activity ceased when one of the boys was killed by a cave-in.[79]

Luigi Caligiuri was involved with the United Mine Workers Union and the labor struggles of the late 1920s and early 1930s. Joe recalls that his dad "was constantly on picket lines. The men carried axe handles and then guns; one boy was accidentally shot. Black strike breakers were brought in from the south." The labor war between the company and the miners' union became more violent, and the miners' wives joined in. "The women went on the picket; one woman carried a razor … a strike breaker drove through the picket line, and the picketers overturned the car. During the night, union men had their houses dynamited—under the porch. They [company men] took furniture from one union leader's house and put it on a hill. The gate from our fence was removed and thrown on our porch."[80]

Luigi and Rosina Caligiuri grew weary of the company-controlled towns, the dangerous work, and the labor violence. When their older sons started talking about working in the mine, Luigi decided it was time to take a different course. "Dad wanted to move so us kids wouldn't have to work in the mines," Joe Caligiuri described how Luigi's sister and brother provided an answer to the family's dilemma.[81]

Giuseppina Caligiuri and her husband, Domenico Schipani, had also migrated from Petrona to West Virginia, where their son Bruno was born in 1920. Ten years later, Guiseppina was a widow living with her son and her brother Filippo in Utica, New York. In about 1932, the three moved to Lackawanna, where Giuseppina married Cassiano Baldassari, a Marchegiano who operated a grocery store. The newlyweds lived above the store with Bruno, and the couple ran the business. Filippo, who was single, bought a house in Bethlehem Park and began work in the billet yard at Bethlehem Steel. Now on sure footing, Giuseppina sent to Pennsylvania for her nephew Louis, who, at age 17, was her brother Luigi's oldest son. He arrived in 1933 to live with his aunt's family and work in the grocery store. Soon after, Luigi moved to the Steel City himself and started working in the steel plant. When he decided it was time to move the whole family, another relative, Tom Fuoco, offered to help. Fuoco transported Rosina and five of her and Luigi's children in his car. The three oldest Caligiuri boys—Louis, Matt, and Joe—traveled the 280 miles to Lackawanna sitting on the tailgate of the rented moving van. The Caligiuris moved in with Filippo at 23 Elm Street.[82]

The Colosimo and Marchio families remained in Dearth for several more years. The eldest of the Colosimo children, Michelina, visited the Caligiuris in 1936 and found Bethlehem Park to be a very pleasant neighborhood. Her five siblings were younger than the children of the Caligiuri family, but when the two oldest boys, Dominic and Jim, neared working age, the same dilemma arose that Luigi Caligiuri had faced earlier. The boys asked their father, Carmine, to help them get jobs in the coal mine. Michelina remembers well their father's response. "So my father said: 'Before you go into coal mining, I'm leaving. You are not going there! You know a coal mine is not for young kids.' " Maria Colosimo wrote her sister Rosina, who invited Dominic and Jim to Lackawanna to live

with her family and work in the steel plant. So in about 1941, the two Colosimo boys journeyed to Bethlehem Park and began long careers in the steel mills. The following year, Carmine and Maria and their three remaining children moved to Lackawanna. Carmine obtained work in the steel plant, then sent for his sister and brother-in-law, Saveria and Tomasso Marchio. They set up a home on Madison Avenue and changed their surname to Marks. Luigi Caligiuri helped Tomasso get a job at the Buffalo Tank Company.[83]

Meanwhile, Michelina Colosimo, now called Madge, had married Sam Bevilacqua in 1940 and was living in Martin's Ferry, Ohio. She missed her family and cried at the thought of her parents and siblings being so far away. She talked to her husband about moving to Lackawanna, but he had 15 years of seniority at Wheeling Steel. He would need a special release to leave a wartime defense plant, plus, all of his family was in Martin's Ferry. Eventually, Madge prevailed, and in 1944, they moved to Bethlehem Park. Soon, Sam's mother, a brother, and a sister moved to Lackawanna or Woodlawn, and another sister moved to Rochester. There were many stories of extended families that, like the Colosimos, provided aid and encouragement to move in search of safe and stable employment as well as the companionship of relatives. This is the path many took to find a permanent home in Lackawanna.[84]

Worldwide Travelers

As noted earlier, some Italian immigrants were truly worldwide travelers, having lived in other countries before coming to the United States at the beginning of the twentieth century. For many years, the lack of jobs in Italian towns had led men to wander throughout Italy, then to other European countries, and finally, to nations in North and South America in search of work (see Figure 2.23). The emergence of restrictive immigration laws in the United States in the early 1920s led Italians to immigrate first to Canada or South America and then enter this country. Nazzareno Baldelli, born in Cuccurano, Marche, in 1873, traveled as a young man to Germany, Holland, and France to find employment as a laborer. Workers were required to take their own shovels to jobs. In about 1914, he migrated to the large Marchegiani settlement in Sioux St. Marie, Ontario, where he worked in a lumberyard. In 1919, Baldelli sent for his wife Gimigliana and two adult sons, Domenico and Giuseppe, who also found work in the lumberyard and in the copper mines in nearby Copper Cliff. Domenico married a *paesana*, Angelina Longhini, in 1921. The following year, the Baldellis traveled to Swan Street in Buffalo, where they lived with *paesani* who found jobs for the men at the steel plant in Lackawanna. The family settled in Bethlehem Park in 1925.[85]

FIGURE 2.22

ITALIANS MIGRATING TO LACKAWANNA FROM OTHER STATES

Hundreds of Italian immigrants first lived in other states before moving to Lackawanna. Some examples of this are listed here.

Connecticut

Antonio Zanzano arrived in New York City from Accadia, Puglia, in 1893, went on to Hartford in 1901, and five years later was living on Ingham Avenue.

Florida

Salvatore DiTommaso migrated from Popoli, Abruzzo, to Florida in 1894. He arrived in Buffalo in 1900, then returned to Italy for his fiancee, Teresa Rico, in 1901. They traveled back to Buffalo, married, and moved to Lackawanna.

Louisiana

Giuseppe and Maria Miceli sailed from Sicily to New Orleans in 1898. Like many other Sicilians, they traveled up the Mississippi River and eventually found their way to Lackawanna in 1901.

Maryland

Giovanni and Maria Olivieri left Tufilo, Abruzzo, in 1913 with their two children to join friends in Baltimore. After Giovanni lost his job, the family moved to Lackawanna in 1915 at the urging of Domenico Mariotti.

Massachusetts

Rocco Marinelli landed in New York City after leaving Cocullo, Abruzzo, worked as a shipper in Quincy for four years, then migrated to Lackawanna in 1919.

Minnesota

Many Italians worked in the mines on the Iron Range in northern Minnesota. Emilio and Filomena Manzetti migrated from Abruzzo to Aurora, then moved to the Steel City in about 1913. Calabrese immigrants Michele Saccomanno, Luigi and Rosina Caligiuri, and Tommaso Marchio all spent time in Hibbing as one of many stops during their journeys to western New York.

Ohio

Frank DiCorpo left Italy in 1894 and married a woman of Irish-English background who gave birth to their first child in Ohio. The family moved to Lackawanna in 1901, and DiCorpo became the proprietor of a hotel on South Park Avenue.

Angelo Marracino emigrated from Vastogirardi, Molise, in 1903, and a decade later, he and his wife were living in Lackawanna. In 1917, the family moved to Columbus, but returned to the Steel City by 1922.

Rhode Island

Many Laziali found their way to Providence and its suburb, Barrington. Sosio Piccirilli, Vincenzo Piccirilli, Antonio Andreozzi, Arcadio DeAngelis, and Antonio Conti, all natives of Falvaterra, migrated from Barrington to Lackawanna between 1910 and 1929.

Washington

Leo and Anna Ginnetti migrated to Northport in 1915 and four years later moved to Lackawanna.

Wyoming

At age 14, Domenico Marinelli left Cocullo, Abruzzo, in 1900 and did railroad work in Wyoming. He moved to Marian, Indiana, by 1903, and five years later settled in Lackawanna. Wyoming made quite an impression on Marinelli; his son recalled that Domenico "always wanted to be a cowboy."

Sources: Ohio: U.S. Census, 1910; Erie County Courthouse (ECC) Petition for Naturalization: Angelo Marracino, October 5, 1922. Massachusetts: ECC, Petition for Naturalization: Rocco Marinelli, November 13, 1923. Rhode Island: interview with Vincent Piccirilli, March 4, 1979. Connecticut: ECC, Petition for Naturalization: March 23, 1906. Minnesota: ECC, Petition for Naturalization: Emilio Manzetti, September 7, 1928; interviews with Joe Caligiuri, April 5, 1994 and Michelina Colosimo-Bevilacqua, October 17, 1996; *Front Page*, December 19, 1984. Wyoming: ECC, Petition for Naturalization: Domenico Marinelli, February 17, 1914; interview with John Marinelli, July 10, 1994. Maryland: N.Y. Census, 1905, 1915, 1925; interview with Flora Paolini-Olivieri, July 13, 1994. Florida: interview with Dan and Claude Thomas, July 12, 1994. Louisiana: U.S. Census, 1910. Washington: N.Y. Census, 1925.

Two men from Lazio journeyed to several countries before coming to the United States. Olindo Rosati left Lenola, worked in Holland then sailed from Rotterdam to Canada. In 1909, he traveled by rail from Montreal to Buffalo. He married Lackawanna-born Mary DiCenzo and settled in the Steel City. About the same time, Domenico Ventre ventured from Settefrati and traveled to France to find work. But he had difficulties living among the French and moved to England, where he worked in London and other cities as an organ-grinder, complete with monkey. He returned to Italy, then followed *paesani* to Newcastle, Pennsylvania, and finally, to Lackawanna.[86]

Some Italians migrated to Central America, and millions went to South America, especially Brazil, Argentina, and Venezuela. A number of Italians made the trip from these three countries to the United States, eventually settling in Lackawanna. Antonio Pacillo literally took a tour of the western hemisphere after leaving his hometown of Castelnuovo, Campania. He journeyed to Brazil and French Guinea, later telling his children that he lost his passport while on Devil's Island. He went to the island of Guadaloupe in the West Indies, then to Panama. In 1903, he sailed from Colon to New York City, then resided in Newark, New Jersey, for a while. His next move was to Niagara Falls, New York, and he finally reached Lackawanna by 1906. His wife and children arrived from Italy the following year.[87]

Alfonso and Irene Ditillio immigrated to Brazil by 1912, then returned to Italy. Coming alone to America in 1914, Alfonso found work at Lackawanna Steel, and Irene and their two eldest children were reunited with him in 1920 in the Old Village. The family apparently left the city after 1925. Filomena Paolozzi and Pasqualina Fresco, both born in Brazil, returned to Italy with their families, and eventually moved to Lackawanna. Giuseppe Leonetti and his son Gennaro left Pedace, Calabria, in 1922 and sailed to Brazil to join *paesani* in Porto Allegro. They worked with a friend who had a truck from which he sold macaroni, salami, and other foods. Gennaro married a Brazilian woman and settled there. Giuseppe left Porto Allegro in 1923, traveled to Niagara Falls, New York, to join *paesani* in the large Calabresi community there, then moved to Lackawanna.[88]

Following the Second World War, many Italians immigrated to Australia, but links to the United States led others across the Atlantic Ocean to North America. Most Italians who immigrated to Lackawanna after 1945 had relatives who had come to the United States during the first four decades of the twentieth century. The typical routes of those departing Italy between 1946 and 1969 included many of the same destinations established by the earlier migrants. Restrictive immigration laws, however, led to a new emphasis on first traveling to other countries in the western hemisphere before migrating to America. The story of one Abruzzese family illustrates a 50-year pattern of immigration that culminated in the postwar period.

Gaetano DelMonaco left Pettorano sul Gizio for Boston in 1903 at the age of 16 and worked constructing rail lines in Maine. To clear the way, he and coworkers used rods and hammers to drill holes in rock beds, then inserted dynamite. Gaetano was illiterate and didn't want to pay the $1 fee to a letter writer, so his only mail to his parents in Italy was an occasional envelope full of money. After 12 years, he returned to Pettorano, only to be drafted into the Italian Army to serve in the First World War. Following the war, he settled permanently in Pettorano, where he married and fathered seven children. His son Carmine was 23 when he completed his tour in the Italian Army in 1950. At the time, there was little work and much poverty in Pettorano. The family survived by raising its own food, but it had no money. When Venezuela was accepting immigrants, a number of Pettoranesi immigrated there, including Angelo D'Amato, a relative of DelMonaco. In 1952, D'Amato agreed to sponsor Carmine. DelMonaco and several *paesani* sailed from Naples to La Cuire, Venezuela, joining D'Amato and other Pettoranesi in Caracas. DelMonaco got a job as a laborer at an auto dealer. Friends helped him master the Spanish language, and he became a salesman. "I sold many American cars and made good money," he recalled.[89]

DelMonaco was corresponding with a *paesana*, Giuseppina Suffoletta, who was then living in Canada. "She wrote that Canada and the United States are better than Venezuela." He returned to Pettorano in 1954, visited for three months while getting his papers in order, then sailed to Halifax. Shortly after arriving in Hamilton, Ontario, he married Giuseppina. DelMonaco had difficulty with the cold winter, and, because he spoke no English, it took him seven months to find a job as a cement finisher. They survived on Giuseppina's meager wages from her job at a canning factory. In 1961, they moved to Lackawanna to join her parents. Delmonaco's inability to speak or read English meant he couldn't get a job at Bethlehem Steel, but he did obtain work with the Amadori Construction Company, and began a 28-year career with the company.[90]

Provincial and Village Migration Chains

Returning to the theme of chain migration, it is important to note some of the details of this process. The Italians who settled in Lackawanna between 1900 and 1924 were the initiators of migration chains from specific areas of Italy. The settlements along each chain from an individual Italian town often remained useful to first- and second-generation Italian Americans for many years, as can be seen in their movements into and out of Lackawanna. These movements strengthened ties between the Steel City, towns in Italy, and other towns in the United States.

Natives of Lazio represented the largest regional group in Lackawanna, but only 65 arrived in the city by 1910. Some 266 Laziali came during the following decade, and another 164 between 1921 and 1930 (see Figure 2.29). Antonio Torella left Giuliano di Roma and settled in the Steel City in 1910, when the steel plant was bustling. When his son Armando joined him in 1932, work at the plant was slow, so his family used its network of Giulianese contacts to find work for him. Armando and Giuseppe DeSantis, a *paesano*, traveled to Montgomery County in eastern New York, where they worked in a coal mine under two Giulianesi foremen. The next year, Torella returned to Lackawanna and worked for a while at Republic Steel before finally getting a job at Bethlehem Steel in 1934.[91]

Alfredo Anticoli also benefited from the network of Giulianesi settlements. He left Giuliano to join *paesani* working on the railroad in Sayre, Pennsylvania. In 1910, he traveled to Bristol, Connecticut, where cousins arranged a job for him with the city water department. After serving in the U.S. Army in World War I, he sent for his mother Rosa, a widow. In 1921, Rosa and Alfredo joined relatives on Germania Street in South Buffalo, and Alfredo began work at Republic Steel. His brother Biagio soon migrated, and in 1924, the three Anticolis moved to Lackawanna, where the men procured jobs at Bethlehem Steel. In the next few years, both brothers returned to Giuliano, married, then permanently settled in the Steel City.[92]

The migration chains from Giuliano di Roma and nearby towns in Frosinone and Latina provinces also had specific destinations in North America (see Sidebar 2-26). Aboard the steamship *Phoenicia*, when it docked in New York City on May 3, 1902, were Pico natives Antonio Carnevale (not the same Antonio Carnevale mentioned earlier) and Angelantonio Vallone. Both men headed to Buffalo to room with a *paesano*, and Carnevale soon moved to Lackawanna. When the *SS Gallia* arrived in New York City in March 1902, there were more than 150 men from Lazio on the passenger list. Most of the 59 men from Morolo gave New York City or Utica as their destination; virtually all of the 41 Giulianesi listed New York City; and the majority of the 31 men from Pofi were traveling to Boston. The fact that they were traveling in groups and had common destinations underscores the theme of chain migration. It also indicates that Lackawanna was not a prime destination at this time. While none of these men can be directly linked to Lackawanna, many had surnames of people who later appeared in the Steel City—Schiavi and Canali from Morolo, DeSantis from Pofi, and Anticoli, Sperduti, Violanti, and Pietrocarlo from Giuliano.[93]

Arcangelo and Giuseppe Colafranceschi left Giuliano di Roma in 1903 and went to Syracuse to join a relative. By 1910, they were living in Lackawanna. As time went on, more of the Laziali began migrating to Lackawanna from their first towns of residence in the United States. Sixteen-year-old Antonio Colello departed from Pico, Lazio, in 1913 and migrated to Pittsfield, Massachusetts, to join *paesani* there. Several years later he traveled to Lackawanna and lived with the family of Antonio Grossi. Leaving Pico in 1923, Erasmo Colello joined his brother Antonio in New York City, and within three years, they had settled in Lackawanna. The Steel City was becoming a more important settlement for the Laziali by the 1920s, as indicated by the greater number of immigrants who came directly to the city from Italy. Antonio Colella (not to be confused with Antonio Colello mentioned

above) and Carmine Grossi left Pico in 1922, sailed from Naples on the *SS. America*, then headed for Ingham Avenue to join relatives boarding at the Grossi home.[94]

Natives of eight towns in Lazio formed settlements in common geographical areas in America, as provincial and regional destinations were typical features of chain migration (see Figure 2.26). The destinations of immigrants from these towns formed three clusters: the first included Pittsburgh and other towns in western Pennsylvania and nearby Follansbee, West Virginia, and Steubenville, Ohio; the second focused on towns in Massachusetts and Connecticut; and the third, the Detroit-Flint area in Michigan. One indication of the many Laziali in Michigan was an Italian organization there called the *Ciociari di Detroit*, based on the ancient name for the people in the southern part of the province of Frosinone. Street names in Italy offer another indication. To honor its many citizens who migrated to Connecticut, the town of Settefrati named streets for the cities of Stamford and Darien.[95]

Immigrants from towns in Abruzzo, mostly in the province of Aquila, settled in Lackawanna and had their own network of settlements. Pettorano sul Gizio sent 135 immigrants to Lackawanna, the second largest number from any single town. Cousins Gaetano and Domenico Tristani arrived in Buffalo in about 1895, and while they did not remain long, they were part of a small settlement of Pettoranesi on Swan Street in Buffalo. The migration chain from Pettorano included 15 American and Canadian towns (see Figure 2.28). Many Pettoranesi lived in Bradford and Lewis Run, Pennsylvania, before going northward to Lackawanna.[96]

Natives of Campania composed the third-largest regional group of Italians to locate in Lackawanna. Some 71 Napolitani had settled in Lackawanna by 1910. During the following decade, 81 emigrants from Campania arrived in the Steel City. Like many other immigrants, some followed an indirect

FIGURE 2.23

Countries that have been
First Stops for Lackawanna Italian Immigrants

Europe	The Americas
England	Canada
France	Mexico
Germany	Panama
Holland	Brazil
Austria	Argentina
Spain	Venezuela
	French Guiana

route to Lackawanna that covered a number of years and locales. Giuseppe Basile left Bagnoli Irpino and migrated to Aliquippa, Pennsylvania. His son Lorenzo joined him there in 1915, and they moved to Lackawanna seven years later. Three decades passed and in 1955, another son, Carmine, immigrated to the Steel City, where his wife Gerarda later joined him. Raffaele Palante followed the Bagnoli *paesani* chain first to Aliquippa in 1925, then on to Lackawanna. His wife and son were not able to join him until 1947. Farrell and Sharon are two other western Pennsylvania towns occupied by many Napolitani residents. After Francesco Pallante departed from Bagnoli Irpino in 1912, he wound up in Farrell, then settled in Lackawanna by 1927.[97]

Migrants from 10 towns in Marche made up the fourth largest group of Italian immigrants in Lackawanna. Early arrivals were Giovanni Sambuchi and Benvenuto and Domenico Bracci, all of whom arrived in the Steel City from Fano in 1903 or 1904. Sambuchi initially went to Copper Cliff, Ontario, to join a Marchegiani settlement there and then moved on to the Steel City. Other Marchegiani first went to the textile mills of Massachusetts, such as Lavinio Montanari, who left Fano in 1913 to join his brother Pippo in Framingham. Both men moved to Lackawanna in 1914 after being contacted by the Paolini family. Vittorio Manna was 17 years old when he left Pesaro for Winchendon, Massachusetts. He worked in the cotton mills there for 12 years and married a *Marchegiana*, Iolanda Sbrega. In 1923, the Mannas journeyed to Lackawanna, taking up residence with cousins in the Old Village. Paolo Filipetti emigrated in 1912 from Ancona, Marche, going first to Canada, then joining relatives in New London, Connecticut, where he worked as a fisherman. He moved to Lackawanna when he heard about job opportunities in the steel plant. Enrico Spadoni left Italy for other reasons. In 1914, shortly after he was born in New Haven, his family returned to Cerasa, Marche. Some years later, following an argument with his father, 15-year-old Enrico returned alone to New Haven to live with relatives. After several months, he joined his cousin Frank Lucarelli in Lackawanna and secured a job in the steel plant.[98]

Natives of Calabria composed the fifth largest group of immigrants in the Lackawanna Italian community. People from Soveria Mannelli gathered in six states and one Canadian province, where they usually worked in mines or on railroads. Those in Cumberland, Wisconsin, were part of an Italian farming community whose men also did seasonal railroad work. Like many other Italians, they followed the jobs along railroad lines, often attracted to the more skilled, better-paying jobs in railroad roundhouses and repair shops. Men from

FIGURE 2.24

A TRAGIC SIDE TRIP THROUGH CANADA

Salvatore Macaluso had quite a long and dramatic journey before finally settling in Lackawanna. Born in Racalmuto, Sicily, to an Italian father and a Greek mother, he left his dad in 1912, at age 14, to join his mother and sister in Hamilton, Canada. He sailed from Palermo to New York City, where an Italian labor agent recruited Macaluso and two older Italian youths to work in Canada. He may have responded to the recruiter because he did not have the $25 required by Canadian authorities for entrance into the country. Macaluso, two other young Italian men from the boat, and men of other nationalities then boarded a train for Montreal. Outside the city, armed men boarded the train and told the men recruited for work to leave the train. They were ordered into a boxcar on another train and shipped to a work camp in a remote forest in Quebec Province. The labor agents told the men that they carried guns to protect against bears.

The immigrants were put to work cutting down trees. The camp provided living quarters and food, but it was surrounded by barbed wire. Guards refused to allow Macaluso to leave for Hamilton. After being there close to a year, he and his two Italian companions escaped one night. The three spent the evening running through the forest while being pursued by men with dogs. As the story is told by his daughter, Macaluso's two companions were shot, one of them fatally. Finally, the wounded man and Macaluso were able to hop aboard a logging train. Traveling as hobos, they headed toward Hamilton, encountering many poor people along the way. Later, Macaluso would always tell his children: "Never turn away a hungry person. Feed him." He lived in Hamilton among a group of relatives, then traveled to Buffalo, where another cluster of kinfolk resided. By age 16 he was an auto mechanic. He set up a business in Lackawanna, eventually moving there with his family in 1936.

Source: Interview with Carmella Macaluso-Pawlowski, April 3, 1996.

Soveria Mannelli came to Lackawanna because they heard jobs were available at the roundhouses of the New York Central Railroad and the South Buffalo Railway. Working at a permanent facility alleviated the need for constant migration to railroad construction and repair sites, and the discomfort of living in crude workers' barracks or boxcars.[99]

FIGURE 2.25

ILIO DIPAOLO: FROM ABRUZZO TO WESTERN NEW YORK

A wrestler well known throughout the Buffalo area came from humble roots in Abruzzo. Born in Introdacqua, Ilio DiPaolo was not the first in his family to immigrate to America. His maternal grandparents, Achille and Angelina Volpe, migrated to York, Pennsylvania, in the 1890s. Two children, Gina and Ernesimo, were born there. The family went back and forth to Italy before finally settling in Introdacqua, but Ernesimo remained in America. In Italy, Gina married Parigi (Paris) DiPaolo, and in 1926 gave birth to Ilio. The following year, Parigi left for Argentina and died there. Gina remarried and gave birth to daughter Giannina in 1941. Ilio overcame polio and used the rehabilitation program to build his strength. He helped his grandfather farm, gather wood, and slaughter animals for food. During World War II, Ilio was one of a number of men forced by German soldiers to carry supplies through the Abruzzese mountains during the winter. For the most part, he and his family survived the deprivations of war.

Following the war, DiPaolo did odd jobs and some amateur wrestling, but the lack of economic opportunity led him to join the sizable postwar exodus from Italy. In 1949, accompanied by several *paesani*, DiPaolo went to Venezuela, where he worked as a laborer and carpenter. A large and husky man, he began to wrestle professionally there. In 1950, he branched out to Cuba and the Dominican Republic,

then to New York City, where he was based for two years. He wrestled in Haiti for four months until he received a permanent visa, and in 1953 returned to New York. He had matches throughout the United States and Canada, traveling 10 months of the year. In 1957, he and his wife, Ethel Martinez, settled in Buffalo. DiPaolo worked the local circuits in New York state and Canada, traveling as far as Japan for matches. He held the world tag-team title for two years, and three times drew ties for the world heavyweight championship. Known as the "bruiser from Abruzzi," he retired from professional wrestling in 1965.

The DiPaolos lived in Lackawanna during the 1960s and opened a restaurant there. After a fire, they moved the restaurant to Blasdell, where it has been a landmark business since 1965. DiPaolo became involved in civic activities and was the campaign chairman for Joe Bala's bid for Lackawanna councilman in 1968. The DiPaolos and their four children later moved to nearby Orchard Park.

An enthusiastic sports fan, DiPaolo supported boys' athletics in Lackawanna and Blasdell. He was active in many organizations, including the Lackawanna Boccie League and the Lake Erie Italian Club, as well as charitable events. An outgoing and popular man, DiPaolo was named Man of the Year by at least nine organizations. He died tragically when struck by a car in 1995. His family has continued

Ilio DiPaolo, born in Introdacqua, Abruzzo, was one of the post – World War II immigrants who came to western New York after first migrating to Venezuela. Following an impressive career as a professional wrestler, his family lived for a while in Lackawanna and established a restaurant there.
Photo source: Dennis DiPaolo

to operate the restaurant, and events held in his honor continue to support the charitable causes that he championed.

Source: Interview with Ilio DiPaolo, December 29, 1994.

For some families, it was not until the second generation reached adulthood that the migration to Lackawanna occurred. Antonio Mancuso emigrated from Soveria Mannelli in 1900 to join his brother Tomasso in Wharton, Pennsylvania, where both men were section hands with the Buffalo and Susquehanna Railroad. Two years later, Antonio returned to Calabria, married, then brought his

wife back to Wharton. A foreman by 1913, he was entitled to have his family live in a two-story section house provided by the railroad. In the early 1920s, his oldest daughter, Mary, married Louis Costanzo, a *paesano* living in Lackawanna. The couple settled in the Steel City, where Costanzo had a job on the South Buffalo Railway. Mary's brother Tom worked for his dad but grew tired and

FIGURE 2.26

U.S. and Canadian Settlements Established by Natives of Towns in Lazio

Giuliano di Roma

New York
Buffalo, Lackawanna,
Lockport, New York City,
Niagara Falls, Syracuse,
Tarrytown

Pennsylvania
Aliquippa, Bethlehem,
Bradford, Easton, Milton,
Pittsburgh, Sayre,
Sharpsville, Williamsport

Connecticut
Bristol

New Jersey
Newark

Ohio
Akron, Ashtabula,
Steubenville

CANADA
Ontario
London, Niagara Falls,
Toronto, Woodstock

Quebec
Montreal

Pico

New York
Lackawanna, New York City

Massachusetts
Pittsfield

Rhode Island
Providence

Settefrati

New York
Lackawanna,
White Plains

Pennsylvania
Aliquippa, Newcastle,
Pittsburgh

Connecticut
Stamford, Darien

Michigan
Flint

Falvaterra

New York
Lackawanna, New York City

Rhode Island
Barrington, Providence

Pennsylvania
Sharon, Sharpsville

West Virginia
Follansbee

Michigan
Dearborn

Morolo

New York
Buffalo, Elmira, Hornell,
Lackawanna, New York City,
Syracuse, Utica

Michigan
Detroit

Pofi

New York
Lackawanna

New Jersey
Monachi

Massachusetts
Boston

Pennsylvania
Sharpsville

Michigan
Detroit

Castro dei Volsci

New York
Albany, Lackawanna

Pennsylvania
Sharpsville

Lenola

New York
Lackawanna,
New York City

New Jersey
West Plainfield

Pennsylvania
Connellsville

Connecticut
Bristol

---

disillusioned with railroad work. In 1935, at age 22, he traveled to Lackawanna to live with the Costanzos on Roland Avenue. He lined up a job in Bethlehem Steel's Yard Department, married, settled on Roland Avenue, and worked at the steel plant for 40 years.[100]

One chain of immigrants involved natives from two neighboring towns in the province of Cosenza in Calabria. Immigrants from Marano Principato and Marano Marchesato traveled to a series of American towns, most after making an initial stop in Chicago, a destination of many Calabresi.

As a young man, Ferdinando Cosentino left Marano Principato in 1876 for Chicago. Recruited by a *padrone* to do railroad construction work, his crew was dispatched to sites as far away as Montana. For 35 years, Cosentino went back and forth between his work in Chicago and his wife and children in Calabria. On one of his return trips to America, he was accompanied by Giacinto Moretti, a younger man from Marano Marchesato, who later married Cosentino's daughter.[101]

FIGURE 2.27

LAZIALI MIGRATE FROM PENNSYLVANIA TO LACKAWANNA

Looking at two towns in western Pennsylvania helps to give a flavor of the chain migration from the towns in Lazio. Newcastle was home to a number of Laziali who found temporary work in the city's cement and steel industries. Antonio Marcocci arrived from Arce in 1913, married in Newcastle, and later moved with his wife and three children to Lackawanna. Angelo Panniccia, a native of Settefrati, followed a similar pattern after moving from Dearborn, Michigan, to Newcastle. Two of his *paesani*, Raffaele Policella and Domenico Ventre, also migrated from Newcastle to more secure jobs at Bethlehem Steel in Lackawanna.

Many natives of Castro dei Volsci went to Sharpsville and lived in a neighborhood called Little Castro, where their Catholic Church was named Santa Oliva, the patron saint of Castro. Giuseppe Campoli emigrated from Pofi to Lackawanna, then moved on to Sharpsville, where he was joined by his brothers Felice and Nicola. When the men were laid off by Shenango Furnace, Giuseppe and Nicola moved to Lackawanna, entering the labor force in the mills, while Felice remained in Sharpsville. As time went on, an increasing number of smaller factories shut down, a trend that greatly increased with the onset of the Great Depression in 1929.

Giustino DeSantis, another native of Pofi, had worked at a blast furnace in Detroit. When visiting relatives in Sharpsville in 1924, he was offered a job at the Clare Furnace Company. Accepting the job, he took up residence with his cousin in company housing, learned to read and write English, and started working on the railroad sidings that serviced the furnaces. Eventually, DeSantis was made foreman of the track gang. When Clare closed down its blast furnaces in 1930, the *paesani* network again proved invaluable to him. He and his cousin were called to Lackawanna by townsmen, and DeSantis moved in with another relative, Giulio DeSantis, on Elm Street. A *paesano* lined him up with work in the South Buffalo Railway (SBR) Track Department, where many Laziali worked. DeSantis became part of a track gang, and after a trip to Italy, settled permanently in Lackawanna in 1932. Further plant closings in other areas brought more Italian migrants to Lackawanna, where the mills never shut down during the Depression. Eventually, the Shenango Steel Company in Sharpsville relocated to Buffalo, just north of Lackawanna, which also drew Italians from Sharpsville to western New York.

Source: Interviews with Angelo DeGiulio, December 23, 1994; Rocco Campoli, July 5, 1995; Giustino DeSantis, July 9, 1985; Vince Morga, April 7, 1999; and Lucia Caracci-Cullens, November 20, 2008.

Ferdinando Cosentino came to Lackawanna's Old Village in 1912, and Giacinto Moretti sailed back to the United States and joined him there the following year. In Italy, they had been talking with Bruno Luminera, who had journeyed to Buffalo a few years earlier and worked as a mold maker at Lackawanna Steel. During frequent return trips to his hometown, he spoke of his good wages. Cosentino, Moretti, and other townsmen followed him to western New York. Several Maranesi had been in the steel-plant district even earlier. When Fiore Covelli and Antonio Tenuta landed in New York City in 1907, they traveled straight to West Seneca to join Eugenio Covelli, Fiore's brother. The Covelli brothers soon moved on to Kenosha, Wisconsin, while Tenuta became a permanent resident of Lackawanna and sent for his wife by 1910. When other *paesani* already in the United States learned of the opportunities, they too journeyed to the Steel City. Cosentino's sons Alessandro and Giuseppe joined him there, as did Moretti's wife and children. Ferdinando Cosentino returned to Italy after World War I. Planning on coming back to Lackawanna, he suffered a stroke and remained in Marano Principato with his wife.[102]

A number of *paesani* from Kenosha left their foundry jobs for higher wages in Lackawanna. Fiore Covelli, mentioned earlier, returned to the area in 1915 and worked at Lackawanna Steel while living in Buffalo. He was followed by Eugenio and two of his other brothers, as well as a cousin, Filiberto Covelli. One brother, Arturo, lived in Lackawanna in 1918, then returned to Italy. Both Fiore and Filiberto Covelli moved with their families to Lackawanna in 1928. Like other migrants, these Italians had already acquired industrial skills in America that helped them advance to better jobs in Lackawanna's mills. Their success in Lackawanna drew even more *paesani* to the Steel City. Mariano Savaglio migrated from Marano Principato to Kenosha in 1935 and lived with one of the Covelli families there. A few years later, he visited Calabria, then returned to America with Albert Caira. Both men went directly to Lackawanna to live with kinsmen and start jobs in the steel plant. Other *paesani* used the Steel City as a way station. Carmine Tenuta and Leopoldo Caira had traveled back and forth between Calabria and the United States several times. Each made his final trip to this country in 1930, stopping for one month at Filiberto and Gelsomina Covelli's home in the

Many generations of Spadonis have lived in this house in Cerasa, Marche. Enrico Spadoni, who became known as Harry Spadone, arrived in Lackawanna in about 1931. Pictured here in 2005, the house is still occupied by members of the Spadoni family. Photo source: Ron Spadone

Old Village. They then journeyed to their final destinations—Tenuta to California, Caira to Kenosha.[103]

Lackawanna's Italian community is somewhat unique in its regional origins. The immigrants came from 191 towns located in 17 of the 20 regions in the "old country." Natives of Sicily and Campania have been the two largest regional groups in the United States and predominate in the Little Italys of many American cities. However, Lackawanna has had a more unusual blend, with 36% of the immigrants coming from Lazio and 19% from Abruzzo (see Figure 2.30). There were a few Sicilian immigrants in the city, and the Napolitani (people from Campania) represent the third most numerous regional group. The vast majority of Italian immigrants to the United States have been southern Italians, but definitions of "southern Italy" vary. In this book, everything south of Rome, including the provinces of Latina and Frosinone in southern Lazio, and Abruzzo, Molise, Sicilia, and Sardinia will be considered as the Italian south. It is recognized that the cultural values of northern Italy have been notably different from those of southern Italy, and, given Italy's strong sense of regionalism, the cultural practices of the southerners vary significantly, especially when comparing the

regions of Lazio, Abruzzo, and Molise with those of the deep south—Campania, Puglia, Basilicata, Calabria, and Sicily.[104]

In describing the values of townspeople in Sermoneta, in the Latina province of Lazio, during the 1950s, Donald Pitkin found that they saw northern Italy, with some envy, as more advanced, but at the same time viewed the northern Italian as "too loose in his morality, and evidence of this is the lesser value they place on virginity." On the other hand, the Sermonetani saw the people of the deep south, especially the Calabrese, who moved into their area in the 1930s, in a negative light, referring to them as *cafoni* (boors). Pitkin observed Calabrian life to be "richer in traditional folkways" than that of Sermoneta, and placing tremendous importance on respect "within a framework of social hierarchy." The Calabresi assigned titles to status positions and used these more frequently. They closely guarded the honor of the unmarried females, causing the natives of Sermoneta to criticize them as being too jealous. The Sermoneta regarded the Calabrians as "tradition-bound and backward," while the Calabrians viewed them as "lacking in respect and morality." As one travels north from the deep south, writes Pitkin, there is a gradual de-emphasis

97

FIGURE 2.28

North American Immigrant Settlements for Specified Towns in Italy

ABRUZZO

Pettorano sul Gizio

New York
Buffalo, Lackawanna

Connecticut
Bridgeport

Massachusetts
Boston

New Jersey
Princeton, Lambertville

Pennsylvania
Bradford, Lewis Run

West Virginia
Follansbee

Ohio
Columbus, Mingo Junction,
Steubenville, Toronto,
Youngstown

CANADA
Ontario
Hamilton

CALABRIA

Soveria Mannelli

New York
Buffalo, Lackawanna

Rhode Island
Providence

Pennsylvania
Allegheny, Bradford, Eldred,
Galeton, Keating, Pittsburgh,
Punxsutawney, Smethport,
Wharton, Wesleyville

Wisconsin
Cumberland

Minnesota
Hibbing, St. Paul

Nebraska
Omaha

CANADA
Quebec
Montreal

Marano Principato

New York
Lackawanna, Buffalo

Illinois
Chicago

Wisconsin
Kenosha

CANADA
Ontario
Toronto

MARCHE

Fano and nearby towns

New York
Buffalo, Lackawanna

Connecticut
New Haven, New London

Massachusetts
Framingham, Winchendon

CANADA
Ontario
Copper Cliff,
Sault Sainte Marie

MOLISE

Cantalupo Nel Sannio

New York
Buffalo, Corona,
Lackawanna, New York City

Massachusetts
Boston

Ohio
Akron

Illinois
Chicago

North Dakota
Fryburg, Jamestown

Montana
Forsyth

California
Los Angeles

CANADA
Ontario
Niagara Falls, Toronto

Quebec
Montreal

on female virginity, male protectiveness, the use of titles indicating status, and mutual-aid activity, such as elaborate funeral rituals. To this list can be added other rituals, such as the religious *feste*. In Lackawanna, where the Italian community has been heavily Laziali and Abruzzesi, it appears there was less emphasis on the religious *feste*, which were not always celebrated on an annual basis and were discontinued in the late 1930s. Despite these differences, Pitkin concluded that the culture of the Laziali in Sermoneta had more in common with the deep south than with northern Italy. Also, the three-

way division of Italy into the north, central, and south areas has meant that Lazio, Abruzzo, and Molise are grouped with Marche and Toscana in central Italy. Many Steel City immigrants, when asked what part of Italy they hailed from, answered "central Italy". In Lackawanna, the only significant regional group considered northern Italian is composed of immigrants from Marche. Together, the Marchegiani, Laziali, and Abruzzesi comprise two-thirds of Lackawanna's Italians, a regional mix of central Italy that does not seem common to other American cities. This may account for the willingness of the Marchegiani of the city to live among the southerners, most of whom were from the adjacent regions of Lazio and Abruzzo. In Milwaukee, the Marchegiani, along with the Piedmontesi, lived apart from the southerners, most of whom were Siciliani—from the deep south.[105]

In Buffalo, during the period 1900 to 1906, the total Italian population of 19,630 was dominated by 10,500 Sicilians, 5,000 Basilicati, and 1,500 people with roots in Abruzzo and Molise (the two comprised a single region until 1963). Campania, with 800, and Calabria, with 500, were well represented, but all the other regions had 250 or fewer representatives, and Lazio had only 10. Since hundreds of Italian immigrants moved from Buffalo to Lackawanna, one might assume that similar percentages of regional groups would be found in the Steel City, but this was not always the case. Six of the nine largest Buffalo regional groups—the Abruzzesi, Campanesi, Marchegiani, Molisani, Calabresi, and Pugliesi—are also among the largest groups in Lackawanna. But it is surprising that so few Sicilians and Basilicati moved to the Steel City. Even less predictable is that the Laziali, who numbered only a handful in Buffalo by 1906 (although the hometowns of many people from Campania fell within Lazio when regional borders were changed in the 1920s), became the largest regional group in Lackawanna. There is no evidence to suggest that immigrants from Lazio, Abruzzo, and the other regional groups in Lackawanna had any more experience with steelmaking than did those from Sicily and Basilicata. Indeed, studies suggest that the overwhelming majority of all Italian immigrants in western New York had roots in rural and small-town Italy, where industrial jobs were rare. Perhaps it was simply a matter of the migration chains from Abruzzo and Lazio taking an early hold in Buffalo and Lackawanna, and the following immigration mirroring this precedent. As a function of the size of their groups, the Siciliani and Basilicati provided much of the leadership for the Buffalo Italian community and had the political and economic connections that produced jobs, which provided a strong incentive for natives of these regions to remain in Buffalo's Little Italys.[106]

The regional migration patterns of Lackawanna's Italian immigrants varied by decade as different chains of migrants became more active. For each 10-year period, the regional origins of a significant number of the immigrants was determined, and these figures provide the basis for Figure 2.29. In the first decade of the twentieth century, Abruzzesi and Napolitani were, respectively, the first and second most numerous immigrants in Lackawanna, although the numbers involved are small. But during the 1910s, the number of Laziali arrivals increased four-fold and simply dominated the statistics thereafter. The Napolitani migration peaked in the 1910s,

Giuseppe Leonetti (left) arrived in the United States from Pedace, Calabria, in 1915. His son Armando (right) immigrated in 1930 to join him in Lackawanna.
Photo source: Mary Leonetti

while the Calabrese immigration, which crested in the 1920s, was third in size between 1920 and 1939.[107]

In summary, Lackawanna was somewhat unusual—different from other Italian settlements. Most of the immigrants worked in steel plants, a rarity for Italians in the early years of the twentieth century. Plus, the city's Italian colony had a very high turnover of population into the 1930s. Its regional origins are unique in that the two largest groups were natives of Lazio and Abruzzo. The Italian immigrants who came to Lackawanna represented 17 of the 20 regions in Italy and they came to realize that regional differences, while important, comprised only one issue confronting them. The Italians also faced the daunting task of adapting to an urban, industrial environment in which they were seen as foreigners.

The historical events and cultural traditions of Italy were evident in the experiences of the immigrants and in their attempts to adjust to the new land. Suspicious of formal

Figure 2.29

Regional Origin of Italian Immigrants by Decade of Arrival in Lackawanna*

Region	1900 to 1910	1911 to 1920	1921 to 1930	1931 to 1940	1941 to 1950	1951 to 1960	1961 to 1999	Arrival Date Not Known	Total
Abruzzo	91	138	80	24	7	3	4	31	378
Basilicata	6	7	3	—	—	—	—	—	16
Calabria	33	50	49	9	9	2	1	3	156
Campania	71	81	37	16	7	17	3	40	272
Emilia-Romagna	—	—	2	—	—	—	—	—	2
Friuli-Venezia Giulia	—	1	1	—	—	—	—	—	2
Lazio	65	266	164	50	13	23	9	146	736
Lombardia	1	—	—	—	—	—	—	—	1
Marche	19	98	45	12	6	—	2	12	194
Molise	17	29	38	13	11	5	3	36	152
Piemonte	—	1	2	—	—	—	—	—	3
Puglia	6	19	19	3	—	1	1	18	67
Sardinia	—	—	—	—	—	—	1	—	1
Sicilia	14	22	10	4	1	3	—	3	57
Toscana	—	2	—	—	—	—	—	—	2
Trentino-Alto Adige	—	—	—	—	—	—	1	1	2
Umbria	—	—	—	—	—	—	—	1	1
Region Identified	323	714	450	131	54	54	25	291	2,042*
Region Unknown	314	340	229	19	15	2	3	106	1,028
Total	637	1,054	679	150	69	56	28	397	3,070

*This chart indicates that regional backgrounds of 2042 Lackawanna Italian immigrants, or 67% of the total of 3070, have been identified.

institutions, the immigrants—and later, their children—utilized an informal network of family (*paesani*) and provincial ties in settlements throughout the United States to serve many social functions. Initially, for the immigrants, the emphasis was on finding work, housing, and friends from Italy who could provide a haven for socializing in a familiar dialect, psychological support, and information on how to survive in America. The job-finding function became crucial during economic slumps and depressions, taking on a new emphasis as immigrants began to seek safer or more lucrative employment. This was evident as immigrants left the coal mines of Pennsylvania to seek jobs in the steel mills or railroads of Lackawanna.

Many marriages were the result of matchmaking done via these networks, especially during and after World War I, when Italian immigrants decided on permanent settlement in the United States. For example, Vincenzo Suffoletto, a native of Pettorano sul Gizio, immigrated in 1905, was living in Minnesota 10 years later, and arrived in Lackawanna in 1917. He used the *paesani* chain to meet his wife, Carmela Monaco, who was born and raised in Lewis Run, Pennsylvania. After their marriage, they settled in the Steel City.[108]

The immigrants and their children kept in contact with *paesani* and relatives in towns throughout the United States. Often, this took the form of visits, especially on holidays and during patron-saint festivals. Following World War II, many emigrants from Pettorano settled in Hamilton, Ontario, 50 miles northwest of Lackawanna. Each year, the Pettoranesi in the city celebrate the *festa* of Santa Margherita, which draws their *paesani* from throughout Ontario and western New York.[109]

With the end of mass immigration, the chain of contacts between Italian settlements focused less on the need for jobs and housing, and more on social and recreational functions. Gradually, Lackawanna's Italian families could afford to visit their *paesani* in Ohio, Pennsylvania, and other parts of New York state. By the 1920s, it was common for people to take a train or hire an Italian neighbor to drive them to another *paesano* settlement. In the following decades, many people had their own car, and could more easily visit relatives and attend festivals in distant towns. News about these visits among Italians became more common in local newspapers by the 1930s. For example, the *Lackawanna Leader* in 1938 described the birthday party held on Roland Avenue for Mrs. Mary Chiodo and her twin brother Joseph Pinto of Wesleyville, Pennsylvania. Guests included relatives from Lackawanna as well as Rochester and Gowanda, New York.[110]

The younger generation found another valuable asset of the *paesani* networks. Some young people eloped from a town in western New York, then showed up at the door of a *paesano* in Lackawanna. One such couple, the children of Giulianesi immigrants, went straight from Niagara Falls to the home of Ferdinando Catuzza in the Steel City. Catuzza was an immigrant who enjoyed the respect of other migrants from Giuliano, including the parents of at least one of the eloping youngsters. After hearing the couple's explanations for eloping, Catuzza contacted the families in Niagara Falls and negotiated a peace that preserved the social honor of both clans.

At times, young people in Lackawanna went to an older adult in the Italian community for help, as was the case with Pat Vertalino. In 1927, at the age of 19, he and Grace Valentine decided to get married. "My father didn't care," said Vertalino, "but my mother said I was too young." So the young man approached Bruno Falbo, an immigrant living in the same Roland Avenue neighborhood. While he wasn't a *paesano* of the Vertalinos, Falbo was well known in the community, had a car, and had his own *paesani* in Bradford, Pennsylvania. Falbo drove the couple to Bradford, where an alderman performed the marriage, and the couple returned to Lackawanna. "My mother was mad," reports Vertalino. "We lived for a month at my mother-in-law's before I could go home to get my clothes." Eventually, the Vertalino family accepted the marriage, due in part to Falbo's chaperoning of the elopement.

Contacts and visits between Italians in Lackawanna and other settlements in the United States, though not quite as common as in decades past, continued through the late twentieth century to the present time.[112]

FIGURE 2.30

Regional Origins of Italian Immigrants in Lackawanna*

1900 – 2009

Region	Town Known	Town Unknown	Total
Lazio	664	72	736
Abruzzo	308	70	378
Campania	234	38	272
Marche	162	32	194
Calabria	126	30	156
Molise	132	20	152
Puglia	64	3	67
Sicilia	26	31	57
Basilicata	14	2	16
Piemonte	0	3	3
Toscana	2	0	2
Emilia-Romagna	2	0	2
Friuli-Venezia Giulia	2	0	2
Trentino Alto-Adige	0	2	2
Lombardia	1	0	1
Sardegna	0	1	1
Umbria	1	0	1
Totals	**1,738**	**304**	**2,042**

*The 2,042 immigrants whose regional origins are known represent 67% of the 3,070 Italian immigrants who lived in Lackawanna at one time or another.

This chapter has focused on the journey of immigrants from Italy to the United States and their eventual settlement in Lackawanna. The next chapter will give an overall description of the experience of the first generation of immigrants and their descendants over the past century.

CHAPTER 3

THE LACKAWANNA ITALIAN EXPERIENCE SINCE 1900

A century ago, Italians in Lackawanna and throughout the United States made up a minority group that was the focus of great hostility. Today, Italian Americans are an integral part of mainstream society. For Lackawannans, this long journey began when immigrants left Italy and settled in the small city that had sprung up beside a huge steel plant.

A century later, their descendants can proclaim pride in their humble immigrant forebears and in the knowledge that Italian Americans have made significant contributions to American society. This chapter examines some of the key events that shaped the Italian experience in Lackawanna over the past 109 years. Later chapters will discuss specific aspects of this journey.

The 3,070 Italian immigrants who lived at one time or another in Lackawanna were part of the movement of approximately 5.5 million migrants from Italy to the United States. Most of them arrived between 1890 and 1924, when many other immigrant groups were also coming to the United States, and ethnic minorities were migrating from the southern states to northern cities. People of at least 91 other ethnic groups came to Lackawanna during the last century, many of them from southeast Europe, and the Italian ethnic group was one of the largest.[1]

The Lackawanna Italians forged their own community and ethnic identity, gradually assimilating as they encountered American institutions, other ethnic groups, and national and international events. The most crucial aspects of this transformation occurred during the first half of the twentieth

< Many Italian immigrants worked at outdoor jobs, especially construction projects. Antonio Monaco (circled) is among these men who built the Sears and Roebuck store on Main Street in Buffalo, May 1929.
Photo source: Yolanda Monaco-Bracci

century, so this chapter will look closely at the period from 1900 to 1950, then more briefly at the following six decades. After an overview of the Italian migration to the United States, there will be a discussion of six time periods and the important events within them that shaped Lackawanna's Italian community and its eventual entry into the mainstream of American society.

The New Immigrants of the Early 20th Century

During the period from 1820, when the U.S. government began keeping statistics, to 1955, more than 40 million immigrants arrived in this country, 85% of them from Europe. Prior to the 1890s, most of the immigrants were from northwest Europe, but then a significant change took place. Among the 20 million newcomers who arrived in the United States between 1890 and 1924, the majority came from southern and eastern Europe. Called the "new immigrants," the two largest groups were Italians and Jews. They were not well received by the nativists—people who thought they were the only true Americans and viewed immigrants as a threat—who launched a variety of attacks against them. Nativism was nothing new in America. In the mid-1700s, Benjamin Franklin spoke out against German immigrants, the Alien and Sedition Acts of 1798 were aimed at Irish and French newcomers, and the Know Nothing movement of the 1850s attacked Irish and German Catholics. But by the 1890s, many nativists were more concerned

FIGURE 3.1

JOHN B. WEBER, COMMISSIONER OF IMMIGRATION FOR NEW YORK

John Baptiste Weber was born in Buffalo in 1842 to a French father and German mother. Enlisting in the Civil War as a private in the New York Volunteer Infantry, he eventually attained the rank of colonel of the 89th United States Colored Infantry. Following the war, he purchased a 60-acre farm on Abbott Road in West Seneca, built a mansion that he named Shamokin, and ran a wholesale grocery business. Four decades later, this area became the city of Lackawanna.

Colonel Weber entered politics and served as the assistant postmaster of Buffalo, sheriff of Erie County, grade-crossing commissioner of Buffalo, and two-term congressman, and was considered for a presidential cabinet post. In 1901,

he was named as the commissioner general of the Pan American Exposition in Buffalo.

John B. Weber held the post of commissioner of immigration for the port of New York from 1890 to 1893. When the Ellis Island immigration station was opened in 1892, he presented a $10 gold piece to the first immigrant to pass through the gates. He was instrumental in developing the ship's manifest, which listed all passengers on a steamship. The lists are now valuable tools for genealogists researching their immigrant forebears.

Colonel Weber was active in persuading Lackawanna Steel to locate its plant in West Seneca and in petitioning Albany to endorse the founding of the city of

Lackawanna. In 1904, when nativists were demanding that immigration be limited, Weber stated that "it would be a serious mistake to stop the flow of immigration," adding that America's progress "was due to the fact that immigrants of all nationalities had come here freely and intermingled with the population." He did call for tighter regulation of the naturalization process to weed out aliens who became criminals. A perusal of his writings did not uncover any observations he may have had regarding Lackawanna as a city of immigrants.

John B. Weber died in Lackawanna on December 18, 1926.

Sources: William H. Emerling and John P. Osborne, *The History of Lackawanna*, 1976, p. 6; Mary J. Shapiro, *Gateway to Liberty: The Story of the Statue of Liberty and Ellis Island*, 1986, p. 120; Pamela Reeves, *Ellis Island: Gateway to the American Dream*, 1991, p. 34; *New York Times*, 1/28/1904, p. 11; *Lackawanna Leader*, 12/1/55; *Front Page*, 1/24/2007; U.S. Census, 1900.

about the new immigrants, and now viewed the Irish and Germans as superior to the migrants from southeast Europe. When the Immigration Restriction League was organized by Harvard graduates in 1894, its founder argued that America should be populated by the "historically free, energetic, progressive" people of British, German, and Scandinavian stock, and not by the "historically down-trodden, atavistic, and stagnant" Slav, Latin, and Jewish Asiatic "races" (all ethnic groups were called races at this time). Italians, a Latin people, came under particularly severe attack. History professor and future president Woodrow Wilson wrote in 1902 that Italian immigrants represented the "lowest class from the south of Italy…. The Chinese were more to be desired." Nativists were upset because many immigrants were "birds of passage" who frequently returned to Europe. Between 1900 and 1914, approximately 1.5 million Italian males returned to Italy from the United States, a return rate of about 50 percent. Furthermore, Italians lived very frugally, under spartan conditions, in order to send money back to their families in Italy. Italians in the U.S. and other countries sent more than 369 million *lire* to Italian banks in 1909 alone.[2]

In 1899, the commissioner general of immigration, in keeping with the current theories of superior and inferior "races," adopted a classification scheme that distinguished

between northern and southern Italians. Based on prejudices prominent in Italy, it viewed northerners—those from Piedmont, Lombardia, and Venezia—as superior to those from the southern two-thirds of the peninsula. American sociologist Edward A. Ross helped spread this bigotry when he wrote:

The fact that the emigrants from the north of Italy wander chiefly to South America, where industrially they dominate, while the emigrants from central and southern Italy come to this country, where they are dominated, makes it important to remember that in race advancement, the North Italians differ from the rest of their fellow-countrymen. In the veins of the broad-head people of Piedmont, Lombardy, and Venetia runs much Northern blood—Celtic, Gothic, Lombard, and German. The other Italians are of the long-head, dark, Mediterranean race, with no small infusion of Greek, Saracen, and African blood in the Calabrians and Sicilians. Rarely is there so wide an ethnic gulf between the geographical extremes of a nation as there is between Milan and Palermo.

Like social scientists in Italy, Ross portrayed the southerners as illiterate and possessing little mechanical aptitude. Addressing the steel industry in particular, he claimed "their noteworthy absence from the rolling mills is attributed to the fact that they lack the nervous stability needed for seizing a white-hot piece of iron with a pair of tongs."[3]

Protestant nativists, feeling threatened by the new immigrants, organized societies, such as the Society of Mayflower Descendants, emphasizing their own ancestral origins. Simultaneously, the fading Irish stereotypes were being replaced by negative images of southeast European immigrants. Nativists lamented that the Nordic (white, Anglo-Saxon, Protestant—or WASP) race that had founded America was being mongrelized by the Alpine, Mediterranean, and Semitic races—most prominently, the Italians, Slavs, and Jews. When Poles and Italians achieved the lowest scores in verbal and performance tests given to draftees in World War I, some psychologists claimed this as proof of Nordic superiority and argued that the new immigrants were lowering the overall level of American intelligence. The Italians' unique brand of Catholicism, characterized by anticlericism and street processions honoring patron saints, also brought criticism from Protestants as well as Irish Catholics.[4]

The most damaging stereotype of Italian immigrants has been the criminal image. Labeled as petty criminals or gangsters who could not be trusted, Italian immigrants allegedly had a taste for violence. "The knife with which he cuts his bread he also uses to lop off another dago's finger or ear…. He is quite as familiar with the sight of human blood as with the sight of the food he eats." The United States Immigration Commission claimed that specific types of criminality were "inherent in the Italian race." The commission completed a 42-volume report in 1911, concluding that the "new" immigrants were inferior to the "old" immigrants from northwest Europe. It didn't seem to matter that much of the massive data collected by commission researchers often contradicted their foregone beliefs.[9]

Immigration, Migration, and Survival, 1900–1914

The Italian experience in Lackawanna can be understood by examining specific time periods, each of which had unique factors that affected the lives of the immigrants and their descendants The initial period in Lackawanna began in 1900, when the construction of the steel plant commenced, and concluded in 1914, when the outbreak of World War I brought transatlantic travel to a virtual standstill. During this 15-year period, over two million Italian immigrants arrived in the United States. Many of them went back and forth between America and Italy, and also migrated between cities in the U.S., resulting in a constant turnover of residents in Italian colonies. The huge influx of Italians and their frequent moves fed into the hostility of nativists.

Italian immigrants in the Limestone Hill or "steel-plant district" of West Seneca, which later became Lackawanna, were also in a constant state of motion as they followed migration chains that extended from overseas to locations within the United States. They worked seasonal jobs, going from farms to railroads to construction sites to factories as they migrated throughout western New York and into other states. A network of *paesani* contacts provided housing and job referrals. A number of the lone males periodically returned to Italy to share their savings and renew contact with their wives, children, and relatives. Of the 801 male immigrants present in Lackawanna at some point during the period from 1900 to 1915, only 149 settled permanently in the city. Few had decided to remain in America, or, if they had, were not yet in the economic position to send for their wives or relatives.

This state of flux meant that Italian immigrants began learning skills for survival, such as key English phrases used in getting a job or dealing with the authorities. In the first three years of the new century, many Italians in the steel-plant district lived in a shantytown on the plant grounds, in Italian "hotels" or other large boardinghouses, or they boarded in the homes of Italian families. Most worked in the steel plant's Yard Department, where a majority of their coworkers were Italian and three became foremen by 1906.

American officials and nativists were concerned about the assimilation of the multitude of immigrants in the steel-plant district. Investigators for the U.S. Immigration Commission made a site visit in 1907, commenting in harsh terms on the contrast between the "old immigrant" groups living east of the railroad tracks and the "new immigrants" living west of the tracks, which two years later become Lackawanna's First Ward:

> This community is conveniently divided into two distinct sections: (1) the section in which the native Americans and the Irish, Scotch, and German immigrants of long residence live; and (2) the section in which all of the later immigrants, including Poles, Magyars, Croatians, Slovaks, and Servians (sic), reside. This second section of the community is completely isolated from the first and absolutely out of touch with any Americanizing influences. All of the shops, saloons, and boardinghouses are conducted by immigrants who discourage and oppose American activities among their people.

Prejudice toward and discrimination against the new immigrants were most intense prior to the mid-1920s. However, the Italian peasants, like the Slavs and Jews, had been the victims of discrimination in Europe, so the hostility they encountered in the United States at least was not foreign to them. They endured deadly violence, were driven out of some towns by mobs, and were segregated in the schools of Philadelphia and the southern states, harassed by police, and lambasted in newspapers. More common were the daily acts of hostility and verbal abuse, sometimes described in America's newspapers, which proved so damaging over time.[6]

Many Lackawanna Italians first lived in Buffalo, where the English-language press regularly denigrated their ethnic group starting in the 1880s (see Figure 3.2). Soon after immigrants began arriving in the Limestone Hill district of West Seneca, Italians felt the scorn of Buffalo's tabloids. In June 1902, the foreman of a work gang at the Lackawanna Steel plant fired 40 Italians. When he refused to either immediately pay or rehire the men, a large group of Italians confined him in a hut until they could reach an agreement. The *Buffalo Enquirer* described the incident in sensational terms, stating that "the foreman of the gang is at the mercy of enraged foreigners," and that the Italians threatened to kill him and "became almost frantic with rage;… Several of them screamed and howled…." (See Chapter 7 for more details.)[7]

Fear of violence by Italians was only one of several themes highlighted by the Buffalo newspapers. Another was filthy living conditions. A few months after the foreman incident, the *Buffalo Morning Express* offered an unflattering description of the Italian shantytown on the steel-plant grounds, where the foreman had been detained:

> (They are) herded together so closely that the wonder is, considering the intense factional feeling of those people, that there has been but one murder and not a dozen…. They do their cooking in the open, on curiously constructed ovens, … and their washing is done on the banks of the creek, whose water has turned from a rich green to a stagnant black. Comparatively speaking, there has been little disease among the laborers, and that is another source for wonderment, for a better culture ground for bacilli hardly could be imagined. (See Chapter 5 for details.)

The theme of filthy living conditions again arose in 1903. At a hearing in the state assembly in Albany, the following exchange took place between Assemblyman Cook and attorney Franklin Locke of the Lackawanna Steel Company regarding the Italian shantytown.

> "Isn't the sewage bad under the present conditions?" asked Assemblyman Cook. "Weren't there 100 cases of typhoid there last year?"
>
> "Those cases were among a lot of Italians living in shacks," said Mr. Locke. "The conditions were such that they would have had the typhoid had they been surrounded by sewers."

In 1910, the Lackawanna City Council voiced concern about the "(m)atter of the building near the New Village built by a contractor to house Italians. Dr. Tracy stated that he went to the place and found it sanitary, but the actions and conduct of the occupants were disgraceful. Mr. Widmer stated that inasmuch as the work was being done in the city of Buffalo, the men should be housed in Buffalo." The council then passed a motion: "The police commissioners be instructed to place an inspector over these men, and if they do anything undesirable, they take steps to have them removed."[98]

Italian immigrants also encountered negative attention from other authorities. The police and minority communities have often been at odds throughout American history, and this was true in the steel-plant district. In 1907, three police officers pounded on the door of an Ingham Avenue tavern at 4:30 a.m. Before proprietors Gennaro Panzarella and Pasquale DeBello could get to the door, the officers broke it down and proceeded to rummage through the second-floor bedrooms, roughing up Angelina Maducca in the process. In the tavern, they demanded drinks and cigars of the owners, and broke tables and chairs. The next day, more than 100 Italians gathered in the West Seneca police court as the judge ordered that one officer be arrested for disorderly conduct; soon afterward, one of the other officers was suspended for being drunk. The judge and a police captain promised to investigate the entire incident. That same week, Carlo Rossi was arrested for assaulting a fireman after a fire wagon ran over and killed a coworker.[9]

WASP capitalists were quick to take advantage of the immigrants in other ways. The owners of corporations needed and encouraged the immigration flow that provided millions of workers for their factories, railroads, and other ventures. With the exception of the years of the First World War, the captains of industry had a virtually unrestricted flow of European immigrants until 1922. Unfamiliar with labor practices in America, the immigrants were more easily coerced into accepting low wages and acting as strikebreakers as the steel industry and other corporations battled the rising tide of unionism. To keep the labor force divided, companies hired a variety of immigrants who did not understand each other's languages and cultures—including, later, blacks and Mexicans. The leaders of the steel industry created the most ethnically mixed workforce in American industry, which reinforced the division of the working class into factions, especially along racial lines. Italians and other immigrants started out near the bottom of the working class, but above blacks and other people of color.[10]

Work at the steel plant was sporadic, and the recession of 1907-08 all but closed down Lackawanna Steel, sending many Italians to other states or back to Italy. When the mills were booming, workers endured a high rate of death and injury in

June 26, 1910, New Village. Italian workers play bocce and prepare meals at a fire pit near the dormitory provided by a contractor to house them. The Lackawanna city council instructed police to have these men removed if they did "anything undesirable." Photo source: Hagley Museum and Library, Delaware

business proprietors, while others who had trades in Italy settled for careers in the steel plant. The high rate of population turnover continued, but at a reduced intensity: only 13 percent of the male Italian immigrants arriving from 1900 to 1905 settled permanently in the city, while the rate for those arriving in the 1911–1915 period rose to 24 percent. These developments set the stage for further adaptations needed to survive in the United States.[12]

Settling In, 1915–1929

The outbreak of World War I in August 1914 ushered in a new period for Italians in Lackawanna. Transoceanic travel came to a virtual standstill, ending immigrants' back-and-forth voyages between Italy and the United States. The immigrants had to again adapt to both opportunities and dangers. On the positive side, the steel plant was booming with defense contracts,

the plant, plus lost time from illness. This led Lackawanna's Italians in 1910 to organize the Lake Erie Italian Club, which provided sickness and death benefits as well as a setting for socializing. The shantytown and the Sperduto boardinghouse at the south end of the steel plant grounds were gone by 1905, and Italians were less inclined to live in the hotels and boardinghouses on Gates and Steelawanna Avenues. Instead, they concentrated in three neighborhoods: the Old Village, Ingham Avenue, and Roland Avenue. Former farm laborers started small businesses in Lackawanna—27 in 1900-09 and 63 in the following decade. In the back rooms of many Italian bars and grocery stores, men played familiar card and drinking games. The business establishments, the Lake Erie Italian Club, and the boardinghouses were the first institutions created by the Italian colony. While these institutions looked too foreign to investigators of the U.S. Immigration Commission, they provided immigrants with news about jobs and legal documents as well as a communal way of coping with the harshness of urban America.[11]

From their homes in Italy to their new homes in the United States, the immigrants had changed in many ways. Beginning with their decision to leave Italy, they networked with townspeople and even distant kin with whom they normally would have limited interactions in their native villages. Italian families in Lackawanna took in boarders, something that was rare in Italy. Mediterranean farmers became steel workers or

which provided Italians with steady work and greater access to skilled jobs. Being an ocean away from Europe, Italian immigrants in the United States could ignore Italy's call for overseas subjects to return for military duty. However, some 90,000 immigrants in America returned to their native land to join the Italian armed forces when Italy entered the war in May 1915. Giuseppe Pietrocarlo's brothers Emilio, Antonio, and Luigi left Lackawanna to serve in the Italian Army and never returned to the United States. Old-world loyalties erupted in Lackawanna that September on Gates Avenue, home to many eastern Europeans. As Giuseppe Mescalino walked by a group of Austrian immigrants, verbal insults were traded and the Italian was stabbed to death. Other Italians got caught up in the war when they visited their hometowns in Italy and were nabbed by authorities. Filiberto Covelli made a trip to Calabria to visit his wife and children just before the war began and was drafted into the Italian Army in 1915. An American citizen at the time, he could have protested his induction, as the U. S. government often demanded the release of its citizens. Unaware of this, he served in the Italian Army, then after the war, joined some *paesani* who had moved to Lackawanna to work in the mills.[13]

American authorities made their own demands on the immigrants even before the United States entered the war. The *Lackawanna Daily Journal* in 1916 urged that foreign languages not be taught in the public schools: "Make America for Americans, and anyone here whose heart throbs for a foreign

A prejudiced view of Italians appears in an 1891 newspaper article citing the poverty, dirtiness, and violence of the ethnic group in Buffalo. As an added emphasis, this cartoon depicts Italians practicing stiletto throwing in a rural area outside Buffalo.
Photo source: Buffalo and Erie County Library, *Buffalo Morning Express*, 5/24/1891

land to such an extent that they must talk their language, let them tie themselves to that country and become its subject; we do not need them here." The Lackawanna Social Service Committee held a July 4th rally at the Old Village in 1916 at which there were addresses in Polish, Hungarian, and Italian intended to "awaken our foreign population to the full meaning of a FREE COUNTRY and a LIBERTY-LOVING people and also that they must shoulder a part of that country's responsibilities." When the United States entered the conflict in 1917, the government demanded that immigrants be "100 percent American," register for the draft, and report "instances of disloyalty" to federal officials. Fortunately for Italians, they were among the few groups of new immigrants whose country of birth was an ally of the United States, England, France, and Russia. Italians must have noticed how harshly German Americans were treated at the time and they were quick to rally under the stars and stripes, so as not to incur the wrath of nativists.

At the 1917 Memorial Day parade, which highlighted the patriotism of Lackawanna's ethnic groups, members of the Lake Erie Italian Club marched behind president Tony Amorosi and vice president Tony Turchiarelli, who were mounted on horseback, confident with the knowledge that their native land was in good standing as an American ally. The next year, the parade included Serbian, Hungarian, and Croatian groups marching with an Italian band and the Lake Erie Italian Club. Thirteen Italians, mostly businesspeople, were included on the honor rolls of Lackawannans purchasing Liberty Bonds. Four Italians sat on the Liberty Loan Committee, which organized street rallies, including one in the Italian neighborhood on lower Ingham Avenue. Across the nation, immigrants donated 18 percent of the funds collected in the Third Liberty Loan Drive; German Americans, the biggest donors, gave $87,295,000, and Italian Americans were second with $52,247,000.[14]

After the United States entered the war in April 1917, one of every five servicemen was foreign born, including 300,000 Italian Americans. Lackawanna newspapers carried regular reports of men going off to military camps. Italian Americans constituted four percent of the population but suffered 12 percent of the military casualties. Approximately 20,000 Italian soldiers, including Lackawanna's Domenico Mattone, Antonio Pirri, and Angelo Costanzi, gave their lives during the conflict. The war played a role in the assimilation process, as Italian American soldiers served with men of other ethnic groups in a patriotic cause and won a measure of respect for it. Those who were aliens and had declared their intent to become citizens were automatically naturalized. Also, nativist hostility and notions of Anglo-Saxon superiority were usually suspended as America recruited the new immigrants to join the fight against Anglo-Saxon Germany. When Italian American soldiers complained of being called "wop" and "dago," and blacks of being called "niggers" and "coons," the military ordered that these slurs no longer be used, which had some effect on officers though little on ordinary soldiers.

During the war, many immigrants, unable to leave the country, decided to settle in Lackawanna. They helped create more institutions during this period. St. Anthony's church was completed in 1917, and an Italian priest arrived to serve as pastor. Two church-affiliated societies were founded, one being the Mt. Carmel women's society, and Italians began to hold *feste* and other communal celebrations. In 1918, Little Italy produced its first American-educated professionals, doctor John Fadale and teacher Mary Yoviene.[15]

After the war, nativism returned with a vengeance, focusing largely on hatred toward Catholics, Jews, and southeast Europeans. The demands for 100 percent Americanism led Lackawanna Italians to make patriotic gestures. In 1919, Lake Erie Italian Club members and their wives took part in a League of Nations pageant in which Serafino Mattucci played the role of Christopher Columbus. During this period, the United States was torn by a number of conflicts: urban versus rural, native WASP stock versus immigrant stock, Protestant versus Catholic, capitalist versus socialist or communist, and, with the advent

FIGURE 3.2

THE BUFFALO PRESS ATTACKS ITALIANS

Following an 1888 incident in which one Italian had killed another, Buffalo's police sprang into action, as "forty-two stalwart bluecoats ... were ordered to bring in all male Dago [sic] that looked as if they carried knives." The police took 325 "swarthy-looking, jibbering foreigners" to the station house but found only two knives on members of the group. The police superintendent, in an attempt to justify the wholesale arrests, stated: "The Italians and Poles of Buffalo made a regular practice of carrying concealed weapons; and the public demanded vigorous police action to curtail crime among the city's foreign-born residents." The Italian community protested and appealed to the Italian government for justice.

In May 1907, as members of the Italian Labor Union of Buffalo marched down Main Street as part of a protest, a streetcar motorman drove his vehicle into the parade. The result was "a bloody riot," according to the *Buffalo Courier*, and a battle "between a handful of bluecoats and a score of courageous citizenry against the fearful odds of half a thousand murderously enraged Sicilians and Calabrians." The Italians "swarmed the narrow tenement-lined streets," most of them "armed with the knife weapon of Italy—the Calabrian with his broad-bladed pugnale down the back of his coat between his shoulder blades and the Sicilian with his slender stiletto concealed in his breast."

The Buffalo police chief later said: "I think that the Italians are a dangerous class, for they break the law." The image of the violent, knife-wielding Italian in Buffalo had earlier been sensationalized in an 1891 news article subtitled "Un-American Codes and Modes." One of the accompanying drawings featured the caption "stiletto practice in the country" (see page 108).

The prejudice, discrimination, and stereotypes of Buffalo's English-language press led an Italian newspaper in the city, *Il Corriere Italiano*, to conclude that "there is hatred for us, and bad opinions have in general formed their way in the hearts of the Americans against us." The paper addressed the issue in a 1907 editorial titled "In Behalf of Race Assimilation." The text reads:

Particular stress and characterization seems to be laid by our local Press to accidents, burglaries, murders, and other crimes committed by people of Italian origin. Such scare, large headlines as 'Italian Murder,' 'Italian Robbery,' 'Black Hand in Italian District,' [and] 'Italian in Stabbing Affair,' are often noticed whenever an affair involving those crimes happens.

Only a short time ago, the *Buffalo Enquirer* apparently found great delight in printing with bold type 'Italian Boy Killed By an Elephant.' Now as a matter of fact the boy was born in America and under the United States Constitution is entitled to as much consideration, than our Mayor, who is not a native born, or the proprietor of the Enquirer. In the same issue appeared in big headlines: 'West Seneca Workmen in a Stabbing Affair.' The stabbing occurred among Hungarians; if it had happened among Italians, you would have undoubtedly seen the name 'Italian' in place of 'Workmen.'

Now, we would ask our neighbors why they do not mention in every instance the nationality of those who commit such offenses? Why is the Italian selected for race hatred? Have the newspapers special interest to bring the 'Italian' name before the American people in disgrace and humiliation?

It should be the duty of every American citizen to help to assimilate the foreigners and make good citizens of them. This end will never be accomplished so long as the Press continues to discriminate in this manner.

Now this criticism is not made for the purpose of depreciating in any sense our Italian country, but to lend such aid in furtherance of good citizenship among foreigners. It is hope [sic] that the Press will aid us along these lines, and eventually give the Italian a 'square deal.'

Sources: *Buffalo Daily Courier*, 1/5/1888; *Buffalo Courier*, 5/6/1907; *Buffalo Morning Express*, 5/24/1891; Virginia Yans-McLaughlin, *Family and Community: Italian Immigrants in Buffalo, 1880–1930*, 1971, p. 112; *Il Corriere Italiano*, 12/1/1906; 6/15/1907.

of Prohibition in 1920, came wet versus dry. The rise of socialism and communism abroad led leaders in capitalist America to react harshly against any type of suspected "radical" activity, including newly formed labor unions. Another significant development of 1920 that divided Americans was the granting of voting rights to women. Caught up in this bewildering whirlpool of events, Italians both closed ranks among their co-ethnics and began to recognize, despite the

formidable barriers between ethnic groups, that they shared a common plight with other working people.[16]

In Lackawanna, the Great Steel Strike of 1919 saw many Irish, Slavic, and Italian steelworkers band together in a union and temporarily shut down Lackawanna Steel. These workers witnessed the awesome power of the police forces of the steel plant, the city, and New York state to use violence and intimidation against workers and defeat the strike. These

FIGURE 3.3

ITALIAN AMERICAN PATRIOTISM IN WORLD WAR I

Lackawanna Italians supported the American war effort in 1917 and 1918. A number of them, mostly businesspeople, were included on the honor rolls of Lackawannans purchasing Liberty Bonds: Angelo and Frank Morinello, Mike Falcone, Frank Sirianni, Tony Amorosi, Alfonso Mortellaro, Joseph Amigone, Cleveland John Tarquinio, Nicola Peronace, Vincenza Agliata, Mary Fusco, Adele Bianchi, and Antonio Guadagno. Leaders in the Italian community were part of the Liberty Loan Committee, which arranged street meetings, including one at Ingham Avenue and Holbrook Street. The long list of committee members included Tony Amorosi, Frank Morinello, Rev. Raffaele D'Alfonso, and Margaret Tarquinio.

Local newspapers carried regular reports of men going off to military camps. On May 21, 1918, Vincenzo DiCenzo, Gaetano Carsiggi, and Silvio Pandozzi were on their way to Camp Dix, New Jersey. A month later Vito Frisolone, Onorato Guglielmi, Biagio Baldassari, and Sosio Mattone followed them, accompanied by Nick Falcone, who was listed as an "alternate"— someone who 'd take the place of a man who failed his physical. In July, Ottavio Gabrielli and Augusto Ghiandonni left for Camp Dix, accompanied by alternates Mike Filighera and Paul Blassio. Aliens who had declared their intent to become citizens were automatically naturalized following military service, as was the case for Gino Bartolomeo, Michele Tibollo, Fausto DeSantis, Luigi Petricca, Joe Fox, Eugenio Ziccarelli, and Lawrence Marmineo. Three Lackawanna Italian American soldiers—Domenico Mattone, Antonio Pirri, and Angelo Costanzi—died in the conflict. After Costanzi was killed in France in 1918 his mother Elizabeth never recovered from the loss, mourning his death for 24 years until her own passing in 1942.

Sources: *Lackawanna Daily Journal,* 4/ 16,19,24,25,27,& 30/18, 5/21/18; Lackawanna Library, microfilm reel of *Steel City Press* and *Lackawanna Press* includes a newspaper clipping dated 9/21/18; Alexander DeConde, *Half Bitter, Half Sweet: An Excursion into Italian-American History,* 1971, pp. 156-57; *Lackawanna Leader,* 8/20/42.

Antonio Monaco was one of many immigrants who first served in the Italian Army during World War I before immigrating to the United States.
Photo source: Yolanda Monaco-Bracci

Luigi Violanti came to the U.S. in 1920, after serving in the Italian military. Italy entered World War I in 1915 as an ally of England, France, and Russia.
Photo source: Aldo Filipetti

Federico Marrano, shown with his wife Maria, was in the Italian Army in 1912, when Italy and Turkey battled for control of Libya. He received a medal for his service.
Photo source: Neil Marrano

Italians provided much of the labor needed to maintain and expand railroads 100 years ago. Immigrant Francesco Caferro was one of many sent out in work gangs from Chicago, winding up in Whitefish, Montana (shown above). His son Antonio eventually settled in Lackawanna. Photo source: Tony Caferro

workers also became more aware of the racial pecking order and saw that some groups were more detested than their own. As African Americans migrated to the industrial north, Italians and other immigrants joined native-born whites in attacking them. In 1919, this occurred during the Chicago race riots, and in Lackawanna, when the steel company brought in black strikebreakers during the Great Steel Strike. The arrival of a large number of blacks and a smaller group of Mexicans in the Steel City in the early 1920s brought about an unexpected benefit to the city's new immigrants. By the mid-1920s, nativists and other bigots, reassured that the flood of foreigners had been halted by new legislation, began to moderate their prejudice toward the new immigrants and focus more on the blacks and Mexicans who were migrating north to fill the jobs once reserved for new arrivals from Europe. After living side-by-side with black families in the Old Village, many Italians moved to the new Bethlehem Park housing development, where African Americans were not allowed. This pattern provided a vivid example of America's racial duality, reinforcing the idea that all whites, even immigrants from southeast Europe, were favored over people of color. At the same, time the Lackawanna

English-language press, and even the rabidly anti-immigrant Buffalo press, began offering more sympathetic and even positive news about Italians and other southeast Europeans. While prejudice and discrimination continued, the most violent and belligerent forms of nativism were declining.[17]

The struggles within the American ruling class regarding immigration came to a climax in the early 1920s. Until this time, the barons of industry had successfully lobbied for policies allowing millions of immigrants to enter the country to provide a cheap labor force for their steel mills and other industries. But a competing segment of the ruling WASP elite, the nativists, were finally able in 1921 and 1924 to pass laws that sharply reduced the number of Italian, Slavic, and Jewish immigrants. WASP legislators, academics, and nativist organizations continued to denounce these immigrant groups as inferior, and a revived and expanded Ku Klux Klan aggressively attacked both blacks and southeast European immigrants in the north. In 1927, Italian Americans were again reminded of their minority status when anarchists Bartolomeo Vanzetti and Nicola Sacco were executed in Massachusetts after a decidedly unfair trial. During the 1920s, restrictive covenants became widespread, and while most were

These Lackawannans, most of them immigrants from Marche, registered for the U.S. Army draft on the same day in 1917. Top row, left to right: Michele Filighera, Augusto Ghiandoni, Paolo Filipetti, Odo Revelli, "Jawbone," Emidio Antilli, and Augusto Capodagli. Middle row: Rico Caselli, [Unk], Ermete Silvestrini, Giuseppe Montanari, Stefano Canestrari, Luigi Renzoni, Agosto Dellacecca, and [Unk]. Bottom row: Lavinio Montanari, Pietro Bartolucci, Cesare Renzoni, and Clario Bartolucci. Photo source: Aldo Filipetti

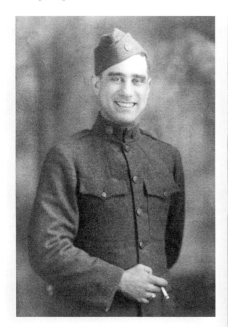

James Sirianni served in the U.S. Army in World War I. He was born in Galeton, Pennsylvania, and his family moved to Front Street in 1905. His parents, Pietro and Caterina, established a grocery store. Photo source: Collection of Frank Chiodo

Nicola Falcone, left, and Antonio Colello, center, were natives of Pico, Lazio. They, along with the unidentified man at the right, served in the U.S. military in the First World War. Photo source: Collection of Lou Colello

Angelo Costanzi was one of three Lackawanna Italians who died during World War I while serving in the American Army. Photo source: Lake Erie Italian Club

League of Nations Day in Lackawanna, September 1919. The Italian group included (lower row, from left): Emidio Zaccagnini, Antonetta Sperduto, Filomena Milano, Serafino Mattucci (as Columbus), Lucia Fadale, Angelo Sperduto, and Angelo Carlini. Upper row: Michele DelBello, Virginia Mattucci, Antonio Amorosi, Michele Tornatore, and Vittoria Carlini. The men were members of the Cooperativa Lago Erie Societa di Mutuo Soccorso (now called the Lake Erie Italian Club), and the society's flag is on the right. Photo source: League of Nations Day booklet; collection of Tina Mattucci Ginnetti and Yolanda Mattucci-Nigro

aimed at people of color, some prohibited Italians from moving into certain neighborhoods in western New York.[18]

Lackawanna's Italians and other white ethnics were welcomed into the new Bethlehem Park housing development, but they continued to feel the sting of prejudice. When Ferrari's Carnival Show appeared in Lackawanna in 1918, the *Lackawanna Daily Journal* remarked on "the crowds of foreigners who were herding themselves into the tents after the manner of the animals who followed Noah into the ark." During the first days of the Great Steel Strike in 1919, Lackawanna Steel Company security guards shot and killed two Polish American strikers. The *Buffalo Commercial* condemned the strikers, many of whom were immigrants, calling them "ignorant foreigners, the scum of their native lands" and "baffled foreigners" with "shrunken heads." During the early 1920s, members of the Ku Klux Klan went through the streets of Buffalo, Hamburg, and Lackawanna putting up posters to recruit members. The Klan, which had a heavily WASP membership, found only a few supporters in Lackawanna, including Herbert Davis, the chief of the steel plant's police force. The KKK held mass meetings throughout western New

York, including one in 1923 in Blasdell, where Klansmen burned a cross and arranged their 500 vehicles into a semicircle with headlights on to illuminate the ceremonies. This alarmed area Italians, including two youths whose families had moved from Lackawanna to Blasdell. Fourteen-year-old Al Croce watched the event from a distance and thought of the fights he had had with boys in Blasdell who called him "guinea." Rose Carestio-Iacobucci was called "dago" by some people, and her family was uneasy knowing that a number of their neighbors were at the cross burning. Some Italians were prepared to defend themselves with firearms if attacked.[19]

The stereotype of the new immigrants as violent criminals was reinforced by Lackawanna police captain Charles Curtin, who described events of the 1920s this way: "During this period there were many conflicts among the recent immigrants to the city. They only understood the law of the gun and the knife and did not look to the police and the courts to settle disputes. This resulted in many murders. These murders seemed to run in cycles and some weeks there would be a murder a day." In the steel-plant, Italians were sometimes harassed by men of other ethnic groups. Nunze Oddy was shunned and called "dago" by some

League of Nations Day, 1919, participants (from left): Vittoria Carlini, Virginia Mattucci, and Antonetta Sperduto. Photo source: League of Nations Day booklet, collection of Tina Mattucci Ginnetti and Yolanda Mattucci-Nigro

coworkers when he started work in the roll shop. Joe Violanti was called "boy" and Alfredo Campanelli "spaghetti bender" by supervisors and other workers in the open hearths. Vincenzo "Jimmy" D'Alessandro ended the constant hazing and intimidation of two coworkers only by threatening to shoot them.[20]

When the Lackawanna Steel Company began its move from Scranton, Pennsylvania, to West Seneca, New York, in 1900, it brought along many of its Irish workers. This large and more assimilated ethnic group, along with some WASPs and Germans, developed political clout. In 1909, it was largely the Irish who founded Lackawanna's political and civic institutions, and they dominated the ranks of leaders and civil servants. They were the plant foremen and supervisors, teachers, policemen, and politicians. Ironically, it was these second-, third- and fourth-generation ethnics, fresh from their own assimilation lessons at the hands of WASP officials, who were now directing Lackawanna Italians and Slavs through their own adjustment to American society. The thousands of southeast European immigrants arriving in the same at the same time did not have the know-how and unity to effectively compete with the northwest Europeans.[21]

Anxious to preserve their newly won status in the city's pecking order, and desiring to rise to loftier positions, some Irishmen and Germans discriminated against the new immigrants in the same way the WASPs had discriminated against them earlier. It must have felt good to no longer be at the bottom of the white ethnic pecking order. Enforcing demands of assimilation upon Lackawanna's Italians and Slavs could also help enhance their legitimacy in the eyes of the WASP elite that maintained control of the economy of western New York

and the fate of the Lackawanna Steel Company. While some Irish and German Catholics worked with WASP nativists to keep the new immigrants in line, others, remembering the sting of discrimination they themselves had endured, sought to treat the newcomers with respect and guide them through the process of learning American ways. Further, since most of Lackawanna's new arrivals were Roman Catholics, it made sense to reach out to them to create a religious and political unity that could further the interests of Catholic ethnic groups and challenge WASP hegemony. The Irish-dominated hierarchy of the Roman Catholic Church in America, while frowning on Italian street processions and other rituals of the new immigrants, realized it must create nationality parishes and tolerate "foreign" rituals to keep these groups within the Catholic fold. In addition to an Irish parish, Lackawanna offered Croatian, Polish, Hungarian, and Italian parishes. The city's Irish elected officials used guile and political maneuvering to maintain their positions but usually avoided the drastic nativist attacks that characterized other cities. Certainly prejudice and discrimination existed in the Steel City, but for Italians, they were not as intense as that faced by their cousins in other locales. Plus, the Lackawanna press was much less rabid than Buffalo's newspapers in reporting on the immigrants. The only European group regularly lambasted in the local press was a band of Gypsies.

While there were many southeast European ethnic groups in Lackawanna, most were relatively small in number except for the Poles. The Italian colony, like that of other groups, was probably not perceived as a large and conspicuous foreign threat, as it was in cities like Buffalo, Boston, and New York. Most of Lackawanna's population in the first 40 years of the twentieth century, when 77 ethnic groups were present, consisted of immigrants or other minorities. Fifty-four percent of the 1910 population and 57 percent of that in 1930 were first- and second-generation ethnics from southeast Europe, the groups designated "inferior" by immigration laws. By 1930, another 10 percent were people of color. Only the northwest Europeans could claim to be "100 percent American" in a city of minority peoples. Any nativist bigot would probably be equally upset by the presence of Poles, Croatians, Serbs, Greeks, Italians, and Macedonians. The large size of the Polish community made it easier to single out, but the Poles were a potent bloc of voters who could retaliate in city elections against bigoted officials. To a lesser degree, this same principle served to protect Italians, who represented one of the larger ethnic groups in Lackawanna and had the potential to coalesce into a voting bloc. Indeed, because the city's population was so heavily composed of immigrants from southeast Europe, the Irish and WASPs usually seemed to avoid any harsh public act that could generate a unified political movement among the new immigrants. Some politicians and civil servants were openly bigoted, but many seemed content to co-opt and bribe ethnic groups with the plentiful money available in the bustling city. In their leadership roles, the Irish taught and enforced the values of the dominant WASP group by both tutoring the new immigrants and keeping them "in line." Throughout the northeastern states, the Irish feared that the southeast Europeans might undermine their control of the Catholic Church hierarchy and challenge their urban political machines. In Lackawanna, their fears were realized in the early 1920s when the Poles, backed by Italians and other ethnic groups, elected a Polish mayor and several Slavic councilmen. But despite the political gains of the southeast Europeans, some city leaders degraded them. A city health official complained in 1924 that "foreigners" were a "menace to public health," noting that "[t]here are instances where several families crowd into a small building and just exist—they don't live."[22]

To teach immigrants and their children the ways of America, northwest Europeans ran three social settlement agencies. The YMCA's Lackawanna Institute, the Lackawanna Community House, and Friendship House offered libraries, handicrafts, industrial arts, sports, recreation, bathing facilities, movies, and classes in English for people of all ages (see Figure 3.4). In 1924, the Lackawanna Community House (LCH) served people of 45 nationalities, including those with roots in "Poland, Hungary, Italy, Ireland, Syria, Bohemia, Ukraine, Russia, and occasionally Arabs and Croatians," which presented challenges to the staff. For the Lackawanna Community House:

> The greatest problem confronting the center at the present moment is, undoubtedly, the variety of nationalities that are included in its membership. 'We have not been able to mix the various groups in the smaller clubs,' Miss Grace M. Laing, the director of the house, stated, 'but we have much better success in our social dances which we conduct weekly and sometimes succeed in breaking up the group clannishness.'

Laing then pondered two classic issues of social work: race relations and whether to emphasize "amalgamation" (assimilation) or the preservation of immigrant cultures.

> 'I have been debating the question with myself whether we should work for the amalgamation of the different foreign groups, or make an attempt to develop their national spirit. We also have a large colored population and will have to meet that problem some day, too.... We have received fine cooperation from the clergymen of the different churches, especially from the Polish priests. There is a great deal of amalgamation needed. So far, our best work has been with the Irish and the Polish. We find we can mix them best in our gymnasium and various

Figure 3.4

THREE AGENCIES WORKING TO ASSIMILATE THE IMMIGRANTS

The Lackawanna Institute was founded by the Buffalo YMCA in 1911 "in the heart of the foreign boardinghouse section," on Steelawanna Avenue. Its goal was to be "a helping hand extended to the foreigner in an effort to help Americanization." The institute offered English classes for men, activities for men and boys, and a recreation camp on Lake Erie. Open night and day, it attempted to be "a permanent moulding influence to create good citizens." In 1915, some 320 Croatians, Poles, Italians, Syrians, and Hungarians attended English classes there. Renamed the Lackawanna Industrial Branch (LIB), the agency moved into a new two-story building constructed by Lackawanna Steel on Hamburg Turnpike. It featured a gymnasium, a boys' club, manual training facilities, sewing classes for girls, games, jitney dances, and a restaurant patronized by steel-plant employees. It was hoped that the LIB could "solve many of the problems of the home, the employer and of the city. It would compete successfully with the saloon for the men's and boys' evenings, which would mean clearer heads and steadier hands." The LIB's membership grew, and the combined attendance at all events in 1919-20 was 52,500. Daily activities, social gatherings, and movies drew large crowds, including the 400 people who attended the Christmas party in 1922. Though the agency helped hundreds of immigrants and their children become acculturated, it ran at a deficit, and Bethlehem Steel shut it down in 1923.

The Lackawanna Community House (LCH) opened in 1910 as a social and recreational center and was funded by Lackawanna Steel and wealthy Buffalonians. By 1914, the LCH occupied a large building on Wilkesbarre Avenue that had a hall/gymnasium and meeting rooms on the first floor, and manual training and carpentry shops on the second. Staff members taught basketball and supervised the playground at the LCH building and other sites in the city. They also maintained a library, gymnasium, and public baths in the Old Village School Annex, where Angelo Croce was the part-time caretaker.

The LCH had a variety of activities for boys and girls, including a kindergarten. Twins Josephine and Patricia Fadale walked from Ingham Avenue to participate in the Girl Scout program. Sara Chiacchia played basketball there, took sewing classes, and joined other girls in making cloth diapers for Father Baker's orphanage. Teenager Joe

(continued)

Cosentino took dance lessons at the LCH and its Old Village site. "I learned to dance there. Mr. Robb taught us the fox-trot and the waltz." Waldo Robb, the agency director, hired Joe Milano and Patsy George to lead a Scout troop and recreational programs at the Old Village playground, and supervise boys on trips to a campground in Woodlawn. Milano and his brother Nick made the newspapers in 1921 when they rescued a three-year-old girl who had fallen into Smokes Creek. The high point in Joe Milano's LCH job was when he and Nick Thomas attended a 1923 conference for social workers in Washington, D.C.

The gymnasiums at the LCH and Old Village were crucial for indoor sports during the winter when school gyms were not always available. An LCH team composed almost totally of Italians won the YMCA basketball league championship for the 1921-22 season by defeating the "Erins," an Irish squad from the New Village. After Bethlehem Steel purchased the steel works in 1922, it reduced its funding of the LCH and donated the building to the city, which procured funds from other industries and continued programs until at least 1939. In addition to sports and recreation groups, the LCH offered teen dances, a baby clinic, Americanization classes, and sewing and canning classes for "the poor."

Friendship House had its origins in 1907, when Presbyterians in Buffalo established a kindergarten class and later a Sunday School program for Hungarian children. When health and hygiene classes,

a nursery school, a women's society, and a Red Cross Auxiliary were added to these activities, Friendship House was born. Ministers and laypeople did outreach work among Croatians, Slovenes, and other ethnic groups, and established the Immigrant Aid Office in 1918 and the Daily Vacation School in 1919. The school enrolled children of the Protestant, Roman and Greek Catholic, and Greek Orthodox faiths. It also held Religious Day school on Saturdays, English classes for immigrants, and film programs. Relocating to a new building on Ridge Road in 1921, the agency addressed the need of men living in boardinghouses with no bathing facilities by providing one shower and six bathtubs for public use. By year's end more than 10,000 baths had been taken. The agency's founders stressed the assimilation of immigrants. "Lackawanna, almost at our doors, was a foreign land, swarming with children and mothers who, not understanding English, were stranded there needing a friendly greeting in this strange land… Through the work we have learned to appreciate more fully the difficulties beset anyone trying to do Christian work in the midst of a foreign people.…"

Between 1920 and 1930, Friendship House established sewing and cooking classes for girls, English classes, a library, an American History Pageant, and a summer-camp program. During the Depression, the agency handed out food and clothing to those in need. By 1940, hundreds of children were involved in athletic leagues, and crafts and educational clubs, and teens participated in social

The Lackawanna Community House, 1915. Located on Wilkesbarre Avenue, its adult and youth programs focused on Americanizing the city's many immigrants and their children.
Photo source: Collection of Joe Milano

groups and dances. Community groups and the fledgling steelworkers union held meetings at Friendship House, and a consumers cooperative store was founded in 1941. People of 20 nationalities, mostly Hungarians and Slavs attended Friendship House programs in 1926 – 27. Caz DePasquale noticed he was one of the few Italians going to these programs in the late 1920s and early 1930s. Friendship House was six or seven blocks from the Italian enclave on Ingham Avenue and in an area populated by east European ethnic groups. Also, DePasquale and other young people at St. Anthony's were told by Reverend Vifredo not to attend Friendship House—for fear they would be converted to Presbyterianism. But DePasquale enjoyed the pool tables, basketball, library, and band practice, and it was there that he learned to dance. In1999, after decades of service to the community, Friendship House closed.

Sources: YMCA: YMCA of Buffalo, *Annual Report,* January, 1912, p. 12 (1st quote); November, 1912, p. 3 (2nd and 3rd quotes); February, 1913 (4th quote); June/July, 1915, pp. 3-4; December, 1922, p. 18; December, 1923, p. 5; Kenneth C. Hausauer, *The Second Fifty Years: A History of the Young Men's Christian Association of Buffalo and Erie County,* 1902-1952, 1970, pp. 47, 52; interviews with Joe Milano, December 28, 1988; Blanche Rice, July 9, 1996; Sara Chiacchia-Kemp, July 12, 1996. Lackawanna Community House: interviews with Patricia Fadale-Pellegrino, July 8, 1996; Joe Milano, April 9, 1988; Joe Cosentino, July 13, 1994; *Lackawanna Daily Journal,* 5/9/23; newspaper clipping, 7/16/21, in scrapbook of Joe Milano. Friendship House: Women's Missionary Society of the Presbytery of Buffalo, New York, Annual Report, 1907–1909; 1916–1917; 1917–1918, 1918–1919; 1921–1922, p. 14 (quote); 1923 – 1924; 1926–1927; clipping, *Buffalo Express,* June 1907, in *Annual Report,* 1907–08; Lackawanna Friendship House, "The Chatter Box," May 1941, May 1942; Mrs. T. L. Bishop, "Friendship House," memo, October 17, 1945; *Lackawanna Daily Journal,* 10/14/21, 11/16/21; *Lackawanna News,* 6/21/28, 7/17/30, 5/12/32, 2/23/33; *Lackawanna Leader,* 10/23/41; Friendship House, "Attendance Report, 1939–1940", interview with Caz DePasquale, December 8, 1977. The building on Ridge Road vacated by Friendship House in 1921 later became the Ebenezer Baptist Church.

athletic activities, although even there we have to step in occasionally and settle a debate whether the basketball suits should be green as the Irish want it, or red and yellow as the Polish desire.'

While a number of Italian families utilized these settlement centers, overall the Italian community appears to have had limited involvement in them. This may have reflected the immigrants' distrust of charity institutions and *Mericani* (American) institutions in general, and their fear that the agencies would undermine family solidarity. Other factors were Reverend Vifredo's admonishments to avoid Protestant agencies, such as Friendship House, and the fact that the three settlement houses were not located within the Italian neighborhoods but in nearby areas populated mostly by Slavic immigrants and people of color.[23]

The anti-immigrant hysteria peaked with the restrictive immigration laws of 1921 and 1924, which labeled southeast Europeans inferior to WASPs on one hand but also clearly certified them as white and acceptable as citizens once they gave up their ancestral cultures. It would be another 20 years before Italians were free of most forms of prejudice and discrimination, but America's belief that southeast Europeans were white folks, and its virulent racism toward people of color, served to aid Italians. In the late 1920s, most Italians still clustered in four neighborhoods in Lackawanna, both because they needed the familiarity of their native language and customs, and they were still discriminated against by the mainstream society. In their ethnic enclaves, Italians accepted each other as equals and provided companionship and encouragement that helped the immigrants and their children preserve their social honor. They also maintained their self-esteem by refusing to recognize the legitimacy of the mainstream culture. One boy overheard his father and other immigrants lamenting many times that "Italians are not given a chance to get ahead in the steel plant," and "the Italians never get a fair break in America because the Mericani all hate us," and then adding "because we are really superior to them." This type of defensive pride was also displayed at times by the second generation.[24]

The passage of time saw Italian immigrants gaining a better understanding of the rules of American society and their children being indoctrinated with American ways in the public schools. Lackawanna's Italian colony was stabilized as more immigrants, including wives and children, arrived from Italy prior to 1922, when restrictions on immigration took effect, or migrated from other parts of the United States. Among the newly arrived Italian males, the portion who permanently remained in the city climbed from 19 percent between 1916 and 1920 to 38 percent between 1921 and 1930. The economic situation of the Italian colony improved after the recession of 1921-22.

Like other ethnics, Italians stoically labored under harsh conditions in the steel-plant. Even in the union's defeat of 1919, however, they learned that workers could unite into a powerful organization. Advancement into the higher-level social institutions—political, occupational, educational, and housing—was gradually taking place. By 1925, many immigrants and even more of their adult children had moved into skilled positions and foremen slots in the steel plant and on the railroads. During the late 1920s, more Italians moved into new homes in Bethlehem Park, the east side of the city, and nearby Blasdell. The number of Italian homeowners in the Steel City grew from 14 in 1910 to 48 in 1920. As Italians became more involved in politics, two were appointed to city commissions, and several more were elected as committeemen— the city dog-warden position alternated between two of them. Italians ran for the city assessor slots, and Joe Milano finally captured one of these seats. The first Italian political group was founded in 1921. Four years later, the Italian community had enough political clout to get its first police officer and firefighter appointed. Among the organizations created during the 1920s were two sports and one social group that were mostly composed of the American-born generation. Italians continued to celebrate patron-saint days with street festivals. More businesses were created between 1915 and 1929 to serve the expanding Italian community, including 35 groceries, seven saloons, 12 barbershops, and seven shoe-repair shops. The immigrants were becoming more familiar and comfortable with the language and customs of the Americans, and a number of them advanced to higher positions in the occupational, business, and political arenas.[25]

Things were gradually getting better for Lackawanna's Italians between 1922 (when a recession ended) and 1929. More Italians were becoming naturalized citizens and feeling more economically secure. The situation changed, however, when the Great Depression hit in October 1929. The following decade held economic hardship for Italians but also saw a series of significant developments in the Italian American experience.

The Crucial Twelve Years: 1930–1941

The years between 1930 and 1941 represented a dynamic time for Italian Americans. It was a period marked by international and national developments that literally changed the world. These events directly influenced life in America and in its Little Italys. The Great Depression began in the last months of 1929 and grew worse in the following years. It did result in the New Deal and a host of federal programs that had significant impact on white ethnics, including the creation of industrial unions, in which many Italians participated. Under the leadership of Benito Mussolini, Italy had become a world power and gained great stature but the armed conflicts that erupted with the Japanese invasions of Manchuria and then China, the invasion of Ethiopia by Italy, and the Spanish Civil War eventually culminated in history's greatest catastrophe—World War II.

By 1930, the Italian colony in Lackawanna had grown to a significant size, and most Italians had decided to remain in the city permanently. Many of the immigrants had been in America long enough to have a better overview of the dynamics of the mainstream society and their place within it. Two-thirds of the second generation reached adulthood during the decade of the 1930s, and many rose to leadership positions in the Italian groups. The number of activities and organizations in Lackawanna's Italian community mushroomed as people continued to cope with the ethnic group's minority status and the pressures to assimilate.

Forging an Italian American Identity and Community

The formation of the Lackawanna Italian American community and its ethnic identity involved four trends. The first two of them focused on events and conditions in the United States, and the third and fourth concerned events in, and perceptions of, conditions in Italy. Trend No. 1—meeting the immediate social, economic, political, and psychological needs of the Italian community—usually served to support a pan-Italian identity, one based on the common bonds and unity of all Italian Americans. Trend No. 2—constructing activities and organizations that incorporated more of the American lifestyle and customs—also supported a pan-Italian identity based on Italian Americans trying to fit into American society. Trend No. 3—the construction of a pan-Italian identity that focused on Italy and its national culture, history, and current status in the world—was based on the prestige of Mussolini's Italy as a world power and the past glories and culture of the nation. Trend No. 4—retaining a provincial Italian identity by maintaining and celebrating hometown and regional roots in Italy—both undercut the pan-ethnic identities by splintering the Italian colony and supported them by mobilizing people to pursue goals in Lackawanna. These trends began soon after the immigrants arrived in Lackawanna but took more definite form in the years 1930 to 1941. All four of them not only interacted with and influenced one another, but were also shaped by the national and international developments mentioned above.

No. 1 Meeting the immediate needs of the Italian settlement in Lackawanna. The informal chain-migration networks continued to assist new arrivals from other parts of the United States in getting to Lackawanna, finding a job, and arranging for temporary housing. The 23 men who founded the Lake Erie Italian Club in 1910 were from six regions of Italy but were united in their desire to provide sickness and death benefits and other mutual assistance to immigrants. Italian men were either looking for a spouse in the new country or gathering the resources to send for their wives and children in Italy as well as locating adequate housing for a family. This process became more intense after the immigration laws of the 1920s restricted travel between the United States and Italy. Political connections were needed in getting visas, naturalization papers, and other needed documents.

Politically oriented Italians established a good relationship with Congressman James Mead, and in 1930, organized the Lady Mead Club to campaign for him at election time. In turn, Mead's office procured documents in Washington that immigrants needed for naturalization, legal issues in Italy, and family-reunification matters. The fact that Italians represented the third-largest ethnic group in the city helped their political fortunes. Four other new political organizations of the 1930s galvanized specific segments of the Italian voters: male Democrats, female Republicans, female independents, and young male progressives. Immigrants who were committeemen became involved in the citywide Republican and Democratic organizations and learned to mix with members of many ethnic groups as they formed alliances and made deals. This attested to a greater sophistication of Italians in dealing with Lackawanna's hard-nosed ethnic politics and in avoiding some of the divide-and-conquer tactics of the politically dominant Irish and Poles. Italian women and men registered to vote in significant numbers and helped elect co-ethnics to the city assessor seats and, in 1933, to the First Ward councilman post. The council controlled many of the city's patronage jobs and its New Deal job programs. The new councilman, Joe Milano, gave half of the jobs at his disposal to fellow Italians. The Italian community was acting as a political interest group that, like the city's other ethnic groups, looked out for its own people. As was the case in Philadelphia and other cities, politics served to reduce the regional divisions among Italians.[26]

Working together to upgrade their neighborhoods became one avenue for building Italian American unity, and the Federation of Italian American Associations of Lackawanna (FIAAL), founded in 1933, provided the vehicle. The group discussed such lofty goals as a public university and also pressured city officials for basic needs in the Italian neighborhoods, such as regulating automobile traffic, increasing winter recreational activities, and improving bus service. FIAAL leaders lobbied the city council and the board of education to hire Italians as teachers and policemen and got results. In 1940, the group publicly charged First Ward Councilman Julius Karsa with offending the Italian community when he failed to get Tony DeMasi appointed as a police officer. The FIAAL also participated in other events that brought public recognition to Italians.[27]

The Depression made full-time and permanent jobs hard to attain. Italian politicians, as well as foremen in the steel plant and on the railroads, were called upon to find jobs for unemployed workers. Informal barbers, shoemakers, and other artisans made additional income by charging moderate fees for services done in the neighborhood, while other Italians bartered services or helped relatives and *paesani* for no charge. Some newly formed Italian societies provided mutual aid via sickness and death benefits. A host of groups sponsored recreational, social, and athletic events, while others organized picnics and carnivals. Group meetings provided social and psychological support, as did gatherings in the taverns, grocery stores, and pool halls owned by Italians. All these activities and networks helped define and unite the Italian community, adding to the sense of common destiny and the "we" of ethnicity.

No. 2 Constructing activities and organizations that incorporated more of the American lifestyle and customs. This trend represented a step in the assimilation process that attempted to bridge the gap between the Italian and American cultures. Many new groups were composed of an Italian membership, while others combined a majority of Italians with a number of non – Italian members. This effort began in the late 1920s, when the Roland Wildcats and the Galanti Athletic Association (GAA) were organized to provide youth with an opportunity to play American team sports: softball, hardball, football, basketball, and bowling. The membership of each group was mostly Italian but included a significant number of non – Italian youth living in the same neighborhood. Some of these males were young immigrants, but most were of the second generation. Six similar groups for males were founded during the 1930s, and, like the two earlier ones, they participated in citywide leagues. In effect, these groups were parallels to mainstream American groups—they had an Italian membership, but the activity was American. Another parallel group was the Boy Scout troop created at St. Anthony's Church, which, again, put ethnic youth into a mainstream activity. The troop was created by the Holy Name Society, most of whose members were second-generation men who did not follow the Italian pattern of anticlericism and nonparticipation in church.

Established organizations, such as the Lake Erie Italian Club (LEIC) and the Italian American Citizens Club, increasingly sponsored American-style dances, picnics, and outings. Beginning in the late 1930s, the LEIC and GAA organized large carnivals, complete with rides and games of chance, and invited the general public to attend. The many new social, recreational, sports, and religious groups created between 1930 and 1941 offered informal gatherings, dances, banquets, and picnics. Some Italian societies gained prestige by holding dances with live big-band music, others by sponsoring civic activities, such as giving awards to Lackawannans of any ethnicity who had achieved athletic or academic success.[28]

Italians increasingly became involved in mainstream organizations to help meet their basic needs. Individuals desiring to advance in the political, civic, and business spheres joined mainstream groups, such as the city's Democratic Party, the Eagles, the chamber of commerce, and citywide associations of grocers and tavern owners. Especially important to the many Italians working in the steel plant was the movement to create industrial unions. The Steelworkers Organizing Committee, or SWOC, set up an office in Lackawanna in 1936, and its paid staff started recruiting members and volunteer organizers. A number of Italians, mostly second generation, became involved in this effort and were active in the 1941 strike that won union recognition at Bethlehem Steel. This paved the way to better wages, fair treatment, and greater access by white ethnics to supervisory positions as well as leadership roles in the locals of the steelworkers union. By engaging with mainstream institutions to meet basic needs, Italians were reinforcing a wider identity as members of the small-business class or multiethnic working class. In this manner, pragmatic decisions about how to meet basic ends and guarantee a better future for one's family worked to assimilate the first and second generations, whether or not this assimilation was consciously willed by individual Italians.[29]

No. 3 Constructing a pan-Italian identity focused on Italy and its national culture, history, and current status in the world. Developments in Italy influenced the emerging Italian American identity of the residents of Lackawanna. Benito Mussolini led Italy's rise to a world power during the 1920s and 1930s. The resulting prestige on the international stage encouraged the development of *Italianita*, or Italianness, among Italian Americans. Discriminated against by mainstream U.S. society, Italians in America fortified their self-respect by showing pride in Italy and the contributions of its culture. A second-generation man in Boston expressed this as he addressed an Italian group: "Whatever you fellows may think of Mussolini, you've got to admit one thing: He has done more to get respect for the Italian people than anyone else. The Italians get a lot more respect now than when I started going to school. And you can thank Mussolini for that." Between 1922 and 1935, many American newspapers and magazines gave glowing reports on Mussolini's policies. In 1933, the *Lackawanna Republic* credited Fascist educational reforms with increasing Italy's literacy rate and encouraging youth "to develop a culture that truly represents the manifold powers of the Italian race."[30]

So, ironically, it was only after immigrating to the United States that Laziali, Abruzzesi, Napolitani, Calabresi, and Marchegiani finally began seeing themselves as Italians—something they had scarcely thought about in Italy. The immigrants and their children had come to realize that American institutions, as well as individual citizens, often viewed them collectively as Italians, and usually negatively. The Lackawanna English-language press usually used the term "Italian" to refer to the ethnic group. But the press in Buffalo and other cities sometimes spoke harshly of southern Italians, who comprised the majority of migrants from Italy. The north/south distinction was encoded in U.S. immigration laws between 1899 and 1924, thus giving official sanction to this view. Many southern Italians were dark complected—an important factor in race-obsessed America. In addition, popular literature since the 1890s and movies since the 1920s have focused on Italian gangsters, often referring to criminal organizations in southern Italy: the Mafia in Sicilia, the *Camorra* in Naples, and the *'Ndranghita* (Honored Society) in Calabria.[31]

In the mid-1930s, the American press began taking a more negative view of Italy's Fascist government. During the Ethiopian war of 1935-36, the press condemned Italy for its invasion of that country. Many Italian Americans, however, proclaimed their support for Italy by organizing Italian Red Cross committees throughout the United States to raise funds for medical supplies for the Italian Army. Lackawanna's Italian Red Cross Committee collected money from more than 300 Italian countrymen, including Reverend Vifredo of St. Anthony's Church and a number of the city's Italian organizations. Dr. John Fadale of Lackawanna sat on the committee of the Federation of Italian Societies of Buffalo that coordinated the drive throughout western New York, and *Corriere Italiano* printed long lists of donors in the Buffalo area, including those from the Steel City. Some Lackawanna Italians who had visited Italy after Mussolini came to power saw the real and ugly face of Fascism and became very anti-Fascist, but there is no record of Italian groups clashing on this matter as there was in Buffalo (see Figure 3.5).[32]

Despite the bad press, many Italian immigrants and their children throughout America continued to honor the cultural accomplishments of Italy in the late 1930s. Some extolled Italian heroes such as Giuseppe Garibaldi, and Lackawanna's Circolo D'Annunzio Dopolavoro was named after Gabrielle D'Annunzio, a nationalist hero from Abruzzo. Cristoforo Colombo represented a sure thing for an Italian American hero. Proclaimed by many European Americans as the "discoverer" of the western hemisphere, Columbus was one of the few Italians honored in American history books and mythology. This was a source of pride to Italian immigrants, who were staging elaborate celebrations of the mariner's exploits by the 1890s. Irish Americans also celebrated him because he was Catholic, and the Spanish Americans because he sailed for Spain. Italian, Irish, and Spanish Americans worked together to get Columbus Day declared a legal holiday in 43 states and, eventually, at the national level. The Italian American Citizens Club of Lackawanna began holding annual Columbus Day banquets in the 1920s, and the Lake Erie Italian Club has sponsored periodic Columbus Day banquets since the 1930s. The FIAAL sent representatives to meetings of the Federation of Italian Societies of Buffalo and to the large Columbus Day parades and other activities sponsored by that group. Perhaps the crowning moment for the FIAAL was the placement of a bust of Christopher Columbus at the entrance to Bethlehem Park in 1940. Carried out with much pomp and circumstance, with representatives from the local Knights of Columbus council present, the dedication of the bust served to announce to all those who entered the neighborhood that it was the largest Italian American enclave in the city.[33]

Lackawanna Italians also proclaimed their cultural pride via religious feasts and processions. They must have rejoiced when the procession of the Mount Carmel Society in 1931 was dubbed the "biggest parade of any church organization in the history of Lackawanna" by a city newspaper. Events highlighting the city's ethnic mix became common, and the combined July 4th and George Washington Bicentennial observation in 1932 featured a parade of 8,000 Lackawannans representing various ethnic groups. Rocco Campoli, Frank Marinelli, and John Grasso enacted the Spirit of 1776 as they led the Italian troupe to win first prize for "best Colonial group." The Old World Pageant in August 1934 drew 10,000 people to Lackawanna Stadium, where more than 15 ethnic groups had displays, including an Italian village scene. The following year at the All Nations Harvest Pageant, performances by Italian dancers and musicians, dressed in native costume, "received great applause," according to the *Buffalo Evening News*.[34]

Despite these well-received displays of ethnicity, Italians were still a minority group. While the period of the most violent and blatant prejudice and discrimination had passed, Italians continued to be viewed as "inferior," and daily life in Lackawanna was often marred by ethnic slurs and negative acts by employers, policemen, and welfare officials. In the steel plant, a foreman told Louie Petrucci that "it will be a cold day in hell before a dago becomes a foreman." When Antonio DiMillo accompanied one of his daughters to downtown Buffalo as she looked for a job, they saw a sign in a department store window that read: "Help Wanted, No Italians." Prejudice and the tough environment in the Steel City caused many male immigrants from Giuliano di Roma to permanently return to Italy rather than bring their families to Lackawanna. Other immigrants, such as Felice Morga, had the same concerns and delayed bringing their families to the United States. Morga had traveled back and forth for many years between Settefrati, Lazio, towns in Pennsylvania, then Lackawanna. He sent for his oldest son in 1938 but didn't bring his other son, wife, and mother until 1947. When the younger son, Vince, asked why Felice waited so long to bring the whole family to America, he replied that he wanted to spare his loved ones the terrible discrimination that Italians encountered prior to World War II.[35]

Some commentators continued to be impatient about the rate of assimilation of Lackawanna's Italians and Slavs. In 1934, Reverend John Botty of the Magyar Presbyterian Church, stated, "There is no real community spirit. Many of the inhabitants still live in the Old World and are suspicious of each other …. There is a tendency for the development of crime and vice, due to such things as the broken home life of people who have come to this country without their families, the presence of saloons, gambling houses, houses of ill fame, etc." Botty also noted that the progress that had been made and the mixture of fears and hopes he expressed seemed an appropriate metaphor for the 1930s. The continued prejudice and discrimination created an impetus for Italians to maintain a strong ethnic identity. Another factor that reinforced the sense of being an Italian American was the immigrant's need to adjust from Italy's small-town agrarian environment to Lackawanna's hectic urban and industrial lifestyle.[36]

No. 4 Retaining provincial Italian identities by maintaining and celebrating hometown and regional roots in Italy. Practicing *Italianita*, or cultivating a pan-Italian identity, is the opposite of focusing on hometown and provincial ties. Yet an ironic aspect of the development of *Italianita* in the 1930s was that it reinforced the conflicting notion of hometown and regional identities in some Italian Americans. At the time of the mass emigration from its shores, Italy had been a nation for a scant several decades. Immigrants, mostly from rural Italian areas, saw themselves as residents of their towns or provinces, and tended to identify with their regions, such as Campania or Abruzzo. Differences in customs and dialects were noticeable by traveling only 15 or 20 miles in southern Italy. Many people had rarely left their provinces before emigrating overseas, and Italian immigrants in the United States often settled near others from their town, province, or region.

In some older Italian settlements, such as Buffalo and Milwaukee, many of the Italian organizations founded during the years 1880 to 1919 were based on hometown and provincial ties. Then, in the 1920s, the trend was toward pan-Italian organizations that honored Italian culture and history, as well as Mussolini's achievements. While this trend continued into the following decade, the 1930s also saw a renewed interest in forming

FIGURE 3.5

ITALIAN AMERICAN GROUPS REACT TO FASCIST ITALY

Italian organizations throughout the United States struggled with how closely to embrace the Mussolini government. When leaders of the Order Sons of Italy in America (OSIA), a nationwide group with hundreds of lodges, signed an accord with Italy's Fascist government, many lodges and leaders were opposed and simply left the order. The seeds of this schism were apparent at the convention of OSIA's New York State Grand Lodge held in Buffalo in 1923. When Italy invaded Ethiopia in 1935, attorney Francis DiBartolo of the East Buffalo Federation of Italian Societies publicly criticized the war as an "unjust, inhuman, and useless sacrifice of innocent victims on all sides." The leaders of the East Buffalo federation supported DiBartolo, which led the Buffalo Federation of Italian Societies to denounce them and applaud the invasion of Ethiopia. Two organizations then withdrew, in protest, from DiBartolo's group. Both federations included lodges of OSIA, the national leaders of which lent Mussolini their "moral support" while at the same time supporting President Roosevelt's declaration of neutrality. With the Italian conquest of Ethiopia completed in May 1936, many Italian Americans celebrated. More than 1,000 Italians gathered in Buffalo, where Dr. August Lascola told them, "The conquest of Ethiopia brings to us, the children of Italian immigrants, the added respect that is the inevitable result of victory." The audience, "with arms extended in the Fascist salute sang 'Giovanezza,' the Fascist hymn." Outside, 30 anti-Facist demonstrators picketed. Lackawanna's John Fadale attended the meeting, but when told he must join the others in giving the Fascist salute, he refused and walked out of the hall.

In 1940, the outspoken DiBartolo condemned Italian and German Fascism and Italy's entry into World War II, accusing pro-Mussolini Italians in Buffalo of distributing Italian-language textbooks that extolled Fascist principles. There is no record of similar divisions in Lackawanna during these years, but in 1938, the newly formed Circolo D'Annunzio Dopolavoro (D'Annunzio Afterwork Club), which had ties with similar groups in Italy, declared itself more representative of *Italianita*—Italianness—than of the Federation of Italian American Associations of Lackawanna, but this potential conflict apparently never developed.

Sources: *Buffalo Evening News*, 10/ 3 & 15/35, 5/20/36, 6/11/40; *Courier Express*, 10/2/35, 11/19/40; *Lackawanna Leader*, 10/13/38; interview with John Fadale, November 23, 1979.

regional and hometown societies. The Italian community in Lackawanna was a newer settlement, initiated in 1900, and all but one of the groups organized prior to 1930 did not stipulate or maintain a regional identity. The founding of the Marchegiani men's group in 1928 set the precedent for this type of organization in Lackawanna. Five other regional societies came into being during the 1930s, one each for Laziali and Calabresi, and three additional Marchegiani groups, as well as a society composed solely of men with roots in Pettorano sul Gizio, Abruzzo. So, like Buffalo and Milwaukee, the Steel City had a series of hometown societies founded in the 1930s as well as many pan-Italian groups. The continued arrival of immigrants from both Italy and other parts of the United States throughout the 1920s and 1930s added to the numbers of people who identified with specific Italian towns and regions. These groups offered immigrants a place to speak their local dialect, practice regional customs, and encounter familiar faces from the "old county." The fact that all but one of the societies focused on the large regional areas, and none on the geographically smaller province identities, may indicate a compromise between the larger pan-Italian identity and the more local provincial and town base loyalties.[37]

These four trends in ethnic identity formation were interconnected. Several of the groups formed in the 1930s had a political purpose, sometimes a stated goal and other times an unstated motive. Politicians sponsored some groups that fielded American-style sports teams, and at election time, these became booster groups that helped get adults in each family out to vote. One reason for forming groups based on regional origins, especially for numerically smaller groups such as the Calabresi or Marchegiani, was to form a block of voters that could lobby both Italian and non – Italian politicians for patronage jobs and other favors. Any organization could provide a launching platform if its president had ambitions to run for political office. The FIAAL focused on bread-and-butter civic issues but also appealed to a pan-Italian ethnic identity by erecting a bust of Columbus in Bethlehem Park. The groups and activities that focused on pan-Italian and provincial identities were usually composed of immigrants and some of the older individuals of the second-generation. Those focusing on Italian American identity and more Americanized activities tended to have second generation memberships with some immigrants, many of whom migrated as children. The second-generation adults, whose numbers had grown by the late 1930s, had little or no direct experience with their parents' provincial ties or pan-Italian identity based on the glories of Italy; they usually emphasized the "American" in Italian American.[38]

The 40 new organizations founded by Lackawanna Italians between 1930 and 1941 provide an indicator as to which of the four trends was emphasized. Of the 19 groups organized from

October 1940. The Federation of Italian American Associations of Lackawanna installs a bust of Christopher Columbus at the Madison Avenue entrance to Bethlehem Park. Photo source: Collection of Tony Grasso

1930 to 1936, seven had second-generation memberships, and six each had immigrant and mixed first- and second-generation memberships. For the 21 organizations created from 1937 to 1941, however, 13 had second-generation memberships, three had combined first- and second-generation rosters, and five were composed of immigrants. The surge of new groups in this 12 year period reached it's crest in 1938-40, when 15 organizations were founded. What the four trends represented was a number of segments of the Italian community, each trying out specific interests, activities, and goals to recalibrate their identities. These ventures often went well beyond the customs of southern Italian towns, such as the formation of two coed societies—the Gamma Kappa Club, a social group, and the Bethlehem Park GOP Club. The maturation of the second-generation, which hungered to fit into American society, combined with mainstream America's increasingly negative view of Mussolini and Italy after 1935, led many Italians in Lackawanna to downplay the trends of pan-ethnic *Italianita* and regional identities. Rather, they focused on the tasks of dealing with daily needs in Lackawanna and assimilating more into American mainstream culture. And there was increasing evidence that assimilation had its payoffs, as more Italians gained national recognition and celebrity status, such as mayors Fiorello LaGuardia of New York and Angelo Rossi of San Francisco, and Joe DiMaggio of the New York Yankees, who was named Most Valuable Player in the American League in 1939. Starting in 1936, the second generation became active in the drive to unionize Lackawanna's steelworkers, which ended in victory in 1941. Many members of this generation wanted to limit conspicuous displays of "foreign" customs, which was one factor in the termination of the *feste* and street processions. The intervention of Italy and Germany in the Spanish Civil War (1936–1939), the outbreak of World War II, Italy's entry as an Axis partner in 1940, and America's entry in 1941 finally quashed the movement toward pan-ethnic Italianita and regional identities in Lackawanna's Italian community. What became strengthened was the pan-ethnic identity that presented Italian Americans as a united ethnic group dedicated to proving themselves loyal citizens of the United States.[39]

Leaders

The leadership class that had developed by the late 1920s included mostly immigrants and a few members of the second generation. Leaders emerged from different sectors of the community at various times, and many were among those who settled in Lackawanna between 1900 and 1915. Umberto Giannotti and Salvatore DiTommaso were officers in societies in part because they were literate. Merchants had frequent contact with other Italians, especially if their shops were gathering spots and had one of the few telephones in the neighborhood. Some of the first Italians to move into the area were experienced merchants who set up businesses, such as Luca Tarquinio, Tony Mauriello, Angelo Sperduto, and Calogero Fadale in the First Ward, and Angelo Morinello on Roland Avenue. They urged others to move to Lackawanna, bought and sold property, made informal loans, and extended credit to other Italians. Being acquainted with many people through their tavern businesses helped get Tony Amorosi and Tony Turchiarelli elected as committeemen and enabled them to mediate between the Italian and mainstream communities. Ferdinand Catuzza, Joe Cosentino, and V. Jimmy D'Alessandro were viewed as leaders by Laziali, Calabresi, and Abruzzesi, respectively, which facilitated their involvement in politics, as did their ability to speak English. Businessmen Fadale and Serafino Mattucci were trustees at St. Anthony's Church, and Mattucci had connections with Italian business leaders in Buffalo. Foremen Benigno and Pietro Oddi, Antonio Grossi, Umberto Barbati and Pietro Fiore held economic power in that they had the ability to hire steelworkers or railroad trackmen.

Teacher Mary Yoviene, who emigrated from Italy as an infant, and American-born Dr. John Fadale earned leadership credentials by obtaining college degrees. Joe Milano, Angelo Grosso, Tony Falcone, and Tony DePasquale were second-generation men who began successful political careers in the late 1920s that culminated in the 1930s and 1940s. During the 1930s, C. John Tarquinio became president of the Italian American Citizens Club, and Nick Thomas leader of the Federation of Italian American Associations of Lackawanna (FIAAL), both powerful groups with heavily immigrant memberships. Nick Milano, a teacher, and Joseph and Edmund Pacillo were among the American-born men who formed the backbone of the Holy Name Society at St. Anthony's. The number and variety of second-generation societies founded in the 1930s allowed men to develop leadership skills and eventually become officers of the Lake Erie Italian Club, the FIAAL, and the Roland Italian American Lodge, or to seek political office or leadership of mainstream groups. A crop of new businesspeople emerged who could more easily relate to the wider community and attract customers. Nick Sperduto opened the first pizzeria in Lackawanna, and Frank Morinello, who arrived from Italy at age three, won recognition by establishing successful businesses outside the Italian enclaves.[40]

First-generation women had a handful of church and secular organizations in which they could act as leaders. Enrichetta Oddi, Alessandrina Sperduti, Carmela Suffoletto, Maria Ricci, and Pasqualina Amorosi were leaders of the Mount Carmel Society. During the years between the world wars, the only Italian female to hold political office was another immigrant, Adele Panzetta. Both she and her husband John were committee persons, and she eventually became a powerful figure in First Ward Republican circles. Adele Panzetta helped found the Italian Republican Women's Club of the First Ward in 1930. Carmela Canestrari, who arrived in America as a young child, headed both the Lady Mead Club and the Marchegiani Ladies Social Club. There was not a women's society included in the FIAAL, but second-generation females gained stature in the Italian community by creating 12 women's and two coed groups between 1930 and 1941, and, as in the case of Jennie Nigro, by starting their own businesses. The resulting leadership experience allowed American-born females to become officers in some of the older religious societies, to organize the expanded social activities undertaken by church groups after World War II, and to lead the five women's auxiliaries founded between 1943 and 1958.[41]

Figure 3.6

THE 1.5 GENERATION

Much of this study focuses on the immigrants, known as the first generation, and their America-born children, called the second generation. There is, however, an important distinction between individuals who immigrate as adults and those who come as children. The adult immigrant is in a very different stage of development than one who is, say, eight years old. Youngsters who are mostly raised in the United States have a greater potential to learn and adapt to complex cultural behaviors, such as language. One study found that children who arrive before age six are more likely to speak English without an accent than those who come after puberty. Children who immigrate prior to age 10 are more capable of learning the language and other cultural components of the new society, therefore have a lot in common with the second generation. In this study, persons 10 through 17 years of age are viewed as the younger segment of the first generation, and those migrating at ages one through nine are designated the 1.5 generation.

In 1930, Lackawanna's Italian population included 646 first-generation individuals (immigrants who arrived by age 10 or older), 101 of the 1.5 generation, 1,016 second-generation, and 76 third-generation. Interviews revealed that many individuals of the 1.5 generation did not have accents, while immigrants who arrived as teens usually had at least a trace of an accent. People of the 1.5 generation usually learned English quickly, if not painlessly, in the city's streets and schools. Some even acquired partial fluency in the languages of their Slavic and Hungarian neighbors. Many individuals in the younger segment of the first generation and the 1.5 generation displayed skill in adapting to life in America. Among the latter group were organization leader Carmella Canestrari; merchants Frank Morinello, Joe Amadori, Armondo Pietrocarlo, and Tony Grasso; skilled workers and foremen such as Louis Olivieri, Tony Palumbo, Charles Sambuchi, and S. John Ceccarelli; church leader Gerald Pacillo; civic leader James Petti; and Louis Morasco, the first Italian engineer on the South Buffalo Railway. Over 200 male immigrants arrived in this country between the ages of 10 and 17, including railroad foremen Phillip Verel and Albert Federici; merchants John Verel and Peter Mazuca; Air Force pilot Arcangelo Carlini; and organization leaders Dan Chiacchia and Natale Chiodo.

Sources: Ruben G. Rumbaut, "Assimilation and Its Discontents: Between Rhetoric and Reality," *International Migration Review,* 1997, Vol. 31, pp. 937, 945, 951; Richard Alba, "Rethinking Assimilation Theory for a New Era of Immigration," *International Migration Review,* 1997, Vol. 31, pp. 830, 849; Joel Perlmann, *Italians Then, Mexicans Now: Immigrant Origins and Second-Generation Progress, 1890-2000,* 2005, p. 67; U.S. Census, 1930.

The Second Generation

The period from 1930 to 1941 saw significant changes, especially for the American-born generation. It was this second generation, the majority of whom entered their teens or early adult years during this period, that accelerated the overall assimilation of Lackawanna's Italians. Newly formed social, recreational, and athletic organizations stressed American-style activities for their members. There were now many women's groups and a few coed societies, and non – Italian neighbors and friends were often invited to join. St. Anthony's parish never established a school, so most Italian youth attended public schools, with a few attending multiethnic parochial schools. It was in the city schools where much of the Americanization of the second-generation took place.

Schools and Education

In Lackawanna's public schools, second -generation Italians learned or perfected their English and the everyday behaviors of American culture. Italian children were concentrated at four public elementary schools in the first half of the twentieth century. Roland Avenue youth went to Washington School, children living on lower Ingham Avenue went to Roosevelt Elementary School, and those residing in the Old Village attended first and second grade in the Old Village Annex School, then went on to Roosevelt. When Lincoln Elementary School was completed in 1925, it accommodated all students from the Old Village and Bethlehem Park until 1929, when an elementary school opened in Bethlehem Park. Other than the Old Village Annex, all schools went up to eighth grade. Just one school, Lackawanna High School, served the older students, but by 1932, it became overcrowded. Lincoln, whose student population had dropped with the demolition of the Old Village, was made into a combination elementary and auxiliary high school. One hundred and fifty First Ward students attended ninth through 11th grade there, then completed their senior year at the high school. When John Fadale graduated from Roosevelt in 1909, he was one of the few Italian students there. This changed by the early 1920s, as more Italian families took up residence on Ingham Avenue. Anne Melillo who attended Roosevelt from 1924 to 1932, noted that many of the students were Italian, including her four siblings. After graduating from the elementary school, Melillo spent three years at the Lincoln Annex, then graduated from Lackawanna High School in 1936.[42]

The eighth-grade graduating classes at three elementary schools in Italian neighborhoods increased in size between 1930 and 1937, as did the number of Italian children (see Figure 3.7). Staff rosters for Bethlehem Park, Roosevelt, Wilson, Franklin, and Washington schools during the period 1934 to 1937 reveal that at least 44 of the 102 teachers had Irish surnames, and most of the rest had roots in other northwest European countries. Of the city's 165 teachers in 1931, 104 resided in Lackawanna, but only seven of them in the First Ward, where most immigrant families lived. Italians interviewed said that the Lackawanna public schools of 60 to 80 years ago had many talented and respectful Irish teachers, and a few who were bigoted. Principals such as Dennis Kane and Edward Gunn were firm disciplinarians, but Italian kids at Lincoln and Bethlehem Park schools did not detect any ethnic favoritism or discrimination. Anne Melillo stated that the Irish teachers at Roosevelt "treated the kids well."[43]

Some teachers, however, did show signs of prejudiced attitudes. One Irish teacher arranged photos of her students in an album by their ethnicity. Occasionally, she asked "my Irish students" to stand up but never invited those of the other ethnic groups to do so. The same teacher had the expectation that Irish students should be model students who excelled beyond the accomplishments of their Italian and Slavic peers, and berated Irish students who did not outdo the others in grooming and grades. Observing this, one Italian girl got the message that Italians and other ethnics "were not quite as good" as the Irish, but she also had sympathy for an Irish girl whom the teacher continually belittled for lack of grooming, a common situation among students during the Depression.[44]

Children born in Italy and second-generation youth living in homes where only Italian was spoken faced a great challenge in school. Learning the English language in itself presented a formidable challenge, but the education practices in force during this period caused many painful moments. In 1921, school superintendent William Breen launched a campaign for grade-school students to speak only English at school, and students who did so wore "I Speak English" badges to reinforce the point. If the students did nothing, or said or did something not in keeping with the teacher's instructions, they were taunted or laughed at by the other students, including some of the Italian children. The humiliation was even greater when the teacher laughed or made insensitive comments.[45]

It was fortunate indeed when another Italian American student who was bilingual could act as an interpreter. When Marie Ceccarelli emigrated from Lazio in 1929 at age six, she had never attended school. Unable to speak any English, she started in kindergarten at Bethlehem Park School and was fortunate to have two neighbors in her class. Anna DePasquale

and Laura Battisti spoke to her in Italian and used hand signals to help Marie grasp what was going on in class. Tom Ventre, who immigrated at age nine, was not as fortunate. "It was hard to learn the language," he said. "The Italian kids knew only a few words in Italian to help out. My father only knew some broken English." One girl, who grew up speaking Italian at home, was put in the back of the classroom and mostly ignored. As Lena Bellagamba struggled to learn English, she discovered that the Italian language had no equivalent of the "th" sound. So she practiced by placing a piece of paper in her mouth; if the paper moved, she knew she was pronouncing the "th" correctly.[46]

Learning basic expressions in English was only the first of many trying tasks in mastering the new language. Florindo "Gene" Covelli, who was seven when his family left Italy, learned some English at Lincoln School, but he could not think in the new language. In his mind, he constantly "translated" ideas and words into Italian, processed them, and then re-translated the new thoughts back into English. It was not until fifth grade that he could successfully read, comprehend, and think in English. As John Novelli learned the new language, he found "it was unclear as to whether I was thinking in Italian or English." When he and other children worked at speaking English, they ran into humiliating situations. Novelli felt this when he was asked to play the role of an Italian immigrant for a St. Patrick's Day stage show. "People laughed at my broken English. It was a horrible feeling." To escape the taunting and

FIGURE 3.7

Graduates of Schools in Italian Neighborhoods: 1930s

Elementary School	Year	Total Graduates	Italian Graduates
Roosevelt (Ingham Avenue)	1930	75	9
	1935	87	16
	1936	80	17
	1937	84	14
Bethlehem Park	1930	25	6
	1935	43	20
	1936	45	20
	1937	44	18
Washington (Roland Avenue)	1930	44	3
	1935	78	4
	1936	69	6
	1937	64	7

Sources: *Lackawanna News*, 6/26/30; *Lackawanna Herald*, 6/20/35; 6/25/36; *Lackawanna Leader*, 6/3/37.

Roosevelt Elementary School, on Odell street, just off Ingham Avenue, was built in 1904. Photo source: Collection of Tony Grasso

humiliation of such incidents, some Italian children worked with a passionate intensity to learn the English language, while others dropped out of school.[47]

Language ability was not the only reason that a child could be stigmatized with the label "foreigner" or "greenhorn." Just before Tom and Tony Ventre departed from Naples in 1929, they had their heads shaved, a standard practice to prevent lice. When the boys and their mother arrived in Lackawanna, she immediately enrolled them at Bethlehem Park School. Tom recalled that on "the first day of school in Lackawanna, our heads were still shaved. The kids laughed and called us 'cumbas' [dialect for *compare*, a title of respect used in regard to the godparent relationship]—the Italians and other kids. And this was not said as a compliment. The kids also called us wop and dago." Lena Bellagamba was also called dago, and some teachers and students teased her about her dark complexion, inability to speak English, and clothing that bespoke her family's poverty.[48]

For older children, like John Novelli, part of the problem of adjusting to school was the practice of placing recent arrivals from foreign countries in first or second grade, apparently with the idea that the basic English spoken by younger children would make it easier for the teens to learn the language. But this was a humiliating set-up for many teens, and even if they were rapidly promoted, as was the case with Novelli, some quickly left school. Their departure also involved family pressure on males to help provide income and the teenagers' desire to have a little spending money. When 16-year-old Romolo Petricca arrived from Italy in 1920, he was enrolled in the first grade at Roosevelt School and had his desk right next to the teacher's. He did well in math and within several months was promoted to seventh grade, but after winter passed and spring jobs became available, he left school to work on a road construction crew and never returned again. Giuseppe Cosentino, another teenage immigrant, attended Roosevelt for one year. "Joe," as he soon was called, knew only the few words of English that his father had taught him. However, he

learned quickly, studying his textbooks late into the night. His teachers liked him, and one told Cosentino he had "a beautiful smile." His stay at Roosevelt was made more comfortable by the presence of Petricca and 14 other immigrant Italian teens. But Cosentino also quit school and went to work.[49]

For Caroline DePaula, the English language and strict discipline at school were not her biggest challenges. DePaula and her four older siblings were all American born, but at home spoke only Italian to each other and their immigrant parents. She first spoke English when she attended Roosevelt, quickly learning the language and how to endure teachers' use of a rubber hose or ruler to exact discipline. Her problem at school involved social stigma. The DePaula children worked in their parents' bakery—Caroline started at age five—and also tended to the livestock in the barn behind the house. At times, the children hurriedly left home and arrived at school with the remnants of bread dough or yeast on their clothing or manure on their shoes, which brought humiliating remarks from teachers and other students. Still, Caroline liked school because it was relaxing compared to the constant chores at home. Her three eldest siblings quit school by sixth grade to work full-time in the bakery, but she and her brother Anthony had the luxury of graduating from eighth grade.[50]

One other factor made the school experience difficult for Italian children and other students. There was an apparent lack of concern by the authorities for the welfare of children in the First Ward. During the period from 1916 to 1919, when the DePaula children were at Roosevelt, the *Lackawanna Daily Journal* reported the school to be in an "unkempt" and "loathsome" condition, with floors unswept and slippery with oil spills, odors from the lavatories, backed-up sewers, and a basement that was unfit for children. The newspaper's editor claimed that schools east of the railroad tracks were clean and well kept, and blamed the school board for ignoring the conditions in which the "foreign children" at Roosevelt received their schooling.[51]

Lincoln School on Dona Street, Built in 1925, it served the Old Village and Bethlehem Park, then was made into a 9th – 11th grade "feeder" school to Lackawanna High School. Photo source: Collection of Tony Grasso

Washington Elementary School was just off Roland Avenue, a few blocks east of the Italian section. Mary Yoviene-Clark, the city's first Italian American teacher, began her career at this school in 1918. Photo source: Romaine Lillis

Despite all these difficulties, the schools taught the children of diverse immigrant groups the language and customs of American society. They also Americanized children in other ways. The playground, gym classes, and athletic teams focused on baseball, basketball, and football, while soccer—an Italian pastime—was a sometimes event, and bocce was not to be found. But the most powerful lesson that Italian and other minority group children learned during this period came in a more subtle manner. Throughout the United States, school curricula taught students that "foreign" cultures were undesirable. Textbooks often presented a false sense of reality to lower-class children. Oscar Handlin explains the effect of a popular textbook, *Good Morning, Mr. Robin*, that describes Jack's idyllic home:

> Blue-eyed and blond, Jack himself stares over the nice white collar and the neatly buttoned jacket. Across the green lawn, from the porch of the pretty yellow house, a miraculously slim mother waves. By the side of the road that dips through the fields of corn, the animals wait, each in turn to extend its greeting. There it all is, real as life. Except that it is all a lie.

> There is no Jack, no house, no brightly smiling 'Mummy.' In the whole room there is not a boy with such a name, with such an appearance. One can walk streets without end and there will be never a glimpse of the yellow clapboards, of the close-cropped grass. Who sleeps like Jack alone in the prim room by the window to be wakened by singing birds? Good Morning, Mr. Robin. The whole book is false because nothing in it touches upon the experience of its readers and no element in their experience creeps into its pages.

Most textbooks subtly taught students that cultures different from that of WASP America were inferior, and that immigrants and their children must learn to speak English, forget their foreign ways, and act like Americans. The books were all in

Bethlehem Park Elementary School was a major institution in the new housing tract built in the mid 1920's. Erected in 1929, the school offered night-school classes for adults, cultural events, and even a branch of the Lackawanna Library. Photo source: Romaine Lillis

The original Lackawanna High School was in Ridge Pond, east of the maze of railroad tracks. The number of Italians completing high school grew slowly prior to 1940, then grew rapidly thereafter. Photo source: Romaine Lillis

English, of course, and said little or nothing about the contemporary cultures of Italy, Spain, or Hungary. If Italy was mentioned, it was usually in terms of the Roman Empire or some long-dead artist. The model citizens in the textbooks rarely had swarthy skin color, brown eyes, or dark hair. And

A classroom at Roosevelt Elementary School on Odell Street, just off Ingham Avenue.
Photo source: Collection of Tony Grasso

In 1930, the girls' basketball team at Lincoln School won the city championship.
Top row, from left: Gladys Farnham, Elizabeth Petti. Middle row: [Unk],
Genevieve Bulka, Miss Sporney (coach), Connie Marinelli, [Unk], Josephine
D'Alessandro. Bottom row: Bridget Ginnetti, Felicia Renzi.
Photo source: Collection of Bridget Ginnetti-Bracci

there were few teachers of southeast European origin to act as role models. Teenager Phil Andreozzi got the message "that if your family wasn't in America for five or six generations, you were not quite good enough."[52]

That fact that there was only one Italian elementary school teacher prior to 1939 spoke loudly to the city's school children, implying that Italians and other "foreigners" were inferior. The

sole elementary teacher was Mary Yoviene-Clark, who became Lackawanna's first Italian American teacher in 1918, and spent her whole career at Washington Elementary School. Fluent in Italian, she translated for many immigrant children, and for their parents when they visited the school. Yoviene-Clark was a source of pride and hope for Italian kids on Roland Avenue, who many decades later boasted: "We had an Italian teacher at Washington." It took 16 years, however, before more Italian teachers joined Mary Yoviene-Clark in the city's schools.[53]

Nick Milano attended college in Buffalo, began substitute teaching at Lackawanna High School, and was appointed to a permanent teaching post in 1934. Two other sons of immigrants, John Yoviene (brother of Mary) and Samuel Conte, joined the high school's teaching staff in the following five years. Theresa Morgan became a teacher at Roosevelt in 1939 and was the first Italian American to teach in the First Ward. Thus, by the late 1930s, Italian American students had three members of their ethnic group as teachers at Lackawanna High School, one at Washington, and another at Roosevelt. During the mid 1940s, Margaret Lombardi and Concetta Russo were hired as teachers at the high school and Rita Montanari was hired at Wilson School in the First Ward. Bethlehem Park Elementary School did not have an Italian American teacher until 1954, but that did not stop Italian students from doing well there; in 1935, half the graduating class had Italian surnames, including John Christiano, the valedictorian.[54]

As Italians were elected to city offices and the school board during the 1930s and 1940s, they were able to get members of their ethnic group teachers' positions and other jobs in the schools. Mary Guadagno, daughter of bakery proprietor Antonio Guadagno, was clerk at Roosevelt by 1934, and Rose Grosso, sister of First Ward politician Angelo Grosso, was secretary to the high school principal in 1931. Soon after Tony Moretti's

Wilson School, 1950s. Principal Aldo Filipetti stands at the left rear. The school's student body was a mix of many different ethnic groups. Photo source: Aldo Filipetti

election to the school board in the 1940s, his sister Carmella became a secretary there. Eventually, as Italians gained more political clout, many Italian widows, such as Augusta Anticoli, were hired as charwomen at the schools.[55]

While most Italian children went to public schools, a few attended Catholic schools. In 1940, youngsters attending school represented one-quarter of Lackawanna's population—3,995 in the public schools and 1,842 in parochial schools. St. Charles, the only multiethnic parish and school available to Italians in the First Ward, was replaced in 1923 by the OLV Mission church and school, and later became Queen of All Saints parish. It was staffed by priests and nuns from Our Lady of Victory parish. Nunze Oddy, born in 1903, attended St. Charles School and noted that most of the students were Irish. He recalled that "the nuns were very strict. I lasted there three years, then went to School No. 3 (Roosevelt)." Frank Amorosi attended the OLV Mission School, completing the eighth grade there. Nine-year-old Iole Schiavi left Roosevelt School in 1931 and enrolled in the OLV Mission School, where most of her classmates were Hungarian. Schiavi did well in school, got along with the teachers, and, after completing eighth grade, went on to graduate from Lincoln Annex and Lackawanna High School. For Gene Covelli, who failed seventh grade at Bethlehem Park

School, the mission school represented his last attempt at completing grade school. It was possible for his family to enroll him there only because there was no tuition charge. Sister Latenchia had a profound effect on him, guiding him to graduate from the eighth grade. In 1932, nine Italians received diplomas at the OLV Mission School, including valedictorian Anna Monaco. Eight Italians graduated in 1935.[56]

When Donato and Lucia Chiacchia moved from the Old Village to Dorrance and South Park Avenues in 1922, they sent their children to church and school at Our Lady of Victory parish. The third of eight children, Sara, was very outgoing, enjoyed school, and "taught the nuns to Charleston." Chiacchia made her First Holy Communion at OLV Church, and "by fifth grade I wanted to be a nun. Mom said 'No, you aren't saintly enough and quiet.' She said I'd ruin the nuns!" Chiacchia completed eighth grade and went on to the OLV Academy but left during her sophomore year. Marie Mauriello was the lone Italian in the academy's graduating class of 1930. The eight children of Joe and Sue Fox attended the OLV schools, where Joe Jr., the second oldest, had some problems with the Irish and Polish students, but it was the teachers that stand out most in his memories. He recalls that "the nuns were strict. One hit me with a ruler, so I broke it over my knee." Despite this encounter, Fox went on to

Figure 3.8
Italian Graduates of
Lackawanna High School, 1930-46

Year	Total Graduates	Italian Graduates		
		Total	Males	Females
1930	52	3	2	1
1931	75	8	6	2
1933	110	12	9	3
1934	126	16	9	7
1935	158	13	5	8
1936	124	12	5	7
1937	132	2	1	1
1938	151	16	5	11
1939	185	21	12	9
1940	228	28	14	14
1941	217	21	10	11
1942	233	28	16	12
1946	198	29	14	15

Sources: *Lackawanna News*, 6/26/30; 6/25/31; *Lackawanna Herald*, 6/22/33; 6/28/34; 6/20/35; 6/25/36; *Lackawanna Leader*, 6/3/37; 6/11/42; *Lackawanna High School yearbook*, 1938, 1939, 1940, 1941, 1946.

graduate from the academy. A number of Roland Avenue Italians attended Our Mother of Good Counsel Church in Blasdell, and a few sent their children to the parish school.[57]

The 1913 graduating class at Lackawanna High School numbered 18, including John Fadale. His sister Lucy was the only Italian among the city's 46 grammar-school graduates that year. Most of their classmates had Irish surnames. Five years later, the 62 high-school graduates included Francis Campanelli, Anna Miceli, Joe Milano, and Nick Thomas. Between 1930 and 1940, the total number of graduates quadrupled, and Italian graduates (aside from a steep drop in 1937) grew from three in 1930 to 28 in 1940. The drop in graduates in 1941 was a result of the availability of defense jobs that paid well, but at war's end, the number of Italian graduates rose to 29 in 1946. The number of female graduates grew significantly during this period, an indication that the Italian tradition of down-playing the importance of educating females was changing (see Figure 3.8). Older Italians attended the city's adult educational night schools, which in 1934 had a student council with Nicholas Yacobucci as president and Anthony Molea as secretary. During the 1930s and 1940s, Italian American youth were increasingly well represented in local newspaper articles listing students who were graduating, on the honor roll, or involved in academic or athletic programs. As the second generation learned American ways at school, it sometimes created conflict at home with their immigrant parents.[58]

Family and Cultural Values

In its encounter with the mainstream culture of America, the Italian family and culture were placed under great stress. The change from a farming existence and life in a small town to living and working in industrial cities in America was a huge one. Part of the Italians' daunting task of assimilation was to bridge the wide gulf between these two ways of life. It fell upon the immigrants and their children to make adaptations to their new situation. The previous sections have addressed this situation at the community level and pertaining to interactions with American schools. This section and the two that follow will examine other areas in which the Italian family and culture changed in America. Chapter 4 will elaborate on this process of assimilation.

In the United States, Italian peasants found jobs more plentiful in urban and industrial areas. To contribute to the family economy, the wife and children had to labor outside the protective umbrella of the father and family, which was quite foreign to Italians. One scholar writes, "The family no longer constituted a tightly knit economic unit, and children were often an economic liability." Some compromises were made—women and children tended to boarders and family businesses, or joined groups of other Italians as farm laborers in the nearby countryside. In Italy, education was more valued for boys than for girls. Most children left school by the fifth grade unless there were aspirations to higher education, something out of reach of most families. In America, most children went to school. It was common, and later required, for them to complete elementary school.[59]

The greatest source of conflict between immigrant parents and their children was the American concept of individualism that was gradually absorbed by Italian youth. Family solidarity was undermined as group goals were challenged by individual aspirations. In America, adult females and their daughters were treated in a more egalitarian way than they had been in Italy. By the 1930s, the females had a wide variety of Italian American societies to join as well as some mainstream groups. Older sons literate in English could sometimes get jobs more easily, and at higher wages, than could their immigrant fathers. Parents less skilled in English were put in the uncomfortable position of depending on, and often deferring to, their children for important transactions with American institutions. The father, especially, was in danger of losing his authority and prestige within the family.[60]

Some members of the second generation had very mixed or anguished reactions to the plight of their ethnic group. Boys saw that their fathers were unskilled laborers in the steel plant who received little respect from mainstream society. One youth pondered the predicament of his family and the Italian community. He saw that immigrants were "downtrodden and held down—look where we are"; in contrast to the Irish, "the Italians are lower. I would do something about it—this injustice would be undone." Yet he also concluded that "there was not much to be proud of regarding the first generation; they were good workers and providers," but, he continued, "my father and his friends didn't have the brains to see how backward they were, and were willing to remain." Angry at their immigrant parents, whom they viewed as too foreign, some teens even referred to them using such derogatory terms as "greaser." Others felt embarrassed by the immigrants' ignorance of American ways. One young man was upset that an immigrant neighbor, who originally was poor, continued to cover his kitchen floor with newspapers, after he was doing well financially. Yet the second generation was also angry at American society for viewing them as "too Italian" and "inferior". Some teens and young men acted out against both their parents and American authority figures in a pattern labeled "oppositional youth culture," which is common in minority communities. Teens formed their own peer networks outside of the family's direct influence. In school and on the street, Italian American youth, in the first four decades of the twentieth century, learned things that were very foreign to their immigrant parents. Trapped between two cultures, the second generation tried to reconcile "Italian" and "American" standards, each of which had its own rewards and consequences.[61]

Language Spoken in the Home

One of the most difficult areas in the relationship between the immigrants and their children revolved around language usage. The lifeblood of any culture is language. To preserve their heritage, Italian immigrants in America needed to speak Italian and have their children follow suit. But to survive, the immigrants needed at least a minimal ability to speak English. Unfortunately, English is one of the more difficult of the major world languages. The challenge of two languages, and the different culture each embodies, set the stage for confusion and conflict between the immigrants and American society, as well as between immigrants and their children. Many immigrants wanted the comfort of speaking their native tongue at home. Jerre Mangione described his family's dilemma in Rochester, New York. "My mother's insistence that we speak only Italian at home drew a sharp line between our existence there and our life in the world outside. We gradually acquired the notion that we were Italian at home and American (whatever that was) elsewhere. Instinctively, we all sensed the necessity of adapting ourselves to two different worlds." [62]

Second-generation men and women in Lackawanna described interesting language accommodations they and their immigrant parents fashioned in the years prior to World War II. Rose Fiore grew up speaking Italian at home because her parents spoke limited English. She noticed that as her parents' English improved, they continued to speak to their children in Italian, but the children responded in English—and everyone understood what was being said. Soon, the younger children needed to know only a handful of phrases in Italian. This was also true in the Morgan household, where Sam and Maria often spoke Italian to their nine kids, who usually answered in English. Mike Morgan and his younger siblings had limited command of Italian, but they could grasp what their parents said in their native language. The older Morgan children were fluent in Italian, a pattern true of other second-generation Italian Americans interviewed. Some families found a different solution to the language issue. Antonio and Annamaria Monaco spoke only Italian in their home, but their two eldest children, Yolanda and Helen, wanted to practice speaking English. This angered Annamaria because she relied on Yolanda to go shopping with her, speak Italian, and act as her translator. Then, in 1939, Annamaria took English classes at Roosevelt and became a naturalized citizen. Her three children were then free to practice their English at home, and Yolanda was relieved that her mother "then went shopping on her own." Other immigrants urged their children to learn the English language, as was the case with Tony Colello, who then himself attended night classes at Roosevelt in the late 1920s, where the Americanization classes focused on English, civics, and U.S. history. By 1929, some 600 men and women of many ethnicities were attending these classes each semester at Washington, Franklin, Roosevelt, Lincoln, and Wilson schools.[63]

Children often served as gatekeepers at the family home by talking with the *Mericani* (the Americans) who called at the door. In Lackawanna, insurance agents came around monthly, and vendors traveled door to door selling cloth, sewing supplies, clothes, and kitchen utensils. Some immigrants depended on their children to greet the visitors, translate for them, and explain the American terms and concepts that were unfamiliar to them. Anne Scarsella, the youngest of the seven children of Luigi and Colomba Scarsella, was nine months old when the family immigrated to Lackawanna and soon learned to speak English. "I had to learn it; my father spoke some and my mother not too well, but my brothers and sisters did not speak it too well, and I was the one pushed into learning how to speak 'American.' By the time I was five, I spoke it really well.

Because I'd answer the door; I'd be the one to translate." One man regularly made his rounds selling coffee, and after the Scarsellas bought a certain amount, he gave them free bowls. Another American peddled pots and pans, and other items not available in local stores. Scarsella continued, "And your insurance agent—of course, he always came to your house. He was a friend…. He was a real nice man, and he'd sit there and have coffee." Anne Scarsella did all the translating between her mother and the Americans.[64]

Many immigrants gained some fluency in English by having their children teach them. The children were bilingual, having learned Italian at home and English at school and in the streets. Sara Chiacchia quickly picked up English in kindergarten at the Old Village School Annex. She remembers the Italian immigrants in the neighborhood always speaking their native tongue during the World War I period. However, her mother Lucia, and her grandmother, Rosabella Fiorella, were eager to have the girl teach them some English. When Chiacchia gave the two adults informal lessons, they referred to her as *la maestra*—the teacher. Jim Oddy, the eldest of four children of Benigno and Giselda Oddi, relayed to his parents and younger siblings the lessons he learned each week at the Old Village School. He was the first in his family to speak fluent English, as Italian had been the language of their home. His informal lessons broadened his parents' vocabulary and introduced his siblings to English. By the time they entered school, his brother and two sisters were fluent in the new language.[65]

When immigrants from different regions of Italy met and married in Lackawanna, English wasn't the only language challenge; they had to get used to each other's dialects, too. It took Pietro Fiore, a native of Cantalupo, and Giulia Violanti, from Giuliano di Roma, a significant period of time to master each other's dialects. Plus, these different dialects sometimes caused the couple's children confusion and woes. Lavinio Montanari was a Marchegiano and his wife Adelina an Abruzzesa. When their son Dewey referred to the soup ladle by its Abruzzese word, *cupina*, Lavinio admonished him to use the "correct', i.e., Marchegiano term: *ramaglillo*. As couples intermixed their dialects and neighbors incorporated words from each other's dialects, there emerged a hodgepodge version of Italian that was spoken in each neighborhood.[66]

The dialects of immigrants from rural Italy lacked words to describe many objects and concepts encountered in America. "Even 'street' had no precise equivalent," writes Joseph Lopreato, "for what one usually walked on in the old community was not really a street but a mud trail leading from the village to the farming plots on the mountain slopes."

So Italian immigrants developed "Italglish," Italianized versions of English words. Some examples are:

English word	Italianized version
shop	shoppa
job	giobba
store	storu
shovel	sciabbella
refrigerator	frigidaria
steel plant	stima planta
backhouse (outhouse)	baccausa
factory	fattoria
girlfriend	ghellafrienda
car	carra
street	streetu
s.o.b.	somma na binccia

The immigrants had their own pronunciations of English words and names: Umberto Barbati referred to his favorite movie star as "Hotta Gabbeans" (Hoot Gibson). Italian immigrants also adopted words of other ethnic groups; taking the Polish and Russian prosit, or "to your health," Italians offered a toast by saying *prosito*. The immigrants also used Italian phrases to capture a certain thought or event, such as *mortu di fam'* (which literally means "dying of hunger") to describe someone who puts on airs, as if to say "he is wearing fancy clothes, but he's really poor." The Italian American blended words represented the immigrant's transition from the Italian to the English language. Sadly, however, American society looked down on those who did not speak English, spoke it with an accent, or used hybrid words. Observing this, many Italian American children quickly learned English to avoid ridicule when communicating with the Mericani.[67]

Adaptations and Changes

Many second-generation Italians who entered adulthood between the late 1920s and early 1940s had to make adjustments to ease their precarious situations. In Rochester, New York, Jerre Mangione felt the deep rift between his generation and that of his immigrant parents. He relates, "It wasn't that we wanted to be Americans so much as we wanted to be like most people." And most people around them were not Italians. Oscar Handlin described how public schools had widened the gap between the generations: "If it did nothing else to the child, the school introduced into his life a rival source of authority. The day the little boy hesitantly made his way into the classroom, the image of the teacher began to compete with that of the father…. He came to believe in a universe, divided as it were into two realms, one for school and one for home, and each with rules and modes of behavior of its own." The schools also brought Italian kids in

Figure 3.9

NAME CHANGES

As they acculturated, some Italian immigrants and their children altered their first name, their surname, or both. One technique was to change the spelling to conform to English pronunciation while maintaining the basic Italian sound:

Oddi	to	Oddy	Iacobucci	to	Yacobucci
Giuditta	to	Juditta	Iovieno	to	Yoviene
Cristiano	to	Christiano	Ginnetti	to	Jennetti

A second method was to drop some letters and make the name appear more English, as in:

Verelli	to	Verel	Russo	to	Ross
Centofante	to	Chentfant	Delmonte	to	Delmont
Manna	to	Mann	Tarquinio	to	Tarquino or Tarquin
Morgante	to	Morgan	Basile	to	Basel
Prosciutto	to	Preshoot	Bellagamba	to	Bell

Related to the dropping-letter method was the technique of dropping one or two syllables to make the name, while still appearing Italian, simpler and easier for English speakers to pronounce:

Vitaterna	to	Viterna
Mastrobattista	to	Battista
Zuccarini	to	Zucca (later to Zaccarine)

A fourth strategy was to translate the name into its English equivalent, or something similar, as in:

Volpe	to	Fox	Di Tomasso	to	Thomas
Giorgio	to	George	DiCenzo	to	Denzel
Antigiovanni	to	Andyjohn			

Some Lackawanna Italians invented surnames having little in common with the original:

Delguercio	to	Welch	Berarducci	to	Blard
Sambuchi	to	Sham	DeSantis	to	Rand

Others adopted northwest European surnames, such as:

Allen	Frank	Downing	Matthews	Williams	Logan	Feneck	Peters

A complete makeover of both first name and surname was sometimes the goal, as in:

Antonio Grossi	to	Jim Paine	Antonio Turchiarelli	to	Tony Costello
Ferdinando Catuzza	to	Jim Jones	Antonio Colello	to	Tony Cole
Giuseppe Miceli	to	Joseph Mitchell			

Changing one's name could allow a man to avoid ridicule, discrimination in hiring, or retaliation for one's actions. Angelo Croce went by the name Tony George in the plant during the steel strike of 1919 to conceal the fact that he worked while others were on strike. The name stuck, however, and he was called Tony George by other workers for the rest of his life.

Officials sometimes took name-changing liberties. In school, Thomas Pepe's teacher asked what his last name meant in English. When he responded "pepper," she said, "That's what your name will be from now on," and for the rest of his life he went by Tom Pepper. The paymaster at the plant where Giustino DeSantis worked couldn't pronounce his first name, so he dubbed the Italian Chester. Other Italians came up with creative translations of their own. Salvatore DiTomasso used the nickname Sullivan. Many men named Vincenzo, instead of translating it to Vince, went by Jimmy, as did Jimmy D'Alessandro and Jimmy Suffoletto. Comillo Ross and Eugenio Galanti also used the name Jimmy. Sosio Ceccarelli was called Sessio by friends and relatives, and John by coworkers and most other people. Eugenio Ziccarelli also went by John.

(continued)

Children born in the "old country" and the United States alike often Americanized their first names:

Concezio Novelli	to	John
Nunzio Oddy	to	Nunze
Duilio Baldelli	to	Doc
Sarabella Chiacchia	to	Sara
Ludovico Paolini, Duilio Montanari	to	Dewey
Filomena Leo	to	Nellie
Giustina Covino	to	Jay

Filomena Andreozzi Americanized her name by spelling it Philomena but was known to most people as Dolly. Leopoldo Covelli went by Leo, and when his parents considered naming his youngest sibling Ermingildo or Anselmo, Leo intervened and steered them to Elmer instead. Luca and Maddelena Tarquinio named one of their sons Cleveland John Tarquinio, in honor of President Grover Cleveland. And some people changed their name for no particular reason. As an adult, Armando Pietrocarlo altered his first name by changing the second vowel to an "o" to get Armondo.

Italian first names and surnames proved in many cases to sound and be spelled much differently from English names. Perhaps the most common surname-altering practice of first- and second-generation Italians was simply to use English pronunciations, as follows:

Name	Italian Pronunciation	English Pronunciation
Chiodo	Key OH doe	Ch-eye OH dah
Pagliei	Pall YEAH ee	Pag glee A ee
Chiacchia	Key AH key ah	CHA cha
Bracci	BRA chee	BRAH key

Lastly, Lackawanna Italians had many interesting nicknames. Some immigrants were nicknamed for their geographic roots in Italy, such as Filberto the Calabrese, or Mike the Sicilian. Some individuals were simply known by the name of their hometowns: Giuseppe Baldelli from the Marche region, was called Senigallia and a Sicilian man was called Palermo.

Other nicknames, in Italian and English, covered a broad spectrum; all but one of the following are for males:

Italian:

U barone (The Baron)	Pipa (pipe, smoking)	Baruff (brawl, squabble)	Pip'Antonio (pipe Anthony)
Piucc' (Little Pio)	Buff" (funny, odd)	U professore (The Professor)	Capobianco (white head/hair)
Sabatucc' (Little Sabato)	Sciurrill' (short)	Carmellun' (f) (Little Carmella)	Corporale (Corporal)
U scupattore (The Sweeper)	Bragon' (baggy pants)	Settecocce (seven heads)	Piccolino (Little One)

English:

Bell, Palle Royal, Charlie Chaplain, Shiek, Josie, Shoo-shoo, the lawyer

Sosio Piccirilli had both an Italian nickname (Pelle, meaning skin or leather) and one in English (Kaiser).

From second-generation Lackawannans came the following nicknames:

Jelly Belly, Curly, Kook, Burly, Chief, Roughhouse, Dynamite, Soup, Butts, Gigi, Tarzan, Cheety, Harpo, Ziggy, Hawk, Ace, Boots, Erie, Pedro, Hook, Spike, Turk, Greek, Zingale (Gypsy, dark-complected), Pappy, Sir Knight, Mambo, Shakes

Sources: Interviews with Al Croce, April 8, 1994; Tom Pepper, 1977; Tony Grasso, November 27, 1981, December 27, 1981, July 12, 1985; Angelo Grosso, April 18, 1989; Mike Morgan, April 18, 1995; Ang Pitillo, April 15, 1994; Frank Chiodo, December 28, 1983, September 20, 2000; Chico Galanti, April 22, 1995; Bruce Tarquino, March 31, 1996; Mary Sperduto-Cuomo, August 8, 1998; Jack Ziccarelli, March 15, 2009; Jay Covino-Masters, July 6, 1996; and John Novelli, April 18, 1995; U.S. Census 1910–1930; N.Y. Census 1905–1925; *Erie County Directory,* 1931, 1941; *Corriere Italiano,* December 13, 1917.

FIGURE 3.10

Name Changes of Italian Entertainers, 1930s – 1980s

Dino Crocetti	Dean Martin
Antonio Benedetta	Tony Bennett
Vito Ferrinola	Vic Damone
Gennaro Vitaliano	Jerry Vale
Luigi Valaro	Don Cornell
Frank LoVecchio	Frankie Laine
Francis Avallone	Frankie Avalon
Roberto Ridarelli	Bobby Rydell
Fabian Forte	Fabian
Dion DiMucci	Dion
Robert Waldo Cassotto	Bobby Darin
Giovanni De Simone	Johnny Desmond
Francis Casteluccio	Frankie Valli
Joseph DiNicola	Joey Dee
Anna Maria Italiano	Anne Bancroft
Gloria Balotta	Kaye Ballard
Concetta Franconero	Connie Francis
Bernadette Lazzara	Bernadette Peters
Madonna Ciccone	Madonna
Alfred Cini	Al Martino
Arnaldo Cocozza	Mario Lanza
William Levise	Mitch Ryder
Frederick Picciarello	Freddie Canon

Sources: Gary Null and Carl Stone, *The Italian-Americans,* 1976, pp. 98-99, 101, 116, 126, 128-29, 145; *Altre Voci/Other Voices,* March/April 2007; Pellegrino D'Acierno, ed., *The Italian American Heritage: A Companion to Literature and Arts,* pp. 785, 789; Robert Connolly and Pellegrino D'Acierno, "Italian American Musical Culture and Its Contribution to American Music," in D'Acierno, pp. 400, 418, 430-31, 437-38, 440-41; Fosca D'Acierno, "Madonna: The Postmodern Diva as Maculate Conception, in D'Acierno, p 492; Joseph Fioravanti, "Pop Singers," in Salvatore J. LaGumina, Frank J. Cavaioli, Salvatore Primeggia, Joseph A. Varacalli, eds., *The Italian American Experience: An Encyclopedia,* 2000, p. 493; Mary C. Kalfatovic, "Bancroft, Anne," in LaGumina, et al., p. 52.

contact with children of other ethnic groups. They too were struggling with the clash of cultures and the stigma of their lower-class status. Children of different southeast European ethnic groups sometimes clashed, but they also shared the common plight of feeling out of place both at school and at home, which helped forge a type of solidarity among them. The second-generation was placed in a sort of no-man's land, sitting on the fence separating the Italian and American cultures. They often viewed their parents as too foreign yet themselves were judged too foreign by American society. In the next chapter, we will see how they adjusted to this dilemma.[68]

The problem of their minority status haunted both the first and second generations into the early years of World War II. John and Nicolina Verel planned to move their family from Lackawanna to Orchard Park at a time when another Italian family was also building a home on the same street. Some of the neighbors circulated a petition protesting the arrival of the two families, fearing they would build "Italian shacks." Observing Italian American men in the north end of Boston during the late 1930s and early 1940s, William Foote Whyte described the difficulty for the second-generation man who desired to climb the ladder of success. "He is an Italian, and the Italians are looked down upon by upper-class people as among the least desirable of immigrant peoples. This attitude has been accentuated by the war. Even if a man can get a grip on the bottom rung, he finds the same factors prejudicing his advancement."[69]

The Americanization of Italian first names and surnames was one method used by immigrants and the second generation as a strategy to avoid the prejudice and discrimination that Italians encountered. A man might improve his odds for a job at the daily round of hiring in the steel plant if his name sounded Irish and rolled easily off the foreman's tongue, as when Collarino was changed to Gallarney. Many of the name changes were made by adult or teenage immigrants, but a significant number were initiated by the second generation in an effort to avoid the ridicule or taunting Italians often received (see Figure 3.9). In some cases, an older child in the family altered the surname while the parents used the original one. Nick DiTommaso used Thomas as his surname to get a job at the New York Central Railroad, and his younger siblings followed suit. But their immigrant parents, Salvatore and Teresa, continued to go by DiTommaso. Likewise, Angelo Grossi and his siblings changed their surname to Grosso, while their immigrant parents always used Grossi. Italian American entertainers often changed their names to avoid prejudice, formulating short, snappy names that the general public could easily pronounce and recognize (see Figure 3.10).

Personal Relationships

An important aspect of the Italian American experience in the first half of the twentieth century was forming personal relationships with non – Italians. These informal relations, which sociologists call primary relationships, include those between friends, members of informal clubs or neighborhood cliques, and couples in marriages. Intermarriage, or the marriage between people of different ethnic groups, is, according to one scholar, the "ultimate measure of social acceptance in any community," representing a blending of ethnic groups. Like Italian immigrants throughout the United States, those in Lackawanna tended to marry within their ethnic group during the early years of the twentieth century. Only three percent of Italian immigrants in the Steel City married outside their ethnic group. Among them were Domenico DiCenzo, who married Frances Kirkmeyer, a German American, in 1900, two years after he arrived in the United States, and Carmella Zitto, who married Jesus Cocina, a native of Spain, in 1923.[70]

The situation of second-generation Italians in Lackawanna was very different from that of their parents in that half of them chose non – Italian spouses. Among the second-generation

Albert Brasch and sons Al, left, and Anthony, late 1930s. Brasch, a German American, married Mary Core, the daughter of Italian immigrants, in 1936. Almost half the second-generation Italians in Lackawanna married non - Italians. Photo source: Roy Brasch

individuals of mixed ancestry (one parent Italian, the other non–Italian), four out of five married people of other ethnic groups. Many of the non–Italian spouses had Polish and other Slavic surnames, and Irish, German, and Hungarian surnames were also common. Some Italian immigrants objected to their children marrying outside the ethnic group, while others approved of their children marrying non – Italians usually focusing instead on whether the person was of good character and a Catholic.

The American ideals of individualism and romantic love were often attractive to young Italian women who were American-born or had emigrated from Europe as children. Many rejected the arranged marriages brokered by relatives and *paesani*, encouraging suitors they found personally attractive. During the 1920s and 1930s, young people met at dances and social events where the women were free from the watchful protectiveness of Italian families. The resulting courtship may have included family chaperones, but the young man and woman had done their own matchmaking, often with the help of friends. Giovanni and Nazzarena Schiavi introduced their daughter Iole to Italian men they felt were good candidates for a husband, many of whom were financially secure and some much older than she. But Iole wanted to make her own choice. She loved to dance, and at a ballroom in Buffalo, she met Bob Murray, a Scottish Canadian, who became her husband.[71]

Many Italian Americans' personal relationships with non – Italians were the result of Italians being accepted into formal institutions or moving to higher levels within them. This happened in the case of some immigrants who entered politics, such as Tony and Lena Amorosi and Ferdinand Catuzza, who then gained access to the informal cliques and friendship networks of Irish and Polish Americans. This process was even more noted among the second-generation, who in most cases could speak English fluently. Dr. John Fadale and teacher Mary Yoviene-Clark, businessmen Frank Morinello, Patsy Pitillo, and Charles Saccomanno, and politicians Joe Milano, Tony Falcone, and Angelo Grosso were involved in formal institutions or organizations that led to personal relationships outside the Italian community. When a city newspaper noted that businessman Nick Sperduto was participating in an informal political club, it indicated that he had become part of the political "in-crowd." In 1934, the Gamma Sigma Lak fraternity, a social group made up of young men from at least eight European ethnic groups, included Ralph Galanti and Dan Monaco, who was treasurer of the group. There was constant interplay between involvement in formal institutions and formation of personal relationships that helped many of the second generation enter the world of the *Mericani*.[72]

FIGURE 3.11

Lackawanna's Italian Households Outside of Little Italy (by Wards), 1910 – 1941

Number of Households and % of Ward Totals

Ward	1910	1920	1925	1930	1941
1	4 (7%)	9 (6%)	2 (1%)	9 (4%)	21 (9%)
2-4:	2 (10%)	6 (16%)	9 (20%)	27 (35%)	71 (55%)
Totals:	6 (7%)	15 (14%)	11 (5%)	36 (11%)	92 (26%)

The First Ward neighborhoods with high concentrations of Italians were Ingham Ave., the Old Village (razed in the early 1930s), and Bethlehem Park. In Wards 2-4 the only Little Italy was Roland Ave. The Ingham Ave. area includes Ingham, Lehigh, Holland avenues, the east-west sidestreets north of Wilson, between Holland and Lehigh, and the sidestreets from Wilson to Dona Street running between Ingham and Wilmuth avenues. The Roland Avenue area includes the area bounded by Warsaw Street on the north, South Park Avenue on the east, Cleveland Avenue on the south, and the railroad tracks on the west. The number of Italian households is approximate, based on Italian surnames and known cases of name changes and Italian women married to men with non-Italian surnames. Italian youth living in the Our Lady of Victory institutions are not included.

Sources: U.S. Census: 1910, 1920, 1930; N.Y. Census, 1925; *Erie County Directory,* 1941.

Advancing up the Social Ladder

Early in the twentieth century a few Italian immigrants began to advance to higher levels in mainstream institutions, and this grew into a significant movement by the 1930s. These formal structures include: political, civic, religious, residential, economic, occupational, media, military, entertainment, and athletic institutions.

Ethnic politics. In the first two decades of the twentieth century, a number of the Irish, German, and English supervisors in the steel plant ran for political office. Some of them ordered Italian and Slavic steelworkers to hand out flyers on company time and expected workers to vote for the "right" candidates. Italian immigrants learned the importance of elections and how to utilize the vote to better their own community. Several immigrants became committeemen in the 1910s, and by the following decade, a number of second-generation men ran for office. Starting in the late 1920s with Joe Milano's election as an assessor, a number of second-generation Italians captured a variety of elected positions at city hall and on the school board. This was a reflection of a process going on throughout the country.

On the national level, the programs of the New Deal opened many doors for white ethnics to enter the structures of society. Public works jobs which helped alleviate the poverty of the Depression, were accessible to Lackawanna Italians through their committeemen and councilman Milano. New mortgage loan programs enabled many immigrants and their children to achieve one of their basic dreams—homeownership. Italian and Slavic immigrants emphasized this goal and committed the family's hard-earned money to that end. By 1930, almost half of all Italian families in the city owned a home. The New Deal initiated public-housing projects, including three in Lackawanna. The first of these was the Baker Homes, completed in 1938. There, many young Italian families found affordable rents; in 1939, the 35 Italian families were second in number only to the 59 Polish families. The Wagner Act indicated the government's support for the formation of unions, and Italians joined other ethnic groups in the campaign to organize steelworkers. Other laws established minimum wages and maximum working hours.[73]

The local and regional political power of the new immigrants had grown, especially in cities like New York, where Fiorello LaGuardia's election as mayor was the result of an Italian-Jewish alliance defeating an Irish political machine. LaGuardia, the son of an Italian father and Jewish mother, and other children of new immigrants could now gain access to and advise WASP federal officials. President Franklin D. Roosevelt created "the first national political alliance critically dependent upon religious and ethnic minorities," and he appointed southeast European ethnics to important government positions. Roosevelt's three predecessors had appointed a total of 207 federal judges—170 of whom were Protestant, eight Catholic, and eight Jewish. FDR's 197 judicial appointees included 52 Catholics and eight Jews. Truman's 127 appointments included 38 Catholics and two Jews. Many of the Catholic appointees were Irish, but in 1936 Roosevelt named Matthew Abruzzo the first Italian on the federal bench. These developments signaled the reduction of prejudice and the growing political power of Italians, which helped to strengthen group identity.[74]

At the local level, Lackawanna Italians voted for FDR and organized the Lady Mead Club to support Congressman Jimmy Mead and cultivate his continued attention to their needs. The women who led the club, as well as committeewoman Adele Panzetta, were now part of the leadership of the Italian community. More Italians were appointed to city commissions or rose to higher civil-service positions. Joe Jennetti became the city's first Italian police officer in 1925, and nine years later, he was promoted to the rank of lieutenant. C. John Tarquinio became an assistant city engineer in 1928, and John Verel Jr. did so 10 years later. At least five Italians were appointed to city commissions between 1934 and 1940. In Italian neighborhoods, some leaders were able to mobilize voters for candidates who addressed their needs. The ethnic group had finally become a political interest group that could successfully compete with other ethnic groups for power and patronage.[75]

Friends gathered at the corner of Roland and Electric avenues, circa 1940. From left, they are: E. Wnuk, John Ciesla, [Unk] Greg Reviezzo, Frank Chiodo, R. Cirello standing behind Chiodo, Bill Eagan, J. Selvaggio, and Nick Acanfora.
Photo source: Collection of Frank Chiodo

Civic organizations. Italians began to enter the civic organizations of the greater community prior to World War I, when Benigno Oddi accepted an offer to join the Fraternal Order of Moose. Following World War I, Italians who served in the American military joined Steel City veterans associations, and their wives and daughters became active in the women's and youth auxiliaries. In 1920, the Knights of Columbus established a free night school on Ingham Avenue for Catholic veterans in the First Ward.[76]

Beginning in the 1930s, many second-generation men became involved in civic groups, such as parent-teacher organizations, the Knights of Columbus, the Eagles, and the chamber of commerce, and several became officers of these groups. In February 1941, the Lackawanna Chamber of Commerce proclaimed Americanism Week to promote programs on citizenship and Americanization. The committee in charge

was headed by James Petti, a 1.5 generation Italian American, (see Figure 3.6) and included a Hungarian, two Poles, and a Russian. Ironically, this Americanization effort was being directed by men from the very southeast European ethnic groups previously branded by nativists as inferior and not 100 percent American.[77]

Religion. During the 1930s and early 1940s, most First Ward Italians and some from Roland Avenue attended St. Anthony's Church. Some of the Roland Avenue families attended mass at Our Mother of Good Counsel Church in Blasdell, a mixed ethnic parish that was closer and easier to reach than St. Anthony's. By the 1920s, a notable number of Italian families moved from the First Ward to the eastern part of the city and attended Our Lady of Victory Basilica. At St. Anthony's Church, a cadre of second-generation men was shedding the anticlericism of the immigrants and actively supporting the church and its functions. The men formed the core of the Holy Name Society, which helped found religious and Scout groups for boys of the parish. In the 1930s, religious-instruction classes in the First Ward often involved the children of several parishes and were usually taught by a priest who had roots in northwest Europe.

Area of residence. The early managers of the steel plant lived in trendy neighborhoods in Buffalo or as far away as New York or Cleveland. In the 1930s, some of them had luxurious homes constructed on Lake Erie south of Lackawanna, with steelworkers unloading the barges ferrying building materials. Ninety years ago, many of the Irish, German, and English foremen and supervisors in the steel plant lived in eastern Lackawanna, away from the air pollution of the mills. But most of the immigrants working in the plant lived in Lackawanna's densely populated First Ward, with its ore dust from the mills and soot from steam locomotives. In America, just as in Italy, the power and privilege of the upper classes were easily visible. The increased movement of Italians into mixed neighborhoods in eastern Lackawanna during the 1920s and 1930s represented the crossing of an ethnic boundary. These neighborhoods, characterized by a greater variety of white ethnic residents, a more stable financial status, and cleaner air had few ethnic markers and symbolized the assimilated working-class community. There, Italians had the opportunity to form friendships with non – Italians and enter the personal cliques of the dominant culture. The number of Italian households outside the Italian neighborhoods went from 7 percent to 26 percent between 1910 and 1941, as shown in Figure 3.11. The high increase in 1920 was due to the fact that many Ingham Avenue residents left for Italy or other parts of the United States, but returned by 1925. Also, the percentage of Italians living east of the railroad tracks in the second, third, and fourth wards grew from 14 percent in 1910 to 38 percent in 1941. These trends became even more pronounced after World War II.[78]

Economic and occupational institutions. Italians set up 120 small businesses between 1930 and 1941, usually within their ethnic neighborhoods, although some were larger and more diverse enterprises that served the general population: restaurants, food markets, beauty salons, barbershops, and automotive and construction businesses. A few of these merchants were small-time capitalists, such as restaurateur Nicholas Mattucci, and grocers Peter Mazuca and Frank Morinello, each of whom had a number of employees. Mazuca and Morinello ran several groceries serving Italian and non-Italian customers, and both were active in the Lackawanna Grocers and Butchers Association. Mazuca, a Mason, helped found the association and was also a member of the city's

credit bureau. In 1941, Patsy Pitillo and Frank Spinelli were among the 17 founding members of the Lackawanna Tavern Owners Association. The small group of Italian professionals by 1941 included two doctors, four nurses, six school teachers, a priest, and two engineers. Two other professionals from Lackawanna had moved away—banker James Oddy (to Buffalo), and lawyer Daniel Monaco (to Washington, D. C.).[79]

Despite the nativist predictions that Italians couldn't work in rolling mills, more men moved to jobs inside the mills, advancing from laborers to skilled workers, and from track workers to train crewmen on the South Buffalo Railway. By 1930, 23 Lackawanna Italians were foremen, and 45% of all Steel City Italian males held skilled or semiskilled jobs. They entered into many departments of the steel plants and railroads, a process that was apparent by 1925. The formation of industrial unions between 1936 and 1941 greatly benefited Italians and other immigrants not only by raising their wages, but also by breaking the ethnic hierarchy in the steel plant and opening up positions that had been dominated by northwest Europeans.[80]

Leonard Giovinetti, who changed his last name to Govenettio, joined the U.S. army in the late 1920s. The military has always acted as an "employer" of working-class and poor people, especially immigrants and other minority groups. Photo source: Dorothy Govenettio

The Civilian Conservation Corps, or CCC, employed young men during the Depression of the 1930s to do construction and forestry projects. Armando Leonetti, shown here at his barracks, was stationed at Camp Dix and then in Loyston, Tennessee.
Photo source: Collection of Phil and Adeline Andreozzi

The press and other media. The Lackawanna press gradually provided more news about Italians. Though historically less derogatory than Buffalo's newspapers, those in the Steel City had propagated some stereotypes about immigrants and initially offered little news about First Ward immigrants. However, by 1917, First Ward Italians running for office and entering into the informal cliques of mainstream society were being mentioned in the journals. That year, Anthony Tarquinio, secretary of the Lackawanna Base Ball Club, penned a brief article about the team, which was probably the first time an Italian American wrote an article for a city newspaper. In the 1920s and 1930s, more announcements about Italian society functions, celebrations, marriages, and births also appeared in the press. In 1934, mechanic Leonard DePaula launched the "Automobile Problems" and also a gossip column, the "Lackawanna Banana Peel," for the *Lackawanna Herald*.

Those reading Buffalo's *Corriere Italiano* found more English-language articles, and beginning in 1937, there was at least one page totally in English.[81]

Both the Italian- and English-language press included advertising, short stories and editorials, information about theater performances and other entertainment, and listings regarding movies and radio shows. Radio and motion pictures greatly expanded advertising and entertainment, accelerating the development of a new American culture. "Between 1890 and 1945," concludes Charles McGovern, "the United States became a consumer society." The middle class learned to buy brand-name goods during the economic boom of the 1920s, and the working class was drawn into the individual consumption that was being promoted. Public life in the urban, commercial, mass culture equated citizenship with being a consumer. Advertising professionals used "American national symbols and political language not only to legitimize their work, but also to unite a nation in a citizenship based on purchasing, ownership, entertainment, and display." American clothes and haircuts made the greenhorn acceptable and less foreign, as "shopping, spending, and acquiring mass-manufactured goods confirmed their identities as Americans. ... Fearful of the ethnic diversity and suspicious of immigrant and working-class culture, advertisers viewed consumption as efficient ... Americanization. Spending and ownership could transform any immigrant or worker ... into a modern, assimilated, unthreatening American." Anecdotal evidence indicates that many second-generation Italians in Lackawanna were drawn to the citizen-as-consumer idea.[82]

Films at Lackawanna's six movie theaters (four of them in the First Ward), as well as those shown at agencies serving the immigrants and their children, taught Hollywood's version of American history and culture, and often included advertisements. Music provided by record players allowed immigrants to listen to opera as well as the latest American pop tunes. The music, entertainment, and advertisements on radio served the same functions, and by 1940, more than 96% of Lackawanna households had a radio set. Some popular songs even focused on Italian immigrants, such as "Where Do You Work - A John?" (see Figure 3.12).[83]

The military, sports and entertainment. Minority groups tend to make their early advancement in these three career paths (as well as in organized crime, which will be discussed in the following chapter). During the years between the world wars, especially after the onset of the Depression, some Lackawanna Italian men followed the military path. Leonard Govenettio, who was an infant when his family left Italy, joined the U.S. army in 1925 at age 17. He returned to Lackawanna about eight years later with his wife, whom he had met while stationed near New York City. Gene Bracci served in the Marines from 1928 to 1948. Ralph Sterlace joined the Civilian Conservation Corps (CCC), which was run by the U.S. Army, in the early 1930s, then enlisted in the Army, after which he secured a job in the steel plant. Caz DePasquale and Gene Covelli also served in the CCC, then joined the military during World War II.[84]

One hundred years ago, the Irish were thought to be natural athletes because so many of them had excelled on amateur and professional teams and in the boxing ring. Soon thereafter, Italians became part of the ethnic succession of sports stars, especially with the maturation of the second generation. Samuel Lubell, himself an immigrant from Poland, wrote of the growing tendency to see outstanding Italian athletes in big-league baseball and on college football teams. "Until 1929 not a single Italian name was listed on Walter Camp's annual all-star football team," he wrote in 1956. "Since then there has been hardly a year in which there wasn't at least one Italian name on the all-star list." Early in the twentieth century, Ed Abbaticchio and Tony Lazzari were baseball stars, followed by Phil Rizzuto

and the three DiMaggio brothers in the 1930s and 1940s. More than eight percent of the players listed in the Baseball Register of 1942 were Italian. Sports pages included the exploits of boxers Tony Canzoneri and Johnny Dundee (Giuseppe Carrora), and later, Carl Furillo, Willie Pep (Guglielmo Papaleo), and Rocky Marciano. Quarterback Vincent Pazzetti of Lehigh University made the second team on the Camp's 1912 list of outstanding football players. Young Italian caddies at Wanakah Country Club, south of Lackawanna, admired Gene Sarazen, a champion professional golfer whose long career began in the 1920s.[85]

Italian pop singers first gained recognition during World War I. Russ Colombo was a popular crooner in the 1920s and 1930s. A long line of singers then emerged: Perry Como, Frankie Laine, Louie Prima, Lou Monte, Don Cornell, Julius LaRosa, Jerry Vale, and Tony Bennett. Early Italian movie actresses were Edith and Mabel Taliaferro and their cousin Bessie Barriscale. Immigrant Rudolph Valentino made his first film in 1918 and became a legend of the silent screen before dying in 1926. Other screen stars followed: Henry Armetta, Jimmy

FIGURE 3.12

A POPULAR SONG OF THE 1920s

"Where Do You Work - A John?" was written by three non – Italians—Mortimer Weinberg, Charley Marks, and Harry Warren—in 1926. It can be viewed as degrading and disrespectful of Italians, especially one chorus that includes the word "wop," but also as an indicator that the ethnic group was slowly being accepted into American culture. Some Italians saw it as a type of recognition of their existence, even if it was also stereotypical and demeaning. The song highlighted the jobs held by many immigrants and their sons on railroads, such as the Delaware and Lackawanna. And for Steel City Italians, it mentioned the name of their new hometown in America. Below are three of the song's nine verses.

Long time a - go, John and - a Joe	*- a - wan - a - wan - a - wan,*	*The Telephone Companee*
Come from sunny It-a-ly,	*The Delaware Lack - a - wan*	*AH - AH - AH! AH - AH - AH!*
to - a try - a to get the dough	*AH - AH - AH! AH - AH - AH AH*	*AH - AH - AH! AH - AH - AH*
Joe go a - way, John he's - a stay	*- AH - AH!*	*Chorus*
When they meet the oth-er day	*Ah - AH - AH! AH!*	*Where do work - a, Joe?*
Here's what - a they got - a say:	*Chorus*	*For the city I shovel snow*
Chorus	*Where do you work, Marie?*	*What do you do - a, Joe?*
Where do you work - a John?	*In the telephone Companee*	*I push - a push - a push*
On the Del - a - ware Lack - a - wan	*What do you do, Marie?*	*What do you push - a, Joe?*
What do you do - a, John?	*I push - a push - a push*	*I push, I push - a da snow*
I push - a, push - a push	*What do push, Marie?*	*For the city I shovel snow o - OH*
What do you push - a, John?	*I push, I push - a da plug*	*o - OH o - OH*
I push, I push - a da truck	*Where do you push, Marie?*	*The city I shovel snow*
Where do you push - a, John?	*In the Telephone Companee*	*AH - AH - AH! AH - AH - AH!*
On the Del - a - ware Lack - a -wan	*- anee - anee - anee*	*AH - AH - AH! AH - AH - AH!*

Source: Songsheet: *Where Do You Work-a, John? (Push - a Push - a Push)*, by Mortimer Weinberg, Charley Marks, and Harry Warren, Shapiro Bernstein & Co., Music Publishers, New York, 1926.

Figure 3.13

POLITICIANS SPEAK OUT IN DEFENSE OF ITALIAN AMERICANS

In November 1939, just two months after the outbreak of World War II, U.S. Senator James Mead of western New York sensed the growing distrust of the American public toward Mussolini's Italy, which had not yet entered the war, and Italian Americans. Mead was popular among Italians for his support of issues important to them, and those in Lackawanna had organized the Lady Mead Club in 1930 to support him and turn out voters on election day. Mead wrote a letter to the public to remind readers of "the traditional friendship between the United States and Italy," and the how voyages of Columbus and Vespucci "wove the first ties between the Old and New Worlds." Praising the cultural and religious contributions of Italy to the United States, he added:

The culminating expression of our deep friendship came in 1917 when the United States joined hands with Italy as Allies in the World War. Italy's ties in Latin America and our own ties with Latin America form a common bond between these two leading neutrals… Although civil and political liberties have been restricted, Italy is fundamentally a religious nation…

Mead pointed out that, in keeping with the Encyclical of the Pope, Mussolini purged from his cabinet "those members having pro – Nazi or pro – Communist tendencies." He urged that both Italy and the United States remain neutral, and reminded Christians in both hemispheres that "Religion begets peace;

peace is the fruition of religion. Let us join hands across the sea in the establishing of a Religious Front against all wars."

Charles Poletti, the lieutenant governor of New York State, weighed in on the issue a few months later at a gathering on American Citizenship Day in New York City. He called for "whole-hearted allegiance to the United States and the equality of all Americans." He continued:

We can be proud of the great strides made by foreign-born Americans and first-generation Americans. They have had greater opportunities accorded them than could be enjoyed in any country in the world. And I am sure that foreign-born Americans and first-generation Americans are alert to those simple facts and that they feel grateful to the United States. Moreover I am certain that foreign-born Americans and first-generation Americans are not going to be seduced by non-American doctrines. They will continue to love and cherish the freedom of a free America.

Some first-generation Americans may think that this opportunity has been restricted because of the mere fact he is a first-generation American. He may on occasion feel that he is a less desirable citizen.

Allow me to say to that young man or young woman that no one who understands the glory and destiny of America can entertain any distinction on such grounds. No true

American seeks to classify his fellow American on the basis of the number of years he or his family has been in this country.

All Americans stand on an equal basis. Each American is the equal of every other. Equal opportunity must be given every American. The descendant of an early President of the United States is no better and no worse than a first-generation American….

Poletti then railed against newly organized groups, such as the Yankee-American Action Organization in Massachusetts.

Who is a Yankee-American? Is he a Mayflower American? You and I know that a Yankee-American is no better than any other American citizen. And let me assure you that the good sense of the average man and woman will kill all of those un-American organizations….

On this American Citizenship Day (w)e pledge ourselves to the full respect of every privilege, right and guarantee contained in the Bill of Rights of the American Constitution; we pledge ourselves to countenance no discrimination or prejudice on the basis of racial or religious background; we pledge ourselves whole hearted and exclusive allegiance to the United States; and we pledge our willingness to defend the United States against all enemies.

Sources: *Corriere Italiano*, 11/9/39, 2/22/40.

Durante, Jerry Colonna, Ruth Roman, Don Ameche, Richard Conte, Robert Alda, Anne Bancroft, and Ernest Borgnine.[86]

The accomplishments of these national celebrities was replicated in Little Italys throughout America. In Lackawanna, many young Italians, most of them second generation, won recognition for their skills in sports, music, and entertainment.

Their work in these areas represented part of the acculturation process—that is, learning the ways of American society. They also helped achieve, for both themselves and the Italian community, a sense of recognition as they excelled in these "American" forms of recreation.

During the early and mid twentieth century, the athletes, singers, and actors at the national level were examples of Italians rising in America's entertainment industry and achieving legitimacy in the mainstream culture. For immigrants, and the second-generation, these men and women were viewed with pride as heroes; their personal success symbolized the good image and upward mobility that many Italian Americans sought. Samuel Lubell referred to this process as "the hunger for middle-class social standing," or "a passion for respectability." The national celebrities helped working-class and poor Italians deal with the minority status of their ethnic group and the continuing social and political turbulence of the 1930s. By the end of the decade, the worst years of the Great Depression were past, and an economic recovery was slowly occurring.[87]

Charitable organizations. Several agencies provided various types of relief to impoverished immigrants. In 1907 and 1908, prior to the founding of Lackawanna, a recession led to a mass layoff at the steel plant. The Hungarian Presbyterian Church provided some clothing and food to the unemployed in an outreach effort that eventually culminated in the founding of Friendship House. Traditional agencies feared that the area could not "harbor a large number of unemployed without menace." This reflected a common belief that poor people and immigrants are dangerous and need to be controlled. So in 1908, the Charity Organization Society (COS) of Buffalo, with Lackawanna Steel footing most of the expense, set up a temporary office to help the unemployed. After many of the men were rehired, the relief work ceased and the COS reported that "There was no disorder as a result." The COS of Lackawanna, founded in 1919, provided temporary aid to families not able to get public welfare, and during the 1920s assisted families with home visits, food, clothing, rent, and utility grants.[88]

The advent of the Great Depression in 1929 stressed the resources of private and public agencies. Friendship House did its part by handing out free milk, flour, and clothing to families in need. The Erie County Welfare Bureau took over public assistance in Lackawanna, and by 1932, some 2,194 families, including 9,900 individuals, were on welfare. The following year, 2,800 families and 10,000 individuals received aid. One city newspaper claimed that "Lackawanna is one of the hardest hit cities in the country." Even as late as April 1942, 1,200 "patrons" received welfare in the city. Italians were reluctant to seek charity, but Tom Pepper, a welfare case worker at the Lackawanna office in 1932, said, "Many people were on welfare … there was a good number of Italians on welfare."[89]

The Italian distrust of charity agencies was reinforced in 1933, when the city's welfare bureau was charged with unfairly distributing aid to families, certifying dirty and unsafe tenements as livable, and neglecting the needs of single men. A committee cleared the department of the charges, but a few months later, several Italians, believing that Francis Eagan of the bureau had discriminated against them, circulated a petition in Bethlehem Park urging Eagan's removal. The bureau's director dismissed these charges, claiming that some of the petition's signatures had been forged. Public welfare reinforced America's stigma against the poor and minority groups, and the powerlessness that accompanies it. In writing an article about the COS of Lackawanna, a school student bluntly but accurately described the process for receiving aid and America's fixation on who is deserving of it:

> To receive assistance a family must reside in Lackawanna for at least one year, and the organization investigates to see that they are not lazy or trying to see how much they can get for nothing. If they find the family is deserving of help they are willing to do all they can to assist them.

Many Italians and other ethnics on the COS or welfare rolls made vows to escape this shaming experience.[90]

A kinder and more respectful form of relief came from the Catholic Church in Lackawanna during the Depression. Prior to his death in 1936, Monsignor Nelson Baker, the pastor of Our Lady of Victory Basilica, headed a number of charitable institutions linked to the parish that extended help to people throughout the city. Lackawannans of all ethnic groups stood in long lines at the OLV institutions waiting for free bread and clothing. There were no forms or interviews to complete, and all were welcome. Teens of the OLV's orphanage and reform school baked the bread, but as the need increased, Father Baker first convinced area bakeries to donate day-old bread and later purchased the bread from them. Father Baker's boys prepared free meals for the poor and unemployed, and by mid-1932, some 30,000 meals per month were being served. The youth repaired clothing and shoes, and gave away clothes and footwear to needy persons. The homeless were allowed to sleep on cots in the OLV buildings, and when room ran out there, Father Baker established lodging houses for men and women.[91]

The city provided several free services to people in need. The police department allowed homeless people to sleep in its rooms in the basement of city hall, which 2,377 "lodgers" did in 1933. The department of public works offered garden plots on a large tract of land off Milnor Avenue as well as free loans of plowing and gardening tools. In the Italian neighborhoods, relatives helped each other, and artisans provided low-fee or free services, such as repairing shoes, giving haircuts, and assisting with winemaking and the slaughtering of pigs.[92]

The length and depth of the Depression forced many Italian families to seek charity. Some were perhaps a little more comfortable doing so in the 1930s, as they had been in America long enough to speak passable English and gained a greater understanding of how the system operated. Many Italians were recipients of aid, but three American-born Italians held higher status positions in the city's charity agencies. Case worker Tom Pepper was an employee of the Lackawanna office of the Erie County Welfare Bureau. A few years earlier, in 1927, the COS of Lackawanna, following a successful fundraising campaign, praised the city's "foreign groups" for their support, making special mention of two young volunteers, Louis Amorosi and Leonard DePaula, "who volunteered their services and who raised more than their quota in a remarkably short time."[93]

World War II: Everything Changed

World War II led to a new phase in the Italian American experience, presenting quite a challenge to the first and second generations. Unlike the situation during World War I, Italy was an enemy of America and its allies this time around. Italian Americans endured much stress during the war, as their loyalty was continually questioned. Mussolini's regime was admired by many Americans until 1935 when Italy's invasion of Ethiopia brought sanctions by the League of Nations and much criticism throughout the world. Between 1936 and 1939, Mussolini fell into more disfavor with the western democracies by sending troops to support the Fascist forces in the Spanish Civil War, passing "racial laws" against Jews, annexing Albania, and entering the Pact of Steel alliance with Hitler. The outbreak of war in 1939 created a difficult situation for Italian Americans, who constituted the largest group of foreign stock (immigrants and their children) in the United States. The federal government feared the presence of an American "Fifth Column" (saboteurs within a country who aid an enemy invader) and was especially suspicious of aliens—immigrants who were not citizens. In 1940, Congress passed the Alien Registration Act, which required all noncitizens over 14 years of age to register, be fingerprinted, carry an identification card, and file a sworn statement listing their associations and political affiliations. Those not complying faced a $1,000 fine and six months in jail. "Persons who cannot speak English are urged to bring interpreters with them," advised the *Lackawanna Leader*.[94]

Italy entered the war in June 1940 by attacking France when that country was about to capitulate to Germany. President Roosevelt termed this action "a stab in the back," words that played on the stereotype of the dangerous, knife-wielding Italian. Many Italian Americans were angered by Roosevelt's remark but quickly came to realize that Italy's foreign policy

The Filipetti brothers met in Belgium during the last year of World War II. Alex, left, was a staff sergeant, and Silvio was a corporal in the 101st Airborne.
Photo source: Aldo Filipetti

Anthony Chiodo receives a medal in the Pacific Theater during the Second World War.
Photo source: Collection of Frank Chiodo

FIGURE 3.14

A NEW RELATION WITH ITALY: 1943

A crucial turning point in Italian American history was realized in September 1943, when Italy surrendered to the Allies, then joined with them in fighting the German troops who had occupied most of the Italian peninsula. With Italy no longer an enemy of the United States, Italian Americans could again identify with their land of origin, but in a different way. Now they focused on humanitarian aid, sending clothing and other needed essentials to their relatives in war-torn Italy. Italian Americans organized a nationwide drive to gather clothing to be sent to Italy. The 25 Italian Catholic parishes in the Diocese of Buffalo, led by Reverend Paschal Tronolone, had two collections of clothing in 1944. Steel City Italian organizations participated in this effort, which was coordinated by St. Anthony's Church. The following year, a national organization, American Relief for Italy, Inc., held a rally in Buffalo that drew more than 1,000 people dedicated to collecting clothes, food, and medicine to send to Italy. These efforts continued for several years. Food donations were especially helpful during Italy's hard winter of 1947; a grateful Italian

Mary Grasso and her children sending a package and Christmas greetings to her husband's aunt in Campania, circa 1944. Photo source: Collection of Tony Grasso

government thanked the people of western New York by sending a small statue of a mother holding an infant. Other national organizations, such as the Sons of Italy and UNICO, lobbied Congress to grant material aid and favorable treaties to war-torn Italy. Italian Americans again proved their patriotism by mailing millions of letters to relatives, urging them to vote against communist candidates in Italy's 1948 national elections. The Federation of Italian Societies in Buffalo mobilized area Italian organizations with the goal of sending 60,000 letters to friends and

relatives in Italy. Into the 1950s and 1960s, Italian Americans in western New York continued to raise funds for orphans and flood and earthquake victims in Italy. Americans came to see Italy as an ally in the last two years of the war, then as a new democracy, a NATO partner, and, finally, a destination for tourists. This encouraged both Italian Americans and Italians to cross the ocean and renew contact with relatives. In 2009, Italian Americans in western New York again responded to an earthquake, this one in Abruzzo, by sending funds to support relief efforts.

Sources: *Lackawanna Leader,* 9/16/43, 7/27/44; *Buffalo Evening News,* 10/13/44, 4/6/45, 3/19/48, 3/24/48, 6/30/52. The statue, titled *Maternita,* was presented to Albright Art Gallery by James Battistoni, Buffalo's Italian consul.

reflected negatively on them. In the Steel City, Luigi Scarsella, who had admired Mussolini and in his home displayed a picture of "Il Duce" adorned with Italian flags, immediately took the picture down after Italy attacked France. The *Lackawanna Leader* had confidence in the city's ethnic groups: "Lackawanna—a melting pot for more than 50 nationalities— is as loyally American as the 48 stars in Old Glory." The article proclaimed "This city of steel stands ready almost to the man to pledge anew its love of freedom and Americanism… In the opinion of the man-on-the-street, 'it will be a sorry day for any fifth-columnist' if the latter attempts to gain a foothold here or rear his ugly head." Old-world loyalties, however, were acted out a few minutes after Italy's attack on France was announced in a Ridge Road restaurant. Elias Amar, an immigrant

from Morrocco, which was under French rule, and Frank Milani, an Italian, began arguing about the war in Europe and got into a fistfight, which police had to break up.[95]

Tension mounted as ethnic groups throughout the country waited to see if the United States would enter the war. The climax came on December 7, 1941, when Japan attacked Pearl Harbor, and its allies Germany and Italy declared war on the United States four days later. Now the ancestral homeland of five million Italian Americans was an enemy of America. The three Axis nations became the targets of propaganda, and immigrants from these countries were suspect. The 600,000 Italian aliens in the United States, along with German and Japanese nationals, were branded by the federal government as "enemy aliens." Over 110,000 Japanese were taken to

Madison Avenue, Bethlehem Park, 1943. Dolly Ceccarelli, with her son John, Jr. in the stroller, points to her husband's name on the display listing Bethlehem Park residents serving in the armed forces in World War II. Photo source: Collection of Jo Andreozzi

internment camps, as were 3,278 Italians, mostly immigrants, suspected of aiding the enemy. In January 1942, German and Italian aliens had to reregister and again be photographed, fingerprinted, and issued new identification booklets to be carried at all times. Now, an alien could neither change addresses without notifying authorities nor travel beyond five miles without a permit nor possess items that could be used to commit sabotage, such as a shortwave radio, a camera, or any type of weapon. In California, a curfew confined so called enemy aliens to their homes between 8:00 p.m. and 6:00 a.m., which affected 50,000 Italians. When most of the state's coastline was declared a prohibited zone, these individuals were not allowed within five miles of the coast. About 10,000 Italian aliens were forced to relocate and find other homes inland.[96]

In Lackawanna, Police Chief Ray Gilson was told by federal officials not to arrest aliens but to report suspicious activities to the FBI. Agents of the FBI interviewed officers of Italian organizations and confiscated their books, looking for any sign of unpatriotic activity. Three agents visited Armando Torella, who had emigrated from Italy in 1932, and altered his shortwave radio so it could not receive broadcasts from Italy. The months following the Pearl Harbor attack were tense as federal agents

interrogated Italians in Lackawanna's Little Italys as well as those throughout the country.[97]

New York Governor Herbert Lehman and Lieutenant Governor Charles Pioletti pressured President Roosevelt to ease the restrictions on aliens and to rescind blanket assumptions about their loyalties to the "Old Country." In October 1942, the U.S. attorney general decided that Italians who were not citizens were no longer enemy aliens, and most of the extra restrictions in California were ended. Of the 3,278 Italians interned during the war, fewer than 200 were held for long periods, and many were released after Italy surrendered to the western allies in September 1943. There were, however, other woes that affected Italian Americans from 1940 to 1943. Some defense contractors refused to hire aliens and even American-born Italians. In New York City, one company hired only workers who were "white, Christian, and not Italian." In 1941, a survey among Italian Americans in Boston found that 80% of those interviewed encountered discrimination in securing jobs. In Buffalo, some homes displayed signs degrading "dagoes" as the enemy. Such job discrimination and displays were not mentioned by the Lackawanna Italians interviewed.[98]

Italian Americans reacted quickly to allay fears about their loyalties. In Indianapolis, the *Societa Italiana di Mutuo Beneficenze Umberto* [The Umberto Italian Mutual Benefit Society] changed its name to Victory Benefit Association and cut its ties with the Sons of Italy. Many organizations bought war bonds, including Lackawanna's Lake Erie Italian Club, which purchased a $1,500 defense bond in February 1942. The club also installed its first American-born president, Charles Nigro, in January. It is estimated that 500,000 to 1.5 million Italian Americans served in the armed forces during the war, perhaps representing the largest ethnic group in the military. When the Allies invaded Italy in 1943, many of the American GIs were of Italian descent. When Jack Ziccarelli, who was born in the United States, was asked in boot camp if he minded fighting against Italians, he said he didn't know any of his relatives in Italy. Soldiers born in Italy were more vigorously interrogated before being sent to the Mediterranean Theater. John Novelli immigrated to America as a teen and was drafted into the army in 1942. When asked how he felt about fighting against Italians, he responded, "I don't like it, but I will fight Fascists." During his basic training, the Army closely observed him, and a sergeant even told Novelli that he was suspected of attempting to be in touch with Italy. Novelli must have passed the test, as he went on to serve in North Africa and Italy.[99]

By June of 1944, Lackawanna's youthful population had provided 3,225 men and women to the armed forces, including many Italian Americans. By April 1943, 31 of the 80 members of the Galanti Athletic Association were in the military or the Maritime Service. Italian American women also joined the armed forces, including Gloria Tarquino and sisters Patricia and Rose Mary Nigro, who served in the Marines. During the war, many Lackawanna Italian men worked in defense plants, as did the women who took jobs at Bethlehem Steel, Curtiss Wright Aircraft, and other plants.[100]

At least 53 Lackawanna GIs were killed in World War II, including Italian Americans Gino Baldelli, Daniel Rosati, Dominic Rosati, Bruno Schipani, and Mario Cipriani, all of Bethlehem Park, Joseph Vertalino of Roland Avenue, and Brondo Capriotti, who lived just south of the city. Ironically, the two Rosati brothers were killed in the Italian campaign—one at sea, the other in ground combat. Some Italian Americans displayed another type of courage. During World War II, 37,000 conscientious objectors of various religions performed noncombatant service within the military or in civilian work camps, and 6,086 men, mostly Jehovah's Witnesses, served prison sentences because they believed in nonviolence and refused to cooperate with the draft. In Lackawanna, immigrant Ludovico "Dewey" Paolini had become a Jehovah's Witness, and when the United States entered the war, he refused to

Neil Marrano joined the National Guard in 1939 because "nothing was happening in Lackawanna." His regiment was mobilized in 1940, and Marrano took part in the landings in Normandy, France. Photo source: Neil Marrano

Ralph Carestio with his father, Antonio, at the family home on Franklin Street. Carestio served in the Marines during World War II and was later elected to the Lackawanna school board. Photo source: Dennis Sterlace

serve in the military. He was tried, then sentenced to two years in a government prison.[101]

Italy's unconditional surrender to the Allies on September 8, 1943, caused rejoicing in Little Italys in the United States. "Throughout Bethlehem Park and in the Ingham Avenue neighborhood, where many Americans of Italian extraction reside here, expressions [of joy] were heard yesterday afternoon and early today," reported the *Lackawanna Leader*. The newspaper also gave the reactions of Italian American political leaders. "News of Italy's surrender to the United Nations," said City Council President Angelo Grosso, "is the best yet received in the war. The Italian armed forces now will be most eager to help the Allies drive Hitler into the ground. Italy's hour of freedom is at hand, and America rejoices!" School-board member Anthony Moretti stated, "The Americans of Italian descent never have sympathized with Mussolini's government or with any country whose hand Hitler held. Italy's unconditional surrender, and her turning on the Axis, will forever be a credit to a nation which had slept too long under the hypnotism of international gangsters." The Circolo D'Annunzio Dopolavoro, which had taken a low profile during the previous three years, held a banquet the following month celebrating the Italian surrender.[102]

Bethlehem Park, 1947. The memorial honors the eight men from the neighborhood who gave their lives during World War II, five of whom were Italian Americans. The project was sponsored by the Bethlehem Park Veterans Association. Photo source: Aldo Filipetti

With Italy joining the United States and its allies in the fight against Germany, Italian Americans could renew their ties to the "Old Country" without raising questions about their loyalty. However, as Mussolini abdicated power and the new Italian government prepared to surrender, the German military rushed in and occupied most of the country, initiating a grinding war of attrition that continued until the war in Europe ended. The Allied armies took Rome in June 1944, and Italian Americans began a series of programs to provide relief to war-torn Italy. A committee of Lackawanna Italians in 1944 canvassed homes to collect clothing "for the needy in liberated Italy." A city truck picked up the donations, and Reverend Vifredo of St. Anthony's Church took in additional contributions. Individual families sent packages of clothing and dry goods to their relatives in Italy. A new era in the relationship between Italian Americans and Italy was beginning (see Figure 3.14).[103]

The entry of the United States into the war at first threatened to worsen the minority status of Italians Americans, but it ultimately allowed the ethnic group to transcend its position of social inferiority. Italy's participation in the war as an Axis partner of Germany and Japan between 1940 and 1943 led many Americans to doubt the loyalties of Italian Americans. Government concern about the use of foreign languages led an FBI agent in Buffalo to report that *Corriere Italiano* was printing its first page in English, but "its editorials and local news as well as most advertisements are printed in the Italian language." Government pressure led to the cancellation of Italian radio programs and to Italian American shopowners displaying signs stating "No Italian Spoken Here for the Duration of the War." These developments fostered "a further

Ed Pacillo, at left center, takes part in the 1947 ceremony dedicating the memorial to Bethlehem Park servicemen who died in World War II. More than 400 Bethlehem Park men served in the military during the war.
Photo source: Aldo Filipetti

stigmatization of Italian Americans and the Italian language," according to one historian. But the war also gave Italians the opportunity to prove their loyalty to the United States, as they stood solidly behind the war effort. Italian American GIs fought against Mussolini's armed forces in North Africa and Italy prior to latter's surrender. Four Italian Americans attained the rank of brigadier general, and servicemen such as Marine John Basilone and pilot Don Gentile became well-known war heroes. Basilone was one of 12 Italians who received the Congressional Medal of Honor during the war, and Italians were among the many Lackawanna GIs decorated for outstanding service. On the home front, many Italian aliens followed the government's urging to become citizens, as did aliens of other ethnic groups. Between 1941 and 1945, the overall number of aliens nationally declined from roughly five million to three million. In Lackawanna, the board of education sponsored an ongoing campaign for Americanization and citizenship. In July 1944, it sent letters to more than 1,000 aliens urging them to file for "first papers," the initial step in the process. The *Lackawanna Leader* explained the process "not only as a help in their own future in this country, but as an outstanding duty towards this country, now at war with the common enemy of their homelands." The high school offered free classes three nights a week that prepared adults for citizenship tests. The largest number of aliens in the city were of Polish origin, followed in order by Italians, Spaniards, Yugoslavians, Canadians, and Austrians.[104]

With the Allied victory in 1945, Italian Americans could rightfully point to their patriotism and devotion to the war effort. By then, few people questioned the loyalty of this large ethnic group that had arrived in the country only a generation or two earlier. The old stereotypes of the recently arrived immigrant from southern Italy were no longer as potent. The Italian American ethnic group had crossed a major milestone in its quest for social acceptance.

From Minority to the Mainstream

The war's end marked an important change in Italian ethnicity that continued into the mid-1960s. The days of systemic prejudice and discrimination had come to an end, and Italian Americans could partake in the relative economic prosperity that came after the war. Along with other white ethnics, they enjoyed greater access to new housing, jobs, and education. The second generation and their children were well acculturated; they spoke English, knew American civic and work customs, and fit in much more easily than their immigrant parents and grandparents. With the employment opportunities of the war and the postwar period, Italians joined other Americans in enjoying the fruits of economic stability that

Holbrook Street and Ingham Avenue, 1945. Three GIs pose with their friend; from left are: Tommy Fiore, Angelo Sperduto, Pete Monaco, and Aldo Canestrari.
Photo source: Mary Sperduto-Cuomo

allowed them to advance in terms of education, income, and housing. Several factors made the war a watershed event for Italian Americans, allowing them to emerge from this traumatic period with a new social standing and to shed their minority-group-status.

The mobilization of millions of Americans for military service, jobs in defense plants, and civil-defense chores helped create a common bond among the diverse array of European ethnic groups in the United States. This was especially helpful in allowing Italians and other south and east European groups to feel they fit in. Thousands of Italian men and women mingled with other Americans of different ethnic groups, and those in the military left their communities and lived among other Americans in camps and bases throughout the world. The common cause created the sense of a unified American people, at least among those of European ancestry.[105]

The formation of industrial unions was another factor in creating common bonds and inclusiveness. By the late 1930s, Italians and other ethnic groups from east and south Europe composed a significant percentage of the country's blue-collar workers. In addition to their similar occupations, financial situations, and neighborhoods, working-class people developed new bonds in the late 1930s and early 1940s through the

Men of the Roland Avenue neighborhood gather at Pitillo's Tavern during World War II. Many had just shaved their beards upon getting their draft notices. Bottom row, from left: [Unk], Dominic Selvaggio, Abe DePerto, George Valentine, Delbert Herkimer. Second row: Bill Russell, Charles DePerto, Marge Pitillo, [Unk], Tony Falbo, Patsy Pitillo. Third and fourth rows: [Unk], [Unk], [Unk], Erie DePerto, Pete Juran, [Unk], John Steffan, Pat Vertalino, Bill Eagan, Jake DePerto. Man at top: Murphy Evans. Photo source: Collection of Frank Chiodo

formation of industrial unions. Labor unions had for decades provided a potential vehicle to assimilate Italians into the American working class, although a number of unions had initially been hostile to immigrants. In Lackawanna, the efforts of the Amalgamated Association of Steel, Iron, and Tin Workers during the 1919 strike helped plant the seed of unionism. Even though that strike ultimately failed, many Italians and other ethnics honored the picket lines, and everyone in the city felt the intimidating presence of state troopers who made it clear that city, state, and federal governments sided with the steel industry. The union movement became a large and significant structure of American society in the mid-1930s when new federal legislation granted the right to organize. The newly founded Congress of Industrial Organizations (CIO) started organizing efforts in many industries and launched the Steel Workers Organizing Committee (SWOC) in 1936. Lackawanna's Italians and other ethnic groups joined SWOC, which actively courted second-generation Italians and Slavs who wanted to

improve their lot in American society. Italians were among the volunteer organizers in Lackawanna, and the turning point in the battle to get the Bethlehem Steel Company to recognize the union came with the dramatic victory in the 1941 strike at the city's steel plant. Unlike, 1919 strike, this one had the support of federal and city officials.

The formation of the United Steelworkers of America (USWA) led the workers from 92 Lackawanna ethnic groups to gain a sense of togetherness and power in the workplace. Italians and other southeast European ethnics joined the Irish as leaders of USWA locals. The unionization of Bethlehem Steel broke both the arbitrary power of the foremen and the plant's ethnic hierarchy, giving white ethnics a better chance at advancing to more skilled and supervisory positions. Soon, Italians became first helpers and melters in the open hearths and general foremen and supervisors in a number of departments. Working men of all ethnic groups no longer had to endure the demeaning conditions that the immigrants had faced in earlier years, and the union's political clout could challenge the strong ties that often developed between steel-plant management and city hall. The meetings of the locals and the associated social and political activities provided a whole new domain of organizational affiliation for Italian Americans. By the mid -1940s, most Italian and other immigrants spoke enough English to function at union meetings. By then, a high percentage of the European ethnics were second-generation men, many veterans of World War II, who were well-versed in how things work in American society.

War production and Lackawanna's bustling steel mills finally ended the devastating economic depression and gave southern and eastern European ethnics greater financial stability. The second generation and emerging third generation now had reason to be more optimistic about their acceptance by mainstream society. During the war, settlement houses throughout the country sponsored by the Presbyterian Church noted the acculturation of young southeast European ethnics. According to one account:

> The second and third generation Italians, Poles, and Czechoslovaks do not stand out as easily identified separate groups in any such manner as did their parents, the first generation 'foreigners'…. Superficially, the Americanization … is thorough and complete. Their speech is … of the American city streets racy with slang and careless of grammar … with not a trace of foreign accent. The dress follows the American pattern. Like other American born youth, their leisure time is largely consumed with the funnies, the pulp magazines, the radio and the movies…. They are rabid sports fans….

The report also points out that those individuals who "have risen in the economic scale … have moved out to more desirable residential sections." After the war, the revived national economy provided jobs that, along with New Deal financial-aid programs, allowed many Italians to afford homes and businesses both inside and outside their traditional ethnic neighborhoods.[106]

Many of the 16 million Americans who had served in the military participated in veterans organizations following the war. Bethlehem Park had sent more than 400 of its sons into the armed forces, and five of the eight neighborhood men who made the supreme sacrifice were Italians. In 1946, the ex-servicemen founded the Bethlehem Park Veterans Association and its women's auxiliary. These organizations were multiethnic, but Italians, the largest ethnic group in Bethlehem Park, comprised a high percentage of their combined membership. The white ethnic memberships of both groups were bound together by neighborhood ties and the recent experience of wartime military service.[107]

Their newly won integration into society had a significant effect on the types of groups Steel City Italians organized and joined. The 12 Italian associations created in Lackawanna from 1942 to 1949 mostly emphasized nonethnic goals, such as American-style sports and social activities. The new groups sponsored by St. Anthony's Church focused on American cultural practices, such as Scouting and other adult and youth social activities encouraged by Reverend Ciolino, the American-born priest who joined the parish in 1946. Many second-generation Italian veterans shunned the Italian American societies and joined nonethnic organizations. Some desired to avoid the stigma of being viewed as too ethnic or old-fashioned, or simply wanted to "fit in" as Americans. They joined the Knights of Columbus, the chamber of commerce, and similar organizations. The GI bill enabled millions of white ethnics to get home mortgages and college degrees through the Veterans Administration. Through both military service and union activities, Lackawanna's Italians had forged common bonds with members of America's other ethnic groups. Their greater economic security and social acceptance meant they could more easily enter mainstream social groups and institutions. Italians continued their advance to the more skilled and professional occupations previously held by old-line ethnic groups. Marie Tarquinio was an employee at the Lackawanna Library by 1941, and James Anzalone, a World War II veteran, was hired as the reference librarian in 1948.[108]

The political gains made by Italians in the 1920s and 1930s continued into the following decades as the ethnic group won important elective and appointive offices. Three Italian Americans held city council seats in the 1950s and two in the 1960s. This success at holding public office helped reinforce a positive Italian American identity as well as integrate the ethnic group into the political and civic structures of the city. In Italian neighborhoods, leaders were able to mobilize voters for candidates who addressed their needs, resulting in a larger number of Italian Americans being elected to office. By the 1930s, the Italians—with their strength centered in the enclaves of Ingham Avenue, Bethlehem Park, and Roland Avenue (the Old Village was razed in the early 1930s)—competed effectively with other ethnic groups. This cohesion weakened after the war, however, as Italians moved to new housing on the city's east side. They became scattered in small pockets away from the pollution and noise of the First Ward with fewer issues to rally people around, although many people still voted for Italian candidates. By 1960, the geographic dispersion of Italians throughout the city and surrounding townships was well under way, in part abetted by the New Deal programs that encouraged mortgage loans in suburban developments and discouraged them in the older neighborhoods where the immigrants had settled. The government wanted to

Construction of Roland Wildcats Hall, 1950, corner of Milnor and Electric avenues.
Photo source: Collection of Frank Chiodo

The Baker Homes under construction. This was the first of three federally financed public-housing projects completed in Lackawanna between 1938 and 1943. A series of buildings that included 271 units, and located in the First Ward, the Baker Homes opened in 1938.
Photo source: Collection of Tony Grasso

The Ridgewood Village was completed in 1943 in eastern Lackawanna, at the corner of Ridge and Abbott roads. Another federal project, the Albright Homes, opened in 1941, in the First Ward, but was torn down three decades later. Photo source: Collection of Joe Milano

disperse these unassimilated "foreign" populations and prevent people of color from taking their place. Often, the original immigrant quarters, such as Lackawanna's Old Village, fell victim to so-called urban renewal.[109]

Throughout the 1940s and 1950s, the younger members of the second generation reached adulthood and married. While the immigrant family was parent-centered, the second-generation family often practiced the child-centered attitudes consistent with those of mainstream American culture. There tended to be a more democratic relationship between husband and wife, although the Italian American husband still maintained greater authority and was found by one study to be a strict disciplinarian. Adult children were usually allowed to choose their own marriage partners. Italian food was prepared, especially holiday delicacies, but the family diet often became similar to that of mainstream Americans. Fewer white ethnics were attracted to foreign-language newspapers and radio programs. Between 1942 and 1948 the number of radio stations in the U.S. doing broadcasts in any foreign language fell from 205 to 126.[110]

Gradually, as Italians dispersed geographically, they affiliated with whatever Catholic Church was nearby, as Reverend Ciolino, who became the pastor of St. Anthony's in the late 1940s, suggested they do. This hastened their religious assimilation, as Italians moved away from the Italian American traditions at St. Anthony's Church and learned that family attendance at services was a mark of respectability in America.[111]

By the latter half of the 1940s and beginning of the 1950s, the Italians, Poles, and other white ethnics were more accepted by society at large, but many retained fresh memories of discrimination and continued to have run-ins with bigots. Their former minority-group status and daily lives in ethnic enclaves had fostered a strong sense of ethnicity and defensiveness that did not vanish, even as they wished simply to be accepted as Americans. Many white ethnics continued to display a defensive pride in their actions, as evidenced by second-generation Italians and their children, who continued to wrestle with the conflicts between their traditional values and those embraced by others in the United States. The religious street processions in Lackawanna had ceased during the 1930s, and the new groups at St. Anthony's Church focused on the involvement of males and females in religious and social activities that seemed foreign to many of the immigrants. Most second- and third-generation Italian Americans gave little credence to the "evil eye" and didn't see any need for the services of a person who administered rituals to remove it. The few Italian societies formed in the 1950s and 1960s, focused on American-style social and recreational activities. Many of the groups founded by immigrants and early societies organized by the second generation declined or folded altogether.

Through the 1950s, Italians continued to rise to higher and better-paid jobs, and many individuals founded business enterprises. Only 12 Italian businesses came into being during the years the United States was involved in World War II, but between 1946 and 1964, more than 240 new enterprises were launched. Food establishments continued to dominate the field, as 23 groceries and 34 restaurants were started. Automobile-related businesses, saloons, and barbershops also showed a sharp increase. In general, the new businesses were larger and catered to the entire Lackawanna community, not just fellow ethnics.

Italian Americans, while no longer encumbered by a minority-group status, still encountered some prejudice and discrimination during this period. A second-generation Italian working at Buffalo Tank in the 1950s was called "dago" by some German American coworkers until he informed them that his wife was of German ancestry. Italians in the political and civic arenas also still encountered some negative attitudes and behavior. Another second-generation Italian who was active in civic groups felt degraded by the way several Irishmen introduced him to others, saying, "he is one of the good Italians," implying that most Italians were not good. Several decades earlier, a number of Roland Avenue Italians had left the Democratic Party and became Republicans after Irish politicos referred to them as "dagos." Frank Chiodo remained in the Democratic party, finding some Irish politicians were strong allies, while others were bigots. Chiodo was campaigning in 1953 for one of the city-wide assessor slots when he was taken by his Irish friend, Mike Dillon, then running for judge, to meet Irish voters in the Second Ward. This upset several of the Irish political bosses, one of whom told Dillon, "If you bring that dago around, you won't get our vote." Both Dillon and Chiodo were defeated in the election. "Joe Amorosi beat me by 25 votes," said Chiodo. "The Irish voters clobbered me; I got 12 votes from the Ridge-South Park area."[112]

Despite lingering stereotypes and occasional challenges from bigots, the city's second- and third-generation Italian Americans again answered the call to bear arms during the Korean conflict, the Vietnam War, and the two Gulf Wars. Unlike World War II, those who served were not questioned about their loyalty, as was apparent in the experience of a Bethlehem Park family. After Lt. Robert DiTommaso's plane went down in Laos in 1966, his mother Mafalda worked for years to locate her son's remains and served as an effective advocate for POW-MIA families and veterans. Though she died in 1991 without learning her son's fate, her family's tragedy highlighted an issue that was deeply felt by many Americans. The public stature of the DiTommaso family symbolized that Italian Americans were well advanced in their assimilation and acceptance by society.[113]

In more recent decades, people have married not only outside their nationality or cultural groups but also outside their religious groups. Sociologist Milton Gordon has stressed that intermarriage is the key to full assimilation, and by the 1950s and 1960s, the intermarriage of various European ethnic groups was in full progress, and marriages between religious groups was commencing. The late 1960s brought changes in America that directly affected Italians and other white ethnics. Between 1900 and the 1960s, Anglo-conformity demanded the demise of ethnic roots, but new developments fostered an acceptance of ethnic identities.

Ethnic Revival and into the 21st Century: 1965 – 2009

In the late 1960s and 1970s, an increased ethnic consciousness sprang up among Americans with roots in southern and eastern Europe. Dubbed the "white ethnics," the category included many Catholics, including Italians, Slavs, Greeks, and also Irish and Germans, living in urban areas. In part, they were reacting to the civil rights movement with both fear and admiration. On the one hand, the white ethnics feared

Anthony Sperduto (center) at the time of his graduation from Lackawanna High School in 1944. Pictured with him are his parents Margaret and Nick Sperduto. Anthony was one of the fortunate graduates whose parents, successful businesspeople, could afford to send them to college.
Photo source: Mary Sperduto-Cuomo

that the demands of racial minorities to be included in mainstream society would be at their expense. But they also wanted to imitate the African American display of ethnic pride and assertive demands for recognition and inclusion in the higher echelons of society. Lastly, some white ethnics felt renewed resentment toward the WASPs who had dominated America's social institutions for 200 years.

Italians and other southeast European ethnic groups had only recently gained significant entry into the seats of political and economic power at the local and state levels, and were still in the process of expanding these inroads. For example, Frank Sedita, the first Italian mayor of Buffalo, was elected in 1957. Suddenly, the civil-rights movement led blacks, Latinos, and other minorities to demand entry into these positions, which had been denied them throughout American history, and these demands were receiving support from federal officials. The white ethnics felt the rules of the game had been changed and that they themselves were being denied some of the rewards they had long worked toward. Often, it was Italians and Slavs who lived adjacent to black and Latino neighborhoods and whose children attended the same schools. This provided ample opportunity for confrontation and conflict, and the new ethnicity was seen by some as a form of white backlash.[114]

The white ethnics had issues with the WASPs, who had long controlled America's halls of power and prestige. For many decades, the White Anglo-Saxon Protestant group had locked out southeast Europeans, as well as northwest European Catholics and Jews, labeling their religions and cultures inferior. In the 1960s, many upper-class WASPs and some academics launched new stereotypes denigrating the working-class white ethnics and depicting them as the worst racists in America. This "respectable bigotry" was expressed via Polish jokes, images of inarticulate blue-collar hardhats, and portrayals of Italians as political buffoons or cunning gangsters. In truth, the white ethnics were no more racist than other whites, and especially the WASPs, who controlled the major institutions that practiced racism. The media was flooded with unflattering images of working-class ethnic hardhats. Attending college in Buffalo in the late 1960s, this author heard a professor and other students describe Lackawanna's working-class ethnics as either knife-carrying, illiterate, or lacking intelligence. One Italian American student at Lackawanna's Baker-Victory Academy felt harassed by classmates who equated organized crime with Italians. There was also racial tension in the Steel City as Polish, Italian, and Irish officials, the voice of the local white power structure, reacted to the demands of blacks and Latinos for equality in housing, jobs, and education (see Chapter 4).[115]

White ethnics admired and wanted to imitate one aspect in particular of the black-power movement: The southeast Europeans were anxious to show pride in the ancestral cultures that American society had forced them to downplay in earlier decades. It had not been considered appropriate for white ethnics to celebrate their heritage except on socially approved occasions, such as St. Patrick's Day or Columbus Day. But when African Americans proclaimed that "black is beautiful" and constantly celebrated their culture, they legitimized ethnic self-consciousness. So, as Andrew Greeley notes, white ethnics said of African Americans, "If they can be proud of their heritage every day of the year and be explicitly proud of it, why can't we?" The white ethnics started demanding more access to the higher echelons of society. Native Americans, Latinos, and Asians also followed the lead of blacks by launching their own civil-rights movements.[116]

Other, earlier factors had been leading up to the white ethnic revival. Congress had passed the McCarran-Walter Act in 1952, which upheld the national origins and quota system, stating that 85 percent of all immigrants must come from northwest Europe. President Truman vetoed the bill, objecting to the quota system and stating that "it discriminates, deliberately and intentionally, against many of the people of the world. The purpose behind it was to cut down and virtually eliminate immigration to this country from Southern and Eastern Europe.... " Congress overrode Truman's veto, and not until passage of the Immigration Act of 1965 was the bigoted national origins and quota system abolished so that each country had an equal share of visas. The act represented full acceptance of Italians, Jews, and other southeast European immigrants as equals. According to historian Aristide Zolberg, it signaled that "the United States definitely abandoned attempts to constitute itself into a 'WASP' nation and redefined itself as a Pan-European one, pledging allegiance to the flag under a deity that was Catholic and Jewish as well as Protestant." Five years earlier, the election of John F. Kennedy as U.S. president marked the breaking of an old religious barrier that was a meaningful event to the white ethnics, the majority of whom were Catholic. The Irish had made great progress in the United States and finally, with the support of millions of southeast European Catholics, gave the country its first Catholic president in 1960.[117]

By the 1960s, the children and grandchildren of southeast European immigrants were more assimilated, more accepted by American society, and had achieved economic and occupational stability. Italians could celebrate their roots because their ethnicity was no longer seen as a problem by other Americans. It was safe to display ethnic pride that had been denied to their immigrant forebears in the early years of the twentieth century. Following the lead of African Americans, many Italians and other European Americans reaffirmed traditional customs. The ethnic revival was in part a search for stability and roots in reaction to a number of

Sign on the house of Louie and Loretta Petrucci, South Drive, 2005. The sign, which in Italian says "the home of Louis Petrucci," is one symbol of ethnic pride in the Steel City. Photo source: The author

forces in American society. A modern technological society imposes many different and complex roles on individuals forcing them into functional and atomized relationships that do not provide recognition or a stable identity. The celebration of ethnicity answered the need for a collective identity that offered stability. The ethnic revival was also a response to the social unrest caused by the unpopularity of the Viet Nam War and the increasingly negative political landscape that culminated in Watergate. At times it was also a reaction to other new social movements: the youth counterculture, women's liberation, gay rights, and environmentalism.[118]

Italians who had worked hard to become assimilated and respected still had to contend with a reinvigorated gangster stereotype in the 1950s and 1960s. Television stations broadcast the hearings of the Special Committee to Investigate Crime in Interstate Commerce in 1950 and 1951. Led by Senator Estes Kefauver, the hearings offered millions of TV viewers sensational testimony portraying Italians as the masters of criminal syndicates throughout the United States. *The Untouchables* series, which focused on Al Capone and other Chicago gangsters of the 1920s, began a long run on TV in 1959 that continues (via reruns) to this day. Starting in 1958, another senate committee, this one chaired by Senator John McClellan, held televised hearings that in 1963 featured Joe Valachi, a low-ranking member of an Italian syndicate in New York City. His sensationalized comments later appeared in book form as *The Valachi Papers*, which hyped the term *La Cosa Nostra* (translation: our thing). After winning the 1964 election, President Lyndon Johnson created a presidential crime commission, whose published report further spread the image of a national criminal conspiracy operated by Italian Americans with ties to gangsters in southern Italy.[119]

Rallying against the Mafia stereotype helped to reaffirm a sense of identity and purpose among Italian Americans. A number of antidefamation groups sprang up around the country. The Order Sons of Italian in America (OSIA), the largest Italian organization in the United States, launched its Commission on Social Justice in 1953, and it is still active today. The Italian American Civil Rights League, although tinged by the involvement of organized-crime figures, helped convince advertisers to drop wording that offended Italians, such as Alka Seltzer's "that's a spicy meatball," and also persuaded the FBI and the *New York Times* to cease using the terms "Mafia" and "La Cosa Nostra" to refer to organized crime.[120]

Italian Americans also rallied around other causes that helped build ethnic group cohesion and identity. The American Committee on Italian Migration, formed in 1951, first lobbied to end the infamous national-origins quota system and pressed for passage of the 1965 act that finally accomplished that goal. The group, with chapters across the nation, continues to work for fairness in immigration policy. Further, Italians in the United States have been sending aid to Italy following natural disasters and war since at least 1905. A more affluent Italian American community continued this tradition after World War II, as national and local Italian American groups continue to send aid to Italy following earthquakes, floods, and volcanic eruptions.[121]

Over the past four decades, the founding of a series of national organizations has highlighted the advancement of Italian Americans in many realms of society. The National Italian American Foundation, the Conference of Presidents of Major Italian American Organizations, and the Italian American Congressional Delegation were formed in the 1970s to pursue political, cultural, and educational goals. The American Justinian Society, organized in 1966 and composed of Italian American judges, functions to improve the administration of justice and expand knowledge of all aspects of law. That same year saw the founding of the American Italian Historical Association, a forum for scholarship on the Italian American experience. The National Organization of Italian American Women supports the advancement of Italian American women and the preservation of their history and accomplishments. A series of local Italian historical and cultural organizations has sprung up throughout the country, and a number of them sponsor festivals, such as *Festa Italiana* in Milwaukee. In Buffalo, the Association of Italian American Women was founded in 1993. The Federation of Italian American Societies of Western New York celebrated its hundred-year anniversary in Buffalo in 2007 with "*La Terra Promessa*—The Promised Land," including a musical show, a documentary film, and a book of family vignettes. During the 1970s, several Italian American magazines were published, and more than a dozen television shows featured Italian characters.[122]

The federal government recognized ethnicity as a positive force in American society with the passage of the Ethnic Heritage Studies

Act of 1972. Italian American congressmen sponsored a law, "The Wartime Violation of Italian American Civil Liberties Act," which was passed in 2000 and resulted in a report on this topic and the government's formal acknowledgement that the violation of civil rights had occurred on the West Coast during World War II. Italians and other southeast European ethnics are now presented more positively in history books, finally displacing the image of "immigrant hordes" and inferior cultures. But the Mafia stereotype has continued beyond The *Godfather* book and movies in more recent publications about Italian gangsters and *The Sopranos* series on cable TV.[123]

The ethnic revival and racial antagonisms in Lackawanna became less violent and overt in the late 1970s. And while white ethnics celebrated their roots, they also became more assimilated through intermarriage. Data from the 1980 U.S. Census revealed that throughout the United States 59% of Italians and 52% of Poles age 60 or older had married within their ethnic group, but for those under the age of 30, the figures were 25% for Italians and 18% for Poles. The 1980 census counted 12 million Italians in the United States, 44% of whom had mixed ancestry, which was the same in Lackawanna, where 1,437 of the 3,291 Italians had mixed ethnic roots. Studies, such as James Crispino's on Bridgeport found that Italians in the late 1970s displayed a high degree of assimilation.[124]

Indeed, the trend to marry outside of one's ethnic group in Lackawanna accelerated in the late twentieth century. Seventy-one percent of the grandchildren of Italian immigrants married non – Italians, and for third-generation individuals of mixed Italian ancestry, the percentage was even higher. Throughout the United States, the percentage of full-blooded Italians marrying Italian spouses fell from 42% in the 1940s to 19% in the 1980s. The triple melting pot phenomenon began to change nationwide as people married not only outside their nationality group but also outside of their religion. Catholic and Jewish Americans have increasingly married spouses of other faiths. Between 1960 and the mid-1980s, the proportion of Jews marrying non – Jews in the United States had increased from a very small number to an estimated 25 to 35%. The interfaith marriage rate of Catholics grew even more quickly, and by the late 1970s, about half of young Catholics married outside their faith—mostly Protestants, who comprise about two-thirds of the American population. For Italian Americans in the late 1970s, overall, 67% were married to Catholics, 29% to Protestants, and four percent to people of other religions. However, for younger Italians, those born after World War II, 49% had Catholic spouses and 49% Protestant spouses. Little data are available on interreligious marriages among Italians with roots in Lackawanna, but since the city and surrounding area have been heavily Catholic until recent decades, it is assumed that many post – World War II marriages have been to Catholic spouses.[125]

On the national level, Italians made significant strides in entering the uppermost strata of social institutions, such as corporate boards, following World War II. For example, second-generation Italians began to rise into the managerial ranks of corporations and banks. By the early 1950s, Joseph Martino had become president of National Lead, producer of Dutch Boy paint. In 1954, Frank Petito, a Princeton graduate and the son of an illiterate immigrant, became the first Italian American partner in the investment banking house of Morgan Stanley; he was named chairman in 1973. These men were exceptions to the rule, as studies done in the 1970s demonstrate that Italians, Poles, and Jews were notably absent in many corporate boardrooms. Sociologist William Domhoff noted that "any male in America" can rise in corporate and professional ranks, but "those that rise do so by becoming less and less Jewish or less and less Catholic or less and less something else."[126]

Since the 1970s, according to Robert Christopher, southeast Europeans have been "crashing the gates" of WASP-controlled corporations. This new era, says Christopher, was launched by two significant events: the election of Irving Shapiro, a Jew, as chairman of E. I. duPont de Nemours & Company in 1973, and the appointment of Lee Iacocca, an Italian, as chairman of Chrysler Corporation in 1979. More people of Italian descent became corporate executives in the 1980s, including Paul Rizzo at IBM, Samuel Fortunato at Metropolitan Property and Liability Insurance, and J. R. Samartini at Whirlpool. Capitalist Jeno Paulucci, after a mediocre start selling Italian American food specialties, did extremely well producing Chinese food. By 2008, five percent of the chief executive officers of the Fortune 500 companies were Italian Americans.[127]

As for holding high political office, in 1950, John Pastore of Rhode Island became the first Italian American to hold a U.S. senate seat. Anthony Celebrezze's appointment to President Kennedy's cabinet in 1962 marked another first for Italians, and he was followed by Joseph Califano, Jack Valenti, John Volpe, and Frank Carlucci. Leon Pannetta was the chief of staff for President Bill Clinton. Italian governors were a rarity until 1945, when John Pastore occupied that office in Rhode Island. Four Italians captured governors' seats in the 1950s, and 10 more followed in the last four decades of the twentieth century. One of them, Mario Cuomo of New York, was considered a likely presidential candidate in the 1980s, and Geraldine Ferraro was the vice-presidential candidate on the Democratic ticket in 1984. Mirroring the national trend, a series of Italians have been Lackawanna city councilmen in the past half-century. During the Watergate investigation that eventually led to President Nixon's resignation, two Italian Americans won notoriety and praise for their performances. Congressman Peter Rodino chaired the Judiciary Committee that voted to impeach the president. John Sirica, chief judge of the federal court in the District of Columbia that dealt with many aspects of the Watergate case, was named Man of the Year in 1974 by *Time* magazine for his work.[128]

The ethnic revival of the last four decades was present in Lackawanna as Italians refocused on customs of the immigrants of the early twentieth century. The men's bocce league expanded and was joined by a women's league in the 1970s. The memberships of the Lake Erie Italian Club, its ladies auxiliary, and several other established Italian groups increased. On the national level, prominent Italian Americans made public displays of their ethnic roots. Auto executive Lee Iacocca was a leader of the Statue of Liberty -Ellis Island Commission and spoke of his parents' immigration from southern Italy. According to Matthew Frye Jacobson, this represented "a seismic shift from the popular Pilgrim-and-Founding-Fathers national legend to the more recent conception of 'a nation of immigrants.'" In the late twentieth century, America finally celebrated the ethnic cultures of all European Americans. The year 1965 not only witnessed the elimination of the national origins and quota system that governed immigration but also the designation of Ellis Island as an immigration museum. The restrictionist mentality of 60 years that had viewed WASPs as the only true Americans finally gave way to full recognition of Irish and other northwest European Catholics and the southeast European ethnics. Italians, Jews, Poles and others could now claim to be true Americans as descendants of Ellis Island immigrants who were a cornerstone of American society. Politicians and CEOs now present their ethnic roots as credentials of true Americanism, and television shows and movies tend to romanticize the immigrant ghettos that were so loudly condemned by nativists in the early 1900s. Even the spate of new Mafia movies, starting with *The Godfather* in 1972, often depicted aspects of immigrant life in Little Italy that went beyond the mobster stereotypes. In essence, the white ethnics had expanded the definition of American identity to include non – WASP European roots and institutions within the "nation of immigrants." This image of the ideal American including all those with roots in Europe grew during the 1970s and 1980s. Now that the humble Ellis Island immigrants stand alongside the WASP founders of the nation in America's self-image, Italians and other white ethnics are more frequently included at the highest levels of the mainstream culture. There is rarely overt, significant value and power conflict between Italians and the WASPs.[129]

The presence of about 100 immigrants who arrived in Lackawanna between 1935 and 1945, and the 90 who came after World War II, enhanced the ethnic revival and extended its duration. Most of the postwar immigrants arrived between 1945 and 1965, and their emigration was basically a continuation

---

FIGURE 3.15

The Decline of Lackawanna's Little Italys: 1960 – 2006

Number of Italian Households*

	1960	1973	1990	2006
In Little Italys				
Bethlehem Park	156	136	126	58
Ingham Ave. Area	131	78	26	14
Roland Ave. Area	81	69	72	55
Subtotals	368 (50%)	283 (31%)	224 (26%)	127 (19%)
In Other Neighborhoods				
	369 (50%)	618 (69%)	651 (74%)	533 (81%)
Grand Totals	**737**	**901**	**875**	**660**

Sources: *Lackawanna City Directory,* 1960; *Buffalo Southeast Suburban Directory,* 1973; *Buffalo City Directory, Including Lackawanna,* 1990; *Buffalo South Suburban Directory,* 2006. The Ingham Avenue area includes Ingham, Lehigh, and Holland avenues, and the east-west sidestreets north of Wilson, between Holland and Lehigh, and the sidestreets from Wilson to Dona Street running between Ingham and Wilmuth avenues. The Roland Avenue area includes the area bounded by Warsaw Street on the north, South Park Avenue on the east, Cleveland Avenue on the south, and the railroad tracks on the west. The number of Italian households is approximate, based on Italian surnames and known cases of name changes and Italian women married to men with non – Italian surnames.

* Does not include Italian youth living in Our Lady of Victory institutions.

---

of the chain migration begun earlier in the century, with people from specific towns seeking relatives and friends already in the city. Due to this relatively recent immigration, the 1990 U.S. Census found that 290 Lackawannans over the age of five spoke Italian, the fourth most commonly used language after Polish, Spanish, and Arabic at home. These newer immigrants infused new energy into the maintenance of the Italian language and customs in the city. A number of them settled in the old Italian neighborhoods and joined ethnic organizations. Active in the Lake Erie Italian Club and its women's auxiliary, they were the core members of the Italian choir and two dance groups formed in the 1980s by the two older societies. These groups participated in Lackawanna's 1984 Diamond Jubilee festivities and other events that celebrated the ethnic traditions of western New York. Also, since the 1980s, a group of postwar immigrants from Cantalupo, Molise, have held a small annual *festa* in honor of Sant'Anna, their patron saint.[130]

The second generation wanted their children to succeed, though this often meant losing many of the vestiges of their Italian origins. Yet they have nevertheless reminded the third

FIGURE 3.16

VISITS TO *PAESANI* IN THE UNITED STATES AND ITALY

After settling in Lackawanna, Italians soon began visiting relatives and *paesani* in other parts of the United States. Patsy Yoviene traveled to Galeton, Pennsylvania, in 1927 to spend several weeks with relatives, and when James Pagona came from Galeton on a visit, Josephine Yoviene had a supper party for him. The following year, Yoviene and her daughter Gladys left for New York City to sail to Europe to spend several months in Italy, France, Switzerland, and England. After Josephine became a widow in 1919, she opened a grocery store with the help of several of her adult children. Her success at business and her daughter's career as a nurse provided the funds that allowed them the luxury of going to Italy to visit, as opposed to most Italians at that time who returned to their hometowns only to marry or make arrangements to bring their families to the United States.

During World War II and just afterwards, many Italian American GIs in the European theater made contact with relatives in Italy. While serving in the U.S. Army in 1945, Matt Suffoletto went to his father's hometown of Pettorano sul Gizio and visited his Uncle Luigi. Matt's father, Vincenzo Suffoletto, made the last of several voyages from Italy in 1913, and Matt became the first member of Vincenzo's family whom Luigi met. In 1952, Luigi immigrated to the United States and for the first time in 42 years saw his brother Vincenzo, who hosted a celebration of their reunion at his home on Dona Street. Luigi settled permanently in Buffalo.

After World War II, as Italian Americans achieved greater financial stability and more lucrative careers, more were able to visit the "old country." In 1947, Rae Spinelli was working in a beauty salon some 12 years after emigrating from Ceccano, Lazio, to the United States. That summer, she sailed on the *SS Saturnia* for a three-month stay in Italy to visit her grandmother. She traveled to Naples and Venice, and in Rome, she was present for the Eucharistic Congress. After her voyage back from Italy, she was met in New York City by Ann Pacillo, and they toured the city before returning to Lackawanna. A few years later, another native of Ceccano, Colomba Scarsella, joined a tour group from Buffalo that flew to Italy. She had first immigrated to Lackawanna 20 years earlier, and this would be her only return visit to her native land.

Armando Leonetti emigrated from Pedace, Calabria, to Lackawanna in 1930. He made his first return trip to Italy in 1954, accompanied by his wife Mary. The couple and their children made many more trips in the following years. Leonetti's relatives enjoyed these visits so much that they even constructed an addition to their home to accommodate the visitors from Lackawanna.

Dominic Sperduti returned to Giuliano di Roma in 1966 to visit his brothers Federico and Giovanni and their families. He hadn't seen his siblings for 40 years. In Giuliano, he met friends and relatives from Lackawanna, Buffalo, and Niagara Falls. His son Joseph accompanied him but returned to Lackawanna after a month, while the elder Sperduti remained five months. A year earlier, Sperduti's brother Armando had visited Giuliano with his daughter Josephine and her husband. When Sperduti returned to Bethlehem Park, he was greeted with a welcome home party by his children, their families, and Armando.

Over the last 40 years, many Lackawanna Italians have reconnected with relatives in hometowns. Many of the travelers are second-, third-, and fourth-generation Italian Americans who had no previous contacts with their Italian kin other than an occasional letter or postcard. Chet Catuzza has visited his father's hometown of Giuliano di Roma a number of times. John and Mary Tiberio also visit Giuliano, where Mary's parents were born, and Ceccano, the hometown of the Tiberios. This author made two trips to Italy, visiting relatives in Rome and Marano Principato, Calabria. Several of the relatives visited have since made trips to western New York. All the Italian Americans mentioned here reported that they were warmly received by their relatives in Italy.

Sources: *Lackawanna News*, 9/29/27, 5/24/28, 6/21/28; *Lackawanna Leader*, 8/7/47, 11/14/47, 4/24/52, 11/10/66. Interviews with Anne Scarsella-Antos, December 26, 1995; Mary Leonetti, December 28, 1994; Chet Catuzza, September 8, 1994; John Tiberio, April 13, 1998.

Relatives from Italy visit the Andreozzi family on Berg Road in 1981. In the lower row, from left, are Stefano Catalucci (from Rome), Jeanette Andreozzi-Brooks, Rosalind Andreozzi-Case, and Jo Andreozzi. Standing are Adeline, Phil Jr, Luigi (from Rome), Phil Sr., Dolly Andreozzi-Ceccarelli, S. John Ceccarelli, John, Nick, and Mike. Photo source: The author

generation of family roots in Little Italy and noted the accomplishments of nationally recognized Italian Americans. Members of the third and fourth generation, while often distant from the immigrant neighborhoods and ethnic institutions, sometimes enact "symbolic ethnicity" by practicing selective aspects of their ethnic heritage, such as preparing holiday foods, visiting the old Italian neighborhood to attend mass and renew acquaintances, or wearing a *cornu* (horn) to ward off the evil eye. These things are sometimes a matter of personal style and not necessarily rooted in passionately held beliefs. Some later-generation Italian Americans have visited Italy and reestablished ties with kin in the hometowns of their immigrant forebears. These trips and reciprocal visits by relatives from Italy have served as tangible links to the old country and encouraged Italian Americans to rediscover the language and customs of the immigrants.[131]

The Italian family has adapted to American ways, but some still maintain aspects of the group orientation of the early immigrants. Many people interviewed spoke of living close to family members and visiting them often. Family picnics are yearly events for a number of extended family networks in Lackawanna. The St. Anthony's Church picnic held in the 1980s and 1990s was designated with the Italian equivalent, *scampagnata*, and while Italian is rarely spoken today at St. Anthony's, statues of San Biagio and San Rocco still remain on the altar.[132]

Over the past 40 years Lackawanna Italians have accomplished much of the assimilation process. They became residentially scattered by moving out of the Bethlehem Park, Ingham Avenue, and Roland Avenue Italian enclaves, where the number of Italian households fell from 368 in 1960 to 127 in 2006 (see Figures 3.11 and 3.15), and settled in the eastern section of the city or in nearby suburbs. Italians joined the informal groups of the general community and became well established in the formal social institutions. Since 1965, they created another 162 businesses, 44 of them Italian restaurants, which marked this industry as an economic niche for Italians. Other than the ongoing stereotype about organized crime, there are few instances of prejudice, and Italians are patriotic and do not contest the basic beliefs of the dominant culture. Many individuals of the second and third generation describe themselves as Italian Americans or Americans of Italian background, a notion reinforced by a handful of Italian organizations, but this does not detract from their stronger identity as Americans. The aging postwar immigrants maintain an attachment to the Italian language and culture, but their children, who as youth were involved in Italian singing and dancing groups, have often lost interest in ethnic customs and organizations as adults. Many of the third- and fourth-generation view their Italian roots as a historical footnote, and the significant amount of intermarriage has further blurred their sense of ethnic identity. This has led to what sociologist Richard Alba describes as the "twilight" or fading of Italian American ethnicity. Along with other white ethnic groups, Italians continue to merge into the broad grouping of Americans of European ancestry that has been shaped by a common culture. For those of us of Italian ancestry, knowing our history can help us make sense of the current dynamics of nationality, religion, and race in the United States, and provide some measure of guidance as our country steps into an uncertain future.[133]

This chapter has offered a general outline of the Lackawanna Italian American experience over the past 109 years. The following chapter also examines the past century, but focuses on the assimilation processes that evolved in the Italian community, compares them with the experiences of some of the city's other ethnic groups, and discusses the ongoing stereotype that equates Italians with organized crime.

Form 2603 A   (see other side)

CHAPTER 4

ETHNICITY AND ASSIMILATION

The Italian American experience of the past 100 years has been one of upheaval, changes, and eventually, significant assimilation into American society. By the year 2000, there were nearly 16 million Italian Americans, approximately half of them of full Italian ancestry.

Italian immigrants and their children endured painful transitions when trying to fit into American society in the first half of the twentieth century. During the last five decades, the second-generation, or American-born, offspring of the immigrants, and the third- and fourth-generations have entered into the final stages of the movement to become fully accepted as Americans. This process, which sociologists call assimilation, has been marked by a series of changes at key moments in American and world history. We will examine the processes of assimilation experienced by Lackawanna's Italians within the wider context of Italian American history, as outlined in the previous chapter. This chapter also discusses the ways our society has treated various ethnic groups, how the Italian experience compares to those of other ethnic groups in Lackawanna, and the ongoing stereotype linking Italians with organized crime.

The ethnic identity of Italians in the United States has changed dramatically during the past century, in a pattern common among immigrant groups. Immigrants who first identified with towns, provinces, and regions in Italy eventually began to see themselves as Italian Americans. While specific national and international events affect how ethnic and minority

< Citizenship certificates of Alfredo and Augusta Anticoli, 1939 and 1938. By the late 1930s the majority of Italian immigrants in Lackawanna had become naturalized citizens.
Photo source: Augusta Anticoli and Rose Anticoli-Wagner

groups are treated, in general, American society has expected each group to shed its ancestral ethnic identity and accept the dominant WASP culture. The only expressions of ethnicity tolerated are those that do not challenge core societal values or undermine the ethnic group's basic American identity. By the mid-twentieth century, people of various white ethnic groups were merging into America's Triple Melting Pot, as people of different nationalities intermarried within the boundaries of their religions—Protestant, Catholic, and Jewish. By the 1980s, even religious lines became less rigid, and racial boundaries had weakened. We now have a Quintuple Melting Pot, in which various nationality, cultural, and religious groups are coalescing into five racial groups: European Americans, Native Americans, African Americans, Latino Americans, and Asian Americans. With the advent of the fourth and later generations, Italians, many of whom are of mixed ethnic background, are now fully assimilated into the European American mainstream culture.[1]

Assimilation in America

Assimilation is the process by which different ethnic groups merge into a unified society, resulting in the sharp reduction or elimination of ethnic differences. Every ethnic group has a common set of cultural traits or guidelines for living in the world. The resulting sense of community, or "we-ness," among an ethnic group's members is based on a common heritage,

FIGURE 4.1
SOME DEFINITIONS FOR ETHNIC RELATIONS

Minority Group: a group defined by the dominant society as different because of physical or cultural traits. All people within the group endure systematic prejudice and discrimination regardless of personal traits or behavior—so individuals cannot voluntarily leave their minority status. A majority or dominant group has superior power, rights, and advantages but need not have greater numbers than a minority group. This study focuses on nationality, religious, and racial minorities, but gender, age, sexual orientation, mental illness, and physical handicap can also define a minority group.

Mainstream Society: the core institutions, organizations, beliefs, rules, and practices established by the dominant ethnic group, such as the WASPs in the United States. Immigrant groups are expected to adopt these core cultural values, which often weakens or undermines their own ethnic identities.

Culture: the values, attitudes, beliefs, customs, and habits shared by members of a society. A subculture is a group that shares in the overall culture of a society while retaining its own distinctive traditions and lifestyle.

Ethnic Group: a group defined by nationality, culture, religion, or race, or any combination of these. There is a bewildering array of formal and informal definitions of all these terms. The three main types of ethnic groups are different and defined as follows. A *nationality* group is usually defined by itself as socially different on the basis of shared kinship,

heritage, and culture. Also, a nationality group may or may not be the dominant political power in its original homeland, and it may or may not be defined by a more powerful group that sees itself as superior. A *religious* group is self-defined based on one of the most important aspects of culture—a belief system, that can also be held by other groups. Both nationality and religion focus on "who we are." *Race* is a classification of people based on genetics and biological traits, such as skin color. It usually is defined by a more powerful group that desires to separate itself from, and portray itself as superior to, others who are less powerful. Race focuses on "who they are and how they are fundamentally different from us." A racial group, such as African Americans, can eventually define its own identity and culture. Over the past 400 years, scholars around the world have defined anywhere from three to 63 races.

Generations: immigration and assimilation often focus on generational factors. The following terms are used in this study. *First generation*: the immigrants. *Second generation*: the American-born children of the immigrants. *Third generation*: the grandchildren of the immigrants, who are followed by the fourth, fifth, and sixth generations. Most European immigrant groups became well assimilated by the third generation. For young children who immigrate prior to age 10, the term *1.5 generation* is used to describe their unique situation.

Ethnocentrism: the belief that one's own ethnic group and way of doing things

are normal and superior to the ways of other ethnic groups.

Stereotype: created when a dominant group selects a few distinctive traits of an ethnic group and exaggerates these to construct a "shorthand depiction" of the group; for example, "Italians are gangsters." These depictions, which can be negative or positive, are "overly simplistic and exaggerated beliefs about a group, generally acquired second hand and resistant to change." The opposite of a stereotype is an accurate generalization about an ethnic group based on facts.

Prejudice: negative prejudgment of an individual on the basis of a stereotype and without first getting to know the person.

Discrimination: negative actions carried out by individuals, small groups, or institutions of the dominant group against a minority group. One example is a real estate company's deliberate practice of steering minority groups into specific neighborhoods. *Indirect institutional discrimination* refers to practices that disadvantage minority groups even though the negative effects were not intended. For example, direct intentional discrimination in the education and training of minority groups has frequently handicapped the groups attempts to compete with dominant group members in the employment sphere, where guidelines for hiring and promotion are often based on educational requirements that were never intended to treat people in an unequal manner.

and one's ethnicity is usually acquired at birth. All aspects of America cultural traits are rooted in traditions specific to certain ethnic groups, so everything is really "ethnic." But the dominant WASP—white, Anglo–Saxon, Protestant—culture was seen as the norm until the 1960s. As mentioned above, the basic WASP traits that have grounded U.S. culture are the English language, the Judeo-Christian religion and ethics, democratic principles, and the capitalist economic system.[2]

American society has been dominated by the English ever since the early European settlers arrived on the Atlantic coast and their descendants established the United States as a country in the late 1700s. The English, who along with the Scots made

Bigotry: intolerant devotion to a particular belief, opinion, or practice. It includes prejudice and discrimination against a specific nationality, cultural, religious, or racial group. A bigot is a person who engages in this behavior.

Institution: a formal system of values and procedures to meet a basic social need. Examples: (1) the family is the institution that provides for emotional needs, sex and reproduction, and child-rearing; (2) the economy is the overall institution for producing and distributing needed goods and services, and includes smaller institutions such as corporations, factories, and banks.

Social Class: a way to designate people's place in the hierarchy or pecking order of a society. It is usually based on income, amount of property, degree of power, status, and lifestyle (see Figure 4.14).

Caste System: an ethnic-stratification system, often becoming rigid and static, in which social mobility is extremely limited by law and custom. Blacks, Native Americans, Asians, and Latinos have experienced caste in various degrees in the United States, especially prior to 1950, in smaller institutions, such as corporations, factories, and banks.

Sources of definitions: **Minority:** Joe R. Feagin, *Racial and Ethnic Relations, 2nd edition,* 1984, pp. 10–11; Martin N. Marger, *Race and Ethnic Relations: American and Global Perspectives,* 1985, p. 27; Vincent N. Parrillo, *Strangers to These Shores: Race and Ethnic Relations in The United States, 5th edition,* 1997, p. 22. **Mainstream:** Richard Alba & Victor Nee, *Remaking the American Mainstream: Assimilation and Contemporary Immigration,* 2003, p. 12. **Culture:** Parrillo, pp. 548, 552. **Ethnic group:** Werner Sollors, *Beyond Ethnicity: Consent and Descent in American Culture,* 1986, p. 39; Milton M. Gordon, *Assimilation in American Life: The Role of Race, Religion, and National Origins,* 1964, p. 27; Stephen Cornell & Douglas Hartmann, *Ethnicity and Race: Making Identities in a Changing World,* 2nd edition, 2007, p. 36; The term "ethnic" was coined in the 1940s to designate European Americans who were not WASPs. **Race:** Marger, pp. 11–12; Feagin, p. 5; Cornell & Hartmann, pp. 16–17, 22, 36. **Racism:** Marger, p. 16; Feagin, p. 5. **Ethnocentrism:** Cornell & Hartmann, p. 32; Stereotype: Marger, pp. 46–47; **Prejudice:** Feagin, p. 11. **Discrimination:** Marger, pp. 54–55. **Bigotry:** *The American College Dictionary,* 1962, p. 120. **Institution:** Charles H. Anderson, *Toward A New Sociology: A Critical View,* 1971, p. 41; Paul Kaplan & Clovis Shepard, *Doing Sociology: A Sociological Experience in the Classroom,* 1973, p. 149. **Social class:** Parrillo, p. 42. **Caste system:** Marger, p. 37.

up 69% of America's white population in 1790, basically set the tone for the national institutions of the United States. At that time, being an American meant to be white, Anglo–Saxon, Protestant, and free. The one exception was a small Catholic settlement in Maryland. Natives of the British Isles and other white, Protestant groups, such as non–Catholic Irish, Canadians, and Germans, as well as the Dutch and Scandinavians, gradually coalesced into a more broadly defined WASP identity by the late 1800s. By 1920, over 41% of white Americans were of English, Scottish, or Welsh ancestry, followed by German ancestry (at least half of German immigrants were Protestant). This block of northwest European ethnic groups constituted the mainstream culture and dominated American society until the late twentieth century. WASPs set the terms for assimilation by regulating the flow of immigrants into the United States and demanding that newcomers accept their basic values.[3]

Any ethnic group is capable of being ethnocentric—that is, displaying the tendency to judge other groups by the standards of one's own group and to feel superior to others (see Figure 4.1 for definitions of terms used in this section). Feeling superior often leads to prejudice against individuals on the basis of their group membership, and prejudice is based on a stereotype, or distorted image of an ethnic group. This leads to negative behavior, or acts of discrimination, toward the group. "Members of minority groups," states sociologist Martin Marger, "occupy poorer jobs, earn less income, live in less desirable areas, receive an inferior education, exercise less political power, and are subjected to various social indignities." On the other hand, members of the dominant, or majority, group in a multiethnic society, such as the WASPs in the United States, "own a greater share of the society's wealth, earn more income, acquire more and better education, work at higher ranking and more prestigious occupations, and generally attain more of the society's valued resources." In the United States, the ethnocentricity of WASPs and their traditional domination of the seats of power have led to prejudice and discrimination against non – WASPs.[4]

Ethnic groups that deviated from mainstream culture were called foreign, greenhorns, or "hyphenate Americans" 100 years ago. To be so labeled in America meant that the particular group was a "problem," or "un – American" and a threat. Many ethnic groups have felt the painful stings of prejudice and discrimination. The experience of Italians and other southeast European immigrants will be our immediate focus, then later in this chapter, we will examine how the situation of European Americans has been significantly different from that of people of color in the United States. Virtually all nationality, religious, and racial groups have encountered the trials of assimilation. There have been three major theories of assimilation that have been applied to immigrants arriving in America—the melting pot, cultural pluralism, and Anglo-conformity. The melting pot concept holds that all the various ethnic groups, or at least those from Europe, will combine into a new and unique culture that includes elements from each group. Cultural pluralism calls for a multiethnic society with a common language and economic and political structure. Within this structure, a variety of ethnic groups function as equals, each maintaining its own cultural practices. The third theory, Anglo-conformity, demands that each new immigrant group quickly shed its unique culture and take on the ways of the core WASP culture. The melting pot and cultural pluralism are idealistic concepts that stress equality and democracy, but the Anglo-conformity model best describes the reality experienced by Italians and other immigrants. It is, writes Martin Marger, the "prevalent ethnic ideology, one expressed most forcefully in government policies in the United States." While some Americans speak in support of the melting pot or cultural pluralism, "they typically expect foreigners to assimilate, as quickly as possible," asserts Vincent Parrillo. "Mainstream Americans often tolerate pluralism only as a short-term phenomenon, for many believe sustained pluralism is the enemy of assimilation, a threat to the cohesiveness of American society." Anglo-conformity describes the basic experience of many immigrants, but it has caused needless suffering and humiliation, and is anything but an ideal model. The more recent theory of multiculturalism has several formats that can emphasize ideas consistent with the melting pot theory and cultural pluralism.[5]

The demands of Anglo-conformity have varied from mild pressure to strong legal action to brutal violence against an ethnic group, depending on the time period, national and international events, and specific regional conditions within the United States. This process has undermined many of the basic ideals of American democracy and caused social strife for several hundred years. A century ago, nativists were confident that by the time the second-generation (American-born children of immigrants) had matured, they would abandon the native culture of their immigrant parents and no longer exhibit behavior or values different from the dominant WASP group. For Italians and some other European ethnic groups, however, this process took three generations as immigrants and their children and grandchildren made vast and painful changes in adopting and adapting to the norms of the WASP core group. Yet they also retained some of their ethnic traditions, and American society has absorbed many cultural practices of immigrant and minority groups. Foods such as bing cherries (Chinese), tacos (Mexican), and waffles (Dutch) are now standard fare in the United States. The influences of the Irish political style, Scandinavian cooperatives, the Jewish focus on human rights, African American music, and the French language are imprinted on everyday American society. The largest immigrant group, the Germans, have given us the traditions of the lighted Christmas tree, drinking alcohol at public venues, Sunday recreational activities, and publicly sponsored athletic contests. Despite the strong rhetoric of Anglo-conformity, assimilation has in some ways been a two-way street.[6]

Two major changes in American culture were brought about by the southeast Europeans in conjunction with Irish and German Catholics. The Roman Catholic, Eastern Orthodox, and Jewish faiths, originally seen as intruders by the Protestant majority, eventually won acceptance as legitimate American religious institutions, although Jews have not received the same level of acceptance as the Catholic Christians. And the definition of the mythical American—the WASP who fought in the Revolutionary War and was a founder of the country—was broadened to encompass all Europeans, including those with humble beginnings at Ellis Island who eventually prospered. As a result, many third- and fourth-generation Italians are now rediscovering ethnic customs and history and visiting ancestral towns and long-lost relatives in the "old country."[7]

The Eight Processes of Assimilation

The assimilation of an ethnic minority group in America can be measured by eight processes that focus on how the group interacts with the WASP mainstream culture, or host society. In 1900, the ideal result of Anglo-conformity, from the nativist viewpoint, was for each new immigrant group to completely absorb the WASP culture, abandoning its ancestral culture as soon as possible. From the vantage point of a century later, it is evident that the Italians, Slavs, and Jews, like earlier European immigrants, were nonetheless able to effect changes in the dominant culture. The eight processes, or stages, of assimilation, defined next, focus on how both the culture of the immigrant/minority group and that of the mainstream WASP host group were changed. The general processes are described with references to the Italian experience in Lackawanna. See Figure 4.1 for definitions of specific terms used in each description.

1. Acculturation: the adaptation by the minority group of the cultural patterns of the WASP group. Culture includes patterns ranging from public behavior—such as language, diet, rules of behavior, and style of dress—to inner qualities like emotional expression, core values, and life goals. Italian immigrants had to learn some English and the basic rules of work and public behavior to get and hold jobs and to avoid trouble with the authorities. As they settled in the city and established families, their children gained fluency in English and learned the fine points of the American culture.[8]

2. Building an ethnic community: the immigrant minority group establishes a new ethnic identity to bridge internal differences and creates institutions to address basic life needs, eventually becoming more assimilated in the process. Utilized by immigrants and minority groups from Colonial times to the present day, it involves the ethnic group defining its own identity, then forming associations for religious expression, fraternal solidarity, and mutual aid. Next, the ethnic group organizes for economic success and political power, and, lastly, it seeks greater rewards from society and defends its gains and interests. To complete the last two steps, the group must form coalitions with other ethnic groups and participate in the civic and economic life of the wider society, thereby becoming better assimilated and more loyal to America in the process. Lackawanna Italians followed this pattern.[9]

3. Large-scale entrance of the minority group into all levels of the formal institutions of the mainstream society, including the economic, vocational, educational, religious, residential, organizational, and political sectors. Prior to the mid-1920s, Italian Americans encountered potent prejudice and discriminatory treatment from the dominant group and had limited access to skilled jobs, higher education, and political clout. But gradually, prejudice and discrimination abated as Italians became more acculturated. They rose to higher levels in the mainstream institutions: from unskilled laborers to skilled workers, foremen, supervisors, and superintendents; from committeemen to assessors and councilmen; from shacks and apartments to houses in Little Italy to newer homes in multiethnic neighborhoods; and from mom-and-pop grocery proprietors in Little Italy to owners of larger businesses catering to the general population. These progressions did not occur on a large scale until the 1930s and 1940s, aided by New Deal programs, the formation of industrial unions, and defense production and military service during World War II.

4. Large-scale entrance of the minority group into personal relationships with members of the dominant group, including those in informal clubs, neighborhood cliques, friendship circles, and intermarriage. The prejudice that blocked entry of Italians into America's social institutions also inhibited their acceptance into personal relationships. Immigrants and their children socialized within the city's four Italian neighborhoods, and friends and spouses were usually Italian. But by the 1930s and 1940s, the continuing acculturation—gradual for the immigrants and more rapid for the second generation—led to friendships, membership in cliques, and, most important, intermarriage with other southeast European ethnics and the Irish and German Americans just above them in the social order. By the late twentieth century, the rate of intermarriage was very high for Italian Americans.

5. Absence of prejudice, by WASPs and others, toward the minority group. Prejudice against Italians in Lackawanna became less intense in the mid-1920s as bigots focused on newly arrived southern blacks and Latinos, and by the end of World War II, it was no longer systematic. The stereotype of the Italian gangster, however, seems entrenched in American culture.

6. Absence of discrimination, by WASPs and others, toward the minority group. As prejudiced attitudes abated, so too did the negative behaviors that flowed from them. Italian-American patriotism during World War I helped in this process and was even more crucial in World War II, when military service and commitment to the war effort removed any doubt about the ethnic group's loyalty. By 1945, Italian Americans were no longer a minority group enduring systematic discrimination. Since then, Italians throughout the United States have slowly climbed to the highest positions in society, becoming corporate executives, candidates for high political office, and Supreme Court justices. Lackawanna's Italians have experienced success in social advancement.

7. Civic assimilation: the absence of major value and power conflicts between the minority group and the dominant group (WASPs). Members of the minority group do not contest the basic structures and beliefs of American society. The nativist view of Italians as inferior certainly fed into a conflict of values. America demanded that Italians maintain and display patriotic values during World War I. After the war, Italian American praise for Mussolini became a source of conflict when Italy invaded Ethiopia in 1935. After proving their patriotism during the Second World War, Italian Americans adhered to U.S. foreign policy toward Italy during the Cold War. Since 1945, there have been several value and power conflicts regarding religion. One pitted Italians against the Catholic Church in the U.S., and others found Italians as members of the growing American Catholic community pitted against Protestant Americans. Italians were participants in the white ethnic revival of the 1960s and 1970s, which mixed ethnic pride, both a fear and imitation of the civil-rights movement, and resentment against the WASP elite. Intermarriage among ethnics of the same religion and across religious lines has increased greatly, blurring the previous nationality and religious differences. As part of the newly solidified Euro–America ethnic group, the mainstream society, Italians now have little occasion for value or power conflict with the dominant culture they helped form.

8. Identity assimilation: individuals of the minority group identify with the larger society, i.e., the dominant WASP group, and think of themselves as just "Americans." Since the 1960s, the significant reduction of value and power conflict has led to a decreased need for group solidarity among Italian Americans. The ethnic group ultimately came to see itself as basically American. But Italians and other southeast Europeans in the last 40 years have broadened the definition of the ideal American, previously limited to descendants of the WASP founding fathers, to include all European Americans. This has allowed all people of European stock to celebrate their humble beginnings, even as ethnicity recedes and religious intermarriage has become more significant.

Processes 3, 4, 5, and 6 focus directly on the thoughts and actions of individuals and institutions of the mainstream WASP society in accepting the minority group, while 1, 7, and 8 refer to crucial changes expected of members of the minority group. Process 2 involves a time of transition for the minority group.[10]

Several underlying assumptions and trends characterized Anglo-conformity in the early twentieth century. Until each immigrant minority group adopted the mainstream WASP culture it could expect to endure prejudice and discrimination. Only as immigrants became more acculturated and abandoned their foreign traits did the prejudice and discrimination of the dominant group decline and assimilation into the social institutions and personal relationships of the host society take place. In other words, ethnic individuals could learn the dominant culture (acculturate), but they could not enter mainstream institutions or personal relations (assimilate) in large numbers without "permission"—that is, the dominant culture had to first curb its prejudice and discrimination. Virtually all European immigrants were eventually given this permission, but that has not been the case for nonwhite groups, as will be discussed later. Once members of the minority ethnic group attained access to higher positions in social institutions and personal associations, then civic and identity assimilation could follow.[11]

The assimilation experience is not a simple, straight-line process, nor one that can be easily put on a time schedule. An immigrant group may voluntarily decide to remain separate from the majority group on a permanent basis, as in the case of the Amish, or during a period when it experiences significant discrimination, as did Italians between the 1870s and 1940s. Progress in assimilation can be reversed by new developments, such as conflict between the United States and the native land of the immigrant group. The arrival rate of immigrants, their numbers, and their geographic concentration can affect the assimilation process. A rapid and large influx of immigrants, especially if they cluster in specific geographical areas, can frighten mainstream society, increase the amount of prejudice toward the newcomers, and reduce the interethnic contact that can aid the assimilation process. The arrival of four million Italian immigrants between 1890 and 1924, and their concentration in urban neighborhoods in the northeastern states, is a case in point. The degree of similarity between the culture and economy of the host society and that of the country sending the immigrants also has great importance, and in 1900, the Italian and American cultures were vastly different. Most immigrants from southern Italy had been farmers or farm laborers living in rural towns. They had little education, were often illiterate, had no fluency in English, brought little money, and few had professional training or technical skills. So in industrial America, most could enter the institutions of the new society only at the lowest levels. Italian immigrants became day laborers in America, gradually learning job skills as they entered the ranks of the working class. Some of them, and many of their American-born sons, eventually became skilled workers. The few immigrants who were professionals or had technical skills could potentially move into the middle class and their children rapidly assimilate into the core culture. They had what is called "human capital," that is, educational and work experience that meant they could individually or as a small family unit enjoy rapid social mobility. The majority of male Italian immigrants did not have human capital. Arriving as sojourner laborers without their families, they possessed a different source of capital, as described by sociologists Richard Alba and Victor Nee:

> The most valuable capital that labor migrants possess is their stock of social capital, the network ties that span the distance from their home villages and towns to their destination point in the United States. The migration network significantly reduces the risks of international migration for labor migrants who rely on word of mouth for timely information about labor market conditions, … finding a first job, and other practical aspects of workaday lives.

These bonds can galvanize individuals or the entire ethnic community to cooperate in solving problems and pursuing common interests. This "social capital" did increase the immigrants' dependence on the Italian community, leading them to congregate in Little Italys, which lengthened the time needed to assimilate. In the United States, assimilation typically involves generational changes and focuses on individuals becoming socially mobile. Nativists expected that the American-born children of the European immigrants would become completely acculturated and be well on their way to full assimilation. But the prolonged stay within the ethnic community and the Italian emphasis on the family unit rather than the individual extended the time needed for acculturation and widespread entry into the social institutions and personal relationships of the mainstream. While this reliance on the ethnic community helped support Italian entrepreneurs, it also served as a rationale for nativists and bigots to criticize Italians, maintain prejudiced attitudes, and commit discriminatory acts against them. The processes of assimilation have taken place at different rates for various groups, families, and individuals within the Italian community. The people interviewed had a variety of experiences and viewpoints regarding the assimilation experience. While some general themes did emerge and are examined in this chapter, this study does not claim to include all the personal and unique encounters of each family and individual.[12]

The Assimilation of Lackawanna's Italians

Acculturation

The presence of millions of Europeans in the United States in 1910 meant that the working class was made up of mostly foreign stock, namely immigrants and their children. In Lackawanna, foreign stock composed over 80% of the population in 1920 and 1930. First- and second-generation Italians and other eastern Europeans eventually blended into the working class, then into the country's expanded white religious subcultures, which a century ago included millions of Catholics and Jews in addition to the Protestant majority. Italians became acculturated as they learned the language and the rules governing everyday living in America. For the early immigrants, this meant gradually learning some rudimentary English, the basic rhythms of the industrial workplace, and guidelines for behavior in public. Periodic articles on the front page of Buffalo's *Corriere Italiano* told readers of "the absolute necessity of learning the English language." Some immigrants, especially those arriving prior to their eighteenth birthday, were able to grasp English and American ways quickly and rise in prominence in both the Italian colony and mainstream community. During World War I, many immigrants decided to settle permanently in Lackawanna and cease traveling back and forth between the U.S. and Italy. They then had a greater need and desire to focus on acculturating, especially if they wanted to maintain steady work and advance in their jobs or business ventures. As they sent for their wives and children in Italy, or married and started families in Lackawanna, it became apparent that their family's future depended on a more thorough understanding of the culture of the *Mericani*.[13]

One measure of acculturation is the citizenship status of immigrants. Taking out "first papers" (declaring one's intent to become a citizen), then obtaining "second papers" (becoming a naturalized citizen), both indicate an attempt at acculturation, as well as civic and identity assimilation. In 1910, only 15% of all Italian immigrants in Lackawanna 18 years of age or older were naturalized. Ten years later, the figure stood at 26%, and this grew to 35% in 1925. By 1930, 64% of the immigrants were naturalized, indicating that Italians were both responding to society's pressure to be "100% American" and committing to permanent residence in the United States.[14]

For many Italians in Lackawanna, acculturation was a difficult and often painful process. This was most apparent when the second generation entered Lackawanna's public schools and learned that the foreign ways of their parents marked both generations as outsiders. The immigrants and

Source: F. R. Kluckholm & F. L. Strodtbeck, "Variations in Value Orientations", 1961, as quoted in Monica McGoldrick, John K. Pierce, & Joseph Giordano, eds., *Ethnicity and Family Therapy*, 1982, pp. 37–43.

FIGURE 4.2

DIFFERING CULTURAL PATTERNS OF THE UNITED STATES AND ITALY

The acculturation of Italians was complex and difficult, because America's cultural patterns in the early twentieth century were notably different from those of Italy. According to one study, the cultures differed on four of five basic values. The Italian culture focused on the present, while Americans valued the future and always seemed in a rush to get there. Interpersonal relationships in America focused on "competitiveness, the striving for upward mobility in jobs, and social contacts," which meant controlling one's feelings and gaining recognition based on accomplishments rather than on internal standards. Italian verbal emotionality and the focus on "spontaneous expression of our inner feelings in any given situation" often clashed with the controlled emotions of task-focused Americans. Individualism has been crucial in the United States, with the autonomy of the individual preferred over responsibility to any group. In contrast, Italian culture required group responsibility, and the well-being of the family unit took precedence over individual desires. The American way of relating to the natural or supernatural environment emphasized mastery over nature and relied on science, technology, and vast resources to solve problems. Their historic poverty and unique type of Roman Catholicism led Italians to feel subjugated to nature and to anticipate suffering as well as a need to be in harmony with nature. For Italian culture, this was most apparent in the tremendous powers attributed to local patron saints and the fear of the evil eye. In one value orientation, the basic nature of man, the American and Italian cultures have been similar, as both view humans as a mixture of good and evil. The differences between the two cultures presented serious challenges for the Italian immigrants. Within the family structure, immigrants and their children struggled to resolve these contradictions.

their children experienced conflict over language usage in the home—whether to speak in English or Italian. The kids learned English during daytime classes, and some taught the new language to their parents and younger siblings. A number of immigrants attained a basic mastery of English at night school as they studied for their naturalization papers. Young second-generation men and women were attracted to the individualism

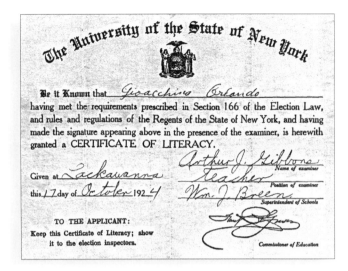

Gioacchino Orlando, like many other immigrants, completed night-school courses on the English language which was required in order to vote in elections. Public schools throughout Lackawanna offered such courses to help acculturate immigrants. Photo source: Charles Orlando

and peer culture of the United States. They desired social activities outside the Italian community and often wanted to follow the American custom of individual choice in finding and courting a spouse. These new values created more intergenerational conflict. The American-born youth were trapped in the classic marginal person dilemma: They were members of two different worlds—the Italian culture of their parents and the American culture of the schools—but not fully accepting or accepted in either.

Most members of the second generation, more than three of every five, became adults in the 1930s. As they married and created families, a crucial turning point in the acculturation process was at hand. Irving Child studied second-generation Italian American men in New Haven, Connecticut, in the 1930s, and found they reacted to their marginal situation in three ways. In the "rebel" adaptation, the individual dropped affiliations with other Italians and did everything possible to act "American" and assimilate. Often full of ambition, he took advantage of any opportunities offered by the dominant society to improve his situation. He had mostly non – Italian friends, limited ties with parents and family members, married a non – Italian, and moved out of Little Italy. The second possibility was the "in-group" reaction, in which a man focused most of his time and affiliations within the Italian community, with the goal of gaining acceptance within his ethnic group. He most likely chose an Italian wife. Some of these men actively promoted Italian causes and political candidates in an effort to challenge discrimination. The in-group person found himself in conflict with things American and sometimes harbored hostility toward

other nationalities, while the rebel battled against things Italian. Each of these two approaches was adopted by only a minority of the second-generation men. The majority followed a third course, accommodation, in which the individual attempted to avoid conflict by using compromise. He downplayed the collision of the Italian and American cultures and denied the effect it had on him. He was open to having non – Italian friends and marrying outside his ethnic group, although he may have favored an Italian spouse "to escape from barriers a non – Italian may impose upon him." He accepted some of the fundamental Italian cultural traits and maintained a respectful attitude toward his parents, thus reinforcing family solidarity. At the same, time he fit in as best he could with the "Americans" and their institutions.[15]

As family heads, second-generation Italians in Lackawanna displayed the adaptations defined by Child—rebel, in-group, and, for most, accommodation. The majority of these parents wanted to become Americanized but desired to do so in a more gradual manner and with less negativity toward their immigrant parents. Joseph Lopreato has described this process.

> The parental culture is rejected as inapplicable, but not condemned. Consequently, though the family is likely to move away from the parental neighborhood and thereby lessen the frequency of communication with the first generation, the emotional bond with the old folks and their ways is not broken. Intimate communication is maintained with the parental household, and relations with all close relatives are marked by affection and understanding. The intimate interaction is, of course, facilitated by the Italian American's tendency to live in close proximity, within the same city or in neighboring towns.

The second-generation spouses were likely to incorporate ideals of the American family model: a patriarchy softened with more democracy, boys and girls treated as equals, the father using less corporal punishment with the children, individuality more emphasized, and the family more child-centered.[16]

The American-born adults often limited their use of Italian to occasions when their parents or other immigrants were present. Many rarely spoke the language to their children other than uttering some favorite phrases in dialect, but would converse in Italian when discussing topics not meant for the children's ears. A 1980 study of Italians in Bridgeport, Connecticut, found that over 70% of the second generation spoke Italian, but only 14% of the third generation, and 10% of the fourth generation. Language is the primary means by which cultural values are transmitted, and there is a strong correlation between the loss of the mother tongue and the degree of cultural assimilation. The price of acculturation in

America has often been to submerge, or even forget, the language and culture of one's forebears.[17]

This chapter and the preceding one describe many changes that occurred in Italian immigrant families in America. It outlines some different traits between families in Italy, first-generation families in America (in which immigrants are the parents), and second-generation families (headed by American-born parents). These comparisons offer a general overview of the three types of families, with a focus on the accommodation process described by Irving Child [see Figure 4.3].

Building an Ethnic Community

The development of an ethnic identity and community influences acculturation and other stages of assimilation. Described as ethnic Americanization, it was utilized by immigrants from England, Germany, Holland, Scandinavia, Ireland, and Northern Ireland in the past and other ethnic groups ever since. A hundred years ago, Italians and other southeast Europeans followed the same general pattern, beginning soon after the immigrants arrived in this country.

Despite the prejudice and discrimination that plagued immigrants, the civic culture of America offered benefits to Italians and other white immigrant groups. The three basic components to this civic culture are: the belief that citizens could govern themselves via elected representatives; the ability of each citizen to participate as an equal; and "voluntary pluralism," which meant immigrants could maintain their religions and customs. This model allows for variation in the "content of American identity"—ethnic religions and customs, which in turn support "the form of American identity"—and respect for individual rights and differences.[18]

The formation of the Lackawanna Italian American community and its ethnic identity involved four trends, as described in detail in Chapter 3. The first two focused on events and conditions in the United States, and the third and fourth on events, and perceptions of conditions, in Italy. Trend No. 1, meeting the immediate social, economic, political, and psychological needs of the Italian community, usually served to support a Pan – Italian or nonprovincial identity based on the unity of all Italian Americans. Trend No. 2, constructing activities and organizations that incorporated more of the American lifestyle and customs, also supported a Pan – Italian identity based on Italian Americans assimilating into American society. Trend No. 3, the construction of a Pan – Italian identity focused on Italy and its national culture, history, and current status in the world, supported a Pan – Italian identity based on the prestige of Mussolini's Italy as a world power and the past glories and culture of the nation. Trend No. 4, retaining a provincial Italian identity by maintaining and celebrating

1929. Vicinity of South Park Avenue and Verel Street. Josephine Yoviene with grandchildren Mary Alice Yoviene, left, and Joan Williams. Photo source: Jim Yoviene

hometown and regional roots in Italy, both undercut the pan-ethnic identities by splintering the Italian colony, and supported them by mobilizing people to pursue specific goals in Lackawanna. These trends began soon after the immigrants arrived in Lackawanna but took more definite form in the years 1930 to 1941. All four of them not only interacted with and influenced one another but were also shaped by the Great Depression and international events. After the Ethiopian War (1935–1936), Italy further alienated the United States by intervening with Germany in the Spanish Civil War (1936–1939), joining the Axis alliance, attacking France in 1940, and, finally, joining Japan and Germany in declaring war on the U.S. in 1941. These developments undercut the focus on Italy involved in trends 3 and 4 and led Steel City Italians to emphasize the assimilation and Pan – Italian identity of the first two trends.

The migrants from Italy were identified by the mainstream American culture as Italians, and the immigrants probably did not dispute that they indeed had been citizens of the nation of Italy that had been created in the 1860s. But they often did not identify in terms of nationality, or did so in a negative way. Political and economic power in Italy was held by those in the northern regions, who were in alliance with the southern aristocracy that exploited the peasants. In the late 1800s, the majority of Italian Army units were stationed in central and southern Italy, where they often brutally repressed uprisings and banditry, and imprisoned many peasants. The national leaders of Italy viewed southern Italy, that area south of Rome,

as backward and inferior, and Italian social scientists described the *meridionali* (southerners) as barbarians and criminals. The racist anthropology of 100 years ago divided Europeans into a hierarchy of three distinct physical types, a system adopted by American authorities preoccupied with the ranking of ethnic groups. The hierarchy was dominated by the "superior" Nordic peoples of northwest Europe, followed by the Alpine race, and finally, at the bottom, the Mediterranean race. The people in the northern-most regions of Italy were classified within the Alpine race, while those of central and southern Italy were included in the "inferior" Mediterranean race. Between 1899 and 1924, each Italian entering the U.S. was labeled as either "northern Italian" or "southern Italian." The national-origins and quota system established in 1924 cast all Italians, along with other southeast Europeans, as inferior and drastically reduced the numbers that could enter the United States.[19]

The immigrants usually defined themselves in terms of their hometown, province, or region in Italy. Each province was named for its capital city, and most immigrants were from small towns unknown outside of the province. As one immigrant met another in the U.S., he or she might say: "I'm from Cosenza (or Roma, or Avellino, or Aquila)," and this provincial identity often appeared on formal documents. This was true in Lackawanna, where some Italians identified themselves by their provincial capital, as in Romani (Lazio) or Napolitani (Campania). Others identified with one of the 20 regions of Italy—as in Marchegiano (from Marche) and Calabrese (from Calabria), and still others, who had many *paesani* in Lackawanna, identified by their hometown: Giulianese (Giuliano di Roma, Lazio), Pettoranese (Pettorano sul Gizio, Abruzzo), or Cilentan' (San Mauro Cilento, Campania).

The formal labels and definitions of identity used by American nativists, and the notions of inferiority associated with them were insulting to Italian immigrants. They had the same feelings toward the ethnic slurs—dago, wop, guinea—hurled at them on the street and in the steel plant. Despite their provincial ties, they were collectively viewed, often in a disparaging way, as Italians, and they recognized their common plight. They soon began referring to themselves more by regional background and, increasingly, as Italians or Italian Americans. The immigrants developed a sudden pride in Italy and its culture and began to honor people and events that they had been indifferent, or even hostile, toward in the old country. Names of organizations reflected the immigrants' new identity, as in the Italian American Citizens Club, the Italian American Social Club, the Italian Social Club of Lackawanna (later called the Stag Club), the Roland Italian American Lodge, and the Federation of Italian American Associations of Lackawanna. Italians of all provinces were welcomed to join the Cooperativa Lago Erie Societa di Mutuo Soccorso (the Lake Erie Cooperative Society of Mutual Aid, now called the Lake Erie Italian Club) when it was founded in 1910 as the city's first Italian organization. Cristoforo Colombo quickly became popular and was honored not only because his voyages connected Europe and the western hemisphere but also because he was one of the few Italian historical figures admired by American nativists. Italians placed a bust of him at the entrance to Bethlehem Park. In the 1920s and early 1930s, many Americans admired Benito Mussolini, who had built Italy into a world power, thus, many immigrants praised *Il Duce* and the sense of social honor and respect he'd gained among the *Mericani*. Religious festivals, street processions for funerals, and other Italian customs were reenacted in Lackawanna as symbols of ethnic identity.

The newcomers also mobilized around common needs, initially forming associations for religious expression, fraternal solidarity, and mutual aid. Italian saloons and boardinghouses in Lackawanna were natural gathering places to converse in one's native language. The founding of the Lake Erie Italian Club provided for sickness and death benefits, and a few years later, the group ran a short-lived cooperative store. St. Anthony's parish, founded in 1917, filled the spiritual needs of many immigrants, and served as a focal point for patron-saint festivals. Gradually, the immigrants turned to organizing for economic success and political power. They helped to elect several Italians as Democratic or Republican committeemen, and in 1921 formed the Italian American Citizens' Club to back both Italian and non – Italian candidates who could provide jobs and other benefits to their growing community.[20]

Figure 4.3
CHANGES IN TRAITS OF THE ITALIAN FAMILY

Family in Italy	First-Generation Family	Second-Generation Family
Patriarchal, father has highest status	Less patriarchal; father loses high status, or it is fictitiously maintained	Somewhat patriarchal to democratic; father shares high status with mother and kids
Mother center of home life; doesn't work for wages	Mother center of home; few work for wages; some belong to clubs	Mother center of home, has active social life; likely to work for wages or may operate a business
Family and community	Some disorganization and conflict; marginal Italian American way of life	Variable; depends on adaptation of individual family to American values, but less marginality
Active in town life	Active in Italian neighborhood, but less so in American community	Active in American community; less active in Italian neighborhood
Culture transmitted only by the family	Italian culture transmitted only by family; American culture, by its institutions	American culture transmitted by family and American institutions
Many functions: economic, recreational, religious, affectional, social, protective	Fewer functions: affectional, social, some economic and recreational	One basic function—affectional—plus some recreational and social
Family has high status and role in community	Family has high status and role in Italian community, but low status and role in American community	Higher status and role in American community; may reject high status and role in Italian community
Women educated for marriage only	Women get some formal education and family education for marriage	General education emphasized; more focus on individual goals besides future marriage
Individual subordinate to the family	Rights of individual increasingly recognized	Family is subordinate to the individual
Children live for parents	Children live more for themselves	Parents live for children
Children are economic asset	Children are economic asset for shorter time	Children are an economic liability
Husband and wife must not show affection in family or in public	Husband and wife are not demonstrative in family or public but tolerate it in their married children	Husband and wife are more demonstrative in family or public
Boys are superior to girls	Boys are regarded as superior to girls	Boys regarded as superior to girls; but status of girls is improving
Boys and girls have separate activities	Separate activities; girls closely monitored, but school is coeducational; peer group is important	School and other activities are coed; less monitoring of girls' activities; peer-group culture is crucial
Chastity rule rigidly enforced by chaperonage	Much less chaperonage, but chastity is expected	No chaperonage; chastity expected, but lack of it may be tolerated
Selection of spouse by parents	Individual selects mate, but with parental consent	Selection of mate by individual regardless of parental consent
No divorce allowed; desertion is rare	Some divorce; small increase in desertion	Divorce is practiced; desertion is relatively rare

Sources: Paul J. Campisi, "Ethnic Family Patterns: The Italian Family in the United States," *American Journal of Sociology*, Vol. 53, 1948, pp. 443–49; Lydio Tomasi, *The Italian American Family*, 1972, p. 23. Campisi's typology includes 53 Italian cultural traits organized into nine categories; Tomasi adapted it to 20 traits in three categories. This study used both typologies, reduced the traits to 17, and modified them to reflect data on Lackawanna's Italian community.

The city's Italians founded 92 businesses between 1900 and 1919, and another 188 during the 1920s and 1930s. Prior to 1945, most Italians were clustered in four neighborhoods (the Old Village, which was razed in 1930, lower Ingham Avenue, Bethlehem Park, and Roland Avenue), and many of their entrepreneurial ventures—such as groceries, barbershops, shoe repair shops, and saloons—continued the pattern of serving mostly Italian customers. Several religious organizations grew out of St. Anthony's Church, and secular associations celebrated Italy and its culture, as well as regional and hometown ties. This multitude of Italian institutions reinforced the notion of a separate ethnic community and served to attract Italian Americans into the social boundaries of that community, which shaped their personal relations. At the same time, Lackawanna's Italians had to increasingly deal with non – Italian employers, merchants, neighbors, customers who patronized the Italian stores, politicians, and union organizers. Some ambitious businesspeople, demonstrating a new found knowledge of American business technology and acumen, founded grocery stores, restaurants, and automotive service shops that catered to the general public. This helped to gradually ease their owners and employees into the mainstream business life of the city.

The Italians were then entering a crucial phase of the community-building phase by seeking greater rewards from society and defending their gains and interests. More political groups were formed in the 1930s to solidify Italian influence in several political parties and to influence legislators in specific offices. The formation of the Federation of Italian American Associations of Lackawanna in 1932 was in large part an effort to achieve civic and political rewards for the Italian community. To gain more prestige in the city, some Italian groups gave awards to individuals of any ethnic group who excelled in sports or academics. Like earlier immigrant groups, Italians were becoming more active in the civic and economic life of the wider society, and gradually assimilating in the process.

One aspect of the Italian adjustment to the new country was interaction with non – Italian neighbors; 91 other ethnic groups have been present in Lackawanna. Italians exchanged respectful if limited comments with neighbors, welcoming them as customers in their stores. Some Italians memorized key phrases in Polish, Ukrainian, Serbo-Croatian, or Hungarian to communicate with neighbors on the sidewalks, at work, in union meetings, or in the local store. Peddler Tony Grasso maintained a multiethnic base of customers by learning the words for specific flowers, fruits, and vegetables in Polish and several other languages. These interactions also served as an incentive to learn English, since the other ethnics were also attempting to master some phrases in the language of the Americans. If nothing else, Italians and other immigrants 100

Figure 4.4

ITALIAN INSTITUTIONS IN LACKAWANNA AND BUFFALO

It is interesting to compare Lackawanna's Italian institutions with those of the large neighboring city. Buffalo's foreign-born Italians numbered 6,000 in 1900 and grew to 16,000 by 1920. Virginia Yans-McLaughlin's study of the Buffalo Italian community focused on the early decades of the twentieth century, when there was a vast system of ethnic institutions: the Italian consular office, a hospital, banks, steamship and ticket agencies, a host of businesses, many professionals, two newspapers, Italian unions, and dozens of mutual-aid and other groups. Several theaters featured Italian movies and opera performances. This array of services and institutions, plus very large Italian neighborhoods, gave Buffalo's Italians a broader and more in-depth community support system than was present in Lackawanna. Yans-McLaughlin's study emphasizes that Italian immigrants preserved their cultural values by not choosing paths that undermined the strength of the all-important family. This made the assimilation process more bearable but also slowed it down so that it took three generations.

In some ways, the presence of Buffalo's Italian population helped support the sense of ethnic identity of Lackawanna's Italians. Steel City Italians utilized the resources available in Buffalo. In 1912, midwives Caterina Nardozzi and Teresa Graticelli assisted Ingham Avenue mothers in giving birth. Nardozzi placed regular ads in *Corriere Italiano*, which had circulation in Lackawanna. Other families who had moved to Lackawanna called on Italian doctors who had treated them in Buffalo to come to their new homes for births and other medical needs. Prior to the 1917 founding of St. Anthony's Church, Steel City Italians went to churches in Buffalo's Italian neighborhoods for marriages, baptisms, and funerals. During the 1930s, they tuned in to an Italian-language amateur radio hour hosted by Buffalonian Emilino Rica. The program offered Italian youth, including some from Lackawanna, the opportunity to broadcast their vocal and musical talents. By the 1930s, Buffalo was home to hundreds of Italian organizations of all types, including some whose members came from the same hometowns or regions as Steel City Italians. A number of Lackawanna Italians, especially those who had originally settled in Buffalo, attended the large street festivals honoring familiar patron saints or became members of the societies there. Italians in each city visited relatives, friends, and *paesani* in the other city. When Lavinio Montanari opened the Fano Restaurant in the Steel City in 1934, many Marchegiani from throughout Erie County came to enjoy foods from their home region, bocce games, and contact with friends from the old country.

Buffalo and Lackawanna Italians had other things in common. Both cities had well-developed and somewhat interconnected migration chains that drew immigrants. According to Yans-McLaughlin, Italian "men flowed in and out of Buffalo until 1924," and on a smaller scale, the number of men arriving in and leaving Lackawanna was notable into the 1930s. Italian families from both cities worked on the farms and in the canneries of western New York, and men traveled throughout the state to work on jobs lined up by *paesani*. Settlement houses seemed to have had a limited impact on both communities, especially on adult and teenage males, though by the time of the Great Depression, Italians were more willing to accept welfare benefits. Owning a home or business was crucial, and by 1930, the number of Italian homeowners in American cities was significant for the immigrant generation: 69% in Philadelphia, 48% in St. Louis, and 45% in Buffalo. In Lackawanna, the 1930 figure was 52%, a substantial increase over the 24% of 1920. Plots of land, both vacant and with structures, owned by Italians in Lackawanna grew from 48 lots in 1910 to 182 in 1930 to 293 in 1940.

One of the basic differences between the two Italian communities was that Lackawanna's Italians worked in a steel plant and by the 1920s were moving from the outdoor work of the Yard Department into the mills. Yans-McLaughlin found that Buffalo's Italians were concentrated in construction, dock, and railroad work, and did not move into heavy industries prior to 1930. Also, the regional mix of Italians was different: In Buffalo, Siciliani and Basilicati were most numerous; in Lackawanna, it was the Laziali and Abruzzesi. While Italian families in both towns took in boarders, the percentage doing so in Lackawanna was much higher than in Buffalo and other cities. In 1920, 12% of Italian families in Buffalo, 10% in Chicago, and 16% in Rochester had boarders. In the Steel City, 37% of Italian families had boarders in 1920, and even as late as 1930, the figure stood at 23%.

Lackawanna's Italian community was one-twentieth the size of Buffalo's in 1910, and had fewer resources to insulate itself from the mainstream institutions that vigorously stressed Americanization. Buffalo's large Italian population was concentrated in several Little Italys, where the public schools had an Italian flavor simply from the high percentages of Italian students, and six Italian Catholic parishes had schools. The highest density in Lackawanna was in Bethlehem Park, where Italian children were 30-40% of the grammar school's student body. The small size of the Lackawanna Italian colony, plus the fact that the four neighborhoods where Italians were concentrated also included many people of other ethnic groups, led to greater intermarriage rates than those found among Buffalo's Italians. In 1930, 71% of all Buffalo Italians married within their ethnic group. Single-year figures are not available for Lackawanna Italians, but decade totals offer a rough comparison. For the years 1920 to 1929, 78% of Lackawanna Italians married Italians, a figure that dropped to 64% for the period 1930 to 1939. Three decades later, the rates for the two cities were more similar: 27% of Buffalo Italians married within their ethnic group in 1960, while the Lackawanna rate was 29% during the 1960 to 1969 period. In regard to nativist hostility, Buffalo's Italians probably suffered more prejudice and discrimination than did Lackawanna's, as indicated by their larger numbers and the harsh attacks by the Buffalo English-language press.

The Lackawanna Italian community, unlike that of Buffalo, had a moderate level of institutional completeness (see page 176); and therefore, Italians had to go outside their ethnic community and into the mainstream society to procure many needed services. Italian businesses, though plentiful in Lackawanna, were usually small, family-run affairs that offered few jobs to people outside the family. Other than the wives and children, who tended to boarders at home or picked crops on Italian-owned farms, most Italians worked in the steel plant, on the railroads, or in other factories of the dominant society. While the Italians had a number of successful political clubs, they did not control a political party and could not successfully unite their fellow ethnics into a single voting block: in this regard the Buffalo and Steel City Italians were similar. The Italian institutions that did exist eventually became more Americanized or simply faded away after World War II.

Sources: Virginia Yans-McLaughlin, *Family and Community: Italian Immigrants in Buffalo, 1880–1930*, pp. 36, 38, (quote) 76, 82, 87, 110, 146–51, 169, 219; interviews with Larry Covelli, 7/14/92; Mary Panzetta-Vertino, 6/9/04; Dewey Montanari, 7/15/94; Gary Mormino, *Immigrants On the Hill: Italian-Americans in St. Louis, 1882–1982*, 1986, p. 117; U.S. Census, 1920, 1930; City of Lackawanna, *Tax Book*, 1910, 1920, 1930; City of Lackawanna, *Births, Book.#3, 1911–12*; *Corriere Italiano*, 6/1/07; 3/12/10; B. R. Bugelski, "Assimilation Through Intermarriage," *Social Forces*, Vol. 40, December 1961, pp. 148–53, as quoted in James A. Crispino, *The Assimilation of Ethnic Groups: The Italian Case*, 1980, p. 103. By 1914, there were six Italian Catholic parishes with schools in Buffalo; Holy Spirit merged into the multiethnic St. Agatha in 1921 leaving five Italian parochial schools in 1929 with a total enrollment of 3,355 students; at that time ,the parishes were: St. Anthony, Francis of Assissi, Holy Cross, Our Lady of Mount Carmel, and St. Columba–St. Lucy (one school serving the two parishes), *Official Catholic Directory*, 1929, pp. 255–58; Erie County, *Official List of Registered Voters*, 1926, 1935.

Giovanni Banchetti, circa 1902. Born in Torino, Italy, he was appointed the Italian Consular Agent in Scranton, Pennsylvania, in 1896, and the next year assumed that role in Buffalo. During his years in Buffalo, he also was an agent for a steamship company whose ships sailed between New York City and Italian ports. Many Italian immigrants gave his office address, 31 Church Street, as their destination. Photo source: Buffalo & Erie County Public Library; *Richmond C. Hill, Twentieth Century Buffalo, Part I, 1902-03,* p. 68

years ago could communicate using a few phrases in English. Laborers greeted each other in the steel plant or along city streets with "Hi, Joe," one of the first English phrases they learned.[21]

As Lackawanna Italians were building their own ethnic identity and community, they were also moving away from *paesani* and regional identities. This was a huge step for the immigrants and their children, as there were significant differences in Italian dialects and customs, which first became apparent in transit to America. When nine-year-old Adelina Covelli and her family embarked on the *SS President Wilson* in Naples Harbor in 1927, she was amazed at the number of dialects, some of them almost incomprehensible, spoken by the other passengers from towns throughout southern and central Italy. On the streets of Lackawanna, first- and second-

generation Italian Americans had difficulty understanding the words and cadence of other dialects. The vocabulary of the Calabresi and Napolitani differed, and were, in turn, noticeably different than those of the Laziali and Abruzzesi. The Arab-influenced words of Sicilian dialects and the quickly spoken Marchegiani dialects presented challenges to people of other regions. To have basic communication, the immigrants in Lackawanna's Italian neighborhoods developed a hodgepodge of dialect phrases, formal Italian (from the people who knew it), and Italianized English phrases.[22]

The formation of ethnic institutions served an important role in helping Italian immigrants and their children survive in American society during the period from the 1870s until 1945, when they were part of a minority group. The institutions of Lackawanna's Italian community eased the pain of fitting into society in several ways. They provided a forum for interacting with people from many towns and provinces in Italy and for forming a common ethnic identity. Little Italy was a refuge in which members could proclaim either a Pan – Italian or provincial identity, preserve their social honor, and nurse the wounds that followed from minority status. The Lackawanna Italian community served as an important middle step in adjusting to American culture. The ethnic institutions provided a place of transition in which immigrants and their children could slowly acculturate, fashioning compromises and bridges between the American and Italian cultures. The societies formed by the immigrants and the second generation gradually introduced more American customs and activities to their members. In sociological terms, Lackawanna's Italians were linked by three bonds. First, there were the shared interests that Italians saw as crucial, such as finding viable jobs, obtaining political clout, and dealing with their minority group status. Leaders bargained with the Irish and Polish officials who dominated the city's political life and demanded patronage jobs, while Italian foremen in the steel plant and on the railroads helped procure jobs for men out of work. Second, the shared institutions of the Italian community—such as St. Anthony's Church and the variety of mutual-aid, social, recreational, and civic groups—were forums for social activity and vehicles for achieving communal goals. Informal institutions such as *paesani* and extended family networks provided communal aid in assisting sick people, slaughtering pigs and preserving meat, purchasing and transporting grapes to Little Italy, and assisting neighbors in making wine. Third, Italian American cultural values provided understanding, interpretation, and expectations that served as a guide to action and a way of making sense of the world. People interviewed spoke of the importance of family unity and the obligation of all members to contribute to economic survival. They described a strong sense of

FIGURE 4.5
'MIDDLEMAN' ETHNIC GROUPS

Occupying an intermediate position between a society's dominant group and the groups at the bottom of the pecking order, 'middleman' ethnic groups often fill a niche, such as traders, money lenders, or independent professionals. They render services to the most downtrodden groups by performing tasks that people in the upper echelons find unpleasant. According to Martin Marger, they "serve a function for both dominant and subordinate groups." Jews have held this role in Europe and the Chinese in southeast Asian countries. Another function of middleman groups is to serve as the instructors and enforcers of the assimilation process for newer arrivals in the United States.

As other European groups became assimilated and left their minority status, they assumed an intermediate status in the ethnic hierarchy, serving as mediators between the WASPS and the newly arrived immigrant minority groups. In the first half of the nineteenth century, the arrival of millions of Irish and German Catholics presented a dilemma for WASPs. Between 1790 and 1860, the number of Catholic Americans grew from 25,000 to three-and-a-half million. The Irish, whose mass immigration began in the 1840s, differed from the WASP culture in more ways than their Catholicism. They were poor and had fiercely resisted centuries of British rule in their home country, neither of which endeared them to the WASP elite in America. The Irish endured poverty, prejudice, nativist violence, and the private agencies that placed Irish orphans with Midwestern farm families who worked them hard and raised them as Protestants. The growing influence of the Irish in the Catholic Church led to the founding of institutions to nurture orphans within the faith. In the part of West Seneca that later became Lackawanna, the St. Joseph's Orphan Asylum was opened in 1851, and St. John's Protectory in 1863. Fifty years after the start of their migration, Irish and German Catholics were rapidly assimilating and transcending their minority status in America. Both groups achieved greater societal acceptance when WASP nativists switched the focus of their attacks onto the "inferior" Italian, Slavic, and Jewish immigrants from southeast Europe. By the 1890s, the Irish dominated the hierarchy of the Catholic Church in America and controlled political machines in many cities, including Buffalo, where they filled the ranks of civil service jobholders. The Irish clerics, politicians, policemen, and social-service officials thus had a large role in assimilating the southeast European immigrants, especially the large number who were Catholic. Their interaction with the Irish provided Italians in Lackawanna and elsewhere with lessons, both caring and harsh, for fitting into American society.

Sources: Martin N. Marger, *Race and Ethnic Relations: American and Global Perspectives*, 1985, p. 32; Roger Daniels, *Not Like Us: Immigrants and Minorities in America*, 1890–1924, 1997, pp. 138–39; Alice M. Pytak, *Our Lady of Victory Basilica and Homes of Charity*, 1986, p. 6.

community, in which Italian adults looked after all children and were allowed to admonish youth who were not following established rules of behavior. It was generally accepted that the honor of females had to be protected, so girls' activities were restricted. There were no coed Italian organizations until 1939, and females could work only in situations where other Italians were present to guard their honor. Mothers basically controlled the daily running of the household, while men were the master gardeners for the vegetable plots that virtually every Italian family maintained. It was expected that females and children would attend church with some regularity, while males would attend only religious festivals and an occasional Mass, and the financial support of St. Anthony's was not a high priority. God-parentage was usually important, and godmothers and godfathers chosen with some care.[23]

The shared interests, institutions, and culture formed bonds that organized a great deal of the individual and collective social life of Lackawanna's Italians. An ethnic bond that is strong and has a significant influence on daily life and activities is designated as "thick" by sociologists Stephen Cornell and Douglas Hartmann, while "a less comprehensive or 'thin' ethnic … tie is one that organizes relatively little of social life and action." Up to the late 1940s, the Lackawanna Italian community displayed a thick ethnic tie. A significant number of people were being Italian Americans, that is, their daily living patterns were based on ethnic cultural standards. This solidarity was enhanced by the clustering of Italians in several neighborhoods close to the major work sites of the immigrants and the city's ethnic politics based on the series of ethnic neighborhoods vying for political offices and favors. While few Italians were employed in Italian businesses, many of the workers were clustered at certain job sites, such as the Yard Department of the steel plant, the Track Department of the South Buffalo Railway, and the roundhouses of the South Buffalo Railway and the New York Central Railroad. These work settings, which often included Italian foreman, helped maintain daily interaction within an ethnic context.[24]

Lackawanna's Italian community was at the height of its institutional strength in the 1930s and 1940s. The 20-year period from 1930 to 1949 witnessed the existence of the greatest number of ethnic organizations, and available documents reveal the extensive participation of Italian Americans in these groups. At least 1,098 adults and teens were members of 39 organizations at some point during these two decades. The 778 teenage and adult men represent approximately 74% of the city's male Italian population in 1930, and the 320 teenage and adult women, about 40% of the females. These are high rates of involvement. An important trend of the Italian organizations founded in the 1940s, as well the older ones, was the greater focus on American-style activities between 1942 and 1949.[25]

The ability of Italians, or any other immigrant group, to stay within their ethnic sphere was largely dependent on the number of these institutions, or the level of "institutional completeness" of the ethnic community, according to Raymond Breton. A very high level meant that the "ethnic community could perform all the services required by its members. Members would never make use of native institutions for the satisfaction of any of their needs, such as education, work, food and clothing, medical care or social assistance." The presence of many institutions could slow down or even prevent the assimilation process if the organizations and agencies stressed the maintenance of Italian cultural patterns, or could accelerate assimilation by encouraging the adoption of the mainstream culture. The Lackawanna Italian colony had a moderate degree of institutional completeness, which initially served to slow down assimilation but eventually to hasten and advocate the adoption of mainstream culture. The Italian colony focused on forming and maintaining ethnic cohesion long enough to stabilize the immigrants and their children in the initial decades of their encounter with American society. The presence of the large Italian colony in Buffalo provided additional and more comprehensive ethnic institutions that Lackawanna Italians could utilize to reinforce their ethnic ties (see Figure 4.4).[26]

Certain forces worked against Italian ethnic solidarity. The restrictive immigration laws of 1921 and 1924 drastically reduced the flow of immigrants arriving from Italy. As the immigrant generation aged and began to pass on, and the second generation matured, there was a growing gap in the knowledge of Italian culture and the experience of actually living in Italy and migrating to the United States. The second generation was torn between the two cultures and pressured to assimilate by the public schools and their own desire to fit in. Indeed, the Italian American community carried a stigma in the eyes of mainstream society, which viewed ethnicity and ethnic neighborhoods as less than 100% American. Italians could rise in society and complete the other stages of assimilation only by making their ethnic community more like the American mainstream, reducing their involvement in the ethnic community, or leaving Little Italy altogether.

With the end of systematic prejudice and discrimination in 1945, there was one less reason for Italians to band together. By 1950, a significant number of people were moving out of the Little Italys, joining nonethnic organizations, and entering the mainstream of society. The arrival of a small post – World War II wave of immigrants, the tendency of in-groupers to remain in the Italian enclaves, and the ethnic revival of the late 1960s all helped support the continued life of several older organizations and the formation of new groups that celebrated Italian culture. But the stream of Italians moving to eastern Lackawanna and nearby suburbs gained more steam in the 1960s and the following decades. Today, only Bethlehem Park and the Roland Avenue area have small concentrations of Italians, and St. Anthony's has become a multiethnic parish. A significant number of the second and third generations, together with the postwar immigrants, are involved in a handful of Italian organizations. A number of the post – World War II migrants also maintain strong ethnic ties beyond the organizations and can be viewed as organizing a significant portion of their lives around their Italian ethnicity. In essence, they are being Italian, while most of the aging second-generation and third-, fourth-, and fifth-generation Italian Americans, many of whom are of mixed ethnicity, may be feeling Italian but not organizing their daily lives around that ethnic identity. Like many Italians throughout the United States, they are merging into the European American group, one of the five large racial groups of the Quintuple Melting Pot, whose official mainstream history now includes the story of humble southeast European immigrants and their descendants.

Prejudice Against Italians

Prejudice involves prejudging an individual based on a negative, exaggerated, and/or inflexible view of that person's ethnic group. These superficial images, or stereotypes, can assign traits—such as being poor, dirty, lazy, unreliable, and dangerous—to one or more ethnic groups. All these negative qualities were part of the stereotype of Italians. In 1902, for example, a Buffalo newspaper quoted a contractor who criticized his many Italians employees because "they absolutely refuse to work in the rain." But one stereotype of Italians has lasted for over 100 years: the criminal and gangster. This can be seen in the newspaper accounts, scholarly studies, and government reports quoted in Chapter 3. The American immigration laws of 1917, 1921, and 1924 reflected bigoted views of Italians and other southeast Europeans, who were declared inferior. In Buffalo, Italians and Jews sponsored a meeting to protest the

1924 bill and were joined by Congressman James Mead and other politicians. But the bill was passed, and the bigoted national-origins and quota system remained in effect and was even reaffirmed by new legislation in 1952. Italians continued to endure ethnic slurs—such as dago, wop, and guinea—often on a daily basis. Real estate practices reflected this bigotry by labeling Italians as undesirable additions to neighborhoods. Over the years, researchers have probed the willingness of Americans to interact with members of 30 specific ethnic groups and charted the "social distance" between groups as one measure of prejudice. Typically, northwest European ethnic groups have been ranked among the top 10 most desirable for relationships ranging from acquaintances to marriage partners, and non – Europeans have occupied the lowest rankings. Italians were rated as 14th of the 30 groups in 1926 and 16th in 1946, then gradually rose to 12th in 1956, 8th in 1966, and 5th in 1977. These findings help illustrate that prejudice against Italians and other southeast Europeans was prevalent from 1900 until the end of World War II.[27]

The negative attitudes toward Italians and other southeast Europeans in the Steel City, were moderated in the mid-1920s due largely to two events. With the flow of migrants from southeast Europe restricted by the new immigration laws, nativists seemed less fearful of the Italians and Poles and more confident that they would assimilate. Given America's pathological obsession with race, the arrival in Lackawanna of large numbers of blacks and a smaller group of Latinos led bigots to make these groups the new targets of their hostility. Niles Carpenter's 1927 study of ethnic groups in the Buffalo area found that job discrimination against African Americans was much more severe and pervasive than that against the new immigrants, and blacks were at the bottom of the occupational hierarchy. Prejudice and discrimination against Italians and other southeast European immigrants in the Buffalo area, while still strong, was less violent and intense than in earlier decades. Some Italians were victims of "petty irritation and persecution" by coworkers and foremen of other ethnic groups—"American," Canadian, German, Polish, and Irish. Men in one factory told an Italian coworker that they "had no use for 'Wops.' " Foremen wielded great power and could easily abuse workers, especially when "the foreman belongs to an ethnic group that feels particular animosity for the worker. Such would seem to be the case when Italians are working under Irish foremen …. " Examining 38 labor unions, Carpenter found that eight excluded immigrants who either did not declare their intention to become citizens or were not naturalized citizens of the United States. Italians and other southeast European immigrants also had two specific handicaps, according to the study: their lack of fluency in English and their agricultural background. "They have been, for the most part, farmers, and

FIGURE 4.6

PREJUDICE AGAINST ITALIAN AMERICANS IN CONGRESS

Vito Marcantonio, the son of Italian immigrants, was the congressman who represented East Harlem in New York City from 1934 to 1950. This was the largest Italian neighborhood in the country at the time, and Marcantonio was a champion of his working-class constituents, who also included blacks and Puerto Ricans. The press often attacked his community supporters as the "scum of the slums" and "lawless," asserting that the "Mafia runs East Harlem." On the floor of the House of Representatives, one member called Marcantonio "an expert on what constitutes racketeering." The Italian congressman vigorously fought back when these types of slurs were made. In 1945, an Italian American woman in Brooklyn wrote Senator Theodore Bilbo of Mississippi and criticized him for being opposed to the Fair Employment Practices Commission (Marcantonio had often pressed the commission to investigate discrimination against Italian Americans). In his letter of response, Bilbo addressed the woman as "My Dear Dago," and Marcantonio demanded an apology. Bilbo refused and responded: "It is through you and your gang, and I dare say many of them are gangsters, from the sin-soaked, Communistic sections of the great metropolis of New York, that practically all the rotten, crackpot, Communistic legislative schemes are being thrown into the Congressional 'mill' … you are a notorious political mongrel." Marcantonio replied that Bilbo was "Hitler's inconsolable male widow." Senator Bilbo then tried to soften his bigotry by focusing on his racism. He explained that his only desire was "to fight against the mongrelization of the two races in America … With the respect and love that I have for Caucasian blood that flows not only in my veins but in the veins of Jews, Italians, Poles and other nationalities of the White race, I would not want to see it contaminated with Negro blood."

Sources: Gerald Meyer, Vito Marcantonio: *Radical Politician, 1902–1954*, 1989, pp. 133–35; David R. Roediger, *Working Toward Whiteness: How America's Immigrants Became White, The Strange Journey From Ellis Island to the Suburbs*, 2005, p. 241; Jerre Mangione and Ben Morreale, *La Storia: Five Centuries of the Italian American Experience*, 1992, pp. 397–400.

primitive peasant farmers at that, and they find themselves thrust into what is probably the most complicated industrial society the world has yet seen."[28]

Prejudice toward Italians continued into the Depression years, when many were poor and on welfare, and the media often depicted them as gangsters. In school, Italian children learned that Italian culture and even their physical appearance made them not quite good enough. During World War II, Italians were among the "enemy aliens" of questionable loyalty because their native land was at war with the United States. But by the war's end, systematic prejudice was greatly reduced, and Italian Americans were no longer a minority group. The abolition of national origins and quotas in America's immigration law in 1965 marked the end of the official notion of southeast European inferiority. Over the past three decades, Italian Americans in Lackawanna and throughout the United States have usually been free of systematic prejudice, except for the continuing stereotype of the Italian gangster.

Discrimination Against Italians

Many behaviors and policies carried out by mainstream society have had a harmful impact on Italians as a group, especially in the 70 years prior to the end of World War II. During that period, the Italian minority group was the subject of systematic discrimination. In its most severe form, it resulted in deadly violence. At least 40 Italians were lynched or killed by mob action in the United States between 1874 and the early 1920s. Two hundred Italians were driven out of Altoona, Pennsylvania, by a mob in 1894, and a similar incident occurred in West Frankfort, Illinois, in 1920. When the mayor of New Orleans led a mob that lynched 11 Italians in 1891, Theodore Roosevelt called it "a rather good thing," and the *New York Times* portrayed the lynching as a solution to the crime problem. The police in many cities treated minorities unfairly and used ethnic profiling and harsh physical treatment against Italians and other southeast Europeans. In 1914, state troopers in Ludlow, Colorado, opened fire on a tent camp of striking mine workers and their families, killing two Italian women and 13 children. Discriminatory actions were carried out by individuals and mobs, and also by institutions, such as law-enforcement agencies, corporations, government agencies, and political machines. The English-language press continually denigrated Italians for their poverty or criminality, and seeing them as fit only for unskilled work. Congress passed bigoted immigration laws between 1917 and 1924 that defined Italians as inferior and limited the numbers admitted to this country. Few Italians were appointed as judges or to other state and federal positions, and upwardly mobile Italians met resistance from realtors and residents when they attempted to move from Little Italy to more affluent communities.[29]

The "Red Scare" began during World War I when the United States government persecuted pacifists and leftists (socialists, anarchists, communists, and radical unionists) opposed to the war. American capitalists became even more frightened when communists took control of Russia, and postwar strikes in the U. S. challenged their power. The federal and state governments renewed attacks on leftist groups in the United States; in response, anarchists set off bombs aimed at government and corporate officials in 1919 and 1920. Immigrants and radicals were linked in the minds of Americans as terrorists, and retribution was demanded. The federal government then arrested thousands of suspects, many of them immigrants from southeast Europe, and deported several hundred to Russia. Among the anarchists arrested were Italian immigrants Nicola Sacco and Bartolomeo Vanzetti, who were charged with the murder of two men in a payroll robbery in Massachusetts. That it was a grossly unfair trial was indicated by comments from two of the key actors during the lengthy proceedings: the judge who bragged to a friend "Did you see what I did with those anarchist bastards the other day?" and the jury foreman who said he wanted all "dagos" kept out of America. The two Italians were found guilty and, despite demonstrations throughout the world, were executed in 1927. In Buffalo, Italians organized protest rallies that decried the legal system of Massachusetts as unjust for sentencing two men to death simply because they were Italians. A year later, America's ethnic divisions were highlighted when Democrat Al Smith, a Catholic, was defeated by Republican Herbert Hoover in the presidential election. "What Smith really embodied," writes Samuel Lubell, "was the revolt of the underdog, urban immigrant against the top dog of 'old American' stock." The campaign underlined the deep chasm between rural, WASP, largely Republican America and the ethnic, largely Democratic, Catholic, urban centers.[30]

At the national level, New York Congressman Vito Marcantonio traded barbs with Washington, D.C. reporters and politicians who defamed Italians (see Figure 4.6). In Lackawanna during the years 1930 to 1941, while Italians didn't experience the rabid discrimination of earlier decades, they endured daily reminders of their low status. An Italian workman in the steel plant was told by one of his bosses that "all Italians are gangsters." Well-educated, English-speaking Italians also encountered discrimination. Frank Scaletta, who was three years old when his family emigrated from Sicily to Farnham, New York, worked a year on the South Buffalo Railway, then studied accounting at colleges in Buffalo. Earning his bachelor's degree in 1930, he looked for an accountant position but soon learned that "many people didn't want to hire Italians—they threw out my job applications." He then worked for a road-construction contractor but was fired because he hadn't become a naturalized citizen. So in 1931, Scaletta returned to the South Buffalo Railway in Lackawanna and went on to complete a 38-year career there. In the steel plant and the Lackawanna public schools, immigrants from Italy and other southeast European countries and their children endured both overt and subtle discrimination. Italian children

FIGURE 4.7

Italian Households Outside of the Little Italys; by Ward, 1941–2006

	1941		1960		1973		1990		2006	
Ward 1	21	9%	19	5%	8	4%	2	1%	1	1%
Wards 2–4	71	55%	350	95%	610	99%	649	90%	532	91%
Total: 4 wards	92	26%	369	50%	618	69%	651	74%	533	81%

Sources: *Erie County Directory*, 1941; *Lackawanna City Directory*, 1960; *Buffalo Southeast Suburban Directory*, 1973; *Buffalo City Directory, Including Lackawanna*, 1990; *Buffalo South Suburban Directory*, 2006.

*The Erie County Directories are much less complete than the census; the total number of Italian households in 1941 was probably significantly higher than listed in the directory.

FIGURE 4.8

Occupations of Lackawanna Italian Males & Females: 1920–1973

MALES	1920		1925		1930		1960		1973	
Professionals	4		5		8		33		91	
Business Proprietors	20		40		46		88		50*	
Skilled, Semiskilled	70		141		255		306		290	
Supervisory	9		23		23		43		60	
Laborers	264	73%	240	55%	285	47%	264	36%	232	25%
Retired/ Widowed	—		—		—		44		227	
Student	—		—		2		38		104	
Military	—		—		—		13		14	
Jobs Not Listed	—		—		—		184		103	
Total	367		444		617		1,013		1,171	
Females (included in total above)	(11)		(20)		(44)		(279)		(346)	

*The decline in Lackawanna Italian business proprietors by 1973 is due in part to a number of people moving their residences and businesss outside the city after 1960. Sources: U.S. Census, 1920, 1930; N.Y. Census, 1925; *Lackawanna City Directory*, 1960; *Buffalo Southeast Suburban Directory*, 1973. Data are not readily available for the 1950s. *The Erie County Directory* of 1941 is incomplete; it lists only 413 Italian adults; for 210 Bethlehem Steel employees no specific occupation is listed, and for another 81 individuals, no job information is given.

heard derogatory comments by a few bigoted teachers and students. Steelworkers were excluded from certain jobs, not assisted by more experienced workers in learning new work assignments, and often referred to as wop, dago, or guinea. Far more destructive was the subtle discrimination, such as the school curriculum teaching that the peoples of southeast Europe were inferior, and that their ethnic groups were not up to the level of the Americans of northwest European origins who had founded the United States. Certain everyday facts of life held subtle messages about Italians and other southeast Europeans not belonging or not being highly valued. There was only one Italian American teacher in Lackawanna's schools until the 1930s. Roosevelt School was in terrible physical condition in 1916, and most of the city's bordellos and illegal gambling dens were in the First Ward, where the majority of Italians lived. Many of the immigrants and second-generation

Italian Americans interviewed stated that they did not experience discrimination on the job or in social situations, but mentioned being called names such as "boy," being laughed at or mocked for their immigrant accents, and hearing "friendly" but demeaning jokes, such as those equating Italians with organized crime. Some individuals were able to ignore these experiences, figuring they were minor compared to more drastic forms of discrimination that minority groups often endure. But these small insults, or microaggressions, could have a devastating effect on one's self-esteem if they occurred regularly enough. The perpetrators of these forms of discrimination did not always do so intentionally. While many offenders were Irish or other northwest Europeans—landlords, politicians, city employees, police officers—others were not. Italians, Poles, Serbs, Hungarians and others often referred to each other using ethnic slurs, following the rules of ethnic competition by treating people of their own ethnic group well and disrespecting those of other ethnicities. At times, it seemed that even the economy was against these ethnic groups. The Great Depression hit just when Italians were beginning to make significant progress, setting the ethnic group back in its advances toward better education, jobs, and income. The outcome of World War II finally changed the situation. Sociologist Milton Gordon measured the progress made by several ethnic groups toward assimilation by 1950. Lumping all European American Catholics into one category, he concluded that these ethnic groups had largely completed the acculturation process. He also found that the Italian and other European Catholics were relatively free from discrimination and had made partial progress in removing anti – Catholic prejudice.[31]

By the 1930s, many Italians were becoming members of mainstream groups that had no official ethnic affiliation. The Bethlehem Park Parents' Association was one of many civic groups in the neighborhood at that time. Costantino Novelli, an immigrant, was very involved in civic and political affairs as well as in Italian organizations.
Source: Mary Novelli-Barone

Widespread Acceptance into Mainstream Institutions

In the decades since the mid – 1920s, Lackawanna Italians have slowly risen from the lower to the upper levels of mainstream social institutions. These developments run parallel to those on the national level. For example, since the 1960s, Italians have been moving into top corporate positions as well as government seats, such as on the Supreme Court and in presidential cabinets.

Ethnic Politics. Involvement in the political process is key to gaining a share of society's rewards and to effectively challenging patterns of prejudice and discrimination. Peasants in southern Italy had little experience with electoral politics and, confounded by America's urban politics, those in the Steel City fell victim to the divide-and-conquer tactics of the Irish and Poles. In the 1910s, Italians had entered into Lackawanna's rough-and-tumble ethnic politics by electing several Democratic and Republican committeemen. Some 31 Italian individuals held this position between 1912 and 1942. Another sign of growing political influence was the number of times Italians were appointed as city-election inspectors, growing from two in the 1910s to 35 in the 1930s.[32]

In 1921, men representing the city's Italian neighborhoods founded the Italian American Citizens Club. Five more political groups organized in the 1930s improved the ethnic group's political clout. Other Italian societies sponsored candidate forums and endorsed candidates. The Federation of Italian American Associations had success in lobbying for jobs and neighborhood improvements. Learning the rules of urban ethnic politics from the Irish and Poles, Italian organizations procured jobs and favors in return for the group's votes. The leaders of Italian societies who sought public office had a natural constituency of voters who could be rallied on election day. The best source of political power and patronage jobs was to elect Italians into office, especially to the city council. Joe Milano's election as a city assessor in the late 1920s and as First Ward councilman in the mid-1930s marked the advancement of Italians in the city's political hierarchy. Angelo Grosso's one term as First Ward councilman, 1941 to 1943, marked another first as his peers elected him council president. Since then, 11 other Italian Americans have served as councilmen.[33]

The growth of Italian political power was dependent on the immigrants and the second generation registering to vote and showing up at the polls. Increasingly, they did so, and Italian females quickly took advantage of that right when women won the franchise in 1920. The number of Italians registered to vote climbed from 157 in 1926 to 910 in 1940, then to 1,017 in 1950. The percentage of females among the Italian voters also increased,

The Lackawanna City Band in 1910 included one Italian, Frank Morinello. On porch, from left: [Unk], Robert Reed. Middle row: Walter Gurstung, [Unk], Carl Robinson, Roy Bloom, Oscar Brown, Ray Menz, Ben Lusich, Ray Trella. Bottom row: Howard McCullough, Ray Bowley, Bernard McCullough, _?_ McCullough, Bill Case, Harry Gallineau, Frank Morinello. Photo source: Collection of Frank Morinello Jr.

from 20% in 1926 to 46% in 1945. Tom Pepper in 1937 was the first Italian elected to the school board. Six years later, Tony Moretti was on the board. This led to the appointment of more Italian teachers as well as secretaries and maintenance people. Since the mid-1950s, Italians have regularly been elected to city assessor and school-board seats. Many Italians have been appointed to city boards and commissions since the first ones broke the ice in 1920. Members of the ethnic group first attained the chairman's seat of the city Republican party in the 1960s and of the Democratic party in the 1970s.[34]

Organizations. Societies of the general community began to attract Italians in the years just prior to World War I. The number of Italians in mainstream organizations increased during the 1930s, with the maturation of the second generation, and blossomed after World War II. By the 1930s, some first-generation politicos and businessmen and a number of second-generation individuals were active in the Eagles, the Young Men's Civic

Club, the chamber of commerce and junior chamber of commerce, school PTAs, and homeowner and taxpayers' associations. More and more American-born men and women joined sports and recreation groups around the city as well as those sponsored by the steel plant. This trend expanded in the 1940s and 1950s as Italians became leaders in resident associations of the Baker Homes and Ridgewood Village, and as those who served in World War II joined a variety of veterans' posts and advocacy groups. Supervisors in the steel plant joined other Catholics in the Anchor clubs which provided peer support and challenged the domination of supervisory positions by Masons. As more Italians enrolled in college following the war, they became involved in student groups along with other Lackawannans. By the 1950s and 1960s, Italians were well represented in a wide variety of mainstream societies and clubs throughout the city.

Religion. St. Anthony's Church was the center of religious life for Lackawanna's Italians since its founding in 1917. In

Students at Roosevelt School, circa 1925. Anne Melillo is at the extreme right in the bottom row.
Photo source: Collection of Anne Melillo-Corvigno

Italy, the religious education of the children was done by the adult women in the home, but in Lackawanna, weekly formal religious instruction began by the 1930s. The Catholic diocese often managed to have an Irish priest instruct public school students at weekly meetings in the nationality parishes of the First Ward. The lessons stressed attending Mass, monetary contributions, and respect for church authority—all of which challenged the Italian traditions of government financing, patron saint-feasts, and anticlericism.[35]

A number of second-generation males were very active in St. Anthony's parish, especially in its Holy Name Society. They involved Italian boys in new groups at the church and provided leadership for the programs. These second-generation leaders were the new role models for male participation in the church, challenging the anticlericism of the immigrant men. Some Italian American girls joined the multiethnic Junior Catholic Daughters of America. By the late 1930s, the *feste*, (religious street processions), were discontinued at St. Anthony's, replaced by card parties and carnival-style events.[36]

As Italians moved out of the ethnic enclaves, they attended other parishes. In 1918, the family of Luca and Maddalena Tarquinio joined what became the Our Lady of Victory parish. John Verel's family and others who moved north

from Roland Avenue also joined that predominantly Irish parish. Italians on Roland Avenue often attended the multiethnic Our Mother of Good Counsel Church in Blasdell, which was closer than St. Anthony's and usually welcoming. A small number of Italians joined Protestant denominations, such as the Jehovah's Witnesses.[37]

Gradually, as Italians dispersed geographically, they affiliated with whatever Catholic Church was nearby. The Italians moved away from the ethnic church and its religious traditions, which hastened their religious assimilation. They learned that family attendance at services was a mark of respectability in America. Those Italians who have remained members of St. Anthony's can still pray to statues of patron saints, but the parish has a new flavor. In 1998, Queen of All Saints Church was closed, and its parishioners, composed of Latinos, blacks, and other ethnic groups, merged into St. Anthony's, which is now a multicultural church.[38]

Area of Residence. After World War II, many Italians moved to new residences in nonethnic neighborhoods. A 1949 directory of homeowners listed 28 Italian families that had moved from Lackawanna to Blasdell, Woodlawn, and Hamburg. In the Steel City, the number of Italian households outside the traditional ethnic enclaves grew tremendously, increasing from 26% in

Sal Yoviene works on the walls of his new house on Orchard Avenue in 1949. His sister-in-law Dorothy Downing looks on. The movement of Italians to the area east of South Park Avenue accelerated after World War II. Photo source: Jim Yoviene

S. John Ceccarelli, pictured here in 1980, became the first Italian to rise to the position of melter in the open hearths of the Bethlehem Steel plant in Lackawanna in 1950. Photo source: Collection of Phil and Adeline Andreozzi

1941 to 50% in 1960. Most of the movement was from the First Ward to the eastern part of the city. By 1960, almost six of every 10 Italian households were located east of the railroad tracks, the majority of them outside Roland Avenue, the only Italian enclave in eastern Lackawanna (see Figure 4.7). During the next four decades, Italians continued to move throughout the city. By 2006, some 81% of Italian households were outside the three Italian neighborhoods, and the original settlements had shrunk greatly. Ingham Avenue had only 14 Italian households, Roland Avenue 55, and Bethlehem Park 58 by 2006. A few small clusters of Italians households formed in the new suburban areas of the city. On Norfred Drive, 22 of the 41 households were Italian in 1973, largely because the Amadori Construction Company, based in Bethlehem Park, had a role in developing the neighborhood. On Fisher Road, relatives and *paesani* from Pettorano sul Gizio established five households.[39]

Economic and Occupational Institutions. Italians gradually gained access to higher levels of economic institutions. Despite the nativist predictions that Italians couldn't perform the more complicated and technical jobs inside the steel mills, it was apparent by 1925 that many Italians were working inside the mills (see Figure 4.8). The formation of industrial unions between 1936 and 1941 greatly benefited Italians and other immigrants not only by yielding better wages and benefits but also by breaking the ethnic hierarchy in the steel plant, opening up skilled and supervisory positions that had been dominated by northwest Europeans. Among all Italian workers in Lackawanna, the number of laborers continually declined,

dropping from 73% in 1920 to 25% in 1973. Skilled and semiskilled workers doubled to 41% between 1920 and 1930, and remained at that mark in the following four decades. Italians holding supervisory jobs rose from 23 in 1930 to 60 in 1973. In the steel plant, Joe Mesi became the general foreman of the South Buffalo Railway's track department in 1926. During the 1940s and early 1950s, several Italians became yardmasters and attained other managerial positions on the railway. In the open hearths of Bethlehem Steel, S. John Ceccarelli became the first Italian to hold the position of melter. Edward Lorenzi became superintendent of No. 1 Open Hearth in 1958 and superintendent of the Steelmaking Division 10 years later. Italians also moved into other sectors of the economy. After graduating from the University of Buffalo in 1950, Lackawanna native Albert Bell held positions at National Gypsum Company and Ford Motors, then moved on in 1966 to the Conax Corporation in Buffalo, where he was named president four years later. Frank Fiore joined Dun & Bradstreet's Buffalo division in 1962, advanced to a higher position in New York City, and in 1976 became the regional vice president of the D & S Marketing Services Division in Los Angeles.[40]

The number of business proprietors more than doubled, going from 42 in 1930 to 88 in 1960, but declined by 1973 as people retired or moved out of the city. Italians established 686 businesses in Lackawanna between 1900 and 2008, more than a third of them were food-related. Of the 379 enterprises created prior to 1950, the leading categories were food (grocery stores and restaurants), saloons, shoe repair and barber shops,

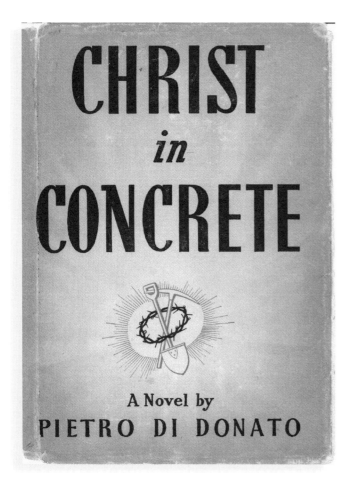

Pietro di Donato's Christ in Concrete *was one of the early English-language novels about life in Little Italy. It was published in 1937 and made into a movie a decade later.*

boardinghouses, and automobile-related services. Among the 307 businesses founded since 1950, food was most numerous, followed by automobile services, construction and builders' supplies, barbers, and beauty salons. The significant number of beauty salons indicated that second-generation women were increasingly becoming business proprietors. The number of Italian professionals in Lackawanna, which stood at 17 in 1941, grew as the second and third generations entered college in large numbers after World War II. From 33 in 1960, the count grew to 91 in 1973, including 33 educators, eight nurses, seven firefighters, and six policemen.[41]

Education. James Oddy graduated from Canisius College in 1928, and Daniel Monaco became a lawyer upon completion of his degree at Southeastern University in Washington, D.C. in 1941. They were among the other professionals who had attained high levels of education. Italians were also making progress in the elementary and secondary schools, with a greater number of them completing eighth grade, then moving on to graduate from high school. Many of these students excelled in their studies and were on the honor roll, accomplishments their immigrant parents could barely conceive

of in Italy. After World War II, more Italians attended college, and between 1946 and 1949, at least 29 were attending college and technical school. In the 1950s, a number of doctors, lawyers, teachers, and other professionals graduated from college. The number of Lackawanna Italian men and women enrolled in college was at least 38 by 1960, increasing to 104 in 1973.[42]

The Press and other Media. The Lackawanna press was slow to print articles about the everyday lives of Italians, and of the First Ward ethnic groups in general. But by the end of World War I, articles by and about Italian Americans began to appear, followed in the mid-1930s by regular columns penned by members of the ethnic group. Ralph Galanti and Armondo Pietrocarlo wrote local interest pieces for the *Rochester Bugle*, and Mike Schiavi had sports and general-interest columns in the *Lackawanna Leader* in the late 1950s. Bill Delmont acquired the *Front Page* in 1958, which today is the only newspaper based in the Steel City. For many years, the paper has carried a column written first by Ralph Galanti and now by his son Chico.[43]

Films at movie theaters in Lackawanna and Buffalo in the early twentieth century modeled the mainstream version of American history and culture. Silent movies emerged at the time millions of Italians and other southeast Europeans were arriving in the United States, and the immigrants became the subject of many films. Director D. W. Griffiths made several films about Italians, such as *Italian Blood* in 1911, in which a jealous and hot-tempered Italian husband is almost convinced by his wife to murder their children. In *At the Altar* (1909), an irrational Italian seeks to get revenge on another man who has found love. Reginald Turner directed *The Italian*, a 1915 movie that was more sympathetic to the main character, a bootblack, but at times portrays him as a crazed animal filled with violent passions, and depicts Italian immigrants in stereotyped ways. Gradually, the movies offered less harsh views of Italians, as in the comedy of Chico Marx's Italian characters in the 1930s, the movie version of Pietro Di Donato's *Christ in Concrete* in the following decade, and *Marty* and *The Rose Tattoo* in the 1950s. But during this same 20-year period, gangster films again reinforced the stereotype of the violent, criminal Italian. While depictions of Italians filled the screen, other types of influence were also being felt by Italians going to the theater. Advertisements and contests for prizes reinforced the notion that being an American citizen meant being a consumer. Music provided by radio and record players allowed Italians to listen to opera as well as learn the latest American pop tunes. The music, entertainment, and advertisements on radio served the same functions. Interview subjects indicated that movies and radio probably helped in the acculturation of some immigrants and a sizable number of the second generation.[44]

Giuseppe Volpe emigrated from Campania and joined the U.S. Army in World War I. Military service automatically made him a naturalized citizen, and he translated his name into English—Joe Fox. Photo source: Anne Fox-Skrzynski

Brothers Brad, left, and Ralph Carestio in early 1940s with nephews and niece, from left: Nelson and Ann Marie Tonucci, and Jerry and Ron Baldelli.
Photo source: Dennis Sterlace

The Military, Entertainment, and Sports. Many Lackawanna Italians, most of them immigrants, served in the U.S. military during World War I, and a number of them obtained citizenship at the completion of their service. Both their service and their naturalization demonstrated patriotism and helped calm nativist fears. During the years between the world wars, especially after the onset of the Depression, some Lackawanna Italians signed up for peacetime stints in the service. In the 1930s, the Civilian Conservation Corps (CCC), run by the Army, offered basic job training and a steady income for the young men who joined. Many Italians entered the CCC, which allowed them to escape the ore dust and poverty of Lackawanna and discover life in rural America, but also required that most of their earnings be sent to their financially strapped families. Military service in the Second World War was crucial

in proving the patriotism of Italian Americans, as Italy was an enemy of the United States from 1941 to 1943. [45]

Military service from 1917 to 1945 also was a great tool in acculturating Lackawanna Italians, who lived with and fought beside people of every European ethnic group in America as well as some people of color. This direct contact helped to dispel ethnic prejudices, as well as to advance the idea of all whites, if not all races, being equal. Many of the Italians serving in World War II were American-born and spoke fluent English, enabling them to more easily rise in rank and encouraging some to make a career of the military. War-time movies celebrated the ethnic diversity of the American military (it seems every film platoon included an Italian American) and a number of Italian enlisted men and officers won national recognition for their exploits on the battlefield. The loyalty of

Figure 4.9

Larry Covelli, Jazz Musician

Larry Covelli was born in Lackawanna in 1928, a few months after his parents and older siblings had immigrated from Italy. He likes to say that he was conceived in Calabria and born in the Old Village. His musical career started in 1934 when he won first prize on Emelino Rica's Italian hour, a weekly radio show featuring a musical talent contest. He sang "Tango della Capinera," and his prizes were a gallon of olive oil and a pair of high-top shoes. A few years later, he sang at his brother Leo's wedding. As a boy, he went with his mother and siblings to pick crops on farms in southern Erie County. He also worked summer jobs at General Mills and caddied at Wanakah Country Club. He gave most of the money he earned to his father. Covelli played clarinet in the Lackawanna High School band, and with the money he saved from his jobs, he bought a tenor sax. He joined Benny Solar's band, which included 15 teens from a variety of ethnic backgrounds. The pianist and drummer was Dick Fadale, who transported Covelli and others in his Model A Ford. The band played at the high school's senior and junior proms, each musician earning $2 or $3 per night.

In 1946, Larry Covelli quit school and joined the Navy. After his discharge, he

Larry Covelli playing the saxophone at Las Hadas Restaurant in Van Nuys, California, 2006.
Photo source: Larry Covelli

learned bricklaying through an apprentice program at Bethlehem Steel. For many years, he alternated between working as a mason and as a musician. He has played saxophone, flute, and clarinet with the bands of Glen Miller, Harry James, Woody Herman, Al Hirt, Chuck Mangione, Louie Bellson, Freddie Martin, and Lloyd Price. One writer called him an "international tenor sax legend." A Covelli hallmark

was his solo on Chuck Mangione's "She's Gone" from the *Friends and Love* album, which he was featured playing during a concert with the Rochester Philharmonic Orchestra in the 1960s. At 80 years old, Covelli continues to play with the big bands, appearing with the Glen Miller band in Singapore and Kuala Lum Pur in late 2008. "I am still able to do it, and I enjoy it more than ever," he said.

Larry Covelli has been married to the former Carol Pastore for 60 years. They live in Southern California near their five children, 12 grandchildren, and great-grandson. They often return to western New York to visit friends and relatives. During the visits, Covelli plays gigs with old friends at the Buffalo Italian Heritage Festival as well as local jazz clubs. The albums on which Covelli has performed include Woody Herman's *Thundering Herd*; Chuck Mangione's *Friends and Love*, *Together*, *Bella Via*, *60 Miles Long*, and *Vintage Mangione*; and Louie Bellson's *Live at Ronnie Scott's* in London, England. Covelli produced his own disc titled *Return to Home*.

Sources: interviews with Larry Covelli, July 14, 1992, and December 29, 2008; letter from Larry Covelli, February 12, 2009; *Il Corriere Italiano*, 10/18/34; Phil Sims, "Three Freakin' Giants of Jazz," *Art Voice*, July 10-16, 2008.

Italian Americans was never questioned again in subsequent conflicts, and members of the ethnic group have served in Korea, Vietnam, the two Gulf Wars, Afghanistan, and other engagements of the American military.

Italian American entertainers who began their careers prior to World War II became even more familiar as the television became a common household item after the war. Perry Como and Dean Martin had their own shows, and Frank Sinatra, Tony Bennett, and others made frequent TV appearances, along with younger rock and roll singers such as Dion DiMucci, Bobby Rydell, and Frankie Avalon. Annette Funicello was one of a number of other Italian TV personalities. Opera and classical singers from Italy, including Luciano Pavarotti and Andrea Bocelli, gained wide American audiences via TV appearances

and stage performances. Italian American athletes continued to gain notoriety in the second half of the Twentieth century. In professional football, Andy Robustelli and Dante Lavelli starred in the 1950s, as did Nicholas Buoniconti and Dan Marino in later years. College football had All-American Joe Bellino and Heisman Trophy winners Gino Torretta and Vinnie Testaverde. Italian American females notable in sports include softball player and coach Donna Lopiano, figure skater Linda Fratianne, and gymnast Mary Lou Retton, who won a gold medal in the Olympics.[46]

In Lackawanna, several American-born Italians had noteworthy athletic, musical, and entertainment careers. Ralph Carestio won a number of awards as an amateur golfer. His brother Brad, an amateur boxer for several years beginning in

Ad for the Crazy Bone night club featuring a mainstay of the Italian diet—pasta fasuli *(pasta and beans in tomato broth).* Photo source: *Steel City Press*, 5/12/48

the late 1920s, later became a trainer and manager of amateur boxers. Jimmy Mandel, of Irish and Italian heritage, was a well-known boxer who had his first professional match in 1941. Other Lackawanna boxers included Joe Capuani, Sam Cardinale, and Mike Schiavi. Mary Orlando graduated from the Sherwood School of Music in Chicago as a classical violinist. Larry Covelli is an accomplished clarinet and saxophone player who has worked with a number of big bands (see Figure 4.9). Dick Fadale was a drummer who had his own group in the 1950s and 1960s and later produced musical tracks. Francis "Caz" DePasquale had a long career in show business beginning in 1936, when he and Sam Milano, Ernest Tenuta, and John Kustreba formed the Harmonics quartet. Dr. John Fadale drove the group to New York City to audition for the Major Bowes radio amateur show; despite their successful audition they were unable to stay in the city until an appearance could be scheduled. DePasquale was involved in many amateur contests in the Buffalo area; he joined the American Guild of Variety Artists, and performed for three months at Lackawanna's Bon-Ton nightclub. Drafted into the Army in 1942, he spent three years acting as master of ceremonies for variety shows at veterans hospitals and military bases. Upon discharge from the service, he worked nightclubs and theaters in western New York, Pennsylvania, and Ohio under the name "Jimmy Caz." In the late 1940s, DePasquale and Kustreba ran the Crazy Bone nightclub where they were joined by Milano, Al LaMarti, Carmen Navarra, Irene DePasquale, and others in performing live shows. DePasquale later became a writer for comedians and speaker and had a column in the *Front Page*.[47]

Charitable Organizations. Early in the twentieth century, relief agencies reflected the common belief that poor people, the unemployed, and immigrants were dangerous and needed to be controlled. Italian immigrants distrusted charity agencies in Italy and later in America. They only reluctantly sought aid from strangers when the survival of their families was in question. They did use the services of the Charity Organization

Society of Lackawanna, the Erie County Welfare Bureau office in the city, and the Our Lady of Victory institutions. With the full employment of World War II and the postwar prosperity, most working class Italians could finally enjoy economic security. One Italian involved in the structure of the Charity Organization Society of Lackawanna was Dr. John Fadale, who alternately served as president and treasurer in the 1940s and 1950s. Fadale and his wife were among a number of Italian doctors and their spouses who were active in committees to raise funds for Our Lady of Victory Hospital. Other professionals were leaders of Red Cross fundraising campaigns.[48]

Widespread Acceptance into Personal Relationships

Even more crucial to the assimilation of Italian Americans was the process of entering into personal relationships with non – Italians—neighbors, friendship circles, social cliques, and, most important, intermarriage. Few of the city's neighborhoods were made up of only one ethnic group, and immigrants formed friendships with neighbors from different ethnic groups. Some of these relationships were more formal

Members of the Schole family, residing in Lackawanna and Blasdell, married non – Italians in the 1920s. Bride Florence Schole and groom Bert Scott are seated, and standing are Jim Burns and his wife Rose Schole-Burns. Photo source: Collection of Frank Morinello Jr.

and grew out of necessity. Women giving birth in Lackawanna were sometimes assisted by Italian midwives from Buffalo, but by 1911, some Italians on Ingham Avenue brought in non – Italian doctors who had offices nearby, or Mrs. M. Zdzienski, a Polish midwife who lived on upper Ingham Avenue. Italian women often exchanged dishes of food or recipes with

Slavic housewives on the same block. Italian men compared wine and liquor-making techniques with Hungarians and Poles, and shared different styles of cigars and pipe tobacco. In the Baker Homes, neighbors Filiberto Covelli and Russian immigrant Joe Kissel often drank wine together, and when Kissel tried his first Parodi cigar, he made the mistake of inhaling—soon coughing and falling out of his chair as an amused Covelli watched. These connections were even more common for their children, who could usually speak English at an early age and were playmates on the streets and classmates at the public schools. In the steel plant, men of different ethnic groups sometimes ate their lunches together, or went to one of Lackawanna's many bars right after work. The United Steelworkers Union also provided a common cause and setting for men to forge friendships. Italians were moving out of the Steel City's Little Italys by the 1920s, a movement that grew more notable after 1945. The second generation intermixed with their peers of other southeast European ethnic groups as well as Irish and German Americans.[49]

Many personal relationships with non – Italians were the result of Italians being accepted into formal institutions, or moving to higher levels of institutions. When Tony Turchiarelli and Adele and John Panzetta became active in political parties, they also gained access to the informal cliques and friendship networks of Irish and Polish politicians. Successful businessmen, such as John Verel and Nicholas Mattucci, had formal relationships with other businesspeople and the chamber of commerce, which enabled them to mix in social circles with non – Italians. Verel and South Buffalo businessman Joe Recchio took boat rides on Lake Erie with non – Italian business and civic leaders. By the 1920s, as more Italians crossed ethnic boundaries by moving into neighborhoods in eastern Lackawanna, they formed friendships with non-Italians and entered the personal cliques of the dominant culture. When a city newspaper noted that businessman Nick Sperduto was participating in an informal political club, it indicated that he was part of the political "in-crowd." There was constant interplay between involvement in formal institutions and forming personal relationships outside one's ethnic group.[50]

Intermarriage represents the highest form of personal relationship. It is the "ultimate measure of social acceptance in any community" and represents a blending of ethnic groups. Data was gathered on marriages involving 4,236 individuals, first- through fifth-generation Italian Americans with roots in Lackawanna, and their spouses (see figures 4.10, 4.11 and 4.12). Like Italian immigrants throughout the United States, those in Lackawanna tended to marry within their ethnic group during the early years of the twentieth century. Of the 1,803 Italian immigrants for whom data is available, only three percent married non – Italians.[51]

FIGURE 4.10

Marriage Partners of Italians with Roots in Lackawanna

ITALIAN
(Unmixed: Full Italian Ancestry)

Generation	Gender	Number	Italian*	Non – Italian
First**	Male	976	935	41
	Female	827	823	4
	Subtotal:	1,803	1,758	45
Second	Male	614	305	309
	Female	908	490	418
	Subtotal:	1,522	795	727
Third	Male	132	42	90
	Female	305	84	221
	Subtotal:	437	126	311
Fourth	Male	6	2	4
	Female	14	2	12
	Subtotal:	20	4	16
	Total:	3,782	2,683	1,099

MIXED ITALIAN
(Partial Italian Ancestry)

Generation	Gender	Number	Italian*	Non – Italian
Second	Male	14	3	11
	Female	40	8	32
	Subtotal:	54	11	43
Third	Male	64	11	53
	Female	239	58	181
	Subtotal:	303	69	234
Fourth	Male	20	7	13
	Female	77	12	65
	Subtotal:	97	19	78
	Total:	454	99	355

ITALIAN AND MIXED

	Grand Total:	4,236	2,782	1,454

*By the third and fourth generations, many of the Italian spouses were probably of mixed ancestry, but data on this were rarely available.

**A total of 2,172 male immigrants and 886 female immigrants were identified as living in Lackawanna for at least a short period of time. Of these, marital partners present in Lackawanna were identified for 976 of the males and 827 of the females. Sources: Compiled from announcements in local newspapers, marriage register at St. Anthony's Church, interviews, U.S. Census 1910–1930; N.Y. Census 1905–1925; Erie Count Directory, 1931, 1941.

The wedding of Rose Fiore and John Pacholczak, 1945. Italians often chose members of other Catholic European ethnic groups as spouses, especially from the sizable Polish and Irish American populations in Lackawanna.
Photo source: Rose Fiore-Pacholczak

The situation of second-generation Italians in Lackawanna was very different from their parents; overall, 49% of them chose non – Italian spouses. The vast majority of second generation individuals married between 1920 and 1959, and the rate of marriages to non – Italians increased: from 23% during the 1920s to 58% in the 1950s. The small number of second-generation individuals who were of mixed ancestry (one parent Italian, the other non – Italian) were even more likely to marry people of other ethnic groups; four out of five of them did so. Many of the non – Italian spouses had Polish and other Slavic surnames. Irish, German, and Hungarian surnames were also common. Italian immigrants sometimes objected to their children marrying outside the ethnic group, as did Aniello Covino when his daughter Jay (Giustina) announced her engagement to a Polish American. Like many of her peers, Jay went ahead with the marriage, while at the same time staying in touch with her parents and showing respect for Italian family customs. Other immigrants approved of their children marrying non – Italians who were respectful and family-oriented. A mixed marriage in many ways hastened the acculturation process, especially if the couple distanced themselves from their parents' ethnic customs. If the couple lived with or felt emotionally closer to one set of parents, the latter set the tone for which traditions were retained in the new family, especially concerning the grandchildren. In a mixed marriage, the spouses had to negotiate about family customs, which sometimes led to a reduction in the number of rituals carried over from both of their ethnic backgrounds.[52]

The American ideals of individualism and romantic love were often attractive to young Italian women who were American-born or had emigrated from Europe as children. Many rejected the arranged marriages brokered by relatives and *paesani*, instead encouraging suitors they themselves found attractive. During the 1920s and 1930s, young people met through friends or at dances and social events, where the women were with a group of peers and free of the watchful protectiveness of family members. The resulting courtship may have included family chaperones, but it was the young man and woman, with the help of friends, who had done their own matchmaking.

Civic Assimilation

The absence of major value and power conflicts between Italian Americans and the mainstream culture is the hallmark of civic assimilation. The hostility of American society toward Italian immigrants between the 1870s and the 1940s certainly

FIGURE 4.11

THE TRIPLE MELTING POT

Sociological studies have found that between 1870 and 1940, members of European American ethnic groups have intermarried but generally within the three major Judeo – Christian religious groups: Protestant, Catholic, and Jewish. Prior to 1976, the vast number of voluntary immigrants were white Europeans. While immigrants from Europe overwhelmingly married within their own nationality or cultural group, their children and grandchildren increasingly found spouses from other white ethnic groups but of the same religion. Will Herberg used the term Triple Melting Pot to describe this phenomenon.

The Triple Melting Pot had its roots in the mid-nineteenth century. There was a steady flow of Protestant immigrants —people from the British Isles, Scandinavia, and at least half of the German migrants— who became assimilated and were included in the enlarged definition of WASPs. The arrival of Irish and German Catholics beginning in the 1840s, however, rapidly expanded the small American Catholic community. The influx of Italian and Slavic Catholics between 1880 and 1924 further swelled their numbers. At the same time, Jewish migrants from eastern Europe joined the smaller group of German Jews who had earlier migrated. The United States became the home of three large religious groups, each composed of a variety of European nationalities. Those who were Protestant could take comfort in being of the same religious background as the WASP host group, but the Catholics and,

especially, the Jews, had a more difficult path to walk.

Looking at Catholics in New Haven, Connecticut, between 1870 and 1940, the number of Irish people marrying within their ethnic group fell from 93% to 45%. Among Italians, the in-group marriage rate fell from 98% in 1900 to 82% in 1940, and that for Poles from 100% to 53%. However, the vast majority of Catholics of all ethnic groups continued to marry Catholics; 80% did so in 1940, only slightly down from 95% in 1870. In the 1930s and 1940s, Irish Americans of marriageable age were likely to be of the third and fourth generations, and to be more assimilated than the Italians and Poles, who were predominantly second generation. With time, however, the number of Poles and Italians who married outside their ethnic group had increased noticeably. About 58% of Italian Americans, of 100% Italian ancestry married within the ethnic group in 1963-64. In Lackawanna, only 30% of full-blooded third-generation Italians marrying between 1960 and 1969 had Italian spouses. Among all the city's Italians who married between 1950 and 1969, 65% chose non – Italian spouses. The European Americans were rapidly blending into a large ethnic grouping based on race, and subdivided into three religions.

As the Triple Melting Pot concept evolved, immigrants of all three religious groupings, assimilated. The Catholic— and to a lesser extent, Jewish— religious institution eventually won acceptance into American society. The Catholics had the

advantages of being Christian and present in huge numbers. The presidency of John F. Kennedy, 1961 to 1963, helped put to rest any lingering Protestant fears that Catholic political leaders were controlled by the Pope. A series of Jewish congressmen and Presidential cabinet members highlighted the greater acceptance of that religious group. Catholics and Jews enlarged and legitimized the religious diversity of the United States. Their transformation into Americanized forms of Catholicism and Judaism marked one passage in their overall assimilation. Writing in 1955, Herberg predicted that the Triple Melting Pot phenomenon was only an intermediate phase, and that Anglo-conformity would prevent any melding of these religious groupings. The national culture, he said, "has always been, and remains, pretty well fixed. It is the Mayflower, John Smith, Davey Crockett, George Washington, and Abraham Lincoln that define the American's self-image, and this is true whether the American in question is a descendant of the Pilgrims or the grandson of an immigrant from southeastern Europe." But by the 1960s, Anglo-conformity was being mediated by the presence of so many southeast European ethnic groups. John F. Kennedy's book, *A Nation of Immigrants*, proclaimed what America had become, at least for the Catholics and Jews who had been denied legitimacy since the 1840s.

Sources: Will Herberg, *Protestant, Catholic, Jew*, 1955 (1960), pp. (quote) 21, 32 –33; Humbert Nelli, *From Immigrants to Ethnics: The Italian Americans*, 1983, p. 180; John F. Kennedy, *A Nation of Immigrants*, 1958.

fed into conflicts between the immigrants and mainstream culture. But gradually, the immigrants accommodated nativist demands. They were patriotic during World War I and increasingly became naturalized during the 1920s. Both mainstream Americans and Italian Americans praised the Mussolini regime from 1922 until 1935. But Italy's invasion of Ethiopia, and other acts of

aggression taken between 1936 and 1939 conflicted with American foreign policy, causing friction between mainstream society and Italian Americans who continued their admiration of *Il Duce*. World War II was very difficult, because Italy was an Axis power and an enemy of the United States. The loyalty of Italians in America was suspect, and the ethnic group endured

FIGURE 4.12

Marriage Partners of Second-, Third- Fourth-, and Fifth-Generation Italians by Decade of Marriage: 1900–2005*

Decade	Total M & F	Spouse Italian	Male	Spouse Italian	Female	Spouse Italian
1900-09	4	100%	—	—	4	100%
1910-19	35	71%	6	67%	29	72%
1920-29	146	78%	52	58%	94	89%
1930-39	369	64%	166	57%	203	70%
1940-49	571	49%	239	51%	332	48%
1950-59	552	39%	202	42%	350	37%
1960-69	415	29%	117	30%	298	29%
1970-79	243	22%	52	29%	191	20%
1980-89	76	21%	21	24%	55	20%
1990-99	33	21%	12	25%	21	19%
2000-05	19	26%	8	25%	11	27%
Total:	**2,463**	**44%**	**875**	**45%**	**1,588**	**44%**

*The second-generation statistics also include immigrants who were nine years old or younger at the time of departure from Italy. Few statistics were readily available for the years 1990 to 2005. Only 97 fourth- and fifth-generation individuals were identified during the period 1950 to 2005.

Helen Downing-Yoviene with her children on Warsaw Avenue in 1936. Mary Alice, in foreground, is making her First Holy Communion. Jim is on the left, Alfonse is on the right and Helen is holding Robert. The photo was taken by Sal Yoviene, the husband/father. Photo source: Jim Yoviene

restrictions and discrimination once the U.S. entered the war. The scene was set for a tremendous power conflict, but Italians quickly made it clear that they were patriotic Americans. Following the war, Italian Americans adhered to U.S. foreign policy, writing millions of letters to relatives in Italy encouraging them to vote against communist candidates in 1948.

In postwar America, several value and power conflicts involved Italians. One pitted them against Catholic teachings, especially regarding birth-control techniques, as many Italian couples used methods banned by the Church. To the extent that Italians had become part of the American Catholic community, they were involved in another type of conflict. As Italians and other European nationality groups were merging into the Protestant, Catholic, and Jewish groupings, it was apparent in the 1950s that American Catholics held beliefs that differed from those of other Americans. These issues concerned birth control, abortion, and church-state issues. The later issue emerged during the Presidential campaign of 1960 but subsided when John F. Kennedy won the election. On issues such as abortion, people began to take positions based less on the three

large religious groupings and more on particular denominations and other demographics.[53]

Intermarriage among second- and later-generation European ethnics had gradually led to a Triple Melting Pot, in which white people married partners of other ethnic groups but of the same religion—Protestant, Catholic, or Jewish. This phenomenon grew tremendously after World War II, and in the last four decades, marriage across religious boundaries has been substantial. This has helped to blur ethnic differences and further reduced chances for power and value conflicts between white ethnics and mainstream society. As religious boundaries were loosened by intermarriage, Italians, other southeast Europeans, and Irish and German Catholics were part of the white ethnic revival of the 1960s and 1970s. In part, they were reacting to the civil rights movement with both fear and admiration. The white ethnics feared that the demands for inclusion in mainstream society by the blacks would come at their expense. But Italians and the other white ethnics also wanted to imitate African Americans by making assertive demands for inclusion in the highest levels of society, being recognized as equals in the

Float in Buffalo parade during World War II. The driver, visible just behind the image of the jeep, is Tullio Paolini, whose trucking company was based in Lackawanna and did much hauling for the Bethlehem Steel Company.
Photo source: Joe Streamer

Night-school naturalization class, Roosevelt School, late 1950s. The class included three Italian immigrants: Orlando D'Alessandro and Maria Fanone, seated at front, and Mario Fanone, standing at right. Photo source: Phil Fanone

Identity Assimilation

This concept, as defined in the early twentieth century, meant that immigrants would completely accept the dominant WASP culture, forget their old world cultures, and think of themselves solely as Americans. What happened, however, is that Italian Americans developed an ethnic identity that, while undergoing changes over the past century, has persisted and is still embraced to varying degrees by many individuals. By 1945, the systematic prejudice against Italians had ended, and in the following two decades, second-generation adults, with the exception of a small number of "in-groupers," usually limited their display of Italian traits in public to avoid negative reactions and stereotyping. Yet in the privacy of their homes, at the Italian church, or in society meetings, they applauded Italian American entertainers, celebrities, and athletes and shared ethnic traditions. This defensive pride was noticeable in the actions of Italians and other white ethnics born prior to World War II who had fresh memories of "being" ethnic in everyday life and enduring discrimination. They retained some of the behavior of "being" Italian as well as the less intense and pervasive state of "feeling" Italian, while at the same time wanting simply to fit in as Americans. Many were becoming more comfortable entering into the wider identities of working-class and lower-middle-class Catholic America. Milton Gordon observed that European American Catholics in 1950 were acculturated but had not completed the process of identity assimilation, which implies that members of an ethnic group will not necessarily shed all key elements of their ancestral culture within two generations, and that religion and some cultural ties are more impervious to assimilation pressures.[54]

The ethnic revival that began in the late 1960s allowed white ethnics to express pride in their roots. Until this time, ethnicity was still viewed as foreign and a trait of blue-collar workers of the lower class (see Figure 4.14). Those who rose in the social-class system were expected to completely submerge their roots, and act more like WASPs. But in the 1970s and 1980s, public

building of the American nation, and displaying pride in the ancestral cultures that assimilation had forced them to downplay for many decades. And so, during the 1970s and 1980s, the image of the European American was born. Standing alongside the descendants of the WASP founders of the nation were the children and grandchildren of Ellis Island immigrants who had made their own patriotic contributions. Value and power conflict between Italians and the dominant culture is now a rarity, as Italians and other white ethnics have become part of mainstream culture and are more frequently included at its highest levels.

Figure 4.13

SOCIAL CLASS AND ETHNICITY

Social class is defined as the hierarchy, or pecking order, based on economic power, political power, and social status (values that define who is superior and who is inferior). Several sociologists described three social classes, each with two subdivisions, that existed in the United States in the first half of the twentieth century.

Upper-Upper: old family aristocrats, especially in large cities; pre – Civil War long-term residents who have a family tradition of wealth and occupy leading social positions in the community that indicate power, privilege, and good taste.

Lower-Upper: newly rich since Civil War who gradually infiltrate institutions of upper-uppers.

Upper-Middle: "solid, substantial citizens" with adequate incomes, but not wealthy or "social"; college education, professionals, or owners of midsize businesses, executives of service agencies, middle levels of power and decision-making, more white collar.

Lower-Middle: lower-rank white collar; skilled blue collar.

Upper-Lower: working class; bulk of blue-collar workers.

Lower-Lower: unskilled manual laborers; poor, often unemployed, on welfare, live in slums.

Both the mainstream society of the United States and specific ethnic communities have always been stratified by social class. Indeed, social class is just as powerful at creating a separate community, or subculture, of values and institutions as are ethnicity, urban or rural residence, or region of the country. Milton Gordon noted these divisions five decades ago and described how they interconnect. Combining the four factors of social class, ethnicity (nationality/culture, religion, and race), region of country, and urban-rural residence can produce the following categorization of one's place in American society (see below).

Gordon went on to combine the two most powerful factors, social class and ethnicity, into his concept of "ethclass" — the subculture created by one's ethnicity and social class. At mid-twentieth century, with regard to cultural behavior, social class was more important than ethnicity—

that is, people of the same social class act more alike and have more of the same values even if they are of different ethnic groups. As to primary relationships, people confine these to their own social-class segment within their ethnic group—that is, the ethclass. So, lower-middle-class Italians tend to seek relationships with other lower-middle-class Italians. Also, an upper-middle-class Italian Catholic has more in common with an upper-middle-class Irish Catholic than with an upper-lower-class Italian Catholic. Ethnicity has usually been associated in the United States with poor people (lower-lower class) and blue-collar workers (upper-lower class), because so many immigrants and their children were from these classes. One expectation of people entering the upper-middle or higher social classes prior to the late 1960s was that their ethnic origins would be muted or discarded. Today, there is more emphasis on social class as the ethnicity of European groups fades, and the ethnic traits of those southeast Europeans entering the three highest social classes can be more consciously displayed, but not to excess.

Social Class	Ethnicity	Region	Urban/Rural
Upper-upper	White-Anglo-Saxon-Protestant	Southern	Rural
Upper-middle	White-German-Jewish	Western	Urban
Upper-middle	Black Protestant	Northern	Urban
Lower-middle	White-Italian-Catholic	Northern	Urban
Lower-middle	White-Polish-Jewish	Midwestern	Urban
Lower-lower	Black Protestant	Southern	Rural

Source: Milton M. Gordon, *Assimilation in American Life: The Role of Race, Religion, and National Origins*, 1964, pp. 42, 51.

figures and people of higher social standing began to declare and celebrate their ethnic roots. During the last four decades, the reaction of whites to the civil-rights movement, the large-scale immigration of nonwhite peoples to the United States, and the pressure from white ethnics to be fully accepted at every level of society have all come together to create the European American as a broad racial group. Now mainstream culture

honors and mythologizes all European immigrants, even as ethnicity recedes and religious intermarriage has become more significant. Italian Americans, along with other white ethnics, are now more free to decide "how much they feel ethnic" and choose behaviors that incorporate ethnicity into their lives.[55]

The Italian ethnic group has come to see itself as basically American while retaining some aspects of its ancestral culture.

The sad price of decades of Anglo-conformity assimilation prior to the 1960s has been the dilution of the ethnic community and, for many, the loss of the ancestral language and culture. Today in Lackawanna, only a few Italians remain in the former enclave of Ingham Avenue, and the number of Italian residents in Bethlehem Park and the Roland Avenue neighborhood is significantly lower. Intermarriage has produced many blended European Americans who are third, fourth, and fifth generation, and a mixture of Italian and other ethnicities. Often, these individuals have little sense of an ethnic culture other than a few Italian foods and the knowledge that one's grandparent was Italian. A number of Lackawanna Italians still participate in several of the remaining ethnic organizations. But as the aging second-generation and post-World War II immigrants pass away, the future of Italian American ethnicity seems uncertain. While Italians are accepted members of the new European American group, they face the risk of completely losing their Italian ethnic identity. This may well be the "twilight" of ethnicity that sociologist Richard Alba has described, but that remains to be seen. In Lackawanna, the issue is not yet settled and will continue to be affected by "the most powerful and persistent group boundary in American history"—race.[56]

Several trends are currently in process that pose questions and challenges for Italian Americans. White ethnics in Lackawanna and around the country continue to assimilate into the new European American ethnicity based on race. There has been significant intermarriage among Catholics and Protestant Europeans, and both groups are now intermarrying with Jews on an increasing basis. While notable prejudice against Jews continues, a white, Judeo – Christian melting pot has taken form over the last four decades. This European American grouping usually excludes Turks, Iranians, and Arabs, who are officially classified as white but are mostly Muslim and have encountered significant prejudice, especially since some of their Middle Eastern homelands are defined by American foreign policy as hostile or supportive of terrorism. Indeed, it may well turn out that Americans with roots in the Middle East and of the Muslim faith become a sixth grouping in the new order of the Quintuple Melting Pot described below.

Racism has been the major unaddressed problem of the United States. Prior to World War II, there was not an official goal or any real hope for racial minorities—nonwhites—to move beyond the processes of acculturation and the formation of an ethnic community. A racial caste system built on strict segregation, bigoted laws and customs, and the threat of violence ruled out any hope of full assimilation into mainstream society. When America faced racist enemies in World War II, the country's leaders proclaimed the equality of all peoples. There followed the Cold War and the civil-rights movement, during which the United States tried to win allies in the Third World by demonstrating that it could put its own ethnic house in order. As a result, the old racial caste system began to break down. The immigration law of 1952 allowed all Asian migrants to become naturalized citizens. Immigration legislation passed in 1965 welcomed immigrants from all lands into American society on an equal basis and in greater numbers. By 1976, European arrivals were less than half the total, and people of color and mixed races from Asia, the Philippines, the Caribbean, and Latin America made up the bulk of the newcomers. The immigrants of the past four decades, while including many Catholics from Mexico and the Philippines, also included a significant number of Buddhists, Sikhs, Hindus, and Muslims, adding to America's diversity. The proportion of non-Hispanic whites in America's population fell to 74% in 1995 and is projected to fall to 53% in 2050, further increasing the fears of European Americans who maintain nativist or bigoted postures. Unlike the pre – World War II European immigrants, half the non – Europeans arriving by 1976 were professionals, and one of four attained professional or technical skills that prepared the way for upper-middle-class ranking. The trend toward worldwide migration has been accelerated by the movement toward economic and cultural globalization.[57]

The racial caste system in America has been at least partially dismantled over the past five decades by federal immigration and civil-rights legislation mandating equality and full participation of all ethnic groups in the society. It is now official doctrine that full assimilation of all racial groups in America is the desirable outcome. The increasing number of nonwhite peoples and their growing political power have aided this process. Blacks, Asians, Latinos, and Native Americans have more participation in mainstream society and are now able to interact with white people to a degree that was unheard of 100 years ago. While racial boundaries and discrimination are still strong, especially for African Americans and Native Americans, they have been gradually weakened. A crucial step toward assimilation into the personal relations of the mainstream came in 1967, when the U.S. Supreme Court struck down all state statutes barring whites from marrying nonwhites. Since then, the number of interracial marriages has increased tremendously. Marriages between blacks and whites increased from 65,000 in 1970 to 422,000 in 2005. During the same period, the number of all marriages that were interracial jumped from 300,000 to 2.3 million. These are preliminary signs that America can potentially become a melting pot that incorporates all ethnicities—nationality, religious, and racial—into a unified people.[58]

The Triple Melting Pot is being replaced by the Quintuple Melting Pot of five racial groups: European Americans, African Americans, Latino Americans, Asian Americans, and Native Americans. Like the European Americans, the other four racial groupings are made up of a variety of nationality and religious groups. African Americans who are the descendants of slaves can trace their lineage to 30 nations; American Indians to 540 tribal groups; Latinos to Mexico, Cuba, Puerto Rico, and the many other mixed-race countries in the western hemisphere; and Asians to a dozen countries and cultures of eastern and southern Asia. These five categories are just as vague and confusing as all previous classification schemes. But the terminology based on geographical areas implies that all groups are hyphenated-Americans of equal standing. At one time, the use of the hyphen, as in Italian-American, was demeaning, but in the term European American or Native American, while the hyphen is only implied, it has become "almost a mark of status." These new terms do not change the fact that "Whiteness … has been consistently privileged over non-Whiteness" throughout American history, but they do challenge the way our country has focused on the diversity of European ethnic groups while ignoring the diversity among Native Americans.[59]

The challenge for Italians and other European Americans is to find common ground with the four other racial groupings in the United States. The Columbus Quincentennial of 1992 displayed how people of color, especially Native Americans, could demand recognition of past exploitation by whites and acceptance into society. European Americans—especially the Italians, Irish, and Spaniards—found their celebrations of Columbus were challenged and sometimes upstaged by Native Americans and Latinos throughout the western hemisphere who desired to "highlight their grievances and their history of oppression under the European yoke." Just as the southeast European ethnics fought to have their story included in the history of America, so too do people of color struggle to be heard. The Quintuple Melting Pot can potentially lead to the greater equality among all ethnic groups and their assimilation into America's mainstream—or, on the other hand, to greater ethnic divisions and conflict. It is important that we European Americans not only understand the history of our own specific ethnic groups, and how our whiteness enabled our assimilation, but also that we acknowledge the long and tragic history of race relations in the United States.[60]

The Racial Pecking Order

In the early twentieth century, Italians and other immigrants were not alone in facing hostile forces in the United States. As bad as the southeast European immigrants had it, the fate of people of color—Indians, Africans, Latinos, and Asians—was far worse. A century ago, warfare had banished the Indians to reservations, segregation and violence made Africans second-class citizens, immigration laws denied entry to Asian laborers, and mixed-race Latinos, especially Mexicans, were wanted as temporary laborers but not welcome to remain

permanently in the U.S. In the 1920s, America finalized a system of ethnic hierarchy based on race, religion, and nationality that was encoded into its immigration and naturalization policies. The pecking order, or what sociologists call social stratification, refers to the way groups of people are ranked and how different groups are assigned different amounts of power, political clout, wealth, privilege, and respect. Race has been the most crucial variable in this system, with whites placed at the top of a three-layer hierarchy, people of color—blacks, American Indians, and Asians—at the bottom, and mixed-race Latinos as well as Arabs and Gypsies in the middle. Each of these layers had its own internal hierarchy according to religion, nationality, and some racial features (see Figure 4.14). This racial pecking order is presented as a general description; the rankings of groups within the three racial levels is intended only as a rough approximation of the stratification present in the early twentieth century.[61]

Whites constitute the first racial category. Europeans were encouraged to immigrate to the U.S., but with priority going to the "superior" groups of northwest Europe. Southeast Europeans were labeled as "inferior" whites who, after 1921, were allowed to immigrate only in small numbers and with the expectation that they would assimilate quickly. Protestants from northwest Europe topped the white groups, followed by Catholics, then Jews. European immigrants always had the right to become naturalized citizens; the first naturalization law in 1790 opened the door to any "free white person."[62]

The second racial category had two subsections. The first was composed of mixed-race Latino groups. Mexicans represent a mixture of Spanish and Native American heritage, and Puerto Ricans a combination of Spanish and African roots. In 1897, a U.S. district court ruled that Mexicans "could be classified neither as white, nor as being of Asian or African descent," but they could be naturalized in Texas. The usual practice, however, was to urge Mexicans to enter the U.S. when farm labor was needed, then to pressure them to return to Mexico when the need was absent. In 1930, a nativist academic told a congressional committee that " 'mixed breed' Mexicans were even more undesirable than Polish Jews or southern Italians." Puerto Ricans, whose island became a U.S. possession during the Spanish American War, were granted American citizenship in 1917. In the second subsection were Arabs and Gypsies, whom white Americans have had difficulty classifying by race and who often have been viewed as not fully white. In 1870, aliens of African nativity were made eligible for naturalization; this included Arabs and Hindus from Africa, but not necessarily those from Asia. In 1910, Syrians, Palestinians, Turks, and Armenians were classified as "Asiatics" and often denied citizenship. The immigration act of 1917 excluded laborers and denied citizenship

FIGURE 4.14
America's Ethnic Pecking Order: Early 20th Century

White	Legal Status, Restrictions, Other Factors
NW European Protestants	Immigrants allowed to become naturalized citizens; absence of systematic legal barriers, but prejudice against Catholics.
NW European Catholics	
SE European Catholics & Eastern Orthodox	Immigration of SE Europeans severely reduced by national-origins and quota laws of 1921 and 1924.
NW European Jews	
SE European Jews	Prejudice against Jews

COLOR LINE

Mixed-Race and Uncertain Classification

Mixed Race: Latinos (Hispanics)	
Mexicans	1924 law placed no restrictions on immigrants from countries in the western hemisphere. Repatriation program forced 500,000 Mexicans in the U.S. to return to Mexico in the 1930s.
Puerto Ricans	Became citizens of the U.S. in 1917.
Uncertain Classification	
Arabs	Some lived in Asiatic barred zone; citizenship often denied.
Gypsies	Roots in India, arrived in Europe in 1300s.

Nonwhite Races

Asians	
Indian	Asiatic barred zone, 1917; citizenship denied.
Japanese	Exclusion agreement, 1907; citizenship denied, unable to own land.
Chinese	Exclusion, 1882; citizenship denied, unable to own land.
American Indians	Forced onto reservations; most denied citizenship until 1924.
Africans	Most were slaves until 1865, made citizens in 1866; Jim Crow laws, lynchings, and segregation begun in the 1870s; denied basic rights.

to people from the Asiatic barred zone, which included most areas from Arabia and Afghanistan to the East Indies and the Pacific islands. The Gypsies, who were originally from India, began migrating to Europe in the 1300s and usually adopted the religion of the country in which they lived. They immigrated to America in relatively small numbers, and many continued their nomadic ways, living in tents until the 1920s.[63]

The third layer of the racial pecking order consisted of nonwhite ethnic groups—Asians, American Indians, and Africans. Asians are placed at the top of this stratum because of their small numbers prior to 1970. The violence and abuse they endured, while significant, seems less intense than that inflicted on Indians and blacks. East Indians are placed at the top of the Asian category because they have some physical features similar to Caucasians, and their immigration, as well as that from most Asian countries, was not completely barred until 1917. The Japanese were excluded by the negotiated agreement of 1907-08, whose racist terms were less harsh than those earlier directed at the Chinese in the

exclusion act of 1882. Those Asians who were allowed to enter the U.S. were "aliens ineligible for citizenship." Native Americans were next to the bottom of the pecking order, as they frequently were enemies of the European settlers in wars (often genocidal in nature,) from the 1500s until the 1890s, and were then banished to reservations. So-called civilized Indians were allowed to become citizens in 1887, but most Native Americans were not granted citizenship until 1924. Many of their children had to endure boarding schools and other coercive attempts at acculturation. At the very bottom of the pecking order were Africans, who endured slavery from the 1600s to 1865, then were subjected by European Americans to the most severe violence and discrimination since the end of the Indian wars. Until late in the twentieth century, blacks were the nation's largest minority group, and in the American scheme of race relations, "blackness" seems to represent the ultimate social distance from "whiteness." The 1924 immigration law excluded the descendants of slaves from the calculation of the national origins baseline, which drastically limited the number of Africans allowed to enter the U.S. All of these factors created a rigid social boundary that has separated white European Americans from the people of other races or of mixed-race lineage, as indicated by the solid "color" line in Figure 4.15.[64]

Italians and other European immigrant groups experienced intense hostility and discrimination from nativists. But unlike people of color in America, their constitutional rights, based on their classification as whites, were seldom denied. Being a white immigrant in the United States has always indicated the possibility of becoming a fully assimilated American, but being of a nonwhite race has always meant being a problem and not eligible to be fully American. This racial duality has plagued America's social fabric for 500 years. Until the mid-twentieth century, our society insisted that people of color acculturate and learn the basics of American culture but refused them permission to assimilate into the institutions and personal relationships of white society. Over the past 50 years the arrival of Arabs, Cubans (many of whom were white), blacks from Haiti and Africa, and Asians (including Koreans, Vietnamese, Cambodians, Filipinos, and Hmong), have added new groups to the pecking order, but the basic format remains the same.[65]

Following race, religion has been the second most important criterion in the American pecking order. Protestant Christians have been given the highest status, followed by Roman Catholic and Eastern Orthodox Christians, and then Jews. In recent years, the growing number of Middle Eastern migrants and the war on terrorism have left Muslims at the bottom of America's religious pecking order. Lastly, nationality or culture is rated as the third most crucial marker in this hierarchy. It is the least permanent component in this scheme, as people can learn the language and other cultural traits of the dominant group, downplay their ancient culture, and more easily blend into society.

The pecking order described above is intended to provide a general overview of the standing of ethnic groups in the United States in 1900 and, specifically, to understand the position of Italians in American society. It is not intended as a systematic explanation of ethnic relations; there are vague areas and exceptions to this pattern. For example, Middle Eastern peoples, such as Yemeni and other Arabs, alternately classified as Caucasian and Asian until 1952, have occupied a hazy position in America's racial pecking order. Appalachian whites, many of whom are WASPs, live in one of the poorest regions of the country and when they migrated to northern cities were stereotyped as "hillbillies."

White ethnic groups such as Italians "have experienced historically considerable deprivation and discrimination in America but not the kind of exclusionary and dehumanizing treatment that deprived racial minorities of even the most basic rights and amenities for much of U.S. history." The southeast

Europeans were most always extended constitutional rights that "provided basic legal rights that kept channels of mobility open." These themes and the ethnic pecking order have been reflected in Lackawanna and have made it possible to compare the situation of Italians and other white ethnics to that of racial minorities in the city.[66]

Assimilation and Racial Stratification in Lackawanna

The processes of assimilation continue in the United States for a variety of ethnic groups, both for recent arrivals and those present in America for hundreds of years. Comparing the Italian American experience with that of other groups in Lackawanna helps clarify the ethnic pecking order, explain the white ethnic revival that began 40 years ago, and examine the Quintuple Melting Pot that has taken shape. Because of America's racial duality—which places whites at the highest level in the social hierarchy—blacks, American Indians, Asians, and Latinos fare most poorly in the assimilation process. In Lackawanna, these groups, along with Arabs and Gypsies, have been outnumbered by the southeast European ethnics. During most of the twentieth century, Italians have been the city's third- or fourth-largest ethnic group. In 2000, they climbed to second most numerous. Poles have been the largest group in Lackawanna, as well as in Erie County. The German, Irish, black, Hungarian, and Yugoslavian groups have, at various times, been among the five largest groups in the city. Many of Lackawanna's 92 ethnic groups have been small in number. In 1920, the total number of East Indians, Japanese, Chinese, and other Asians in the city stood at 53, with 13 of the European groups each including fewer than 90 individuals in 1930.[67]

Lackawanna eventually became home to many people of color. Early in the twentieth century, African Americans were the only sizable group of nonwhites in the city, numbering 197 in 1910, with many more arriving in the 1920s. Some Latinos, Asians, and Arabs arrived prior to World War II, and their numbers increased significantly during and after the war. This demographic change was seen in 1940 at Friendship House, where the clients were classified into 24 ethnic groups: 16 European nationalities as well as "American Negro, West Indian Negro, Mexican, Cuban, Moroccan, Ethiopian, East Indian, and Chinese." A few American Indians lived in the steel-plant district of West Seneca in 1900, including 19 Mohawk boys residing at St. John's Catholic Protectory. By the 1930s, a number of Indian families lived along Hamburg Turnpike.[68]

A European group that had origins in India encountered significant discrimination as it migrated in and out of the Lackawanna area. The Gypsies—because of their nomadic lifestyle, closed society, and unfamiliar ways—were often banished from towns in Europe and were at the bottom of the social order in Italy. Their renegade image is projected in the following passage about the 1890s written by a Blasdell historian.

> Gypsies in their semi-annual migration added color to those days as they made camp each Spring and Fall in the woods opposite Salisbury's Store, or in a field in the Hamburg Rd. (South Park Avenue). ... Their entourage consisted of several wagons loaded with drab-looking men, brightly-dressed women, and scantily-dressed children, followed by strings of poor bony nags running loose. During their stay in town, children did not need the warnings of their elders to stay near the protection of home.
>
> One boy, now to manhood grown, recalls that his father was in the habit of sleeping with an axe under his bed during the sojourn of the gypsies.

In 1915, a Lackawanna judge forced four Gypsy women to return $25 they had received for reading a man's fortune, then told them to leave the city. Two years later, a band of 250 Gypsies arrived in nearby West Seneca in five automobiles and 25 horse-drawn wagons and set up a cluster of colorful tents along a stream. After six weeks, authorities suspected the band was involved in some minor thefts and made them leave. In Lackawanna, officials continued to treat the Gypsies harshly. In 1932, following reports that 200 Gypsies on Gates Avenue were swindling residents out of money, the police chief warned that "they could expect drastic police action on the slightest complaint." During World War II, when many Gypsies crowded into First Ward apartments, city health officials declared that sanitary laws were violated and ordered them to leave town. Although their numbers were small, Gypsies endured frequent acts of discrimination in the Steel City. Some Lackawanna residents had heard stories of Gypsies kidnapping young children, and Italian housewives warned their children to stay in the house when Gypsies rented houses on Ingham Avenue for several days at a time. When Maria DiMillo and her son Tony walked up Ingham Avenue, she told him to put his hands over his eyes so that the Gypsies wouldn't give him the evil eye. One Italian family reported an attempt by Gypsies to kidnap a young boy during the 1940s.[69]

Mexican migrants came to Lackawanna in the early 1920s, and the need for laborers during World War II led more Latinos to the city. Sixty-nine Mexican immigrants were living in Lackawanna in 1940, and a few years later, some were housed in railroad cars situated on sidings along Lehigh Avenue. Apparently, several of these men frequented a bar on Ingham Avenue and became involved with female patrons. This led to tensions with local white males, which erupted into a street brawl. The small Mexican settlement established the Centro Social Mexicano Club on Ingham Avenue, and by 1980, there were 130 Mexican

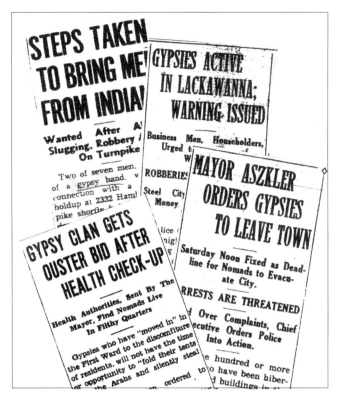

Collage of newspaper articles demonstrating the prejudice and discrimination toward Gypsies in Lackawanna. Photo sources: Lackawanna Library, *Lackawanna Leader*, 4/15/37, 5/6/37, 9/16/43, 8/20/53

Americans in the city. Puerto Ricans began arriving in Lackawanna during the 1950s, numbering 676 in 2000.[70]

Lackawanna's early Arab population included Syrians and Palestinians, many of whom were Eastern Orthodox Christians. A handful of Muslims, mostly from Yemen, came to the city before World War II. American law prevented the immigration of laborers from the Asian Barred Zone, which included Yemen, until 1952, and Yemeni officials did not allow family members to join their breadwinner overseas prior to 1962. Many Yemeni families then migrated to Lackawanna; the 1990 census counted 403 Arabs in the city, and by 2000, the number grew to 1,111. The Yemenite Benevolent Association was established in the 1950s, and the Lackawanna Islamic Mosque in 1965. Many Yemeni and other Arabs now live on the side streets off Ridge Road in the First Ward.[71]

A small number of Native Americans have lived in Lackawanna, mostly in the First Ward. In 2000, there were only 118 Indians residing in the Steel City. Italians interviewed told stories of the limited contact they had with this ethnic group. Lucia Risio, who had only one child of her own, took it upon herself to help others in time of need, including providing food to a homeless Indian man who had an artificial leg. Several of the neighbors of the Macaluso family on Hamburg Turnpike were Native Americans, mostly of the Seneca tribe. Young Carmela Macaluso, who had an uncle with the name of Seneca Raddio Macaluso, assumed that she was related to the Indians. Victor "Dick" Seneca and his family had taken up residence in Bethlehem Park by 1931, the only people of color to do so prior to the 1970s. Bethlehem Steel may have allowed this because Seneca was a foremen in the Iron Workers Department, whose workers, most of them Native Americans, did the iron work on large buildings. Al Croce, who worked for Bethlehem's Real Estate Department, became friends with Seneca. On a repair call to Seneca's house, Croce saw Seneca shaving and jokingly said, "Hey, Dick, I thought Indians didn't shave." Seneca responded, "If that goddamn Italian Christopher Columbus would have left my ancestors alone, I wouldn't be shaving today!" South of Lackawanna, many Native Americans and Italians lived in or near Silver Creek. Some Italian families were reported to have shunned the Native American women who married Italian men.[72]

African Americans began to arrive in the steel-plant district soon after the turn of the century. In 1902, when Gaetano Milano and Antonio Grossi were cutting down trees to clear the land for the new steel plant, their foreman was African American Joseph Moon. William Muller, a steelworker in Sparrows Point, Maryland, arrived in 1904 and was "one of the pioneer colored citizens of Lackawanna." As more blacks came, the *West Seneca Bulletin* carried inflammatory headlines: "Steel Plant Importing Negroes. Two Carloads Brought In and People Do Not Take Kindly to It. Undesirable Residents Hurt Real Estate Values." The town board concocted a scheme to stop the migration: "Each carload of Negroes will cost the plant $1,000,000 more in their assessed valuation." It was during and after the Great Steel Strike of 1919 that the city's African American community grew quickly. Steel companies in Lackawanna and Buffalo brought in southern blacks as strikebreakers, and the restriction of European immigration in 1921 led to recruitment of more blacks to work in the mills. In 1920, there were 1,164 blacks working at the steel plant in Lackawanna (although not necessarily living in the city), and there were 1,709 black residents in the city by 1940. Virtually all of the city's African Americans resided in the First Ward, most near the intersection of Ridge Road and Hamburg Turnpike. A number also lived on Ingham Avenue and its side streets, which was mostly Polish north of Wilson Street and mostly Italian to the south. In 1925, upper Ingham Avenue was home to 161 Polish, 12 black, and three Italian families, while lower Ingham Avenue had 53 Italian, 26 black, and 10 Polish families. One Italian family on Ingham Avenue had a black servant living in the home. Thus, in these two areas, many Italians and blacks were neighbors. Italians who lived there recalled having good relationships with their African American neighbors.[73]

African American businesses existed on lower Ingham Avenue as early as the 1910s, when "Kid" Daniels operated a pool room; "All nationalities hung out there," according to Nunze Oddy. During the 1930s, there were at least three black businesses on lower Ingham Avenue and Dona Street. Many Italians worked side by side with blacks and Mexicans in the steel plant's Yard Department and the South Buffalo Railway's Track Department. At the Old Village Annex, Lincoln, and Roosevelt schools, blacks, Italians, and children of other ethnic groups were classmates. There were many sports teams in Lackawanna, and during the 1940s, the Vagabonds, a group of Bethlehem Park Italian youth, competed against other ethnic squads. Jerry DePasquale remembers playing baseball at the Dona soccer field against the Albright Court squad, which was all black. "We could draw fifteen hundred or more to those games." His father, team manager Tony DePasquale, later recruited two black players for the Vagabonds, which apparently was an early attempt at integrated teams.[74]

A series of events marked the separation of the European ethnic groups from blacks, Latinos, and Arabs, reinforcing "racial duality" in Lackawanna. In one of the early racial encounters, black strikebreakers were attacked by white ethnic strikers in the 1919 steel strike. As Italians in the 1920s were becoming part of an American working class that was divided by nationality, and even more deeply by race, they realized that blacks were more negatively perceived than their own group. The rapid and large influx of blacks in 1922 helped to draw the focus of nativists and bigots away from Italians and other southeast Europeans. When some Italians complained about the new black arrivals, saying they were more rowdy than the original black residents, they were probably echoing comments they heard from native-born whites and sensing that blacks were lower in the pecking order than Italians.[75]

African Americans, along with Italians, were often housed in the deteriorating row houses of the Old Village. In 1925, 174 units, or 43%, were occupied by blacks, and 98, or 24%, by Italians; in 1930, the figures were 60% and 32%, respectively. In both years, three of the row houses had black or Italian residents in virtually all units. The demolition of the Old Village's nine large row houses began in 1930, and as residents were moving out, racial inequalities became very apparent. Many of the Italians moved into the detached homes in the new Bethlehem Park development, but blacks were not allowed to live there. A 1939 newspaper ad listing homes for sale described Bethlehem Park as a "restricted neighborhood." Prior to the 1970s, no people of color lived in Bethlehem Park, with the exception of an American Indian family.[76]

African Americans in Lackawanna became increasingly segregated in the 1930s. The city operated 10 outdoor playgrounds—nine for use by the "White Race" and one for "Negroes." Friendship House was then focusing much of its

FIGURE 4.15

AN ITALIAN AMERICAN GI STRUGGLES WITH RACIAL STRIFE

First Lieutenant Ralph Sambuchi, U.S. Army, who grew up in Bethlehem Park, wrote a letter to the editor that was printed in the *Lackawanna Leader* on February 29, 1968.

Since leaving Lackawanna, some seven years ago, I have had the opportunity to observe the workings of overt discrimination and racial prejudice in many forms, from the beating of a Negro soldier in Georgia, to the harassment of myself and a Negro soldier in Oklahoma, because we were together in a section of a city reserved, unofficially, for whites only. When I became subjected to these and other similar circumstances, I had one overpowering compensation: I grew up in Lackawanna and I am proud of it because we weren't like that at home. Now, I am beginning to wonder and worry.

Despite the now popular cliche, "Some of my best friends are," I often like to think that not some, but many of my friends are Negroes, both in the service and out. Often I remember the names … of other Americans who happened to be born a darker color than was I. Often, I wonder to myself how they are doing and if I'll get to see them on my next leave. I often say to myself, "It sure would be nice to reminisce with John … or Larry … about our days together on the Track team at Lackawanna High." The old high school has brought back several fond memories to me. Now, it brings a rotten taste to my mouth, "Brawl, with Racial Overtones, at L. H. S," was the headline on my "Leader," this morning.

So, the bigotry and backwardness of our age has finally struck home. Now, what happens to my friendships with … my Negro, Lackawanna friends? Do I start to use the (word), "Nigger," and they, the words "Honky," and "Whitey" or do I begin to appraise the thoughts behind the words which led to this disgrace? I choose the latter. Words have no meaning until one is affixed to them. Thoughts and actions have no direction until one is affixed to them. Every adolescent passes through two stages: the learning stage, where meanings are affixed to words, and the action stage, where the apron strings are severed and a course of action for life becomes directed.

If the parents reacted to the recent idiocy in Lackawanna, by saying, "Well those Niggers are really acting up," or by saying, "Those poor colored people," or even, "Those rotten honkies," remember, you affixed the meanings to the words and you laid out the course of thought and action. The degradation, through your children, is yours.

When they were throwing trays and punches at one another, it might just as well have been you. Everyone, both black and white, can scream, "police brutality," but if your thoughts and actions weren't brought to the surface by your children, the police would not have been necessary.

Oh, yes, I know that many of you will say, "I never taught my children to act that way." But, how many of you taught them to step in and see that no one else did? A complacent attitude is just as dangerous as overt hostility.

I have not attempted to hide racist words from my children. Instead, I have attempted to teach them the malice and harm behind them. I have attempted to teach them that America has not and cannot survive in a name-calling contest, which leads to bloodshed and hostility. I have attempted to teach them that their friends who name-call and take the first step toward prejudice, are wrong and should be helped toward understanding their mistakes. I hope my children never choose the path of prejudice ….

So, Lackawanna, I hope you have not destroyed my friendship with my Negro contemporaries. I hope that in June, when I come home, I will not have to look a Negro in the face and wonder, "Am I still his friend?"

Ralph A. Sambuchi

***

Sambuchi had a positive response from his African American friends when he visited Lackawanna. At the invitation of a former teacher, he spoke to a class at Lackawanna High School about race relations. Later, he recalled that the only time he saw blacks in Bethlehem Park was when other teams in a baseball league came to play against his neighborhood team, the Hawks. In recent years, he first learned of the clause in the deeds of Bethlehem Park homes forbidding African Americans, other than servants, from living in the neighborhood.

Sources: *Lackawanna Leader*, 2/29/68; interview with Ralph Sambuchi, March 30, 2009.

programming on African Americans. A medical clinic for "colored" persons was held three mornings a week at the Catholic Charities Center, with free services provided by Dr. S. Calvin Johnson, an African American. A 1934 study refers to a segregated housing policy in the section of the First Ward along Hamburg Turnpike, south of Ridge Road:

In the 'melting pot' district because of economic conditions the one-time segregated Nationality plan has been disrupted and as a result one finds in some instances Negro and white tenants under the same roof (across the hall from one another) sharing the same lavatory. Because of this situation there is some intermarriage between the black and white races, and loose morals.

For many years, blacks continued to attend their churches on Ingham Avenue and Dona Street, where Italians were the majority. Some Italians remember parades of blacks going down Ingham Avenue, probably to one of these churches. One African American stated that Italians did not bother blacks who walked to the churches, but "neither were they overly cordial." While blacks established a number of Protestant churches in the First Ward, one source reports that Monsignor Nelson Baker was credited with converting more than 600 blacks to the Catholic faith in the early 1930s. These individuals apparently attended the OLV Mission Church, which later became Queen of All Saints.[77]

The absurdity of racial classifications gradually became more apparent in Lackawanna. While Arabs had been officially classified as Caucasian for decades, some European American authorities viewed them differently. The Arab "race" was the focal point of a 1938 court decision in which Lackawannan Abdullah Hadgea, a native of Saudi Arabia, was denied citizenship by federal judge John Knight. "The judge held that Arabians are not whites and are therefore denied naturalization. Although he 'may come within the broad term 'Caucasian,' he doesn't come within the term 'white person,' the judge concluded." The census also demonstrates the confusion of racial categories. In 1925, census takers in Lackawanna classified some men born in Arabia and India as being of the "Negro" race. The 1930 census had a new classification system for race. As in the past, all blacks were of the "Negro" race and all Europeans of the "White" race, and Arabs were also considered "White." The race classification of other people of color was equated with their country, geographic area of origin, or religion, as in "Mexican," "Filipino," "Chinese," "Hindu," etc. Census takers in Lackawanna reflected America's doubts about people born in Arab lands, as some were listed as "Arab" and others as "White."[78]

The New Deal programs initiated during the 1930s were a great boon to Italians and other white ethnics but were less generous to people of color. One writer called the programs affirmative action for whites. The Social Security program did not cover domestic workers or farm laborers, which meant that large numbers of blacks in the south and Latinos in the southwest states were left out. The practice of denying loans to people in "red-lined" neighborhoods was built into federal mortgage programs, thereby excluding many blacks and Latinos. The pattern of racial segregation in public-housing projects was common and present in Lackawanna. The city's first federal housing project, the Baker Homes, was completed in 1938. The following year, its 272 resident families included only three Mexican and nine black families, the latter living in a designated section of the complex. Nearby, the Albright Court Project, constructed in 1941, offered 200 units that were in demand by new defense workers arriving in the city. Twenty five of the units were set aside for blacks.[79]

In August 1943, African American ministers complained that black workers were unable to find housing and demanded that the Federal Housing Authority (FHA), in keeping with the federal policy of separate buildings for blacks and whites, designate more units of either the Baker Homes or Albright Court for black only residents. The FHA officials made Albright Court a blacks-only project, attempting to steer white families to the newly opened Ridgewood Village project on the city's east side. At a community meeting in St. Anthony's Church, chaired by union leader Alex Nigro, white residents protested this move. They grilled Mayor Michael Hughes and Council President Angelo Grosso, who said they had no prior notice of the FHA decision and no authority to challenge it. Nigro and other speakers said they found the black tenants recently arrived from the south to be of an "undesirable class." Timothy Smith, an African American and officer in the steelworkers union, "said the reason the housing authority wants to evict the white tenants from Albright Court is to fill Ridgewood, a 400-unit project in the city's Fourth Ward, thus preventing Negroes from moving into the latter project. Rents in Ridgewood are higher, but its facilities are not nearly as good as those of Albright Court. When white families, after they have been forced to move into Ridgewood, discover this, they will blame the Negroes instead of the housing authority."[80]

Nigro then read a petition from the Lackawanna Workingmen's Welfare Committee demanding that the FHA not compel anyone to move from Albright Court, that its units be open to all races and the policy of blacks-only be withdrawn, and, most interesting, that "all new applicants, regardless of race, creed or color, be permitted to enter Ridgewood Village." This was an appeal by union men to end segregation in Lackawanna's public housing. The local FHA housing manager later agreed to the first two demands but not the third, stating, "Negroes have equal rights with all other races in the occupation of Albright Court," and that whites in the project have the option of either moving to another section in Albright Court or to the Ridgewood Village. What the manager didn't directly say was that blacks could not live in the Ridgewood Village because the eastern part of the city was for whites only. By October 1943 all but 45 of the 170 Albright Court white families had moved to the Ridgewood Village. According to several people interviewed, Councilman Grosso's defeat in that fall's election was partly due to white voters holding him responsible for the increased number of Albright Court units allocated to black residents.[81]

Several years later, another incident suggested that white ethnics were upholding the racial pecking order. An Occupational Educational School was established in Albright Court in 1947 for the student who is a "slow learner," or what is now referred to as developmentally delayed. In September 1951, the school and its 69 students, 39 of whom were black, were moved to Bethlehem Park School. A meeting at the school drew many Bethlehem Park parents who protested that there was not enough room at the school and apparently voicing concern about the need for separate restrooms for the occupational school students. Reverend Charles Sanders, director of Friendship House, responded, " 'It's a plain case of discrimination, racial underneath, to say that children regardless of race or color, shouldn't use the same drinking fountains and restrooms,' he asserted. 'There are adequate facilities here for these children and they should be permitted to remain here.' " Following the meeting, 200 parents organized the Bethlehem Park Parents Association, elected Edwin DiCenzo as chairman, and initiated a "strike" that kept 200 children at home for two days. School officials pacified the group by locating the Occupational School on the ground floor, ensuring that its students were "completely separated" from the others, and promising parents that these quarters were only temporary. With this, the strike was ended and attendance returned to its normal level.[82]

Some Bethlehem Park residents recalled that the strike was more a reflection of fears about mental retardation, as opposed to racial prejudice, but race seemed to be a significant aspect of the issue. Around this same time, when an Italian girl was visited in Bethlehem Park by one of her African American classmates from Lincoln School, her mother said to send the girl home, implying that blacks don't belong in the neighborhood. The residents apparently became more tolerant of the occupational school situation, as it remained part of Bethlehem Park School for at least 10 years.[83]

The African American migration to Lackawanna continued, and by 1960, their numbers had grown to 2,971, or 10% of the city's population. A white resident observed discrimination toward blacks and Latinos in "various public places, such as cafes and taverns where Negroes cannot be served," and noted that "whites are unwilling to allow the Negro mobility to achieve better housing and improve his standard of living." Two years later, "(w)hen a respected colored physician proposed to set up his offices 'across the bridge' in the second ward," wrote Reverend Julius Szabo, "there was a noisy storm of protest." Blacks and Latinos were limited to housing on the side streets off Ridge Road and in the New Village, which had changed from an enclave of foremen and skilled workers to one of lower-income, unskilled laborers of all races. This was in the northern part of the First Ward, where in 1950, the population was 40% "nonwhite," while the southern part was only 14%. Bethlehem Steel owned much of the housing in the First Ward, and one writer asserts that the company let its housing deteriorate—first the Old Village, then the New Village. In 1940, only five percent of the ward's housing units needed major repairs, but by 1950, 29% in the northern part of the ward and 19% in the southern portion were dilapidated. The steel company had other plans for its First Ward property; in 1932, the new Spring Perch plant was constructed on part of the Old Village site. The widening of Hamburg Turnpike led to the destruction of more residences. During the 1950s, there was a housing shortage in Lackawanna, but Bethlehem Steel leveled many homes south of Ridge Road and built four large parking lots, despite the protests of the mayor and many citizens. Blacks, Latinos, Arabs, and poor whites were confined in an even smaller area near Ridge Road, where over half of the housing had become dilapidated by 1960. Meanwhile, throughout the 1950s and 1960s, hundreds of white ethnics had moved over the bridge to new homes on the east side of the city.[84]

In 1968, First Ward blacks and Latinos decided it was their turn to move across the tracks, despite the challenges involved. They were well aware that only three black families were residing east of the bridge and that a fourth family had endured vandalism and death threats while building a house there. Their group, the Kennedy Park Homeowners Association (KPHA), made arrangements to purchase 25 acres of land on Martin Road from the Catholic Diocese of Buffalo. There, it would construct 138 homes to sell to black, Latino, and white families. The KPHA had the support of several First Ward Puerto Rican, Yemenite, and black organizations. The diocese and Federal Housing Administration backed the plan, but Third Ward whites organized a group, Taxpayers Interested in Civic Affairs, that filed petitions against the development, urging the city's Catholics to withhold contributions to their churches. The group was supported by the mayor and four of the five councilmen, who maintained that poor sewers made new housing unfeasible, then passed an ordinance zoning the vacant land exclusively for parks and recreation. At a packed council meeting, First Ward resident Delores Perez told council members, "You owe the First Ward something; please do not forget us." Council President Mike DePasquale responded, "I am doing the First Ward a favor … by not exposing them to raw sewage." The ensuing uproar among the city's minority groups led the archdiocese to urge the city council "not to let racial prejudice guide their considerations." A month later, the council condemned the land and announced plans to build a multipurpose recreational center there. Some Italians who were now part of the city's political power structure, along with other white ethnics, were upholding America's pecking order that deemed people of color less than equal.[85]

The diocese and the First Ward groups filed a suit in December 1968 charging that the city restricted blacks to "certain unhealthy geographic portions of the city" and promoted "overcrowding, racial segregation, and racial strife." An Erie County coalition of religious congregations passed a resolution stating that Lackawanna's actions "prevents black and Puerto Rican citizens from developing new housing which would give them better living conditions." The Justice Department joined in the suit, and in 1970, a federal judge ruled against the city. The city of Lackawanna challenged the decision, lost, then took the case to the Supreme Court, which refused to review the city's appeal. After three years of delays and costly legal proceedings, the KPHA was drained of resources and money and the project was abandoned.[86]

At the same time the city was blocking minority housing in the Third Ward, it was planning a housing project near the steel plant. "We expect to redevelop a large part of the first Ward for housing," said Frank Cipriani, Lackawanna's director of development, in 1968. The sector south of Ridge Road along Hamburg Turnpike, according to the *Courier Express*, "is in the midst of one of the largest industrial complexes in the state and is an area which the State Health Department has identified as having one of the highest levels of air pollution in the state." Cipriani acknowledged the pollution problem but said, "as a city we are caught in the middle. Where do you put the people?" It was obvious that some city leaders did not welcome the possibility of nonwhites moving to the new housing developments in the eastern part of Lackawanna. Some 148 housing units were built in the First Ward along Gates Avenue, most inhabited by people of color.[87]

For white ethnics, it was a different story. A significant number of Italians moved from Bethlehem Park and Ingham Avenue "across the bridge" to the east side. Many Italians did remain in Bethlehem Park, located at the far south end of the First Ward, and on Ingham Avenue, located at the far east end of the ward. These areas were the most distant from the densely populated, heavily polluted zone around Gates Avenue and Ridge Road. Bethlehem Park residents had endured soot from steam engines until the late 1940s, when all South Buffalo Railway

locomotives were replaced by diesel engines. Since 1936, they had dealt with noise from the strip mill. As one person explained, "after a while you just don't hear it anymore." This changed in 1964, when the neighborhood became exposed to air pollution from Bethlehem Steel's new basic oxygen furnace located just to the west. Gradually, more Italians and other white ethnics left for the pollution-free neighborhoods on the east side. Among the white ethnic groups that rebuilt their churches, only the Italian community did not relocate its church across the tracks. In 1964, a new St. Anthony's edifice was built next door to the site of the original church on Ingham Avenue.[88]

Race relations in Lackawanna, as in other northern cities, had become strained as blacks steadily migrated from the southern states. In 1933, after a black man allegedly accosted a white woman on the Ridge Road bridge, he was cornered by "a posse of about 100 indignant citizens … armed with clubs and stones" and had "narrowly escaped lynching" by the time a police officer arrived at the scene. Racial animosity grew worse, both across the nation and in Lackawanna. In July 1967, some 250 black men and women were leaving a fashion show at the steelworkers union hall when a white man in a passing car hurled a bottle that struck a black youth. A hundred whites exiting local bars at the time got involved and a brawl erupted. Lackawanna police needed help from three other police departments to restore order.[89]

Beginning in the late 1950s, confrontations occurred between whites and blacks at Lackawanna High School and Lincoln School. Racial violence at the high school in 1968 led to a two-day boycott of the city's schools by minority groups who felt school officials and the police had reacted in a biased manner. Police presence in and near the school was increased, but a fight after a dance at Baker-Victory High School resulted in the fatal stabbing of a white teenager by a black youth in 1970. This led to racial violence in the high-school cafeteria, and when police officers were stationed in the school the following day, about half of the 115 black students started a boycott. With the help of faculty and students from the University of Buffalo, classes were held at Friendship House and were attended by 70 black students. Black leaders had not only objected to the police presence at the high school but also called for more black teachers (there was only one in the city), more black literature in the school library, and a state and federal investigation of the school system. A biracial student committee agreed with most of these demands. Many white parents, fearing more conflict, kept their children at home. Students eventually returned to school, and an uneasy coexistence between the races set in, monitored daily by three police officers—two white and one black. A grand-jury investigation found nepotism in hiring and many irregularities

FIGURE 4.16

COMPARING THE SITUATIONS OF BLACKS AND ITALIANS IN THE U.S.

Irish Catholics, Italians, Slavs, and eastern European Jews were treated harshly when they arrived in the U.S., perhaps worse than any other white immigrants. People of color, however, received a far more brutal reception, and African Americans have endured the worst prejudice and discrimination of all. In the past 40 years, many whites have compared and contrasted the experience of the southeast European immigrants with that of blacks and asked: "Why can't they be like us?" In other words, the Italians and other white ethnics have achieved social mobility and acceptance into mainstream culture in three generations, so why haven't blacks done likewise? What follows is a comparison of the African American and Italian American experiences that attempts to illuminate the significant differences between them.

1. Worth in the eyes of society. While Italians were viewed as less worthy than northwest Europeans, they were allowed and encouraged to enter the U.S.; some 4 million entered between 1880 and 1924. Many were dark complected but still considered white, and they came to the U.S. voluntarily. Blacks were brought to

America against their will as slaves in the 1600s, and 1700s, and by 1880, their descendants had been freed from slavery for only 15 years. The African American population in 1900 included only 84,000 foreign-born individuals, most from the West Indies. To many European Americans, blacks represented the exact opposite of whiteness, and their immigration was not welcome. The immigration act of 1924, which seriously reduced the number of arrivals from Italy, virtually prohibited migration from Africa and Asia.

2. Visibility. Blacks could not change the biological features that distinguished them from whites. Light-skinned immigrants, or certainly their children, could change their style of dress, mannerisms, and names, and learn English to blend into white society. Acculturated Italians could easily intermarry with other whites, but blacks were legally forbidden to do so by many states until the late 1960s.

3. Self-definition. Racial differences were defined in terms of European superiority by whites, who imposed on people from many African nations and cultures the label "black." Italians often had little allegiance to Italy, defining

themselves based more on their provincial origins, but knew they lived in that nation. American officials used this nationality label but also differentiated between northern and southern Italians from 1899 to 1924.

4. Goal of assimilation. Italians were viewed as inferior to northwest Europeans, and the flow of their immigration was restricted, but the dominant society felt they could be fully assimilated once they shed their "foreign" culture. So Italians, like other Europeans, were encouraged to go through all eight processes of assimilation. With few exceptions, the U.S., granted Italians full legal rights, such as voting and intermarrying. Blacks, on the other hand, were kept in a rigid caste system and denied the basic rights of citizens. Insisting that blacks acculturate, the dominant culture allowed them, eventually, to form their own ethnic identity. It was seen as appropriate for Italians to strive to enter the mainstream culture, but for blacks to make such efforts was viewed as "getting out of their place." Full assimilation was never a stated and accepted goal for blacks until after World War II. Italians and other Europeans

---

in financial transactions of the school system. Indictments were handed down against ten defendants, two of whom were Italian Americans. A state overseer was assigned in 1971 to monitor the Lackawanna School Board's compliance with recommendations made by the State Department of Education. School integration became a contentious issue, marked by a variety of strategies and debates. Wrote one newspaper reporter, "The truth is— though no official will say it publicly— it was more politically acceptable to bus minority than white children." Many whites east of the railroad tracks did not want their children bused to the First Ward. The school board pursued a plan to close the four schools in the First Ward and bus those students to the eastern side of the city. This led to a loud protest from First Ward residents. Parents of black children, who made up 90% of Roosevelt School's 432 pupils, demanded that

Roosevelt School be spared, while whites in Bethlehem Park wanted that elementary school saved. The Bethlehem Park parents, with active spokespersons such as Rose Marchese, were particularly effective in advocating for their school, as they didn't want their children leaving the neighborhood. The school board finally decided to close and demolish Wilson, Roosevelt, and Bethlehem Park schools, and eventually to close the recently renovated Lincoln School. To appease the white ethnics in Bethlehem Park, the board promised to bus their children to the newest school in the city, Truman School on Willet Road. By 1977, there were no schools functioning in the First Ward. All students living there, most of them members of minority groups, were bused across the tracks.[90]

Conditions in the First Ward continued to deteriorate. By 1970, many stores on Ridge Road were boarded up, housing

assimilated and escaped minority group status within three generations. African Americans have been in America hundreds of years and remain a minority group that still endures systematic prejudice and discrimination. In the 1950s, while Italians were elected governors, congresspeople, and mayors with increasing frequency, blacks were still struggling to achieve basic voting rights.

5. Home countries. Italians were free until 1924 to travel back and forth between the U.S. and Italy in response to economic opportunities. This "escape valve" was crucial when the American economy was depressed. The Italian government did exert pressure on American officials for better treatment of the immigrants, especially since the money sent back to their hometowns was important to Italy's economy. Blacks had long since left their homelands, most of which were part of European colonies, and were unable to influence how blacks in the U.S. were treated.

6. Location in the United States. A century ago, most Italians were concentrated in northern cities, where jobs and upward mobility didn't depend on advanced education. Blacks were located mostly in rural southern areas, and those in the north, such as barbers, were often displaced by Italians and other white immigrants. The migration of blacks to cities of the north didn't peak until the mid twentieth century, when jobs became more scarce and dependent on a higher level of education.

7. Culture. America's culture is basically a European one—specifically northwest European. But certain proper elements of U.S. culture owe a great debt to southeast Europe, such as classical music and opera from Italy, and the legacy of the Roman empire recorded in textbooks. The jazz and blues musical styles basically developed by African Americans were not recognized as respectable until later in the twentieth century.

8. Degree of hostility endured. As a minority group until 1945, Italians suffered heavily from discrimination, including violence, especially between the 1870s and the 1920s, when at least 40 Italian Americans were lynched. African Americans have been continually subjected to discrimination and violence for more than 300 years. Between 1882 and 1951, there were 3,437 blacks lynched, while 1,293 whites were lynched in the same period. Institutional racism in America continues to afflict blacks with higher rates of infant mortality, disease, poverty, incarceration, and substandard housing.

9. Segmented assimilation. "Refers to the fact that immigrants assimilate to particular sectors of American society: some become integrated into the white middle class, and others assimilate into the inner city underclass." Over the past three decades, immigrants who are black, such as Haitians, and other people of color have arrived in America in large numbers. Some sociologists claim that those who settle in inner-city areas near underclass minorities often find that their children, unlike the second-generation Italians of the early twentieth century, will experience downward assimilation into poverty. Thus, the poverty of native-born blacks becomes the lot of many black immigrants.

Sources: Stanley Lieberson, *A Piece of the Pie: Black and White Immigrants Since 1880*, 1980, pp. 31, 35; Stephen Cornell and Douglas Hartmann, *Ethnicity and Race: Making Identities in a Changing World*, 2nd Edition, p. 48; Grimshaw, *Racial Violence in America*, p. 57; Nancy Foner, "The Immigrant Family: Cultural Legacies and Cultural Changes," in Charles Hirschman, Philip Kasinitz, & Josh deWind, editors, *The Handbook of International Migration: The American Experience*, 1999, p. 260; Gerald Jaynes, "Immigration and the Social Construction of Otherness: 'Underclass' Stigma and Intergroup Relations," in Nancy Foner & George M. Frederick, editors, *Not Just Black and White*, 2004, p. 111.

was in poor condition, and the air pollution was "stifling." Most residents were people of color: 42% black, 10% Latino, and nine percent Arabian. "Blacks who have money move to Buffalo," stated Reverend Peter Carter of Queen of All Saints Church. "They either can't move to other Lackawanna wards or wouldn't feel welcome if they did." One black resident said, "There's no communication between the First Ward and city hall. We have no blacks in city hall and have to take whatever scraps the politicians throw us …. We're like a city, within a city or an island that is completely cut off from the rest of the world." [91]

Racial divisions were perhaps most apparent at Bethlehem Steel. The growth of defense industries during World War I, the Great Steel Strike of 1919, and the restrictions on European immigration in the 1920s led northern factories, including the plant in Lackawanna, to recruit black and Latino workers from the south. Donato Chiacchia was a labor agent with some involvement in Lackawanna's recruitment process. By 1925, a pattern of discrimination had emerged at Bethlehem Steel—one endured by people of color for many years. A study of the First Ward residents listed in the 1925 census found that native-born and immigrant blacks held 64% of the steel plant's "hot jobs"—that is, the most dangerous jobs, which involved constant exposure to molten metal, overhead cranes, and stockpiles of raw materials and scrap metal. Among white immigrants, Yugoslavs had nine percent of the hot jobs, Poles eight percent, and Italians five percent. Native-born whites had only three percent. The European immigrants also fared better than blacks in skilled jobs, with 18% of Poles and 12% of Italians in these positions, but only six percent of blacks. A few miles south in Blasdell, the Seneca Steel Company had a variety of white ethnic groups in its workforce, but an Italian employee working there during the 1930s never saw any black workers.[92]

One could argue that because the bulk of Lackawanna's black residents began arriving during the early 1920s, which was later than many of the European immigrants, it would make sense that they still occupied the lower rungs of the economic ladder in 1925. However, the pattern continued throughout the following decades, as blacks continually found themselves working in the coke ovens, blast furnaces, and other dangerous departments. A 1927 study of ethnic groups in the Buffalo area concluded that Italians and other new immigrants fared worse than other whites, but whites as a group held a convincing "occupational superiority" over African Americans. A "racial-economic caste system" put blacks at a tremendous disadvantage in all job categories the study concluded. During the organizing effort from 1936 to 1941, the Steel Workers Organizing Committee stressed equality for blacks, but the locals of the United Steelworkers eventually fell into discriminatory practices. Arabs, who entered the plant's workforce in larger numbers after World War II, also were frequently given the most dangerous jobs, usually in the coke ovens or blast furnaces.[93]

Strip-mill superintendent Albert Schonkwiler did not like blacks in his mill, and allowed black bricklayers to reline the furnaces only after being directly ordered to do so by the plant manager. Schonkwiler insisted that the blacks not be allowed to go beyond the furnaces into other parts of the mill. In 1945, he became the assistant general manager of the plant, and was later promoted to general manager. Finally, in 1970, a suit filed against Bethlehem Steel charged that for many years, its discriminatory practices had forced blacks, who were 2,600 of the plant's 18,000 workers, to work in 11 of the "less desirable departments in the plant solely on the basis of race." The plant was found to have "discriminated against blacks in hiring, job assignment, apprenticeship and selection of supervisory personnel.... " The seniority system and other practices locked blacks into their jobs by making it possible for them to transfer into a white department only by forfeiting their seniority. "The fact is that the Lackawanna plant was a microcosm of classic job discrimination in the north," the charge stated. It also named the five locals of the United Steelworkers of America as defendants, alleging "that portions of the collective bargaining agreement between Bethlehem and the unions perpetuated discrimination." Some white unionists formed a group called Rights for Whites to contest the charges, but to no avail. The court in 1971 ruled in favor of workers from racial minority groups and ordered Bethlehem Steel to take corrective actions. The victory was short-lived, however, as the plant declined

quickly and all but closed in 1983. These civil-rights issues in Lackawanna and other cities began during the 1960s, and set against the backdrop of increasing racial strife were the beginnings of the white ethnic revival.[94]

Across the United States, a series of crucial developments expanded the civil rights of nonwhite citizens and immigrants. These began modestly in the 1940s. With China as an ally in World War II, Congress reopened emigration from that country, established a small quota, and, finally, made Chinese immigrants eligible for naturalization. In 1946, India and the Philippines were extended the same access. The War Brides Act allowed wives and children of American servicemen to immigrate, free of the usual quota restrictions, and become naturalized. With the wartime manpower shortage, short-term Mexican contract workers were allowed to temporarily enter the U.S. as farm laborers, as had been the case during World War I. The new program was maintained for 20 years. The Displaced Persons Act of 1948 was the first of many legislative acts that allowed refugees to enter the United States, including many Asians. In 1952, the McCarran-Walter Act continued the existing quotas for specific countries and the policy of no quotas on immigrants from the western hemisphere, and increased the combined quotas of northwest European countries from 82% to 85% of the worldwide total. It also abolished the Asiatic barred zone and established the Asian Pacific Triangle, assigned a quota to each country or colony that previously had none, and made all immigrants eligible for citizenship. While the act removed the barriers of exclusion and ineligibility for naturalization of Asians, it also represented tokenism, as each newly assigned quota was for only 100 immigrants. This was seen as an attempt to limit immigration by people of color, especially blacks from the British West Indies and Asians. While the law was a blow to southeast Europeans, whose quotas remained small, its main concern was the "preservation of whiteness" in America.[95]

The civil-rights movement increased America's awareness of racism and brought about profound changes after World War II. President Truman desegregated the armed forces in 1948. Congress passed laws on equal access to schooling (1954), housing, and public accommodations as well as guaranteeing voting rights (1964-68). The Immigration Act of 1965 abolished the restrictionist policies of the national-origins and quota system and the Asian Pacific Triangle designation. The cap on total immigration was raised to 290,000, with 120,000 visas available each year to countries of the western hemisphere and 170,000 to the eastern hemisphere, with no country getting more than 20,000. Applicants were processed on a first-come, first-served basis. Politicians assumed that most of the immigrants would be white, as was the case from 1920 to 1960, when 60% of immigrants came from Europe,

35% from South and Central America, and 3% from Asia. But by 1975, they were surprised that Europe accounted for only 19%, South and Central America 43%, and Asia 34%. With the new civil-rights laws and a population that was more tolerant of differences, government officials, if not the general public, finally proclaimed in the 1960s that people of color must be allowed to fully assimilate into American society. Over the past 40 years, there have been serious attempts to allow people of color to complete the eight processes of assimilation, just as white immigrants had done in the past. Racism has certainly not been laid to rest, and many Americans, including white ethnics, have reacted negatively to the country's growing nonwhite population and its demands for equality. But there has been progress as the new concept of multiculturalism challenges the Anglo-conformity model and advocates tolerance and acceptance of America's ethnic mosaic. Prior to the 1960s, America had believed only in the acculturation of nonwhites, but since then, for the first time in U.S. history, there has been the stated goal of full assimilation for people of color. Intermarriage between races has increased, and several studies have found that Asian Americans, many of whom were professionals when they immigrated, ranked at the same level of assimilation as southeast European Catholics and Jews. The election of President Barack Obama in 2008 marked another important turning point in the assimilation of blacks and other people of color.[96]

In Lackawanna, there were some bright spots in mid-twentieth-century ethnic relations that offered hope for achieving racial harmony. Father Nelson Baker insisted that the Our Lady of Victory programs be open to everyone, including people of color. The OLV Mission Church, which later became Queen of All Saints, encouraged African Americans to join the parish, and many did. St. John's Protectory, a home for delinquent boys at OLV, was open to all races. In the late 1920s, when most delinquent black youth were sent to penal institutions, the protectory was the only agency in the Buffalo area to accept black youth. In 1942, Friendship House sponsored a Boy Scout troop that included both white and black youth. Individuals often bridged the gaps between ethnic groups. Abdul Nashir, who migrated from Yemen in 1959, worked alongside Italian and Hungarian immigrants in the steel plant and felt a common bond with them because they all spoke with an accent. The Italians' family values and spicy foods also bore some similarity to those of Yemen. Several Lackawanna Italians married people of Arab ancestry.[97]

Some community organizations helped improve race relations in the city. In 1953, the Neighborhood Council of the First Ward brought together representatives from Bethlehem Park, Albright Court, the Baker Homes, and Ridge Road to work "toward the solution of common problems of the neighborhood," such as more recreational facilities for children. A few years later, Monsignor Szabo of Assumption Church organized a branch of the Christopher Movement to help deal with problems in the First Ward. Seeing the vast scope of the task, the National Conference of Catholic Charities in 1956 stepped in as a sponsor and brought in Nicholas von Hoffman, a professional organizer from the Industrial Areas Foundation. He spoke with residents and found that the city government "was corrupt and inept, the result of many years of paternalistic control by the steel company." Von Hoffman concluded that Lackawanna was "a city with an inferiority complex," but its residents had learned, from the organizing efforts of the steelworkers union, what people can accomplish when united. The result was the founding in 1957 of the Lackawanna Neighborhood Cooperative Committee (LNCC). The organization assisted more than 100 families, mostly blacks and elderly whites, in getting help from the city housing authority when their homes were condemned prior to the construction of the Father Baker high level bridge. The LNCC successfully lobbied for a city ambulance service, helped push through a long-needed flood-assistance project, and assisted Fourth Ward residents in fighting for better city services. The group renamed itself the Citizens' Federation of Lackawanna (CFL) at its first convention in 1958, which was attended by representatives from 90 organizations, including the Lake Erie Italian Club and its Women's Auxiliary, the Vagabond Club, the Roland Italian American Lodge, and St. Anthony's Church. The CFL had more than 600 members from many of the city's ethnic groups. Among those involved with the eight standing committees were Reverend Ciolino of St. Anthony's, Larry Christ, Charles Saccomanno, Frank Fiore, Nicholas Colello, Anthony Monaco, John Suffoletta, and Peter Rand. Fiore was elected president of the organization in 1962. The CFL began to fade out in the early 1960s because the financial support of Catholic Charities ebbed, local churches were afraid to get embroiled in controversial issues, the steelworkers' union showed limited interest, and Bethlehem Steel maintained its tight grip on local politics. Still functioning in 1967, the CFL did bring together diverse ethnic groups, had blacks and whites working side by side on projects, and taught members to unite to bring about changes in the city.[98]

Following several episodes of violence at Lackawanna High School in 1968, students and staff made efforts to solve the problems in a peaceful way. A committee of the school's student council, made up of six black and six white students and advised by guidance counselor Nick Milano, met to draw up recommendations. A month later, the student council sent an open letter to the *Lackawanna Leader* that expressed the group's thoughts and conclusions.

A great many things have been said and written about the recent racial disturbance at Lackawanna Senior High

School. There has yet to appear, however, an unbiased statement by us students, both White and Negro, of L. H. S. concerning the ways in which our problem has affected us. Let it suffice to say that the near-riot we experienced on February 9 has taught us that all incidents must be dealt with immediately; delayed or neglected action can easily lead to disaster. It has taught us that violence can never be stopped by more violence. And most importantly, it has taught us that all men must learn to live together in peace, there is no other way.

Perhaps then, this racial disturbance has served a useful purpose. We students have been forced to search for a solution to the pressing problem that has been thrust before us. In so doing, we have all come to better understand our own individual feelings on the racial problems of today.

In spite of all these things, however, we cannot bring ourselves to accept the violence. The riot was wrong and we are shamefully aware of it. But we know that something can be done to ease tension and stem further problems. Our newly-formed Inter-Racial Committee has already began to ease tension among the students. This first step toward the attainment of inter-racial understanding may be a small one but it is a beginning nevertheless.

Thus, it can be seen that the past few weeks have been a trying and challenging time for the members of the LHS community. We feel sure that the challenge can be met and that our ultimate goal of mutual understanding will someday be realized.

LHS Student Council

In the following years, there was more racial violence and tension in the school. During the 1971-1972 school year, a student committee planned and carried out a day long conference at Friendship House. Several hundred students attended as well as a number of teachers and administrators. There was a panel discussion followed by small group meetings, and the tone and ideas of the students showed a great deal of maturity and insight regarding race relations at a time when some people in Lackawanna were clamoring for more strident approaches.[99]

Today, Lackawanna seems to have less overt ethnic strife and violence, but racism remains a problem. The city's history demonstrates that many white ethnics, including some Italians, have adopted the racial prejudice that has existed in American society for several hundred years. It is important for the descendants of southeast European immigrants as well as other whites to recognize that the prejudice and discrimination endured by the immigrants and their children prior to 1945 usually lasted only two or three generations. They have not been as severe as the prejudice and discrimination suffered for many generations by blacks, Latinos, Native Americans, and Asians. Lackawanna's Italians have done well for themselves and are now part of the city's power structure and cultural mainstream.

The pressure by people of color to be more fully included in society and the passage of civil-rights legislation over the past five decades have finally given official approval to the goal of complete assimilation of all racial groups. The large-scale immigration of many people of color to the United States has expanded the numbers of nonwhite people and accelerated the melding of different nationality and culture groups into the African American, Latino American, Asian American, and Native American racial groups, as well as stimulated many whites to embrace the European American identity. This Quintuple Melting Pot has the potential to build a truly integrated society that allows all peoples to assimilate into the mainstream. On the other hand, it could lead to increased racial strife resulting from several sources. In one scenario, the United States would fail to develop a fair and consistent immigration policy that reconciles the capitalists' demand for unskilled laborers, the rights of American workers, and the nativists' demand for a legal and limited influx of immigrants. Second, a worsening national and international economy could lead to competition for resources that could arouse civil and racial conflict in this country. Lastly, increased international friction, such as the further escalation of the war on terror, could place nationality, religious, and racial groups in the United States in a heightened state of tension and social conflict.

European Americans throughout the country can potentially find common cause with blacks, Latinos, American Indians, and Asians as well as Arab Muslims. Lackawanna remains a rust-belt city, and its population is rapidly declining as younger white ethnics seek job opportunities elsewhere, and their aging parents and grandparents face the closing or consolidation of the old-nationality churches. But the city's ethnic mosaic is in some ways continuing to develop as many Arab Muslims from Yemen and other countries settle in the First Ward with their young families. Lackawanna Italians and other white ethnics are now part of the European American community and must contend with the Quintuple Melting Pot and the challenge of dealing with America's racism. Italian Americans must face another challenge as they complete the final stages of their assimilation. A crucial aspect of preserving their ethnicity is to challenge the stereotype linking Italians with organized crime, which is more than a century old and remains an unfair smear on the history and culture of the ethnic group. As they take on this stereotype, they become better able to challenge the stereotypes regarding blacks, Asians, Latinos, Native Americans, and Arab Muslims.

Organized Crime: an American Institution

"The underworld performs many services which respectable members of society call for," wrote journalist Walter Lippmann in 1931. To understand organized crime in a city such as Lackawanna, it is helpful to view it first on the national level. Organized crime has been an established American institution since the 1830s. By the 1860s, crime syndicates were forming coalitions with urban political machines. In the early twentieth century, criminals in organized syndicates provided illicit services and goods including prostitution, drugs, political control of minority-group voters, and brute force against "undesirable" groups, such as radicals and union organizers. But it was not only gangsters who organized the criminal activities. In 1904, Minneapolis Mayor Albert Ames and his brother, the police chief, had detectives organize pickpockets, prostitutes, and other criminals, then demand payoffs in return for permission to ply their trades. "It was generally understood," writes Michael Woodiwiss, "that criminal networks could and often did include the active involvement of police, politicians, lawyers and other judges, professionals, and ostensibly legitimate businessmen."[100]

In the second half of the nineteenth century, as American cities grew quickly and political machines became wedded to syndicate activity, Irish Americans were the predominant group in organized crime. The most visible segment of organized crime, the gangs that actually commit the crimes, have typically been composed of people from minority groups. American society has often blamed ethnic gangs for the presence of the whole organized-crime network, conveniently overlooking the respectable citizens and institutions that enable the syndicates. In the 1870s, Irish immigrants were portrayed as the source of organized crime, but as the Irish assimilated and entered more respectable careers, they gradually turned over the role of the ethnic criminal gang to newer arrivals. Some of the Irish then assumed other roles in organized crime, becoming the lawyers and public officials who monitored and set boundaries for criminal activity on behalf of the institutions of the dominant society. For immigrant and minority groups organized crime has always been an informal "ladder of social mobility"—a proven way of gaining wealth and investing in a more respectable future career. And for powerful individuals and institutions, organized crime has been a tool for achieving greater wealth and power.[101]

The large influx of Italian immigrants during the 1880s and events in Louisiana around that time made Italians the new alien threat. Many Sicilian immigrants had settled in New Orleans, and when police chief David Hennessey was murdered in 1890, Italians were suspect. The following year, the 19 Italians indicted for the crime were in the process of being tried when a mob stormed the jail, tracked down 11 of the Italians, and lynched them— committing the single worst known lynching incident in the United States to date. The mob, led by prominent citizens, was convinced that the Sicilians were part of a Mafia plot and that their vigilante action was righteous. Newspapers of the time proclaimed a Mafia conspiracy, and Italian Americans have been stereotyped as gangsters ever since.[102]

Italians and eastern European Jews learned the ropes from Irish gangsters and soon rose in many crime syndicates. During Prohibition (1920 to 1933), criminals of these three ethnic groups provided much of the illicit alcohol that so many "respectable" Americans desired. Often, the government agents pitted against these criminals were WASPs, such as Thomas Dewey (who prosecuted gangsters in New York City) and Eliot Ness (who battled syndicates in Chicago). Beginning in the late 1920s, Italians dominated organized crime in many American cities, although their syndicates often included Jews, Irishmen, and others. The ascendancy of Italians in organized crime coincided with the advent of talkies (motion pictures with sound), and the gangster movies of the era provided vivid images that imprinted the stereotype of Italian criminality on the minds of millions of Americans. Movie newsreels and radio provided ready notoriety for publicity-seeking gangsters such as Al Capone, who boasted of his assimilation: "The American system of ours, call it Americanism, call it Capitalism, call it what you like, gives each and every one of us a great opportunity if we only seize it with both hands and make the most of it.... My rackets are run strictly on American lines and they are going to stay that way." Capone, Lucky Luciano, Frank Costello, and many other Italian American gangsters had emigrated from Italy as children or were born in the United States and learned their criminal ways on the streets of America. It appears that relatively few of the Italian immigrants who led American crime syndicates had been gangsters in Italy.[103]

In the first two decades of the twentieth century, small Black Hand extortion groups and modest crime syndicates functioned within the Little Italys but rarely went outside their boundaries. In 1920, the advent of Prohibition allowed young gangsters such as Luciano to tap the wealth beyond New York City's Italian neighborhoods. The gangs of Luciano, Capone, and Costello included Italians with roots in many regions— especially Sicily, Campania, and Calabria, the home regions of these three criminals. These men and other gangsters eliminated their competitors, made alliances with Jewish and Irish syndicates, and came to dominate organized crime syndicates in many cities. Luciano was allied with Jewish gangster Meyer Lansky, and similar Italian – Jewish cooperative efforts existed in Chicago, Cleveland, and Detroit. The gangsters succeeded because they were allied with segments of the law-enforcement, political, legal, and business institutions. In addition to providing alcohol, drugs, gambling, and prostitutes to so-called respectable Americans, the syndicates ensured that minority groups voted for the "right" candidates. Businessmen hired syndicate thugs to harass competitors, break up workers' strikes, and squelch union-organizing efforts. Henry Ford so frequently employed gangsters to fight unions that a federal agency labeled his tactics as "organized gangsterism." Some politicians actively sought alliances with gangsters. For example, when Mayor LaGuardia's anticrime campaign of 1935 drove Frank Costello's slot machines out of New York City, Governor Huey Long invited Costello to move the machines to New Orleans, where payoffs would guarantee police protection.[104]

Coalitions of gangsters were forged regionally and nationally for such endeavors as drug smuggling, but these arrangements were often shifting and temporary. In 1917, the cocaine trade in New York City was conducted by 22 small gangs, for which the ethnicity of about half of the 263 criminals involved is known: 83 Jews, 23 Italians, eight Irishmen, five blacks, and three Greeks. In Chicago in 1930, of the "108 top crime figures … 30 percent were Italian, 29 percent were Irish, 20 percent were Jewish, and 12 percent were Negro." The warfare and alliances led to some expansion of syndicates and the forging of loose associations with other gangs during the following three decades. However, there was no centralized, permanent national crime confederation, Mafia or otherwise, in the United States. Italian and other ethnic syndicates usually focused on their own local turf. Spotlighting an evil Mafia conspiracy only served to hide the criminal behavior of American institutions.[105]

Prior to the late 1930s, reformers and muckrakers described how "respectable" sectors of society worked directly with not only informal gangs but also with organized crime. After the repeal of Prohibition, attention shifted away from defects in social institutions and focused on how gangsters were a threat to America's institutions. Woodiwiss writes, "The consensus of opinion that emerged among politicians, law enforcement officials, and the press changed the perception of organized crime from one that demanded honest and effective local law enforcement to one that demanded much more nationally coordinated action."[106]

With the advent of the Cold War and America's battle with the international Communist conspiracy, the Mafia conspiracy was a ready-made formula for explaining the corruption of government, the police, and business in America. In the 1950s and 1960s, congressional investigations, government reports, and television programs highlighted an organized crime conspiracy said to include 24 Italian American syndicates ruled by a national council and linked with syndicates in Italy. One source writes, "Understood in such terms, the problem of

organized crime had a very simple solution: give the government more power to get the bad guys." Agencies such as the Federal Bureau of Narcotics promoted the idea that "the Mafia was a super-criminal organization that controlled both the worldwide drug traffic and the core of organized crime in the United States." But like its predecessor, the Bureau of Narcotics, the Federal Bureau of Narcotics was abolished in 1968 because of systematic corruption. Yet the focus of government efforts remained on Italian American criminals.[107]

A more objective view of organized crime breaks through the stereotype of foreign conspiracies. Woodiwiss defines organized crime as "systematic criminal activity for money or power" as practiced by "the powerful and respectable — or those on their way to power and respectability— in those societies, both ancient and early modern, that we usually associate with the centre of 'civilized' development…." Organized crime is a part of society's institutions, not a threat to them, and America's legal and criminal-justice structures provide openings for systematic criminal activity.

High-level politicians and respectable members of business and professional communities have gained more from organized criminal activity than any other group and, for the most part, stayed out of prison. Countless scandals have indicated that the bribe and the fix are still features of U.S. criminal justice and the problem of police corruption is as acute as it ever was.… In sum, after decades of intense efforts against gangsters, U.S. organized crime control measures have done little to control organized criminal activity in either legal or illegal markets.

One study found that the fundamental cause of racketeering—running an illegal business or fraudulent scheme—in America has been cut throat competition, not foreign-born criminals.[108]

After World War II, as Italians assimilated and left behind their minority status, young, able Italians, unlike their forebears, could more easily find legitimate careers. Italian crime syndicates were unable to recruit them, a situation that grew acute by the 1960s. In a desperate bid to retain ethnic dominance, some Italian gangsters recruited young toughs from southern Italy during the 1970s to battle the encroachment of other ethnic gangs. But only in cities with large Italian populations—such as Chicago and New York City, the latter with five entrenched syndicates—did Italians continue to dominate organized crime beyond the 1970s. Since then, most Italian syndicates have given way to the process of ethnic succession and been replaced by blacks, outlaw motorcycle and prison gangs, and immigrants from China, Vietnam, Colombia, Russia, Cuba, and Haiti. The strong stereotype of Italian criminality still exists, however, perpetrated by government agencies and the media.[109]

Organized Crime in Buffalo and Lackawanna

Organized crime in Lackawanna was an offshoot of activities in Buffalo. During the early decades of the twentieth century, local papers were filled with accounts of Black Hand crimes in Italian communities in Buffalo, Albion, and Batavia. One Italian businessman in Lackawanna apparently was the victim of these Italian extortionists, who wounded him. Some of these criminals preyed on Italian laborers working on the main railroad lines running through Blasdell and Lackawanna, and foreman Raffaele Schole carried a rifle to scare the thugs away. Four Italians attempted to extort money from a Lackawanna Italian businessman, when their plan failed, they shot and seriously wounded the merchant. It was immediately labeled a Black Hand incident by the police, and the four extortionists went to prison. As with similar episodes throughout the country, they were the work of small, loosely organized bands of small time thieves. Organized crime syndicates, on the other hand were large operations that provided ongoing "services."[110]

Lackawanna's First Ward had been the site of illegal activity since the first decade of the twentieth century. Even before the city was founded, a Buffalo newspaper called this part of West Seneca "wide open" when the sheriff received "reports of roulette, faro, keno, and bunco running in several saloons," as well as five-cent slot machines at South Park Avenue and Ridge Road. In 1909, the Common Council was presented a petition "in regards to foreigners running and conducting saloons contrary to state excise laws, and also some citizens running bawdy houses and houses of ill repute." Indeed, for much of the past century, the First Ward had houses of prostitution, speakeasies, unlicensed pinball and slot machines, and gambling venues. Several interviewees reported that Irish, Lebanese, Serbian, and African Americans individuals were involved in the city's numbers racket up until the late twentieth century. It appears that many Lackawanna gambling enterprises and houses of prostitution were ultimately controlled by the Buffalo Italian mob.[111]

Lackawanna's illicit activities always had a direct relation to the big city just to the north, Buffalo. During the 1920s, big-city gangsters throughout America found it easier to ally with officials in smaller cities and towns than to deal with complicated big-city governments and changing administrations, some of which attempted to carry out reforms. Notable examples were Al Capone and John Torrio, who reestablished their criminal operations in Cicero after the newly elected mayor of Chicago promised to prosecute leaders of crime syndicates. In western New York, the *Lackawanna News* in 1930 reported that "gangsters and racketeers … driven from some of the larger cities are staying in this city." A 1938 Erie County grand jury found that vice and gambling were "organized" by a syndicate and "protected" by politicians and law-enforcement agencies in Tonawanda, Lancaster, and Lackawanna. Slot machines, bookmaking establishments, and houses of prostitution flourished in all three towns, according to the investigation.[112]

Some of the Italian men involved in Buffalo's Black Hand groups early in the twentieth century apparently later moved on to form organized crime syndicates. *Corriere Italiano* claimed that the Buffalo police cooperated with Italian gangs. Angelo Puma settled in the Hooks, the Italian enclave on Buffalo's waterfront, and by 1910, he was the leader of an Italian gang involved in extortion, theft, prostitution, and gambling. A few years later, Angelo "Buffalo Bill" Palermo became the leader of Buffalo's Italian syndicate, and a relative, saloon owner Giuseppe DiCarlo, was thought to be an accomplice. But it was DiCarlo's sons Joseph and Sam who won notoriety as gangsters. While the immigrant gangsters victimized their fellow Italians, the DiCarlo brothers and other young, American-born gangsters took advantage of Prohibition to spread their illicit activities into the community at large.[113]

Joe DiCarlo's syndicate grew in the 1920s, and the press labeled him the head of "an invisible league of the lawless in Buffalo and Erie County." His brother Sam operated in the counties along the New York and Pennsylvania border. When Joe DiCarlo was described as "Buffalo Public Enemy No. 1," he said, "I can't see why I rate anything like that. Suppose I am mixed up in the slot-machine business? Just for the sake of argument, say I angle on booze and gambling too. What of it? I am only trying to give the people what they want. Nothing but harmless amusement. You can't call a guy a public enemy for that, can you?" DiCarlo was involved in labor and union racketeering as well as the distribution of alcohol, narcotics, and lottery tickets. Pressured by the police, he left Buffalo in the 1950s, then operated out of Youngstown, Ohio, and Miami, Florida.[114]

Less publicity-oriented than DiCarlo, Stefano Magaddino had become the behind-the-scenes leader of the Buffalo syndicate by the late 1920s. Magaddino, a gangster in Sicily before settling in Buffalo, made fabulous money smuggling liquor from Canada. By the 1950s, his gang based in Niagara Falls and Buffalo had ties with criminals in Rochester as well as in Ohio and Canada. Following the process of ethnic succession, the Magaddino mob eventually lost ground to new ethnic syndicates. In the 1960s, blacks negotiated a deal with Magaddino in which they took control of numbers gambling in Buffalo and paid 10 percent of the profits to him. But when the FBI and local police cracked down on Magaddino's gang, the black mobsters refused to pay anything. Still, while there was ethnic competition among criminals, there was also cooperation and accommodation. By the early 1960s, there were seven non – Italian associates in the

Buffalo Italian mob, and the Magaddino syndicate was listed in government reports as one of the 24 major crime "families" in the United States. Long before this time, the Buffalo syndicate was involved in Lackawanna.[115]

During Prohibition, bootlegging was so common in the Steel City that 1,200 of the 2,000 homes owned by Bethlehem Steel had "moonshine stills." In 1924, an Erie County grand jury recommended that Lackawanna pass a law to license the 155 bars that had supposedly been transformed into "soft drink" establishments. When the police were criticized by citizens on this issue, Charles Ellis of the *Lackawanna Daily Journal* defended the Lackawanna police, stating: "you should jump on the guys higher up"—the city councilmen who had stalled any licensing effort. "The alleged councilmen," quipped Ellis, "are on record for allowing disorder to run rift here and then censor the police for not doing things for which there is no law… Crime only flourishes where the authorities want it to."[116]

People of many ethnic groups were involved in producing and selling alcohol, including Italians on Ingham Avenue, in Bethlehem Park, and on Roland Avenue. Walking in certain blocks of these neighborhoods, one could easily smell the alcohol. Businessmen with access to large volumes of sugar set up stills in basements and garages, as did their relatives and neighbors. There was no evidence of organized crime in these small ventures, but larger enterprises may have had such ties. Charles Sorrento of Buffalo was arrested in 1934 for running a distillery in a barn on Abbott Road, in Lackawanna's sparsely settled eastern section. During Prohibition, raids were conducted by government agents, many of whom were WASPs. A 1921 raid on a Ridge Road liquor establishment was carried out by five federal agents, four with WASP surnames, and one Italian, William Martini.[117]

Other illicit activities had definite links to Buffalo and organized crime. In 1924, a newspaper declared that "Lackawanna has been endangered by undesirable women and dope peddlers from Buffalo soliciting on the streets." Five years later, County Sheriff Zimmerman planned to raid 45 gambling joints and disorderly houses in the First Ward. During the late 1920s and early 1930s, there were six to nine houses of

prostitution operating in Lackawanna at any one time. One of them was operated by Nicholas and Rose Matre at their Hamburg Turnpike home. Nicholas Matre, an Italian born in Buffalo, had moved to Lackawanna in the late 1920s. In 1932, after he was shot and killed by two policemen who had been drinking with him, the press highlighted Matre as an underworld figure who had paid off the police. Two years later, his widow, Rose Felice, was arrested for "keeping a disorderly house"; she may have been the brothel operator known by some Lackawannans as Dago Rose. Around the same time, Ed Magini and Buffalonian George Barone were also placed under arrest for operating disorderly houses. An Italian American couple, Nicholas Rogers of Buffalo and his wife Mary, a Lackawanna native, ran a nightclub and bordello on Gates Avenue. Two other bordellos, one on Hamburg Turnpike and the other on O'Dell Street, were operated by Steel City Italians. An Italian on Roland Avenue ran a small gambling and prostitution business for a time, apparently working on his own and generating only modest revenue. In addition to Italians, some of the individuals managing bordellos were eastern Europeans and blacks.[118]

In the early 1940s, two young Italians learned that the Buffalo Italian syndicate was behind a number of these Steel

Joe DiCarlo, named "Buffalo Public Enemy No. 1," was a leader in the Buffalo Italian crime syndicate from the 1920s to the 1950s, when police pressure forced him to move his rackets to Youngstown, Ohio, and Miami, Florida.
Photo sources: Buffalo & Erie County Public Library; *Town Tidings,* September, 1933

Stefano Magaddino was one of the relatively few Italian American gangsters who was also a gangster in Italy. He fled Castellamare del Golfo, Sicily, came to Buffalo in 1927, and became the leader of the Italian crime syndicate in western New York.
Photo source: *Time Magazine,* 8/22/66

City brothels. Amateur journalists Armondo Pietrocarlo and Ralph Galanti were paid seven cents per word to write a Lackawanna gossip column for the *The Bugle*, a Rochester newspaper that was circulated in the Buffalo area. In one column, they wrote of Steel City bordellos and mentioned Patsy Lee's place, which was managed by an African American. They soon were contacted by a Buffalo Italian who told them to visit Joe DiCarlo in Buffalo and "explain things to him." DiCarlo informed Pietrocarlo and Galanti that they had erred in mentioning a place by name, something for which the two young men quickly apologized and assured DiCarlo they would never repeat. DiCarlo told them he would take care of things, and the journalists returned to Lackawanna with a new understanding of the underworld links between the Steel City and Buffalo.[119]

Crime and corruption continued to flourish in Lackawanna, as was revealed in hearings by the New York State Investigation Commission in 1968. The commission found that politicians meddled in the police department, favors were done for police officers and others who helped elect the mayor, and some policemen associated with underworld figures. Lackawannan Sam Cardinale was said to have ties with the Buffalo syndicate and the Lackawanna mayor. After pleading the Fifth Amendment 25 times before a grand jury, Cardinale served a prison term for gambling and conducting unlawful card games in Lackawanna. When interviewed for this book, he spoke with pride about his silence regarding mob activities but with much sadness about his father's reaction. Giuseppe "Josie" Cardinale, who had worked for 48 years on the South Buffalo Railway and was well respected in the community, told his son in Italian, "You didn't speak to the grand jury, then you don't speak to me." The relationship between organized crime and gambling activities in Lackawanna was the topic again in 1969 when a county grand jury interviewed John Cammillieri, a leader in the Buffalo syndicate. Steel City political boss and police commissioner Tom Joyce, according to journalist Ray Hill, "put his house up for bail when John (Fats) Green got himself jailed on a minor charge." Green ran illegal activities in Lackawanna, reportedly had connections with the Italian American syndicate in Buffalo, and eventually was sentenced to 120 years in prison for "crime involving the morals of children."[120]

It appears that only a handful of the Lackawanna Italians were directly linked with the Buffalo Italian syndicate. In the 1950s and 1960s, several Buffalo gangsters moved to homes in eastern Lackawanna, but it is unclear if they had dealings directly in the Steel City. A small number of individuals of other ethnic groups were involved with the illegal activities that had ties to Buffalo's Italian syndicate. In the 1930s, Buffalo Italian mobsters attempted to look after their Steel City enterprises by directly contributing funds to political campaigns, and by including Serbs, Irishmen, Poles, blacks, and Lebanese among their Lackawanna associates. The demise of the steel industry and the rapid decline in population in the 1970s and 1980s in both the Steel City and Buffalo meant that the First Ward was no longer fertile ground for organized crime.

Nonetheless, the stereotype of the Italian gangster continues to hound Italian Americans. During the 1990s, Lackawanna Mayor Kathleen Stanizlewski, in an appearance at the Lake Erie Italian Club, angered the members when she remarked that sitting at the head table with the club's board of directors felt like being at a meeting of the Mafia. When this author mentioned his work on this book in casual conversations, many people, including some Italian Americans, immediately responded with remarks about organized crime. As if to reinforce the stereotype, reruns of *The Untouchables*, *The Sopranos*, and the *Godfather* movies are constantly shown on television.

The Italian American experience of the past 100 years has been one of upheaval, changes, and eventually, significant assimilation into American society. By the year 2000, there were nearly 16 million Italian Americans, perhaps half of whom are of full Italian ancestry. That would mean that the other half is of mixed ancestries, which is one sign of the high degree of assimilation of Italian Americans. While the nativists of a century ago demanded that immigrants and their children abandon their ancestral culture, that attitude has changed as white ethnics have influenced mainstream culture and won greater acceptance over the last four decades. Today, Lackawanna's Italians are part of the European American segment of the Quintuple Melting Pot. They display a sense of peoplehood based on the core culture of the United States, while a significant number also acknowledge their Italian heritage.[121]

By understanding both America's rich ethnic history and its tragic pecking order, Italians and other whites in Lackawanna can become open to the full assimilation of people in the other four racial groupings and accept their unique contributions within a renewed definition of mainstream. A first step is for Italian Americans to gain a greater appreciation of our own history and struggle to assimilate, including our continuing battle against the Mafia stereotype.

To better understand our Italian roots, it is important to look at the day-to-day events that shaped the lives of the immigrants and their children, our forebears, who were trying to fit into American society. During the first half of the twentieth century, that transition took place in the four Lackawanna neighborhoods where Italians clustered—the focus of the next chapter.

CHAPTER 5

FROM SHANTY TOWN TO NEIGHBORHOODS

In 1900, the Lackawanna Steel Company employed experts to design and build the huge plant in West Seneca but did little to plan for workers' living quarters. While the company did construct the Old Village row houses a few years later, it was left to laborers and real estate speculators to improvise a variety of dwellings.

etween the steel plant and the network of railroad tracks, a new town sprang up along the rim of a swamp. East of the tracks, the farmlands gave way to streets and houses. Here, the earliest Italian residents, the Morinello family, settled near the foot of Roland Avenue.

By 1902, Italian laborers had built a shanty town along the northern bank of Smokes Creek, just inland from Lake Erie. This was located on steel company property (see Figure 5.1). The *Times of Buffalo* described these "picturesque" shacks this way in 1903:

> Wood of any old kind was used and then tar paper was put on the sides and roofs of the shacks to keep out the wind and water. The shacks are not over six feet long. One group rests in a hollow and to get to the shack in the middle of the bunch one has to travel through a sort of mystic labyrinth. There are no floors in the shacks and the sleeping places of the occupants usually are hard planks. The shacks are built by Italian laborers at the plant and still occupied by them. Thus, they escape paying rent and, bare and uninviting as these strange abodes are, the occupants seem to be just as well satisfied as any other group of inhabitants in Lackawanna City.[1]

Among the shacks was a larger dormitory structure erected by Charles Vincennes, a contractor who supplied laborers to the steel plant. It was "a cheap, half-story shanty eighteen feet wide and about fifty feet long. Here the Italians slept in two

< Area residents convinced engineers of Lackawanna Steel to leave this large elm tree standing on Second Street. Native Americans in earlier years had meetings under the tree. Pollution eventually killed the tree in the 1930s. Photo source: Steel Plant Museum

tiers of bunks. The bunks are of the cheapest character and only wide enough for one man to sleep in them. The shack is dimly lighted with a small lamp at either end." Typically, 75 to 100 men were housed in the structure.[2]

A lengthy article in the *Buffalo Express* (see Figure 5.3), while describing the shanty town in the stereotypical and bigoted manner typical of the period, identified characteristics of Italian immigrants that helped shape their experience in America, such as their regional loyalties, frugality, and tolerance of difficult living conditions. The strong regional identities and differing dialects posed challenges to Italian American unity. The Italians saved as much money as possible in order to send steamship tickets to other family members or return to Italy to buy a plot of land to farm. As farmers, shepherds, and migrant laborers, they were used to living in huts in the mountains and forests of Italy, where they had tended to flocks, gathered firewood and chestnuts, or cut wood and produced charcoal in earthen furnaces. While such spartan habits may have offended the urban sensitivities of a Buffalo newspaper reporter, they made perfectly good sense to humble Italian laborers.

Across the creek from the shanty town was an old farm house and two barns where Angelo and Maria Sperduto lived with their son Nick. They took in a number of boarders, including relatives such as Gaetano and Maria Giuseppa Milano; other couples such as Pietro and Enrichietta Oddi; and sojourners like Antonio Grossi, Antonio Carnevale, and Giovanni Martino. Like the shanty town, the house was on the grounds of the Lackawanna Steel Company's plant. The construction of the Old Village, which was completed in 1903, spelled the end for the shanty town and the Sperduto boardinghouse. Between 1903 and 1905, a number of the people residing along Smokes

1904. The farmhouse and barns just south of Smokes Creek in which Angelo and Maria Sperduto established their boarding house in 1901. Photo source; Paul Pietrak

Creek moved into standard housing, and by 1910, there was a dormitory for contract workers east of the New Village. In 1907, the Immigration Commission interviewed 79 Italians living in the steel-plant district, 48 of whom were from the northern-most regions of Italy. Most of these men soon left the district, but one former shanty town resident, Ruta Pellegrino, brought his family from Italy in 1903 and had an apartment on Ingham Avenue in 1905. The Sperdutos also moved to Ingham Avenue and took in six boarders. Pietro and Enrichetta Oddi left the Sperduto boarding house and walked a few hundred feet across Hamburg Turnpike to take up residence in the Old Village. Gaetano and Maria Giuseppa Milano moved into the Morinello boardinghouse on Roland Avenue and later to the Old Village. Antonio Grossi followed a similar course, going to Roland Avenue to board with the Falcone family. He then married Nicolina DePaula, and the couple rented a unit in the Old Village.[3]

Some Italians clustered at Gates Avenue and Church Street near the juncture of Ridge Road and Hamburg Turnpike. Luca Tarquinio and Antonio Mauriello served 80 males and several families in their hotel and restaurant, but they put the business

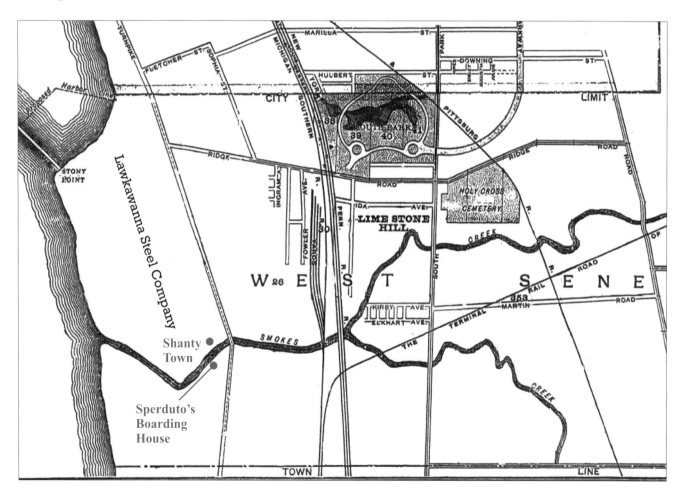

Figure 5.1 The Limestone Hill section of West Seneca in 1901. This area became the City of Lackawanna in 1909. On the lower left are the Italian shanty town and the Sperduto boardinghouse, which were on the grounds of the steel plant.
Source: Lackawanna Library

up for sale in 1903. The Tarquinios continued to live on Gates Avenue for at least two more years. Also living on that street was the Fusco family with their six boarders as well as seven other Italian males who boarded with an Austrian family. Tony Mauriello relocated his family to nearby Steelawanna Avenue, where they took in 13 countrymen as boarders and also ran a grocery store and then a tavern. Others avoided this congested area, with its barracks-type rooming houses and bars, and congregated in significant numbers on the eastern and southern boundaries of the swampy new development, where there was a little more breathing room and small plots of land for gardens.[4]

During the first three decades of the twentieth century, four distinct concentrations of Italian residents emerged in Lackawanna. In the First Ward, Italians gathered on lower Ingham Avenue, in the Old Village, and, later, in Bethlehem

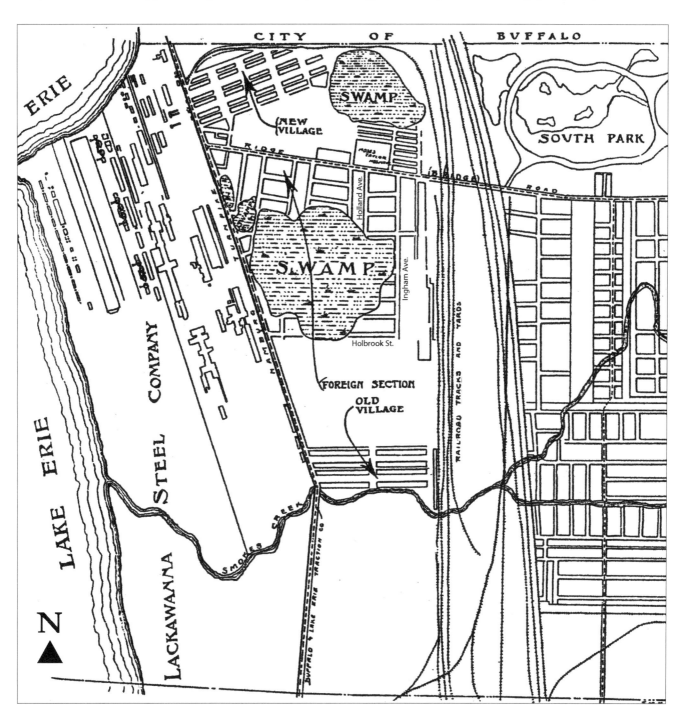

Figure 5.2 1911 Lackawanna's First Ward, to the left of the railroad tracks, had a number of swamps and low-lying areas. Most of the land from the Old Village north toward Ridge Road was too wet to be developed until it was filled in during the 1920s. Source: The Survey, October 1911, p. 931.

FIGURE 5.3

ITALIAN SHANTY TOWN AS DESCRIBED IN THE *BUFFALO EXPRESS*, 1902

Strange People, Strange Customs

At the junction of Smokes Creek and the Lake Shore Road (Hamburg Turnpike) is a small village of steel-plant laborers which is well worth a visit. The population is exclusively Italian and in it are to be found representatives of every province of Italy and Sicily. There was a double murder in that village one night last summer and the officers found that the various dialects in use among the Italians there made it difficult for the inhabitants to understand one another. Calabrese, Sicilians, Neapolitans, Tuscans, Romans and Venetians are jumbled and herded together so closely that the wonder is, considering the intense factional feeling of those people, that there has been but one murder and not a dozen. The men live in little wickiups and shakedowns, constructed by themselves of boards taken from abandoned box cars or cast up on the beach by the surf. They sleep on blankets. They do their cooking in the open, on curiously constructed ovens, built in the earth and their washing is done on the banks of the creek whose water has turned from a rich green to stagnant black.

Comparatively speaking, there has been little disease among the laborers and that is another source of wonderment, for a better culture ground for bacilli hardly could be imagined. The average cost of living under these conditions never has been figured, but it is safe to say the amount could not exceed $2 a week.

Foreign Population
Italians Clannish,
Poles Retain Old Country Customs

The Poles are perhaps a trifle more cleanly than are the Italians, though the difference is so slightly marked as hardly to be apparent. The Italians cannot be said to have a settlement in the village of West Seneca, for those employed at the plant live in huts bordering Smokes Creek and practically within the limits of the company's property. There are few Italian families in the village itself, so that the main increase in the foreign population itself is from the Poles. The Italians are split into little cliques whose membership is regulated according to provincial nativity.

Source: *Buffalo Express*, 11/11/1902.

Park. East of the railroad tracks, they settled along Roland Avenue. In 1899, this western-most area of West Seneca, called Limestone Hill, was mostly farmland and swamps. There were few roads in the area; only three north-south thoroughfares crossed the site: Hamburg Turnpike, South Park Avenue, and Abbott Road. Ridge Road intersected and connected these three roads and served as the only east-west roadway (see Figure 5.1). There were only four other streets west of the railroad tracks, and six in the larger area to the east. But the construction of the steel plant brought thousands of workers to this part of West Seneca, which was also known as the steel-plant district. In 1909, it became the City of Lackawanna. Most residents lived in the First Ward, the area just inland from the steel plant, west of the railroad tracks. The crowded conditions there were a result of the presence of several large swamps in the First Ward and the fact that 38% of the city's land was occupied by the steel plant, small factories, and the railroads by 1924. This put severe restrictions on land for housing.[5]

Over the first two decades of the twentieth century, Lackawanna's temporary Italian settlement became a permanent colony. One indicator of this is the proportion of females in the Italian population, which had climbed to 43% by 1915 and then held steady (see Figure 5.15). There was a corresponding decline in the percentage of male boarders and men living alone. In 1905, about a quarter of the Italian men lived with their wives, while 70% were boarders. Ten years later, the percentage of boarders was half of that. During 1917 and 1918, when America was involved in World War I, many Italians flocked to Lackawanna's job opportunities, and soon 60% of the Italian males were boarders. After the war, the number of boarders in 1920 dropped almost to the 1915 levels (see Figure 5.16).

World War I brought a fluctuation in the number of Italians present in Lackawanna. The war, which began in 1914, drew many immigrants back to Italy to be close to their families and, in some cases, to respond to the Italian draft after May 1915. Others—transatlantic nomads—just happened to be in Italy when the hostilities broke out and were forced to stay. Yet Lackawanna's Italian male population increased after America entered the war, as the demand for steelworkers grew. Of the 490 Steel City Italian men who registered for the U.S. military draft in 1917 and 1918, 345 of them had just arrived in the city. After the war, almost 70% of these newcomers quickly left the city.[6]

Many Italians living in Lackawanna during World War I decided on a lengthy or permanent residence in United States, which furthered the establishment of a permanent Italian colony in the city. This was not only the result of the wartime curtailment of transatlantic travel and mushrooming job opportunities. Average wages doubled, and the federal government enforced an eight-hour work-day. A strong Americanization campaign encouraged naturalization and commitment to the new land. At least 36 Lackawanna Italian immigrants served in the American armed forces, which afforded them the benefit of automatically becoming naturalized citizens at war's end.[7]

The resumption of immigration between 1919 and 1924 brought stability and growth to Lackawanna's Italian neighborhoods as families were reunified and new immigrants arrived. Despite the departure of some workers at the close of the First World War, Lackawanna's Italian population grew with the new flow of immigrants, going from 726 in 1915 to 1,323 in 1925. One indication that Italians intended to remain in the city is that 85% of Italian couples in 1925 had children. With the restrictive immigration law of 1924, the flow of immigrants from Italy again fell off, but the number of Italian adults increased due to internal migration within the United States and the maturation of the second generation. During the 1930s, a significant number of the American-born generation married and set up homesteads. This increase in the Italian American population led to the expansion of the four neighborhoods in Lackawanna.

The same growth was experienced by other European ethnic groups. This, plus the arrival of significant numbers of Mexicans and African Americans in the 1920s, added to the city's housing needs. As we'll see, Bethlehem Park provided new housing for whites, but the razing of the Old Village removed more than 400 low-cost rental units for workers. Still, the First Ward remained the city's most densely populated section for many years. The lack of transportation options coupled with the onset of the Great Depression led most workers to remain in the First Ward's ethnic neighborhoods and their short walk to the steel plant. Many first- and second-generation Italians simply wanted the comfortable feeling of living among coethnics. Also, Italians and other southeast Europeans encountered ethnic barriers in some neighborhoods east of the railroad tracks, while people of color were simply not allowed there. Thus, from 1905 until 1941, most Italians remained clustered in their three ethnic enclaves in the First Ward, or in the Roland Avenue neighborhood.

For many years, lack of housing was a problem in the city. In fact, many steel-plant employees were living in Buffalo and wanted to move to the Steel City. The *Lackawanna Journal* claimed in 1914 that "nearly every day sees a Buffalo family moving into Lackawanna." And things were worse two years later, according to the newspaper: "At no time since Lackawanna has been incorporated has there been such a shortage of houses for rent or for sale." With the flood of defense-industry workers into the city in 1917 and 1918, "this city is 100 per cent short on dwellings," declared the *Lackawanna Daily Journal*. During this time, more than 60% of the steel plant's workforce lived

in Buffalo. Following World War I, however, more usable land was gained as the large swamp was gradually filled in, a process completed by 1929. As each section of swamp was reclaimed, new side streets were laid out west of Ingham Avenue, and homes subsequently constructed. In the 1920s, new streets and homes were added in the eastern section of the city in the Ridge Road – Abbott Road area, near Abbott Road and Willett Road, and east of South Park Avenue near Martin Road. John Verel, funded by his mother-in-law, Giuseppina Yoviene, built new homes at the latter site on a street that bore his name and drew more Italian families. In 1927, the number of building permits issued by the city increased to 128, and the following year, the *Lackawanna News* proclaimed a building boom in the city.[8]

Some Italians eagerly left the ethnic neighborhoods in the 1910s and 1920s, but the significant movement from ethnic enclaves didn't begin until 1938, when the first of two federally funded housing projects arose in the First Ward next to the steel plant (see Figure 5.14). The Father Baker Homes included 271 low-income units on reclaimed swampland just off Hamburg Turnpike, with average monthly rents of just $20. Second-generation families lived there, mostly Poles and Italians, with half the residents under 18 years of age. A block to the south, Albright Court was completed in 1941, giving the city another 200 units of affordable housing. Across town, at Ridge and Abbott roads, a third federal housing project was erected in 1943. Ridgewood Village was composed of wooden townhouses that totaled 400 living units.[9]

After the war, more housing was built off Abbott Road, South Park Avenue, and other sections of eastern Lackawanna. By then, more steelworkers could afford cars, and greater ethnic tolerance made these neighborhoods seem more welcoming to Italians. The enclaves on Roland Avenue, Ingham Avenue, and Bethlehem Park remained central to Italian American life until the 1960s. The process of residential dispersal, which began in the 1920s and became significant in 1938, really mushroomed in the 1940s.[10]

As time went on, more First Ward land was devoted to the expansion of the steel plant and new industries: The Buffalo Tank Company was erected just east of Bethlehem Park in 1929, and the Spring Perch Company was built on the western half of the Old Village site in 1932. In the empty fields south of Bethlehem Park, the steel company constructed its huge strip mill in 1935. Bethlehem Steel razed many homes and old barracks-type structures between Holbrook and Iron streets to create four large parking lots east of Hamburg Turnpike in 1951. Five years later, the 38 homes on the south side of Lincoln Avenue were moved to make way for the expansion of the strip mill (see Figure 5.14). The three public-housing projects helped ease housing shortages during World War II, and while

1902. Italian laborers lived in this shanty town on the steel plant grounds, along Smokes Creek. Photo source: Buffalo & Erie County Public Library, "Lackawanna Steel Company" scrapbook, p. 103

1901. Another view of shanty town on the grounds of the steel plant. Photo source: Buffalo & Erie County Public Library, "Lackawanna Steel Company" scrapbook, p. 58

dwellings continued to sprout up on vacant lots, the amount of housing didn't meet the need.[11]

Into the 1950s, many Italians continued to find housing with relatives, and the Italian settlements expanded on Ingham Avenue, Roland Avenue, and especially in Bethlehem Park. In earlier decades, the decision by an immigrant family to settle in Lackawanna did not necessarily mean an end to movement. Some families moved frequently. The experience of the Milano family typifies the transitory lifestyle of early immigrants adapting to new circumstances. After immigrating in 1900, Gaetano and Maria Giuseppa Milano briefly lived in New Jersey and Pennsylvania before coming to West Seneca in 1902 to board with the Sperduto family. They moved to Morinello's boardinghouse on Roland Avenue, then had a brief residence in Buffalo's waterfront district in 1904 before returning to the steel-plant district to live in the Old Village. They resided at 245 Ingham Avenue in 1910, at 227 Ingham in 1912, and at 598 Odell Street in 1915. Three years later, Milano had a house erected at 222 Ingham, but not until 1925 did the family settle in their permanent home at 208 Ingham.[12]

Lackawanna's Italian Neighborhoods

Ingham Avenue

At the eastern edge of the swamp, Ingham Avenue sloped southward from its intersection with Ridge Road. On the lower end of this street, on the periphery of the cluster of rooming houses and businesses, an Italian enclave began to form between Wilson and Holbrook streets. When the Fadale family moved to 194 Ingham in 1904, it was little more than a dirt path. There were few houses and no buildings south of Holbrook, but the area had both open land and many trees. Calogero and Serafina Fadale liked the peaceful setting; the corner of Ingham Avenue and Wilson was almost a half-mile from the steel plant. In the nearby fields, the Fadale children found many Indian artifacts.[13]

By 1905, 108 Italians lived in 15 households on Ingham Avenue, and three Italian males boarded with a Polish family. There were six businesses run by Italians: Antonio Grossi, Michele Gatto, and Ruta Pellegrino were boardinghouse keepers; the Fadale and Milla families ran grocery stores; and the Manzettis operated a confectionery shop. By 1909, lower Ingham Avenue was lined with 20 homes and two barns, all wood-frame except for one brick home. A year later, there were 29 Italian families in the neighborhood, making it the second largest Italian enclave during the first two decades of the twentieth century (see Figure 5.2). Although it grew rapidly between 1905 and 1910, the area lost about a quarter of its Italian residents, mostly transient men who had boarded in the

larger homes and barracks-type buildings, between 1915 and 1920. These men were the most likely people to migrate from Lackawanna to other sites in the United States or back to Italy. By 1910, nine Italians were homeowners. Antonio and Nicolina Grossi bought the property at 201 Ingham Avenue in 1906; its four apartments began serving as a first stop for immigrants during the next 20 years.[14]

Antonio Grossi helped his brother-in-law, Antonio DePaula, build a one-story house at 226 Ingham using salvaged lumber. With no basement or running water, the DePaula family drew water from a well in the backyard and emptied chamber pots into a 50-gallon barrel behind the house. Another single-story building in the backyard housed the family bakery. Later, DePaula added a second story with three bedrooms and constructed a barn. Other Italian homeowners also improved their property: adding woodsheds, digging cellars, and opening storefronts. By 1920, 17 Italians owned buildings in the lower Ingham Avenue neighborhood, whose southern anchor was St. Anthony's Church and Rectory. By 1925, the number of Italians had doubled on Ingham Avenue as new homes rose south of Holbrook, but there was little growth during the following years, as Bethlehem Park drew many Italians seeking their own homes (see Figure 5.4).[15]

In 1911, Ingham Avenue was unpaved and had a deep ditch on one side that served as an open sewer. Raw sewage and garbage found its way into Smokes Creek and the swamp west of Ingham, leading the board of health to declare the swamp "a public nuisance and a menace to public health." The "swamp district," according to the city council, extended from Hamburg Turnpike to Ingham Avenue, and from Bethlehem Street south past Holbrook Street, to the location where Point Street was later constructed. Some men even traveled across the swamp in small rowboats. When Lake Erie was turbulent, it sometimes backed up into the swamp, bringing lake fish with it. Nunze Oddy recalled that when the swamp flooded to a depth of three or four feet, Johnny Beard launched his homemade, steam-powered boat. He invited other African American youths, as well as Italians such as Oddy, to join him in fishing off the boat as he maneuvered it through the swamp.[16]

From Ingham Avenue, steelworkers walked westward to their jobs along an elevated wooden sidewalk. For years, lower Ingham Avenue had only elevated wooden-plank sidewalks enabling pedestrians to escape the mud and sewage. Nick Falcone told a young immigrant that some people built their own wooden sidewalks in front of their homes, and each "brought it in at night" to prevent theft! When Ridge Road was paved with brick and lined with sidewalks in 1911, 20 Ingham Avenue residents, including Charles Fadale and Antonio DePaula, petitioned the city for their own concrete sidewalks, but to no avail. One Italian

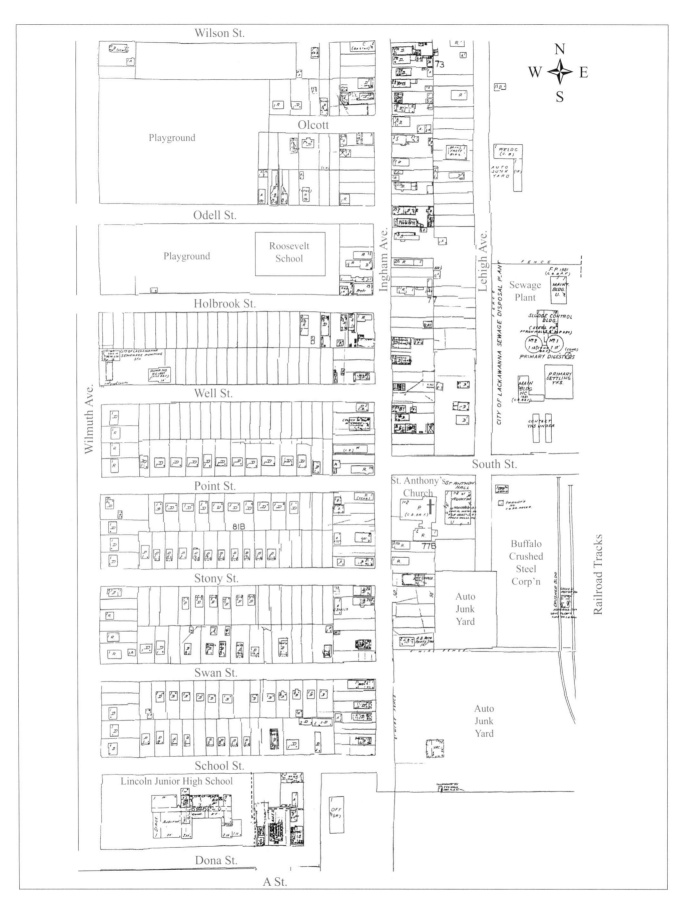

Figure 5.4 Map of Lower Ingham Avenue, South of Wilson Street it was heavily Italian and the site of St. Anthony's Church. Photo Source: Lackawanna City Engineer's office

Ingham Avenue in 1911, with the ditch serving as an open sewer that eventually emptied into the swamp or Smokes Creek. Photo source; The Survey, October 1911

merchant (it may have been Sam Morgan), grew frustrated when politicians did nothing to upgrade Ingham Avenue, and in protest, he blocked the street with his horse and wagon. Ingham Avenue was finally paved in the mid-1920s. The workmen paid Giustina "Jay" Covino and other children to stack the asphalt blocks. By 1926, curbs and cement sidewalks lined the street.[17]

Several large houses were constructed on Holbrook Street just west of Ingham Avenue, on the eastern edge of the swamp. This also was the case on Odell Street, where six buildings were erected, several of them large, barracks-type buildings built on stilts and straddling the swamp. The city continued the process of filling in the swamp and wetlands during the 1920s using ashes, rubbish, construction debris, and slag from the steel plant. As the land was reclaimed, side streets off Ingham Avenue actually became usable roads, and the elevated wooden sidewalks disappeared. Italians helped incorporate these areas into the neighborhood by removing bulky debris used as fill, building houses and small structures, and cultivating gardens.[18]

In the early 1920s, a number of houses were erected south of St. Anthony's Church as Ingham Avenue was extended to Dona Street. South of Holbrook Street were areas where the land rose a few feet in elevation and rarely flooded. Here, the Benson family, immigrants from Sweden, had a home. They took in several boarders of their own ethnic group and maintained a small farm of at least five acres, planting crops and tending to chickens, pigs, and cows. Nunze Oddy was sent to the farm daily to purchase a gallon of fresh milk for his family. Eventually, Ermelindo Marrano bought the farmhouse, which was then situated on Swan Street, and settled there with his family. The city installed new east-west streets south of Holbrook, including Well, Point, Stony, Swan, School, and Dona streets, where Italians purchased or built homes and businesses (see Figure 5.4).[19]

Elevated sidewalks such as this one were common in the First Ward in 1911. Workers used them to walk west to the steel plant from Ingham Avenue. Photo source: The Survey, October 1911

The Italian residents on Holland and Lehigh avenues, which run parallel to Ingham Avenue, and Wilson Street, which connects Holland and Ingham avenues, are included in statistics on Ingham Avenue Italians in this chapter. These streets and avenues were home to several Italian families, a number of whom took in boarders. In 1930, Giuseppe and Rosa Scarlotta had nine boarders at their Wilson Street home. Giovanni and Anna DeCarolis lived in a large three-story building on Lehigh Avenue and rented out apartments and rooms to families and lone males. The structure had previously been a workers' barracks that DeCarolis somehow moved from a site next to the New York Central Railroad's roundhouse in the middle of the maze of railroad tracks just east of Lehigh.[20]

"Ingham Avenue was the nicest place to live," according to Jay Covino-Masters. "People were friendly and helped each other out; kids played together. If someone was sick, the ladies brought in food and watched the kids." She added that the Covino home, like others, "was an open house; the doors were never locked." Nick Canali recalled people gathering on front porches and sidewalks, in driveways and backyards. Often the visitors were *paesani* or relatives, as when the Schiavis or Turchiarellis visited their cousins at the Canali home. These families all lived on Ingham Avenue, just a few blocks from each other.[21]

The Roosevelt School, on Odell Street, was a community hub; many children learned English there, and their parents studied citizenship and English in night-school classes. In 1922, *Corriere Italiano* advised Lackawanna readers that Roosevelt and three other city schools offered English classes on Monday, Wednesday, and Friday evenings. The school's playground was popular with children, as were sidewalks and nearby streets. Girls and boys often played on Lehigh Avenue, a short block to the east, which had fewer homes and many open lots. Yolanda Monaco remembers playing kick the can with her friends, the goal being to propel the can the farthest distance. In another tin-can game, children broke old cans open and wore them on their feet like clogs.[22]

Italian boys explored the nearby fields and played baseball on the small lot just south of St. Anthony's Church. At the far end of the lot was Peter D'Amico's home, which often suffered broken windows thanks to young, would-be Joe DiMaggios. Older boys sometimes played baseball and football at the soccer field at Dona Street and Hamburg Turnpike. In the early 1930s, Charley Orlando and his friends played in the basements of the demolished Old Village row houses nearby. During the winter, the boys found other entertainment. "We broke barrels and used the wood for skis; we tied these to our boots and skied down the railroad embankment at Smokes Creek." Parents were also good at recycling cast-off items for children to use as playthings. Antonio Monaco occasionally found a discarded bicycle and fixed it up for his children. A man who worked with Monaco in the steel plant gave him a small horse, which Monaco presented to his son Gino. The boy kept it on the family's Holbrook Street garden plot but had to give it up when the animal became too wild.[23]

Girls were given less latitude to roam, as Audrey Spagnolo and her sisters learned. "Girls had to be in by 9:00 p.m. Dad was strict." Teenage girls formed informal groups and met at each other's homes to socialize. Rose Fiore was one of 10 girls, mostly Italian Americans, in such a group that got together outside of school to play cards. Rose was also an avid reader, and was among many youngsters who regularly traveled to the Lackawanna Library. Both boys and girls went to programs offered at Friendship House on Ridge Road. Parents often couldn't afford toys during the Depression, so Yolanda Monaco and other girls made dolls by stuffing cotton or rags into old socks, sewing on arms, and embroidering facial features.[24]

Men had their favorite hangouts on Ingham Avenue, usually bars or grocery stores. The grocery store of the Spagnolo family was in the front of their building at Odell and Ingham, connected directly to the family's kitchen. There, Carmine Spagnolo socialized with customers and sold them his homemade wine. Men who frequented Nick Sperduto's tavern during the 1930s played craps near the garage out back. Mike Morgan and other kids were paid a quarter to act as lookouts and alert the men if the police approached. Tony DiMillo remembers dice games

In 1910, this Ingham Avenue building was owned by Gaetano Milano. Tony Turchiarelli, at right with shovel, had his saloon on the first floor, and the Milano family lived on the second floor. The boy standing near Turchiarelli is 7-year-old Joe Milano. The men in the background include "Settecocce," at left, and Angelo Croce, second from left.
Photo source: Collection of Joe Milano

played alongside the Lackawanna Laundry, where onlooking children made side bets as the teens and men rolled the dice. On one occasion, a motorcycle policeman literally broke up the game by driving right through it.[25]

As Lackawanna grew, a number of theaters emerged to bring the novelty of the movies, a new American pastime, into Steel City neighborhoods. Prior to this, and often afterwards, Lackawanna Italians had visited Buffalo theaters to see live performances or view Italian movies. The Academy Theater, for example, ran *Giuseppe Musolino*, the story of the Calabrese bandit, and *Bellezze d'Italia*, a travelogue of beautiful locations in Italy, in September 1931. The Erlanger Theater was another popular destination for Steel City Italians. Enrico Caruso's 1908 appearance at the Convention Hall in Buffalo no doubt drew Italians from throughout western New York. Theaters located in the First Ward of the Steel City included the Ridge, Liberty, Hollywood, and Shea's Lackawanna, all located on Ridge Road, providing a variety of entertainment for both adults and children. Tony DiMillo was eight years old when Shea's opened in 1939 with *Wuthering Heights*. Some theaters offered bingo during the intermissions, and people were given cards as they entered. After each round, the winner went up front to the silver "prize board" and chose one of its numbered panels. An usher then flipped the panel over to reveal the prize: either goods or cash ranging from $5 to a grand prize of $100.[26]

Bingo was offered at other venues, such as VFW Post No. 63, which Tony DiMillo attended with his mother Maria, translating the numbers from English to Italian for her. He liked the comic books given as prizes, while Maria and the other women were drawn by the dishes and other household items awarded to winners. Another resident of Ingham Avenue, Assunta DePasquale, played bingo at the Ridge Theater, taking along a grandchild to translate. "She loved bingo," recalls Jerry DePasquale. "That was her thing. Every week, we had to take Grandma to bingo. And we used to walk … from Ingham Avenue to Ridge Road, down to the shows and back."[27]

Sundays were important days for socializing. Luigi Petti went to the house of his *paesano* Sam Morgan every Sunday after Mass to sing Italian songs and make jokes, to the delight of Anna and the other Morgan children. After church, Nick Canali visited his Grandmother Turchiarelli's house, just down the block, for a snack. Later, the family sat down for a big dinner. Anna DeSantis and her family walked from Highland Street down Ingham Avenue to visit her sister, Enrichetta Oddi, and her children. Oddi served her guests soda pop and cookies, sometimes inviting them for dinner. When the eldest DeSantis child, Theresa, attended Lincoln Junior High School during the 1930s, she lunched at the Oddi's each day and especially enjoyed her aunt's fried potatoes.[28]

In 1926, paesani *and relatives from Accadia, Puglia, have a party in the field off Ingham Avenue that was formerly a large swamp. The ladies (top photo, left to right) are Olmitella Schiavone, Antonetta Capozzi, Maria Giuseppa Tibollo, and Ripalda Giordano. The man with the mandolin (lower photo) is Domenico Schiavone; the "couple" on the left are Antonio Capozzi and Pasquale Tibollo; in the center are Joe Capozzi and Tony Colella; and Mike Tibollo (?) and Tony Giordano are on the right.* Photo source: Collection of Tony Grasso

Helen Hrabocsak-Dankovich was born and raised on lower Ingham Avenue in the 1930s. Her father, John Hrabocsak, a Ukrainian immigrant, ran a store at the corner of Ingham and Holbrook. Theirs was one of the few non – Italian families there. Hrabocsak learned to speak a little Italian, and his wife Mary became an honorary member of the Mount Carmel Society at St. Anthony's Church. Helen Dankovich uses three words to summarize her Italian neighbors: "friendship, giving, love." Once her grandmother "accidentally put out the fire in

The new home of the Schiavi family on Olcott Street in 1938. From left are Giovanni, Iole, and Nazzarena Schiavi. At far right is Mario Infante, a recent arrival from Italy who boarded with the family.
Photo source: Iole Schiavi-Murray

The home of Domenico Antonio and Marietta Marinelli at 359 Ingham Avenue.
Photo source: Jack and Mary Panczykowski

the pot-bellied kitchen stove while her husband was at work. She was so upset that she went outside and sat on the steps crying as she waited for him to return from work. An Italian woman came along and, speaking no English, gave my grandmother some food to console her." When Mike and Rose Gaglia moved next door and started a huge garden, Helen recalls, "she shared the produce with us. Rose only spoke Italian, and was called *zia* (aunt) by Italians." When Maria Giuseppa Tibollo was too ill to assist her husband Pasquale at their grocery store, teenager Helen helped him out. The roof of the three-story Hrabocsak building offered a panoramic

view of lower Ingham Avenue to Helen and her family. Weddings at St. Anthony's Church "usually took place on Saturdays at 10:00 a.m. My family would always watch for this from our building, and then we went down to the front of the church to pick up almond candy and coins that were thrown at the bride and groom as they left," states Dankovitch.[29]

In the late 1940s, Ingham Avenue was home to some 80 businesses: dry goods, clothing, laundry, and dry-cleaning businesses as well as taverns, barber shops, shoemakers, and confectioneries. Many of these were Italian establishments. In the 1930s, the Covino family bought its groceries at Monaco's,

February 6, 1928. Looking east toward Ingham Avenue, with St. Anthony's Church on the left. The spot where the workman is standing was previously in the middle of a large swamp. To fill in the swamp, the city used it as a trash dump and had Bethlehem Steel bring in slag. Photo source: Collection of Frank Rozwood.

Antonio Risio, an immigrant from Casale, Abruzzo, on Ingham Avenue, circa 1940. Photo source: Jack and Mary Pancyzkowski

Another photograph taken by Tony Grasso who purchased his first camera in the mid 1920s. "Palermo" Seidita probably got his nickname because he was an immigrant from Palermo, Sicily. Photo source: Collection of Tony Grasso

Tony DiMasi, left, and Nunze Oddy outside the Milano home at 208 Ingham Avenue, 1920s. Photo source: Collection of Nunze Oddy

The wedding of Antonio Colello and Maria Civita Grosso (middle of second row) in 1922. Photo source: John Mecca Jr.

The yard between the home and the storefront of the Mattucci family, 1924 on Ingham Avenue. Parties, dances, informal theater, and celebrations in honor of San Pio delle Camere, the patron saint of Serafino Mattucci's hometown, took place here. He is standing in the center with the bow tie, and his wife, Virginia Lalli, is to the right of him. To the right of them are Lavinio Montanari and his wife, Adelina Lalli, Virginia's sister. Most of the other people are members of the extended Lalli family.
Photo source: Collection of Tina Mattucci-Ginnetti

Pasquale and Maria Giuseppa Tibollo moved to Blasdell after retiring from their Ingham Avenue grocery business in the late 1940s. Photo source: Patsy Giordano

Tibollo's, and Amorosi's, and its clothes at Pliss Brothers at Ingham and Odell. As noted earlier, grocery stores were often gathering places for men who conversed, played cards, and enjoyed a glass of wine in the back room or in the owner's kitchen. At the corner of Ingham Avenue and Dona Street, men played *morra* for glasses of wine in the back room of Vincenzo Suffoletto's store. Saloons also served this purpose, as Italian men played drinking games and the traditional card games: *scopa*, *briscola*, and *tre-sett*e. Nick Sperduto allowed teens 16 years and older to frequent the combination saloon and restaurant that he and his wife Margaret ran. It was there that teenager Clyde Capasso and his friends learned card games such as "boss" from the old-timers. The winner of the boss round decides who does and doesn't have a drink. When the teens lost, as was common among newcomers, they went without a drink, but as they caught on to the rules of the game, they sent the old-timers "dry," thus earning the unflattering name of "black birds."[30]

Other neighborhood entrepreneurs, too, were friendly to youth. Yolanda Monaco was a teenager in the mid-1930s when her family rented a flat from Santo DePasquale at Ingham and Stony. Charles Barone had a barber shop in the storefront. When Yolanda's long hair became tangled, her mother cut it.

"I refused to go to school," Yolanda reminisced, "because it looked bad. Charley trimmed my hair; he was a very nice man." In earlier years at a nearby site, there was a small pool hall run by Kid Daniels, an African American who welcomed all comers, including Nunze Oddy and his friends.[31]

In 1918, Serafino Mattucci built a hall at 229 Ingham, next door to his home. Here, he and his wife Virginia at various times ran a grocery, a dry goods, and an import store as well as a saloon. In 1919, the Mattuccis had a concrete slab laid between the two buildings and began holding "open air dances on the concrete," said Nunze Oddy. In the newer building, "he first showed movies, then used it as a dance hall. He and his wife dressed well, and she was called La Regina (the queen)." The wives of other Italian businessmen were also admired for their wardrobes and stature. According to one teenage Italian girl, Virginia Melillo "was beautiful, dressed elegantly, spoke well, and wore white gloves as she walked on Sunday afternoons with Mrs. Mattucci and Mrs. Guadagno; they were the elite of the neighborhood." Enrichietta Oddi, a widow who ran a grocery store, traveled to downtown Buffalo each year around Memorial Day to purchase a new hat and shoes. Like the other ladies, she proudly displayed these on her Sunday walks to St. Anthony's Church.[32]

The 1929 Ingham Avenue funeral procession for Alessandro Guglielmi, the former leader of immigrants from Giuliano di Roma. At right are Ferdinand Catuzza, who assumed the leadership role, and, with top hat, John Panzetta, a funeral director at the time. Photo source: Mary Panzetta-Vertino

The October 1929, funeral procession for Mary Panzetta, looking south on Ingham Avenue. The clock in the center of the wreath gives the time of death. Following Italian tradition, the next female infant in the Panzetta family was given the name Mary. Photo source: Mary Panzetta-Vertino

St. Anthony's Church, circa 1932, was an institution that marked lower Ingham Avenue as an Italian neighborhood. Photo source: Collection of Tony Grasso

The funeral for a member of the Marsillo family at St. Anthony's Church in the 1920s. Many of those gathered are paesani *from Cantalupo nel Sannio, Molise.* Photo source: Yolanda Monaco-Bracci

Work and family life in this neighborhood also had its less attractive side. Families living on Ingham and Lehigh avenues contended not only with railroad noise and soot but also the city's sewage-treatment plant. By 1950, the plant's odor was a community issue. Assessor Joe Pacillo suggested that a new treatment plant be constructed in an area "where the least number of people will be subjected to its odors." According to the *Lackawanna Leader*, "Rev. T. N. Ciolino, pastor of St. Anthony's Church, explained that 'although we get the dirty end of it, it's not the First Ward's problem.' His parishioners

The first-grade class at Roosevelt School in 1938. Top row, from left: Vera Gudzi, Camella Macaluso, Rose Capasso, [Unk], Rosemary Monaco, Dorothy Lichon. Middle row: [Unk], [Unk], Linda Priljevo, [Unk], [Unk], Dot Androff, Helen Cruz, Mary Panzetta, Gerry Kuzdale, Millie Tyree, Catherine Panoff. Bottom row: Gino Monaco, [Unk], Ed Marinelli, [Unk], Chris George, [Unk], [Unk], Tony DiMillo, [Unk], Dick McCann, Mike Grasso, Steven Check, Anthony Cellini. The teacher is Mrs. O'Connor. Photo source: Mary Panzetta-Vertino

The Grasso family in front of their home and grocery store at 276 Ingham Avenue in 1926. From left: Rosa, Jenny, Sammy, Michele, Mariuccia, Yolanda. The eldest offspring, Tony, was most likely taking the photo, as he bought his first camera in the mid 1920s. Photo source: Collection of Tony Grasso

Arcangelo and Michelina Cervoni, circa 1950. The couple's house was on Holbrook Street, just off Ingham Avenue. Photo source: Lake Erie Italian Club

are chiefly affected by the plant's odors. Father Ciolino urged members of the Council to prepare for the needs of an expanding city." Nick Sperduto, owner of the AA Restaurant on Ingham Avenue, warned that the problem would worsen in warmer weather. "There are small flies—so small they easily crawl through regulation screens," he proclaimed. "The odor is terrible. It's not only the First Ward, it's the whole city. We have only begun to fight. Something has got to be done." But the problem continued for another 25 years.[33]

Lower Ingham Avenue was distinctly Italian; a majority of its residents were first- and second-generation Italian Americans. In addition to many Italian-operated grocery stores and other businesses, the presence of the Lake Erie Italian Club's meeting hall and St. Anthony's Church contributed to the neighborhood's ethnic identity. Funeral and religious processions as well as other public events also contributed to this area's Italian flavor.

The Spagnolo family in 1920. From left: Jenny, Audrey, Angelina, Carmine, Lucy, and Mafalda. They maintained a grocery store at Ingham Avenue and Odell Street from 1918 to 1960, when Carmine and Angelina retired and moved to Bethlehem Park. Photo source: The Amadori family

Young men were welcome at Sperduto's, circa 1940. From the left are: (1)Anthony Sperduto, (2)Arcangelo Carlini, (3)Pete Monaco, (4)Mike Morgan, and (5)Dominic Ungaro. Photo source: Mary Sperduto-Cuomo

Three friends outside Sperduto's restaurant, circa 1940. From left: Ed Morgan, John "Hopper" Grasso, Ugo Scarsella. Photo source: Lake Erie Italian Club

The Giordano home on Ingham Avenue in 1926. From left: Ripalda, her husband Tony, and Maria Giuseppa Tibollo, (Ripalda's sister). All three were immigrants from Accadia, Puglia. Tony Giordano was a merchant like so many of his paesani in Lackawanna and Buffalo. Photo source: Collection of Tony Grasso

Outside Sperduto's in the early 1940s are, from left: Anthony Sperduto, Al Suffoletto, Clyde Capasso (being carried), [Unk] , [Unk]. Photo source: Mary Sperduto-Cuomo

Circa 1920. Paesani *from Molise; from left: Tony DiRe, Antonio Monaco, Antonio Monaco.* Photo source: Yolanda Monaco-Bracci

Friends and neighbors Giovanna Viglietta-Fanone, on the left, and Giulia Violanti-Fiore. Both were immigrants from Lazio—Fanone from Sora, and Fiore from Giuliano di Roma. Photo source: Rose Fiore-Pacholczak

The water-filtration plant on Lehigh Avenue, circa 1926. It eventually caused many woes for Ingham Avenue residents.
Photo source: Collection of Tony Grasso

The Milano family in the 1950s. Row 1 (on floor), from left: Jeanie, Dick Topinko, Walter Topinko Jr., Viola (wife of Joe), Arlene. Row 2 (sitting in chairs): Carol Topinko, Florence Milano-Cuomo, Maria, Gaetano, Joe, Amy. Row 3: Ann (wife of Nick), Anna Milano-Mattucci, Virginia Milano-Topinko, Mary, Dorothy, Rose (wife of Sam), Sam. Row 4: Nick, John Mattucci, Neal Cuomo, Walter Topinko, Frank Cuomo, Joe Mattucci, Dorothy Cuomo.
Photo source: Collection of Joe Milano

Ingham Avenue, 1920s. [Unk], Yolanda, Inez, and Ida DiMillo. Photo source: Tony DiMillo

The Fadale family moved from Buffalo's westside to Ingham Avenue in West Seneca in 1904. Sara Fadale (front and center) is pictured in the 1950s with her daughters, from left, Helen Costello, Lucy Killingbeck, Mary Brockto, Patricia Pellegrino, Josephine Ippolito.
Photo source: Collection of Helen Fadale-Costello

The Ruggeri-Melillo family, circa 1915. Seated: Antonio and Maria Ruggeri. Standing, from left: Mary, Guglielmo, Felice, Virginia Ruggeri-Melillo holding Santina, Antonio Melillo. Photo source: Collection of Anne Melillo-Corvigno

Enrichetta Oddi. She and her husband
Pietro were among the early Italian
immigrants arriving in the Limestone
Hill section of West Seneca. When
Pietro died in 1917, Enrichietta opened
a grocery store that she ran with the
help of her children. Photo source:
Theresa DeSantis-DiBlasi

FIGURE 5.5

Italian Enclaves in Lackawanna:1905 –1930

Number of Households [HHs] and Individuals [Inds]

	1905 HHs/Inds	1910 HHs/Inds	1915 HHs/Inds	1920 HHs/Inds	1925 HHs/Inds	1930 HHs/Inds
1st Ward						
Ingham Ave[a]	12 / 95	32 / 220	43 / 244	33 / 226	62 / 348	83 / 507
Old Village	25 / 131	30 / 150	67 / 343	111 / 668	106 / 642	70 / 352
Bethlehem Park	—	—	—	—	17 / 103	83 / 478
Other	3 / 26	4 / 29	6 / 23	8 / 20	2 / 6	12 / 39
East of Tracks						
Roland Ave[b]	7 / 30	16 / 97	24 / 109	29 / 160	40 / 196	51 / 318
Other	0 / 0	2 / 17	1 / 7	7 / 18	11 / 31	36 / 148
Totals:	47 / 282	84 / 513	141 / 726	188 / 1092	238 / 1326	335 / 1842

a) The Ingham Avenue area includes Holland, Ingham, and Lehigh avenues, extends from Ridge Road on the
north to Dona Street on the south, and includes side streets as far west as Holland Avenue and, for those
south of Wilson Street, to Willmuth Street.

b) The Roland Avenue area is bounded by Warsaw Street on the north, Cleveland Avenue on the south, South
Park Avenue on the east, and Front Street on the west.

Sources: U.S. Census, 1910, 1920, 1930; New York Census, 1905, 1915, 1925.

Italian youth living in the Our Lady of Victory institutions are not included.

Friends gather at the Schiavi home, 158 Olcott Street, 1952. From left: Paolo and
Bombina Liberta, Nazzarena and John Schiavi. Photo source: Iole Schiavi-Murray

Margherita Marinelli, Ingham
Avenue, 1951. Photo source: Jack and
Mary Panczykowski

Circa 1950, Anna Core and her husband Antonio emigrated from Penne, Abruzzo, to Pennsylvania, moved to Lackawanna's Old Village, then settled on Ingham Avenue. Photo source: Mary and Roy Brasch

Mary Morgan, on left, with her daughters Theresa, Angie, Sue, and Anna in 1941. The little girl is Emilia Cardoni. Photo source: Emilia Cardoni-Cutre

Sosio Vitaterna in front of Grasso's grocery store on Ingham Avenue, 1926. Photo source: Collection of Tony Grasso

1926, Pasquale Tibollo. He emigrated from Accadia, Puglia, and operated a grocery store on Ingham Avenue. Photo source: Collection of Tony Grasso

Ingham Avenue, 1944. From left: Carmen Corvigno, Ed Morgan, and Al Nigro. Photo source: Anne Melillo-Corvigno

The Old Village

In 1902, Lackawanna Steel responded to the need for workers' housing by beginning construction of the Smokes Creek Village, 445 units in nine block-long row houses. Located south of a large swamp and along the north bank of the creek, it was completed in 1903. When a second housing development, the Ridge Road Village, was built by Lackawanna Steel a short time later, residents dubbed it the "New Village" and the Smokes Creek Village the "Old Village." For most years over the next three decades, the Old Village had the largest concentration of Italian households in the city (see Figure 5.5).

The Old Village's identical row houses lined First and Second Streets, running east for two blocks from Hamburg Turnpike, then intersecting A and B Streets. One row house paralleled B Street, adjacent to the maze of railroad tracks (see Figure 5.6). A distinctive numbering system helped people locate homes in this tightly planned neighborhood. Though armed with their carefully drawn blueprints, the engineers who designed the straight and orderly lines of the Old Village gave in to area residents who insisted that a huge elm tree jutting into Second Street be left standing. In June 1902, the *Buffalo Express* reported that "the tree used to be the site of open air counsels [sic] of Indians, more recently it sheltered tramps and hobos." Sadly the huge tree, which had a circumference of 20 feet and branches that spread 100 feet, finally succumbed to industrial pollution in the 1930s.[34]

Each of the nine row houses was 760 to 900 feet long and one-and-a-half stories high with a brick front and chimney, and a sloping slate roof. Wooden clapboards covered the rear exterior walls. Every unit had a front yard with a lawn. In six of the row houses, each unit had a kitchen and a living room downstairs and two bedrooms on the second floor. Those in the 200, 300, and 400 rows were somewhat larger, with three

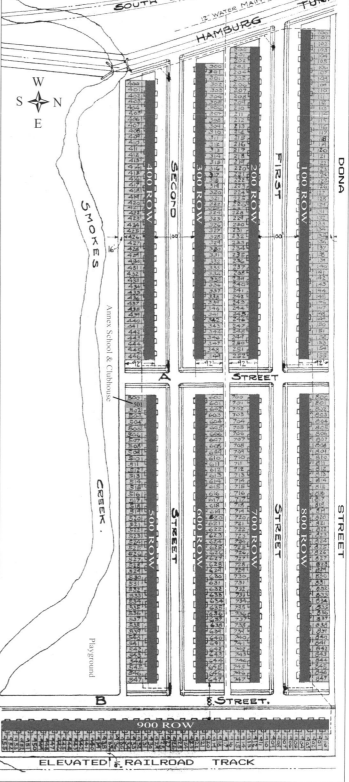

Figure 5.6. The Old Village consisted of nine row houses, each up to 900 feet long and having its own numbering system. The units of the 200, 300, and 400 rows were slightly larger than the others. Source: Steel Plant Museum

The Old Village was completed in 1903. This is the view looking down First or Second Street in the early 20th century. The photographer was standing on A Street, looking east toward B Street. Photo source: Steel Plant Museum

The original caption of this photo was "Foreign children, Old Village, 1916." Most residents of the Old Village that year were immigrants, and many of their children were also born in Europe. The label "foreign" in that era meant inferior, not up to American standards. Prejudice and discrimination against people from southern and eastern Europe were common. Photo source: Hagley Museum and Library, Delaware

bedrooms upstairs. All the units had a front porch covered by a sloping roof that was shared by adjacent homes, with a railing separating the two sections.[35]

Each kitchen had a sink, a cold water spigot, and a cooking stove fueled by wood or coal. This stove, and sometimes a second one in the living room, was the only source of heat.

Kerosene lanterns were used until electricity was brought in during the 1920s. A small pantry and a water closet with a metal toilet extended from the kitchen onto the rear porch, which also had an open area that served as an outdoor porch for adjacent units. A small fence separated each home's section. The backyard was a garden plot.[36]

In 1905, 24 units were occupied by Italian families, and 10 Italian boarders were living in non – Italian households (see Figure 5.8). Tenants occupied the houses on month-to-month leases, and the Lackawanna Steel Company reserved the right to evict them "at any time for any reason." Rents were deducted directly from the workers' wages, and company men inspected the homes at least once per month. If a home was found to be "dirty," the occupants were ordered to clean it up within three days or risk eviction. Such evictions were common in the earliest years of the Old Village, but rare when journalist John Fitch visited Lackawanna in 1910. He described the Old Village as well built, with excellent sanitary conditions, in contrast to nearby boardinghouses. However, he reported more than 100 unoccupied units, which was probably due to several factors. At that time, the Old Village was somewhat isolated from the rest of the First Ward, being more than a quarter-mile south of the nearest cluster of homes on Ingham and Holbrook. Many single workmen, including Italians, preferred the boardinghouses run by their countrymen, though as they married or brought their families from Italy, they found the low-cost units in the Old Village more attractive. In at least one case, Lackawanna Steel told an employee to move his family into the Old Village or lose his job. Fitch found that most Old Villagers were immigrants, African Americans, or the more poorly paid native-born whites.[37]

As the Italian population grew, more families settled in the Old Village. By 1915, some 65 Italian families were residents in the row houses, almost all of them on Second Street. World War I brought an influx of workers, including Italians, to the steel plant. Of the 490 Lackawanna Italian males who registered for the draft, almost half were from Old Village households. The number of Italian families in the row houses grew to 106 in 1925, as Second Street continued to draw immigrant families from Italy. Indeed, throughout most of the first 30 years of the century, the Old Village was the city's largest Italian enclave, home to about half of the Italians in the area between 1915 and 1925. There were comparatively few lone male immigrants or boarders until 1917-1918, when Old Village Italian families took in at least 130 boarders involved in defense work (see Figure 5.16). The number of boarders in the row houses dropped to 53 in 1925, and 21 in 1930.[38]

This photo captures "domestic education in the home" in the Old Village in 1915. The social worker is standing over the immigrant woman and directing her in basic cleaning tasks, reinforcing the image of the ignorant foreigner whose proper place is taking orders from a native-born American.
Photo source: Hagley Museum and Library, Delaware

There were several businesses in the Old Village, including this store in the 700 row on First Street at the corner of A Street. Photo source: Steel Plant Museum

FIGURE 5.7

SOME DETAILS ABOUT THE OLD VILLAGE

The units in the Old Village were modest in size but much bigger than the homes most immigrants had left in Italy. In six of the row houses, each unit had four rooms, including two bedrooms on the second floor, and measured 16 feet in width and 23 feet in length from front to back. The units in the 200, 300, and 400 rows were larger, with three bedrooms upstairs, and measured 16 feet in width and 28 feet from front to back. Both the larger and smaller units had a living room up front and a kitchen to the rear. The front door opened into the living room, and across from the doorway were stairs that led to the second floor. A dormer with a double window was located in the front bedroom, and two smaller dormers with single windows were at the rear of the second floor. Tony Grasso recalls that the common walls between units were about eight inches thick. In 1910, the smaller apartments rented for $6 per month, the larger ones for $7.50.

The living room in the four-room homes was 12 feet square, and the kitchen was 11 feet from front to back, and 16 feet wide.

The stairway leading upstairs from the living room—and underneath that, the one going to the basement from the kitchen—accounted for the remaining four feet of width. Two bedrooms upstairs paralleled the dimensions of the living room and kitchen. In the larger units, the living room measured 15 feet long by 12 feet wide; the kitchen, 13 feet long by 16 feet wide. Upstairs, the front bedroom measured 15 feet by 16 feet, including a closet. Two smaller bedrooms were at the rear, totaling 13 feet long by 16 feet wide.

The kitchen sink had only a cold-water faucet. Adjacent to the kitchen was a 7-by-5-foot pantry and a water closet that was 5 square feet and featured a conical metal toilet. Ralph D'Amore, born in the Old Village in 1910, recalls the metal rod that had to be pushed down to flush the toilet and how cold both this and the toilet were in winter. This tiny room had a small window located near the ceiling. Both the toilet and pantry were accessed by doors from the kitchen. Exiting the kitchen and descending the porch steps, one entered the garden plot, bordered by a wooden

picket or wire fence. The garden extended 50 feet to the rear fence and gate. The front yard extended 25 feet from the front porch. An alley or roadway ran along the back fence, one between First and Second streets and another along the north bank of Smokes Creek, behind the 400 and 500 rows of Second Street.

In the kitchen, opposite the door leading to the rear porch, another door led to the cellar steps. The cement-lined cellar extended completely under each unit; one small window provided the only sunlight into the dark cavern. As Tony Grasso remembered it, an open, cement-lined drain across the rear of the cellar was about one foot wide and eight to ten inches deep. This drain, which ran the entire length of each row house, was "flushed" once a month. The trough also informed neighbors that Italians were making wine when they saw the grape residue that flowed through it. Lackawanna Steel furnished a covered garbage can and also maintained the houses and cleaned the streets and alleys.

Sources: U.S. Senate, *Labor Conditions in the Iron and Steel Industry, Volume III, Working Conditions and Relations of Employers and Employees*, pp. 436-37; John A. Fitch, "Lackawanna – Swamp, Mill, and Town," *The Survey*, October 7, 1911, p. 932; interviews with Ralph D'Amore, April 20, 1995; and Tony Grasso, November 27, 1981; Tony Grasso—untitled "reflections and observations," unpublished, no date.

After 1919, there was an increase in Italians living in the larger units of the 200, 300, and 400 rows. The three-bedroom apartments were needed due to the increase in relatives and job-seeking boarders, the creation or reuniting of families, and the greater number of children. Cesidio and Rosina D'Amore, who had four children when they settled at 639 Second Street in 1910, moved to 232 First Street in 1920 following the birth of their seventh child. The rows bordering Hamburg Turnpike were also more desirable because they were closer to the plant and the streetcar lines, although there was more noise. By January 1920, federal census takers counted 68 Italian homesteads in the 200 through 400 rows. This may have been partially a result of the 1919 Great Steel Strike, during which some Italians continued to work; when strikers left or were evicted, non – striking Italians may have rented the vacated units.[39]

One instance of this involved a turnover in storekeepers in the Old Village. In August of 1919, Peter Mazuca, an immigrant living in Buffalo, was one of many men hired as special police officers by Lackawanna Steel, and he soon attained the rank of captain. In October, a month after the strike began, the company threatened employees with eviction if they did not show up for work and warned storekeepers not to do business with striking employees. A grocer named Mees disregarded this warning, extended credit to the strikers, and was evicted. The company then allowed Mazuca to take over the grocery store at 701 First Street, which he did by January 1920, and he and his family moved into the unit at 703.[40]

Backyard on Second Street in the Old Village, showing gardens, residents, and a police officer.
Photo source: Steel Plant Museum

Looking northwest from the railroad bridge over Smokes Creek toward the backside of the 900 row of the Old Village on B Street, 1924. Photo source: Hamburg Historical Society

Figure 5.8
Italian Households in the Old Village: 1905–1930

	1905	1910	1915	1917–18*	1920	1925	1930
First Street							
100 row	0	0	0	0	1	3	3
200 row	1	0	0	4	14	18	13
700 row	1	1	2	3	4	2	1
800 row	4	1	1	5	0	1	0
Second Street							
300 row	1	0	9	12	24	25	22
400 row	2	2	15	22	33	28	8
500 row	9	15	15	16	11	14	7
600 row	1	10	23	22	17	15	16
B Street							
900 row	5	0	0	1	0	0	1
Total Families:	**24**	**29**	**65**	**85**	**104**	**106**	**71**
Units Occupied by Italian Families:**	**24**	**29**	**64**	**85**	**103**	**98**	**70**

*World War I draft registration cards list only adult males, ages 18 to 45, and in some cases omit the name and residence of spouses or parents. No information is offered about the families with whom Italian men boarded.

**In several cases, two families lived in one unit.

Source: U.S. Census, 1910, 1920, 1930; New York Census, 1905, 1915, 1925; World War I Draft Registration Records.

Mazuca's store and several others were located at the intersections of First Street and Second Street with A Street. Joe Milano recalled grocery stores run by William Kirsch and Joseph Donowick. There was a clothing store at the end of the 200 row, a saloon on the 800 row, and a maintenance shop on the 300 row. The Annex School occupied the first floor of units 500–504; the dividing walls had been removed, and two sets of sliding doors created three classrooms. The 505–509 units were used as meeting rooms on the first floor. The second floor of the nine units had walls removed and was known as the Old Village Clubhouse. It included a library, gymnasium, and shower room. Al Croce, whose father was the custodian, remembers that a yearly membership fee of 25 cents allowed males to play pool, wrestle, box, and take classes to learn shoe repair. Five cents purchased use of the shower room and soap and a towel. Females used the clubhouse facilities on Saturdays, mostly for showers. Virginia Croce was employed to hand out soap and towels. Dances and movies were held in the clubhouse. Downstairs, the school rooms were used at night for classes in sewing, knitting, and crocheting for females. Sara Chiacchia remembers that a priest or minister offered religious services and Sunday school in the meeting rooms on both Saturday and Sunday. In the backyard, a fenced-in playground extended toward Smokes Creek. The 500 row also included a police substation in 1910.[41]

Despite its long, monotonous rows and tightly engineered lines, the Old Village was warmly recalled by former residents. It served the Italians and other immigrant and minority peoples well for the 30 years of its existence and became a springboard, at least for white ethnic groups, to better housing in Bethlehem Park and other neighborhoods. Italians arriving in Lackawanna had a variety of reactions to the Old Village. When the Covelli family moved to 406 Second Street in 1928, 10-year-old Adelina, who soon Americanized her name to Adeline, was impressed by the long row houses, which were 10 times the length of the Covelli row house in Italy. The Covellis had lived for several months with relatives in Buffalo whose house had central heating, flush toilets, and hot-water spigots. They were sad to learn that the Old Village had none of these conveniences.[42]

Gene Covelli recalls his family's first winter in the Old Village. "There was that ... stove, and no matter how much you stoked that stove during the wintertime, two hours after you went to bed [it got chilly]." Rats and other vermin infested the basement, and Adeline, after peeking down the stairs, was so scared that she never descended them. When bedbugs emerged, Filiberto and his eldest son Leo removed the bedroom baseboards and applied chemicals, but they could not get rid of the pests. However, Antonio and Anna Core and their children, who moved to First Street in about 1918, had better luck. To ward off cockroaches, Anna made a paste of flour, water, and powdered insect repellent and applied it at every opening along the baseboards. Her daughter Mary reports that her mother's technique got rid of the insects.[43]

Giuseppe Violanti and several family members moved in with his sister and brother-in-law on Second Street in 1919. Violanti, too, noted the rats living in the basement. He reported that with no electricity, the women heated laundry water in huge copper kettles on the kitchen stove. When storms agitated Lake Erie's waters, sand came out of the faucets. A filter helped, but it had to be cleaned constantly. Despite these factors, Violanti felt that "the Old Village was better than what we had over there," referring to his hometown of Giuliano di Roma.[44]

Former residents of the Old Village described it as a neighborly small town. Ralph D'Amore tells of friendly relations with a neighboring black family who shared their telephone and whose boys were pals with D'Amore's older brothers. Adeline Covelli remembers warm relations among the Italian families and also between Italians, Croatians, blacks, and other groups. Sometimes, however, friction developed between the children. Following a fight between her brother Gene and a black lad, the parents of the boys met over glasses of wine and discussed steps to end their sons' conflict. Al Croce recalls Italian, Polish, and black playmates, but during 1916 and 1917, Irish boys living in the 300 and 400 rows of Second Street ganged up on Italians who walked down their block toward Hamburg Turnpike. To avoid the Irish toughs, Croce and other Italian boys took the alley along Smokes Creek. Croce, who lived at 511 Second Street, explained that he felt safe on his block because "the Italians made sure no one messed with you."[45]

The Old Village offered exciting possibilities to youngsters. Although Smokes Creek had been a virtual cesspool since the first decade of the century, Gene Covelli found it and the Old Village a wondrous place. "I found my Mississippi River," he reminisced, "right in the backyard—Holy Christ! Once in a while there was a backup in the lake, and the fish go into the different streams, in the creeks, … I mean there were fish jumping all over, in Smokes Creek!" He was delighted, too, with the cottonwood trees. "They got inside the inner chambers of my soul—the wind playing in those leaves that I had never seen before. The strength of them," he recalls, "even then, 40 to 50 feet high. This was an impact moment for me. I went out of my door at 406 Second Street. It was October 1928, the sun was on those cottonwoods, the colors were just starting to change. The wind through those trees was just like a symphony. I was spellbound for a couple of minutes. It's something that I will never forget."[46]

At the southeast corner of the Old Village, Smokes Creek meandered southward and created an open field. This recreation

Residents of Second Street and a police officer, 1917. Many Italians rented units on this street, especially in the 500 and 600 rows.
Photo source: Hagley Museum and Library, Delaware

Umberto Barbati with nephews and children. From left: Ilario Covino, Mike and Rina Barbati, Aniello Covino (standing), Umberto holding Silvio Barbati, Gemma and John Barbati, Donato Covino. Photo source: Carl Covino

The southern end of B Street, with bandstand and playground, July 4, 1916. Smokes Creek is off to the left, the backside of the 500 row of Second Street is on the right. Photo source: Hagley Museum and Library, Delaware

area was supervised by youth workers based at the Lackawanna Community House. Along the creek bank stood a bandstand, and there were tennis courts and a baseball diamond separated by a chain-link fence. Nearby was a building containing restrooms. Playground equipment included slides and a foot-powered merry-go-round made of an old wagon wheel. When Al Croce played baseball on the diamond near the intersection of Second and B streets, he noticed Ingham Avenue children there, too. Recreation supervisors ran slingshot contests that Croce and his friends enjoyed. Joe Milano or another supervisor placed a target on the side of the shelter house, and the boys tested their marksmanship.[47]

Ralph D'Amore and his friends of various nationalities found many opportunities for recreation in the Old Village. The

Virginia Croce with her sons Vito, on the left, and Al. Because he was big for his age, Al was called "Elephant." They are standing at the back of their unit at 511 Second Street in 1926. Photo source: Collection of Tony Grasso

windowless end walls of the 200, 500, and 700 row houses offered surfaces against which the boys could play handball. The youth also drew circles in the cinder streets and played marbles, often getting sore knuckles from the coarse edges of the cinders. D'Amore and his buddies also played a game called "nip." Using part of a broomstick that was tapered at both ends, the team on the inside of a circle hit a three-inch dowel into the air. Another team of boys on the outside of the circle attempted to catch the dowel. When they did, their team went to the inner circle. For their games, the boys made use of the playground behind the school at Second and A streets. They even used the open drainage trough that ran through the basements of the Old Village. After launching a little boat into the trough in one basement, they raced into their friends' basements to follow the craft as it flowed the length of the row house.[48]

Before Bethlehem Park was built in 1924, the tract of land south of Smokes Creek was surrounded by a wooden fence. Armondo Pietrocarlo and other Old Village children crawled under the fence and explored the vacant farmhouse formerly occupied by the Tobias family. The boys often picked strawberries there and speared fish in two nearby ponds, where sturgeon spawned. Like the girls of Ingham Avenue, the girls of the Old Village weren't free to roam, as protective parents set many restrictions. Young Jay Covino, who lived at 225 First Street, looked up to the older girls of the Barbati family next door and attended Mass with them. She was most impressed by Gemma, who worked in the office at Our Lady of Victory Orphanage. One winter, Gemma collected newly fallen snow in a bowl, mixed in homemade jelly, and shared the treat with Covino and other neighborhood kids. Mary Core remembers that she and other girls were often made to stay at home. Some teenage girls managed to convince their otherwise strict parents to let them go to the playground. There, 15-year-

FIGURE 5.9

THE OLD VILLAGE GOLF COURSE

Newspaper clippings from the 1920 to 1923 period provide a series of snapshots of Old Village youth playing golf.

"The Old Village three-hole golf course is in the open field between Ingham Avenue and A Street, Old Village. Number one is three hundred and twenty-five yards and the distance between two and three is one hundred and sixty yards. Fifty-six is par, made by Frank Sumka in six rounds. Mickey Verog, Jimmy Oddy and Bill Fazekas are among the best. They play every evening and are certainly attaining a great style in this most interesting game."

Golf Match

"Frank Smith won on the Old Village three-hole course after a strenuous play of six rounds through rain last Friday afternoon. (Joe) Milano and Oddy also handed in good cards. The cards:

Frank Smith	33	29	62
Jas. Oddy	33	32	65
Jos. Milano	33	34	67
Al Riggs	37	32	69

The Old Village boys are planning to improve and add a few more holes to the course, which is getting very popular in the district.

Caddies' Tournament

Mr. Carroll, caddy master at Wanakah Golf Club, and his assistant, James Oddy, are arranging the annual caddies' tournament to be held the first week in September. Prizes will be given to caddies according to their medal play. These prizes are all sorts of golf clubs and are being awarded by the Wanakah Golf Club members. All caddies taking part in this tournament are Lackawanna boys."

Source: The papers of Joe Milano, unlabeled news clippings from the 1920 to 1923 period.

old Margaret Monaco, who enjoyed using the swings, met 17-year-old Nick Sperduto. He courted her under the watchful eyes of her parents, and they were married two years later at St. Anthony's Church.[49]

The Grasso family lived on the 500 row of Second Street, and Tony Grasso later wrote this description of neighborhood life in the early 1920s: "Living in this colorful place my father enjoyed some of the happiest years of his life with these fellow immigrants who all spoke the Italian mother tongue with so many variations and dialects. At times it was hard for them to comprehend each other, but they invariably did with hand gestures

and signs." Michele Grasso and other Italians walked home from the plant along the dirt road that ran along Smokes Creek. Grasso sometimes invited his companions in for glasses of wine, a welcome respite for the Roland Avenue men before their treacherous walk across the maze of busy railroad tracks.[50]

One summer night, the Grasso's neighbor Pipp' Antonio Marchetti—so called for the pipe he smoked—passed out on his parlor floor after drinking too much wine. Michele and Tony Grasso helped haul the burly six-footer upstairs to his bedroom. Tony and Michele pushed from the bottom while Pipp'Antonio's stepsons lifted his arms and head. "After going up two stairs in this fashion with a great effort, we were stopped momentarily by the dead weight of this man; then, all at once, like an avalanche, we all slid down to the landing," recalled Tony. "I was trying to push Dad from behind to give leverage, while at the same time pushing at one of the legs hanging over my father's shoulders. While I was doing this, my dad was yelling for help to bear up, with mixed cuss words. At this point I erupted in laughter, letting go the little help I was giving. At this my father used more cuss words, which made me laugh louder." They finally got Pipp'Antonio upstairs and onto his bed. "During all this ordeal Pipp'Antonio never uttered a sound or twitched a muscle." His wife Carmela summoned Dr. Fadale. "He barely said a word, only nodding his head to one side, he walked up to the bed, took off one shoe and stocking, lit a match and applied the flame to the bare foot. In a flash Pipp'Antonio pulled up his leg. The doctor picked up his bag, said only two words—'He'll live', and went outside. I followed him with my hand over my mouth, holding back the pent up laughter."[51]

The cool air of summer evenings often provided relief to the men, after grueling shifts in the steel plant, and to the women, after cooking supper and "washing and boiling clothes in a copper kettle over a hot coal stove," writes Tony Grasso. "They sat in swings to cool off, while others sat on the stoop that led into their apartments, chatting with next-door neighbors, drinking wine and beer. … They drank till the evening shadows enveloped the whole area, the children playing hopscotch on the uneven and broken sidewalks while it was still light, and when darkness began to descend, they ran around playing 'hide and seek' until the parents ordered them to bed." Sometimes Vincent Delgatto played the mandolin, while his brother-in-law, Louis Pilla, played the cithara (a stringed instrument similar to a lyre). Grasso "enjoyed greatly the music and free entertainment till late at night." The Fistola family had a player piano around which family members and neighbors gathered to sing and drink wine. Concerts at the bandstand, too, filled the Old Village with popular music of the era.[52]

An Italian organ-grinder from Buffalo regularly visited the neighborhood. Standing his box organ on its wooden prop, the

No.3 Annex School, located at A Street and the 500 row of Second Street. The first 9 units of the 500 row were converted into classrooms for kindergarten and first-grade classes, meeting rooms, a gymnasium, a library, and public showers. Prior to the construction of Lincoln Junior High School in 1925, the Old Village school was considered an annex of Roosevelt School, which was also known as No. 3 School. Photo source: Hagley Museum and Library, Delaware

Three classrooms were separated by folding partitions in the Old Village school. This classroom, circa 1922, had a number of Italian students. In the row on right: Clementine Ranalli 1st seat, Ed Manzetti, 2nd seat; Angelo Cole, 4th seat. Second row from right: _?_ & _?_ Carestio, 1st seat; Anna Bracci, 2nd seat; Elizabeth Petti, 4th seat. Row on left: Aurora Palmisano, 3rd seat; Fred Rosati, 4th seat. The teacher is sitting in the back of the room, center left. Photo source: Collection of Bridget Ginnetti-Bracci

Salvatore and Adelina Ginnetti and their adult children in 1946. The family lived in the Old Village from 1903 to 1924, moved to Ingham Avenue, and finally settled on School Street by 1930. From left (with the females' married surnames) are: Nina Amrozowicz, Loretta Jagiello, Alfred, and Bridget Bracci; Dominic, Salvatore, Adelina, Josephine Zaccaria; Jennie Houle, and Mary Monaco. Photo source: Collection of Bridget Ginnetti-Bracci

man cranked out a series of tunes while a small monkey perched on his shoulder picked fortune cards from a tray, handing them to each purchaser. Tony Grasso described his neighbors' response this way: "Their eyes seemed to pop out of their heads seeing this performance; young and old were thrilled by this routine in the open air, free of charge." In the early 1920s, another itinerant Italian announced his arrival in the Old Village by ringing a bell. Grasso recalls being awakened by this sound. "I went to the window," he writes, "and looked down. What I saw astounded me: a man carrying a small stand on his back, a round wheel bolted on it, and from it a peg-like spindle a foot from the ground gave the impression that the man had three legs when he turned." Women took knives and scissors to the fellow, who unstrapped the contraption from his back, stood it on its peg leg, and "vigorously pumped a foot pedal which turned the grindstone, and kept turning it a little faster, scattering sparks all around himself as he applied pressure on the wheel with the dull knife."[53]

Among the street peddlers was a Jewish fellow who sold linen. "The man with the heavy bundle on his back walking on the uneven sidewalks of the Old Village projected an image of a displaced person," recalls Tony Grasso, "with his belongings neatly packed on his shoulders—of someone looking for a place to lodge." The Italians dubbed the peddler "Giammarone," although some used the ethnic slur "Sheenie." Each week, Giammarone rode the streetcar from Buffalo to Lackawanna carrying bedsheets, tablecloths, towels, handkerchiefs, lingerie, and other cloth products. These were especially important items for Italian women who prepared dowries for their daughters' future marriages. When he arrived, Tony Grasso recalls, "the cry went out: 'Here comes Giammarone!'" He took orders and then returned within a week to deliver his goods, sometimes making two trips in the same day if business was brisk. The Grassos and the Pacillos next door were among his regular customers. Tony Grasso, who would later wed Mary Pacillo, noted that "when Bethlehem Park was constructed he [Giammarone] followed the Pacillos and the other customers to this new community. He knew my wife since she was a child, and when I married her, he knew who she had married. When I began my produce business I met him on the streets of the Old Village numerous times. If we had some time to spare we compared notes. It was a pleasure to talk with and listen to this patriarch of business acumen and shrewdness."[54]

Another traveling merchant captured young Tony Grasso's respect and admiration. After he moved to the Old Village, Grasso noticed that many homes had white cards in the windows. At first, he thought these were "for rent" signs, but on closer inspection, he saw the word "ice" written on the top section of the card and below it, the number "25." "I saw a truck pull

Gilda, Adeline, and Gene Covelli in the backyard of their home at 406 Second Street, circa 1929. Their family arrived from Calabria in 1927, spent a few months with relatives in Buffalo, and moved to the Old Village in early 1928. Photo source: Collection of Phil and Adeline Andreozzi

up in front of one of the apartments with the card in the window," writes Grasso. "The driver came out, went to the rear, pulled a big cake of ice with the tongs towards the tailgate, cut off a big chunk with a pick." He then "hooked it with the tongs, heaved it over onto his shoulder, where a burlap bag, dripping wet, cushioned the blow, and carried the piece of ice dripping water all the way to where the card was displayed." The iceman was Saverio Morgante, better known as Sam Morgan. "I saw Sam more often and spoke to him as he carried ice to my family's small wooden icebox—there wasn't much room in either the front room or kitchen to have a larger one. I noticed his wet shirt in front, and more so in back, dripping cold water down to his trousers." Grasso marvelled at Morgan's strong constitution and that he never caught pneumonia.[55]

During summer, school children "gave him a hard time, getting in his way, milling around when he cut a piece of ice, in the hope of snatching a sliver of it broken off in the process. It was a hassle trying to chase them away; they were back as soon as he returned from delivering the piece of ice." Grasso, who a few years later himself became a huckster, "took a great liking to this man, for his guts and will power to feed his large

Galanti's store on Dona Street, 1940s. Left to right: Paul Petti, Carl Selice, Armondo Pietrocarlo, Walter Topinko, Vince Jennetti, Carl Morgan holding Eileen Petti, Pete Suffoletto, Mike Munich.
Photo source: Booklet, "Testimonial Roast: Ralph J. Galanti, Sr.," 11/24/1984

Galanti Athletic Club members and friends, 1937.
Photo source: Booklet, "Testimonial Roast: Ralph J. Galanti, Sr.,"
11/24/1984

brood of children, clothe them decently, and, above all, [give them] an education to be proud of—enduring discomfort and pain. I never thought or conceived in my mind that someday I would follow in his footsteps, in a different field of endeavor, but with the same goal to be achieved."[56]

Other merchants served the Old Village community as well. Al Croce recalls helping his Ingham Avenue friend Lenny DePaula deliver bread to the Old Village in a horse-drawn covered wagon. Filiberto and Gelsomina Covelli, during their brief stay in Buffalo, had been pleased with the foods at the

Curtis Import store. When they moved to Lackawanna, they gave weekly orders to an Italian fellow who worked for "Curtis the Greek" and delivered the goods from Buffalo. Antonio and Anna Core were among the other Italians who utilized this delivery service. Mrs. Mirad, a member of the city's Syrian community, peddled sewing implements: the cloth, thread, and needles so necessary for many Italian housewives. Mary Core recalls that the only other source of these goods was Serafino Mattucci's store on Ingham Avenue. [57]

As Ingham Avenue was extended southward in the early 1920s, and Dona Street was built parallel to First Street, new homes and stores appeared, such as Vincenzo Suffoletto's grocery and Eugenio Galanti's confectionery. These businesses drew customers from the Old Village, and many Italian teens and young men hung around Galanti's store. This informal, multiethnic group was the nucleus of the Galanti Athletic Association. The Old Village community had its future decided in 1930, when the Bethlehem Steel Company, which purchased Lackawanna Steel in 1922, announced that the row houses would be razed. A February 1930 article in the *Courier Express* began with the headline: "Steel Plant to Raze Squalid Old Buildings." The article continued, "Razing will start immediately. Lots will be sold to employees and new houses built according to designs selected by purchasers with the Steel Company." However, new homes were never constructed at the site.[58]

By April 1930, more than 100 units were vacated, over half of them in the 400 and 500 rows on Second Street. The nine rows of the Old Village were slowly dismantled by the Buffalo Housewrecking Company, which called off work during the winter. By July 1930, the Depression was nine months old, and weary residents were beginning to prepare for the coming winter. As reported by the *Lackawanna News*, "A small army approached First Street Saturday and trailing behind each member of the gang was improvised wagons, boxes, crates and burlap bags." In addition to seeking firewood, private citizens carted off building materials used in constructing or enlarging homes, garages, and utility sheds throughout the First Ward. At night, the units that remained standing were taken over by drifters and the homeless, who quickly disappeared at dawn before workmen or the police arrived. In 1931, the residents of the 100, 200, and 900 rows were moved out. Seventeen Italian families were among the remaining residents of the Old Village, and the Stags Club held meetings in the community rooms of the 500 row. The 300 and 400 rows were soon torn down to make way for the new Spring Perch Company facility, which was erected in 1932. However, according to *Official List of Registered Voters* in Erie County, a large number of residents remained in the 500, 600, 700, and 800 rows until at least 1933, and a handful of families were still living there in 1935.[59]

The razing of the Old Village in the early 1930s symbolizes the fate of many of America's original Italian neighborhoods. Second Street in Lackawanna's Old Village, the Hooks in Buffalo, Boston's west side, and Milwaukee's Third Ward were among the Italian enclaves in the United States that fell to the wrecking ball between 1930 and 1960. In each instance, Italian Americans had to relocate to new areas. In Lackawanna, the detached homes in Bethlehem Park provided a new gathering point for many Old Village Italians.[60]

Bethlehem Park

From the backyard of her family's Second Street home in the Old Village, 10-year-old Sara Chiacchia looked across Smokes Creek at the wooden fence erected on the south bank. It was 1921, and Sara couldn't see beyond the high fence. She knew that horses were raised there and that the farm of the Tobias family was located some distance beyond the fence. Italian girls weren't allowed the freedom to roam that their brothers enjoyed, and it would be another three or four years before Sara learned what was transpiring south of Smokes Creek.[61]

In May 1923, the Niagara Coke Company sold 60 acres of land south of that fence to the Bethlehem Land Improvement Company, a steel company subsidiary that soon took out a building permit for a new subdivision called Bethlehem Park.

Felice and Maria Pepe and children: James, left, Tom, and Elvira. In school, Tom's teacher asked him what "Pepe" meant. He said Pepper, and the teacher told him that would be his last name from then on, and it was.
Photo source: Tom Pepper Jr.

Its frame houses were to average 24 by 28 feet. A contractor erected 278 such homes, many of which were occupied by the autumn of 1925. Businessmen also moved in: Peter Mazuca had a large brick building constructed at 76 Jackson in 1924; the following year, Peter and Louis Williams, Syrian Americans, had a two-story brick building constructed that housed a movie theater and several small shops. A pedestrian bridge was built across Smokes Creek joining Spruce and A streets, allowing residents to walk north through the Old Village site and on to Dona Street and Ingham Avenue (see Figure 5.4). This bridge took on additional significance, as many Old Village families used it between 1925 and 1931 to move to new homes in Bethlehem Park.[62]

One occasion that symbolized this process was the September 1929 opening of Bethlehem Park Elementary School. The teachers at the Old Village Annex School lined up all six kindergarten, first- and second-grade classes, and marched with them across the Smokes Creek bridge to their new school. Over the years, the Bethlehem Park school grew to be a focal point of the neighborhood. In addition to educating the youngsters, the school provided evening classes for adult immigrants such as Maria Marrano, who attended night-school

Figure 5.10 Street plan for Bethlehem Park, which was constructed in 1923-24. When the Old Village demolition began in 1930, many residents moved to Bethlehem Park. Source: Lillian Colafranceschi-Bracci

classes and became a citizen. Community meetings were held in the auditorium, and the school even included a branch of the Lackawanna Public Library, which opened in 1931. Cultural activities were also held there, such as the June 1932 presentation of *The Slave of Santo Domingo*, a play by an Italian theater group direct from Naples, Italy. In 1957, the Bethlehem Park school had the unusual distinction of being struck by a basketball-size meteor that burned a hole in its roof.[63]

When New York State took its 1925 census, Nick Sperduto was the enumerator for District Two of Lackawanna's First Ward. His data showed 16 Italian families living in Bethlehem Park, with all but four of the 50 adults there having been born in Italy. Most were from Lazio and Marche (see Figure 5.11).

Fourteen of the couples had a total of 53 children, an average of almost four per family. Vincent and Elizabeth Rosati accounted for 10 of those youngsters, and an eleventh child was later born. More Italians continued to move into Bethlehem Park during the late 1920s as new houses were constructed. In 1930, the total number of families living in there had grown to 255, 82 of whom were Italian. The following year found 100 Italian families in "the Park." At least 62 of the Italian families who moved to Bethlehem Park between 1925 and 1931 had previously lived in the Old Village. During the 1930s, some families—such as the Zaccarinis, who relocated from Jackson Avenue to Woodlawn—continued the trend of moving to the suburbs that had started a decade earlier. The number of Italian households

September 10, 1923: The view from Hamburg Turnpike looking southeast at the Bethlehem Park development under construction. In the foreground is Smokes Creek, at center left are homes on Jackson Avenue, and at far right are houses on Lincoln Avenue. Note the railroad cars, right of center, used to deliver construction materials, and to the right of them, the outline of Madison Avenue. Photo source: Hamburg Historical Society

decreased slightly by 1941, but Bethlehem Park again grew in the following years. In 1958, Italians owned over half of the homes and commercial buildings in the neighborhood. Two years later, with 149 Italian households, Bethlehem Park surpassed Ingham Avenue's Italian population.[64]

Italian families clustered on certain streets along regional lines. In 1958, they owned the majority of homes on Elm, Jackson, and Madison. Most of these homes were owner-occupied. Laziali predominated on Jackson Avenue, and Marchegiani on Elm Street. Overall, Laziali were the largest regional group, followed closely by Marchegiani during the years 1925 to 1960. Together, the two groups comprised about 60% of the neighborhood's Italian residents. The majority of the Laziali were from Giuliano di Roma, and at least 30 Giulianesi families lived in Bethlehem Park during the 1930s. Several families from Lazio who were neighbors in Buffalo had moved to adjoining houses in Bethlehem Park.[65]

Many Italians began purchasing the Bethlehem Park homes they had rented in the early 1930s. Brothers Alfredo and Biagio Anticoli bought the six-room house at 99 Elm Street to share with their mother, Rosa, at her insistence. The house cost $4,000, and Alfredo continued the payments after Biagio and his family moved to a rented unit on Lincoln Avenue. Bethlehem Steel deducted the payments from his paychecks, and with slack work during the Depression, Alfredo was lucky to have $10 left each week. During one slow week in 1935, he cleared only six cents! Sadly, Bethlehem Steel foreclosed on the house, but the family stayed on as renters. Eventually, the Anticolis repurchased the house, sold it in 1939, and moved to 28 Elm Street. Other families had similar experiences—purchasing their homes in the late 1920s, then enduring foreclosure in the 1930s. Residents banded together in 1937 to protest against a new proposal by Bethlehem Steel. The company had earlier refused to accept the $12 per month rent payment offered by the Emergency Relief Bureau but allowed the unemployed tenants to remain in the homes it owned. The company then tried to collect back rent from the tenants who were off welfare and employed in the plant. It is unclear how this matter was resolved. The negative effect of the economy on homeowners and renters in Bethlehem Park continued into 1941, when 68 homes there were vacant, some no doubt due to foreclosure. The vacancy rate underscores how the Depression struck Italians and other southeast Europeans just as they were making significant economic and social progress. Things finally began to improve, and by November 1940 there were more than 300 individually owned homes in the development, 250 of which had been sold by Bethlehem in the previous year. At that time, 11 new homes were being erected, all of which were sold.[66]

Looking east down Madison Avenue from Walnut Street, 1930.
Photo source: Hamburg Historical Society

The opposite view: looking west down Madison Avenue from Pine Street, 1930.
Photo source: Hamburg Historical Society

Looking north down Elm Street from Madison Avenue, 1930.
Photo source: Hamburg Historical Society

View from Beech Street, looking west down Adams Avenue, which intersects Hamburg Turnpike in the distance, 1930. Photo source: Hamburg Historical Society

Despite the economic woes of the period, from 1929 to 1941, Bethlehem Park remained an inviting neighborhood. "The people in Bethlehem Park were warm and loving," states Marie Ceccarelli-Rosati, who lived for many years at 40 Jackson Avenue. "They helped when someone was ill; they brought food. If people didn't see you for a couple of days, they'd drop by and see how you're doing and say 'Let's have coffee.' " Aldo Filipetti is even more emphatic: "Bethlehem Park was one of the best neighborhoods in the world—it was a safe community. Every family showed warmth and love …. a lot of love, clean clothes, good food, and respect." Lifetime resident Celestino "Chet" Catuzza recalls that people regularly came to visit. "People helped each other to put up a garage, to make wine."[67]

As in the Old Village and on Ingham Avenue, the sidewalks, driveways, and small yards in Bethlehem Park were used for socializing. There, the men shared homemade wine and garden produce, while the women exchanged foods and looked after one another's children. Men set up card tables and invited their neighbors to indulge in Italian card games. Wearing hats and smoking Parodi or DeNobili cigars, they often "serenaded" each other with a combination of jokes, cussing, and teasing remarks in Italian dialect. The wine and root cellars, which often shared space under the houses' front porches, were easily accessible, and basements offered relief from the summer heat. Basements, too, provided room for cooking and entertaining.

Emilio Miniri, an immigrant from Lazio, would stroll down Jackson Avenue in his black suit with an air of dignity, often with a cigar in a holder that he'd fashioned from chicken bones. Twice widowed by 1940, Miniri had married Frances Eposito from Buffalo. In the working-class neighborhood of Bethlehem Park, Esposito stood out as a woman who dressed quite elegantly. Another notable character was an Abruzzese immigrant, Giuseppe Bassi, better known as "Bragon," (baggy pants) who wore a cowboy hat. When he encountered a woman or girl on the sidewalk, he took off his hat, swooped it down before him, and bowed his head, exclaiming, "Howdy, ma'am!" He made quite an impression on some of the girls.[68]

This warm community life continued into the 1960s. Joe Ceccarelli lived the first 13 years of his youth in Bethlehem Park before his family moved to eastern Lackawanna in 1961. Both sets of his grandparents and other relatives also lived there. "For me and John [his older brother] our childhood in Bethlehem Park were the best years of our lives; the family was there, all the things you needed were there. You could just walk into any house if you needed to use the bathroom." In general, children were disciplined by any adult in the community. "Neighbors disciplined kids who broke rules," said Chet Catuzza. "Respect was very important."[69]

Home life reflected the emphasis Italians placed on family. Ferdinand and Rosa Catuzza saw to it that their four boys did chores regularly. Chet Catuzza recalls washing the stairs and bathroom floor on Saturday to earn money for the Sunday movie. His father always dressed in a shirt and tie, examined and initialed all the boys' homework and demanded that his sons wear shirts and ties for Sunday dinner. But another youth, Duilio "Dewey" Montanari, had a different experience. He described his father as unusually lenient and "very democratic. He asked all us kids for our opinions." Even on issues such as trading stocks or properties, Lavinio Montanari consulted with his wife and four children. As owner of the Fano Restaurant, he entrusted his family with important responsibilities. "He had a safe in the house," Dewey reports, "and all the kids had the

The photographer is in the intersection of Spruce Street and Lincoln Avenue. The view is toward the Hamburg Turnpike, looking down Lincoln Avenue, 1930. Photo source: Hamburg Historical Society

The north side of Madison Avenue, between Pine and Spruce streets, 1930. Photo source: Hamburg Historical Society

House on a street corner with garage in back (off the side street), Bethlehem Park, 1930. Photo source: Hamburg Historical Society

A 1931 photo of gardens in the fields just south of Bethlehem Park, looking east from Hamburg Turnpike. In 1935, the Strip Mill was constructed on this site. Photo source: Hamburg Historical Society

Giuseppe "Pepe" Guglielmi doing yard chores at his home, 47 Elm Street, circa 1957. He had migrated to Lackawanna with his father Alessandro in 1920 and decided to remain permanently even though his father had planned on returning to Giuliano.
Photo source: Joe and Rose Guglielmi

Backyard of Pacillo home at 101 Spruce Street, late 1920s. Caterina (middle) and Antonio Pacillo, with Caterina's mother, Maria Antonia Cuzzarella, on the left.
Photo source: Collection of Tony Grasso

Gathering of the Colosimo and Filipetti families, circa 1950. From left are: Maria Colosimo, Jackie Gerace, Silvio Filipetti and his wife Rose Colosimo, Jim Colosimo, Domenico Colosimo, Antoinette Colosimo (wife of Alex Filipetti), Adele Filipetti, Paul Filipetti, Carmine Colosimo. Photo source: Aldo Filipetti

Spruce Street, 1929. Mary Pacillo stands next to her brother's Nash. Photo source: Collection of Tony Grasso

combination. He called home to have us bring money to the Fano. We never had to 'sneak' to do things. He allowed me to drink—to take liquor he stored in the wine cellar. My dad smoked cigarettes. He told me and the kids we could smoke if we wanted."[70]

After work, men usually tended to their gardens, had dinner with their families, and sipped wine on their front porches. Sunday was a day for visiting, or for drives and picnics if a family were fortunate enough to own a car. Paolo Filipetti had a Model A Ford, and his son Aldo recalls Sunday afternoon family drives to Chestnut Ridge, for a macaroni picnic. Sometimes they went to the cemetery to take care of the graves of friends and relatives, or to Swan Street in Buffalo to visit relatives. On Friday or Saturday nights, the Filipettis walked a block south to visit Vittorio and Iolanda Manna, fellow Marchegiani and godparents to Aldo. The adults usually played cards in the kitchen, while the children sat on the living-room floor and listened to the radio. Girls in their teens found a social outlet in

Bethlehem Park, circa 1928. Ada and Enrico Lucarelli and their daughter Dolores.
Photo source: Dolores Lucarelli-Sambuchi

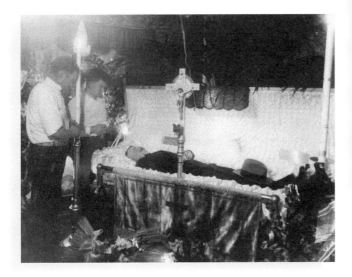

1929. The wake of Alessandro Guglielmi in a Bethlehem Park home. Photo source: Joe and Rose Guglielmi

Alessandro Guglielmi was the recognized leader of the immigrants from Giuliano di Roma. He had planned to return to Italy in 1928, but when he learned that a bank failure in Giuliano had wiped out his savings, he decided to remain in Lackawanna just long enough to replenish the money. Tragically, he was killed in a steel plant accident in 1929. Photo source: Ennio Guglielmi

Figure 5.11

Italian Regional Groups in Bethlehem Park

Region of Family Head	Number of Family Heads by Year:				
	1925	1930	1931	1941	1960
Lazio	6	24	45	46	58
Marche	5	22	25	21	31
Abruzzo	4	13	13	13	15
Calabria	1	4	7	6	16
Campania	0	6	6	6	8
Other	0	5	3	4	4
Unknown	1	8	9	12	17
Totals	**17**	**82**	**108**	**108**	**149**

Sources: New York Census, 1925; U.S. Census, 1930; *Erie County Directory*, 1931, 1941; *Lackawanna City Directory*, 1960.

Jene and Robert Amadori, circa 1929.
Photo source: The Amadori family

Eighth-grade classes at Bethlehem Park School, 1935-36. Bottom row, kneeling, from left: Mike Hacic, Harold Blattenberger, Dan DePasquale, Jacob Cwick, Bill McCluskey, Dan Ranalli, Jess Ferrelli, Larry Gangloff, Steve Turkovich, Anthony Rosati, Norm Sambuchi. Second row: Angeline [Unk], Regina Stelmach, [Unk], [Unk], Caroline or Margaret (?) Policella, _?_ Pietrocarlo, _?_ Rosati, Rose Delgatto, Dora Bartolucci, [Unk]. Third row: Alfred O'Donnell (teacher), Sue Bellagamba, Emma Brennor, Anna Poliseno, Mary Sperduti, Mary Stone, Marie Zaccaria, Anna or Helen? Matuszic, Gerald McMahon – teacher. Fourth row: Lillian Kalenda, Edith or Elizabeth Cushner, [Unk], Connie Antonelli, [Unk], Dorothy Nichols, Genevieve Simon, Mary Ribivich, Nada Atansoff, Wilma Stone. Fifth row: Grace Marrano, Frank Danch, Alex Filipetti, Dennis Kane (principal), John Yelich, Joe Bandish, Eli Rushnov, Joe Bellagamba. Photo source: Collection of Jene Amadori

Gustavo Amadori on Jackson Avenue in 1938. Father of businessman Joe Amadori and grandfather of Jene and Robert, Gustave was born in Cuccurano, Marche. He came to the U.S. in about 1906 and was living in Lackawanna four years later. His wife Teresa joined him there around 1912.
Photo source: The Amadori family

Marchegiani hunters, circa 1922. Top row, from left: Charles Sambuchi, Attilio Lorenzetti. Middle row: Enrico Lucarelli, Bruno Santi, Liso Mattioli. Bottom row: "Fly" the hunting dog, Joe Amadori.
Photo source: Collection of Jene Amadori.

Dominic and Alessandrina Sperduti at their home, 94 Elm, 1939. Photo source: Collection of Yolanda Sperduti-Tobias

Emilio Miniri and his daughter, Clementine Miniri-Cardoni, at Emilio's home on Jackson Avenue, 1938. Photo source: Emilia Cardoni-Cutre

Charles Sambuchi and Paul Filipetti attending a basketball game at Bethlehem Park Elementary School, 1946. In addition to all its other activities, the school at one time housed a branch of the Lackawanna Public Library. Photo source: Norm Sambuchi

friendship circles or groups such as the Parkettes Club, which held occasional card parties at the Park Grille.[71]

A few of the immigrants and many in the second generation discovered the joys of reading at the Lackawanna Public Library on Ridge Road, just east of the railroad tracks. Italian youngsters walked from as far away as Bethlehem Park to borrow books. Most of these were in English, but the library also had small collections in Polish, Hungarian, Italian, and other languages. Every two weeks, Dolly Andreozzi and Adeline Covelli walked from Bethlehem Park to the library and left with an armful of their favorite books. At times, the girls' parents provided a dime for the two-way bus trip to the library. The girls each saved a nickel by walking there, then using it to purchase ice cream before riding the bus back home.[72]

Bethlehem Park boys romped in the swampy area south of Lincoln Avenue, where the strip mill and bar mill were later built. There were many cattails and a six-foot-deep water hole called the Lily Pond, where the boys skinny-dipped. When mud and ashes were stirred up from the bottom of the pond, it was impossible to see underwater. Some youth caught crayfish or crabs in the swamp, roasted them over open fires, and ate

Alessandrina Sperduti, holding flowers, lost her first husband in 1920, and later married Dominic Sperduti, third from left. Photo source: Yolanda Sperduti-Tobias

Reception at the Park Grille following the 1949 wedding of Elga LaMarti and Orlando Moretti, center. Both the bride and the groom were raised in Bethlehem Park. Photo source: Collection of Jo Andreozzi

flying tackles sometimes landed on cow dung. Boys worked doing odd jobs, delivering newspapers, or caddying at Wanakah Country Club. Don Grosso had a paper route in the early 1950s, and when he made his weekly collections on Saturdays, Lucy Amadori offered him *pastatese*, a soup with noodles made of cheese and bread crumbs that was a Marchegian' specialty. At age 12, when Grosso discovered that the $5 a week he made delivering papers could be earned in one day of caddying, he quit his route and joined other boys in hitchhiking to Wanakah.[73]

Within Bethlehem Park, there was a small ravine along the north side of Jackson Avenue, east of Spruce Street, where neighborhood boys roasted potatoes along the creekside. Some of the teens and young men played craps behind Saccomanno's store, while others played in the abandoned wire mill at the east end of the neighborhood or hopped railroad freight cars and rode them to Blasdell. The many youth sports teams utilized the playground at the Bethlehem Park school, and some boys organized informal baseball games at the east end of Madison Avenue. When the Bethlehem Park Hawks baseball teams were organized in 1953, coach Harry Sambuchi brought in loads of dirt, which the boys spread out and planted with grass. When the Hawks disbanded a few years later, older men began playing bocce there.[74]

Prior to World War II, the men also played bocce on the vacant lots in Bethlehem Park and in fields around the site of the Old Village. The field near the Buffalo Brake Beam Company was favored by the men,

them. There was a second pond east of the elevated Pennsylvania Railroad tracks, near the South Buffalo Railway's roundhouse, and a third pond south of Smokes Creek, just west of the Pennsylvania Railroad embankment. Called the Sunny Pond, the latter had a clear swimmable area about the size of a modern swimming pool. Further to the south of Bethlehem Park, near Woodlawn, were fields in which teens played baseball and football. Unfortunately for the boys, some people also allowed their livestock to graze there, and sandlot football players making

as was the cinder bocce court behind the Fano Restaurant, where the losing team often bought the winners a round of drinks. In the mid-1950s, bocce courts were constructed on the field where the Hawks had played. "The Bethlehem Steel retirees tossed the Argentine-imported spheres 7 days a week and often used car headlights to illuminate the courts in the evenings," stated the *Front Page*. The bocce courts were enclosed in a permanent structure in 1960 and named for Joe "Pappy" Amadori, a longtime resident of "the Park." Bocce was one of three favorite pastimes of Luigi "Gigi" Violanti, the other two being the Italian card games *briscola* and *tre-sette*. "Card games for drinks were prominent among the Romans, but for Luigi, it was not vino, or beer or pop whenever he won. He invariably ordered spearmint gum. John Grasso and the late Earl Collareno always kidded Luigi about his love of spearmint gum. Good-naturedly he dallied between *briscola* and *bocce* ... " Violanti and his friends competed daily on the *bocce* courts during warm weather, sometimes until the middle of the night. A resident of Bethlehem Park since the 1920s, Violanti passed away in 1973.[75]

As a boy during the 1950s, this author accompanied his family on weekly trips to Bethlehem Park to visit my grandparents, Tony and Jenny Andreozzi, and a number of aunts, uncles, and cousins. Everyone gathered at my grandparents' house at 42 Jackson. We sat on an assortment of pastel-colored benches and chairs that ringed a large table in the basement kitchen. Food was prepared on an antique stove that Grandma Jenny must have bought in the 1920s. A garland of garlic braided by my grandfather hung in the next room. During the meal or snack, the adults talked mostly in Italian but addressed the numerous children around the table in English. After a while, we kids were allowed to play in other rooms during winter or outside during warmer months. As we played hide-and-go-seek, we found crannies behind trees or shrubs facing Jackson Avenue, in the garage, or in my grandfather's lush garden along the shore of Smokes Creek. Some Sundays, we were elated to each be given 15 cents to go down the block to the Park Theater or get candy at Wicky Bacchus's shop.

The Park Theater provided ready entertainment for both adults and the many children in the neighborhood. Frank Moretti recalls that in the 1930s, the movie house offered a variety of entertainments. The five-cent admission to the theater bought not only a film but such extras as a turkey raffle, group singing with lyrics on the screen, and attention-grabbing lobby decorations. "A wax figure, full size, of a cowboy was displayed," said Frank Moretti. "It was then put in a hearse and carried to the next theater." [76]

A number of part-time and informal artisans added a village flavor to Bethlehem Park. Domenico Carducci, a track laborer on the South Buffalo Railway, also worked as a barber during the Depression, charging 25 cents for a haircut. Phil Andreozzi remembers Carducci coming to the family home and cutting his hair. Carducci spoke broken English as he instructed Andreozzi to "close-a da high" (close your eyes) and then "open-a da high" (open your eyes). Carducci was called *u scupatore* (the sweeper), because he swept up the fallen hair, singing as he did so. Other residents also had enterprises that augmented the family income. Armando Torella repaired shoes in his garage, and Angelina Poliseno sold snails imported from

1925. Audrey Spagnolo, age 16, practices her music. She took lessons from Miss Heinz on Ridge Road.
Photo source: Collection of Audrey Spagnolo-Surgenor

Italy and was known as *la ciamutara* (the snail merchant). The snails were cooked in their shells, and boys later played with the shells and traded them.[77]

A series of businesses and peddlers added to the social interactions and lively atmosphere of Bethlehem Park. Joe the Popcorn Man, also known as Peanut Joe, regularly brought his two-wheel push wagon to Bethlehem Park. There, he popped corn and roasted peanuts; he also shaved ice from a block into a paper cup and flavored it with syrup for three cents. He traveled throughout the First Ward. Born Jimmy Maginas, he was a Greek immigrant who lived on Lehigh Avenue and spoke broken English. But after his death in 1955, police found $4,500 in coins and dollar bills "hidden among the trash and garbage of the rented garage where he slept on boards without a mattress."[78]

Peter Mazuca moved his Old Village grocery to a new building he had constructed at Jackson and Spruce in 1925; he ran it there until 1934. His son Joseph made quite an impression when he drove down Jackson Avenue in a Stutz Bearcat; few Italians had cars then, let alone such an expensive model. Mazuca's second wife, Lucy, went house to house each week during the early 1930s, collecting a dollar toward each family's debt at the grocery store. As a girl, Aldina Manna noticed that Lucy Mazuca dressed very nicely and carried a little book in which she recorded payments. When Charles Saccomanno, Mazuca's nephew, took over the grocery store, he and his wife recorded each family's purchase "on the book." At the end of the week, it was often the oldest child in a family who came to pay the bill. Upon receiving payments, Anna Saccomanno offered a small gift, such as cigars or pipe tobacco for the head of the house.[79]

Joe "Pappy" Amadori opened the Park Grille at 64 Jackson in 1933. His wife, Lucy, prepared fish fries and occasionally venison for the patrons; her sister, Audrey Spagnolo, also worked there. Customers were entertained on weekends by floor shows, which sometimes included comedians, one who went by the name Popeye, and strippers. Local entertainers also performed there; a Marchegiano named Turiddu played his clarinet for patrons. At times, the customers got rough. When a group of Ohio Italians arrived in the area in 1936, "There were fist fights, local Italians versus Steubenville guys from Ohio—they got good jobs at the strip mill and took girls away from the locals at the Park Grille," recalls Pappy's son Jene. Eventually, the Ohio men were accepted into the community. In 1939, Audrey Spagnolo met Ohio transplant David Surgenor at the Park Grille, and they were soon married. For many Bethlehem Park men, the tavern was simply a place to share drinks with friends or play cards. Many a lengthy game of "boss" was played there. The pensioners occupied the back room during daylight hours, passing the time playing cards. Like other saloons and taverns in Lackawanna, each payday saw many men cashing their checks at the Park Grille. The tavern had a hall that was often rented for wedding receptions. Pappy Amadori left the tavern business in early 1945, when he bought the large building across the street that housed the Park Theater and several storefronts. Amadori refurbished the building and ran the movie theater, with sons Jene and Bobby often staffing the projection room. Jene recalled that the reels of film had to be changed every 17 minutes, which, he added, limited the amount of time he could spend making out with his girlfriend. If the many children in the audience became too boisterous, Lucy Amadori would stop the film and scold them. In addition to movies, Pappy Amadori occasionally brought in live entertainment, including an appearance by the Ink Spots, a nationally known singing group.[80]

Lavinio Montanari's Fano Restaurant, just north of Bethlehem Park, was a favorite gathering spot for Marchegiani of all ages, including some from Buffalo. On Sundays, the families ate dinner there, after which the men played bocce. Each week, the Baldassari family walked from

Charles and Anna Saccomanno in front of their grocery store on Jackson Avenue at Spruce Street, circa 1940. They operated the store from 1932 to 1967. Photo source: Joe Saccomanno

Anna Saccomanno was widowed in 1915 when her husband, Francesco, was killed in a railroad accident in Cranberry Lake, New York. She lived with her son Charles and his family and helped out in the grocery store. Photo source: Joe Saccomanno

Winter on Pine Street; the home of Paul and Adele Filipetti is on the right. Photo source: Aldo Filipetti

Lucy Amadori in 1938, standing next to the Park Grille Bishop's Grocery is in the background.
Photo source: The Amadori family

Paolo and Ortenza Zaccarine and their children. From left: Joe, Ortenza holding Rose, Louise, Dan, Paolo, Romeo. The family moved from Bethlehem Park to Woodlawn in the late 1930s. Paolo's surname was most likely Zuccarini originally; he also went by Zucca before deciding on Zaccarine. Photo source: Collection of Jo Andreozzi

First Holy Communion, late 1940s. John Ceccarelli Jr. with three of his grandparents. At left is Filomena Ceccarelli, and Jenny Andreozzi is on the right. Standing behind them on the lawn of his home at 42 Jackson is Tony Andreozzi. The grandparent not appearing in the photo is Arduino Ceccarelli. Photo source: Collection of Jo Andreozzi

Friends at 20 Elm in the 1940s. Standing, from left, are: John and Dominic Masocco, and Sam Conti. Sitting is Frank Tobias. In the rear right is Domenico Nannucci, the maternal grandfather of the Masocco brothers.
Photo source: John Masocco

Bethlehem Park to the Fano as a group, with Giuseppe in the lead, followed by Lena and the children. Vittorio and Iolanda Manna also took their daughters to the restaurant. "My father Vittorio sang and danced with me and my sister in the kitchen of the restaurant," recalls Aldina Manna. "Gino Tonucci played the squeeze box and

Dedication of the Columbus monument on the medium strip of Madison Avenue, October 1940. Charles Saccomanno, chairman of the event, addresses the large gathering. Photo source: Joe Saccomanno

The Columbus bust on its pedestal at the dedication in 1940. At right is Charles Saccomanno, and on the left is Ferdinand Catuzza, president of the Federation of Italian American Associations of Lackawanna, the group that raised funds and successfully lobbied the city for a site at which to place the monument. Photo source: Joe Saccomanno

a Polish guy played the drums. Later Mario Sorbini and his two sons, who lived in Blasdell, played music at the Fano." Card parties and dances were also held at the restaurant.[81]

The neighborhood endured some difficult times besides the unemployment and house foreclosures during the Great Depression. In the post – World War II years, the steel plant kept encroaching on the neighborhood. In 1950, the homes on the south side of Lincoln Avenue were removed to make way for expansion of the Strip Mill. After the Basic Oxygen Furnace was erected just west of Bethlehem Park in 1964, air pollution and increased noise became issues for the residents. Smokes Creek became heavily polluted with industrial waste and actually caught fire on two occasions during the 1960s. A decade earlier, the creek was the source of other woes. In 1953 and again in 1955, it was swollen with springtime water and overflowed its banks. In the second flood, Bethlehem Park was the hardest hit, as it is in a low-lying area, especially at the Lincoln Avenue end. Bethlehem Park school was closed for the day, and Red Cross workers established an evacuation center there. More than 40 families were evacuated from their flooded homes by coastguardsmen and two volunteers using rowboats. One of the volunteers, Al Ginnetti, borrowed a boat and, with help from Joe Moretti, spent five hours assisting marooned neighbors in getting to safety. Officials estimated that damages throughout Lackawanna ranged from $500,000 to $1 million.[82]

Bethlehem Park had a strong Italian flavor for many years due to at least a third of its residents being of Italian American. In addition to Italian stores, there were other ethnic markers in the neighborhood. A home on Elm Street known as the Italian Hall was rented by several Italian organizations and used for meeting rooms in the late 1930s. The city's Italians erected a bust of Columbus at the Madison Avenue entrance to the neighborhood and had an elaborate ceremony at the unveiling in October 1940. Seven years later, a monument was erected and dedicated to the eight Bethlehem Park servicemen, five of these men were Italian Americans, who gave their lives in World War II. Late in the twentieth century, one could still hear Italian or a combination of English and Italian spoken, but Bethlehem Park's Italian population has dwindled in recent decades.

Roland Avenue

In the early years of the twentieth century, plenty of land lay undeveloped in the eastern half of Lackawanna. Some tracts just east of South Park Avenue were held by the Catholic Diocese of Buffalo. In 1899, the only side streets running off South Park Avenue in this area were Kirby and Elkhart avenues. Within a few years, Roland Avenue and other streets were installed to the south, and many homes were built.

In 1900, Angelo Morinello and his family were the first Italians to live in what was then the Limestone Hill, or steel-plant district of West Seneca. Morinello ran a saloon on Milnor Avenue and, after buying several more properties in 1902 and 1903, had a three-story brick building erected at Roland Avenue and Front Street. He opened a dry-goods and grocery store on the first floor and rented out rooms on the other floors. In 1905, Morinello moved his family to 38 Roland, and reestablished his saloon there.[83]

At the same time, other Italians—including young Frank Morinello, Francesco Falcone, and Francesco Sirianni—were buying and selling homes in the Roland Avenue area. Bruno Falbo purchased the home at 91 Roland from Angelo Morinello, and Natale Chiodo bought the house at 35 Milnor from Francesco Sirianni. Over the next generation, the neighborhood's Italian population grew tenfold—from 29 in 1905 to 318 in 1930 (see Figure 5.5). Some of these families were related. The Siriannis were blood relatives of the Chiodos, Morascos, and Falbos, and like the Bonaccios and Costanzos, had their roots in Soveria Mannelli, Calabria. The Bevilacqua, Cardamone, and

FIGURE 5.12

ROLAND: A VILLAGE WITHIN LACKAWANNA

By 1904, the newly developed Roland Avenue area was dubbed Roland, and its residents took pride in the Roland Volunteer Hose Company formed that year, the first fire company in the western part of West Seneca. They informally proclaimed Roland a municipality and appointed Richard E. Hyland its honorary mayor. After the city of Lackawanna was founded in 1909, Roland remained a distinct "village," although Hyland gave his honorary position to Councilman Joe Bouley in 1914. The *Lackawanna Daily Journal* proclaimed in 1923 that "Roland Village is now part of Lackawanna City" after Lackawanna finally filled in holes in the area's streets and sidewalks. The neighborhood's strong identity was reinforced by the large number of railroad workers who lived there.

Sources: *Lackawanna Journal*, January 12, 1914; *Lackawanna Daily Journal*, January 26, 1923, *Buffalo Evening News*, February 6, 1924.

Figure 5.13 Italians were concentrated along Roland Avenue and its side streets, west of Electric Avenue.
Source: Office of the Lackawanna City Engineer

Domenico Giovinetti and his wife Maria Grazia emigrated from Baselice, Campania, in about 1908 and arrived in Lackawanna six years later. Photo source: Dorothy Govenettio

Leo families also had Calabrian roots. Many of their neighbors were from Salerno province in Campania; Angelo and Caterina Morinello, Biagio Vertalino, and Joe Fox all were born in Acquavella. Fonsina Vertalino, the Cennamos, DeMarias, Margaruccis, Pintos, and Pitillos were Cilentan', or natives of San Mauro Cilento.[84]

The small Italian community was concentrated at the western end of Roland Avenue, between Electric Avenue and the railroad tracks. While many Italians eventually settled in the Roland Avenue neighborhood, the area never had the heavy concentration of Italians found on lower Ingham Avenue or Second Street in the Old Village, or Bethlehem Park. Rather, the neighborhood had a greater number of residents from other ethnic groups. The Italians were soon spread over a six-block area, and although Italian businesses were present, no Italian statue, church, or other institution provided a physical symbol of ethnic identity. The Roland Wildcats building, erected in 1950, symbolized a multiethnic athletic club that happened to have a sizable Italian membership.

Many men in the Roland Avenue area, including Italians and those of other ethnic groups, worked on the mainline railroads and at the nearby South Buffalo Railway and New York Central Railroad roundhouses; indeed, the neighborhood abutted a network of tracks. By 1920, the Italian enclave had spread to Wood Street and Myrtle and Mitchell avenues, just off Roland. Five years later, it extended to South Park and Warsaw avenues, and Pierce and Verel streets. But the neighborhood remained mixed: Anglo-American Protestants lived on Roland east of Electric; Cleveland Avenue was Irish and German; Keever and Warsaw were heavily Polish.[85]

The rooming house and general store that Angelo Morinello had built in 1902 at 1 Roland Avenue at the intersection with Front Street.
Photo source: Collection of Frank Morinello, Jr.

Angelo Morinello with customers and neighbors at his general store. Morinello is second from right, standing. Bernardo "Bosco" Schole is seated at the right. Morinello had the store and rooming house from 1902 until 1910, when he moved his business to a building just down the block on Roland Avenue.
Photo source: Collection of Frank Morinello, Jr.

Maria and Natale Chiodo with their son Sam at the family's Milnor Avenue home, 1935.
Photo Source: Collection of Frank Chiodo

Friends and paesani, *1930s. Angelo Antigiovanni, left, and Michele Spirito, both immigrants from Lenola, Lazio, socialized often.* Photo source: Constance Antigiovanni-Bauer

Margaret and Mary Cardinale state that "it was a nice area to live. There were many Italians, and the ethnic groups all got along." Frank Chiodo agreed, saying, "There was no ethnic friction. We had all nationalities mixed—Poles, Irish, Ukrainians. The same was true at Washington School." Among boys, occasional ethnic tensions were minor. "The boys fought, called each other names, and then made up," recalls Frank Sanak, a Polish American. Tony Falbo observed that when someone had to appear in court, the neighbors chipped in money so that a lawyer could be hired. The court usually provided a translator. The immigrants often went to older *paesani* for advice. Biagio Vertalino, for example, sought out Angelo Pitillo when he needed to consult about an issue. Other natives of Campania approached Angelo Morinello, John Verel, or Tony Welsh. Among the Calabresi, Natale Chiodo, Francesco Sirianni, and Pietro Sirianni were viewed as leaders.[86]

Relatives and *paesani* visited each other often. Sisters Mary and Margaret Cardinale recall the visits of Angelo Antigiovanni and their uncle, Michele Spirito. Giuseppe and Luisa Cardinale welcomed these callers, as they were all natives of Latina province, and Luisa was the sister of Michele. Antigiovanni and Spirito often visited after drinking some wine; they played banjo or guitar, and everyone sang. Some men were less restrained than others when celebrating and drinking; after a night of partying one man woke up to find himself on the roof of a neighbor's house. More formal entertainment was available

by the late 1910s at the A. C. Theater, located at Kirby and Electric avenues. Later, the Franklin Theater on Ridge Road offered movies. Several Roland Avenue residents socialized in the First Ward. Bruno Falbo played cards at Nick Sperduto's tavern on Ingham Avenue. His son John was visiting Bethlehem Park by age 14, crossing over the railroad tracks to the foot of Madison Avenue. [87]

Italian men gathered at Morinello's store at the foot of Roland Avenue, and socialized and played cards at his saloon that had been relocated at 38 Roland Avenue. By 1916, the Falbo family lived above the saloon, and young Tony Falbo was often sent downstairs with a nickel to purchase a bucket of beer for his father. Tony Welsh, born Antonio Delguercio, also established a tavern on Roland Avenue, which, as Tony Falbo described it, served as "headquarters where the men played *briscola*, *scopa*, and *tre-sette*." Some Italians also frequented Trella's bar on Milnor Avenue, which was owned by a Polish American.[88]

The Washington Elementary School, earlier known as School No. 2, was located just off Roland Avenue. Like other Lackawanna schools, it had evening courses for adult immigrants. The school also had one other feature important to Italians: Mary Yoviene-Clark, the first Italian American teacher in the city, who began her career in 1918. Her fluency in Italian was crucial in communication with immigrant parents, and she was a strong role model for Italian kids. When interviewed, many elderly

A neighborhood gathering at 1 Roland Avenue, circa 1928, to celebrate the baptism of the daughter of Giovanni and Evelyn Carroccia. The infant is being held by her godmother, Giuseppina Pitillo, wearing a white dress and hat and seated under the "Salada Tea" sign. Sitting to the left of Pitillo are the baby's parents.
Photo source: Collection of John Falbo

The members of the Roland Wildcats constructed their clubhouse in 1950 at the corner of Electric and Milnor avenues. Shown here in 2005, it has continued to be the center of the club's activities. Photo source: Paul Pasquarella

members of the second generation noted with pride that Mary Yoviene-Clark was one of their teachers at Washington Elementary School. When a fire damaged the school, Yoviene-Clark and several other teachers taught classes at the fire hall at Electric and Milnor avenues for a year.[89]

Roland Avenue Italians usually attended St. Anthony's Church in the First Ward or Our Mother of Good Counsel in Blasdell. Some later joined the Our Lady of Victory parish at Ridge Road and South Park Avenue. The Chiodo family attended Our Mother of Good Counsel, but the oldest son, Frank, switched to St. Anthony's in the late 1940s to get to know the new pastor, Reverend Thomas Ciolino. Later, Chiodo joined the OLV parish. Other families divided their loyalties; Biagio and Fonzina Vertalino went to St. Anthony's, their children attended Our Mother of Good Counsel, which was closer and a shorter walk. Several other types of religious activities were offered in the neighborhood. A group of women organized the Madonna della Carmine Society of Roland, which met in members' homes. A number of Italians became involved with Gesu the Monk, who had his own church in North Collins and a strong following among western New York Italians (see Chapter 6). Individual families practiced other Italian traditions. Giuseppina Pitillo set up a table with meatless food every March on St. Joseph's Day to give thanks for her husband's recovery from the Spanish flu, the same illness that claimed her brother's life. The Pitillo and Chiodo children acted the roles of Mary and Joseph.[90]

Wedding receptions and other gatherings were often held at the fire hall. The marriage of James Sirianni and Rose Morinello in 1911 linked many Calabresi in the neighborhood with the Napolitani, or natives of Campania. At the reception, the Siriannis were joined by the Chiodos and other *paesani* from Soveria Mannelli. The Morinello extended family included the Pintos, who at the time lived near Jamestown, and other natives of Acquavella and San Mauro Cilento. Natale Chiodo and Maria Pinto met at the reception and were married the following year.[91]

Baptisms, too, were social celebrations in the Roland Avenue neighborhood. A photo taken in the late 1920s shows some 35 adults and children in front of Morinello's store at 101 Roland Avenue (see page 266). Seated in the middle is Giuseppina Pitillo, holding her infant godchild, Mary Carroccia, who had just been baptized, and nearby are the girl's parents, Giovanni and Evelyn Carroccia. Funerals provided another type of social event, sometimes grand in style. When Angelo Morinello died in 1940, his family brought in undertaker Pasquale Rubino from Buffalo to arrange the wake in the Morinello house. The funeral began with a procession led by a band that marched two blocks to Electric Avenue. Those who could afford $2 per seat then traveled by limousine to Holy Cross Cemetery, where the casket was interred in the family's impressive mausoleum.[92]

At any given time, there were eight grocery stores on Roland Avenue, at least half of them run by Italians. In 1905, three

The children of Natale and Maria Chiodo, Milnor Avenue, 1930. Sam stands front center, and behind him, from left, are Frank, Carmen, Angeline, and Tony.
Photo source: Collection of Frank Chiodo

Friends circa 1934, at Electric and Milnor avenues. From left are: Michael Pitillo, George Valentine, and Joe "Pedro" Angotti. Ang Pitillo is the boy in the foreground.
Photo source: Ang Pitillo

years after Angelo Morinello opened his grocery and general store at 101 Roland Avenue, Pietro Sirianni established a grocery on Front Street, which he operated until at least 1920. Morinello maintained his store even after he built his new home and saloon at 132 Roland. Later, his son Frank briefly had a grocery at Roland and Electric avenues, in addition to a second one some blocks north. But Angelo Morinello resisted other competition. In 1911, when Giuseppina Pitillo—whose family rented from Morinello—started a grocery store to serve the boarders of their friends the Falcones, Morinello evicted the Pitillos. The Pitillo family moved further down Roland where Giuseppina setup another grocery store. Finally, the family settled at 1651 Electric Avenue, at the corner of Milnor. Earlier this storefront had been an ice cream parlor; Giuseppina Pitillo again established a grocery store.[93]

The storefronts at the corner of Roland and Electric housed four Italian groceries between 1927 and 1947. Italian peddlers came through the neighborhood, too: Tony Grasso sold fruit and vegetables from his truck, calling out, "Tomatoes! Potatoes!" During the 1930s, Grasso also sold bottles of wine, and, for a period of time, boxes of pasta he and Nick Delgatto had acquired at wholesale prices. Another First Ward Italian, Antonio Guadagno, delivered bread from his bakery on Ingham Avenue.[94]

Patsy Pitillo's bar eventually became a bar/restaurant, which he ran until 1974, when his son Angelo took it on for another 13 years. Angelo, who likes to be called Ang, had worked there as a boy. Once, while his dad was at a funeral, 12-year-old Ang was left to tend bar by himself. When he needed some advice on mixing a certain drink, he went next door to ask his grandfather, leaving the bar untended. Nothing was taken, but Ang's father and grandfather impressed upon him the importance of always having someone present at the bar. Growing up in the bar, Ang mingled with the neighborhood men at both their most jovial and most gross moments. One Italian patron, for example, "ate raw eggs, shell and all, as he drank the beer," recounts Pitillo. One day, his grandfather put a live egg—one with a chick about to hatch—with the other eggs. "The man ate it, with the legs hanging out of his mouth, and a foul look on his face!"[95]

Many Italian men liked to play boss, the card game in which glasses of wine or beer served as ante, and the winner decided who could drink the "pot." In one incident, an Italian man had been playing the game for quite a while and was losing. The winners, or bosses, had continually denied him any drinks. When he finally won, the man denied the previous bosses any drinks, and he then proceeded to consume all the glasses of liquor that he had won. "He drank for eight hours," said Pitillo, "threw up, and then he drank more to

Fonzina and Biagio Vertalino in about 1905. He is holding their son Nick. The couple met in Buffalo after emigrating from towns in Salerno province in Campania. They moved to Lackawanna in 1912. The family name was originally Bertalini. Photo source: Collection of Nick Vertalino

punish the men who left him 'dry' earlier." Men frequenting Pitillo's Tavern, many of whom were steel workers or railroad laborers, often let off steam in other ways. Sometimes fistfights broke out between Italian men, or between the Irish and Italians. Even brothers might get into brawls. Patsy Pitillo, Ang's father, would get out his billy club and use it to break up the contests.[96]

Boys played sandlot baseball between the two railroad embankments near where they crossed Electric Avenue. The Roland Wildcats teams also practiced there, and the Wildcats entered teams in baseball, football, and bowling leagues. East of South Park Avenue, there was a swimming hole known as "Tomaka's woods" on the south branch of Smokes Creek. Dominic Selvaggio and other boys swam there, even though the water was polluted by fluids leeching from the city dump. Natale Chiodo wouldn't allow his sons to go there for fear they would drown. Like youngsters in the First Ward, Roland Avenue teens went to the railroad sidings off Front Street to obtain coal and lumber to bring home or sell to businesses or other families. The money Sam Cardinale earned in this way was all handed over to his mother.[97]

The Pitillo family, circa 1918. Front row, from left: Michael, Katie, Angelo holding Anthony, Josephine, Louise, Millie. Standing in back are John, Pasquale, Frank. The boys had interesting nicknames: Pasquale was known as "Hook," John as "Spike," Michael as "Greek," and Anthony as "Turk."
Photo source: Ang Pitillo

Pitillo's tavern, 1941. Bob Eagan is in the lower foreground. In the center row, from the left, are: Sam Cardinale, Joe Ziccarelli, Joe Angotti, Eddie Wnuk, Ang Pitillo. In the back row are: [Unk], Walter Lebeck, Patsy Pitillo, George Delmont, Charley DePerto. Photo source: Collection of Frank Chiodo

Like most Italian neighborhoods, Roland Avenue did not lack for barbers. The first Italian barber was Andrea Berarducci, better known as Andrew Blard, who was in business by 1915 at 39 Roland. By the 1920s, he was joined by Anthony Falcone, Donato Selvaggio, and Angelo Antigiovanni, all with shops near Roland and Electric. Thomas Miceli and Anthony Gustello established their businesses in the 1930s. Vincent Antigiovanni started up some years later. Despite these barbers' usually reasonable prices, some frugal Italians, such as Natale Chiodo, regularly cut their own family members' hair.[98]

Italian shoe-repair businesses, too, were plentiful. Francesco Sirianni established the first in 1910 on Milnor Avenue, later moving to 105 Roland. When he died in 1926, his nephew Eugenio Morasco took over the business. Thomas Cennamo started a shop in 1920, across the street from Sirianni, making the two men active competitors. In 1925, Cennamo moved to a new shop a few blocks north on Electric Avenue. Two of the barbers, Anthony Falcone and Andrea Berarducci, also repaired shoes. Across Roland Avenue from Berarducci was his main competitor, Domenico Giovinetti, who ran a shoe-repair shop into the 1930s, after which his sons Leonard and John took it over. Joseph Antigiovanni and Dominic Papaleo had shoe-repair businesses on Electric Avenue in the early 1940s.[99]

The Roland Avenue enclave had Italian saloons and groceries that served as ethnic markers but did not have an Italian church or meeting hall to lend the strong ethnic flavor of Ingham Avenue or Bethlehem Park. The Roland Wildcats eventually put up a building in 1950, but the group, while heavily Italian at first, has always been multiethnic. The fact that Italian family members often attended different churches—St. Anthony's, Our Mother of Good Counsel, and Our Lady of Victory—also helped dilute the

The Morinelli-Sirianni wedding party at Front Street and Roland Avenue, 1911.
Photo source: Collection of Frank Morinello Jr.

Rose Morinello and James Sirianni at Our Mother of Good Counsel Church, Blasdell, on their wedding day in 1911.
Photo source: Collection of Frank Morinello Jr.

Italianita of the neighborhood. In the family homes, Italian businesses, and meetings of several Italian organizations, however, there did exist an ethnic culture.

Italians in other Neighborhoods

Aside from the four enclaves— Ingham Avenue, the Old Village, Bethlehem Park, and Roland Avenue—Italians also settled elsewhere in the city. The Scarsellas lived in the First Ward on Wasson Avenue, a neighborhood that some scoffed at because it included a house of prostitution. Anne Scarsella saw it differently. "It was a nice neighborhood. We never had any trouble.… It was a lot of friendliness." The neighbors had common issues to commiserate about. "We'd sit out there at

Salvatore and Maria Calzone, immigrants from Calabria, settled on Milnor Avenue.
Photo source: Collection of Frank Chiodo

night in the hot weather and talk of Bethlehem Steel, with their shooting off that stuff [ore dust] they did. Everyone had screens in the summer, and you covered them with cheesecloth or ripped up old sheets to catch the red ore dust. Otherwise you'd be a mess."[100]

On Hamburg Turnpike, a few other Italian families had homes and businesses, including a confectionery, a haberdashery, and a popular restaurant and nightspot. Salvatore Macaluso ran an auto-repair garage at the corner of Odell Street and moved his family from Buffalo into the apartment on the second floor. His neighbors reflected Lackawanna's ethnic mix: American Indians, an Italian-owned building housing Puerto Rican and Arab families, and a Jewish-owned fruit stand offering 24-hour service. American Indians lived in a rear apartment next to the store. Sal Macaluso, while not a churchgoer, respected anyone who believed in God. On the first Christmas following his family's move to Lackawanna, he invited all his neighbors over for a celebration, even though most were not Christians. Carmella Macaluso remembers that her parents shared lamb and freshly baked bread with their Arab, Puerto Rican, and Jewish guests. "No one ate the bread

Circa 1923, 87 Spruce Street. Eugenio Ziccarelli in the family garden holding Jack, his oldest son. During the 1930s he also had a garden in between the railroad tracks off Front Street and another on Electric Avenue.
Photo source: Jack Ziccarelli

The Ziccarelli family on Roland Avenue, circa 1930. From left are Jack, Nellie holiding Carol, Joe, and Tony. At upper right are Eugenio "John" Ziccarelli and Sam.
Photo source: Jack Ziccarelli

until my father broke the bread; he broke it in half. And then he gave it to everybody; and when he went to the Jewish family the wife broke the bread for her husband, and the Arabs did the same. Oh, see," Carmella reminisced, "wasn't this an education for a young kid like myself?"[101]

East of the railroad tracks, Italians were settling near the intersection of Ridge Road and South Park Avenue. In 1910, Luca and Maddelina Tarquinio owned a home in the Irish enclave on Victory Avenue, and hotel proprietor Frank DiCorpo and his family were living on South Park Avenue. Seven years later, two other Italians were located on Victory Avenue—two in the Polish neighborhood on Center Street, and barbers Antonio Agliata and Joseph Corbo settled with their families on Parkview, across from the South Park Botanical Gardens. Corbo eventually had his barbershop at the busy corner at Ridge and South Park.[102]

Hard Times in Little Italy

Countless stories, ranging from suffering and toil to community togetherness and economic advancement, have been enacted on Lackawanna's streets over the past century by individuals and families of 92 ethnic groups. In the city's Italian neighborhoods, residents dealt with illness, crime, death, poverty, the Depression, being "on relief," and having to rely on boarders for income during the first half of the twentieth century.

Many of Lackawanna's Italian immigrants knew poverty both in the Old Country and as newcomers to American cities. They were deeply affected by the Great Depression, which struck just as they had begun to enjoy some longevity and economic stability in the new country. It meant a return to hard times for many people. Steelworkers were lucky to work one or two days a week as production fell at Bethlehem Steel and many were laid off. One Easter during the 1930s, Vittorio Manna received a paycheck for seven cents, which he misread as $7. "He went to Tomaka's bar, ordered a fifteen cent beer," recalls his daughter Aldina, "and

1935, 91 Roland Avenue. From left are Bruno and Rosamaria Falbo, Michelina Mazza, Carmela Falbo holding her nephew Jerry Falbo, and her niece, Micolina Falbo. The dog, Spotty, was Micolina's pet. Photo source: Ben Falbo

waited for change. Tomaka explained that the check was for seven cents, and there would be no change. My father was heartbroken because he could not buy Easter presents for his two daughters"— his custom in the past. "He came home, sat on the steps outside the door and sobbed. My mother wouldn't let us girls see this, but she did promise to bake us cookies as presents."[103]

Lackawannans adopted many survival tactics. One Italian man scavenged glass shards from First Ward landfills and sold them to scrap dealers for a few pennies. Other men gave haircuts, repaired shoes, or did minor construction, concrete, or carpentry jobs. Adults and children sold rabbits, chickens, goats they had raised. After the Old Village was condemned and partially razed in 1930, nearby residents informally finished the demolition of the unoccupied units over the next five years. For $15, one could purchase the right to strip a unit of all its materials, including the valuable metals. Many struggling families ignored such formalities and collected bricks, lumber, and metal from the derelict row houses, with only occasional intervention from the Lackawanna police. Indeed, they probably saved the city huge demolition expenses. Sam Morgan was hired to pull down chimneys with his delivery truck. Tony Grasso used his truck to haul slate roofing, which he used in the construction of his garage. Antonio Carmillone and other men salvaged concrete sidewalk slabs and installed them in their Bethlehem Park yards. [104]

Government welfare, called "relief" at that time, came in the form of bulk supplies of basic foods, vouchers for shoes and clothes, and small cash allotments. Many Italians and other Lackawannans depended on the Erie County Welfare Department

and the institutions of Our Lady of Victory for assistance. Father Baker, pastor of the OLV parish, became a revered figure for the many free services his institutions offered to all ethnic groups, especially during the Depression. The steel plant and the railroads provided heating fuel and other necessities, in both intended and unintended ways. Occasionally, Bethlehem Steel dumped scrap wood, coal, or coke from a railroad car in a spot where people could help themselves—in Bethlehem Park or Woodlawn, just south of Lackawanna. Luigi Pilla used a makeshift cart, whose wheels were salvaged from discarded wheelbarrows, to haul coke, which he placed in burlap bags. Other men and boys simply loaded and hauled several bags of coke by hand, and some went door-to-door selling them.[105]

Many families gleaned fallen coal and coke from the railroad sidings east of Ingham Avenue and Bethlehem Park. Even the waste materials tamped under railroad ties contained some reclaimable hunks of coal or coke. Parents and their children could be seen walking the tracks in search of combustible materials to fuel their stoves. In other instances, boys and young men climbed on railroad cars and tossed down usable materials, such as slabs of wood used to stack steel. Other more venturesome youth visited the coal hoppers. Each day, the Pennsylvania Railroad spotted 40 or 50 laden hoppers on a siding that ran along Lehigh Avenue and the Old Village. Men, as well as boys who skipped school for the occasion, climbed up on the hoppers, pushed off soft coal chunks, some up to a foot in length, packed it into burlap bags, and took them home or sold them to other families. In the early 1930s, children at Lincoln School observed this practice on a daily basis.[106]

Colomba Scarsella, center, at her Wasson Avenue home with two paesane *from Buffalo: Faustina Tiberio, left, and Elisabetta Mastrantoni, right.* Photo source: Anne Scarsella-Antes

Tony DiMillo watched teenagers knock coke off the cars and gather it up for the family furnace; they even carried off railroad ties for fuel. People broke into boxcars and made off with all types of goods—DiMillo remembers kids distributing watermelons along Ingham Avenue one day. Occasionally railroad police caught the pilfering boys and escorted them home to their parents. In at least one case, they shot a man. The greatest danger, however, was that of falling under the wheels of a moving train. As a child, John Fadale saw one of his friends killed this way. In another incident, Vito Casciano, a 15-year-old living on Roland Avenue, was killed when run over by a train in 1916.[107]

Indeed, death and disease were everyday features of life as immigrants lived in sometimes squalid housing next to swamps and surrounded by steel mills and railroad tracks. An outbreak of typhoid fever along Smokes Creek in 1903 affected many Italians. In 1907, one doctor estimated that up to 60% of immigrants in the steel-plant district were infected with tuberculosis. The city health department reported 91 cases of pneumonia in 1911; 21 of the people died. "The high rate of death in this disease is partially accounted for by the fact that many of the deaths were among foreigners, who usually wait until the patient is nearly dead before calling in a physician." The influenza (Spanish flu) epidemic of 1918 found many victims in Lackawanna's crowded First Ward. The usual

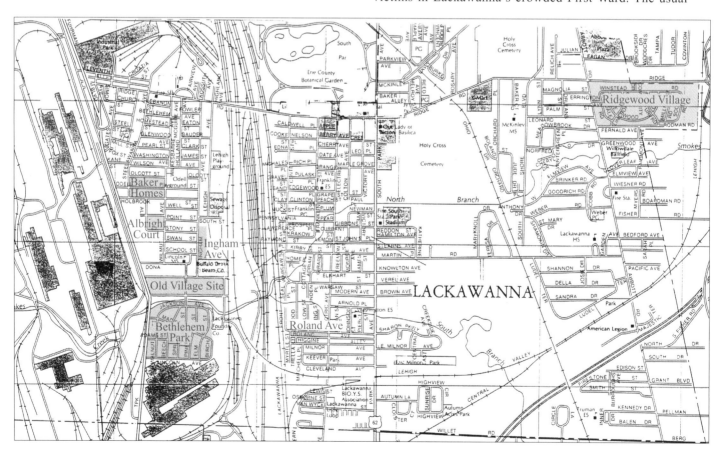

Figure 5.14 Lackawanna showing Italian neighborhoods and public-housing projects in 1945. Source: *Front Page*, 3/17/1993

citywide monthly death toll of 32 increased to 68 during each of the last three months of year. Among the victims were 33-year-old Maria Baldassari of the Old Village and 23-year-old Italia Berarducci of Roland Avenue. Mary Pacillo and other Old Village children wore masks to avoid contracting the disease. The Annex School on Second Street was closed to classes for a month and used as a hospital; bodies were removed at night. Sara Chiacchia watched as mattresses and the clothes of the deceased were burned in the school yard. In 1922, the city's health department, fearing an outbreak of typhoid fever, advised residents to boil tap water before drinking it.[108]

Children were most vulnerable to disease, generally, and many Italian families lost at least one child, often a newborn. City records indicate that the 54 Italian Americans who died in Lackawanna

Luca Tarquinio and sons, circa 1905. From left are Tony, Luca, Luke, C. John, and Leo. Photo source: Bruce Tarquino

between 1911 and 1917 included nine adults, two teens, a two-year-old, and 40 infants. This trend continued into the 1930s, as records at St. Anthony's Church list 83 funeral services for Italian Americans between 1918 and 1935; 31 of the deceased were children, and 36 infants. Surveys in the early 1930s found that Lackawanna had a "high tuberculosis death rate"—in fact, "alarmingly higher than other communities in Western New York"—and this was deduced to be the result of congested housing conditions in the First Ward. Carmine Spagnolo contracted the disease and went to a sanatorium in Perrysberg, New York, for treatment that eventually healed him.[109]

Violence and street crime were present in various forms throughout the city, including in the Italian neighborhoods. Lackawanna had numerous taverns and thousands of immigrant steelworkers to patronize them, a combination that fed into a rough-and-tumble atmosphere. In bars on Ingham Avenue, in Bethlehem Park, and on Roland Avenue, steelworkers and railroad men, many young and energetic, often argued and sometimes came to blows. Since many of them went directly to the bar after work without stopping at home to eat, the wine and beer had an even more dramatic effect. A youthful Angelo Grosso witnessed an example of this heightened effect on Ingham Avenue. "A bunch of Abruzzesi got off their 12-hour shift and came to Tony Amorosi's tavern to play cards and drink wine," said Grosso. "Eventually, they got drunk, especially since they hadn't eaten, tempers rose, and when some guys didn't get to drink during games of boss, fights

would erupt. Chairs would fly as the Abruzzesi fought among themselves, and Tony Amorosi pulled out his nightstick and started cracking heads."[110]

Sometimes the violence escalated into deadly force. As a boy in the first decade of this century, John Fadale witnessed the activities at a tavern on Ingham Avenue run by an Italian immigrant named Pasqualino. Italian ruffians hanging out at the bar tormented any men who walked by, including fellow Italians from Buffalo who were visiting friends or relatives. Pasqualino himself was known to have beaten many men, and one of his victims eventually found revenge by shooting and killing him, then quickly leaving town. In 1917, the *Lackawanna Journal* reported another murder near the same intersection. Antonio Ricci, a 28-year-old laborer, was killed by Vincenzo DiCenzo, who claimed he shot in self-defense after Ricci stabbed him. Four years later, Aniello Carpentieri, an employee of Lackawanna Steel, was murdered when someone struck him in the ribs with a steel wedge. Fred DePaolis, an Italian immigrant who resided on Olcott Street, was convicted of killing two men in Angola in 1941.[111]

The Italian sense of honor sometimes led men to avoid going to the authorities and to personally avenge insults to family honor. When a First Ward man received a deep cut on his head during a confrontation, he refused to give police any information about the incident. In another case, an immigrant learned that the man who had married his sister in Lackawanna also had a wife and children in Italy. He went to his brother-

Marianna Pinto, in chair, with daughters and granddaughters. Standing, from left, are Angeline Cennamo, Anne Fox, Sue Fox, and, at lower right, June Fox.
Photo source: Anne Fox-Skazynski

Vincenza Agliata, left, and Rosabella Fiorella at the Apple Street home of the Agliata family.
Photo source: Sarah Chiacchia-Kempf

FIGURE 5.15

Lackawanna's Italian Population*, By Gender, 1905–1930

Year	Total Italians	Males	(%)	Females	(%)
1905	288	212	(74)	76	(26)
1910	551	402	(73)	149	(27)
1915	766	448	(58)	318	(42)
1920	1,215	723	(60)	492	(40)
1925	1,336	763	(57)	573	(43)
1930	1,902	1,105	(58)	797	(42)

Sources: New York Census, 1905, 1915, 1925; U.S. Census, 1910, 1920, 1930.

*Italian youth living in the Our Lady of Victory institutions are included

in-law's house in the Old Village, confronted the man with this information, and asked if it was true. When the brother-in-law responded in the affirmative, gunplay ensued, and the brother-in-law was killed. A jury found the man not guilty of murder, as he claimed he shot in self-defense.[112]

It was common for men to carry firearms and other weapons, especially in the sometimes hard-nosed environment of the First Ward. Nick Falcone told one man that "everyone carried a gun" early in the twentieth century. This included people living on Ingham Avenue who were often approached by hobos from the nearby railroad tracks. Some of the latter aggressively sought contributions of money or food, and a few were prone to criminal acts. Antonio DePaula, who ran a bakery, kept firearms on the premises. One day, Giuseppina DePaula heard her husband Antonio yelling from the street. She grabbed a gun and went out to discover that two men were attempting to mug Antonio and take the roll of bills he had just collected from customers. She was able to scare the men away before they grabbed the money.[113]

It wasn't only outsiders who posed a danger to Italian families. One day, Caroline DePaula returned from school and entered her parents' bakery to find a scary scene. Angelo Sperduto and Antonio Turchiarelli were having a fierce argument regarding the politics involved in the position of city dog warden. Caroline's mother, Giuseppina, was trying to calm them down when each man drew a gun and threatened to shoot the other. That's when Caroline walked in. Giuseppina begged them not to shoot and told Caroline to flee the building. But the child was confused and instead walked into the middle of the room. Giuseppina's frantic pleading finally caused the two men to lower their weapons and leave the bakery.[114]

Despite the sometimes chaotic and violent events in Lackawanna, Italian families functioned as best they could and struggled for economic survival. To supplement their income both before and during the Depression, many Italian

Adult Male Italian Boarders* by Neighborhood

Neighborhood	1905	1910	1915	1917-18	1920	1925	1930
1st Ward							
Ingham Avenue	53	100	33	138	24	57	49
Old Village	45	26	39	130	88	53	21
Bethlehem Park	—	—	—	—	—	7	40
Other	13	14	0	8	7	0	5
East of Tracks							
Roland Avenue	6	42	9	24	11	7	7
Other	0	0	0	0	2	3	1
Totals:	117	182	81	300	132	127	123

*Not blood relatives of the host family.

There was also one female boarder in both 1915 and 1930.

Sources: U.S. Census, 1910, 1920, 1930; New York Census, 1905, 1915, 1925; World War I Draft Registration Records, 1917-1918

families took in boarders, which was an outgrowth of their traditional values. In Italy, every family member over the age of five had an economic responsibility to help out with farm chores. However, Italians took a dim view of women working outside the home, so any tasks performed my females were allowed only if relatives or neighbors were present to preserve their social honor. These practices continued in American cities, as Virginia Yans-McLaughlin found in her study of Buffalo's Italians, and the same was true in Lackawanna. Italian women and children in both cities worked in family units alongside trusted friends and *paesani* on farms in western New York. In their homes the housewives and older children abetted the family economy by taking care of boarders (see Figure 5.16).[115]

Hosting boarders was a full-time business for some Lackawanna families. Between 1905 and 1915, the city had 18 Italian-run boarding houses or hotels, most on Ingham Avenue. In 12 cases, the proprietors were women. For many families, however, it was a more informal practice, with two to four boarders being typical. In Bethlehem Park, the Andreozzis, a family of eight, took in a series of boarders for 20 years, beginning in the late 1920s. Tony and Jenny shared one bedroom with their youngest child, Tony, Jr. Daughters Dolly and Josie shared another, and the three older boys—Phil, Nick, and Paul—plus any boarders slept in two beds in the master bedroom. The first boarder, a carpenter named Massimino, built a bathroom cabinet for the family that lasted more than 80 years. The next man was John, a baker; when his brother died, the Andreozzis

Antonio Carestio relaxes at his home at 174 Franklin Street, circa 1940. He was one of the handful of Italians who moved out of the Italian neighborhoods in the late 1920s. He moved his family from the Old Village to this neighborhood, where few Italians resided.

Photo source: Dennis Sterlace.

Gladys Yoviene with nieces Joan Williams, on left, and Mary Alice Yoviene, 1929. Josephine Yoviene, who was widowed in 1919, had moved to South Park Avenue with her eight children by 1925. Photo source: Jim Yoviene

Four of the seven Carestio sisters pose on Franklin Street in the 1940s. At top are Assunta, on the left, and Sally, and below them are Mary and Quintina. Photo source: Dennis Sterlace

offered their house for the wake. Then came Paul—who Phil Andreozzi remembers as a quiet, distinguished man—and two brothers from Calabria, Mario and Carlo Cuozzo. Vince Piccirilli, a *paesano* of Tony's, boarded with the family and there met his future wife, Jenny's sister, Rose Limongiello. In 1930, Francesco DeAngelis, another *paesano*, moved in. He stayed in Lackawanna for 18 years, then returned to Lazio.[116]

Giovanni and Nazzarena Schiavi took in six boarders at a time at $8 each a month in their Olcott Street home during the late 1930s. Their daughter Iole helped with cooking, and doing dishes, laundry, and ironing. On Ingham Avenue, the Covino family of eight lived on the second floor of their building; the first floor storefront was rented to a businessman, and the apartment behind that was home to 11 boarders. The three

eldest children—Jay, Carl, and Al—helped with the chores, such as scrubbing floors and making bread and pizza. Not counted as boarders were relatives of the host family (see Figure 5.17). The number of these expanded from 10 in 1910 to 36 in 1930, reflecting the increasing stability of the Italian community, as both individuals and couples decided to settle permanently in the United States and sent for their parents, siblings, in-laws, and other relatives.[117]

While the presence of boarders meant extra family income, it also placed certain strains on the family: extra work, scant privacy, and the potential of a male boarder attempting to seduce the woman of the house or one of the daughters. The fact that many boarders were relatives or *paesani* of their hosts, in combination with Lackawanna's small-town familiarity,

FIGURE 5.17 Male and Female Relatives* Living with Families							
Gender	1905	1910	1915	1917-18	1920	1925	1930
Male	7	6	16	NA	25	27	36
Female	3	1	3	NA	5	5	10
Totals:	10	7	19	—	30	32	46

*The relatives included parents, grandparents, siblings, cousins, nieces, nephews, in-laws, and unspecified relatives.

Sources: U.S. Census, 1910, 1920, 1930; New York Census, 1905, 1915, 1925.

FIGURE 5.18

ITALIANS IMPROVE THEIR PROPERTY

As Italians decided to settle permanently in Lackawanna, they bought homes, made improvements to their houses, added other structures, and, in some cases, purchased more property. Calogero Fadale constructed a woodshed on his original lot in 1910 and purchased three other lots on Ingham Avenue. Pietro and Enrichetta Oddi purchased the home at 219 Ingham Avenue for $2,000 in 1914, and soon afterwards acquired the vacant lot next door. The Oddi house did not have a basement, so Pietro and his 12-year-old son Nunze dug out the cellar by hand. In 1916, Antonio Guadagno erected a frame building at 195 Ingham, and in the following year, Marco and Elisabetta Costanzi built their home at 183 Ingham Avenue. In the Roland Avenue area, Natale Chiodo constructed a two-story addition to his house, and

Santo Mancuso had a store built in the early 1920s.

Between 1920 and 1924, Italian homeowners increased from 44 to 73, and the number of barns they owned jumped from 14 to 47. Most Italian homeowners possessed one or two lots and structures, but several had larger holdings. Antonio and Maria DePaula held the deeds to six properties, Frank Morinello to five, and Charles Fadale to four during the 1910s and early 1920s. John Verel and his mother-in-law, Giuseppina Yoviene, jointly owned 86 lots along South Park Avenue, where Verel started constructing homes in 1922. As homeownership increased, Italians were gradually constructing more structures of various types. During the 1920s and 1930s, many Italians erected toolsheds, barns, and chicken coops. Garages were an indication of homeownership and plans

for purchasing a car. Even during the Depression year of 1930, 13 garages were erected by Italians, most in Bethlehem Park. Some men constructed their own homes, and nine storefronts were put up by Italian merchants in the city in the early 1920s. Aniello and Carmella Covino had a house built on Ingham Avenue in about 1923. A horse-drawn scoop was used to dig the cellar, but when the sides of the hole became too steep to use horses, recalls Albert Covino, the parents and older children finished the excavation with hand shovels. Many of these projects involved friends or relatives who either contributed free labor or, on larger tasks, were paid. When Michele Grasso erected a house on Ingham Avenue in 1925, he was assisted by his son Tony and three hired hands with carpentry skills—Charley Ross, Joe Bernardi, and Sam Ginnetti.

Sources: Interviews with Nunze Oddy, April 12, 1982; Tony Grasso, December 23, 1987; Albert Covino, unpublished, untitled memoirs, no date; City of Lackawanna, Tax Books, Building Permits, 1910–1939.

---

for the most part discouraged inappropriate behavior. There were, however, several unhappy endings. When a husband found his wife in bed with a boarder, the two males scuffled for a gun, and the boarder was shot and killed. Two other accounts describe the woman of the house abandoning her family to run off with a boarder. In one instance, an Ingham Avenue woman left her house saying she was going to the store. Instead, she sneaked off to another city with one of the family's boarders never to return. Her husband and children

were sick with grief, and her brother, furious at the betrayal, tracked her down. Despite his angry demands to return to her family, she remained with her new partner.[118]

The number of Italian boarders in Lackawanna peaked during World War I, dropped by half in 1920, and remained at roughly the same level for the next decade. When immigration was dramatically curtailed in 1924, the number began to dwindle. Then the Great Depression caused lone men and families to travel, looking for jobs. As work fluctuated at the steel plant and on the railroads during the 1930s, many men moved in and out of the Italian neighborhood. As the economy improved in the late 1930s, the number of boarders again dwindled because people were buying homes.[119]

Lackawanna's European American population had become more stable prior to the onset of the Great Depression. Among Italians the ratio of males to females was becoming more even; in 1930, 57 of every 100 Italians were males to 43 females. Among the foreign-born Italians, 63% were male, a reflection of the many lone men who had migrated to the city in the previous three decades. The second generation, which had a more equal gender ratio, now greatly outnumbered the first. Indeed, about a fifth of all the city's

FIGURE 5.19

Lackawanna Italian Families as Homeowners and Renters

Year	Total	Homeowners	Renters
1910	75	14	61
1920	182	44	138
1930	327	145	182

A family is defined as any residence with an Italian listed as family head, or with an Italian wife and non-Italian husband.

Sources: U. S. Census, 1910, 1920, 1930

FIGURE 5.20

ADAPTING TO AMERICAN TECHNOLOGY

Marchegiani males gather around Louie Giuliani and his car on Madison Avenue, late 1920s. The boys on the sidewalk at left are, Alex Filipetti and John Sambuchi. Standing on the far side of the car are, from left, Alfred Campanella (with hat), Albert Tonucci, and _?_ Montanari. Seated in the car are Bruno Santi, Paul Filipetti (in back), Joe Amadori (in hat), and Louie Giuliani, wearing glasses. The boy sitting on the dashboard in the foreground is Norm Samuchi. Photo source: Collection of Jene Amadori

Ingham Avenue at Holbrook Street, circa 1940. Ed Morgan, right, polishes the car as others admire the vehicle which belonged to Mike Giordano. When he went into the military, he entrusted the car to Pete Monaco. From left are: Mike Giordano, [Unk], Ugo Scarsella, Pete Monaco, Concetto Monaco, Charley Nigro (sitting on hood), Ed Morgan, Kenneth Nigro (sitting on hood), and Antonio Giordano. Photo source: Frank and Mary Cuomo

Before leaving Italy, many of the immigrants had never seen, let alone owned, the new machines and gadgets, that would become available to Americans in the first four decades of the twentieth century. Running water, indoor plumbing, electricity, and paved roads weren't part of rural southern Italian towns until the 1930s. Automobiles, telephones, record players, and radios were even more scarce. Tom Ventre recalls only two cars in Settefrati, Lazio, a town of more than 3,200 inhabitants in the 1920s. In the United States, the immigrants encountered these mechanized items in large numbers and had to adjust to them. Indeed, adapting to American technology was a significant part of the assimilation process for immigrants. Italian workmen were often mesmerized by the pneumatic tools and other machinery in the steel plant and on the railroads.

Immigrants who were hard-pressed to save money to send back to Italy, or to finance their family's trip to America, were in no position to purchase an auto. Some of them relied on the streetcar or bus. Many led a lifestyle that focused on work, family, and neighborhood, all reached by foot. Giuseppe Baldassari simply used a bicycle for longer trips.

Eventually, some immigrants and their children started buying motor vehicles. One of the first to do so was Michael Falcone of Roland Avenue, who bought a new motorcycle in 1913. Falcone, however, disapproved of his daughter Camille driving a car in the 1930s, but she drove anyway. In 1918, Mary Fusco, whose parents ran a confectionery store on Hamburg Turnpike, was driving her own car, a 1917 Oakland. Antonio DeSantis owned a motorcycle but never had a car. A small number of Italians possessed cars, but the vehicles were used in vastly different manners. Calogero Fadale used a horse and buggy to get food products

Serafino Mattucci enters his car at his Ingham Avenue home. Photo source: Collection of Tina Mattucci-Ginnetti

Molly Caferro stands near the family car in Bethlehem Park in front of her home at 21 Spruce Street. Photo source: Tony Caferro

in Buffalo to stock his Ingham Avenue grocery store. He did buy an Oldsmobile but apparently decided not to drive it after his son Cosmer smashed a fender in an accident. Fadale went back to the horse and buggy for grocery deliveries, allowing all his sons, except Cosmer to drive the Oldsmobile. Carmine Spagnolo rarely drove his car, which remained a semipermanent fixture on Odell Street. In Bethlehem Park, Luigi Filipetti used his large Buick to drive many family members and other Marchegiani to social events. In the late 1930s, young Al Baldassari was elated when he was allowed to sit next to the gearshift as Luigi transported people to picnics. When, at age five, Baldassari had appendicitis, several of his friends in the Baldelli family convinced the reluctant youth to go to the hospital—to which he was transported, of course, in Filipetti's Buick.

Paolo Filipetti drove his family to picnics and to the cemetery to tend the graves. The car also came in handy for transporting boxes of grapes or 50-pound sacks of flour or sugar to stock the family pantry. Umberto Barbati, a foreman in Bethlehem Steel's Yard Department, was able to buy a Model T Ford.

Tony Deramo was the first Italian in the Old Village to own a car. In 1919, when Tony Andreozzi was boarding with Patsy Ricci's family in the Old Village, the two men bought and shared an automobile. One day, Andreozzi was driving down Hamburg Turnpike when one of the car's narrow tires got stuck in the space between the streetcar rail and the pavement. He was attempting to free the wheel when he saw a streetcar bearing down on him. He jumped up, pulled out his handkerchief, and waved it wildly until the motorman stopped the streetcar. Several people then helped Andreozzi free the car. The exasperated Italian drove the vehicle back to the Old Village and told Patsy Ricci that he could be its sole owner. After this experience Tony Andreozzi said he would never drive a car again, and he kept his word for the remaining 45 years of his life.

Antonio Monaco had his driver's license and owned his own car by 1929. Many of his *paesani* from Cantalupo, Molise, did not have cars, so he was often called on to provide rides. Shortly after moving from Buffalo to Ingham Avenue, he and Tony DiRe drove to Warsaw Street in the Third Ward to visit their friend, Angelo Marracino.

The three men shared a lot of wine, and when it came time to leave, Monaco backed his car down the driveway and right into a tree. The vehicle was wrecked. Fed up with automobiles and transporting people, Antonio Monaco vowed never to drive again, and he didn't.

Italian immigrants who wanted a car often could not afford it, especially during the Depression. But some businessmen had a steady income and were able to save up enough funds. Joe Mazuca worked at his father's grocery store in Bethlehem Park and business was good. The father purchased a Stutz Bearcat for Joe in the late 1920s. Shoemaker Gioacchino Orlando was of more limited means, but in 1934, he bought his first automobile, a 1930 Model A Ford. Tony Grasso in 1924 bought a 1920 Ford touring car for $40. The convertible roof folded down but had many rips in it, and Grasso kept the car only a year.

Certain Italian immigrants had very distinctive driving styles. Serafino Mattucci drove his car very slowly down Ingham Avenue. Eugenio Galante always drove his vehicle down the center of the street, perhaps to maintain a better view of his surroundings.

Adapting *(continued)*

Lavinio Montanari arrived in this country in 1913 and soon learned to drive. He obtained work as a beer-truck driver in 1920 and as a chauffeur for the U.S. Post Office by 1925. Nunze Oddy and Bruno Falbo each had large touring cars and earned money by driving Lackawanna Italians to visit relatives throughout western New York.

Pasquale "Shorty" Tibollo never learned to drive. The grocer relied on his Ukrainian neighbor, John Hraboczak, to drive him to markets in Buffalo to purchase meat and provisions. In Italy, Mario Fanone got around on a bicycle, but soon after his arrival in Lackawanna, he was able to purchase a 1956 Ford Fairlane. Cesare Cardi arrived in the U.S. in 1957. When he moved to Lackawanna two years later, he bought a red Cadillac.

Other Gadgets:

In the early years of the twentieth century, telephones were a luxury beyond the reach of many poor and working-class Italian Americans. Businesspeople whose livelihoods depended on rapid communication were the first to utilize the electronic contraptions. Grocery stores, already popular places to gather and socialize, took on more importance with the arrival of telephones. Often, the local store had the only telephone in an area of several blocks or more. Important messages and emergency calls brought many Italians into the businesses and created additional demands for storekeepers, especially in the case of after-hours emergencies.

Gradually, telephones and other appliances were purchased in greater numbers. Opera and music lovers bought phonograph players. By 1930, a total of 1,529 Lackawanna families, including many Italian homes, had radios. This device brought Italian-language programs, including music and talent contests hosted by Buffalo's Emilino Rica, into the homes of Steel City Italians. Many broadcast programs helped acculturate immigrants and their children by bringing the English language and American folkways directly into the home.

Italian women who for years had washed their families' laundry in the streams of southern Italy were amazed by the washing machine. Speranza Spadoni remained impressed into her old age. She told her granddaughter, "It's a miracle, I can say my rosary while the clothes are being washed."

Mario Cardamone in his customized car, Roland Avenue neighborhood, 1940s.
Photo source: Collection of Frank Chiodo

Mario Fanone polishes his new 1956 Ford Fairlane, Ingham Avenue, circa 1956.
Photo source: Collection of Phil Fanone

Sources: *Lackawanna Journal*, June 5, 1913; Lackawanna Library, vertical file, "People," U.S. Census, 1930. Interviews with Phil Fanone, November 28, 2008; John Barbati, July 9, 1995; Yolanda Monaco-Bracci, July 9, 1996; Tom Ventre, September 23, 1994; Al Baldassari, April, 1994; Audrey Spagnolo-Surgenor, March 29, 1996; Theresa DeSantis-DiBlasi, July 1, 1996; Carol Camillone-Daley, April 3, 1982; Tony Falbo, February 25, 1978; Dewey Montanari, July 15, 1994; Helen Hraboczak-Dankovich, October 24, 1996; Cesare Cardi, April 3, 1997; Patricia Fadale-Pellegrino, July 8, 1996; Tony Grasso, March 24, 1986 and September 20, 1995; Camille Falcone-Schwan, April 5, 1996;

families were headed by individuals born in the United States. Lackawanna had a youthful population in 1930; about half of the inhabitants were 20 years old or younger.[120]

The European immigrants and their children had progressed in the economic sense, also. This is revealed by information in the 1930 census which, while it was gathered several months after the onset of the Depression in October 1929, still reflected the growth during the previous decade. Foreign-born whites in 1930 represented 71% of homeowners in the city. Their second-generation children clocked in at 17%, indicating that Poles, Croatians, Serbs, Italians, and others planned to settle permanently. In the Italian community, 44% of families owned their homes in 1930 (see Figure 5.19). Also, the overall number of properties owned by Italians in the city, both with and without homes or other structures, had increased dramatically, from 48 lots in 1910 to 189 lots in 1929. After 1910, Italians not only purchased more homes and vacant lots, but they improved their houses and added other structures on their properties; from woodsheds, chicken coops, and barns they progressed to tool sheds, garages, houses, and stores.[121]

Making Wine

Una cena senza vino e come un giorno senza sole (A meal without wine is like a day without the sun) – Italian saying.

Given their roots in one of the world's great wine-producing countries, the Italian immigrants tended to love wine. It was a staple of family meals, imparting friendship and community. A basement wine cellar and winepress were part of the good life for immigrants. Wine making, which many immigrants commenced in the 1920s, was another indication that Italians planned on settling permanently in Lackawanna. By that time, many either owned their own homes or rented a dwelling with a basement, as was the case in the Old Village units. In the heyday of Lackawanna's Italian community, boxes of grapes from California as well as upstate New York vineyards were delivered every fall and stacked high on the sidewalks of the city's four Italian neighborhoods. Some men pooled their money and bought 250 crates at a time, discounted, from the Clinton-Bailey market in Buffalo. One way or another, the wine makers purchased their grapes, helped each other haul them home, launched into production, and celebrated with a festive meal. Fathers and sons worked side by side, typically making 30 to 200 gallons a year. While some immigrants engaged in the American custom of guzzling beer or wine at local bars, many followed Italian custom and savored wine during and after dinner at their homes. If they became high or inebriated, it was over a period of time, in the privacy of their homes—perhaps with a few friends and rarely involving raucous behavior.[122]

At first, Gaetano Milano crushed the fruit the old-fashioned way, stomping it in a tub, while his son Joe continuously added pails of grapes. Later, Milano got a winepress with a ratchet, which he shared with his neighbors. Some wine-making setups were elaborate. Domenico Canali bolted his press to the basement floor to provide greater stability when tightening it down on the grapes. His Ingham Avenue neighbor, Antonio Core, did the same, and also dug a three-foot well in the basement floor for storage. Antonio Grossi raised his first floor so the basement could accommodate a press. Luigi Caligiuri and other Italians made their own winepresses, some using gears and assorted metal parts from the steel plant. Many Italian families dug wine cellars under the front porches of their homes.[123]

There were other ways of procuring grapes and making wine that did not involve the laborious process of crushing and pressing the fruit. Giuseppe Pietrocarlo and some of his *paesani* from Giuliano tended a vineyard in Eden owned by two teachers. The Italians harvested the grapes, gave a portion of the produce to the owners, then divided the rest among themselves. Lavinio Montanari was a more modest wine drinker. He transported enough grapes for three gallons of wine to a cider mill in Blossom, New York, where, in exchange for a new filter for the mill, the owner crushed the grapes. This was done under heat so that the color immediately was drawn from the skins. This process was later followed by many an aging wine maker who wanted to avoid the labor of pressing the grapes and tending to the juice-and-mash mixture until the color of the grape skins transferred to the juice.[124]

Some Italians produced other beverages, too. Paolo Filipetti made both green and red anisette, while Luigi Scarsella concocted rum-and-cherry cordials each Christmas. Natale Chiodo produced his own beer, as did Maria Morgan. *Strega*, an almond liqueur, was also brewed in Italian American cellars, and some families made root beer. Italians enjoyed sharing their wine, beer, and other "nectars," and produced large amounts to serve visitors, bottle, and give as gifts. During Prohibition (1920 to 1933), many Italians continued to make wine, and some brewed more potent beverages. A number of families in Bethlehem Park made whiskey, putting up some for sale. On Ingham Avenue, baker Antonio DePaula made beer in his garage until law enforcement agents raided it and smashed the barrels. "I came home from school," states Caroline DePaula-Silvaroli, "[and] heard my father screaming as I'm coming around Mrs. Oddi's house. And there was beer. They were making moonshine and beer in the back of my father's garage. There's beer running into our driveway and on Ingham Avenue." DePaula's neighbor, Serafino Mattucci, sold liquor in bottles imprinted "S. Mattucci, 605 Ingham, Lack."[125]

FIGURE 5.21

MAKING WINE

The first stage of wine making, as initially practiced by Lackawanna's Italian immigrants involved crushing the grapes. In the early years of immigration this step had family members literally walking on grapes in large tubs. Soon, many Italians found the money and space to acquire a crusher—a small wooden bin with a hand-powered handle that turned a roller with square knobs on it. This was placed directly over an open barrel, into which the mash and juice dropped. The pulpy output was allowed to sit for about a week so that the juice could take on the color of the skins. The juice was then drained through a spigot at the bottom of the barrel and placed in other barrels and sealed. The pulpy residue (mash) was subsequently loaded into the round cylinder of the press, a cap was placed on top of it, and the large screw mounted over the cylinder was turned to compress the pulp and extract more juice, which emerged on the tray-like platform at the bottom of the press. Sometimes two or more men were required to turn the screw, each man pushing on a hefty steel bar or piece of wood fit onto the top of the screw (see diagram at right). Sometimes the grape pulp, called *vinacc*, was pressed three separate times to extract every ounce of juice. After the first and second pressing, the solid mass of pulp was broken on the floor with a shovel, then loaded back into the press with some water and sugar for the next effort. The product from the second and third pressings, referred to as *vinello* by the immigrants, was dubbed "jerk wine" by more contemporary wine makers.

The juice was loaded into barrels that were usually sealed with a water tap, allowing air from the fermentation process to escape but preventing outside air from entering the barrel, as this would spoil the wine. Fermentation requires sugar and yeast, and vintners checked the level of each in their juice, adding more as necessary. The wine sat in the barrels for three to six months, until the fermentation process ceased. It was then tapped and transferred to bottles.

Many Lackawanna Italians had wine cellars in their basements, especially under the front porches, where it was cool year-round. Some energetic Italian brewers used all types of fruits and vegetables to make wine, including potatoes, beets, dandelions, cherries, strawberries, and plums. Before moving to Lackawanna, Luigi Caligiuri used elderberries found near his home in Pennsylvania to make wine. Whatever type of wine was produced, it was shared with friends, neighbors, and relatives. At the Lake Erie Italian Club, wine-tasting ceremonies have been held over the years and prizes presented to the members who produced the best homemade vintages.

Western New York is known for its grape vineyards, and many Italian Americans eventually owned good-sized ones. The grape plants native to New York State, such as the Concord, are hardy and can survive cold winters, but have a low sugar content that produces a tart wine. Vintners in the Finger Lakes region developed a process for grafting the sweet California and European grapevines onto the hardy New York State stock. This produced a series of hybrid grapes that were sweeter than native grapes and could endure the cold winters. Many Italian American wine makers now utilize the hybrid varieties.

There have also been mechanical advances in wine making. Hydraulic presses are now available for basement breweries. A commercial process of crushing grapes under heat causes the color of the grape skins to immediately transfer to the juice. This saves much time and labor. Many wine makers, especially senior citizens, simply transport their grapes to a cider mill and leave with a quantity of juice that then can be placed in barrels or five-gallon bottles to age.

Wine presses like the one shown here were present in many cellars of Italian homes in Lackawanna. Often, a home's basement was expanded to the space under the front porch, which was then used to store the wine as it aged.
Illustration by Patricia Murtaugh

Sources: Interviews with Phil Andreozzi, January 30, 2004; and Joe Caligiuri, April 5, 1994.

Merchants had the advantage of buying sugar and other liquor-making ingredients in bulk. On Roland Avenue, the Falcone and Falbo families helped produce moonshine in grocer Santo Mancuso's garage. At times, Mancuso's truck was so laden with sugar it could barely move. Tony Welsh bought two to three truckloads of grapes every fall, made wine in his garage, and sold it. Nearby, Paul Tomaka's lumberyard was also used for making moonshine. This and the Italian enterprises were raided at least once by government agents. Patsy Pitillo had a still in the basement of the family's grocery on Electric Avenue and reportedly ran a speakeasy in the basement of Verel's block factory on South Park Avenue.[126]

Gardens and Livestock

Gardens and livestock were of vital importance to Lackawanna Italian families in the first half of the twentieth century. These two sources of food were essential to a family's economic survival, as was apparent in the comments of people interviewed. "He canned the best eggplant that you'd ever want to taste; with the oil and the garlic," said Anne Scarsella about her father. Luigi Scarsella grew his eggplant on a friend's lot, having no tillable land with the house he rented. Lackawanna Italians used every available bit of city ground to grow vegetables, often the same ones they and their forebears had grown in Italy: eggplant, tomatoes, peppers, potatoes, greens, and more. Plots behind the homes on the east side of Ingham extended all the way to Lehigh Avenue, accommodating the Canalis', DePaulas', and Fiores' large gardens. Antonio DeMillo's garden was on a plot of land he rented from the Pennsylvania Railroad for $1 per year. Swampland west of Ingham, reclaimed by the city in the 1920s, soon filled with Italian vegetables tended by Antonio Monaco, Pietro Gemmati, and others, who first had to clear the debris from the plots. Antonio Melillo's family maintained a huge garden on Holbrook Street. On Sunday mornings in May, his wife and children rushed to get the planting done so they could attend Mass at 7:00 a.m. Garden plots lined the dirt road leading to the pump station at Well Street. Camillo Capasso helped feed his family of 10 by cultivating a garden at this site and two in Woodlawn. By transplanting celery into a sandbox in his basement and storing green tomatoes to ripen in the attic, he provided fresh produce year-round. Adele Filipetti made a mixture of eggplant, garlic, and oil that she stored in crocks. Many Lackawanna Italians spread such a mixture on a cold-cuts sandwich.[127]

Early on, the steel company cleared land for 200 employee-garden plots in Woodlawn. The company plowed the land and for a time installed water pipes with spigots at intervals. In 1917, Italians, many of them from Lackawanna, tended 16 of the plots. Gaetano Milano had a Victory Garden there in 1918. While he was at work, his son Joe's job was to haul water from the pipe and do other chores at the garden. "I went by streetcar and carried a shovel and rake," recalls Joe Milano. "I hated going there; I was embarrassed." Milano sometimes hid the tools in bushes near their garden plot instead. There were no watchmen, and the Milanos' tools as well as vegetables were pilfered. Gaetano Milano gave up the garden after one year, much to Joe's relief.[128]

Some families, such as the Oddis in the Old Village, kept plots both at home and at the Woodlawn site. Benigno and Giselda Oddi and their children walked to their garden in Woodlawn to harvest potatoes and other vegetables. "I can remember the harvest of the potatoes on Columbus Day," recalls Margaret, "because we had the day off from school. It was also my birthday and my brother Don and I would have to go with my mother.... Don would dig up the potatoes, my mother would cull' em, and they'd put them on this blanket where I sat, and I put them in a bushel." When the family moved to South Buffalo, they continued their treks to Woodlawn, sometimes pulling two wagons. They left at 7:00 a.m. on Sunday morning, right after Mass, arriving at the garden site two hours later. As the Italian population in Lackawanna grew during the 1920s, more Italian families tilled gardens in Woodlawn. It was one of many sites in and around Lackawanna where frugal Italians practiced their centuries-old gardening skills.[129]

In Bethlehem Park, Arduino Ceccarelli was an ambitious gardener who had up to four gardens annually in the early 1930s. In addition to the small plot he tended behind his Jackson Avenue home, he had a garden at the Old Village site, one in Woodlawn, and a fourth along Hamburg Turnpike, south of Lincoln Avenue. The steel company allowed families to garden there before the Strip Mill was built in 1935. Marie Ceccarelli remembers planting beans and potatoes at their Woodlawn garden. Her father made a two-wheeled cart that he used to transport manure from the pigs he raised behind his home or from the filtration plant on Lehigh Avenue. The cart was also used to carry produce.[130]

Italian men were usually the main gardeners in the family, but they depended on their wives and children to help out. While Michele Grasso was at work, his son Tony tended to the garden behind their Old Village home. In a few families, women oversaw the garden. Nunzia Orlando, with help from her son Charley, did most of the work on their family's garden in the First Ward. Vincenza Novelli maintained a Victory Garden at her Bethlehem Park home during World War II. After the war she made it into a rock garden and planted flowers. While she did the gardening, her husband Costantino busied himself with many construction and improvement

FIGURE 5.22

GARDENS EVERYWHERE

Bethlehem Park residents Salvatore DiTomasso, Vincent Rosati, and Filiberto Covelli all had gardens at their homes and in Woodlawn. Luigi Caligiuri established a garden in his backyard, two in the Old Village, and one behind the bar mill in Woodlawn, a mile south of his home. Italians also gardened on Bethlehem Steel land just east of Bethlehem Park, between the South Buffalo Railway tracks and the embankment of the elevated Pennsylvania Railroad tracks.

During the 1930s and 1940s, Jimmy Ross had a garden behind his Jackson Avenue house (on the bank of Smokes Creek), a second plot across the creek at the Old Village site, and two in Woodlawn. One of these latter was at the Bethlehem Steel communal site, the other on the east side of the Hamburg Turnpike, on the land of his former neighbor, Paolo Zaccarine. Ross often walked across the railroad tracks to Roland Avenue to visit his son Attilio and his family, then returned to Bethlehem Park with his grandsons Dick and Jim. Dick recalls that his grandfather would load a wagon with his garden tools then have the boys help him pull it to Woodlawn. After working the two plots, they returned to Bethlehem Park with a wagon load of produce.

On Ingham Avenue, Joe Schiavi's backyard garden featured bean plants that were two stories high. Down the street, Tony Marinelli had a large garden alongside his house and also maintained four other gardens in which he produced virtually all the greens needed for the family's meals. Gardens, like homes, came in all sizes. One elderly man known as Zi Gaetan' (Uncle Gaetano) lived in a shack in a field off Holbrook Street where he had a garden and raised chickens and goats.

Sources: Interviews with Gene Covelli, July 17, 1990; Dick Ross, June 29, 1997; Charley Orlando, October 16, 1996; Annette Schiavi-Iafallo, June 7, 2005; Anne Melillo-Corvigno, April 17, 1998.

projects in the house and garage. Roland Avenue Italians had gardens in their backyards and also on vacant land off the foot of that street. "Italians had gardens everywhere," says Frank Sanak, a Polish American who grew up on Roland Avenue. A number of Italians hired a Polish man who used a horse-drawn plow to turn over their garden plots. In between the Erie Railroad tracks (just west of Front Street), and the busy New York Central tracks, there was an open space in which a number of Italian families had gardens. This was railroad property, but the companies did not seem to mind the presence of the garden plots. Luigi Bevilacqua and Giuseppe Nasso had gardens there,

and each year, Molly Nasso canned enough tomatoes and peppers to last through the long winter. John Carroccia got permission from Polish neighbors to plant gardens in their yards, then shared the produce with them.[131]

Angelo Pitillo had a garden near his home on Milnor Avenue, as did the Calzone family. Pitillo also farmed two plots on First Street in Blasdell, on land owned by Our Mother of Good Counsel Church, the home parish for many Roland Avenue Italians. The Chiodo family had a huge garden that extended from the back of their Milnor Avenue home and covered three empty lots. Natale and Maria Chiodo assigned their five children specific chores. "I had to do the tomatoes," recalls Frank Chiodo, "450 tomato plants! I dug the ground, planted them, put in the sticks, tied them up, and weeded them." Grapevines and cherry, apple, and plum trees were scattered throughout the garden. "The plum tree was so full of fruit that we had to hold the branches up with sticks." As if this were not enough, the family had another plot in Woodlawn. Sometimes Louie Morasco, Natale's cousin who rented a room on the second floor, drove them to Woodlawn; otherwise, they walked. Maria Chiodo's sister and brother-in-law, Sue and Joe Fox, owned a garden plot next to the Chiodos'. At times, the whole Fox family made trips from their home near McKinley and South Park Avenue to visit their relatives and work their garden. Often, Joe Fox came to tend the garden with one of his children. His daughter Anne liked accompanying her dad, as she could both spend time with him and get away from housework. Frank Chiodo remembers that all Roland Avenue Italians had gardens, but families of other ethnic groups were less inclined to do so.[132]

The crowded conditions in the First Ward and the presence of so many youth prior to World War II did create challenges for Lackawanna gardeners. Children in the immediate neighborhood, especially those of the same ethnic group, usually had temptation to raid gardens squelched by parental and community pressure. However, teenage boys from other neighborhoods and of different ethnic groups were at times tempted to take some fruit or vegetables from gardens. Fiore Covelli, who lived on Ingham Avenue, used diplomacy in addressing some Polish American boys who took a liking to his grapes. He told the youth that he didn't mind if they ate some of the grapes but asked that they not injure the plants themselves, and the boys honored Covelli's request.[133]

Many gardeners started their seedlings in hot boxes—wooden frames one or two feet high topped with windows, and called a *piantolaro* or *piantata* by some Italians. In Bethlehem Park, Tomassino Mazzucchi lined his hot box with fresh horse manure and covered it with dirt that had been sterilized by burning. During the cold spring months, as early

Maria and Mario Fanone came to the United States in 1955 and rented an apartment above Sperduto's restaurant. Mario then built the grape arbor in the backyard. Photo source: Phil Fanone

Circa 1926. Michele Grasso tends his garden at the family home on Ingham Avenue. This large hoe is similar to the zappa, *the tool of Italian farmers.*
Photo source: Collection of Tony Grasso

Ralph Sterlace tends the garden at his house on Franklin Street, with his wife Assunta and son David, circa 1940.
Photo source: Dennis Sterlace

Josie Cardinale in his garden in the Roland Avenue neighborhood. Photo source: Sam Cardinale

as mid – March, seedlings could grow in the warmth of the sunlight and manure. Pietro Fiore started his seedlings under glass in early spring, at a certain phase of the moon. He asked his daughter Rose to consult a calendar with lunar forecasts and provide the exact date. He and other Ingham Avenue Italians procured fertilizer at the sewage-treatment plant on Lehigh Avenue after the material had dried and been purified by city workers. In Bethlehem Park, Arduino Ceccarelli, Antonio Andreozzi, and Filiberto Covelli each had large *piantate* that were four- to-five feet square and up to two feet high. As the weather became warmer, they opened up the glass top slightly, and in really warm weather, removed the top altogether. When a cold night was predicted, they covered the hot box with old coats. Jimmy Ross and Tomassino Mazzucchi often started plants in their hot boxes for some of their neighbors. Years later Mazzucchi died tragically when his clothes caught fire during the process of burning the dirt to sterilize it. Tony Marinelli not only used his hot box to start seedlings in the spring, but in the fall it was put into service to age celery. He wrapped each celery stalk in newspaper and placed layers of these, separated by dirt, in the hot box. This caused the celery to bleach and become more tender.[134]

A few Italians managed the remarkable feat of growing fig trees that survived the area's harsh winters. In Bethlehem Park, with the onset of winter, Luigi Caligiuri bent his fig tree over, tied it down, and buried it under tarps and dirt. Giuseppe Baldassari dug a trench, bent his tree over into the trench and covered it with leaves and dirt. Each spring, the tree was unearthed and allowed to stand tall and produce small green figs. Jimmy Ross loosened the dirt around the base of his tree so that it could bend more easily. In the spring, he tied it to his neighbor's fence to straighten the trunk. Ross's tree outlived him, surviving into the 1980s. Domenico Cellini had a fig tree along with apple, plum, and sweet and sour cherry trees in his yard on Dona Street. He also had a grape arbor, roses, and lilacs.[135]

The open fields and empty lots of Lackawanna provided Italians with greens. During the late 1910s and early 1920s, Lucia Chiacchia, her children, and her mother plied the fields near the Old Village in search of *cardunni*, a rhubarb-like plant, and *mezzareddu*, a mustard green with yellow flowers, both used in *minestrone*. Colomba Scarsella went to the field on Odell Street to pick *ciccoria* (dandelions) and *cardunni*. "Odell was the prime place to go and she knew exactly when to go before the dogs got there," states her daughter Anne. "The *ciccoria*, she knew … when to go and it was tender, because for the salad you need the inner, tender part. For cooking, you can use the other one." Before the Strip Mill was built there in 1935, many a Bethlehem Park Italian went to the fields south of Lincoln Avenue to pick *ciccoria* and other greens. Paolo and Adele Filipetti picked dandelions wherever they could find them and went to the country to pick mushrooms. As the mushrooms were boiled, a silver quarter was dropped into the pot. If the quarter turned black, the mushrooms were considered poisonous and not eaten.[136]

Alessandro Cardoni tends his garden on Milestrip Road in Woodlawn, 1940s.
Photo source: Emilia Cardoni-Cutre

Several Italians had farms in or near Lackawanna. Sam Monduori works his land on Sheldon Road (near Abbott Road and Southwestern Boulevard) in the 1930s. His sister, Rosa Grasso, lived in Lackawanna's First Ward.
Photo source: Collection of Tony Grasso

Preserving produce was an art in itself. Many families made *conserv'* by sun-drying crushed tomatoes spread on boards. The resulting paste was then put in crocks, covered with oil, and placed in a root cellar in the basement. Lackawanna Italians joked that the *conserv'* also had a little extra "spice" from the ore dust and soot that descended on many parts of the city. The practice of sun-drying tomato paste was discontinued during the 1930s, when efficient home-bottling techniques became available. Some families had a simple, hand-powered gadget that crushed the tomatoes. Colomba Scarsella, however, rapidly sliced up the tomatoes with a knife while her daughter Anne watched in amazement. "You didn't know how she didn't cut her finger," said Anne Scarsella-Antes. Recycled soda-pop bottles that had been collected throughout the year were filled with the finely cut or crushed tomatoes. Children poured the semifluid mixture into the bottles forcing the solid pieces down the narrow neck using a small wooden dowel. A contraption that looked like a car's jack stand was then used to seal each bottle with a metal cap. Maria Morgan and her children canned 30 bushels of tomatoes every fall in this manner. Collectively, Lackawanna Italian families must have prepared thousands of such bottles. Throughout the year, the crushed tomatoes were used to make tomato sauce. Many families bottled tomatoes, corn, beans, fried peppers with tomatoes, and prepared pickles. Most families stored the jars and crocks in the basement. The DePaula family did not have a basement in their home, so the *conserv'*, bottled goods, and some items needed for their bakery were stored in a hole in the backyard that was covered and had a door and steps as an entryway. The family referred to this cellar as *la puzz'* (the stink).[137]

Next to his garden plots on Holbrook Street, Antonio Monaco had a shack for two goats, a pig, and several chickens. "Nobody bothered them," recalls Yolanda Monaco-Bracci. Monaco sold goats' milk, and one customer, an African American man suffering from an ulcer, purchased a quart of the milk from him for $1 daily. Monaco butchered baby goats for Easter, and each fall he, his wife, and several *paesani* slaughtered a pig at the shack. Many Italians kept livestock in their yards. When the Milano family lived at 227 Ingham, their backyard adjoined the Roosevelt School lawn. To feed the goat, the oldest child, Joe, led it through a loosened board in the fence to the school lawn, pounded a stake in the ground, and tethered the goat. When the animal had nibbled the grass within reach, Milano led the goat to some fresh grass and pounded in the stake again. "The school janitor never objected," Milano observed. Both he and his mother, Maria, milked the goat, and she made ricotta cheese from its milk. The Milanos also raised chickens that were prized for their eggs. Occasionally, Maria slaughtered one of the egg-producing chickens for a family

Giovanna Fanone, Peter Fiore, and Mario Fanone look over Mario's garden on the Ingham Avenue plot he rented. He and a friend later shared an even larger garden.
Photo source: Phil Fanone

meal. When it proved difficult for the children to feed the animals regularly, and the fowl didn't lay eggs reliably, Maria got rid of them.[138]

Antonio Giordano had six or seven goats in the backyard of his Ingham Avenue home. "They used to break away," recalls Patsy Giordano, "and eat Father Vifredo's flowers." In one instance, when Patsy ran to the rectory to retrieve the livestock, an angry Reverend Vifredo grabbed him by the ear and scolded him. The goats also got the young Giordano into other trouble. "The billy goat saw a Russian woman wearing a heavy fur coat. He got excited, broke free of the rope, and chased her up Lehigh. The goat nudged her with his nose and tried to mount her. I finally got the goat; the woman yelled in Russian and hit me and the goat with her purse." Goats' milk was prized by many Italians for its curative effects; sick people were often given a warmed cup of goats' milk to drink. Many Italians considered baby goat a delicacy and served it for their Easter meal. This was true for Augusta Anticoli and many other Giulianesi who purchased baby goats from a farmer in Springville if none were available from neighbors in Bethlehem Park. Giulio Maturani, who lived next door to the Anticolis, often raised goats and sold them to families at Easter time. Pat Bonitatibus sadly remembers that each spring Maturani brought

Goats of the Scarlotta family graze along Wilson Street near Holland Avenue, 1926. Many Italians believed that goats' milk helped cure illnesses.
Photo source: Collection of Tony Grasso

FIGURE 5.23

URBAN LIVESTOCK

The Giordano family made *casa ricotta* (house or basket cheese) from goats' milk and sold both the cheese and the milk. The Scarlotta family raised goats in the field at Holland Avenue and Wilson Street. Francesco Canali went to this family to purchase young, milk-fed goats to be used for important meals. Aniello Covino raised a pig each year, as well as rabbits, and a goat for its milk. The goats' milk was given to sick children who could not digest cows' milk.

Antonio DePaula's barn housed pigs and chickens as well as two horses used to pull his bakery delivery wagon. His five children took turns feeding the animals and pitching the hay. During the early 1930s, Leo Covelli raised rabbits in his parents' garage and sold them as they matured. Paolo Filipetti raised both chickens and rabbits, and his family regularly ate the meat from the animals he slaughtered in their backyard.

In his enclosed front porch, Arduino Ceccarelli installed wire bins that held up to 24 chickens. Later, he maintained a smaller flock of chickens, along with some rabbits, in his garage. Behind the garage, along the banks of Smokes Creek, the Ceccarellis kept one or two pigs. Santo and Donata Bonitatibus raised chickens in their backyard following their move to Bethlehem Park in 1941. Other Italian families raised pigs and had chicken coops in their backyards, near their gardens. The chickens not only provided eggs but also the main course for occasional meals.

Sources: Interviews with Pat Bonitatibus, July 6, 1995; Pat Giordano, July 3, 1996; Caroline DePaula-Silveroli, October 13, 1996; Marie Ceccarelli-Rosati, July 8, 1996; Albert Covino, unpublished, untitled memoir, n. d.

Maddalena Iafallo feeds geese at her Verel Street home, circa 1938. Italians and people of other ethnic groups in Lackawanna raised goats, pigs, chickens, and rabbits— even in the crowded neighborhoods of the First Ward.
Photo source: Collection of Tony Grasso

a baby goat to his parents' home. The goat, perhaps sensing its fate, cried continually. The young Bonitatibus couldn't bear it, so he went to Wicky's Candy Store for two hours until the goat had been dispatched.[139]

In a communal effort reminiscent of Italy, families who owned pigs helped each other slaughter and prepare the meat. Every spring, just prior to Easter, Tony Giordano slaughtered two pigs. With four friends holding a pig, Giordano first stunned the animal by hitting its head with a sledgehammer, then slit its throat. Blood sausage, or *sanquinacc'*, was made and the heart, lungs, and other organs were cut up and fried with pickled peppers. Tomassino Mazzucchi was the "official" pig slaughterer for a number of Bethlehem Park Italians, working free of charge. He used a stake to puncture the pig's heart: sometimes he botched the job and a squealing animal ran off through the yards of Bethlehem Park, pursued by a group of shouting Italians. After the pig was dispatched, the neighbors worked together to place it on a wooden platform, pour boiling water over the body to disinfect it, hang the carcass on a hook, and dismember it. Every part of the pig was utilized for food or

Olcott Street, circa 1939. Paul Guadagno, left, and Peter Schiavi sit next to the garden behind the Schiavi House. This view, toward the northwest, shows the steel plant in the background. Photo source: Iole Schiavi-Murray

other purposes. The densest internal fat was used for lard, while other fats were boiled to make soap.[140]

On Elm Street, brothers Alfredo and Biagio Anticoli bought a pig each year and slaughtered it, just as they had done in Giuliano di Roma. Rose Anticoli remembers that when her father and uncle got the pig into the basement, they got drunk and rode the animal like cowboys prior to putting it to death. They made sausage and some *prosciutto*, drying it in Alfredo's attic. He also had chickens and a nanny goat in his yard. A few blocks away on Pine Street, Paolo and Adele Filipetti made *prosciutto*, *capocola*, and *lonza*, a fennel-flavored Marchegian' sausage, which were hung to dry in their combination wine and fruit cellar. On Ingham Avenue, an annual event for the Covino family was the slaughtering of their pig, which had usually grown to weigh 200 to 250 pounds, in the late fall. Albert Covino described this process in his memoirs:

> The pork was cured by a salting process up in the attic
> area above the second floor flats during the winter months.
> We left the windows partially open because there were no
> freezers as we have them today. The pig provided many
> kinds of meat, especially delicious homemade sausage. The
> small and large intestines were taken out of the pig, then

1989. Phil Andreozzi, the author's father, ties tomato plants to wooden stakes in his garden. He grew up in Bethlehem Park and settled with his family in the house he built on Berg Road with the help of relatives.
Photo source: Robert L. Smith, *Buffalo News*

Maria Fanone making pasta in her Ingham Avenue home, late 1950s. Photo source: Phil Fanone

drained, washed and soaked to clean them thoroughly. Filling the intestines with air enabled us to find the best sections for the sausage. Pork … was sliced into small pieces, ground up, mixed with flavorings, and stuffed into smaller sections of the pig's intestines. Six to eight inch lengths were tied off and the sausage was hung in the attic for curing. The larger section of the intestine was used to make blood sausage. All the pig's blood was saved and processed … [and] ingredients [of] … rice, spices, and organ meats ground up. After stuffing, these firm sausages were hung in the attic next to the other curing meats. When cured and aged, they were very good for sandwich making all year long!

Many Italian immigrants believed that only in America could they afford to eat meat on more than an occasional basis. Then came the Depression, and once again a complete diet became a luxury.[141]

Italian Food

During the 1920s and 1930s, the DePaula family, like many others in Lackawanna, ate mostly macaroni (the generic name for pasta at that time), *pasta-fasule* (pasta and beans in a thin sauce), and greens. Many Italian women and girls often worked long hours to produce homemade macaroni for Sunday feasts, holidays, and special events. For other meals, pasta was purchased in large boxes at Italian groceries and import stores; some Italians referred to this as "bought-made pasta" to distinguish it from homemade. *Acini de pepe*, or pastina, was one of many types of pasta consumed in Italian homes. Ravioli also came in many

versions and sizes. Some Italians stuffed them with only ricotta cheese, others with both cheese and meat. People from Pettorano combined mashed chickpeas, nuts, and nutmeg in a ravioli dish they called *ceci di ripina*. The Spagnolos often ate pasta or chicken soup. Another staple was a thick stew Calabrese families called *minestra*, made of many vegetables and greens as well as pasta and meat, if these were available. Gelsomina Covelli prepared macaroni at least twice a week. Her son Larry loved the homemade noodles and sauce, sometimes accompanied by meatballs, spare ribs, or hard-boiled eggs. While pasta (macaroni) was a common staple, the tomato sauces of different regions in Italy varied from sweet to hot and spicy, with some regional groups preparing a sauce of oil and anchovies or other fish. The Calabresi preferred spicy *sopressata* sausage, while the Marchegiani usually favored a milder *lonza* sausage but also prepared a spicy *porchetta* pork roll. For meatless meals on Fridays, natives of Lazio, such as Maria Ricci and Colomba Scarsella, prepared snails covered with sauce. "No one ate sliced bread," said Phil and Adeline Andreozzi. "This was called 'American bread' and was only for 'rich' people."[142]

Families avoided wasting food. For breakfast, Tony Andreozzi often put stale bread in a bowl, covered it with coffee, and drank the mixture. When Jenny Andreozzi cooked a chicken, she used every part of the bird, claiming that the feet and eyes that appeared in her chicken soup were enjoyed by her husband, Tony. During the Depression, many Italian families received relief from the county government in the form of clothes and food staples—such as flour, canned milk, oatmeal, and cornmeal, the last of which some families made into *polenta*, a cornmeal mush covered with tomato sauce.[143]

Christmas called for special foods according to regional traditions. On Christmas Eve, families from most parts of Italy had meatless dinners that included various types of fish. The Sambuchi family and others from the Marche region had fried smelt and a *brodetto* made of squid, shrimp, and *merluzzi* (a white fish) cooked in a tomato sauce and eaten with bread. The family of Charles Barone followed Sicilian custom, dining on seven types of fish: *calamari* (squid), *baccala* (dried and treated cod), octopus, haddock, perch, shrimp, and smelt. Angelina Spagnolo prepared *baccala*, eel, and other fish. Giuseppe and Ada Pietrocarlo, natives of Giuliano, had seafood dinners on Christmas and New Year's Day that included potatoes, greens, and stuffed eels. Chet Catuzza, whose parents were Giulianesi, recalls that the family fasted on Christmas Eve, attended midnight Mass at St. Anthony's Church, then gathered with relatives at 1:00 a.m. for a feast that included both fish and meat dishes. Augusta Anticoli prepared the same Christmas treats in Lackawanna that she had known in Giuliano. On Christmas Eve, the family ate *baccala*, *lupini* (treated

Maria Cellini, left, and her daughter Nazzarena Schiavi in the kitchen of the Schiavi's home, 158 Olcott Street, 1959.
Photo source: Iole Schiavi-Murray

Basement of the Schiavi home, circa 1952, preparing tomatoes. From the left are Nazzareno Schiavi; behind her is John Schiavi (a cousin), Dominic Cellini, John Schiavi (Nazzarena's husband), Iole Schiavi-Murray holding her son Rob, Paolo Liberta, and Bombina Liberta. Photo source: Iole Schiavi-Murray

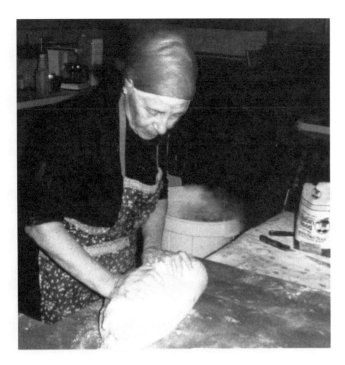

Adeline Andreozzi kneading dough for Easter bread in her Berg Road home, 1996. Photo source: the author

yellow flat beans), and roasted chestnuts. Josephine Ferrelli prepared eels, *baccala*, other fish, and turkey. The Scarsella family, with roots in Ceccano, Lazio, ate eels and *baccala* on Christmas Eve, while the Cardinale family, from another province in Lazio, had fish on Christmas Eve and homemade pasta on Christmas Day. Rosina Caligiuri, a native of Calabria, made squid and *baccala* with cabbage.[144]

A seemingly endless variety of sweets for Christmas and other occasions was prepared in kitchens throughout Lackawanna. The Giulianesi made *ciammele* sweet rolls, *molarri* (fried bread dough covered with sugar and honey), and *gnucchetti*, small-fried potato dumplings covered with honey. Immigrants from Ceccano made *ciammallone* sweet bread, flavored with anisette and dried fruits, and bow-shaped cookies. On Christmas morning, their tradition was to eat *pizza fritt'*, deep-fried balls of dough with raisins and sugar. The Cardinale family had their own version of fried sweet dough called *zeppole*. For Pettoranesi, there was *crispelli*, donuts of fried potato and flour with salt on top, and *crostolla*, fried bread dough with rosemary and powdered sugar. Many Abruzzesi made *pizzelle*, sweet wafers baked in metal molds and sprinkled with powdered sugar. The Siciliani favored cannoli and *cuccidaddi* fig cookies. The Caligiuri family and other Calabresi made a sweet roll with nuts and honey called *pintachiusa*. Another group of Calabresi from Marano Principato and Marano Marchesato made several deep-fried treats. Bread dough in flat shapes, *vecchiareddi*, or donut-shaped, *cuddieddi*, was browned in oil, then covered with honey or powdered sugar. Of the sweet dough variety were

turdiddri, which was spiked with homemade wine, and *scaliddre*; both were soaked in honey. Many Italians bought boxes of *torrone* nougat candy at import stores.[145]

Other seasons of the year called for special foods. For the pre – Lent, or Carnevale, period, people from Lenola, Lazio, baked *struffoli*, round loaves of bread sweetened with sugar. Marchegiani prepared *castagnioli*, made of sweet dough, flavored with anise and lemon, fried in oil, and sprinkled with sugar. For Easter, people of this region enjoyed *crescia*, a loaf of bread consisting of eggs, black pepper, and grated cheese. As mentioned earlier, many families, especially the Giulianesi, ate baby goat for Easter. There were several types of Easter bread. People from Ceccano and Pettorano made *panettone*, with the former group including a hard-boiled egg in the recipe, while the latter did not. The Pettoranesi also prepared *fiattone*, a pastry filled with orange rinds and ricotta cheese; *cioffre*, deep-fried, flaky ribbons of dough sprinkled with sugar; and another type of fried dough, *cresscia*, that was seasoned with salt. On St. Lucy's day, December 13, some families prepared polenta with tomato sauce to celebrate the feast, but Gelsomina Covelli followed Calabrese custom and made *cuccia*, a vegetable porridge of chickpeas, white beans, barley, and lentils.[146]

The traditional foods, gardens, wine making and other customs of Italy flourished in Lackawanna's Italian neighborhoods. Immigrants and their children both maintained Italian values and adapted American ways as the assimilation process took place on Ingham Avenue and Roland Avenue, in the Old Village

Andreozzi home, 1996. Loaves of Easter bread cooling off after being removed from the oven. Each loaf held a hard-boiled egg at one end. The final step was a thin coat of icing. Photo source: the author

up to its demise in 1930, and in the new Bethlehem Park development after its completion in 1925. The era of the lone Italian male immigrant living in a shanty town and migrating to other sites in America, or returning to Italy, gave way to the reunification of families and their permanent settlement in Lackawanna. After 1930, the three Italian enclaves continued to maintain their ethnic flavor, especially on Ingham Avenue and in Bethlehem Park, where St. Anthony's Church in the former and a statue of Columbus and a bocce court in the latter were physical symbols of Italian roots. Home ownership grew as did families, and Italian dialects interspersed with English could be heard on the streets of Bethlehem Park and along Ingham and Roland avenues.

After the razing of the Old Village in 1930, the remaining three Italian enclaves stayed strong into the 1960s, when the gradual process of moving to new locations, begun four decades earlier, surged into an exodus to new housing tracts in the eastern portion of the city and nearby suburbs. In the first six decades of the twentieth century the ethnic neighborhood was one of many social forces that shaped the lives of the first and second generations and influenced the ethnic identity of many third generation Italian Americans. One of the key institutions in these communities was church and its affiliated religious rituals, both of which are examined in detail in the next chapter.

Family gatherings at the Andreozzi home often saw 15-20 relatives gathered in the dining room. Homemade ravioli, sauce, and wine await the family on Christmas Eve 1999.
Photo source: the author

September 2000. Homemade ravioli filled with ricotta and Romano cheese were a favorite of the Andreozzis. Meatballs, roasted peppers, salad, and homemade wine rounded out the meal.
Photo source: the author

CHAPTER 6

ITALIAN RELIGIOUS LIFE

Lackawanna's Italian Roman Catholic church began in 1917 when a mission was established in a rented, one-story building on Ingham Avenue near the corner of Holbrook. The building had formerly been the location of a poolroom, and, prior to that, a horse stable and a fish store. The first altar was constructed of empty spaghetti boxes covered with a cloth.

Early Italian arrivals in the steel-plant district of West Seneca had to travel to Buffalo to attend an Italian church. St. Anthony's Church, located just west of Buffalo's city hall, became the first Italian church in the Buffalo area when it opened in 1891. It was staffed by priests of the Scalabrinian Order, created in Italy to minister to Italians living abroad. The priests were soon traveling throughout western New York to celebrate Mass to Italian farm workers, perform baptisms, and celebrate the feasts of patron saints in Farnham, Fredonia, and Chautauqua. Occasionally, they made Sunday visits to Lackawanna to offer Mass, although it is not known where this occurred.[1]

Steel City Italians traveled to St. Anthony's for baptisms, weddings, funerals, and holiday Masses in their native language. In September 1903, Pietro and Enrichetta Oddi took their infant son Nunzio to be baptized there. When Our Lady of Mount Carmel Church opened in 1906 in the Hooks neighborhood, half a mile south of St. Anthony's, some Lackawanna families journeyed there for important occasions. Aniello and Carmela Covino's eldest child, Giustina, was baptized there in 1915. But for many Italians, the journey was too far and expensive. They instead attended the St. Charles Church, which was built in 1903 on Ridge Road, just east of the steel plant. While many Irish

< Reverend Joseph Vifredo celebrating wedding Mass at St. Anthony's Church, circa 1940. The church was built in 1917 and was replaced by the current structure in 1964. Photo source: Collection of Mike Morgan

families from the New Village attended the church, it was not strictly aligned with one ethnic group, as it was situated in the midst of thousands of immigrants from dozens of countries.[2]

Italians went to St. Charles Church for baptisms and funerals, if only because it was so close. One hundred and three Italian infants were baptized at the church between 1904 and early 1917, and it was the site of the funeral service for Giovanni Sambuchi in 1913. Only one Italian couple was married at St. Charles during this same period, however, as it appears that Italians wanted their wedding Mass said in their native language. When a number of Italians settled in South Buffalo to work on the nearby railroads and at New York Steel (later Republic Steel), a new Catholic parish was established at the corner of Germania and Mystic streets. Built in 1909, the Church of Anime Sante (literally Holy Souls, but translated as All Souls) had an Italian pastor, Reverend Antonio Clemente, and was located just two miles north of Lackawanna's Ridge Road. Since it was much closer than the other Italian churches in Buffalo, it soon drew Italians from the Steel City. On July 9, 1909, Domenico and Maria Mariotti took their infant son Pietro to the church to be baptized. Reverend Clemente baptized five children from Lackawanna Italian families in 1910, and in each of the following five years, he performed this sacrament for 10 to 19 more. Beginning with the marriage of Dominick Marinelli and Margaret Ginnetti in 1910, a number of Lackawanna Italians took their vows at All Souls. It is likely that Clemente also started visiting Italian homes in Lackawanna.[3]

The funeral of Giovanni Sambuchi at St. Charles Church, August 1913. Built in 1903 on Ridge Road, just east of Hamburg Turnpike, it was the only Roman Catholic church in the First Ward until 1910, when St. Hyacinth's, a Polish church, was constructed. By 1917, other churches had been founded, to serve the Croatian, Hungarian, and Italian communities. While largely Irish, St. Charles had a multiethnic congregation. Photo source: Ed Sambuchi

The Founding of a Parish

The origins of Lackawanna's own Italian Roman Catholic mission and church are obscure. According to several accounts, a group of Lackawanna Italians approached Bishop Dennis Dougherty of Buffalo in 1916 or early 1917, asking that a church be established in their community. This group probably included Gaetano Milano, Tony Amorosi, Angelo Sperduto, Serafino Mattucci, Angelo Carlini, Pietro Oddi, Antonio Grossi, and Emidio Zaccagnini. According to Angelo Grosso (he changed his last name from Grossi), the group met at Roosevelt School to discuss the idea of forming a parish and later canvassed Italian homes to raise money. A mission was established in a rented, one-story building on Ingham Avenue near the corner of Holbrook. The building had formerly been the location of a poolroom, and, prior to that, a horse stable and a fish store.

In the tiny mission hall—measuring approximately 25 feet by 30 feet—folding chairs were set up for parishioners. The first altar was constructed of empty spaghetti boxes covered with a cloth made by Enrichetta Oddi and Virginia Melillo. This altar was later replaced by a standard wooden one.[4]

According to church history, in June 1917, Reverend John Boland, then assistant pastor at St. Bridget's in Buffalo, was appointed rector of the Lackawanna mission, and was replaced by Reverend Clemente within a month. Elizabeth Rosati and Joe Milano, however, recalled that Clemente was the original pastor. Milano believed that Clemente was replaced by Boland, then brought back to the mission when Boland was given another assignment. In either case, it is known that on June 6, 1917, Reverend Boland was directed to establish a church to serve Steel City Italians. He said the first Mass on June

17. An Irish American from Buffalo, Boland was fluent in Italian and offered Masses in that language. A number of Boland's former parishioners from St. Bridget's visited him one Sunday at the Ingham Avenue mission to congratulate him on his appointment as rector of the newly created Italian parish. However, Boland's stay in Lackawanna lasted only a few weeks; on July 11, 1917, he was appointed the new pastor of St. Lucy's Church in Buffalo's near-eastside Italian community. Reverend Clemente left All Souls Church that same month, found living quarters on Hamburg Turnpike in Lackawanna, and began offering Masses at the Ingham Avenue mission on Sunday, July 15. At some point, that year one of the priests took a census of the Italians living in Lackawanna and found 150 families in the city.[5]

Both Boland and Clemente were assisted by altar boys Joe and Jerry Pacillo, Joe Milano, Nunze Oddy, Tom Pepper, and Angelo Grosso. The boys helped clean the mission on Saturdays, after which the priest treated them to dinner. Also helping to maintain and clean the chapel were Donata Monaco, Nicolina Grossi, Maria Giuseppa Milano, and Caterina Pacillo. Most of the worshipers were elderly women, but enough male wage earners were involved to ensure the success of the Italian mission. Nunze Oddy recalled that "the chapel was packed and everyone donated money."[6]

Clemente and a committee of parishioners, most notably Angelo Sperduto and Antonio Amorosi, visited all Italian breadwinners in the city seeking contributions to build a new church. Any person making a $25 pledge was considered a founder of the new parish. They raised $2,500 and in the summer of 1917 purchased five lots at the corner of Ingham and South avenues. Reverend Clemente obtained a building permit on October 13, 1917, for a "temporary one story building … at the foot of Ingham," and continued raising money to finance both the structure and its furnishings. The bishop of the Buffalo diocese procured a contractor, and construction began on a wooden-frame building designed to seat 300. Men of the parish, including Antonio DiMillo, assisted in the project. Nunze Oddy remembered that Brother Laglori, a non – Italian cleric, helped Clemente gather money for the church windows and interior. For $25, a sponsor could purchase a window made of inlaid, leaded, and colored glass; Gaetano and Maria Giuseppa Milano purchased one of these.[7]

Work on the new church edifice and attached house was completed that winter at a cost of $1,200. The name St. Anthony was chosen, perhaps, as had been the case with St. Anthony's in Buffalo 26 years earlier, to avoid squabbles over which of many local patron saints should be the namesake. The Church of St. Anthony of Padua was formally dedicated on Sunday, December 16, 1917. Prior to the High Mass at 10:30 a.m., the

St. Anthony of Padua.

Lake Erie Cooperative Society (today called the Lake Erie Italian Club), bearing American and Italian flags, marched in a procession to the site. Bishop Dougherty blessed the building, and the Mass was celebrated by Reverend H. Gerlack, assisted by Reverend Leo Medic, pastor of the city's Croatian church, and Reverend Joseph Vifredo. The bishop gave a sermon in English, which was translated by Reverend Clemente, who also served as master of ceremonies. The new church soon had its first trustees—Calogero Fadale and Antonio Guadagno—and a bell. Antonio Amorosi, Serafino Mattucci, and other men raised $600 to purchase the bell. "They wanted a 'godmother' and 'godfather,'" Nunze Oddy recalled, "to christen the bell; each would pay. They had an auction and started bidding—$5, $10, $100—until they got to $300" contributed from each prospective godparent. Giovanni Battista Felici, a native of Giuliano di Roma, was the high bidder and became the *compare*, or godfather, and Marietta Risio-Marinelli of Cocullo was named the *comare*, or godmother. The bell was blessed by Monsignor Nelson Baker in 1919.[8]

In July 1918, Clemente was suddenly transferred from St. Anthony's, and rumors circulated in the Italian community about the cause of the transfer. About Reverend Clemente and Brother Laglori, Nunze Oddy heard that "on the side, they built and sold homes outside of Lackawanna." Joe Milano was told that Clemente "was removed" because of "something to

Figure 6.1

EARLY PASTORS AT ST. ANTHONY'S MISSION AND CHURCH

Photo source: Catholic Center of Buffalo

Photo source: *Corriere Italiano*, 8/25/08

Photo source: Archives of the Detroit Diocese

Rev. John P. Boland (1888-1968), an Irish American, had studied at a seminary in Rome and was fluent in Italian. Ordained in 1911, he was an assistant pastor at St. Joseph's New cathedral and St. Bridget's in Buffalo, then was transferred to St. Anthony's mission in 1917. He was there only a month before he was appointed pastor of St. Lucy's, an Italian parish in Buffalo. He later became a monsignor and served at St. Thomas Aquinas Church in Buffalo. Rev. Boland wrote a prayer book in Italian for working men, taught at the labor college of the Buffalo Diocese, and gained wide recognition as a labor negotiator. He was vice president of the Catholic Industrial Conference of America, and by 1941 was chairman of the New York State Labor Relations Board. After World War II, he was an administrator of the National Recovery Relief Association in Italy, Greece, and the Balkan states. Rev. Boland was the principal speaker at the 1948 testimonial banquet for Rev. Thomas Ciolino, the new pastor at St. Anthony's after Rev. Joseph Vifredo's long tenure.

Rev. Antonio Clemente was born in Bugnara, Abruzzo, in 1881. He became a priest and completed training to be a high school teacher. In 1907, he earned a degree in letters and philosophy from the University of Rome. Coming to the United States in early 1908, he quickly acclimated himself to his new surroundings and was appointed pastor of a new Italian church in South Buffalo, *Anima Sante*, which later became St. Agatha's parish. He served as pastor of St. Anthony's Mission and Church in Lackawanna from July 1917 to August 1918, then was sent to Portville in Cattaraugus County to serve as rector of Sacred Heart Church. By 1922, he was in Hulberton, New York, where he was rector of St. Roche, an Italian church. He continued to live in that area until 1929, when he apparently passed away or returned to Italy.

Rev. Raffaele D'Alfonso was born in 1882 in Campobasso, Molise. He immigrated to the United States in 1914, served in a parish in New Haven, Connecticut, and arrived in Lackawanna in August 1918. After five months at St. Anthony's Church, he moved on to Kansas City, Missouri, then to Boston. By 1925, he was pastor of St. Joseph's, an Italian parish in Detroit. He became very ill in 1935, resigned his pastorate, and returned to Italy, where he died in 1940.

Sources: *Steel City Press*, 8/25/48; *Il Corriere Italiano*, 11/14/1908; *Official Catholic Directory*, 1916–1935; U.S. Census, 1910; World War I Draft Registration Records; "Silver Jubilee of St. Joseph's Church, Detroit Diocese" booklet, 1948; "A Living Edifice to God: St. Anthony and His Parish, Past, Present, Future," booklet, 1964.

The bell installed in the original St. Anthony's Church in 1917, when Rev. D'Alfonso was pastor. The bell is still kept on the church grounds. Photo source: Paul Pasquarello

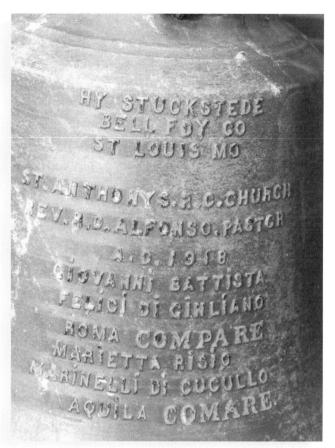

Close-up of the church bell, which was made in St. Louis and had its own godparents: Giovanni Battista Felici of Giuliano, in Roma province (which became part of Frosinone province in the 1920s), godfather, and Marietta Risio-Marinelli of Cocullo, in Aquila province, godmother. Photo source: Paul Pasquarello

do with finances" and the "construction of a church on Steelawanna [Avenue]." In fact, available records indicate that in 1917 the Catholic Diocese gave permission to Reverend Boehm to organize a Hungarian church in Lackawanna, and in June 1918, he in turn authorized Clemente "to seek bids and to close the contract for the building of a church." Clemente was issued a building permit on July 1 to erect a "one story frame building for a church" on Steelawanna Avenue that had the same dimensions as St. Anthony's. This became the Assumption Magyar Church, and Clemente apparently had a major role in beginning its construction. Whatever the reason, Clemente was transferred to Portville, New York in July of 1918.[9]

Reverend Raffaele D'Alfonso, a priest sponsored by the Scalabrinian Order, succeeded Clemente at St. Anthony's. Described as an "excellent preacher" by his successor, D'Alfonso was popular with his parishioners, according to Joe Milano, who had become an altar boy in 1917. At a parish meeting, Milano recalled, the priest explained that "he was like a missionary; he was just there to organize the parish." Under the leadership of Clemente and then D'Alfonso, St. Anthony's became a busy parish. The church's records list complete data

starting only in August 1918, but during the last six months of 1918, nine funeral services and 27 baptisms took place there. The first baptism that took place at the mission church was recorded on August 26, 1917. It was for Brigida Ginnetti, the infant daughter of Salvatore and Adelina Ginnetti; Vincenzo and Carmella Suffoletto were the godparents. The first wedding occurred on September 1, 1918, when Domenico Antonio Marinelli and Marietta Risio took their vows. The initial funeral service took place on August 6, 1918, for Francesco Monaco, a native of Pettorano sul Gizio. In December 1918, only six months after his arrival, Rev. D'Alfonso left St. Anthony's for a post in Kansas City, Missouri. It is possible that he, and perhaps Reverend Clemente before him, had been intended as short-term fill-ins as the diocese searched for a permanent pastor. That pastor was Reverend Joseph Vifredo, appointed on December 5, 1918, by Monsignor Nelson Baker, the administrator of the diocese. Vifredo was to remain at St. Anthony's for 29 years, during which he guided the parish through many difficult times.[10]

The establishment of St. Anthony's parish marked a milestone in the development of the Italian community in Lackawanna. It was founded during World War I, when many Italians had decided to settle permanently in the United States. Committees of Italian men and women worked hard to raise funds and maintain first the mission, then the new church. Some men helped construct the new structure. It appears that the archdiocese sponsored half of the construction costs, while the parish assumed a mortgage for the remaining $6,000. Located in the midst of the Italian neighborhood on Ingham Avenue, St. Anthony's became a focal point for the weddings, baptisms, and funerals that served as landmarks in family and community life. No longer did people have to journey to non – Italian churches in Lackawanna or the more distant churches of their countrymen in Buffalo. As in other ethnic communities, the church was a vital institution that linked Italian Americans in celebration and consoled them in grief. It not only filled basic spiritual and social needs but also fostered group solidarity.[11]

FIGURE 6.2

REV. JOSEPH VIFREDO

Rev. Joseph Vifredo was pastor of St. Anthony's from 1918 to 1947. Photo source: Collection of Mike Morgan

Joseph Benoit Louis Vifredo was born in Lanslebourg, in the French province of Savoie, on April 2, 1881. One of five children, his parents had emigrated from Piedmont in northwest Italy, which has a common boundary with Savoie. Vifredo attended elementary schools in Lanslebourg and received a teacher's diploma in Valence, France. After teaching for two years in Marseilles, he went to Spain to teach French at the Catholic Circle in Cartagena. In August 1904, he followed his parents back to the Piedmont region of Italy and entered the Little Seminary of Suse in Torino. Vifredo was ordained as a priest at the Cathedral of San Giusto on December 12, 1912, then was given permission to finish his study of moral theology at the Convitto della Consolata. Two of his classmates there, Rev. Giuseppe Gambino and Rev. Teofilo Zutta, also came to western New York.

Upon completion of his schooling in October 1914, Rev. Vifredo sailed for the United States at the request of Bishop William Colton. He served as assistant pastor at St. James Church in Jamestown, New York, and in September 1916, was sent to St. Lucy's Church in Buffalo to work with Rev. C. Maxwell and Rev. John Boland. His next assignment was at St. Anthony's in Lackawanna. Two of his siblings remained in Europe, and two came to the United States. His brother Celestino became a Christian brother in Valence, France, and his sister Anna Chiabaudo raised a family in Susa, Italy. The other brother, Vincent, was living in Endicott, New York, by 1947; the other sister, Maria, emigrated from France in 1920 to work as Vifredo's housekeeper at St. Anthony's Church.

Rev. Vifredo died on December 6, 1947, after serving as pastor of St. Anthony's for 29 years. Reverends Gambino and Zutta joined Bishop John O'Hara in celebrating the funeral Mass on December 10. Rev. Vifredo's devotion to the Church was evident in the terms of his will. He left $4,000 to Pope Pious XII, some property and war bonds to his sister Maria, and other funds to Catholic organizations and charities.

Maria Vifredo, sister of Rev. Joseph Vifredo, served as his housekeeper in the rectory. After her brother's death, she continued in her job under Rev. Ciolino. Photo source: Lolly Suffoletto

Sources: *Lackawanna Leader*, 1/9/47, 12/11/47; *Buffalo Evening News*, 12/8/47; *Steel City Press*, 12/10/47, 1/21/48.

Catholics in a Protestant Country

Prior to 1840, the United States was overwhelmingly a Protestant country. The arrival of millions of Irish and German Catholic immigrants after 1840 altered this equation. While Protestants were still in the majority. The Catholic Church was a strong presence by 1890. By that time, the nation's Roman Catholic Church was dominated by Irish clerics who had worked hard to make the Church accepted and legitimate to other Americans. The arrival of the southern and eastern European immigrants presented the Irish with a dilemma. The Catholic Church in America wanted to present itself as unified and thoroughly assimilated, but the large numbers of immigrants from a variety of ethnic groups undercut this image. The previous challenges to the Irish leadership by German and French Catholics were now exacerbated by the large numbers of southern and eastern Europeans, all of whom wanted to follow their own cultural traditions. "Official Catholicism saw the various nationality groups as a temptation toward isolation from the surrounding society," sociologist Silvano Tomasi suggests. "The remedy proposed was ... Americanization of the Church and acceptance of national ideas and priorities." But allowing nationality or ethnic parishes in the United States was a difficult compromise for the Irish prelates. As Tomasi writes:

> The Church officially accepted and considered herself a pluralistic society only as an unavoidable and temporary condition while working to shape Southern, Eastern Europeans and non-Latin rite Catholics into "true Americans." At least at the time of mass emigration from Italy, the Catholic hierarchy was struggling to reassure itself of being a "monocolor," monolithic group completely American.

While the WASP—white Anglo-Saxon Protestant—elite that controlled America was often hostile to the Irish Catholics who arrived in the mid-1800s, it viewed the new immigrants as an even greater menace. The steel and railroad tycoons needed the unskilled labor provided by the southeast Europeans to continue the process of industrializing the United States, but their Protestant peers saw the immigrants as a "threat to America's free institutions." According to Tomasi, "this fear was tempered only by the conviction that the alien population could be evangelized and properly Americanized." In the eyes of many American Protestants, the Italians and other new immigrants were inferior not only because they were Catholic but also because their ethnic cultures were inferior to those of WASPs and the Irish. In turn, the Irish-dominated Catholic Church assumed a middle-man position, claiming it would assimilate the "ignorant and superstitious" groups such as the Italians by turning them into patriotic Catholics who held the same basic social values as did the WASP Americans.[12]

The Church criticized Italians for their "pagan" street processions, their lack of religious education, and the limited number of priests who migrated from Italy to tend to their religious needs. These complaints were lumped together and referred to as the "Italian Problem." In some cities, the Church leadership attempted to forbid the *feste* and processions that

---

FIGURE 6.3

Contributions of Lackawanna Catholic Churches to the Annual Catholic Charity Drive

Parish	Location		1924	1932	1944
St. Patrick's (replaced in 1926 by Our Lady of Victory)	4th Ward	(Irish)	$3,426.50	$4,266.25	$8,887.05
St. Anthony	1st Ward	(Italian)	127.25	37.50	154.75
St. Barbara	2nd Ward	(Polish)	969.07	1,090.12	2,451.65
Assumption	1st Ward	(Hungarian)	250.00	220.00	604.50
Sacred Heart	1st Ward	(Croatian)	153.50	75.13	123.25
St. Michael	3rd Ward	(Polish)	72.62	704.03	3,812.50
St. Hyacinth	1st Ward	(Polish)	402.00	716.20	1,519.55

Sources: *Catholic Union Times*, 6/5/24; *Lackawanna News*, 3/19/31; 3/24/32; *Lackawanna Leader*, 3/30/44.

were so abhorrent to Irish leadership, but not so in Lackawanna, where four of every five residents were Catholic. The Church did demand that priests in all nationality parishes maintain the stability of their communities by indulging the religious practices of the immigrants, and at the same time building an allegiance and connection to the greater Catholic community. For the immigrants, the Italian parish, according to Tomasi, "made them a 'people' in the social context of American society, where belonging to an ethnic group was a condition for adjustment and mobility." The challenge for Rev. Vifredo at St. Anthony's, and for hundreds of other priests, was that Italian immigrants identified with their towns or regions back home more than with Italy at large. Most Laziali, Abruzzesi, Napolitani, and others did not think of themselves as "Italian." Not only were the Italians' styles of Catholicism different from that practiced by the Irish, but they were characterized by historical tensions between the peasants and the clergy.[13]

An Italian Priest and his Anticlerical Parishioners

Like the pastors of other Italian churches in America, Rev. Vifredo had his work cut out for him when he arrived at St. Anthony's. The economic and working conditions endured by the immigrants in Lackawanna during the early decades of the twentieth century were in sharp contrast to living and working conditions in rural Italy. Life in an industrial city was very harsh. Strikes, layoffs, recessions, and the Great Depression meant that Italian families had irregular income and scant money to donate to the church, or to any other cause. Even when they did have sufficient income, southern Italians were not known to be generous in giving to the Church. In Italy, the peasants contributed little to the financial well-being of the Church, while the main support came from government bodies, the wealthy, and property holdings of the Church itself.

Up to the early 1920s, when the steel plant was in full production, the workers labored seven days a week in 10-, 12-, or 14 hour shifts. Depending on the department, the day shift started at 6:00 or 7:00 a.m. and typically ran 10 to 12 hours; the night shift, 12 to 14 hours. Usually, workmen had to switch from day to night shift every two weeks. On the day of the shift change, often over a weekend, one group of steelworkers worked 24 hours straight, while the other had a rare day of rest. Such an all-consuming schedule did not allow for regular attendance at Sunday morning Mass. Low church attendance by the men was also the result of historic class conflicts and cultural values. Italians, especially those from the southern provinces, were often anticlerical. In both the old country and the new, it all added up to low church attendance, especially by men. These attitudes were evident among the Italian immigrants in Lackawanna. During the 1920s, altar boy Joe Milano noticed that few Italian

men attended Mass and that the people attending the brief evening benediction were usually those from the immediate Ingham Avenue neighborhood. Only a few came from the more distant Old Village or Bethlehem Park neighborhoods. Francis "Caz" DePasquale lived on Ingham Avenue and became an altar boy in 1924, at age seven. He noticed that women, especially those who were members of the Church societies, were the most frequent attendees of Mass. Only a handful of men—including Serafino Mattucci, Gaetano Milano, Tony Turchiarelli, and Antonio Pacillo—attended regularly.[14]

The meager weekly contributions by St. Anthony parishioners meant that Rev. Vifredo was constantly scrambling for basic economic survival. In August 1921, he wrote to Rev. Murphy, the vice chancellor of the diocese, asking for financial aid. Rev. Vifredo explained that he had to support both his sister, who served as his housekeeper, and himself, and that he had "not taken a penny in salary this year." He reported that the parish had only $10 in the Church fund, plus $12 he'd collected the previous week for 12 intentions of Masses. Vifredo listed the bills he had paid using his personal money during the previous six months: $110 for altar wine, $80.78 for candles, and $61.90 for interest due on two notes. He concluded his letter, "It is impossible to pay $30.40 due this month for interest to the Lackawanna National Bank." It is not known how the archdiocese responded, but the letter illustrates Vifredo's difficulties. It also reveals Italians' tendency to light candles and request Masses for deceased family members. These practices brought in small contributions, but not enough to significantly improve the parish's financial standing.[15]

During the 1920s and 1930s, weekly Sunday collections at St. Anthony's often totaled no more than $4 to $5. On one occasion, a Polish priest from St. Hyacinth's Church said Mass. "In the sermon," recalls altar boy Caz DePasquale, "he said Italians were poor givers and Poles gave more. He said he went to the bank with two bags of money; Father Vifredo went with a handful." The chastising remarks of the Polish priest apparently fell on deaf ears. Indeed, Vifredo annually read from the altar each family's total yearly donations to St. Anthony's. People recall that the totals were often embarrassingly low; for several families, the priest called out a total of "cinque centesimi," or five cents. Vifredo's public recitations and admonitions to give more were not well received by many parishioners.[16]

The combination of Italians' meager finances and reluctance to give to the church was evident in other areas. Each Roman Catholic Church participated in the yearly Catholic Charities fund drive, and a layman was appointed to chair the effort. In 1931, immigrant Luigi Petti, one of the handful of immigrant men to attend Mass regularly, served as St. Anthony's campaign chairman. The shortage of men willing to assist in this effort meant that altar boys, such as Joe Milano, were often recruited to go door-to-door collecting money. "It was hard: the immigrants seemed to be against the church," Milano recalled of his attempts to gather funds in the Old Village and Bethlehem Park during the 1920s. When the annual results for the city's churches were reported, the total from St. Anthony's was one of the two lowest in the city, as seen in the 1924, 1932, and 1944 Catholic Charity drives (see Figure 6.3). Our Lady of Victory and St. Barbara were much larger parishes, but others were roughly the same size as St. Anthony's. Some of the differences may have been the result of higher unemployment in some First Ward churches during the Depression year of 1932. But the disparity, at least for the Italian Church, was partly the result of differing cultural values, as well as the nature of ethnic relations in the United States.[17]

Italian immigrants often had run-ins with the Irish, who dominated the positions of civic, political, and religious power in Lackawanna and other American cities. And the appeals from Irish diocesan officials for money didn't register well with Italians. Cultural differences between Italians and the Irish are significant when attempting to understand Italian attitudes toward the Church. In countries such as Ireland and Poland, the Catholic Church was a mainstay of ethnic identity, and its priests were leaders of nationalistic movements. But this was not the case in Italy. Prior to 1860, the Papal States included what later became the regions of Lazio, Abruzzo, Umbria, Marche, and the eastern provinces of Emilia-Romagna (see Figure 1.19). Italians in those regions remembered the often harsh rule of the papal authorities and their French and Austrian allies, who crushed several revolts in the first half of the nineteenth century and assisted the Pope in combatting the Risorgimento, the movement spanning the early to mid-nineteenth century that created the nation of Italy. When Italian nationhood was finally achieved in 1870, the Church lost the vast tracts of land it had controlled, and the Pope considered himself a "prisoner" in the Vatican. This situation was not resolved until 1929, when the Vatican and the Mussolini government signed the Lateran Treaty. Some Italian immigrants in America who had a sense of Italian patriotism were keenly aware of this aspect of Italian history, and this fueled their anticlericism. Most immigrants were impressed by neither the Church, the demise of the Vatican States in 1870, nor the new Italian nation formed that year. Both the foreign troops defending the Vatican States and the northern Italian soldiers of the new national government were harsh in suppressing dissent and rebellion in central and southern Italy.[18]

Generally speaking, many Italians carried to the U.S. a deep distrust of the Church based on their experiences in their native country. In Italy, often only the wealthy could afford to send

Rev. Vifredo at the altar saying Mass, St. Anthony's Church.
Photo source: Lolly Suffoletto

their sons to the seminary, so sharp economic class lines in small Italian towns contributed to the social distance between priest and parishioners. Further, the Church owned significant tracts of land throughout Italy and was viewed as an antagonistic landlord by the typical farmer or agricultural laborer. Italian men, ever protective of the honor of their wives and the chastity of their daughters, were wary of priests. On the one hand, a cleric wore dress-like garments and took a vow of celibacy, which made him less than a man in the eyes of many *contadini*. On the other, the *contadino* suspected that the priest might attempt to act out repressed sexual urges with his wife or daughter. The stories of such transgressions were recited in Italian American communities. Teenager Virginia Marrano left Capriglia Irpina, Campania, with her brothers and immigrated to Lackawanna, in part to avoid being violated by the local priest, who was said to have had affairs with a series of 18-year-old housemaids, by whom he had fathered several children.[19]

Stories circulating in Lackawanna's Italian community told of other alleged improprieties committed by priests. While serving in the Italian Army during World War I, Gaetano Paolini had two experiences that turned him away from the Catholic Church. The first occurred when he was stationed in his native Abruzzo and witnessed a priest kissing a nun. The second incident, more related to the war, had graver consequences.

Audrey Spagnolo making her First Holy Communion, circa 1917. Photo source: Collection of Audrey Spagnolo-Surgenor

Near the front lines, Paolini was among a large group of soldiers attending an open-air Mass, their attention focused on the priest. Suddenly, an enemy plane dropped bombs on a nearby ammunition dump, and the ensuing explosion killed most of the soldiers at the religious service. Following these events, Paolini made a few visits to his local church to light candles, but after immigrating to western New York in 1920, he never again set foot in a church.[20]

Several immigrants from Giuliano di Roma told the story of townspeople putting their savings into a cooperative bank, the Banca Cattolica, which included at least one priest among its leaders. Various versions of this episode have it that either the bank folded or the leaders fled with all the money. In one version, the bankruptcy was a hoax perpetuated by priests to defraud the peasants of their savings, while in another, an individual priest was said to be the main culprit. Romolo Petricca, whose family farmed land in Giuliano that was rented from an elderly priest, the only cleric respected by the young Petricca, expressed another reason to be wary of priests. As an altar boy, he observed several clerics eating meat on Fridays, something they had told the peasants not to do. He concluded that most priests were dishonest men who "duped the poor uneducated peasants." When interviewed in 1986, he sang a bawdy Italian song that ridiculed the hypocrisy of priests. Other immigrants, too, claimed to have seen priests eating poultry on Fridays. In Ceccano, Luigi Scarsella, visited the church rectory, and observed

a priest eating chicken; he told his children that this was the reason he didn't attend church. Even altar boy Nunze Oddy was surprised, during several visits to the St. Anthony's rectory, to find Rev. Clemente eating chicken soup on Fridays.[21]

The brief tenures of Clemente and D'Alfonso during 1917 and 1918 provided fuel for other rumors among the immigrants. Tony Grasso hinted at impropriety when he wrote that he wondered why D'Alfonso had left Lackawanna so hurriedly. Joe Milano and Nunze Oddy heard stories, mentioned earlier, suggesting that Clemente had been transferred because of questionable financial doings. Whether the stories of transgressions by priests were real or imagined, their effect was to reinforce the anticlericism of Italian men. In Italy, churchgoing was seen as the domain of poor people, especially women and children. When men did attend Mass, they often stood in the back of the church or just outside the door, socializing and occasionally mocking the priest or other parishioners. Some Lackawanna men also showed disrespect in church. However, most immigrant men simply avoided church, except for Easter and Christmas services or to attend baptisms, weddings, and funerals.[22]

Italians' strong provincial and regional loyalties were another source of friction. For many years, those from the regions north of Rome have looked down on the southern Italians, often referring to them as *terrone,* or people of the earth. Tony Grasso, who attended St. Anthony's from its founding, recorded some of his impressions in writing. He noted that Rev. Vifredo, who attended seminary in northern Italy and whose parents were from the Piedmont, displayed some of this prejudice toward his southern Italian parishioners in Lackawanna. Grasso felt this was most evident during the difficult Depression years. In Italy, northern Italian priests often were appointed pastors of churches in the south, and southern Italians in the United States sometimes had bitter memories of priests' condescending attitudes. The only group of northern Italians in Lackawanna, the immigrants from Marche, were just as anticlerical as the southerners if not more so. Joe Milano observed that a number of the Marchegiani avoided church altogether because they felt the priests were dishonest and not to be trusted. Some Marchegiani, who were said to be atheists, would not allow Rev. Vifredo to enter their homes. While other regional groups celebrated patron-saint days or procured a statue of their hometown saint, the Marchegiani did neither. Social-class sensitivies were also present in Lackawanna, as in the case of a female resident who described Rev. Vifredo as somewhat aloof and presumably from a well-to-do family.[23]

All these factors suggest that Italian Catholicism was characterized by a tenuous relationship between priest and parishioners. Most Irish and Polish Catholics automatically respected a clergyman simply for the culturally honored position he held, which made it easier to overlook his personal shortcomings. The anticlericism of the Italian, however, meant that each priest, based on his individual attributes, had to earn respect. Only a handful of immigrant men were inclined to simply accept the legitimacy of the cleric based on his formal station. Thus, a priest such as Rev. Vifredo had a limited reserve of cultural acceptance upon which he could rely to soften the judgments of parishioners when his personal shortcomings became apparent.

Language and politics posed more challenges for Rev. Vifredo. St. Anthony's offered at least one Mass per day, three on Sunday, and vespers at night. At each Mass, Vifredo gave the sermon in both English and Italian. While it was a plus that he spoke Italian, his vocabulary and cadence were influenced by his Piedmontese dialect, which immigrants from Lazio, Abruzzo, and the more southern regions found hard to understand. On top of that, Vifredo's English was poor, which undermined his rapport with children of the parish. He humbly apologized from the altar for his limited ability at public speaking.[24]

The Church hierarchy expected priests in nationality parishes to solidify their flock in their ethnic identity and, at the same time, gradually steer parishioners toward the values demanded by American society. This sometimes led to tensions. The Church, striving to be patriotic and appease demands for assimilation, took strong stands against socialism and communism. In working-class parishes during the early twentieth century, however, the messages of socialist candidates were often popular. When Rev. Vifredo denounced Calogero Fadale, one of the church's first trustees, for backing a socialist political candidate, Fadale and his wife stopped attending St. Anthony's, although they continued sending their children to Mass there. When Fadale died in 1931, Rev. Vifredo offered only a pauper's Mass. An infuriated Serafina Fadale held her husband's funeral service at St. Paul's Episcopal Church in Buffalo. Thereafter, she and her younger children attended services at the Episcopal church. This event was also the final straw for the Fadales' eldest son, John, who then joined in his family's exodus from St. Anthony's. A doctor, John Fadale had continued supporting St. Anthony's after his parents had stopped, but he ceased being active when he concluded that "Vifredo wanted all the credit." Years later, as Serafina Fadale was dying from a stroke, Rev. Ciolino of St. Anthony's prayed at her deathbed, but her funeral service, was held at St. Paul's Episcopal Church.[25]

During the first three decades of the twentieth century, Catholic Church leaders were concerned that Protestant missions and social agencies were making inroads into Italian communities. In keeping with this concern, Rev. Vifredo forbade Italian children

FIGURE 6.4

Regional Roots of St. Anthony's Founders, Trustees, and Altar Boys: 1917

Region/ Surname	Immigrants	American-born Children
Campania		
Amorosi	Antonio	
Guadagno	Antonio	
Milano	Gaetano & Maria	Joe
Pacillo	Caterina	Joe, Jerry
Pepper		Tom
Sperduto	Angelo	
Lazio		
Carlini	Angelo	
Felici	Giovanni Battista	
Grossi	Antonio	
	& Nicolina	Angelo (Grosso)
Abruzzo		
Mattucci	Serafino	
Marinelli	Maria	
Melillo	Virginia	
Monaco	Donata	
Oddi	Pietro	Nunze (Oddy)
Zaccagnini	Emidio	
Sicilia		
Fadale	Calogero	

*Sources: Interviews with Joe Milano, July 12, 1996; Nunze Oddy, April 12, 1982; Angelo Grosso, November 22, 1977.

from attending recreational activities at Friendship House, which was run by the Presbyterian Church. This irritated some Italian adults and children, and Caz DePasquale was one of many children who ignored the priest's pronouncements and frequented Friendship House on Ridge Road.[26]

Every Easter, Rev. Vifredo traveled throughout Lackawanna to bless Italian homes on the day before and after the holiday. According to Caz DePasquale, this process began after morning Mass on Holy Saturday, and included a trek by the priest and three altar boys across the maze of railroad tracks to Roland Avenue. There, John Giovinetti and another youth met the entourage and guided Vifredo to every Italian home. Bearing a water font, the priest entered and blessed every room of the homes, and even the car of any family fortunate enough to own one. DePasquale observed that "The priest blessed the house until people gave a donation." The majority of time was spent in the First Ward, where the priest and altar boys started at Wilson and Ingham, then proceeded house by house down

Ingham Avenue, through the Old Village, and into Bethlehem Park. This went on until as late as 9:00 p.m. each day and was followed by the altar boys joining Vifredo for a big meal. "He would bless all the Italian houses in Lackawanna," stated DePasquale. Usually the woman of the house greeted the priest at the door. Augusta Anticoli recalls the major effort that many housewives and their children put into thoroughly cleaning all rooms of their homes before the blessing. When the priest had completed blessing all rooms, typically the housewife handed him an envelope with the family's donation. Some, such as Lucia Risio, gave him eggs instead of money.[27]

Men who didn't attend church often hid from the priest as he did this annual blessing of Italian homes at Easter. Indeed, some men seemed to fear the priest, while others ridiculed him. Charles Barone, an altar boy from 1937 to 1947, observed, as did others, that during these visits Rev. Vifredo was not always treated with respect. "People treated him shabbily," DePasquale said, "and believed that he was a drunkard." In fact, some Italians habitually offered the priest a glass of homemade wine. Old-timers tell of the priest getting drunk after visiting a number of homes and tasting the homemade wine offered him. Whether these stories are true or not, it is apparent that priests were easy targets for scorn by some Italian immigrants.[28]

Rev. Vifredo had to endure other woes as he desperately attempted to raise funds, alienating some families in the process. A number of men did start attending church as their children grew up and needed Rev. Vifredo to perform weddings and baptisms. The priest often made the heads of families pay past dues before he performed such religious ceremonies for their family members. In other cases, Vifredo told some immigrant women that they could be deported to Italy if their families didn't support the church. A frightened Virginia Croce once gave $3 to the priest, money that her son Al had been saving for a Boy Scout uniform. When he found out, the teenager was furious with the priest. Rev. Vifredo also sometimes delivered offering envelopes to the homes of people who were lax in their contributions or attendance. One example involves the DePaula family, whose five children regularly went to Mass, though the mother rarely did, and Antonio DePaula never attended. One day Vifredo walked into the bakery behind their home and attempted to hand Antonio DePaula a box of envelopes, explaining the need for weekly church contributions. DePaula became enraged, grabbed the box of envelopes, and flung it into the flames of the oven. Joseph DePaula later begged Vifredo to forgive his father for this crude act. In another sad episode Rev. Vifredo was struck on the head and robbed near the Old Village; he had to be treated in the hospital for minor head injuries. Incidents in which Italian priests were physically attacked also occurred in other American cities, and, in a few instances, priests were even killed.[29]

The sparse giving of his parishioners forced Rev. Vifredo to conserve fuel in the winter; thus, the church and rectory were very cold. During the winter of 1927-28, some parishioners organized a special event at Lackawanna's Memorial Hall to raise funds for heating fuel. Special collections by parishioners, or "coal drives," became regular occurrences. The proceeds of the Holy Name Society's picnic in 1934 went to support the church. Leaders of church societies took individual initiatives. Alessandrina Sperduti went house-to-house seeking funds from parishioners. Women of the parish held a card party and dance to benefit the church in 1932. Four years later, a card party was organized and carried out by a committee of 44 ladies, about evenly divided between immigrants and American-born women. Vifredo also was able to collect some small change two or three times per year at nighttime vespers services. Arcangelo "Arc" Petricca, an altar boy in 1942 and 1943, recalled passing the basket at these services when given the verbal cue by Vifredo. Petricca noted that no other churches took such a collection.[30]

In the 1920s, the Lake Erie Italian Club supported the church by paying rent for its meetings there and making donations for the use of church property for festivals and picnics. The society made a few outright gifts to the church, such as providing $25 for repairs in 1936. The church held various fund-raisers, including a lawn fete and picnic in June 1927, with a special Mass, food, dancing, and fireworks. Two years later, an actors group composed of young parishioners staged the play *Backfire* in the high-school auditorium. The profits were applied to improvements on the church's interior. These activities fostered a sense of unity and common purpose.[31]

The communal activities sponsored by the church helped bridge the regional differences among parishioners. Despite the anticlerical attitudes, the Laziali, Abruzzesi, Napolitani, Calabresi and others slowly congealed into a parish community. The Napolitani seemed very active in founding the church, numbering 10 of the 23 people identified as early church leaders and activists (see Figure 6.4). But even the Marchegiani, viewed by some as the most alienated from the church, became more involved. Stephan and Carmela Canestrari and Alphonse Bracci were active in church societies by the early 1930s. The Ladies Social Club, made up of women with roots in Marche, was identified in 1939 as a group affiliated with St. Anthony's Church. The founding of the church led directly to the creation of two of the city's earliest Italian organizations between 1918 and 1920, and to a number of others in the following decades. Some of the secular Italian groups, such as the Lake Erie Italian Club, not only held their meetings at the church but, as stated earlier, actively supported church activities and made monetary contributions. Parishioners came to tolerate, if not fully accept, Rev. Vifredo's northern Italian roots and Piedmontese dialect.

The grave of Giuseppina DePaula in Holy Cross Cemetery, 2002. It is an Italian tradition to place a photo of the deceased on the gravestone Photo source: The author

The church helped immigrants develop an Italian identity, rather than their regional ones, which was new to them. By welcoming the statues and ceremonies honoring a variety of patron saints, Rev. Vifredo won a degree of acceptance and legitimacy for St. Anthony's.[32]

Despite the tension between the pastor and his flock, a number of parishioners actively supported and befriended Rev. Vifredo. These included children, such as Yolanda Monaco, who lived near the church and observed Rev. Vifredo to be "a good priest who was strict." The first trustees at St. Anthony's, Calogero Fadale and Antonio Guadagno, were stalwarts of the parish who worked closely with Vifredo, although Fadale and the priest eventually had a falling-out. Serafino Mattucci, who later became a trustee, was a friend and supporter of Vifredo and often assisted with the parish's bookkeeping. His daughter Yolanda became the church organist in 1936, a position she held for at least 30 years. Mattucci and Sam Baratta, both immigrants, as well as American-born men such as Ed Pacillo and Louis Mauro, who later became trustees, regularly served as ushers, passing the collection baskets during Mass. A senior citizen, Antonio Ruggeri, attended church daily and sometimes served as an altar boy. He took collections of nickels and dimes with which he purchased a manger set for St. Anthony's. Prior

to his death in the early 1920s, Ruggeri was a friend of Vifredo's, and the priest regularly visited him at home. On his walks along Ingham Avenue, Vifredo visited such friendly parishioners as Serafino and Virginia Mattucci, John and Adele Panzetta, Tony and Jenny Turchiarelli, and Frank and Donata Monaco. The priest also befriended immigrant men who did not attend church. Luigi Scarsella, who regularly invited Vifredo to his Wasson Street home for food, drink, and conversation, was never pressured by the priest to make an appearance at St. Anthony's. Scarsella's daughter Anne recalled that the priest "liked his drink. But he was a wonderful man. These little old ladies would go there [to St. Anthony's]—the widows—and they'd say to him: 'We don't have any money to put into the basket.' He would take it out of his pocket and give them the money. He was really a saint." Salvatore Macaluso and Vifredo were cordial friends who talked as they sipped homemade wine at Macaluso's home on Hamburg Turnpike. As a girl, Carmella Macaluso observed their interactions and remembers Vifredo as a warm hearted man.[33]

It was predominantly the women who were active in the church, and according to Tony DiMillo, "many Italian women wailed when Father Vifredo died." A handful of the more church-minded parents, usually at the lead of the mother, encouraged their sons to be altar boys. Three of Antonio and Caterina Pacillo's sons—Ed, Joe, and Jerry— were altar boys, as were Santo and Assunta DePasquale's son Caz and two of their nephews, Nick and Joe DePasquale. Calogero and Maria Barone attended Mass with their children, and their son Charles Jr. was an altar boy. Jennie Andreozzi, who prayed the rosary five nights a week at church, had her son Tony become an altar boy by age seven in 1935. He remained at the church as an altar boy until 1947, and was joined by several Bethlehem Park neighbors: Al Ceccarelli, Fred and Tony Rosati, and Dominic Sperduti. The priest, sometimes gave the boys a quarter for serving Mass. Vifredo also had some support from other priests. During the early 1930s, Brother Liguori of St. John's Protectory, an Our Lady of Victory institution in Lackawanna, helped coordinate the activities of the Holy Name Society.[34]

Throughout his tenure, Rev. Vifredo was open to non – Italians, and invited their participation in St. Anthony's parish. The priest was able to speak Italian, French, Spanish, and, to a lesser extent, English. A newspaper notice in 1933 announced that the priest was available to hear confessions in Spanish, Italian, and French before each Sunday Mass. This helped to draw a number of Spanish-speaking people to St. Anthony's, especially since Lackawanna had no Spanish church. Immigrants from Spain, as well as from Mexico, Puerto Rico, Cuba, and Chile were involved in more than 100 marriages, baptisms, and funerals at the church between 1919 and 1946. During the 1920s and 1930s three sons

Figure 6.5

Festa at St. Anthony's Church, June 1919

The following article from the *Lackawanna Daily Journal* in 1919 describes a celebration honoring St. Anthony:

ST. ANTONIO CHURCH
Big Celebration Today

Today the Italians of this city celebrate what is, in their former country, our 4th of July.

This morning at 9:30 o'clock a gigantic parade was held in which the native and foreign born participated to a man.

High mass was celebrated by three Priests as the beginning of church festivities. The entire day and evening will be given over to this annual affair and a special $700 fire works display will be set off, after dark tonight, the work being in the hands of specialists from New York City.

A full brass band and an orchestra furnish music at the picnic grounds where refreshments were served all day and will be served this evening.

Tonight dancing will be the chief amusement after the fireworks.

This celebration is one of the biggest annual events of the year in this city, work and business operations are practically suspended the entire day and evening in the Italian section of the city and everyone simply turns in today to out-do the event of last year.

Source: *Lackawanna Daily Journal,* 6/13/19.

Santa Lucia, or St. Lucy, St. Anthony's Church, 2005
Photo source: Paul Pasquarello

of Porfirio and Louise Castro were altar boys at St. Anthony's, and Louise Castro sang in the church choir. Anne Hurley, who lived on Electric Avenue, got to know Vifredo around 1920. To help support her family she became the organist at St. Anthony's, a paid position, which she held for five or six years. Her sister Cecelia befriended the Fadale family and the two young women went to outdoor summer dances at St.Anthony;'s.[35]

Patron Saints and Religious *Feste*

In southern Italy, the epitome of religiosity is the annual celebration of a town's patron saint. These *feste* involve two- or three-day celebrations featuring a High Mass; the carrying of the saint's statue through the streets amidst a long procession of the faithful; and entertainment, food, and fireworks. People pin money on the statue, adorn it with jewelry, and place food offerings on the vada (the wooden platform the statue rests on), all as offerings to thank the saint for past divine interventions or to beseech it for future ones. In larger towns, such as Giuliano di Roma, a number of saints and Madonnas are honored. In addition to San Biagio, the patron saint, there are festivals for Assunta (the Assumption), San Rocco, Madonna della Speranza (Our Lady of Hope), San Giuseppe, San Antonio, and Sacro Cuore (the Sacred Heart). Italian immigrants in Lackawanna carried on these *feste* in the early twentieth century.

The first known religious festival held by Lackawanna Italians took place in 1909 to honor San Pio delle Camere. Serafino Mattucci opened his home at 229 Ingham Avenue on Sunday, July 11, to celebrate the saint for whom his hometown in Abruzzo was named. Priests from St. Anthony's Church in Buffalo said Mass for this event, and musicians entertained the crowd. During the 1920s, Mattucci organized more elaborate celebrations in honor of San Pio and convinced Rev. Vifredo to procure two other priests to help him celebrate a High Mass on the saint's day. Mattucci, who had served in the Italian military, loved music, especially marches, and always hired a band for the *feste*. During the religious service, the band played numbers at selected times. When not playing, the band members were served liquor as they stood outside the church. Afterwards, there were festivities in the lot separating Mattucci's home and the tavern hall. People danced to the band's music, and a lean-to sheltered the musicians from inclement weather. The Mattucci family strung lights across their yard, and relatives helped them prepare huge tables of food for the festival. Serafino Mattucci held this *festa* every year up to 1935.[36]

Lackawanna Italians held festivals celebrating St. Anthony of Padua, the saint for whom their church was named, beginning in 1918. The second year, there was a big, one-day *festa* that included a Mass celebrated by three priests, a parade, band music, dancing, food, and fireworks (see Figure 6.5). The organizing committee invited the Lake Erie Italian Club to march in the procession under its own banner and to display flags. The celebration of June 19, 1927, was similar, but there was no procession or parade, and the event was billed in the *Lackawanna News* as a "lawn fete and picnic." During the 1930s, the Lake Erie Italian Club apparently took an active role in the festivals honoring St. Anthony. "As a band marched down Ingham Avenue," Joe Milano reminisced, "Tony Amorosi, Anthony Zaccaria, and Serafino Mattucci collected money" from onlookers. Sometimes the procession went as far as Bethlehem Park, and the three men walked the distance, extending their plates to people for donations. This was followed by a picnic on the church grounds.[37]

A *festa* in honor of San Biagio was held on August 25, 1918, under the direction of a committee of immigrants from Giuliano di Roma. It began with a Low Mass at 8:00 a.m. followed by a band marching through the streets of the district from 10:00 a.m. to noon. There was a High Mass at noon, after which the band again paraded through the streets. From 8:00 a.m. until midnight, people were entertained by a band concert and fireworks. A similar *festa* was organized by the Giulianesi in August 1920. Throughout the 1920s and 1930s, Lackawanna Italians regularly paid homage to other patron saints. Domenico and Rosina Tripoli, immigrants from Calabria, organized festivals to honor San Rocco. There was a Mass followed by festivities, including food booths, games of skill, musicians, and dancing on an outdoor platform installed on the church grounds. Prior to the *festa* the Tripolis canvassed the Italian community, collecting donations and renting out food booths. Grocer Antonio Melillo usually rented a booth where his wife and daughters sold grapes. Other booths offered lemon ice and ice cream.[38]

The women of the Mount Carmel Society paid homage to one of the most popular Italian patron saints. During the 1920s and 1930s, the society annually held a weekend festival, that at times included a procession marching north on Ingham Avenue to Ridge Road, then back to St. Anthony's Church.

Statue of San Biagio at St. Anthony's Church, 2005. The patron saint of Giuliano di Roma, he is believed to have the power to prevent people from choking. Photo source: Paul Pasquarello

The ladies carried two banners—one bearing an image of the Madonna and the society's name, and the other devoted to St. Anthony. Two long streamers flowed from the banner of Mount Carmel Society. While an adult carried the pole supporting the banner, two youths each held a streamer; Anne Melillo and Anne Monaco did this as girls. Along the route, the procession frequently stopped to allow people to pin money on the banner. The arrival of the procession back at the church grounds marked the start of a picnic, but entertainment and fireworks were not offered every year. In July 1931, however, the society sponsored an elaborate procession that meandered throughout the First Ward. *The Lackawanna News* described it as:

> ...the biggest parade of any church organization in the history of Lackawanna. Blocks long, white clad children, and other loyal members of the parish, as well as hundreds of local friends, paraded through the streets of the community, including Ridge Road, Hamburg Turnpike, and Bethlehem Park. With colors flying and bands playing, the marching hosts drew the attention of thousands of motorists including hundreds of tourists.

In July 1933, this event included games for children and dancing for adults. Its organizing committee included Carmela Suffoletto, the chairperson, Carmela Marchetti, Alessandrina Sperduti, Rosa Delgatto, and Maria Ricci, all of whom were immigrants.[39]

Even more impressive was the annual *festa* in honor of Montevergine, Our Lady of the Mountain. Some Italians remember this as the event of the year during the Depression. John Panzetta, under the auspices of the Italian American Citizens Club, of which he was an officer, regularly organized the festival. In the province of Avellino, Campania, where Panzetta and his wife were raised, there is a mountaintop abbey dedicated to the Madonna. In Italy she was often referred to as the Black Madonna, or, in Italian, Madonna Bruna. Tony Grasso, from the same province as the Panzettas, described this *festa* as a two-day event that included a Mass at St. Anthony's, during which "Panzetta had a man in the rear of the church. A few seconds before the elevation of the Host, he would run out, hands held high…. The band immediately struck up a martial song; at the same time the man in charge of fireworks lit a couple rounds of mortars, the blast making an infernal noise." This was followed by a street procession, led by a banner depicting the Virgin and accompanied by a band. "Starting at the lower end of Ingham Avenue," wrote Grasso, "Panzetta led the procession, [which] stopped at every business place, side street, and at homes. Panzetta hirelings with small wicker baskets went around soliciting donations from bystanders, reminiscent of the way it was done in the old country." The weekend festivities included music, songs, dancing, and fireworks on the church grounds. During the several years when Panzetta and Rev. Vifredo had a falling out about the disposition of the funds collected during the procession, the *festa* was held a few blocks from the church, at the Odell Street playground. There, Panzetta had a bandstand and gazebo set up, and tents erected for food booths and games. In 1933, the celebration was held on September 16 and 17, and included "sports, Italian dances and songs, a band concert, and a grand display of fireworks."[40]

Although the *feste* represented the high point of Italian religious and social expression, they at times had a downside that underscored the traditional tension between priest and layman. This conflict concerned the distribution of monies raised at the events. The struggle for control of the activities and purse strings of Italian-society-sponsored religious celebrations has a long, sad history at many Italian American parishes. In one frequent scenario, the priest wanted the sponsoring society to turn over all proceeds to him. During the two-day *festa* in honor of Montevergine, John Panzetta and other members of the Italian American Citizens Club collected donations, but the only money that went to St. Anthony's was the fee for Rev. Vifredo saying the Mass. Panzetta did send

some proceeds to the Montevergine Abbey in Avellino, but Vifredo was bothered that St. Anthony's saw so little profits. However, "what disturbed Father Vifredo most," wrote Tony Grasso, "was the way Panzetta operated. Father Vifredo, year after year, never fully supported the fireworks, saying, 'It's a waste of all that money—going up in smoke.'" This was the cause of the falling out between the priest and Panzetta.[41]

The Lake Erie Italian Club helped carry out some of the festivals in honor of St. Anthony and also occasionally used the church grounds for its own events in the years prior to World War II. On Sunday, August 26, 1928, the society held its annual festival. Afterward, the membership attended a special Mass given by Rev. Vifredo. They then proceeded to the activities on the church grounds. The society sometimes gave half the proceeds of these events to St. Anthony's. The ladies of the church's Mount Carmel Society were committed solely to the financial well-being of their parish; all proceeds from their two-day *festa* in July 1936 were earmarked for the repair and modernizing of the church's interior.[42]

Madonna Della Speranza, Our Lady of Hope, along with St. Anthony and St. Nicholas were important in the religious life of Giuliano di Roma.
Photo source: Paul Pasquarello

Other religious events involved street processions. In 1938, all five societies of St. Anthony's parish, as well as a contingent of Father Baker's Boys, paraded through the streets of the First Ward to honor the Sacred Heart. The following year, the Blessed Virgin of Mary Sodality marched in the procession for First Holy Communion exercises and performed a crowning ceremony that evening for the statue of the Blessed Virgin. When Monsignor Nelson Baker, a beloved figure in Lackawanna, died in 1936, a procession of St. Anthony's parishioners, mostly women and children, walked to Our Lady of Victory Basilica (OLV). There they joined thousands of other mourners standing in a long line on Ridge Road, waiting to glimpse the body of the saintly priest.[43]

Funerals often involved processions from St. Anthony's Church to Holy Cross Cemetery, a distance of a mile-and-a-half. Mourners, accompanied by a band, slowly marched up Ingham Avenue, then went east on Ridge Road to the cemetery. Some people rented cars to drive them back to the First Ward. Members of the Lake Erie Italian Club and other societies were fined if they did not take part in the funeral service and procession of a deceased member, or send other persons in their places.[44]

By the late 1930s the Italian funeral processions and religious festivals were no longer held. Many second-generation Italians had little interest in these traditions from the "old country." Instead, Italians flocked to more secular summer carnivals sponsored by the Lake Erie Italian Club, the Galanti Athletic Association, and other groups. However, the devotion of Italians to local patron saints did persevere over time. This is evident when one enters St. Anthony's, where a statue of San Biagio, purchased by natives of Giuliano di Roma, stands to the left of the altar. The Giulianesi have a Mass said every year to honor their patron saint, and they collect money to maintain the statue. The church has also held statues of St. Joseph, the Blessed Mother, St. Lucy, San Bonifacio, Sacred Heart, Our Lady of Hope, and Our Lady of Mount Carmel. The saintly icons were well cared for by parishioners; for example, Alessandrina Sperduti gave money to have the statue of the Sacred Heart repainted.[45]

The *feste* in Lackawanna differed from those in Buffalo and other large Italian settlements. Those in the Steel City did not involve huge displays of electric lights, and statues of the honored saints were not always carried in the street processions, although banners and large drawings depicting the saints were. Apparently the statue of St. Anthony was carried by four men during some of the June celebrations in his honor. Many Italian communities had at least one men's religious organization that sponsored a *festa*, but such a group was not present in Lackawanna. Instead, a political group, the Italian American Citizens Club, sponsored the Montevergine *festa*. Indeed, some of the festivals were

Montevergine, or Our Lady of the Mountain, was an important saint with a mountain-top shrine in the Avellino province of Campania. Festivals in her honor were held in Lackawanna. Photo source: Neil Marrano

somewhat secularly described as fairs and picnics, both in the press and by Italians. Interestingly, no photos of these religious events could be located. It is surprising that there were not more *feste* held by the Giulianesi, the largest township grouping, and that apparently none were held by the Pettoranesi, the second most numerous group of *paesani*. Several factors may have mitigated against the development of institutions that could regularly sponsor *feste*. Italians arrived in Lackawanna in a piecemeal manner; the constant moving in and out of the city continued well into the 1930s, leaving only a small group of permanent settlers. Plus, the Italian mission and parish were not established until 1917. The town's proximity to Buffalo and its huge *feste* may have overshadowed those in Lackawanna's, especially since a number of Steel City Italian men belonged to societies in the larger city. Lastly, it is possible that the celebration of *feste* is emphasized more in the deep-south regions of Italy as opposed to Lazio and Abruzzo, which have been home to over half of the Lackawanna immigrants.

Lackawanna Italians demonstrated their faith in other small but significant ways. Aldo Filipetti remembers that his mother, Adele, was a member of one of the women's groups at St. Anthony's, and that she "had the rosary hanging on the bedpost and every night she'd say her rosary. I remember she always had those beads and she'd be able to push those beads through her fingers like it was programmed.... Like most of the other Italians in Bethlehem Park, they all had their candles with their statues in the house, and they'd light these for certain occasions like holidays." The small statues of the Madonna, often in the form of the Infant of Prague, were popular among Italian American women, who also were fond of lighting votive candles both at home and in church. Maria Ross showed her faith and dedication by helping to clean St. Anthony's Church; she walked to church from her Bethlehem Park home every day until she reached the age of 88.[46]

The Roland Avenue Italians

Italians living east of the railroad tracks in the Roland Avenue neighborhood had few options about which Catholic church to attend. Prior to 1917, there were two parishes a mile to the north, on Ridge Road. St. Barbara's, a Polish parish founded in 1905, stood at Ridge and Center, and the Irish parish of St. Patrick's was at Ridge and South Park. Twenty years later, St. Michael's church was constructed on Electric Avenue, a few blocks north of Roland Avenue, but it was a Polish parish and therefore not viewed as a potential church by Italian immigrants. However, Our Mother of Good Counsel, organized in 1906, was less than a mile to the south in Blasdell and was not a nationality parish for any ethnic group. When St. Anthony's Church came into being in 1917, the Roland Italians, as they came to be called, found it inconvenient to travel there. It was only slightly over a half-mile walk, going west across the railroad tracks, then up Ingham Avenue, but maneuvering through the maze of tracks was always a dangerous venture, especially for families with children. Even a safe journey couldn't protect their Sunday clothes from getting soiled. Taking a streetcar meant going north on Electric Avenue, transferring to a west-bound Ridge Road trolley, then walking about a half-mile south on Ingham Avenue. The time, expense, and bother involved in the trek usually made it prohibitive. It appears that some of the Roland Italians went to St. Anthony's, some simply ignored church altogether, and a significant number went to Our Mother of Good Counsel. There was even a Roland Catholic Club with apparent ties to the church in Blasdell. In 1933, the group sponsored a dance that was held at the church.[47]

Our Mother of Good Counsel, unlike most Catholic churches in Lackawanna, was not a nationality parish but did have many Irish members who had moved to the area from Scranton, Pennsylvania. The church's baptismal register for the period 1906 to 1936 also lists dozens of Italian families. Some were residents of Blasdell (including a number who had recently moved from Lackawanna), others lived in Woodlawn, and at least half lived along Roland Avenue. Frank Chiodo remembers that most of the Roland Italians, including his family, regularly attended Our Mother of Good Counsel. He also witnessed Rev. Jacobs of the church reaching out to the community in a unique manner. "He used to ride around on a horse and give the kids candy."[48]

In the early 1940s, the Madonna del Carmine Society was organized by Italian women on Roland Avenue. In July 1941, the group celebrated the saint's day by receiving communion at the High Mass and presenting a small statue of their patroness to Our Mother of Good Counsel Church. The society served to reinforce the separation between that neighborhood and St. Anthony's Church. Perhaps this is why Rev. Vifredo took pains at Easter time to cross the railroad tracks and bless the Italians' homes on Roland Avenue. A number of Roland families did have baptisms, marriages, and funerals at St. Anthony's, and the heightened ethnic consciousness of the 1930s drew more of the Roland Italians to St. Anthony's. In 1937, the Roland Italian American Lodge had its flags blessed there. The impressive ceremony included the appointment of godparents for each flag— Michele and Maria Selvaggio for the American flag, and Santo and Ursala Mancuso for the Italian.[49]

As Italian families settled along South Park Avenue and moved northward, some began to attend the new OLV Basilica that was completed in 1926 replacing St. Patrick's Church. By the late 1920s, families headed by Joe and Susan Fox, Nicola and Filomena Delvecchio, Vito and Josephine Pacillo, and Maddelena Tarquinio lived a few blocks north of the imposing edifice and considered OLV their parish. Tarquinio, a widow living with one of her adult children, was a devout Catholic who attended mass every morning and devotions each evening. Further south, John Verel lived on the street named after him, just off South Park Avenue. He moved his builders supply business to Ridge Road, and his family attended services at OLV. As his enterprise prospered and he began to move in higher social circles, he received the recognition afforded only a handful of people. On Sundays, Verel drove up to the church, exited the vehicle with his family, and had his car parked by the ever-present Irish policeman.[50]

Gesu the Monk

Some of the Roland Avenue Italians found their religious leader in an unusual man known as Gesu (Jesus) the Monk. Jesus John Alvarez arrived in the United States in early 1913 and began studies at St. Anthony's College, a Franciscan school in Catskill, New York. He was born in Spain but spoke fluent Italian and had previously worked in the West Indies. He left the Franciscan school after a few months and, though never ordained as a priest, began to preach in Italian agricultural communities in western New York. In June 1913, he established the Chapel of the Most Holy Mary in North Collins, and *Corriere Italiano* referred to him as the "Monaco Miracoloso," the miraculous monk. Gesu lived in a tiny building and constantly prayed there before a small altar featuring statues of the Madonna and the crucifixion. In 1925, he was accused of molesting a teenage girl who was associated with his chapel, but most of his followers stood by him and raised money for his legal defense. Gesu's congregation continued to expand, the small chapel was replaced by a modern building, and by 1941, Gesu had organized another church in Niagara Falls, New York, and a third in Philadelphia. Italians from western New York, Philadelphia, and Vineland, New Jersey, made regular pilgrimages to the North Collins church. Gesu was a popular figure who had insight into the ways of his Italian followers. "In a unique and charismatic way," Secondo Casarotto observed, "Jesus John Alvarez had understood certain traits of the Italian religious, cultural, and social traditions."[51]

In the early 1920s, Gesu was preaching to Italians in Niagara Falls and Lackawanna. By 1924, Catholic leaders in Buffalo were concerned about the self-proclaimed monk. Gesu reportedly approached Rev. Vifredo and asked permission to offer Mass at St. Anthony's. According to some stories, he actually said several Masses there. Vifredo, however, refused to allow the monk to preach when he could not produce the credentials indicating he was a priest. Gesu nevertheless established a long-lasting relationship with Italians in the Roland Avenue neighborhood. Frank Chiodo was a boy of 10 in 1925 when he attended a prayer meeting held at 105 Roland Avenue, the home of his uncle and aunt, Francesco and Michelina Sirianni. Twenty people, mostly immigrants, were present at this gathering, which was followed by weekly sessions held at different homes. "Gesu went into a trance, he'd predict the future, and he cured people," according to Chiodo, who noted the preacher's fluent Italian. People gave him money as well as food and occasional lodging.[52]

Gesu looked like an archetypal preacher. Millie Pitillo-Savarese saw him arrive on Roland Avenue dressed in sandals and a dark robe, walking with a staff. "He gave me the

Gesu the Monk was born Jesus John Alvarez in Spain. Although never ordained, he developed quite a following in western New York, especially among Italians. Gesu spoke fluent Italian and regularly visited families on Roland Avenue. Photo source: Collection of Frank Chiodo

chills—he looked like God, but not in a scary way," reports Dolores DeMaria-Antecki. In Lackawanna, the monk had a following of perhaps 20 women and several of their husbands, all of whom contributed money to his work. One of the devotees, Michelina Sirianni, was widowed in 1926 and soon remarried Santo Mazza, a *paesano* from Calabria. Gesu left the imprint of his hand in fresh plaster on a wall in her house. She was one of three Lackawanna housewives "ordained" by the monk in about 1930; the others were Maria DeMaria and Maria Miceli. The three "nuns" dressed in brown and black habits. Earlier, in 1919, Gesu had "ordained" two women as the first members of the Order of the Most Holy Blood of Jesus. Apparently, Gesu lived for short periods within each of the communities where he preached. He lodged at the home of the Pascuzza family in Niagara Falls for two weeks, moved on to Lackawanna for a two-week sojourn at the Miceli or DeMaria house, then returned to Niagara Falls. When his new church was completed in North Collins during the mid-1930s, the Lackawanna "nuns" brought food to the Italian congregation.[53]

During the late 1940s, Rev. Anthony Bilotta, then stationed at St. James Church in Jamestown, heard neighborhood Italians talk of the pasta dinners prepared at the North Collins church by Gesu's "nuns." Some of these Italians displayed photographs of Gesu on their walls and wore rings with mini-photos of the monk. "He looked like Christ—with his beard, long hair, and robes," said Bilotta. The priest had heard that busloads of Italians from Erie, Buffalo, Jamestown, and Lackawanna were traveling to Gesu's North Collins church. Tony Grasso, who had contact with most Italian families in the Steel City, heard that Italian women from Roland Avenue, and some from Bethlehem Park, made regular pilgrimages to North Collins from the mid-1930s until the 1950s. They occasionally rented a bus that transported 30 to 40 people for a visit. Gesu often held his masses on Saturday evenings, and it was said in Lackawanna that part of his Easter ritual was to ride around his church on a donkey. Rev. Bilotta heard from his Jamestown parishioners that Gesu's elaborate Masses included incense, candles, and singing.[54]

Gesu approached Italians in other urban areas of western New York. In South Buffalo, he tried to convert Mrs. Bettina Casciani, a Jehovah's Witness, but she only conceded a monetary donation. His activities and the size of his following obviously was of concern to Catholic prelates. Rev. Hunt of Our Mother of Good Counsel attempted to discourage the Roland Avenue Italians from having any involvement with Gesu. Catholic officials even attempted unsuccessfully, to have the monk arrested during the 1930s. Gesu's handful of Lackawanna devotees were loyal for about 30 years, from the 1920s to the 1950s. Giuseppe and Maria Miceli purchased two cemetery plots near the monk's church in North Collins. When they moved to Florida in 1947, they gave the plots to Pasquale and Maria DeMaria, who were interred there when they passed away.[55]

Italian Protestants

In many American cities, Protestant proselytizers of various denominations made serious efforts to attract Italians into their ranks. In Buffalo, Milwaukee, and other cities, a significant number of Italians attended Protestant services and activities. This was not the case in Lackawanna, however, where only a handful of Italians entered the Protestant fold. An Italian Protestant minister did make a brief appearance on Roland Avenue. From 1918 to 1920, Rev. Salvatore Musso lived at the parsonage for the Roland Methodist Church. He is described in the 1920 census as a 45-year-old widower who migrated to the United States in 1902 and became a citizen 16 years later. He was able to speak, as well as read and write, in English,

his second language. While the census listed his occupation as "Pastor, Methodist Church," Musso was not the pastor of the Methodist church on Roland Avenue. He may have been sent there as an assistant pastor in an attempt to convert some of the Roland Avenue Italians clustered a few blocks to the west. However, longtime members of the Roland Methodist Church state that the congregation was always a mix of English, German, and Scottish Americans, with the addition of some Poles and Serbs during the last six decades. If Rev. Musso had tried to convert the local Italians, he had little luck. By 1921, he had moved on to another assignment.[56]

At this time, Buffalo had five Italian Protestant churches and a number of missions, including several formed by immigrants from Abruzzo. There is no evidence of a Protestant mission in the smaller Italian colony in Lackawanna. In the early 1920s, Salvatore DiTommaso, an immigrant from Abruzzo, was asked by an Italian from Buffalo to assist in organizing an Italian Protestant church in Lackawanna by urging other Steel City Italians to join. DiTommasso refused to get involved. It is probable that the recruiter was from the Abruzzese community in the Kensington district whose residents had become Baptists in Italy and founded an Italian Baptist church in Buffalo in 1896.[57]

Beyond the self-styled "Catholicism" of Gesu the Monk, the only other believers that drew any Steel City Italians away from the Roman Catholic Church were the Jehovah's Witnesses. After Donato Andrisani emigrated from Abruzzo to Buffalo, he became a Jehovah's Witness. When he moved to Lackawanna, he drove to a church on Myrtle Avenue in Buffalo for Sunday services. Several other Abruzzesi, perhaps influenced by *paesani* in Buffalo, also joined this denomination. Maddalena Iafallo, a widow with 10 children, was a Jehovah's Witness, and her family rode with the Andrisanis to the Myrtle Avenue church. Her son Angelo recalls the Buffalonians who provided Bible study classes to the Iafallo family in its Lackawanna home. Another immigrant, Ludovico "Dewey" Paolini, lived in Springville before moving with his family to Lackawanna. While working at Bethlehem Steel, he befriended several non – Italians who were Jehovah's Witnesses. He studied the Bible that his friends gave him and joined their denomination in the early 1940s. Paolini, who lived with his sister and brother-in-law, in turn gave his sister a Bible. Flora Paolini-Olivieri studied the scriptures herself, and ceased attending Catholic services, and became a Jehovah's Witness. Her husband, Pasquale, remained a Roman Catholic. Like the other Lackawanna Italians who became Jehovah's Witnesses, Dewey Paolini and his sister Flora traveled to Buffalo to attend church. By the 1950s, there were enough people of this denomination, including Poles from Lackawanna and other Italians from South Buffalo, to establish religious

FIGURE 6.6
GODPARENTS AND THE EVIL EYE

Two unique practices brought to the United States by Italian immigrants that other Catholics, as well as Protestants, found strange and superstitious were: the strong emphasis on godparents, and the belief in the evil eye.

Godparentage

The institution of godparentage was central to Italian life. It was a way of bringing people not related by blood into the family circle. Candidates for godparents were usually respected people in the community who were trusted friends of the parents and who could be depended on. The parents knew that the godparents would help raise the child if one or both of them should suddenly die or become incapacitated. In Lackawanna, the godparent sometimes exchanged gifts with the godchild and took a special interest in the child's development and growth into adulthood. Even St. Anthony's church bell and the flags of some organizations had godparents.

Titles demonstrating respect and intimacy were utilized by the parents, child, and godparents. These names varied among the regions in Italy, with the focus here being on southern Italy.

The parent and the godparent address:

- the father and the godfather as compare, *cumpa*, or *cumpadi*
- the mother and the godmother as *commare*, *cumma*, or *cummadi*
- the godson as compare, *comparello*, or *comparuccio*
- the goddaughter as *commare*, *comparella*, or *commarella*

The godson and goddaughter address:

- the godfather as *padrino*, compare, *cumpa*, or *cumpadi*
- the godmother as *madrina*, *commare*, *cumma*, or *cummadi*

The dialect terms *cumadi*, *cumma*, *cumpadi*, and *cumpa* are still used today, especially by first- and second-generation Italian Americans. Others have used the terms in a more general way to address close friends and others whom they respect. Such customs have varied by region and province. In Calabria, some families in that patriarchal society chose only a godfather for the children and no godmother.

During the first three decades of the twentieth century in Lackawanna, prominent Italians as well as common laborers were asked to be godparents. John and Nicolina Verel, Angelo and Caterina Acanfora, and Michelina Sirianni were often sought as godparents by Roland Avenue Italians. In the First Ward, Angelo and Vittoria Carlini, John and Adele Panzetta, and Amedeo and Giulia Catuzza were often asked to fill this role. In Italy and among Italian immigrants in the United States 100 years ago, the practice was to choose non-relatives as godparents. As time went on, the second and third generations altered the practice and often chose siblings of the parents or other relatives to be the godparents of their children.

The Real Godfather

Movies depicting Italian Americans as gangsters have promoted a mistaken idea about the meaning of godparents to Italians. The institution of the godparents in Italian culture involves a close and honored relationship.

Family is all-important in Italian culture, and the godparent becomes an extension of the immediate family. Italian immigrants and their children have valued godparents and given this institution a prominent position in the community. In Italian neighborhoods

Maria and Nicola Manzetti with their godson, Ralph Maninelli, in 1913.
Photo source: Jack and Mary Panczykowski

throughout the United States, leaders and respected individuals can be identified by the number of godchildren they have.

While assimilation and the passage of time have made godparentage less vital in the lives of Italian Americans, it still remains a respected part of community life. The next time you see a film portraying Italians as gangster godfathers, remember the role and relationship of *real* godfathers.

The *Mal'occhio* or Evil Eye

Many Italian immigrants believed in the *mal'occhio*, or evil eye. "People talked about the mal'occhio," recalls Frank Chiodo, who grew up on Roland Avenue. Children, especially babies, were held to be vulnerable to the spell of the evil eye. Giuseppe and Molly Nasso had each of their offspring wear a clove of garlic on a chain around their neck. Horns, red ribbons, and scissors-shaped amulets were pinned to clothes or suspended from a chain around the neck. These amulets it was believed, could ward off or cut the gaze of the mal'occhio. Women were often seen with such items pinned to their dresses. Italians who believed in the evil eye were always on the alert for people who gave compliments, as these statements were viewed as a cover for jealousy or envy, typically seen as root causes of the malady. An adult offering a compliment regarding a child would immediately follow it with the phrase "God bless him/her" to indicate that no ill will was intended.

Italian women had various means to diagnose and treat the evil eye. Maddalena Basel dropped oil into a bowl of water, if it spread, this indicated that the evil eye was present. She then said prayers to remove the spell. Another Roland Avenue resident, Rosamaria Falbo, said prayers to remove the evil eye and cried as she did so. Pauline Antigiovanni could remove the evil eye either in person or over the telephone.

Anna Fistola taught her technique to other Ingham Avenue women, including her daughter Carmela and granddaughter Giustina. The ritual consisted of anointing the head of the stricken person and dropping some of the oil into a dish of clean, cold water. If the oil spread, this indicated the evil eye was present. A brief prayer was then said nine times, with the healer making the sign of the cross on the person's forehead with each repetition:

Occhiu e occhiettu, cornett' ca sambi,

Occhiu crab la media, e sciatta u mal'occhiu

(Translation: Eye and gaze, horns which heal; eye be the cure and get rid of the evil eye.)

More oil was dropped into the water, and the sign of the cross was made in the oil. If the oil spread, indicating the hex was still present, the phrase *sciatta u mal'occhiu* was uttered two or three more times.

To maintain one's healing powers often involved certain rituals. In Pettorano sul Gizio, one lady repeated certain secret prayers on Easter and Christmas to maintain her ability to remove the mal'occhiu. Some women such as Maria Olivieri of Bethlehem Park, could remove the evil eye and also cure other maladies. When Jenny Andreozzi had headaches, she often called on Maria to remove the hex. Maria put oil on "the victim's" forehead and placed some of it in a bowl of water to determine if the evil eye was in effect. She then said prayers in Italian as she stood over her "patient." Tony and Jenny Andreozzi also sent their daughter Dolly to Maria when the girl had a headache. On one occasion Dolly asked her friend Adeline Covelli to accompany her. Not wanting to be left out, Adeline told Maria that she also had the evil eye cast upon her, and both girls were involved in the ceremony to remove the hex.

Rosabella Fiorella lived with her daughter Lucia, son-in-law Donato Chiacchia, and their children in the Old Village. Her granddaughter Sara observed Rosabella carrying out the healing practices she had learned in Sicily. Rosabella set sprains by soaking a cloth in a mixture of egg whites and sugar, then wrapping this around the affected area. When the cloth dried, the result was a hardened cast. To make a salve, she mixed chopped leaves, sugar, and laundry soap and placed them on cloth sterilized by boiling. This was applied to boils and infections to draw out fluids. During the influenza epidemic of

1918, Fiorella used her own technique to protect her family from the deadly disease. "My grandmother," states Sara Chiacchia-Kempf, "rubbed garlic on the stove, on the flat part where water was boiled, and under the covers. It burned and protected our family from the flu." On Roland Avenue, Anna Maria DePerto and Carmela Falcone were midwives who also tended to sprains and broken bones. Anna Maria applied casts made of egg whites to sprains. When 10-year-old Frank Chiodo had a swollen arm that he could not bend, his parents contacted Carmela. "I was afraid that I wouldn't have been able to make my First Holy Communion … I couldn't cross myself," Chiodo recalls. Carmela made a poultice that included raw eggs and charred pig's ears. She applied it to the boy's arm and wrapped it with a towel. "Overnight the swelling went down," recalls Chiodo, and the relieved boy was able to make his First Holy Communion. Carmela's husband Francesco was sometimes called on to set broken bones.

Rosina Tripoli, a resident of Ingham Avenue, had a knack for removing the evil eye and treating injuries. The Covelli family, which also had roots in Calabria, called Tripoli to their Bethlehem Park home when one of their children sprained her wrist. Adeline Covelli remembers Rosina going through quite a ritual in tending to her. Mrs. Tripoli first said prayers to her patron saint (San Rocco), did a treatment with oil and water, wrapped the wrist in a cast made of egg whites, and then put the girl's arm in a sling.

Sources: Interviews with Frank Chiodo, December 28, 1983; Joe Nasso, December 28, 1994; Jay Covino-Masters, July 6, 1996; John Novelli, April 18, 1995; Adeline Covelli-Andreozzi; Margaret Battista and Mary Mastrobattista, April 5, 1996; Sara Chiacchia-Kemp, July 12, 1996; Gallatin Anderson, "Il Comparaggio, the Italian Godparenthood Complex," *Southwestern Journal of Anthropology,* Vol. 13, 1957, pp 32-53

meetings in Lackawanna. At first, the group rented space at the Chuck Wagon Restaurant on Abbott Road; later, they had a brick structure built on South Fisher Road. By the 1990s, the congregation had 85 members of many ethnic backgrounds.[58]

Teaching the Faith to the Children

While Italian immigrants had a variety of religious experiences,—attending Catholic churches, following Gesu the Monk, or simply ignoring church altogether—many of their children were being taught Catholic doctrine. The American Catholic Church, wanting to de-emphasize the Italian *feste* and other folk customs of eastern and southern European immigrants, took every opportunity to instill children with the formal beliefs of the Catholic Church in the United States. In Italy and America, according to historian Leonard Covello, "religious education was almost entirely the prerogative of the older females within the family. It involved no church tenets or Christian dogma, but included primarily the memorization of prayers and stories from the life of the saints." This gradually changed in Lackawanna's Italian neighborhoods. While many men ignored church, their wives sent their children to St. Anthony's or Our Mother of Good Counsel for Sunday Mass. An increasing number also had the youngsters attend religious instruction classes. By the 1930s, the public schools in New York State dismissed all students an hour early on Mondays for this purpose. By this time, church volunteers were offering this instruction to the youth of St. Anthony's parish. Sometimes, all Catholic children at a particular public school attended classes at one parish. During the late 1930s, Nick Canali and his Catholic classmates at Roosevelt School went to religious instruction at St. Charles Church. Five years later, Arc Petricca and other First Ward youth went alternately to St. Anthony's, St. Hyacinth's, and Assumption for classes, which were usually taught by a priest from St. Charles (which later became Queen of All Saints).[59]

The Italian children went to St. Anthony's for instruction prior to their First Holy Communion and Confirmation. Adeline Covelli remembers that the instructors for her Confirmation classes were a woman from St. Anthony's parish and a religious brother from Our Lady of Victory Church. When Yolanda Monaco attended classes prior to making her First Holy Communion in 1936, Dolly Andreozzi was one of the group of teenagers and young adults who served as instructors. Rev. Vifredo also took a role, questioning youngsters who were preparing themselves for confirmation to test their knowledge. Aldo Filipetti vividly recalled his preparation for Confirmation in the early 1940s.

I remember Father Vifredo. I had studied and studied and studied, and then they call you up there to take the test. Father Vifredo was very strict and tough. I remembered going in there, and I knew all the questions except one, and I failed. He told me that I failed and I cried all the way home … because my mother had bought a suit for me for the confirmation, and now I couldn't make it. … There was an Italian woman next to the church, she saw me crying. She brought me in the house, and gave me an orange to settle me down. She knew who I was; I didn't know who she was. … This woman said, "Don't worry about it. It'll all work out." Sure enough, the next day the priest called us back and then he asked us a couple more questions. And we passed. It was a very trying couple of days.

Another Italian youth followed a different course. Iole Schiavi was an independent-minded girl who decided on her own to attend St. Anthony's, as her father never went to church and her mother's attendance at Mass was irregular. When it came time for her First Holy Communion, she concluded that the Sacred Heart of Jesus, a Croatian church, would be appropriate for her, and she made her Communion there. Later, when Rev. Vifredo learned of this, he confronted Schiavi in St. Anthony's Church and scolded her.[60]

Occasionally, St. Anthony's hosted missions, which began on Sunday afternoon and lasted for a week. Visiting priests addressed the children during the afternoon and the adults at evening time. During the early 1930s, teenager Adeline Covelli enjoyed going to these missions. She recalls one Italian priest in particular, a silver-haired man who was kind and smiled a lot. He spoke to the young people in both English and Italian, telling them, "Be proud of your heritage," and "Don't change your names. Be proud of who you are—don't focus on names." He taught the children two Italian hymns in honor of the Blessed Virgin and gave each attendee a religious medal.[61]

The children of Lackawanna's Italian immigrants were gradually learning a new form of Catholicism, and such involvement gained one respect in America. Girls and especially boys, despite their fathers' indifference to church matters, were becoming involved in the Church and learning religious doctrine prescribed by Irish American clerics. This process became more pronounced in the late 1930s and grew after World War II. The new pastor at St. Anthony's as of 1946, Rev. Ciolino, founded the Bishop's Committee, which visited homes and gave children religious pamphlets to increase their knowledge of Catholic teachings. During years just after the war, the number of organizations and activities at St. Anthony's Church increased dramatically.[62]

Leaders of the Mount Carmel Society celebrated the 60th anniversary of the group's founding with Rev. Bilotta in 1978. From left are: Tony and Mary Grasso, Jo Andreozzi, Dolly Ceccarelli, [Unk], Laura Canali, Rev. Bilotta, Anna Fistola, Sabatino Fistola, Mary Covino-Kurnik, Walter Kurnik. Photo source: Collection of Rev. Anthony Bilotta

Church Societies

The first society at St. Anthony's Church was Congrega Madonna del Carmine, [Our Lady of Mount Carmel Congregation], founded in 1918. Better known as the Mount Carmel Society, this women's group offered death benefits to families of deceased members. The society supported church functions and raised funds via dues and raffles. Every month, a Mass was said at St. Anthony's for society members, both living and dead. According to the group's bylaws, the members were "obliged to perform their Easter duty in a body, … and also on the feast of Our Lady of Mount Carmel, which feast shall be celebrated with solemnity." Any member who failed to appear at one of these events without a legitimate excuse was fined $1. The annual society dues were $2, and new members paid a $1 initiation fee. Each member was also assessed $1 upon the death of any member so as to replenish the society's treasury. The designated beneficiary of a deceased member received $100, and the society furnished a wreath of flowers and paid for a High Mass. All members were required to say the rosary as a group at the house of the deceased member.[63]

Every August, the Mount Carmel society took part in a pilgrimage to a shrine in Cheektowaga dedicated to the Feast of the Assumption. Busloads of women, many of them Italian American, from throughout western New York gathered at Our Lady Help of Christians Church at Union Road and Genesee Street in Cheektowaga. At an old chapel and grotto on the church grounds, the faithful attended Mass, performed the stations of the cross, and offered prayers to the Madonna. Some Italian women walked barefoot, or with only stockings on their feet, from the Buffalo city line to the church. Others, such as Maria Ross of Lackawanna, "walked" on their knees from the chapel door to the altar and the statue of the blessed mother, thanking her for answering prayers or beseeching her to cure afflictions or grant other requests. A bus took St. Anthony's parishioners and members of the Mount Carmel Society to the shrine. Usually composed of women and children, the group took lunches and stayed for the day.[64]

Banner of the Ladies Society of Madonna del Carmine at St. Anthony's Church. The organization folded in 1990. Photo source: Paul Pasquarello

The Holy Name Society of St. Anthony's parish had a slow start but became very active in the 1930s when a number of the American-born men became members. In 1939, the society sponsored a performance of the play Trail of the Lonesome Pine. *The cast included Tony Moretti (standing, 3rd from left) and (seated) John Christiano, at left, Julia Cologgi, 3rd from left, and Olivia Capodagli, 2nd from right.* Photo source: Collection of Mike Morgan

American-born, took turns occupying the president's office from 1932 to 1940. No immigrants were listed in the available rosters of society leaders after 1941.[65]

Many second-generation men active in the Holy Name Society were also active in the civic life of Lackawanna, both within and outside the Italian community. Through involvement in St. Anthony's Church, they joined the American trend of achieving respectability and status through participation in one's church. Traditional southern Italians had seen church involvement as the province of women, children, and the poor, and with the highest expression of religiosity the *festa*, the religious festival. However, attitudes were changing among Lackawanna's Italians. While a significant number of second-generation men adopted the anticlerical stance of their fathers, the young men in the Holy Name Society reflected a dramatic shift in values. In 1937, the Holy Name Society celebrated the 25th anniversary of Rev. Vifredo's ordination with a banquet at the Hotel Lackawanna. In addition to the monthly Communion breakfasts, the society hosted theatrical productions at the church. In 1939, the Lackawanna Players, an amateur theater group including many Italian Americans, presented *Trail of the Lonesome Pine*. Two years later, the troupe staged a comedy, *Tish*.[66]

St. Anthony's parish reached out to boys in the Italian community in 1939 by sponsoring Boy Scout Troop No. 20, with Samuel Conte of the Holy Name Society acting as scoutmaster. The boys organized a Mother's Day ceremony in May 1939 and presented gifts to their mothers. During the 1930s, the Holy Name Society encouraged males age 15 and over to join in the group's activities. In 1940, it founded the Junior Holy Name Society for 12- to 17-year-old boys, who received Communion on the third Sunday of the month. This junior organization did not last long, as many of its members were drafted into military service during World War II.[67]

The Sodality of the Immaculate Conception was founded by 1934. At that time, it was composed of 30 members, mostly second-generation women. The Blessed Virgin Mary Sodality, also was in existence by 1934, and made up of the daughters of immigrants who engaged in a variety of activities. In December 1938, the society held a Christmas party at St. Anthony's Church and collected gifts for children at the Our Lady of Victory Orphanage. The group was inactive for a period during World War II but reorganized in 1945.[68]

The founding dates of the Sacred Heart Society is uncertain, as it had already been in existence when it was incorporated in 1933 as the Pio Unione de Sacro Cuore di Gesu, the Pious Union of the Sacred Heart of Jesus. Alessandrina Sperduti and Augusta Anticoli were the principal founders of the group, which focused on offering prayers and also cleaning the church. Sperduti encouraged her daughter Yolanda to join at age 14 by paying her 10-cent dues. The St. Anthony Society, formed in 1920, was probably the first attempt at a holy name society in the parish. Joe Milano remembered that the group had trouble attracting members. The 10 to 15 male members were teased by other Italian men, and the society eventually folded. As Milano observed, "The old-timers weren't religious." The Holy Name Society was functioning by 1932 and held an after – Communion breakfast that July. Three months later, the monthly breakfast featured realtor James Privitera of Buffalo as the speaker. This was received well, and two years later, the members "approved a plan to stimulate interest in and create a better understanding of local affairs by inviting prominent business or professional men to attend each meeting during the year as a guest speaker." Immigrants such as Steve Canestrari, Luigi Petti, and Joe Juditta held leadership positions, but the majority of officers were of the second generation. Joseph Pacillo and Nick Milano, both

World War II was a pivotal period for ethnic groups in the United States, and this was equally true for the assimilation of Italian Americans. After the war, activities at St. Anthony's Church increased dramatically. Existing groups became more active, and new societies were founded. The gradual involvement of young Italian men in church programs was boosted by the arrival of the youthful Rev. Ciolino as assistant pastor in 1946. The Rosary Society was functioning by this time and held what turned out to be its first annual masquerade party at Memorial Hall in February 1947. The following year, the society had a membership of 100 first- and second-generation women. Within a few years, the group's name was changed to the Rosary Altar Society. A Mothers Club was functioning in the parish by 1950, with the apparent purpose of raising funds to help the parish Boy Scout troop organize a drum corps. The group sponsored a card party toward this end, assisted by the Lake Erie Italian Club.[69]

The return of many veterans following World War II reactivated the Holy Name Society. In 1946, with the assistance of the Rosary and Blessed Virgin Mary societies, it held its first (later, annual) dance at the Dom Polski Hall. The following year, it joined with its counterparts in four other parishes to sponsor a rally at Albright Court, then began sponsoring its own annual rally. These usually began with Mass and Communion at St. Anthony's Church, followed by breakfast at the Albright Court community hall or Lincoln School. Keynote speakers included Judge Christy Buscaglia in 1948 and, during the early 1950s, Congressman Anthony Tauriello of Buffalo and banker James Oddy, who was raised in the Old Village. Three hundred members attended these rallies.[70]

In 1946, Rev. Ciolino organized the Campus Youth Club, a group for high-school boys and girls. The club met every Thursday evening for dancing, games, basketball, and other sports. As early as 1928, the parish sponsored a football team, the St. Anthony's All-Stars. After World War II, recreational activities quickly grew as Anthony DePasquale became sports director and business manager of the parish in 1947. He appointed John Palumbo to manage the baseball team, the St. Anthony's Saints, and John Marinelli to manage its softball team.[71]

Dances and other events sponsored by individual church groups slowly grew more inclusive. In 1948, the first Annual Spring Dance was sponsored by the Blessed Virgin Mary Sodality and the Sacred Heart Society. The women's societies held card parties and spaghetti dinners to raise money for the parish. In May 1947, they organized a Mother's Day breakfast and program at which the men of the Holy Name Society served the food. The following year, the women sponsored a father-and-son banquet at which the women and their daughters served breakfast to the men and boys following Sunday Mass.

The Society of the Sacred Heart of Jesus was founded at St. Anthony's by 1933. Photo source: Paul Pasquarello

The June 1949 breakfast was sponsored by four women's groups of the parish as well as the Lake Erie Ladies Auxiliary Society. The males were treated to breakfast at the Lincoln School auditorium, then led by toastmaster Ralph Fiore through a program that included guest speaker Thomas Glass of Seneca Vocational School. These annual celebrations of mothers and fathers underscored the importance of the family in Italian American life.[72]

The men's and women's societies of St. Anthony's joined forces for other parish events. In October 1947, the Holy Name Society sponsored a ball, with refreshments served by members of the women's sodalities. The next year, the parish societies hosted a Christmas party that was cosponsored by several of the sectarian groups: the Lake Erie Italian Club and its auxiliary, the Stag Club; the Galanti Athletic Association; and the Roman Independent Club. Two plays, *The Christ Child* and The *Christmas Story*, were put on by members of the church societies. In January 1947, actors from the Catholic Youth Council put on a comedy, *Where Is That Report Card?*, which won first place in a contest held at Our Lady of Victory Academy.[73]

This level of participation by Italian men marked a definite change from the experience of their immigrant fathers, in both

Italy and Lackawanna. Strengthened by postwar economic prosperity and greater acceptance of Italians in society, this newly emerging Italian American religious experience was one sign of the ethnic group's assimilation. The Italian pastor and his parishioners, no longer constantly at odds, could now experience a greater sense of common purpose. Some attitudes, predictably of course, were slow to change. Many second-generation men, including businessman Nick Sperduto, did not attend Mass. Sperduto did support St. Anthony's financially, however, and his children attended Mass. When Rev. Ciolino confronted him, saying, "Nick, I never see you in church," Sperduto responded, "Don't worry about me, Father, worry about those guys in the front pews." In a more serious vein, an old anticlerical attitude was demonstrated in an incident that harkened back to the traditional tension between Italian priests and male parishioners. The basement of the church had been refinished by the Lake Erie Italian Club, and Rev. Ciolino then had the church painted and a new furnace installed. Nick Thomas, president of the Holy Name Society, stated that the society planned to pay the contractor for this work. When Rev. Ciolino asked that the money be paid directly to him, Thomas refused. This impasse lead to a temporary dissolution of the society. A similar situation arose several decades later, but these incidents were exceptions rather than the rule in postwar years.[74]

The Parish Grows and Changes

In 1917, Lackawanna had about 150 Italian families who were to be served by the new St. Anthony's Church. By 1946, the parish had grown to include 1,283 parishioners in 251 families. During Rev. Vifredo's 29-year tenure, he enlarged the rectory, bought two side altars, and in 1945 paid off the mortgage. Vifredo's health was obviously failing by 1944, and in December of that year, Bishop John O'Hara sent Rev. John McCarthy to serve as temporary assistant pastor. On June 13, 1946, the bishop appointed a new assistant pastor, Thomas Ciolino. Upon his arrival in Lackawanna, Rev. Ciolino was put in charge of the altar boys and had good relations with them. According to Armondo Pietrocarlo, the new priest was "outgoing and a good Ping-Pong player." Following Vifredo's death in December 1947, Ciolino became the pastor of St. Anthony's, officially taking on this role on June 6, 1948. A youthful and energetic man, Rev. Ciolino brought new life to the parish. "He was able to relate with young and old alike," Tony Grasso wrote. "His charming personal qualities projected him into immediate favor with the people of the parish. Taking the reins of our church as pastor, this young shepherd was a remarkable experience for St. Anthony's. It was like a transfusion of new blood in a sick body." Ciolino attracted the second generation to church activities and organized several new

FIGURE 6.7

REV. THOMAS CIOLINO

Born in Buffalo on August 4, 1911, Thomas Ciolino was the son of Nicola and Caterina Salemi, immigrants from Montemaggiore Belsito, Sicily. He grew up in St. Anthony's parish in Buffalo, was baptized and confirmed there, and attended the parish school from 1916 to 1924. Graduating from Buffalo's Canisius High School in 1928, he then studied for two years at Canisius College before completing his seminary studies at Our Lady of Angels College and Seminary at Niagara University in 1936. On June 6 of that year, he was ordained as a priest at St. Joseph's New Cathedral in Buffalo. Years later, he explained to a news reporter that the ceremony was almost " 'postponed indefinitely because I did something I shouldn't have done. I sent out invitations. We weren't supposed to. The chancellor blew his stack.' But the president of Niagara University spoke with the chancellor and he was forgiven."

Rev. Ciolino remained in New York State throughout his career, first as assistant pastor at St. Anthony's in Batavia, where he remained two years. From 1938 to 1940, he served brief assignments as an assistant at St. James in Jamestown, St. Anthony's in Fredonia, and St. Francis of Assissi in Buffalo before returning to St. Anthony's in Batavia. All these were Italian parishes. On June 22, 1946, he was assigned to St. Anthony's in Lackawanna as assistant pastor, and became the church's pastor two years later. He transferred in 1960 to Our Lady of Mount Carmel in Silver Creek, where he became pastor. Sixteen years later, he became pastor of Our Lady of Mount Carmel in Brant, N.Y. He retired from the priesthood on September 1, 1986.

Rev. Ciolino was a member of the Knights of Columbus and served as coordinator for Region 22 of Diocese Parish Groupings. He also belonged to the Italian Commission on Vocations, an organization that encouraged young men to enter the priesthood. Rev. Ciolino died in Dunkirk, New York, on April 13, 1987.

Sources: Archives of the Buffalo Diocese, clergy data sheet on Rev. Ciolino; *Buffalo News*, 4/15/87.

societies. The son of immigrants, he spoke some Italian but usually conversed with parishioners and gave his sermons in English. By this time, the late 1940s, many immigrants were fairly comfortable with the English language, and the need for priests to speak Italian had diminished. Also, seminary training, especially at diocesan seminaries, encouraged priests to focus on assimilation and the abandonment of old-world ways. Some

FIGURE 6.8

LACKAWANNA ITALIANS IN RELIGIOUS ORDERS

Rev. Louis Manzo, ordained in 1966, grew up on South Park Avenue, attended the OLV Basilica, and graduated from Father Baker High School.
Photo source: *Lackawanna Leader*, 12/16/65

Italian immigrants believed in marriage and childbearing for their children and sometimes discouraged young people from entering seminaries and convents. As a result, only a handful of Lackawanna Italian American men and women entered religious orders. Joseph Fiore, once an altar boy at St. Anthony's, was the only member of the parish to enter the priesthood. Louis Mauro Jr., whose father was a trustee at St. Anthony's, could not enter the seminary because of poor eyesight. He did become a Jesuit brother and later a deacon. Nick and Angela DePasquale were raised in Lackawanna, attended St. Anthony's, and later joined Our Mother of Good Counsel parish when they moved to Blasdell. Their son Leonard became a priest in 1971 at a ceremony attended by Rev. Ciolino and Rev. Bilotta of St. Anthony's. Rev. DePasquale is in the Consolata Missionary Order, which was founded in Turin, Italy. Another parishioner at Our Mother of Good Counsel, Vincent Pierino, whose parents ran a business in Lackawanna for many years, also became a priest. Two members of the Our Lady of Victory parish were ordained as priests—Michael DelVecchio in 1954, and Louis Manzo in 1965. Rev. Manzo studied for his doctor of theology degree in Rome. Rose Panzetta became a nun in a cloistered order in New Jersey. Antoinette Calzone, whose family lived on Roland Avenue and attended Our Mother of Good Counsel, became Sister Mary Goretti when she joined the Order of St. Francis and lived in a convent in Joliet, Illinois. Linda Talbot, daughter of Lackawanna native Mary DePasquale, a cousin of Rev. DePasquale, became a Sister of St. Joseph. Mauro, Manzo, DePasquale, and Talbot are all third-generation Italian Americans, the others named here are second-generation.

Source: Interviews with Joe Ceccarelli, June 9, 2005; Rev. Anthony Bilotta, September 24, 1994; Rev. Larry Burns, June 6, 2005; Rev. Leonard DePasquale, July 24, 2005; Chet Catuzza, September 8, 1994; *Lackawanna Leader*, 3/30/61, 12/30/65, 10/27/66, 8/24/67; *Front Page*, 11/14/90; U.S. Census, 1930; *Buffalo Suburban Directory of Householders*, 1949.

of the immigrants, however, disapproved of Ciolino, thinking him too modern. He was criticized for blessing only specific homes, upon request, at Easter time instead of automatically going to all parishioners' homes, as Rev. Vifredo had done. Assunta DePasquale, a parish stalwart who attended Mass daily, was at first very leery of the new priest.[75]

Rev. Ciolino brought in other priests and nuns to assist in parish projects. During the early years of his tenure, the Society of St. Paul opened a high school and a home for the faculty priests in Derby, 10 miles south of Lackawanna. "This religious order supplied St. Anthony's with priests to care for a great number of people in the parish." One of these young priests, Rev. Bernard Paterniti, became very involved in life at St. Anthony's. In 1955, four nuns of the Missionary Sisters of Mercy, whose mother house was in Bahia, Brazil, came to St. Anthony's. The parish purchased a building across the street from the church to house the nuns. While Rev. Ciolino was disappointed that the nuns did not speak Italian, he welcomed their assistance in teaching religion to the children of the parish. After 18 months,

Rev. Ciolino with church trustees Serafino Mattucci, on left, and Louis Mauro, on right, in 1955. Photo source: *"Dedication Booklet: St. Anthony's New Hall,"* 1955

the nuns moved to Leroy, New York, and later to Buffalo. In 1958, eight nuns of the Sisters of Social Service came to Lackawanna to work at Assumption Church, a Hungarian parish.

FIGURE 6.9

ITALIAN PRIESTS VISIT LACKAWANNA

Several priests from Italy visited their relatives in Lackawanna following World War II. In 1952, Monsignor Edmondo Catuzza, a nephew of Ferdinand Catuzza, traveled from Giuliano di Roma to renew ties with *paesani* in Aliquippa, Pennsylvania; Steubenville, Ohio; and Tarrytown and Lackawanna in New York. He lived for four months in Bethlehem Park with his cousin, Chet Catuzza. Rev. Catuzza said Mass at St. Anthony's, where a special collection was taken to support his orphanage at Lobigo, near Rome. Another priest from Giuliano, Leone Fabi, traveled to the Steel City in about 1960 to visit Domenico Sperduti and other cousins. A member of the Franciscan order, he had been a missionary in Africa. Rev. Ernesto Leonetti made several trips from Pedace, Calabria, to visit his brother Armando in Lackawanna. A priest from Santacroce, Molise, came to the Steel City to spend time with relatives and said Mass several times at St. Anthony's. Rev. Dante Gemmiti of Sora, Lazio, visited his aunt and uncle, Mario and Maria

Fanone, and grandparents, Angelo and Giovanna Fanone, in Lackawanna in 1966. He said Mass at St. Anthony's, and 200

parishioners attended a testimonial dinner for him at the church.

St. Anthony's Hall, where Rev. Gemmiti is honored at a banquet attended by 200 parishioners. From left are Michael Morgan (at the podium), Rev. Bilotta, Rev. Gemmiti, and Maria Fanone (standing at right).
Photo source: Phil Fanone

When Rev. Dante Gemmiti traveled to Lackawanna in 1966 to visit relatives, he said Mass at St. Anthony's. Mario and Maria Fanone, his aunt and uncle, as well as Angelo and Giovanna Fanone, his maternal grandparents, lived on Ingham Avenue.
Photo source: Phil Fanone

Source: Interviews with Joe Ceccarelli, June 9, 2005; Rev. Anthony Bilotta, September 24, 1994; Rev. Larry Burns, June 6, 2005; Rev. Leonard DePasquale, July 24, 2005; Chet Catuzza, September 8, 1994; and Phil Fanone, November 24, 2008; *Lackawanna Leader*, 3/30/61, 12/30/65, 10/27/66, 8/24/67; *Front Page*, 11/14/90; U.S. Census, 1930; *Buffalo Suburban Directory of Householders*, 1949

This order, founded in Hungary, had established communities in Cuba, Canada, and the United States. All natives of Hungary, the nuns needed a place to live, and Rev. Ciolino invited them to stay at the then-vacant convent on Ingham Avenue. There were no Italian-speakers among them, but the nuns taught catechism to the children of the parish. Loretta Nicometo, who lived just across Point Street from the convent, remembers that the women wore a distinctive gray habit. During the 1960s, the nuns were also working with the Spanish Apostolate at Assumption Church in Lackawanna and at Immaculate Conception parish in Buffalo. The Sisters of Social Service moved to their mother house in Buffalo by 1971.[76]

The parish continued to grow, and by 1955 there were 350 families enrolled in St. Anthony's. The improved economic conditions and a different attitude toward charity drives was reflected in the monies collected for the annual Catholic Charities drive. In the 1950 appeal, St. Anthony's parishioners

gave $4,217, an offering second only to that of Our Lady of Victory Basilica among the eight parishes in Lackawanna. This was a far cry from the 1932 drive, in which St. Anthony's contributed the least. The new attitude of giving was again displayed in 1958, when seven societies of St. Anthony's pledged $1,000 toward the construction of a new wing at Our Lady of Victory Hospital. When the parish decided to build a center to hold classes and gatherings, a committee of men, chaired by John Galanti, canvassed the neighborhoods and asked each family in the parish for $100. A total of $82,000 was raised, which included contributions from the Rosary Society, the Holy Name Society, the Lake Erie Italian Club, the Galanti Athletic Association, and the Stag Club. The ground-breaking for the building took place on December 5, 1954, and the hall was completed the following year. Located behind the church, the center included a kitchen, religious-instruction classrooms, utility rooms, and a hall with a capacity

Rev. Ciolino celebrating May Day, Circa 1959. The nun at right is one of eight Sisters of Social Service who lived in the convent across the street from St. Anthony's. Photo source: St. Anthony's Church

In 1958, seven St. Anthony's Church societies pledged $1,000 toward the construction of a new wing at Our Lady of Victory Hospital. Seated, left to right, are Yolanda Sperduti-Tobias, Rev. Thomas Ciolino, and Donata Monaco. Standing, left to right, are: Leonard Pasiecznik of the fund drive, John Galanti, Anna Suffoletto, Kenneth Bracci, and Ed Rosinski of the fund drive. Photo source: *Front Page*, Bill Delmont

of 300. There was space for banquets and social events, church society meetings, community group meetings, and even to store athletic equipment for the parish youth. The dedication ceremony was held on November 20, 1955, followed by a dinner and dance in the new hall. Rev. Bernard Paterniti gave the invocation, Rev. Donato Valente, pastor of St. Francis of Assissi Church in Buffalo, offered the benediction, and Rev. Ciolino presented a history of the parish. Another speaker, Monsignor Joseph McGuire, praised the spirit of the parishioners. "Love, devotion, loyalty—of such was the new parish hall of St. Anthony's constructed." Things had definitely changed since the pre – World War II days.[77]

The church continued to prosper in both its social and economic functions. The Rosary Altar Society and Holy Name Society raised funds with frequent card parties. In 1958, when bingo became legal in New York State, the parish hosted the game in its new hall. Parishioners spent a lot of money on bingo, enough to loan the diocese $50,000. Meanwhile, volunteers helped the parish save money. John Galanti, Vince Madar, and Essio "Ace" Baldelli freely gave of their time to make repairs on the aging church edifice. Ida Monaco-Madar and many other women worked hard on all aspects of church functions, including cleaning. Millie Sambrotto and Jo Andreozzi handled the church envelopes and recorded the weekly collections. The second generation was very amenable to this more open and participatory style of parish life, and many eagerly joined the church societies. Parishioner Albert Suffoletto went on to become the Youth Director of the Catholic Youth Council of the Diocese of Buffalo. He received the 1958 National Pro Deo et Juventute [to God and youth] award for his work at St. Anthony's and other parishes. Suffoletto was raised on Dona Street in Lackawanna's First Ward.[78]

Rev. Ciolino remained a popular pastor throughout his 14 years at the church. When John Galanti married in his wife's home state of California, he paid to have the priest travel to the West Coast and perform the ceremony. Ciolino left St. Anthony's in early 1960 and was replaced on March 7 of that year by Rev. Anthony Bilotta, who remained as pastor for 16 years and led the parish in a number of important projects (see Figure 6.11). His first day in Lackawanna boded well for the new pastor. As his car turned from Hamburg Turnpike and headed east on Holbrook Street, children waved and shouted "Hi, Father!" Bilotta thought to himself, "There must be a lot of Catholics in Lackawanna."[79]

By the early 1960s, St. Anthony's had grown to more than 450 families, and it was obvious that a new church and rectory were needed. When Rev. Bilotta requested permission to build a new church, the bishop asked a question that reflected a 75-year issue for the Catholic hierarchy: "How come Italians don't form Catholic schools?" Bilotta could respond only with generalities. Certainly, the Poles, Irish, and Germans had formed hundreds of Catholic schools in parishes around the country. But Italian parishioners in Lackawanna and elsewhere were less likely to take an interest in such endeavors, reasoning that their children could go to public schools or existing parochial schools. Second generation Italians were more open to financing schools than were their parents, but Italians in general remained leery of committing to such financial investments and displays of religiosity. The bishop's question notwithstanding, Bilotta received permission to build a new edifice. A large fund-raising campaign committee was created, with Anthony Moretti as general chairman and John Galanti as administrative chairman. Four teams of solicitors canvassed Lackawanna and neighboring areas; each family in the parish was assessed $200, and by spring of 1963, $133,000 had been raised. On April 7, 1963, a large group of parishioners watched Rev. Bilotta and church trustees Serafino Mattucci and Louis Mauro break ground for the new structure on the lot just south of the original building. Fund-raising progress was indicated on a huge barometer placed on the outer front wall of the old church. By May 19, the barometer reading was $40,000, and a June 9 bulletin announced that $104,000 had been pledged. The Lake Erie Italian Club was cited for its "most generous gift," and parishioners were reminded to pick up their "fair share" envelopes. Yellow placards proclaiming "St. Anthony's Church: We Gave a Fair Share!" were placed in windows throughout Lackawanna. Eventually $302,000 was raised, the construction was completed, and the congregation moved into the new building on April 16, 1964. Two months later on June 13, the feast of St. Anthony, bishop James McNulty dedicated the new church. Another dedication ceremony and banquet took place on August 15.[81]

This house was purchased by St. Anthony's parish in 1955 and used as a convent until 1971. The building is directly across the street from the church.
Photo source: St. Anthony's Church

Sister Mary Agnes and Sister Mary Cross, Superior, were among four nuns of the Missionary Sisters of Mercy who lived in the convent purchased by the parish. The nuns remained at the convent from 1955 to 1956. Photo source: "Dedication Booklet, St. Anthony's New Hall," 1955

These women, all immigrants from Giuliano di Roma, were active in St. Anthony's Church. In the photo, taken in the late 1940s or early 1950s, are (from left): Mary Petricca, Alfreda Petricca, Ada Guglielmi, and Augusta Anticoli. Photo source: Joe and Rose Guglielmi

FIGURE 6.10

ITALIANS' CONTINUING DEVOTION TO SAINTS

The late 1930s marked the end of religious *feste* and street processions at St. Anthony's, but Lackawanna Italians have expressed traditional religious practices in several other formats during the past four decades. In 1965, Jimmy and Frances D'Alessandro organized the Lackawanna chapter of the Our Lady of Fatima Guild, a Catholic group that traveled each year to Lewiston, New York, to attend Mass at the shrine honoring the Madonna. The spacious grounds of the shrine have walkways lined by dozens of statues of saints, including one of San Biagio. The names of donors are inscribed on many of the statues; a good number of them are Italians from Lackawanna and other western New York towns.

The devotion of Italian Americans to the Madonna has found other expressions. Postwar immigrants from Cantalupo, Molise, went house-to-house on Ingham Avenue collecting money to send to their hometown for the *festa* of Sant'Anna. Relatives of Ida Liberta then brought a large picture of the patron saint from Italy, and in 1984, the Cantalupani placed the photo on a vada with a canopy and had a procession on the grounds of St. Anthony's. The small *festa* included a Mass and a dinner at the church hall. This was repeated the following year, but friction then developed between the group and the pastor. A concrete bust of Sant'Anna was purchased and stored at Mike Liberta's house in Eden, and the *feste* were held at the nearby Immaculate Conception Church from 1986 to 1988. The next year, the site of the *festa* was Our Lady of Victory Basilica, and in 1990, it was moved to Our Lady of Bistricca, a Croatian church on Abbott Road near the homes of many of the Cantalupani. Fifty to 100 people came to the yearly Mass and procession, and up to 300 attended the dance that usually followed. In more recent years, there was simply a meal after the religious service. In 2004, the group was invited to hold its festival at St. Anthony's and did so for several years. The *festa* was held on the grounds of the Lake Erie Italian Club in 2008. The founding of a group with roots in a specific Italian town typifies the resurgence of ethnicity that began in the late 1960s.

Sources: Interviews with Jimmy D'Alessandro, April 9, 1985; Ida Liberta, October 16, 1996; Tony Monaco, June 8, 2005; Guy Iannarelli, November 11, 2008.

Natives of Cantalupo in Lackawanna and nearby towns had a statue of Sant'Anna made and have held a yearly festa *in her honor since 1984. The celebrations have taken place at various sites throughout the city; the 1989 event, pictured here, was held at Our Lady of Victory Basilica. The men are carrying the statue down South Park Avenue.* Photo source: Elio and Ida Liberta

Soon a new organ was purchased, and extra classrooms, Plexiglas front doors, and a canopy awning for the front entrance were added. The total of $350,000 spent for the church, rectory, and furnishings was completely paid off by 1970. Enjoying the postwar prosperity, Lackawanna Italians generously supported the church's special projects.[81]

Despite their apparent assimilation of the values of the Catholic Church in America, Italians in Lackawanna maintained some traditional attitudes. Rev. Bilotta noticed a number of characteristics. The second and third generations did not give lavishly to the weekly collections. During the 1960s, individuals who made good salaries often put only $1 in the collection basket at Sunday Mass and gave mediocre donations to Catholic fund drives. The parishioners were also still not interested in building a Catholic school. Rev. Bilotta noticed that Italians continued the practices of lighting candles, having Masses said for the deceased, and carefully tending cemetery plots. He observed that "the women had strong faith, the men not as much," and only a few Italian men and women joined religious orders. While the women's church societies gave most of the funds they raised to support the church, the Holy Name Society dedicated most of its proceeds to events and gave little toward the church's upkeep. Nationwide studies done in 1960s and 1970s demonstrated significant differences among Catholic ethnic groups throughout America. Compared to Irish, Polish, French, and German Catholics, Italians and Latinos were much

FIGURE 6.11
REV. ANTHONY J. BILOTTA

Born on November 28, 1919, in Hinsdale, New York, Anthony Bilotta was the son of immigrants from Cortale, Calabria. His father worked on the Pennsylvania Railroad. In 1923, the Bilottas moved to Olean, where Anthony completed his education in public schools. He attended St. Bonaventure University for two-and-a-half years in an accelerated program, then entered Christ the King Seminary. He was ordained into the priesthood on September 22, 1945, at St. Joseph's Old Cathedral in Buffalo. Rev. Bilotta served New York parishes throughout his life, first as a weekend assistant pastor at St. James Church in Jamestown. In June 1946, he was appointed to the Buffalo Missionary Apostolate, which served the missions of St. Ann's in Sinclairville, and was also appointed the acting Catholic chaplain at Newton Memorial Hospital in Cassadaga.

In 1947, Rev. Bilotta returned to St. James Church in Jamestown as an assistant pastor. In June of the following year, he was transferred to St. Joseph's Church in Lockport, again as an assistant. He moved on to St. Joseph's New Cathedral in Buffalo to serve as an assistant administrator in 1952. Three years later, he was transferred to Sheridan, where he became the administrator at St. John Bosco's Church. He was pastor of St. Anthony's parish in Lackawanna from 1960 to 1976, and served as chaplain for the Lackawanna Police Department for 16 years. Active in diocesan activities, Rev. Bilotta was a moderator of the Pope Pius X Chapter of the Buffalo Choirmasters Guild and was the moderator of the Lackawanna Deanery of Holy Name Societies in 1970. He passed away in Dunkirk, New York, on August 17, 1997.

Rev. Anthony J. Bilotta, the sixth pastor of St. Anthony's Church, guided the parish during the period of construction of a new church edifice, which was completed in 1964. Photo source: Chico Galanti

Sources: Interview with Rev. Anthony Bilotta, September 24, 1994; *Front Page*, 8/23/95; *Buffalo News*, 8/18/97; papers of Loretta Nicometo, "Silver Anniversary Honoring Father Anthony J. Bilotta," program brochure, 9/20/70.

---

less likely to attend Mass, receive Communion, or be involved in church organizations and schools. Two-thirds of Irish wives adhered to Catholic doctrine and did not use artificial methods of contraception, while two-thirds of Italian wives did just the opposite. One woman in the Steel City said that she and her husband did not follow the "rhythm method" advocated by the Church because it wasn't reliable, stating, "The Pope isn't going to pay for raising a child when the rhythm method doesn't work."[82]

Following completion of the new church and rectory, things were going well at St. Anthony's. In 1965, Rev. Bilotta was named chaplain of the Lackawanna Police Department and was involved with the Protestant-funded Friendship House, something that wouldn't have happened 30 years earlier. His parish had the only new church edifice in the First Ward, as several congregations founded by eastern Europeans had relocated to the east side of the city. But while the church graced Ingham Avenue, its surroundings were not pleasant. There were several scrap yards along Lehigh and Ingham avenues. Just behind St. Anthony's, Roblin Steel had a car crusher and shredder. Old cars were dragged through the street,

and such combustible material as seat stuffing and paint were burned at the facility, causing noxious odors and irritation to the eyes.[83]

Just north of the church, on Lehigh Avenue, the city's sewerage-treatment plant often emitted foul smells. When a 1972 federal law mandated secondary treatment of sewage

St. Anthony's Church and the church hall, right, which was completed in 1955. Photo source: St. Anthony's Church

and a state law called for phosphate removal, one county proposal included a six-acre expansion of the treatment plant to handle sewerage from Lackawanna, West Seneca, Hamburg, and Orchard Park. This plan would have brought the sewerage-treatment process within close proximity of St. Anthony's. Rev. Bilotta and some of his parishioners were active in the groups that fought this plan, a risky stance for Bethlehem Steel employees, as the company favored the county plan. Eventually,

the plant was located at another site. For his work on this issue and his involvement in Friendship House, Rev. Bilotta received citations of praise from several First Ward citizens' groups. He also received the 1974 Award for Outstanding Service from the Lackawanna Human Rights Commission.[84]

While the sewage problems were resolved, the intrusions from the Roblin Steel car crusher only worsened over the years, taking their toll on both parishioners and pastor. Tow trucks

Rev. Bilotta, second row center, stands among parishioners after the 8:00 a.m. Mass on May 5, 1963, at the original church edifice. At center right is the parish hall. Photo source: Mike Morgan

"We Gave" signs were placed in the windows of parishioners' homes to indicate donations had been made for the construction of the new church hall building, 1955. Photo source: St. Anthony's Church

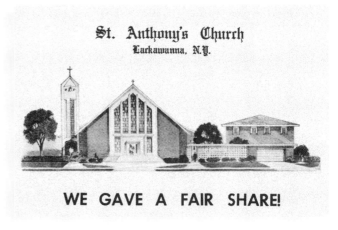

The drive that raised funds for building a new church edifice at St. Anthony's had donors place a yellow card in their windows to indicate they had contributed. The new church was completed in 1964. Source: Collection of Jo Andreozzi

Rev. Bilotta and presidents of the parish societies in the early 1960s. The outline of the thermometer on the wall indicates progress made in the drive to raise funds for the new church edifice. In the first row, from left, are: Donata Monaco, Ada Guglielmi, Rev. Bilotta, Mary Panzetta-Fistola, Charles Fistola. In the rear row, from left, are: Larry Colello, Tony Moretti, Mike Morgan.
Photo source: Mary Panzetta-Vertino

The Holy Name Society has continued a tradition of father-and-son breakfasts that began in 1948. At the 1976 event, from left, Larry Colello, Ralph Fiore, and Mike Giordano worked the griddle. Photo source: Don Grosso

Holy Name Society members in the kitchen in 1976 are, from left, Rudy Rusczyck, Guy Angilello, and Mark Pacillo. Photo source: Don Grosso

Lou Saban, Buffalo Bills coach, was one of the featured speakers at the 1976 breakfast. Photo source: Don Grosso

FIGURE 6.13
ST. ANTHONY'S PASTORS SINCE 1976

Rev. Paul Coppola was born in Buffalo. His father and four grandparents were immigrants from Poggio Marino, Campania. He attended the Little Seminary, Franciscan Major Seminaries, and was ordained in 1951. Rev. Coppola became the pastor of St. Anthony's Church in 1976.

Rev. Frank Barone first came to St. Anthony's as the temporary administrator of the parish and rose to the position of pastor in 1985. He was raised on Buffalo's west side, in Holy Cross parish, the son of Calogero Barone and Wyktoria Durzewski. He attended Public School No. 1 and Holy Cross Elementary School. He studied for the priesthood at the Diocesan Preparatory Seminary and St. John Vianney Seminary in East Aurora, New York, and was ordained in 1967. Rev. Barone then was sent for advanced studies at the Catholic University of Puerto Rico. His first parish assignment was in the Capuchin Shrine of San Antonio in Rio Piedras. Following this, Rev. Barone returned to Holy Cross, the church where he was baptized, then went on to serve at six other parishes in western New York before coming to Lackawanna. At St.

Anthony's, he organized a series of events, including a *scampagnata* (picnic) in 1993. He also was a part-time chaplain of the Wende Correctional Facility, where he became full-time chaplain when he left St. Anthony's in January 1998. He passed away a few months later.

Rev. Peter Drilling, a native of Queens, New York, came to Lackawanna in 1998. He attended Our Lady of Good Council Elementary School in Darien Center, New York, then commenced on a scholarly path. Starting at the Diocesan Preparatory Seminary in Buffalo, he moved on to St. John Vianney Seminary; the Gregorian University and North American College in Rome; the State University of New York at Buffalo; and the Toronto School of Theology at the University of Toronto. He was ordained in 1967 at St. Peter's Basilica in the Vatican City. Rev. Drilling then served at four parishes in western New York. He joined the faculty of Christ the King Seminary in 1982 and was the director of formation there in the early 1990s. A month after becoming the pastor of St. Anthony's, he guided the merger of Queen of All Saints Church into St. Anthony's. In the process of this successful

blending of Italian and Hispanic cultural traditions, he also reached out to area Protestant churches. In 1993, he held an ecumenical service at St. Anthony's and invited the ministers of three nearby African American churches to participate. He also initiated a program in which Sister Geri, of the Sisters of Mercy, did outreach to families in the parish. In January 2005, Rev. Drilling left the parish to become a full-time instructor at Christ the King Seminary.

Rev. David Glassmire, who was born in Lackawanna and adopted as an infant, became St. Anthony's next pastor. His biological parents have roots in Sicily and England, while his adoptive parents are of English, Irish, and German heritage. After serving in the Navy from 1979 to 1986, he studied for the priesthood and was ordained in 1994. Rev. Glassmire was assigned to five Buffalo-area parishes prior to 2005. He has been in the Naval Reserves since 1988, serving first as an intelligence officer and then as a chaplain. Since 2003, he has had periods of active duty as the chaplain to a Marines unit. At St. Anthony's, he continued the development of a multicultural parish prior to leaving in August 2008.

Source: *Front Page*, 5/13/92, 7/28/93, 1/14/98, 2/7/98, 4/22/98, 1/16/2002, 1/5/2005; letter from Rev. Paul Coppola, Feb. 2003; interviews with Rev. David Glassmire, June 8, 2005; Rose Anticoli-Wagner, November 1, 2008.

dragging old cars occasionally cut across church property. "This was the final straw," recalled Rev. Bilotta. "That's when I left." When Betty Ungaro heard that the pastor was departing from St. Anthony's, she angrily wrote the bishop, accusing him of "taking Father Bilotta away." The bishop replied and explained that Rev. Bilotta had made the decision. Rev. Paul Coppola replaced Bilotta in March 1976. A native of Buffalo, he was described by one parishioner as a scholarly man. When financial difficulties appeared, another Buffalonian, Rev. Frank Barone, became temporary administrator of the church in 1981 and assumed the pastor's position in 1985 when Rev. Coppola departed.[85]

As the immigrant generation passed away, Italians moved from the First Ward to eastern Lackawanna or nearby towns, and Italian membership at St. Anthony's declined. While many

Italians who moved attended churches in their new neighborhoods, some returned to St. Anthony's for important events. The old issue of control of church society funds again arose during Rev. Barone's tenure, as the pastor and the Holy Name Society locked horns. The priest refused to give Communion to members of the society and limited the group's activities, causing a number of them, and other parishioners as well, to leave the parish. The ex-members of the Holy Name Society and a few who remained active in the church, began to meet socially. In early 1998, Barone left St. Anthony's to become chaplain at the Correctional Facility in Wende, New York. Since then, the Holy Name Society has resumed its usual programs, and a number of exiled members have returned. But the independent social meetings continue on a monthly basis

Rev. Paul Coppola was pastor of St. Anthony's from 1976 until 1985. Photo source: Collection of Paul Coppola

Rev. Frank Barone, son of an Italian father and a Polish mother, was the eighth pastor of St. Anthony's, filling that role from 1985 to 1998. Photo source: St. Anthony's Parish Book, 1992

Rev. Peter Drilling, pastor from 1998 to 2005, guided the merger of the St. Anthony's and Queen of All Saints parishes. Photo source: Rev. Peter Drilling

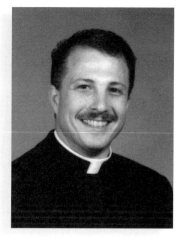

The last pastor of St. Anthony's, Rev. David Glassmire, led the parish from 2005 to 2008, when Sister Barbara Riter became the pastoral administrator. Photo source: Rev. David Glassmire

at the Lake Erie Italian Club hall, where most of the 30 men are also members. The group is now known as the 3200 Club, after the street address of the meeting hall.[86]

St. Anthony's becomes a Multiethnic Parish

Over the years, the number of non – Italian parishioners at St. Anthony's has grown. After becoming the pastor in 1918, Rev. Vifredo invited people of French, Spanish, and Hispanic background to receive sacraments at the church, and many responded. As a significant number of second-generation Italian Americans married outside their ethnic group, the non – Italian spouses, usually husbands, became parishioners. By the mid-1930s, Thomas Houle, Joseph Schmidt, and John Morrissey were officers in the Holy Name Society. After World War II, it became common to see people of other ethnic backgrounds as members and officers of Lackawanna church organizations. At least 19 non – Italian men were active in parish leadership roles between 1947 and 1964. As Lackawanna ethnic neighborhoods dispersed, some non – Italians attended St. Anthony's simply because it was near their homes, others because the new edifice, completed in 1964, was the most modern of the First Ward's Catholic Churches. The congregation, once heavily Italian, had gradually become more ethnically diverse. In 1998, it became truly multiethnic.[87]

Rev. Peter Drilling, the church's second non – Italian pastor, assumed the leadership of St. Anthony's in January 1998. By that time, Lackawanna's population had declined significantly, the city's European American population was elderly, and there

were too many Catholic parishes. The diocese made plans to close Queen of All Saints Church on Ridge Road, which served about 200 households, and combine its parishioners with St. Anthony's congregation of 225 families. On February 15, 1998, Bishop Henry Mansell conducted a closing prayer service at Queen of All Saints, after which the parishioners drove the

---

FIGURE 6.13

PASTORS OF ST. ANTHONY'S MISSION AND CHURCH: 1917-2008

June – July 1917	Rev. John P. Boland
July 1917 – August 1918*	Rev. Antonio Clemente
August – December 1918	Rev. Raffaele D'Alfonso
1918 – 1947	Rev. Joseph Vifredo
1948 – 1960	Rev. Thomas Ciolino
1960 – 1976	Rev. Anthony Bilotta
1976 – 1985	Rev. Paul Coppola
1985 – 1997	Rev. Frank Barone
1998 – 2005	Rev. Peter Drilling
2005 – 2008	Rev. David Glassmire

*According to two people interviewed, Rev. Clemente may have led religious services at the Italian mission in Lackawanna prior to the arrival of Rev. Boland.

The Altar and Rosary Society, formerly known as the Rosary Altar Society, was founded in 1946. Members in 2008 included, from left: Angie Jiammarino, Christina Baratta, Jean Borgogelli, Helen DeSantis, Lucy Pietrocarlo, Mary Marks, Marge Ziccarelli, and Velma Borgogelli.
Photo source: "*St. Anthony's Parish 90th Anniversary Book,*" 2008

Voices of St. Anthony, formed when St. Anthony's parish merged with Queen of All Saints church in 1998. Bottom row, from the left: Christina Baratta, Josephine Saldana, Migdalia Nowak, Kathleen Mateja, Diane Paolini. Middle row: Crucita Diaz, Andrea Haxton, Dawn Quinn, Elvia Celotto, Catalina Castillo. Top row: John Nowak, Daniel Torres, Karen Hernandez, Edward Dean, Michael Quinn, Auria Delgado, Elizabeth Mobley. Photo source: "*St. Anthony's Parish 90th Anniversary Book,*" 2008

patron saints and celebrated the festival of Our Lady of Guadalupe. Groups established at Queen of All Saints were welcomed into the St. Anthony parish: the Young Christian Choir, Sagrado Corazon (Sacred Heart) Society, the Spanish Choir, the Youth Group, and Cub and Boy Scouts. The Young Christian Choir from Queen of All Saints merged with St. Anthony's choir to become St. Anthony's Voices, which then included men and women of Mexican, Puerto Rican, African American, Polish, and Italian heritage. Latino men joined Italian Americans in the Holy Name Society. At his farewell banquet, attended by 300 parishioners and friends, Rev. Drilling was "credited with providing the leadership and guidance to merge St. Anthony's and Queen of All Saints parishes smoothly and efficiently into one thriving parish." Appropriately enough, the event was cochaired by an Italian American, Don Grosso, the president of the Holy Name Society, and a Puerto Rican American, Luz Rivera, the church secretary.[89]

In January 2005, Rev. Drilling left St. Anthony's and was replaced by Rev. David Glassmire. The new pastor was fluent in Spanish and traced his own roots to Sicily, England, Ireland, and Germany. He found that St. Anthony's parish included Italians, other European Americans, Puerto Ricans, Mexicans, African Americans, and several Vietnamese and Guatemalans. Rev. Glassmire initiated the Hands Across the Bridge program to support the work of the Lackawanna Food Pantry and Catholic Relief organizations. He left St. Anthony's in August 2008, and the diocese then appointed a pastoral administrator, Sister Barbara Riter, who guides the parish as it becomes home to many ethnic groups. Lackawanna's shrinking population has recently led to the closing of more parishes. Annunciation Church was closed and torn down. The city's three Polish Roman Catholic churches—St. Hyacinth's in the First Ward, and St. Barbara's and St. Michael's in the Second Ward, have combined with

half-mile to St. Anthony's, where the bishop celebrated the merger Mass in English, Spanish, and Italian.[88]

Like St. Anthony's other non – Italian pastor, Rev. Boland, Rev. Drilling could speak Italian. Also fluent in Spanish, Drilling worked closely with all members of the parish to integrate the Hispanic and other ethnic customs of Queen of All Saints with those of the Italians. He led prayers to Italian

Father Baker with the Blessed Mother and Children, *an original painting by artist John Novelli who immigrated at age 13 from Abruzzo to Lackawanna.* Photo source: John Novelli

Our Lady of Grace in Woodlawn to form a new parish called Queen of Angels, which is housed in the former edifice of St. Michael's. This leaves St. Anthony's as the only Catholic parish in the First Ward. Visiting priests now offer Mass in English and Spanish, and the parish has formal links with the Our Lady of Victory parish. As Lackawanna's population continues to decrease, it is unclear if the parish has enough of a base to maintain the church edifice; a possible merger with Our Lady of Victory parish has been discussed. But for now, the parishioners of St. Anthony's church worship Our Lady of Guadalupe at the same altar on which the statues of San Biagio, San Rocco, and Santa Lucia have stood for many decades.[90]

Over the years, the daily lives of Lackawanna's Italians have been strongly influenced not only by religious institutions but also by the workplace. It was the industrial jobs in the steel plant and on the railroads that drew Italians to the city in the first place, and the neighborhoods in which immigrants clustered were sandwiched between steel mills, small factories, and a maze of railroads. For many male immigrants, their work sites were the main arenas of their interactions with American society and had a tremendous influence on their adjustment to the new country. These work environments and their considerable sway in immigrants' lives are the subject of the next two chapters.

CHAPTER 7

WORK IN THE MILLS
AND ON THE RAILROADS

*Many of the steel operators today consider that
the district in which this community is located is
the future iron and steel center of the country.*

– U.S. Immigration Commission, 1911[1]

When its construction was finished at the dawn of the twentieth century, the Lackawanna Steel Company's new facility in West Seneca was the world's largest steel plant. It was proclaimed the "eighth wonder of the world," and Buffalo streetcar lines began to offer tours to the site by 1902. One newspaper proclaimed that the steel plant and other new industries in the area meant that "South Buffalo will become a second East Chicago, a second Homestead," while another journal boasted of "a new era of prosperity for Buffalo; the Manchester of America.[2]"

The steel plant was the most dramatic episode of accelerating industrialization in the Buffalo area. Between 1890 and 1905, some 412 new factories were built in Buffalo alone. Now, the new steel plant acted as a magnet for more workers. Thousands of people, many of them immigrants, migrated to the area from throughout the Northeast, hoping to be among those employed by the plant. The western-most part of West Seneca, where the steel plant was located and which had been called Limestone Hill, became the City of Lackawanna in 1909. This chapter will examine the occupational trends among Lackawanna's Italians, focusing on the two areas where they clustered most, the steel mills and the railroads. The main time frame will be

the years 1900 to 1945, with some discussion of the postwar years up to the demise of steelmaking in western New York in 1983.[3]

Early Arrivals: 1900 – 1905

Large-scale immigration to West Seneca's Limestone Hill district began in 1900 with the construction of the Lackawanna Steel Company mills. Among the 1,500 workers employed to clear the land and construct the mills were a large number of southern Italians. The area was mostly swamp and woodland, and by July 1900, many of its trees had become ties for the plant's railroad. The Lathrop, Shea, and Henwood Company was hired to build the South Buffalo Railway (SBR), a subsidiary of Lackawanna Steel. On July 16 of that year, a work crew of 16 Italians excavated land opposite the foot of Roland Avenue for an intersection of the new SBR railway with the New York Central Railroad. The Lackawanna Steel Company promised many jobs for western New Yorkers in 1900 but never delivered the number it projected. In 1903 and 1904, as the company was about to start producing steel, it laid off its initial laborers, including the southern Italians. Hiring new workers to produce steel, it gave jobs to some 2,000 men, mostly Irish, who had moved to West Seneca from Scranton, Pennsylvania, where Lackawanna Steel had shut down its original plant. By 1904, 70% of the plant's workforce was made up of Scrantonites. And Limestone Hill became known to many as the steel-plant district.[4]

< View of the Bethlehem Steel Company plant in winter looking northwest, circa 1950. The structural shipping yard is in the foreground, No. 3 Open Hearth at center left, and ship canal at the upper right. Photo source: Paul Pietrak

Laborers started clearing the land at Stoney Point in 1900. Antonio Grossi and Gaetano Milano had their first jobs sharing a two-man saw to cut off the tops of tree pilings.
Photo source: Buffalo & Erie County Public Library, *Lackawanna Steel Company* scrapbook, p. 25

which collected its data between 1907 and 1909, interviewed a sample of 79 Italian male adults, most of whom were described as "northern Italians," a term used by American officials to designate natives of the regions of Italy north of Tuscany and Liguria. Most of these northerners must have soon left the area, as few people from the northernmost regions of Italy were later to be found in Lackawanna's population. One reason people left the steel-plant district was the severe depression of 1907, when production at Lackawanna Steel dropped by 40%, and two-thirds of the plant's 6,000 workers were unemployed for a prolonged period. Another factor in the continual turnover of Italians was their unfamiliarity with steel production; many resorted to this type of work as a temporary measure when outdoor railroad and construction jobs were scarce. Buffalo and western New York offered a great array of seasonal and temporary jobs, from foundry work to road construction to agricultural labor, and the steel plant was just one more stop for itinerant Italian workmen. The turnover in laborers was a general trend that involved many ethnic groups. In the years prior to World War I, the steel company employed more than 7,000 men, and there was a weekly turnover of 1,500 men. The continual coming and going of Italian males in Lackawanna went on through the 1930s.[5]

In 1900, the only Italians known to be residing in the steel-plant district were the four members of the Morinello family and 38 boys living in St. John's Protectory. Within two years, many Italian workers were living in a shantytown along Smokes Creek as they labored to construct the steel plant. The Italian construction workers left the community when their work was done, presumably in 1904, when the plant was in full production. Others arrived, and in 1905, there were 288 Italians in the steel-plant district. It is clear that Italians, mostly lone men without families, arrived and left in significant numbers. Of the 176 Italian male adults listed in the 1905 Census, only 72 appeared in later censuses. The U.S. Immigration Commission,

In 1910, Lackawanna Steel and two nearby plants, Seneca Steel and Rogers Brown Iron Company (the forerunner of Hanna

View of the north end of Lackawanna Steel Company's plant in 1917. The main office building is center right, No. 2 Open Hearth is the large structure with 12 smokestacks, and No. 1 Open Hearth is at center left with 14 smokestacks. The specialty shops are in the center, and the houses of the New Village are on the right. Photo source: Larry Platz

Shift change in 1902. At this time Lackawanna Steel employed roughly 6,000 workers. Photo source: Buffalo & Erie County Public Library, *Lackawanna Steel Company* scrapbook, p. 117

Furnace), employed 90% of Lackawanna immigrant men, but the majority of the plants' workers lived in Buffalo or nearby towns. The wages, averaging $1.50 to $2 per day for unskilled laborers, were equal to those paid in the Pittsburgh steel plants, where Yard Department laborers and trackmen averaged 16-17 cents per hour. Most laborers worked 12-hour shifts seven days per week, but some departments put in 10 hour shifts six days per week. Seneca Steel in Blasdell eventually employed up to 500 men, as did the Rogers Brown Iron Company, which was erected in 1906 across the street from the main office of Lackawanna Steel. The workforce of each plant varied according to economic conditions. In 1912, there were 5,041 factory workers, all males, at 13 sites in the Steel City, 4,700 of them at Lackawanna Steel. In Blasdell, 306 men worked in factories, the vast majority at Seneca Steel. In addition to the factory and railroad jobs, other factors also attracted immigrants to Lackawanna, as the U.S. Immigration Commission noted. The city's proximity to Buffalo offered an array of schools, churches, and alternate work options during layoffs. The large immigrant population in Lackawanna and Buffalo drew fellow ethnics, some of whom, referred to as "higher class" by the commission,

saw a ready market for their trades: saloons, restaurants, jewelry stores, and other businesses.[6]

A study of Italians throughout the American steel industry in 1910 indicates that prior to emigration 58% had been farmers or farm laborers, 20% general laborers, and less than four percent had been involved in any type of manufacturing. In 1907, Italians made up less than four percent of the workers in all Carnegie Steel plants in the Pittsburgh, Pennsylvania, district, and 93% of them were unskilled laborers. Likewise, the Italian immigrants entered Lackawanna Steel and the two smaller plants as unskilled laborers. Sixty-two percent of all Lackawanna's male European immigrants had been farmers or farm laborers in the old country, and only 11% had jobs in the manufacture of iron and steel. The Croatian immigrants in Lackawanna also lacked steelmaking experience; only 1% of them had done this type of work in Europe. However, other Steel City ethnic groups had a greater level of steelmaking experience in the old country: seven percent of the Irish and Slovaks, and 10% of the Poles. Inside the mills at Lackawanna Steel, most workers were Polish, other eastern Europeans, or Irish. Eastern Europeans were similarly concentrated in other American

FIGURE 7.1

Occupations of Lackawanna Italian Males in Steelmaking, Railroad, and Other Settings: 1905 – 1930

	1905	1910	1915	1917–18	1920	1925	1930
Professionals							
Steel	—	—	—	—	—	—	1
Railroad	—	—	—	—	1	—	—
Other	—	—	—	3	2	3	4
Business:	9	16	22	15	18	34	42
Skilled, Semiskilled							
General							
Steel	1	12	16	91	38	91	166
Railroad	—	—	4	19	20	27	32
Other	—	2	6	8	8	12	34
Supervisors							
Steel	—	3	4	21	8	13	14
Railroad	—	1	1	2	1	10	8
Other	—	—	—	—	—	—	1
Laborers:							
Steel	166	171	162	289	241	168	202
Railroad	4	53	4	27	17	49	26
Other	—	9	5	1	2	17	43
Totals:	180	267	224	476*	356	424	573

* World War I Draft Registration Records include only males 18-45 years of age.

Sources: U.S. Census, 1910, 1920, 1930; New York Census, 1905, 1915, 1925; World War I Draft Registration Records, 1917-18.

steel mills, such as the Carnegie Steel plants in the Pittsburgh area. The central fact was that immigrants and their children dominated the ranks of steelworkers in the nation; during 1907-08, the foreign-born were 58% and the second generation 13% of the 86,000 steelworkers in the United States.[7]

Occupational Patterns: 1905 – 1930

Most of Lackawanna's Italians worked in the steel mills or on railroads, but others had their own businesses or were employed in nonindustrial work. Figure 7.1 summarizes the occupational patterns of Lackawanna Italian males from 1905 to 1930, and Figure 7.2 for females. Each table focuses on adults working outside the home and classifies them in five categories:

1. Professionals: artist, doctor, nurse, engineer, police officer, fireman, school teacher, clergyman

2. Business operators: contractor, store or saloon proprietor, hotel owner, peddler

3. Skilled and semiskilled workers:
   A. Carpenter, machinist, plasterer, boilermaker, baker, printer, roll turner, heater, clerk, accountant
   B. Foreman, section boss, yardmaster

4. Laborers: day laborer, section hand, track laborer, ironworker or steelworker

Several trends emerge in the occupational patterns of Lackawanna Italians during the first three decades of the twentieth century. First, the number of Italian laborers in the most menial jobs steadily decreased, especially in the 1920s, as they advanced into skilled and supervisory roles. Second, Lackawanna's Italians were moving from their outdoor jobs and going into the mills, dispersing throughout the many departments of the

Figure 7.2

Occupations of Lackawanna Italian Females in Steelmaking, Railroad, and Other Settings: 1905 – 1930

	1905	1910	1915	1917–18	1920	1925	1930
Professionals:							
Steel	—	—	—	—	—	—	—
Railroad	—	—	—	—	—	—	—
Other	—	—	—	—	1	2	3
Business:	1	3	—	—	2	1	4
Skilled, Semiskilled:							
General:							
Steel	—	—	—	—	—	—	—
Railroad	—	—	—	—	—	—	—
Other	—	—	1	—	4	11	23
Supervisors:							
Steel	—	—	—	—	—	—	—
Railroad	—	—	—	—	—	—	—
Other	—	—	—	—	—	—	—
Laborers:							
Steel	—	—	—	—	—	—	—
Railroad	—	—	—	—	—	—	—
Other	—	—	6	—	4	6	14
Totals:	1	3	7	NA*	11	20	44

* World War I Draft Registration Records include only males 18-45 years of age.

Sources: U. S. Census, 1910, 1920, 1930; N.Y. Census, 1905, 1915, 1925; World War I Draft Registration Records, 1917–18.

Lackawanna Steel Company. A third trend was Italians' movement into jobs outside the railroad and steel-plant domains in nonindustrial settings, or operating their own businesses. Fourth, Italian women began to work outside the home, although in very small numbers, and most of those doing so were born in America (see Figure 7.2). Finally, these trends were accentuated by the maturation of second-generation men and women and their entries into the workforce. The experiences of Italian men and women working nonindustrial jobs and operating their own businesses will be discussed Chapter 9.[8]

Early Italian immigrants were known to prefer outdoor labor, especially the construction and railroad work that was readily available. Indeed, nationwide in 1920, railroads employed 2,236,000 workers. The data summarized in Figure 7.1 indicates that 54 Lackawanna Italian men, 20% of the total,

performed railroad work in 1910. Many of these men were probably employed by the Yard Department (Yard, for short) of Lackawanna Steel, which handled virtually all track maintenance until 1922. At that time, the Bethlehem Steel Company purchased the plant and formed the Track Department of the South Buffalo Railway, transferring a number of track laborers from the Yard to fill its ranks.[9]

The 1925 New York State census offers more details than do other censuses taken from 1900 to 1930 about occupations in specific steel-plant departments. It shows that 86 Italian men were employed by railroads, at least 30 by the South Buffalo Railway (SBR), while others worked in locomotive and car-repair shops of the steel plant's narrow-gauge railroad, and the remainder on the main-line railroads running through Lackawanna (see Figure 7.1). Looking at the 272 Italians

March 1902. This was the original employment office and gate. The building was painted red, and the wooden fence surrounded the entire steel plant. Photo source: Buffalo & Erie County Public Library, "Lackawanna Steel Company" scrapbook, p. 84

censuses of the twentieth century listed each worker's job type but not the name of the employing company. The 1914-15 Lackawanna City Directory, however, did indicate employers, and listed 129 adult Italian males, 94 of whom were employed at Lackawanna Steel. The World War I Draft Registration Records of 1917 and 1918 list 476 Italian males, ages 18 to 45, living in Lackawanna. Nine of every 10 of these men worked for Lackawanna Steel or its subsidiary, the SBR. This confirms the claim of many interviewees that most Italian men in Lackawanna during the first three decades of the twentieth century were steel-plant employees.[11]

In 1905, 99% of all Lackawanna Italians working in the steel mills and on the railroads were laborers, but by 1930 the Italian workers were about evenly split between laborers and semiskilled and skilled positions (see Figure 7.1). While crane operator Anthony Barone was the only skilled or semiskilled worker in 1905, 221 Italians were in this category in 1930. By 1910 in steel plants throughout the nation there was a trend to recruit semiskilled workers, such as handymen and machine operators, mostly from the ranks of the many unskilled immigrant workers. In Lackawanna, the number of skilled and semiskilled workers rose slowly between 1905 and 1915 but expanded rapidly in 1917-18, when America's involvement in World War I saw the rapid expansion of defense production, opening up these positions to 30% of Lackawanna Italian workers in industrial and railroad settings. The end of the war saw these numbers plummet in 1920. With the economic boom of the 1920s, the number of Italian skilled and semiskilled workers increased, reaching almost half in 1930. The number of Italian crane operators, for example,

holding jobs at Bethlehem Steel and the two smaller steel plants, more than 40% worked in the Yard. Added together, the Italian Yard and railroad workers represent half of all Italians working in these settings, which means they labored mostly in the outdoors. While this is a significant percentage, it is smaller than it was in the previous 20 years.[10]

Industrial and Railroad Workers

From 1900 to 1915, Lackawanna's Italian workforce basically consisted of males holding jobs at Lackawanna Steel and its railroad or on other railroads in the area. The early

In 1904 a second building was added at the company's employment office just north of the 1902 office. During the early 20th century most workers were hired on a daily basis at Lackawanna Steel. Photo source: Hamburg Historical Society

grew from one in 1905 to 41 in 1930.

The variety of positions held between 1917 and 1930 indicates that Italians were working in many mills and departments of the steel plant and the SBR. The Yard and SBR employed many Italians over the years, but more and more Italian men found jobs in other departments and mills where indoor work was the norm. In the period 1925 to 1930, there were roughly 52 mills, departments, and shops in the plant. Slightly more than half of the Lackawanna Italians employed by Bethlehem Steel worked for the Yard and SBR, and the rest in 33 other departments, including the open hearths, blast furnaces, coke ovens, rolling mills, and specialty shops. The process of gaining different and more skilled jobs in departments throughout the steel plant was accelerated by the arrival of the second-generation Italian Americans in the workforce (see Figure 7.3).

Men waiting for work near the employment office on Hamburg Turnpike, circa 1905. Here the South Buffalo Railway crosses over the road to service what later became the Hanna Furnace Company. Photo source: Hamburg Historical Society

The Second Generation Enters the Workforce

The second generation—those individuals born in this country of immigrant parents—began to mature and enter into the workplace during the 1920s. One of every nine Lackawanna Italians holding jobs outside the home in 1920 was of the second generation, a proportion that grew to one in four in 1930. By 1925, there were 10 second-generation males working on the railroads, and 26 others held jobs in the steel mills. The majority of these men held skilled and semiskilled positions, including three foremen, six machinists, and four accountants. In 1930, the number of second-generation workers in these settings rose to 115, two-thirds of whom were in skilled and semiskilled positions. This represents a truly significant advance as compared to the first-generation Italian males, 16% of whom held skilled or semiskilled positions in 1925 and 43% in 1930.[12]

Many second-generation males entered the steel plant as messenger boys and advanced into skilled jobs through apprentice-training programs. In early 1918, Joe Milano, in what was a common practice of the time, claimed he was 15 years old when he was actually 14 and became a messenger boy. In traveling throughout the plant, he got to know the supervisors and, in 1919, was hired to work in No. 6 Mill, perhaps the first Italian American employee there. As a checker, the fourth highest position in the mill, Milano counted out steel bars of different lengths to fill customers' orders. Other Italian teenagers followed similar courses. Fourteen-year-old Brownie

Leo used a fake birth certificate provided by Milano to become a messenger boy in 1924. During two summers between high school terms, he earned $45 per month, then left school to work in the Inspection Department, where his father was a janitor. Dan Thomas delivered mail from the main office to many mills, within a year he becoming an electrician's helper and participant in the construction of new mills.[13]

Nunze Oddy became a messenger boy in 1917 and later an apprentice. Working 10 hours per day, six days per week, he became familiar with the foremen and supervisors. "I kept after the superintendent of the Roll Department about getting a job for six months, but he said I was too small." In 1919, Oddy finally got the job, but only after the intervention of another superintendent, a friend of Oddy's deceased father, who realized that the youth helped support his mother and five siblings. Soon after entering the Roll Shop, Oddy began five years of apprentice schooling. Each workday, he and 100 other apprentices from throughout the plant attended morning classes in the main office, then worked six hours in their respective departments. The young men learned math, blueprint reading, and other skills from instructor George W. Davis, who Oddy remembered as a fair man "who was good to the apprentices." As time progressed, Oddy worked eight hours per day in the Roll Shop. He earned 18 cents per hour, and when he completed the program in 1925, his wages doubled. That year, Ralph D'Amore began a two-year apprenticeship in the Roll Shop at 25 cents per hour.[14]

Figure 7.3

Occupations of Lackawanna Second-generation Italian Males in Steelmaking, Railroad, and Other Settings: 1905 – 1930

	1905	1910	1915	1917-18	1920	1925	1930
Professionals							
Steel	—	—	—	—	—	—	1
Railroad	—	—	—	—	1	—	—
Other	—	—	—	2	—	1	—
Business	—	2	1	1	1	—	5
Skilled, Semiskilled							
General							
Steel	—	1	1	2	8	16	63
Railroad	—	—	2	2	6	8	8
Other	—	—	2	—	4	4	—
Supervisors							
Steel	—	—	—	2	1	2	4
Railroad	—	—	—	—	—	1	2
Other	—	—	—	—	—	—	—
Laborers							
Steel	—	3	2	2	10	8	32
Railroad	—	1	—	—	1	1	5
Other	—	1	1	2	—	2	1
Totals	**0**	**8**	**9**	**13***	**32**	**43**	**121**

* Includes only males 18–45 years of age.

Sources: U.S. Census, 1900, 1910, 1920, 1930; N.Y. Census, 1905, 1915, 1925; World War I Draft Registration Records, 1917–18.

Other Italian Americans had taken advantage of the steel plant's apprentice programs as early as 1910, the year 20-year-old Julius Orsini became an apprentice. In the mid-1920s, after completing one year of high school, Pat Vertalino got a job in Bethlehem's Tool Shop, entered the apprentice program, and then transferred to the Blacksmith Shop. He later became a blacksmith and then a millwright at Seneca Steel. Armondo Pietrocarlo joined Vertalino in the Blacksmith Shop in 1927; after a four-year internship he became a clerk there. During the 1930s, more second-generation Italians came of age and joined Bethlehem's workforce. This influx of young men and women into the ranks of industrial and nonindustrial workers began a new era in the Italian American experience in Lackawanna, as elsewhere in the nation. It coincided with the dramatic international and national forces that would change their lives over the next two decades: the Depression, the birth of industrial unions, the Second World War, and economic recovery.[15]

Occupational Patterns: 1931 – 1983

The Great Depression, which had begun in October 1929, deepened in the early 1930s and seriously disrupted the occupational and economic gains that Lackawanna Italians had worked so hard to attain. The passage of the Wagner Act, in which the federal government endorsed union organizing, led to the birth of the Steel Workers Organizing Committee (SWOC) and the unionization of Lackawanna's Bethlehem Steel plant in early 1941. This legislation ended the absolute control of plant foremen, undercut the plant's ethnic hierarchy, and enhanced opportunities for Italians and other ethnics to get promotions. Meanwhile, World War II reinvigorated the steel industry, bringing jobs and increased prosperity to the Steel City. The war also called many Italian American men to take up arms against enemies that included the nation from

Young apprentices in 1928 at Bethlehem Steel's main office building, where they attended classes for half the day, then worked in the mills for the remainder of their shifts. Armando Pietrocarlo (who later spelled his first name Armondo), is at the far right in the bottom row. Photo source: Collection of Armondo Pietrocarlo

which they or their parents had emigrated. As Italians took part in the war effort, postwar economic development, and union activities in Lackawanna, they became more fully included in the community's social and economic fabric.

The trends that had begun in the first three decades of the century were more apparent after 1930. Despite Depression setbacks, Italians continued to rise through the ranks. In the Yard, for example, there were 22 Italian foremen during the 1940s. Italians also continued to find more positions at the heart of steelmaking, inside the mills, and even in professions outside the steel industry and railroads. Detailed census data are not currently available for the years after 1930, but other sources provide information on vocations. The 1941 *Erie County Directory* listed 414 Italian American adults who lived in Lackawanna and worked outside the home. More than three-quarters of the men had jobs in steel plants or other industrial settings, and 17 worked on railroads. During World War II, jobs became plentiful in Lackawanna. Not only did second-

generation men enter the workforce in large numbers, but teens and women were recruited for work at Bethlehem Steel and other defense plants. Males between 16 and 18 were hired at Bethlehem as "commandos," legally allowing them to work while technically underage, although a commando did not begin to accrue seniority until his 18th birthday. Women entered the plant as steelworkers for the first time.[16]

Mary Core-Brasch was one of several women who worked in the No. 3 Boiler Shop at Bethlehem Steel. Her job, which lasted one year, was to test water in the laboratory. During the war Sara Chiacchia-Kempf first worked as a punch-press operator at a Buffalo defense plant, then as an inspector at Bethlehem's bar mill. Donata Bonitatibus was working in the steel plant in 1943 when she encouraged Augusta Anticoli to follow suit. Anticoli, whose husband had died the previous year, worked as a chipper for two years. Along with other women, she used a small pneumatic chipping gun to remove imperfections from steel billets. Angelina Mazzucchi joined her husband,

FIGURE 7.4

BETHLEHEM STEEL AND SOUTH BUFFALO RAILWAY
DEPARTMENTS WITH ITALIAN EMPLOYEES, 1920 – 1930

Early Italian workers clustered in the outdoor jobs of Bethlehem Steel's Yard Department then the Track Department of the South Buffalo Railway. Beginning in 1920, Italians spread to other divisions of these departments and into the mills and departments where indoor work was the norm. During this decade, Italians were present, as indicated by a double asterisk (**), in 39 of the following 52 departments, mills, and shops:

MILLS AND SHOPS	Structural Fabricating Shop	NARROW-GAUGE RAILROAD
** Coke ovens	** Bridge Shop	** Car shop
** Blast furnaces	** Foundry	** Locomotive shop
Open hearths:	** Erection Department	** Train crews
** No. 1	** Inspection Department and	** Real Estate
** No. 2	Laboratories	Engineering
Rolling mills:	** Power House	** Main Office
** No. 1	** Gas House	** Plant Security
** No. 2		Yard Department:
No. 3	SPECIALTY SHOPS	** Locomotive cranes
No. 4	Babbit	** Garage
** No. 5	** Pattern	** High Drop
** No. 6	** Blacksmith (Forge)	
** No. 7	** Pipe	SOUTH BUFFALO RAILWAY
** No. 8	** Carpenter	** Track Department
No. 9	Plate	(Maintenance of Way)
No.10	** Electrical	** Roundhouse
No. 11	** Roll	Yard Clerks
No. 12	** Machine	** Car Department – Inspectors
No. 13	Paint	** Train Crews
** No. 14		
** No. 15		

** Italians present in these facilities

Notes: While census records name a position, such as millwright, they often omit the exact job site. It is probable that Italians worked in a number of the other rolling mills. The Babbitt Shop produced babbitt, an anti-friction alloy made of tin, antimony, lead, and copper that is used for bearings and other products.

Sources: interviews; Bethlehem Steel Company (BSC), "A Visit to the Lackawanna Plant of Bethlehem Steel Company, " Booklet 104, 1939; BSC, "Lackawanna Plant, Telephone Directory," 1948, 1974.

Tomassino, working in the open hearths. At a ramp just outside the mill, she and other workers used long metal rods to break the baked clay molds that shaped rounded projections called "hot tops" on special ingots. Carmela Coviello was a wartime worker in the steel plant, and a number of Italian women worked in the Yard. Some women took up the call of Rosie the Riveter. After graduating from Lackawanna High School in 1943, Jo Andreozzi wanted to work at the main office of Bethlehem Steel. When her father vetoed this idea, female neighbors working at the Curtiss-Wright aircraft factory made the connections that landed Andreozzi a job. She and Gina Capodagli rode to Curtiss-Wright with a woman who commuted from Angola to the plant located next to the Buffalo airport. Anne Melillo-Corvigno also worked at Curtiss-Wright during the war, rising to the position of inspector. Iole Schiavi, because of her petite size worked as a riveter inside the aircraft wings.[17]

World War II brought full employment to Lackawanna and other industrial centers, and despite some slack times and labor-management strife, the next 25 years were relatively prosperous. A 1949 directory lists 284 Italian male heads of households who owned their homes in Lackawanna. Two-thirds of them worked at Bethlehem Steel, and over half of the total number held skilled and semiskilled positions. A little over half of these men were immigrants, many of them with several adult children living in

1 H. J. Kelley.............Assistant M. M.
2 R. Hodges....Asst. Foreman Bricklayers
3 J. B. Fitz-Gibbon..Mechanical Engineer
4 L. H. Cocke...Asst Foreman Pipe Fitters
5 W. G. O'Malley.........General M. M.
6 T. Brocklebank.Chief Engr.,Power Houses
7 P. E. Parker........Supt. of Shops
8 P. McMahon.Asst. Foreman Blast Furns.
9 W. H. Gasset.......Electrical Foreman
10 W. J. Hillery.........
   Electrical Foreman, Nos. 2 and 3 Mills
11 J. Barret..............Elec. Line Foreman
12 J. J. Purrie..Elec. Foreman Open Hearth
13 E. Lawler..........
   Foreman B. E. H. No. 3 and Pump Sta.
14 E. A. Comstock....................
   Millwright Foreman O. H. Steel Works
15 E. J. Carey.......................
   .....Millwright Foreman, Mill No. 1
16 T. Brown..Night Foreman of Plate Shop
17 S. H. Greanoff.......................
   Gen. Foreman, Plate and Bridge Shops
18 J. Dundon.Asst. Foreman, B. E. H. No. 3
19 P. Reed...Asst.Foreman, B. E. H. No. 3
20 J. W. Brophie.......................
   Millwright Foreman, No. 6 Mill
21 C. Brooklyn.Asst.Foreman Boiler Houses

22 C. W. Mackay.......................
   .....Mech. Foreman, Blast Furnaces
23 W. H. Gilman....Foreman, Iron Workers
24 C. Nelson........Foreman, Pipe Fitters
25 W. Fennesey.......................
   Elec. Foreman, Bessemer Steel Works
26 T. Hughes.............Electrical Foreman
27 J. W. Stoklrantz......Foreman Riggers
28 C. Mundt....Asst. Foreman, Plate Shop
29 Z. A. Cooke...Foreman, Pattern Shop
30 H. Bennet.Asst. Foreman Boiler Houses
31 E. Abplanalp....Asst. Foreman, Foundry
32 P. Smith........Asst. Foreman, Foundry
33 A. Haldeman....Asst. Foreman, Foundry
34 F. Greanoff.......................
   .....Asst. Foreman, Plate Shop
35 L. Miller.......................
36 C. Jacobson...Supt. Docks and Harbor
37 H. Knapp.......................
   Asst. Foreman, Bridge Shop
38 D. A. Russ.......................
   .Mech. Foreman, Docks and Harbor
39 H. Black.......................
   Electrical Foreman, Nos. 4 and 5 Mills
40 P. Smith......Gen. Foreman Bricklayers
41 A. Johnson....Asst. Foreman Riggers
42 L. Wolf......Asst. Supt. Blast Furnaces

43 R. A. Stewart...............Draftsman
44 E. Mahon..Asst. Foreman Pattern Shop
45 J. H. Parsons.......................
   .... Foreman Electric Shop
46 P. Best.......................
47 H. Hester............N. G. Yardmaster
48 T. Reil..........Elec. Foreman, Cranes
49 R. Coleman.......................
   Elec. Foreman, Mill No. 1
50 E. Smith....Asst. Elec. Foreman Cranes
51 Geo. Gee....Foreman Outside Machinist
52 L. A. Gooch...........Electrical Foreman
53 R. Payfair......Gen. Electrical Foreman
54 W. Cook..Asst. Foreman, Machine Shop
55 P. Eagan.....Asst. Foreman, Carpenters
56 H. Jansen.....Asst. Foreman, Tool Shop
57 W. J. Bissett......Foreman, Tool Shop
58 G. P. Anderson......Foreman, Painters
59 M. J. Walsh,Foreman Loco. Repair Shop
60 P. Tickner.............Supt. Foundry
61 P. Leuthner, Sr..........Supt. Foundry
62 J. Wilkins.......................
   Millwright Foreman, Mills Nos. 2 and 3

63 A. V. Patterson.......................
   .... General Foreman Boiler Houses
64 Geo. Burcke..Asst. Foreman, Forge Shop
65 E. Dwyer...........Foreman, Forge Shop
66 J. W. Hemberger...................Clerk
67 L. Goette.................Gantry Foreman
68 F. C. Pratt...............Chief Clerk
69 W. E. Burke....Foreman, Machine Shop
70 G. M. Sturgess.Electrical Superintendent
71 H. M. Hurd..Asst. Elec. . Superintendent
72 J. O'Brien.Asst. Foreman, No. 2 B. E. H.
73 P. H. Gast.............Assistant M. M.
74 C. Venhrem.......................
   Foreman P. H. No. 1 and B. E. H. No. 2
75 H. Kloten.Elec. Foreman, Blast Furnaces
76 W. M. Hartnett...................Clerk
77 J. Nelson.Asst. Foreman, Carpenter Shop
78 J. P. Campbell.........Foreman, Bridges
79 M. Briggs....Asst. Foreman, Carpenters
80 E. G. Slater............Stenographer
81 J. Byrnes.........Foreman, Carpenters
82 F. Bell......Asst. Foreman, P. H. No. 1
83 J. B. Cullen............ Civil Engineer

1908 *LACKAWANNA STEEL CO. MASTER MECHANICS DIV.* "BI-MAC"

The surnames of the master mechanics pictured above in 1908 represent virtually all northwest European countries. There are no apparent Italian names and only a few that might indicate roots in southeast European countries. All but a few Italians were unskilled laborers at this time. Photo source: Hamburg Historical Society

the household. If the directory had included the occupations of children over 16 years of age living with their parents, it is assumed that there would be many more skilled, supervisory, and professional positions listed. The 1960 *Lackawanna City Directory* was more thorough and included the names and occupations of 734 Italian American men and women. About two-thirds of them held skilled and semiskilled positions, while only 36% were laborers or unskilled workers (see Figure 7.6). The 401 Italians employees at Bethlehem Steel plus another 48 in other industrial settings made up almost half of the Italian workforce. Job titles reveal that the workers were located in a variety of mills, shops, offices, and departments throughout the steel plant, as was true of the 37 individuals holding supervisory positions. Railroad work had become less common among Lackawanna's Italians, with only 27 people in this category, most of them South Buffalo Railway employees.[18]

The decade of the 1960s was the high point for the steel industry in western New York, and Bethlehem's workforce grew to over 20,000. America's economic power had remained virtually unrivaled until the 1960s, when foreign countries began to seriously compete with the United States in the world market. It then became obvious that aging American steel plants, such as the one in Lackawanna, were no longer economically viable. Bethlehem Steel reduced its workforce and urged many men to take early retirement. Production wound down, and the plant all but closed in 1983. Both young and middle-aged people moved from Lackawanna to other parts of the country, especially the South, to look for jobs. Joining the exodus were some fortunate steelworkers with enough seniority to be transferred to other Bethlehem plants. The population of Lackawanna, like that of neighboring Buffalo, dropped dramatically. After eight decades of operation, the steel plant was now a huge skeleton, leaving the Steel City an economic wasteland.[19]

Making Steel in Lackawanna

Lackawanna's location on Lake Erie offered many advantages for steelmaking. There was a ready supply of water as well as easy access to the freighters that transported iron ore over the Great Lakes from mines in Michigan and Minnesota. A long breakwater in the lake protected the approaches to the steel plant's canal, which was 3,900 feet long and 200 feet wide. Here, lake freighters delivered iron ore, limestone, tar, and fuel oil, and then took on board finished steel. The land under Lake Erie provided a place to dump slag, although at a terrible cost to the environment. Eventually the shoreline of Lake Erie was extended out at least a half-mile from its original location. The Niagara Falls power generators provided inexpensive electricity, and the many railroads that converged on Buffalo provided ready transportation for bringing in coal mined in Pennsylvania and shipping out finished steel. Lastly, there was a large workforce of immigrants residing in Buffalo and western New York, and more immigrants and migrants from other states could be drawn to the area. This is why the Lackawanna Iron and Steel Company moved from its original site in Scranton, Pennsylvania.[20]

When the Bethlehem Steel Company purchased the plant in 1922, it began a modernization process. In 1924, the Lackawanna plant had three new batteries of coke ovens, each including 57 individual ovens. Between 1925 and 1927, three new mills were added: No. 12, No. 14, and No. 15 (see Figure 7.7). An additional 10 mills, open hearths, and other facilities were constructed from 1930 to 1974. Earlier, the plant had initiated a series of acquisitions; by 1921, Lackawanna Steel had purchased the Lackawanna Bridge Works. After Bethlehem took over the plant, it acquired the Seneca Steel, Kalman Steel, McClintoc-Marshall, and Buffalo Tank plants. The old Seneca Steel facility was used as a galvanizing mill for a period and eventually became the home of Buffalo Tank. The magnitude of the plant's operation can be more fully appreciated by noting some of the auxiliary functions. There were two power houses, five boiler houses, and a steam plant that provided energy to the mills. Two pump houses brought in water from Lake Erie, and pollution-control facilities were later added as concern about the lake increased. A dispensary, fire department, security unit, and series of food concession stands also served the plant. The 17 "welfare" buildings added in 1939 provided lunch and locker rooms, showers, and lavatories for workers.[21]

A Look at Specific Departments in the Steel Plant

Men from Lackawanna's 92 ethnic groups composed much of the workforce at the steel plant, which dominated the local job market. Lackawanna's steel plant was the largest in the world in 1903 when it began producing iron. It was surpassed in 1914 by the huge United States Steel complex in Gary, Indiana, and later by other plants. With continued expansion, the Lackawanna plant in 1956 became the third-largest steel works in the United States, surpassed only by that in Gary and the Bethlehem plant in Sparrow's Point, Maryland. This section provides a detailed look at where Italians worked in Lackawanna's steel plant, highlighting the occupational trends discussed earlier and giving some flavor of the working conditions throughout the complex. The attempt here is to touch on the departments that employed a few Italians and to focus on those with many. While the period from 1920 to 1930 is emphasized, there is also information about the presence of Italians in various departments in later years.[22]

Italians in the Mills

By 1930, in addition to working in the Yard and on the SBR, Italians worked in at least eight of the steel plant's mills, in 20 shops and departments, and in the open hearths, blast furnaces, and coke ovens (see Figure 7.4). At this time, the trend of Italians to work inside the mills and shops became notable, and it accelerated during the following years. The Bethlehem plant, with a workforce that peaked in 1965 at 21,500, drew workers from throughout Erie County, adjacent counties, and even Canada. This included a significant number of Italians who lived outside Lackawanna. Information on these non–Lackawanna Italians is incorporated because it helps demonstrate the general trends regarding Italians in specific departments of the steel plant. Each Italian not residing in Lackawanna is identified by his town or city of residence, when known.[23]

Among the first Italians to work in the blast furnaces was Cesidio D'Amore in 1910. Several years later, Donato DePasquale and Eugenio Galanti were laborers in the engine Blowing House which provided the surge of air—"the blast" for which the furnaces are named. Jerry Omicioli was a machine operator in the blast furnaces by 1919. After immigrating from Calabria in 1938, Albert Caira worked in the blast furnaces, then transferred to the Ladle House, cleaning the ladles that carried molten iron from the furnaces to the open hearths. A hook was used to clear excess iron that had adhered to the spout and lining of the ladle. After being thoroughly cleaned, it was lined with fire-brick.[24]

No. 1 Open Hearth was operational by the end of 1903, and included several Bessemer furnaces, an early type of open hearth. When No. 2 Open Hearth, sometimes called "two shop," was completed in 1912 it too, included several Bessemer furnaces as well as electric furnaces which were used for making special types of steel. No. 3 Open Hearth became operational in 1937, and, like two shop, it incorporated

FIGURE 7.5
Lackawanna Italian Industrial and Railroad Workers*: Percentage Laborers and Skilled/Semiskilled

Year	Total Industrial & Railroad Workers	Laborers No.	(%)	Skilled & Semiskilled No.	(%)
1905	171	170	(99)	1	(1)
1910	240	225	(94)	15	(6)
1915	191	166	(87)	25	(13)
1917-18	449	316	(70)	133	(30)
1920	326	258	(79)	68	(21)
1925	358	217	(61)	141	(39)
1930	449	228	(51)	221	(49)

*Left out of these statistics are workers in nonindustrial and non-railroad vocations that are listed in Figure 7-1. Sources: U.S. Census, 1910, 1920, 1930; N.Y. Census, 1905, 1915, 1925; WWIDRR, 1917–1918. In 1910 semiskilled workers were those who "acted as helpers to the skilled workmen," and also men who had "been taught to perform relatively complex functions, such as the operation of cranes and other mechanical appliances, but who possess little or no general mechanical or metallurgical knowledge" that would come from a special course of training or long experience in the occupation." Skilled workmen had a "knowledge of some trade or technical process." Skilled workers were paid 25 cents or more per hour, semiskilled received 18 to 24 cents per hour, and the unskilled paid under 18 cents per hour. It proved difficult to classify many of the jobs at the Lackawanna plant, so skilled and semiskilled were combined into one general category for this study. U.S. Senate, *Report On Conditions of Employment in the Iron and Steel Industry, Volume III, Working Conditions and the Relations of Employers and Employees*, 1913, pp. 80–81.

FIGURE 7.6
Occupations of Lackawanna Italians, 1960

	Total	Industrial	Railroad	Non-Industrial
1. Professional	33	—	—	33
2. Business Proprietors	88	—	—	88
3. Skilled/Semiskilled				
A. General	306	207	11	88
B. Supervisory	43	37	4	2
4. Laborers/Unskilled	264	205	12	47
Totals:	734*	449	27	258

* A total of 962 adult males and females with Italian surnames were listed, but occupations were not given for 228 of them.
Source: Lackawanna City Directory, 1960.

improvements and greater capacities. By that time, the Bessemer furnaces had been eliminated and the open-hearth furnaces and hot-metal mixers, which maintained molten iron until it was poured into the furnaces, were larger. In 1964, a new shop featuring the basic oxygen furnace (BOF) was constructed, greatly increasing the plants steelmaking capacity. Italian workmen were present in all four shops. As early as 1910, Joseph Rauve was a foreman at the Bessemer furnace in No. 1 Open Hearth. Several immigrants from Abruzzo began working on the Bessemer. Donato, Domenico, Antonio,

Giovanni, and Giuseppe Iacobucci as well as Angelo Croce—all related—worked on the railroad steam cranes of the Yard that sometimes did lifting chores inside the mills in the early years of the steel plant's operation. Donato Iacobucci had become an overhead crane operator by 1914, as had Angelo Croce by 1920.[25]

As more electric overhead cranes were incorporated into the structure of the open hearth mills, more Italians were operating them. Marchegiani had been connected with the open-hearths since 1912, when Giovanni Sambuchi, a Yard employee, had a part in constructing Two Shop. His eldest son Daniel, who started as a messenger boy in 1909 at age 15, was soon laboring in the open hearths and became a crane operator in No. 1 Open Hearth by 1915. Later, as a stockyard foreman, he directed the preparation of the scrap steel that was sent to the charging floor of the open hearth. The next oldest Sambuchi,—Carlo or "Charley"—rose from the position of clerk in 1914 at age 17 to labor foreman the following year. By the 1920s, he also operated an overhead crane. In 1925 the youngest Sambuchi son, Enrico, or "Harry," was working on the open hearth weighing scales, and then became a foreman. At least 18 other Italians were employed in the open hearths in the early 1920s, most of them Marchegiani. Upon arriving from Italy in 1920, Alfredo Campanelli first worked in the Yard and then in the coke ovens, where he had few Italian coworkers. Campanelli convinced his supervisor to allow him to transfer to No. 1 Open Hearth where he could work with other Marchegiani. After working briefly as a sample carrier and then a nozzle setter, Alfredo Campanelli wanted to escape the intense heat and asked his foreman to try him out as a crane operator. By 1925, Campanelli was operating a crane far above the extreme heat of the pit and charging floor. Four other Marchegiani crane operators were in the open hearths as well, and there were 10 more by 1931 (see Figure 7.10). Many of these men were lined up with open-hearth jobs by Giuseppe

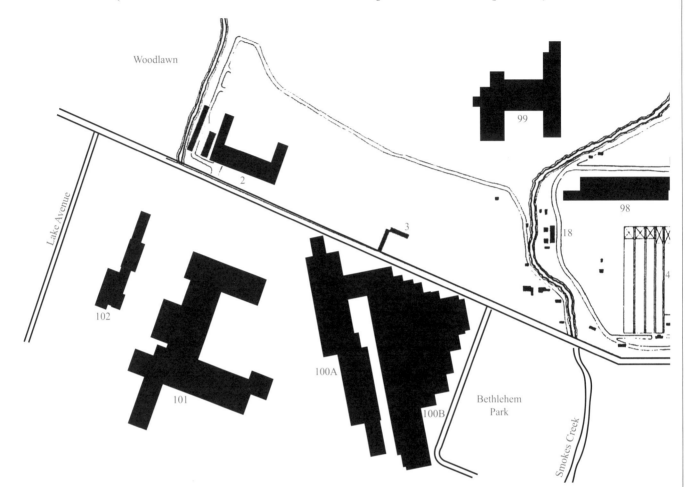

FIGURE 7.7

Ground Plan of Bethlehem Steel Company Plant, 1930
(with mills constructed after that date [numbers 96-102] added)

1	Brick shed #1 & #2	19	Office: calcining plant	37	Stock yard dept #1
2	Narrow-gauge locomotive house	20	Car-repair shops	38	Gas producers tar storage
3	Pattern storage	21	Cold saw house	39	Offices yard dept #1
4	Structural shipping yard	22	Rail mill #1	40	Storehouse
5	Runways 1-10, runways 10-15	23	Drop test mill #1	41	North office plant
6	Mill building #15	24	Hot scale on NQ	42	Structural repair shop
7	Motor room #12 & #15 mill	25	44" Blooming/rail mill	43	Roll shop
8	Mill building #12	26	Blooming mill #7	44	Storehouse
9	Mill building #14	27	Billet yard	45	Pipe tool shop
10	Billet yard #12	28	Billet mill #8	46	Blacksmith/forge shop
11	Shear building	29	Two crane runways	47	Electric repair
12	Plate mill #5	30	Physical laboratory shipping	48	Boiler shop/plate shop
13	Slabbing mill #4	31	Bar mill #8	49	Mechanical repair shop
14	Billet yard	32	Bar mill #6	50	Carpenter shop
15	Structural mills #2-#9	33	Bar mill #10	51	Pattern shop
16	Pig-casting machines #4-#5	34	Open Hearth #1	52	Pattern storage
17	Scrap-reclaiming plant	35	Covered mold yard O.H.	53	Foundry
18	Thaw house	36	Stripper building	54	Open Hearth #2

Illustration source: *Thomas E. Leary and Elizabeth C. Sholes,* From Fire to Rust, *1987, p. 60*

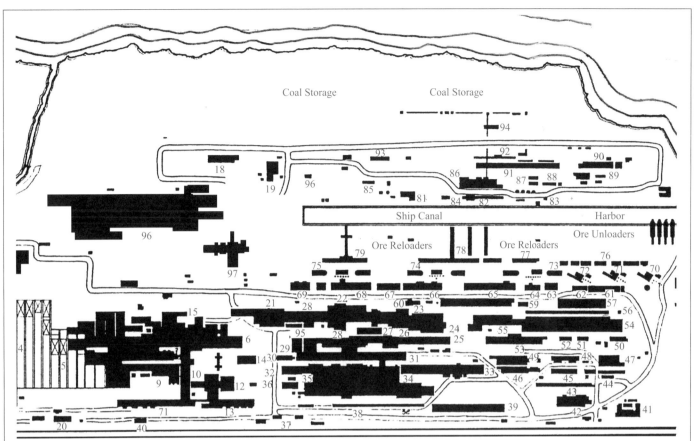

Coal Storage   Coal Storage

Ship Canal   Harbor

Ore Reloaders   Ore Reloaders   Ore Unloaders

Hamburg Turnpike

55	Bessemer dept	73	Blast furnace F	91	Coppers ovens 3 batteries
56	Gas producer dept #2	74	Blast furnace G	92	Coke wharf
57	Stockyard OH dept #2	75	Blast furnace H	93	Quenching station (coke dept)
58	Power station #2	76	Ore limestone bins	94	Screening station
59	Power house #1	77	Ore bins	95	Hellhole

POST 1930

55 Bessemer dept
56 Gas producer dept #2
57 Stockyard OH dept #2
58 Power station #2
59 Power house #1
60 Narrow-gauge repair shop
61 Blowing Engine House #4
62 Ladle house
63 Boiler house #1
64 Brick storage
65 Blowing Engine House #2
66 Boiler house #2
67 Pumping station
68 Blowing Engine House #3
69 Boiler house #3
70 Blast furnace A
71 Blast furnace B
72 Blast furnace C

73 Blast furnace F
74 Blast furnace G
75 Blast furnace H
76 Ore limestone bins
77 Ore bins
78 Coke limestone bins
79 Ore bins
80 Traveling boat unloaders
81 Booster house
82 Benzol building
83 Storage tanks
84 Rail unloader
85 Boiler house
86 Condensing & ammonia house
87 Settling basin
88 Circulating pump houses
89 Tar storage
90 Car dumper

91 Coppers ovens 3 batteries
92 Coke wharf
93 Quenching station (coke dept)
94 Screening station
95 Hellhole

POST 1930

96 Open hearth #3 (1936)
97 Sintering plant (1950)
98 Basic oxygen furnace (1964)
99 Slabbing mill (1961)
100 Strip mill: A. Hot mill (1936)
                 B. Cold mill (1936)
101 Bar mills:
    12" (1940)
    10" (1947)
    13" (1976)
102 Galvanizing mill (1962)

FIGURE 7.8

THE STEELMAKING PROCESS

The steel plant of the twentieth century was like a small, crowded city where everything was interconnected. These plants were huge, covering anywhere from two to seven miles along a lake or river. The basic process of steelmaking was developed in the nineteenth century and used a tremendous amount of energy and materials. Moving and processing these materials, plus maintaining the machinery and operations, involved the intricate choreography of thousands of workers and machines.

Producing a ton of finished steel in 1940 consumed 30,000 gallons of water, four tons of air, and five tons of raw materials. At Bethlehem Steel's Lackawanna plant, two pumping stations brought in 135 million gallons of water each day. Among the raw materials needed were half a ton of pig iron and half a ton of scrap steel. Making one ton of iron called for a ton of coke, two tons of iron ore, half a ton of limestone, and four tons of air. Coke, which is coal that has been superheated so that it burns rapidly and develops tremendous heat, was produced by distilling crushed coal in long rows of vertical ovens called coke ovens. It required 1.4 tons of coal to make one ton of coke. Once the molten iron was produced, other ingredients were added to produce steel—scrap metal, manganese, silicon, and small quantities of phosphorous and sulphur. Other elements—such as nickel, chromium, vanadium, tungsten, and cobalt were sometimes added to make steel with specific properties.[26]

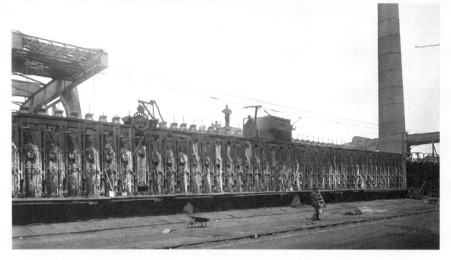

Battery of coke ovens. Coke is coal that has been superheated so that it burns rapidly and develops tremendous heat. Photo source: Hamburg Historical Society

The complicated process of making steel was, and basically still is, accomplished in several steps. The first occurs at a blast furnace, where iron is produced. A blast furnace resembles a huge vase; it is a vertical, brick-lined steel cylinder that in the 1940s usually measured 100 feet high and 27 feet in diameter (see Figure 7.9). Iron ore, limestone, and coke are carried to the top of the furnace by a skip car running on an inclined track. The materials are dumped, or "charged," into the furnace. After the raw materials have been added, air that has been heated to 1700 degrees F is blasted through nozzles at the base of the blast furnace, burning the coke and melting the iron, which collects in a pool in the hearth at the bottom. At the same time, the limestone combines with impurities in the ore and coke to form a molten slag that also drips into the hearth and floats on top of the heavier iron. The

The coke ovens machine shop, circa 1930. Four of the men on the right are Italian, including Antonio DiMillo, top row, second from the right.
Photo source: Tony DiMillo

(continued)

slag is drawn off, emptied into ladles mounted on railroad cars, and dumped into Lake Erie. In the early years of the twentieth century, iron was often cast into 40-to 100-pound bars called "pigs" to be used for future steelmaking or in the production of iron castings. By the 1930s, the molten iron was commonly tapped into hot-metal cars and transported to an open-hearth mill, where hot-metal mixers kept the iron at a steady temperature until needed. Iron, which lacks the strength and malleability of steel, is transformed into steel in the next process.[27]

The second stage of steelmaking involves the open-hearth furnace, in which 90% of American steel was produced in the early 1940s. The open-hearth furnace ranged from 70 to 100 feet in height and 20 to 26 feet in width (see Figure 7.9). An open-hearth mill consists of a row of furnaces that face the charging floor, where a machine places raw materials in each furnace when its door is opened. First limestone is added which removes impurities by congealing them into slag. Equal amounts of scrap steel, which is prepared in a "stockyard," and molten iron are then added, along with iron ore and other ingredients, depending on the type of steel being made. Metal is held in the shallow hearth of the furnace, which has a port at each end. Gas or liquid fuel and preheated air are blown through ports, causing a flame to sweep across the hearth directly over the materials—thus the name open hearth. The flames melt the ingredients, then, during the refining process, heat the molten metal to 2900 degrees F. Samples are rushed to labs for analysis, the resulting data being used to control the refining process. In the 1940s, one "heat," or batch, yielded 100 to 175 tons of steel.[28]

Tapping an open-hearth furnace is spectacular. The back of the furnace faces

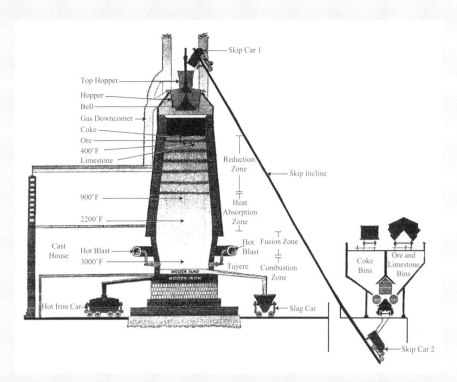

Figure 7.9. Blast furnace
The first step in steelmaking is to make iron in a blast furnace, which is shown in this cross section. Illustration source: Bethlehem Steel Company, "A Visit to the Lackawanna Plant of the Bethlehem Steel Company." booklet 104, 1939

the pit, which is one level lower than the charging floor. When the clay plug is removed from the tap hole, molten steel bursts out with explosive force producing a giant fireworks effect. The molten metal pours down a spout and into a huge ladle. The floating slag flows out last and goes into a slag pot, which is placed on a railroad car for dumping. The steel-filled ladle is carried by an overhead crane across the pit to the pouring platform, where a row of ingot molds atop narrow-gauge railroad flat cars stand ready for pouring. The ladle is moved from mold to mold as a worker uses a lever to control the flow of steel into each mold. Ingots vary in size to accommodate the subsequent rolling process, ranging from five to 25 tons. Each ingot mold tapers slightly toward the top so it can later be easily lifted away. Just outside the open-hearth

mill is a stripper house where the molds are pulled off the hardened ingots.[29]

After leaving the open hearths, the ingots are processed into steel products. In this third stage, the ingots are taken to a semi-finishing mill, where they are lowered into soaking pits for reheating to a temperature that allows them to be rolled. Rolling involves passing the ingot between two horizontal cylinders that are mounted in a stand, one above the other, and held in position by large screws. Each trip through the rollers is called a pass. As the steel goes through the series of stands, it is gradually reduced to the desired thickness. In semi-finishing mills, ingots are rolled and flattened into three shapes: blooms, billets, or slabs (see Figure 7-11). These are inspected for defects, and all surface flaws are removed by grinding, chipping, or scarfing. The

(continued)

353

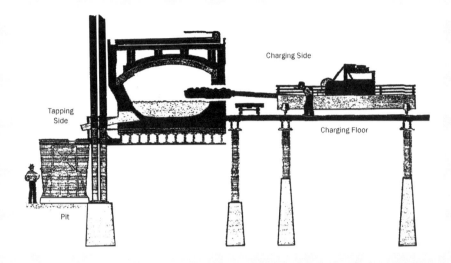

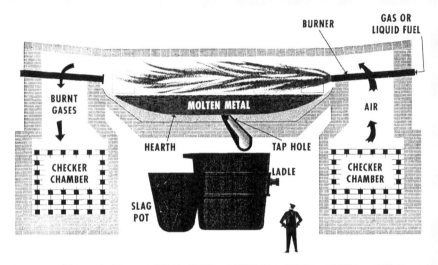

Figure 7.10 Open-hearth furnace
Top: Side view. Iron is transported from the blast furnace to an open-hearth mill,
where it and a number of ingredients are placed into a furnace from the charging floor.
Bottom: View from the pit, or tapping side. After the materials have melted
together, the steel is tapped from the pit, the lowest level in the mill. The steel
fills up the large ladle, then the waste material, or slag, floating on top drains
into the slag pot.
Illustration source: Bethlehem Steel Company, "A Visit to the Lackawanna Plant of the
Bethlehem Steel Company." booklet 104, 1939.

fourth stage is accomplished in finishing mills, where the blooms, billets, and slabs are rolled into the final products, such as bars, rods, rails, beams, and strip steel. The huge strip mills introduced in the 1930s represented one type of finishing mill that allowed for rapid production of many tons of light-gauge steel used for automobiles and appliances. A strip mill actually consisted of two mills built side by side. In the Hot Mill, a hot slab passes through four roughing stands and, gathering speed, travels nearly 1,000 feet through six finishing stands, emerging several minutes later as a roll of 1,000 feet of coiled steel.

In the Cold Mill, smaller gauges of steel, below .05 inch, are produced. A strip of steel is uncoiled, run through sulfuric acid in a "pickler" to remove scale, then rolled to the specified thickness. The finished metal is then either cut into sheets or rolled back into a coil. Some steel products, such as structural beams fashioned in a mill, need a fifth processing stage, in which a protective coating of zinc is added to steel in a galvanizing mill. Scales at key locations weighed both raw materials and finished steel. At Bethlehem Steel, a dozen specialty shops tended to the needs of the mills by retooling rolls, producing molds, fashioning tools, and repairing machinery. Standard and narrow-gauge trains as well as trucks moved raw materials and finished products throughout the expanse of the plant.[30]

Sources: Bethlehem Steel Company (BSC), "A Visit to the Lackawanna Plant of the Bethlehem Steel Company," booklet 104, 1939, pp. 7-9, 12-13, 29; BSC, "Steel in the making," booklet 136-c, 1942, pp. 8-19, 22-39; interview with Phil Andreozzi, June 10, 1994.

Note: Flue dust is produced in a blast furnace, where the fine particles of ore are trapped in a funnel and then loaded into tightly sealed railroad hopper cars. A ladle car is virtually a frame on trucks—railroad wheels—onto which a large cone-shaped pot, or ladle, was placed. This was used to haul molten iron and slag from a blast furnace and molten slag from an open hearth. The slag from the blast furnaces was usually dumped in Lake Erie, although some was reclaimed by the Buffalo Slag Company, which crushed it and sold it for roadbed construction. Open-hearth slag, which had many particles of steel mixed in, was first broken up at the High Drop, the steel removed by a magnet, and then used in the open hearths. The remainder was dumped on a hill at the northwest end of the plant. Especially noted by environmentalists was the small mountain of slag on the western edge of the grounds that over the years extended further and further into Lake Erie and fouled nearby Woodlawn Beach. Molten iron was later transported by large "submarine cars," named for their resemblance to the underwater naval craft and having a small opening at the top. When iron was not needed at the open hearths it was made into pigs for future use. At the Lackawanna plant in 1922 there were two semi-finishing mills and eight finishing mills; in 1942, there were three semi-finishing mills and ten finishing mills. Among the finishing mills were the Spike Mill, Rail Mill, and several bar and structural mills. Blooms, slabs, and billets brought to a finishing mill, such as the strip mill, were laid flat into a shallow soaking furnace, entering at one end and exiting on the other end through hinged doors prior to rolling.

Paolini, an immigrant from Marche and the father of Garage Department foreman Mickey Paolini.[26]

Domenico Bracci, another Marchegiano, worked in one of the scrap yards, where he was promoted to foreman in 1925. Each open hearth had its own scrap yard, where scrap metal was loaded into oblong pans placed on special rail cars called charging

Each open-hearth mill had a stripper building where the molds were pulled off the solidified ingots. This photo was taken on December 15, 1939. Photo source: Paul Pietrak

buggies. In 1930, Lavinio Montanari was operating an overhead crane loading the buggies for No. 1 Open Hearth. A highline locomotive pushed a line of buggies and other cars filled with materials such as manganese up the trestle to the charging floor, where a charging machine placed one pan at a time through the furnace door and dumped its contents. Luigi Montanari, Lavinio's brother, was one of the charging machine operators.[27]

The open-hearth furnaces were tended by crews with specialized functions. The unskilled third helper was like an apprentice hoping to rise up the line of skilled positions: second helper, first helper, and finally, melter. The third helper did cleanup chores and shoveled dolomite into the furnaces after the steel was poured; this filled in any holes in the brickwork. The second helper crushed various ingredients, or "stock," such as sulfur or manganese, in a wheelbarrow and shoveled these into the furnace. Alfred Olivieri was a third helper in 1931, and a decade later, Dominic Antonio was a second helper. Earlier, in 1915, Dimitri Papo was a "helper," the forerunner of either position. The first helper directed the work of the third helpers, monitored the furnace, and took steel samples by inserting a long-handled "spoon" into a hole in the furnace door. These were carried to a laboratory by a test sample carrier, a semiskilled position that was held by six Marchegiani between 1910 and 1924. The test results were used by a lab specialist or the melter to give further instructions to the second helper. The melter oversaw the operations of several furnaces and

FIGURE 7.11

BLOOMS, BILLETS, AND SLABS

An ingot is a large piece of raw steel created when molten steel is poured into a mold in an open-hearth mill. In a semi-finishing mill, an ingot is rolled into a flat configuration that can take one of three rough dimensions:

1) Blooms are either square or rectangular in cross section, measuring six inches or more in width and height, and many feet in length.

2) Billets are blooms that are further reduced to one-and-a-half to six inches in height and width, with square, rectangular or round cross sections.

3) Slabs are much flatter than blooms, with widths that are three, four, or more times their thickness

In finishing mills the blooms, billets, and slabs are rolled into finished products. Blooms are processed into structural steel and railroad rails. Billets are fashioned into bars or rods, the latter being used to make wire. Slabs are fashioned into very thin products such as plates, coils of strip, and sheets.

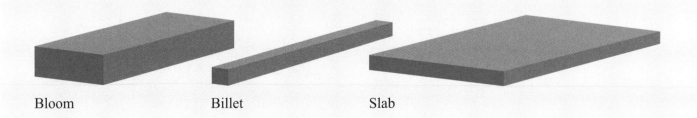

Bloom   Billet   Slab

Sources: Bethlehem Steel Company, "Steel in the Making," booklet 136c, 1942, pp. 63, 68; Bethlehem Steel Company, "Steel In the Making," Booklet 479A, n. d., p. 17.

decided when each furnace should be tapped. An open-hearth furnace took eight to 14 hours to complete a "heat," and then the molten steel was ready to be "tapped" into a ladle. On the pit side of the furnace, the second helper positioned himself three to five feet away from the tap hole and used a high-pressure air hose or an explosive to break the clay plug in the furnace. The molten steel at first exploded like fireworks out of the tapping hole as tremendous heat was released. After this initial burst, the liquid metal flowed down a trough into a huge vessel, or ladle, on the "pit" floor below the furnace. An overhead crane, such as the one Amerigo Bracci operated, then lifted the vessel across the pit to a line of narrow-gauge flatcars, each carrying two upright molds. A skilled worker known as a pourer stepped along a catwalk operating a 10-foot lever that allowed molten steel in the vessel to flow into the molds; this process produced more "fireworks." In 1925, Latino LaMarti was a pourer, and Anthony DePasquale a pit foreman who oversaw the pouring and insured that the vessels and molds were in proper order.[28]

Open-hearth employees assumed the role of crewmen on the standard-gauge, "highline" locomotives that pushed railcars bearing materials up to the charging floor. It was challenging work to negotiate the steep grades on the trestles of these short sections of railroad that went from the stockyard into each open-hearth mill. In 1921, after 18 months in the scrap yard,

A blast furnace viewed from the deck of the highline. Bethlehem Steel had 6 blast furnaces in operation in 1930. Photo source: Paul Pietrak

The charging floor of No. 3 Open Hearth in 1941. The man kneeling, front left, is Louie Patrucci, who became a first helper in 1949. Photo source: Collection of Louie Patrucci

Giuseppe "Joe" Violanti convinced a foreman to make him a fireman on the highline engine. A German American engineer named Bill first taught Violanti how to tend the fire, clean the flues, and monitor the boiler pressure, then how to actually run the 75-ton engine. Within six months, Violanti was filling in for engineers on the smaller steam engines. Bill was not only a good teacher but also a considerate man who referred to Violanti as "Joe" instead of the belittling "boy" used by some other workers. Violanti worked 12-hour shifts as an engineer for about two years. During slack hours, he practiced operating the overhead crane in the stockyard, then asked Superintendent Viller if he could become a crane operator in No. 2 Open Hearth. Viller simply asked, "Can you run the crane?" When Violanti responded with a firm yes, Viller commanded the master mechanic to "get the 'boy' on the crane." The mechanic told Violanti to "stay there [on the crane] until I tell you to stop." He remained there for 10 years, until Two Shop temporarily closed down in 1933. Other Giulianesi also worked on the open hearths' locomotives. Giuseppe Petricca was a highline engineer by the early 1920s. His nephew, Romolo Petricca, who was working on a Yard railroad steam crane, in 1926 became a fireman on the highline in No. 1 Open Hearth. By 1937, he was engineer on a full-sized engine in No. 3 Open Hearth. Petricca then followed his *paesani,* the Violanti brothers, to Hanna Furnace, where he was an assistant engineer for the boiler house steam engine. Like Giuseppe Violanti, he too met a friendly German American engineer who taught him all the facets of maintaining the steam engine. After a year, Petricca returned to Bethlehem Steel as a highline engineer.[29]

In 1905, 15-year-old Antonio Barone was the first Italian known to become a crane operator at Bethlehem Steel. He was joined by John Cole and Joseph Faranti in 1910, and seven other Italians were crane operators by 1915. During the full production of World War I, 12 Italians operated cranes in the mills and nine were on the Yard's railroad steam cranes. The number of Italian crane operators continued to increase, and by 1930 there were 41. The following year, Paolo Zaccarine,

Tapping a heat of steel from an open-hearth furnace. The molten steel is about 2,000°F and flows into the vessel on the right. The slag or waste matter, comes out last and goes into the smaller vessel at the left. Photo source: Bethlehem Steel Company, "Lackawanna Plant," Booklet 309-A, 1952.

an Abruzzese, and Agosto Capodagli, a Marchegiano, were operating cranes in No. 1 Mill. Several years later, Albert Covino became one of the few non–Marchegiani Italians working as an open hearth crane operator.[30]

Between 1903 and 1940, 14 rolling mills were put into operation at the steel plant, and three more were added by 1974 (see Figure 7.7). Eventually, Italian workers became scattered throughout most of these mills, some of them working as millwrights. A key person in every mill, the millwright was a general handyman who serviced the machinery and equipment. Between 1910 and 1926, documents mention eight Italian millwrights in unspecified mills, plus Emilio Miniri in No. 1 Mill and Domenico Marinelli in No. 2 Mill, where a variety of plates and light structural shapes were produced. A coworker of Marinelli, Joseph Florino, was a splice bar recorder. Recorders, or clerks, took inventory of raw materials and finished products in each mill; many of these men were American-born and literate in English. During the 1920s, Tom Pepper and Vincent George had such jobs, and Joe DePasquale was a recorder, then chief clerk in No. 7-8 Mills in the 1930s. Other second-generation men who entered the mills in the 1940s as clerks were Joseph Leo in the 12" Bar Mill and A. Mancuso in the Finishing Department of the 44"-32" Mill.[31]

Italians gravitated to other skilled and semiskilled positions in the plant. Dan George, Vincent's older brother, worked as a weigher, and Joseph Mingarelli as a mill inspector. Most large mills had an electrical crew, while other electricians were based in the plant's Electrical Shop. These positions required literacy in English and were a natural entry point into skilled jobs for the American-born generation and for young immigrants who could quickly learn English. Alex Cosentino emigrated as a teenager from Calabria in 1914 and became an electrician six years later. Lackawanna-born Mike Pacillo was an electrician's apprentice in the mid-1920s. There were thousands of machines in the plant, and skilled machinists were located in many mills, with the largest concentration in the Machine Shop. Domenico Aloisi and Antonio Delguercio were machinists in 1910, and three more Italians became machinists by 1917. Several immigrants switched from one skilled position to another: Donato Chiacchia moved from a weigher's job to that of machinist by 1918, and the following year, Ferdinando Catuzza vacated his millwright job and enrolled in the Machine Shop's apprentice program. Sixteen-year-old Tony Grasso started working in the Machine Shop in December 1919 as the steel strike was waning. There were 15 Italian machinists in the early 1920s, and by the end of the decade, Vincenzo Carnevale and others joined their ranks. More Italian machinists emerged during the 1930s, most of them second–generation men, such as Romeo Zaccarine, who started his career in the Foundry in 1934 and soon moved to the Machine Shop.[32]

Among the many Italians who started as laborers in the mills, some eventually moved up into skilled positions. For several Italians, the huge No. 1 Mill was the best setting for advancement. It was a third of a mile long, and the southern end of it housed the rail mill. Pasquale Olivieri, who started working in the plant

Loading charging boxes with scrap metal and other materials. Special railroad cars carried the boxes up to the charging floor of an open hearth where a charging machine emptied the contents of the boxes into the furnaces.
Photo source: Hamburg Historical Society

A highline engine pulling buggies with charging boxes up to the charging floor of the open hearth. Photo source: Paul Pietrak

in 1919 at age 16, transferred to No. 1 Mill and became a machinist. By 1931, he was operating a crane. Agosto Aleggi was also a laborer in the mill, but later he and Agosto Capodagli became pulpit operators, who controlled the complex process of rolling steel. This represented an important advancement by Italians to a key position. Earlier, V. Jimmy D'Alessandro was one of the first Italians to rise to this level. D'Alessandro had mastered the mechanics of rolling steel in the Roll Shop and in 1928 became a pulpit operator in No. 1 Mill, the fifth-highest position. In this job, he operated the rolling controls from an elevated booth, or pulpit. He moved up to second, then first guide setter, jobs in which he adjusted the guides on each role stand that shaped the steel. He then became the First Guide Setter for rollers, the mill's third-highest position. Another immigrant, Donato Andrisani, started as a mill laborer, became a recorder in No. 12 Mill in 1925, and later was a Gauger. In this last role, Andrisani set the equipment that trimmed the excess from each side of the steel as it passed through the roll stand.[33]

In the rolling mills, the Heater was among the top positions. Pasquale Ricci was one of several men from Falvaterra, Lazio, who worked in No. 7 Mill, and in 1922, he became a Heater. In this job, he had to decide when the ingots in the storage ovens, or soaking pits, were at the proper temperature to be rolled. If he misjudged and the center of the ingot was not hot and malleable, then the rollers and roll stands would be damaged. During the 1920s, the heater was the third-highest position in the mill; it paid well, and Ricci was the first Italian to attain it at the Lackawanna plant. Pasquale Olivieri continued his advance into a series of skilled positions and became a heater in No. 9 Mill during the 1930s.[34]

The careers of two American-born men demonstrate the increasing importance of this generation to both family income and the overall advancement of Italians in the steel plant. The jobs held by some second-generation men were often essential to the economic survival of Italian families, as their fathers were underemployed or incapacitated. Carl Covino was the eldest son of Aniello Covino, who had lost a leg in an open-hearth accident. The family looked to Carl to become its breadwinner, and he began working in the steel plant in 1934 at the age of 17. He labored as a hooker—attaching cable loops to the hook lowered from a crane—in the billet yard of No. 12

FIGURE 7.12

MARCHEGIANI OPEN–HEARTH CRANE OPERATORS

Immigrants from Le Marche and their sons seemed to have a penchant for the position of crane operator in the open hearths. Between 1925 and 1931, at least 15 Marchegiani performed this work:

Emidio Antilli

Giuseppe Baldassari

Giuseppe Baldelli

Clario Bartolucci

Amerigo Bracci*

Alfredo Campanelli

Enrico Lucarelli

Vittorio Manna

Lavinio Montanari

Luigi Montanari

Enrico Sambuchi**

Carlo Sambuchi*

Bruno Santi

Alfredo Tonucci

Gino Tonucci

Fourteen of these men were immigrants, two of them (*) coming to the U.S. as young children; one man (**) was born in the U.S.

Sources: U.S. Census, 1920, 1930; N.Y. Census, 1925; *Erie County Directory*, 1931.

Ingots marked with batch numbers. The large pieces of steel ranged in weight from 5 to 25 tons. Photo source: Hamburg Historical Society

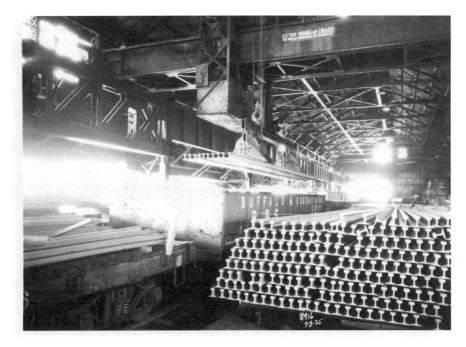

1925. No. 1 Mill produced rails that were sold throughout the country. Photo source: Paul Pietrak

A Bethlehem Steel rolling mill in 1936. Photo source: Paul Pietrak

of steel ordered. After steel was rolled, put in a cooler bed, and straightened, it was then cut to order by the crew according to the slipmaker's instruction, bundled and weighed. In the 1960s, Covino was a subforeman at the finishing end of No. 14 Mill, and then went on to the mill's Shipping Department, and finally, worked in the position of stock-shearman. He recalls that No. 14 "was a hand-operated mill; there was much bull work." Many blacks and Poles as well as several other Italians worked there.[35]

Frank Rosati's 39-year career in the steel plant reflects the rise of second-generation Italians through the ranks as well as the adaptation of steelworkers to the changing technology of the industry. In 1940, Rosati was having trouble finding a job, so he went to the Lackawanna City Hall and talked to the mayor and then to a neighbor, City Assessor Angelo Grosso, who helped Rosati get a laborer's job in No. 9 Mill. After military service, Rosati returned to the mill in 1945, where his coworkers included Poles, blacks, Hungarians, Spaniards, and other Italians. In 1947, No. 9 Mill was shut down and the workers were transferred to the new 10" Bar Mill, where flat and round bars were rolled. The steel was then shipped to customers who fashioned the metal into bars, reinforcing rods, and springs. Rosati, a semiskilled cradleman, operated a cradle, a U-shaped machine that bundled and weighed newly rolled steel. "This could be dangerous work," Rosati reported, "because the bars can whip around." In 1950, he began work as a chainman, placing chains or cables around each end of a bundle of 30-foot billets, which a crane then lifted into a vertical storage rack. Each bundle contained elongated "loaves of bread"—that is, billets that were 2 1/2 to 4 inches square and 30 feet long. He and the other chainmen were always on the alert for frayed cables that were about to snap.[36]

In 1952, Rosati's foreman sent him back to the main part of the mill to become a roll builder. In this skilled position, Rosati set up and took down roll stands as dictated by the type

Mill, but was laid off within three months. He then found work in No. 14 Mill but only for two to three days per week. When Covino worked the second shift, 3:00 to 11:00 p.m., an African American crane operator taught him how to use the machine and during slow periods allowed Covino to practice running it. In 1937, Covino became a crane operator himself, a job he resumed after military service in World War II. He later became a slipmaker, making sure each customer got the exact quantity

Workers in No. 7 Mill in 1936. Photo source: Jack and Mary Panczykowski

of bar being produced. A billet was continuously reduced in height and width as it traveled through the 18 roll stands and gradually assumed the desired shape. Rosati was fascinated by the process in which the billet was stretched into a 300 to 400-foot-long ribbon of steel. He soon advanced to Guide Setter, which was the third position from the top in the mill hierarchy. Some guides were comparatively light and could be installed by hand, while others necessitated an overhead crane. Rosati did this type of work for three years, then returned to the roll builder position. In 1976, he went to the new and very modern 13" Bar Mill, where he spent the last three years of his career as a Mill Adjuster. Unlike a Guide Setter who physically placed the guides, the Mill Adjuster simply pressed buttons, and adjustments were made automatically.[37]

In 1932, the Bethlehem Steel Corporation purchased Seneca Steel of Blasdell, which was an early version of a strip mill. Prior to this, Bethlehem had only one strip mill among its nine plants, the one in Sparrows Point, Maryland. The No. 8 Mill in Lackawanna had been supplying semifinished sheet bars to Seneca Steel since 1907, but with this purchase, Bethlehem acquired Seneca's 150,000-ton capacity for automotive and furniture sheets. As one writer noted, "Absorbing the Blasdell operation gave Bethlehem quick entry into the sheet market at a time when sales in heavier product lines were particularly slow." But the technology and machinery in the Seneca plant were dated, and to compete on the market, Bethlehem needed to duplicate the large, automated strip mills innovated by other companies. These were "hot strip mills that produced long, wide, and uniform sheets and strips. A complimentary cold-rolling process permitted even greater reductions in thickness while simultaneously improving the surface and mechanical properties of the steel used for auto body stampings and other mass-production industries."[38]

In March 1935, a new strip mill began to rise on a 67-acre tract just south of Bethlehem Park; it opened a year later. Some 200 men from the Seneca plant, about a quarter of them Italians, were transferred to the new mill to help set up the machinery. Among them was millwright Al Croce, who recounts that they worked closely with Luigi Paolini and other iron workers of Bethlehem's Erection Department, who were under the direction of Croce's friend, Native American Dick Seneca. Carl Covino was working two or three days per week in No. 12 Mill in 1935 and 1936. At times a blue "loan slip" from his supervisor allowed him to work in other departments. Usually, he joined his uncle Umberto Barbati's track-laying crew at the Strip Mill. Sections of track were built at one site, loaded onto railroad flatcars, moved to the construction area, and unloaded by a Yard steam crane. Antonio Carestio, a crane operator, was involved in this work.[39]

Before the Strip Mill opened, the newly hired general superintendent, West Virginia native Albert Schonkweiler, sent

Workers in No. 9 Mill. The sign provided monthly information on two types of accidents: "minor" ones that involved no loss of work time, and "lost time" accidents that forced a worker to leave his job for a period of time due to injury. Photo source: Hamburg Historical Society

These bars, called "Japanese sheet bars," were produced at No. 8 Mill, then transported to the Seneca Steel plant in Blasdell to be made into strip, or thin-gauge steel, circa 1930. Photo source: Hamburg Historical Society

FIGURE 7.13

TEMPORARY WORK AND CHANGING JOBS

A notable trend in the development of the Italian workforce in Lackawanna was the continual switching of jobs both within and outside the steel plant. This process went on into the early 1940s, as many Italians changed jobs five or more times before settling on a career. Seventeen-year-old Joe Cosentino first worked at a tannery in Gowanda, New York, in 1921. The following year, he entered the steel plant, working in the blast furnaces, on the cranes at the ore docks, and in the Power House. With the help of his brother, an electrician, Cosentino became an electrician's helper and then an electrician in the late 1920s. He worked in a variety of settings in the plant, at one point, he took a six-month leave of absence to work on a construction job that paid $140 per week compared to $56 the per week, he made in the steel plant. Cosentino finally settled into an electrician's position in the Structural Shipping Yard, where he enjoyed the outdoor work. Some men changed jobs for more personal reasons. When annoyed by a foreman's style or feeling that he demanded too much, these men simply looked for jobs in other departments. Antonio Pacillo often did this during the early days of his career in the steel plant.

Railroad workers also changed jobs, as illustrated by the careers of three immigrants. James Valentine began working for the Yard in 1922, and the following year he transferred to the SBR's Track Department. In 1928 he moved to the Billet Yard, but again went back to the railroad job. In a similar vein, Lorenzo Coviello joined the Yard in 1920, transferred to the SBR Track Department three years later, went to work in No.1 Open Hearth in 1925, then returned to the SBR within five months. Amedeo "Mike" Catuzza was a section hand for the Lake Shore and Michigan Southern Railroad in 1915, then became a crane operator in the steel plant's mills five years later. From there he went to the Yard, where he alternated between jobs. He was a locomotive crane engineer in 1921, a construction laborer in 1925, and again a locomotive crane engineer the following year.

The same pattern could be found among workers who immigrated as children or were born in the U.S. Tony Grasso arrived in Lackawanna in 1916 at the age of 13 and was soon working as a waterboy for a Lehigh Valley track gang. Grasso found many other Italians working the rails, including his Calabrese foreman, and Philip Verel, foreman of another track gang. He continued this work for three years, with some temporary work in No. 5 Mill at Lackawanna Steel in 1917. By the end of 1919, he was a machinist's helper in the Machine Shop. When Grasso was laid off in 1921, he found several road construction jobs in western New York and Syracuse. He returned to the steel plant in 1922, this time working with the Bricklaying Department, relining the open-hearth furnaces. Grasso worked 10 hours per day seven days per week for two months. His wages were 22 cents per hour. He then returned to the Machine Shop, working with apprentice Tony Gallarney. They worked 12-hour shifts, but Grasso's pay was higher now. After three or four months, both men secured employment at Donner Steel (later Republic Steel) in South Buffalo. They worked 10-hour shifts at an even better wage. By 1925, Grasso had became a machinist and Gallarney a night foreman.

The Great Depression played havoc with jobs. Many men were laid off, while others had their hours reduced. Men were hired for a brief period of time, then let go, and later hired again for short spans of time. The daily hiring of laborers at the plant office made everything uncertain for prospective employees. Amerigo Bracci recalled, "in the Depression, I was laid off 10 different times in six or seven years." Until the plant was unionized in 1941, many workers were hired on a daily basis, a practice that led to frequent job changes. Men appeared in the morning and representatives from each department picked the number needed for that day's work. Many men found that their nationalities, lack of personal acquaintance with the foremen, and other arbitrary factors meant they were seldom hired in certain departments. When a mill was down for repairs, all but those men needed for the maintenance were sent home. Also, workers were paid wholly or in part on a piecework basis. Sometimes the recorder or foreman made biased decisions about how much was produced by a specific worker. Frank Scaletta (Angola), who worked for the SBR's Track Department, remembered that a piece-rate man stationed at the office came around and allotted prices for laying ties, installing switches, unloading materials, and so on. With no fixed rates, the piece-rate man could arbitrarily set these; if a track gang was very productive, he might lower the rate. If work was simply slow, the employees received less take-home pay. Because of these factors, men often sought stopgap jobs in other departments.

Sources: Interviews with Joe Cosentino, July 14, 1995; Tony Grasso, December 23, 1987; Frank Scaletta, April 4, 1988; South Buffalo Railway Company, "Seniority Roster—Maintenance of Way Employees," 1942; *Buffalo News Magazine*, June 5, 1983. Piecework means that a worker's pay is based on the number of items he produces, such as the number of iron pigs produced or railroad ties installed..

out recruiters to seek experienced Strip-Mill workers in the mill towns of Ohio, Pennsylvania, Indiana, and West Virginia. John Savarese, who had worked in the Ashtabula Sheet Steel Plant until it closed, traveled with his brother and four other men from Ohio to Woodlawn, where they were quartered in a hotel. After starting work at the steel plant, Savarese and three of the men then moved to Roland Avenue. Bethlehem recruiters also gathered 200 Steubenville, Ohio, steelworkers and 100 others in Indiana Harbor, Indiana. Most of these men were German, Irish, Polish, or Russian, but there also were 25 Italians in the group. Among them were three Abruzzesi from Steubenville, immigrant Pietro Suffoletta, and American-born brothers Jack and Ralph Meta. The Metas had worked in the Wierton Steel Company, across the Ohio River in West Virginia, but were laid off in the early 1930s. Arriving in 1936, they took up residence in Blasdell and Jack started work as a "catcher" in the mill. He later moved to Lackawanna, and his brother to Pittsburgh. Suffoletta, who had arrived in the United States in 1929 and worked in Steubenville's mills, took up residence in Bethlehem Park. Another trio of Abruzzesi—Domenico Vittorini, Antonio Pavone, and Antonio Logan (Laconne)—had come to Lackawanna a few years earlier. They had immigrated to Niles, Ohio, in the 1920s and

worked in steel mills. In the early 1930s, jobs at Seneca Steel brought them to Lackawanna, where they boarded with Italian families. When the Strip Mill was completed, these men were among the 200 workers transferred there from the older plant in Blasdell.[40]

The Strip Mill drew other transfers from within the Bethlehem plant. V. Jimmy D'Alessandro transferred from No. 1 Mill in 1935 to operate a crane: "a good job—it was safe, clean, and easy." That same year, a former open-hearth crane operator, Nick Sperduto, returned to the plant to join the Strip Mill's workforce. In 1934, Nick DePasquale and Fred Rosati entered the steel plant and soon were working in the Strip Mill's slab yard. Both became crane operators, and Rosati was later a foreman. A number of other Italians rose to skilled and supervisory roles in the 1940s. John Falbo was one of the transfers from Seneca Steel to the Strip Mill, where he rose to assistant roller. Millwright foreman Leonard Luciano supervised 30 millwrights in the Hot Mill division, where Al Verel was a General Finishing and Shipping Foreman. Verel, originally of Seneca Steel, went on to become Superintendent of the Hot Mill.[41]

Several other areas in the steel plant had functions directly related to the rolling mills. In the Structural Shipping and

FIGURE 7.14

THE HELLHOLE

No. 1 Mill was about 2,000 feet long, and just east of it and running parallel was another lengthy structure that housed No. 7 Mill and No. 8 Mill. The space between the two structures, the Hellhole, was approximately 100 to 150 feet wide (see Figure 7.7). Three overhead cranes spanned the area. A standard-gauge SBR track ran through it, as did a narrow-gauge track. Worst of all, both tracks curved through the Hellhole and crossed each other in two places. In addition, there were a number of railroad sidings, or stubs, serving the mills. On a short stub next to No. 7 Mill, the SBR spotted three gondolas which received "butts," the jagged ends of blooms or slabs that were cut off in the mill and sent tumbling down a chute. If the SBR engine was late in picking up the loaded gondolas and

spotting more empties, then either the mill shut down, the gondolas were dangerously overloaded, or the butts fell to the ground and were later picked up by a crane. Either of the two latter options was usually chosen, and each meant increased danger for steelworkers.

On the other side of the Hellhole, ingots were rolled into slabs or billets at the north end of No. 1 Mill. Some continued down the line to be rolled into rails, while others were diverted to one side. The latter billets were loaded onto narrow-gauge flatcars. Nearby, on the SBR track, hot slabs were loaded onto a line of seven special flatcars with insulated floors. The loading operation was performed by the overhead cranes, and whenever one of them moved, a clanging bell gave warning to workers below. The

SBR track went to the north end of the mill, where it terminated as two stubs, each spotted with a railcar to receive rubble or roll scale.

Finished rails emerged in the south part of No. 1 Mill and were loaded onto SBR gondolas spotted on a stub in the mill. One other stub was just long enough to hold a gondola, into which rail butts, steel trimmed off the end of rails, were dumped. SBR and narrow-gauge engines continually shuttled cars in and out of this area. The engineers alerted each other with toots on their whistles to avoid collisions at the two spots where the tracks crossed. All this activity helped to create the chaotic and dangerous working environment that gave the Hellhole its name.

Source: Interview with Phil Andreozzi, July 20, 2002.

Storage Bed Yard, located near No. 15 Mill, rolled bars were assembled, cut, and shipped after being sorted into a series of bays, each with two overhead cranes. SBR gondola cars transported the steel either to mills within the plant or to customers. Dominic Sperduti and Cristoforo D'Alessandro labored there in the 1920s, as did at least five other Italians in the early 1930s, including American-born Alfonso Bracci, who later became a foreman. A saw operator in 1920, James Sirianni likely worked at this site cutting steel with three- to five-foot circular blades. As well as tremendous displays of sparks, the saws produced loud noises audible in the Old Village and Bethlehem Park. Art Sambuchi began his career at the plant in 1953 and spent much time in the Structural Shipping

The area near the 54" mill circa 1930. Photo source: Hamburg Historical Society

1940s. The Strip Mill actually consisted of the Hot Mill, on the left, and the Cold Mill. In the Hot Mill, which was approximately 2,100 feet long, large slabs were gradually reduced in thickness to a 1,000-foot ribbon of thin metal that was then rolled into a coil. In the Cold Mill, the surface was treated and any rough scale removed. Photo source: Paul Pietrak

The Strip Mill, 1950. This is the Cold Mill's cutting room, where the ribbon of metal was cut to the customers' specifications. Photo source: Jack and Mary Panczykowski

Yard. He reports that it was "the most dangerous part of the plant"—outdoors, exposed to heat, cold, snow, and high winds that came off Lake Erie. "Hot sawing, cold sawing, recondition welding, cooling beds, and loading were some of the jobs," he said. During the 1960s, 1,800 men worked there, of whom about 10% were Italian, including one of Sambuchi's foremen, Joe Amorosi.[42]

Before the billets could be rolled into finished products, they had to be inspected for flaws. This was done both in the mills and in the General Billet Yard, where gantry crane operators loaded billets onto metal supports and turned them over as inspectors looked for imperfections. These were marked with chalk, and workers with pneumatic chisel guns chipped away the flawed sections. During the 1920s,

1950s. View of Lackawanna looking north, with the tree-lined Lake Avenue running horizontally at the bottom of the photo, and Hamburg Turnpike positioned vertically through the middle of the photo. The village of Woodlawn is at the bottom of the photo. The numbered sites are as follows: (1) the structural fabrication shop; (2) the 12" and 10" bar mills; (3) the strip mill; (4) the older part of the Bethlehem Steel facility; and (5) Bethlehem Park. Photo source: Paul Pietrak

366

Biagio Anticoli, Salvatore DePasquale, Benedetto DiManno, and Rocco Marinelli were chippers, and Antonio Diranio, Michael Miceli, and Aldo Aleggi were inspectors. After arriving from Italy in the 1930s, Armando Torella worked in the General Billet Yard, where most of his coworkers were Irish, Greek, Serbian, Spanish, Macedonian, and Italian immigrants. Of the 100 men on his shift in the mid-1930s, approximately one-third were Italians. Joe Florino was a first inspector during this time, but the Billet Yard's Superintendent and many of the foremen were Irish. After emigrating from Calabria, Armando Leonetti worked on various construction jobs and then sought work at Bethlehem Steel in 1937. When told the plant needed a chipper, he claimed he had experience handling a chipping gun, which was not the case. Still, he got the job, quickly learned to use the gun, and worked in one of the billet yards for five or six years.[43]

Specialty Shops

The steel plant had at least 14 specialized shops, most of which were located at the north end of the complex. Parallel to the line of shops was the Gantry Yard, named for the large gantry crane that moved materials to specific shops. In 1925, Domenico Mariotti was a gantry foreman there. At the Roll Shop, where the large rollers from the rolling mills were repaired, the ethnic hierarchy was similar to that of other departments: German, English, and Irish supervisors, and many of the 200 men working there were members of these ethnic groups or Polish. In 1918, Jimmy Ginnetti became the first Italian to work in the Roll Shop and was joined the following year by Nunze Oddy. At first, the other workers called Oddy "wop" and refused to explain things or help him carry out chores. It helped to have more Italians entering the shop's workforce. In 1920, Joseph Ginnetti, Jimmy's brother, and Joseph Pacillo arrived, and all three men held the skilled position of roll turner. Two years later, V. Jimmy D'Alessandro came on board; he was a recent immigrant from Pettorano sul Gizio, hometown of the Oddy and Ginnetti families. In the Roll Shop, D'Alessandro learned to speak

The Structural Shipping Yard looking east toward Hamburg Turnpike, 1930.
Photo source: Hamburg Historical Society

The Structural Shipping Yard; men grinding out imperfections in the steel, 1972.
Photo source: Art Sambuchi

English and read blueprints. He became a tool apprentice by 1925, and from there moved on to No. 1 Mill. By that time, 11 Italians were working in the roll shop, including foreman Arcangelo Cervoni, roll turner Luigi Corsi, and four laborers, one of whom, Ferdinand Catuzza, moved up to the skilled position of Roll Burner. Jimmy Ginnetti spent his 50-plus years in the plant within the Roll Shop. His half-brother, Ralph D'Amore, like Nunze Oddy and Charley Nigro before him, came to the shop via the plant's apprentice program. James Petti was a roll turner by 1931 and Dewey Cervoni an apprentice roll turner when he entered the Army in 1941. After working in the Billet Yard, Armando Leonetti transferred to the Roll Shop and became a foreman there.[44]

Among the other departments in the steel plant were a series of laboratories, which in the 1930s included three metallurgical and chemical labs for the Blast Furnace, Open Hearths, and Mill Departments, a chemical lab for the Coke

FIGURE 7.15

ITALIANS IN THE STEEL PLANT SPECIALTY SHOPS

Italians worked in Bethlehem Steels's Machine and Roll shops and several other specialty shops:

Forge Or Blacksmith Shop: While there were blacksmiths throughout the steel plant, most of them worked in the Forge Shop. The 1920 census lists three Italian blacksmiths and one blacksmith's helper. By 1926, Angelo Fiore, Domenico Mattioli, and Leone Ginnetti were blacksmiths, as was Filiberto Covelli, who joined the men in the Forge Shop after learning the blacksmith trade in the foundries at Kenosha, Wisconsin. When Armondo Pietrocarlo entered the Forge Shop in 1927, his foreman and 80% of the workers were German Americans. In his 23 years of service there, Pietrocarlo saw the proportion of German workers drop to about 25% and that of Italians grow to 10%. Many of these Italians were relatives from Giuliano di Roma or friends, such as Ralph Galanti, whom Pietrocarlo himself recruited as he rose to clerk and then higher positions.

Foundry: There were several foundry shops in the plant by 1939. They were equipped to produce brass, iron, bronze, and steel castings for outside sale, but most of the products were used within the steel plant. Chief among these were the large molds into which liquid metal was poured. Between 1912 and 1925, Gaetano DiPronio, Vito Pacillo, and Nick Delvecchio were molders, and Saverio DiTommasso was a molder's helper.

Pipe Shop: Pipes carrying water and gas crisscrossed the steelmaking complex and necessitated their own maintenance crews. Pasquale Volpe was a pipefitter by 1919 and during the next 15 years was joined by eight more Italians, including pipefitters Carlo Capuani, Frank Bernardi, and Arduino Ceccarelli.

Tool & Die Shop: Joe Amadori was a 17-year-old machinist in the Tool and Die Shop in 1920 and remained four more years before going into private business. In 1925, the shop's workforce included toolmaker Sebastian Fistola and several Italian American apprentices.

Sources: Interviews with Armondo Pietrocarlo, March 24, 1986; Tony Mingarelli, July 11, 1994; Phil Andreozzi, April 17, 1995; Chet Catuzza, September 8, 1994; and Joe Cosentino, July 14, 1995.

and By-Products Division, and a physical lab for performing general functions. Brothers John and Louis Core, both American-born, arrived at the steel plant in the 1930s and spent their working years in the Metallurgical Lab. Paolo Filipetti, an immigrant, spent most of his 50 years of plant service in the Chemical Lab. His oldest son, Alex, graduated from high school in 1940 and gathered written references from Rev. Vifredo, a teacher, and a lawyer. This impressed his Bethlehem interviewer and Filipetti was hired to work in the Inspection Department. Starting out as an inspector in the Bar Mill, he moved on to the Physical Lab, the Chemical Lab, and to observer positions in the open hearths and rolling mills. Filipetti and other second-generation teenagers who entered the plant in the 1930s and early 1940s were more likely to have completed high school than were those who preceded them. Following their graduations, Dewey Montanari became an Alloy Chemist in the Chemical Lab in the Main Office, where he was soon joined by Nick Andreozzi and Anthony Rosati. Dario "Doc" Baldelli took his education further. He got a mill job in 1945, moved on to the Chemical Lab, took classes at Erie County Technical Institute, became a supervisor, and concluded his 36-year career at the steel plant as a chemist, supervising the analysis of water samples.[45]

The Erection Department handled the construction or expansion of large buildings in which steel or iron girders were involved. Riggers were men who actually walked on the girders and secured them in place. In 1910, Domenico Marco held this job, and during the early 1920s, nine other Italians worked there. Many areas of the steel plant utilized natural gas, which was stored in a tank on the west side of the plant grounds. Some gas was produced in the coke ovens, and gas houses supplied the fuel to each open hearth. In 1910, Ralph Tenuta worked in the steel plant as a gas man. Five years later, Tony Rongo and Mike Filighera were "gas makers," and seven Italians worked on the plant's gas lines in the 1920s.[46]

Lackawanna Steel produced special bridge and structural steel after taking over the Lackawanna Bridge Works and another small factory in South Buffalo. The two plants became known as No. 1 and No. 2 Specialty Shop, and in 1926 had a combined annual capacity of 60,000 tons of structural steel. Lackawanna Italians worked in the shops as early as World War I, when Giovanni Andreozzi was employed as a crane operator, Joseph Di Rosa and Luigi Petti as helpers, and Emilio Lucarelli as a laborer. The steel plant's Structural Fabricating Department was located in a building on the south end of the grounds, in Woodlawn, that housed facilities for the making special sections, such as columns. As it was expanded in the 1920s, more land was purchased, and after the steel plant purchased Kalman Steel and the McClintoc-Marshall Company in the 1930s, it incorporated these operations into the department.[47]

Excavation for the extension on No. 5 Shear Building, April 26, 1917. The man at left in the foreground is most likely Antonio Grossi, a foreman in the Yard Department since 1906. Photo source: Hagley Museum and Library, Delaware

Lackawanna Steel Company had crews to maintain its housing units in both the Old Village and the New Village. After Bethlehem Steel acquired the plant, it formed the Real Estate Department to service its new housing development in Bethlehem Park. A small office was set up on Madison Avenue, and crews based there in 1930 included carpenter-painter Peter Ranalli, plumber Al Croce, and five of their countrymen. The plant's private police force staffed the gates, patrolled the grounds, and performed other security tasks. Gabrielle Marosi was an officer in 1914, followed in the next six years by Peter Mazuca and two other Italians. These men were Buffalo residents, but Mazuca later moved to Lackawanna. During the late 1920s, brothers Amicare and Tulio Paolini did brief stints as security officers. When the steel plant beefed up its police force to confront union organizers in 1937, five Buffalo Italians were among the new hires. The force grew to 120 officers by 1960, including Pat Bonitatibus, who said that officers investigated accidents and incidents such as fights, and conducted Breathalyzer tests.[48]

One worker in constant demand in virtually all departments was the cutting torch operator, or "burner." At least six Italians were burners between 1920 and 1930, and Salvatore Baratta had the more specialized job of electric welder. A small number of Italians held office jobs in Lackawanna Steel's early years.

Alfonso Serio started as an office clerk in 1903, and 10 years later was promoted to assistant accountant-paymaster. An article in *Corriere Italiano* praised the young man for achieving a position of "responsibility and trust … given the difficulties our people are put through." Tony Casazza worked in the Payroll Department in 1911 and the Timekeeping Department in 1914. Later, more and more Italians rose to office and administrative positions. Italian workers were scattered throughout the steel plant by the 1920s, but during the first four decades of the twentieth century, they were most concentrated in two departments: the Yard Department and the South Buffalo Railway's Track Department. This was especially true of the immigrants.[49]

The Yard Department

Employees of the Yard Department (or Yard, for short) carried out an array of functions that touched all aspects of steelmaking. Workers removed slag from the blast furnaces and open hearths, and reclaimed iron and steel from this waste material. The department reclaimed scrap steel and prepared it for the open hearths. Its crews constructed small buildings and bridges, maintained roads and water lines, removed snow, and did daily cleanup duties throughout the steel plant. Yard personnel built

The Yard Department had crews, such as this one in 1929, that constructed or repaired small buildings. Photo source: Hamburg Historical Society

John Schiavi, left, and Rocco Giannicchi in the Yard Department office in the 1930s. Schiavi was seriously injured in 1929 when a pile of steel fell. He was then given the job of delivering mail throughout the steel plant.
Photo source: Iole Schiavi-Murray

up stockpiles of materials, unloaded coal and iron ore from lake freighters, and loaded freighters with finished steel. The Yard also served the steel plant's vast network of railroads. Crews unloaded materials from rail cars, operated the self-propelled railroad cranes, and, until Bethlehem Steel bought the plant in 1922, handled all track maintenance. Thereafter, workers in the Yard maintained only a few standard-gauge tracks, such as the highlines for the stockyards and the coke ovens, ladle sidings, and some of the narrow-gauge tracks.

During the first half of the twentieth century the workforce in the Yard was heavily Italian, especially during the 1920s and 1930s. John Barbati, who started working there in 1934, estimates that about two-thirds of his coworkers were fellow ethnics, most of them immigrants. For many steelworkers, the Yard was synonymous with Italians, and some called its large work crews the "Italian Army," perhaps a derogatory remark that emerged during World War II. During the first four decades of the century, Italian Yard foremen actively recruited their *paesani.* In 1925, some 109 Lackawanna Italians were Yard workers, including seven foremen and 14 steam-crane crewmen. This group represented 41% of the 264 Italian steel workers residing in Lackawanna at that time. Many relatives worked together in the Yard, as evidenced by father-and-son combinations—Felice and Anthony DiPronio, Giovanni and Christopher D'Alessandro, Luigi and Giovanni Violanti, Sosio and Vincenzo Piccirilli, and Antonio and Dominick Risio. When Charles Hinman started working in the Yard in 1942, more than half of the 42 foremen were Italian Americans. During his 30-year career, he observed that the Yard workforce averaged 500 employees per year, with Italians as the largest group— about half of all employees—and blacks with 30%. Among the Italians in the Yard in

1925, the largest regional contingent—38%—was from Abruzzo, followed by Lazio at 30%. These were the two largest Italian regional groups in the city, and while the Abruzzesi were more numerous in the Yard and Roll Shop, the Laziali were more prevalent among SBR workers and highline engine crews.[50]

In Lackawanna Steel's early years, construction workers built the plant southward along the Lake Erie shoreline. When Giuseppe Pietrocarlo arrived in Lackawanna in 1911, he joined a 10-man Yard crew that blasted tree stumps in the swampy areas of the grounds. He later told his son Armondo that some men lost their lives in the quicksand. Undeterred, the elder Pietrocarlo went on to become an operator and conductor on a railroad steam crane, one of the many Italians on the steam-crane crews that functioned throughout the plant. Domenico A. Marinelli was a steam-crane operator by 1923. Just two years later, Italians working on these machines numbered seven crane operators, six conductors, and one repairman. When Giulio Maturani became a steam-crane operator in 1940, most of his coworkers were Italian. Maturani's usual task was loading and

Loading and unloading lake freighters and railroad cars were among the many duties carried out by the Yard Department. This freighter is docked in the canal of the Bethlehem Steel plant in Lackawanna in 1930.
Photo source: Hamburg Historical Society

unloading scrap steel, and he welcomed the arrival of diesel locomotive cranes because they did not require the shoveling of coal and tending of fires.[51]

Among the many chores carried out by Yard workers was cutting up scrap metal. The SBR hauled cobble (a ribbon of

At the High Drop, worn-out molds, rolls, and other metal objects were broken into smaller pieces by dropping a metal ball, or other heavy object, from a magnet. This scrap was then loaded onto railroad cars and taken to the open hearths.
Photo source: Buffalo and Erie County Historical Society

Self-propelled steam cranes such as this were part of the equipment used by the Yard Department.
Photo source: Paul Pietrak

Dumping slag could be one of the more dangerous tasks done by Yard Department workers. If the molten slag being poured out of special railroad cars hit a pool of water or Lake Erie, it resulted in an explosion. Photo source: Paul Pietrak

steel that splits off as steel is rolled) in gondola cars to one of the work areas located just south of Smokes Creek. Using massive magnets, locomotive steam-crane operators unloaded the scrap onto the ground, where burners cut it into shorter lengths, and laborers then reloaded it. Scrap was also cut up by large and small alligator shears near the Breaking Drop. A baler compressed Strip Mill scrap into bales that were then taken to the open hearths. In 1930, Sosio Piccirilli was a foreman who worked the baler and was also in charge of the shears. The scrap was then sent to the three open-hearth stockyards.[52]

The Yard also maintained the High Drop at the center of the steel-plant grounds. This steel structure supported huge overhead cranes that straddled a large hole in the ground. SBR tracks on each flank carried railroad cars loaded with liquid slag from the open hearths, worn-out rolls, old molds, and 10-inch-thick iron floors of narrow-gauge flatcars. These, along with other discarded pieces of iron and steel, were dropped into the hole. When a string of about 10 rail cars arrived, workers such as John Barbati made sure the steam hoses for the brakes were connected to the switch engine. To empty the

The 1940 annual picnic of the Yard Department took place in Ebenezer. Photo source: Lucy Pietrocarlo and Concetta Risio

special ladle cars holding liquid slag, Barbati turned a wrench on the car, engaging a piston that tipped the ladle. The men dove for a three-sided steel shelter that protected them from the explosion resulting from molten slag hitting water that had gathered in the hole. After the liquid slag had cooled and solidified, a crane lifted a large metal ball or an old roll and dropped it onto the heap, shattering the metal. Next, a large magnet attached to the overhead crane loaded the scrap onto gondola cars, which were moved to the open hearth stockyards. The workers then attached a bucket to the overhead crane to scoop up slag and other nonmetallic debris and load it into Clark cars (railroad cars that tipped to empty their contents), which were moved to low areas and dumped. In 1919, Luigi Scarnecchia worked at the High Drop as a "blockbreaker." A few years later, Domenico DiCenzo was a laborer there.[53]

The men in the Yard did strenuous and exhausting work, but many Italians spent much of their careers there. Antonio Torella began his 36-year career in 1915. Laborers like Giuseppe Gabrielli performed backbreaking work on the ore docks, and Ferdinando Cosentino labored on the trains that dumped flue dust—fine particles of iron ore from the blast furnaces—into Lake Erie. The demanding physical work led many Italian Yard laborers to move on to other jobs. Alfredo Campanelli shoveled coal on the boat docks and from railroad cars before moving on to the Coke Ovens and Open Hearths. Eugenio Galanti, Michele Grasso, and Santo Mancuso started in the Yard but left the steel plant in the 1920s to run independent businesses. Jimmy Ross left the Yard in 1925 for the blast furnaces, as did his son Attilio. Salvatore

This group of Yard Department employees photographed in 1939 included Dick Buscaglia, standing second from left, and Dominic Gennetti, kneeling second from right, and John Schiavi, kneeling at right.
Photo source: Iole Schiavi-Murray

Leo first worked on a mainline railroad, then in the Yard, followed by janitor work for the Shipping and Order Department, and then for the Inspection Department.[54]

Mario Infante was another man who disliked the arduous pick-and-shovel work and vowed that he would not remain a laborer. Arriving in Lackawanna in 1939, he became a Yard laborer, unloading dolomite and coke breeze—fine particles

Bethlehem Steel fire engines, 1940. These vehicles were driven by men of the Garage, who received an extra dollar for each fire. Photo source: Paul Pietrak

A 1929 photo of a truck used by the Garage Department, formed in about 1923 as an offshoot of the Yard Department. A decade later, the number of the department's vehicles and workers had greatly expanded, and half the workers were Italian Americans. Photo source: Joe Streamer

Mike Selvaggio, an immigrant, stands next to the truck he drove in 1938. Many of the drivers in the Yard Department were Italian, but most were second-generation—that is, born in America. Photo source: Collection of Dominick Selvaggio

created as coke is handled—from rail cars. At the trestle adjacent to the coke ovens, Infante unlatched the bottoms of hopper cars to dump the contents into bins. He choked on the dust, and the winter snows made his job even more unpleasant and dangerous. But Infante eventually found a way to escape his laborer's job. The Whirley steam crane often worked in conjunction with Infante's crew, and he carefully observed its operator. One day when the operator was sick, Infante convinced his foreman to allow him to run the machine. In 1941, he became a fireman on the Whirley, then a conductor on a tracked crane that unloaded materials in areas not accessible to railroad cranes. At Lackawanna High School, Infante took night-school courses, including machine shop, and in 1942, he was made a blacksmith's helper, working in the building that housed the cranes. There he and the blacksmith, also an Italian, made repairs, welded chain links, and sharpened picks and shovels. Infante was happy his laborer's role had ended.[55]

The heavy-duty trucks developed for the military during World War I proved useful to the steel plant, which acquired some trucks during the war. After the company bought two trucks in 1922 and an ambulance the following year, it established the Garage Department. When Angelo Grosso was hired as a truck driver in 1925, the Garage had two drivers and a dispensary man who drove the ambulance. Four other Italian men worked at least temporarily as truck drivers in the late 1920s. Storehouse clerk Amicare "Mickey" Paolini started in the plant in 1922 as an apprentice in the electrical shop, transferring to the garage two years later. He delivered goods by truck throughout the plant, and in 1929 was made the Garage's first foreman because he knew how to repair the vehicles. For many years, the Garage also maintained the company's limousine and cars, and Paolini served as chauffeur for the plant manager during the 1920s and 1930s. He wore a black uniform and cap, and his duties extended to driving on trips outside the plant. In 1930, Paolini drove plant manager Timothy Burns and his wife to Florida, and the following year to South Dakota. Joe Streamer, who later worked under Paolini, remembers his boss as a large man, six feet tall, 250

Amicare "Mickey" Paolini, left, drove a truck and became the first foreman in the Garage Department in 1929. He also served as chauffeur for plant manager Timothy Burns, right, and his wife, whom he drove to Florida one year and South Dakota the next. Photo source: Joe Streamer

Mickey Paolini, left, and plant manager Fred A. Daggart in the 1970s, admiring the limousine that Paolini drove to transport the 1930's plant manager to other states. Photo source: Joe Streamer

pounds, who was "straightforward" and could speak with "some bluster."[56]

As trucks became more rugged and reliable, the Garage expanded, as did the number of Italians working there. Mike Barbati began work there in 1931, and his brother John transferred to join him five years later, thanks to Mickey Paolini's skills of persuasion with the Yard superintendent. In the mid-1930s, Barbati was making 44 cents per hour. He drove trucks, pumped gas, washed the vehicles, and procured his chauffeur's license. In 1936, about 20 men worked in the Garage, most of them on the first shift. The two men on the second and third shifts had the task of driving the ambulance. Half of the workers were Italians, all second-generation, and the rest were Irish and German. During the first two decades of its existence, the Garage utilized flatbed trucks to shuttle machinery and materials from the Mechanical Shop to various departments in the plant and to the old Seneca Steel plant. John Barbati hauled shafts and gears from millwrights to the Machine Shop then back to the mills. The Garage had five cars, which were used to transport men with minor injuries to the dispensary, to pick up visitors, and to chauffeur supervisors. The men in the Garage also drove the fire engines at that time, receiving an extra dollar for each fire. The Yard also had a variety of specialized vehicles and equipment, including bulldozers, whose operators included Art Giannicchi and John Grasso.[57]

Bethlehem Steel contracted with private companies for heavy-duty dump trucks to haul materials within the plant, and up to 100 such vehicles could be at work on any given day.

The company also contracted with trucking companies for shipping to distant customers. Tulio Paolini, who had earlier worked at the Garage under his younger brother Mickey, founded Paolini Trucking by 1941, and for the next two decades was one of Bethlehem's contractors. John Barbati recalls that the Garage had 20 trucks in 1948 when it purchased its first dump truck, of which he was one of the first drivers. When Mike Morgan was hired in 1952, there were 40 to 50 trucks in the Garage. Sixty men, 40% of them Italian Americans, worked on one shift. During his 32-year career, Morgan saw the department expand, and by 1969, the Garage had 375 workers plus 200 trucks and other vehicles.[58]

The South Buffalo Railway

Many Lackawanna Italians, especially those living in the Roland Avenue section, worked on railroads in the area. A number of these men were employees of the South Buffalo Railway (SBR). The railway was incorporated on April 25, 1899, and construction completed in 1902. A terminal switching line, its tracks extended from Lackawanna to Buffalo and connected with the 26 mainline railroads that ran through the area. Its tracks were later extended along the lakefront into Woodlawn and further inland to the Seneca Steel plant and the Ford Stamping Plant (see Figure 7.17). The SBR Track Department was created in 1922, when Bethlehem Steel purchased the Lackawanna Steel Company and shifted most of the maintenance chores for the standard-gauge rails from the Yard to the new department. In addition, 74 railroad men from the Yard, almost

FIGURE 7.16

SOUTH BUFFALO RAILWAY

A subsidiary of Lackawanna Steel, and later Bethlehem Steel, the South Buffalo Railway (SBR) grew along with the steel plant and eventually served dozens of other factories from Woodlawn to South Buffalo. It tied into the mainline railroads that ran through Lackawanna, and the railway's locomotives were serviced in a roundhouse located in the maze of tracks in the city's rail yards. The SBR had up to 20 passenger cars that were used in the four daily commuter trains that it ran between Lackawanna Steel and the Delaware, Lackawanna, and Western Railroad train station in downtown Buffalo from 1902 to 1915. The 35 miles of SBR standard-gauge track in 1908 grew to 108 miles over the following 20 years. The tracks ran among the mills and into them as well as in open areas on the plant grounds. As the railroad expanded, its roster of employees grew from 274 in 1911 to 400 in 1919 to 700 in 1927, and finally, to 1,200 in 1971. In 1908, the railway operated 24 locomotives and 217 freight cars; within two decades there were 30 steam engines handling close to 1,700 rolling stock that carried 5.1 million tons of steel products. The steam engines eventually gave way to diesels. In 1939, the SBR operated nine diesel and 26 steam locomotives; 10 years later, all 34 locomotives were diesels.

South Buffalo Railway Switcher No. 20 in the late 1930s. The engine entered service in 1906 and was retired in 1941. Few Italians were train crew members at this time. Photo source: Collection of Frank Chiodo

In addition to serving the mills of Lackawanna Steel Company, which was purchased by Bethlehem Steel Company in 1922, the SBR served dozens of other industries in the area. Its customers included Spring Perch, Buffalo Brake Beam, Buffalo Tank, and Buffalo Slag in Lackawanna; Seneca Steel in Blasdell; Kalman Steel, Federal Portland Cement, and the Ford plant in Woodlawn; Bethlehem's two bridge shops: and Donner-Hanna Coke, Hanna Furnace, Shenango Ingot Mold, Buffalo Sintering, Republic Steel, and Bliss and Laughlin Steel in Buffalo. With the demise of Bethlehem Steel. the railway struggled and was bought in 2001 by Genesee & Wyoming Industries, which owns 22 other railroads.

Sources: Edward T. Dunn, *A History of Railroads in Western New York*, 2nd edition, 2000, pp. 166, 238; *Lackawanna Press*, December 2, 1949; *BSC*, "A Visit to the Lackawanna Plant," p. 28; Stephan Koenig, *South Buffalo Railway: Bethlehem Steel Company Railroad Operations in Lackawanna, New York*, 2004, pp. 9, 17; interview with Phil Andreozzi, August 15, 1999.

two-thirds of them Italian, were transferred to the Track Department. There were relatively few members of the ethnic group working in the other SBR departments, which were dominated by the Irish and other northern Europeans. By 1946, Italians comprised 12% of the Yard clerks and 10% of the roundhouse workers, but were few and far between on the train crews and among the car inspectors. This pattern of specific ethnic groups dominating a mill or department was common in the steel plant.[59]

At least 74 Lackawanna Italians were doing railroad work by 1925, many of them on the SBR. Those living in the Roland Avenue area made up about half this number. For many years, a roundhouse, located in the maze of tracks just east of the Old Village, serviced the SBR's engines. A roundhouse is a semicircular building in which locomotives were repaired. A circular turntable allowed engines to move from the main tracks into one of the many work areas in the large structure. Located several hundred feet northwest of the terminus of

Louie Morasco, on left, who emigrated from Calabria at age five, was the first Italian to become an engineer on the South Buffalo Railway. In 1923, he was an engine fireman and became an engineer in 1928. Photo source: Lou Morasco, Jr.

Roland Avenue, the roundhouse was a short walk for neighborhood residents, although the men had to cross a number of busy tracks along the way. When 13-year-old Natale Chiodo arrived in the Roland Avenue neighborhood in 1901, he worked on railroad construction on the main lines coming into the Buffalo area. Four years later, he was one of the first Roland Italians employed at the SBR roundhouse. He went on to become a stationary engineer, boiler fireman, and machinist's helper. Later, as a carpenter, he repaired roundhouse buildings and locomotive cab woodwork, such as window frames, armrests, and footboards. During the period from 1917 to 1925, at least 15 other Italians were employed at the roundhouse, four of whom, including boilermaker Mike Falcone, held skilled positions. When he started work in 1919, Falcone was the first of the American-born men to join the workforce. During the 1920s, other young men of the second generation arrived, including 15-year-old Tony Falbo, who became an apprentice

at the roundhouse after Natale Chiodo made arrangements with the superintendent. Three immigrants from the First Ward also worked there in the early 1920s: Olindo and Vincenzo Rosati, and Giuseppe Conti, all of whom became machinists. By 1946, Italians comprised 10% of the roundhouse workforce.[60]

In its early days, the Track Department was headed by General Foreman L. J. Campbell, who directed six foremen, two of whom were Italian and three Polish. The railway's seniority lists from 1900 to 1945 reveal that Italians comprised at least 53% of the Track Department workforce. This was confirmed by Frank Scaletta, who recalled that in 1931, half his fellow workers on the track gangs were Italians, the rest a mixture of Poles, Mexicans, Irishmen, and African Americans. The presence of so many Italians created a situation where members of the ethnic group could rise to leadership positions. Joe Mesi was hired as a foreman by 1926. Born in Buffalo to Sicilian immigrants in 1903, he was raised in Angola, and worked as a track foreman for the Nickel Plate

1911. The South Buffalo Railway roundhouse was in the middle of the maze of railroad tracks that ran through Lackawanna. Many Roland Avenue Italians worked there. Photo source: Paul Pietak

South Buffalo Railway foremen dine on "chicken in the pan" at Perro's Restaurant in Brant, circa 1934. At the far end of the table are new Track Department Superintendent _?_ Royer, left, and General Foreman Joe Mesi. On the left side of the table, starting in foreground, are: Joe Sack, Joe Ceroni, [Unk], _?_ Judson, Peter Fiore, _?_ Gullo, Tony Urbanczyk, [Unk], [Unk]. On the right, starting in the foreground, are: Carl Capponi, Dan Monaco, Al Federici, Sam Plumber (Plumiere), Frank Scaletta, Dominic Colello, Josie Cardinale, Phil Polackowitz, _?_ Marsillo, [Unk].
Photo source: Collection of Frank Scaletta

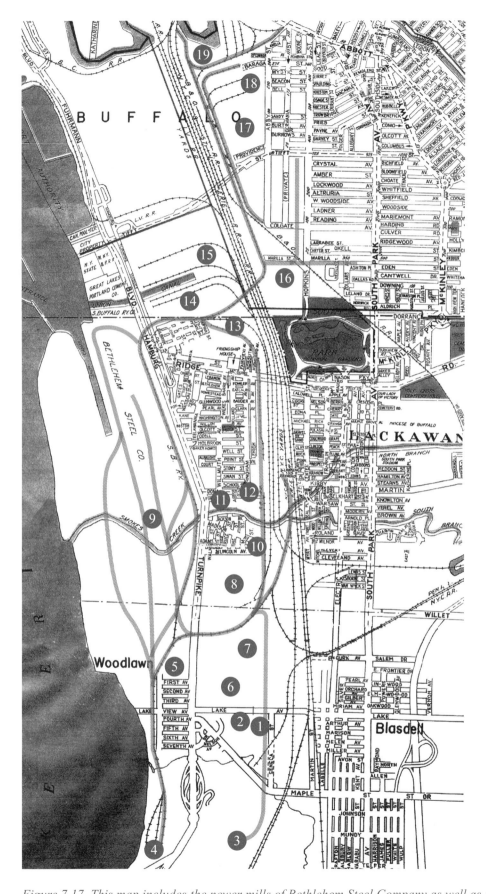

Key:
1 Seneca Steel Company
2. Kalman Steel
3. Ford Stamping Plant
4. Federal Cement
5. Structural Fabricating Shop (BS)
6. Galvanizing Mill (BS)
7. Bar Mill (BS)
8. Strip Mill (BS)
9. Basic Oxygen Furnace (BS)
10. Buffalo Tank
11. Spring Perch
12. Buffalo Brake Beam
13. Buffalo Slag
14. Hanna Furnace
15. Shenango Ingot Mold
16. Buffalo Sintering
17. Donner Hanna Coke Corporation
18. Bridge Shops #1 and #2 (BS)
19. Republic Steel Company

BS = Bethlehem Steel

Figure 7.17. This map includes the newer mills of Bethlehem Steel Company as well as other factories served by the South Buffalo Railway, ranging from the Ford Stamping Plant on the south to the Republic Steel Company on the north.

The Track Department (also known as the Maintenance of Way Department) of the South Buffalo Railway (SBR) included many Italians in 1931. Standing at the far right (next page) is General Foreman Joe Mesi. The office is the wooden building at the right, >

1904. Looking west toward the steel plant across the maze of railroad tracks of the Seneca Yard running under the Ridge Road bridge, at right. Soot from steam engines as well as ore dust from the production of steel were daily facts of life for many >

Federal Cement was located just south of Woodlawn on the Lake Erie coastline. It was one of many industries in the south towns area and was served by the South Buffalo Railway. Photo source: Collection of Tony Grasso

and the Structural Shipping right, and the Structural Shipping Yard is in the background. In 1942, the SBR moved its offices to a new brick building on Hamburg Turnpike, just south of Dona Street. Photo source: Collection of Frank Scaletta

Lackawannans, especially in the First Ward. At this time, five years before the City of Lackawanna was founded, there were few houses on Lehigh and Ingham Avenues on the far side of the tracks. Photo source: Buffalo and Erie County Public Library, "Lackawanna Steel Company" scrapbook, p. 202

Railroad previous to his job in Lackawanna. When Mesi became General Foreman of the Track Department in 1926, he began hiring Italian railroad men he knew from Angola and Buffalo as well as new acquaintances from Lackawanna's Italian colony. For workers who lived in Angola and nearby towns, he arranged automobile transportation to the plant, charging a fee comparable to the streetcar fare.[61]

While Italians worked on the Yard's self-propelled steam cranes and the open hearths' highline locomotive crews, it took many years for them to get jobs as train crewmen on the SBR. Olindo "Rocco" Rosati was an operator on one of the two SBR locomotive steam cranes in 1925, but the majority of engines were switchers that seldom included Italian crewmen. In the

cab of the typical steam locomotive was an engineer who directed the movement of the locomotive and a fireman who fed coal into the fire and observed the train's path from the other cab window. Three switchmen, often called trainmen, rode on the locomotive or freight cars and stepped to the ground to manually throw switches; they used hand and arm motions to signal the engineer in daytime and a lantern at night. The senior switchman was the conductor, who was in charge of the entire train.

The booming defense work of World War I provided an opening for Domenico Tripoli to become the SBR's first Italian train crewman. In 1918, he was a locomotive fireman, but with the end of the war, Tripoli was soon back to the role of laborer.

In 1923, Louie Morasco was an engine fireman; five years later, he became the first of his ethnic group to advance to the engineer's job. (Frank Columbus was an engineer by 1906, but it is unclear if his ancestry was French or Italian.) Ignazio Caito and Patsy Yoviene became firemen in 1936, and each moved up to engineer in the early 1940s. Between 1947 and 1965, nine other Italians achieved engineer status. Tom Mesi and A. Privitera entered the fireman ranks in the late 1930s, and four more Italians became diesel helpers in the 1960s. Tony Colello in 1920 became the first Italian to work as a switchman, followed seven years later by Jack Lanza. The Depression apparently closed any openings for new switchmen, but between 1937 and 1945, a dozen Italian Americans attained this position. Some Italians got to work on the SBR locomotives as hostlers, men who moved engines during shift changes. Mike Militello moved from Brant to Lackawanna in 1934 after Joe Mesi lined him up with a SBR job, and he later became a hostler. John Andrisani was a hostler in 1945 but was laid off a few years later because the widespread use of diesel locomotives, which handled more work than steam engines, reduced the number of train crewmen needed.[62]

SBR train crewmen faced many dangers in the steel plant, as Phil Andreozzi, a switchman from 1939 to 1952, recalled:

> So many tracks and stubs. The Hellhole was well named—anyone experiencing it can attest to that. What a job servicing No. 1 Open Hearth's

Diesel switchers began to join the South Buffalo Railway's locomotives in 1936. Diesel No. 56, shown here, arriving in 1937 was one of the first diesels purchased by the railway, Photo source: Paul Pietrak

Francesco Saccomanno, standing at left, an immigrant from Calabria, became foreman of a crew that traveled throughout New York State and Pennsylvania, building new railroad spur lines. He died tragically in Cranberry Lake, New York, in 1915 when struck by a locomotive. His widow Anna and their son Charles eventually settled in Lackawanna. Photo source: Joe Saccomanno

old stock yard was. Anyone working on our railroad in the 1930s and 1940s and prior can tell you of obstacles and curves, of the clearances of the smokestacks of our locomotives. Everyone had to be on their toes every moment. The open hearth pits were another place for absolute concentration and watching overhead for cranes, to the sides for narrow-gauge trains of molds and ingots, checking the loads of kish and skulls (large pieces of iron or steel), especially in tight spots, to make sure you weren't buried or hit by falling rubble. And

often times the impending tap of an open hearth furnace; the steel sparks it shoots out across the vast width of the pit area when its tap is opened.

Railroad cars, constantly subjected to heavy-duty use in the steel plant, were repaired at the SBR's "cripple" car yard. Luigi Petti worked there in 1925, and Paul DeLallo was part of the wrecking gang that rerailed locomotives and cars; later, as a car inspector, he directed crews doing these cleanup jobs. During the early 1930s, Mike Caito became head clerk to the SBR's

The summer of 1948, 4:00 pm to 12:00 am shift. This diesel and its crew of H.R. Finley, Phil Andreozzi, and John Doty standing, and Charles Wanser and Arthur McGowan kneeling, worked a job in the bar mill area. When Andreozzi became a switchman in 1939, he was only the twelfth Italian to become a trainman on the South Buffalo Railway.
Photo source: Collection of Phil and Adeline Andreozzi

superintendent, and his nephew, Tony Sardina, was named director of personnel. In 1939, Italians broke into the ranks of the yardmasters when Jack Lanza was added to the roster. Each section of the SBR had a tower from which the yardmaster directed rail traffic in that area. Tony Colello worked briefly in this capacity, but it was not until a decade later that other Italians would follow in Lanza's footsteps. His son, Steve Lanza, as well as Tony Sardina and Frank Baressi each began limited tenures as yardmasters in about 1950. Then, two Italians each began a 24-year career as yardmaster; Phil Andreozzi in 1952, and George Fox in 1954. Petti, DeLallo, Colello, Andreozzi, and Fox were Lackawannans, while the others were from Buffalo.[63]

Other railroad men worked on the narrow-gauge lines that crisscrossed the grounds of the steel plant. During the 1920s, at least a dozen Italians worked in the narrow-gauge shops, and Valentino Mariotti was a locomotive engineer. In 1939, there were 18 locomotives operating on 12 miles of narrow-gauge track. The following three decades saw expansion to 25 miles of track on which 24 locomotives and 960 rail cars operated. Most of the narrow-gauge rolling stock consisted of flatcars, each able to carry two upright ingot molds, which were taken into the open-hearth mills, filled with molten steel,

FIGURE 7.18

ITALIANS KILLED OR INJURED IN THE STEEL PLANT*

1910 – Rosario Bracco, age 45, died when he suffered a crushed chest in a railroad accident. A laborer, he had been in the United States for 17 years at the time of his death.

1913 – Peter Corvodi, a locomotive craneman with the Yard Department, was killed when accidentally struck by a lever that ruptured his liver.

1913 – Giovanni Sambuchi fell to his death while working at the top level of the ore crusher.

1917 – John Difonzo, while working as a Yard conductor, met his death when he became caught between a platform and a railroad car, and his pelvis was crushed.

1918 – Francesco Monaco, age 38, and a resident of the Old Village, died when a crane fell on him and broke his back.

1919 – Nunzio Collarino, a laborer in the steel plant, was killed when he was scalded.

1920 – Salvatore DiMiceli suffered a terrible death in a rolling mill when he was crushed by a twisting piece of steel that broke off during the rolling process.

1927 – Samuel Ardizzone, a 21 year old wire inspector, was electrocuted in the steel plant.

1936 – Luigi Conte was crushed to death by an electric crane on the ore docks.

1944 – Steve Canestrari was killed while coupling railroad cars near the open hearths.

1947 – Bruno Lorenzetti was burned by molten metal when a mold exploded. One of his legs was amputated above the knee.

1950 – Electrician Mike Pacillo was electrocuted while testing electric motors.

* This is only a partial list.

Source: Interviews with Sam Violanti, December 29, 1987; clipping from unidentified Buffalo newspaper, 8/1913, provided by Art Sambuchi; City of Lackawanna, Deaths, Book 1, 1909-10, Birth and Deaths, Book 5, 1912-13, Deaths, Book 9, 1916-18, Deaths, Book 10, 1918-20; *Corriere Italiano*, 8/8/1918; *Labor Press*, 7/28/50; *Lackawanna Leader*, 7/27/50, 3/25/54; *Lackawanna Daily Journal*, 6/7/23, 6/9/23

then moved to rolling mills. The engines and rolling stock were serviced by the Car Shop and Locomotive Shop, where heavy repair and maintenance work were done.[64]

A Dangerous Place to Work

Economic and physical dangers were part of daily life in the steel plant, for both the workers in the mills and the railroad personnel within the plant. Unemployment and under-employment, especially in the preunion years, were ongoing features of life in Lackawanna. Steel industry practices resulted in the irregularity of work even during periods of relative prosperity, according to the U.S. Commissioner of Labor, who wrote in 1913:

It is a fixed and characteristic policy of the iron and steel industry to operate each producing unit to its fullest capacity and for the maximum number of working hours during a period of active demand, and then as soon as there is a decline in the market to shut down completely and wait for an accumulation of orders or the development of better prices.

His report went on to explain that, while these policies affected all steelworkers, the largest fluctuation in hours was experienced by workers in the Yard, docks, and miscellaneous operations,

precisely where most Lackawanna Italians were concentrated during the early years of the twentieth century. Between the spring of 1909 and the spring of 1910 in Lackawanna, some 52 Italians, about a fifth of the city's Italian workers, were unemployed for three or more weeks. Throughout the American steel industry in 1910, only 63% of steelworkers were employed for as long as 44 weeks. In addition, the average steelworker in America lost four days per year due to accidents and at least 10 days because of sickness.[65]

Economic recessions and depressions had severe effects on the steel industry. In 1907, a depression led to the layoff of most Lackawanna Steel workers. The plant all but closed down during another economic slump that began in November 1913. Not until March of the following year was a full workforce again in place. Many men were laid off during the slump of 1921-22, and the plant's workforce was dramatically reduced with indefinite layoffs during the Great Depression of the 1930s. Some men were fortunate to work one to three days per week, as No. 2 Open Hearth and various mills were temporarily shut down. Major events revived the economy, such as defense spending in World War I and World War II, which stimulated full employment at Bethlehem Steel by 1940.[66]

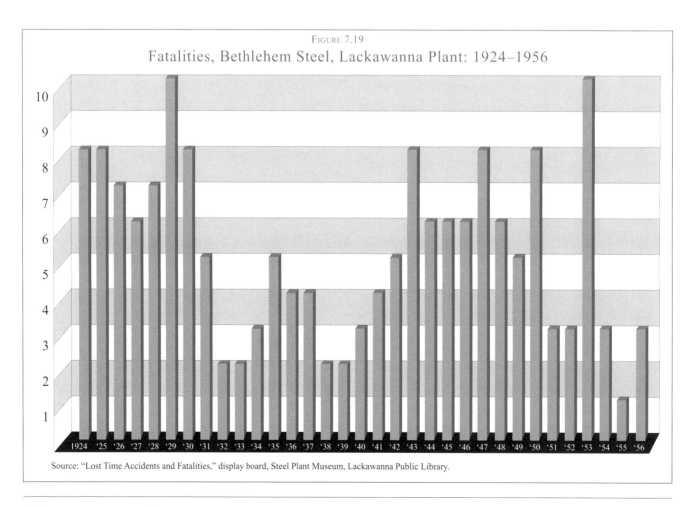

FIGURE 7.19
Fatalities, Bethlehem Steel, Lackawanna Plant: 1924–1956

Source: "Lost Time Accidents and Fatalities," display board, Steel Plant Museum, Lackawanna Public Library.

The ethnic hierarchy involved in the plant's daily hiring practices also left many Italians in an unfavorable situation, as there was only a handful of Italian foremen, and it was the foremen who either did the hiring or told the employment office whom to hire. Another factor limiting income was the sick time workers often took due to the working conditions. Virtually every job in the plant, not just those inside the mills, exposed workers to intense heat and dust. The fine dust in the pit of an open hearth, blast furnace, or rolling mill was often six inches deep and quickly lined a worker's nose and throat. The presence of furnaces, soaking pits, and hot metal meant that workers often had to endure great heat. Added to these factors was the extreme variation in weather conditions in the northern part of the United States. Most workers were exposed to severe heat in the summer and severe cold and snow in the winter as mills typically had huge openings for railroad and vehicle access, reducing protection from the weather. Ten- to 14-hour shifts further aggravated these factors, as did lax safety standards and a largely immigrant workforce with limited ability to speak English. The saloons were a favorite reprieve for many men after work; the strong beverages washed away the dust and stress, and the closed doors protected patrons from inclement weather. Eventually, the establishment of the eight-hour workday, locker rooms, and increased safety standards provided some relief.

The formation of the United Steelworkers Union in 1941 solidified these gains, removed arbitrary hiring practices, and curtailed some of the most devastating effects of unemployment and underemployment.[67]

The most basic concern of Lackawanna steelworkers and railroad men was the ever-present physical danger. Throughout the United States, 3,382 railroad workers were killed and 95,671 injured in 1910 alone. Between 1890 and 1920, a total of 86,600 railroad workers died on the job. A study of accidents in the country's major steel plants found that for the year ending on June 30, 1910, there were 36,038 accidents: 274 steelworkers died, 400 suffered permanent injuries, and 35,364 had temporary injuries that resulted in losing at least one day of work. The highest fatality rates were among workers in the blast furnaces, Yard, and open-hearth Bessemer furnaces. The leading cause of death was "crushing injury," especially for workers in the Yard Departments, which included railroad switchmen and general laborers, who together accounted for 80% of Yard fatalities. The study concluded that "the greatest dangers of the steel mills are connected with the operation of means of transportation, including especially cars and cranes." These trends were evident in Erie County, where 168 men died in industrial accidents in 1907 and 1908, including 49 at

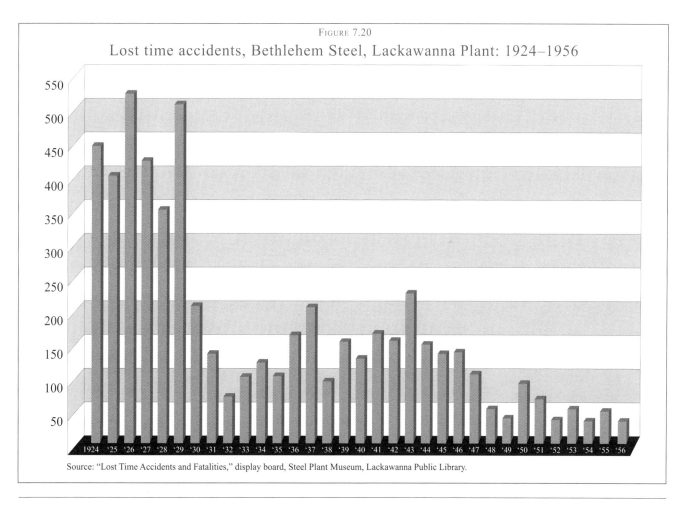

FIGURE 7.20

Lost time accidents, Bethlehem Steel, Lackawanna Plant: 1924–1956

Source: "Lost Time Accidents and Fatalities," display board, Steel Plant Museum, Lackawanna Public Library.

FIGURE 7.21

Lackawanna Italians in Supervisory Positions
at Specific Times: 1906–1930

	Total	Steel Plant	South Buffalo Railway*	Mainline Railroads
1906	3	3	0	0
1910	4	3	0	1
1915	5	4	0	1
1917-18	23	21	0	2
1920	9	8	0	1
1925	22	15**	4	3
1930	21	13	5	3

* The Yard Department handled all track maintenance until 1922, when the Track Department of the South Buffalo Railway was created; many Italians worked in the new department.

** One of these men worked at the nearby Hanna Furnace Company.

Source: U.S. Census, 1910, 1920, 1930; N.Y. Census, 1905, 1915, 1925; WWIDRR, 1917-18.

Lackawanna Steel, and 50 on mainline railroads. The casualties at Lackawanna Steel began during the construction phase, which in itself was harsh and risky. In a single incident, as many as 12 Italian workmen were said to have perished in quicksand. In 1902, Tony Russo and Giuseppe Quamatiello were killed by a train, and Antonio Corotici fell to his death. The following year, Pasquale Lavinia was near death after being hit in the head with a shovel during a fight with another worker. The *Buffalo Express* reported an incredible 4,000 accidents in 1905, and was probably exaggerating when it claimed "Fatalities average one per day" among the steel plant's 8,000 to 9,000 employees. On March 17 alone, 52 men were injured before 11:30 a.m. In the following year, there was a decrease in incidents: 1,147 lost-time accidents and 21 fatalities in 1910, dropped to 719 and seven, respectively, in 1911. Data for the years 1924 to 1956 (see Figures 7.19 and 7.20) show a steep decline in accidents when the workforce was reduced during the Depression, and an increase during the full employment of the 1940s. Overall, however, the number of injuries and fatalities decreased as time progressed and safety procedures were established.[68]

Frank Scaletta, an SBR employee from 1926 to 1956, recalled that 70 to 80 steelworkers and SBR employees were killed in the steel plant during his tenure. Sam Castiglia, a switchman, was killed on the job, and 19-year-old Gino Silvestrini died in 1952 when a locomotive struck the truck in which he was riding. Other men, such as Carmelo Amadori, sustained serious injuries in the steel plant. During the 1940s, Louis Camarotta was working at Station O, an SBR area on the west side of the plant, when he was struck and run over by a railroad car. With one of his arms cut off, Camarotta got up, took hold of his severed limb, and walked to the Station O tower for help. He survived this incident, and later was given the job of manning a signal light shanty.[69]

The Violanti family learned first-hand the dangers of working in the steel plant. In 1926, Giovanni Violanti, a Yard steam-crane conductor, slipped on the snow as he attempted to board a moving train, and his foot was crushed under the wheels. His leg had to be amputated below the knee, but he was fitted with an artificial limb and eventually returned to the plant as a janitor. His brother Joe was never injured while working in the plant but witnessed two serious accidents in the open hearths. The first occurred in 1924, when Joe Violanti and Natalino Sperduti were working as switchmen on the highline that went up to the open-hearth charging floor. Some improperly loaded scrap steel hung over the side of a railroad car and struck Sperduti, crushing his chest. Violanti picked up his friend, placed him in the highline locomotive, and took him to the dispensary. Sperduti died the next day in the hospital. He had recently arrived in the United States and had worked in the steel plant for only two months at the time of his death.[70]

The second incident took place in 1930 and involved Aniello Covino, who, after a layoff had returned to work as a car checker in the open hearths. While recording the numbers of railroad cars loaded with scrap, he stepped between two cars for a closer look at a number just as the locomotive pushed the line of cars. Covino was struck and his left leg completely severed, yet he had the presence of mind to use his belt as a tourniquet. Joe Violanti observed the scene from his crane operator's position, yelling to Covino when he saw the locomotive lurch, but the distance and noise drowned out his call. Violanti climbed down from his crane, told several men to get a stretcher, then rushed to Covino. They put the stricken man on the stretcher, then placed it in the highline engine, which Violanti guided to the dispensary at No. 1 Gate. "I was really shaking," he later recalled. The tourniquet and the cold weather slowed the victim's loss of blood, and Violanti's prompt action getting Covino to the dispensary helped save the man's life. When his shift ended at midnight, Violanti walked to the Old Village to alert Covino's relatives.[71]

Different locations in the plant presented unique dangers. Sometimes the raw materials charged into the top of a blast furnace got lodged in the upper part of the furnace, causing a "slip," in which ore and flue dust (fine particles of ore) blow out of the top of the stack, raining debris on workers below. Many incidents occurred in the pits of the mills, located on the ground level, or at outdoor unloading sites. Nazzareno Baldelli was working in the pit of a mill when he was struck

Figure 7.22

Lackawanna Italians in Foreman and Supervisory Positions, by Generation: 1906–1949

Department	1st	2nd	Unknown	Total
Yard	37	3	—	40
Open Hearths	7	5	—	12
Blast Furnaces	2	2	—	4
Rolling Mills	3	3	1	7
Specialty Shops	2	4	—	6
South Buffalo RR:				
Track Dept. **	9	2	1	12
Other Depts.	—	4	—	4

*1st generation = immigrant; 2nd generation = American-born child of immigrant.

** The Yard Department handled all track maintenance until 1922, when the Track Department of the South Buffalo Railway was created and began to perform most of the standard-gauge rail maintenance. Many Italians worked in the new department, including a number transferred from the Yard.

Sources: U.S. Census, 1910, 1920, 1930; N.Y. Census, 1905, 1915, 1925; WWIDRR, 1917-18; interviews; naturalization papers.

Italians in Supervisory Positions

Supervisory positions constitute an important subcategory of skilled/semiskilled employees. The number of Italian men in such positions rose from three in 1906 to 21 in 1930 (see Figure 7.21). The 1905 census does not indicate any Italians in supervisory positions, but the following year, Angelo Sperduto, Antonio Grossi, and Pietro Oddi were made Yard foremen. Prior to his death in 1913, Giovanni Sambuchi had also become a Yard foreman. The number of Italian foremen had increased only to five by 1915, but that changed during World War I, when 21 Italians held supervisory positions in the plant's expanded workforce, and two others were foremen on the mainline railroads. With the return to a peacetime economy, the size of the workforce decreased but rose again in 1925, when 22 Lackawanna Italians were working as supervisors in industrial settings. Within Bethlehem Steel, the Italian foremen were clustered in three departments: five in the Yard, three in the Open Hearths, and four on the SBR. Three others worked on the mainline railroads. During these years, the Italians enjoying the highest supervisory positions were Pasquale Ricci, who by 1922 was a Heater in No. 7 Mill, and Anthony Falcone, a Yardmaster for the New York Central Railroad.[73]

In the Yard, Pietro Oddi was a foreman until his death in 1917, and Antonio Sperduto and Antonio Grossi until the mid-1920s. The five censuses taken between 1905 and 1925 often

by a chain swinging from an overhead crane; luckily, he was not seriously injured. In 1928, Yard employee Giovanni Schiavi was unloading a freighter docked in Bethlehem Steel's canal. He was standing next to a pile of off-loaded steel when the steel shifted, crushing his legs. He spent the next two years in Moses Taylor Hospital, where he endured many operations and had a steel plate placed in his leg.[72]

A loopers outing in 1929. Loopers are college-educated men who attain leadership positions without having to come up through the ranks. Laborers often felt resentment toward these men, especially if they were required to teach the "leaders" the everyday skills of the mills. In the early twentieth century, some workers were laid off after sharing their job knowledge with a looper. Photo source: Joe Saccomanno

FIGURE 7.23

FOREMEN AND THE ETHNIC HIERARCHY

The tremendous power of foremen in pre-union years, their ethnic ties, and the steel plant's practice of hiring sons and relatives of reliable employees helped cement the ethnic makeup of specific departments and job categories. When George Clark was head of the Car Inspection Department of the South Buffalo Railway (SBR), he found new hires by contacting Boy Scout leaders in heavily Irish South Buffalo and asking for the names of reliable young men. Joe Parker was an 18-year-old in 1936 when he was hired in this manner to be a car checker. When Clark was promoted two years later, Parker was made a foreman. This process brought in many other Irish Americans. The same was true for Italians concentrated in the Yard and SBR Track departments, where Italian foremen hired friends, *paesani*, and relatives. These ethnic lines had become less rigid by the 1920s but were still present up to 1941 when the plant was unionized. Louis Patrucci found few Italians in No. 3 Open Hearth in 1937, as the Irish dominated the mill. "You had to know a foreman real good to get 'on the floor,' as a third helper, then second helper." However, Italians did slowly spread throughout the steel plant, including the mills and specialized shops.

The younger immigrants and American-born Italians found that some foremen and supervisors did hire men solely on merit. Some Italians did advance to skilled and supervisory jobs in mills dominated by Englishmen, Germans, and Irishmen. Superintendent Benning of the SBR probably hired Joe Mesi to head his Track Department not only because many of his laborers were Italian but also because Mesi was an experienced railroad man. One observer stated that another of Mesi's advantages was that he "did not look Italian." Benning also hired Mike Caito, who was born and raised in Buffalo, as Head Clerk, an important position traditionally held by non–Italians. Mesi in turn hired his Italian friends, as did Caito, who brought in his nephew Tony Sardina.

Italians had made significant strides in advancing to more diverse and skilled positions by 1930, but several obstacles blocked further progress. Many foremen continued to practice ethnic discrimination. And with the advent of the Great Depression's many layoffs, the scarcity of jobs served to reinforce the ethnic hierarchy, thus barring the full integration of southern and eastern Europeans and people of color into Bethlehem Steel's workforce.

Department superintendents—mostly English, German, and Irish—often hired foremen of similar lineage, giving them full power to hire, promote, and fire laborers. The foremen were the key to regular work and advancement in the plant. Aspiring workers often encountered rigid systems with little chance for repeal or redress of a foreman's decisions, unless one had a personal connection with either the foreman or the superintendent. To help gain the favor of a foreman, some Italians discovered that their homemade wine could be used as an asset. Angelo Croce kept wine in the coffee thermos in his lunchbox and invited his Irish foreman to help himself. Croce and other Italians told their foremen, "have some coffee," and the foremen understood what this meant.

Some foremen dealt fairly with workers, while others exercised their power arbitrarily. There were foremen who strongly favored members of their own ethnic group, especially if they themselves spoke poor English, while others made it known that they disliked certain ethnic groups. One supervisor told Louie Petrucci that it would be "a long day in hell before a Dago becomes a foreman!" Despite this, Petrucci persevered and eventually became a foreman. In the late 1920s, Al Croce and three other men were temporarily laid off from Bethlehem Steel's Real Estate Division, where they did maintenance work on company-owned homes in Bethlehem Park. Their supervisor, Henry Sylvester, told the men to ask a Carpenter Shop foreman, a Polish

listed these men as laborers, but it is likely that Oddi and Grossi were called to be foremen at specific times of need, when work was booming, then were released into the general labor pool during slowdowns. This may also have been the case for Felice Pepper, who was listed in census records as a laborer but was a lead man or assistant foreman for a Yard work gang during the 1910s. It is possible that at times, the supervisors of these Italians may have been interested in promoting men of their own ethnic group, or those who had more political connections, over the Italian immigrants. Grossi's experience illustrates one way of coping with ethnic

favoritism. After working in mill construction for his first several years in Lackawanna, he moved to the Yard and changed his name to Jimmy Paine with an eye toward making himself more acceptable to the Irish bosses who did the daily hiring. Soon he gained enough experience to be considered for a foreman's slot. With the growing number of Italian laborers, his supervisor may have seen the advantage in naming an Italian to be foreman, if only to facilitate communication.[74]

When Grossi was a foreman and hiring Italians, he told them: "It's safer digging ditches than working in the mills." Some must

immigrant, if he needed more workers. The foreman spoke to each of three Poles in Polish, then motioned them into the shop; there was work for them. "Then he looked at me," states Croce, "and I said: 'I'm Italian.' He said: 'Sorry, I no got job for you. Get out!'" No doubt, this scene was repeated many times, with men of various ethnic groups in the roles of both foreman and job-seeker.

Some foremen were more concerned with the informal "benefits"—kickbacks and favors—that could be elicited from workers newly hired or promoted. An SBR General Yardmaster had his clerk hire conductors and switchmen for train crews from among the men who appeared each morning at 8:00 a.m. Usually those hired had previously placed an envelope with money under the General Yardmaster's door. Men who wanted to work regularly were expected to attend two trainmen stag parties, paying $10 per ticket, an expensive proposition in the 1930s. One common form of petty graft throughout the steel industry was the foreman who borrowed money from his laborers and never repaid it. The Italians, Poles, Croatians and other new immigrants fared poorly in this system because they were not familiar with the language and nuances of the plant's social system, and had few people to guide them, as only a handful of their co-ethnics had risen to supervisory positions by 1930. And some of the Italian and Polish foremen were guilty of the same abuses as were the Northern Europeans. Only with the advent of union organizing in the late 1930s was the great arbitrary power of the foremen and supervisors curbed.

Sources: Interviews with Frank Scaletta, April 4, 1988; Al Croce, April 8, 1994; Joe Parker, July 17, 1986; and Louie Petrucci, December 28, 1984; U.S. Senate, *Report on Conditions of Employment in the Iron and Steel Industry, Volume III: Working Conditions and the Relations of Employers and Employees,* 1913, p. 148.

have agreed, and at times, the Yard workers labored outside in areas relatively free of railroad and vehicle traffic. But steel-industry statistics demonstrate that the Yard was just as dangerous as the blast furnaces and open hearths; much of the time, workers were in or near the mills or in the midst of busy rail traffic or overhead cranes as they moved throughout the plant grounds. Yet the Yard drew Italian workers for many decades because of their familiarity with outdoor pick-and-shovel work, the presence of Italian coworkers, and the basic fact that it was one of the few departments in which jobs were available to them—their ethnic niche in the plant, as it were. This is demonstrated by the case of the Petrucci

family. Michele Petrucci and his family emigrated to Clyde, New York, but ten years after he and his son Louie found themselves unemployed. Cousins in Lackawanna then lined up jobs for both men. Louie Petrucci vividly recalled that he and his dad arrived in Buffalo by train at 2:00 a.m. on July 3, 1932, and that he started work in the Yard at 3:00 p.m. that same day. Michele, who first had to resolve some citizenship questions, joined his son several days later. Louie Petrucci worked with several crews—maintaining tracks, unloading materials, doing construction work—before joining a work gang that loaded material by hand and received higher pay. Laid off in 1938, he returned to the steel plant the following year as an oiler in the blast furnaces, then went back to the Yard, where he became a labor gang leader and was put in charge of a scrap-burner yard.[75]

Indeed, the Yard Department offered Italians the best opportunity for promotion to supervisory positions. In 1915, Umberto Barbati and his nephew, Aniello Covino, both became foremen, Covino in the brick sheds stocked by Yard personnel. When Bethlehem Steel purchased the Lackawanna plant in 1922, the maintenance of South Buffalo Railway tracks was handed from the Yard to the railway's newly created Track Department. Yard foremen Luigi Conti and Cesidio D'Amore were transferred to the new unit. Abruzzesi such as D'Amore made up one-third of the 40 Italians who were Yard foremen between 1906 and 1949. In the second half of the twentieth century, the Italian presence in the Yard remained strong. Mike Morgan became a foreman and Bruno Mariani a supervisor in the Garage. In the early 1970s, the Yard was combined with General Services to form the Plant Services Department, with Mickey Paolini as its first superintendent. Paolini named Sam Longo of Buffalo as head clerk of the department. Overall in the mid 1970s, the Plant Services roster listed two Italian general foremen and seven foremen, including Alphonse Mortellaro and John Marsillo of Lackawanna.[76]

Salvatore DiTommaso, Pietro Fiore, and Romolo Sperduti were laborers when they transferred from the Yard to the SBR Track Department in 1922, but all were foremen three years later. Along with Giuseppe Cardinale, Luigi Conti, Cesidio D'Amore, and general foreman Joe Mesi, they constituted the majority of the department's foremen in 1926. While the department was heavily Italian, it was also a melting pot of many ethnic groups. When Giustino DeSantis began there in 1930, his work gang was led by a Polish foreman who spoke broken English to his crew of 11 laborers that included Poles, Italians, Mexicans, blacks, and Hungarians. DeSantis soon discovered that most of his colleagues were Italian; he estimated that 60% of the 300 track laborers during the 1930s were Italian. Three more Italians became track foremen during the 1930s, and Giustino DeSantis himself became a foreman in 1943.[77]

Kalman Steel was located in Blasdell on Lake Avenue, where it produced structural beams. It was bought out by Bethlehem Steel in 1931. Just behind it, partially obscured by smoke from its stacks, is the Seneca Steel Company. The view is toward the southeast; Lake Avenue is directly under the aircraft from which this picture was shot.
Photo source: Hamburg Historical Society

Regional roots also played a role in the SBR Track Department: of the 12 Italian foremen from 1922 to 1943, four were Laziali and three Abruzzesi. Among the 30 Italians identified as SBR employees in 1925, the Laziali composed 30% and the second largest group, the Napolitani, 14%. The trend of Laziali to cluster on the SBR and other railroad jobs in Lackawanna continued after World War II when Al Federici, a native of Giuliano, became a foreman. Pete DelPrince and Jim Corsaro, who did not live in Lackawanna, each rose to the position of general foreman. Italians advanced more slowly in the SBR Roundhouse, where for many years most supervisors were Dutch or Irish. Michael Falcone was made a foreman in 1941, and Tony Falbo became a boilermaker, then rose to the rank of foreman in 1965.[78]

A third grouping of Italians became open hearth foremen, beginning with Joe Rauve in 1910. He was followed by 10 others over the next four decades, seven of whom were Marchegiani. It took some men a long time to attain the foreman's position: Domenico Baldelli, a Marchegiano, began his career in 1923 and finally became a Stockyard foreman in No. 3 Open Hearth by 1941. Carl Presciutto, a Yard employee, lined up a job for his stepson, Louis Patrucci (a different person from Louie Petrucci, mentioned earlier) in 1933. The 18-year-old soon joined the CC gang installing firebrick in furnaces. He did much of his work in the newly constructed No. 3 Open

Hearth, and in 1937 he transferred there, soon becoming a third helper. He rose to the skilled position of Second Helper, a job he resumed after a stint in the army, and in 1949 became a first helper. Patrucci was later offered the job of Melter but refused because the position involved tremendous pressure, yet was accompanied by only a modest pay increase. He did become a Turn Foreman and later moved on to the new Basic Oxygen Furnace (BOF).[79]

Sosio "John" Ceccarelli emigrated from Lazio as a child and was 16 years old when he graduated from eighth grade at Bethlehem Park School in 1937. He started working as an open-hearth laborer, studied metallurgy books and the steelmaking process, and became a Third Helper in No. 2 Open Hearth in 1941. After being discharged from the Marines in 1945, he returned to the steel plant, soon becoming a turn foreman and a second helper. In 1948 he became a first helper. Ceccarelli broke new ground for Italians in 1950 when he became a melter in No. 2 Open Hearth, the first Italian American to do so. His rise through the ranks was assisted by his expertise in golf: during the 1930s at the Wanakah Country Club, Ceccarelli was both a caddy and an informal instructor for Open Hearth superintendent Frank Gregory and later became a golfing companion of Gregory's. By 1974, Ceccarelli was an assistant general foreman in the BOF, where Dominick Grasso and Joseph Mecca were assistant pit foremen.[80]

Edward Lorenzi completed his education at Pennsylvania State University and joined the Bethlehem plant in Lackawanna in 1946. Unlike those who worked their way up through the ranks, Lorenzi was what was know at the plant as a "looper," a college-trained man who immediately assumed a supervisory role. In 1950, he became the assistant supervisor of No. 1 Open Hearth, the superintendent eight years later, and superintendent of the steelmaking division by 1974. Essio "Ace" Baldelli joined other Marchegiani in the Open Hearths while attending Lackawanna High School. He lost a hand in a work-related accident there, but went on to Lehigh University to study metallurgy, simultaneously working at Bethlehem Steel's home plant in Bethlehem, Pennsylvania. He returned to Lackawanna in 1942 and eventually became a chief metallographist in the steel plant during his 42-year career.[81]

Four generations of the Paolini family worked in the steel plant. Giuseppe Paolini came to western New York from Marche in 1905, and bringing his wife and two eldest children over four years later. The family was living in the Old Village in 1915, at which time Paolini was a laborer in the Yard. The family moved to Buffalo, but Paolini worked for more than 25 years in the steel plant, as a subforeman for part of that time. He was instrumental in getting many of his *paesani* jobs there, including his son Mickey, who had a 50-year career and was a Yard supervisor. Mickey Paolini's son, Gregory F. Paolini, attended the University of Pittsburgh, did his "internship" as a looper at the Sparrows Point plant in Maryland, and was superintendent of Blast Furnaces and Technology in the Lackawanna plant from 1975 to 1983. In 1979, his son became the fourth generation of the family to work in the plant. Gregory M. Paolini was superintendent of the Galvanizing Mill, one of the few mills still functioning at Bethlehem Steel's Lackawanna plant, until 2003, when the company went bankrupt and was sold.[82]

Italians first became foremen in the blast furnaces, rolling mills and specialty shops between 1917 and 1925. One young, second-generation Italian found it to his advantage to change his name. Tony Collarino started to use the surname Gallarney so that Irish foremen would hire him. Apparently his plan worked, as in 1920 he was a machinist and went on to became a night foreman in the Machine Shop. Some Italians rose in the ranks to discover that not only their nationality but also their religion was held against them. In 1956, Alex Filipetti became an assistant inspector foreman. The chief inspector was a Mason, and Filipetti, as the only Italian and Catholic, was the target of jokes and taunts at supervisory meetings. He endured and went on to serve as assistant chief inspector in the Mechanical Department from 1964 to 1966.[83]

Other Industrial Companies and Railroads

A number of other industries, much smaller than the huge steel plant, were also located in or near Lackawanna. The Buffalo Brake Beam plant was founded in 1907 at the southern end of Ingham Avenue on land acquired from Lackawanna Steel. The company designed and produced rail-car braking systems, its name referring to the steel beams to which the brake shoes were attached. In 1912, the company employed 70 workers, and a number of Italians eventually worked there. The plant finally closed down in 2001. The Shenandoah Steel Wire Works, which later became Wickwire and then the Lackawanna Foundry, was functioning by 1909. It stood along the south bank of Smokes Creek, adjacent to the area that became Bethlehem Park. Just to the south, the Buffalo Tank Company was established off Lincoln Avenue in 1929 (see Figure 7.17). Lackawanna was the site of the car-repair shop of the LS&MS Railroad (later absorbed by the New York Central Railroad); Trimble, Mudge and Company, which cut up scrap iron; the Hazard, Coates, and Bennett Company; and a silk factory. Just north of Lackawanna, within the city of Buffalo, were Hanna Furnace Company, the Buffalo Sintering Company, as well as McClintoc-Marshall Company and the Lackawanna Bridge Shop. The last two shops were eventually purchased by Bethlehem Steel.[84]

Corrugated Bar, built in 1909 on Lake Avenue in Woodlawn, fabricated concrete reinforcing bars. Within 10 years of its opening, it employed 184 men, including Tony DePasquale, Tony Deramo, and Natale Chiodo. By the late 1920s, the company was taken over by Kalman Steel, which was in turn purchased by Bethlehem Steel in 1931. Kalman Steel produced structural support beams, also known as "H" beams, and Bethlehem eventually moved the operations to Hamburg Turnpike in Woodlawn. It was then referred to as the Kalman Steel Division, and later the Specialty Products Shop. Joe Milano, Angelo Iafallo, and George Schole were listed among the 143 employees there in 1934. The Seneca Iron and Steel Company was established in 1906 in Blasdell, just east of the Kalman site. It employed more than 300 workers, including a number of Italians from Roland Avenue (see Figure 7.24). Both Buffalo Tank and Seneca Steel were purchased by Bethlehem Steel in 1932.[85]

In 1902, industrialists William Rogers and Frank and Charles Goodyear combined resources to found the Buffalo and Susquehanna Furnace Company, across from Lackawanna Steel's main office building, on the east side of Hamburg Turnpike. The Goodyear Canal, now known as the Union Ship Canal, was dug eastward from Lake Erie, allowing for lake freighter access. The first blast furnace was completed and

FIGURE 7.24

SENECA IRON & STEEL COMPANY

The Seneca Iron and Steel Company was established in 1906 in Blasdell. Its two buildings, known as the east and west plants, each grew to 500 feet in length by the early 1930s. At that time, 23-year-old Al Croce, whose family had moved from the Old Village to Blasdell, was unemployed. A neighbor told him of an opening for a laborer at the plant, and Croce was soon cleaning furnaces and shoveling ashes. He discovered that both the east and west plants included a hot and cold mill section. In the hot mill, sheets of steel were hand-fed and manually pushed on skids through the furnace. When the heated steel emerged from the other end of the furnace, men called rollers grasped one sheet with tongs and brought it to their roll stand. The East Plant had six to eight stands, while the West Plant had four to five. Each stand was five-and-one-half-feet high; the roller stood on one side, and the catcher (or roller assistant) on the other. Using tongs, the roller passed a sheet of hot steel through the stand. Each sheet was three feet across, five feet long, and 1/32 of an inch thick. The catcher grasped the sheet with his tongs as it came through to his side, then passed it back over the top of the stand to the roller. In the few seconds while the steel was picked up by the catcher, the roller tightened the gauge on the rolls by turning a wheel. After two or three passes, the sheet was compressed into the desired thickness. The men repeated this physically exhausting process over and over. They wore mitts with steel staples to protect their hands.

The finished sheets were then taken to the cold mill section and put through a machine called a leveler, which had 12 rollers on both the top and bottom that straightened out the steel. From there, the steel was cut to size, packed, and shipped. In the 1930s, Bethlehem's No. 7-8 Mills rolled 30-foot-long "Japanese sheet bars" that the SBR transported to the Seneca mills, where they were cut into shorter lengths and then rolled.

When Al Croce started at Seneca Steel, there were perhaps 200 men on each shift. When men reported each morning hoping to be hired, an English American foreman had them line up against a wall and used ethnic slurs, such as "guinea" or "Polack," as he selected men for that day. This so insulted Croce that he complained to the foreman. "I was always sent home after that," he lamented: "If a foreman didn't like your looks, he sent you home." Eventually, Croce was hired occasionally, and his luck improved when a foreman in the machine shop needed a toilet installed at his home and heard of Croce's plumbing experience. Exercising his sense of privilege, the foreman asked Croce to do this chore free of charge, Croce was rewarded by being hired to operate lathes, roll grinders, and shapers in the machine shop of the east plant. The foreman was strict and insisted that his employees "work and keep quiet," as Croce later recalled. Gaining much experience as a machinist, Croce became a millwright, then moved on to become an overhead crane operator.

Seneca Steel was nicknamed the "farmers mill," because many employees were farmers who worked at the plant from late fall, after the harvest, until plowing and planting time. From spring to fall, "city" men from Lackawanna, Blasdell, and Woodlawn comprised the bulk of Seneca's employees. When the farmers returned they brought bushels of fruit and vegetables to help persuade the foremen to hire them. Some city men who fished on Lake Erie brought their catch to foremen in hopes of avoiding a layoff. But many lost their jobs at this point and went on welfare. There were a number of Italian employees at Seneca, but none were foremen. Croce noted that Italians and Poles "were at the bottom of the barrel" in the plant hierarchy.

When Bethlehem Steel purchased Seneca Steel in 1932, it insisted that workers be available year-round, thus ending the seasonal work pattern. Most of the Seneca workers were transferred to the new Strip Mill in 1936; the old plant was maintained as a standby facility, then converted into a galvanizing operation. During World War II, part of the site was used to house Bethlehem's Car Repair Shop when its original location was temporarily used as a billet yard. In the 1950s, the Buffalo Tank Company took over the Seneca facility when it moved from Bethlehem Park.

Source: Interview with Al Croce, April 20, 1995.

operating in 1904. The plant then changed hands several times and in 1930 was merged with the Hanna Division of the National Steel Company and became known as Hanna Furnace. Hanna's iron was sent to various steel mills, including Bethlehem, to meet its World War II production quotas. Many Italians worked at Hanna Furnace, especially during slack periods across the street at the Bethlehem plant. One of the earliest was Paul Giuditta, who in 1907 was working at Hanna as a railroad conductor when he was killed while attempting to couple cars. Antonio Carnevale emigrated from Pico, Lazio, to Lackawanna in 1901 and within the next decade was working at the plant. When he returned to Pico, he told his grandson Santino of "the rivers of molten metal" he viewed in the blast furnaces.[86]

Lackawanna Italians also worked at the Buffalo Sintering plant, formerly known as Rogers Brown Sintering, in South Buffalo, just north of Lackawanna (see Figure 7.17). Waste

Seneca Steel Company, built in 1906, was an early producer of small pieces of thin-gauge steel that were used in producing storage tanks, automobiles, and appliances. The view here looks northeast, with Mile Strip Road in foreground and Blasdell and Lake Avenue in the distance. The plant was purchased by Bethlehem Steel in 1932.
Photo source: Steel Plant Museum

materials from iron and steel production, ore dust from blast furnaces, coke breeze, and roll scale were collected and taken by rail to the plant, where iron was reclaimed from them. The resulting product, called sinter, was then sold back to the iron and steel companies. During World War I, Charles Roncalli and Santo Crescenza worked there. In 1925, Giuseppe Basile was foreman of a crew that worked on reclaiming iron from flue dust. The crew included his son Lawrence, and Antonio Gargano, Antonio Selice, and Aniello Infante, all of whom were lodgers in the Basile home and immigrants from Bagnoli Irpino. Lawrence Basile became a foreman by 1927.[87]

A significant number of Lackawanna Italians worked on the mainline railroads that passed through the city and into Buffalo. Early in the twentieth century, these included the Erie; Pennsylvania; Lehigh Valley; New York, Chicago, & St. Louis (later, the Nickel Plate); New York Central (NYC); Lake Shore and Southern Michigan (LS&MS); and the Buffalo, Rochester and Pittsburgh Railroad (BP&R). The LS&MS was absorbed into the New York Central in 1914, and the BP&R later became part of the Baltimore and Ohio Railroad, which had a passenger station near McKinley Parkway and South Park Avenue. The maze of tracks was adjacent to the Roland Avenue neighborhood, so the numerous railroad workers who lived there enjoyed easy access to their jobs. Between 1905 and 1930, many of the city's Italian railroad workers lived along Roland Avenue. Some of the Calabresi and Napolitani in the neighborhood had worked

on railroads in other parts of the United States before coming to Lackawanna, and it was railroad work, not the steel mills, that drew them to the Steel City. Bruno Falbo was working in a Pennsylvania coal mine when he heard that the NYC was hiring at its Seneca Yard in Lackawanna. At least 21 other Italians, most of them Roland Avenue residents, were employees of this rail line between 1910 and 1929. The huge Seneca Yard had 32 parallel tracks, with a combined length of 42 miles, that could handle 1,600 cars per day. There was an NYC passenger station accessible by steps from the Ridge Road bridge, as well as offices and an ice house. The railroad's large roundhouse in the maze of railroad tracks between Kirby Avenue and Dona Street was a short walk from the Italian neighborhoods to the east and west. Italians found opportunities to move into skilled positions at the roundhouse. Pasquale DeMaria became a machinist; Joseph Orlando, a machinist's helper; Michael Orlando, a boiler washer; and Cleveland J. Tarquinio, an instrument man. Bruno Falbo started working there as a laborer, then became a boilermaker, and finally a boiler inspector. All of them were Roland Avenue residents, as was Domenico Bulone, a laborer at the ice house who helped replenish the ice in refrigerator cars carrying food products. Nick Thomas from Bethlehem Park was 15 years old in 1919 when he started as a messenger boy in the Seneca Yard and soon became a clerk, then a bookkeeper. His brother Oliver joined him there in 1922 and was also a bookkeeper. In the late 1920s, the Seneca Yard was shut down and reestablished in

FIGURE 7.25

BUFFALO TANK COMPANY

The Buffalo Tank Company had its origins in Sharon, Pennsylvania, where the Youngstown Sheet and Tube Company manufactured large gasoline-storage tanks and boilers. These vessels were made with rivets, and several engineers at the plant realized that welded tanks would soon replace the riveted type. Four of them decided to produce welded tanks, and located their new business near one of the few sources of sheet metal in the nation: the Seneca Steel Company in Blasdell. Many Italians in Sharon worked at Youngstown Sheet and Tube, including Antonio Palumbo, who was a boy when his family immigrated from Campania in 1902. Palumbo learned machine skills at the Erie Railroad roundhouse and at a Westinghouse plant. In 1928, he was hired as a machinist at Youngstown Sheet and Tube, where he became familiar with burning and welding.

In 1929, the four foresightful engineers started their new business in Lackawanna, purchasing land in Bethlehem Park. They asked Antonio Palumbo and four other skilled workers at Youngstown Sheet and Tube to join them. At the east end of Lincoln Avenue, the workmen used recycled materials to erect a spartan structure in which they were soon building 550-gallon tanks. It was slow going from 1929 to 1932, but the business succeeded

and the workforce grew to 20 men. An old boxcar served as the lunchroom, and additions were tacked onto the main building in a piecemeal fashion. Palumbo acted as millwright and took care of all the machinery as well as other chores. He boarded with the Galanti family until 1932, when he brought his wife and six children from Sharon and settled in Bethlehem Park.

Seneca Steel sent sheets of strip metal to the Buffalo Tank Company, a practice that continued after Bethlehem bought the Seneca plant in 1932. Tullio Paolini's trucking company was often hired to haul the increasing tonnage of metal demanded by the expanding business. Buffalo Tank began making 4,000-gallon tanks, and became a subsidiary of Bethlehem Steel in 1940. With the advent of World War II, the company prospered and its workforce grew to 50 men. Soon the workers were building and erecting large smokestacks, and the plant was modernized and expanded; a real lunchroom replaced the old boxcar. Palumbo's youngest son, 18-year-old John, joined Buffalo Tank in 1942, earning 60 cents per hour. When he returned following military service, the workforce had grown to 65 employees, and John worked on lathes and transported materials from Bethlehem Steel's storehouse by pickup truck. His father

continued as a foreman, a position he had gained in 1934, and encouraged his son to learn welding and electrical work. "I hated wearing the mask," recalls John Palumbo, "but welders got more pay and respect." During the late 1940s, all welding was done by hand. In addition to Antonio and John Palumbo, eight other Italians worked at Buffalo Tank during the 1940s and 1950s. When Antonio Palumbo retired as Maintenance Foreman in 1959, his son John filled this position.

In 1948, Bethlehem Steel moved its Buffalo Tank subsidiary to the old Seneca Steel site in Blasdell to make room for the Strip Mill expansion. By this time, Buffalo Tank was constructing tanks with up to a 16,000-gallon capacity. During the summer, the workforce grew to 120 men as new tanks were erected, then shrank to 60 in the slack winter months. Buffalo Tank Division discontinued its costly field services in 1950 and subcontracted this work to Bethlehem Steel's Erection Department. In 25 years, the small business had expanded dramatically, as it sent John Palumbo and other Lackawanna employees to six other states to establish eight new plants. By 1964, Palumbo had become superintendent of the Buffalo Tank Division in Blasdell, and he became plant manager in 1981. He retired the following year, and the Blasdell plant closed down a few years later.

Sources: Interview with John Palumbo, September 22, 1995. The four engineers were R. F. Johnson, W. C. McGraffic, R. B. Taylor, and R. I. Morrison. Buffalo Tank initially expanded by establishing plants in Dunnelin, New Jersey, and Baltimore, Maryland. This expansion was followed by new facilities in Charlotte and Raleigh, North Carolina; Jacksonville and Hollandale, Florida; Worcester, Massachusetts; and Romulus, Michigan.

Gardenville, some five or six miles northeast of Lackawanna, and out of walking range from Roland Avenue. Bruno Falbo acquired a seven-passenger car—first a Lincoln, then a Pierce Arrow, and finally, a Hudson—in which he transported neighbors and coworkers to the Gardenville roundhouse.[88]

Alfonso Yoviene had been a section foreman for the Buffalo and Susquehanna Railroad, directing wrecking crews first in Galeton, Pennsylvania, then in Sardinia, New York. In about 1915, the line folded, and his future son-in-law, John Verel,

lined him up with a railroad job in Lackawanna. It is unclear if he held a supervisory position, but his career ended abruptly in 1919 when he was accidentally electrocuted near his Roland Avenue home. But railroad work itself was the main hazard faced by workers. For example, Augusto Madalona, a Roland Avenue resident and section hand on the LS&MS, was killed in a 1913 work accident.[89]

All but three of the 54 Italian railroad men listed in the 1910 census were designated as laborers, but by 1917-18, they

The Buffalo Tank Company was established at Birch Street and Lincoln Avenue in Bethlehem Park in 1929. It manufactured large storage tanks and smokestacks. The company became a subsidiary of Bethlehem Steel, and the facility was moved to the old Seneca Steel site in Blasdell. Photo source: Hamburg Historical Society

had diversified. Half those men had a variety of skilled and semiskilled jobs, including crane and stationary engineer, car repairer, blacksmith helper, and two foremen. Over half the 39 railroad workers in 1920 also held skilled/semiskilled jobs, including a crane operator and four crewmen—two switchmen and two firemen. Pasquale Pitillo was a "caller," which meant he was a crew clerk who contacted trainmen to replace men who were absent. C. John Tarquinio had become a civil engineer and Peter Mastrobattista a yard foreman in 1925. The highest position was attained by Anthony Falcone, who was a yardmaster with the New York Central Railroad. In this capacity, he directed all rail traffic within the part of the Seneca Yard under his control. Carlo Riccio and Joe Fox became foremen on the Lehigh Valley Railroad between 1917 and 1930. Earlier, Phil Verel began a 67-year career that started on that railroad and touched many facets of track work. He was 10 years old upon arrival in the United States in 1891 and soon found work as a waterboy on the Lehigh Valley Railroad, then as a section hand. In 1900, he went to the PS&N Railroad as a section foreman. Nine years later, he returned to the Lehigh Valley and worked as a track foreman or section foreman until his retirement in 1959. He served as vice president and local

chairman of Lodge 1473 of the Brotherhood of Railroad Maintenance Men.[90]

For many years, the majority of Lackawanna Italians were employees of industrial companies such as Bethlehem Steel and the railroads that served them. By 1930, Italians were claiming more skilled jobs and working in many mills and shops throughout the steel plant. They had also begun to obtain more positions in the railroad train crew, roundhouse, and office rosters. This process of integration into different departments and levels of the workforce was integral to the assimilation of Italians into America's working class. And the struggle to unionize the workplace between 1919 and 1941 touched the lives of all the workers in Lackawanna's multiethnic workforce. For Italians and other ethnic groups, this effort became a watershed event in the assimilation of both immigrants and their adult children.

CHAPTER 8

UNIONS AND STRIKES

The Lackawanna Steel Company is a large employer of labor. They have always opposed organized labor, even from the year 1901, when they took the contracts from the American Bridge Company for erecting their structural steel frames at the plant and did it themselves with non – Union labor.[1]

The struggle between unions and the business community has been a dominant theme in America since the mid-nineteenth century. Corporations have been ruthless and often violent in suppressing worker's attempts at forming unions. Indeed, until the late 1930s, the federal government as well as state and local governments regularly sided with businesses, dispatching military troops and police forces to break strikes. Going back even further, American industrial corporations in the late 1800s attempted to break the hold of skilled workers and their unions while increasing the productivity of workers. New technologies and machines were used to displace many skilled workers, and other skilled positions were broken down into routine basic tasks, most of which could be performed by unskilled laborers. Even the number of semiskilled and unskilled laborers needed to operate a steel mill was reduced by the installation of sophisticated machinery and procedures. As a result of these developments, the expansion of the steel corporations involved a huge increase in capital investment to retool existing plants and build new ones, as was the case in Lackawanna. Only a moderate increase was seen in the number of steelworkers, and most of the new positions were for unskilled workers.[2]

< Steel strike, February 26-28, 1941. Picketers near No. 3 Gate include Bill Mingarell (waving) and Joe Vertalino, to the right. The success of their strike in Lackawanna led to unionization of all steel companies in the U.S.
Photo source: Collection of Frank Chiodo

The primary source of unskilled laborers after 1890 for industries manufacturing products such as steel were the millions of peasants from southern and eastern Europe who immigrated to this country. The American steel industry deliberately hired immigrants, imagining them to be easily managed and unlikely to join unions. In fact, by 1907-08 some 58% of steelworkers in the United States were foreign-born, and another 13% were the sons of immigrants. That same year the U.S. Immigration Commission sampled 441 foreign-born workers at Lackawanna Steel and two neighboring steel plants and found only two men, both Polish, who were affiliated with trade unions. The commission's report concluded that the "immigrants, who are in the majority among the workers, seem to take no interest whatever in trade unionism."[3]

Throughout the United States from 1900 to 1918, unions and management struggled incessantly, and the number of annual strikes varied from 315 to 4,450. At Lackawanna Steel during this period, there were no major strikes, just as the Buffalo industrialists had predicted in 1899. The company's managers emerged from World War I with burgeoning profits and the confidence they could handle any potential labor unrest. They were in for a rude awakening.[4]

During the Great Steel Strike of 1919, immigrants in Lackawanna and other mill towns shocked the steel barons by participating in a nationwide strike. The workers were eventually defeated, and the steel companies resumed absolute control over their laborers for nearly two more decades. The labor scene again shifted in the late 1930s, when immigrants and their American-born sons responded to the new industrial unions sponsored by the Congress of Industrial Organizations (CIO). They began to organize and fight against company unions, a campaign that started in Lackawanna and other locales in 1936. The largest steel corporation, United States Steel, agreed to recognize unions in 1937, but Bethlehem, which bought the Lackawanna plant in 1922, and other smaller companies—collectively known as "Little Steel"—stubbornly battled against the effort to unionize their workforces. The turning point in labor's struggle with Little Steel was the strike at the Lackawanna plant in 1941, which forced Bethlehem Steel to recognize the United Steelworkers Union.[5]

While no major strikes occurred at Lackawanna Steel prior to 1919, a series of labor actions and small strikes took place in the early years of the twentieth century that foreshadowed later events. In August 1900, 11 workmen from Buffalo walked off the job, demanding a wage increase from 25 to 40 cents per hour (the union rate). The men involved, who were nonunion, had been advised of the wage difference by a business agent of the Bricklayers' Union. Another walkout occurred in May 1902, when 100 bricklayers employed by contractors learned that Lackawanna Steel had independently hired other masons under a different pay formula. At the same time, 200 plumbers were on strike, and carpenters and ironworkers had also staged work stoppages. Three months later boilermakers struck for two days after hearing reports that some plant foremen discriminated against union men. In October, 400 boilermakers and their helpers went on strike in an attempt to gain time-and-a-half pay for overtime work, to end the practice of men being fired for refusing to work on Sundays, and to support the discharge of the foremen who had discriminated against union men. The company had begun to hire replacements and set up 60 cots in the plant to accommodate them. Other trade unions of skilled workers in the steel plant promised a sympathy strike in support of the boilermakers. One newspaper speculated, somewhat naively, "A great problem that promises to arise soon at the steel plant will be the question of unionism. The attitude of the great corporation toward union labor is yet to be defined. Today, both union and non-union men are employed. A man is not asked whether he is a member of a union or not when he makes application for work." This reporter seemed unaware of the steel magnates' great animosity toward unions, and, indeed, that one of the primary reasons for Lackawanna Steel Company's relocation to western New York was to find and hire more nonunion workers.[6]

The result of these and other early labor actions was that by 1905, some 400 bricklayers in the plant were unionized, and some train crewmen on the South Buffalo Railway (SBR) were represented by railroad unions. Newspaper accounts of the strikes did not indicate if the union workers were foreign born or members of specific ethnic groups, but since these unions represented skilled trades, they probably included few Italians, Poles, or other recent arrivals. Italian laborers at the steel plant, however, were at the center of a spontaneous labor action in the summer of 1902. While most workers at the plant were Lackawanna Steel hirees, a number of Italians were employed by Lathrop, Shea & Henwood, a subcontractor with offices across the street from the plant. On June 16, when a foreman fired some 30 to 40 Italian workmen, 100 other Italians spontaneously ceased their work and took up the cause of their countrymen. The men demanded that the fired workers be rehired or immediately paid and that other Italians now desiring to leave the job be paid as well. When the foreman stated that he couldn't pay all the Italians who had been fired or wanted to quit the job, the workers shouted at him angrily and locked him in one of their shanties at the south end of the plant grounds. After two hours of negotiations, the two parties reached an agreement, the foreman was released, and the fired men received their pay. The others were to either report to work the next day; or if they didn't, they would then be paid and, like those fired, told not to report for future work. Buffalo's Italian newspaper, *Corriere Italiano*, told the story in a relatively short article under the lead "A Foreman in a Swindle." The piece criticized the foreman, who had "made excuses, saying he only had enough money for the fired workers," and commented on the overly detailed account given earlier in the *Buffalo Enquirer*. Under the sensationalized banner, "Laborers Make Foreman a Prisoner," the *Enquirer* had described "a hundred infuriated Italians, who … sought to avenge themselves on the foreman." Building up the drama, the article continued:

'If you don't pay us we'll kill you,' said one Italian in a frenzied tone. At this many voices cried out, 'We want our money! Kill him! … The Italians became almost frantic with rage as they dilated over their fancied wrongs … Several of them screamed and howled.

"Cooler counsel" prevailed, the article went on to say, and the leaders among the Italians calmly talked to the foreman until "a compromise was reached." Besides belittling the workers' grievances as "fancied wrongs," the *Enquirer* even doubted their right to act as a group, noting that "the men are unorganized and have no affiliation with any of the Buffalo labor bodies."[7]

Corriere Italiano often criticized the mainstream press in Buffalo for being biased against Italians and ignoring their dangerous and difficult working conditions. The *Enquirer*, guilty as charged, had earned its reputation for sensational articles that often condemned and attacked immigrants. Other local English-language newspapers also failed to report the dangerous conditions at Lackawanna Steel that often resulted in tragedy for Italians and other employees.

During the economic depression of 1907, two-thirds of the steel plant's workers were laid off, then the whole plant was shut down for several weeks. In mid – December, individual departments began to reopen, and by April 1908, the plant had called back a total of 4,600 men, leaving at least 1,500 men still laid off. Noting that the depression and slow recovery had created hardships for Italians in Buffalo and Lackawanna, the editors of *Corriere Italiano* wrote: "We hope that the financial crisis will be completely over so that Italians can have peace of mind." But these hopes weren't met, as other woes followed for steelworkers.[8]

In 1909, the Lackawanna Steel Company reduced the pay of its office personnel by 10% and cut its steelworkers' hourly wages, which had previously ranged from 13.5 to 17 cents, to a flat 12 cents. Nationwide, the steel industry relentlessly fought unionization, defeating the efforts of the American Federation of Labor (AFL) and the Amalgamated Association of Iron, Steel, and Tin Workers (AAISTW) during the period from 1910 to 1913. The workers at the Seneca Steel Company in Blasdell, apparently mostly American-born men of northwest European ethnic groups, staged a series of strikes between 1910 and 1912, eventually leading to the formation of an Amalgamated local in 1915. But immigrant and African American laborers were often snubbed during the AAISTW's organizing drives. The pages of the *Amalgamated Journal* carried articles titled "Aliens—A Menace to Labor" and "Sidelight on America's Immigration Problem," noting that "the influx of Southern Italians continue [sic] in one unbroken deluge." An article titled "Grasshopper Immigrants" lamented "these tramp immigrants who come like the grasshopper and the locust to eat up our green fields of glorious opportunity, and then in the first arid season to skip away with full bellies to some far country from which they come." This attitude came to haunt the union. In 1903, a strike by workers at the Buffalo Structural Steel Company to gain recognition of the union was defeated when Polish, Hungarian, Italian, and black strikebreakers were brought in.[9]

The union was rightly concerned about the manner in which steel corporations manipulated immigrants against native-born workers. The *Amalgamated Journal* commented on a 1911 letter written by Fred F. Graham, secretary of the Lackawanna Steel Company, to two men seeking jobs. According to the *Journal*, the letter "practically states in so many words that if the two men are foreigners, they can get employment at once, but if not, they are courteously requested to call." Similarly, the *Buffalo Republic* noted that steel companies "have made a successful effort in employing foreigners of different nationalities, in order that there may not be free-speaking intercourse between them." The corporations divide-and-conquer

ITALIANS PUT FOREMAN IN SHACK

Row at Steel Plant Over Discharged Men Followed by Strike and Imprisonment of Foreman in Tenement.

With a band of nearly 100 infuriated Italians surrounding him, muttering curses and threatening every form and style of punishment, a foreman for Lathrop, Shea & Henwood, sub-contractors at the Lackawanna Iron & Steel Company's plant in West Seneca, was confined in a shack for two hours yesterday afternoon. He was in the same building where the murder of one Italian and the serious injury of another recently took place.

Italian laborers went on a spontaneous strike when a foreman treated them unfairly. Photo source: Buffalo & Erie County Public Library, *Buffalo Courier*, 6/17/1902

FIGURE 8.1

THE MAN-KILLING SYSTEM

Until 1923, the average length of a shift for many steelworkers was 12 hours. The 24-hour swing shift occurred every two weeks, when day-shift workers changed to the night shift and vice versa. On the day this switch occurred, one shift put in a full 24 hours on the job, while the other one enjoyed a day off. In many plants, the daytime shift lasted 10 to 11 hours, and the slower nighttime shift put in 13 to 14 hours. At the Lackawanna plant, many departments had a day shift of 10 hours and a night shift of 14 hours. These long hours in combination with the harsh working environment led to illness and injury for many a steelworker and resulted in death for others.

tactics often worked, as the AAISTW tended to blame the unskilled immigrants and African Americans instead of inviting them to join the union. Without an industrial union open to both skilled and unskilled steelworkers, the men could not effectively act on their accumulating grievances. There was, however, some support for workers from a handful of journalists and state governments.[10]

Reformers for years had been publicizing the terrible conditions in the nation's steel mills, especially the abuses of the seven-day week, the 12-hour workday, and the 24-hour swing shift, referred to as "the man-killing system" (see Figure 8.1). John Fitch wrote a landmark article on the effects of long work hours, its title, "Old Age by Forty," became a national rallying cry for change. U.S. Steel, the nation's largest steel producer, voluntarily went to an eight-hour day in 1907 but stuck with this policy only when the economy was slow and the mills were not operating at full capacity. In 1912, the corporation finally ended the seven-day work week at its mills. Lackawanna Steel and several other smaller companies accepted this plan only for some of its departments, omitting others, such as the blast furnaces. In 1913, the Industrial Commission of New York State forbade the seven-day work week, and by 1915 this was a nationwide practice. Also, during this period the 12-hour work day was somewhat restricted. The advent of World War I in 1914 cut immigration to a trickle, and the steel companies soon had labor shortages. Two years later, Lackawanna Steel petitioned the commission for permission to reinstate the seven-day work week. While this request was initially denied, the continuing labor shortage and the urgency of defense production led to the full reinstatement of the seven-day work week and the 12-hour workday throughout the nation. By 1916, large numbers of blacks were recruited from the South to work in the steel plants. The war brought some benefits to workers—full employment in the mills and, to retain workers, increased wages. In addition, important help came from an influential new ally. The entry of the United States into the World War I in 1917 saw President Wilson eager to unite working Americans behind the war effort. He traveled to Buffalo in November 1917 and addressed the American Federation of Labor convention. The President voiced his support of the AFL's principles of workers' rights, including the right to organize unions without interference by employers, and he soon appointed union representatives to the War Labor Board. Wages, hours, and working conditions were standardized in war industries, and the eight-hour day was instituted in October 1918, in effect requiring that additional hours had to paid at a time-and-a-half rate. The board was also empowered to settle labor-management disputes in defense industries, in at least one case making an unusually assertive decision. After hearing the issues of machinists at one Bethlehem Steel plant, the board ordered the company to institute shop committees and to stop interfering with union activities. While the steel magnates felt threatened by this intrusion of the federal government and the increased power of their employees, the workers and union organizers realized that they at last had some muscle.[12]

Still, the steel corporations did well during the war. Lackawanna Steel's net earnings skyrocketed from $8 million in 1915 to $17 million in 1916 to $33.8 million in 1918. After the war, the War Labor Board was disbanded and the federal government no longer provided assistance to organized labor. Lackawanna Steel and the other companies were free to return to their authoritarian ways. Throughout the country in 1919, almost half the steelworkers, including those in Lackawanna, continued to suffer the 12-hour workday and the seven-day work week. One study calculated the average work week for all steelworkers to be just under 69 hours. While the wages of steelworkers increased by between 25% and 45% during the war, the cost of living had risen by 70%. Unionists in Lackawanna and throughout the country, encouraged by their wartime gains, prepared to organize the steelworkers. In 1919, the steelworkers of Lackawanna displayed an energy and solidarity for the union movement that would have dumbfounded the western New York industrial magnates of 1900.[13]

"The year 1919," according to one historian, "was the worst year for industrial strife that the United States had ever known." Throughout the nation more than 4 million workers were involved in 2,665 strikes. Most of these were local struggles, such as that of 16,000 harbor workers in New York City who struck in January of that year. Other strikes, however, had nationwide effects. In February, a strike of metal workers in the shipyards of Seattle, Washington, led to a general strike that paralyzed the city for five days. In Boston, policemen struck for higher wages, but state troopers were called in and the strike was defeated. Later that month, steelworkers throughout the nation went on strike, and in November, the coal miners followed suit. Conservative Americans came to view the number and scope of the strikes as threatening to the nation and condemned all unionists as radicals. Corporations and local and state governments set out to defeat the rise of working-class unions, and the Great Steel Strike of 1919 was the epic battle fought in this contest.[14]

The Great Steel Strike of 1919

In 1918, representatives of the AAISTW and 23 other unions met in Chicago and, under the AFL umbrella, set up the National Organizing Committee for Iron and Steel Workers. The committee divided the steel industry into 11 districts, including one for the Buffalo area, and established a steelworkers council in each. By January 1919, organizers were active in each district. Lackawanna Steel reacted by suddenly cutting its production by half, shutting down several blast furnaces, and limiting some workers to three- or four-day weeks while laying off others. The pro-labor *Lackawanna Daily Journal* observed, "But the situation looks to us as tho [sic] these men will go back to work at a VERY much lower wage than they laid off under and much lower than they have received in the past three years." Lackawanna Steel further attempted to destabilize the plant's workforce by dismissing experienced workers and keeping on newer people who could be more easily manipulated. Employees told the *Daily Journal*:

> If you have been working at the 'Plant' 17 years you are laid off, out right.
>
> If you have been there 8 years you work 3 days a week.
>
> If you are a foreigner only in this country a few years you work steady, you become a part of the retained force.

In March, pressured by the U.S. Labor Department and the AFL, Lackawanna Steel and other companies returned to the eight-hour day, but this lasted only briefly. Lackawanna's April layoffs brought the total of unemployed men to fully half its workforce of 12,000. The *Daily Journal* saw this as an effort to "bring the unemployed to their knees."[15]

The steel plant used its political leverage to prevent union meetings in Lackawanna. Organizers were denied use of a rental hall, and their advance payment was returned. So on February 20, the organizers held a mass meeting of Lackawanna workers in South Buffalo. There was no mention of the event in the *Lackawanna News*, the city's official organ. When workers attempted to distribute handbills announcing union meetings, Lackawanna Steel's police officers confiscated the papers and destroyed them. A local of the International Switchmen's Union, whose membership included 150 SBR switchmen, invited all Lackawanna steelworkers to attend its regular meeting in the city. The Lackawanna police, however, stating that the hall's owner saw this as a violation of the union's lease, allowed entry only to card-carrying members of the switchmen's local. Despite this harassment, 1,500 workers at Lackawanna Steel and 500 at the nearby Donner Steel and Wickwire plants signed up for the union by early March, and the Seneca Steel plant in Blasdell, unionized in 1915, became 100% union.[16]

Four AFL organizers, including I. Liberti, visited Lackawanna to protest the city's blocking of meetings. They vowed that the AFL would back a "union workingman ticket" in the city elections that fall. The union leaders later petitioned the Lackawanna Common Council for permission to hold public meetings in the city, but the council avoided the issue by referring the matter to the police department. In addition to the city government, many businesspeople were also against the union drive, fearing labor conflict would cause the plant to retaliate against the whole city. When AAISTW organizer, William Griffiths, arrived in Lackawanna, he avoided the snooping of company spies by registering in a series of boardinghouses under assumed names. Aware that immigrants composed 80% of the plant's workforce, and that Poles were the largest ethnic group in the city, Griffiths brought in a Polish-speaking colleague, and they secretly met with workers in bars, rooming houses, and social clubs. In July, the union

set up an office at 16 Ingham Avenue, just off Ridge Road in the heavily Polish section north of the Italian colony. Several Amalgamated locals were formed in Lackawanna—Loyalty Lodge No. 15, Blast Furnace Workers No. 290, and, a while later the Queen City Lodge No. 16 in South Buffalo, composed of workers at Donner Steel.[17]

With fewer obstacles from the city council, the union organizers initiated a series of mass meetings at the A. C. Theater, located at the intersection of Kirby and Electric avenues in a Polish neighborhood east of the railroad tracks. Even the *Lackawanna News* announced the first gathering, held on August 2. Polish speakers and translators were usually on the agenda, and hundreds of steelworkers attended and joined the union. William Z. Foster, secretary treasurer of the national organizing committee, spoke at the August 23rd meeting. Some meeting notices in the *Daily Journal* were in Polish, and the paper printed several articles by William Griffiths. The organizers sought to allay fears of company spies, called "spotters," by placing a spotlight on the stage of the A. C. Theater "and as fast as a Steel Plant 'spotter' is located in the audience the 'spot' will be turned on him." In August, the Lackawanna Steel Plant laid off 600 men under the pretense of slack orders for steel. This helped union recruiting, and in mid-September, an estimated 80 to 90% of the unskilled and semiskilled steelworkers had joined the union and voted to strike unless the following 12 demands were met:

1. The right of collective bargaining
2. The reinstatement of men discharged for union activities
3. An eight-hour workday
4. One day's rest in seven
5. The abolition of the 24-hour shift
6. An increase in wages sufficient to guarantee an American standard of living
7. Standard scales of wages in all trades and classifications of workers
8. Double rate of pay for all overtime, holiday, and Sunday work
9. A check-off system of collecting union dues and assessments
10. The principle of seniority to apply in maintenance, reduction, and increase of working forces
11. The abolition of company unions
12. The abolition of physical examination of applicants for employment

When the steel barons refused to negotiate, the union called for a nationwide strike to commence on September 22, 1919.[18]

Anticipating the strike, Lackawanna Police Department Chief Gilson had his men raid all the city's saloons, arresting

The union office at 16 Ingham Avenue was set up in July 1919. The union held many small meetings at the A.C. theater at Electric and Kirby avenues. Both neighborhoods were heavily Polish. Photo source: Buffalo & Erie County Public Library, Buffalo Evening Times, 9/13/19

On September 22, some 17,000 workers in the Buffalo area—including 4,000 of the 7,000 at Lackawanna Steel and all 500 at the Rogers Brown Iron Company—walked off the job. Seneca Steel in Blasdell was not struck, because the workers who had organized an AAISTW local four years earlier honored their contract with the company. On September 23, another 2,000 Lackawanna Steel workers joined the strikers, and 50 SBR switchmen went home because there was no work for them to do. The plant all but closed down. On that same day, 3,000 strikers confronted company security forces at Three Gate. Mary Fusco, who with her mother operated a confectionery store on Gates Avenue, witnessed strikers throwing rocks and yelling as two plant policemen emerged from Three Gate and headed toward a streetcar. One of them, Buffalonian Angelo Giobbetti, testified that when the crowd moved toward him and the other officer, other plant-security officers opened fire, and he himself drew his revolver and fired into the air "just to scare the people." Plant policemen posted at openings behind the tall wooden fence that ran along Hamburg Turnpike fired 50 to 100 shots. Police chief Gilson, who with his men was standing among the strikers and trying to calm them, ordered the plant officers to stop shooting, but not before two Polish American strikers were killed by gunfire and two other men and a three-year-old boy were wounded.[20]

Tony Grasso was among the teenagers who went to Three Gate to support the strikers and watch the action. As things heated up, they threw rocks at the company security guards. When the company police opened fire, Grasso and his companions hid behind several buildings. Another teenager, Joe Milano, was walking near the intersection of Gates Avenue and Hamburg Turnpike when he saw Police chief Gilson and his men trying to stop strikers from throwing rocks at men entering the plant grounds. After Milano heard the shots ring out, he too ran for cover behind a store. He recalls that the Lackawanna police were trying to protect the people gathered on the east side of Hamburg Turnpike. Following the shooting incident, Grasso ceased his involvement with the pickets, as both he and Milano had learned a lesson about the power of violence. Milano also noted the power of political connections when he found out that Harry Kelley, a mill superintendent and the city's

several saloon keepers in the process—likely one of the few times the police strongly enforced ordinances regarding drinking establishments. The chief also increased his force from 20 to 70 men by hiring special officers. Lackawanna Steel hired two former police chiefs to lead its own 80-man police force and added 100 more special officers through the Washington Detective Agency. Across the street from the Lackawanna plant, the Rogers Brown Iron Company plant had 35 officers. The National Guard and the county sheriff were put on alert. Lackawanna Mayor John Toomey displayed his antiunion sentiments when he spoke of businessmen being fearful: "Many of these merchants have been openly threatened by the Bolshevik elements we have out here … The foreigners told them when the strike begins they will help themselves to everything in the stores unless the merchants permit them to have everything they want, whether they pay for it or not." No such looting came to pass, but three days before the strike, new members of the AAISTW marched through the streets of the city despite Mayor Toomey's consistent refusal to grant parade permits. The Lackawanna Steel Company confidently predicted that no more than 15% of its workers would strike. On the day before the strike, a mass meeting of steelworkers was held at the Labor Temple in Buffalo, with many Lackawannans attending. According to the Buffalo Express, the overflow crowd included " [sic], Poles, Italians, Spaniards, Bulgarians, Russians, Hungarians and many other nationalities."[19]

A collage of photos showing the huge turnout of strikers for the funeral of one of the two men killed by Lackawanna Steel police officers. Photo source: Buffalo & Erie County Public Library, *Buffalo Evening Times*, 9/26/19

Democratic party boss, was instrumental in calling in the state troopers to subdue the strikers.[21]

The *Buffalo Commercial* was outraged by "the riot" and criticized the city for not providing more policemen to contain the large group of strikers—

> particularly in view of their being for the most part ignorant foreigners, the scum of their native lands transported here without any real knowledge of American ideas of liberty or law observance, and as such easily, and certain to be, incited to violence of the worst order.

Pressing on with its tirade, the article further condemned Lackawanna's immigrants as "baffled foreigners" with "shrunken minds ... who can be counted upon to continue the present reign of lawlessness until they meet a show of overwhelming force, and see what happens to their type of thug in this land of individual freedom...." Most of the other Buffalo newspapers were also hostile to the strikers, one claiming that the first shot in the September 23rd incident was "fired by a striker." But the editor of the *Lackawanna Daily Journal*, socialist and ex-steelworker Charles Ellis, was solidly behind the union movement. He challenged Mayor's Toomey's

WANTED

IRON STEEL AND TIN WORKERS
Carpenters Laborers Machinists and Craftsmen of all kinds to keep Away From Lackawanna

STRIKE ON HERE

"Strikers wanted" ad. Source: Lackawanna Library, *Lackawanna Daily Journal*, 10/23/19

LACKAWANNA
is composed of
AMERICAN (loyal)
CITIZENS
— not —
FOREIGNERS
CURRAN

An ad by union supporter. Source: Lackawanna Library, *Lackawanna Daily Journal*, 12/17/19

characterization of the September 23rd shootings as a riot, claiming "there has never been a riot in this city and the mayor knows it." Ellis covered events that were barely noted in the Buffalo papers, including the funeral of one of the slain strikers, Casimer Mazurek, a decorated World War I veteran. The service included a procession of 7,000 mourners marching behind the horse-drawn wagon carrying Mazurek's coffin. The Polish consul and Lackawanna Post No. 63 of the American Legion, of which Mazurek had been a member, demanded an investigation into the incident. When labor radical Mother Jones visited Lackawanna on October 2, she met with strike leaders in an attempt to boost the morale of strikers and also visited Ellis's newspaper office. Fifteen strikers were charged with inciting the September 23rd "riot," but these charges were later dropped. Later in October, strikers battled with strikebreakers traveling to the plant by trolley from Buffalo, and many men on both sides brandished weapons. Buffalo police with shotguns began to ride the trolley cars, and the Lackawanna police and state troopers strictly enforced laws and cleared the streets. Strikers like Angelo Calabrese and Joseph Mangino as well as men who continued to work were charged with disorderly conduct for carrying weapons.[22]

The strikers received encouragement when the Lake Erie seamen went on a sympathy strike, and ore boats were idled in both Buffalo and Lackawanna. In November, a brief strike by the United Mineworkers Union offered another momentary image of increased worker solidarity. Father Baker, head of the Our Lady of Victory institutions, provided aid for workers evicted from company housing, and a union commissary passed out food and other essentials to the striking men and their families. Rallies continued to draw up to 3,000 union men at the newly opened Dom Polski hall, but time was on the side of Lackawanna Steel and the other steel companies.[23]

The *Daily Journal*, which had attacked Lackawanna politicians as lackeys of the steel plant, supported socialist candidates for office, including John Gibbons, an SBR engineer, who was running for mayor. Ellis exhorted his readers, "If you do not protect your own interests the steel plant will not." Lackawannans agreed, especially immigrants in the First Ward, and Gibbons won office in the November 4 election. This was a morale booster for the strikers; "immediately we could feel and see the stock in the steel strike rise," said one organizer. The mayor-elect declared his support of the strike, saying steelworkers could look forward to fair treatment by the city's new power structure. After the election in November Gibbons held many meetings to solicit aid for the strikers, but he did not take office until January, too late to help them.[24]

The continual pressure from all sides began to erode the ranks of the union men, though press reports differed onto what extent. In late September and into October, several major newspapers in the area reported that hundreds of strikers were returning to work at Lackawanna Steel, later claiming that the number of strikers in the Buffalo-Lackawanna district fell from 12,000 in September to 5,000 in December. On the other hand, the *Amalgamated Journal* reported in late October that the "men are standing like a rock …" and that "things here are still tied up like a drum, notwithstanding newspaper stories to the contrary." In mid – December, the journal claimed that 9,500 men were still on strike in the Buffalo area. Nationwide, however, the strike was failing; the National Strike Committee counted 365,000 strikers on September 29 but only 109,000 on December 10. Reports by FBI agents operating in the Steel City on November 22 indicated that only 1,500 to 2,000 workers, most of them Russians and Poles, remained on strike. Inside the steel plant, a coal shortage and the inexperience of many strikebreakers reduced production.[25]

The union tried to shore up the morale of the strikers by urging the wives and daughters of strikers to walk the picket lines, as was done at other steel plants. Some Lackawanna merchants offered to extend credit to the strikers and to ask the governor to investigate the deaths of the two strikers in September. By November, however, it was apparent that the strike was doomed and many workers returned to the plant. Lackawanna Steel served eviction notices to about 400 strikers' families in the Old Village and New Village settlements in late October, and on November 1 began the process of evicting workers still on strike. More men then returned to work, and the number grew in December. Following up on its wartime recruiting in the South, Lackawanna Steel and plants in Buffalo brought in 2,000 African American strikebreakers, playing on racial tensions to taunt the strikers to return to work. A number of the blacks apparently quit soon afterwards, some either because the plant paid them less than half the promised hourly rate, some due to the volatility of the strike in Lackawanna.[26]

Despite opposition from city officials, state troopers, and some business and religious leaders, the strikers in Lackawanna held out longer than steelworkers in many other cities. William Z. Foster, national leader of the strike, wrote:

Nowhere in the strike zone was there a more bitter fight than in the Buffalo district. … All the important plants were affected, but the storm centered around the Lackawanna Steel Company. This concern left nothing undone to defeat its workers. For eight months it had prevented any meetings from being held in Lackawanna, and then, when the workers broke through this obstruction and crowded into the unions, it discharged hundreds of them. This put the iron into the workers' hearts, and they made a heroic struggle. So firm were their ranks that when the general strike was called off

With Lackawanna's working men strongly united at the start, mass parades and rallies took place to support them.
Photo source: Lackawanna Library, *Lackawanna Daily Journal*, 10/26/19

on January 8, they voted to continue the fight in Lackawanna. But this was soon seen to be hopeless.

By early January 1920, only 100,000 strikers remained nationwide, and steel production was at about 70% of normal rates. The strike remained active only in Pueblo, Colorado; Joliet, Illinois; scattered mills in Pittsburgh and Cleveland; and Lackawanna, New York. The strike was broken and called off by the national committee on January 8, 1920. None of the workers' demands had been met, and 20 strikers had been killed nationwide. The New York State Troopers left Lackawanna on December 24, but a small detachment returned in early January 1920. Strikers in the city had voted to maintain the picket lines despite the decree of union leaders that the strike was over. In South Buffalo, Donner Steel workers in the Queen City Lodge of AAISTW also voted to continue the strike. The Lackawanna workers continued to picket into late January, but apparently ceased their efforts sometime in February. The Donner Steel strikers were still active at the end of May 1920.[27]

The Italian workers found the strike challenging and confusing, at best. On the one hand, jobs meant security, and they feared losing them. On the other, they recognized the practical benefits of the union. Because many of them could not speak English and their numbers were relatively small, the Italians, as Joe Milano observed, "were in the background, more neutral." The Poles, with their great numbers, and the Irish, with their command of English and greater familiarity with the American workplace, became the leaders of the action. Joe Cosentino, a teenager when he arrived from Calabria,

observed that many Italians honored the strike, some were scabs, and some occasionally sneaked into the plant to work. Indeed, the Italian community did not take a unified stance on the strike. One reason for this was the apparent absence of Italian-speaking organizers in Lackawanna. A daunting challenge for the national strike committee was effectively communicating with the majority of steelworkers who were immigrants and had a limited command of English. The lead union organizer in Gary, Indiana, noted that Romanian and Greek immigrants in that city were not active in the strike because of a lack of organizers who spoke their languages.[28]

One union tactic was to focus organizing efforts on the largest ethnic groups in each plant's workforce. In some cities, such as Youngstown, Ohio, Italians were among the major ethnic groups and were active in the strike. In Lackawanna, eastern Europeans composed the majority of the workforce, so union organizers concentrated on the huge Polish population and brought in Polish-speaking staff. The union office and most meeting sites were in Polish neighborhoods. When Loyalty Lodge No. 15 was founded, its 1,000 members voted in 11 officers, 10 of whom had eastern European surnames. Therefore, Italians could well have felt like outsiders. In a display of ethnic solidarity, striking Polish, Croatian, Serbian, and Hungarian workers announced plans in December to form a cement block company in the First Ward. There was no mention of Italians in this enterprise. Several *Lackawanna Daily Journal* articles in Polish and other eastern European languages urged the strikers on. One article in Italian, which appeared in late December, besieged Italians not to be scabs.[29]

Many Italians did honor the strike, for a variety of reasons. Gaetano Milano, who lived on Ingham Avenue, feared the potential for violence near the steel plant, so he kept his distance. As noted earlier, his son Joe had seen strikers on Ridge Road throwing stones at streetcars carrying scabs. Other Italians feared the wrath of their numerous eastern European neighbors who were in many cases staunch supporters of the strike. When a Lackawanna Steel representative told Michele Grasso to report for work or move out of his company-owned dwelling, Grasso moved his family from the New Village to Buffalo, as did Antonio Core and his family. In so doing, each family avoided, on the one hand, being evicted and, on the other, being branded strikebreakers by their Slavic neighbors. Michele Grasso and his son Tony were among the many strikers who took jobs in Buffalo and surrounding towns. Gaetano Milano found temporary work on a construction job in Buffalo; his 16-year-old son Joe was a waterboy for the crew. In September 1919, teenager Nunze Oddy had just transferred from a messenger-boy job in the plant to one in the roll shop in addition to helping his mother run the family grocery store. He and two other Italian American youths honored the strike and secured temporary work in nearby Bayview. Another alternative for foreign-born steelworkers was simply to leave the country. One newspaper reported that 20 to 30 local immigrants were returning to Europe each day, wanting no part of labor strife. True to this trend, many Italians left Lackawanna for Italy between November 1918, when World War I ended, and January 1920, some no doubt because of the strike.[30]

A number of Italians continued to work in the plant and, along with other nonstrikers, crossed picket lines or sneaked into the plant. Some of them, like Antonio Pacillo, lived inside the plant and occasionally went home to visit their families. In late September, police chief Gilson stated that men in the Old Village wanted to work and that his officers would protect them as they entered the plant. The steel company, which had already threatened striking skilled workers in the New Village with eviction, later made similar threats to striking unskilled workers in the Old Village. Some Italian residents there were intimidated and reported for work throughout the strike. The Croce family lived on Second Street, and 10-year-old Al Croce watched as "company goons" went to strikers' homes and threw their furniture into the street. New York State Troopers were stationed at Second and B streets in the Old Village to patrol the area. Croce recalls troopers on horseback escorting a column of workers down Second Street and right into Four Gate. Among the men entering the plant were his father, Angelo Croce, and other Italian and Polish residents of the Old Village. During the strike, the elder Croce changed his name to hide the fact that he was a strikebreaker, and for the rest of his life,

his fellow workers knew him by his assumed name, Tony George. Francesco Ginnetti, who also lived on Second Street, observed that when strikebreakers entered and exited the gate to the plant, the wives of Polish strikers blew black pepper from their palms into the men's faces.[31]

For Italians who did work, the usually dangerous mills became even more so as men were assigned unfamiliar jobs, making accidents more common. The *Daily Journal* reported that scab laborers were producing a "great lot of scrap" that was "unfit for manufacturing purposes." The laborers were "completely demoralized" by the strike, according to one account by a union leader who went on to say,

> The Negroes are quarreling and all the scabs are jealous of one another. The Italians who are going in to work stay a few hours and walk out again. When they get inside they line up for coffee and rations consisting of two sandwiches. … After eating it they beat it outside. There is no semblance of discipline among the men in the mill whatever.

Often the Italians who honored the picket lines had a long and sometimes difficult wait for the strike's outcome. In the Old Village, Giacinto Moretti and his brother-in-law, Alessandro Cosentino, honored the picket lines despite the company's threats of eviction, and they endured the mounted state troopers who were quick to use their batons. By November and December, Italians and others who supported the strike saw that it was in serious trouble and began reporting back to work. Gaetano and Joe Milano and Michele and Tony Grasso were among them. When Joe Milano returned to the plant, he reported to the storehouse, where a large supply of sandwiches was stored for strikebreakers living on the plant grounds. He and other returning workers were allowed to help themselves to the food.[32]

Life in Lackawanna during the strike was tense and unpredictable for all the city's inhabitants. State troopers, labeled "cossacks" by the eastern Europeans, were ever present. They established a strike zone near the plant where only residents of the area were allowed to enter. The troopers patrolled the streets, ensuring that no more than two people gathered at a time. They even attempted to prohibit discussion of the strike in saloons and pool halls. While helping at his mother's grocery store, Nunze Oddy recalled four state troopers coming into the store to warm up as the winter weather set in. He observed them patrolling the streets on horseback, always in pairs of two, breaking up any type of public gathering and going to great lengths to keep men off the streets. Joe Milano, who heard the troopers threaten to use their clubs on anyone who was slow to respond, and them drive men back into Amorosi's and Turchiarelli's taverns by spurring their

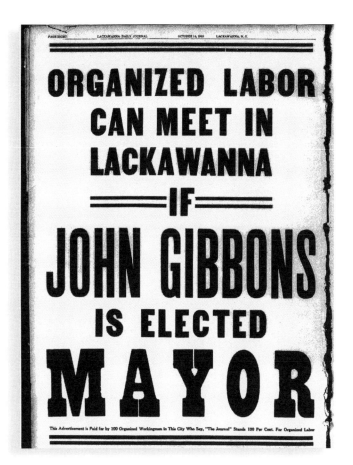

ORGANIZED LABOR CAN MEET IN LACKAWANNA ═IF═ JOHN GIBBONS IS ELECTED MAYOR

In the November 1919 election, Lackawanna working men elected Socialist John Gibbons as mayor, but the strike was lost by the time he took office. Photo source: Lackawanna Library, *Lackawanna Daily Journal*, 10/14/19

horses right into the front doors of the establishments. News and rumors spread quickly through Lackawanna. Nunze Oddy heard that when strikers turned over a streetcar and state troopers intervened, two strikers died of gunshot wounds. Al Croce was told that a woman walked up to a mounted state trooper at Three Gate and offered him a glass of water. When he leaned over to accept it, she threw the contents of the glass—hot pepper—in his face. As the woman fled up some nearby stairs, so the story went, the trooper shot and killed her. No verification could be found for either of these incidents in the local newspapers.[33]

The strike did provide some Italians with unexpected opportunities. When nine-year-old Ralph D'Amore, who lived with his family in the Old Village, observed the state troopers stationed nearby, he and some enterprising friends sneaked wine from their parents' basements and sold it by the quart to the troopers. Peter Mazuca was one of the special security officers hired by Lackawanna Steel. After a Polish grocery-store operator in the Old Village was evicted for extending credit to the strikers, Mazuca convinced company officials to allow him to take over the store. He and his family moved in

next door to the shop and established a successful business. Some of the nonstriking Old Village residents living in the two-bedroom units east of A Street apparently moved into the larger units west of A Street as strikers were evicted.[34]

The Great Steel Strike had brought home to Italians the tough realities of industrial work and the power of large corporations and the government. An immediate consequence for some men who had been strikers was that they were not allowed to return to work after the strike ended. Natale Chiodo was not called back to work by the South Buffalo Railway for a long time. Plus, there were long-term consequences of the strike that affected workers' attitudes. One study, concluding that many workers came to believe that local government officials tried to break strikes and that most newspapers exerted a strikebreaking influence, reported: "The steel strike made tens of thousands of citizens believe that our American institutions are not democratic or not democratically administered." In Lackawanna, there was also a positive lesson about democracy. Ethnic voters helped elect a Socialist mayor that November who pledged to respect workers and their unions. Whatever their positions during the strike, Italians gained a heightened sense of being part of the multiethnic working class that was at the mercy of local and state police forces backing corporations such as Lackawanna Steel—a point literally driven home by state troopers riding their horses into bars and freely using batons on anyone who didn't move quickly. Despite the roller-coaster ride from wartime job opportunities to antiforeigner agitation by the American power structure to the bitter strike following the war, many Italians decided to settle permanently in Lackawanna. Ralph D'Amore recalls hearing the whistles blow at the plant when the strike ended—a sound marking the passing of one era into another. His generation would be instrumental two decades later in finally winning the right to collective bargaining. But the time between the demise of the steel strike and the formation of the Congress of Industrial Organizations in 1936 was a long, tough period for industrial workers.[35]

Italian steelworkers in Lackawanna heard of the defeat of other local and national strikes in the early 1920s, and, like other working people, were reminded that local police, state troopers, and the federal government invariably sided with the corporations. The AAISTW lost credibility and by the early 1930s was competing with other unions to sign up steelworkers, in addition to contending with company unions. The Great Depression added to the poststrike sense of malaise, devastating working-class communities and leaving many unemployed. A commission that investigated the Great Steel Strike noted that the steel industry had used every means possible to fill the mills with immigrants since the 1890s. It noted, "When the large corporations put these foreigners in they thought they

FIGURE 8.2

STATE TROOPERS BATTLE AGAINST UNIONS

The New York State unit of the National Guard, like those in other states, had often been called out when local authorities seemed inadequate to handle situations, such as during strikes. The New York National Guard, in an attempt to anticipate labor unrest, made plans for intervening in a possible strike at the Lackawanna Steel plant while the facility was being constructed. However, calling out the National Guard or state militia, a regular occurrence until early in the twentieth century, was an expensive proposition and sometimes raised the ire of local citizens. Further, corporation heads feared that working-class militiamen might be loyal to their striking brothers.

State police forces were formed to replace the militias. The first such force, founded in 1905, was the Pennsylvania State Police, whose motto was "one state policeman should be able to handle a hundred foreigners." This exaggerated boast accurately conveyed the antiforeigner and antiunion sentiments of state police forces. A proposal by the New York State Chamber of Commerce led to the founding of the New York State Police in 1916. The leaders saw strike-handling as part of their duties and recruited only men with horseback experience who were trained in using horses to break up strikes. The state police soon showed its mettle, intervening in strikes more quickly and

effectively than the state militia had in the past. In the 1919 strike by metal workers in Rome, New York, state troopers on horseback charged at groups of strikers to disperse them. "The state police," wrote Gerda Ray, "destroyed the entire strike's organization by forbidding people from congregating, but they concentrated on the Italian workers who made up about half of those on strike. Almost all the people arrested were Italian, and they received severe sentences." Two months later, the State Police were in Lackawanna riding their horses into saloons. The state troopers and the steel plant's police were under joint command, and "the state police colluded with private forces to avoid prosecution of the company detective who had shot and killed a striker."

Attempting to anticipate conflict in advance, the State Police sought information during its daily patrols, sending officers to survey potential trouble spots. On August 29, 1919, four mounted troopers appeared in Lackawanna, prompting the *Daily Journal* to ask, "Why are the state police here in numbers?" Continuing, the article observes, "Our [police] department has not yet signified that the city was beyond their control. No trouble of any sort has followed the wholesale lay-off at the plant." At the same time, the steel plant hired Michael Regan, ex-police chief of Buffalo, to lead

its private police force, an act that the *Daily Journal* said was "like putting a red flag in front of a bull … There will be no fighting in Lackawanna unless the plant fires the first shot," which is what occurred three weeks later.

In 1922, the state police sent in plainclothes officers prior to the strikes of the Buffalo streetcar workers and the railway shopmen, which occurred at the same time. The state troopers worked directly with railroad detectives, who shot and killed one striker and wounded a woman and two children in Buffalo. State troopers drove through city streets in a truck mounted with a machine gun and freely used their batons. When troopers were criticized for breaking one man's arm and fracturing the skull of another, State Police Superintendent George Chandler responded that his troopers were "teaching respect for the law." The State Police continued to be allied with the corporations' private police forces and increased these alliances in the following years. "By the 1940s, New York State Police were attending meetings in plainclothes, taking photographs of organizers, gathering detailed intelligence about union and radical activity, and exchanging information with private police on a regular basis." The State Police took on an expanded role in highway patrol but retained its function of policing labor relations.

Sources: Gerda W. Ray, " 'We Can Stay Until Hell Freezes Over': Strike Control and the State Police in New York, 1919 – 1923," *Labor History*, Volume 37, No. 3, pp. 404 (1st quote), 413, 417, 419 (2nd quote), 420-21 (3rd & 7th quotes), 422-23, 424 (6th quote); *Lackawanna Daily Journal*, 8/30/19 (4th & 5th quotes)..

had a class of men who wouldn't strike. Now they want to get rid of some of them." By 1920, the steel corporations were again able to control their workers, and that May, Lackawanna Steel discharged some employees who attempted to honor a strike by railroad switchmen. When railroad shopmen launched a nationwide strike in 1922, concerted action by the railroad magnates and the federal government defeated them. State police, federal militia, and U.S. marshals protected the strikebreakers entering the rail yards, and federal court

injunctions charged the strikers with conspiracy. At the same time, a strike by Buffalo streetcar workers was broken, with state troopers causing many casualties with their batons. It must have been very clear to Italian and other steelworkers in Lackawanna that President Harding's administration, and that of the state government, was willing to use overwhelming force to battle strikers.[36]

As new federal laws in 1921 and 1924 curtailed European immigration, the steel plant in Lackawanna, purchased in 1922 by Bethlehem Steel, brought in more black and Mexican workers to fill the gaps. This further ethnic diversification of the workforce served the company's goal of undermining worker solidarity. Secure in their 1919 victory over union agitators but with new respect for the potential of their immigrant workers, to unite, the steel corporations launched a series of programs to placate workers and prevent any further effort to create unions. Dubbed "the American Plan" by industry leaders, it included such steps as increasing wages, forming cooperative clubs, and building new employee housing. These benefits could be withdrawn at any time by the steel executives, however, as the workers had no organization through which to protest. In early 1921, for example, most steel companies slashed wages by as much as 20%, leaving steelworkers earning 30 cents per hour. In January 1922, Lackawanna Steel made another wage cut, this one a 15% reduction, then awarded a 20% raise in August. One long-standing grievance of the workers, however, was pursued by the federal government. In 1922, President Harding urged steel executives to abolish the 12-hour workday. The steel magnates dragged their feet for a year, but public outrage fueled by newspapers and religious organizations forced them to abolish the 12-hour day. These and other changes were felt in Lackawanna, where Bethlehem Steel began to modernize the mills, construct the Bethlehem Park housing development for workers, and offer other worker "welfare" programs.[37]

The Company Union

At the heart of the steel industry's so-called American Plan was the company union. Such an organization is "a union in name only because it is fostered, financed, and dominated by management to discourage a bona fide union from being organized." Bethlehem Steel introduced its version of a company union, called the Employee Representation Plan (ERP), at all its plants by 1919, and brought it to Lackawanna when it took over the plant there in 1922. Under this plan, employee representatives elected from each department met regularly with company superintendents to discuss a variety of topics. In November 1924, Joe Milano was elected to sit on the ERP by Unit 6 of the mechanical division, which included the blacksmith, babbitt, and mechanical repair shops. The next year, he was one of 37 men chosen to represent the entire plant, each speaking for 200 workers. Most of the employee representatives had Irish, English, or German surnames, but at least one other seemed to share Milano's Italian roots. Frank Columbus, who claimed to be a direct descendant of Christopher Columbus, was one of three employee representatives of the South Buffalo Railway from 1923 until at least 1926. A skilled

public speaker, he was elected chairman of the general body of employee representatives, sometimes concurrently acting as its spokesman (ironically, Columbus, a locomotive engineer, was at the same time an official in a real union, the Brotherhood of Locomotive Firemen and Enginemen.) The annual ERP conference featured a dinner and series of speakers, most of whom were Bethlehem Steel administrators. In 1926, the 10 speakers included ERP chair Frank Columbus and two other employees. Among the seven administrative speakers were plant manager Timothy Burns, the lead-off speaker, and Eugene Grace, the president of Bethlehem Steel, who gave the final address.[38]

Each Bethlehem steel plant had an industrial relations manager, such as N. B. Ludlum at the Lackawanna plant, who acted as a liaison with the ERP group. The workers' representatives and superintendents were divided into committees, whose intricate titles promised more than the structure of the company union could deliver:

1. Appeals
2. Rules, Ways, and Means
3. Wages, Piece Work, Bonus, and Tonnage Schedules; Practice Methods and Economy; Employment and Working Conditions
4. Safety and Prevention of Accidents; Health and Works Sanitation; Pensions and Relief; Athletics and Recreation
5. Transportation, Housing, Domestic Economies, Living Conditions, Education and Publications, Continuous Employment and Condition of Industry

The committees reported on their deliberations at the monthly meetings of the general body. *Iron Age*, the magazine of the steel industry, boasted of the trusting atmosphere in the plants due to the American Plan and claimed that the majority of the 2,365 "cases" discussed by the committees between 1918 and 1923 were settled in favor of the employees. But the basic concerns of workers were rarely discussed, and the workers knew the process was a sham. Employee representatives never met alone; company representatives were always present. Both during the workday and in the taverns after work, foremen and company spies monitored employees' actions and conversations. One worker said of the ERP, "Too much boss, not enough union," while another stated that he "found out that the ERP was nothing but something to keep track of the men. It was no benefit." Joe Milano and other employee representatives did bring up issues related to safety, seniority, overly strict actions by foremen, and the lack of lunchrooms and showers. Milano felt the ERP was instrumental in getting "welfare buildings" constructed to provide washing and eating facilities for workers. The wage committee discussed tonnage

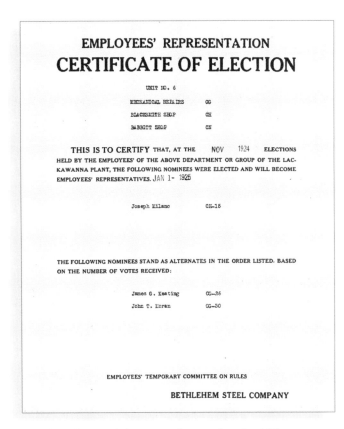

EMPLOYEES' REPRESENTATION
CERTIFICATE OF ELECTION

UNIT NO. 6

MECHANICAL REPAIRS	CG
BLACKSMITH SHOP	CH
BABBITT SHOP	CN

THIS IS TO CERTIFY THAT, AT THE NOV 1924 ELECTIONS HELD BY THE EMPLOYEES' OF THE ABOVE DEPARTMENT OR GROUP OF THE LAC-KAWANNA PLANT, THE FOLLOWING NOMINEES WERE ELECTED AND WILL BECOME EMPLOYEES' REPRESENTATIVES. JAN 1- 1925

Joseph Milano   CH-15

THE FOLLOWING NOMINEES STAND AS ALTERNATES IN THE ORDER LISTED. BASED ON THE NUMBER OF VOTES RECEIVED:

James G. Keating   CG-26

John T. Moran   CG-50

EMPLOYEES' TEMPORARY COMMITTEE ON RULES

BETHLEHEM STEEL COMPANY

This certificate of election indicates that Joe Milano was duly elected to represent Unit 6 of the Mechanical Division with the ERP. Photo source: Collection of Joe Milano

The Employee Representation Plan (ERP) was one of the tools Bethlehem Steel used to discourage a true union. The representatives were often picked by foremen or superintendents, and important matters such as wages could never be discussed. Joe Milano (second row, 3rd from left) was actually elected by coworkers to the ERP, and he served in this role in 1925. Also involved with ERP that year was Frank Columbus (front row, 4th from right), who claimed to be a direct descendant of Christopher Columbus. Photo source: Collection of Joe Milano

and piecework rates, but no employee representative actually checked the daily calculations of the weighmen or foremen. Both Milano and Frank Scaletta, who represented South Buffalo Railway track workers, recalled that the worker-superintendent discussions might have addressed safety and new buildings, but not wages. The company did not share information on wages or other financial matters, and it was only through workers migrating from one district to another that Lackawanna steelworkers learned their wages were lower than those at many other plants. The men in Lackawanna saw no wage increases between 1923 and 1926. In the latter year, a proposed wage cut in one department was deadlocked in the wage committee. All employee representatives on the committee voted against it, fearing it foretold a plant-wide wage cut; all company superintendents voted for it. The plan was finally sent to Bethlehem's president, Eugene Grace, who eventually instituted a series of actions that nibbled away at piece rates, one department at a time.[39]

The Bethlehem Steel brass made much of the fact that most company workers participated in ERP elections; 87% of them voted in the 1923 election. A Polish immigrant explained why participation was so high: " 'Foremen make us vote, Got to go to 'lection. Boss say, You vote or you no good.' " Workers were often reluctant to get involved in the ERP; Frank Scaletta said he was virtually appointed by his foreman as the representative from the SBR Track Department. As it pushed for the Americanization of its workers, Bethlehem appeared to favor those born in the United States. In 1927, the company bragged that 90% of the 306 workers on all its ERP councils were American-born and that the remainder had declared their intentions to become citizens.[40]

The American Plan of Bethlehem Steel and other steel companies included other strategies to pacify workers and discourage any attempts to form real unions. In 1923, Bethlehem started a pension plan for employees with a minimum of 25 years of service and who were at least 65 years old. President Eugene Grace, at the annual meeting of the Lackawanna plant's ERP in January 1924, announced that Bethlehem would offer workers the opportunity to buy shares of company stock. The corporation pushed the program, but only 29% of Bethlehem's 70,000 employees nationwide

FIGURE 8.3

FRANK COLUMBUS, A DESCENDANT OF CHRISTOPHER COLUMBUS?

Frank S. Columbus (1885–1972) was born in Buffalo. He assisted his father in the hotel business, then, at age 16, started working as a wiper for the Buffalo, Rochester, and Pittsburgh Railroad. Three years later, he joined the South Buffalo Railway as a locomotive fireman. He was promoted to engineer in 1905, a job he kept until his retirement in 1960. Columbus joined the Brotherhood of Locomotive Firemen and Enginemen (BLFE) in 1905, was secretary of the Allied Railroad Organizations during the 1920s, and was chairman of the New York State Legislative Board of the BLFE from 1934 to 1958. He was a mediator for the National War Labor Board during World War II and served on the New York State Anti-Discrimination Commission. Columbus was the first labor leader named as a trustee of Cornell University and was a member of the Central Railway Club of Buffalo.

His grandfather, Alexius Columbus, was born in 1789 in Montreal to a French family. He married Mary Pomelia Dairy, and in about 1840, they settled in South Buffalo, where they raised 11 children. Alexius Columbus worked as a carpenter in a shipbuilding yard and lived to be more than 111 years old, dying in 1901. Family members later found records that traced their lineage back to the marriage of Jacques Colombe and Boemie Drieu in Normandy, France, in about 1640. Louis Colombe, the son of this couple, was living in Montreal by 1670. When he died, his daughter, Mrs. Elizabeth Baker, claimed that he was the great-great-great-great-grandson of Christopher Columbus. She stated that the lineage went back to Diego Columbus, the son of the famous explorer, whose descendants learned the shipbuilder trade and passed it on, with Alexius being the final recipient. This scenario assumed that one of the Columbus family members eventually moved from Spain to France. These claims, however, could be not confirmed through documents.

Source: Interviews with Tony Grasso, July 16, 1990; and Joe Milano, December 27, 1989

had purchased stock by the end of 1925. Four years later, Bethlehem claimed that half its nationwide workforce of 60,000 had purchased stock since the program began. Modest yearly bonuses were given to employee stockholders, but with the notice of earnings, each man received a voting proxy form to sign. Realizing that President Grace and his cronies would cast the proxy votes to benefit themselves, many workers came to question the company's motives, withdrew their investments, and deposited the money in the bank.[41]

Bethlehem's Relief Plan, launched in 1926, required every employee to make monthly contributions ($1 to $2.50, depending on annual earnings), which yielded a sick benefit of $10 to $12 per week and a death benefit of $500 to $1,500 for the family. Bethlehem Steel boasted that in its first three years, the

Members of the Employee Representation Plan (ERP), the company union, 1926. Frank Columbus (front row, 3rd from right) also belonged to a real union—the Brotherhood of Locomotive Firemen and Enginemen – throughout the time he was in Bethlehem Steel's employer-controlled company union.
Photo source: Steel Plant Museum

plan had paid out more than $2 million in benefits. However, the plan had a big catch: "Injury is one of the serious problems in the life of the steel worker. It is his chief dread. ... But in his compulsory policy, he is informed that this plan does not apply to any injury covered by the various compensation acts." Workers in Lackawanna knew that the steel company took in more than $6,700 per month in 1926, when the workforce totaled 6,700 men, but questioned whether an injured man would receive any of the money he paid in. For an employee in the lowest income group, the monthly payments could equal 1% or more of his wages.[42]

Another project that the steel plant hoped would win over its workers was the Bethlehem Park housing tract, built in 1923 and 1924. Here, workers could purchase relatively inexpensive detached homes in an attractive neighborhood. The homes were paid for by regular deductions from workers' paychecks, as a type of rent with an option to buy. If a worker left the employment of Bethlehem, however, he lost all credit toward the purchase. The company also initiated an accident-prevention and first-aid-training program that featured competitions and prizes. Sadly, none of these programs met the most basic needs of the workers. After interviewing many Lackawanna steelworkers in 1926, Louis Budenz, managing editor of *Labor Age* magazine, summarized what the men really wanted:

1. The right to join the Amalgamated Association of Iron, Steel, and Tin Workers

2. The abolition of the labor spy system, including the firing of the Pinkertons, the Corporation Auxiliary Company, and your own private operatives

3. The immediate right to meet in departmental meetings, or in plant meetings, without the presence of the representatives of the Company

4. A union check-weighman for tonnage workers, and a public written guarantee that men will not be fired for membership or activity in unions affiliated with the American Federation of Labor

5. No wage cuts—such as have been threatened—but a marked wage increase, based on the increased productivity of the workers at the Lackawanna Plant[43]

Union advocates in 1926 could point to only a small number of unionized workers at the Lackawanna plant—400 bricklayers, and the South Buffalo Railway engineers, firemen, and switchmen—who were unionized prior to the Great Steel Strike. The AAISTW local at Seneca Steel did continue to function, and even resolved an issue with a one-day strike in 1929. However, the unionization of the vast majority of steelworkers and the basic changes they desired would not take place for another decade. The workers had to endure a harsh situation, including the nasty behavior of Bethlehem Steel's police force, which "treated [the] men worse than dogs." The situation was only made worse by the advent of the Great Depression in 1929. A New York State study found that during 1932, part-time employment was greatest in the iron and steel industry, where 45% of workers fell into this category. The steel corporations lowered wages in 1931 and again in 1932. Bethlehem and other companies also made indirect cuts during this period by firing skilled piece workers,

then rehiring them at a lower rate. The steel financiers had planned another wage cut in March 1933 but postponed it because thousands of auto workers in Detroit had struck in February when their wages were cut. The previous month, 200 workers at the two plants of the Lackawanna Steel Construction Company, a subsidiary of Bethlehem Steel in Buffalo, went on strike when their wages were reduced by 16 cents per hour. The strikers protested that four pay cuts in two years had reduced their income by two-thirds. Two days later the strike was called off after the company president threatened to close down the plants unless the men returned to their jobs. In July of that year, steelworkers' wages nationwide actually rose, but increases in the cost of living left real wages below the 1929 level.[44]

Company unions—at Bethlehem Steel and other plants, such as Republic Steel in South Buffalo—were less active during the Depression. As the economic crisis continued, however, a variety of groups, including many leftists, fought tenant evictions, demanded more relief for the unemployed, and sought to organize workers. In the winter of 1932-33, large parades and protests were held at the lower end of Ridge Road by the Citizens' League of the Unemployed. The group, which had 1,000 members and was strongly communist, had demanded food and clothing from the Temporary Emergency Relief Administration. The league was active in a May Day celebration in 1933, carrying the red flag alongside the stars and stripes. *Steel Struggle*, a newsletter issued by the Communist Party Nucleus of Bethlehem Steel in Lackawanna, urged steelworkers to "organize and strike against wage cuts," referring them to the Metal Workers Industrial League in Buffalo for assistance in drawing up demands and organizing a grievance committee. One worker wrote that "we are forced to slave ten hours a day around the yards for $4.20," noting that 50 men had been laid off the previous week. "We used to get $1.25 an hour," said an iron worker at Bethlehem. "Recently the boss cut our wages to 80 cents an hour and told us that if we didn't want to work for it we could stay at home, that they could get plenty men [sic] who would work for even less."[45]

The AAISTW union had attempted to rally workers several times after the defeat of 1919 but ran into competition from another union. The Metal Workers Industrial League was organized in Pittsburgh in 1929 by workers unhappy with the practices of the AAISTW. The new organization was an industrial union—that is, all crafts and occupations in each plant were combined in a single local. By 1933, the new union boasted a national membership of 14,000. The following year, under its new name—the Steel and Metal Workers Industrial Union (SMWIU)—the union attempted to organize in both light and heavy industries and led workers in six successful strikes,

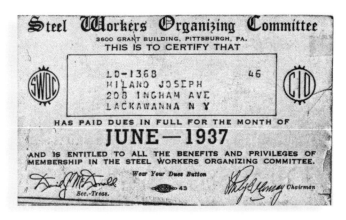

The Steel Workers Organizing Committee (SWOC) membership card of Joe Milano. Organizing workers and getting them to sign up as members of a real union were big challenges in the late 1930s. Company spies were everywhere, and union organizers and members, if caught in action, were often punished by company foremen and superintendents. Photo source: Collection of Joe Milano

including one in Buffalo. Like the AAISTW, it tried to organize workers at Republic Steel in the Buffalo and at Lackawanna's Bethlehem plant. The SMWIU did succeed in organizing a strike at Republic Steel in the fall of 1933, but according to the Buffalo Evening News, it "ended when the workers accused the leaders of Communism." The AAISTW continued its efforts, and in late 1933 its vice president, John Miller, gave speeches in Buffalo, and came to Lackawanna, where workers gave him a respectful, but cool reception. By the following spring the steelworker members of the SMWIU joined the AAISTW, and soon 1,200 men in Bethlehem's workforce of 6,000 were claimed as members by the AAISTW. The AFL had called for a general strike on June 16, 1934, but this apparently never came to pass. The failure of the organizing efforts of the AAISTW and the SMWIU was partially due to the numbing effects of the Depression, as many steelworkers did not want to endanger their part-time or full-time jobs. Also, by actively competing with each other prior to 1934, the two unions negated any chance for success. Meanwhile, the company unions, in the Buffalo area used intimidation tactics to curb the workers. At the Bethlehem plant's annual election of ERP delegates, the ballot that each employee received six days in advance of the vote included a statement indicating that casting the ballot signified approval of the ERP and disapproval of any other union. Department superintendents and foremen made participation in elections compulsory. On payday, men had to go through the voting booth before going to the pay line. One man who bypassed the booth was told by the paymaster to go and vote if he wanted to get paid. Not surprisingly, 95% of Lackawanna steelworkers cast their ballots. The failed organizing effort by the real unions had several effects.

Bethlehem and Republic reenergized the activities of their company unions. The union movement learned that it could not afford divisive competition, and the limited successes of the SMWIU pointed to the industrial style of union for the future. As it turned out, that is exactly what occurred with the arrival of the Steel Workers Organizing Committee in 1936. Despite Bethlehem Steel's efforts to resuscitate its ERP, the tide finally began to turn in the late 1930s. Finally, Lackawanna's steelworkers started winning the types of rights they had fought for in the Great Steel Strike of 1919 and could only wish for in the 1920s.[46]

The Coming of SWOC

The Great Depression and new policies of Franklin D. Roosevelt's administration marked an end to the unchallenged control of the workplace enjoyed by steel companies and other corporations. The federal government changed its position from hands off—leaving businesses to fashion their own labor policies—to recognizing the right of workers to form unions. The National Labor Relations Act, passed by Congress in 1935, established the right of unions to organize and the obligation of employers to bargain with organized labor. This signaled a new era in which federal- and state-government troops were no longer sent to break up strikes. In 1936, as during World War I, the actions of the federal government helped launch a new union drive. This time, the crisis was the Great Depression and President Roosevelt's desire to win workers over to his programs. As in 1918, existing unions created a new entity, founding the Congress of Industrial Organizations (CIO) to organize workers within each basic industry. In turn, the CIO created the Steel Workers Organizing Committee (SWOC) to focus on the steel industry. Union organizers courted the many second-generation ethnics who had entered the workforce after 1925. The American-born workers were acculturated, and they wanted their share of the American pie.[47]

The composition of the workforce in the steel plants had changed over the years. In 1907-08, 58% of steelworkers in the United States were foreign-born whites, 13% were the sons of immigrants, some 24% were the sons of native-born whites, and four percent were black. By 1930, foreign-born whites made up 31% of the workforce, native-born whites 58%, and African Americans some 9%. As late as 1938, 30% of the nation's 500,000 steelworkers were foreign born, with Italian immigrants composing the largest group, followed by Poles. A few plants, such as those in Aliquippa, Pennsylvania, and Lackawanna still had workforces in which foreign-born workers were the majority. Some of these workers, such as Antonio DiMillo, though weary of unions after the failure of the 1919 strike, thought president Roosevelt a god for recognizing unions. The American-born sons of these immigrants were an important element in the union campaign of the late 1930s. Indeed, the CIO's organizing successes of this period—especially in the steel, auto, electric appliance, and meat-packing industries—were largely based on the mobilization of ethnic workers, that is, immigrants and their sons. The assimilation of Italians and other ethnics was hastened by the sharp decline in new arrivals caused by the immigration-restriction laws of the 1920s as well as by the rise of the CIO unions.[48]

By the 1930s, the American-born east European and Italian ethnics knew the language and the rules of daily living in America. Lackawanna Italian youth went to public schools and St. Charles Catholic School with children from dozens of other ethnic groups. They had more than a few non – Italian neighbors in the Old Village, in Bethlehem Park, on Ingham Avenue, and on Roland Avenue. In the 1920s and

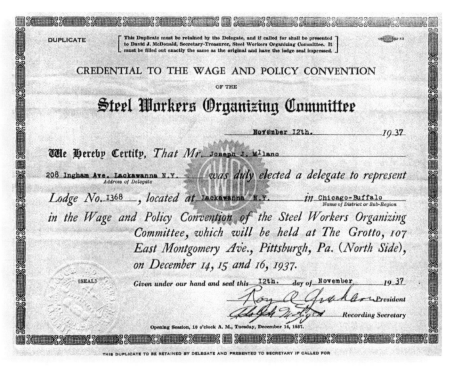

Joe Milano attended the 1937 SWOC convention in Pittsburgh. This credential certificate is what he showed at the door. Photo source: Collection of Joe Milano

1930s, many Italians married people of other nationalities and joined associations with multiethnic memberships, be they political groups, the Eagles, or even such heavily Italian organizations as the Galanti Athletic Association and the Roland Wildcats. The athletic teams of the last two groups had rosters with diverse ethnic names, but the sports they played were the American games of football, baseball, and basketball. A number of Italians were moving from the heavily Italian enclaves into other neighborhoods in Lackawanna. The 1920s brought significant social mobility, and the Italian community began to stratify into different social classes as some businesspeople grew prosperous, more people entered the professions, and more men achieved skilled occupations in the steel plant. Italians as a group were no longer simply common laborers.[49]

The second generation was eager to advance in American society, and many took steps toward the individual model of mobility that is characteristic of the United States. They found that alliances outside the Italian community often boosted them in occupational, business, and political realms. The Depression, however, undercut these gains, triggering downward mobility. Individuals first looked to family and ethnic networks for survival, just as immigrants had done earlier in the chain-migration process. But the challenge of the Depression was beyond the scope of these primary institutions, and ultimately, families depended on federal programs such as the Federal Emergency Relief Administration and the Civilian Conservation Corps as well as the emerging union movement.[50]

The American working class had more potential for unity in the 1930s, both socially and culturally. The dramatically reduced flow of new immigrants plus the fact that many of the earlier immigrants had been in the United States for 10 or 20 years meant that many immigrants were better acquainted with the language, customs, and power relationships of their adopted country. Their children were better educated and eager to gain social respect and advancement. The common foe of the Depression unified people, and in mill towns like Lackawanna, Italians and steelworkers of other ethnic groups realized they were all in the same boat when it came to dealing with the formidable power of the Bethlehem Steel Company (BSC). The lowering of ethnic boundaries was most notable among European Americans, but even the strong American racial caste system began to show cracks. In Lackawanna's First Ward, where most Italians lived, many European ethnics lived next door to or near blacks, Mexicans, Puerto Ricans, and Yemeni as they all suffered through the Depression. One historian notes that ethnic tensions actually decreased in America during the Depression.[51]

For young, second-generation adults, the industrial union advocated by the CIO offered a means to civic and economic equality. Italians and others wanted to escape the discrimination their immigrant parents had endured and achieve a sense of dignity and power. They wanted to be fully accepted as equals in American society, and the CIO catered to this image, billing its program in terms of inclusiveness and true Americanism. Ethnic ties were still strong, and most second-generation Italians maintained a loyalty to their families and fellow ethnics, but they were willing to work together with the vast array of other ethnic groups in the union's organizing effort. Indeed, ethnicity at times helped forge greater support for the unions, as businesspeople and professionals united behind the steelworkers who shared their roots. Another factor that assisted in the organizing of Lackawanna's steelworkers was the presence of workers familiar with unions. Many of the older workers had been active in the Great Steel Strike of 1919. In 1932, Bethlehem Steel purchased Seneca Steel, whose workers had formed an Amalgamated local in 1915 and maintained a strong union consciousness. In addition, as Bethlehem Steel expanded its Lackawanna plant, it brought in many workers from other states, a number of whom had experience organizing unions and participating in strikes.[52]

"Steel Labor War Is Watched Here" proclaimed an article in the July 2, 1936, edition of the *Lackawanna Leader*, noting that "thousands of steel workers in the Buffalo-Lackawanna area were watching developments in the announced war between the steel industry and the Committee for Industrial Organization [sic]." In the same issue, a full-page ad from the American Iron and Steel Institute, speaking for the steel corporations, warned that the union organizers will "employ coercion and intimidation of employees in the Industry and foment strikes" and "endanger the welfare of the country." Three weeks later, SWOC sent Charles Payne, an experienced United Mine Workers (UMW) organizer, and five other staff people to organize steelworkers in the Buffalo area. Payne's team founded six SWOC locals in plants in western New York and Ontario, including one at Bethlehem Steel in Lackawanna.[53]

The first mass-organizing meeting in the Steel City, held on October 18, drew 200 people, half of them steelworkers. At Friendship House, the speakers included Rev. Francis Hunt, pastor of Our Mother of Good Counsel Catholic Church in Blasdell; Rev. Lewis Holley of the National Negro Council; and two union leaders. Learning from the painful lessons of the 1919 steel strike, SWOC sought alliances with the established churches as well as with African Americans and other ethnic groups. *Steel Labor*, the semimonthly national publication of SWOC, offered information to stir potential members to action and tried to demonstrate that ethnic and racial divisions could be overcome. In one article, under the lead "Prominent Negroes Push Steel," SWOC President Philip Murray pledged that there would be "no discrimination" toward blacks. Another, titled "Steve, Angelo, and Tom Talk it Over," portrays a dialogue in which an Italian immigrant speaking broken English and two other men agree they need a union. The paper also illuminated Bethlehem Steel's profits and executive salaries. After showing a loss of $8 million in 1933, the company's nine plants netted $5.5 million in 1934 and more than $13 million in 1936. Western New York steelworkers were angry to learn that BSC board Chairman Charles Schwab earned $226,500 per year, and President Eugene Grace got $180,000.[54]

UMW organizer Charles Payne had links with the Communist party, as did many labor organizers nationwide during this period. Payne recruited many volunteers from party ranks, as they were experienced and skilled organizers. "Some of these party members worked in the Bethlehem plant in Lackawanna and busied themselves spreading the word of the CIO. They did so by forming what they called 'Bethlehem Clubs.' These clubs, located in many of the main departments of the plant, met in the homes of their members." SWOC leadership eventually toned down its radical pronouncements and dismissed outspoken communist organizers. Remembering the hard lessons of the Great Steel Strike, the union wanted to avoid the label of "red" or "radical" as it appealed to traditional religious and political leaders for support.[55]

In early 1937, a union local had been established in the Bethlehem Steel plant and in each of its two subsidiaries, McKaig-Hatch and Seneca Steel. These three plants in the Lackawanna area employed more than 10,000 men. Bethlehem Steel tried to sabotage the organizing effort, as *Steel Labor* reported:

At a meeting of the Seneca Lodge of the Bethlehem Steel, a company stooge made several attempts to break up the meeting. Upon being ousted from the union hall by the workers, he admitted having received $3 from the company to break up the meeting. After a meeting of the McKaig-Hatch employees, when officers were elected, 14 men were dismissed. But the company was made to put them all back to work and a general increase in wages was granted. The plant is now 100 per cent unionized.

SWOC proclaimed it had 5,000 members in 10 locals in the Buffalo district, noting that "the union is now strong enough to hold open meetings, there is no longer the need to secretly visit workers' homes." In addition to building its membership base, SWOC also had a strategy for dealing with company unions in western New York, as described by James McDonnell:

They decided to capture the already existing workers groups. The tactics of take over were simple; where the company unions resisted the SWOC they would work to discredit them as pawns of the corporation and where they were not hostile, the SWOC would follow a plan of "boring from within." They would work to fill the leadership with SWOC members and transfer the company unions into the SWOC-CIO.

Unlike previous years, when workers were coerced by supervisors into voting, many workers were now eager to vote for different reasons. In March 1937, some 94% of the 9,375 eligible workers voted in the election of ERP representatives at the Bethlehem plant. SWOC claimed that half the men elected were their members, including James DePasquale, who later became a United Steelworkers officer. That month, the three Lackawanna SWOC lodges savored several victories: their success in overcoming management's efforts to sabotage their founding, getting their candidates elected to at least half the positions in Bethlehem's company union, and a victory of their colleagues in the autoworkers union. The Lackawanna SWOC lodges celebrated with a parade, a mass meeting, a card party, and a dance. To counteract SWOC's gains, the company announced a wage raise to a minimum of $5 per day and began sponsoring picnics for various departments. And SWOC had even more adversity to overvome.[56]

Many of the SWOC organizers were Irish, English, and Scotch, and Julian Bruce was a Native American. Italians were also involved in the SWOC campaign; in April 1937, they made up about 13% of the 288 members of SWOC Local No. 1024 at the Bethlehem plant and 15% at Seneca Steel's Local No. 1119. In that same year, while working at Bethlehem's Kalman Division, Joe Milano joined SWOC Local No. 1368 and was a steward for the next two years. The leaders of this local were Roy Graham and Adolph Miska, both of whom Milano admired. He and other SWOC stewards met outside the plant, often in Blasdell. Bethlehem Steel police tried to locate the meeting halls, reading attendees' license-plate numbers to identify the members. If SWOC men were identified at SWOC meetings, they were assigned jobs "pushing brooms," harassed, or laid off. Milano recalls that the union men changed meeting halls frequently, gathering at the Liberty Theater on Ridge Road and various bars in the area. The harassment by the company no doubt helped curtail union membership. SWOC ledgers indicate that Local No. 1024's membership dropped from 288 in April to 144 in May, where it remained through September.[57]

The spring-summer season of 1937 was a rough period for union organizers. The economy, which had been making a gradual recovery since 1934, faltered and put millions of people out of work again. While United States Steel, the country's largest steel corporation, decided to recognize the SWOC union, the smaller steel conglomerates (Bethlehem, Republic, Inland, Weirton, Jones and Laughlin, and Youngstown Sheet and Tube), collectively known as Little Steel, vowed to fight against the union. In May and June of 1937, SWOC called for strikes at several of the Little Steel companies. The strike at Jones and Laughlin Steel in Pennsylvania was successful, and SWOC was elected as the workers' bargaining agent. SWOC then struck Republic Steel after two volunteer organizers were fired at the company's Cleveland plant. Each Republic plant had an enormous

arsenal of weapons, and in South Chicago, Illinois, police killed 10 strikers in the infamous Memorial Day Massacre. In South Buffalo, the sparse SWOC membership at the Republic plant was harassed by mounted Buffalo policemen. The strike was a bitter defeat for the fledgling union. SWOC tried to regain its momentum with a strike at Bethlehem's plant in Johnstown, Pennsylvania, but this effort also failed. The failure of these Little Steel strikes served to deflate the organizing effort in Buffalo, Lackawanna, and throughout the country.[58]

SWOC activities continued, if at a more sluggish pace, at the Bethlehem plant in Lackawanna. A SWOC women's auxiliary was formed, and the union's lead organizer in the city, Charles Doyle, claimed that 8,000 of the 10,000 to 12,000 workers at Bethlehem had joined the union by the close of 1937. Joe Milano went to the December SWOC convention in Pittsburgh. "I drove all the way. I went alone, by the way. No one else wanted to come. They didn't want to take the time off—they were only working part time." Once there, he met up with Edward Boyle, and together they represented workers at Bethlehem's Lackawanna plant. As the union grew in strength, the supervisors in the specialty shop offered Milano supervisory jobs to draw him away from the rank and file and union activities. This presented a dilemma, as Milano had friends in management who appreciated his political acumen, while his union friends wanted him to stay with SWOC. In 1939, he accepted the position of relief foreman with the inspectors, with the promise that he would be soon made a general foreman. But he felt he was slighting his union friends, and in 1940, Milano resolved the dilemma by leaving Bethlehem Steel and taking a position with the city. Other Italians at the plant remained active in the union-organizing drive.[59]

In December 1937, Jack Meta, one of some 200 men transported to Lackawanna from the Midwest to work at the new Strip Mill, suffered a broken leg when struck by a 10-ton roll of metal. During his four-month stay at Moses Taylor Hospital, he met Joe Sluso, a SWOC organizer, who gave him a union brochure. Meta signed up. In addition to the $1 initiation fee, he paid 11 months' dues in advance, for a total of $12—a significant amount of money in the 1930s. By late 1938, Meta and seven other union members were meeting in the back room of a cab stand on lower Ridge Road, where they strategized leafleting and other recruitment plans. This group, which included Buffalonian Ed Mastrangelo, attempted to organize both the hot- and cold-mill sections of the Strip Mill. The task proved difficult, and they signed up only 50 of the 3,000 workers by year's end. Superintendent Schonkwiler gave favored treatment to the several hundred men he had recruited from Indiana and Ohio, and they were loyal to him. While the superintendent didn't permit overt retaliation against the unionists, the foremen regularly passed them over for promotions. "Meanwhile," Meta stated, "across the street in the old plant [Seneca Steel] workers are being signed up for the union — five times more than in the Strip Mill." In disgust and frustration, Meta and other organizers stopped trying and didn't pay their union dues for the first half of 1939. Still, SWOC membership rose from 52 in January to 125 in May before dropping to 102 in August.[60]

Meta and the others reapplied themselves in the second half of 1939 and were encouraged by the transfer of many former Amalgamated members from the Seneca plant to the hot mill. Occasionally, the union called meetings for each plant department, but those in the Strip Mill attracted only some three dozen workers. Mass meetings of all Bethlehem workers drew crowds of 300, but again, few from the Strip Mill. Things looked better in 1940 when about one-third of the Strip Mill's workers were union members. Many of the Hot Mill's 1,000 workers had signed union cards, but the larger workforce in the Cold Mill was strongly antiunion. Meta and other organizers tried to convert these men by arguing that with a union, there would be no favoritism such as Schonkwiler displayed toward his Midwestern recruits. In his union pitch, Meta also claimed that SWOC activities had forced Bethlehem Steel to: 1) give all men with 10 years' seniority a week of paid vacation each year; 2) remove the authority to fire from the previously all-powerful

foremen and vest it only in mill superintendents; and 3) hear the complaints of workers. If the union were their official bargaining agent, Meta and other organizers argued, the workers could get even more. Throughout 1940, the Strip Mill organizers and stewards struggled to maintain their ranks and collect dues, giving union men new membership books in which each month's paid dues were indicated by a stamp. They urged members to wear a button, a different color each month, proclaiming "Dues Paid." It was tough going. Another factor mitigating against the organizers was that the brand-new Strip Mill, while certainly dangerous at times, was viewed as safe and clean by workers in other mills and departments. Indeed, workers in the blast furnaces, Coke Ovens, and open hearths referred to the Strip Mill as "the playground."[61]

While union movement was slow in the Strip Mill, Italians helped bolster the organizing effort in other mills. Joe Iafallo and Joe Baldo rallied men in No. 2 Open Hearth, Angelo Manna and Bill Petrangelo in the coke ovens, and Vince Lojacano in the Bar Mill. In the Electrical Department Rocco LaPenna and Dom Galluch volunteered as SWOC organizers, as did Gus Tenuta in No. 10 Mill. Joe Fiorella, Jim Nappo, and Charles Saldi were recruited by John McCann to help organize the No. 7 and No. 8 mills. The son of Sicilian immigrants, Fiorella first worked as a longshoreman and teamster in Buffalo, carrying a union card in each of these jobs. In March 1937, he began

Leo's Grove in Ebenezer, September 12, 1937. The first outing of the Garage Department, which employed many Italian American workers. Among them are: 1)Angelo Grosso, 2) Amicare "Mickey" Paolini, and 3) Armondo Pietrocarlo.
Photo source: Don Grosso

The first annual picnic of the Yard Department in 1937. Bethlehem Steel tried to discourage workers from joining the Steel Workers Organizing Committee (SWOC) union both by granting benefits, such as picnics and pay raises, and by punishing SWOC organizers and intimidating would-be members. Photo source: Collection of Louie Petrucci

work in Bethlehem's No. 7 Mill, where he stamped hot steel with a heat number. His labor gang included a slipmaker, a checker, four samplers, two hookers, and a man who pushed the newly rolled steel off the line. As to the group's ethnic mix, there was a Spaniard, a Hungarian, a Jew, and three other Italians: Joe, Mike, and Tony DePasquale. Fiorella quickly learned that "to advance in the plant depended on what you could provide outside of the plant," i.e., favors to the foremen, which were often monitored by the chief clerk of the mill. When recruiters John McCann and Solly Rosenthal promised Fiorella that SWOC would end the patronage system, he signed up.[62]

SWOC's organizing effort in Lackawanna focused on the main grievances of the workers: vacation time, a uniform rate for piece work and per-ton wages, paid down time when repairs prevented steel production, and promotion based on seniority. Workers in the blast furnaces, open hearths, and coke ovens, where conditions were worst, swarmed to the union. To offset SWOC's thrust, Bethlehem Steel gave vacation time to long-term employees and awarded five-cent-per-hour raises three times between 1936 and 1941. The company also organized yearly picnics and departmental outings, and many foremen stopped pressing for informal favors from the workers. The company was slow to rehire union activists following layoffs, however, as Fiorella found out in 1939. Union organizing ebbed and flowed, and membership varied with conditions in each mill or department; in No. 7 Mill, Fiorella and other organizers signed up 70% of the workers in 1937.[63]

Keeping the lessons of the 1919 strike in mind, SWOC continued to court political and religious leaders, and to avoid a radical image by letting go of some communist organizers. Charles Doyle, the lead staff person in Lackawanna, was eventually replaced by the more conservative Julian Bruce. In 1937, the union endorsed a candidate who as elected Buffalo's mayor. The following year, priests in Buffalo and Lackawanna endorsed SWOC, and Rev. Francis Hunt, the Catholic priest from Blasdell, addressed several more mass union meetings. SWOC organizers filed charges with the National Labor Relations Board (NLRB), citing Bethlehem's unfair labor practices. In 1939, the NLRB found Bethlehem Steel guilty of violating the Wagner Act and instructed it to disband the ERP in all its plants and to cease interfering with SWOC. Bethlehem appealed the decision and continued operating the ERP until the Circuit Court of Appeals upheld the decision on May 12, 1941.[64]

While SWOC continued to organize locals and win bargaining rights at many small factories in western New York, its efforts in the large plants, such as Bethlehem, were bogged down during 1938 and 1939. Across the country, Bethlehem and the other companies that comprised Little Steel continued to thwart SWOC's organizing efforts. The American steel industry could not be successfully unionized until these companies recognized SWOC, as U.S. Steel could renege on its recognition of labor unions if Little Steel defeated SWOC. In 1940, SWOC initiated a national drive that focused solely on the largest corporation in Little Steel. Directed by Van Bittner of the national SWOC staff, the campaign targeted

all 11 plants of the Bethlehem Steel Corporation. More SWOC organizers came to Lackawanna, working to expand the corps of volunteer organizers among the mill workers. An issue of the *Buffalo Union Leader* featured a photograph of 27 paid and volunteer organizers at the Lackawanna plant, including Alessandro DeSantis, Frank DePasquale, and Russell DePasquale. In No. 1 Open Hearth, Gene Covelli was one of a dozen volunteer representatives who listened to the complaints of fellow workers and pointed out that membership in the union was the best way to act on the issues. In September 1940, a 30-hour walkout by 4,000 ore dock and blast furnace workers persuaded the company to reinstate two men who insisted they retain their union membership while acting as straw bosses. While the union drive was turning up the heat at Bethlehem Steel, even more dramatic repercussions were felt across Hamburg Turnpike at the former site of the Old Village, where a small factory had been erected.[65]

At the Spring Perch Company, which had moved from Connecticut to Lackawanna in 1932, most of the 185 employees walked off the job on November 4, 1940. The strike was into its third day when the company agreed to recognize SWOC Local No. 2267. The local gained exclusive bargaining rights for all maintenance and production employees, a raise of at least five cents in the minimum hourly wage, a 40-hour week with time-and-a-half for overtime and double time for holidays, paid vacations, seniority protection, grievance procedures, and compulsory dues checkoffs for all employees. Anthony Costantino, secretary for SWOC in Lackawanna, was a prominent figure in these actions, and Lackawannans Alex Nigro and Art Thomas each served as president of the Spring Perch local in the early 1940s.[66]

SWOC had brought to Lackawanna one of its most colorful organizers, Smoile "Smiley" Chatak, to help with the recruiting drive at Bethlehem Steel. The experienced coal miner from Pennsylvania attracted new members by telling stories of the confrontations between union men and the security forces of the coal companies. He organized wear-your-button days, during which members in a department sported their metal SWOC buttons, something that foremen hadn't encountered previously. If a few men had done so, a foreman could easily have sent them home, but this punishment wouldn't work with so many men, as it would curtail production. In mid-1939, Chatak began organizing "quickies"—brief strikes in the blast furnaces, coke ovens, or open hearths that usually lasted just a few hours. The purpose of these tactics "was to irritate management but also to demonstrate to the workers that SWOC was, in fact, present in the plant and willing to challenge the company." In November 1940, Smoile Chatak and Lorne Nelles led 40 workers from the coke ovens, blast furnaces, and mechanical departments into a conference with C. L. Baker, personnel director for Bethlehem Steel. SWOC spokesman Anthony Costantino said that " 'the major object' of the meeting 'was to present the vigorous demands of the workers for more pay. Most insistent,' he declared, 'were those of the mechanical departments.' " In December, SWOC geared up for further action by increasing the Lackawanna organizing staff to six, and moving its office into a larger building, one with three meeting halls, at Ridge Road and Hamburg Turnpike.[67]

After a mass meeting in January 1941, *Steel Labor* reported that 40% of the plant's 16,000 hourly workers joined the union ranks. The following month, the publication noted that the

Fabricating Department was 95% organized. There were more "quickie" strikes in the plant, especially among coke-oven workers. SWOC lead organizer Lorne Nelles explained that the stoppages were spontaneous. "The whole issue centers around the company's refusal to recognize union stewards as a grievance committee for the coke-oven workers, and the workers' refusal to accept the Employee Representatives as their representatives." At the beginning of each shift, the grievance committee attempted to meet with the superintendent. When he refused to talk, the men protested by stopping work for one hour. On February 12, the resultant coke shortage caused No. 14 and No. 15 mills to shut down and three other mills to slow their operations. Company police ordered 550 coke-oven workers and 350 mill employees to leave the plant during the protests, but the men ignored them and sang union songs; Nelles denied charges that the songs were "communistic." After two weeks of stoppages, Bethlehem Steel responded on February 19 by locking out 300 union members from the coke ovens. This was followed by the layoff of 1,000 union men. SWOC "had succeeded in goading management into a mistake," writes historian Jim McDonnell. "The union, confident in its leadership and satisfied with its membership in three departments (blast furnaces, coke ovens, and open hearth) decided to call for a strike vote." Following Bethlehem's refusal to negotiate with the union, the men voted to strike and did so at 9:00 p.m. on February 26, 1941. SWOC brought in a group of experienced organizers to assist. The plant was immediately surrounded by pickets, with an estimated 12,000 men joining the strike. "Even the company's claim," reported *Steel Labor*, "showed less than 2,000 men in the plant during the strike, most of them officials." The overall momentum was all for the union, and even a fifth of the reluctant Strip Mill workers honored the picket lines. Among the strikers walking the picket lines were many Italians including Joe Cosentino, Bill Mingarell, and Joe Vertalino.[68]

Van Bittner arrived in Lackawanna to direct the strike and announce the union's demands:

1. All workmen, including those locked out by Bethlehem, returned to their jobs with full seniority
2. Immediate conferences with management to settle grievances which arose in the plant
3. A Labor Board election

Bethlehem Steel deliberately had strikebreakers enter through No. 1 Gate at the far north end of the plant, which was actually within the city of Buffalo. In that way, the resources of the Buffalo Police Department, which was much larger than Lackawanna's, could be brought to bear on the strikers. On the second day of the strike, violence erupted as strikers attempted to prevent autos from entering the gate. The police used clubs and horses when strikers refused to let cars pass, and injuries and arrests ensued. Strike leaders, who had earlier attended unsuccessful meetings with the Buffalo police chief, called on Mayor Holling of Buffalo to intervene. New York City Mayor Fiorello LaGuardia happened to be visiting Holling at the time and heard the union men's description of the violence at No. 1 Gate. Holling then asked LaGuardia for his advice. According to one source,

LaGuardia told Buffalo's Mayor that he had handled a similar situation in New York. He explained that he avoided violence by closing off the city street, thus keeping autos from approaching the gates of the struck plant. Holling took LaGuardia's advice and ordered

SWOC's strike at the Lackawanna plant of Bethlehem Steel lasted from February 26-28, 1941. The photos above and the four that follow were taken at No.3 Gate, where thousands of striking steelworkers walked the picket line. In the upper right photo are Bill Mingarell (left) and Joe Vertalino, crossing Hamburg Turnpike. In addition to the Lackawanna police with their billy clubs, there were deputized SWOC workers carrying nightsticks (upper left photo). Photo source: Collection of Frank Chiodo

Fuhrmann Boulevard closed from Tifft Street to the city line. This act removed the Buffalo Police force a full quarter mile from the troubled plant gate and left control of the gate in the hands of the strikers.

Mayor John Aszkler of Lackawanna, a SWOC member who worked at Bethlehem Steel, further assisted the union by closing Hamburg Turnpike (the name for Route 5 in Lackawanna; the Buffalo section is known as Fuhrmann Boulevard), prohibiting access to other gates, and deputizing 100 SWOC members as special policemen.[69]

The federal government also came to the aid of the strikers. The Office of Production Management of the National Defense Commission, led by Secretary of Labor Frances Perkins, informed Bethlehem that President Roosevelt wanted to avoid a halt in production at the plant and recommended that Bethlehem accept the union's terms, which it did two days later. The strike ended at noon on February 28. It might not have succeeded without the intervention of the federal and local governments, and the active backing of the Roman Catholic archdiocese and several Protestant denominations. Steelworkers supported the strike in overwhelming numbers, even though there were only 1,200 men on the SWOC membership rolls in October 1940. That number had risen to 5,300 just before the February strike. The SWOC organizers had learned from the sad lessons of the 1919 strike and achieved a

Many strikers dressed in their Sunday best, perhaps to indicate the seriousness of their action, to make a good impression on the general public, and to reduce the chance of men getting into altercations. The first day of the strike, the Buffalo Police and strikers got into a physical confrontation at No. 1 Gate (which was within the Buffalo city limits) when scabs tried to enter the plant there. Photo source: Collection of Frank Chiodo

On the advice of New York City Mayor Fiorello LaGuardia, the mayors of Buffalo and Lackawanna closed Hamburg Turnpike to auto traffic, and there was no further violence. SWOC's victory in the Lackawanna strike spelled defeat for the Little Steel companies that had fought unionization. Photo source: Collection of Frank Chiodo

On February 28, some 3,500 men in Lackawanna's Memorial Hall cheered as they officially approved the terms of the agreement that ended the strike. Van Bittner was carried through the hall on the shoulders of his steelworkers. "From the hall, the SWOC members marched down to the plant and paraded past each gate. Pickets on duty and thousands of other union steelworkers joined the parade until there was a marching throng of men nearly two miles long." The article in *Steel Labor* continued: " 'This is the beginning of the end of tyranny, of spies, of espionage,' declared Mr. Bittner at the meeting. 'This is the beginning of the end—I repeat, this is the beginning of the end of non-unionism in the plants of Bethlehem Steel.' " Philip Murray, SWOC national chairman, sent a telegram that Bittner read aloud to the steelworkers of Lackawanna. " 'Please convey to the membership, the staff and the officers my deepest appreciation for the solid backing they gave to bring about this victor—one of the greatest victories in the history of SWOC. The capitulation of the Bethlehem Steel Company to our demands after a two-day strike is a great tribute to the union men of Lackawanna. This marvelous display of strength brings *that* much nearer the day when Bethlehem Steel must sign a contract with our union.' "[71]

A week after the strike SWOC petitioned the NLRB for an election at the Lackawanna plant, and the board issued an order to this effect on April 7. The company tried to form an independent union, the Bethlehem Lackawanna Independent Union, but BLEWY, as the workers called it, signed up few people. SWOC held three mass meetings at Memorial Hall prior to the election. In sharp contrast to the 1919 strike, mayors John Aszkler of Lackawanna and Thomas Holling of Buffalo welcomed the national SWOC leadership to a May 12 gathering and "wished the steel workers 'complete success' in the election." Preceding the meeting, SWOC and other CIO unions organized a miles-long parade through the streets of the Steel City. As the election neared, a powerful propaganda campaign was waged via

remarkable victory in Lackawanna. African American workers were actively recruited and made to feel welcome by the union. SWOC continued to fight the labels of "radical" and "communist." The union's cultivation of a political and civic agenda for the three preceding years had won the backing of governmental leaders.[70]

'Cheers Signal End of Strike at Bethlehem Steel Plant

Workers cheer outside Memorial Hall on Ridge Road after a vote to accept the agreement to end the strike and return back to work. They then marched through the streets of Lackawanna.
Photo source: Buffalo State College Courier-Express Collection, *Courier Express*, 3/1/41

newspapers, meetings, and flyers. The *Lackawanna Leader* ran half-page SWOC ads urging workers to vote for the union:

> What does SWOC mean to you?
> 1. 10c per hour wage increase
> 2. job security
> 3. vacations with pay
> 4. machinery to settle all grievances peacefully

The Fair Election Committee, founded by Bethlehem Steel, ran a number of full-page ads against the union:

> Think before you vote! Vote No
> If you vote yes:
> - communists will welcome your yes
> - fifth columnists will know they have succeeded
> - Hitler will appreciate it. … it will help him win

Many workers, such as Marius DeCarolis, signed petitions and spoke out publicly against the tactics of the committee.[72]

Several days before the election, the headline on the front page of the *Lackawanna Leader* read: "Nation Eyes City; Battleground Wednesday in SWOC's Campaign to Organize Bethlehem; NLRB Election May Seal Fate of Either Side." The May 13 election drew 11,184 of the 12,445 steelworkers eligible to vote. By an almost three-to-one vote (8,223 to

2,961), SWOC won the right to be the collective bargaining agent for the Lackawanna plant. It was indeed a great victory for the steelworkers and their union, and the first major steel strike in the twentieth century in which the workers achieved success. Following Lackawanna's lead, workers at 10 other Bethlehem Steel plants elected SWOC, soon renamed the United Steelworkers of America (USWA), as their bargaining agent by October 1941. Other plants in the Buffalo area, such as E. T. Weir Steel and Donner Hanna Coke Corporation, also followed suit. At Bethlehem's Lackawanna plant five USWA locals (nos. 2601-2605) were established in the spring of 1941 and a sixth (No. 2613) by January 1942. As a result, the 40-hour work week was instituted, workers were paid time-and-a-half for overtime, men on the job more than five years received two weeks of vacation, and seniority and grievance systems were installed. The arbitrary decisions of management and the tremendous informal power of the foremen finally came to an end.[73]

The ongoing meetings and activities during the steelworkers' five-year struggle to win recognition of the union helped foster a solidarity that reduced the ethnic divisions in the plant. But ethnicity remained an important factor in the early days of the USWA in Lackawanna, most steelworkers were immigrants or children of immigrants, and there was a historic pattern of department workforces being dominated by specific ethnic groups. In 1941, 12 of the 19 SWOC stewards at the SBR were Italians, and Mike Speranza was chairman of the grievance committee. In 1956, all six stewards for the Yard Department division of Local No. 2602 were Italian Americans. Some locals followed a pattern of ethnically mixed tickets in elections to ensure that the leadership reflected the ethnic composition of the membership. Local No. 2603 usually elected ethnic tickets that included an Irishman, a Pole, and an Italian. In the 1950s and 1960s, No. 2603, with 6,600 workers, had the largest membership of any local in New York State. Some 35 to 40% of the workers were Polish, while Italians constituted approximately 10%. However, in locals representing newer mills, such as the Strip Mill, the ethnic factor was less important, and the passage of time served to break down ethnic boundaries where they had existed. John McCann, who joined the USWA

FIGURE 8.4

Hourly Wage for Laborers in U.S. Steel Plants: 1905 – 1947

Year	Cents Per Hour	Related Events
1905	15	
1910	17	
1916	25	Increased production World War I
1918	42	Defense production U.S. in the war
1920	46	Decreased immigration worker shortage
1921	37	Depression layoffs
1922	30	Depression layoffs
1925	44	
1930	44	Early stages of Great Depression
1932	39	Depression worsens
1933	33	Depression worsens
1934	43	
1936	47	SWOC union founded companies begin to court
1937	53	workers with wage and benefit increases
1940	63	World War II defense contracts bring full production
1941	73	Strikes win union recognition U.S. enters war
1942	78	Union contract but voluntary wartime wage freeze
1946	97	Postwar strike raises wages
1947	109	Unions continue push for better wages and benefits

Source: *Steel Labor*, June 1947.

staff in 1942, remembers that men sat with fellow ethnics at union meetings in the early 1940s but later congregated with those who worked in the same mill, regardless of ethnicity.[74]

The union provided a new structure for occupational advancement for Italians and other southeast Europeans and, for a while, for blacks and other nonwhite minorities. Italians became involved in leadership and staff roles in the USWA locals of Bethlehem Steel soon after the union started organizing. Marius DeCarolis, active in SWOC since 1938, was a delegate at two SWOC conventions, secretary of the general stewardship, and an official checker at the NLRB election. In the first election of officers in 1941 (see Figure 8.5) Joe Manzella was elected financial secretary of local No. 2605 and Russell DePasquale the vice president of Local No. 2603. DePasquale became president of his local in 1945, and Manzella joined the District No. 4 union staff in 1944. Virtually all these men were second-generation Italian Americans, and as time passed, more men of their generation became officers in the locals.[75]

Italian steelworkers continued to rise to leadership positions in the following years, both in the Lackawanna locals and at higher levels of the union. In 1968, Mike Mazuca (Buffalo) became director of District 4 of the USWA, which took in all

of New York State. The district's heaviest membership was in the industrial area in and around Buffalo, and Lackawanna's seven locals included No. 3734 at the Buffalo Tank Division of Bethlehem Steel. Other unions represented a variety of industries and occupations, including the trainmen of the South Buffalo Railway. While most SBR employees were represented by Local No. 2613, the train crewmen were divided into traditional railroad unions. The engineers and firemen had been represented by the Brotherhood of Locomotive Firemen and Enginemen (BLFE) since at least 1905, while the switchmen were affiliated with the International Switchmens Union in the 1910s and in the late 1930s with Lodge No. 758 of the Brotherhood of Railroad Trainmen (BRT). The membership was heavily Irish, but Italian Steve Lanza (Buffalo) was secretary of the BRT local in the 1950s and later became the state legislative representative. Lanza and other union leaders exerted great pressure on Bethlehem Steel to improve safety standards, which, he said, the company "slowly implemented." When the BRT joined forces with the BLFE, they could virtually shut down the steel plant by idling the SBR locomotives. In 1951, both unions went on strike to force a resolution to accumulated grievances and by the fifth day, steel production was at a standstill, and some 12,000 steelworkers were idled. In 1969, the BRT merged with the BLFE and two other railway brotherhoods to form the United Transportation Union. Eventually, a ticket of southern and eastern European ethnics, including Tony Zuppa (Buffalo), was elected to union offices traditionally held by Irish trainmen. After 1941, the surge of union organizing influenced even supervisors; SBR yardmasters were represented by the Railroad Yardmasters of North America, and steel-plant foremen organized a chapter of the Foremen's Association of America.[76]

The formation of the United Steelworkers of America and the other industrial unions of the CIO helped produce a redistribution of wealth in America. The base hourly wage for laborers in steel plants (see Figure 8.4) rose only 32 cents between 1905 and 1936, as pay rates were spurred upward by manpower shortages and lowered by economic depressions—but rarely influenced by workers, themselves. However, the

11 years of union activity following SWOC's founding in 1936 saw steelworkers win an increase of 62 cents per hour—twice the increase of the preceding three decades. In the 18 months prior to the Pearl Harbor attack, the victories of SWOC and other fledgling industrial unions led to the CIO's gain of about 1.5 million new members. SWOC was victorious at Republic Steel, which had violently defeated the union's efforts just four years earlier. And the United Auto Workers finally won recognition at Ford, the last holdout in the auto industry, despite the repressive tactics of 3,000 thugs employed by the company. With huge government defense spending and full production at factories, many unions endeavored to improve wages, benefits, and work rules, resulting in 4,200 strikes in 1941 alone. Unions grew as the workforce expanded during the war years. By 1945, there were 14.5 million union members, including 708,000 steelworkers. The CIO and AFL unions voluntarily agreed to a no-strike pledge during the war but after 1942, as the tide of battle turned in favor of the Allies, the number of strikes grew. Unions fought for better wages, increased safety standards, and fair work assignments, and against the slow machinations of the National War Labor Board. Lackawanna steelworkers flexed their union muscle to settle conflicts with their longtime arch enemies: the foremen. In February 1943, 125 electrical workers walked out for three days to protest a foreman's order, and in April, some 240 of the bar mill's billet yard workers first did a sit-down strike, then a walkout to contest a foreman's actions. Both were wildcat strikes that didn't have formal union support, but union leaders stepped in to negotiate the issues with plant managers.[77]

Following World War II, workers nationwide struggled to make up for the large drop in earnings due to reduced production, layoffs, curtailment of overtime pay, and the lifting of government price controls. In 1946, which recorded the greatest number of strikes in U.S. history, the walkout by steelworkers was the first national steel strike since 1919. This time, however, private security forces and state troopers did not bludgeon the workers; the event was peaceful, and the steelworkers finally won pay raises. Unlike the strikes from 1919 to 1941, in which steelworker unions fought for basic survival, those in the mid-1940s focused on improving the contract terms and did not endanger the very existence of unions. The wave of strikes and the resultant victories indicated that the industrial unions of the CIO were now established institutions.[78]

The successful strikes by industrial workers did not, however, signal the end of labor-management struggles. Later in 1946 the steel corporations more than recouped the higher wages paid to workers by raising their prices and purchasing the mills built by the federal government during the war for half their original cost. Business interests focused on turning

THINK BEFORE YOU VOTE

If You Vote "YES" —

The Communists Will Welcome Your "Yes."
Fifth Columnists Will Know They Have Succeeded.
Hitler Will Appreciate It---- It Will Help Him Win!
There Will Be More Delay in America's Defense.
There Will Be Picket Lines Formed.
There Will Be Strikes For Unfair Demands.
There Will Be Sympathy Strikes.
Your Dues Will Support Highly Paid Organizers in Luxury, and You Will Get Nothing.
Your Grievances Will Not Get Immediate Attention From Uninterested Outsiders Who Are Only Interested in Your Dues.
Your Demands Are Settled by Strikes Which Means Violence, Brutality and loss of Pay.

If You Vote "NO" O"—

All America Will Know You Are 100% American.
You Will Not Be Forced to Go Out in Sympathy Strikes.
You Will Build America's Defenses for the Safety of Your Wives and Children.
Your Money Will Be Spent for You.
Your Grievances Will Be Handled by Fellow Workers Who Know Your Problems.
Your Problems Will Be Handled Without Strikes, Brutality and Loss of Pay for You.
Honorable Dealings With the Company Will Prevent Loss of Time and Wages.
Strikes Will Not Be Called at the Whim of a Professional, Highly Paid Labor Organizer.
Working Conditions Will Be Improved.

FELLOW WORKERS:-

On May 14th you will be called on to vote upon your future.

To protect that future you must vote. In no other way can you guarantee your American way of life except by making it your duty on that day to go to the Polls and VOTE NO.

A vote against the CIO is a vote

FOR

1 National Defense.
2 Personal Security.
3 Local Labor Representation.

AGAINST

1 Labor Dictatorship.
2 Radical Leadership.
3 Waste of YOUR Money.
4 Strikes Called By Outsiders For Outsiders.

FAIR ELECTION COMMITTEE.

VOTE "NO" ON MAY 14th

The so-called Fair Election Committee, created and funded by Bethlehem Steel, took out ads such as this one. The committee used scare tactics to convince steelworkers to vote against SWOC, part of the Congress of Industrial Organizations (CIO), and for a company union. But on May 14, 1941, workers voted by a nearly 3-to-1 margin, to have SWOC represent them in collective bargaining. Workers throughout the city celebrated the victory. Photo sources: Lackawanna Library; *Lackawanna Herald*, May 9, 1941

back the tide of union advancement of the previous 10 years. The USWA, with locals in both the U.S. and Canada, and the steel corporations had continual face-offs in the late 1940s and throughout the following decade. The strikes of 1946, 1949, 1952, and 1959 were enormous—involved some of the largest in North America—sometimes witnessed drastic actions. In 1946, union pickets sealed off the Lackawanna Bethlehem Steel plant prohibiting strikebreakers from entering or leaving the plant. The company responded by having airplanes drop parachutes with bags of food to those who remained in the plant; a bag that missed its target landed on Pine Street in Bethlehem Park.[79]

During the lengthy strike of 1949, union leaders at the Lackawanna plant listed the two basic CIO demands in a local newspaper: "(1) a general and uniform change in wage rates,

Strike picketers at 1 Gate, 1946. Many of the union men were World War II veterans.
Photo source: William H. Emerling and John P. Osborne, *The History of Lackawanna*, 1976, p. 32

Following the 1941 election, SWOC became the United Steelworkers of America. The union organized six locals at Bethlehem Steel and many more at other factories in western New York. The USWA called a nationwide strike in January 1946, and these pickets were stationed in Bethlehem Park, near the Strip Mill.
Photo source: Collection of Tony Grasso

and (2) a program for life, accident, health, medical, and hospital insurance benefits." As a result of the strike, the USWA secured pension and insurance terms that were free from employer control. The striking workers had the support of Lackawanna businesspeople, who placed a moratorium on union members' installment payments for the strike's duration. The city's USWA locals and Bethlehem managers constantly struggled over the rules that dictated working conditions in the mills. Wildcat strikes were a regular occurrence. In 1950, there were at least five—three of them in the Strip Mill, which had become a hotbed of activity—with each walkout involving 150 to 1,000 workers. In 1953, carpenters and coke-oven and blast-furnace workers left their jobs. The Strip Mill was again the center of controversy when 2,500 hot- and cold-mill personnel walked out in March, and 1,035 were idled in August after 26 crane operators left their jobs.[80]

In 1959, the steel industry sought to freeze wages and change job-assignment practices to reduce its workforce. This led steelworkers to launch one of the longest strikes in U.S. history, lasting four months. In the end, the USWA was victorious in maintaining job-assignment rules and getting a wage increase. But the victory was short-lived, as an economic recession, automation, and imports from abroad led steel corporations to lay off one of every five steelworkers by 1962. The year 1959 was the first in the twentieth century in which American steel imports surpassed exports, setting the stage for a trend that became pronounced during the 1960s. The opening of the St. Lawrence Seaway made it easier for imported steel to enter the Midwest, the largest American market for steel and one traditionally dominated by domestic steel companies. By 1964, more imports were arriving in the Great Lakes than any other area of the U.S. This gradually had its effect on the Bethlehem plant in Lackawanna, where the workforce declined from a peak of 21,500 in 1965 to 12,000 in 1972. The USWA had few tools to avert the massive layoffs; as court rulings after 1947 had curtailed options such as wildcat strikes, which were routinely being countered with court injunctions by the 1970s. The situation in Lackawanna gradually deteriorated as Bethlehem opened its new plant in Burns Harbor, Indiana, to serve its Midwest customers. Operations at the Lackawanna plant were reduced, and the huge plant was all but shut down in 1983.[81]

In 80 years, the Lackawanna facility went from being the largest steel plant in the world to just one more rust-belt relic. The union that had been so strong since it won recognition at Bethlehem's Lackawanna plant during the 1941 strike was beset by a huge calamity 40 years later. The USWA locals continued to advocate for their members as the layoffs and closings of individual mills proceeded. Many men took early retirements, and a number were able to transfer to other

FIGURE 8.5

Italian Officers in Lackawanna Locals of
The United Steelworkers of America: 1941 – 1994*

Local No. 2601: open-hearth, blast-furnace, and coke-oven workers

Joe Ventura (Buffalo)	President	1940s

Local No. 2602: yard, mechanical, and electric departments

Marius De Carolis	Financial Secretary	1941
Carmine Lagana (Buffalo)	Financial Secretary	1945
Mike Pacillo	Trustee	1945
Armand Capodagli	Treasurer	1956-58
Dominic Galluch (Blasdell)	Financial Secretary	1956-58
Rocco LaPenna (Buffalo)	Trustee	1956-58
Pete Yacobucci (Blasdell)	Trustee	1956-58
	Guide	1967-69
Salvatore Amarante (Buffalo)	President	1966-69
	Vice President	1977
Peter Schiavi	Trustee	1967-69
Benny Vertalino	President	1970s
Salvatore Corsi	Treasurer	1977

Local No. 2603: rolling mills, billet yard, and structural shipping department

Frank DePasquale (Buffalo)	Outside Guard	1941-42
Russell DePasquale	President	1945
Joe Fiorella	Trustee	1940s
	Vice President	1956-58
	President	1958
Anthony Iafallo	Trustee	1956-58
Ralph Carestio	Trustee	1958
Mike DePasquale	Treasurer	1950
	Financial Secretary	1950s
	President	1962-67
Tulio Antonio	President	1968-69
Art Sambuchi	President	1976-94

Local No. 2604: Strip Mill and specialty shops

Edwin Mastrangelo (Buffalo)	Vice President	1949-50
Jack Meta	Trustee	1944-48
	President	1964-78
Tony Iafallo	Treasurer	1964-67
Ralph Carestio	Vice President	1967
Tom Cervolia (Angola)	President	1980s

Local No. 2605: structural fabricating shop

Joseph Manzella (Buffalo)	Financial Secretary	1941-42
Louis DiRosa (Buffalo)	Trustee	1945
	Treasurer	1956-58
Anthony Anticola	President	1956-58

Local No. 2613, all South Buffalo Railway employees other than train crewmen

Joseph Scarpello (Buffalo)	Vice President	1941
Tony Falbo	Financial Secretary	1943
Charles DePerto	Trustee	1942
Leonard Govenettio	President	1944
Frank Sardina	Financial Secretary	1946
John Govenettio	President	1950-54
Frank Pasqualetti (Buffalo)	Vice President	1950
	Financial Secretary	1953
Justino Christiano	Trustee	1950
	Vice President	1953
Joe Bavaro (Cheektowaga)	Financial Secretary	1950
	Financial Secretary	1956-58
	Recording Secretary	1954
	President	1960-62
Bart Graziadei (Buffalo)	Vice President	1956
	Vice President	1960-62
Dominick Nasso	Trustee	1956-58
Jack Gardina	Treasurer	1958-62
Leonard Verrastro	Financial Secretary	1960-62
Luigi Costanzo (Buffalo)	Trustee	1960
Albert Ceccarelli	President	1960's
Frank Militello (Angola)	Recording Secretary	1962

*This is not a complete list of the Italian American officers for this time period.
Sources: Compiled from various interviews, newspaper articles, and union records.

Leonard Govenettio, a member of Local No. 2613, which included all South Buffalo Railway workers except train crewmen, was elected president of his local in 1944. Photo source: Dorothy Govenettio

John Govenettio, brother of Leonard, was president of Local No. 2613 from 1950 to 1954. He and his brother grew up on Roland Avenue. Photo source: Dorothy Govenettio

Armand Capodagli, of Bethlehem Park, was treasurer of Local No. 2602 from 1956 to 1958. Photo source: "St. Anthony's Holy Name Society, First Annual Dance," booklet, 11/30/46

Bethlehem plants. The Bar Mill and the Specialty Shop were sold to other companies, and the Hot Mill section of the Strip Mill, the Basic Oxygen Furnace, and many other buildings were razed. Soon the Galvanizing Mill, the Cold Mill department of the Strip Mill, and the Coke Ovens were the only units functioning, serviced by a greatly downsized South Buffalo Railway. In 2001, the railway was purchased by Genesee and Wyoming Industries. The Coke Ovens were shut down, and in 2001, the Bethlehem Steel Corporation filed for bankruptcy. The Cold Mill and Galvanizing mill eventually were purchased by Arcelot-Mittel, an international steel cartel. During the last 20 years, the aging steelworkers, even in retirement, faced new challenges. Union leaders such as Art Sambuchi, whose grandfather was immigrant steelworker Giovanni Sambuchi, continued to seek settlements owed by the steel company to open-hearth workers and chippers who became ill from the selenium and lead in automobile steel. Even more dangerous were the effects of rolling billets made of uranium that the government sent to the Lackawanna plant between 1949 and 1951. Some steelworkers developed cancer decades later, and Sambuchi's union local attempted to get settlements for the families of workers who died as a result.[82]

At the turn of the last century in Lackawanna, the struggle to gain workers' rights began with small actions taken by Italians and other workers. The baby steps taken in 1902 grew to a huge movement to form a union in 1919. Many Italian immigrants took up the union banner and suffered the trauma of defeat in the Great Steel Strike of 1919, then endured the

total control of the steel corporations from 1920 to 1936. In the late 1930s, immigrants and their sons joined with other ethnic blue-collar workers to take part in SWOC's organizing campaign. Their determination led to the union's crucial victory at the local Bethlehem plant in 1941. Whereas Lackawanna Steel had boasted of its recruitment of "docile immigrants" 40 years earlier, in the struggle to win recognition for the union, the Slavic and Italian ethnics displayed a strong fighting spirit. The formation of the United Steelworkers of America marked a new era for the workers. The immigrants, especially the second generation, won the respect and social advancement they so desired through their involvement in the union movement. For Italians and other ethnic groups, this was a pivotal moment in history. Historians have noted that World War II marked the end of minority status for Italian Americans, who proved themselves to be patriotic workers in defense industries and loyal soldiers in U.S. military. What is often overlooked is another battle that Italians and other southern and eastern European ethnics successfully fought in the late 1930s and early 1940s—the struggle to gain union recognition for millions of industrial workers. The strike at Bethlehem Steel's Lackawanna plant in 1941 proved to be the turning point in the fight against "Little Steel" and led to the creation of the United Steelworkers of America. For Lackawanna Italians, participation in union organizing was a crucial part of their assimilation into the working class and their attainment of social honor in American society.

Marius DeCarolis was one year old when his family immigrated to the United States. He was active in SWOC from its beginnings, and in 1941 was elected financial secretary of Local No. 2602, which included the plant's yard, mechanical, and electric departments.
Photo source: "St. Anthony's Holy Name Society, First Annual Dance," booklet, 11/30/46

Tony Falbo worked at the roundhouse of the South Buffalo Railway and was elected financial secretary of local No. 2613 in 1943. Like the Govenettio brothers, he had roots on Roland Avenue. Photo source: Collection of Frank Chiodo

Art Sambuchi began a 40-year career at Bethlehem Steel in 1954. He became a union steward in 1960, and went on to be chief steward, chief grievance man, and president of No. Local 2603 of the United Steelworkers of America for 18 years. A strong voice for workers, he was respected as a negotiator, an advocate for health and safety, and for his ability to creatively solve long-standing issues. Photo source: *Front Page*, 1/26/94

One hundred years ago, corporations encouraged mass immigration from Europe and migration within the United States to bring more workers to their plants, thereby undercutting the fledgling union movement. Today, it is often the corporations that migrate, establishing plants in third-world countries offering wages and benefits that are miniscule by American standards, and where unions are unknown. One hundred years go American corporations made fabulous profits, paid low wages to their employees, fought tooth and nail against unionization, and wielded massive political and economic power. Our country has been in a similar state for the past several decades. Once again the American union movement, under increasingly potent attacks since 1980, has been struggling against corporate dominance. By looking at the history of unions, and the tremendous efforts of steelworkers in 1919 and the late 1930s, today's workers can draw on the strength of their fathers' and grandfathers' struggles, and gird themselves for the future. Those of us with roots in Lackawanna can take great pride in and hope from the immigrants who participated in the Great Steel Strike nine decades ago and the first- and second-generation ethnics who won the decisive battle against Little Steel fought in Lackawanna's mills in 1941.

The union movement has been presented in some detail in this chapter because of its significant role in incorporating southeast European ethnics into America's working class. The assimilation of Italians and other ethnic groups, especially in blue-collar towns such as Lackawanna, took place to a significant degree at the work place. The formation of industrial labor unions such as the United Steelworkers of America is linked to the sweat and tears of the immigrants and second-generation workers who fought for workers' rights throughout the twentieth century.

In Chapter 9 other aspects of the Italian work experience in Lackawanna will be explored. Small businesses, tending to boarders, and the gradual rise of a professional class were important developments in the early twentieth century.

CHAPTER 9

BUSINESSES, PROFESSIONS, AND OTHER WORK

*Luca Tarquinio came to the United States from Italy in the early 1880s.
Within the next decade, his wife Maddalena and daughter Carmela had joined him
in Buffalo, where he ran a saloon and restaurant in the Hooks. As their family grew,
he opened a saloon on Genesee Street, near the Buffalo City Hall. Tarquinio then
discovered some enticing business opportunities just south of Buffalo.*

After 1900, Luca Tarquinio focused on business opportunities in West Seneca, where many Italian workmen, some of them living in shacks along Lake Erie, were helping construct the new Lackawanna Steel Company complex. By 1902, Tarquinio and his son-in-law, Antonio Mauriello, had set up a hotel on Gates Avenue and advertised that it was designed to serve the needs of Italians working at the steel plant. The two men included a restaurant in their establishment, which was called the *Albergo Italiano* (Italian Hotel), and claimed to have 80 residents in their building. Soon Luca and Maddalena and six of their children, plus Antonio and Carmela Mauriello and their son Luca, were among the residents.[1]

In 1903, Antonio Mauriello branched out on his own, opening a grocery store a few blocks away at 200 Steelwanna Avenue. The Mauriellos remained in the First Ward for several years, then moved back to Buffalo. Luca Tarquinio continued to run a boardinghouse on Gates Avenue, then moved his family to Victory Avenue in the Irish section of Lackawanna's Second Ward. He died in 1918, and his family members went on to become active in Lackawanna's business and civic life. Like Angelo Morinello before them, Tarquinio and Mauriello were

< Antonio Melillo in his grocery store on Holbrook Street, circa 1925. With him are his daughters, from front to back: Josephine, Rose, Anne, and Santina. The store featured a walk-in refrigeration unit for meats. Photo source: Collection of Anne Melillo-Corvigno

businessmen in Buffalo's Italian quarter who were drawn to the opportunities in the steel plant district that became the city of Lackawanna. They were followed by Calogero Fadale and Antonio George, who moved their businesses from Buffalo to West Seneca. As more Italians settled in the area, a number of them established other businesses.[2]

These businesspeople were among the handful of Italian immigrants in Lackawanna not engaged in steelmaking and railroad work during the first half of the twentieth century. This small but significant portion of Italian breadwinners increased from 11 in 1905 to 173 in 1930 (see Figure 9.1). Several trends were part of this process. The proportion of women in this group gradually rose from 8% in 1910 to 25% in 1930, and the vast majority of these females were American-born. Both women and men of the second generation began entering the workforce during the 1920s, and their proportion among Italian Americans in the nonindustrial sector increased from one in six in 1910 to almost half in 1930. Another trend: the occupations of people engaged in these work settings grew more diverse between 1905 and 1941. Some men and women worked in small factories making boxes or aluminum pans, packing candy, or stitching shirtwaists, while others became clerks in stores or offices. Twenty men worked in construction, a typical job for Italians in 1930, while others held jobs that were more unusual for Italians. In 1910, Dominick Ricci was a sailor on the Great Lakes, and five Italian American women were domestic servants in 1915. In a pattern similar to that of

A 1903 ad in a Buffalo Italian newspaper on the Italian Hotel on "The Avenue" (now Gates Avenue) that offers "all the amenities for Italians who work in the steel plant." Photo source: Buffalo & Erie County Historical Society, *Corriere Italiano*, 2/21/1903

A 1902 ad for the Fadale grocery on Buffalo's west side, offering "generic foods of every type." Calogero and Sara Fadale moved their family and business to Lackawanna's Ingham Avenue two years later. Photo source: Buffalo & Erie County Historical Society, *Corriere Italiano*, 6/7/1902

steel and railroad workers, Lackawanna Italians in nonindustrial vocations increasingly attained semiskilled and skilled positions as time progressed. Gradually, their occupations expanded to include truck drivers and chauffeurs, mechanics, waitresses, seamstresses, salespeople, and hotel employees. While the steel plant and railroads were the most crucial employers of Lackawanna Italians until late in the twentieth century, the nonindustrial vocations became an important part of Italian community life.[3]

This chapter will focus on several segments of nonindustrial work done by Italian men, women, and children, and how each was influenced by the structure and values of the Italian American family. In addition to entrepreneurial business, a small but important class of Italian American professionals appeared in Lackawanna during World War I, gradually growing to 17 in 1941. Several of these people worked for the city's police, fire, or engineering departments. Also of note, the

number of nonprofessional people employed by the city grew to 10 in 1941, a signal of the rising political power of Italians in the Steel City.

Italian men as well as women and children provided secondary sources of family income. Some men brought in extra money from part-time jobs, such as transporting people in their cars or occasionally serving as neighborhood shoemakers or barbers. Important sources of family income were provided by women and children in jobs that were usually not recorded by census takers. In addition to doing housework, raising children, tilling gardens, and canning foods, many women and their older children tended to the needs of boarders (see Chapter 5). Second, a significant number of women and children worked long hours in the family business—often times a storefront within the same structure as the family home. While the husband was usually listed as proprietor of the family business, his wife often functioned as business partner, bookkeeper, and manager of the enterprise, especially if the man was out making deliveries or holding down a job in the steel plant. A third area of endeavor for women and children was agricultural labor on farms south of the city. This work was usually done on a daily basis throughout the summer, but in some cases, whole families lived in crude shanties at a farm for the entire growing and harvesting season. A fourth form of family income was provided by boys and teenagers who did odd jobs—maintained newspaper routes, peddled various goods, or journeyed to Wanakah Country Club to work as caddies. While Italian girls and young women were rarely allowed to go into work situations without protective relatives or *paesani* present, young males were given great autonomy in their occupational ventures. Children, especially girls, also assisted their mothers in many functions, including that of caring for their younger siblings. All of these informal jobs were important aspects of the economic survival of Italian American families in Lackawanna.[5]

Businesspeople

In 1905 and 1910, the majority of Lackawanna Italians in nonindustrial occupations were self-employed businesspeople. Although this percentage dropped some after 1915, businesspeople remained the single largest segment of this category up to 1941. Italians throughout the United States were quick to start independent ventures; in 1905, they operated 10,000 stores in New York City alone. In addition to grocery stores, Italians were notable for providing personal services, especially as barbers and shoemakers. The first Italian business in Lackawanna, was the saloon opened by Angelo Morinello in 1900. Within a few years, Morinello was running a combined saloon-dry goods-grocery store-rooming house on Roland

FIGURE 9.1
Lackawanna Italian Workers Not Engaged in Industrial or Railroad Work

	1905	1910	1915	1920	1925	1930	1941*
Business Proprietor	9	20	23	21	35	47	55
Professional	—	—	—	3	6	7	16
Wage Earner (includes skilled)							
– Store clerk/salesperson							
a) In family business	1	—	1	8	—	7	3
b) Other	—	—	1	2	7	12	3
– Clerk, office	—	—	—	2	2	1	2
– Laborer, small factory	—	2	2	5	2	22	—
– Bartender	—	1	1	—	—	—	2
– Stenographer/secretary	1	—	—	—	1	2	2
– Bookkeeper/accountant	—	—	1	1	4	—	—
– Domestic servant	—	5	—	—	—	1	2
– Driver/chauffeur	—	—	—	2	3	2	1
– City employee	—	—	1	—	1	4	10
– Other	—	1	2	3	16	68	11
Totals:	**11**	**29**	**32**	**47**	**77**	**173**	**107**

*The *Erie County Directory* is much less complete than the censuses; thus the 1941 totals for wage earners are significantly lower than those provided in the 1930 census.

Sources: U.S. Census, 1910, 1920, 1930; New York Census, 1905, 1915, 1925; *Erie County Directory*, 1941.

Avenue. He acquired real estate and sold a number of Roland Avenue lots to other Italians. His son Frank established three grocery stores and eventually bought property in both Lackawanna and other parts of Erie County. Frank Jr. later took over his father's grocery store and ran it for several years. Other Lackawanna Italian families also launched a series of businesses over three generations (see Figure 9.19).[6]

The 686 business ventures founded by Lackawanna Italians between 1900 and 2008 are divided into two time periods, pre- and post-1950, with 55% in the former and 45% in the latter (see Figure 9.2). The businesses were identified through interviews and a variety of documents. While not exhaustive, the Figure 9.2 listing probably includes the majority of enterprises created by Lackawanna Italian immigrants and their descendants during the past century. Divided into seven general categories, the table makes it apparent that food-related businesses comprise the largest category, and service businesses the second largest. Combined, these two sectors account for nearly 60% of the business totals. Focusing on specific types of businesses, the seven most numerous are: restaurants (101), groceries/delicatessens (94), automobile-service businesses (60), saloons (49), barber shops (45), construction and building supply firms (33), and shoemakers (29).

Among the businesses founded by Lackawanna Italians, more than a third are concentrated in the food industry. The food of an immigrant group offers a potential business opportunity for a group member who would venture to open a restaurant, deli, or food stand. This is especially true if the ethnic group's food is noticeably different from the standard meat-and-potatoes fare of northwest Europe that dominates many regions of the United States. A century ago, Italian cuisine was a novelty that appealed to many Americans. This is one reason for the great number of Italian-food-oriented businesses, especially restaurants, which were often patronized by non – Italians. It was not until after World War II that a large number of Italians, especially members of the second generation, had the financial resources to establish restaurants and that the American public could afford to eat out more often. Early in the twentieth century, selling basic foods to Italian immigrants, both lone males and housewives, was another matter. The foods and spices favored by Italian immigrants were often unavailable at non – Italian groceries, a void that fueled the rapid growth of Italian groceries that carried olive oil, cod fish, and other products that met the needs and tastes of immigrant households. Starting a grocery store, produce stand, or confectionery usually

FIGURE 9.2

Lackawanna Italian Businesses, by Decades of Founding 1900-2008

	Total	1900s	1910s	1920s	1930s	1940s	1950s	1960s	1970s	1980s	1990s	2000s
I. FOOD												
1. Confectioners	13	—	3	3	5	—	—	2	—	—	—	—
2. Peddlers, Food Distributors	12	—	1	2	3	6	—	—	—	—	—	—
3. Produce & Poultry Stands	10	—	—	1	3	2	2	1	1	—	—	—
4. Bakeries	3	1	2	—	—	—	—	—	—	—	—	—
5. Groceries, Delicatessens	94	9	10	29	13	12	9	8	4	—	—	—
6. Caterers	6	—	1	—	—	1	2	—	—	1	—	1
7. Restaurants	101	1	—	4	16	14	14	12	20	2	10	8
8. Other Food	3	—	—	—	1	1	—	—	—	—	—	1
SUBTOTALS	**242**	**11**	**17**	**39**	**41**	**36**	**27**	**23**	**25**	**3**	**10**	**10**
II. ALCOHOL/ BEVERAGES												
9. Saloons	49	8	13	3	3	9	5	3	3	—	1	1
10. Liquor Stores	6	—	—	—	—	2	—	3	—	1	—	—
11. Soft Drinks	3	—	—	—	2	—	—	1	—	—	—	—
SUBTOTALS	**58**	**8**	**13**	**3**	**5**	**11**	**5**	**7**	**3**	**1**	**1**	**1**
III. SERVICE												
12. Shoemakers	29	1	5	6	9	3	1	4	—	—	—	—
13. Barbers	45	—	8	9	6	5	5	9	3	—	—	—
14. Beauty Parlors	25	—	—	—	5	3	3	6	4	2	1	1
15. Boardinghouses, Hotels	28	7	11	2	2	—	3	1	2	—	—	—
16. Clothing, Tailors	10	—	1	1	3	1	—	2	1	—	—	1
17. Cleaners & Laundries	3	—	—	—	1	2	—	—	—	—	—	—
18. Insurance & Accounting	7	—	—	—	1	1	2	1	1	—	—	1
19. Undertakers, Monuments	6	—	1	—	2	—	2	—	—	—	1	—
20. Realtors	10	—	2	1	1	1	1	1	1	1	1	—
SUBTOTALS	**163**	**8**	**28**	**19**	**30**	**16**	**17**	**24**	**12**	**3**	**3**	**3**
IV. RETAIL STORES												
21. Dry Goods, Hardware	5	—	—	2	1	—	—	1	—	1	—	—
22. Furniture & Appliances	13	—	—	—	1	3	1	3	3	1	1	—
23. Gift & Floral Shops	5	—	—	—	—	1	2	1	—	—	—	1
SUBTOTALS	**23**	**—**	**—**	**2**	**2**	**4**	**3**	**5**	**3**	**2**	**1**	**1**

Figure 9.2

Lackawanna Italian Businesses, by Decades of Founding: 1900 – 2008 *(Continued)*

	Total	1900s	1910s	1920s	1930s	1940s	1950s	1960s	1970s	1980s	1990s	2000s
V. AUTOMOTIVE, TRUCKING, DELIVERY												
24. Auto: Gas Stations, Repair, Parts, Dealers	60	—	—	3	10	10	7	16	5	3	1	5
25. Trucking, Excavation	19	—	—	3	4	4	4	4	—	—	—	—
26. Ice & Coal Delivery	7	—	1	5	1	—	—	—	—	—	—	—
SUBTOTALS	86	—	1	11	15	14	11	20	5	3	1	5
VI. CONSTRUCTION, LIGHT INDUSTRY, ETC.												
27. Construction, Building Supplies	33	—	—	5	1	7	10	6	—	—	2	2
28. Manufacturing	6	—	—	1	—	—	3	1	1	—	—	—
29. Scrapyards	5	—	—	—	—	2	—	2	—	—	—	1
SUBTOTALS	44	—	—	6	1	9	13	9	1	—	2	3
VII. OTHER												
30. Home Decorating	11	—	—	1	1	2	2	2	1	—	2	—
31. Recreation	15	—	—	1	4	5	2	3	—	—	—	—
32. Other	40	—	4	6	1	2	3	7	6	2	2	7
33. Type Unknown	4	2	—	—	—	—	1	—	—	—	1	—
SUBTOTALS	70	2	4	8	6	9	8	12	7	2	5	7
GRAND TOTALS:	**686**	**29**	**63**	**88**	**100**	**99**	**84**	**100**	**56**	**14**	**23**	**30**

1900–1949: 379   **1950–2008: 307**

Sources: Interviews; Lackawanna and Buffalo city directories; Buffalo suburban directories; Erie County directories; newspaper articles and ads.

required minimal outlay of capital. Most of the businesses established were small concerns that easily supported and used the resources of the central institution of Italian culture—the family. About six of every 10 grocery stores operated by Lackawanna Italians were founded between 1902 and 1939. For Steel City Italian immigrants in the first half of the twentieth century, grocery stores served as the single most important expression of the trend to establish independent family businesses, one that was noted in Italian settlements throughout the United States. In 1931, about 23% of Buffalo's 1,552 grocery stores were run by Italians. Many an Italian merchant probably shared some of the traits of Calogero Fadale, whose daughter described him as "independent, hard-headed; he never worked for others."[7]

Throughout Lackawanna, many small grocery stores served the array of ethnic groups, and those operated by Italians constituted a significant proportion of the total. In 1931, Italians were the proprietors of 20, or 19%, of the city's 104 grocery stores. This figure is significant when one considers that Italians comprised only seven percent of Lackawanna's population at that time. The first Italian grocery was established by Angelo Morinello in 1902 on Roland Avenue. Three years later, Peter Sirianni had a grocery on Front Street, a block north of Morinello's business. In 1903, Antonio Mauriello founded the first Italian grocery store west of the tracks, in what soon became Lackawanna's First Ward. A year later, Calogero and Sara Fadale opened their grocery on Ingham Avenue. The Fadale's business became a general store that lasted many years. As a boy, the eldest Fadale child, John, would go to the Old Village to take orders, then deliver the groceries the following day. The very first day he did so, he gathered 42 orders.[8]

In the following two decades, many Italian grocery stores opened. *La Cooperativa*, launched by the Lake Erie Italian Club in 1917 as a cooperative store for members, was managed by Angelo Carlini and located in a storefront owned by Enrichietta Oddi. Like many other business ventures of its

FIGURE 9.3

Statistics on Lackawanna Italian Businesses

I. Total number of Italian businesses   **686**

1) Located in Lackawanna

    Proprietor(s), Lackawanna resident(s)   517

    Proprietor(s), not Lackawanna resident(s)*   92

2) Located outside of Lackawanna

    Proprietor(s), Lackawanna resident(s)   77

II. Total number of proprietors, including all partners   **654**

		Italians	Non–Italian Partners
1) Residency	Lackawanna residents	504	37
	Non – Lackawanna residents	108	5
	Total	612	42
2) Gender	Male	407	30
	Female	105	12
	Total	612	42

III. Generation

First (immigrant)	44%
Second (child of immigrant)	44%
Third (grandchild of immigrant) or later	12%
Total	100%

*In addition to those who regularly came to Lackawanna to sell goods, other Italian merchants occasionally did so. Filippo Balistriri of South Buffalo carved tombstones for Holy Cross Cemetery and also made small plaster statues that he took to the OLV institutions and even sold at the gates of Bethlehem Steel.

Some proprietors started multiple businesses; nine is the greatest number. There were 156 individual businesses that had two, three, four, or 10 proprietors or partners. In 31 cases, the two partners are husband-wife teams; in 39 others, the owners are relatives. Of the 602 Italian proprietors, 376, or 62%, were identified by generation and regional roots. Businesses are calculated on the basis of ownership, i.e.— the proprietor. For example, if the original owner of a saloon sold it to another person, this was counted as two different businesses. If two partners owned a business and one died or left the business, this was counted as one business. However, if a child or other relative of the original proprietor purchased or inherited the business, this was counted as two different businesses.
Source: *Steel Labor*, June 1947.

time, it lasted only briefly. After it failed, Oddi set up her own grocery in the storefront, a business with a lifetime of about 12 years. Between 1904 and 1925, Italians founded 23 groceries along Ingham Avenue and its side streets, an area heavily populated by Italians (see Figure 9.4). Larger grocery stores also provided employment opportunities for the Italian community. Peter Mazuca took over a grocery in the Old Village in 1920, then as Italians moved into Bethlehem Park, he followed them. He had a building constructed at 76 Jackson in 1925, moved his family into the second-floor apartment, and ran his store on the first floor. Charles Saccomanno, Mazuca's cousin, and Cassiano Baldassari were among the nine or 10 employees at the large store. In the grocery section of the building, customers ordered at a counter and clerks then filed through the shelves gathering the orders. Saccomanno and Baldassari worked as butchers in the store's back room, which people could enter either from a side door or via an arch from the grocery. Saccomanno also drove Mazuca's truck to deliver groceries to customers throughout Lackawanna, but most of his stops were in Bethlehem Park.

The Mazucas did well in their business and in 1931 expanded their operations. Mazuca's son Joseph ran a second grocery store on Arnold Place, near Roland Avenue, and the family opened a restaurant in Athol Springs. Mazuca retired in the early 1930s. When he passed away in 1936, his widow closed the Jackson Avenue store. Charles Saccomanno took over the Arnold Place grocery and ran it for several years with the help of his cousin, Mario Cozzo. He then acquired the vacant store and apartment at 76 Jackson Avenue and reopened the grocery there. The small cluster of commercial buildings at Jackson and Spruce streets housed the majority of storefronts within Bethlehem Park and were prime locations. In the 1930s, Cassiano Baldassari established his own grocery at 75 Jackson, which his widow, Josephine, operated after his death. Tony DePasquale then took over the store for a year, and in the early 1950s, brothers John, Bill, and Joseph Moretti were its proprietors.[9]

East of the railroad tracks, the number of Italian grocers had also grown, and there was some competition among them. In 1910, Angelo and Giuseppina Pitillo moved from Buffalo to Roland Avenue, where they rented an apartment from Angelo Morinello. Mrs. Pitillo soon started a grocery business that attracted boarders from the nearby home of Francesco and Carmela Falcone, who, like Morinello, were *paesani*. Morinello, angry over losing some of his customers, told the Pitillo family to find lodging elsewhere. After moving with her family to a nearby apartment, the undaunted Giuseppina Pitillo opened another grocery. In 1912, the family bought a house and reestablished the store there. Finally, in 1925, the Pitillos settled in a storefront at the corner of Electric and Milnor, again maintaining a grocery store/confectionery, which Pitillo operated until her death in 1931. Her son Pasquale then ran the store until 1933, when, with the end of Prohibition, he established a saloon. A block to the north, the ideally located storefronts at 105 Roland were home to a succession of Italian groceries, beginning with Joseph Miceli's store in 1922 (see Figure 9.5).[10]

Many grocery stores operated by immigrants had unique features that attracted customers. Some stores—such as Antonio Melillo's store, which featured a large, walk-in meat refrigerator,

The grocery store of Michele and Rosa Grasso on Ingham Avenue, circa 1926. Several of the Grasso children are standing out front. The large building which included the store and family living quarters, was always painted green.
Photo source: Collection of Tony Grasso

FIGURE 9.4

ITALIAN GROCERS ON INGHAM AVENUE AND SIDE STREETS,
by Approximate Date of Founding

Calogero & Sara Fadale	194 Ingham	1904
Antonio Milla	[Unk] Ingham	1905
Antonio Melillo	187 Holbrook	1907
Ermete DeMasi	[Unk] Ingham	1908
Sam Morgan	201 Ingham	1908
Carminantonio Picariello	231 Ingham	1910
Pasquale Tibollo	245 Ingham	1910
Cesare Tucci	194 Odell	1911
Francesco Monaco	245 Ingham	1914
Salvatore Ginnetti	192 Odell	1915
La Cooperativa	219 Ingham	1917
Serafino Mattucci	229 Ingham	1917
Carmine Spagnolo	211 Ingham	1918
Enrichetta Oddi	219 Ingham	1919
Tony Amorosi	245 Ingham	1920
Cassiano Baldassari	201 Ingham	1920
Ermete Silvestrini	201 Ingham	1921
Vincenzo Suffoletto	16 Dona	1921
Steve Canestrari	211 Ingham	1922
Antonio Giordano	194 Odell	1925
Rosa Grasso	276 Ingham	1925
Tony Turchiarelli	209 Ingham	1925
Eugenio Galanti	22 Dona	1921
Ersilia Bracci	123 School	1928
Sam Marinaccio	205 Ingham	1935
Gennaro & Adele Panzetta	194 Odell	1930s
Mariano Savaglio	65 Dona	1940

[Unk] = information not available.

Note: Street numbers are those of the numbering system instituted in 1938; in earlier years, the numbering system was different.

Sources: Interviews; newspaper ads; U.S. Census, 1910, 1920; New York Census, 1905, 1915, 1925; *Buffalo telephone book,* 1912 – 1930; *Erie County Directory,* 1931 – 1941.

carried fresh meat. At his Dona Street grocery, Mariano Savaglio sold chicken which he advertised with a sign that combined English and his native Italian: "Gallina for sale." Specialty products catered to regional tastes. Ersilia Bracci's homemade sausage, seasoned with the milder spices favored in Marche, drew many fellow Marchegiani to her store. Customers were also drawn to stores whose owner spoke their own dialect of Italian, or a similar one that they could easily understand. Some proprietors, including Frank Morinello, Virginia Mattucci, and Pasqualina Amorosi—spoke enough Polish or other languages to accommodate patrons of different ethnic groups. The earliest telephones in the city were often those of local store owners, which attracted people who reasoned that they might earn phone rights by becoming regular customers (see Figure 9.7). This was an important issue when the steel plants and railroads began using the telephone to call in substitutes for ill workers. Some male proprietors, such as Carmine Spagnolo and Vincenzo Suffoletto, offered a back room in their stores where males could socialize, play cards, and drink homemade wine; in turn, the men's wives shopped at these stores.[11]

As indicated previously, a number of Italian grocers visited customers to take orders, then made deliveries to the homes. Deliveries were usually done by the male head of household, or the older sons, who at first walked their routes carrying large baskets, then used horse-drawn wagons; some eventually had trucks. Tony Ziccarelli remembers the "rickety, shaky old truck" in which Antonio Melillo delivered groceries to his First Ward customers during the 1940s. Merchant Serafino Mattucci had a truck by 1916. One of the first grocers to use a delivery truck was Frank Morinello, who bought a vehicle

Businesses in Bethlehem Park at the intersection of Jackson Avenue and Spruce Street, 1930s. The grocery store is that of Charles and Anna Saccomanno; next to it is the barbershop of Charle's cousin, Mike Saccomanno.
Photo source: Joe Saccomanno

FIGURE 9.5

ITALIAN GROCERS OPERATING IN THE ROLAND AVENUE AREA
by Approximate Date of Founding

Angelo Morinello	1 Roland	1902
Peter Sirianni	22 Front	1905
Giuseppina Pitillo	67 Roland	1910
Joe Miceli	105 Roland	1922
Michele Orlando	60* Milnor	1922
Antonio Delguercio	105 Roland	1922
Sam & Ursala Mancuso	26 Roland	1922
Tony Welsh	105 Roland	1927
Phil Verel	63 Roland	1928
Giuseppina Yoviene	3096* South Park	1929
Joseph Mazuca	21 Arnold Place	1931
Michael Sirianni	3049* South Park	1931
Giuseppe Reviezzo	83 Roland	1938
_?_ Gennari	83 Roland	1940s
Santo & Michelina Mazza	105 Roland	1930s
Frank Chiodo & Ralph Cirello	105 Roland	1945
Tony Falbo	105 Roland	1947

_?_ = first name not known.

* Exact street number uncertain; Addresses on some streets changed several times; all street numbers given conform to system instituted in 1938.

Sources: Interviews; newspaper ads; U.S. Census, 1910, 1920; New York Census, 1905, 1915, 1925; *Buffalo telephone book*, 1912 – 1930; *Erie County Directory*, 1931 – 1941.

Anna Morinello holds her son John while her daughter Katherine stands at left, circa 1920. The grocery store they are standing in front of—run by Anna's husband, Frank Morinello—is located at the corner of Electric and Kirby avenues. Photo source: Collection of Frank Morinello Jr.

in 1922 and constructed a brick garage for it next to his Kirby Avenue store.[12]

Most of the grocers extended credit to their customers who were strapped for cash. Caterina Pacillo started shopping at the Melillo grocery because both families were from Campania. But Melillo won the undying loyalty of the Pacillos during the depression of 1907, when Antonio Pacillo was laid off from the steel plant and Melillo hired the family's eldest son, Vito, as a helper and paid him with groceries that fed the family.[13]

The Great Depression took its toll on Italian groceries; only 14 were counted among the city's 100 grocery stores in 1938. As the American economy recovered in the early 1940s, more grocery stores were established by Italians outside the three Italian settlements. This was a reflection of the significant exodus from the old neighborhoods by members of European ethnic groups who were willing to live in mixed-ethnic communities. After World War II, second- and third-generation Italian Americans set up grocery stores or delicatessens in the Italian neighborhoods as well as other areas of the city. The stores tended to be on main traffic routes, such as Ridge Road, where in the late 1940s Salvatore Butera opened a small supermarket in the First Ward, and Daniel Zaccarine established a delicatessen in the Second Ward. The trend toward larger stores and more centralized locations were apparent as Italian businessmen from Buffalo established branches of the Columbia Market, the Federal Market, and F. & J. Perna Produce in the newly developed Abbott Road Plaza during the 1950s. This pattern, plus the advanced age of many immigrant proprietors, marked the demise of many neighborhood grocery stores.[14]

The majority of the Italian groceries were small mom-and-pop stores. Some were short-lived, as was the case with Salvatore Ginnetti's grocery store on Odell Street, which functioned for several months in 1915. Other groceries were in business for decades: Tony Melillo's store lasted from 1907 to 1948, Carmine and Angelina Spagnolo's from 1918 to 1960, and Sam and Ursala Mancuso's from 1925 to 1979. Calogero and Sara Fadale maintained their grocery store on Ingham Avenue from 1905 until Calogero's death in 1929. Sara then ran the grocery until her passing in 1958, and her son Louis and his wife operated it until about 1985. Many stores struggled to make a decent profit, and the family survived economically only through additional sources of income. Charles Saccomanno prolonged the life of his Bethlehem Park grocery when he joined the Red and White grocery chain in 1960. The centralized buying helped him cut costs, as a truckload of food products was delivered weekly. Saccomanno further improved his business viability by seizing on the idea of precut meats that could be wrapped and quickly sold to customers.[15]

This grocery store on the corner of Ingham Avenue and Odell Street, circa 1920, was operated by Carmine and Angelina Spagnolo, who opened it in 1918.
Photo source: Collection of Jene Amadori

Carmine Spagnolo in his grocery store in 1959. He and his wife Angelina ran the store from 1918 to 1960, then retired and moved to Bethlehem Park.
Photo source: Audrey Spagnolo-Surgenor

Salvatore Yoviene and his daughter, circa 1929. Yoviene creatively decorated his car to advertise either his own business or the grocery store run by his mother and sister, Josephine and Margaret Yoviene. Photo source: Jim Yoviene

The novelty of Italian food to Americans and the tendency of Italians to found independent businesses combined to foster the growth of Italian restaurants throughout the United States. This trend was present in Lackawanna, although it developed slowly. Unlike a grocery store, a restaurant usually called for more start-up capital. It wasn't until the 1930s that a series of Italian-operated eating establishments was founded. The majority of early Italian restaurants were established by immigrants, but eventually, two-thirds of the proprietors were the children of immigrants. As discussed at the start of this chapter, the first known Italian restaurant in Lackawanna was opened in 1902 by Luca Tarquinio and Antonio Mauriello in their Gates Avenue hotel (see Figure 9.11). Nicholas Mattucci was the most successful of the early Italian restaurateurs, becoming owner of the New Colonial Restaurant in 1928 and later opening five other restaurants in the Buffalo area (see Figure 9.14). Italians were operating only three of the 70 eating establishments in Lackawanna in 1929, but during the 1930s, they established 15 others. A number of these were launched by Italians who had accumulated capital through earlier business ventures. Mary Fusco-Rogers, who inherited a confectionery from her mother, later operated a restaurant-nightclub on Hamburg Turnpike. Peter and Joe Mazuca, who ran grocery stores, each established a restaurant. Nick Sperduto, like Mary Fusco-Rogers and Joe Mazuca, a second-generation Italian American, was running a tavern and clam parlor at 235 Ingham by 1931. As was the case with a number of Italian businessmen, he also maintained a job in the steel plant or with the city.

Ads, 1922. Photo source: Lackawanna Library, *Lackawanna Daily Journal, 5/1/22*

Sue Fox and her husband Joe operated this grocery at South Park Avenue and Parkview Street from 1929 to 1943. Photo source: Anne Fox-Skazynski

When Sperduto and his wife Margaret opened a restaurant in 1933, she ran the business much of the time, preparing roast-beef dinners for WPA workers and charging them 50 cents for the food, a nickel for beer, and a dime for mixed drinks. The Sperdutos remodeled the building in 1948, making it into a pizzeria with a bar and renaming it the AA Restaurant in honor of their two sons, Angelo and Anthony. The first pizzeria in Lackawanna, it was patronized by people of diverse ethnic groups and many politicians.[16]

A number of other restaurants also grew out of successful saloon businesses during the 1930s and 1940s. The Ingham Avenue saloon operated by Luigi and Caterina Conti became the Lone Star Restaurant. In Bethlehem Park, Joe Amadori expanded the Park Grille into a restaurant featuring homemade spaghetti and ravioli. Pasquale Pitillo followed a similar course at his Electric Avenue establishment, and his wife and children all worked in the business, which Pitillo ran until 1974, when his son Ang took over. Lavinio Montanari established the Fano Restaurant, named after his hometown in Marche, on Hamburg Turnpike in 1934. He persuaded his brothers Giuseppe and Luigi to work for him, and Giuseppe

Frank Chiodo, pictured here, and his cousin Ralph Cirello ran the grocery and imports store at Roland and Electric avenues from 1945 to 1947. Photo source: Collection of Frank Chiodo

FIGURE 9.6

ITALIAN GROCERS WHO BRANCHED OUT

Some Italian businesspeople ventured into neighborhoods dominated by other ethnic groups. Frank Morinello worked in his father's store, then in 1915 established his own grocery at Kirby and Electric avenues in a predominantly Polish neighborhood. It helped that Morinello could speak some Polish. In 1928, he purchased a tract of land on the east side of South Park Avenue, had a large building constructed just north of Martin Road, and moved his business there. (About the time he did so, Mellie Verel set up a grocery store on Kirby Avenue, just a few doors down from the site Morinello had vacated.) Morinello, his wife, and their five children all worked in the new store, as did four employees, two from the Acanfora family. In addition to the long hours of work, the family and store staff endured a more formidable stressor. In 1931, a gas leak caused an explosion that

demolished the store and severely burned Morinello, Sal Acanfora, and two customers. Morinello persevered and had a new storefront built at the corner of South Park Avenue and Martin Road. In 1955, Morinello sold the business to his son, Frank Jr., who operated it for another six years.

Italians also ventured into other neighborhoods closer to Ridge Road. Two of the Tarquinio brothers maintained a grocery on Electric Avenue, which was the dividing line between Polish and Irish neighborhoods. Joe Fox, who had previously worked in a grocery store in Arcade, New York, and his wife Susan established a grocery on South Park Avenue, just south of the Buffalo city line, in an Irish neighborhood. They operated it from 1931 until 1943, and for a brief period, Fox also ran a second store around the corner on Parkview. Among the Foxes'

customers were two neighborhood families, the DelVecchios and the Pacillos. Susan Fox's parents, Biagio and Mariana Pinto, operated a grocery at the corner of South Park Avenue and Maplegrove from 1925 into the 1930s. Immigrants who spoke very little English, the Pintos were somehow able to maintain their business in this heavily Irish neighborhood. Charles Fadale branched out from the family business on Ingham Avenue and had established a second grocery store at the corner of Ridge and Abbott roads by 1922. Pat Fadale remembers that it was a treat for her and her twin sister Josephine to go all the way from Ingham Avenue to the store on Saturdays to help their father. Fadale operated the store for two years, closed it, then opened another in South Buffalo that was closed by the family when he died in 1929.

Sources: Interviews with Frank Morinello Jr., December 26, 1983 and July 7, 1996; Anne Fox-Skrzynski, March 31, 1996; Joe Fox Jr., March 31, 1996; and Patricia Fadale-Pellegrino, July 8, 1996; Arcade Sesquicentennial and Historical Society, *Progress with a Past: Arcade, New York, 1807 – 1957*, 1957, p. 151.

FIGURE 9.7

ITALIANS WITH TELEPHONES IN LACKAWANNA: 1912 – 1925

Businesspeople were often the first in an area to obtain telephone service, which made their stores or offices even more important as community hubs. From 1912 to 1917, the *Buffalo Telephone Directory* had a separate section for Lackawanna. The 1912 edition lists 186 telephones in Lackawanna and Blasdell, most of them at government offices, factories, institutions, and businesses. Three Italian businessmen were included:

	Businesspeople	Business/Residence	Address
1912	Mattucci, Serafino	saloon	229 Ingham Ave.
	Morgan, Sam	grocery	205 Ingham Ave.
	Verel, John	residence	1 Roland Ave. (saloon)

During the following years, more Italians obtained phone service and were listed, including:

1913	Guadagno, Antonio	residence	195 Ingham Ave. (bakery)
	Amorosi, Antonio	saloon	219 Ingham Ave.
	Turchiarelli, Antonio	saloon	227 Ingham Ave.
1916	Fadale, Charles	grocer	194 Ingham Ave.
	Mauriello, Antonio	saloon	200* Steelawanna Ave.
1917	Monaco, Paolo	saloon	219 Ingham Ave.
1918	Fusco, Mary L.	residence	2240 Hamburg Turnpike (confectionery)
	Monaco, Frank	residence	226 Ingham Ave. (grocery)
	Morinello, Frank	residence	179 Kirby Ave. (grocery)
	Oddi, Enrichetta	residence	219 Ingham Ave. (grocery)
1920	Fadale, John D., MD	office	231 Ridge Rd.
	Silvestrini Co.	grocer	201 Ingham Ave.
1921	Mazuca, Peter	residence	702 First St. (grocer)
	Pitillo, Josephine	confectionery	1783 Electric Ave.
	Sirianni, Peter	residence	3049* South Park Ave. (grocery)
1922	Canestrari, Stephen	grocer	211 Ingham Ave.
1925	DePaula, Anthony	residence	218 Ingham Ave. (bakery)
	Falconio, Antonio	barber	191 Roland Ave.
	Galanti, Eugenio	grocer	22 Dona St.
	Pacillo, Anthony	residence	516 Second St.
	Sirianni, James A.	batteries	954 Ridge Rd.
	Yoviene, Josephine	residence	3096* South Park Ave. (grocery)

These listings are reproduced as shown in the original telephone directories. Where a listing indicates a "residence," the type of business is added in parentheses after the street address.

All of these people except Anthony Pacillo and Dr. John Fadale operated businesses.

* Exact street number uncertain; Addresses on some streets changed several times; all street numbers given conform to system instituted in 1938.

Source: *Buffalo Telephone Directory*, 1912 – 1925.

prepared a well-seasoned pork specialty called *porchetta* several times a year. The building was expanded to accommodate a band and a dance floor, and an outdoor bocce court was added. The restaurant drew customers not only from Lackawanna but also from Buffalo and other nearby towns; many of the patrons were Marchegiani. The financial resources acquired during

World War II and the immediate postwar years allowed Italians to open 59 restaurants including 21 in nearby towns during the three decades following the war, Perhaps the most well known of these was founded by wrestler Ilio DiPaolo in Lackawanna in 1960, which he soon relocated to Blasdell. Since then, Ilio DiPaolo's Restaurant, still a popular dining and gathering spot,

In 1908, Antonio and Giuseppina DePaula opened an
Ingham Avenue bakery that all of their children helped
run. When Giuseppina died in the early 1920s, the
business was sold to the Diaz family. In this 1923 photo,
Mrs. Diaz is sitting with her daughter. Standing are
Caroline DePaula, on the left, and Anna Monaco.
Photo source: Collection of Caroline DePaula-Silvaroli

FIGURE 9.8

THREE ITALIAN BAKERIES AND THE BUFFALO CONNECTION

Buffalo Italians figure prominently in the story of three
Lackawanna bakeries. By the time Antonio and Angelina
Giorgio established the first Italian bakery in Lackawanna
in 1908, their family had completed a series of migrations.
The couple had married in their hometown of San Fele,
Basilicata, and soon had three children. In 1892, Antonio
joined his older brother in Niagara Falls, New York, and
Angelina and the children followed six years later. In 1900,
the family moved to the lower Main Street area of Buffalo,
just a few blocks from "the Hooks." Four more children
were born, and the family name was Americanized to
George. Antonio ran a bakery on Burwell Place for several
years, then the family moved to 195 Ingham Avenue in
Lackawanna. Reestablishing his bakery in the new location,
Antonio was assisted by his oldest son, Frank. When
Antonio George died in 1912, the family sold the business,
and the older sons took jobs at the steel plant to support
the large family.

Antonio Guadagno had immigrated from Campania to
Buffalo, where he ran a shoe-repair shop. His brother, an
Erie County sheriff's deputy, informed him that the George
bakery was for sale, and Guadagno purchased it and moved
his family to Lackawanna. For a while, he operated the
business with Pasquale Tibollo, another former Buffalonian,
but the latter left to start a grocery store a few blocks down
Ingham Avenue in 1925. Guadagno operated the bakery
for another 25 years, assisted by his sons, who became
baker's helpers as teenagers.

The third Italian bakery in Lackawanna was operated
by Antonio DePaula, who arrived in the city in 1905, and
five years later started a bakery at 224 Ingham. His wife,
Giuseppina, and all their children assisted in the bakery,
with his two eldest sons, Joseph and Leonard, serving as
baker's helpers. Following the death of Giuseppina, DePaula
sold the bakery to a Spanish family in 1925.

Sources: *Buffalo City Directory*, 1904-1908; interviews with Elizabeth
George-Rosati, September 8, 1984; and Tony Grasso, November 27, 1981.

has been operated by his son Dennis following DiPaolo's death
in 1995. By the 1980s, ethnic restaurants represented 10% of
all restaurants in the United States; Chinese, Italian, and Mexican
accounted for 70% of the ethnic establishments.[17]

Lackawanna Italians founded a variety of food businesses,
including 11 confectioneries and three bakeries. In 1928,
V. Jimmy D'Alessandro and Nunze Oddy gathered $1,200 to
purchase four acres of land on a sparsely settled stretch of
Abbott Road. The men planned to raise chickens and sell the
eggs for less than the prevailing rate. They constructed a coop
and began the operation, but the chickens soon died because
the structure was not heated to the needed temperature.
Undaunted, D'Alessandro then lived alone in a rented house
at the site and raised sheep for two years.[18]

Other Italians joined the ranks of food peddlers who traveled
through the city streets. The first was Celestino Nigro, who
began selling ice cream from his horse and wagon in 1915.
Nigro continued this business into the 1940s, by which time
he had several competitors, including Mariano Savaglio (see

Figure 9.12). Lackawanna Italian peddlers, including two
females, also sold other types of food. Angelina Poliseno
delivered snails to her customers in Bethlehem Park, and Maria
Giuliani took orders for snails and fresh fish, then delivered
these orders by car to First Ward Italians. Both women lived
in Bethlehem Park and each was sometimes referred to as *la
ciamutara* or *la ciammarughe* (the snail seller). One of their

FIGURE 9.9
AN ICE CREAM PEDDLER AND A 1940 TRAGEDY

Mariano Savaglio was born in Marano Principato, Calabria, and immigrated to Lackawanna with a *paesano* in 1939, and immediately began work in the steel mills. A year later he purchased a pony and a white wagon. For the next 22 years Savaglio's wagon was a common site in Lackawanna and South Buffalo. In 1951 he sent to Calabria for his son Carlo, who assisted him with the ice cream business. Both men had full-time jobs, but at night they made ice cream suckers in their Dona Street home, and then they took turns on the afternoon and evening runs peddling routes. Typically the route included stops along Ingham Avenue, Holbrook Street, in Bethlehem Park, the New Village, the Ridgewood Village, and along Tifft Street in Buffalo. Carlo could complete the route in three hours, and on hot days he or Mariano did a second run. The ice cream suckers sold for 10 cents, and children were readily attracted by the bells worn by Pete the horse, the chance to pet the friendly pony, and the bright wagon bearing the sign: "Mariano Savaglio & Son, Ice Cream." Mariano and Carlo Savaglio gave up the business in 1961.

For 20 years the Savaglios' wagon was drawn by a pony named Pete, but originally Marianno Savaglio had a different pony. That pony and Mariano Savaglio were involved in a sad but memorable incident that occurred on a exceptionally warm day in November

1940, as recalled by Michael Langan. President Roosevelt was touring Lackawanna and its steel plant, and crowds gathered along Ridge Road to get a look at the motorcade. At Ridge and South Park, Savaglio had parked his pony and wagon along the curb so he could sell ice cream and candy on the hot day. Meanwhile an iceman was trying to pass through with his horse and wagon, but he was slowed by the crowd. As the ice wagon moved past Savaglio's cart, the two peddlers exchanged greetings. A policeman shouted to the ice man to speed it up, and suddenly an official car drove up and screeched to a stop. Langan recalls, "The horse and pony both reared up as the car stopped just short of them. The ice wagon shuddered and almost tipped … as ice slid off the back, doing a skeetering dance in all directions onto Ridge Road. The small pony was less lucky. As he reared up he got caught in his harness and fell sideways. The candy cart toppled. The pony became entangled in the wooden rigging and the weight of the cart crushed his leg." Langan continues, "I have a vivid memory of the poor animal lying on the street and looking ahead in narrow terror, blinders blocking a broader view. Candy and ice cream spilled across the pavement." Langan and other children feasted on the spilled candy as Savaglio "chased us away and looked after his pony at the same time." Desperate

to clear the wreckage as the motorcade approached, the police had a tow truck drag the injured pony to a nearby field, while Savaglio tried to comfort the animal. "There in a field of sunflowers a fat policeman wearing white gloves looked half away. He shot the pony and the animal shuddered. The patriots who wanted to see the smiling face of Roosevelt saw the shooting instead. Children were sick to their stomachs, I could barely swallow my candy. It was terrible. As the pony's breathing ceased and his teeth clenched in a final grimace, blood pooled in the matted, coarse grass and flowers underneath its head. Flies were everywhere. The pony's owner tried to shoo them away, but couldn't. He was sobbing. 'Get away, you no-good kids!' he cried. It was then I felt ashamed." Soon the motorcade drove through, and the president made his appearance. "But most children stood mute, caramel drool escaping the corners of their mouths, sick from seeing the pony shot. The president looked bemused. His car travelled over ice cakes, blood and penny candy that day. Residents of our town looked on the pageantry in a profoundly numb state, sick or distracted. The president didn't know about the pony. He bit his cigarette holder tighter and gave the crowd one last fighter's grin. But the pony had beaten him to us."

Sources: Interview with Carlo Savaglio, July 3, 1995; Michael D. Langan, "The President and the Pony," *Buffalo Magazine, Buffalo News*, 5/22/94.

neighbors, Gaetano Masocco, also became a peddler. In 1941, at the age of 41, Masocco retired from the steel plant due to health problems. He bought a small used school bus and converted it into a vehicle to transport produce. Every morning, Monday through Saturday, Masocco went to the Clinton and Baily Market in Buffalo at 4:00 a.m., purchased produce, and returned with it to his home in Bethlehem Park, where he sorted it in the backyard. By 7:00 a.m. the truck was reloaded, and

Masocco was off making deliveries to customers in Lackawanna and surrounding towns. In the summer, he did not finish his route until 9:00 p.m. When his sons John and Dominic each turned seven, they rode along in the truck and helped out year-round. During the school year, Masocco picked up the boys at 3:00 p.m. and continued on his rounds. John Masocco recalls the small seat at the front of the vehicle where he and his brother sat. Near the back door there was a scale suspended

FIGURE 9.10
CONFECTIONERY STORES

Confectioneries, like grocery stores, were small businesses that required little start-up capital. Lackawanna, with its large number of children, had 68 such stores in 1929. Ermete DiMasi, who established a confectionery on Ingham Avenue by 1905, was probably the first Steel City Italian in this field of business. Celestino Nigro had a street confectionery on Ingham Avenue in 1910, where he also sold ice cream, pickles, and peanuts he roasted in a hand-turned steel drum. His proximity to the Roosevelt School no doubt increased his business. Some stores apparently vacillated between being confectioneries and groceries. As business improved, a small confectionery would expand into a grocery, later reducing its offerings to those of a confectionery as economic conditions worsened. This was true of both Josephine Pitillo's store on Electric Avenue and Angelo Morinello's on Roland. During the 1920s and 1930s, Eugenio Galanti's store on Dona Street sold only candy and soft drinks at times, adding groceries and cigars at other times. The store's back room was a gathering spot for young men from the Old Village. Soft drinks and penny candy were draws for students from Lincoln School, and this demand spawned a number of similar stores in the area, including the one owned by Salvatore Ginnetti on School Street.

Sources: Interviews with Ralph D'Amore, April 20, 1995; and Tony Grasso, September 21, 1994; *Erie County Directory*, 1938.

Chick's Swing Bar, shown in 1941, was a popular nightclub and restaurant on Hamburg Turnpike owned by Louis Ciccarelli. Photo source: Collection of Frank Chiodo

from three chains. Just inside the door were stored radishes, celery, cucumbers, and tomatoes. By the late 1940s, Masocco's health had further deteriorated, forcing him to give up his produce business. Another Italian, Tony Grasso, had a remarkable 52-year career as a peddler, or huckster (see Figure 9.13).[19]

Saloons were the fourth most common type of Italian business in Lackawanna. The city, with its numerous male immigrants and the daily presence of thousands of steelworkers from outside the city, never suffered for a lack of saloons. It is no surprise that the first Italian business venture in the city was the saloon opened by Angelo Morinello in 1900. It was in the First Ward of Lackawanna that most of the population and saloons were concentrated. John Daniels, the Buffalo secretary of the North American Civic League for Immigrants, deplored the existence of "approximately 200 saloons" in Lackawanna. By 1902, Antonio Mauriello was running a saloon and restaurant within the hotel that he and Luca Tarquinio operated on Gates Avenue. In the next 10 years, Thomas Fusco

Pitillo's Tavern was a neighborhood gathering spot. In this 1941 photo are: Bob Eagan, kneeling; seated, from the left: Sam Cardinale, Joe Ziccarelli, Joe Angotti, Ed Wnuk, Ang Pitillo; standing in back, from left: [Unk], Walter Lebeck, Patsy Pitillo, George Delmont, Charley DePerto. Photo source: Collection of Frank Chiodo

Lavinio Montanari arrived in Lackawanna in 1913 from Fano, Marche. In 1934, he established the Fano Restaurant on Hamburg Turnpike. The restaurant drew Marchegiani patrons from throughout western New York.
Photo source: Collection of Tina Mattucci-Ginnetti

By 1948, Francis "Caz" DePasquale and J. B. Kustreba were managing Mattucci's Crazy Bone restaurant and, with their friends, providing much of the entertainment. Pasta fasuli, a popular dish among Italian Americans was the featured speciality in this 1948 ad.
Photo sources: Lackawanna Library, *Steel City Press*, 5/12/48.

FIGURE 9.11

EARLY RESTAURANTS RUN BY LACKAWANNA ITALIANS
By Approximate Founding Date

	Proprietor(s)	**Address**	**Business Name**
1902	Luca Tarquinio & Antonio Mauriello	35 Gates Avenue	Albergo Italiano (Italian Hotel)
1926	Gennaro & Adele Panzetta	Buffalo*	Florence Restaurant
1928	Nicholas Mattucci	728 Ridge Road	The New Colonial Restaurant
1928	Luke J. Tarquinio	200** Steelawanna	[Unk]
1929	Jimmy Guglietti	1870 Hamburg Turnpike	[Unk]
1930	Serafino Mattucci	2618 Hamburg Turnpike	[Unk]
1930	Concetta Caitrone	1666 Hamburg Turnpike	[Unk]
1930	James Williams	13 Modern	[Unk]
1931	Peter Mazuca	Athol Springs*	Lake Shore Paradise
1931	Nick Sperduto	235 Ingham Avenue	[Unk]
1933	Nick & Margaret Sperduto	235-37 Ingham Avenue	Italian Gardens
1933	Joe Amadori	64 Jackson Avenue	Park Grille
1933	Patsy Pitillo	1738 Electric Avenue	Pitillo's Tavern
1934	Lavinio Montanari	2618 Hamburg Turnpike	Fano Restaurant
1935	Tony Colello	[Unk] Ingham Avenue	[Unk]
1936	Gennaro & Adele Panzetta	169 Ingham Avenue	Bright Spot
1938	Francesco Spinelli	169 Ingham Avenue	Spinellis
1938	Joe Mazuca	55 Wasson Avenue	[Unk]
1938	Mary Rogers	2240 Hamburg Turnpike	[Unk]
1930s	Luigi & Catarina Conti	349 Ingham Avenue	Lone Star Restaurant

[Unk] = information is un available

* = located outside of Lackawanna.

** Exact street number uncertain; Addresses on some streets changed several times; all street numbers given conform to system instituted in 1938.

Sources: Interviews; U.S. Census, 1930; *Erie County Directory*, 1931, 1941; *Lackawanna Street and Business Directory*, 1938.

established a saloon on Hamburg Turnpike, and Antonio Campanelli opened one on Wasson Avenue. It was, on Ingham Avenue, however, with its concentration of Italian residents, that the majority of saloons opened for business.[20]

Antonio Zanzano, an immigrant from Puglia, arrived in Lackawanna in 1905 and soon owned the building at 227 Ingham, where he ran a saloon. He sent to Italy for his niece Jenny, who married a *paesano*, Antonio Turchiarelli, and the couple lived with Zanzano. When Zanzano moved to Buffalo in 1911, he sold the saloon to Turchiarelli. At first he rented it to Nicholas Welsh, but by 1913, Turchiarelli was running the business, and the following year, he moved his family and the saloon to 219 Ingham. This process of changing business sites was common in this period, as families first rented then purchased a building, only to sell it then either purchase or rent again, depending on their economic circumstances. This was the case of the saloon at 219 Ingham Avenue, which was operated by Salvatore Ginnetti in 1910, then by Tony Amorosi. Turchiarelli took it over in 1914, causing Amorosi to move his saloon to 245 Ingham. The following year, the building was purchased by Pietro and Enrichetta Oddi, putting an end to Turchiarelli's business. After temporarily returning to work at the steel plant, Turchiarelli then opened a grocery store. Oddi, who wanted to own the saloon and work in the steel plant, convinced a relative, Paolo Monaco, to move from Lewis Run, Pennsylvania, to manage the saloon. Following Oddi's death in 1917, Monaco returned to Lewis Run to establish his own saloon.[21]

Many saloon businesses started by Italian immigrants in Lackawanna were very short-lived, as was the case with

FIGURE 9.12

ITALIAN SALOONS ON LOWER INGHAM AVENUE
by Approximate Founding Dates

Guglielmo Gallo	[Unk] Ingham Ave.	1905
Antonio Zanzano	227 Ingham Ave.	1905
Daniele Cristiano	327 Ingham Ave.	1906
Guglielmo Ghetto	[Unk] Ingham Ave.	1906
[Unk] Panzarella	[Unk] Ingham Ave.	1907
Salvatore Ginnetti	219 Ingham Ave.	1910
Serafino Mattucci	229 Ingham Ave.	1910
Nicholas Delguercio	227 Ingham Ave.	1911
Antonio Amorosi	219 Ingham Ave.	1913
Antonio Turchiarelli	227 Ingham Ave.	1913
Salvatore DiTommaso	[Unk] Ingham Ave.	1914
Antonio Cortello	[Unk] Ingham Ave.	1915
Domenico Marinelli	201 Ingham Ave.	1915
Pietro & Enrichetta Oddi	219 Ingham Ave.	1915
[Unk] DiCarlo	327 Ingham Ave.	1924
Aniello Covino	327 Ingham Ave.	1926

[Unk] = Information was unavailable. The date given is the earliest known for the existence of the business.

Sources: U.S. Census, 1910; New York Census, 1905, 1910, 1915; *Lackawanna City Directory*, 1914-15; *Il Corriere Italiano*, 11/18/1905, 10/6/1906, 12/1/1906, 8/7/15.

ANNOUNCEMENT

BEGINNING

FRIDAY EVENING, MAY 16th

at

Angelo's Taproom

1511 ABBOTT ROAD   LACKAWANNA, N. Y.

STEAK — CHICKEN — FISH DINNERS

Sandwiches of All Kinds

Friday, Saturday & Sunday Nights

Music by Angies Orchestra

ANGELO OREFICE, Prop.   HOWARD STONE, Mgr.

Angelo Orefice, who lived in Buffalo, operated a tavern at the corner of Ridge and Abbott roads. He placed this ad in a local newspaper in 1941. Photo sources: Lackawanna Library; *Lackawanna Herald*, 5/9/41

Pasquale "Patsy" Pitillo ran Pitillo's Tavern from 1933 to 1974, when his son Ang took it over. The whole family helped in the business, a common practice in the Italian American community. Photo source: Ang Pitillo

FIGURE 9.13

TONY THE HUCKSTER*

Most notable among Lackawanna's Italian peddlers was Tony Grasso (1903 – 1995). His career actually was launched by his father, Michele, who in 1925 bought a horse and wagon from the Lackawanna Fire Department and began to peddle fruit and vegetables when he wasn't working in the Yard Department at the steel plant. The white horse was a gentle creature, according to Tony Grasso, but "it went running every time the fire siren went off!" When Michele grew ill in 1927, his son took a six-month leave from his machinist job to help him. Afraid of horses, Tony Grasso disliked having to harness the family horse and tend to it. So he used all his savings to buy a new Dodge truck for $2,000. He then built a garage for the vehicle behind the family home. The father and son worked together, but Michele's health continued to deteriorate. In 1928, he had to quit his job in the steel plant and could offer only minimal assistance to his son as they peddled produce. At this point, Tony began doing the route on a full-time basis. Michele died in November 1929.

The original route established by Michele included stops in the First Ward and across the tracks on Roland Avenue. Tony continued with these customers, most of whom were Italian, and began to expand the business. In the spring of 1928, he started to sell plants—tomatoes, peppers, and celery—to the many gardeners in

Tony Grasso and his Stewart truck in the mid-1930s.
Photo source: Joanna Grasso-Swiercz

Lackawanna. That spring he sold 200 flats, or boxes, of plants, then an equal amount following an unusual July frost. Grasso's amiable manner and hard work won more customers. He learned the Polish words for various flowers and focused on the Poles in the Second Ward when he commenced selling potted flowers in 1930. Many of the elderly Polish women who did not speak English appreciated Grasso's ability to converse with them, and Grasso was soon lashing 16 crates of flowers onto the tailgate of his truck. He used his knowledge of the Serbo-Croatian language to win Croatian customers in the First

Ward. On Lebanon Street, he sold fruit to Hungarians, who were especially eager to buy prunes, which they boiled down and made into a jam called *lagwar*. Polish and Ukrainian families purchased four or five bushels of cabbage to use for making sauerkraut. The east Europeans also bought many bags of potatoes and bushels of cucumbers. Grasso, who spoke a little Spanish, had several Spanish families and one Mexican family as customers. He also cultivated Irish customers on Parkview Avenue, near Our Lady of Victory Hospital, where some friends and relatives lived.

immigrant-operated saloons in other cities. The successful proprietor maintained strong social connections to his patrons, who were usually fellow ethnics. However, this strength had a downside that reduced profitability; fellow Italians had little spending money and often expected to buy drinks on credit. Profit margins were thin, and most Italian saloon businesses in Lackawanna didn't last long. For example, in 1914, Salvatore DiTommaso moved his family from the Old Village into an Ingham Avenue building he rented. The saloon he established there did not work out, and the family returned

to the Old Village the next year. Only so many Italian-run businesses geared to customers of the same ethnic group could survive the competition. To keep up with the competing saloons down the block, proprietors offered patrons free food; Tony Amorosi, for example, served peppers and cheese. This apparently worked; among the early Italian saloons, Amorosi's business had the greatest longevity, operating from 1913 to about 1928. Amorosi, Serafino Mattucci, Tony Turchiarelli and others on Ingham Avenue survived as independent businessmen by using the saloon as a springboard to other

To accommodate his expanding business Grasso, in 1932, bought a Stewart truck with a roof rack that accommodated many boxes of produce. It also helped that he got to know the merchants at the Clinton and Baily Market in Buffalo, most of whom were Italian or Jewish, who taught him how to procure high-quality fruit and vegetables. Interesting, up until the late 1930s, Grasso used metal containers of various sizes, rather than scales, to measure out his produce to customers.

Grasso catered to the culinary needs of his many Italian customers. During the fall canning season, he sold large quantities of produce to his countrymen. On a typical day, he might sell 10 bushels of cauliflower, 10 of eggplant, and 15 of various types—sweet, bell, hot, cherry, yellow, etc—of pepper. One year, he sold more than 200 bushels of tomatoes in two days. He carried the baskets on his shoulders, and during his younger days, he bounded up the staircase, traversing two or three stairs with each leap in the large apartment building at 11 Lehigh Avenue.

Some Italians preferred pimento peppers, which had a delicious taste when roasted. Artichokes were a favorite of Italians, as was *finocchio* (fennel) during the Easter and Christmas seasons. But Grasso did not like selling fennel. People preferred the female plant because it had a large round head and was very sweet. This left him with the difficult task of trying to sell the longer, less sweet male fennel stalks. The Romans, or natives of Lazio, loved mustard greens, which they referred to as *broccoli di rapa* or *rapini*. Sicilian customers favored another type of greens, *carduni*. Other Italians ordered *ciccoria* (dandelions), some favoring the late-blooming type grown in Texas that had a blue flower and tough texture, while others preferred the more tender variety grown in Florida. Curly endive, regular figs, and spiny figs were also demanded by Italian customers.

Throughout his long career, Tony Grasso continued to diversify his business. As his career progressed, he sold produce to a restaurant, the Lincoln School, Baker Hall, and the OLV Infant Home. At times he sold chickens that he had either raised in his own coop or purchased from farmers. During the 1930s and 1940s, he and Nick Delvecchio purchased bulk quantities of spaghetti and olive oil from Buffalo importers, stored them at Delvecchio's house, then made deliveries to Italian customers in Lackawanna. He also used his truck to do various chores for customers. Some men purchased large quantities of grapes at the markets in Buffalo, then hired Grasso to transport the cargo to their wine cellars in Lackawanna.

In addition to catering to the tastes of his customers, Grasso also recognized their financial situations. One Italian widow with a large family always ordered a half bushel of tomatoes, which Grasso accommodated. He refrained from doing a large markup on the prices he paid for his goods. And his customers showed their appreciation for his years of service. After transporting boxes of grapes to the Manna and Filipetti homes on Pine Street and helping the men unload the fruit, he was treated to a large spread of food in the Manna home. Paolo and Bambina Liberta regularly gave Grasso a gallon of wine. Other people had him in for coffee or tea. As stories were exchanged about life in Lackawanna or relatives in Italy, Grasso glanced out the window to be sure his truck was secure.

During his long years as a peddler, many families remained Grasso's customers, and he often served three generations within the same family. When the Schiavi, Monaco, and other families moved from the First Ward to neighborhoods east of the railroad tracks, Grasso delivered produce to their new addresses. Tony Grasso retired in 1979, at the age of 76, ending a 52 year career as a full-time peddler.

* The term "huckster," while having negative connotations in some areas of the United States, seems to have only a positive meaning in Lackawanna.
Sources: Interviews with Tony Grasso, September 23, 1983, December 23, 1987, July 11, 1994, September 21, 1994, April 18, 1995, September 20, 1995.

ventures. Amorosi delivered ice and ran a grocery store, Turchiarelli started a grocery store, and Mattucci had several businesses. On Roland Avenue, Angelo Morinello maintained a saloon for 10 years, then focused on his grocery and confectionery businesses. John Verel had a saloon for a year or two, then sought more profitable ventures. [22]

Nine Italians enhanced their operations by expanding a saloon into a restaurant business. Joe Amadori ran the Park Grille from 1933 to 1945. His wife and sister-in-law prepared Italian meals for patrons, but the work was demanding, and only one of the five Italian owners who succeeded him lasted as long in the business as Amadori. Leonard and John Govenettio, both having the nickname "Boots," established Boots Brothers Tavern on Steelawanna Avenue in 1953, and expanding it into a bar and restaurant when they relocated to Ingham Avenue. Others successfully combined a bar with entertainment. In the 1930s and 1940s, five such bar/nightclubs were established along Hamburg Turnpike by Italians, most of whom were second generation. These businesses focused on attracting the general public as opposed

GRAND OPENING
AT THE
ITALIAN GARDENS
FREE SPAGHETTI   MUSIC-DANCING

SATURDAY, MAY 13

611-613 INGHAM AVENUE, LACKAWANNA
(USE REAR ENTRANCE)   NICK SPERDUTO, PROPRIETOR

Nick Sperduto established a clam bar at 235-37 Ingham Avenue, at the corner of Holbrook, in 1931. It was the building his parents had owned. The business was expanded into a restaurant and nightclub, as seen in this 1933 ad. Photo sources: Lackawanna Library, *Lackawanna Herald*, 5/11/33

Marge and Nick Sperduto at their clam bar. Marge usually worked longer hours there because Nick also worked for the city or steel plant. Photo source: Mary and Frank Cuomo

The Sperdutos changed their business to a pizzeria and renamed it in honor of their sons, Anthony and Angelo. Photo source: Mary and Frank Cuomo

FIGURE 9.14
NICHOLAS MATTUCCI

Born in 1898 in San Pio delle Camere, Abruzzo, Nicola Mattucci completed a four-year course in food preparation in Florence and served as a commissar for the Italian Red Cross. He immigrated to the United States in 1920 and lived in Buffalo's east-side Italian community, where he worked as a cook. Americanizing his name to Nicholas, he did some informal catering by loading the sidecar of his motorcycle with bundles of sandwiches and peddling these to workers as he drove through the Lackawanna Steel complex. By 1921, he was the cook at Flessel's Restaurant, across the street from city hall, and soon married the head waitress.

Three years later, Mattucci became manager of the New Colonial Restaurant at the corner of Ridge Road and South Park Avenue, and by 1928 he was its owner. Mattucci continued to run the business for the next three decades, eventually opening three additional restaurants—in Blasdell, Hamburg, and Buffalo. In 1960, he sold the Lackawanna restaurant but continued in the business until his retirement in 1968. He became a staunch Republican and was friends with Walter Lohr, a prominent businessman and politician in Lackawanna.

Mattucci cemented his relationship with the area's business elite via memberships in St. James United Church of Christ, Lackawanna Lodge No. 887 F&AM, the Buffalo Consistory of the Scottish Rite, and Ismalia Shrine Temple. An active member of the National Restaurant Association, he attended the group's national conventions. Mattucci's prosperity allowed him to move his family to Hamburg in 1941 and to purchase a cattle farm six years later. At his Colonial Hill Farm, he gathered a herd of 40 purebred Guernsey cattle and was inducted into the American Guernsey Cattle Club, a national organization of cattle breeders.

Sources: Interview with Blanche Rice, July 9, 1996; Erie County Courthouse, naturalization papers of Nicholas Mattucci, 6/25/26; *Lackawanna Leader*, 2/27/47, 12/29/49, 5/3/51, 4/28/55, 8/4/55, 6/27/74; *Courier Express*, 6/24/74.

to the relatively small Italian community, and, located on a main thoroughfare and across the street from the steel plant, they had a large pool of potential patrons.[23]

Service-oriented businesses provided a significant niche for Lackawanna Italians; the 163 enterprises in this category represent the second largest cluster of Italian businesses. More than 60% of these have been barbershops, shoe-repair shops, or boardinghouses. In the densely populated First Ward, boardinghouses quickly grew prior to 1920, and then all but disappeared within a 10-year span. Seventeen Italian

Clementine Miniri-Cardoni sat in the driveway of the Morgan house at 208 Ingham Avenue where her family rented an apartment in 1941. In the background is Tony Grasso at the back of his truck, weighing produce for a customer. Photo source: Emelia Cardoni-Cutre

Calogero "Charles" Barone, an immigrant from Roccapalomba, Sicily, ran a barbershop on Ingham Avenue for more than four decades. Photo source: Lake Erie Italian Club

boardinghouses or small hotels operated in the First Ward between 1902 and 1918, 10 of them run by females. Two of these "boarding mistresses" rented out sections of the large structure at 242 Ingham Avenue, which housed 50 to 60 people. The term "boardinghouse" could easily have been applied to other situations where individuals had large buildings that housed many tenants. By the 1920s, the barracks-style dormitories that had been popular with lone male immigrants were less in demand as men married or were reunited with their families.

In 1900, almost 10% of all male barbers in the United States were Italian, and in New York City, Italians made up over half the total. A similar pattern was found in Lackawanna, where 44 Italian barbers had shops, most of them during the first half of the twentieth century. By 1941, there were 39 Steel City barbershops, 11 of them run by Italians. Three decades later, Barbers Local No. 141—which covered South Buffalo, Lackawanna, and nearby towns—represented 57 shops, two-thirds of which had Italian proprietors. Salvatore Messoma established the first Italian barbershop in Lackawanna in 1910 on Gates Avenue, and within a few years, three other Italian barbers had shops nearby. In 1914, Constantino Marchi was the first of seven Italian men to open barbershops on Ingham Avenue, and the following year, Andrew Blard became the first on Roland Avenue. Several barbers left the First Ward; Joseph Corbo relocated to Parkview Avenue in 1920, and Carl Selice moved to Blasdell in the 1940s. Seven other Italian Americans set up barbershops in the three decades following World War II. These included John Tiberio, who grew up in

South Buffalo and to this day sometimes plays tapes of Italian music and sings along as he cuts hair.[24]

The beauty shops established by Lackawanna Italians, most of them second-generation females, marked the greater independence of Italian American females. Audrey Spagnolo established a beauty salon in Bethlehem Park during the late 1930s, and a decade later, Virginia Verel was an instructor at the Lackawanna Beauty School. Most of the 24 beauty shops founded by Italians were located east of the railroad tracks. Between 1938 and 1963, six women, including Frances Valentine, the proprietor of the Salone di Bellezza (Salon of Beauty), operated salons on Electric Avenue. For second-generation Italian women, the beauty salon represented not

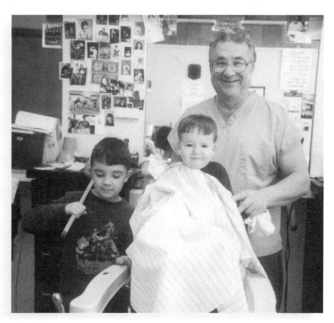

John Tiberio grew up in South Buffalo, the son of immigrants from Ceccano, Lazio. Since 1962 he has lived in Lackawanna and operated Johnny's Barber Shop at 3056 South Park Avenue. Photo source: John Tiberio

Thomas Cennamo ran a shoe-repair shop from 1920 until 1941. He and relatives are standing in front of his shop at 1528 Electric Avenue. From left are: Thomas Cennamo, Irene Fox, Joe Fox, and Angelina Pinto-Cennamo.
Photo source: Anne Fox-Skrzynski

Francesco Sirianni had his shoe-repair shop at the corner of Roland and Electric avenues from 1910 until his death in 1926. His nephew, Eugene Morasco, pictured here, took over the shop and ran it for 10 years.
Photo source: Collection of Frank Chiodo

only an independent avenue to employment but freedom from some of the strict traditions of Italian family life. In more recent decades, Italian American men have also operated salons.[25]

As was true across the United States, Italians in Lackawanna were overrepresented as operators of shoe-repair shops; in 1931, four of the city's 14 shops were run by Italians. Most of the city's 29 Italian shoe shops were founded by immigrant proprietors prior to 1950. Ruta Pellegrino, who had a shop on Ingham Avenue in 1908, was the first Italian in Lackawanna to establish this type of business. Within two decades, Ingham Avenue was home to five other Italian shoe-repair shops, and two were established in Bethlehem Park. Frank Sirianni established a shop in 1910 and later moved it to the corner of Roland and Electric avenues. Thomas Cennamo established a shoe business in 1920 at the same intersection but moved to a location further up Electric Avenue. By 1941, Italians had established seven other shoe-repair shops in the neighborhood. In later years, four others were opened along Abbott Road and South Park Avenue.[26]

To immigrants who had rarely encountered automobiles in rural Italy, American city streets of the early twentieth century must have been astonishing. The motor vehicles in American cities, with their many maintenance needs, offered business opportunities to Italian Americans, especially with the mass production of automobiles after World War I. The development and increased use of motorized trucks offered further potential for business enterprise. Young immigrants and the children of

immigrants in Lackawanna had more opportunities to understand the workings of automobiles and trucks. Not only did they grow up in the presence of motor vehicles, they also could typically converse in, and read, both Italian and English to gain further information. Two-thirds of the Italian men who founded automotive-service, trucking, and excavation businesses were second or third generation, and several of the immigrants, like Joe Amadori and Salvatore Macaluso, were youngsters when they arrived in the United States. As these men reached adulthood in the 1920s and 1930s, they began to enter this field of business. Repair shops, auto-parts stores, and firms that sold or rebuilt batteries and generators first appeared in the mid-1920s, when James Sirianni started his battery business and Alfred Conte and Tony Welsh opened their auto-repair shops. In Lackawanna, the number of gas stations quickly grew from six in 1929 to 19 in 1935. Italians ran four of these during the 1930s and established another 27 gas stations between 1940 and 1977. Second-generation men who gained mechanical skills from their steel-plant jobs and military service in World War II were among the Italians who started 42 businesses related to automobiles after 1945.[27]

Italians entered the trucking and excavation business in 1926 when 10 men, most of them Marchegiani, incorporated the Lackawanna Trucking Company. This business was short-lived, and in 1927 three of them—Joe Amadori, Ermete Silvestrini, and Emidio Antilli—incorporated a new entity, the Lackawanna Trucking and Excavating Corporation, based on

Robert Amadori at his desk in the offices of Amadori Construction Company in 1985. The business was located in the former Park Theater building on Jackson Avenue. Photo source: Amadori family

Dona Street. In the business of road construction, the company failed in 1929 due to the Depression and the unreliability of the new inflatable truck tires. Amadori was able to retain the steam shovel and in the 1930s formed the Joseph Amadori Construction Company. His sons Gene and Bobby, who gained valuable construction experience as Navy Seabees during World War II, purchased surplus military equipment after the war and founded their own company. Their father eventually joined them, and the new business was called Amadori Construction Company, Inc. The family hired many Italian immigrants, some on a full-time basis and others who worked part time with the Amadoris and full time at Bethlehem Steel. Carmine DelMonaco, an Abruzzese immigrant, worked full time for the company from 1961 to 1989, the last 14 years as a foreman. The company did excavation, street paving, and construction of sidewalks and sewers throughout western New York. After 1983, it was hired to demolish some of the mills shut down by Bethlehem Steel. Mickey and Tulio Paolini had very successful careers in trucking—Mickey as a foreman in the steel plant's Garage Department, and Tulio as a trucking contractor. Bethlehem Steel hired private trucking companies to transport finished products over the highways, and one of these firms was Paolini Trucking. Founded by Tulio in the 1930s and based across the street from the steel plant, Paolini Trucking worked for Bethlehem for 20 years until the steel company decided to purchase its own fleet of large trucks.[28]

Italian immigrants to the United States were found at construction sites throughout the nation. Many Lackawanna

Cleveland John Tarquinio, the son of immigrants, was the first Lackawanna Italian known to work as an engineer. This ad appeared in a 1921 newspaper. Photo source: Lackawanna Library; *Lackawanna Daily Journal*, 4/2/21

Italians learned the basics of construction through outdoor jobs at building projects, work in the steel plant's Yard Department, or as railroad laborers erecting and repairing bridges along the right of way. Thirty-three Italians set up construction, plastering, roofing, and home building businesses. In 1918, John Verel became the first Lackawanna Italian to organize a business enterprise in this field; he was followed by two other immigrants in the 1920s, contractors Marco Costanzi and Robert Delmont. Thereafter, the field was dominated by American-born Italians, starting with contractor Phillip Dolce in 1930. During the 1940s, Robert Delmont's son Victor became a masonry and plaster contractor, and another plaster mason, John Pitillo, founded a construction company. Alex Nigro and his sons Ken and Charles began doing home construction in the 1950s, while Louis Christ moved from Buffalo to Lackawanna, where he erected many houses in tracts off Abbott Road. Other men, such as Salvatore Yoviene, engaged in light manufacturing businesses. Yoviene founded the Lackawanna Insulation

FIGURE 9.15

JOHN VEREL

Giovanni Verrilli came to the United States in 1908 at the age of 16. He joined his older brother Filippo, who had emigrated from Italy in 1892 and changed his name to Phil Verel. In 1910, Giovanni, then going by John Verel, was a railroad laborer and one of eight Italians boarding at the home of Joseph Kinczar near Roland Avenue. Phil Verel, a track foreman, probably lined up his brother's job and also introduced his brother to Alfonso Yoviene, a railroad section boss who lived with his family in Sardina, New York. In 1913, John married one of Yoviene's daughters, Nicolina, at Our Mother of Good Counsel Church in Blasdell. They settled at 1 Roland Avenue, formerly Angelo Morinello's building, and lived above the saloon that John established. The Verels became well known and respected, as they were godparents at nine baptisms during the following five years. In about 1916, they set up a home in Fredonia, where they managed the Fredonia Wine Company. They also maintained their home in Lackawanna and spent part of the year living in each city. The winery was purchased in 1917 by Verel's in-laws, who soon sold the company to Verel. Meanwhile, Verel founded a builders' supply business in Lackawanna in 1918, using a horse and buggy to transport his goods. The family

sold the winery and resumed permanent residence in Lackawanna in 1920.

Verel began to construct homes on a small street running off South Park Avenue that was soon named Verel Street. The family took up residence at the corner of South Park Avenue and Verel Street, where they lived on the second floor of the cinder-block building. The building's exterior featured a stone with the name "Verel" carved into it. Here, Verel established a concrete-block factory, in which the blocks were manufactured one at a time in a small machine operated by Patsy Pitillo and other employees. In July 1921, Verel signed the incorporation papers for the Lackawanna Concrete Block and Builders Supply Company. Five years later, the concrete-block manufacturing apparently came to an end, as Verel changed the name of his business to Lackawanna Builders Supply. During this period, the company had 250 shares of stock and a board of directors composed of three non – Italians from Buffalo— George L. Grobe, Samuel Ginsburg, and Esther Smolev.

John Verel continued to build homes on the street bearing his name. By 1922, he and his mother-in-law, Giuseppina Yoviene, owned 86 lots, totaling more than 14 acres. (According to one source, nearby Brown Street was originally named

Yoviene Street.) Verel won a series of municipal contracts, and his work crews constructed sewers and sidewalks in Lackawanna and Blasdell. Lackawanna Builders Supply grew rapidly; starting in 1928, it sold and delivered coal and coke to homeowners and institutions in Lackawanna, Buffalo, and Orchard Park. Five trucks transported materials, and a manager supervised the large warehouse. By 1938, Verel had moved his business to larger facilities at 880 Ridge Road.

In the early 1940s, John and Nicolina Verel moved their family to Orchard Park. The Verels and another Italian family each had a house constructed on the same street. Some neighbors, worried that Italians would live in shacks and bring down housing values, circulated a petition protesting the arrival of the newcomers. Concern quickly faded as neighbors admired the substantial homes and good manners of the Italian families.

Nicolina Verel always worked with her husband, keeping the books and making sales, and was the vice president of the company. Many of the 12 Verel children, both as teens and adults, worked in the family business. After John Verel died in 1955, his wife and then their children ran the company before closing it in 1971.

John Verel and his wife ran a number of successful businesses, including the manufacture of concrete blocks, and the Verel Park development. These newspaper ads are from the early 1920s. Photo source: Lackawanna Library; Lackawanna Daily Journal, 7/18/21, 4/30/23

Sources: U.S. Census, 1910, 1920; N.Y. Census, 1915; interviews with Mary Yoviene-Clark, December 29, 1983; James Yoviene, September 17, 1997; and Gene Verel, September 23, 1994; information from business and mortgage records in the Chautauqua County Courthouse provided by Doug Shepard, Baker Historical Museum, Fredonia; *Baptismal Register*, 1906 – 1936, Our Mother of Good Counsel Church; Erie County Courthouse, *Assumed Business Names*, I-M, 1900 – 1933, certificate nos.# 10902, 17358, and 16773.

Company in 1938. Operating out of a building on South Park Avenue, he and his workers did home insulation for another two decades. In 1954, Yoviene and his wife, Helen, established Sellmore Industries, which manufactured aluminum windows and other home-construction supplies. Later, the plant was moved to Buffalo and subsidiaries were set up in Pennsylvania and Maryland. When Salvatore Yoviene retired as board chairman in 1977, his sons James and Robert became leaders of the company.[29]

Lackawanna Italians have established other businesses that cover a great variety of services and products. In 1910, Caterina Tarquinio, a dressmaker who operated out of her parents' home, established the first of 14 Italian businesses in the clothing and cleaning field. Philip Faraci was the city's first Italian tailor, opening a shop on Ingham Avenue in 1927. The Lackawanna Laundry was founded on Ingham Avenue in 1937 by brothers Anthony and Russell Mesi and their partner Helen Bauer. The business expanded, was moved to a larger building on Lehigh Avenue, and several delivery trucks were procured. The laundry had one of the largest workforces of any Italian business in the city; it included 30 employees, most of whom were female and Italian, but also included Poles and African Americans. A number of immigrants, such as Nunzia D'Alessandro and Carlo Savaglio, had their first jobs at the laundry.[30]

The first Italian recreation business was the Ingham Avenue poolroom, founded by Santo DePasquale in 1925. Armondo Pietrocarlo, a noted pool player in Lackawanna's First Ward, ran a poolroom on A Street and a bowling alley in Buffalo. Taking his father's advice, he left these ventures, bought land in Woodlawn, and set up a restaurant and tavern. Other Italian businesses focused on specialty niches. James Cheroti and Donato Chiacchia were labor contractors from 1915 to 1925, while Isadore Mattioli was a self-employed landscape gardener. Mattioli carefully maintained a business diary from 1927 to 1941 in which he listed customers of many nationalities, the fees he collected, and the number of hours he worked each day; 10-hour days were not uncommon.[31]

The Italian businesses run by immigrants were mostly grocery stores and other food businesses, saloons, barbershops, shoe-repair stores, and boardinghouses and hotels. There were only a few retail stores in the Old Village and a handful in Bethlehem Park; over the years, however, 148 Italian businesses were on located Ingham Avenue and its side streets, and another 79 in the Roland Avenue area. During the past century, the many Italian businesses found in these two ethnic enclaves included: 49 grocery stores, 19 saloons, 20 shoe-repair shops, and 18 barbershops. Also, 23 of the early Italian restaurants were located in the Ingham Avenue or Roland Avenue neighborhoods.

As a satellite city of Buffalo, Lackawanna had many connections with the larger city at its northern border. In the first decade of the twentieth century, Italian immigrants who originally settled in Buffalo and opened businesses moved to the Steel City. Other Italians residing outside of Lackawanna, most of them in Buffalo, established 87 enterprises in the Steel City, 23 of which were food-related. Early in the twentieth century, some Italian businesspeople moved to Lackawanna to escape the congestion and crime in Buffalo.

Biagio and Marianna Pinto left Buffalo's Hooks neighborhood after Biagio, a peddler, encountered too much street crime. Serafino and Rosa Capriotto departed to find cleaner air to breath in the less settled areas east of the railroad tracks in Lackawanna and then in adjacent Orchard Park township (see Figure 9.18). Lackawanna Italians also looked outside of their city for good business sites. One of the first to do so was Serafino Mattucci, who had earlier lived in Buffalo. In 1918, Mattucci and Buffalonian Samuel DiGiuseppi jointly operated a saloon on Seneca Street near downtown Buffalo. Eventually, Lackawanna Italians established 77 enterprises beyond the city's boundaries, most of them in nearby Buffalo, Blasdell, and Hamburg. Restaurants, food stores, and automotive services accounted for half of these enterprises. The majority of the businesses were founded between 1950 and 1999, when

FIGURE 9.17

SAM MORGAN, ICE AND COAL MAN

There were six Italian ice and coal delivery businesses founded between 1917 and 1923. Tony Amorosi eventually turned his business over to his son Luciano. John and Dominick Grasso, following the example of their father and older brother, Tony, both produce peddlers, founded an ice and carting business in 1934. Most of these ventures were short-lived except for those of John Verel (see Figure 9.15) and Sam Morgan.

Saverio Morgante, better known as Sam Morgan, founded the first Italian ice and coal delivery business in Lackawanna in 1917. He had been operating a grocery when a visiting relative who ran a successful landscaping business in Cleveland suggested the idea he start an ice business. That winter, Morgan and several helpers went onto the frozen Lake Erie and cut blocks of ice. Using a horse (named Nellie) and wagon, they hauled their cargo to a neighbor's yard, where they buried it in a hole in the ground and covered it with sawdust. The ice was retrieved with the arrival of warm weather and sold to customers. The horse and wagon had a home in the Morgans' Ingham Avenue garage, which was equipped with

a hay loft. When Walter Lohr built an icehouse on Ridge Road in the 1920s, it was no longer necessary for Morgan to endure the frozen waters of Lake Erie to acquire his product. He bought a series of trucks and was assisted in the ice business by all four of his sons, while his wife, Mary, and their three daughters tended to the family's grocery store.

Morgan occasionally hired other young men, including Nick Sperduto and Angelo Grosso, to help him with deliveries, though most of the labor was provided by his sons. Pat Morgan started driving one of his dad's trucks by age 11. Blocks of wood were fastened to the clutch, brake, and gas pedals so the youngster could reach them with his feet. His younger brother Mike started working on the trucks in 1937, at age 10, and three years later was driving one of the three vehicles. Mike's route included 20 saloons and a number of grocery stores. During World War II, the enterprising teen claimed 300 customers at the newly constructed Ridgewood Village. Many clients entrusted the Morgans with the keys to their houses to ensure they didn't miss ice deliveries. At each stop, one of

the Morgans hauled a 25-, 50-, or 100-pound block of ice into the customer's house or store. In 1940, fewer than half of Lackawanna's homes had refrigerators, and it was around this time that the family's business tripled and the customer base reached 1,000.

Mike Morgan recalls that on one August day during World War II, he and his dad sold and delivered 101 tons of ice. Monday through Thursday were the busiest days. During the winter, Sam Morgan and his sons delivered coal to customers. On weekends and during the winter, they also used their trucks to cart people's furniture when they moved. During the 1930s, Morgan delivered sacks of flower, corn, and other foods for the Welfare Department. Mike Morgan was paid $15 per week, of which he kept $3 for himself and gave the rest to his mother. When he went into the armed forces in 1945, his brother Eddie took over his route. After his discharge, Mike again worked delivering ice, but the availability of refrigerators soon made the ice business a thing of the past. The Morgan's business came to an end in the early 1950s.

Source: Interview with Mike Morgan, April 8, 1995.

Sam Morgan's business card in 1908. He was one of the first Italians in the steel-plant district of West Seneca to have a telephone. The mistakes in spelling and grammar on the card (including Sam's last name) are typical of immigrants recently arrived in this country, whose fluency in English was limited. Photo source: Collection of Mike Morgan

Sam Morgan's customers bought packets of tickets in advance and used them to pay Morgan or one of his sons for deliveries of ice or coal. In 1938, the city's new numbering system changed the address from 205 Ingham Avenue.
Photo source: Collection of Mike Morgan

autos and buses provided more mobility and small neighborhood stores were on the decline.[32]

Lackawanna Italian families who ran successful businesses also produced opportunities for their children. Sometimes this was in the form of the second generation inheriting the family business, such as when Frank Sirianni died in 1926 and his nephew, Eugene Morasco, took over his shoe-repair shop. Twenty-four other Italian Americans inherited family businesses, 21 of them from parents or in-laws, and three from uncles and aunts. In Joe Mazuca's case, his father opened a second grocery store in 1931 and gave it to him to run. Some children and teens picked up skills in the family business that enabled them to launch their own ventures. Robert Delmont, a contractor mason, employed five of his sons as helpers, two of whom later became contractors. Eighty Lackawanna proprietors were the children of businesspeople, and a number of them founded establishments that were larger than those of their parents.[33]

Many Lackawanna Italian businesses had one proprietor, and some were operated by two or three partners. The business with the largest number of partners was the Lackawanna Trucking Company, founded in 1926 by Joe Amadori and nine copartners, all but one of them Italian. Several individuals created a number of businesses; Serafino Mattucci launched nine enterprises, including two with his wife and one with a friend. Altogether, there were 612 Italian men and women, plus 42 non – Italian partners, who founded the 686 businesses included in this book. Approximately 44% were immigrants, 44% second generation, and 12% third or fourth generation (see Figure 9.3).[34]

Women were very active partners in many family grocery stores, though they were rarely listed in documents as co-owners and often held subordinate roles to their husband. Several, including Giuseppina Pitillo, ran the family business without the involvement of their husbands, and a number of widows operated businesses, usually with the help of their children. While many immigrant Italian housewives tended to boarders, only 10 were listed in records as proprietors of boardinghouses between 1905 and 1914. Italian tradition usually demanded that women work outside the home only if under the protective eye of relatives or *paesani*. But there were exceptions, such as Angelina Poliseno and Maria Giuliani, who ran part-time food-distribution businesses out of their homes. For the second-generation females, raised in the more liberal tradition of the United States, greater opportunities became available. Mary Fusco had a confectionery business and later a bar-restaurant. Margaret Yoviene managed the meat section of the family grocery store for several years, and her sister Mary ran an appliance-repair shop. Beauty salons established by Italian women represented the most significant business niche for second-generation females.[35]

Tony Mesi's son Sal was a driver for the Lackawanna Laundry. The business employed about 30 people.
Photo source: Sal Mesi

The Mesi brothers, Tony, on the left, and Russell in the 1920s. They and Helen Bauer were owners of the Lackawanna Laundry, which opened for business on Ingham Avenue in 1937, then moved to 319 Ridge Road.
Photo source: Sal Mesi

Figure 9.18

SERAFINO CAPRIOTTO

Serafino Capriotto migrated from Abruzzo to Oswego, New York, where he worked in a feed mill, then moved to Hopkins Street in South Buffalo and again found work in a feed mill. In 1926, Capriotto incorporated the Lackawanna Feed Company, which was located at 821 Ridge Road. He married Rosa Orefice, and the couple was living in Buffalo when she developed tuberculosis and was instructed by the family doctor to "move to the country." Capriotto, who by then went by the first name John, procured money from a *paesano* in Buffalo and bought land on Abbott Road at Lakeview Avenue. He built a store and house there, and in 1927 the couple moved into the home and John Capriotto moved his feed store there. This area was once called the town of East Hamburg and is now part of the township of Orchard Park. A number of Italian American farmers and laborers had earlier settled along this stretch of Abbott Road, which is just south of Willett Road, Lackawanna's southern boundary.

Capriotto established a coal trucking and moving company in 1928. He gave up the feed company and by 1940 had established a general store and the Lackawanna Fuel Oil Company next to his home. He was a member of the Lackawanna Chamber of Commerce. During World War II, he operated a tire-recapping business in his building. He and Rosa suffered the loss of their oldest son, Biondo, who died while serving in the military. With his other sons, Carmen and John, Capriotto founded John Capriotto & Sons auto parts, which is still in business today.

Sources: Interview with John Capriotto, September 22, 1999; Erie County Courthouse, *Assumed Business Names*, I-M, 1900-1933, certificate # 17347; *Lackawanna News*, 8/11/27, 6/7/28; *Courier Express*, 11/22/69.

In the first half of the twentieth century stores were often small, neighborhood-focused businesses. Most people got about on foot, and on well-populated streets such as Ingham Avenue there were one or two grocery stores on most blocks. These stores usually catered to the owner's ethnic group, plus some customers from other ethnic groups. There were non-Italians living in each of the Italian enclaves in Lackawanna, and as time went on, immigrant Italian business people learned English phrases which enabled them to have at least basic communication with people of each cultural group, as English, however broken or imperfectly spoken, increasingly became the common language of the 92 ethnic groups in Lackawanna.[36]

The Italian-run businesses often involved jobs for a small number of Italians outside the family circle. The data provided in Figure 9.1 most likely underreports the number of people in this category. The large Bethlehem Park grocery store run by Peter Mazuca employed several clerks and butchers who were not relatives. Frank Morinello hired two Italian Americans to help maintain his large market on South Park Avenue in the 1930s. Serafino Mattucci, who had a fruit stand on Hamburg Turnpike in the 1930s, employed Ralph Marinelli and Paul Petti to take his truck throughout western New York to procure fresh fruit from farmers. The Lackawanna Laundry and the Amadori Construction Company each had dozens of employees, most of them Italian Americans. The Italian stores also provided opportunities for neighborhood children to earn money—some gathering greens growing in local fields and selling them to grocers. As a young boy, Lou Colello cleaned up at Leonard DePaul's auto-repair shop for five to 10 cents. He also picked a bushel of dandelions and took it to Morgans' grocery, where Mary Morgan paid him five cents for it.[7]

The Italian businesses enumerated in this study do not include those founded by second- and third-generation Italians who followed in their parents' footsteps as businesspeople but moved out of Lackawanna. Tony Giordano's sons, Mike and Patsy, followed this course, as did Emidio Chiacchia, the son of businessman Donato Chiacchia. Jennie Nigro was a 14-year-old student at a business school in 1924 when her teacher told her that the Lunghino Italian Bank in Buffalo was looking for workers. Nigro fixed her hair to appear older, interviewed for the job, and soon was an employee at the bank. Three years later, and without her mother's knowledge, she opened a hair salon on Main Street in Buffalo. She married Nick Vertalino in 1929, and they lived in Buffalo for 48 years, where she ran several beauty salons and a children's clothing store, and also was a realtor. The couple returned to live in Lackawanna after retirement. The management skills and financial resources acquired from family businesses provided a foundation for the advancement of members of the second generation. While many children of immigrant businesspeople went on to become store proprietors, others went to college or trade schools and embarked on professional careers.[38]

A look at the regional origins of Lackawanna business proprietors reveals some interesting patterns (see Figure 9.20). Among the 376 Italian proprietors of all generations for whom regional origins are known, the Napolitani are the largest group, at 22%, and the Calabresi, at 15%, are tied for third largest. This is surprising, as the Laziali, the largest Italian regional group in the city, comprise the second-largest group of proprietors, while the Abruzzesi, the second most numerous in the total population, are tied with the Calabresi for the third

FIGURE 9.19

ITALIAN FAMILIES WITH A KNACK FOR BUSINESS

In some Lackawanna Italian American families, members of the first, second, and third generations have all been involved in a series of businesses. Among these are the following families.*

Surname	Generation	First Name	Type Of Business
COLELLO	1st	Antonio	clam stand
	2nd	Angelo	income tax returns, insurance, blacktop
		Louis	gas station, used cars, lawnmowers-snowblowers
		Nicholas	realty
		Richard	gas station
	3rd	Bruce (& Louis)	golf driving range
DELMONT	1st	Robert	masonry, plaster contractor
	2nd	Charles	gas station, contractor, builder
		Robert	gas station
		Victor	mason and builder
	3rd	Gerald	pizzeria
		James	pizzerias
		William	printing, newspaper
FADALE	1st	Calogero & Sara	groceries
	2nd	Cosmer	restaurant, contractor
		Helen	restaurant, beauty salon
		James	signs
		John	real estate, candy shop
		Josephine	beauty salon
		Louis	awnings, scrapyard, grocery, transmissions
	3rd	Charles (& John)	electroplating
		Dick	musician, musical tracks producer
		Dolores (& Helen)	restaurant
		Louis, Lois, Charles	transmission repair
MORINELLO	1st	Angelo	saloon, grocery, rooming house
	2nd	Frank	groceries
	3rd	Frank Jr.	grocery
NIGRO	1st	Celestino	confectionery, peddler
	2nd	Alex	home construction, appliances
		Jennie	beauty shop
	3rd	Charles	insurance, home construction
		Kenneth	home construction
PITILLO	1st	Giuseppina	grocery/confectionery
	2nd	John	shoe repair, home construction
		Marie	beauty salon
		Pasquale	grocery, bar-restaurant
		Sue	beauty salon
	3rd	Ang	restaurant
YOVIENE	1st	Alfonso & Giuseppina	winery, grocery, meeting hall
	2nd	John	interior decorating
		Margaret (& Giuseppina)	grocery
		Mary	radio and TV repair
		Salvatore	cheese distributor, restaurant, roller rink, furnace and heating, window and door manufacturer
	3rd	James & Robert	window and door manufacturer
		Paul & Ronald	interior decorating

*This is not intended as a complete list of all such families.
Generation: 1st = immigrant; 2nd = child of immigrant; 3rd = grandchild of immigrant.
Sources: U.S. Census, 1900, 1920; N.Y. Census, 1915; *Erie County Directory*, 1931, 1941; *Lackawanna Leader*, 6/10/48; interviews with John Fadale, November 23, 1979; Dick Fadale, April 24, 2000; Patricia Fadale-Pellegrino, July 8, 1996; Helen Fadale-Costello, April 25, 2000; Frank Morinello Jr., December 26, 1983; Angelo Pitillo, April 15, 1994; Mary Clark-Yoviene, December 29, 1983; James Yoviene, September 17, 1997; and Paul and Ronald Yoviene, April 4, 1996.

largest number of business proprietors. In addition to the Napolitani and Calabresi, other regional groups from the deep south of Italy—Basilicati, Pugliesi, and Siciliani—have a higher-than-expected percentage of businesspeople. The Laziali, Abruzzesi, and Marchegiani comprise almost two-thirds of Lackawanna's Italian population but account for less than half of the city's Italian businesspeople. These statistics take in four generations of Italian Americans, ranging from immigrants to their great-grandchildren. Looking at just the immigrant businesspeople, who constitute 44% of all the city's Italian merchants, the regional percentages are generally similar, with the Napolitani in the lead, followed in order by the Abruzzesi, the Laziali, and the Calabresi. Again, the six regions of the deep south produced business proprietors far beyond their percentage of the city's Italian population, especially the Siciliani. Looking at the total group of proprietors, regional clusters can be seen in certain types of businesses. Abruzzesi, Laziali, and Napolitani make up the majority of saloon operators. Siciliani accounted for more than one-fifth of the Italian barbershops in Lackawanna, while the Laziali, Abruzzesi, and Napolitani together operated at least half the city's restaurants. Napolitani also owned about one of every four groceries, followed by the Abruzzesi and the Calabresi, with the Laziali accounting for only four percent. The Marchegiani, the only large regional group in Lackawanna that is not from southern Italy, are modestly represented among saloon, restaurant, and grocery proprietors. In Lackawanna, as in Buffalo, a significant number of immigrants from Accadia, Puglia, ran businesses.

Information on how Italians obtained start-up financing for their businesses is sketchy, but some patterns are discernible. Many of their enterprises were small neighborhood shops that called for little initial outlay of capital. Beer companies often provided the basic equipment, furniture, and signs needed to open a saloon. After working in the steel plant for several years, a man could save up enough money to embark on a modest business venture. Antonio Turchiarelli and Nick Sperduto followed this course in establishing saloons, as did Angelo Antigiovanni, who worked in the steel plant while starting a part-time barbering business, then left the plant to be a full-time barber. Some people who wished to start new businesses went to friends or *paesani* who had already launched successful enterprises and asked for loans. Angelo Morinello was the "banker" for Italian immigrants living on Roland Avenue as well as Italian railroad workers maintaining the nearby tracks. In his store and saloon, Morinello cashed paychecks, held money for people in his safe, extended credit, loaned money, sold homes, and sent money to Italy for immigrants. He taught his son Frank the grocery business by employing him in his original store, then no doubt provided some financial backing

when the young man launched his own grocery business. After his father's death in 1940, Frank Morinello backed other Italian business ventures, including the tavern opened by John and Leo Govenettio in the 1950s. Sal Yoviene went to Morinello for loans during rough economic periods, in turn, Yoviene later helped finance his nephew's radio and television repair shop. Pasquale Pitillo made loans to Italians who wanted to start businesses. Tony Amorosi's friend and *paesano*, Tony Mauriello, helped him get his saloon business started in 1913, a year after Amorosi arrived in the city. The Lake Erie Italian Club occasionally loaned money to members, including those who used it for business ventures. Some of the immigrants did not trust banks and preferred instead to go to individuals or small loan businesses. A Serbian businessman named Milosevich made loans to many Bethlehem Park Italians.[39]

Serafino Mattucci used a combination of techniques to underwrite the business ventures that he and his wife embarked on. Mattucci had briefly worked in the steel plant, then he and his wife launched a series of businesses. Apparently, funds generated by one enterprise served as a basis for starting another. Mattucci, however, on occasion borrowed money from the Lake Erie Italian Club and his neighbor, Antonio DePaula, who had a successful bakery business. The Mattuccis also adapted to situations as they arose. In 1930, they had a brick building constructed on South Park Avenue in Buffalo where Virginia, Serafino's wife, ran a grocery business, but with the Depression, it fared poorly. The Mattuccis then divided the building into two storefronts and rented them out to several businesspeople before finally selling the building in 1935. Some entrepreneurs provided

Donato Chiacchia had a variety of careers during his lifetime. Here, he stands in front of the City Line Inn, at South Park and Dorrance avenues, which he ran from 1921 to 1923. His family lived on the premises, then moved to Apple Street in 1923. Photo source: Sara Chiacchia-Kempf

FIGURE 9.20

Regional Groups and Lackawanna Businesses

Region of Italy (ranked by percentage of city's Italians)	% of City's Italian Population	% of Immigrant Italian Proprietors	% of All Italian Proprietors
1. Lazio	36%	14%	19%
2. Abruzzo	19	18	15
3. Campania	13	22	22
4. Marche	10	10	9
5. Calabria	8	12	15
6. Molise	7	5	3
7. Puglia	3	6	6
8. Sicilia	3	11	10
9. Basilicata	1	2	3

Of the 612 Italian business proprietors in Lackawanna, the regional roots and generation of 378 were established. Seven other second- and third-generation males with mixed regional backgrounds were also identified but were not factored into these statistics.

the late 1940s, automobiles were affordable for many people. These developments, plus the increased residential mixing of European ethnic groups, meant the decline of small neighborhood businesses that had focused primarily on customers of one ethnic group. Proprietors began to establish their businesses on main thoroughfares, relying on larger stores and a greater selection of products to draw a diverse customer base. After World War II, however, the steel plant expanded and its workforce grew, as did the city's population. Lackawanna had 410 retail businesses in 1948, two-thirds of them "food stores" and "eating and drinking establishments," of which 10% were run by Italians. Overall, Italians operated at least 12% of all the city's businesses that year.

other resources. Sam Morgan, who had one of the only safes on lower Ingham Avenue early in the twentieth century, allowed other businesspeople to use it for storing their important papers and cash. Frank Morinello usually drove his father, Angelo, to procure fruit and produce in Buffalo, both when he worked for his dad and later when each man had his own store.[40]

Successful businesspeople had funds available to purchase property, an important goal of many immigrants who had owned little or no property in Italy. Among the 32 Italian landowners in Lackawanna in 1910, 10 were businesspeople. In 1920 and 1930, business proprietors made up one-third of the Italian landowners, who numbered 69 in 1920 and 128 in 1930. The largest landholdings usually belonged to merchants, and in 1910, the leading Italian property holders were businessmen Frank Morinello and Calogero Fadale, each of whom owned four lots. In 1922, John Verel and his mother-in-law, Giuseppina Yoviene, combined the resources earned in their respective businesses to purchase 14 acres of land, upon which Verel began to construct homes to sell. Frank Morinello increased his holdings to three acres along South Park Avenue and Martin Road, where he had several houses constructed. Within a few years, Morinello had also purchased property in East Aurora, Tonawanda, and Fort Erie, Ontario.[41]

Lackawanna's small ethnic neighborhoods slowly began to decline in the 1920s, a process that accelerated in the following two decades. As permanent sidewalks were installed, people could walk longer distances. Intercity travel was further aided by expanded streetcar lines and the advent of buses. By

This encouraged postwar immigrants from Italy to establish business ventures in their new environs. Cesare Cardi set up a tailor shop that employed members of his family, and Egino and Lelio DeSantis opened a gas station. Christina DeSantis-Coviello established a beauty salon, Victor Liberta a barbershop, and Carlo and Rosa Provinzano set up an interior decorating store, as did Ida Liberta.[42]

Other forces limited the feasibility of the small family businesses that Italians usually favored. The pattern of centralized buying in large specialty stores was firmly established in 1950 with the construction of the L. B. Smith Plaza on Abbott Road. The number of businesses in Lackawanna dropped from 410 in 1948 to 327 just six years later. The housing in ethnic enclaves such as Ingham and Roland avenues began to deteriorate, and the overall housing situation in the First Ward was negatively affected by greater pollution from the steel plant and increasing racial tensions. The development of the eastern portion of Lackawanna proceeded rapidly, with the construction of Ridgewood Village in 1943 and other housing tracts, after the war. During the 1950s, many businesses were located east of the railroad tracks as European ethnics moved out of the First Ward and, along with newcomers from Buffalo, bought homes in the suburban-type developments east of South Park Avenue. Italian merchants had to adjust to these changes and adopt business strategies very different from those utilized earlier. As the steel plant began to reduce operations in the late 1960s, all but shutting down in 1983, Lackawanna's population fell dramatically, as did business opportunities.[43]

WISHING ALL OUR PATRONS A VERY
PROSPEROUS AND HAPPY NEW YEAR

Get In The Fun Join

Our New Year's

Eve Party With The

MASON DIXON RAMBLERS

HATS — NOISEMAKERS — ENTERTAINMENT
CHICKEN DINNERS — PIZZA

VIOLANTI'S CANTINA

3292 SOUTH PARK AVE.
Corner EAST MILNOR

Joseph and Louie Violanti, Props.
ALL NIGHT LICENSE
OPEN HOUSE or CALL SO. 9456
And Reserve a Table

Joe Violanti operated Violanti's Cantina first in partnership with his son-in-law, Eugene Kusmierz, and later with his son Louis. Violanti earlier raised chickens and had a stand on South Park Avenue where he sold the birds plus produce. Photo source: Lackawanna Library; *Lackawanna Leader*, 12/30/54

In 1950, Frank Chiodo started an accounting business at 105 Roland Avenue. His nephews Sam and Michael Chiodo took over the enterprise in 1977 and it remains in business today. Photo source: Paul Pasquarella

Mariano Savaglio used this horse and cart to peddle ice cream bars in Lackawanna and South Buffalo. He started the business in 1940, shortly after arriving from Calabria, and was joined by his son Carlo, who immigrated to Lackawanna in 1951. In this photo, Russell Mesi is sitting on Pete the horse in front of the boy's McKinley Avenue home. Photo source: Sal Mesi

Mirroring the values of American society, the Italian American community paid respect to those who earned their livelihood independently and didn't have to endure the hardships and dangers of work in the steel plant or on the railroads. The extension of easy credit to customers added to the appeal of businesspeople in the daily lives of Italian families. The confectionery, grocery, or saloon was often the neighborhood gathering spot and informal community center. Early in the twentieth century, the only telephone in the neighborhood was often the one at the local store, which served to elevate the importance of these businesses (see Figure 9.7). The high status often accorded businesspeople was most noticeable for those who achieved a comfortable financial status and other symbols of success from their businesses. Funeral director Nick DelBello and construction company proprietor Joe Amadori won recognition and attracted new customers by sponsoring sports teams whose uniforms carried the names of their businesses.

Many merchants held leadership positions, both in the city at large and within the Italian community. Active in the Democratic party, Peter Mazuca was secretary of the city's Civil Service Commission in 1931-32, a member of the chamber of commerce, and a founder of the Lackawanna Grocers and Butchers Association. Calogero Fadale and Serafino Mattucci became trustees of St. Anthony's Church. Mattucci, Carminantonio Picariello, Tony Amorosi, Tony Turchiarelli, and other early presidents of the

Lake Erie Italian Club were all businessmen. Gennaro Panzetta and John Verel were among the founders and leaders of the Italian American Citizens Club. For men interested in appointments to political jobs or in holding public office, running a business and being the leader of a society with many potential voters was a plus in a small, politically active city such as Lackawanna. Businessmen learned to cultivate political contacts to win city purchases or contracts. The Lackawanna Charities Commission regularly purchased food for needy families at a number of local grocery stores, presumably matching recipients with a nearby merchant who was often of the same ethnic group. In 1918 and 1919, Peter Sirianni and Sam Morgan each received six payments from the commission for groceries given to families in need. Contractors such as John Verel and Marco Costanzi captured city sidewalk and sewer construction jobs in the 1920s, as did Eugenio Galanti, who used his truck to haul materials for the city.[44]

The immigrants formed small businesses that served the needs of other Italian newcomers to the United States. For the Italian immigrant, running a business allowed him or her to overcome discrimination and cultural and language barriers within American society. Operating a grocery or saloon did not require formal education, training, or hiring practices, and knowledge of Italian culture and language were a plus in dealing with Italian patrons. Differing regional dialects and foods created additional niches for businesspeople who were from a region that was well represented among the Italian immigrants in Lackawanna. The Italian family structure and work ethic, which called for everyone from the youngest child to the elderly grandparent to contribute time to the family business, served to maximize hours and minimize overhead costs. This work setting also protected Italian females, who did not have to risk dishonor by laboring outside the home. While the work was often long and demanding, in many cases it paid off for the family, especially the children, when the business brought a profit and helped launch a young adult into his or her own business or paid for a college education. These business ventures helped create a middle class of Italian Americans who served in many leadership roles. It was the money from the family business that propelled the rise of a small upper class of professionals in Lackawanna's Italian community.

FIGURE 9.21

MARY YOVIENE-CLARK, LACKAWANNA'S FIRST ITALIAN AMERICAN TEACHER

Born in Boscoreale, Campania, as Maria Iovieno, Mary Yoviene was an infant when she arrived in the United States with her family. Her father, Alfonso, was a railroad section foreman whose jobs took the family to several towns in western Pennsylvania and then to Sardinia, New York. Mary Yoviene completed high school there in 1913, then entered the Normal School in Buffalo (Buffalo State Teachers College). This was possible because she had two older sisters who could help their mother do house chores and care for the three youngest children, and her father arranged for her free rail transportation to Buffalo. For several years, Yoviene daily took the 7:30 a.m. "milk train" from Sardinia to Buffalo, a route that made frequent stops to pick up milk cans; she then would catch the same train at 5:20 p.m. for the return run. When the Yoviene family moved to Roland Avenue in Lackawanna, Mary took the streetcar to school.

After graduating from college, Yoviene started teaching at the Washington School, just off Roland Avenue. Her typical fifth-grade class had 38 students. After a few years, she was assigned the "slow" students by Principal Hennessey and had the special class moved to Franklin School where there was more room. She visited the homes of these students, nurturing close relations with the community. Yoviene often translated for Italian parents whose children attended Washington School, and Principal Hennessey assigned Italian students to her class until they learned enough English to be placed in another classroom. For a short time, Yoviene taught adult night-school classes at Lackawanna High School, usually instructing recent immigrants in language skills. Her career spanned 35 years at the two schools. In 1935, she married Bob Clark. The couple purchased a home on Verel Street, where Yoviene remained until her death in the 1984.

Source: Interview with Mary Yoviene-Clark, December 29, 1983.

Joe Jennetti, the city's first Italian police officer, was appointed by Mayor Walter Lohr in 1925. He rose to the rank of lieutenant before retiring in 1945.
Photo source: Collection of Frank Rozwood

Sebastian Fistola became the first Italian firefighter in the city in 1925. Mayor Lohr appointed Fistola and Joe Jennetti because fellow Republican Tony Turchiarelli helped deliver the Italian vote at election time.
Photo source: Mary Panzetta-Vertino

In 1939, Theresa Morgan became the first Italian American teacher at Roosevelt Elementary School, where she taught for 42 years.
Photo source: Emilia Cardoni-Cutre

Professionals

The first Italian professionals in Lackawanna emerged during World War I. Three Italian priests arrived in the city in 1917 and 1918. Rev. Antonio Clemente came in July 1917 to serve as pastor of St. Anthony's Church but was transferred after one year. His successor, Rev. Raffaele D'Alfonso, left at the end of 1918 and was replaced by Rev. Giuseppe Vifredo, who began his long tenure as the church's pastor. Mary Yoviene graduated from college in Buffalo in 1916, applied for a teaching job in Lackawanna the following year, and was hired in February 1918 as an elementary school teacher (see Figure 9.21). John Fadale graduated from the University of Buffalo Medical School and in 1918 began his practice in Lackawanna. By 1920, he had an office on Ridge Road, not far from his parents' home and grocery store on Ingham Avenue. C. John Tarquinio had become a civil engineer by 1920. Several other professionals had brief stays in Lackawanna. A Methodist minister, Rev. Salvatore Musso, lived in the rectory of the Roland Methodist Church from 1918 to 1921, then moved on to his own congregation in central New York State. During the 1920s, Gonippo Raggi, a painter from Florence, Italy, lived at 1141 McKinley Parkway as he labored at painting the ceiling murals in Our Lady of Victory Basilica.[45]

The traditional route for immigrant and minority groups to enter the professions was through public-service jobs. The Irish certainly used this method, and they dominated the ranks of Lackawanna teachers, nurses, police officers, and firefighters. The large Polish community used its numbers to gain political clout and to get city jobs early in the twentieth century. With the election of Walter Lohr as mayor in 1924, Polish Americans came into their full political power. The Polish politicians were quick to court other ethnic groups to help them overthrow the Irish hegemony at city hall, and a significant number of Italians, Croatians, and other east European ethnics supported the Poles. To reward his supporters, Lohr appointed members of these ethnic groups to city positions. For Italians, this resulted in the 1925 appointment of Joseph Jennetti as the city's first Italian police officer and Sebastian Fistola its first Italian firefighter. In another area of professional advancement, Buffalonian Valentino Amarante became the pharmacist at Skudwick's Drugstore in Lackawanna in 1926 and remained in the position for more than 20 years.[46]

In addition to Mary Yoviene and John Fadale, a small number of other Italians were able to attend college in the early twentieth century. Several of Fadale's siblings did so, as did James Oddy, who became a successful bank administrator after graduating from Canisius College (see Figure 9.25). Many second-generation Italian Americans gravitated to the nursing and teaching professions. Gladys Yoviene, Mary's sister, was 19 years old in 1925 when she became a nurse; within three years, she was working for the Lackawanna Health Department. In 1930, Frances Cuozzo and Carmela Villoni were student nurses at Our Lady of Victory Maternity Hospital. As more members of the second generation entered adulthood in the 1930s, the number of Italian American professionals in Lackawanna continued to grow. In the late 1930s and early 1940s, Aurora Palmisano became a public-health nurse for the city, and Angeline George, Rose and Mamie Fiore, Virginia and Josephine Marrano, Cecile Marinelli, Mary Guercio, and Gloria Tarquinio also

FIGURE 9.22

EARLY ITALIAN SCHOOL TEACHERS IN LACKAWANNA

Following in the footsteps of Mary Yoviene-Clark in 1918 was Mary Martin, who taught at a Catholic school in 1930. Nick Milano joined Lackawanna's high school faculty in 1934, teaching social studies and eventually becoming a guidance counselor. He retired after more than 40 years of service. Theresa Morgan became an instructor in adult Americanization classes in 1936 and three years later secured a full-time teaching position at Roosevelt Elementary School, where she taught for 42 years. She actively helped young postwar Italian immigrants such as Guy Iannarelli, spending extra time tutoring and sharing a book written in English and Italian. John Yoviene, the brother of Mary and Gladys, entered the school system as a teacher of high-school mathematics and science in 1938. He became vice-principal at Lackawanna High School in 1967, retiring four years later. Samuel D. Conte began his teaching career in 1939 following his graduation from the Buffalo Teachers' College. After several

years as a math teacher at Lackawanna High School, he entered the armed forces in 1943 and was a teacher at an army university in France three years later. After his discharge, Conte taught at Wayne State University in Detroit, then completed a doctorate of applied mathematics at the University of Michigan in 1950. He joined the faculty at Purdue University, became chairman of the computer department, and authored a book on software engineering. Conte retired from teaching in 1993; four years later, Purdue named its new computer center after him.

Second-generation Italian Americans continued entering the teaching profession during the 1940s and 1950s. John Costanzo was a teacher by 1941, and Caroline Fiore and Mildred Montanari-Grabowski were teaching by 1947, the latter at Wilson School in the First Ward. Montanari-Grabowski eventually rose to an administrative position in the schools, one of the first Italian Americans to do so. Aldo Filipetti began teaching at his childhood

school, Bethlehem Park School, in 1954. That same year, Dorothy Milano, daughter of politician Joe Milano, became a school teacher in western New York and spent a year teaching in Japan. After graduating from Canisius College, Frank Saccomanno worked at the Ford Stamping Plant, then at his father's grocery store as a butcher. He returned to school, received a teaching degree, and in 1959 began his new career at Roosevelt Elementary School. He was also chief negotiator for the teachers union. Another First Warder, Mike Schiavi, started his career as a health teacher and coach at the high school, and in 1990 published a book titled, *Coach's Guide to Athletic Training*. Loretta Barreca-Petrucci, a native of Silver Creek who married Lackawannan Louie Petrucci, taught third and fourth grade at Our Lady of Victory School from 1955 to 1978. Josephine Fadale-Ippolito operated a beauty salon, then taught future beauticians at Fosdick Masten Vocational High School in Buffalo.

Sources: *Lackawanna Leader*, 1/3/46, 12/4/47; *Buffalo News*, 12/24/91; *Front Page*, 12/24/97; *Erie County Directory*, 1941; *Lackawanna City Directory*, 1960; Lackawanna School Board Minutes, 9/21/36, 9/29/38, 2/9/39, 10/5/39, 5/2/40; interviews with Guy Iannarelli, April 7, 1994; Iole Schiavi-Murray, March 31, 1997; Patricia Fadale-Pellegrino, July 8, 1996; Nick Milano, June 24, 1997; Frank Saccomanno, April 2, 1996; Jerry Baldelli, November 26, 2008; and Loretta Barreca Petrucci, December 27, 1984.

became nurses. It is interesting to note that a number of second- and third-generation Italian American women were encouraged by their parents to attend college, but, unlike their brothers, they were not allowed to attend out-of-town schools. The Italian tradition of closely guarding the honor of females meant the women had to live at home and make the daily commute to a local college until they were married.[47]

The ranks of Italian American teachers began to expand in 1930, when Mary Martin became a teacher at the St. Joseph's Boy's Orphan Asylum, one of the institutions under the direction of Father Baker, pastor of the Our Lady of Victory parish. Nick Milano was the second Italian teacher in the Lackawanna public-school system. After graduating from the University of Buffalo, he applied for a position at Lackawanna High School. Unfortunately for Milano, his brother Joe was a Democrat and an outspoken critic of Republican powerhouse Walter Lohr. So, for three years,

Nick Milano was able to work only as a substitute teacher, despite the lobbying efforts of the Federation of Italian American Associations of Lackawanna. He was finally hired as a full-time high-school teacher in 1934. In the late 1930s, three more Italian teachers joined the Lackawanna Public Schools system: Theresa Morgan at Roosevelt Elementary School, and John Yoviene and Samuel Conte at the high school (see Figure 9.22).[48]

In the 1930s and 1940s, three Italian American doctors from Buffalo moved to Lackawanna, where two of them established practices. Gustave DaLuiso began his career at Our Lady of Victory Hospital in 1931, permanently settling in Lackawanna seven years later. Sam Balisteri, an oculist, was living in the Steel City by 1941 and maintaining a practice in Buffalo. Dr. Carl Faso, an ear, nose, and throat specialist, established his office on Ridge Road in about 1942 and practiced in Lackawanna until he retired in the early 1980s. Second-generation Italians

FIGURE 9.23

JOHN FADALE, MD

Photo source: Collection of Helen Fadale-Costello

John Fadale (1895–1980) was born in Geneseo, New York, the eldest of seven children. His parents, immigrants from Valledolmo, Sicily, moved the family first to Buffalo, then to Lackawanna in 1904. He remembers being the only Italian student both at Roosevelt School, from which he graduated in 1909, and the original Lackawanna High School, where he won his diploma in 1913. Attending the University of Buffalo Medical School from 1914 to 1918, he finally had a number of Italians as classmates.

While in medical school, Fadale lived at the family home and commuted to the university. After classes, he helped his father at the family store, delivering groceries to customers' homes. He married Nina Mayne, a French American, and they settled at 231 Ridge Road, where Fadale also had his office. Right next door was Dr. John Tracy, whom Fadale described as "my hero."

John Fadale served as the doctor for Wilson and Roosevelt schools, and for 55 years was on the staff of Our Lady of Victory Hospital. He made rounds at the hospital each morning, then returned home and had office hours from 1:00 to 3:00 p.m. and again from 7:00 to 8:00 p.m. He made many house calls, for which he charged $3 (later increased to $5). He sometimes took one of his sons along. "When my dad went on house calls, he took me with him, to spend time with him," said Dick Fadale. "I locked myself in the car while dad was inside with a patient." The doctor was constantly on call, and sometimes at very inconvenient times. "People with sick family members would wait for the father to come home from the plant before calling a doctor. Therefore, I had to make many night calls," said John Fadale. He also did a lot of "clerical work" for immigrants, writing letters and serving as an unofficial court interpreter.

Fadale had a number of Italian patients, but most of his clientele were of other ethnic groups. Some of the factors involved in this were described by his sister Patricia:

> John never sent out bills. Often people didn't pay; they were ashamed to face him and went to other doctors. Italians often went to Dr. Fisher because he was Irish and 'smart.' John would tell patients that nothing was wrong with them; they would then go to Dr. Fisher to get sugar pills.

Other factors besides Fadale's direct style may have kept Italians away. During the 1930s, a young Italian woman died while under his care, though probably through no fault of Fadale's. Some Italians felt Fadale was responsible for the death, however, and switched to other doctors.

Fadale ran as a Republican for city assessor in 1917 and 1921 at the urging of Italian friends, but success eluded him. He ran a candy store and financed another person's furniture store. Fadale invented a solution used to polish stainless steel, then he and his son Charles started the Electro Process Company on Lehigh Avenue to incorporate this invention.

He was active in local civic organizations, and in 1918 was one of the founding members of the Lackawanna Tuberculosis Association. He was appointed to the Lackawanna Board of Health in 1920, and for several years was the doctor for the Lake Erie Italian Club. Much of his organizational activity focused on his work at Our Lady of Victory Hospital and the Lackawanna Charity Organization, where he sat on the board of directors. He did emergency-room work at OLV Hospital prior to retiring in 1974. John Fadale was a member of the Erie County Medical Association, the Odd Fellows Lodge No. 187, and St. Paul's Episcopal Cathedral in Buffalo.

Sources: Interviews with Patricia Fadale-Pellegrino, July 8, 1996; Dick Fadale, July 24, 2000; John Fadale, November 23, 1979, and Helen Fadale-Costello, April 25, 2000; *Lackawanna Daily Journal*, 11/6/17; 7/10/18; *Lackawanna Leader*, 11/14/46.

FIGURE 9.24

GUSTAVE DALUISO, MD

John D'Alessandro, shown here upon graduation from medical school, was born and raised in Lackawanna's First Ward. He settled in Detroit, where he established his medical practice. Photo source: John D'Alessandro

Gustave DaLuiso (1905–1993) was born in Vastogirardi, Abruzzo. At age two, he traveled from Italy with his mother and older brother to join his father in the United States. The family moved from Pennsylvania to Troy, New York, then settled in Buffalo in 1913. Graduating from the University of Buffalo Medical School in 1931, DaLuiso joined the medical staff at Our Lady of Victory Hospital. For two years, he lived in the hospital, receiving $50 per month in addition to room and board. He was constantly on duty, and his only reprieve was Sunday dinners at his parents' house. From 1933 to 1936, he practiced medicine in Brocton, New York, then received specialized training at the New York Eye and Ear Infirmary in New York City.

Returning to Lackawanna in 1938, DaLuiso rented a home and office at 678 Ridge Road. In 1940, he married Florence Simini, and four years later the couple moved to 2660 South Park Avenue, just north of OLV Hospital. Fluent in Italian, DaLuiso served many Italians in his office and at the hospital. A member of the Bacelli Medical Club of Buffalo, he was also involved in the Lake Erie Italian Club for several years and the chamber of commerce.

Sources: Interview with Florence Simini-DaLuiso, July 14, 1994; Thomas S. Bumbalo, MD, "Gustave A. DaLuiso: Physician, Gentleman, and Scholar," n. d., unpublished paper, provided by Florence Simini-DaLuiso.

Angelo D'Alessandro, like his brother John, grew up in the First Ward and became a medical doctor. He established his home and career in Tulsa, Oklahoma.
Photo source: Angelo D'Alessandro

raised in Lackawanna entered medical professions in the postwar period. John D'Alessandro completed his studies in osteopathic medicine in Philadelphia in 1956, going on to settle in Detroit and establishing a practice in radiology. His brother, Angelo D'Alessandro, graduated from the University of Buffalo School of Pharmacy in 1956, and, after completing studies at the Chicago School of Osteopathic Medicine in 1960, settled in Tulsa, Oklahoma. During the same period, Mario Campanelli completed medical school and established his podiatrist practice in Buffalo. Ross L. Guarino became a cardiothoracic surgeon and, eventually, president of the Medical Society of Erie County. David Novelli set up a general practice in Lackawanna in 1980. Anthony Grasso Jr. was a dentist practicing in Rochester, New York, until his untimely death in 1965. After military service in World War II, Carl Morgan received a doctorate in experimental medicine and in 1955 was appointed Associate Cancer Research Director of the St. Anthony's Guild Research Institute in Lafayette, New Jersey. Joseph Saccomanno became a pharmacist in the 1950s.[49]

Vatican City Rome, 2008. David Novelli, MD, (left) had his first office in Lackawanna and now has his practice in West Seneca. His father, John, at right, is a noted artist.
Photo source: David Novelli

Gladys Yoviene was most likely the first Italian in Lackawanna to become a nurse, which she did at the age of 19 in 1925. Within three years, she began a long career as a public-health nurse for the city of Lackawanna.
Photo source: Jim Yoviene

The first Lackawanna Italian to attain a law degree was Daniel Monaco, who, in 1941, graduated from Southeastern University in Washington, D.C. Apparently he did not return to the Steel City to practice his profession. Richard Buscaglia, a native of Buffalo, set up a law office in Lackawanna in 1948 and maintained the practice there until his death five years later. He frequently served as an acting judge in the Lackawanna City Court. Another second-generation Italian, Arcangelo Petricca, grew up in Bethlehem Park and became a lawyer in 1955, sharing his Lackawanna office with attorney Carlo Perfetto of Buffalo. Since 1958 Petricca has served as municipal judge and been appointed to several other city positions.[50]

A significant number of second-generation Italian Americans in Lackawanna joined the ranks of business professionals. For many, their military experience in World War II and the opportunity to attend college under the GI Bill helped launch their careers. For example, Louis Marrano, after leaving the military in 1946 began a long career as a security officer with the U.S. State Department. He has held posts in Belgium, Holland, Denmark, France, Argentina, Taiwan, and Washington DC. John Novelli studied electronics after his discharge, and in 1948 he and classmate Dominic Zignossi became the first TV cameramen in Buffalo. He pursued his life-long interest in art by studying sculpture, etching, and lithography in Buffalo and two local art schools, and three art academies in Italy. He continues to paint and has won many awards, including silver and bronze medals from the Buffalo Society of Artists for monotype oil paintings. This trend was seen in Italian communities throughout the country, as Italian Americans made significant gains in income and choice of occupation following World War II. By 1960, second-generation Italian Americans had an above-average occupational level and a significantly higher average income than reported for all native-born white Americans.[51]

Some of the Italian professionals, like the Italian businesspeople, took an active role in the organizational and civic life of the Steel City. In the 1930s, C. John Tarquinio was president of the Italian American Citizens Club, and Nick Milano served several terms as president of the Stags Club. These men were the exceptions, however, as most Italian American professionals were not very active in the city's Italian groups—at least, not in leadership roles. Instead, professionals seemed to be attracted to community-wide organizations and professional societies. John Fadale was active in the affairs of Our Lady of Victory Hospital and was involved for many years in the Lackawanna Charity Organization. Gustave DaLuiso participated in hospital-related groups and, after a brief time in the Lake Erie Italian Club, was active in the junior chamber of commerce. The wives of these doctors were involved in the hospital guild, and Florence DaLuiso was founder of the

Rose Fiore was one of several Italian women to complete studies as a nurse in the late 1930s and early 1940s. Photo source: Rose Fiore-Pacholczak

Josephine Marrano started her nursing career in the early 1940s, working as a city public-health nurse, then for 25 years at Our Lady of Victory Hospital. When she visited some elderly Italian immigrants to give them free shots, the families gave her a plate of spaghetti to show their appreciation. Photo source: Josephine Marrano-Fistola

Lackawanna Garden Club. Teacher Samuel Conte was president of the Lackawanna Junior Chamber of Commerce in 1942. Like some of the successful businesspeople, successful Italian American professionals crossed ethnic lines and mixed with others who had attained a similar occupational and social status. Some Italian professionals, such as James Oddy and Dan Monaco, left blue-collar Lackawanna to pursue careers in larger, more occupationally diverse cities. A significant number of the American-born professionals were the children of immigrants who had operated successful businesses that provided funds for college tuition. Four of Sam and Mary Morgan's nine children —Theresa, Patrick, Carl, and Sue—went on to college, as did Mary, Gladys, and John Yoviene. Dr. John Fadale and engineer C. John Tarquinio were both the sons of immigrant entrepreneurs. Frank and Joseph Saccomanno were the sons of second-generation Italian American businesspeople who maintained a successful grocery store. In more recent years a number of third-generation Italian American women attended college and entered the teaching profession. Linda Cipriano began a 36-year career teaching in elementary schools, rising to an administrative position in the second half of her tenure with the Lackawanna schools. Both Sandra Marinelli and Lois Ginnetti-Hooper have taught for three decades in the city's

Louis Marrano attended college after World War II under the GI Bill and in 1948 began a long career with the U.S. State Department. He is pictured here, on the right, speaking with a cleric. Photo source: Neil Marrano

FIGURE 9.25

JAMES J. ODDY, BANKER

Born Giacomo Oddi in the Old Village, James Oddy (1907–1993) was the eldest of four children of Benigno Oddi and Giselda Luigia Monaco. He first learned English when he attended the Annex School in the Old Village, and at home taught it to his parents and siblings. He completed elementary and high school study in the Lackawanna Public Schools and worked as a caddy at the Wanakah Country Club. In 1924, he won the Western New York Junior Golf Championship. Oddy attended Canisius College, financing his education by working as a tutor of Spanish. Upon graduation in 1929, he worked as a messenger for the Marine Trust Company. He joined the Niagara National Bank in 1938. "I was supposed to handle the credit department when I went to Niagara National from Marine," said Oddy, "but on my first day there Herb Vogelsang came up to my desk and said: 'You are our lending officer,' so I took care of loan operations during the day and took the credit department work home with me at night."

Oddy initiated policies to help the small-business person, including "granting loans on inventories, accounts

Source: Margaret Oddy-Guastaferro

receivable, and purchase orders. In those days the bigger banks were wary of extending loans based on such terms." Recounting the early days of his career, Oddy said, "It was hard to get a $1,000 loan back in the late 1930s. Most customers were checked, rechecked, and then had to get cosigners." After World War II, the bank granted loans for equipment that allowed many contractors to launch their businesses.

Niagara National later became First National Bank, and Oddy had risen to executive vice-president by 1955. That year, the M&T Bank acquired First

National, and Oddy was named senior vice-president, presiding over the busy branch on Main and Genesee streets in Buffalo. Living with his family in Eggertsville, James Oddy was very active in community-service activities. He was general chairman of the Catholic Charities fund drive in 1953, chairman of the 1954 March of Dimes campaign, and community division chairman of the United Jewish Fund in 1969. President of the Canisius College Alumni Association in the 1950s, Oddy also served on the board of Rosary Hill College for 15 years, and was awarded a doctor of humane letters degree by that college in 1966. Oddy was president of the 250 Club, a fund-raising offshoot of the Erie County Democratic Party that in the 1960s helped underwrite the successful mayoral campaigns of Frank Sedita in Buffalo. In 1972, James Oddy retired after a 43-year career in the banking industry.

Oddy, whose family had moved to South Buffalo in 1924, was involved in Lackawanna Council No. 2243 of the Knights of Columbus in the early 1930s. Eventually, he bought a home in the well-to-do suburb of Eggertsville, just north of Buffalo, where he lived with his wife and daughters.

Sources: Interview with Margaret Oddy-Guastaferro, May 7, 1996; collection of newspaper clippings provided by Margaret Oddy-Guastaferro, including: *Buffalo Evening News*, 12/13/52, 12/13/68; *Courier Express*, 9/28/67, 1/31/69, and other undated, clippings.

---

schools and been involved in politics as committee persons in their neighborhoods.[52]

The early professionals occupied a type of upper-class status in the Lackawanna Italian community, a ranking that also included successful Italian businesspeople like John Verel and Nicholas Mattucci. Most of the businesspeople were akin to an upper-middle class (see Figure 4.13 in chapter 4), and to their ranks can be added politicians and some of the men holding skilled and supervisory positions at the steel plant and on the railroads. After 1941, Italian labor leaders also entered this grouping. In blue-collar Lackawanna, it was these two strata that filled a variety of leadership roles

throughout the community. The upper elite represented Italians in the key professions and institutions of Lackawanna: hospitals, business institutions, schools and other public institutions. If they could make no other claim, these people at a minimum provided role models for Italian American youth and a claim to status for Italian immigrants within American society. Members of the upper-middle class were leaders of many Italian organizations, including those that focused on civic and political themes. They also guided the interaction between the predominantly blue-collar Italian community and institutions such as labor unions, political parties, and the educational system.

FIGURE 9.26

LATER-GENERATION PROFESSIONALS

Many Lackawanna Italians born since the late 1930s have had distinguished careers in a variety of fields. A significant number of these individuals live outside of western New York or in other states. Some have remained in the Lackawanna area and are active in the community and in Italian American circles. Among them are four individuals, three raised in the First Ward, who have excelled in the fields of education and civic involvement.

Gerald Baldelli
Photo source: Gerald Baldelli

Gerald Baldelli grew up in Bethlehem Park, and his family has its roots in Marche and Abruzzo. Baldelli was president of his graduating class at Lackawanna High School in 1956, attended the University of Buffalo on a scholarship, and later received a master's degree from Canisius College. In 1961, he began a 35-year career in the Frontier School system and became chairman of the high school mathematics department and the director of adult education. He was named Hamburg's Outstanding Young Educator by the Hamburg Jaycees in 1969. Two years later, Baldelli was appointed principal of Amsdell Heights Junior High School, then served as high-school

principal from 1973 to 1984. He expanded his career in 1990 when he started as a part-time mathematics instructor at the south campus of Erie Community College (ECC). When he retired from the Frontier School system in 1996, Baldelli was assistant superintendent for personnel and could look back on a long list of accomplishments: coaching basketball and volleyball; chairing the 1991 and 1996 Marketing Bond Issue Committees, which raised millions of dollars; and serving as president of the Erie County High School Principals' Association, the Erie County Interscholastic Conference, and the Western New York Association of School Personnel Administrators. His retirement proved very short indeed, as he not only continued teaching at ECC but also served for three years as the principal of the Southtowns Catholic School.

In 1967, Baldelli and his wife Marie, settled in Lakeview where they raised their four children. He became president of the parish council of Our Lady of Perpetual Help Parish in Lakeview and was chairman of the Building Committee for the new church. During the 1960s, Baldelli was elected to two terms as a Democratic committeeman in Bethlehem Park, and four decades later, he again ran for public office. In 2004, he won a seat on the Frontier Board of Education, and two years later, he was elected as board president.

Gerald Baldelli has maintained his ties to Lackawanna through his involvement in St. Anthony's Church and the Galanti Athletic Association. Commenting on his ethnic roots, he said:

I have particularly cherished our Italian culture primarily because the Italian American people value and appreciate so many very basic traditions in life: … they love and take

pride in the preparation of Italian cuisine which is continually handed down to their children…; they cherish their music and dance customs; they take pride in the artists, sculptors, scientists of Italian history. The entire Italian experience and existence are two of God's greatest gifts to me.

Anne Ginnetti-Spadone
Photo source: Anne Ginnetti-Spadone

Anne Ginnetti-Spadone is the daughter of an Italian American father and a Polish American mother. She was raised on Berry Street, and her family later moved to Shannon Drive. John Ginnetti, her father, worked in the steel plant, eventually earning a graduate degree and teaching night school. Her mother, Esther Kaznowski, worked as an executive secretary. After graduating from Lackawanna High School, Anne completed a bachelor's degree at D'Youville College in 1972 and a master's degree in business education two years later. Married to Ron Spadone, she worked part-time while raising five children. She taught high-school business courses in Perry, West Seneca, and Lackawanna. In 1980, she was an instructor of community- and adult-education courses in the Steel City, and in 1982, she began a five-year stint teaching secretarial science at ECC. Moving on to the Board of Cooperative Educational Services (BOCES), she specialized in workforce development for 10 years. Returning to the Steel City schools, she taught business and computer courses in the middle and high schools. Since 2000, she has worked full-time at BOCES in several capacities: as coordinator of curriculum and staff development; as coordinator of programs to attract middle-school children; and, most recently, as assistant principal at Potter Career and Technical Center.

Anne has been involved in the Lake Erie Italian Club Auxiliary, has been actively involved in her husband's political campaigns, and has written literature for a number of campaigns and politicians. She enjoys her mixed-ethnic heritage and preparing the Polish and Italian food specialties that go along with each holiday. She feels that her two ethnic heritages are "a nice blend" and honors the traditions of both her Italian father and her Polish mother.

Chico Galanti
Photo source: Chico Galanti

Ralph Galanti Jr., better known as **Chico**, is a third-generation Italian American whose family origins are in two towns in Campania. Long involved in the fields of education and recreation, he graduated from Lackawanna High School in 1963, where he was active in athletics. He completed a bachelor's degree at SUNY at Buffalo in 1967, then a master's degree, both in health, physical education, and recreation. After teaching for two years in the Lackawanna schools, Galanti in 1969 began a 36-year career at ECC. Serving as the school's athletic director from 1975 until his retirement in 2005, he developed the "one-college concept" for athletics at the school's multiple campus sites, established the women's sports program, implemented academic monitoring and tracking of athletes, and founded and coached the successful ECC varsity hockey team. Many honors have been bestowed upon him: International Collegiate Hockey League Coach of the Year (four times), National Junior College Athletic Association Region III/JUCO Coach of the Year (five times); election to the National College Hockey Coaches Association Hall of Fame (2002),

the Greater Buffalo Sports Hall of Fame (2004), and the Lackawanna High School Wall of Fame (1997). In addition, Galanti received the Erie Community College Outstanding Achievement Award in 1976 and 1984, and won the SUNY Chancellor's Award for Excellence in Professional Service in 1998. More recently, he was inducted into the Erie County College Athletic Hall of Fame and the National College Hockey Coaches Association Bowling Hall of Fame (2006), and he received the Buffalo Bison Ilio DiPaolo Humanitarian Award that same year. Although he is now retired, Galanti has become the local chairman for the 2010 Empire State Games.

Chico Galanti was elected to one term on the Lackawanna School Board and served as board president. He has lived his whole life in Lackawanna, where he and his wife Diane raised their three children, one of whom (Ralph III) is now the chief of the Lackawanna Fire Department. Chico Galanti remains active in the Galanti Athletic Association, founded at his grandfather's grocery store eight decades ago. Galanti writes:

> I feel … very proud to be an American. But I also have deep pride in my Italian Heritage. I attribute much of my success to my parents and grandparents. Through their Italian ideals of family, work ethic, compassion and traditions, they taught me the values of life that have guided me throughout my private and professional career. To them and my Italian heritage, I will always be grateful.

Today, he continues to write his weekly column in the *Front Page* in which he reminisces about the many individuals and organizations that have contributed to Lackawanna's community life.

Lucia Caracci-Cullens
Photo source: Lucia Caracci-Cullens

Lucia Caracci-Cullens was born in Castro dei Volsci, Lazio, the daughter of Emilio and Maria Rossi. In 1954, Emilio immigrated to Lackawanna to join relatives and eventually obtained a job in the steel plant. When Maria and Lucia immigrated four years later, they were met in New York City by Emilio and Patsy Ricci, who drove them to Lackawanna. The family took up residence in Bethlehem Park, and Lucia entered second grade at the elementary school there. Prior to immigrating, Lucia and her mother studied an Italian-English book that Emilio had sent. Like many other children who immigrated before age 10, Lucia quickly picked up English. When she graduated from eighth grade and enrolled at Lincoln Junior High School, the family moved to Ingham Avenue, then to Sandra Drive when Lucia entered senior high school. Maria worked in the kitchen at Our Lady of Victory Hospital, and the family's strong commitment to volunteer work led 15-year-old Lucia to volunteer there.

Lucia attended the State Teachers College at Buffalo and completed a master's degree in secondary education. She then worked as a substitute teacher. Remembering how the International Institute in Buffalo had helped with the paperwork that allowed her older sister's family to come to the United States, Lucia signed up for volunteer duties there. Quickly impressed by her credentials—fluency in English, Italian and Spanish, and first-hand knowledge of the immigration experience—the institute offered her a job in 1973. Lucia taught classes in English and other subjects, did case work for immigrants from many countries, and organized activities and resources. She established a group of volunteer interpreters who could assist immigrants in any of a number of languages. Lucia traveled to camps in southeast Asia to work out plans for refugees' resettlement in the United States. She eventually became program director at the International Institute, and her hard work there was well known.

Lucia never applied for a job, "the jobs always came to me," she said. Rev. Secondo Casarotto of St. Anthony's Church in Buffalo hired her in 1992 to help revitalize the parish. Founded in 1891, it is the oldest Italian church in Buffalo, and Rev. Casarotto wanted to maintain an Italian presence and sponsor activities that would foster a positive identity for local Italian Americans. Lucia went to work and organized dances, concerts, and lectures on Italian and Catholic culture. She utilized the new hall built in the 1970s for bingo and after-Mass socials, as a meeting place for Italian

societies. In 2002, Lucia established the Camerata Sant'Antonio (chamber orchestra) and two choirs, and there is now a Parish Life Committee and the Friends of St. Anthony, the latter consisting of nonparishioners and non – Catholics who support the programs of the church. St. Anthony's Church also has photographs and cultural displays in the church basement, and Rev. Casarotto has prepared a series of papers that document aspects of Italian American history in western New York. The parish now has 500 families, half of whom have roots in Italy. There are daily Masses and three Masses on Sunday—one each in English, Italian, and Latin.

Lucia has accomplished all of this with the help of only a maintenance man and a part-time secretary. In 1992, she was appointed honorary vice consul of Italy, a nonpaid job that involves a lot of work. Her office is located in the rectory of St. Anthony's. Lucia seems to love her work and remains energetic and devoted to the many activities in which she is involved. And Lucia Caracci-Cullens is very proud of and knowledgeable about Italian and Italian American history and culture.

Sources: *Lackawanna Leader*, 6/21/56, 2/6/69, 7/15/71; *Front Page*, 6/19/96, 12/25/96, 11/12/2003, 2/11/2004, 5/26/2004, 8/30/2006, 11/21/2007; "Retirement Roast of Ralph 'Chico' Galanti, Jr.," booklet, 11/26/2005; interviews with Anne Ginnetti-Spadone, October 26, 2008 and November 23, 2008; Jerry Baldelli, November 26, 2008; Chico Galanti, November 25, 2008; and Lucia Caracci-Cullens, November 22, 2008.

Mario Fanone with his son Phil, photo on the left., and with his wife Maria, photo on the right, 1956. The Fanone family harvested crops on the Zittel farm south of Lackawanna. Like the earlier Italian immigrants, the Fanones found that summer farm labor provided a reliable source of income for the family. Photo source: Phil Fanone

Women and Kids: Farm Labor, Housework, and Odd Jobs

Like many other Italians in Buffalo and western New York, those in Lackawanna often supplemented their family income prior to World War II by doing farm labor. Usually, it was the children and their mothers who harvested vegetables and fruits on the large farms in Eden, North Collins, Farnham, and Brant. Children and young adults, sometimes accompanied by their mothers, traveled to the farms on a daily basis. Trucks came around early in the morning hours to pickup points in the First Ward and Roland Avenue, then returned the laborers to Lackawanna at dusk. Gene Covelli remembers that the driver went through the streets of Bethlehem Park until his truck had a full load of 30 to 35 people. The trucks appeared on each day that the farmers needed laborers. Some families stayed on the farms the whole summer living in shanties. The husband/father might join them on weekends, or, if work was slow at the steel plant, remain with his family for the summer. This pattern continued well into the 1950s. Saggio, Thomas, Mecca, Catalano, and Sessanna families, and most of the other farm-owners were Italian Americans.[53]

In 1924, during a slack period at Bethlehem Steel, Michele and Rosa Grasso and their children spent the summer at Catalano's farm in Brant picking beans and other crops. The Grassos' oldest son, Tony, was working on the Lehigh Valley Railroad, and was fortunate enough to own a 1920 Ford touring car. Several times he drove out to help his family pick vegetables, but he didn't care for the work and soon ceased the trips.

Beginning in 1929, Anna Core and her four children, ages four to 14, spent five seasons working on the Mecca and Catalano farms. They lived in a two-room shack; nearby were a manual water pump and outhouses. One shanty was equipped with stoves for communal cooking, and Anna baked bread in outdoor ovens at night. During the long workday, Anna earned seven and one-half cents per hour for hoeing. The children picked strawberries, which brought five cents per quart, and beans paid one-half cent per pound. Most of the other farm laborers were also Italian, many of them from Buffalo. At times, Anna and Mary Core worked at a tomato cannery in Farnham. Pans of preboiled tomatoes would come down a conveyor line, and the female workers removed the skins. Paid by volume, the women worked at a feverish pace. The workers took turns being at the beginning of the line, where one had access to a greater number of tomatoes. Anna gave her turn to Mary, as the younger woman was very adept at this work and could quickly peel the skins. Beginning in 1934, the Cores went to the farms on a daily basis, catching a truck early in the morning along Ingham Avenue. Although she married that year, Mary continued to accompany her family to Brant and Farnham. Later, from 1948 to 1951, she took her four boys with her to do daily work at the farms.[54]

Many Italian children and teenagers made the daily farm trips. Margaret Marinelli and her two sisters did farm work in Brant during the late 1930s and early 1940s. They usually worked at the Thomas farm, owned by an Italian family that had Anglicized its name. All wages earned by the girls were

Picking crops on a farm in western New York, just as they did in Italy. The workers include Giulia Fiore, seated at left, and Giovanna Fanone, standing at left. Photo source: Rose Fiore-Pacholczak

given to their parents. One year, Giovanni and Annaregina Marinelli rewarded their daughters by buying a two-wheel bicycle for the girls to share. Roland Avenue residents were often picked up by trucks from the Sessanna farm in Eden. Filomena Ziccarelli regularly took her younger children to harvest crops at this farm. Her son Tony recalls that Ben and Frank Gruppo, the men who drove the truck in which the family rode, also had jobs in the Strip Mill at the time.[55]

Women, children, and the elderly all helped perform the many home chores as well as those in family stores. The housework in a typical home included tending the stove, preparing meals, cleaning, washing the laundry, raising children, feeding livestock, tilling gardens, and canning foods. Many families had boarders, and it was the mother and her older children who cooked the boarders' meals, washed their laundry and made them bag lunches to take to work, among many other chores (see Chapter 5). While the girls usually were kept close to home, Italian American boys started out early in life to supplement the family income by doing work outside the family home. Eleven-year-old Nunze Oddy, who was the second of

six children, became a newspaper delivery boy. The following year, he and Jimmy Ginnetti worked at a scrapyard on Ingham Avenue. The two boys broke bolts off old rails using hammers and chisels. Oddy then had a job with several other boys hauling rods and other materials at Buffalo Brake Beam. At age 14, he became a messenger boy operating out of the main office building at Lackawanna Steel. Eugenio and Filomena Ziccarelli had seven children, five of them boys. Beginning in the late 1930s the four oldest boys, whose ages ranged from 10 to 16, journeyed each week to a store at Broadway and Bailey Avenues in Buffalo and purchased three large bags of peanuts. Back at their Roland Avenue home, they divided the peanuts into small bags, loaded these onto a wagon, then walked a mile and a half northward to the corner of McKinley Parkway and South Park Avenue, across from the Botanical Gardens in South Park. There, each Sunday, they sold peanuts to passersby for 10 cents a bag, or three bags for a quarter. When they returned home, all the money was turned over to their father.[56]

Lou Colello, who as a boy went to local businessmen to get temporary work doing chores, continued this practice as a

A CADDIES' STRIKE AT WANAKAH

In 1937, Gene Covelli and several of his friends felt they should be better paid for the four hours of work involved in caddying a round of golf. Covelli, Frank Polisella, Dan DePasquale, and a few others thus organized a strike of 210 caddies on the busiest golf day of the year. "At nine o'clock on the morning of July 4th," Covelli reports, "I marched 210 caddies down the road, who vowed, to the man, that we would not go up [report for work] until we had our dollar—that massive twenty-five cent raise! The moral of that is very simple. At 11:30 a.m. there were only three people [strikers] left—Frank Polisella, Dan DePasquale, and yours truly. Everybody else was gone. Now that economic lesson I never really forgot." The other boys saw golfers arriving who needed caddies, and the economic needs of their families and themselves overshadowed the commitment to the planned strike.

Source: Interview with Gene Covelli, July 22, 1990.

teenager. He approached his godmother's husband, Joe Jennetti, and worked at his gas station greasing cars, and changing oil and tires. Shortly afterwards, Colello went across the street and became a waterboy for the contractor constructing Ridgewood Village. Many other boys in Lackawanna made money for their families by caddying at Wanakah Country Club, located five miles south of the Steel City, along Lake Erie. Waldo Robb, the director of the Lackawanna Community House, encouraged youth to pursue this course and in 1921 had a clubhouse built for the 200 Lackawanna youth who served as caddies. That year Robb traveled to Wanakah twice a week to supervise the boys and confer with the two caddy masters. Prior to 1933, some youth traveled there via the Erie Car, a trolley that ran along the Lake Erie shoreline, for 15 cents per round trip. Those who wished (or needed) to avoid this expense walked or hitchhiked to Wanakah, then hitched a ride home with golfers. Also several of the older caddies had cars and charged others a nickel for a ride. Gene Antonelli and Gino Fini both packed 10 or 11 other Italian American teens into their cars and drove from Bethlehem Park to the golf course.[57]

At Wanakah, the caddy masters directed the activities of the caddies. A modest caddy house had small, numbered bins in which the youth stored their lunches. Tony Moretti often served as an informal helper to the caddy masters, directing activities in the caddy house. Most of the caddies were boys from Lackawanna's First Ward neighborhood's, and many of the city's varied ethnic groups were represented among their ranks. Some of the boys were very young, age 10 or 11, when they started caddying. In the mid-1930s, a caddy earned 75 cents for a full round of golf, which was good money to youth from families of humble means. Prior to the Depression, the rate was closer to $1. It was common for the boys to give all their earnings to their parents, who in turn might hand back a nickel or dime for an ice-cream cone or a movie. At Wanakah, working-class and poor Italian American boys got their first glimpse of the lifestyles of wealthy, white Anglo – Saxon Protestants. Corporate executives from all over western New York were members of the private club. To the youth from Lackawanna's First Ward, it must have been an eye-opening experience. Some of them used the caddying outings as an opportunity to connect with the steel-plant superintendents who golfed at Wanakah.[58]

The men in the family often performed odd jobs in addition to their full-time work. Prior to World War II, when automobiles were relatively scarce in the Italian community, men fortunate enough to own a vehicle transported others for a fee. This could mean driving people to weddings, christenings, or funerals, or to visit relatives or *paesani* in Buffalo, Lockport, Niagara Falls, or other towns in western New York. One of the first Lackawanna Italians to own a car was Nunze Oddy. Just after World War I, he used $2,000 he had saved up from his many jobs to purchase a Buick sedan that accommodated seven passengers. He charged $10 to drive someone to Buffalo and $25 to go to Niagara Falls. To transport people to a local funeral or christening, he levied a fee of $2 per passenger. Eugenio Galanti and Vincenzo Suffoletto also owned cars at this time and made money chauffeuring people.[59]

In addition to jobs in the steel plant and railroads, Steel City Italians entered into nonindustrial vocations. Italians found a variety of jobs in stores, small factories, and offices. A significant number of the Lackawanna Italian Americans established independent businesses. As they gained more political power, a number of Italian Americans were able to get jobs with the City of Lackawanna, including civil-service and professional positions that marked the immigrants' first steps into more secure, higher-status vocations. This process of founding businesses, entering professions, and gaining access to government jobs was accelerated as the second generation matured and became businesspeople, attained college educations, and entered professions. Many times, the family business served as a foundation for this advancement in social status, providing financial resources as well as experience in operating an enterprise and dealing with the public. A similar pattern evolved in Birmingham, Alabama, where Sicilians were entering the steel mills in the first decade of the twentieth century, just as Italians in Lackawanna were doing. Many of the Birmingham Sicilians also opened grocery stores and other businesses that aided their advance into the middle class.[60]

While the United States offered Italians and other immigrants greater opportunities for prosperity than their native lands could, some aspects of the new country also seriously challenged them. The urban, industrial America of the early twentieth century could be severe and unkind. Discrimination, unemployment, the lack of protective labor unions, and economic depression greatly taxed the immigrants

and their children. The pursuit and performance of nonindustrial jobs by men, women, and children were crucial aspects of the economic equation that allowed most Italian American families to survive and eventually prosper.

The organizations founded by Lackawanna Italians helped them to survive the difficult years of the early 20th century and to gather the skills and resources that slowly brought about their social and economic advancement. Chapter 10 will focus on the role of these 76 societies in the assimilation of the Steel City's Italians.

Salvatore Macaluso, standing, and his son Charley, seated, circa 1955. An immigrant from Racalmuto, Sicilia, Macaluso established an auto collision shop on Hamburg Turnpike, and later a gas station and auto parts store. His daughter Carmella Pawlowski won a scholarship at age 18 to study at the Albright Art School. She has worked in many mediums including oil and watercolor, pen and ink, print-making, and pottery. Carmella has done artwork on commission and taught art classes at Mt. Mercy Academy and Trocaire College.
Photo source: Carmella Macaluso-Pawlowski

CHAPTER 10

ORGANIZATIONS

A popular young immigrant arrived in Lackawanna from Italy in 1907. Although history does not record his name, we know that he quickly earned the respect and friendship of many Italians. Several years later, this man became seriously ill and spent all of his savings on medical care.

At the time of his death, he was single and destitute, and his friends, including Umberto Giannotti, got together and raised enough money to provide him with a decent burial. Following this sad episode, Giannotti told the other Italians that the communal effort they had made for their departed friend could be available to everyone, on an ongoing basis. He spoke to other Italian steel workers about forming a society that would provide its members with sickness and death benefits. This led to the founding in 1910, of the Lake Erie Cooperative Society the first Italian organization in the city of Lackawanna. Umberto Giannotti was elected its first president.[1]

Since the 1820s, when the Unione e Fratellanza Italiana (Italian Union and Brotherhood) was founded in New York City, Italian immigrants and their descendants have formed an estimated 16,000 to 26,000 organizations in the United States. Over this 180-year period a fascinating variety of groups has evolved, groups whose goals have changed over time to meet the emerging needs of each generation. Their activities represent

< Members of the Lake Erie Cooperative Society of Mutual Aid (now called the Lake Erie Italian Club) and their female relatives represent the Italian community in the 1919 League of Nations Pageant. In the front row: Lucia Fadale, Angelo Sperduto, and Antonio Carlini; Behind them: Michele Tornatore and Vittoria Carlini. Photo source: "League of Nations Day, 1919" booklet, from the collection of Tina Mattucci-Ginnetti

an important segment of the communal life of Italians in the United States. Of course, all ethnic groups, especially immigrant and minority populations, have formed organizations in the United States during the past 200 years. Lackawannans have created more than 1,000 organizations since 1900, many of them founded by the city's 92 ethnic groups, which range from the Irish to the Yemeni. In particular, Lackawanna's Italians have founded or been the mainstays of 76 organizations between 1910 and 2004.[2]

The area that became the City of Lackawanna began to be heavily settled in 1900, and its Italian colony took shape comparatively late, several decades after those in Buffalo and other major centers. By 1910, only 551 Italians lived in the new city, a small community in terms of the huge Italian migration to the United States. Therefore, the development of Lackawanna's Italian organizations was in some ways different from that of earlier Italian settlements, such as Buffalo's, although the general trends outlined next were similar.[3]

The first Italian organization in Lackawanna, La Cooperativa Lago Erie Societa di Mutuo Soccorso (the Lake Erie Cooperative Mutual Aid Society), was organized in 1910 and still operates today. At the all-male Lake Erie Italian Club, as it is now called, men could speak Italian and enjoy some of the basic cultural traditions familiar to all members. As laborers low in the steel-plant hierarchy, members counted on modest financial benefits from the society during times of illness and were secure in the knowledge that a deceased members' family would receive a

Members of the Lake Erie Italian Club, circa 1918, most likely standing in front of an Ingham Avenue saloon where they held their meetings. In the front row, 5th from left, is president Serafino Mattucci; 2nd from right is Antonio Amorosi. Photo source: "The Lake Erie Cooperative Society, 50th Anniversary, 1910-1960" booklet, 4/30/60.

death benefit. The society focused on members' immediate needs for social contact and financial stability, as did the original Italian organizations in Buffalo and other cities decades earlier. Unlike the first organizations in some cities, the Lake Erie Italian Club was open to immigrants from many regions in Italy, the founders had roots in Abruzzo, Campania, Lazio, Molise, Sicilia, and Toscana.[4]

The 76 associations created by Lackawanna Italians between 1910 and 2004 are described in Figures 10.1, 10.2, and 10.3. The first figure summarizes the types of groups founded in each decade, while the second summarizes membership gender, and age data by decade. Figure 10.3 lists for each organization, the year founded, function and membership characteristics at the time of founding—gender, generation, age, and ethnic and regional ties—as well as name changes, sponsoring institutions, and incorporation data.

Following the Lake Erie Italian Club, the next three groups organized by Steel City Italians focused on religious matters. In 1917, Serafino Mattucci founded a group that bore his name, and most likely focused on celebrations of his hometown saint, San Pio. Mattucci and his family organized an annual *festa* in honor of this saint during the two following decades. The establishment of St. Anthony's Church led to the formation of two organizations. The Mount Carmel Society, a women's group founded in 1918, supported church functions and celebrated the Madonna, who was popular among southern Italians. The

St. Anthony Society, created in 1920, had a small membership composed mostly of young, American-born men whose immigrant parents had actively supported the formation of the parish. The society appears to have had a short existence, but it served as the forerunner of the Holy Name Society, which began functioning a decade later. Italians founded five other groups in the 1920s. The Italian American Citizens Club was organized by immigrant men in 1921 to unite the city's Italians into a voting block. Its creation marked the immigrants' growing awareness of urban politics. The Roland Wildcats and Galanti Athletic Club were sports organizations, each with a multiethnic membership dominated by Italians. The members, children of immigrants, initiated a prototype for athletic organizations, just as the predominantly second-generation members of the Stag Club established a precedent for social groups. The Italian American Social Club, better known as the Marchegiani Men's Club, was created by immigrants from Marche in 1929 and was the first group with a definite regional or hometown focus.

The nine Italian groups organized in Lackawanna prior to 1930 served as models for groups formed in the following decades. While the three societies of the 1910s were created by immigrants, this was the case for only two of the six groups founded in the 1920s. Two of the groups had both immigrants and second-generation founders, and the last two were started by American-born Italians and youths of several other ethnic groups. Other than the Mount Carmel Society, all nine were men's organizations,

The Italian American Social Club, better known as the Marchegiani Men's Club, was founded in 1929. The members who posed for this photo in 1948 include, seated in the first row, from left: Joseph Baldelli, Luigi Montanari, Frank Lucarelli, Primo Battista, Jimmy Bracci, Emidio Antilli, Dominick Baldelli, Ermete Silvestrini, Rico Caselli, Anthony Antilli. Second row: Enrico Lucarelli, Agosto Dellacecca, Gino Tonucci, Alfredo Campanelli, Charles Sambuchi, Giuseppe Baldelli, Paul Filipetti, Isodore Mattioli, Terso Tonucci, Luigi Filipetti. Third row: Lavinio Montanari, Giuseppe Baldassari, Vittorio Manna, Alex Montanari, Attilio Montanari, Nazzareno Paolini, Ermete Ghiandonni, Bruno Santi, Dominic Capodagli, Pete Zaccarini. Photo source: Leo Baldelli

and their functions varied widely, focusing on mutual aid, religion, social activities, sports, and politics.

During the 1930s, another 32 organizations came into being, displaying an even greater range of functions and characteristics than the first nine. Recreation and mixed-gender groups first appeared, and 12 more women's societies were launched. The Italian Red Cross Committee, along with the Circolo D'Annunzio Dopolavoro and its auxiliary, identified with the contemporary situation in Italy, while six other societies celebrated roots in Marche, Lazio, Abruzzo, and Calabria. Civic associations were formed—most notably, the Federation of Italian American Associations of Lackawanna—in an attempt to look after the broad interests of the city's Italian colony. The immigrant generation organized nine of the societies

STATUTO

DELLA

Cooperativa Lago Erie

Società di

-- Mutuo Soccorso --

Lackawanna, N. Y.

Incorporata il giorno 30 Settembre 1910.

TIPOGRAFIA COOPERATIVA ITALIANA
127 W. Eagle St., Buffalo, N.Y.
1917

Certificato di Ammissione.

No. d'ordine..............

Noi qui sottoscritti certifichiamo che il Signor

Ferdinando Catuzza

Figlio di......*Celestino*

Nato a......*Giuliano di Roma*

Provincia di......*Roma*

domiciliato......*340 2ndo St*

è stato ammesso in questa Società come Socio Effettivo il giorno......*1*......del mese di......*Agosto*......nell'anno *1919.*

ed è stato iscritto nel registro di Matricola al No..............

Lackawanna, N.Y......*9 settembre 1919.*

IL PRESIDENTE......*A. Amorosi.*

IL SEGRETARIO......*V. Giuditta*

At left: Cover of the Lake Erie Italian Club bylaws, printed in 1917. At right: Ferdinando Catuzza's certificate of admission, indicating that he joined the society on August 1, 1919. It was signed by president Antonio Amorosi and secretary Vincenzo Giuditta. Photo source: Chet Catuzza

FIGURE 10.1

Founding Dates of Lackawanna Italian Groups, by Decade and Basic Function: 1910 – 2008

Basic Function	1910–1919	1920–1929	1930–1939	1940–1949	1950–1959	1960–1969	1970–1979	1980–1989	1990–1999	2000–2008	Total
Civic	—	—	3	—	—	—	—	—	—	—	3
Cultural	—	—	—	—	—	—	—	3	—	—	3
Mutual Aid	1	—	2	1	—	—	—	—	—	—	4
Political	—	1	5	1	—	—	—	—	—	—	7
Recreational	—	—	1	1	1	1	1	—	—	—	5
Religious	2	1	4	3	—	1	—	1	—	—	12
Social	—	2	12	10	4	—	1	1	—	1	31
Sports	—	2	5	4	—	—	—	—	—	—	11
Totals:	3	6	32	20	5	2	2	5	—	1	76

Function:	Civic	involvement in community-betterment projects
	Cultural	preservation of Italian traditions and folkways
	Mutual Aid	provision of sickness, death, or other benefits
	Political	involvement in some aspect of the political process
	Recreational	involvement in hobbies, hunting, bocce
	Religious	support of church, organization of religious festivals
	Social	sponsorship of activities for social interaction
	Sports	sponsorship of one or more sports teams or leagues

Youth outing sponsored by the Stag Club in the 1930s. In addition to social functions, the organization was involved in civic functions, such as sponsoring youth sports teams and presenting an annual award to the Lackawanna High School graduate with the highest grade average. Photo source: Collection of Tony Grasso

Figure 10.2

Founding Dates of Lackawanna Italian Groups, by Decade, Gender, and Age Group: 1910 – 2008

	1910–1919	1920–1929	1930–1939	1940–1949	1950–1959	1960–1969	1970–1979	1980–1989	1990–1999	2000–2008	Total
MALE											
Adult	2	4	12	3	1	—	—	1	—	—	23
Adult & Youth	—	—	1	—	—	—	—	—	—	—	1
Youth	—	2	6	6	—	—	—	—	—	—	14
(subtotal)											(38)
FEMALE											
Adult	1	—	7	9	3	1	2	—	—	1	24
Adult & Youth	—	—	2	—	—	—	—	—	—	—	2
Youth	—	—	3	—	—	—	—	—	—	—	3
(subtotal)											(29)
COED											
Adult	—	—	1	1	—	1	—	3	—	—	6
Adult & Youth	—	—	—	—	—	—	—	—	—	—	—
Youth	—	—	—	1	1	—	—	1	—	—	3
(Subtotal)											(9)
Totals:	3	6	32	20	5	2	2	5	—	1	76

created in the 1930s, and also joined with second-generation Italians to form eight other groups. Signaling that they were well on their way to assuming leadership positions in the Italian community, the young adults of the American-born generation created 15 organizations of their own.[5]

The Steel City Italian societies not only represented many functions among them, but individual associations were often involved in several activities. This was especially true of the large groups, such as the Lake Erie Italian Club, which during its first three decades displayed all eight functions listed in Figure 10.1. In addition to providing mutual aid, social, and cultural functions, it raised funds for St. Anthony's Church and cosponsored church events, organized picnics and carnivals, represented the Italian community in city events, sponsored youth athletic teams, and informally counseled members on political matters. Over the past century, the emphasis of the club's functions at any particular time has changed according to the needs of the Italian community. The Italian American Citizens Club, which had 200 members in the 1930s, was mainly a political group that also sponsored an annual Columbus Day ball and a

religious festival honoring Montevergine. This club had a 20-year life, while the Lake Erie Italian Club is now going strong at 99 years. Several other societies were very short-lived. The existence of the Gamma Kappa Club and the Italian Good Time Club came to light only via a single newspaper article about each group. Other societies lasted many decades; some had large memberships, while others included only five or 10 people. There were groups with formal structures and articles of incorporation, while others were informal and loosely organized. Information on many groups was scant, but nine decades' worth of documents about the Lake Erie Italian Club were made available to the author. Incorporation papers, newspaper articles, and interviews provided valuable information about many of the groups.[6]

Figure 10.3

Societies of Italian or Majority Italian Membership; Year Founded, Membership Characteristics, and Functions

[See page 487 for key to chart.]

Organization	Year Founded	Gender	Generation	Age	Ethnicity	Basic Function
1. La Cooperativa Lago Erie Società di Mutuo Soccorso aka: Lake Erie Cooperative Mutual Aid Society nc: Lake Erie Italian Club Inc. 9/26/10	1910	M	1	A	It	Mutual Aid
2. Serafino Mattucci Italian Society	by 1917	M?	1	A	It.	Religious?
3. Congrega Madonna del Carmine (St. Anthony's) aka: Mount Carmel Society Reorganized 3/27/38	1918	F	1	A	It.	Religious
4. St. Anthony Society (St. Anthony's)	1920	M	1, 2	A	It.	Religious
5. Italian American Citizens Club Inc. 8/4/21	1921	M	1	A	It.	Political
6. *Roland Wildcats Inc. 9/18/45	by 1924	M	2	Y	Mix	Sports
7. Italian Social Club of Lackawanna nc: Lackawanna Stag Club, 1928 aka: Stags Club, 1928	1925	M	1, 2	A	It.	Social
8. Italian American Social Club aka: Marchegiani Men's Club Inc. 7/29/30	1929	M	1	A	Marche	Social
9. *Galanti Athletic Association Inc. 1/24/39	1929	M	2	Y	Mix	Sports
10. Lady Mead Club	1930	F	1, 2	A,Y	It.	Political
11. *Milano Athletic Club	1930	M	2	Y	Mix	Sports
12. Lackawanna Republican Women's Club of the First Ward nc: Italian Women's Republican Club of the First Ward, 1932	1930	F	1, 2	A	It.	Political
13. *Bethlehem Park Ladies Aid Club	by 1931	F	1,2	A	Mix	Civic
14. Roman Independent Club Inc. 9/10/36	1932	M	1	A	Lazio	Mutual Aid
15. Roland Italian American Lodge aka: Italian American Mutual Aid Society of the Third Ward	1932	M	1	A	It.	Mutual Aid
16. Holy Name Society (St. Anthony's)	by 1932	M	2	A	It.	Religious
17. Pia Unione de Sacro Cuore (St. Anthony's) aka: Sacred Heart Society Inc. 1933	1933	F	1, 2	A	It.	Religious
18. *Pitillo's Social Club	by 1933	M	2	A,Y	Mix	Social
19. Federation of Italian American Associations of Lackawanna	1933	M	1, 2	A	It.	Civic

(Continued)

Organization	Year Founded	Gender	Generation	Age	Ethnicity	Basic Function
20. Giuditta's Athletic Club aka: Robin Athletic Club	by 1933	M	2	Y	?	Sports
21. *Park Athletic and Social Club of Lackawanna Inc. 8/28/33 nc: Park Rod and Gun Club, 1938 Inc. 7/29/49	1933	M	1,2	A	Mix	Recreation
22. Silver and Black Club	1933	F	2	A,Y	It.	Social
23. Ladies Social Club aka: Marchegiane Ladies Social Club	by 1934	F	1	A	Marche	Social
24. Sodality of the Immaculate Conception (St. Anthony's)	by 1934	F	2	Y	It.	Religious
25. Blessed Virgin Mary Sodality (St. Anthony's)	by 1934	F	2	A	It.	Religious
26. Pettorano Sul Gizio	1935	M	1	A	Abruzzo	Social
27. Italian Red Cross Committee of Lackawanna	1935	M	1	A	It.	Civic
28. Roosevelt Club	by 1935	M	1	A	It.	Political
29. Young Italian Progressive Club of Lackawanna	1937	M	2	A	It.	Political
30. *Pappy Softball Club	by 1937	M	2	Y	Mix	Sports
31. Italian Good Time Club	1937	M	1	A?	Marche	Social
32. *Young Ladies Gold Star Society	1938	F	2	Y	Mix	Social
33. Circolo D'Annunzio Dopolavoro (D'Annunzio Afterwork Club)	1938	M	1	A	It.	Social
34. Circolo D'Annunzio Dopolavoro, Ladies Chapter	1938	F	1	A	It.	Social
35. *Amici Athletic Club	1938	M	2	Y	Mix	Sports
36. Boy Scout Troop #20 (St. Anthony's)	by 1938	M	2	Y	It.	Social
37. Social Union Calabrese	1939	M	1, 2	A	Calabria	Social
38. *Ladies Independent Club	1939	F	1, 2	A	Mix	Political
39. Social Debs	1939	F	2?	Y?	?	Social
40. Eaglettes	1939	M	2	Y	Marche	Sports
41. *Gamma Kappa Club	by 1939	M, F	2	A	Mix	Social
42. Jolly Boosters Club	1940	F	1	A	It.	Social
43. Bethlehem Park GOP Club	1940	M, F	2	A	It.	Political
44. Madonna del Carmine Society (Roland Avenue)	by 1940	F	1	A	It.	Religious
45. *Gymnistici Club	by 1940	M	2	A	Mix	Sports
46. Alpha Beta Gamma Sorority	by 1940	F	2	A	It.	Social

Organization	Year Founded	Gender	Generations	Age	Ethnicity	Basic Function
47. Junior Holy Name Society (St. Anthony's)	1941	M	2	Y	It.	Religious
48. Knick-Knacks	by 1941	F	1, 2	A	It.	Social
49. *Park Athletic Club	by 1941	M	2	Y	Mix	Sports
50. Model Airplane Club	1942	M	2	Y	It.	Recreational
51. Lake Erie Ladies Auxiliary	1943	F	1, 2	A	It.	Mutual Aid
52. Vagabond Athletic and Social Club Inc. 10/10/44	1944	M	2	Y	It.	Sports
53. Texans Athletic Club	by 1945	M	2	Y	It.	Sports
54. *Bethlehem Park Veterans Association	1946	M	2	A	Mix	Social
55. Campus Youth Club (St. Anthony's)	1946	M, F	2	Y	It.	Social
56. Rosary Society (St. Anthony's) nc: Rosary Altar Society	by 1946	F	2	A	It.	Religious
57. *Bethlehem Park Veterans Ladies Auxiliary	1947	F	2	A	Mix	Social
58. Good Time Club	1947	M	2	A	It.	Social
59. Get Together Club	by 1948	F	2	A	It.	Social
60. Cub Scout Pack No. 20 (St. Anthony's)	1949	M	2, 3	Y	It.	Social
61. Mothers' Club (St. Anthony's)	by 1949	F	1, 2	A	It.	Social
62. *Roland Wildcats Ladies Auxiliary	by 1951	F	2	A	Mix	Social
63. *Galanti Athletic Association Ladies Auxiliary	1954	F	2	A	Mix	Social
64. Lackawanna Bocce Association nc: Lackawanna Recreation Bocce League (1958) (Lackawanna Recreation Dept.)	1954	M	1, 2	A	It.	Recreational
65. Catholic Youth Council (St. Anthony's)	by 1956	M, F	2	Y	It.	Social
66. Vagabond Athletic and Social Club, Ladies Auxiliary	1958	F	2	A	It.	Social
67. Amadori Marchegiani Club	1961	M	2	A	Marche	Recreational
68. *Our Lady of Fatima Guild, Lackawanna Chapter	1965	M, F	2	A	Mix	Religious
69. *Lackawanna Ladies Bocce League	1976	F	2	A	Mix	Recreational
70. Lake Erie Women's Auxiliary	1977	F	2	A	It.	Social
71. Coro Italiano (Lake Erie Italian Club) aka: Italian Chorus	1982	M, F	1	A	It.	Cultural
72. Junior Italian Dance Group (Lake Erie Italian Club)	1982	M, F	2	Y	It.	Cultural
73. St. Anna Cantalupo Club	1984	M, F	1	A	Molise	Religious
74. Senior Italian Dance Group (Lake Erie Italian Club)	1985	M, F	1, 2	A	It.	Cultural
75. 3200 Club	1985	M	2, 3	A	It	Social
76. New Beginnings Italian Group	2004	F	1, 2	A	It.	Social

The process of group formation in Lackawanna's Italian community between 1910 and 2004 includes the following 11 patterns:

1. The original immigrants formed 16 organizations, all but two of them prior to 1940. Most of these groups focused on meeting the basic needs of economic security, socializing within an Italian cultural setting, establishing civic and political power, and sponsoring religious festivals.

2. Beginning in the 1930s, the second generation entered adulthood and eventually created 39 organizations. This generation and their immigrant parents joined together to found an additional 14 groups between 1920 and 1954.

3. The creation of more religious groups at St. Anthony's Church between 1932 and 1956, most of them by the second generation, played a key role in Italians' adoption of a more Americanized form of Catholicism, and a less anticlerical attitude.

4. The period from 1930 to 1941 was a fascinating time during which more than half of the Italian societies were founded, and a high percentage of Italians were involved in ethnic organizations. The many societies, and the different goals and activities they pursued, were a reflection of the struggle by immigrants and the second generation to construct several types of ethnic identity to preserve their social honor, including:

   a. developing an identity based on Italian roots and a sense of ethnic pride by:
      - constructing a pan–Italian identity—that is, a nonregional sense of Italianness focused on Italy's culture, history, and status as a world power
      - continuing, at the same time, to honor and celebrate regional and hometown roots

   b. developing an Italian identity focusing on the ethnic group's situation in the United States and how to adapt to American culture by:
      - pursuing activities typical of American culture, sports, and founding chapters of American-style organizations, such as the Boy Scouts
      - seeking political and civic power in Lackawanna by uniting the city's Italians and addressing the needs of the Italian colony.

5. America's involvement in World War II from 1941 to 1945 quickly ended the Italian community's active phase of identification with Italy. Groups fostering these activities folded or fell into decline. Because Italy was an ally of Germany and Japan from June 1940 until September 1943, patriotism and assimilation were demanded of all Italian Americans.

6. Between 1943 and the early 1960s, the Italian American identification with Italy was based on providing aid or lobbying for American policies to help Italy recover from wartime devastation, and assisting the new wave of immigrants.

7. After proving their allegiance to America during the war and partaking in the resurgence of the economy, Italian Americans finally transcended their minority group status. The second generation began to join so-called American organizations in large numbers, causing a decline in Italian groups.

8. As time passed, more women's groups as well as coed organizations were founded, and these 36 groups accounted for almost half the Italian societies in Lackawanna.

9. There was an increasing trend toward creating social, recreational, and sports organizations, which collectively accounted for the majority of the Italian groups organized between 1940 and 2004.

10. The groups formed by the second generation displayed a greater tendency to include people of other ethnic groups as members.

11. The arrival of new immigrants after World War II, together with the ethnic revival that began in the late 1960s, led to the creation of new groups that preserved Italian traditions.

< **KEY to chart.**

Gender:
   M = male
   F = female

Generation:
   1 = first generation or immigrant
   2 = second generation, children of immigrants
   3 = third generation, grandchildren of immigrants

Age:
   A = adult
   Y = youth

Ethnicity:
   It. = Italian – all or vast majority of members Italian; or name of region if all or most members share common origins
   * ; Mix = mixed ethnic backgrounds, but majority Italian

Function:
   see Figure 10-1 for definitions of the eight types of societies

Miscellaneous:
   ? = lack of data, or unsure of information.
   by - followed by a date = organization may have been founded at an earlier date
   ( ) = enclose the name of the organization or institution sponsoring a group
   Inc. = incorporation papers, followed by date
   aka = also known as
   nc = name change

Immigrant Organizations: Meeting Basic Needs

The early groups formed by Italian immigrants in Lackawanna focused on mutual aid, civic, political, and religious functions. These organizations tried to recreate familiar cultural and religious events of Italy or assist in basic survival tasks in the new country. These types of societies represented half of the 41 organizations founded between 1910 and 1939. Addressing economic security, the most pressing task of the immigrants, was the central goal of the city's first Italian group, the Lake Erie Italian Club. In 1916, the organization even formed a short-lived food cooperative (see Chapter 9), but its main forms of financial relief were sickness-and-death benefits. In 1910, a member who was ill and unable to work collected $7 per week, while the family of a deceased member received an amount equal to $1 from each member of the organization. A member whose wife died received $25. By 1918, the death benefit given to the family of a deceased member was set at $50, then raised to $100 in 1925. During the 1940s, a man who was ill collected $15 per week for up to 16 weeks, provided that the illness extended beyond seven days and was verified by a doctor's certificate. When a member died, his family received $260 from the organization's treasury, an assessment of $1.50 from each remaining member, and $15 for a wreath. The associations created during the 1930s included all the civic groups and most of the mutual-aid, political, and regional associations organized by the city's Italians during the last century.[7]

The sickness-and-death benefits were crucial to the immigrant families, and other societies provided these benefits. In 1932, Italians on Roland Avenue founded their own mutual-benefit association, the Roland Italian American Lodge. Each man paid a $1 initiation fee and $.50 for monthly dues, which entitled him to a sick benefit of $5 to $7 per week, and his family to a $50 to $100 death benefit. The Roman Independent Club provided sick benefits of $10 per week, a death benefit of $150 plus $1 from each member, and $50 upon the death of a member's wife. The Mount Carmel Society of St. Anthony's Church gave $100 to the family of a deceased member, furnished a wreath of flowers, and paid for a High Mass. The Lake Erie Ladies Auxiliary Society, founded in 1943, paid $200 plus $1 from each member to the family of a deceased member, as well as $10 to purchase a wreath or Mass. The auxiliary also awarded $25 to a member upon the death of her spouse. The charter of Circolo D'Annunzio Dopolavoro (D'Annunzio Afterwork Club) stated the group would furnish "pecuniary protection … to members from losses caused by accidental or natural death." Even one of the sports organizations, the Galanti Athletic Association, had a stated goal in 1939 of assisting members "who through circumstances may become indigent."

A different type of material benefit was provided by the Stags Club, which during its first three years presented a gift to each member upon his marriage. Tony Grasso claimed that his wedding gift in 1930, a small piece of furniture, was the last one given.[8]

Just as important as the financial benefit in times of loss were the social and psychological support these groups provided. The members of the Mount Carmel Society were required to say the rosary as a group at the home of the deceased member. The Lake Erie Italian Club sent two-man teams to sit with the body around the clock for the several days of a wake, usually at the departed member's home, and dispatched an honor guard of four to six men who carried out a burial ritual at the funeral. The general membership was part of the funeral procession which walked from St. Anthony's Church to Holy Cross Cemetery; 100 men did so for the 1940 funeral of Dominick Marinelli. Some societies sent members to visit the bereaved family and offer consolation, food, and other help. Following a meeting of the Circolo D'Annunzio Dopolavoro, the entire membership "proceeded in a body to the home of a fellow member, Gaetano DeMilio, 357 Ingham Avenue, as a mark of respect and to extend sympathy over the death of Mrs. DeMilio."[9]

Dispersing sick benefits involved more complicated procedures. Doctor John Fadale was one of several practitioners retained by the men's societies to give physical exams and verify reported illnesses. Most groups had a sick committee to oversee the validity of claims and award benefits, although the Lake Erie Italian Club (LEIC) sometimes assigned such responsibilities to only one man. Much time was spent at society meetings discussing the merits of individual requests for sick benefits. At the LEIC there were many long-winded and heated debates regarding reports that a member was seen working in his garden at the same time he was receiving sick benefits. In such cases, it was helpful if the member claiming benefits had a good relationship with the chair of the club's sick committee. The provision of sickness-and-death benefits was especially crucial in the years prior to World War II, when adequate policies from insurance companies were either unavailable or unaffordable.

The Second Generation Organizes Societies

The second generation burst into the organizational life of the Italian community during the 1930s, when a large number of them came to maturity. The American-born men and women founded half of the 32 new Italian associations, cofounded another eight with the immigrant generation, and soon captured leadership positions in many of the city's Italian organizations. By 1939, the second generation dominated the process of

FIGURE 10.4

HONOR AND DISCIPLINE AT SOCIETY MEETINGS

Honor was important to the immigrants in the Lake Erie Italian Club (LEIC). When it was learned that one member's wife tore up a notice mailed by the club, the other members voted to scold that member "so that in the future, respect will be shown to the letters of the society." LEIC members were infuriated when the Buffalo Italian organization, in its collection for the Italian Red Cross in 1936, did not list the club's $100 donation in its reports to the media. In the minutes book, the secretary wrote: "Our honor is offended." Even after a representative of the Federation of Italian Societies of Buffalo came to a LEIC meeting to apologize, the club appointed a committee to "retrieve our honor." The LEIC also had difficulties with the Federation of Italian American Associations of Lackawanna (FIAAL) and dropped out of the organization several times. "Our club has been made fun of many times," said Tony Amorosi at a 1938 meeting. "It's difficult for the society to be part of the Federation again. The society is honorable, the oldest in the city, and must be respected." Only after a special meeting with the FIAAL did the club rejoin as a member group. In January 1939, another question of honor arose when the club met at the Ukrainian church. Tony Colello stated that the group couldn't meet at St. Anthony's, "because the basement of the Italian church is too cold." But Fausto

DeSantis and Vincenzo Suffoletto protested, saying it is an "affront to the Italian colony and a shame to have our meeting in a different church than our own Italian church." The group returned to St. Anthony's for its February meeting and voted to pay for the installation of a cement floor in the basement meeting room.

The meetings of Italian societies could sometimes be rowdy, and the LEIC's early sergeant-at-arms, Angelo Croce, literally carried a billy club at all meetings. The group usually imposed penalties for bad behavior. For speaking out of turn at a 1924 meeting, Michele Tibollo was suspended for three months, fined $1, and warned that one more infraction would mean expulsion from the society. Two months later, Michele Grasso was fined 25 cents for leaving a meeting early. In 1929, Joe Santoro had to pay a $1 fine for bringing his dog to a meeting. At times meetings of the Italian societies got very tense and serious. As the membership debated ideas about its annual carnival in 1940, angry words were exchanged, and LEIC President Tony Amorosi threatened to resign. At the following meeting, the assembly discussed the "disorder at meetings—people talk without permission and get up and walk belligerently towards the president." Things were even more extreme at a 1938 meeting of the FIAAL. Costantino Novelli, a representative of the

LEIC, and Pasquale Ricci, a representative of the Stags Club, engaged in a heated debate that escalated into a physical fight. The men, both 44 years old, were arrested and released on $500 property bail. Each man charged the other with third-degree assault and obtained the services of an attorney. The board of the LEIC decided that Patsy Ricci was the instigator, but Judge Joseph McCann had the last word. At a city court session crowded with 250 spectators, McCann "was forced to use his gavel many times to keep the courtroom in order." After hearing four hours of testimony, he ruled that there was insufficient evidence to determine guilt, and he dismissed both charges.

Michele Grasso continued to incur fines at LEIC meetings following the 1924 incident in which he left early. Two years later, he made a motion that members must walk, not ride, to the cemetery for the funeral of a deceased group member, otherwise a fine would be imposed. The club members voted and passed the measure, but the new ruling soon came back to haunt Grasso. Several weeks later, he and Serafino Mattucci were fined $5 each for riding back from the cemetery after a funeral. Grasso's son Tony found this hilarious and joked about it six decades later.

Sources: Lake Erie Italian Club meeting minutes from 4/10/17, 5/7/24, 10/30/26, 11/10/26, 12/2/29, 3/26/36, 1/25/38, 4/5/38, 1/11/39, 2/1/39; LL, 1/20/38, 1/27/38; interviews with Al Croce, April 8, 1994; and Nunze Oddy, April 12, 1982.

forming Italian groups; after this point, only a few societies were founded by the aging immigrants who had arrived in the United States during the first quarter of the twentieth century. From the 1930s onward, it was the second generation and the post – World War II immigrants who created organizations. The younger generation was familiar with the English language, mixing more easily with people of other ethnic groups in their neighborhoods and schools. As the second generation joined groups established by their immigrant parents, a number of

changes occurred. Bilingual members of the Lake Erie Italian Club translated discussions into English to assist younger men with limited fluency in Italian. Although one person quipped that the results of a vote could quickly change with the shifts back and forth between Italian and English, holding bilingual meetings did serve to welcome the American-born generation. The Federation of Italian American Associations of Lackawanna in 1939 had two secretaries: Louis Corsi recorded the minutes in Italian, and Joseph Pacillo, in English.

Figure 10.5
A PLACE TO HOLD MEETINGS

A significant aspect of the lives of organizations was arranging for a venue for meetings and activities. For many of the smaller social groups, members' homes sufficed for meeting places. Groups with larger membership rolls used a variety of sites. In the Roland Avenue neighborhood, the young men of Pitillo's Social Club no doubt held meetings at the Electric Avenue storefront run by Pasquale Pitillo. The members celebrated the repeal of Prohibition in 1933, and Pitillo soon converted his store into a bar and restaurant. The women in the Madonna del Carmine Society of Roland Avenue usually gathered in private homes but occasionally met at the Odd Fellows Hall on Electric Avenue, where the Roland Italian American Lodge usually met. The Roland Wildcats convened at 105 Roland Avenue and held banquets and dances at the Hotel Lackawanna, Memorial Hall, Dom Polski, and Our Mother of Good Counsel Church. In 1950, the group erected its own clubhouse, which was also used by the Roland Italian American Lodge and other groups.

The members of the Lake Erie Italian Club constructed this building in 1920 but sold it after a windstorm damaged it. After St. Anthony's Church was built in 1917, the club utilized its meeting rooms for many years. Photo source: *The Lake Erie Cooperative Society, 50th Anniversary*, booklet, 1910-1960, 4/30/60.

St. Anthony's Church, built in 1917, immediately became a community hub and meeting site for the large First Ward Italian colony. Religious societies as well as the Lake Erie Italian Club and social groups gathered there. The Stags Club which sometimes met in Santo DePasquale's poolroom or Nick Sperduto's restaurant, usually gathered in the Old Village community rooms in the late 1920s and early 1930s. The Stags and Lady Mead clubs also held dances at the Old Village site. Beginning in 1934, several Italian societies, including the Federation of Italian American Associations of Lackawanna, met at Italian Hall, the house at 39 Elm Street in Bethlehem Park that was rented by the societies. The Pettorano sul Gizio Club held its masquerade ball there in February 1938. The house was sold to a family in late 1938, and the LEIC, after one meeting at the Ukrainian church, relocated to St. Anthony's Church. Other groups, such as the Circolo D'Annunzio Dopolavoro, also met at the Italian church. The Galanti Athletic Association had access to the hall attached to Eugenio Galanti's store until the owner's death in 1977, and other groups met there too. Nearby, in the basement of Jimmy Suffoletto's store, the Pettorano sul Gizio Club held its gatherings. The Bethlehem Park School and the Park Grille were popular meeting spots for the many Bethlehem Park associations. The LEIC in 1942 purchased a hall on Hamburg Turnpike for holding events and renting out to other groups, but the building was torn down in 1950 when the road was widened. After the Old Village was razed, the Lady Mead Club held meetings at both Monaco's Hall and Covino's Hall

on Ingham Avenue, St. Anthony's Church, and the Hungarian Hall. Italian restaurants, such as Nicolas Mattucci's Colonial Kitchen and Serafino Mattucci's establishment on Ingham Avenue, were used for society banquets. When Marche native Lavinio Montanari opened the Fano Restaurant in 1934, complete with an outdoor bocce court, the four Marchegiani societies had a site for all their activities. The Bethlehem Park Veterans Association and auxiliary in 1950 acquired club rooms at the former tavern on A Street, just off Dona Street.

Throughout the first half of the twentieth century, there was never one central Italian meeting hall other than the cramped facilities at St. Anthony's Church. The LEIC briefly had a building on Ingham Avenue in 1920 and operated a Hamburg Turnpike hall for eight years before returning to St. Anthony's Church for its meetings. The parish hall built in 1954 and the new church edifice completed 10 years later provided larger meeting rooms for the Italian societies. In 1967, the LEIC acquired a clubhouse in neighboring West Seneca, but it was destroyed by a fire in 1973. Three years later, the club finally acquired a permanent home at the former shoe store at 3200 South Park Avenue. This large building was a site for many of the city's Italian activities. Had such a venue been available in the First Ward in earlier years, when Italians were concentrated in that area, it could well have helped to encourage and maintain a greater level of organizational functions.

Sources: *Lackawanna News*, 11/21/29, 10/30/30, 12/11/30, 2/5/31, 9/10/31; *Lackawanna Herald*, 1/13/34, 4/11/35, 4/18/35, 9/3/36; *Lackawanna Leader*, 11/3/38, 4/30/42, 5/17/45, 1/17/46, 10/10/46, 4/21/49, 6/1/50, 6/21/51; undated clipping on Pitillo Social Club; *Lake Erie Co-operative Society, 50th Anniversary, 1910–1960*, souvenir booklet, 4/30/60; *Second Annual Masquerade Ball, Pettorano sul Gizio Club*, souvenir booklet, 2/27/38; Lake Erie Italian Club meeting minutes from 1/11/39, 2/1/39; interviews with Tony Grasso, November 27, 1981, December 27, 1982

By the 1940s, the second-generation individuals led many of the groups and founded most of the 20 societies created in that decade. As a result, the official language of several existing societies changed from Italian to English. The meeting minutes were usually written in Italian if the secretary was an immigrant, and in English if he or she was born in the United States. Language preference was not the only difference between the immigrants and their adult children. The American-born Italians focused on different organizational goals than did their parents, tending more toward social and athletic activities. The first social group, the Lackawanna Stag Club, was organized by immigrant Costantino Novelli in 1925 and soon had many second-generation members on its roster and in leadership positions. Half of the 16 social groups founded between 1928 and 1941 had second-generation memberships, as did the majority of those formed in the years 1942 to 1949. Italian females became very active in organizations during the 1930s and 1940s, composing 10 of the social groups formed that decade, such as the Silver and Black Club and the Jolly Boosters Club. Three other groups of that decade had both male and female members.[10]

Religious Groups and a New Catholicism

Religious organizations played an especially crucial role in the assimilation of Lackawanna's Italians. Given Catholic traditions in Italy, it is not surprising that eight of the 12 religious groups were women's societies. St. Anthony's Church sponsored not only eight of these societies but also five secular groups, most targeting the parish's youth. Because women of that era were usually more involved in church than men were, one of the most notable developments at St. Anthony's was the founding of societies for men and boys. These groups spawned a noticeable involvement of males in parish life—a real departure from southern Italian tradition. The church's eight religious societies included three for men, and four of the secular groups sponsored by St. Anthony's focused on young males. By 1932, the Holy Name Society had replaced the defunct St. Anthony Society, with a majority of its members second-generation men active in other organizations and civic affairs. A number of them, including schoolteachers Nick Milano and Samuel Conte, were professionals. The Holy Name Society organized various programs and initiated a level of male involvement in church activities that was rare in Italy. The members also involved younger males by organizing the Junior Holy Name Society, a Boy Scout troop, and a Cub Scout pack that were officially sponsored by the church. Second-generation activists in St. Anthony's also brought Italian American boys and girls into the church by forming the Campus Youth Club and the Catholic Youth Council. This strong involvement by a core of

The Lake Erie Italian Club purchased this building on Hamburg Turnpike and Dona Street from Eugenio Galanti in 1942 and leased out its bar and restaurant. The facility attracted many younger men who became LEIC members but was torn down for the widening of Hamburg Turnpike in 1950. Photo source: Lake Erie Co-operative Society, 50th Anniversary, 1910–1960, booklet

male leaders (more than 100 men were members of the Holy Name Society at some point during the 1930s and 1940s) demonstrated a significant break from the anticlericism of the male immigrants and ushered in an Americanized-style of Catholicism. While the *feste* of the immigrants were fading in the mid-1930s, the church organizations grew more numerous, and this continued into the 1940s. The second-generation men and women sponsored many dances, socials, card parties, and other celebrations that brought more parishioners, especially males, into the religious fold (see Chapter 6).[11]

Four other religious societies were not directly connected with St. Anthony's Church. The Serafino Mattucci Italian Society, an informal group organized in 1917, held an annual festival in honor of San Pio at Serafino Mattucci's home, which also included a Mass at St. Anthony's Church. The other groups were the Madonna del Carmine Society of Roland Avenue, founded in 1940 by immigrant women living in that neighborhood, and, in later decades, the Lackawanna chapter of the Our Lady of Fatima Guild and the St. Anna Cantalupo Club.[12]

The Crucial Events of the 1930s

The large number of Italian organizations founded during the 1930s, and their wide range of functions and activities, reflected the dynamic forces that directly influenced Italian American communities at that time. These included Italy's stature as a world power, the Great Depression, the approach of World War II, the continued minority status of Italian Americans, the opposing trends of ethnic cohesion and assimilation within the Little Italys, and the maturation of the second generation. These factors, as described in Chapter 3,

A Stags outing in the 1930s. Standing, from left, are: Dan Thomas, Tony Grasso, Tony DePasquale; kneeling are Nick Thomas and Tony Ranalli. Many club members, like four of these men, were of the second generation—that is, they were born in this country to immigrant parents. Grasso emigrated from Italy with his family when he was about 10 years old. Photo source: Collection of Tony Grasso

made the 1930s a crucial time in the formation of Italian American associations.

By the 1930s, Italian Americans were immersed in the process of moving from a conglomeration of immigrants from specific towns and regions of their home country to an ethnic group with a somewhat cohesive general identity. In hundreds of locales throughout the United States, Italian Americans were struggling to build an ethnic identity. In Lackawanna, this process of determining "who we are" involved four trends, three of which focused on defining a pan-Italian core—that is, a nonregional sense of Italianness that meant identifying with Italy as a country and organizing to increase civic and political power in America (see Chapter 4). By 1930, most Italian immigrants had decided to remain in Lackawanna permanently and sought the strength in numbers to meet their needs. To maintain their social honor, they continued to display pride in their hometowns and regional roots, but they also proclaimed their common roots in the nation of Italy. Ironically, it was only after immigrating to the United States that Romani, Abruzzesi, Napolitani, Calabresi, and Marchegiani finally began seeing themselves simply as Italians, something they had rarely done in Italy. The immigrants and their children had come to realize that many American institutions, as well as many individual Americans, viewed all Italians negatively. Because federal immigration laws of the 1920s, had branded Italians inferior to

northwestern Europeans, daily life in Lackawanna for Italian Americans often meant enduring ethnic slurs and discrimination by supervisors in the steel plant, policemen, and individuals of other ethnic groups. Steel City Italians attempted to preserve self-respect and build social respect in the 1930s. This led them to maintain ties with Italian organizations in Buffalo and to found organizations that focused on the nation of Italy, hometown and regional origins, and civic advancement in Lackawanna.

After 1920, a number of Italian immigrants arrived in Lackawanna from both Italy and other parts of the United States, adding to the numbers of people who identified with specific regions or hometowns in Italy. A pattern in the older Italian American settlements in Buffalo and Milwaukee, during the years 1890 to 1920, was to found societies composed of people with roots in specific towns, provinces, or regions of Italy. This trend reemerged in the dynamic 1930s. The founding of the Marchegiani men's group in 1929 set the precedent for this type of organization in Lackawanna, and five similar societies came into being during the 1930s. Marchegiani women organized the Ladies Social Club, and the men who created the Roman Independent Club were largely from the province of Frosinone, Lazio, many of them from the town of Giuliano di Roma. The Social Union Calabrese was founded by male immigrants from Calabria and their sons, most of them with roots in Marano Principato, Soveria Mannelli, and nearby towns. The only society focusing exclusively on a hometown membership was organized by male immigrants from the town of Pettorano sul Gizio, Abruzzo, who founded the society bearing that name in 1935. These groups offered immigrants a place to speak their local dialect, practice regional customs, and encounter familiar faces from the old county. In terms of numbers of organizations, the Marchegiani displayed the strongest regional spirit over the years. In addition to the two groups already mentioned, they comprised most of the membership of the Italian Good Time Club and the Eaglettes, each organized in the late 1930s, and founded the Amadori Marchegiani Club some two decades later.[13]

The presence of a large Italian population in Buffalo helped support the sense of ethnic identity of Lackawanna's Italians. In the first half of the twentieth century, many Italian immigrants in the Steel City utilized institutions in Buffalo's Italian neighborhoods that were not present in their own community (see Chapter 3). Buffalo was home to hundreds of Italian organizations of all types, including some whose members came from the same hometowns and regions as Steel City Italians. A number of Lackawanna Italians joined organizations that existed in Buffalo, where many of them had originally settled. Pietro Oddi, Antonio Zaccaria, and Angelo Sperduto were members of Buffalo's San Giacomo (St. James) Society,

STAGS CLUB LEADER

NICHOLAS J. MILANO

MILANO IS ELECTED HEAD OF STAGS CLUB

Committees for Year Also Are Announced.
1935

Nick Milano was active in the Stags Club and served as president from 1935 to 1937. Nick Thomas was president the previous four years. The two men were also active in leadership roles in other Italian organizations.
Photo source: Clipping from Buffalo newspaper, collection of Joe Milano

Badge and ribbon worn by members of the Roland Italian American Lodge. The group was founded in 1932.
Source: Collection of Frank Chiodo

of the first society, and Michele and Pasquale Tibollo and Antonio Giordano were also active in these groups. Some immigrants, such as Abruzzo native Donato Chiacchia, became members of the hometown societies of their spouses' families. Following his marriage to Lucia Fiorella, who was born in Vallelunga Pratameno, Sicilia, Chiacchia joined her brothers in the Vallelunga Club of Buffalo. While many Lackawannans, including Italians, have often proclaimed their independence from the large city to the north, there exists a long history of connections between the two cities and their ethnic institutions. This was especially true during the 1930s, when Italians in both cities were developing a sense of ethnic solidarity that often focused on events in Italy.[15]

The power and prestige that Mussolini's Italy achieved on the international stage during the 1920s and 1930s fostered the development of Italianness, or *Italianita*, among Italian Americans. Newspapers and magazines in the United States often praised the Fascist regime of *Il Duce*, who built Italy into a world power. Mussolini emerged as a leader to be reckoned with, even though he was condemned by the Western press for his 1935-1936 invasion of Ethiopia. Identifying with this newfound respectability, Italian Americans often proclaimed their Italian identity by participating in organizations. The Italian Red Cross Committee of Lackawanna, one of dozens organized throughout the United States in 1935, collected money for medical supplies for the Italian Army during the Ethiopian War. *Corriere Italiano* printed long lists of donors that included dozens of Steel City Italians as well as the Roman Independent Club, the Stags Club, and the Italian American Citizens Club. The Lake Erie Italian Club gave $100 to the Italian Red Cross in 1936 and was still making donations as of April 1941.[16]

The Roman Independent Club, while composed mostly of immigrants from Lazio, encompassed a wider Italian identity. The club celebrated the date September 20, 1870, when Rome and the surrounding provinces were freed from French and Vatican rule, and the city was made the capital of the newly unified Italian nation. In 1938, Donato Chiacchia organized

and Oddi was often seen wearing the society's gold pin. Salvatore DiTommaso joined the group when he lived in Buffalo and held the office of secretary. The organization, which provided members with sickness-and-death benefits, met at St. Anthony's Church in Buffalo. In 1918, enough Lackawannans had joined the mutual-benefit group that, in addition to the doctor designated for Buffalo members, a second was named for those in Lackawanna. Dr. John Fadale was one of the founding members of the Ausonia Club, a group for professionals and businessmen in the Buffalo area.[14]

Serafino Mattucci belonged to an Abruzzese group that gathered in the Italian community along East Delevan Avenue in Buffalo. Several Lackawanna immigrants from Accadia joined Buffalo's Accadia Duca Degli Abruzzi Society, Circolo Accadia, and San Vito Society. Tony Turchiarelli was a lifelong member

Figure 10.6

LACKAWANNA AND BUFFALO ITALIANS
PROCLAIMING ETHNIC PRIDE PRIOR TO WORLD WAR II

In addition to individual Lackawanna Italians belonging to societies in Buffalo's Italian enclaves, events in the larger city attracted Steel City Italian groups' participation. Lackawannan involvement in Buffalo's Columbus Day festivities had begun by 1927, when Rev. Vifredo of Lackawanna was one of four priests offering Mass at Mount Carmel Church. With the formation of the Federation of Italian American Associations of Lackawanna (FIAAL), representatives were sent to Buffalo's annual Columbus Day celebration. Ferdinand Catuzza was on the planning committee of the 1933 event. In 1934, more than 15,000 people in the Columbus Day parade marched down Niagara Street, and Rev. Vifredo was one of eight priests who said High Mass at St. Anthony's Church in Buffalo. The following year, Joe Cosentino was on the planning committee of the celebration, while John Panzetta sold Lackawannans tickets to other festivities of the Italian Federation of Buffalo. In 1936, FIAAL members were involved in organizing the festivities and sent a delegation to march in the parade.

Identifying with Christopher Columbus was an important ritual for Italian Americans. Recognized by many European Americans as the "discoverer" of the western hemisphere, Columbus was one of the few Italians honored in American history books and mythology. This was a source of pride to Italian immigrants, and their descendants have celebrated Columbus for over a century. In Buffalo, 21 societies were named after Columbus. Although Lackawanna's

Italians did not name a group for the mariner, they have honored Columbus as an ethnic hero over the years. The Italian American Citizens Club began holding annual Columbus Day banquets in the mid-1920s, and the Lake Erie Italian Club has sponsored occasional Columbus Day banquets since 1938.

Perhaps the crowning moment for the Federation of Italian American Associations of Lackawanna was the placement of a bust of Christopher Columbus on Madison Avenue, at the entrance to Bethlehem Park. FIAAL's member groups raised money to match the amount of funding contributed by the city for the stone column and bronze bust, debating long hours about where to place it. The initial proposal located it in front of the Lackawanna Library, but the sidewalk was too narrow. Others suggested the grounds in front of city hall, but a bust of Abraham Lincoln was already there. The entrance to Bethlehem Park was finally selected, probably because the neighborhood had the greatest concentration of the city's Italians. The final decision was preceded by much debate, as the *Lackawanna Leader* noted: "Distraught and harassed city fathers have asked the Italian societies to come to an agreement and say when and where." A strong contingent of Ingham Avenue Italians wanted the memorial on their street. The Italian and Spanish Committee, representing the two ethnic groups with the closest connections to Columbus, protested the location, saying the bust should be placed on public property, such as Memorial Hall, "where people

of all nations are able to see it." One Ingham Avenue advocate, Marco Costanzi, was said to be so infuriated with the choice of Bethlehem Park that he struck the bust with a crowbar just before its unveiling. Despite this outburst the memorial remained intact.

The public dedication of the Columbus bust on Sunday, October 13, 1940, was marked with great festivity. A parade of Italian organizations, the Knights of Columbus, the American Legion, and First Assembly drum corps marched from St. Anthony's Church to the entrance of Bethlehem Park. After federation president Ferdinand Catuzza unveiled the monument, Rev. Joseph Vifredo gave the benediction, and Charles Saccomanno formally presented it to Mayor John Aszkler. Margaret DiCenzo presented a ribboned wreath bearing the federation's name. This was followed by addresses from John Osborne of the Knights of Columbus, District Attorney Leo Hagerty, City Judge John McCann, Italian Consul Rocco Spano, and John Montana, president of the Federation of Italian Societies of Buffalo. The bust of Columbus still stands at the entrance to Bethlehem Park, and in 2000 the Lake Erie Italian Club erected a black granite monument in front of their building that commemorates the Italian navigator.

Sources: Interview with Ralph Galanti, 9/22/83; *Lackawanna Herald*, 3/6/36; *Lackawanna Leader*, 8/17/39, 9/12/40, 10/3/40, 10/10/40; Front Page, 11/1/2000; *Corriere Italiano*, 10/20/27, 10/19/33, 10/18/34, 4/18/35, 9/13/35; *Buffalo Evening News*, 10/8/35; 10/12/36; Lake Erie Italian Club, meeting minutes, 9/28/38, 10/4/39; Lackawanna School Board, minutes, 10/7/40.

The Pettorano sul Gizio Club, made up of men with origins in that town in Abruzzo, provided a place where immigrants could speak in their dialect with people they had known in Italy. They often met in Vincenzo "Jimmy" Suffoletto's grocery store on Dona Street but held their events in the house on Elm Street that Italian organizations rented in the late 1930s. Photo source: Booklet from the collection of Josephine Ferrelli

The softball team sponsored by the Roland Italian American Lodge made an appearance at the Civic Stadium in Buffalo in 1940. In the first row, from left, are Stanley Kumiega, Tony Falbo, [Unk], Ralph "Murphy" Evans, Frank Chiodo. Just behind Evans and Chiodo are Jake DePerto and Louis Cambria, and at the upper right are Erie DePerto, Ed Spyhala, and Ted Bernas. Photo source: Collection of Frank Chiodo

the Circolo D'Annunzio Dopolavoro (D'Annunzio Afterwork Club) and a women's auxiliary, based on the nomenclature and corporate laws of this international workers' fraternity. He also claimed that the state headquarters of the group would reside in the Steel City. The Lackawanna chapter was named after Gabriele D'Annunzio, the Italian poet and nationalist who, like Chiacchia, was a native of Abruzzo. The 72 men in the club, mostly immigrants and a few American-born members, had roots in many Italian provinces. In early 1939, the club was preparing to elect a delegation to go to the world convention of the fraternal group, but the advent of World War II later that year led to the cancellation of the gathering. Chiacchia may have been among the thousands of Italian Americans throughout the United States who, in 1935 and 1936, donated their gold wedding rings to the Italian government to support the war in

Ethiopia and in return received steel rings with Mussolini's name engraved on them.[17]

The pan-Italian identity based on pride in Italy's status as a world power coincided with Lackawanna Italians' perception of their common interests on social issues in their American community. Like earlier immigrant and minority groups, Italians throughout the United States grasped the importance of closing ranks to achieve goals that benefited the ethnic group. This realization culminated in 1933 with the creation of the Federation of Italian American Associations of Lackawanna (FIAAL), a coalition of seven large men's groups that addressed issues specifically affecting the city's Italian neighborhoods. The federation's leaders lobbied the city council and the board of education to meet the Italian community's needs and to hire Italian Americans as teachers and policemen. One goal of the

FIGURE 10.7

FEDERATION OF ITALIAN AMERICAN ASSOCIATIONS OF LACKAWANNA

The federation of seven of the largest Italian groups in the Steel City had the goal of "promoting the welfare of the Italian citizens of Lackawanna." The group organized in 1933 with a governing body made up of three representatives from each of the five founding organizations: the Stag Club, the Lake Erie Italian Club, the Roman Independent Club, the Italian American Citizens Club, and the Marchegiani Men's Club. A few years later, the Roland Italian American Lodge and the Pettorano sul Gizio Club also joined. In 1933, the officers of the federation and the groups they represent were:

> *Chairman:* Nicholas Thomas
> (Stags Club)
> *Vice Chairman:* Anthony Zaccaria
> (Lake Erie Italian Club)
> *Secretary:* Ferdinand Catuzza
> (Roman Independent Club)
> *Treasurer:* Ettore Spadoni
> (Marchegiani Men's Club)
> *Hall Marshall:* Angelo Monaco
> (Italian American Citizens Club)

All officers were immigrants except for the chairman, American-born Nick Thomas.

The federation stressed unity among Lackawanna's Italian groups and participation in events that brought public recognition to the Italian community. In July 1933, a contingent led by John Panzetta marched in the city's parade during Prosperity Week. The federation and other groups rented a house at 39 Elm Street in Bethlehem Park from 1934 to 1938. Known as the "Italian Clubhouse" or "Italian Hall," this location hosted many of the member organizations' meeting and events.

By 1938, the federation had four standing committees that delivered the issues and concerns of the Steel City Italian neighborhoods to public officials.

The hazards of automobile traffic in Italian neighborhoods was one FIAAL priority. The group, in a 1936 letter to the city council, requested that a traffic light be installed at Dona Street and Hamburg Turnpike to relieve congestion during shift changes at the steel plant and that dividing lines be painted on Ingham Avenue, Dona Street, and School Street. Two years later, the federation petitioned for the installation of stop signs at the intersections of various side streets off of Hamburg Turnpike and Ridge Road, emphasizing the particular dangers where Madison Avenue and other Bethlehem Park streets intersected Hamburg Turnpike. At the same time, the federation appealed to both the Buffalo and Lackawanna city councils to reduce the speed limit to 18 miles per hour along South Park Avenue.

The group took up a number of other causes. In January 1937, it requested that the city flood the playground in Bethlehem Park to allow ice skating. A year later, the group urged the city council to petition the Buffalo and Lackawanna Traction Company to resume bus service along Hamburg Turnpike, from the Buffalo city line to Ridge Road. Matters regarding city schools were also important. Communications to the Lackawanna School Board sometimes addressed mundane matters, such as ice on school sidewalks or the condition of the lawn at Bethlehem Park School. The federation in 1935 requested that the board provide transportation for Bethlehem Park students attending the public high school and Our Lady of Victory school, and also proposed a plan for a public university.

A more charged issue arose shortly after the organization's founding. Nick Milano had applied for a teaching position in 1931 but for what the federation deemed

political reasons had not been hired on a full-time basis. In September 1933, a letter was mailed from FIAAL officers to the school board:

Dear Sirs:

At the last meeting of the Federation of Italian Societies of Lackawanna it was resolved to petition the School Board as follows:

We have a candidate for the position of high school teacher, namely Nicholas J. Milano, whom we know has tried the examinations required, and passed satisfactorily and we petition your honorable body to give his application due consideration.

His teaching abilities are well known to both the Principal and Superintendent. He has substituted as high school teacher of Latin for some time, and he is the only local teacher who has taken and successfully passed the examination in Latin. He has been the first and only local teacher on the Latin list for more than two years, and although he was twice recommended by the Superintendent for an appointment because a vacancy for a Latin teacher existed, he has nonetheless been unjustly disregarded.

We feel that he is just as much a credit to the school system as he is to our own group. We pride in having him as our representative and your disposition of his application shall affect us very deeply.

Nicholas J. Thomas, President
Fred Catuzza, Secretary

A petition signed by 503 people accompanied the letter. Thomas and others attended that month's board meeting and demanded to know why Milano was not being considered; several people argued with board members, and "considerable confusion" ensued. When the appointment was given to another Latin teacher, the federation demanded a private meeting with representatives of the board. Their efforts paid off; the following August, Nick Milano was appointed a full-time teacher at the high school. That same month, Nick Thomas ran in a field of 12 candidates for three school board seats; he lost, ending in fifth place.

The FIAAL made the front page of the *Lackawanna Leader* in 1939 when it charged that First Ward Councilman Julius Karsa had "embarrassed the city's Italian population." The federation held Karsa responsible for the city's failure to appoint Anthony DeMasi to the police force. At a Common Council meeting, Karsa pleaded for "pure Americanism," stating "I have endeavored to serve my citizens and neighbors as one body, as one American mass, not as many individual races, creeds, or colors." He did move that DeMasi be placed on the civil service list for a future position. In 1940, Anthony DeMasi was appointed to the city's Fire Commission.

The entry of the United States into World War II brought the demand that Japanese, German, and Italian organizations in America display unwavering loyalty to their adopted land. This marked the beginning of the demise of the FIAAL in Lackawanna, which was heavily first-generation in membership. After the war many second-generation Italian Americans were not interested in civic groups created solely on the basis of ethnicity, but the federation was in existence until at least 1954.

Sources: *Lackawanna Republic*, 4/14/33; *Lackawanna Herald*, 6/22/33, 4/11/35; *Lackawanna Leader*, 12/10/36, 1/7/37, 4/28/38, 6/30/38, 3/30/39, 5/13/54.

FIAAL was to protect the image of Italians and to proclaim pride in Italian heroes. The federation became affiliated with the Federation of Italian Societies of Buffalo, sent delegates to meetings, and took part in Columbus Day celebrations and other Italian functions held in Buffalo (see Figure 10.7). It seemed the federation had a rival when Circolo D'Annunzio Dopolavoro leader, Donato Chiacchia did not seek FIAAL membership, declaring "We are the true Italian federation," but there is no record of this potential factionalism developing.[18]

Some Italian organizations launched projects that sought to achieve status and respect outside the Italian colony, in the general Lackawanna community. The Stags Club not only held its annual banquet and ball in an upscale and respectable venue, but in 1929 it donated the proceeds of its annual dance to the Lackawanna Charity Campaign. A number of years later, the club began the practice of presenting a gold medal to the graduating senior at Lackawanna High School (regardless of the student's ethnic background) who attained the highest four-year grade-point average. The annual ceremony was started by the Stags in 1935 and continued until at least 1950, when Dorothy Milano was the recipient. Other ethnic groups had similar functions—for example, the American Serb Club gave an annual citizenship medal to a deserving graduating senior. This type of civic activity accelerated in the late 1940s, when the Galanti Athletic Association began awarding an annual trophy to the outstanding high-school athlete in the city, and the Roland Wildcats annually presented a plaque to the outstanding contributor to Lackawanna sports that year.[19]

The founding of five political groups in the 1930s indicated that Italians had become seriously involved in Lackawanna politics and sought to improve their ethnic group's situation. This process was initiated in 1921 with the creation of the Italian American Citizens Club by six immigrants who represented the Italian neighborhoods in the First and Third wards. They recognized the importance of the political arena, encouraged fellow Italians to participate in city elections, and did some direct advocacy for their members; for example, in 1940, the club sent a letter to the city council urging that Marco Costanzi, who was unemployed, be hired as a city worker. The Lady Mead Club, a women's group founded by Tony and Lena Amorosi in 1930, was a booster organization for Democratic Congressman James Mead, who was supportive

Roman Independent Club

Lackawanna, N. Y.

The logo of the Roman Independent Club featured the wolf who nurtured Romulus and Remus, the founders of Rome. The name of the organization refers to the date, September 20, 1870, when Rome was made the capital of the newly unified country of Italy. The club—whose members were all from Lazio, the region in which Rome is located— celebrated with a feast every year. Photo source: Letterhead stationary of Ferdinand Catuzza, provided by Chet Catuzza

Members of the Italian Social Club of Lackawanna pose on April 18, 1928. That same year, the group changed its name to the Lackawanna Stag Club. Seated on the floor, from left, are: Nick Christiano, [Unk]. Seated on chairs in the second row from left are: Joe Amadori, Erasmo Colello, Anthony DiPronio, Costantino Novelli, Tony DiPronio, Edmund Jennetti, Louis Corsi, Joe Cosentino, Tito Paolini. Standing from left are: Joe Milano, Tony DePasquale, Tony Colello, Patsy Ricci, Tom Pepper, Leonard DePaula, Patsy George, and "Piccolino" (little one), a visitor from Newark, New Jersey, who had roots in the same Italian town as the Milanos and Sperdutos. Photo source: Collection of Joe Milano

498

The Lackawanna Stag Club, better known as the Stags, was organized in 1925. It was the first true social club founded by Lackawanna Italians and sponsored an annual ball that was one of the highlights of the year for many Italian Americans in the area. Pictured here is the fifth ball, held in 1932 at the New Palms Royal on the Lake, one of the region's fancier nightclubs of the era. Politics often made an appearance at the event. Here, city treasurer Paul Tomaka (circle at left), Angelo Grosso (circle above Tomaka), and Joe Milano (circle at right) partake in the festivities. Photo source: Theresa DeSantis-DiBlasi

The second annual outing of the Roland Italian American Lodge, July 14, 1940. The 100-plus people pictured here include lodge members as well as their family members and neighbors. Outings such as this became very popular in the 1930s, and Lackawanna Italian groups held many of these events per year.

Photo source: Collection of Frank Chiodo

The annual outing of the Galanti Athletic Association, September 3, 1945, Kudara's Grove in Hamburg. Seated on the ground, from left, are: Frances DiCenzo-Myzel, Frank Marinelli, Irene DePasquale-Szymanski. Seated in the second row from left are: Lucy Amadori, Filomena Galanti, Grace Galanti, Bridget Bracci, Loretta Pietrocarlo, Margaret Kubiak, Marion D'Alessandro, Mary DiCenzo, Hazel Rushnov, Mary Petti, Connie Staniszewski, Carolyn Cswaykus, Dolly Rushnov, Mrs. John Livsey; Virginia Topinko, Mary Core, Mary Hacic, Mrs. Jack Russell, Jo Galanti, Mrs. Walter Widmer. Standing in the third row from left are: Eleanor Hojsaw Huziak, Dorothy Kollender, Jean Spiker, Dan Cipriani, Alvira Cipriani, Clementine Bracci, Ann D'Alessandro, Arnold D'Alessandro, Sis Renzi, John Panczykowski, Stan Rushnov, Armondo Pietrocarlo, Eugene Staniszewski, Nick DelBello, Adam Rushnov, John Livsey, Walter Topinko, George Hacic, Leo Kujawa, Louis Venturi, Evy Juran, Jack Russell. Standing in the fourth row from left are: Ed DiCenzo, Joe Amadori, Amerigo Bracci, Mike Tobias, Joe Spiker, Vince Jennetti, Lena Bellagamba, Ralph Marinelli, Fermino Pietrocarlo, Paul Petti, Armando Jennetti, John Cswaykus, Phil "Snyder" Becker, John Core, Judge Joseph McCann, John "Doc" Kollender, John Diane, Anthony Moretti, Arcangelo Claroni, Councilman Walter Widmer, Eugene Galanti. A Front Page article dated 6/28/76 provided the names. Photo source: Lolly Suffoletto

501

Baseball outing for members of the Galanti Athletic Association, August 22, 1938. Sitting on the ground, up front, is John Core. The men kneeling, from left, are: Carl Covino, Ed Manzetti, Victor Giancaterino, James Conti, [Unk], Armondo Pietrocarlo. Standing are: Carmen Moretti, Adolph Giancaterino, George Hacic, Orlando Collarino, John Cswaykus, Joe Juran, Brad Carestio, Louis Marinelli. Photo source: Chico Galanti

meetings. Vincent Tauriello, a county supervisor from Buffalo, gave a speech in Italian to the Lady Mead Club in 1930.[21]

Joe Milano's terms as assessor and councilman in Lackawanna during the late 1920s and mid-1930s served as a catalyst for the formation of some Italian organizations. In certain cases, politicians organized sports or recreational societies that also served as booster clubs during campaigns. Many Italians had learned a powerful rule of Lackawanna political life: anyone with a small following could approach politicians and request favors in return for the group's votes. Organization leaders had a natural constituency of voters who could be rallied on election day, and heads of Italian organizations were no different. Furthermore, officers in charge of an association's activities were known not only by the group's membership but also by the Italian community and the general public at large via word of mouth, posters, and newspaper articles. Finally, even when political issues were not officially part of meeting agendas, they were present in informal discussions. For many leaders of Italian organizations, the groups served as springboards for their own political endeavors. Not only did these individuals seek advantages for their groups' memberships, but they also often sought official political recognition for themselves.

In addition to forming political and civic associations that mimicked those of other ethnic groups, Italians were founding branches of such "American" organizations as scouting groups. Boy Scout Troop No. 20 was organized in 1938 with the help of Ed Pacillo, a leader of the multiethnic Bethlehem Park troop established several years earlier. The Gamma Kappa Club, founded in 1939 as the first coed Italian organization in the city, had a name that suggested college fraternities and sororities, and its members were mostly young Italian men and women of the second generation. Within a year, Italian females organized the Alpha Beta Gamma Sorority.[22]

Other trends made the 1930s a period of change for Italians, influencing the types of organizations they formed. Economic issues were crucial during the Great Depression, and several groups followed the Lake Erie Italian Club's lead in providing sickness-and-death benefits. In another realm, 18 new organizations were oriented toward sports, recreation, or social activities. The five sports groups with second-generation memberships focused on American sports. Six

of Italians and working-class people in general. Mead helped such politicians as Tony Amorosi and Joe Milano secure services from federal bureaucracies, including obtaining legal documents for their immigrant constituents.[20]

The year 1930 also witnessed the founding of what would later be renamed the Italian Women's Republican Club of the First Ward, led by Adele Panzetta, a committeeperson who was very active in Republican politics. The group's membership consisted mostly of immigrants living along Ingham Avenue, as did the roster of the Roosevelt Club, a men's group. Second-generation men in that neighborhood launched the Young Italian Progressive Club in 1937, although the club's officers also included immigrant Carl Selice and a non – Italian, Stephen Soroka. In Bethlehem Park, the Ladies Independent Club, created in 1939, had a heavily Italian membership, comprising mostly by second-generation women. The Bethlehem Park GOP Club, founded a year later, was led by American-born men and women. Other Italian groups also participated in the city's political events, including the Circolo D'Annunzio Dopolavoro, which in 1939 held a forum open to political candidates of all parties. The Roman Independent Club occasionally endorsed candidates seeking political office. Two of the group's leaders, Ferdinand Catuzza and Biagio Sperduti, were Democratic committeemen who aggressively lobbied to secure city jobs and other benefits for club members. The Italian community also held banquets to honor its successful politicians; Joe Milano was recognized this way in 1935, and Buffalo politicians were invited to address

new associations had mixed-ethnic, though predominantly Italian, memberships. The fertile organizing ground of this important decade led to the creation of 32 Italian associations, a trend that continued into 1940 and 1941, when eight more societies were founded. The high point in this period was 1938 to 1940, when 15 organizations were formed. On December 7, 1941, however, the situation for Italian Americans and their organizations was drastically altered.

World War II and Italian American Organizations

When the United States entered World War II in December 1941, it was at war with the three Axis powers—Germany, Japan, and Italy. The FBI immediately interrogated the officers of Italian American organizations and confiscated many of their books, including those of several Lackawannans. Italians in the United States were under great pressure to prove their loyalty to Uncle Sam. The intensity of events just after Pearl Harbor led the Roman Independent Club to cancel meetings for three months before reconvening in March 1942. A number of Lackawanna groups, such as the Circolo D'Annunzio Dopolavoro, became inactive or lost a significant number of members. The Lake Erie Italian Club displayed only the American flag at its events, reprinted its bylaws and constitution in both Italian and English, and had LEIC Vice President Armondo Pietrocarlo translate meeting discussions into English for the group's younger members. Lackawanna's Italian groups, like their counterparts throughout the country, proclaimed their allegiance to the United States and actively supported America's entry into the war. In early 1942, the Lake Erie Italian Club purchased a $1,500 defense bond, and the Marchegiani Men's Club bought one for $500. This patriotic spirit continued throughout the war. In 1943 the members of the Roman Independent Club bought $700 worth of war bonds, and the Stag Club purchased a $1,000 war bond in 1944. Although it donated money to the Italian Red Cross in 1935 and 1941, the Lake Erie Italian Club contributed only to the American Red Cross during the following years.[23]

Italian American men and women comprised a significant percentage of American military personnel during World War II; estimates range from 500,000 to 1.5 million. Lackawanna was well represented in the armed forces, with one writer claiming it was the American city with the highest percentage of its population in uniform during the war. Often, Italian groups sponsored farewell events for departing soldiers and honored them when home on leave or upon discharge. When Brad Carestio was home on military furlough, he was welcomed at a meeting of the Lake Erie Italian Club with a round of applause. During the war, the club reduced active soldiers' monthly dues by half and waived their payments

into the death-benefit fund. Several Italian organizations waived annual fees for GIs during the conflict and reinstated the returned servicemen to full membership at war's end. Young men in the Roland Wildcats grew beards before receiving their draft notices, at which time they shaved, posed for group photos, and celebrated this rite of passage. The Roland Italian American Lodge and the Galanti Athletic Association (GAA) sent cigarettes, cigars, and reading materials to their members overseas. In addition, the GAA sent all proceeds from its 1944 festival to its 44 members in the armed forces. When these men returned to Lackawanna, each was presented with a special ring.[24]

After the war, many second-generation Italian veterans were drawn to nonethnic organizations, shunning the ethnic societies formed by their immigrant parents. Some wanted to avoid the stigma of being viewed as too ethnic or simply wanted to fit in with other Americans. Others were not fluent in Italian, or were uncomfortable with meetings held in Italian or a combination of Italian and English. Still others viewed the old-country ways as old-fashioned or irrelevant. Lou Colello noticed that men from the same regions in Italy sat together in small clusters at Lake Erie Italian Club gatherings. A number of second-generation men complained about the long debates concerning sick benefits and other seemingly endless arguments that characterized the older groups' meetings. Colello was bothered at first because he couldn't enter into the discussions; new men weren't allowed to speak at meetings until they had been members for six months. During the 1930s, Tony Grasso joined the Lake Erie Italian Club, paid the fee for a physical exam, and started attending meetings. But he was soon upset by the continual bickering among some immigrant members. "Arguing, my God," Grasso recalled, "you thought they were going to come to blows. I said to myself, 'I have to come and listen to this?' I didn't go back, so the $5 paid to the doctor went down the drain." Grasso joined and quit the organization three times, but with his fourth try, he remained a member. The net effects of such situations were that Lackawanna Italians formed few new groups after 1947, and many of the societies created by the immigrants and second generation folded in the 1950s and 1960s as their original members gravitated to nonethnic organizations or died off.[25]

The period 1930 to 1949 was one of profound changes nationwide caused by a series of social movements and upheavals. These forces led to the creation of two-thirds of Lackawanna's Italian organizations, groups that reflected the societal changes at hand. The most significant of these was the entry of the United States into World War II. That historical marker alone caused the functions of the Italian associations founded from 1942 to 1949 to differ significantly from those of the previous 12 years. The dozen Italian organizations created

Members of the Lake Erie Italian Club (LEIC) were part of the procession marching down Hamburg Turnpike to Bethlehem Park in August 1947 for the dedication of the monument to eight Bethlehem Park servicemen who gave their lives during military service in World War II. Photo source: Collection of Tony Grasso

The LEIC contingent marches down Madison Avenue in Bethlehem Park. Photo source: Collection of Tony Grasso

Closeup of the LEIC section of the parade marching in Bethlehem Park, 1947. Photo source: Aldo Filipetti

in the post – Pearl Harbor 1940s emphasized nonethnic goals, focused on American-style sports and social activities, and established new settings and formats. The Bethlehem Park Veterans Association and its women's auxiliary were the first veterans groups that Italians had a major role in organizing. The new groups' mixed-ethnic memberships were based on neighborhood ties and the shared experience of wartime service in the armed forces of the United States. The Vagabond Athletic and Social Club was made up largely of teenage males, but with an unusual format: a number of their fathers acted as a governing board, some serving as officers and program chairmen. Previously, immigrant adults and their offspring had this type of experience only when the father persuaded the son to join the Lake Erie Italian Club or the Roland Italian American Lodge, or when immigrant mothers convinced daughters to join the Mount Carmel Society at St. Anthony's. Only the Lake Erie Ladies Auxiliary had a strong ethnic tie, but its inception also marked the adoption of the American pattern of male groups organizing female auxiliaries; the Lake Erie Italian Club was only the second Italian group to do so.[26]

The four new groups sponsored by St. Anthony's Church represent a more deliberate step toward American practices than those formed in the 1930s. This pattern was no doubt encouraged by Rev. Ciolino, the American-born and educated priest who joined the parish in 1946. The single religious society among the four groups, the Rosary Altar Society, quickly became the city's largest women's Italian organization, attracting two immigrants for every American-born member. The program leaders were usually second-generation women, and the group focused on support of the church and raising funds through a variety of social activities. Shortly after its founding, the society held its first annual masquerade dance. Each

FIGURE 10.8

Membership Totals of Italian Societies for Selected Years: 1930 – 1948

Men's Societies	1930s	1940s
Italian American Citizens Club	1930: 200	
Lake Erie Italian Club	1936: 130	1942: 240
Circolo D'Annunzio Dopolavoro	1938: 66	
Galanti Athletic Association	1938: 59 (+ 48 non – Italians)	1948: 69 (+ 21 non – Italians)
Stag Club	1939: 62	
Roland Wildcats		1946: 75 (+ 75 non – Italians)
Good Time Club		1947: 90
Holy Name Society (St. Anthony's)		1948: 150
Women's Societies		
Immaculate Conception Sodality	1934: 30	
Mount Carmel Society		1947: 61

of its events took place at the city's Memorial Hall and featured a big-name band. The Rosary Altar Society united with other parish groups to organize Christmas parties for children and programs honoring mothers and daughters and fathers and sons. Unlike previous groups, the Rosary Altar Society did not focus on patron saints and processions. Two of the new groups initiated by the church sought to bring more youth into parish life with activities that were the hallmark of either American civic life [Cub Scout Pack No. 20] or American Catholicism [the Campus Youth Club]. The latter group sponsored dances, games, and sports for high-school boys and girls. The Mothers Club raised funds with card parties to support the activities of the parish's two scouting groups.[27]

The distinct movement toward American activities exhibited by the societies founded between 1942 and 1949 set an important trend for Italian organizations created in the following three decades. It went hand in hand with the movement of Italian Americans into the nonethnic societies of the general Lackawanna community after World War II. All this was happening in the latter part of the two-decade period (1930–1949) when Lackawanna's Italian organizations were plentiful and enjoyed robust memberships. Before moving on to the organizational developments in the second half of the twentieth century, it is helpful to examine the significant involvement of Lackawanna Italians in the associations during the 1930s and 1940s and the large-scale entry of Italians, especially those of the second generation, into "American" organizations.

Italian Societies at their Peak: The 1930s and 1940s

There were more active Italian societies and larger membership rosters in the years from 1930 to 1949 than in any other period. The 52 societies founded during these two decades represent two-thirds of the total of all the city's Italian groups. Similar surges in group formation occurred in Buffalo and Milwaukee, with half of each city's Italian groups created during this period. In Lackawanna, membership numbers for 10 societies show the extent of organizational involvement by the city's Italian community during the 1930s and 1940s (see Figure 10.8).

Using available documents, partial membership lists for 22 Lackawanna men's groups and 17 women's societies were assembled for the period 1930 to 1949. During this time, 778 Italian American males and 320 females were, at one time or another, involved in at least one of the city's Italian organizations (see Figure 10.9). No doubt there were members who were not mentioned in the accessible sources, but the 1,098 individuals named represent a high percentage of Lackawanna's Italians. The 1930 U.S. census listed 1,105 Italian American males and 797 females of all ages living in Lackawanna. Since complete figures are not available for the 1940 and 1950 censuses, the 1930 figures can be used as an approximate baseline for the period 1930 to 1949. The youngest among the 1,902 Italian Americans living in the city in 1930 would have reached their mid-teens by 1945, when they could have joined several of the Italian organizations. While the 39 groups were predominantly composed of adults, youths in their mid-teens were sometimes recruited into these societies by parents and older siblings. Yolanda Sperduti was only 14 years old when her mother persuaded her to join the Sacred Heart Society, and

FIGURE 10.9

Members of Forty Lackawanna Italian Organizations: 1930 – 1949*

| Generation | Total | Number of Organizations in Which Each Individual Held Membership | | | | | | | | |
		1	2	3	4	5	6	7	8	9
MALES										
1st	362	221	80	38	13	8	2	—	—	—
2nd	369	198	108	36	17	6	1	2	—	1
3rd	10	3	4	3	—	—	—	—	—	—
Unknown	37	35	1	1	—	—	—	—	—	—
Subtotals:	**778**	**457**	**193**	**78**	**30**	**14**	**3**	**2**	**—**	**1**
FEMALES										
1st	120	80	28	11	1	—	—	—	—	—
2nd	182	137	34	11	—	—	—	—	—	—
3rd	1	1	—	—	—	—	—	—	—	—
Unknown	17	16	1	—	—	—	—	—	—	—
Subtotals:	**320**	**234**	**63**	**22**	**1**	**—**	**—**	**—**	**—**	**—**
GRAND TOTALS:	**1,098**	**691**	**256**	**100**	**31**	**14**	**3**	**2**	**—**	**1**

KEY:

1st = immigrant

2nd = American-born, child of immigrants

3rd = American-born, grandchild of immigrants

Unknown = no information on generation status

*These numbers are not complete; they represent the information gathered from local newspapers, the minutes book of the Lake Erie Italian Club, and brochures and booklets from specific events.

the Vagabond Athletic and Social Club was made up largely of teenage males.[28]

The 1,098 males and females active in organizational life of the Italian community in the 1930s and 1940s represent the equivalent of 60% of the city's 1930 Italian population. Breaking this down by gender, two of every five Italian females and three of every four males were on the groups' membership rolls at some time during this 20-year period. It is important to remember that the women's organizations in Lackawanna typically were created later than those of the men. Eleven of the 17 women's groups for which data are available were founded between 1938 and 1947, while this was true for only seven of the 23 men's groups. The rapid growth of female societies during these two decades is exemplified by the Rosary Altar Society, which was founded in 1946 and had at least 96 members by January 1948.[29]

The percentage of Lackawanna Italian males involved in organizations was significantly greater than that reported in larger cities. In the 1910s, when Chicago and New York had the large numbers of mutual-aid societies, about half of each city's adult Italian males were members. In New York City's Greenwich Village Italian colony, the proportion of male society members fell rapidly—from 50% in 1910 to 30% in 1920 to 10 to 15% in 1930. The number of provincial mutual-aid societies peaked in New York and Chicago prior to World War I, but in Lackawanna's small Italian colony, which didn't begin to form until 1900, only in the 1920s did the number of associations start to grow. In the two following decades, membership peaked. Of all the individual immigrants and families who arrived in Lackawanna between 1900 and 1925, only 330 remained in the city after 1930; thus, it took some time for the number of permanent Italian settlers to reach a critical mass that would support a number of organizations. These core

FIGURE 10.10

Individual Italian Males Holding Membership in Lackawanna Italian Organizations: 1930 – 1949*

Organization	Year Founded	Males in Membership at Some Point From 1930 to 1949, by Generation				
		Total	1st	2nd	3rd	Unknown
Lake Erie Italian Club	1910	318	174	127	—	17
Galanti Athletic Association**	1929	107	8	97	2	—
Holy Name Society St. Anthony's	1932	104	20	79	5	—
Bethlehem Park Veterans Association**	1946	73	8	59	5	1
Circolo D'Annunzio Dopolavoro	1938	73	62	8	—	3
Lackawanna Stag Club	1925	69	22	46	—	1
Italian American Citizens Club	1921	66	56	9	—	1
Roland Wildcats**	1924	63	6	57	—	—
Vagabond Athletic and Social Club	1944	62	20	39	3	—
Federation of Italian American Associations of Lackawanna	1933	61	44	17	—	—
Roland Italian American Lodge	1932	55	34	18	—	3
Pettorano sul Gizio Club	1935	47	33	5	—	9
Roman Independent Club	1932	44	40	1	—	3
Pappy Softball Club	1937	42	5	36	—	1
Marchegiani Men's Club	1928	32	32	—	—	—
Park Athletic & Social Club	1933	29	7	19	1	2
Eaglettes	1939	15	4	10	1	—
Social Union Calabrese	1938	12	7	5	—	—
Park Athletic Club	1941	8	—	7	1	—
Good Time Club	1947	6	—	5	1	—
Pitillo's Social Club	1933	5	—	5	—	—
Roosevelt Club	1935	5	5	—	—	—
Young Italian Progressive Club of Lackawanna	1937	5	2	3	—	—
Total Memberships:		**1,301**	**589**	**652**	**19**	**41**
Number of individuals represented in total memberships:		778	362	369	10	37

KEY:

1st = immigrant

2nd = American-born, child of immigrants

3rd = American-born, grandchild of immigrants

unknown = no information on generation status

*These numbers are not complete; they represent the information gathered from local newspapers, the minutes book of the Lake Erie Italian Club, and brochures and booklets from specific events.

**Group with multiethnic membership but Italian majority; the number given is Italian members only.

FIGURE 10.11

Individual Italian Females Holding Membership in Lackawanna Italian Organizations: 1930 – 1949*

Organization	Year Founded	Females in Membership at Some Point From 1930 to 1949, by Generation				
		Total	1st	2nd	3rd	Unknown
Rosary Altar Society (St. Anthony's)	1946	96	60	31	—	5
Mount Carmel Society (St. Anthony's)	1918	77	49	28	—	—
Lady Mead Club	1930	59	16	40	—	3
Marchegiane Ladies Social Club	1934	37	18	11	—	8
Lake Erie Ladies Auxiliary	1943	31	3	27	—	1
Blessed Virgin Mary Sodality (St. Anthony's)	1938	27	3	24	—	—
Sacred Heart Society (St. Anthony's)	1933	20	8	11	1	—
Bethlehem Park Veterans Ladies Auxiliary**	1947	13	—	12	—	1
Young Ladies Gold Star Society	1938	13	2	11	—	—
Jolly Boosters Club	1940	9	3	6	—	—
Silver and Black Club	1933	8	—	8	—	—
Gamma Kappa Club**	1939	7	—	7	—	—
Madonna del Carmine Society (Roland Avenue)	1940	7	3	4	—	—
Ladies Independent Club	1939	6	—	6	—	—
Italian Women's Republican Club-1st Ward	1930	6	5	1	—	—
Get Together Club	1948	6	1	5	—	—
Alpha Beta Gamma Sorority	1940	6	—	6	—	—
Total Memberships:		**428**	**171**	**238**	**1**	**18**
Number of individuals represented in total memberships:		320	120	182	1	17

KEY

    1st = immigrant
    2nd = American-born, child of immigrants
    3rd = American-born, grandchild of immigrants
    Unknown = no information on generation status

*These numbers are not complete; they represent the information gathered from local newspapers, the minutes book of the Lake Erie Italian Club, and brochures and booklets from specific events.

**Group with multiethnic membership but Italian majority; the number given is Italian members only.

families and their adult children provided a notable percentage of the associations' founders and leaders. Buffalo's large Italian community and its many established institutions and organizations were also accessible to Lackawanna Italians.[30]

Male immigrants tended to cluster in the societies they originally organized, including the Lake Erie Italian Club, the Italian American Citizens Club, the Federation of Italian American Associations of Lackawanna (FIAAL), and the Roland Italian American Lodge. They were also concentrated in groups that focused on ties with Italy, such as the Circolo D'Annunzio Dopolavoro, the Marchegiani Men's Club, the Roman Independent Club, and the Pettorano sul Gizio Club. The three male organizations with the highest membership totals were of very different types: the Lake Erie Italian Club (a social and mutual-aid group), the Galanti Athletic Association (sports), and the Holy Name Society (St. Anthony's; the only adult-male religious

The Bethlehem Park Veterans Ladies Auxiliary was created in 1947, a year after the Bethlehem Park Veterans Association was founded. Among the group's many activities was this outing to the Town Casino in Buffalo. Seated in foreground, from left to right, are: Gina Capodagli, Rose Olivieri-Conti, Delfine Rosati. Second row left to right: Betty Tan, Gladys Valetta-Schiavi, Eleanor Rosati, Jo Andreozzi. Third row left to right: Vincenza Novelli, Mrs. Reed, Olivia Capodagli-Hund. Fourth row left to right: Margaret Cipriano, Mrs. Madar, Mrs. Tan, Edith Ranalli-Pavone. Fifth row left to right: Mary Giuliani, Frances Christiano-Hughes, Christine Ricci-Florino, Helen Tan, Mary Trotta. Sixth row left to right: Theresa Christiano, Mary Christiano, Lulu Mae Christiano, Dorothy Kresconko-Christiano, Josephine Turkovich, Mrs. Madar, Ann DePasquale-Bellagamba, Ginny Martin, Katie Turkovich-Juran, Margaret Danch.
Photo source: Collection of Jo Andreozzi

group). Second-generation men comprised the vast majority of Holy Name members and also dominated the rosters of the Bethlehem Park Veterans Association, the Stags, the Galanti Athletic Association, the Roland Wildcats, and other sports societies. The two largest female groups were the Rosary Altar Society and the Mount Carmel Society at St. Anthony's Church, while the Lady Mead political club had the third highest women's group membership. Overall, about half the female memberships were in religious societies, one-third in social groups, and one-fifth in political clubs. For the male memberships, one-third were in mutual aid, one-quarter in sports and recreation, and one-quarter in social groups, although it should be remembered that mutual-aid organizations by this time had other functions, especially social and recreational.

A number of Italian individuals had high membership rates—that is, each was involved in several groups during the 20-year time span considered here, often at the same time. The total number of memberships involved is 1,301 for the men's societies and 428 for the women's, with the actual number of individuals estimated at 778 men and 320 women (see Figure 10.9). About 40% of the immigrant males belonged to two or more organizations; for second-generation men, the figure approached one-half. For the women, the proportions concerning multiple membership were one-third for immigrants and one-fourth for the second generation. The individual men and women who held the most memberships were active in all institutions of the Italian community. Females, especially the immigrants, focused their involvement in the religious societies. Maria Giuseppa Milano and Anna Maria Ricci were both in the Rosary Altar and Mount Carmel societies. Milano's third group was the Lady Mead political club, Ricci's, the Lake Erie Ladies Auxiliary. Three other immigrants—Augusta Anticoli, Rosa Delgatto, and Alessandrina Sperduti—each were members of three sodalities at St. Anthony's Church. Carmella Canestrari, the only Lackawanna woman to belong to four societies, was active in diverse areas: two religious societies, the Lady Mead Club, and the Marchegiane Ladies Social Club. Eleven American-born women were in the high-membership

During the 1930s and 1940s, yearly carnivals sponsored by organizations such as the Galanti Athletic Association (GAA) were important social events in Lackawanna. Between 1938 and 1951, the GAA held annual carnivals lasting from three to 11 days. These events were typically located at the soccer field at the corner of Dona Street and Hamburg Turnpike, which is the setting of this photo, circa 1940. Standing next to one of the children's rides are, from left: Ralph Marinelli, Judge Joseph McCann, and Paul Petti. Photo source: Jack and Mary Panczykowski

Members attending a Roland Wildcats meeting at 103 Roland Avenue, circa 1950. First row, at bottom, from left to right, are John Evans, Frank Vertalino, Bobby Eagan, Gene Alimonte, Mike Nasso, Ben Vertalino, Norm Blaird. Second row: Helim Solomon, B. Leo, William Eagan, Moe Selvaggio, Nick Acanfora, John DePerto, Sam Cardinale. Third row: Bill Russell, Frank Chiodo, Erie DePerto, Ted Demitroff, Don Bonitati, Peter Juran, Joe Krause. Fourth row: Joe Cardamone, Tony Cardamone, Richie Wnuk, Tony Falbo, Tony Leo. Photo source: Collection of Frank Chiodo

category, but only Anne Melillo-Corvigno and Anne Pacillo were enrolled in two sodalities at St. Anthony's. This was consistent with their family patterns; Melillo's grandfather was very active at the church, as were Pacillo's two sisters and four of her brothers. Among the nine other second-generation women with triple memberships, most belonged to one religious group, a social or political group, and the Lake Erie Ladies Auxiliary. Like Melillo-Corvigno, Anna Saccomanno and Angeline Morgan were among the many people active in organizations whose families ran successful businesses.

Men were much more likely to have multiple memberships in Lackawanna organizations; 50 were high-membership individuals active in four to nine groups. Eighty percent of these men held membership in the Lake Erie Italian Club (LEIC), which has always been the dominant society in Lackawanna's Italian American community, and 60% were in the FIAAL and 44% in the Stags Club. These three groups played pivotal roles in the social, civic, and political sectors of the Italian colony; it was natural for those involved in politics to be active in organizations. Immigrants Tony Amorosi, Ferdinand Catuzza, Constantino Novelli, Louis Corsi, and V. Jimmy D'Alessandro all held memberships in four or five groups, as did the American-born Ralph Galanti, Angelo Grosso, and Joe Milano. More numerous memberships were held by Joe Cosentino, Joe Pacillo, and businessman Joe Amadori, each enrolled in six groups, and Brad Carestio and Tony Ranalli, who were in seven. Cosentino immigrated as a teenager, Amadori as a nine-year-old, and the others were second generation. Tony DePasquale, active in both sports and politics, outdid his contemporaries by being involved in nine Italian American groups. Some businessmen did much networking through their memberships in Italian societies. Antonio Giordano and Camillo Spagnolo, of the first generation, Armondo Pietrocarlo of the 1.5 generation, and Nick DelBello and John Govenettio of the second generation, all had memberships in four to six organizations.

The high-membership men were also likely to hold officer positions during the 1930s and 1940s. The presidential post was held by Tony DePasquale (LEIC and Vagabonds), Joe Pacillo (Holy Name Society), Brad Carestio (Stags), and Joe Cosentino (FIAAL and the Social Union Calabrese). Armondo Pietrocarlo and Frank Renzi each belonged to four groups and

Roland Wildcats bowling team, 1945-46 season. From left, they are: [Unk], Joe Angotti, Pat Vertalino, Frank Vertalino, Erie DePerto, Cy Michalek.
Photo source: Collection of Frank Chiodo

was president of two of those organizations during the 1940s; Pietrocarlo of the Lake Erie Italian Club and the Galanti Athletic Association, and Renzi of the Stags and the Galanti Athletic Association. In Buffalo, some men assumed the presidency of an Italian society for several decades, a pattern that occurred on a more limited scale in Lackawanna. Tony Amorosi was elected president of the LEIC for 19 of the years between 1917 and his death in 1944; Ferdinand Catuzza headed the FIAAL for four years and was president of the Roman Independent Club for more than a decade; and Natale Chiodo led the Roland Italian American Lodge for the seven years prior to his death in 1939. In Lackawanna it was more common for a variety of individuals to rotate through the leadership positions of a society. Since 1910, 33 men have been president of the Lake Erie Italian Club; seven Italian Americans held the presidency of the Roland Wildcats between 1945 and 1955; and the Galanti Athletic Association had 16 Italian and four non – Italian members in the president's office between 1936 and 1971.[31]

Leaders and activists in the Italian societies acquired skills and confidence that enabled them to move beyond the small Italian community and into the larger organizations of the city that were becoming accessible to the general population. Holding leadership positions in one of the Italian societies could readily enhance the possibilities for people to advance in political, professional, and business circles. In the 1940s, Frank Chiodo was an officer in the Roland Wildcats when he was first elected as a committeeman, and Bill Delmont was on the club's board of directors when he was elected Third Ward councilman in 1955. Being a well-known leader in the Italian community did not ensure success, but it certainly could help. In 1937, Tom Pepper—who was active in the LEIC, the Stags, and the Galanti Athletic Association—became the first Italian elected to the school board. Since World War I, presidents of the Lake Erie Italian Club have sought appointments to city positions and election to committeeman, councilman, and school-board posts. These men include Tony Amorosi, Tony Turchiarelli, Vincenzo Suffoletto, Tony DePasquale, Costantino Novelli, Ralph Fiore, Charles Nigro, Ed Pacillo, Charles Fistola, Jerry DePasquale, and Joe Carnevale, most of whom met with success. A number of the second-generation men who were active in Lackawanna's Italian American organizations were also involved in the union movement that began in the late 1930s. Marius DeCarolis, Mike Pacillo, Armando Capodagli, Al Ceccarelli, Ralph Carestio, Tony Falbo, Charles DePerto, John and Leonard Govenettio, Art Thomas, Alex Nigro, and Jack Gardina all became officers in locals of the United Steelworkers of America in the two decades after 1941. Throughout the 1930s and 1940s, especially after World War II, many Italians also became active and gained leadership positions in mainstream civic and community organizations previously closed to their ethnic group.[32]

Italian Americans in Mainstream Organizations

The movement of Lackawanna Italians into nonethnic associations and the organizations of other ethnic groups began earlier in the twentieth century. This was especially true of the second generation, which, through formal schooling and community life, had learned the English language and the customs of the United States. They often wanted to belong to "American" groups, to fit in with the general population. Other factors motivated Italians to join non – Italian organizations. While large Italian colonies, such as the one in Buffalo, guaranteed enough interested individuals to form an all – Italian branch of a typical American group, such as the Eagles or Foresters, this was not the case in small settlements like Lackawanna. So Lackawanna Italians joined groups that had multiethnic memberships or were dominated by another ethnic group. Frank Morinello was the only Italian member of the Lackawanna City Band in about 1910, and A. J. Tarquinio, a member of one of the few Italian families living in the Fourth Ward, was secretary of the Lackawanna Baseball Club in 1916. During this period, Pietro Oddi was asked to join the Moose, which had a largely Irish membership. The invitation was likely extended because the group wanted to build a Catholic

organization that could challenge the Masons, who held many supervisory positions in the steel plant, and Oddi was a foreman who could read and write English as well as speak it with some fluency. Two decades later, Ferdinand Catuzza became a member of the group. The Knights of Columbus, a Roman Catholic organization reacted to the Masons' domination of many supervisory jobs by forming Anchor Clubs throughout the country for its members holding supervisory positions. Two Anchor Clubs were established at the Bethlehem plant in Lackawanna, and John Galanti was treasurer of one in 1954. Some Italians were drawn to organizations established by other ethnic groups. Angelo Grosso and Nick Sperduto joined the Spanish Welfare Association for political reasons and for access to its meeting hall and generous sickness-and-death benefits (up to $1,000 for the latter). Dances and social activities apparently drew Italians into other organizations. Guy Schiavi, Joseph Cellini, and Charles Fistola were active in the Castilliana Club, a First Ward Spanish group, in 1947. Sometimes, joining a group was simply a matter of wanting to socialize with friends and neighbors. The Sisters Eight, a women's social group that included several Italians, started meeting monthly in members' homes in 1945, continuing to do so into the late 1990s.[33]

One aspect of the assimilation of European ethnic groups was the development of solidarity among Protestants, Catholics, and Jews. Called the "Triple Melting Pot," it involved the uniting of different nationalities by a common religion. In Lackawanna, because 84% of the population in 1958 was Roman Catholic, this was most visible in the Catholic sphere. By the 1930s, intermarriage gradually increased among individuals of Polish, Italian, Croatian, Irish, and other ethnic backgrounds who shared the Catholic religion. An early form of interethnic communication was the Catholic tradition of visiting seven churches on Christmas Eve. For First Ward Italians, this meant going from their home parish of St. Anthony's to visit St. Hyacinth (Polish), Assumption (Hungarian), Sacred Heart (Croatian), and St. Charles (multiethnic) in the First Ward, then crossing the Ridge Road bridge to stop at St. Barbara (Polish) and Our Lady of Victory (Irish). Catholics also came together in organizations. The Knights of Columbus (K of C), created by Irish clerics in 1882, gradually accepted other Catholic ethnics. In addition to the Anchor Clubs organized by the group, there was also Father Baker Council No. 2243 of the K of C in Lackawanna. James Oddy and Nick Sperduto were among the few Italian members of the council in 1931. Less than a decade later, Ross Guarino, Joe Milano, Harry Agliata, and John Verel were members of the committee that organized the group's annual Columbus Day dance. Italian American youth socialized with Catholics of other nationalities in several venues. Ellen Monaco was a member of the First Ward court, or chapter, of the Junior Catholic Daughters of America in 1937. Nine years later, Margaret DePasquale was president and Rita Montanari secretary of the Monsignor Baker Court of this girls' organization, while Margaret Suffoletto was a member of the St. Theresa Court. In the 1950s, the Catholic Youth Organization chapters formed at St. Anthony's and other churches led to increased interaction among youngsters in several Lackawanna parishes. Catholics also united in other domains.[34]

First- and second-generation Italian Americans who were interested in civic, political, and business connections also expressed this through affiliations outside the Italian community. The presence of 92 ethnic groups in Lackawanna brought home the need to form alliances to attain political and community-wide goals. In 1933, Joe Pacillo, Tony Amorosi, and Jimmy Guglietta were members, the latter two as officers, of the First Ward Democratic Club, a predominantly Irish group. Twenty years later, Daniel Thomas was elected president. Italian business and professional men became active in groups such as the Lackawanna Chamber of Commerce (see Figure 10.12), while others became involved in a variety of organizations, including veterans, civic, recreational, and charity groups. Members of the second generation began to participate in civic groups when they joined the ranks of the city's married couples, parents, and homeowners. Renters in public-housing projects took part in resident councils, and the increasing number of Italian Americans who purchased homes were often involved in homeowner associations. With the advent of parent-teacher organizations in the late 1930s, Italian Americans were well represented among their founders and leaders (see Sidebar 10.13).[35]

Women's Societies and Mixed Gender Groups

During the 1930s and 1940 there was a significant increase in Lackawanna's women's and mixed-gender groups. Women's societies were less common in the old country, but Italian American women eventually enjoyed more freedom of expression than their predecessors had experienced before leaving Italy. The American-born generation had learned a somewhat more expansive view of a woman's place from other ethnic groups, popular culture, and the public schools. The Mount Carmel Society, founded by immigrant women in 1918, was the only female group created prior to 1930. The decade of the 1930s witnessed the formation of 12 women's groups, and in an even more dramatic break from Italian tradition, the new Gamma Kappa Club became the first Italian organization to include both male and female members. The women's groups included not only those with religious and social functions but also those with political and civic missions. American-born women formed such groups as the Knick-Knacks, the Social Debs, and the Young Ladies Gold Star Society to sponsor social

FIGURE 10.12

ITALIANS IN THE LACKAWANNA CHAMBER OF COMMERCE

One important milestone in the civic assimilation of Italians was their involvement in the Lackawanna Chamber of Commerce and the Junior Chamber of Commerce (JCC), two organizations that played pivotal roles in the business and political life of the city. Restaurateur Nicholas Mattucci was elected to the chamber's board of directors in 1936. Soon, younger Italians became involved in the JCC, including Samuel Conte, who chaired one of the group's dances in 1939. Edmund Pacillo was awarded the organization's Distinguished Service Key in 1938 for his civic achievement. "Lauded by his selectors as a worker in [the] Boy Scout organization and for aiding persons of foreign extraction to gain citizenship papers, Mr. Pacillo is a typical young American." Soon Pacillo, Bradley Carestio, James Petti, and Dr. Gustave DaLuiso were active in the JCC. During the 1940s, Petti, Conte, and Alphonse Verel were elected to the president's office, and Frank Chiodo and Joseph Barone were named recording secretary. In 1950, school teacher Anthony Bevaque held the office of JCC recording secretary, and six other Italian Americans were active in the organization's leadership roles.

The Verel family, prominent in Lackawanna business circles, was well represented in the city's chamber of commerce. John Verel was an early member, and three of his sons later became members. In addition to Alphonse Verel, who was active in the JCC, Rocco was on its board of directors during the 1950s, and Gene was elected chamber president in 1970. Fred Catuzza Jr. served as the president from 1978 to 1988 and was the first recipient of the Silvio Filipetti Award "for his hard work and diligent efforts on behalf of the Chamber." This annual award, honoring the member who had most expanded the chamber's ranks, was named for Bethlehem Park native Silvio Filipetti after his death in 1975. An employee of the Niagara Mohawk Power Company, Filipetti designed and installed the lights that illuminate Our Lady of Victory Basilica. As a "loaned executive" from Niagara Mohawk, he also helped the Lackawanna Chamber of Commerce recruit members engaged in civic and government projects. When he passed away in 1975, the chamber decided to present an annual award in his name to the member who had recruited the most new members.

Sources: *Lackawanna Herald*, 5/30/41; *Lackawanna Leader*, 1/27/38, 5/9/40, 7/18/40, 10/22/42, 7/11/46, 6/5/47, 2/5/48, 6/8/50, 2/28/57, 12/14/67, 1/18/68, 12/25/69, 12/22/77; *Steel City Press*, 1/29/47, 6/11/47; *Lackawanna Press*, 4/28/50; letter to author from Aldo Filipetti, 2/97.

FIGURE 10.13
ITALIANS JOIN 'AMERICAN' GROUPS

An important aspect of the assimilation of Lackawanna's Italians was their involvement in groups outside the domain of the Italian American community. The following examples of this process are arranged by the group types.

POLITICAL: Joe Milano joined the Knights of Columbus in the late 1920s to help his chances in the citywide election for an assessor position. Angelo Grosso became a member of the Spanish Welfare Association to strengthen his political base in the First Ward. During the 1930s, Nick Sperduto, John Panzetta, and Vincent Suffoletto were active in the Grant Republican Club, of which Anthony Falcone became president and Anthony Turchiarelli, the sergeant at arms. Ralph Galanti was elected vice president of the First Ward Independent Club. Pasquale Pitillo became president of the Roland Republican Club in 1936, when at least five other Italians were members. Three Italian American housewives held officer slots in the Roland Ladies Independent Club in 1940: Margaret Pitillo; president, Anna Falcone, vice president; and Catherine Delmont, treasurer. That same year, Patrick Vertalino was secretary of the Third Ward Democratic Club. Ferdinand Catuzza, by virtue of being a dog warden, was a member of the Judges and Police Executives Conference of Erie County, one of 16 Italian Americans on the 1939 roster.

BUSINESS: Restaurateur Nicholas Mattucci was one of the 21 original members of the Lackawanna Retail Trade Council, founded in 1933. Storekeeper Peter Mazuca was one of the founders of Lackawanna Grocers and Butchers Association, and merchants Charles Saccomanno, Frank Morinello, and Frank Monaco became members by 1937. Vincent Lojacano was vice president in 1952, when

the group was known as the Lackawanna Food Merchant's Association.

CIVIC: By 1936, 17 Italian Americans were members of the Eagles, Aerie No. 2231, and more joined during the next five years. Pasquale Pitillo and Leonard DePaula each served as president, and Brownie Leo, Patsy Yoviene, Paul Mortellano, and Louis Corbo also were officers. Harry Agliata, active in a number of groups, chaired the Young Men's Civic Club's Athletic Commission in 1937. He was the first Italian to join the Irish-dominated Limestone Club. Mike Morgan became the club's second Italian member, serving two terms as president and helping to initiate the annual "World's Shortest St. Patrick's Day Parade" in the early 1950s.

VETERANS: Italians became active in veterans organizations after World War I, during which a number of immigrants and several of the American-born generation served in the American armed services. A large number of Italian Americans served during World War II, and they not only comprised the bulk of the membership of the Bethlehem Park Veterans Association and its auxiliary but also participated actively in other veterans groups after the war. Joseph Barone was executive secretary of the Lackawanna Veterans Administration, and Ralph Guadagno was elected president of the Lackawanna Interested Veterans Association in 1948. In the following years, Guadagno served as second vice commander of the Matthew Glab Post of the American Legion. In the late 1940s, Harry Agliata managed the softball teams of American Legion Post No. 63; Elizabeth Rosati was on the executive board of the women's auxiliary of the post; and Angelina Guglielmi and Caroline Fiore were members of the junior auxiliary. Angelo "Bing" Colello was elected post

commander in the 1950s, and Anthony Selvaggio and Simon Palumbo became officers of the Bett-Toomey Detachment of the Marine Corps League. Chet Catuzza became commandant of the League and was succeeded by his brother, Fred Catuzza Jr. Rose Capriotto and Florence Vertalino were officers in the local branch of the Gold Star Mothers, whose members' sons had died while serving their country. Years earlier, Elizabeth Costanzi, who lost her son Angelo in France during World War I, had been a member of the group.

PARENT-TEACHER: Throughout Lackawanna, Italian American parents became active in their children's schools during the years 1939 to 1941. Joe Cosentino was president of Franklin Orthopedic (Handicapped) School's PTA, the first such group in the city, and Tony Colello served as first vice president. Joe Milano was founding president of the Roosevelt School PTA; the following year, Frank Fiore and Samuel Conte became officers. Six other Italians were on the association's executive committee, which was chaired by Armondo Pietrocarlo. Bridget Corsi was a leader in the Bethlehem Park PTA in 1940. Twelve years later, the Bethlehem Park Parents Association was created, and Edwin DiCenzo became the first president. The group actively petitioned elected officials and Bethlehem Steel to clean up the plant's discharges into Smokes Creek.

RESIDENTS AND HOME-OWNERS: Like the Old Village and the New Village in earlier years, housing projects built in the 1930s and 1940s attracted people of many ethnic groups, including Italians. In the 1940s, Samuel Marinaccio and Peter Sartori were active participants in the Baker Homes Parents Association in the First Ward. Anthony Ranalli served as president of the

Bethlehem Park Homeowners group and also the Bethlehem Park Tax Payer's Association. Many Italians were involved in the Tenants Council and the Home Bureau Unit of the Ridgewood Village.

LABOR UNIONS: In addition to the United Steelworkers of America and the various railroad unions, Italians were involved in other labor organizations. As more Italians became employees of the city, they helped organize other groups. Sebastian Fistola served two terms in the late 1940s as president of the Lackawanna Firemen's Benevolent Association. Leonard DePaula became the financial secretary of the city's new Department of Public Works Benevolent Association in 1954.

SPORTS AND RECREATION: Sue Bellagamba was elected president of the Lincoln Annex Theater Guild in 1938. Sports groups and leagues drew Lackawanna youth from the city's many ethnic enclaves. In 1941, the Bethlehem Park Basketball League was organized by Peter Juran, Bill Russell, and two Italians: Essio Baldelli and Joe Christiano. The five teams vied

for a most valuable player award, donated by Frank Chiodo, and a sportsman's medal donated by boxer John Sacco. Frank Iafallo was president of the Second Ward Basketball Club in 1937. At the end of World War II, the United Steelworkers union at the Bethlehem plant in Lackawanna launched the Steelworkers Recreational Organization. Armondo Pietrocarlo was president, and five other Italians were department representatives.

COLLEGE: As Steel City Italians began attending local colleges, they developed bonds with other students from their hometown and participated in sororities and fraternities. In 1947, the Lackawanna Club was organized at Niagara University by 12 students from the city, including Camillo Campoli, the group's treasurer. The *Lackawanna Leader* listed the names of 51 Lackawannans attending the University of Buffalo (U.B.) in 1946, including: Angelo Colello, Nicholas Monaco, Angelo Sperduto, Cosmo Covino, Guido Galfo, Joseph DePasquale, Silvio Filipetti, Carl Renzi, and John Ginnetti. When the Lackawanna

U.B. Club was organized the following year, Angelo Sperduto was elected its treasurer. Caroline Fiore was vice president of the Theta Chapter of Theta Sigma Upsilon sorority at the time of her graduation from the Buffalo State Teachers College in 1946.

CHARITY: Italians have participated in civic and charitable organizations for many years. In 1940, the Galanti Athletic Association was one of five young men's organizations that sponsored the annual appeal for Our Lady of Victory Hospital. Italian professionals and their spouses, such as Dr. and Mrs. John Fadale and Dr. and Mrs. Gustave DaLuiso, were active on committees at Our Lady of Victory Hospital. John Fadale was president of the OLV Hospital Guild in 1939 and active for many years in the Lackawanna Charity Society. Edward Morgan, a World War II veteran, directed the Lackawanna Red Cross fundraising campaign in 1947.

Sources: Interviews with Joe Milano, October 16, 1996; Angelo Grosso, November 22, 1977; Chet Catuzza, September 18, 1994; and Mike Morgan, December 27, 1995; *Directory: Judges and Police Executive Conference of Erie County, N. Y.*, 1939, p. 17; *Lackawanna Republic*, 3/24/33; *Lackawanna Herald*, 12/7/33, 1/16/36, 1/30/36, 7/2/36, 11/5/36; 1/7/37, 10/21/37; 3/16/39, 4/13/39, 11/9/39, 4/18/40; 11/20/40, 8/29/41; *Labor Press*, 10/21/49; *Lackawanna Leader*, 1/7/37, 11/18/37, 10/27/38, 2/29/40, 4/4/40, 9/19/40, 10/25/40, 11/20/40, 11/27/41, 8/20/42, 3/22/45, 7/19/45, 12/27/45, 5/2/46, 6/20/46, 11/7/46, 12/24/46, 2/6/47, 3/13/47, 4/24/47, 2/5/48, 4/1/48, 9/15/49, 10/20/49, 2/1/51, 1/3/52, 1/17/52, 4/10/52, 10/23/52, 11/16/52, 12/11/52, 3/26/53, 6/25/53, 11/5/53, 4/29/54.

activities. Founded in the early 1940s, the Jolly Boosters Club on Roland Avenue included second-generation females as well as their immigrant mothers. Altogether, 28 women's societies, more than a third of all Italian organizations, were created, mostly during the 1930s and 1940s. As proof that the segregation of sexes was still a potent factor in the mid-1930s, the seven member organizations of the newly founded FIAAL were all male societies. Things began to change in the 1940s with the founding of two more groups with combination male and female memberships: the Campus Youth Club at St. Anthony's and the Bethlehem Park GOP Club. The younger-generation men seemed more willing to share power with females; the first president of the Bethlehem Park GOP Club, William Petti, was succeeded the following year by Aurora Palmisano-

Green.[36]

St. Anthony's Church spawned 13 groups over the years but only two for adult males; the remainder were for women and youth. On one hand, the fact that the church sponsored six women's societies, three for boys, and two for boys and girls reflects the southern-Italian perception of religion as the domain of women and children. On the other hand, it demonstrates the increased importance of the church in community life and at least a slight departure from the anticlericism of the male immigrants (see Chapter 6). Of the secular female groups, six were auxiliaries to men's societies, and few enjoyed a lengthy existence. Only one mention of the auxiliary of the Circolo D'Annunzio Dopolavoro appeared in newspapers; the group likely never got off the ground. The ladies auxiliary of the

Roland Wildcats, formed in 1951, was defunct within 10 years. That of the Galanti Athletic Association folded after four years, and the Vagabonds auxiliary also seems to have had a brief existence. The Lake Erie Italian Club has had a series of three different auxiliaries between 1943 and 2009.[37]

It is interesting to note that among the more recent Italian organizations, those founded between 1950 and 2004, six are women's organizations, three are men's groups, and six have combined male and female memberships. The 36 other men's and boys groups were founded prior to 1950, while more than a third of the women's groups and a majority of the mixed-gender societies were created since that date. The mixed-gender groups include the Catholic Youth Council, founded at St. Anthony's in the mid-1950s, the Lackawanna Chapter of Our Lady of Fatima Guild organized in the 1960s, and four of the five groups created in the 1980s. The establishment of 28 women's societies and nine mixed-gender groups underlines the trend of Italian American females gradually gaining more independence as well as the easing of the traditional Italian practice of segregating activities by gender.

The Growth of Social, Recreational, and Sports Groups

By the late 1910s, Italian teens were playing sandlot sports, and a few were on teams that were part of organized leagues. Al Croce, who lived with his family in the Old Village, recalled

Members gather in the basement of the Wildcats' clubhouse during the 1950s. Standing are, from far left to right: Pat Vertalino, John Pitillo, and Del Herkimer. Dominic Nasso is seated at left, facing the camera. Seated on the bench are Harold Girdlestone (wearing the plaid shirt), [Unk], Jim Vertalino (in the dark shirt with white letters), and John Pitillo (in the white shirt and hat). Standing at right are [Unk], Tom Tomilo, and [Unk].
Photo source: Collection of Frank Chiodo

a Sunday in 1923 when, he encountered some Roland Avenue Italians crossing the railroad tracks and heading for St. Anthony's Church. Among them was Al Verel, manager of the Roland Wildcats football team, who quickly asked Croce to join his team. One of the first squads they played was the St. Anthony's team. At the time, about half the Wildcats football players had names such as Falbo, Pitillo, DePerto, and Vertalino. Croce joined the team and the new Roland Wildcats athletic club that soon emerged.

Many Italian Americans of the second generation reached their teenage and early-adult years during the 1920s and 1930s. This collective coming-of-age was a crucial factor in the formation of social, recreational, and sports groups, which together account for three of every five Italian organizations in Lackawanna. Three such groups were founded in the 1920s, and 18 in the following decade. Italian youth, mostly males, participated in a wide variety of activities—be they the social functions of the Stag Club, the recreational interests of the Model Airplane Club, or the hardball, softball, basketball, or volleyball teams of the Vagabonds. The country's gradual return to economic security, which began in the late 1930s, also accelerated the growth of leisure and recreational activities, some of which became increasingly elaborate. The Park Athletic & Social Club, founded by young immigrants and second-generation males in Bethlehem Park, sponsored baseball, football, and other sports teams. Renamed the Park Rod & Gun Club in 1938, the group added skeet shooting, hunting, and fishing expeditions to its list of activities. At the time, the group included such successful businessmen as Joe Amadori, and the members often hunted on land he owned south of Lackawanna. In 1949, the club purchased a cottage on Georgian Bay in Canada and later bought a plot of land in Ellicotville, New York. To raise money to build a hunting camp and lodge on the latter, the group organized a variety show at the Park Theater featuring music by the nationally known singing group, the Ink Spots.[38]

As time progressed, social and athletic functions grew more important to other Italian organizations, including some of the earliest groups founded by immigrants, and they began to sponsor picnics, sporting events, dances, and other celebrations. The Pettorano sul Gizio Club, for example, held a pre-Lenten costume festival in February 1938. Such activities represented an attempt by immigrants to provide family recreation, induce the second generation to become members, raise funds, and increase their respectability in the eyes of both the Italian colony and the general Lackawanna community. The Marchegiani Men's Club sponsored baseball and basketball teams for their sons and other youth, as did the Lake Erie Italian Club, which also organized a bowling league. These sports-and-recreation events had a multigenerational appeal and were often the highlight of the year's social calendar for Lackawanna Italians, especially between 1920 and 1950.[39]

The LEIC began holding an annual summer outing in 1918, an event that grew progressively more sophisticated. The 1928 affair was held on the grounds of St. Anthony's Church, opening with High Mass attended by the society's membership and closing with a fireworks display. The outings grew to include dances, games, food booths, and raffle prizes, while the pyrotechnics became "monster fireworks" displays. The 1936 celebration, held at the Dona Street soccer field, featured a parade led by an Italian band as well as sports and entertainment. In 1939 and 1941, the outing was held at the Hamburg Fair grounds, to which the club provided free bus transportation from the First Ward. Five hundred people, including a number of Lackawanna politicians, gathered there in 1939. The Roman Independent Club, which began staging an annual one-day outing at the Dona Street soccer field in 1933, bused people to a picnic and lawn fete at the Hamburg fair grounds in 1939 and at Chestnut Ridge Park the following year. The club sponsored fewer activities during World War II, but in July 1945 it held a five-day festival in the First Ward. Three years later, it hosted a six-day festival on a South Park Avenue playground. The Roland Italian American Lodge sponsored softball and bowling teams for young men and held several large picnics between 1939 and 1948. These two groups attracted only a handful of younger members, however, and both disbanded by 1961.[40]

Not to be outdone by the predominantly immigrant societies, second-generation groups also organized lavish social and recreational events. The banquets and dances sponsored by the Stag Club grew larger and began featuring regionally or nationally known bands. Lackawanna politicians sometimes attended these events. In the mid-1930s, the Galanti

Members of the Roland Wildcats Auxiliary, circa 1959. From left are: [Unk], Rita Leo, Mary Leo-Evans, Mary Chiodo, Claudia Kuclich-Chiodo, Marie Gugino-Pitillo, Lillian Leo, Kate Pitillo-Delmont.
Photo source: Collection of Frank Chiodo

Women of the Lake Erie Ladies Auxiliary at a restaurant in Buffalo, October 30, 1944. The group was founded the previous year. Seated, from left, are: Ida Kolenko, Vera Pecora, Marie Costello, Rose Marinaccio, and Rose Laggio. Standing are: Rose Mecca, Anne Corvigno, Anne Vollaro, Louise Mecca, Carmela Ross. Photo source: Anne Melillo-Corvigno

On March 2, 1948, the Roland Wildcats began giving an annual award to the Lackawannan who did the most for sports in the city. At a ceremony held in the Dom Polski hall, the first award was presented by Brownie Leo, center, to Arthur Michalek, at left, for his work in organizing American Legion Junior Baseball competition in Lackawanna in 1947. The award was named for Joe Vertalino, a club member who was killed during the final days of the European campaign in World War II. Photo source: Collection of Frank Chiodo

Since the 1940s, the Galunti Athletic Association has given an annual award to the most valuable athlete at Lackawanna High School. In 1952, the trophy went to Zeke Gobolos. Presenting it are Al Ginnetti, at left, and Ralph Marinelli. Photo source: Jack and Mary Panczykowski

Athletic Association (GAA) initiated annual spring and fall dances, and in 1938, an annual summer festival. The first festival was a three-day event that commenced with a long parade from Roland Avenue to the soccer field in the First Ward. The next year, the event grew to five days, then to six days in 1941, and finally, to 11 days in 1944, when it was publicized as a carnival. Two days after the GAA event ended, the Lake Erie Italian Club commenced its own 11-day carnival. This schedule must have put Armondo Pietrocarlo in a challenging situation as the president of both societies at the time. Apparently, he and other LEIC members decided that Lackawanna was too small for two large festivals, and the LEIC ceased sponsoring this type of activity. The GAA continued to hold these annual events, drawing thousands of people immediately after World War II. The crowds soon grew thinner and the festival had been reduced to six days by the time the last one was held in 1951.[41]

The Lake Erie Italian Club was able to recruit second-generation men as members in the early 1940s, a major draw being the new clubhouse and bar it acquired in 1942. The club purchased the

hall on Hamburg Turnpike at Dona Street, remodeled it and installed a 30-foot mahogany bar. An active recruiting drive brought in more than 80 new members during 1942, about evenly divided between first- and second-generation men. By April 1943, the club's membership stood at 200, including a number of South Buffalo residents. The GAA also tried to attract more second-generation men into its ranks, especially since so many members were entering the armed forces. This attrition was less an issue for the LEIC, many of whose immigrant members were beyond the age of conscription. The club's new bar and meeting hall were effective draws for new recruits, and a larger membership base was desperately needed to support the new facility. Monthly dues were raised from $1.00 to $1.50 to supplement the building fund. The LEIC was one of the few immigrant societies able to attract second-generation members.[42]

Second-generation activists continued to form large and active social-recreational groups following World War II, when returning servicemen enjoyed stable jobs at the steel plant and better pay won by the new United Steelworkers union. The 90 members of the Good Time Club met monthly at Sperduto's Restaurant on

The Galanti Athletic Association's annual installation of officers and sports night, January 23, 1955. Seated at the head table (the top of the "T"), from left to right, are; [Unk], Nick DelBello, Anita and Dan Carnevale (manager of the Buffalo Bisons and featured speaker), Judge Joseph McCann (master of ceremonies) and his wife, Rev. Thomas Ciolino, Rev. Bernard Paterniti, [Unk], Ralph Marinelli (banquet chairman). In the first row of people at the right, the fourth person is Matt Suffoletto. Seated at the center table, the second row of people from right are (starting in the foreground): Lou Fistola, Josephine Marrano-Fistola, Neil Marrano, Adeline Marrano, Grace Marrano-Galanti, Ralph Galanti. The row of people on the left of the center table are: Carl Covino, Sally Covino, Josephine Monaco, Nick Monaco, Evelyn Cocina-Marrano, Ralph Marrano. The last row of people at left are: John "Doc" Kollender, Dorothy Kollender, Amerigo Bracci, Clementine Bracci, Adeline Bracci, Harry Bracci. Photo source: Chico Galanti

Ingham Avenue, had cookouts and parties, and watched sporting events. The Bethlehem Park Veterans Association and its women's auxiliary raised funds to erect a monument to the eight GIs from the neighborhood who died in World War II. The two groups held a series of annual events for at least 10 years after their founding in 1946-47. The activities included spring and fall dances, picnics, New Year's Eve parties, card parties, communion breakfasts at St. Anthony's Church, dinners, three-day lawn fetes, bazaars, and St. Patrick parties for adults. The groups also focused on Bethlehem Park youth, organizing field days and Christmas parties for children and dances for teenagers, and sponsoring a drill team and a Cub Scout pack.[43]

The activities of most of the sports and recreational groups usually focused on American, not Italian, pastimes. Other than bocce, these young Lackawannans played the games they learned from the *Americani*: baseball, softball, football, basketball, and bowling. These games brought the recognition and approval of the general Lackawanna community. When the Galanti Athletic Association team participated in the softball playoff games in 1947, 6,000 fans watched. The GAA's yearly summer picnic featured softball games and other recreation; up to 200 men,

women, and children attended these outings in the late 1940s and early 1950s. In addition, the GAA and the Stag Club both sponsored pinochle tournaments, choosing the American card game over the traditional Italian *scopa*, *briscola*, and *tre-sette*. This was another small indicator of the assimilation process for the immigrants and their children. Many of the organizations pursued the dual mission of reinforcing an Italian American identity and encouraging the adoption of American ways. The formal written goals of several societies included statements about encouraging U. S. citizenship, discussing civic and governmental issues, and leading members to "a better understanding of citizenry." The focus on recreation, sports, and social activities was evident among the nine new groups founded between 1950 and 1979.

Associations with Mixed Ethnic Memberships

Blossoming after 1930 was the formation of associations that had a majority of Italian members plus people of other ethnic groups. This trend began in the 1920s with the creation of the Galanti Athletic Association and the Roland Wildcats, each of which included young men of other ethnic groups who were the neighbors of Italian American families. Overall,

At the 1955 GAA banquet, some friends gather at the bar. From left: Al Ginnetti, Evy Juran, Walter Topinko, Leo Kujawa, Ralph Marinelli, Eugenio Galanti, Ralph Galanti, John Faraci, Lou Fistola. Photo source: Chico Galanti

18 of the 76 Italian groups fall into this category, and all but two of them focused on sports, social, or recreational functions that drew the interest of the American-born teenagers and young adults who comprised the membership. The Gymnistici Club was made up of young men of Italian and Hungarian lineage who had been classmates at Our Lady of Victory Mission School. It was an exercise club that trained in the weight room at Lackawanna High School and occasionally sponsored a social function to raise funds. The Pappy Softball Club, sponsored by Joe Amadori, included 44 Italian Americans among its 67 members. Another group in 1938 with mixed-ethnic membership, the Amici Athletic Club, not only was active in sports but also sponsored annual skating parties and picnics. The membership of the Park Rod & Gun Club had grown to 52 men, half of whom were non – Italians. Two groups were sponsored by men involved in political and civic affairs—the Milano Athletic Club (Joe Milano), and Pitillo's Social Club (Pasquale Pitillo). The first female group with a mixed-ethnic membership, the Bethlehem Park Ladies Aid Club, also had a political connection. Half the club's executive board members were males, many of them prominent political leaders, including Tony Amorosi, Tony DePasquale, and Joe Milano. A number of the women's groups sponsored dances, and the Young Ladies Gold Star Society helped Bethlehem Park females "pass their leisure time by learning popular dance steps." The Lackawanna Chapter of the Our Lady of Fatima Guild and the Lackawanna Ladies Bocce League—

created in 1965 and 1976, respectively—both had mixed-ethnic memberships. Overall, half the mixed-ethnic organizations had male memberships and were organized for the most part, by 1940, while the majority of those with female or coed memberships came into being after 1944.[45]

The societies with multiethnic memberships served as a key transition agent from a single ethnic focus to a neighborhood grouping that highlighted the common American experience of all European ethnic groups. In the four neighborhoods in which Lackawanna's Italians were concentrated prior to 1945—Ingham Avenue, the Old Village, Roland Avenue, and Bethlehem Park—Italians were usually the most numerous, but by no means the only, ethnic group present. The memberships of 55 (out of 76) Italian groups resided in the First Ward, while 15 Italian societies had citywide memberships. The Roland Avenue neighborhood had six Italian groups. Among those in the First Ward, 14 were in the lower Ingham Avenue neighborhood, and 19 were in Bethlehem Park. In the 1930s and 1940s, many an Italian group included at least a few non – Italian neighbors in its membership. The ideas of neighborhood and inclusiveness even affected groups dominated by Italians with roots in a specific region of Italy. The Eaglettes of Bethlehem Park, known as a Marchegiani group, included six members out of the 15 who were sons of immigrants from Calabria and Lazio.[46]

Ethnic Revival:
the Preservation of Italian Traditions

Several organizations, one created in each of the three decades after 1945, preserved an Italian recreational custom. The Lackawanna Bocce Association, the Amadori Marchegiani Club, and the Lackawanna Ladies Bocce League all focused on the game of bocce. The Lackawanna Bocce Association held its first games at the Old Village site and a field near Roland Avenue, but soon all its first games were moved to the ball field at the foot of Madison Avenue in Bethlehem Park. Games attracted as many as 350 spectators, and team members included elderly immigrants as well as their sons and grandsons. For many years, Lackawanna teams dueled with squads from the Italian neighborhoods of Buffalo, Lockport, and Niagara Falls. The group was renamed the Lackawanna Recreation Bocce

League when the city's recreation department became its sponsor, which led to the construction of an enclosed bocce court in Bethlehem Park, that is still in use today. The structure is named for businessman Joseph "Pappy" Amadori, a bocce enthusiast who sponsored many teams during his lifetime. For the several decades of its existence, the Lackawanna Ladies Bocce League also played its matches at this site.

Italian men and women continue to play bocce on the courts in both formal summer leagues and informal winter tournaments. For many years, Gene DeSantis has coordinated the scheduling of and access to the Bethlehem Park bocce courts. In 2008, Joe Carnevale was president of the Lackawanna Recreation Bocce League, and Tom Collana, vice president and treasurer. The formation of the three bocce groups over three decades was, at least in part, an expression of the ethnic revival that began in the 1960s and continued into the 1980s. Other expressions of this movement were also seen in the Lackawanna area. The Lake Erie Ladies Auxiliary formed a tarantella dance group that put on several performances during the 1960s, then again in 1979 and 1980. A number of Steel City Italian men joined the Volpe Club in nearby Blasdell when it was organized in the 1970s.[47]

In Lackawanna, four of the five groups founded in the 1980s represented a new effort to maintain Italian traditions. Three of these groups were projects of the Lake Erie Italian Club and its women's auxiliary. The *Coro Italiano* (Italian Chorus), which began in 1982, had a membership of mostly postwar male and female immigrants organized by Guy and Delia Iannarelli. Rose Marchese was the director during the first two years, then Guy Iannarelli assumed that role. In 1983, the Iannarellis founded the Junior Italian Dance Group, made up of young people ages 10 to 21, most of them second

Alfonso Bracci, right, is awarded the Galanti Athletic Association's annual golf trophy by Ralph Carestio, circa 1951. Standing at left is Frank Renzi, and Vince Jennetti is seated at the table. Photo source: Collection of Bridget Ginnetti-Bracci

The Lake Erie Ladies Auxiliary had a tarantella dance group for a period during the 1960s. The dancers in the lower row, from left, are: Frances Zawacki, Lorraine Nigro-Katra, and Mary Panzetta-Vertino. Standing are: Rose Guido, Connie Marinelli-Staniszewski, Tina DiTommaso-Camilloni, Shirley Nigro, Antoinette Zelli. Photo source: Mary Panzetta-Vertino

FIGURE 10.14

BOCCE AS RECREATION

For many years, immigrant men in Lackawanna played informal games of bocce on fields in Bethlehem Park and the Old Village as well as along Ingham and Roland avenues. The Fano Restaurant on Hamburg Turnpike had outdoor courts that drew many Marchegiani bocce enthusiasts and their friends. When the restaurant closed down in the mid-1950s, the games again took place in the nearby fields, with the teams usually pitting the Marchegiani against the Romans, the natives of Lazio. Many matches took place on the field at the foot of Madison Avenue. The improved economic situation of Italians, the aging of the immigrant generation, and increased leisure time encouraged the creation of a formal bocce league, the Lackawanna Bocce Association. Liso Mattioli, Nick DelBello, and Lavinio

and Luigi Montanari, some of the group's primary organizers, in 1958 persuaded the Lackawanna Recreation Department to sponsor the association. Operating under the new title of Lackawanna Recreation Bocce League, the Park Grille Romans, Amadori's Marchegiani, Paesanos, and DelBello's DPs (for displaced persons, made up of recent immigrants from Italy) began competing in July, when Mayor Ogarek tossed the first jack ball to open the initial tournaments at the Madison Avenue ball field. First Ward Councilman Aldo Filipetti served as judge. Amadori's Marchegiani team won the championship that year. The Marchegiani and the runner-up team, the Romans, then played matches against the Perseverance Club in Buffalo and the Century Club in Niagara Falls. At the end

of the season, all teams from the three cities attended a banquet at the Park Grille, where city officials and dignitaries handed out a series of trophies. The next year, two additional teams, Amigones and Roland, joined the league. Ralph Galanti, director of the Lackawanna recreation department, was instrumental in convincing the city to build an enclosed bocce court at the Madison Avenue site. Completed in 1960, the structure was named after businessman Joseph "Pappy" Amadori, founder of the Amadori Marchegiani Club. The number of teams grew rapidly, most of them sponsored by businesses or organizations. During the 1960s, the teams included: Ilio DiPaolo's, Boot's, the Lake Erie Italian Club, L & B, Stags, DiCenzo's, and DePasquale's. By 1965, Galanti was appointing a bocce league director. That year, Philip Fanone was the designee, and in 1967, it was Louis Montanari. A full set of officers was elected each year. Angelo Grosso was president in 1965, and Nick DelBello assumed the office two years later. The annual competitions grew more intense as Lackawanna's best players took on those from Niagara Falls and Lockport in quest of the Tri-City Trophy, donated by the city of Lackawanna. Each season concluded with an elaborate banquet hosted by the Lackawanna and Niagara Falls teams on an alternating basis. The hosts tried to outdo each other at these events, and Phil Fanone recalls the Lackawanna team really impressing its opponents one year by wheeling out a roast pig with an apple in its mouth. The Lackawanna bocce teams also traveled to tournaments in Pennsylvania and Las Vegas as well as to the World Championship of Bocce held in Rome, New York.

The Lackawanna Ladies Bocce League was founded in 1976 by Yolanda Mazzucchi-Culver. The league soon had 40 or 50

The outdoor bocce courts in Bethlehem Park in 1958. Teams from the Lackawanna Recreation Bocce League look on as five others get close to the ground to take measurements for points. The men squatting down are, from left, Al Colafranceschi, Lavinio Montanari (with the measuring string), Aldo Filipetti, Gino Fini, and Art Sambuchi. Photo source: Aldo Filipetti

members, mostly Italian Americans, and teams with interesting names, such as Yola's Yoyos, the Seven Dwarfs, and the Baccalas. The organization became inactive for a period, then reorganized in 1989. Some team names were changed during the downtime; the Baccalas became the Sunflowers, and the Seven Dwarfs were transformed into the Jennie-Lites. During the 1990s, the two other teams in the league were the Golden Girls and the Parkettes. Bocce has become a popular family sport, with many games played in the backyards of Italian American homes. Some families have even installed their own bocce courts. When Armando and Mary Leonetti had a new house constructed on Fisher Road in West Seneca in 1958, the couple did the landscaping work themselves, including the installation of a gravel bocce court, complete with sideboards.

Al D'Alessandro and his brother Carmine, near left, played on Del Bello's bocce squad in 1958. Both men were recently arrived immigrants from Campania.
Photo source: Collection of Al D'Alessandro

Sources: Interviews with Gene DeSantis, December 29, 1994, April 20, 1995, December 17, 2005; Ruth Catuzza, December 30, 1994; Dora Sambuchi-Grosso, July 18, 1986; Phil Fanone, November 28, 2008; and Mary Leonetti, December 28, 1994; *Lackawanna Leader*, 6/5/58, 6/26/58, 7/17/58, 7/31/58, 9/4/58, 10/9/58, 3/19/59, 7/1/65, 7/22/65, 7/6/67; *Front Page*, 4/14/93, 10/19/94, 9/6/95, 11/8/95.

With the Strip Mill as backdrop, Al Colafranceschi, third from left in plaid shirt with arm raised, has apparently just thrown a bocce ball. To the right of him, waiting to make their tosses, are Lavinio Montanari (in white shirt), Councilman Aldo Filipetti (in shirt and tie), and Carmine D'Alessandro (in striped hat and T-shirt saying Nick DelBello DPs). Nick DelBello, whose funeral business sponsored the team and its uniforms, stands at far right. To the left of DelBello, wearing his team's uniforms are: Joe Leone, Al D'Alessandro, [Unk], Sam Violanti, Gino Fini, [Unk]. Most of the team's members were recent immigrants from Italy, and the DP stands for "displaced persons," a term coined after World War II, when many fled war-ravaged Europe to live in the United States. Photo source: Aldo Filipetti

A bocce tournament in Niagara Falls featuring Lackawanna versus the Century Club, circa 1960. Larry Colello of the Lackawanna squad (in striped shirt) and others try to determine which team's balls have landed closer to the jack (also called the polino or palletta) – the small ball that each team attempts to get as close to as possible. Photo source: Chico Galanti

Ilio DiPaolo, (in dark shirt), and other men discuss which team scored points in this photo from the 1960s. The setting for this annual match between Niagara Falls' Century Club and the Lackawanna team was the courts along the Niagara River in Niagara Falls. Photo source: Dennis DiPaolo

generation. In late 1985, the Iannarellis were asked by LEIC leaders to form an adult dance group to participate in the annual folk festival in Buffalo. They gathered 37 men and women, many of them first and second generation, and launched the Senior Italian Dance Group. Delia Iannarelli and Carmella Monaco made costumes for the dancers, and the group procured the services of John Andreff, a dance instructor. Both the junior and senior dancers participated in the festival, and within a few months, all three groups appeared at another folk festival, then at the large Ethnic Festival at the Buffalo Convention Center. The LEIC underwrote the full cost of the three groups until 1989. Since then, the club's bingo committee has made donations to the groups, and the dancers and singers have held fund-raisers, such as pancake breakfasts at the club hall. The three groups gave 15 performances per year together during the 1980s and 1990s, appearing at the New York State Fair, and at ethnic celebrations, Italian festivals, and churches throughout western New York, from Buffalo to Syracuse to Olean. In years past, the groups' leaders organized Italian-language classes. The Junior Italian Dance Group was reconstituted in 1993, drawing as members boys and girls from five to 14 years of age, many of them children or grandchildren of the two adult groups' members. In the past decade, the same people have made up the membership of both the *Coro* and the senior dancers group. The three cultural groups combined have made eight to 10 annual appearances at nursing homes, hospitals, sports events, and public-park concerts during that time. In 2003, the aging senior dancers could no longer perform, so the group disbanded. However, these 24 men and women have expanded their activities to include singing with the *Coro Italiano* at the funeral Masses of members of the LEIC and its auxiliary.[48]

Sign on the outside wall of the Pappy Amadori Memorial Bocce Court, constructed in 1960.
Photo source: Mike and Julie Andreozzi

The indoor bocce court at the east end of Madison Avenue in Bethlehem Park, 2009. Photo source: Mike and Julie Andreozzi

Interior of bocce court, 2009. From left are Joe Carnevale, Egino DeSantis, and Angelo Lattanzo. Carnevale is the current president of the Lackawanna Recreation Bocce league, and DeSantis has coordinated activities at the court for many years.
Photo source: Mike and Julie Andreozzi

April, 2009. Inside the Pappy Amadori Memorial bocce Court, Bethlehem Park. From left, the players are: Cesare Cardi, Dean Ziccarelli, Carmen Iuliano, and Remo Fischione. Photo source: Mike and Julie Andreozzi

At the 2005 bocce tournament at the Lake Erie Italian Club, the champion women's team consisted of [Unk], Antoinette Monaco, Carmella Cardero, Marge Ziccarelli.
Photo source: Lake Erie Italian Club

The outdoor bocce courts behind the Lake Erie Italian Club in 2005. The men's champions in that year's tournament were, from left to right: Gerry Giannicchi, Tony Monaco, Angelo Muscarella, and Nick Liberta.
Photo source: Lake Erie Italian Club

Members of the Lake Erie Women's Auxiliary at the St. Joseph's table they prepared in 2001. From left are Delia Iannarelli, Carmela Monaco, Anita Marrocco, and Chris Coviello. Every year on March 19, Italian tradition calls for a table of meatless food to be prepared and shared with the poor. Photo source: Don Grosso

2008. Linda Masella-Perry, left, president of the Lake Erie Women's Auxiliary presents Member of the Year award to Wanda DeSantis, who became the president in 2009.
Photo source: Lake Erie Italian Club

April 2009. The large outdoor sign in front of the Lake Erie Italian Club. Photo source: Mike and Julie Andreozzi

The fifth annual banquet of the Lake Erie Italian Club drew 265 people on April 12, 1958, in St. Anthony's parish hall. Nick Sperduto was toastmaster and Aldo Canestrari general chairman of the event. Photo source: Gerarda and Carmen Basile

Postwar immigrants from Cantalupo, Molise, organized the St. Anna Cantalupo Club in 1984 and continue to honor the town's patron saint and pass the tradition on to their children (see Chapter 6). The annual ritual has been held at a number of churches in Lackawanna and Eden, including St. Anthony's. The 2008 festa, which took place at the Lake Erie Italian Club, featured a Mass, a procession on the club's grounds, a dinner, and a dance. Approximately 100 people attend the event each year.

The last three decades have witnessed a trend toward the independence of Italian American women. Most of the women's auxiliaries formed by men's groups have long since folded, while the auxiliaries of the Lake Erie Italian Club have developed a more independent stance, sometimes challenging the traditional power of Italian males. The original Lake Erie Ladies Auxiliary, founded in 1943, eventually had disagreements with the men about membership criteria, decision making, and finances. In 1977, the men's club severed relations and the women's group pursued its own course until it disbanded in 2000. A new group, the Lake Erie Women's Auxiliary, was formed in 1977. The group eventually admitted the daughters of members into the group and its membership grew to 70 in 2004. In that year, some of the old issues again came to a head, and more than half the auxiliary's members left to form an independent organization. Since then, the Lake Erie Women's Auxiliary has reorganized, increased its membership to 50, and continued to assist the men's group in organizing installation banquets, big-band nights, and family and children's programs. The women run a series of raffles to raise money for the LEIC hall, the Our Lady of

Victory Infant Home, and the YMCA. One of the group's creative fund-raising projects is selling baked goods on election day at the LEIC building, a voting site. Members take trips to casinos, and their monthly meetings include a social hour and bingo. The women who left the auxiliary in 2004 founded the New Beginnings Italian Group, which has grown to 80 members, most of them postwar immigrants and second-generation Italian Americans, plus a number of non – Italians. The club has a full slate of officers and each year sponsors a family picnic, bocce matches, a St. Joseph's table, and a Befana party at Christmas. Members take trips to other cities and raise funds for cancer research, children's programs, women's shelters, and area food pantries.[49]

A handful of Lackawanna's Italian organizations still function, but over the past half-century, many Italian societies have folded. The most recent loss was the Sacred Heart Society at St. Anthony's Church, whose members had been meeting only annually before the group was disbanded in January 2008. The society had been unable to attract younger members   a problem for Italian societies for many decades. Likewise, the Roman Independent Club and the Marchegiani Men's Club went out of existence in the 1940s due to their inability to draw in second-generation members. The Stags Club, which never tried to recruit members from the third generation, and the Roland Italian American Lodge both disbanded in the early 1960s as their second-generation members aged and membership numbers fell. The Milano Athletic Club, founded in 1930, broke up within the decade as men moved on to other teams or

HAPPY 25TH ANNIVERSARY
CORO ITALIANO
2007

A portrait taken to commemorate the 25th anniversary of the Coro Italiano (Italian Chorus) of the Lake Erie Italian Club in 2007. Seated, from left to right, are: Diana Santarelli, Chris Coviello, Delia Iannarelli, Guy Iannarelli, Phyllis Russo, Anita Marrocco, Rita Violanti. Standing: Barbara Russo, Carmela Monaco, Tony Monaco, Clara Masella, Antoinette Monaco, Aldo Monaco, Mary Carmella Marsillo, Victor Santarelli, Marge Ziccarelli, Angelo DeGiuli, Teresa DeGiuli, Tina Liberta, Michelina Palmeri, John Tiberio, Ida Liberta, Margaret Battista. Photo source: Guy Iannarelli

The Senior Italian Dance Group (under the auspices of the Lake Erie Italian Club) shortly after its inception in 1985. First row kneeling, left to right, are: Jamie Macri, Diana DiBacco, Cathy; Butera. Second row: Maria Riccardi, Rosanne Carroccia, Rosemarie Alimonti, Dawn Guz, Debbie Alimonti, Rita Iannarelli. Third row: Diana Monaco, James Butera, Maryanne Monaco, Russell Carroccia, Gemma DiCristofero, Nora Canestrari, Marie Palante, John Andreff, dance instructor. Fourth row: Maria Tiberio, Jenelle Marchese. Photo source: Lake Erie Italian Club

Veteran members talking at the Lake Erie Italian Club, 2005. From left: Jerry DePasquale, Lou Colello, Frank Cuomo, and Sam Angrisano. All except Cuomo were past presidents of the club. Photo source: Lake Erie Italian Club

In 1960, on the 50th anniversary of the founding of the Lake Erie Italian Club, two of the club's founders are honored by its officers and Lackawanna's mayor. Seated at the table, from left, are: Ed Pacillo, Bing Colello, Mayor John Ogarek, Serafino Mattucci (a founding member), Angelo Croce (a founding member), and Nunze Oddy. In the second row are: Charley Conti, Bill Monaco, Frank Cuomo, John Mecca, Nick DelBello, Charles Fistola, Mike Morgan, Clyde Capasso, Mike Giordano, Ralph Fiore, Aldo Canestrari, Sam Angrisano. In the third row are: Louis Corsi, Angelo Sperduto, Alex Nigro, Mike Militello, Sam Butera. Photo source: Lake Erie Italian Club

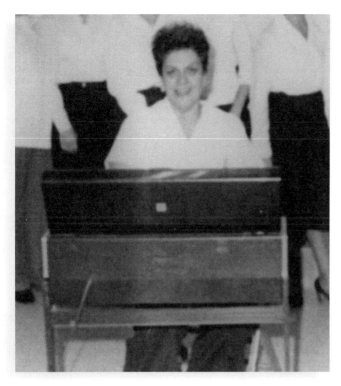

Rose Marchese at the keyboard, 1982. Following her two years as director of the Coro Italiano, *Guy Iannarelli assumed the director's role.* Photo source: Guy Iannarelli

A Coro Italiano *performance featuring Frankie Reino on accordion. Delia Iannarelli, a chorus member is on the right.* Photo source: Guy Iannarelli

New York Supreme Court Justice Michael Catalano, speaker at the 1958 Lake Erie Italian Club (LEIC) banquet, left, is presented a gavel by Aldo Canestrari, at right. Second from left is Nick Sperduto, and second from right is president of the LEIC, Ed Pacillo.
Photo source: Lake Erie Italian Club

The Junior Italian Dance Group of the Lake Erie Italian Club in March 1982. Bottom row, from left to right, are: Amy Claroni, Tommy Nicometo, Lia DiBacco. Second row: Nicole Pacillo, Jamie Macri, Dina Claroni. Third row: Tony Nicometo, James Butera, Russell Carroccia, Joey Butera. Photo source: Guy Iannarelli

The Lake Erie Italian Club in recent years has added a picnic shelter, left, and a food and beverage pavilion, right, in the large lot behind its clubhouse. Photo source: Mike and Julie Andreozzi

married. The club's early members had reunions until 1978, when 15 of them gathered.[50]

Some of the 13 surviving Lackawanna societies have become less Italian in membership and more broadly inclusive of other ethnic groups—so much so that Italians are now a minority in the Roland Wildcats. The Galanti Athletic Association, the Vagabonds, and the Wildcats have experienced a decline in membership and sporting activities as their members age. The Vagabond Athletic & Social Club members, about 80 members strong in 1950, dropped to 45 members in the late 1950s and even lower 10 years later when there were fewer activities. Today, the 20 aging members, half of whom are Italian, socialize monthly, but no longer partake in sports activities. The Roland Wildcats—now 50 in number, about one-third Italian—is predominantly a social club that has monthly meetings and allows members open access to their clubhouse and bar on Milnor Avenue. The club also sponsors a bowling group that includes many nonmembers. The Galanti Athletic Association has 50 members, of whom about 30 are Italian American. The group's activities include a yearly children's party, the annual presentation of the Leo Joyce Memorial Award to the city's best athlete, and bowling outings that include an ongoing match against a team from the Lake Erie Italian Club. Since the 1998 merger of the St. Anthony's parish and the largely Hispanic Queen of All Saints parish, the Holy Name Society now has a multicultural membership of 25 men; a little more than half are Italian Americans, the rest Latino Americans. The Rosary Altar Society currently has 20 members, most of them Italian, who meet monthly.[51]

Two of the cultural groups nurtured by the Lake Erie Italian Club, the *Coro Italiano* and the Junior Italian Dance Group, remain active today. Among the 20 youngsters in the dance group, only seven have Italian roots, and these individuals are of mixed ethnic heritage. These two groups have participated

Board member Fred Palumbo, left, and recording secretary Lou Mustillo at January 2009 meeting of the Lake Erie Italian Club. Photo source: John Marchinda

in the South Park Italian Festival, an annual event that began in 2005. LEIC board chairman Rich Angrisano was on the planning committee for the 2008 festival. The junior dancers have also appeared at the annual Italian American Festival held on Hertel Avenue, which has become Buffalo's new Little Italy. Postwar immigrants and their children in the St. Anna Cantalupo Club continue holding their annual religious *festa*. The 30 members of the Lackawanna Recreation Bocce League now carry on the 50-year tradition of bocce matches at the Pappy Amadori Memorial Courts in Bethlehem Park. Leagues are organized each summer, and informal matches are held in the winter, with men and women from other Italian groups taking part. The Lake Erie Italian Club has given more impetus to the game by erecting outdoor bocce courts, well used during the summer, at its clubhouse. Italian Americans at the Lackawanna Senior Center organize mixed-doubles bocce games for men and women every summer at the Martin Road facility.[52]

The Lake Erie Italian Club continues to prosper, and about a third of its members are third- or fourth-generation Italian

FIGURE 10.15

LAKE ERIE ITALIAN CLUB

A 1950s banquet of the Lake Erie Italian Club. Seated on the left, from foreground to rear, are [Unk], Mike Giordano, Antonio Giordano, Ripalda Giordano. On the right, from foreground to rear, are: Flora Paolini-Olivieri, Patsy Olivieri, Joe Milano, Carmen Corvigno, Anne Melillo-Corvigno, Florence Giordano-Butera, Sam Butera.
Photo source: Lake Erie Italian Club

Umberto Giannotti was the principal architect behind the founding of the Lake Erie Cooperative Society of Mutual Aid, as it was originally called. Joe Milano remembers Giannotti as "an aggressive fellow who wanted the Italians to stick together." As noted earlier, a tragic death provided the impetus for the society's formation. Giannotti gathered 23 Italian immigrants at Serafino Mattucci's saloon on Ingham Avenue in 1910 to discuss the founding of a mutual aid society but one that also served a social function. In his account of the first meeting, Tony Grasso writes: "A heated discussion ensued among the group; some wanted a social club, a place where they could get together and have a good time." The name was the main obstacle to be surmounted. After reviewing

many suggestions, the group settled on a name based on the function and location of the organization—providing mutual aid—and the proximity to Lake Erie. The logo of two hands grasping in friendship and unity was adopted, and Lackawanna's first Italian American organization came into being. The society has been Lackawanna's oldest and most enduring Italian American organization.

The group's first official meeting took place on July 8, 1910, and its incorporation papers were completed on September 26, 1910. The society's stated goals were the social improvement of its members, the promotion of social activities, and encouraging fraternity and mutual activities among Italians in the Steel City and the nearby vicinity.

The first slate of officers, elected in 1910, included:

President: Umberto Giannotti
Vice President: Antonio Grossi
Secretary: Carminantonio
                Picariello
Treasurer: Serafino Mattucci
Trustees: Gaetano Milano
                Antonio DelGuercio
                Cesidio Fistola
Counselors: Angelo Sperduto
                Domenico Aloisio
                Carmine Spagnolo
                Paolo Zucca (Zaccarine)

The club extended sickness-and-death benefits to its members and their families, offering some security during an era when insurance was basically unavailable to working people. By January 1917, the

Lake Erie Italian Club *(continued)*

membership stood at 79. That year, the group opened a cooperative grocery store on Ingham Avenue, but it functioned for only a short period. In 1920, the members themselves built a meeting hall on Ingham Avenue. They later repaired it after a windstorm, but eventually sold it and returned to St. Anthony's Church.

Throughout its long life, the Lake Erie Italian Club (LEIC) has maintained a high profile in Lackawanna. During World War I, the membership marched in patriotic parades, and in 1919, members and their wives constituted the Italian contingent in the city's League of Nations Pageant. By the 1920s, the group was sponsoring an annual picnic, and the 1933 event held on the St. Anthony's Church grounds was reported by the *Lackawanna Herald* as "one of the largest events in the organization's history." Festivities included a raffle, with first prize being a lamb and second, a dozen spring chickens. To celebrate its 26th anniversary in 1936, the club had a parade that started at Italian Hall on Elm Street, marched up Ingham Avenue and along Ridge Road, then back down to the Dona Street soccer field. The members, in club uniform, were accompanied by Messori's Band and several other Italian groups from Lackawanna. At the soccer field, participants were treated to a picnic with a program of sports and entertainment. A couple years later, the club organized an annual carnival that served as its chief fund-raiser from 1938 until 1944.

With more second-generation members on the LEIC roster in the 1940s, social events became numerous. The Columbus Day dance held at Memorial Hall in October 1941 featured the music of Bob Armstrong's NBC Orchestra for a 50-cent admission fee.

Celebration of the Diamond Jubilee of Lackawanna's founding, 1984. The float of the Lake Erie Italian Club in the parade moving west on Ridge Road past the Our Lady of Victory institutions. On the back of the float are members of the Junior Italian Dance Group. Photo source: Lake Erie Italian Club

When the Diamond Jubilee parade periodically came to a stop, the junior dancers did a quick tarantella on Ridge Road. Photo source: Lake Erie Italian Club

Men of the Lake Erie Italian Club and women of the club's auxiliary march in the parade behind the club's banner. Photo source: Lake Erie Italian Club

While meetings had been conducted in Italian up to this point, some of the second-generation members were limited in their command of the Italian language or preferred to speak English. This, plus the Americanization pressures of World War II, resulted in a compromise: the club's secretary, Louie Petrucci, read the minutes of the previous meeting aloud in both English and Italian. Prior to 1941, all chief officers of the LEIC had been immigrants. That year, American-born Charles Nigro became the club's vice president and, the following year, its president. Armondo Pietrocarlo, who immigrated to America as a young boy, became president when Antonio Amorosi died in 1944. Within two years, four of the club's top six officers were second-generation men. Costantino Novelli, president for four years during the 1950s, was the last immigrant to hold this office in the twentieth century. In that decade, as the second generation swelled the LEIC ranks and rose to its top offices, English became the language spoken at meetings and used to record the minutes.

In 1942, the LEIC purchased Eugenio Galanti's brick building on Hamburg Turnpike, at the corner of Dona Street. The building was remodeled and a 30-foot bar installed. Judge Buscaglia of Buffalo spoke at the inauguration dinner for the new clubhouse, an event also attended by Lackawanna city officials and civic leaders. With its own hall, the club increased its activities, holding Christmas and New Year's Eve parties, and the LEIC membership quickly grew to 240. The club organized a bowling league that often held tournaments at Floss Palace Bowling Alleys in Buffalo, owned by Armondo Pietrocarlo and Christy Monaco. In 1950, the club's building was purchased by the state for the widening of Hamburg Turnpike, and the LEIC once again returned to St. Anthony's

for its meetings. The move did not, however, slow down the organizations activities or growth. In 1950, it sponsored a baseball team, which was managed by Anthony DePasquale. Soon thereafter, it began holding an annual basket picnic for members and their families as well as annual installation banquets for newly elected officers. By 1957, the membership roster had grown to 450.

In 1965, the LEIC acquired a new clubhouse—on Fisher Road, in neighboring West Seneca—where it held picnics and

clambakes. A fire destroyed that facility in 1973. Three years later, the society purchased the building formerly occupied by Kinney Shoes at 3200 South Park Avenue. The building has been renovated and expanded—bocce courts, a pavilion, and a picnic shelter constructed out back—and a stone monument bearing the likeness of Columbus was installed on the front lawn. The renovated facility remains the center of the club's activities. Though club membership declined as the immigrant generation passed on, during the later

The 2008 officers of the Lake Erie Italian Club. From left are: Ned DiPasquale, financial secretary; Rich Angrisano, treasurer; Phil Fanone, Joe DiStefano, sergeant-at-arms; Vince Morga, president; Dean Ziccarelli, vice president; Lou Mustillo (seated), recording secretary; Tony Masella, hall manager.
Photo source: Lake Erie Italian Club

The 2008 board members of the Lake Erie Italian Club. From left are: Louie Petrucci, Louie Pacifico, Joe Gangarosa, Fred Palumbo, Guy Iannarelli, Peter Vince, Tony Nicometo, John Mariano. Photo source: Lake Erie Italian Club

2007, in front of the Lake Erie Italian Club. Rev. Peter Drilling, former pastor of St. Anthony's Church, blesses the monument to deceased members as well as the Columbus monument. Earlier, the priest celebrated Mass inside the hall to honor the club's deceased members. Photo source: Lake Erie Italian Club

decades of the twentieth century it usually ranged from 200 to 300 members.

In 1977, the LEIC began sponsoring the annual Lake Erie Italian Open Golf Tourney and also started weekly bingo games. The club has used the proceeds from both activities to award scholarships to students and to support a host of other charitable causes. In the early and mid-1980s the club launched three cultural groups: the *Coro Italiano* (Italian Chorus), the Junior Italian Dance Group, and the Senior Italian Dance Group. In Lackawanna's 1984 Diamond Jubilee parade, the LEIC entered a float and a contingent of marchers, and the Junior Italian Dance Group performed along the route. The three groups have performed

at many cultural events since that time.

The Lake Erie Italian Club's expanded building, which includes several meeting rooms and a banquet hall, has functioned for three decades as a gathering place for the Italian American community. Ongoing activities include bocce tournaments, raffles, excursions, wine-making contests, pancake breakfasts, dinners, dances, and band concerts. Each year, the club sponsors a Christmas party for handicapped children, another for the members' children, a New Year's Eve party, an installation banquet for officers, an Italian Night, and a Mass and breakfast in honor of deceased members. The club's 2006 calendar listed 28 events and activities. Members also meet informally at the hall;

a common scenario involves several dozen men gathering around the television to watch Monday-night football and share a potluck dinner. The current membership includes 45 immigrants, many men of the second generation, and a significant number of third- and fourth-generation Italian American men, which bodes well for the club's future.

The club's presidents during the past 99 years have often been prominent individuals in the Italian community. These men are listed next with information on their generation, regional roots in Italy, and years in the office.

President	Generation	Regional Roots	Years in Office
Umberto Giannotti	1st	Toscana	1910-12
Carminantonio Picariello	1st	Campania	1913
Domenico Aloisi	1st	[Unk]	1914
Serafino Mattucci	1st	Abruzzo	1915, 1916, 1918
Antonio Amorosi	1st	Campania	1917, 1919, 1920, 1922-30, 1932-33, 1936-37, 1940, 1944
Antonio Turchiarelli	1st	Puglia	1921
Angelo Carlini	1st	Lazio	1931

President	Generation	Regional Roots	Years in Office
Ettore Spadoni	1st	Marche	1934
Vincenzo Suffoletto	1st	Abruzzo	1935
Arcangelo Cervoni	1st	Lazio	1938-39
Erasmo Colello	1st	Lazio	1941
Celestino Nigro	2nd	Puglia	1942-43, 1948-49, 1951, 1955-56
Armondo Pietrocarlo	2nd	Lazio	1944
Santo Bonitatibus	1st	Abruzzo	1945
Anthony DePasquale	2nd	Abruzzo	1946
Frank Amorosi	2nd	Campania	1947
Charles Nicometo	2nd	Sicilia	1947
Ralph Fiore	2nd	Molise, Lazio	1950
Costantino Novelli	1st	Abruzzo	1952, 1953, 1954, 1959
Edmund Pacillo	2nd	Campania	1954, 1957-58, 1960-63
Charles Fistola	2nd	Abruzzo	1964-65
Sam Angrisano	2nd	Basilicata	1966-68, 1979-80, 1996-98
Larry Colello	2nd	Lazio	1969-78, 1987-90
Aldo Canestrari	2nd	Marche	1981-82, 1985
Al Billi	3rd	Sicilia, Abruzzo	1983-84
Lou Colello	2nd	Lazio	1986
Angelo Bellittiere	2nd	Sicilia	1991
Jerry DePasquale	3rd	Abruzzo	1992-95
Joe Carnevale	2nd	Lazio	1999-2004
Tony Angrisano	3rd	Basilicata, Puglia	2005
Paul Fino	3rd	Sicilia	2005-07
Vince Morga	1st	Lazio	2007-08
Dean Ziccarelli	3rd	Calabria, Abruzzo	2009

Most of the club's current members live in Lackawanna and nearby towns, but many are scattered throughout western New York. As of July 2007, the residences of the 294 LEIC members were as follows:

Lackawanna	89
Adjacent towns and cities (Buffalo, Blasdell, West Seneca, Orchard Park, Hamburg)	141
Other towns in western New York	58
States other than New York	6

Sources: Interviews with Joe Milano, April 20, 1979, July 12, 1996; Nunze Oddy, April 12, 1982; Louie Petrucci, December 27, 1984; and Ernie Leonetti, December 17, 2005; group interview with Vince Morga, Paul Fino, Guy Iannarelli, Rich Angrisano, Pete Marrocco, Matteo Sassarelli, Joe Pallante, and Tony Monaco, November 22, 2006; Tony Grasso, "Bridging the Bitter Years," October 1984; Erie County Courthouse, incorporation papers, Lake Erie Co-operative Society of Lackawanna, N.Y., 9/29/10; *Lake Erie Co-operative Society, 50th Anniversary, 1910 – 1960*, souvenir booklet; 4/30/60, "Lake Erie Italian Club Banquet," brochure; 3/6/99, Lake Erie Italian Club, meeting minutes, 1910, 1/15/17, 8/19/20, 6/13/33, 6/3/36, 6/3/42; "Lake Erie General Membership," 7/11/2007; Community Service Commission, Lackawanna, N.Y., "League of Nations Pageant, Official Souvenir Program, Labor Day 1919"; *Lackawanna News*, 8/20/28; *Lackawanna Herald*, 8/17/33; *Steel City Press*, 1/7/48; *Lackawanna Leader*, 6/18/36, 7/20/39, 7/17/41, 10/2/41, 6/11/42, 6/8/44, 4/13/50, 5/22/52, 12/12/57, 6/29/67, 8/17/67, 2/15/73; *Front Page*, 8/5/92, 8/23/2000, 11/2/2000, 9/25/2002, 1/31/2007.

The bingo workers of the Lake Erie Italian Club, 2008. First row, seated, from left to right, are: Clyde Capasso, Vince Morga, Guy Iannarelli, Louie Lorenzetti, Alex Coviello, Larry Riccardi, Dean Ziccarelli. Second row: Peter Vinci, Tony LaForte, Vittorio Santarelli, Egino DeSantis, Phil Fanone, Ralph Pallante, Carlo Savaglio. Third row: John Marchinda, Jim Alimonti, Guy Godios, Ron DiCioccio, Tony Monaco, Norm Lucarelli, Louie Pacifico, Frank Carroccia, Pete Marrocco, Larry Schiavi.
Photo source: Lake Erie Italian Club

January 7, 2009. New board members being sworn in at monthly meeting of the Lake Erie Italian Club. From left are: Peter Vinci, Dominic Vicaretti, Joe Cino, Fred Palumbo, Lou Pacifico, and Lou Petrucci, Jr. Photo source: John Marchinda

Installation banquet for new officers, April 12, 2009, showing interior of the clubhouse of the Lake Erie Italian Club.
Photo source: Lake Erie Italian Club

April 12, 2009, installation dinner for new officers. Vince Morga, president, in 2008, congratulates the newly elected 2009 president, Dean Ziccarelli.
Photo source: Lake Erie Italian Club

Lake Erie Italian Club scholarship winners, 2008. From left are: Sean Hasset, West Seneca West High School; Nicolette Liberta, Hamburg High School; Steven Marrocco, St. Francis High School; Pete Marrocco, chairman of the LEIC Bingo Committee, which raises funds for the club's scholarships and other worthy causes.
Photo source: Lake Erie Italian Club

Americans. Although several other Italian societies have brought in some younger members, most groups seem to be declining, drawing fewer members of the younger generations than needed to survive. While few statistics are available, it appears that most grandchildren and great-grandchildren of Italian immigrants do not participate in Italian organizations. Today's young people are more likely to enroll in health clubs and social, recreational, and civic organizations with no ethnic ties. The increasing number of intermarriages between ethnic groups over the past four decades has blurred ethnic lines, serving to undermine a once strong sense of ethnic identity. Further, as a rust-belt city, Lackawanna has lost almost half its population as families move elsewhere in search of jobs. Whereas immigration from Italy helped to rejuvenate the city's Italian organizations in the past, it has all but disappeared during the last three decades. One source of membership for the Lackawanna Recreation Bocce League and the Lake Erie Italian Club has been second- and third-generation Italian Americans from Buffalo and nearby suburbs who do not have Italian organizations in their own communities.[53]

Many members of the contemporary Italian organizations are aging, postwar immigrants or second-generation men and women. It is likely that more Italian groups in Lackawanna will disband and that those that do continue will have a more multiethnic membership and character. However, the Lake Erie Italian Club, with its hall and expanded facilities, appears geared to prosper and to continue to draw many members from outside of Lackawanna. The city's current 13 Italian organizations have a combined membership of about 700, with at least 115 of these individuals not of Italian lineage. Since many of these individuals belong to more than one organization, the actual number of Italian Americans involved is more in the range of 300 to 450. Perhaps half of these Italian Americans actually live in Lackawanna, but judging from the Lake Erie Italian Club's membership, most live in adjacent towns and cities. The Italian groups, plus the nonmembers who annually attend the St. Anna Cantalupo *festa* and the annual picnic for people with roots in Giuliano di Roma, reflect the rich variety of societies created by the Italian American community over the past century. These organizations and their events and activities help maintain Italian ethnicity and a sense of community in a rust-belt city that is rapidly declining in population. When asked why they stay involved in the Lake Erie Italian Club, Pete Marrocco responded, "pride in our ethnic history," and Vince Morga, likely speaking for many LEIC members, past and present, said, "We are family here."[54]

Some members and officers of the Roland Wildcats, 2008. Seated, from left, are: Dan Welsh, vice president; Ben Falbo, president; and Chris Monaco, member. Standing: Al Monaco, board of directors member; Randy Evans, sergeant-at-arms; Vince Cala, treasurer and board of directors member; Patrick Welsh, member; Hank Klubek, financial secretary. The Wildcats still meet in the clubhouse they built in 1950. Photo source: Ben Falbo

The St. Anthony Holy Name Society, 2008. Seated from left, are: Fred Bauer, Angel Torres, Tito Paolini, Rev. Henry Orzulak. Standing: Vince Morga, Frank Nowak, Don Grosso, Jerry Borgogelli, Marino Chini, Carlo Savaglio, Iano Clarone, Joe Schiavi. Photo source: Vince Morga

Officers of the New Beginnings Italian Group, the newest Italian American society in Lackawanna, August 2008. Standing, from left, are: Mary Ann Notto, Chris Coviello, Anita Marrocco. Seated are Viola Syta, Pat Billi, Rose Anticoli-Wagner. Photo source: Mary Ann Notto

Some members of the New Beginnings Italian Group, August 2008. Right hand row, from foreground to rear, are: Viola Syta, Viola Liberta, Maria Carducci, Carmela Monaco, Teresa DeGiuli, Margaret Battista. Left row, foreground to rear: Kathy Vaughn, Toni Smolkovich, Delia Iannarelli, Mirella Ventre, Ann Schieda. Photo source: Mary Ann Notto

People with roots in Giuliano di Roma at the 1987 reunion picnic. The event is still held every year at Evangola State Park, south of Lackawanna, on the shores of Lake Erie. Photo source: Collection of Lelio DeSantis

The 2008 bowling tournament between the Galanti Athletic Association (GAA) and the Lake Erie Italian Club (LEIC). Kneeling, from left to right, are: Dom Vicaretti (LEIC), Joe Calderon (GAA), Darryl Ziccarelli (LEIC), Jim Ziccarelli (LEIC). Standing are: Vince Morga (LEIC president), Mike Mrak (GAA president), Dennis Ziccarelli (LEIC), Chris Grzbowski (GAA), Joe DiStefano Jr. (GAA), Mark Smith (owner of bowling alley), Gene Olivieri Jr. (GAA), infant Tessa Olivieri (GAA), Dave Olivieri (GAA), Brandon Ziccarelli (LEIC), Bill Crappo (GAA), Dave Szpara (GAA), Brian Grzbowski (GAA). Photo source: Vince Morga

SOCIETA' CO-OPERATIVA LAKE ERIE
DI MUTUO SOCCORSO -- LACKAWANNA, N. Y.

Ottobre 7.   1942

Received from _Oddi Nunzi_ $25⁰⁰

Venticinque   Dollars

for which the SOCIETA' CO-OPERATIVA LAKE ERIE agrees to pay three per cent (3%) annually for the use of the above amount. Verification of this transaction must be signed by the following officals, viz:

Charles Nigro
President

James D'Alessandro
Treasurer

Antonio Amorosi
Vice-President

_____
Recording Secretary

(NOT TRANSFERABLE OR NEGOTIABLE)   32

To raise funds, the Lake Erie Italian Club sometimes sold promissory notes to its members. Nunze Oddy purchased this $25 note in 1942; it yielded annual interest of 3%. Photo source: Collection of Nunze Oddy

CHAPTER 11

POLITICS

National newspaper columnist and radio commentator Walter Winchell, when interviewing James Farley in the 1930s, asked the national Democratic Party chair: "What would you tell an aspiring young politician?" Two versions of Farley's response are now Lackawanna legend: "I would send him to Lackawanna to get basic schooling," or "I'd rather be the mayor of Lackawanna than the president of the United States."[1]

Lackawanna has an interesting and colorful political history, as suggested by Democratic Party Chair Farley's comments some seven decades ago. As earlier chapters have conveyed, the small section of mostly rural land along Lake Erie was transformed between 1900 and 1909 into a crowded city centered around a huge steel plant. Populated by immigrants and migrants of 92 ethnic groups struggling to accommodate each other and acclimate to mainstream American culture, the new city drew a variety of speculators and entrepreneurs. The mix included wealthy investors in the steel plant, small-business people, realtors catering to the needs of immigrant steelworkers, and criminals providing illegal activities such as gambling and prostitution. A was the case in many American cities of the time, Lackawanna's political system reflected all these factions and had its share of political bosses, ward politics, and corruption. As a company town dominated by the Lackawanna Steel Company, which later became part of Bethlehem Steel, it was the scene of significant labor strife, as steelworkers battled for the right to form a union. The Italian immigrants who entered this setting as rural agricultural laborers were transformed into industrial workers forced to learn the rules of urban, ethnic politics. They and their children formed one of the city's largest ethnic groups and gradually acquired political power.

A City is Born

Even before its construction began in 1900, the steel plant was the major player on Lackawanna's political scene. Lackawanna Steel Company had major financial and political backers in Buffalo, such as John Milburn and John Albright, who acquired lakefront land cheaply or persuaded governments to donate it. This rural area of West Seneca, called Limestone Hill, was quickly populated as the steel-plant construction began. A Buffalo newspaper reported in 1902 that "there are now about 2,000 more people living [sic] than a year ago, and from day to day the demand for homes increases." By July of that year, a movement had begun to incorporate a self-governing village east of the steel plant as far as Abbott Road. The following January, it was reported that the settlement's population had grown to 6,000 or 7,000 and that its residents opposed being annexed by the City of Buffalo. That same month, Assemblyman Burke, representing this area, drew up a "new bill to create Lackawanna city, which will provide for

< Incoming and outgoing members of the Lackawanna City Council following the election in November 1957. In the lower row are the newly elected councilmen, from left to right: Aldo Filipetti of the 1st Ward, Walter Seres of the Second Ward, and Edward Drozdowski of the Third Ward. The outgoing councilmen, in the upper row, are: Joe Amorosi of the 1st Ward, Leo Kaczor of the 2nd Ward, Bill Delmont of the 3rd Ward, and Walter Tomjanovich of the 4th Ward. Not included in the photo are outgoing mayor Chester Struski, and incoming mayor John Ogarek and 4th Ward councilman Paul Jagiello. Photo source: Aldo Filipetti

five wards, three Democratic and two Republican." The West Seneca Taxpayers and Businessmen's Association drafted a charter for the new city, alternately referred to as "Little Scranton" and "Lackawanna." However, steel-plant spokesman John Milburn stated that it was too early to incorporate. In 1904, John Albright said the steel plant "wouldn't object to being a part of Buffalo, but opposes to incorporate a new city." This may have been a delaying tactic, or the company may have reasoned that its powerful patrons in Buffalo could ensure a favorable tax rate, plus Buffalo's large police force would be an asset in case of labor strife.[2]

At a 1904 state assembly hearing on incorporation, it was noted that Lackawanna Steel was markedly underassessed; the valuation of $2,150,000 should have been more like $5,000,000. While the company had political cronies in West Seneca, it feared that the incorporation of a new city was an untested situation that could undermine its privileged position. West Seneca town officials and steel-plant attorneys led the movement to kill the legislation to incorporate Limestone Hill as a city. The local Democratic Party—composed largely of American-born, skilled workers—was very pro-company, according to historian William Scheuerman. The skilled workers were paid on a sliding scale, based on the market value of the steel they produced. This link between wages and corporate profitability created a common interest between management and skilled workers. The political power of local Democrats was enhanced by a state law allowing voters in unincorporated towns to register without showing up in person. "Local Republicans, who constantly accused the Democrats of registering illegal voters from Pennsylvania, sought to end this practice by incorporating the steel district into a city," Scheuerman said.[3]

Underassessment of the steel plant meant that West Seneca did not have the revenue to pave streets or provide adequate sewers in the new district along the lake, and political leaders seemed to concentrate resources in other areas of town. "The district we want incorporated as a city pays 80 per cent of the taxes of the township, but it doesn't get the benefit of more than 50 per cent," said a supporter of incorporation. This agitated residents, including Italians, who had endured outbreaks of typhoid fever and other diseases. Many people in the thickly populated area adjacent to the steel plant, especially small-business owners, continued to press for incorporation. By 1904, a group of businesspeople signed a petition for incorporation, and their leader, tavern owner Michael Joyce, accused the West Seneca town board and the steel plant of being in complicity to deny services to small businesses, despite the significant taxes paid by this group. The issue of assessing the true value of the Lackawanna Steel plant continually arose. In 1908, when the West Seneca assessors suggested that the steel plant's assessment

be increased from $3,200,000 to $4,700,000, there was such a strong protest from the steel plant and many prominent citizens that the assessors let the $3,200,000 figure stand. The struggle to incorporate the steel-plant district went on until 1909, when a West Seneca town supervisor was imprisoned for misuse of public funds, and the Democratic Party and Lackawanna Steel Company acquiesced to public pressure.[4]

With the incorporation imminent, Lackawanna Steel attempted to assert influence over the structure of the new city. The original charter of the City of Lackawanna was written by company lawyers. Members of the pro-company Democratic Party captured public office, and company officials held key positions. Michael O'Mara, one of the West Seneca assessors who had undervalued the steel-plant holdings, became city treasurer, and John Monaghan, one of the three tax assessors. By maintaining the low assessment of the steel plant, the officials of the new city reduced the amount of revenue that could be used to make the public-service improvements citizens had long demanded. Thus, the tone was set for combative city politics for many decades to follow. The steel plant, whether owned by the Lackawanna Steel Company or Bethlehem Steel Corporation, played a critical role in the political and civic life of the city. Questions regarding the steel plant's assessed value and its tax liability remained issues of contention throughout the twentieth century.

Popular stories among western New Yorkers and in the media, including comments from interviews by nationally known commentators such as Walter Winchell, suggest that Lackawanna politics during much of the twentieth century were more corrupt than those of other American cities. While these claims may be exaggerated, a combination of factors did make Lackawanna's political life unique during most of the twentieth century. The city has always been a small one, with a population that never exceeded 30,000 and a land area of roughly five square miles. Yet, great wealth was centered along its two miles of lakefront. The huge steel plant provided millions of dollars in property taxes to the city, despite assessments that were often too low. According to some estimates, the steel plant paid 60-70% of the taxes collected by the city. Thus, local politicians had access to large numbers of tax dollars to spend on all sorts of public projects that were contracted out, with kickbacks often expected from those winning the bids. Lackawanna politicians also got away with creating nonessential city jobs to reward supporters; in some cases, the employees didn't even have to show up for work.

The steel plant provided another source of political capital: its large workforce, which peaked at 21,500 in the 1960s, and included most of Lackawanna's working men as well as others from throughout western New York. The plant's large number of jobs gave city politicians who struck deals with steel executives a second source of employment to hand out to supporters. It was common practice for city employees and politicians to hold second, paid jobs in the steel plant. Politicians found lucrative positions for people who backed their election campaigns and also lined up steelworker jobs for other Lackawannans as a means of cultivating support. The combination of plentiful jobs and a relatively small population meant that many Lackawannans could look forward to receiving patronage jobs and other rewards from the political system. This scenario created a strong incentive for residents to be actively involved in the political process.

In 1941, 83% of the 12,010 eligible voters in Lackawanna actually took part in that year's elections; by comparison, only 55% of Buffalo voters went to the polls. The 1953 showing was even more impressive; 92% of Steel City's voters went to the polls. Lackawannans knew that jobs and careers were at stake come election time. The votes of even one extended family were important, and politicians cleverly utilized and rewarded the ethnic, familial, and neighborhood ties present in Lackawanna. Political activists took note of who put up lawn signs or passed out flyers for opponents; one could lose a city job if a relative publicly backed the wrong candidate. After lining someone up with a city job, some politicians expected an envelope filled with money, while others demanded an ongoing portion, up to 50%, of the employee's weekly paycheck. During the Depression, one Italian committeeman was said to collect 50 cents per week from each man he had helped to get a job. In more recent decades, newly elected officials or city jobholders were expected to donate the equivalent of 10% of their annual salary to the coffers of the political party that supported them or to buy expensive tickets for party fund-raisers. The unusually large number of city jobs was noticeable early in the city's history. In 1922, the *Buffalo Evening News* said of Lackawanna that "the civil list is high for a third class city," pointing out that city workers got $3 per day, comparatively high pay.[5]

The concentration of working men—city residents and nonresidents, in the city seven days a week, 24 hours per day—was another factor that gave rise to the accumulation of money in Lackawanna. After long shifts of hard and dangerous work in the mills, many men needed to unwind. These factors made Lackawanna a natural for all sorts of entertainment and recreation, both legal and illegal. In 1904, there were 80 saloons in the area that became the First Ward, and by 1917, the entire city had 139 bars. Gambling was available via racetrack betting, numbers, pinball, and slot machines, and five to nine houses of prostitution were typically open for business in the First Ward. The plentiful nightclubs, restaurants, small hotels, and rooming houses dovetailed with these activities. During the early decades of the twentieth century, many immigrant men without wives or families to provide companionship turned to these sources for entertainment. The surplus of men in the city, especially in the densely settled First Ward, continued as late as 1940, when males comprised 53% of the city's 24,058 inhabitants.[6]

The speakeasies that emerged during Prohibition were continued after its repeal by people eager to bypass licensing fees and other expenses of legitimate establishments. In November 1941, Lackawanna Police Chief Gilson appointed two detectives to check into complaints of "nearly 200 speakeasies" operating in the city. Seven years later, William Eagan, a Democratic Party spokesman, charged that "vice and gambling are rampant" in the First Ward, noting "speakeasies, policy slip racketeers, and a disorderly house on Wasson Avenue." Other illegal operations flourished east of the railroad tracks. And the number of potential customers continued to grow. Sailors from lake freighters that docked at the steel plant, Hanna Furnace, or on the Buffalo waterfront sought recreation in the Steel City. As the steel plant expanded and other industries moved to Lackawanna or nearby towns, more workers were drawn into the city. The entertainment and recreational activities brought more money to Lackawanna, both to legitimate businesspeople, who purchased city licenses and permits, and to illegal entrepreneurs, who paid off some of the local officials to maintain their trade. At various times, some of the city's police officers, committeemen, councilmen, party bosses, and the mayor were directly involved in the illicit operations. Other officials did not take part, or were excluded because they were at odds with the mayor or party chiefs. The First Ward's underworld included individuals of several ethnic groups, and an Italian American crime syndicate in Buffalo apparently controlled or was heavily involved in, prostitution and gambling.[7]

One other factor fed into Lackawanna's reputation for tarnished politics and illegal activities. The immigrant and second-generation ethnics of Lackawanna started out as humble working-class people. They did not have access to the techniques and institutions that enabled "respectable" folks to be discreet about their questionable enterprises and political corruption. In the often gruff ward politics of Lackawanna, little pretense was made to maintain good public relations. Money, jobs, and political opportunities were there to be seized, and poor or working-class people often did so in an unprotected, unvarnished manner that quickly drew media attention. Political corruption and vice were present throughout America in the early twentieth century. Buffalo and its other satellite cities were also plagued by these issues. Lackawanna's unique scenario was due to its high concentration of money sources and jobs in such a small city.

Ethnic Politics in Lackawanna

Many of the people who moved from Scranton, Pennsylvania, to Lackawanna were Irish. Lackawanna's Irish community has historically wielded great political clout. Early in the twentieth century, most of the city's elected officials and civil-service workers were from this ethnic group. Having arrived in America before the southern and eastern European immigrants, who composed the majority of Lackawanna's population, the Irish had learned the skills of urban politics. The dominance of Lackawanna's elective offices by Irish Americans began to wane in 1922, however, when eastern Europeans were elected to two of the four councilmen positions. Poles, who made up about half the city's population, demonstrated their political muscle when Polish American Walter J. Lohr was elected mayor of Lackawanna in 1924. Though the Irish then had to share political power, they retained leadership positions in the Democratic Party and maintained a strong influence on Lackawanna politics.

The Steel City's Poles were mainly Republican, while the Irish were solidly Democratic. Groups such as Croatians and Serbians, mostly Democratic, were small in number. The third-largest ethnic group in the city, the Italians, was heavily Democratic with a significant minority of Republicans. It was to the benefit of both the Irish and the Poles to keep the Italians divided, and each group worked at reinforcing the differences that seemed ever-present in the Italian community. As a result, separate factions of Italians—cultivated by the Irish-dominated Democrats and the Polish-dominated Republicans—wrestled over elective and appointed positions. Some Italians, including Giuseppe Pietrocarlo, became Republicans because they felt Irish Democrats treated them with contempt.[8]

Charles Ellis, editor of the *Lackawanna Journal* and then the *Lackawanna Daily Journal*, was an independent voice in the city who continually attacked politicians at city hall and their allies at the steel plant. A former Lackawanna Steel employee, Ellis purchased the *Lackawanna Journal*, the city's official newspaper in 1913. By 1916, his outspoken articles had led the common council to designate a rival paper, the *Lackawanna News*, as the city's official organ. This change initiated a long feud between the publisher and city government. For seven years, Ellis used his newspaper to attack the power of the steel executives and political bosses as well as to advocate for Lackawanna's working-class immigrants. He ran for mayor in 1919, losing in the primary then eagerly supporting Socialist John Gibbons, who was elected in the midst of that year's Great Steel Strike. The political corruption exposed in Ellis's newspaper foreshadowed a number of trends that continued to bedevil the city for decades to come.[9]

Ellis described Harry J. Kelley as "Boss Kelley … Assessor and political boss for the Lackawanna Steel Company." Kelley held one of the city's three assessor positions from 1909 to 1919, serving throughout that time as chairman of the assessors and also as head of the city's Democratic Party. An employee of Lackawanna Steel, Kelley became superintendent of the Rail Mill in 1917 and superintendent of all rolling mills at the company five years later. In his newspaper, Ellis described how Kelley and his fellow assessors continually underassessed the steel plant, noting in 1916 that the Donner Steel plant in Buffalo was assessed at 100% of its value, while Lackawanna Steel was assessed at about 8% of valuation. That same year, Lackawanna Steel and its subsidiary, the Stoney Point Land Company, paid $9,000 less in taxes than in 1915, leaving the total tax load for city homeowners to increase from $21,000 to $31,000. In one article, Ellis vowed that " 'Kelleyism' will be driven from politics."[10]

Ellis put his spotlight on other forms of political wrongdoing and Kelleyism, too. In 1916, when the newly elected city officials appointed three of their fellow Democrats as civil-service commissioners, the *Lackawanna Journal* cried illegal and threatened to take the case to the state. This prompted Kelley to engineer a quick switch; the secretary, a Republican, was made a commissioner, and one of the commissioners was made secretary. Ellis wrote nonstop about how the steel plant got its candidates elected into political office, even quipping that "it would save the taxpayers considerable money if the steel plant were allowed to appoint our city officials." At the time of the 1916 school-board election, he claimed that "the steel plant has 7 men on the school board now, and they want to keep them there." He condemned these men as "carpetbaggers" and "the builder's trust" as he disclosed how the board exaggerated repairs needed at school buildings and rigged a special election to appropriate money for these "repairs". Following the election, grand jury overturned the vote after finding that 158 people had voted illegally. In a subsequent election, the public turned down the appropriation. But not before Ellis put in print what the board did prior to the second election:

> The school board in the meantime had let the contracts to the highest bidder (on a technicality) and they sold bonds to the lowest bidder … The Journal, thru [sic] a New York lawyer and a firm who lost the bonds, secured an injunction restraining the school board from delivering the bonds to the firm they intended to. The firm who were [sic] to get the bonds have their offices in the same building, in New York City, as the Lackawanna Steel Company … Considering that the school board is under the direct control of the Steel Co., you may think as you like, we do not want to offer any thots [sic].

Ellis's articles lambasted the city council for not making its expense vouchers open to the public. He claimed that reported street repairs were not made and that city wagons often collected the garbage, yet the city continued to pay a private contractor hired for garbage collection. He wrote that the city squandered money on dozens of unneeded workers and assistants to office-holders. When a Scranton, Pennsylvania, newspaper exposed election fraud in that city, the former residence of many Lackawannans, Ellis reprinted the article, concluding that "Lackawanna politicians inherit their proclivities."[11]

Prior to the 1919 city elections, in which Ellis was one of four candidates for mayor, the *Lackawanna Journal* listed nine relatives of two-term incumbent John Toomey who held city jobs. The immigrants in the heavily populated First Ward, said Ellis, received few of the city jobs handed out by Toomey and Harry Kelley, describing the latter as "the Steel Plant's political boss." He asserted that Toomey "owes his original election to the mighty Steam Roller of the Steel Plant" and contended that at each election, steelworkers were handed a list of candidates by their boss and told "'vote that ticket or your job will be gone.'" Unfortunately political bossism did not end with Harry Kelley. Michael Mescall, elected Lackawanna mayor in 1921, regularly met with other political power brokers in his First Ward tavern. His son, a political power in later years, held similar meetings. In the 1930s, another Irish American boss, Tom Joyce, had emerged. Joyce taught a generation of Italian and other ethnic politicians all about playing political hardball. And the issues of nepotism, bribery, hiring of unnecessary workers, creation of do-nothing jobs, and falsification of repair-and-construction costs continued for decades.[12]

Pound Keepers, Committeemen, and Assessors

Lackawanna Italians slowly but gradually entered the realm of politics and ranks of elected officials. One way of gaining entry into the political process, they discovered, was to petition the common council to remedy problems. In 1910, Tony Mauriello asked for help preventing his property from flooding, and the following year, for a streetlight near his Steelawanna Avenue store. Other Italians learned the importance of the middleman role and were hired by the city as interpreters between 1910 and 1925. Among them were Joseph DeSantis, John Fadale, Dominic Monaco, Tony Turchiarelli, Tony Mauriello, Mary Yoviene, Frank Deramo, and Patsy Ricci. Josephine Barone, who may have been a nurse, translated at city health clinics in the 1920s. Italian merchants learned that the city bought food for people in need at neighborhood stores, and many Italian grocers were paid by the city to provide this service. By the 1920s, other

FIGURE 11.1

ITALIAN AMERICAN POLITICIANS

Italians have been involved in American politics since the Revolutionary War, when Filippo Mazzei influenced the ideas expressed by Thomas Jefferson in the Declaration of Independence, and William Paca was one of the document's signers. John Phinizy became mayor of Atlanta, Georgia, in 1837. Andrew Longhino was a member of the Mississippi State Senate, then was governor from 1900 to 1904. In New York State, Antonio Rapallo was Justice of the Court of Appeals, and Francis Spinola in 1887 became the first Italian elected to Congress. Three years later, California's Anthony Caminetti became a congressman and in 1913 was appointed commissioner general of immigration. The huge Italian colony in New York City helped elect Fiorello LaGuardia to Congress in 1916, and in 1933, he began the first of his three terms as mayor. In 1926, Baltimore's Vincent Palmisano went to Congress. Within a few years, he was joined by Peter Cavicchia of Newark and Peter Granata of Chicago.

Angelo Rossi became mayor of San Francisco in 1931, and Robert Maestri, mayor of New Orleans in 1936. In Rhode Island, John Pastore was elected governor in 1945; he became the first Italian elected to the U.S. Senate in 1950. Anthony Celebrezze was mayor of Cleveland prior to becoming the first Italian to serve on a president's cabinet; John F. Kennedy named him secretary of health, education, and welfare in 1962.

Lackawanna Italians in the early twentieth century could look to Buffalo for models of successful Italian politicians. John Lunghino became the first Italian county supervisor in 1911, followed in the next two decades by Vito Christiano, Joseph Panzarella, Vincent and Anthony Tauriello, and Tommaso Serio. During those years, John Montana and Zachariah Gentile were elected to the city council, and Charles Martina, Charles Gimbrone, and Joseph Nicosia were elected to the state assembly. Anthony Tauriello later became the first Italian American Congressman from western New York.

Sources: Salvatore J. LaGumina, "Politics," in Salvatore J. LaGumina, Frank J. Cavioli, Salvatore Primeggia, and Joseph A. Varacalli, editors, *The Italian American Experience: An Encyclopedia*, 2000, pp. 480-82; *Corriere Italiano*, 11/4/11, 10/11/23, 11/29/23, 11/4/26, 11/11/26, 11/10/27, 11/7/28, 12/31/31, 6/8/33, 10/12/33, 11/1/33, 9/27/34, 10/24/35; *Buffalo Sunday Times*, 9/4/27; *Buffalo Evening News*, 2/12/72.

Italian merchants had received city payments to provide meals for prisoners, mechanical and automotive repairs, trucking, and construction services. More directly related to politics, citizens were paid to sit at polling sites and monitor elections; Joseph Mezzera was a poll clerk in 1912, John Fadale an election inspector in 1918.[13]

John Fadale was the first Lackawanna Italian to run for a position beyond that of committeeman. Born in the U.S. and the first Italian doctor in the Steel City, he made his initial attempt at one of three assessor slots in 1917 but came in sixth among nine candidates. Other Italians, all of whom were immigrants, fared better in the races for committeemen. Two

Lackawanna   1935

Pair Divides City Post 12 Years

❖   ❖   ❖   ❖   ❖

Amorosi Is Present Dogcatcher

Democrat Tony Amorosi, left, and Republican Tony Turchiarelli alternated as the city pound keeper between 1922 and 1935, depending on which party captured the mayor's office. The Democrats and Amorosi were in office from 1922-23, 1930-31, and 1934-35. Republican mayors appointed Turchiarelli in 1924-29, and 1932-33. In 1936, Ferdinand Catuzza was appointed by the Democrats, and the job became a civil-service position that he held until 1963. In the last quarter of the twentieth century, Jack Migliore and Dan DiVito both worked as Animal Control Officers. Photo source: Clipping from the *Buffalo Evening News*, 1/25/35, provided by Loretta Amorosi-Nicometo

committeepeople from each party were elected in each district of the four wards. Available records indicate that Ferdinando Catuzza, who usually went by Ferdinand or Fred, may have been elected as a Democrat as early as 1916, and Tony Amorosi in 1919. Tony Turchiarelli was active as a Republican and

probably was first elected as a committeeman in the early 1920s. All three men were connected to Tony Mauriello, who lived in Lackawanna for a number of years before moving back to Buffalo. Mauriello served as a translator in both cities and was a witness in naturalization hearings for many Lackawanna Italians, including Catuzza and Turchiarelli. He appeared to be well connected politically and may have been a mentor to the three Italian committeemen in Lackawanna. Turchiarelli was also connected to Daniel Christiano, who had business ties in both Buffalo and Lackawanna, and whose brother Vito was elected in 1920 as county supervisor in Buffalo. Catuzza was affiliated with Gennaro Panzetta, who was a translator and involved with Italian American political leaders in Buffalo. When Panzetta and his wife Adele moved to Lackawanna in the 1920s, they became very active in the Republican party. Adele was soon elected as committeeperson, and Gennaro, who went by John, became a committeeman during the 1930s. Catuzza went back to Lazio for a year or so in the early 1920s but upon his return to the Steel City became very active in the Democratic Party. Ten more First Ward Italians, most of them immigrants, became committeemen in the 1930s (see Figure 11.2). As the number of districts grew in each ward, the greater number of committeemen seats allowed more Italians the opportunity to run for this position. The First Ward grew from two districts in 1931 to five in 1940, then to seven by 1950.[14]

Citywide candidates, such as the mayor and assessors, were keenly aware of the value of committeepeople in the First Ward, where the largest number of voters resided. Newly elected mayors rewarded workers for getting out the vote. When Democrat Michael Mescall succeeded Socialist John Gibbons in 1922, he named Tony Amorosi city pound keeper. Republican Walter Lohr won the next three mayoral elections, installing Tony Turchiarelli as pound keeper. With a Democratic mayor in office in 1930, Amorosi was returned to the job; but with Lohr back two years later, Turchiarelli again had the post. In 1934, Democrat Paul Tomaka reinstated Amorosi, and two years later, Fred Catuzza was appointed pound keeper and it became a civil service job.[15]

Younger Italians became involved in politics between 1925 and 1928, when Nick Sperduto, Cosmer Fadale, Vincent Ginnetti, Joseph Pacillo, and Nick Thomas were election inspectors in the First Ward. Others were appointed to city commissions and boards. In 1920, Donato Chiacchia joined the Civil Service Commission, and John Fadale, the Board of Health.

The establishment of the Italian American Citizens Club in 1921 was a landmark event in the evolution of the ethnic group's political development. The nine founders, all immigrants, included two from Roland Avenue and six First Ward residents.

Most of the men were Democrats, including Tony Amorosi, but soon Republicans such as John Panzetta became involved. They all realized the importance of mobilizing Italian voters to back candidates, especially those from their own ethnic group, who could then address the needs of the Italian community. The office of city assessor was more promising and powerful than that of committeeman, and it offered a stepping stone to running for councilman. The three assessors were elected on a citywide basis until the 1960s, when these became appointive positions. The assessors oversaw the adjustment of the tax base. Between 1917 and 1931, a number of Italians made unsuccessful bids for this post, including Republicans John Fadale, Dan Chiacchia, and Leonard DePaula, Independent Liberal V. Jimmy D'Alessandro, and Socialist Joseph Fusco. The first Italian candidate elected to this position was Joe Milano, a Democrat. He had lost his first run for assessor in 1925 but was successful in the two subsequent elections and served from 1928 to 1931. Tony Falcone of Roland Avenue won an assessor's seat as a Republican candidate in 1931 and again in 1933. Democrat Angelo Grosso served three terms between 1936 and 1941, and Ralph Galanti was appointed to fill a vacant assessor's position in 1936. During this period and for the next three decades, it was common for the three assessor positions to be divided among the three largest ethnic voting blocks—the Irish, the Poles, and the Italians.[16]

As Italians became more involved in politics and captured political offices, this translated into more city jobs for members of the ethnic group. The presence of Italians became noticeable in the early 1920s when Tony Amorosi and Tony Turchiarelli exercised power as committeemen and took turns as city pound keeper. The year 1925 was a pivotal one for Italians, as Mayor Lohr appointed Joseph Jennetti as a police officer and Sebastian Fistola as a firefighter—the first Italians to enter these professions in the city. Tony Turchiarelli was instrumental in obtaining these appointments. Italians had earlier gained less prestigious jobs with the city, mostly with the Department of Public Works (DPW). Peter Sirianni was a laborer in 1915, and within the next four years, Vito Pasquarella became a driver and Domenico Tripoli a laborer. Five other Italians had similar jobs in the 1920s, and Ferdinand Catuzza became a street inspector in 1930. As the city received federal funds during the Depression, many unemployed men were hired. In November 1931, there were 18 Italian DPW laborers, most putting in one to three days per week. Democrat Edward Malone, the mayor at the time, was defeated in that month's election by Republican Walter Lohr. Throughout his two-year term, the DPW employed about 20 Italian workers, but as the 1933 election approached, Mayor Lohr apparently attempted to court the heavily Democratic Italian community. In October of that year, the

FIGURE 11.2

Italian Committeemen, 1916 – 1950

	Democrats	Republicans
Ingham Avenue	Tony Amorosi Tony Giordano Joe Bernardi Tony DePasquale Frank Marinelli	Tony Turchiarelli Adele Panzetta John Panzetta Vincenzo Suffoletto Gioacchino Orlando Amerigo Bracci Armondo Pietrocarlo Carl Chentfant
Bethlehem Park	Costantino Novelli Ferdinand Catuzza Biagio Sperduti Edwin DiCenzo John Falbo Joe Bellagamba	Angeline Poliseno Louis Corsi Anthony Zaccaria Patsy Ricci
Roland Avenue	Patrick Vertalino Anthony DePerto Dominic Selvaggio Joe Leo Frank Chiodo	Tony Falcone
Eastern Lackawanna	Joseph Mendola	Emedio Chiacchia

Sources: Erie County Election Commission, Primary Elections, 1947–1956; *Lackawanna News*, 3/24/32; *Lackawanna Leader*, 2/29/40; *Lackawanna Herald*, 4/5/40; *Steel City Press*, 1/29/47; *Lackawanna Press*, 8/26/49.

number of Italian DPW workers increased to 41, then to 55 in November. The men, mostly part-time laborers, included First Ward residents and a significant number from the Third Ward, where many Roland Avenue residents were Republicans. However, Lohr lost the election to Democrat Paul Tomaka. Italians continued to gain more skilled city jobs. In 1941, the DPW roster included foreman John Panzetta, inspectors Daniel Conti and Vincent Suffoletto, machine operator Tony Turchiarelli, and truck driver Anthony Pitillo.[17]

C. John Tarquino was among the first of his ethnic group to attain a professional position with the city, becoming an assistant city engineer in 1928. John Verel (nephew of the businessman of the same name) gained this position a decade later. Important appointive positions also became open to Italians. Nick Sperduto was named secretary to the board of assessors in 1932. Four years later, councilman Joe Milano was unable to get Tom Pepper appointed as city clerk, but

Tony Giordano, Democrat, committeeman on Ingham Avenue, 1930s. Photo source: Collection of Tony Grasso

Vincenzo "Jimmy" Suffoletto, Republican, committeeman on Ingham Avenue, 1930s. Photo source: Lolly Suffoletto

Amerigo "Mickey" Bracci, Republican, committeeman on Ingham Avenue, 1940. Photo source: Mary Panzetta-Vertino

Edwin DiCenzo, Democrat, Bethlehem Park committeeman, 1940. Photo source: Jack and Mary Panczykowski

Joseph Leo was a Democratic committeeman for many years, a member of the Board of Health, 1946 and chairman of the city's Civil Service Commission, 1948-66. He was raised on Roland Avenue. Photo source: Eugene Leo

Louis Corsi, Republican, committeeman in Bethlehem Park, 1940. Photo source: Lake Erie Italian Club

Ferdinand Catuzza, Democrat, became a First Ward committeeman in 1916, and was the city's pound keeper from 1936 to 1963. Photo source: Aldo Filipetti

Pat Vertalino, Democrat, committeeman on Roland Avenue, 1938. Photo source: Collection of Frank Chiodo

Anthony "Erie" DePerto, Democrat, Roland Avenue committeeman, 1946. Photo source: Collection of Frank Chiodo

Dominic Selvaggio, Democrat, committeeman on Roland Avenue, 1950. Photo source: Collection of Frank Chiodo

Emidio Chiacchia, Republican, committeeman in eastern Lackawanna, 1940. Photo source: Sara Chiacchia-Kempf

Donato Chiacchia was appointed to the Civil Service Commission in 1920 by the newly elected Socialist mayor, John Gibbons. Photo source: Sara Chiacchia-Kempf

Pasquale Pitillo became active in the Republican Party and was named to the Civil Service Commission in 1936. Photo source: Collection of Frank Chiodo

Tony DiMasi was named to the Fire Commission in 1940. Photo source: Collection of Nunze Oddy

Mike Morgan joined the Fire Commission in 1954. Photo source: Lake Erie Italian Club

Pepper did become secretary to the board of assessors. Another first for Italians occurred in 1934, when Mayor Tomaka appointed Nick Milano as his secretary. Anne Monaco was hired as a clerk in the city auditor's office in 1938 and was then appointed commissioner of deeds. Every time citizens went to vote, election inspectors were hired by each political party to observe the polling sites. From 1912 to 1935, only one to three Italians were assigned to fill these slots each year, but their numbers increased rapidly thereafter, and during the early 1940s, nine to 15 inspectors each year were (see Figure 11.3). Many of these individuals were First Ward residents and Democrats, but by 1937, a few Republicans and Roland Avenue residents were gaining these appointments. Most of these 35 individuals were of the second generation, and the first of the 11 females in the group, Betty DeLallo, became an inspector in 1939. Alex Nigro and Dan Thomas were appointed for seven years each, while most others were inspectors for one or two years.[18]

The growing political clout of Italians was further demonstrated by the leadership positions held in the city's political organizations during the 1930s. The First Ward Democratic Club's officers included Financial Secretary Jimmy Guglietta and Treasurer Tony Amorosi. The officers of the Roosevelt Club of Ingham Avenue were Steve Canestrari, Ferdinand Catuzza, Antonio Giordano, Francesco Cologgi, and Ettore Spadoni. Tony Falcone was president of the Grant Republican Club, and east of the tracks, Pasquale Pitillo was president of the Roland Republican Club. In a sign of increasing political know-how, Italian Democrats solidified their relationship with Congressman James Mead by founding the Lady Mead Club, a women's group that backed Mead's electoral campaigns. Carmela Canestrari was president, and Lena Amorosi also served as an officer.[19]

The First Phase: Immigrant Politicians

The process of entering Lackawanna's political system was built on steps taken by successive generations of Italian Americans. The first phase involved Italian immigrants laying the foundation for access to political power, and that was soon exploited by the second generation, who won important elective offices. The immigrant generation was able to win political recognition and leverage via their committeemen positions, and a number were appointed to city jobs and commissions. Several individuals typify the career of the immigrant involved in urban politics, none more than Antonio "Tony" Amorosi. He formally began his political career in 1919, seven years after he and his wife had arrived in Lackawanna. Amorosi was elected one of two Democratic committeemen from the second district of the First Ward. He apparently worked hard to turn out the Italian vote, and in January 1922, Mayor Joseph Mescall appointed him to his first term as city pound keeper. As a committeeman, Amorosi helped select Democratic candidates, especially those who ran in his ward. In the 1930s, a committeeman such as Amorosi received about $250 to hire people to sit at the voting sites and check off voters' names on lists. He also had some leverage in getting people appointed to city positions and jobs. This influence may have extended to Republican officials hoping to make inroads into the Italian community. Republican Walter Lohr, Lackawanna's first Polish American mayor in 1924, launched an ambitious civic-improvement campaign that included paving Ingham Avenue, something strongly supported by Italians, especially businesspeople. Al Croce recalls Democrats such as Tony Amorosi and other businesspeople supporting Lohr at rallies and encouraging Croce's father to back Lohr. Amorosi may have done this in exchange for Lohr's promise to help the Italian community. Amorosi could take some credit for the

TONY AMOROSI – WARD COMMITTEEMAN

Tony Amorosi (1883–1944) was born in Sant'Andrea di Conza, Campania, and in 1904 migrated to Newark, New Jersey, where his brother Giuseppe joined him. There he met Pasqualina "Lena" Fresca, whom he married in 1907. Lena Fresca's family had emigrated from Campania to Newark in the early 1890s, returned to Italy, and soon after migrated to Argentina. Lena was born in 1894 in either Europe or South America. By 1899, the Fresca family was again living in Newark. As a girl, Lena worked as a house cleaner. Since many of her customers were Polish Jews, she learned to speak some basic Polish.

The couple soon had two children, Luciano, born in 1909, and Pietro, who died as an infant. Antonio Amorosi was employed at the Ballentine Brewery in Newark, but when work slowed down, a *paesano* in Lackawanna, Antonio Mauriello, advised him to move to the Steel City. Lena, whose parents and eight siblings all lived in Newark, was very reluctant to leave. Her mother convinced her to move, partly by pointing out that Lena would have a chance to see Niagara Falls, which was only 40 miles north of Lackawanna. The Amorosi family arrived in Lackawanna in 1912 and moved into the Mauriello home on Steelawanna Avenue, which included a grocery store on the ground floor and 14 other boarders. Tony Amorosi worked for Mauriello, but by 1913, he and his family had moved to 219 Ingham Avenue, where he opened a saloon. By 1920, Amorosi owned four lots and one structure on Ingham Avenue and had opened a grocery store. The following year, he had a home constructed at 289 Ingham to accommodate a family that then included four more children: Joe, Thomas (Guy), Frank, and Loretta. The grocery store in the front of the structure was minded by Lena and the older children, while Tony delivered groceries to customers' homes. Amorosi gave up his saloon business in 1928, and for the next five years, he and his son Louie (Luciano) ran an ice-delivery business using the same truck they'd used to cart meats and groceries to First Ward Italians. Tragically, Louie died at age 24 in 1933.

Tony Amorosi remained a committeeman until his death in 1944. According to Joe Milano, "Amorosi was clever and had guts. He had a lot of competition for his committeeman job. He talked people out of running against him, and soothed over feelings." He was involved as a founder or leader of several major Italian American groups, including the Lake Erie Italian Club, the Stags, the Italian American Citizens Club, and the Federation of Italian American Associations of Lackawanna.

Sources: Interviews with Loretta Amorosi-Nicometo, December 29, 1977; and Joe Milano, November 23, 1977; *Lackawanna Leader*, 3/9/44.

---

paving of Ingham Avenue and Lohr's appointments of the first Italians to the police and fire departments. Perhaps he even earned some political favors from Lohr; when Amorosi started his ice-delivery business in 1928, he was supplied by Lohr's icehouse on Lehigh Avenue.[20]

Tony Amorosi was involved in several political organizations and was also president of the Lake Erie Italian Club for much of the period between 1917 and 1944. Involvement in organizations was an important aspect of his political base. Tony and Lena Amorosi were always entertaining political leaders and tending to the needs of constituents. Their youngest child, Loretta, recalls a constant stream of visitors to the Amorosi home for dinner. Conspicuous among them were Irish Democrats, including police chief Gilson, patrolman Charles Curtin, mayor Mike Hughes, and party leader Tom Joyce. At times, the Amorosis were asked to prepare a meal and take it to the home of a Democratic official who was hosting a get-together. Loretta Amorosi-Nicometo remembers the great demands this placed on her parents, especially her mother. Because many of his guests wanted to drink alcohol during the Prohibition era, Tony Amorosi made wine and Strega in his basement. Italian friends and neighbors, such as Tony Colello and Joe Cosentino, were also frequent guests at the Amorosi house. Tony Amorosi was a mentor and sometimes rival of Joe Milano. When Republican Tony Turchiarelli was the pound keeper, he didn't have a driveway, so he parked the city dogcatcher truck in the Milano driveway. This angered Amorosi, who accused Joe Milano of favoring the Republicans. In 1936, after another falling out with Amorosi, Milano appointed Ferdinand Catuzza instead of Amorosi as pound keeper. However, Milano did name Amorosi as a foreman in the Street Department.[21]

Amorosi provided basic services that were essential to the survival of poor Italian immigrants, especially during the Depression years. During the 1930s, Catholic Charities distributed food to the poor via middlemen such as Amorosi, with the understanding that all sacks of flour that weren't immediately given away would be returned. Amorosi took his extra sacks, buried them under his garage in protective coverings,

FIGURE 11.5

GENNARO (JOHN) AND ADELE PANZETTA

Adele Amattucci was born on April 24, 1886, in Capriglia Irpino, Campania, as the second or third youngest of 14 children, all but two of whom migrated to the United States. Her father, twice a widower, remained in Italy. Her eldest brother escorted her to New York City in 1904 after arranging her marriage to a *paesano*, Gennaro Panzetta. Born in 1885, Panzetta had emigrated in 1902, joining his uncle, a barber, in New York City. The young Panzetta soon changed his first name to John.

John and Adele were married in 1905. Several of the Amattucci brothers had established groceries in Brooklyn and offered to set up the new couple in a similar business. But Panzetta was apparently jealous of the power that Adele's older brothers had and disliked living in New York City. So the couple moved to the Buffalo area, where John worked at Lackawanna Steel. They then moved to nearby Lockport, where John worked on the Erie Canal and Adele operated a large boardinghouse. When the building burned down in 1916, the Panzettas moved to Buffalo, where Adele ran a saloon and John sold real estate. Later, the couple ran a restaurant, a soft drinks parlor, and an imported-foods store in Buffalo.

In 1926, the Panzettas finally settled in Lackawanna where they owned three buildings on O'Dell Street. They had a building erected at 169 Ingham Avenue, and established a bar-restaurant there. As was the case with their previous businesses in Buffalo, Adele served as the bouncer while her more soft-spoken husband took a managerial role. She gave birth to four children; tragically, daughter

John and Adele Panzetta early in the twentieth century.
Photo source: Mary Panzetta-Vertino

Mary died at the age of 18 years in 1923. Following Italian custom, the next female born was given the name Mary. The couple's other two children were Rose, who became a nun in New Jersey, and John Jr.

Adele Panzetta helped others in a number of ways, including loans of money that often were not repaid. Councilmen, mayors, and other politicians visited the Panzetta home. The Panzettas loved music and had their own box at Buffalo's Erlanger Theater, where they attended Italian operas and musical events. Emelino Rica, who had his own radio show and was master of ceremonies at the Erlanger, was a friend of the Panzettas, and the two families often had dinner together. Mary Panzetta learned opera at the Erlanger, and Rica addressed her as "Signorina Maria" (Miss Mary). Anthony Greco and his family also were regular visitors from Buffalo.

Mary Panzetta-Vertino describes her mother as a friendly woman who apologized for not having a formal education and for speaking broken English. While Adele Panzetta could not write in English, she did boast, "I can write my name beautifully on a check." The death of John Panzetta in 1943 was acknowledged by *Corriere Italiano* with a lengthy and glowing obituary, but the long illness leading to his passing left the family in financial trouble. Adele took out mortgages on their three houses and went to work as a supervisor of charwomen at city hall. Over the years, many Lackawanna Italians paid homage to John and Adele Panzetta by asking them to be godparents of their children.

Sources: *Buffalo Evening News*, 4/9/43; *Corriere Italiano*, 4/15/43; *Buffalo City Directory*, 1916–1925, U.S. Census, 1930; interviews with Mary Panzetta-Vertino, August 9, 1977, April 21, 1995, June 9, 2004.

and gradually distributed them, much to the gratitude of these poverty-stricken constituents. The Amorosis had other ways of building rapport with voters. Lena Amorosi's ability to speak Polish drew her neighbors of that ethnic group to the family grocery store. Tony rented out apartments in his building at 287 Ingham at very cheap rates. When he was in the store, he either gave people food or extended them credit. Not only was this politically astute, but it also helped him compete with Tibollo's grocery store, located nearby. His daughter Loretta described her father as a "soft touch" for people in need and her mother as the "backbone" of the family grocery, who made the hard decisions that kept the store in business.[22]

Political and charitable activities placed a strain on the Amorosi family, but the result was that Tony Amorosi maintained a strong political base in the community. Many Italian families were grateful for his distribution of food, easy credit terms, and connections with city hall that produced jobs. Politicians could count on Amorosi to turn out many Italian voters on election day. To his daughter Loretta, the end result of all her father's activities was that the family had income and food on the table during the Depression. The political involvement of Tony and Lena Amorosi must have influenced their son Joe, as he later became active in politics.

Several blocks away from the Amorosis lived another immigrant couple who also had a strong role in the political life of Lackawanna's Italian community. Gennaro "John" Panzetta and his wife Adele had both migrated from Campania to western New York, eventually settling in the Steel City. John served as a Republican committeeman in the 1920s and early 1930s. With the advent of women's suffrage in 1920, Adele won a committeewoman's seat in the First Ward by 1922 and served in this position for most of the next 50 years. It is said she was the first Republican committeewoman in New York State. Her power and influence were citywide, and both she and her husband had strong connections to politicians in Buffalo. While John Panzetta was involved both in politics and business, it was Adele who became a powerful political presence in the First Ward. Her career in politics and his in business reinforced one another. John, who had a high-school education and spoke English well, was a court interpreter for Italians and assisted immigrants in sending remittances to Italy via the Lunghino bank and Vito Marinaccio's travel agency in Buffalo. He sold real estate in Lackawanna and had many business connections, one of them with Anthony Greco, an undertaker in Buffalo. In 1931, the two were partners in an undertaking business operating out of Panzetta's home on O'Dell Street in the Steel City. John Panzetta was a member of the Lake Erie Italian Club and the Spanish Welfare Association in Lackawanna as well as the Principe Ereditario Society in Buffalo.[23]

Adele Panzetta was active in St. Anthony's Church and maintained regular contact with numerous Italian women. She won the admiration of many by serving as a midwife, setting broken bones, and performing rituals to remove *mal' occhio* (the evil eye). She helped organize the Italian Republican Women's Club of the First Ward in 1930 and was one of six women to serve on its first board of directors. She had close ties with Lackawanna Republican Party Chairman Steve Vukelic, and her approval was needed for anyone seeking election on the party's ticket in the First Ward. Armondo Pietrocarlo, a First Ward committeeman, attended meetings at the Panzetta home in which political strategies were discussed with Tony Turchiarelli, Gioacchino Orlando, Sam Morgan, Amerigo Bracci, and others. Following the election of 1937, the Panzettas treated the Republican mayor, councilmen, and other party officials to a 12-course Italian dinner at their home, over which they discussed strategies for the coming year.[24]

Nick Canali grew up on Ingham Avenue and became involved with the Republican Party in the early 1950s. As a committeeman, he worked very closely with Adele Panzetta, going door to door along Ingham Avenue and asking Italian Americans to vote for Republicans. "Mrs. Panzetta," he stated, "always gave gifts to people—silk stockings, cigarettes, combs." Adele Panzetta was a shrewd politician, and this was not deterred by her inability to read or write. Her daughter wrote out the ballots that Panzetta used for voting on candidates at endorsement meetings. At one such meeting of Republican committeemen in the 1950s, Nick Canali was pressed into service as Adele's scribe. "Paryz and Szczgiel were running for mayor. She told both she was for them. She had me write down Paryz's name on the ballot, and she told Paryz she voted for him—'Ask Nick'—then told Szczgiel that she had told me to write down his name but that I had wrote [sic] Paryz!"[25]

According to the *Front Page*, "Adele Panzetta had a natural instinct for politics and it became a tradition for aspiring politicians to come to 'Ma' Panzetta's First Ward domain to seek her support and advice. She was a deciding factor in many mayoral elections. Many city policemen and firemen, long retired, can credit their jobs to 'Ma' Panzetta." She also cleared the way for Italian constituents to get licenses, permits, and other essentials at city hall. Panzetta arranged for Michele Grasso, and later his son Tony, to get peddler licenses without paying a fee. In gratitude, the elder Grasso asked her to be the godmother of one of his children and urged his son Tony to show her respect by voting for Republican candidates, even though both men usually backed Democrats.[26]

Adele Panzetta could be as hard-nosed as her male counterparts. At a voting site, she was reported to have told voters not to cast their ballots for a Democratic rival. As she

FIGURE 11.6

FERDINANDO CATUZZA

Ferdinando Catuzza (1893–1970) was the youngest of six children of Celestino Catuzza, a farmer in Giuliano di Roma, Lazio. Amedeo, his eldest brother, emigrated in 1908, joining *paesani* in West Virginia and Ohio who worked on the railroad. Ferdinando migrated in 1909 and took up railroad work with Amedeo in West Virginia. They lived in a boxcar that had four steps leading up to the door, and Catuzza later told his children that the men ate so many potatoes, the peeled skins were piled as high as the top step.

Catuzza did not like the toil of railroad work, especially tasks such as hauling the heavy railroad jacks. In 1911, he joined *paesani* in Niagara Falls, New York, while his brother settled in Lackawanna. Within a year, Catuzza was living in the Steel City with Amedeo and their sister Gertudda, who had emigrated two years earlier. Catuzza, who usually went by Fred or Ferdinand, took up tool and die making in trade school, then became a journeyman in the machine shop at Lackawanna Steel. In 1923, he returned to Italy and worked for a period on the streetcar lines in Rome. In Giuliano di Roma, Catuzza married Rosa DeSantis, and they traveled to Lackawanna in 1924. They had only 25 cents to their name when they arrived at the train station in Buffalo, and John Panzetta gave the couple a ride to Lackawanna. After living with Amedeo Catuzza's family in the Old Village, the couple bought a house in Bethlehem Park. Rosa gave birth to seven children; tragically, three of them, including the first two, died as infants.

Catuzza always wore a shirt and tie, and insisted that his four sons do so for Sunday meals. His son Celestino, better known as Chet, recalls that his father was strict but was a questioning person and encouraged this quality in his offspring. "He taught us boys wine making, plumbing, and electrical work," states Chet. His children worked alongside him as he did his political chores, such as passing out signs and stickers and registering voters. Chet went on to become First Ward councilman in the 1970s, and another son, Roman, was a Democratic committeeman during the 1960s.

Fred Catuzza knew many people involved in political and civic affairs and often visited congressman James Mead. He remained active in the Roman Independent Club and took his family to the annual picnics the group held at Chestnut Ridge Park. He worked as the city pound keeper from 1936 until his retirement in 1963.

Sources: Interview with Chet Catuzza, September 8, 1994; *Lackawanna Leader*, 4/9/70.

spoke to the people, she nodded toward her opponent and said, "Look at him, he has a dirty face! How could you vote for him?" At this point a heated argument erupted, and Panzetta stood her ground against her male adversary, each threatening the other with bodily harm. Panzetta's long political career had several highlights. She traveled to New York City in 1940 to attend the Republican Convention in which Wendell Wilkie was nominated as the presidential candidate. Governor Nelson Rockefeller presented her with a gold elephant at a Lincoln Day dinner. The highlight of her political life, according to her daughter, was a personal invitation to tour Sing Sing Prison with Governor Dewey.[27]

Ferdinand Catuzza was another political leader among the immigrant generation. He was born in Lazio, migrated to the United States in 1909, and became politically involved in 1916 when he was elected as a Democratic committeeman, a post he held until 1937. He took an active part in the Great Steel Strike of 1919, and, like many steelworkers, backed Socialist John Gibbons in his successful bid for mayor. A month after the election, Catuzza formally joined the Socialist Party but rejoined his old party in 1922 when the Democrats regained the mayor's seat. He held a number of skilled jobs in the steel plant between 1912 and 1929, but asthma forced Catuzza to leave the plant in 1930. He worked for several years as a county social worker in Lackawanna, and in 1936, councilman Joe Milano named him city pound keeper. Catuzza successfully lobbied to have his job made a civil-service position and remained in it for close to three decades.[28]

Fred Catuzza was the leader among the Giulianesi, the numerous immigrants from his hometown of Giuliano di Roma. In 1932, he was a founder of the Roman Independent Club, composed mostly of Giulianesi, and he served seven terms as its president. In Lackawanna, being the leader of any organization was a tremendous political asset, as one could influence members to vote as a block. He was also an officer in the Federation of Italian American Associations of Lackawanna, which meant he could potentially get the attention of the members of seven participating organizations. Because he could speak and write in English as well as Italian, he was sought for help in translating, securing legal papers, and interpreting. As his political career of Democratic committeeman developed, he was able to help people, especially the Giulianesi, find jobs with the city. Besides being active in St. Anthony's Church, Catuzza was a member of the Stags, the Lake Erie Italian Club, and the Italian American Citizens Club. He was also involved in the Moose, the First Ward Democratic Club, and, via his police powers as pound keeper, the Judges and Police Executives Conference of Erie County. Catuzza seemed to relish political activity, as witnessed by his attendance at the President's Highway Safety Conference in Washington, D.C. in 1949.[29]

Immigrants including Tony Amorosi, Adele Panzetta, and Fred Catuzza had long careers in politics, as did their peer, Tony Turchiarelli, who held his committeeman position into the 1940s. These four individuals participated in the first phase of the political and civic assimilation of Lackawanna's Italian American community. Despite often warring among themselves, they learned the basic lessons of ethnic and ward politics. One instance of this occurred in 1919, during Prohibition, when laws allowed only one tavern (which could serve only soft drinks) on each block. Tony Amorosi convinced the Democratic mayor to award him instead of Tony Turchiarelli the license, which was the beginning of two decades of competition between the two men. Nonetheless, the immigrant politicians helped the Italian community to understand and utilize the rules of political life in the new country. Mobilizing their fellow ethnics to vote, they got themselves elected as committeepeople and worked to leverage jobs and favors from the political party bosses. At times, these were self-serving efforts—as when Amorosi, Turchiarelli, and Catuzza all pursued the dogcatcher position—but they also helped procure jobs for friends and relatives in the Italian community. These individuals mustered blocks of voters via organizations, such as the Italian American Citizens Club, the Roman Independent Club, and the Lady Mead Club, as well as through special events. In 1928, Lackawannans formed a Smith-Mead Club to back the re-election of James Mead as congressman and Alfred E. Smith as president. Smith, a Catholic [and claimed by some to have one Italian grandparent], was well-regarded in Catholic and immigrant Lackawanna. At a big rally, Edward Malone was chosen as president of the organization, Patsy Ricci as one of seven vice presidents, and Joe Milano as financial secretary. The club's large executive committee included Tony Colello and Anthony Falcone. While the leadership was heavily Irish, there were also a number of Poles and other eastern European ethnics in addition to the four Italians. This united front displayed a more comprehensive grasp of American politics by the Italians and others, and, although Smith lost the election, the Italian community honored mayor-elect Edward Malone and other victorious Democratic candidates. Tony Amorosi and Patsy Ricci were the chairmen of the huge celebration at St. Anthony's Church. Immigrants Amorosi, Ricci, and Colello, and second generation leaders such as Milano and Falcone assisted in developing a sense of Italian identity that went beyond the town and regional mindsets of the immigrants.[30]

Eager young men of the second generation observed these politicians and their varied mix of personal styles as they developed their own political skills. Angelo Grosso learned to remain neutral when immigrant politicians, such as Republican

Adele Panzetta and Democrat Tony Amorosi, were battling each other. While the immigrants sometimes locked horns with upstarts of the American-born generation, they also offered aid and encouragement at crucial times, recognizing this was necessary to develop the political power of their ethnic group. The maturation of the second generation and their involvement in politics marked the second phase of the political assimilation of Lackawanna's Italians. Their arrival on the political scene signaled the full entry of Italians into the Steel City's political life, a process vividly dramatized in the career of Joe Milano.[31]

FIGURE 11.7

POLITICS WITH A SENSE OF HUMOR

Despite the competitive and tense political activities in the city, some Italian politicians in Lackawanna maintained a sense of humor. When the Republicans won important seats, Adele Panzetta had a procession of youth dressed as altar boys carry a mock casket past Tony Amorosi's house to remind him of his party's defeat. In the strongly Democratic city, however, it was often Amorosi who sent a "procession" to the Panzetta home. During the 1920s and early 1930s, Amorosi and Republican Tony Turchiarelli alternated in holding the city pound-keeper's position, depending on which party had won the mayor's seat. Each man "honored" the one who had temporarily lost the pound-keeper slot by sending a procession to march around his home.

Two younger Ingham Avenue Italians took party competition to an even more humorous level in the 1930s. Carl Chentfant, a Republican activist, and Jimmy Guglietta, a strong Democrat, were friends who placed wagers on elections. They agreed that the man whose party lost must take the other for a buggy ride. In 1934, Walter Lohr lost the congressional election to Democrat James Mead, so the men procured a vintage buggy, and Guglietta sat proudly in the driver's seat as Chentfant assumed the horse role pulling the buggy throughout the Ingham Avenue neighborhood. Signs on the buggy and Chentfant explained to onlookers what was going on. Chentfant, whose motto was "never say die," got his revenge the following year when Republican John Aszkler was elected mayor. This time, Chentfant sat like a king in the buggy as Guglietta, bedecked with signs announcing that Aszkler had won and his candidate had lost, played the role of the horse. Many neighbors enjoyed these political antics.

Sources: *Lackawanna Herald*, 11/7/35; interviews with Joe Milano, November 23, 1977

The Second Phase:
Enter the American-Born Generation

Joe Milano's political career was a ground-breaking event for his age group. He was among the children of the immigrants born between 1890 and 1919 who represented the elder group of that generation, and the first to reach adulthood. Other second-generation men who were peers of Milano—John Fadale, Joe Fusco, and Leonard De Paula—made bids for an assessor's post between 1917 and 1931, but none succeeded. Milano was twice elected to an assessor's seat and twice to the First Ward councilman's post.

Born and raised in Lackawanna, Joe Milano attended public school and went to work in the steel plant in 1918 at age 15. His knowledge of politics began with lessons learned from his father, Gaetano, who had been involved in local campaigns.

FIGURE 11.8

JOSEPH MILANO, 1903 – 2000

The story of Joe Milano's political career begins with the immigration of his parents to America. Gaetano Milano and Maria Giuseppa Sperduto left their hometown of Teora, Campania, in 1900. After short stays in Newark, New Jersey, and Scranton, Pennsylvania, they moved to the steel-plant district of West Seneca in 1901 or 1902. Upon arrival there, Gaetano was hired by a contractor engaged in erecting No. 1 Open Hearth. After living in the Sperduto's rooming house in the First Ward, the Milanos rented a room in Angelo Morinello's boardinghouse on Roland Avenue. It was there, in 1903, that Maria gave birth to Joseph, the first of her seven children. Dr. Ira Trevett traveled by horse and buggy from his office on Nason Parkway to assist in the delivery. Returning to the First Ward and by 1905 settling on Ingham Avenue, the Milano family grew to include two more sons and four daughters.

As a youth, Joe Milano rubbed shoulders with individuals from the many ethnic groups in the First Ward. He attended public school, and in 1918, at the age of 15, he began work in the Lackawanna steel plant as a messenger boy. In this position, he traveled throughout the plant and got to meet the supervisors, including the man who was in charge of No. 6 Mill. The following year, he became a checker in the mill, counting steel bars of various

Circa 1927. Joe Milano as a candidate for city assessor. Photo source: Collection of Joe Milano

lengths and filling orders. Milano was one of the first Italian American employees in this mill. His foreman was named Hoff, and most of his coworkers were German and Irish. Milano befriended these men by inviting them to his father's house for a glass of wine following their 12-hour shift in the plant.

Laid off from the steel plant in 1921, Milano turned his focus to his second job, at the Lackawanna Community House on Wilkesbarre Avenue, which he began in November 1920. The center had a satellite in the Old Village where Milano led various recreational programs on the playground and supervised boys on trips to a camp in nearby Woodlawn. In July 1921, Joe and his brother Nick made the newspapers when they rescued a 3-year-old girl who had fallen into Smokes Creek. Joe pulled her from the water, and Nick administered first aid. During his tenure at the recreation center, Milano attended a 1923 conference for social workers in Washington, D.C.

Joe Milano married Viola Kusmierczyk in 1929, and the couple had three daughters: Mary, Dorothy, and Arlene. Milano's political career often took him away from his family, which Mary said had a significant emotional impact on all members. Milano served two terms as a city assessor, then two as First Ward councilman (from 1934 to 1937). After being defeated in his third bid for councilman, Milano focused on his work at Bethlehem Steel, becoming involved in the newly formed Steel Workers Organizing Committee. In 1939, he left the steel plant to take a job with the Lackawanna Department of Public Works, soon rising to the position of assistant commissioner. Milano later was appointed foreman of the Traffic Signs Department and resident manager of the Ridgewood Village. During the 1950s, he made one last attempt to gain elective office but lost his bid for mayor.

Sources: Interviews with Joe Milano, November 23, 1977, April 9, 1988, December 28, 1988, July 17, 1989, December 27, 1989; papers of Joe Milano, unlabeled news clipping, 7/16/21.

In 1911 and 1913, Peter McGovern successfully ran for the First Ward councilman position with the backing of Bernard McDonnell, a foreman in the steel plant who himself was later the First Ward councilman. On election day, McDonnell had two of his employees, Gaetano Milano and Antonio Grossi, go to the polling place at Roosevelt School and pass out McGovern cards to Italians as they entered. This was done on company time and pay. Gaetano Milano's observations helped his son Joe learn that political power in Lackawanna was directly connected with the steel plant. Joe and other second-generation individuals used this knowledge to advance the political skills of the Italian community to a higher level.[32]

In 1923, Joe Milano became a notary public and was soon assisting immigrants in completing legal documents for the sale of their land in Italy or instructing them on how their wives should proceed in applying for the immigration quota and visas needed for them to come to the United States. He assisted immigrants with their income-tax returns, helped them apply for naturalization papers, and acted as a witness for immigrants seeking their "second papers." Congressman James Mead helped in the procure documents in Italy by communicating with the Italian ambassador in Washington, D.C., and the American consul in Italy. Mead's tutoring was invaluable to Milano's ongoing political education.

Milano's political career formally began in 1925 when, after being encouraged by an Irish American politician, he ran for Lackawanna's board of assessors on the Democratic ticket. Milano lost that election but gained the support of many Italians, even Republicans such as John and Adele Panzetta, who appreciated the significance of a member of their own ethnic group running for this position. In 1927, Milano again ran, this time winning one of three assessor slots. The fact that he was the first Italian to hold this position in Lackawanna was celebrated in an article in *Corriere Italiano*, Buffalo's Italian newspaper. Toward the end of his two-year term, an English-language newspaper reported that Milano was seeking reelection and planning "an intensive campaign among the Italian voters." The article continued: "Milano has engaged in Americanizing immigrants. It is as a result of his efforts that a series of Italian-American clubs have been chartered in the city ... His work in the organization of the Italian immigrant also includes the villages of Blasdell, town of Hamburg and Highland Acres." Milano won reelection as assessor in 1929, also becoming commissioner of deeds by that time. In that same year, he was named by Governor Franklin D. Roosevelt a New York delegate to the annual conference of the National Tax Association held at Saranac Lake, New York.[33]

During the time Milano was an assessor, the steel plant gave him a job with the Inspection Department, whereby he filled in for men on vacation or leave. A permanent plant position was not possible at the time because he and the other assessors were busy for three to four months each spring, with pay, to make a survey of properties. Bethlehem Steel provided the assessors with an engineer's appraisal of new construction and other changes to its physical plant as well as a recommended amount for a fair assessment. Milano and the other assessors usually added $500,000 to $1 million to this figure to arrive at the official figure. This arrangement enmeshed the assessors with the steel plant, enabling the company to get a very favorable assessment. When a steel-plant employee was elected to public office, the company usually provided him a "soft" job and hired men referred by him. Thus, the public official became indebted to the private company. If Bethlehem Steel executives did not like the public official's actions, they might punish him by refusing to hire the people he referred, altering his job duties at the plant to include unpleasant work, or laying him off. Milano later got a taste of such punishing treatment.[34]

In 1931, Milano was defeated in his fourth bid for assessor, with Tony Falcone and two other Republicans capturing the seats. He was then assigned to work for Bethlehem Steel's Real Estate Division, and, after being laid off a few years later, procured a work-relief job with the city in 1933. Under this program, he collected $15 per week in relief in exchange for compiling tax bills for city treasurer Paul Tomaka, a Democrat.[35]

Milano ran for First Ward councilman in 1933 after his name was proposed to the Democratic Party by committeeman Tony Amorosi. Many Italians were Democrats, but those who were Republican had to follow the party line. Milano later recalled that some Italian Republicans, including committeewoman Adele Panzetta, who had supported him in his previous bid for assessor, could not do so when it came to the important office of councilman. Whereas the office of assessor was considered politically "neutral" because it involved no control over city patronage jobs, the councilman position brought with it patronage jobs, coveted by both parties to use in rewarding the faithful. So while Milano did not get the entire Italian vote, he did have the support of a significant number of non – Italians. His wife, Viola Kusmierczyk, was Polish American, and her brother Walter was a committeeman in the First Ward. The other Democratic committeeman from this district, Polish American Stanley Wojcik, was also a friend of Milano's. In the heavily Irish New Village, Milano counted on his friend Joe "Dutch" Reuther and his Irish wife to court votes for him. These ethnic connections had helped Milano win his two assessor victories and were even more crucial in the councilman race.[36]

Milano and the other candidates for councilman promised to straighten out a perennial problem in Lackawanna politics:

the city's financial viability with regard to the assessment of the steel plant. The previous council and assessors, elected in 1931, had raised the plant's assessment, partly because the city treasury was drained by numerous civic projects and couldn't meet its payroll. Bethlehem Steel refused to pay the increase, and the issue went to court. During the 1933 election campaign, incumbent Republican Mayor Walter Lohr blamed the previous Democratic assessors, including Milano, for underassessing the steel plant and causing the valuation of city properties to go up. Milano countered by charging that the Republican-controlled board of assessors had underassessed Lohr's home. The contentiousness between these two men had begun during Milano's campaigns for assessor, when he attacked Lohr at the urging of Democratic leaders, and emerged again in the current election. Lohr enlisted the aid of Italians he had assisted, such as Sebastian Fistola, appointed by Lohr as the first Italian fireman in Lackawanna. Fistola and other Italians aligned with the Republican incumbents and campaigned against Milano. Despite their efforts, Lohr lost the 1933 election, as did three of the four incumbent councilmen.[37]

In January 1934, as the newly elected First Ward councilman, Joe Milano had a number of patronage jobs to give out. Though the mayor controlled a portion of these positions through appointments, he looked to the councilmen for recommendations on many of these. For example, the pound-keeper post had traditionally been allocated to a First Ward resident, and Milano and Mayor Tomaka agreed that it should again go to Tony Amorosi. Tomaka also approved Milano's nominees for five clerk-typist jobs at city hall—a Ukrainian, a Pole, a Croatian, and Italians Clara Thomas and Rose Grosso. Half the 100 positions in the Department of Public Works (DPW) were distributed in the heavily populated First Ward. When Milano was elected, some 15 to 20 of these jobs were already occupied. He gave half the remaining slots to Italians and the rest to Democrats from other ethnic groups—Poles, Serbs, Croatians, Hungarians, Ukrainians, blacks, and Spaniards. In addition, there were work-relief positions created by the Works Progress Administration (WPA), the Public Works Administration (PWA), and other federal agencies. Here, too, Milano gave roughly half the slots to Italians and divided the rest among members of other ethnic groups.[38]

Under previous councilmen, few Italians had been given city jobs, but Milano appointed fellow ethnics to laborers' posts at the pump station, DPW, and the garbage-collection department. He rewarded Democrat activists by naming Tony DePasquale as a DPW foreman, Joe Cosentino as electrical foreman at the pump station, and Joe Bernardi as a carpenter at the city's barns. With Milano in the councilman's office, the Italian community also gained greater access to the political

process and a certain amount of status and pride at having one of their own on the city council. In 1935, the Italian American Citizens Club held a testimonial banquet to honor Joe Milano. In attendance were Rocco Spano, the Italian vice consul in Buffalo, Italian politicians from Buffalo, Lackawanna Mayor Paul Tomaka, and Congressman James Mead.[39]

The personal rewards to Milano of being the first Italian councilman and enjoying a new level of political power were more than balanced by the demands of urban politics. Milano and the other newly elected councilmen began their terms in 1934 by lowering the tax assessment on the steel plant and resolving the impasse that existed concerning that matter. The development of this issue marked his full initiation into the rough-and-tumble style of Lackawanna politics. During the course of the city's lawsuit with Bethlehem Steel, Mayor Paul Tomaka had, unknown to the councilmen, hired a special lawyer, promising him $10,000 in fees. When Tomaka asked Milano to second the motion to appropriate city funds for the attorney's fees, he refused, reasoning that the city attorney should be adequate to handle the court case. Because Milano and the single Republican on the council voted against the motion, making it a two-two split, Mayor Tomaka had to cast the deciding vote. For breaking party ranks on the issue, the mayor decided to punish Milano. When it came time to pay the special attorney, Henry Sylvester—head of Bethlehem Steel's Real Estate division and the company's political point man—personally called on Milano, urging him to sign the voucher. Milano, who had recently resumed working at the steel plant in Sylvester's department, got the message that is, he could lose his job in the plant if he did not go along with the alliance of party bosses and Bethlehem Steel executives. On another occasion, Bethlehem Steel pushed for the hiring of a city auditor to monitor the council's spending. Milano agreed but thought the job should be awarded on the basis of a civil-service exam. Sylvester told Milano that a certain man was a "natural" for the job and that an exam was not needed. Milano failed to be persuaded by this logic, inferring that Bethlehem Steel simply wanted to get their man in the position. Shortly afterward, the councilman was summoned to the office of Timothy Burns, general manager of Bethlehem's Lackawanna plant. Milano recalled the discussion:

"Mr. Milano," he says, "I've got a request to make. I understand that you're opposed to giving Jerome McGee the job of auditor. We've got to have the auditor's job created." I said, "I'm not opposed to creating a job. In fact, the only thing I'm against [sic] is picking the man out before the examination." Well, he says, "Nobody can pass that examination except McGee … We would like to see McGee appointed to that job. We have trust in him."

Campaign card for Joe Milano's successful bid for reelection in 1935. Photo source: Collection of Joe Milano

Campaign card of Ralph Galanti, who was seeking the First Ward councilman's slot, 1941. Galanti claimed, half in jest, that the Democratic party boss had his cronies register under the names of deceased persons, and they all voted against Galanti. Photo source: Chico Galanti

Republican Ralph Galanti was appointed to fill a vacant assessor's seat in 1936 but was defeated in the 1937 election. In the citywide election, the three highest vote-getters won the three assessor posts. By this time, Polish Americans, such as Galanti's two running mates on this campaign card, dominated many of the political offices because theirs was the largest ethnic group in the city. Photo source: Collection of Joe Milano

Appointed to the city council seat for the First Ward in 1941, Angelo Grosso ran for reelection later that year and won. Photo source: Collection of Angelo Grosso

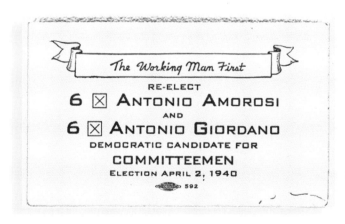

Campaign card for Tony Amorosi and Tony Giordano, 1940. Photo source: Loretta Amorosi-Nicometo

Campaign card for Mike DePasquale's 1975 bid to retain his seat on Lackawanna's city council.

Once again, the councilman got the message and reluctantly told Burns he would go along with McGee's appointment.[40]

During their conflicts, Mayor Tomaka harassed councilman Milano in several ways. Tomaka, who had appointed Tony Colello to the fire commission, convinced Colello that Milano had opposed his appointment. Tomaka also enlisted Tony Amorosi to pressure Milano on several issues. Despite this antipathy, Milano felt constrained to be loyal to fellow Democrat Tomaka, which brought on more problems. Milano usually backed the mayor when Tomaka and Democratic councilman James Galligan feuded, which angered party boss Tom Joyce, a foe of Tomaka. Some Democrats and Bethlehem's Henry Sylvester approached Angelo Grosso to run against Milano in the 1935 primaries, but Grosso refused to run against his boyhood friend. Both Grosso

and Milano were then on Sylvester's bad side, and Milano was laid off from his two-year job at Bethlehem's Real Estate office. By the time he won his second term as councilman, Milano was again working for Bethlehem's Inspection Department.[41]

When Joe Milano won reelection in 1935, he did not give the pound-keeper job to Tony Amorosi but instead appointed Fred Catuzza. The newly elected Republican mayor, John Aszkler, encouraged Catuzza to pressure Milano to make the dog warden-job a civil-service position, thus ensuring Catuzza would have the job indefinitely. When Milano said no to this proposal, he incurred Catuzza's wrath. Aszkler and his allies on the city council passed the proposal. What Milano didn't realize at the time was that Democratic Party boss Tom Joyce had conspired to back the Republican Aszkler in an attempt to defeat Tomaka. Joyce had also been against Milano in the 1935 elections; after Milano's victory, he further conspired with the Republicans to pressure the Italian councilman. When Joe Milano was reelected councilman in 1935, Aszkler asked him to resign. The mayor wanted to gain greater control over

The nasty side of Lackawanna politics, 1937. A brochure circulated by "the Real Democrats of this City" included this cartoon playing on the stereotype of the Italian organ-grinder, (here, former mayor Paul Tomaka) and his trained monkeys (councilmen Joe Milano and Walter Ogarek). Milano later found out that he lost his 1937 bid for reelection because Democratic Party boss Tom Joyce secretly plotted against him. Photo source: John Masocco

A 1936 letter to councilman Joe Milano from the secretary of the Russian Mutual Aid Society demanding jobs for members of that ethnic group. Of the many ethnic organizations that sought jobs and other services on their population's behalf, Italians were the most aggressive in pressuring their countryman Milano for tangible actions. Photo source: Collection of Joe Milano

the city council and probably had an arrangement with Tom Joyce to have Milano replaced by a less independent-minded Democrat. If he resigned, Milano would have been given a civil-service position, but he refused to do so.[42]

During his first campaign for councilman, Milano had promised to attack the vice present in the First Ward including seven brothels that functioned openly in the evenings. After he was elected, Milano was approached by a Lackawanna policeman who explained that the prostitutes served a useful function: by meeting the carnal desires of customers, he explained, the brothels prevented men from raping "respectable" women. Milano asked that the police more closely control the brothels and their hours of operation, but he knew that the illicit-entertainment industry in the First Ward was the domain of the mayor and involved an organized-crime syndicate from Buffalo. Years later he stated, "I would have lost my political career if I crusaded against the rackets in the First Ward."[43]

At times acting differently than the Democratic power brokers desired, Joe Milano got an education on who ran Lackawanna. He witnessed the great power of the steel company through run-ins with plant general manager Timothy Burns and Henry Sylvester, who eventually became a special assistant to the general manager. As a teen, Milano had witnessed the power held by Democratic Party boss Harry Kelley, and as councilman, he ran head first into thc raw power of the new Democratic boss, Tom Joyce. Journalist Ray Hill wrote of Joyce: "His power became absolute in the mid-1930s and lasted into the '70s." Using his leverage as superintendent of the steel plant's narrow-gauge railroad, Joyce gained political power. "Gradually, in exchange for jobs, Joyce gained absolute control over the city's governments," wrote Hill. Another journalist wrote of Joyce, "He represented Bethlehem in Lackawanna politics and Lackawanna politics at Bethlehem." Joyce was chairman of the city's Democratic Committee for many of the years between 1938 and 1951.[44]

When Joe Milano ran for reelection as First Ward councilman in 1937, party boss Tom Joyce again worked with the Republicans to defeat him. Joyce and the Republicans approached Italians who had grievances with the councilman and fanned the flames of discontent. Milano had appointed Tony DePasquale and Joe Cosentino to foreman positions, after which DePasquale complained to Milano that Cosentino received a higher salary. When it became apparent that his pay scale could not be revised, DePasquale refused to support Milano in future elections. DePasquale's friend Tony Colello had held a grudge against Milano since several years earlier, as then-mayor Tomaka had convinced Colello that Milano had opposed Colello's appointment as fire commissioner. Tom Joyce had cronies rekindle this issue, pressuring Colello to

FIGURE 11.9

A POLITICIAN HAS NO PRIVACY

During the mid-1930s, Joe Milano served two terms as First Ward councilman. He and his family quickly learned that a person holding an important city office was besieged by constituents looking for information, contacts, and jobs. Requests came from leaders of many ethnic groups but were frequently from fellow Italian Americans who assumed he would meet their demands. Italians continually telephoned Milano or dropped by his Ingham Avenue home to talk with him. But there was one type of visit that Milano hadn't expected.

Fred Catuzza was a committeeman who had a strong role among the First Ward's Italian political activists. One day he stopped by the Milano house and was greeted at the door by Viola Milano. She invited him in and asked him to have a seat, explaining that her husband was in the bathroom. As soon as she uttered these words, Catuzza walked past her, went straight to the bathroom, where he opened the door, entered the room, and sat on the edge of the bathtub. The startled Milano, who was seated on the toilet, yelled at Catuzza, telling him to wait in the living room. Catuzza refused, saying he had to talk with him immediately about an important issue. Not in a position to change the situation, Milano simply listened as Catuzza explained he needed a part-time job for one of his *paesano's*. The visitor left only when Milano assured him he'd do his best to find a job for the man.

Sources: Interviews with Joe Milano, December 27, 1989, April 9, 1994.

urge DePasquale to run against Milano in the 1937 Democratic primary. DePasquale did so but lost the primary. Milano became the Democratic standard-bearer and faced Republican Julius Karsa, a Hungarian American, in the election for First Ward councilman. Democrats Joyce and James Galligan struck a deal with Karsa and Republican Mayor John Aszkler: They would help finance Karsa's campaign to defeat Milano in return for the mayor's and councilman's votes on key contracts. Joyce and Galligan visited Karsa's home and gave him $1,000 in cash. Putting this money toward the time-honored practice of buying votes, Karsa had it distributed to Italians in Bethlehem Park. As a result, he defeated Milano by 52 votes and became the new First Ward councilman. Milano knew nothing of the alliance between the Democratic bosses and the Republicans, finding out about the donation to Karsa's campaign only years later when Karsa himself told Milano "your friends beat you in the election."[45]

FIGURE 11.10

Registered Italian Voters in Lackawanna, by Ward
1926 – 1950

Ward	1926	1930	1935	1940	1945	1950
1st	113	248	538	662	691	705
2nd	8	9	32	52	29	43
3rd	25	37	95	122	133	107
4th	11	17	33	74	115	162
% of Total:	4.5%	8.1%	8.2%	8.9%	9.2%	9.9%

Sources: Erie County, *Official List of Registered Voters*, 1926, 1930, 1935, 1940, 1945, 1950.

FIGURE 11.11

Registered Italian Voters in Lackawanna by Gender
1926 – 1950

Gender	1926	1930	1935	1940	1945	1950
Male	124	255	497	571	526	583
Female	33	56	201	339	442	434
Total:	157	311	698	910	968	1,017

Sources: Erie County, *Official List of Registered Voters*, 1926, 1930, 1935, 1940, 1945, 1950.

During Milano's two terms as councilman, he was continually frustrated by the constant demands made upon him, especially by the Italian community. He received a barrage of letters and petitions from members of First Ward ethnic organizations looking for jobs and favors, but it was the leaders of several Italian societies who pressured him most. Milano felt he could never satisfy all the demands and was angry that some Italian Americans could not accept the limits of his influence. He had only so many patronage jobs to give out, and half of those had to be given to people from other ethnic groups. Milano had to deal with an Italian community that was divided into small regional and family groups, each with its own narrowly focused agenda. Criticized by many Italians for not providing more, Milano felt overwhelmed. The Lackawanna Italian community had the Italian American Citizens Club and the Federation of Italian American Associations, which provided some direction, but neither served as an effective central structure that consistently set broad-based goals for the entire Italian colony. The leaders of these groups were often the same people who hounded Milano with their individualistic and narrow demands. He regretted that there was no person or association in the Italian community able to provide him with consistent guidance through the city's political quicksand. As

Lackawanna's first Italian councilman, he did he break new ground for the city's Italians, and his election successes encouraged younger, second-generation Italians to claim a larger share of political positions. Milano made a final run for First Ward councilman in 1939 but was again defeated by Julius Karsa, who was returned to office along with fellow Republican and mayor, John Aszkler. During the campaign, Milano asserted: "The city government is now being run by the most ruthless band of politicians in the history of the city. The question before the people is whether the citizens and taxpayers are willing and able to endure two more years of Aszkler's rule." While this type of rhetoric was typical of Lackawanna politics, it did foreshadow events that occurred two years later. Mayor Aszkler, Karsa, the three other councilmen, and several city employees were all removed from office in 1941 following a grand-jury investigation. Milano assumed that these men did the "dirty work" but that Tom Joyce and Jim Galligan were behind some of the schemes.[46]

Other Second-Generation Politicians

Joe Milano's career in public office overlapped with that of Tony Falcone. Born in Buffalo to parents who emigrated from Campania, Falcone was 19 when his family moved to Roland Avenue in 1910. Running for assessor as a Republican in 1931, Falcone received the third-highest number of votes, narrowly defeating Joe Milano. Receiving the Republican, Socialist, and Labor endorsements in 1933, Falcone again came in third, this time topping Angelo Grosso by a scant two votes. In Falcone's 1932-33 term, the two other assessors were also Republicans and Falcone was elected chairman of the group. During his tenure, the board of assessors raised the assessment on the Bethlehem Steel plant from $21 million to $34 million. In 1932, the assessors did a thorough inventory of plant holdings, something that had not occurred for many years. "We did not let anything pass by, and after many months of this hard work we got a(n) assessment, after taking off twenty per cent for depreciation, of $58,000,000," Falcone told a meeting of taxpayers. In view of the impact of the

Angelo Grosso, the second Italian to serve on Lackawanna's city council, was elected president of the council during the 1942-43 term. Photo source: Collection of Angelo Grosso

Flyer encouraging Italians to vote for Angelo Grosso in 1941. Translation:

ITALIANS
Tuesday September 16 do not forget to vote and give your vote to the one who for 6 years has represented the Italian Colony, with fidelity and honesty, in the position of Assessor.
This time he was chosen by the Democratic Party as the candidate for Councilman of the 1st Ward.
This person who merits your vote, is the friend of all, Mr. Angelo M. Grosso.
We are united in voting for him who we all need for our Colony.
He has all the abilities and experience of the business of the city, to administer, to be up to date on all the problems of the public
The timetable for voting is from noon to 9:00 P.M.
The number on the ballot is 19 . . . .
The Committee
Nicholas Falcone
Paul Monaco
Source: Collection of Joe Milano

Depression, the assessors reduced the figure to $34,006,388, and met with steel-plant representatives a number of times. Falcone continued: "I explained to them work of past assessors when one board a few years past put on a large increase and then, after a meeting with plant officials and a visit to a large city for a good time, came back to our city and took off the raise they put on the plant and spread it over the working class people—like you and I. I was willing to compromise with them between 30 to 34 million, but they lost their chance." He noted that Bethlehem Steel had paid $67 million for the plant in 1922, and that plant general manager Timothy Burns himself had stated that, with the improvements made, the facility was worth $115 million. "And they only cry," said Falcone, "that they have been overassessed and they got sore because our assessors would not play with them in their back yard—like some of the past assessors."[47]

The company protested, refused to pay the taxes, and took the matter to court. Without the revenue from Bethlehem Steel's taxes, which made up more than 60% of the city's income, Lackawanna couldn't meet its payroll and seemed headed for bankruptcy. Some unpaid city workers blamed Falcone for this situation; they marched in front of his home and threw rocks. The 1933 elections brought the Democrats back to power in the

FIGURE 11.12

VOTING AND POLITICS IN ITALY AND AMERICA

Italians immigrating to America 100 years ago found both similarities and differences in the political scenes of Italy and the United States. The unification of Italy, which occurred between 1861 and 1870, led to voting rights for the citizens of the new nation. At first, only men who were literate and owned a certain amount of property were allowed to vote—which was about 8% of men over the age of 24. In 1882, the franchise was expanded to include one of every four adult men, but the literacy criteria, which southern landowners insisted on, drastically curtailed the number of peasants entitled to vote. This number was further reduced in the 1890s, when peasant revolts in the south led the government to disenfranchise even more poor people. In 1918, however, the franchise was extended to all Italian men, and in 1946, to women.

Immigrants found a different situation in America, where all men could vote, and women won the franchise in 1920. Newcomers to the country were often courted by ward politicians who rushed them through the naturalization process, took them to the polls, told them who to vote for, and often handed out money, food, or jobs to keep their loyalty. Another new experience for immigrants was ethnic politics. Lackawanna had 92 ethnic groups competing for political and economic resources, although Italians soon learned that the "bosses" were usually of Irish or other northern European stock. Italians from rural towns were accustomed to absentee landowners and a few wealthy families controlling elections and the economy, plus the accompanying nepotism and corruption. Lackawanna had these same basic features: a huge steel plant whose owners and managers lived outside the city, and political bosses and the well-to-do who usually lived east of the railroad tracks. Family was the criterion for hierarchy in Italy; ethnicity, the criterion in Lackawanna. Italians soon figured out that they needed to attain a degree of ethnic unity to advance politically.

Sources: Christopher Duggan, *A Concise History of Italy*, 1994, pp. 136, 168, 188, 195.

Two friends—Joe Cosentino on the left, and Tom Pepper— in 1926. Both men were very active in the Stags and other Italian organizations. In 1937, Pepper became the first Italian elected to the Lackawanna School Board.
Photo source: Collection of Joe Cosentino

mayor's office, on the city council, and among the assessors. Falcone now had two Democrats on the assessors' board with him. The Democratic majority voted to lower the plant's assessment to $27 million, ending the impasse. Falcone stated that the two new assessors had "sold out," adding, "I feel that as the city has reduced the steel company assessment 20 percent, it should give each individual property owner an equal break by reducing the valuation on all other property similarly." Mayor Tomaka responded, "that might be a good idea," but it never came to be. Falcone could take such outspoken and independent stands because he was impervious to Bethlehem Steel Company pressure; being a yardmaster for the New York Central Railroad, he was among the small minority of Lackawanna men who did not work at the steel plant. A Republican committeeman for a number of years, Falcone made unsuccessful runs for the Third Ward council seat in 1925 and 1941.[48]

Angelo Grosso, the son of immigrants from Lazio and Campania, began his political career with an unsuccessful bid for city assessor in 1933. Two years later, again running as a Democrat, he won an assessor's seat, a feat he repeated in 1937 and 1939. In the latter year, he had the highest vote count of all candidates for the three assessor positions. Grosso served

FIGURE 11.13

RALPH GALANTI SR. (1915 – 1993)

Ralph Galanti Sr. became an institution in Lackawanna during his long job tenure as city recreation director. He was born in the Old Village, the eldest of four children of Eugenio Galanti and Filomena Paolozzi. By 1920, the family had moved to 22 Dona Street, where Eugenio had opened a grocery-confectionery business. He encouraged young men to gather there and provided a club room for them behind the store, which led to the founding of the Galanti Athletic Association in 1929. The values in the Galanti home emphasized athletics and group activities among neighbors.

Ralph Galanti became involved in politics in the 1930s and worked in the steel plant from 1939 to 1941. After military service in World War II, he received a master's degree in recreation administration and a teaching certificate from the University of Buffalo. In 1946, Galanti began his 47-year tenure as the recreation director of Lackawanna. The *Buffalo News* described him as "one of the most colorful figures in that colorful city." From the paper's 1993 obituary:

> Galanti, 77, had been Lackawanna's recreation director for 47 years—widely regarded as the longest tenure in New York State. Over that time, he served 11 mayors. Six of them tried to oust

him, but he always survived on his political wits and the good will of generations of Lackawannans who had played on his municipal leagues and had received their first balls and bats free from his storage room. He was noted for sponsoring innovative recreation programs, including a bocce league, yoga lessons for middle-age women, arts and crafts programs for children, and the nation's first youth roller hockey league. Over the years, thousands of high school and college students earned their first paychecks working for Galanti as summer recreation aides or games officials. He was known as the kind of bureaucrat who liked to bend rules rather than enforce them. If money needed to be raised for a dying child, he would lease Ron Jaworski Stadium free of charge to stage a fund-raiser. If a poor child couldn't afford a basketball, Galanti would give him one. He had adversaries—but no enemies. His political battles—efforts to cut his staff or budget or to replace him or appoint someone over him—he referred to as 'funzies.' He never took politics or himself so seriously as to find lasting enmity in anything anyone said about him in the heat of political battle. After

Bethlehem closed its plant, tossing the City of Lackawanna into financial crisis, Galanti voluntarily retired but remained on the job for a salary of a few thousand dollars—the difference between his full pay and pension.

Galanti was inducted into the Western New York Softball Hall of Fame and Distinction. In 1992, the Lackawanna Chamber of Commerce gave him its Citizen of the Year award.

For more than 30 years, Ralph Galanti wrote a weekly column, "Reading Between the Columns," for the *Front Page*. Always joking about the rough edges of Lackawanna politics, Galanti used to say, "Mayors come and mayors go, but my feet will still be on my desk."

Several weeks before his death, Galanti was speaking with Erie County Executive Dennis Gorski, an old friend. "In a sober tone Galanti told Gorski he was getting on in years and had one final favor to ask the county executive. 'You know Dennis, when I die, I wanna go to heaven, but I wanna be buried in Lackawanna,' he said. 'Why?' Gorski asked. 'Because I still wanna vote,' Galanti said.

When he died, his son Chico continued the *Front Page* column, sharing stories about his dad.

Sources: Interview with Ralph Galanti, September 22, 1983; U.S. Census, 1920; *Front Page*, 9/15/93; *Buffalo News*, 9/13/93, 9/17/93, 9/26/93.

as chairman of the board of assessors for four years. He solidified his political base through memberships in Italian groups and other First Ward ethnic organizations, such as the Spanish Welfare Association. These affiliations helped pave the way to his appointment to the vacant First Ward council seat in 1941 following the scandal that forced Mayor Aszkler and all four councilmen out of office. That November Grosso ran on the Democratic slate to retain his council seat and won, becoming the second Italian American to be elected to this position. During his term, 1942-1943, he was elected president of the council. This was a prestigious position, and Grosso was the

first Italian to attain it. The booming wartime economy made it easy for politicians to provide city and steel-plant jobs for supporters, but the role also brought some challenges with it. As the Italian American holding the second highest office in the city, Grosso had to embody the loyalty and patriotism of the city's Italian community during the period, December 1941 to September 1943, when Italy was at war with the United States. As a busy councilman who lived in Bethlehem Park, Grosso had little time to visit his parents on Ingham Avenue. One day his father Antonio admonished him not to forget his boyhood home and to pay the proper respects to his parents.

Grosso made time to stop by his parents' home, even as he found greater political challenges, including a growing racial divide in the First Ward that centered on blacks having access to the new Albright Court public-housing project. This issue and his differences with Democratic powerhouse Tom Joyce, likely contributed to Grosso's defeat by Republican John Panczykowski in the 1943 election.[49]

In the late 1930s and 1940s, other young Italians, born after 1910, were entering the realm of politics. When assessor Thomas Murphy left his position in December 1936 to become city treasurer, Republican Ralph Galanti was appointed to fill the vacancy. Galanti ran to retain the seat in 1937 but came in fourth, just 61 votes behind the third-place finisher, and he again lost two years later. In 1941, he ran for the First Ward councilman's post but was defeated by 25 votes in the Republican primary. Decades later Galanti recalled, in his own humorous way, his struggles with the city's political bosses:

> In 1937, I ran for City Assessor. I was a Republican and the Democrats held a 4 to 1 plurality in the city. Because I was Italian, Tom Joyce and Andy Eszak, two powerful Democratic political figures, were worried that I might win if the Italians crossed party lines and voted for me. At the polling place in the First Ward, Eszak and Joyce hired two guys to stage a fist fight in front of the building. Everyone ran out to see the fight and that's when they switched ballot boxes. I lost by three votes. In 1939 I ran for City Assessor again. Tom Joyce and Andy Eszak were still worried and again staged a fight in front of the polling place. I had Steve Popich watching the ballot box and told him that no matter what happens, he should not leave the ballot box out of his sight. The staged fight was so good and the crowd was so large that Steve's curiosity got the better of him and he ran to the front of the building. This time I lost by 13 votes.

> In 1941, I ran for City Councilman and I was determined to win. I had 12 people watching the ballot box at the polling place. This time, Tom and Jim Joyce went to the Lackawanna cemetery the night before the election. They took all the names off the tombstones and they all voted—against me. I lost by 11 votes. This ended my political career and I remember working in the steel plant until I joined the service during the war.

Galanti did seek a recount, and his father contacted the political bosses, threatening to call the Erie County District Attorney. It was then that Galanti was promised a city job. After returning from military service, he became director of the Lackawanna Recreation Department, a position he held until his death in 1993. During his long career, Ralph Galanti became a popular and respected figure in Lackawanna (see Figure 11.13).[50]

Between 1943 and 1955, no Italians served on the Lackawanna City Council, but other developments led to the advancement of Italians in the city's political system and to a virtually constant Italian presence on the city council from 1956 to present. One factor in the growth of the ethnic group's political power was that more Italians were becoming registered voters. While the total number of city voters tripled between 1926 and 1950, the actual number of Italian voters grew more than sixfold, and as a percentage of total city voters Italians went from 4.5% in 1926 to just under 10% in 1950 (see Figure 11.10). Concentrated in the First Ward, Italians made up more than 15% of the voters there in 1950, were more than half of Bethlehem Park voters, and comprised 41% of voters on Ingham Avenue. Italian women registered to vote in increasing numbers, constituting 43% of the ethnic group's electorate in 1950, double what it had been in 1926 (see Figure 11.11). The maturation of the second generation in the 1930s accounts for much of the increase in voter registration in the Italian community. Those born in America comprised more than half the city's Italian population in 1930.[51]

The increased number of Italian voters was important in citywide elections, such as those for school-board members. A seat on the school board was another entry point into Lackawanna's political and patronage system. There were often many candidates for these unpaid positions—25 people ran for three open seats in 1938—and great interest was shown in the school-board elections. The board's appeal and power resided in awarding contracts for many services, including repairing and remodeling existing structures and erecting new schools, and in hiring staff, including teachers. Teaching was a gateway career by which many working-class people made it into the professional ranks. Awarding contracts and jobs was a good way of reinforcing political ties, and for some, a mode of getting kickbacks from contractors and the newly hired. Stories are legend in Lackawanna about people being instructed to place an envelope of money in the pocket of a specific coat hanging on the wall at a school-board meeting. In the first half of the twentieth century, it was typical for a board member who advocated for the hiring of a person from his or her ethnic group to approach that person (or a family member) just before the decision was to be made and say something like, "I don't want anything from you, but those SOBs (from the other ethnic groups) won't support your hiring unless you pay a certain amount of money. It's not for me, I don't want nothing." In truth, this "friend" on the board often got his share of the payoff. Such was Lackawanna politics.[52]

Newspaper editor, Charles Ellis's 1916 charge of crooked politics, nepotism, and unnecessary repairs echoed for many decades in Lackawanna. The issue of nepotism was again heard in 1939. James Petti, who ran for the school board in that year's

FIGURE 11.14

Italians Appointed to Lackawanna Commissions and Boards: 1920 – 2002*

Civil Service Commission

Donato Chiacchia	1920
Peter Mazuca, secretary	1930
Pasquale Pitillo	1936
Joseph Leo	1948
Charles Barone, secretary	1972
Bill Delmont, chairman	1984
Cesare Cardi, chairman	1994

Board of Health (Health Commission)

Dr. John Fadale	1920
Louis Corsi	1940
Edwin DiCenzo	1943
Joseph Leo, chairman	1946
Constantino Novelli	1946
V. Jimmy D'Alessandro	1946
Anthony Selvaggio	1956

Fire Commission

Tony Colello	1934
Louis Corsi	1930s
Patsy Ricci	1930s, 1946
Anthony DiMasi	1940
Biagio Sperduti	1942
Constantino Novelli	1948
V. Jimmy D'Alessandro	1949
Michael Morgan	1954
Ralph Fiore	1958

Zoning Board of Appeals

Anthony Falcone	1940
Louis Corsi	1958

City Planning Commission

Anthony DePerto	1949

Municipal Housing Commission

Bill Delmont, chairman	1960
Tony Mingarelli	1992
Salvatore Monaco, chairman	2002

Commissioner of Deeds

Anne Monaco-Warren	1943

Stadium Board

Angelo Licata	1953

* This is not intended as a complete listing.
Sources: City of Lackawanna, *Oaths of Office, Books 2-7, 1920-46*; *Lackawanna Leader*, 6/24/43, 2/5/48, 5/14/53, 4/15/54, 1/5/56, 8/2/56, 1/9/58, 2/1/84; *Front Page*, 12/18/02; *Lackawanna City Directory*, 1960; *Buffalo Suburban Directory of Householders*, 1949; *Buffalo City Directory*, 1984; interviews with Cesare Cardi, April 3, 1997; and Tony Mingarelli, July 11, 1994.

---

election, stated that he wanted to correct whatever irregularities that may exist in the administration of Lackawanna's education department. Aware of the public's distrust of candidates' motives, he added, "I have no brothers, sisters, or other relatives looking for jobs." But Petti's stance against nepotism didn't translate into votes, and his campaign was unsuccessful. Two years earlier, a number of candidates—including Nick Thomas, Emedio Chiacchia, Pasquale Ricci, and Tom Pepper—vied for three school-board seats. Only Pepper won a seat, becoming the first Italian to serve on the school board, which was then composed of nine members. The son of Italian immigrants, Pepper had earlier gained public recognition while serving as secretary to the board of assessors. With his election, the ethnic composition of the 1937 school board was four Irishmen, two Poles, one Hungarian, one Croatian, and one Italian. In his position, Pepper was instrumental in getting tenure for Nick Milano and hiring new teachers of Italian extraction. He also helped members of his ethnic group acquire other jobs connected with the schools. For example, Alex Nigro was one of nine clerks appointed by the school board in 1938 to assist with registrations and the canvass of students. While service on the board did not involve a salary, it did lead to political and economic power via jobs and contracts.[53]

Pepper's success in getting elected to the school board encouraged other Italians to seek this position, but his fate was a stern reminder of how one's political future could be quickly undermined. Bethlehem Steel and Democratic Party boss Tom Joyce, who began a 26-year tenure on the school board in 1936, conspired to seal Pepper's fate.

> When Bethlehem Steel signaled it no longer wanted school trustee Tom Pepper re-elected to the board, Tom took on the assignment, and Pepper lost the election. 'That deal was cooked right in my office in the plant,' recalled Ziggie (Armondo) Pietrocarlo … 'The company told Tom to see to it that Pepper was not elected, and Tom told the big boss not to worry.'

The lesson was not lost on Tony Moretti, who was successful in his second try for the school board, winning a seat in 1943. He held the position until his death in 1968. Whereas Milano and Pepper had sometimes challenged Bethlehem and Joyce, Moretti became Tom Joyce's understudy. A popular young man, Moretti was a good choice for Joyce's link with the Italian community and its significant number of Democratic voters. The extended Moretti family was based in Bethlehem Park, which had the controlling block of First Ward voters and where at least a third of the residents were Italian. The political influence of the Moretti family was enhanced in the mid-1950s when Tony's brothers Orlando and Joe Moretti became Democratic committeemen in Bethlehem Park. After graduating from high

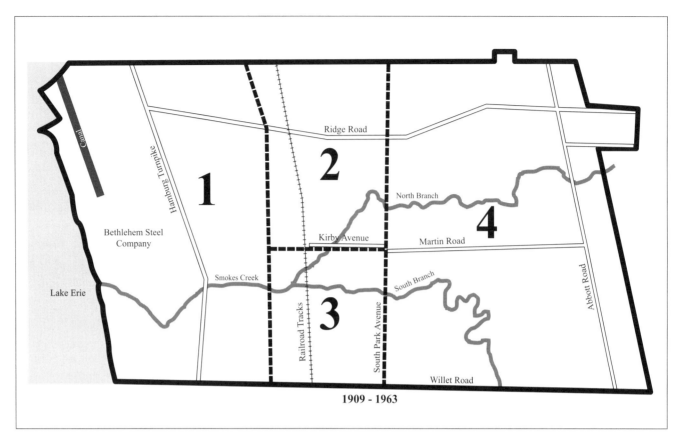

Ward boundaries for the City of Lackawanna, 1909 – 1963.

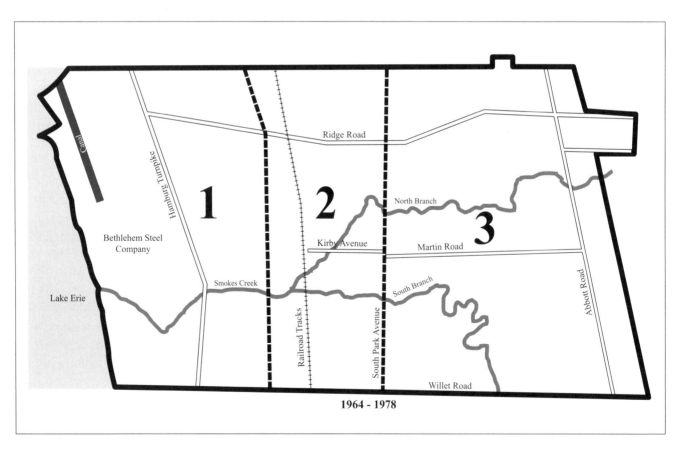

Ward boundaries for the City of Lackawanna, 1964 – 1978.

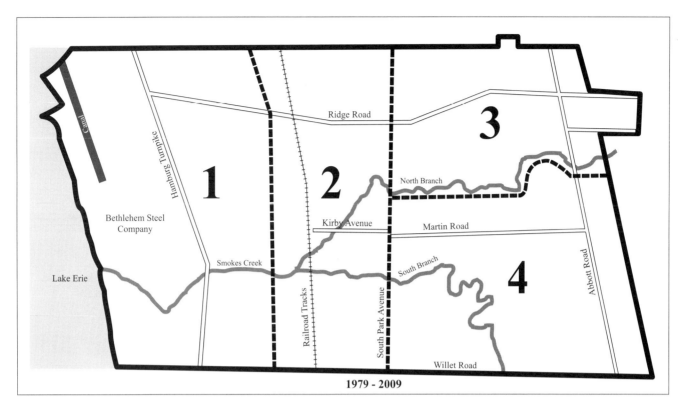

Ward boundaries for the City of Lackawanna, 1979 – 2009. The city's shrinking size recently led to extending the First Ward's eastern boundary to Center Street and the small sliver of land between that street and the railroad tracks. Photo source: Lackawanna City Clerk

school, Tony Moretti procured a job in the Forge Shop at the steel plant, then moved to the Electrical Machine Shop, where he became a general foreman. Like Tom Joyce, who was president of the school board, and Tom Cusack, who was elected to the board in 1949, Tony Moretti held two important spots in the political and economic life of the city: a seat on the school board and a supervisory position in Bethlehem Steel. All three men were able to line up jobs or contracts for supporters in these two spheres.[54]

Ralph Carestio, like Moretti, had been president of the Galanti Athletic Association and was active in the city's social and civic circles. Carestio was elected to the school board in 1947 and became its president the following year. Unlike Moretti, he was not part of the political establishment, and his career on the board followed a different course. In 1949, Carestio was elected to a five-year stint on the board, but it proved to be a challenging position. "There is no place for 'politics,' " Carestio told the *Lackawanna Leader*, "in the administration of a school system and, in my opinion, there has been too much 'politics' to suit me. The board has been operating under a policy with which I cannot agree and it is better that I step out." Carestio resigned in 1952, and Tony DePasquale was appointed to fill the remaining two years of his term. But Carestio had a change of heart, ran in the election

of 1953, and won a one-year seat on the board. Later that year, he fought to stop a school-construction campaign until a comprehensive survey of school-system needs had been completed. He ran for the board again in 1958, teaming up with Walter Andzel to call for reforms: an end to "boss rule," "the elimination of all employment contracts based upon a commission salary," and promotion of teachers and other employees "on the basis of seniority and merit and not on their political capabilities." However, neither man was elected.[55]

Italians continued to align on both sides of the struggles involving the school board. In 1958, the Citizens Federation of Lackawanna (CFL) investigated the board's construction program and campaigned against its referendum to increase school-bond issues. The CFL education committee, led by Edward Lorenzi and Frank Fiore, was instrumental in defeating the referendum and continued to monitor board actions. Tony Moretti was board president in 1960 when the board sold the land adjacent to McKinley School to developers. Many citizens were angered by this sale, and Frank Fiore wrote articles for the *Lackawanna Leader* condemning it. A letter of protest signed by Fiore and McKinley School PTA officers James Speciale and Louis Colello was sent to the state education commissioner. Concerned citizens then formed the Lackawanna League for Efficient Educational Development, or LEED, and

FIGURE 11.15

ALDO FILIPETTI

Aldo Filipetti is the son of Paolo Filipetti and Adele Pascucci, immigrants from Marche. Born in 1930, the youngest of the couple's three sons, he completed eighth grade at Bethlehem Park School and graduated from Lackawanna High School in 1948. After working at the A&P market on Ridge Road, Filipetti got a job in the steel plant's Specialty Shop, operating the shears. Two months later, a young coworker had his arm severed, and Filipetti decided the steel plant was not for him. He attended Buffalo State Teacher's College from 1949 to 1954, working throughout that time at Mirabella's gas station on Hamburg Turnpike. With the help of neighbor and school-board member Tony Moretti, Filipetti was hired to teach developmentally delayed children at the Occupational Educational School located within Bethlehem Park School. In 1962, he became principal of Wilson Elementary School, then went on to the principal's position at Washington School, and, in 1980, at Franklin Elementary School. "I was their trouble shooter, whenever they had a problem. I was a disciplinarian. I always believed in firm and fair. And I always said the three R's were Respect, Responsibility, and Religion."

In 1962, Aldo Filipetti, shown here with some of his students, became the principal of Wilson School in Lackawanna's First Ward. Photo source: Aldo Filipetti

In 1982, Filipetti went to the city's central office where he served first as principal in charge of pupil/personnel, then as head of special education and transportation, and finally, as director of elementary curriculum and instruction. In 1989, he was appointed acting superintendent of Lackawanna schools and the following year, when Superintendent McDonald passed away, became interim superintendent. Filipetti retired from the school system in 1991. He served as First Ward councilman from 1958 to 1961.

Sources: Interview with Aldo Filipetti, July 11, 1996.

ran three candidates for the school board, including Colello. After Colello lost the election by 11 votes, he was approached by the city Democratic chairman who guaranteed Colello a victory if he ran again for the school board. Colello knew there would be strings attached to such a deal, and he refused the offer. A few years later, other Italians were successful in capturing seats on the board. A year after the death of Tony Moretti, Ralph Fiore was elected to the board in 1969, and Bill Mariani won a seat a few years later. Ron Spadone served as a school-board member for all but two of the years between 1969 and 1986. Lawrence Catuzza was appointed to the board in 1995 to fill a vacated seat for a year. More recently, two Italian Americans were elected to the board. Annette Iafallo, who grew up on Ingham Avenue, was a member of the parent teacher student organization at her children's school when she became concerned about school-board infighting. Her son finally said: "Mom, you got to run for the school board," which she did, winning a seat in 2001. Reelected in 2004, Iafallo was board president for two years. Chico Galanti was elected to a three-year term on the board in 2002 and became president in 2004.[56]

Appointed Positions and a New Wave of Italian Councilmen

One avenue to political power in Lackawanna resided in the appointed positions on the city's commissions and boards. For Italians, these began in 1920, and the growing number of Italian Americans who held these seats as time progressed was an indication of the political assimilation of the ethnic group. Figure 11.14 outlines a partial listing of Italian appointments, and their approximate years. Many of these appointees were actively involved in politics as committeemen, former councilmen or assessors, or members of the city committee of one of the political parties. Businessman Peter Mazuca, for example, chaired the Democratic victory dinner following the elections of 1929. The strong Italian presence on the Fire Commission, helps explain the greater number of Italian firefighters compared to policemen, of which there were few prior to 1970.[57]

Following Angelo Grosso's single term as councilman in 1943, more than a decade passed before another Italian was elected to the city council. In the fall of 1955, Joe Amorosi was elected First Ward councilman, and Bill Delmont won the Third Ward councilman's seat. Amorosi, an Ingham Avenue resident and the son of Tony and Lena Amorosi, had earlier made a convincing entry into city politics by being the leading vote-getter among the candidates for assessor in 1951 and 1953. Amorosi was well known as a star football player at Lackawanna High School and Canisius College. In 1957, both Amorosi and Delmont were defeated in their reelection bids, Amorosi losing to Aldo Filipetti. The election of Amorosi and Delmont in 1955 marked the beginning of a 50-year period in which at least one Italian was on the Lackawanna City Council for all but a few years.[58]

Aldo Filipetti's career combined that of professional educator with city politician. In the early 1950s, Filipetti was involved in community projects with his friends John and Joe Moretti, and in 1953, Joe suggested that he and Filipetti run for the two

In Aldo Filipetti's first run for city council, (circa May 1957) his campaign manager was Joe Cellini, center, who was assisted by Steve Witiecki, left, and Walter Gourdine. Photo source: Aldo Filipetti

Democratic committeeman slots in Bethlehem Park. Biagio Sperduti and Edwin DiCenzo had held these seats for most of the preceding 20 years. "They were like the powers-that-be … nothing moved in Bethlehem Park unless they approved it," said Filipetti. The two newcomers were well known and, more important, had the backing of Tom Joyce and Tony Moretti. They both won their bids for election and, following

In their bids for reelection, First Ward councilman Aldo Filipetti and Mayor John Ogarek meet with supporters at the Mexican Club on Ingham Avenue, November 1959. The two men at left are unidentified, third from left is John Ogarek, then (left to right) are: Aldo Filipetti, Frank Balesteros (president of the Mexican Club), Joe Amorosi, and William Eagan. Both Ogarek and Filipetti were reelected. Photo source: Aldo Filipetti

FIGURE 11.16

BILL DELMONT

Bill Delmont, whose family roots are in Abruzzo, was raised in the Roland Avenue neighborhood. He graduated from Lackawanna High School in 1948, then attended Canisius College in Buffalo. He served as a Republican committeeman and one term as Third Ward councilman during the mid-1950s. Staying active in political circles, he held a series of appointed positions at various levels of government: Commissioner, Lackawanna Municipal Housing Authority, 1958-70; Lackawanna Civil Defense Director, 1964-65; Director of Development, Lackawanna, 1971; and New York State Civil Service Commissioner, 1972-91. Delmont also served on the board of directors of Our Lady of Victory Hospital from 1982 to 1998 and was appointed to the board of trustees of Erie Community College in 2002.

From his experience in both elective office and appointed positions, Delmont said he learned it is far more effective to be involved in the behind-the-scenes positions in a political party. "Elected officials come and go, but I'm always here," he said with a chuckle. When he founded the *Front Page* newspaper in 1959, Delmont had at his disposal a powerful political tool. For the last several decades, his has been the only newspaper in Lackawanna. By 1970, he had switched his Republican affiliation to that of Conservative to avoid the city's Democrat-Republican squabbles and lend a more politically neutral flavor to the *Front Page*. Delmont and others slowly built the Conservative Party in Lackawanna and Erie County into a powerful political force. At various times over the past two decades, he's been the party's county (Erie) and city (Lackawanna) chairman. From 1991 to 1995, Delmont was senior executive assistant to the Erie County Executive. Attached to the *Front Page* office is a storefront that serves as the operations hub for the city and county

Bill Delmont. Photo source: Bill Delmont

Conservative Party. Bill Delmont seems to relish his role as the party's master organizer and strategist.

Sources: Interview with Bill Delmont, June 10, 2005; *Front Page*, 11/5/2003.

Lackawanna political tradition, were soon awarded part-time jobs at the city pumping station. At that time, committeemen could command the attention of city hall, and one of the first moves Filipetti and Moretti made was to have the city hire elderly Carmine Colosimo to cut the grass and trim the hedges along Madison Avenue. Filipetti reminisced, "that boulevard was beautiful, and picturesque. And that was his job."[59]

The city's Democratic committeemen elected from among their ranks the chairman of the Lackawanna Democratic Committee. At election time, the chairman urged committeemen to back various candidates and distributed money to them for hiring people to sit at the polls. According to Filipetti, "the chairman would say: ... 'we're going to give you one hundred dollars to spend in Bethlehem Park.' " The committeeman would then hire "ten people at ten dollars a piece or twenty people at five dollars a piece." The poll-sitters, carefully chosen, were typically men and women with five or more other voters in their extended families who were willing to encourage their kin and friends to vote on election day. Bethlehem Park was

crucial in First Ward and city politics. During the 1950s, Filipetti estimates that about 1,200 First Ward Democratic voters turned out. "Bethlehem Park had four hundred some votes. All you had to do was get maybe another two or three hundred out of the rest of the Ward, and you had a majority of the votes." The area around the upper section of Ingham Avenue and along Ridge Road had a large concentration of Poles and other Republican voters.[60]

Filipetti soon became a close associate of Bill Eagan, chairman of the City Democratic Party during the 1950s. Eagan grew up among the Italians on Roland Avenue and was married to an Italian woman from Bethlehem Park. By 1956, he appointed Filipetti as Democratic Party secretary. This was a "stepping stone to get to some sort of district-wide office." In this position, Filipetti could get more things done simply by using his relationship with the chairman. As a committeeman, Filipetti observed, "people would come and they'd say, 'you know my sewer is backed up,' and you'd call and say: 'Hey Billy, send a truck down,' or I call Billy: 'Send a plow down, give it an extra shot in Bethlehem Park.' Or somebody needed a load of dirt or somebody needed a little something, you know, you had your fingers in where you could do favors … Because that's what it's about. It's how many favors you could do for someone."[61]

Aldo Filipetti ran for First Ward councilman in 1957 against incumbent Joe Amorosi in the Democratic primary. Filipetti had the backing of the city Democratic Party, and chairman Eagan called in people of various ethnic groups who were indebted to him for jobs and favors he had rendered. Filipetti's three campaign managers each had a link to an ethnic community: Steve Witiecki to the Polish, Walter Gourdine to the African Americans, and Joe Cellini to the Italians. In addition, campaign workers cultivated supporters among the Mexican, Puerto Rican, and other ethnic communities as well as among some of the Ingham Avenue Italians. Because the First Ward, like the city overall, was predominantly Democratic, the winner of most elections was usually decided in the Democratic primary. Because voting along ethnic lines was a constant in Lackawanna politics, this contest between two Italians created a conundrum. However, Filipetti was from Bethlehem Park, which had a large concentration of Italians, the majority of whom voted for the Italian they knew as a neighbor. With this crucial voting block, Filipetti was able to win the Democratic primary. Adele Panzetta, a Republican powerhouse in the First Ward, did as she had done in earlier elections when an Italian Democrat ran for office. "Mrs. Panzetta supported me indirectly," said Filipetti, "by going easy on the campaign." With this type of support, Filipetti easily won the general election. In 1959, he was reelected to the councilman seat. The previous year, his fellow councilmen had elected him president of the city council, and he was again selected for this role in 1959-60. During a two-month period in which Mayor John Ogarek was ill, Filipetti served as acting mayor. To date, this is as close as any Italian American has come to holding the office of mayor.[62]

As councilman, Filipetti had 40 or 50 patronage jobs to award. Through Democratic Party leaders Tom Joyce, Tony Moretti, and Tom Cusack, who held supervisory positions in the steel plant, Filipetti could line up steelworker jobs for people. He rewarded his supporters, appointing several members of the Puerto Rican club to city jobs, making Joe Cellini (his campaign manager) a foreman in the Sewer Department, and naming Ralph Fiore to the Fire Commission. Eight to 10 jobs were given to Bethlehem Park Italians, including Fred Catuzza Jr., Arc Petricca, and Joe Caligiuri, all of whom had supported Filipetti's campaigns.[63]

Filipetti's second term as councilman proved a challenging one. "The demands by the people and by constituents are so great that … they make you do things you don't wanna do. … great

What I guess I'm trying to say is that politics in general, … you go in there with good intentions, but then because of paybacks and because of the obligations that you have, you can't do what you want to do." In addition to the continual stream of demands from constituents, two issues developed that undermined Filipetti's base of power in Bethlehem Park. The footbridge spanning Smokes Creek, connecting the foot of Spruce Street to the former site of the Old Village, was a handy shortcut for Bethlehem Park residents walking to Lincoln School or Ingham Avenue. The bridge had deteriorated, and Filipetti backed the plan to demolish the span and have a new one constructed. Legal issues delayed the construction of the new bridge, angering many residents. At the same time, many of the elm trees that shaded Bethlehem Park had been infected with Dutch Elm disease and had to be cut down. Residents were very upset at losing the trees that had been part of their neighborhood for four decades. In the election of 1961, an independent Democrat challenged Filipetti, labeling the councilman a "tree hater" and the demolition of the footbridge "Filipetti's Folly." Despite the backing of the Democratic machine, Filipetti lost the primary by 27 votes. Following the campaign, Aldo Filipetti focused on his career in education.[64]

Roland Avenue: Third-Ward Italians

Most of Lackawanna's Italian political activity was focused in the First Ward neighborhoods where the ethnic group was concentrated, but Italians in the smaller Roland Avenue settlement were also active. A definite minority in the Third Ward (an area that became part of the Second Ward in 1964), Italians living there were mostly Democrats but with a significant Republican minority. Tony Falcone, a city assessor in the 1930s, was a Republican, as were some former Democrats including Patsy "Hook" Pitillo, who was offended by Irish politicians who seemed to look down on Italians; he was particularly incensed when an Irishmen made a comment about "Dago voters." In 1921, at the age of 18, Pitillo switched to the Republican party, in which grateful Polish politicians gave jobs to Italians. Pitillo helped round up Italian voters for the Republicans, was a leader of the Roland Republican Club, and in 1936 was appointed to the Civil Service Commission.[65]

Bill Delmont, a Democrat, decided to run for a committeeman post in 1953 but didn't want to run against a friend and neighbor who was also vying for the seat. So he simply changed parties and ran as a Republican. He and Angelo (Ang) Pitillo, the son of Hook Pitillo, won the two committeeman seats for their district. When it came time to select a candidate for the Third Ward councilman post, the Republican city chairman wanted to back the man Delmont had defeated for the committeeman position. Delmont told the chairman, "I could do just as well as he could," but the chairman vetoed this suggestion in an attempt to rein in the young, inexperienced committeeman and his friends. So Delmont and Ang Pitillo got together with a group of their Polish classmates from Canisius College to perform impressive political feats. The two Italians had backed their friend Walter Paryz Jr. in his successful bids for councilman in 1949 and 1951. When it came time to select the Republican candidates for the 1955 election, Pitillo, Delmont, and eight other committeemen held their ranks until Paryz was voted in as the nominee for mayor. Ang Pitillo remembers this meeting of the Republican Party at the VFW hall lasting from 12:00 p.m. until 2:00 a.m. Paryz then joined forces with other young Poles and Italians to get Bill Delmont nominated as the candidate for Third Ward councilman. The Canisius College men, all either Poles or Italians, were a lively group, some even wearing zoot suits to the party meeting. They began an energetic campaign to get their candidates elected, setting up a silk-screen production center to make posters and visiting every saloon in the Third Ward to talk up their candidates. Paryz told Poles that, as mayor, he needed Delmont as Third Ward councilman to help him get things done. Delmont told Italian Democrats that he needed Paryz as mayor to produce results for the Roland Avenue community. In the heavily Polish Third Ward, the Italians were the only other significant ethnic voting block, and if they didn't ally themselves with the Poles, there was little chance any Italian could be elected. Delmont talked with friends whose families had traditionally been Democrats—including the Chiodos, Nassos, Falbos, and Vertalinos—and asked them to get their siblings and parents to support him. Some of the older generation had doubts—including Molly Nasso, who told her son "Delmont's a Republicano"—but they were glad to see someone of their own ethnic group have a chance to become councilman. The Polish-Italian alliance worked; both Paryz and Delmont were elected, and city jobs immediately came to Roland Avenue. Two years earlier, when Pitillo and Delmont were elected as Republican committeemen, only a few city jobs were awarded to Roland Avenue Italians. For example, Pitillo became a garbage inspector in 1954, later worked in the city's Traffic Department, then was employed as a Paint Shop foreman. However, with Delmont's election as councilman and his close ties to the new mayor, many city jobs were awarded to Italian supporters. The councilman's uncle, Charles Delmont, was named commissioner of the Public Works Department, George Yoviene was appointed fire chief, and other young Roland Avenue Italians became city workers. To maintain his rapport with the Polish community, for every job Delmont gave to an Italian, he gave two to Poles.

Tragically, Walter Paryz Jr. died in 1956, and without his strong Polish ally, Bill Delmont was unable to win reelection. He did, however, remain active in city and county politics.[66]

Frank Chiodo was very active in the Democratic Party in his Roland Avenue neighborhood. He was a committeeman for most of the years from 1947 until his death in 2000. Chiodo began a long tenure as clerk to the board of assessors in 1945, eventually becoming chief clerk. He made one unsuccessful run for an assessor's seat and worked for several years as a city real estate agent. A member of the Democratic City Club, Chiodo also was the party's finance chairman.[67]

Italian Americans In Politics Since The 1950s

After World War II, Italians became more prominent in Lackawanna political circles. Those in the Roland Avenue neighborhood captured more committeemen seats, both Republican and Democratic. Others moved into new housing tracts at the eastern end of the city, where Republican Emedio Chiacchia held a Fourth Ward committeeman seat as early as 1940. In the past 59 years at least 46 Italians have held Democratic committeeman slots, 17 have held Republican posts, and 13 conservative Party posts. While only two Italian women began serving as committeepeople prior to 1950, there have been at least 11 others since, four in the Republican, four in the Democratic, and three in the Conservative Parties. A number of Italians switched parties during the past half-century. Gioacchino Orlando was a Republican committeeman in the First Ward from 1930 to 1949, then became a Democrat, serving as a committeeman for that party from 1950 into the 1960s. Others became committeemen in new parties that emerged, such as the Conservative Party. The Lackawanna City Council has included at least one Italian member for most years since 1956. Italians of the second generation as well as those of the third, have held a wide range of other political positions. The career of Don Grosso, the son of former councilman Angelo Grosso, provides a good example of this. Grosso worked for 36 years at Bethlehem Steel, retiring in 2001. He entered politics with an unsuccessful bid for First Ward councilman in 1973 and has since held a variety of political jobs. He was Public Information Officer for the Lackawanna schools and then for mayors Edward Kuwik and Thomas Radich, each in that office eight years. Grosso was principal writer for the campaigns of councilman Robert Surdyke, mayors Kuwik, Radich, and John Kuryak, and, most recently, mayoral candidate Annette Iafallo. During Kuryak's successful campaign, Grosso became the mayor's advisor. After the election, he worked as the city purchasing agent, before becoming Kuryak's personal secretary.[68]

The rules of Lackawanna politics have changed over the past half-century. Ethnic neighborhoods have slowly diminished, and ethnic voting blocks have dissipated. The assimilation process has significantly recast the role of European Americans, and racial divisions have taken on new importance. Carrying less power than in the past, the committeeperson has a reduced role in endorsing candidates. With the reduction of operations at Bethlehem Steel in the 1970s and the closing of most mills in 1983, the main source of taxes and jobs in Lackawanna all but dried up. Without the strong economic base created by the steel plant, city spending and patronage jobs have been drastically reduced, and with them, the political power of committeepersons and other officeholders. Yet some Italians have done well in the political system for many decades. To better appreciate the roles of family and ethnicity in Lackawanna's politics from the early twentieth century through more recent decades, we will examine the political fortunes of one Italian American family.

A Political Family: The De Pasquales

Members of the extended DePasquale family have been very involved in Lackawanna politics for the past eight decades. All of the DePasquales in Lackawanna are the descendants of three brothers and their wives, immigrants from Abruzzo, who settled in the city by 1920. Anthony (Tony) DePasquale, born in the United States, became active in the Democratic party in 1923. He was a Democratic committeeman who represented his Ingham Avenue district from 1934 to 1941 before moving to Bethlehem Park. He served the next six years as an assessor, acting as chairman of the board of assessors for several of those years. DePasquale lost his first bid for First Ward councilman in the Democratic primary in 1937, but 10 years later he had more of a political base, as he was a Bethlehem Park homeowner and very active in civic and athletic groups. DePasquale ran for councilman on the Democratic and Liberal tickets in 1947, won the Democratic primary, but, despite a strong campaign, was defeated in the general election by Republican Andrew Eszak. DePasquale served two years on the Lackawanna School Board during the 1950s. At election time, many a Democratic candidate visited the DePasquale home and received a tour of Bethlehem Park to be introduced to voters. Tony DePasquale remained active in many sports organizations and in the First Ward Democratic Club.[69]

Tony's son Jerry DePasquale was involved in politics by age 14, when he accompanied his father to political meetings and helped put up signs and hand out cards for his father's campaigns. He observed the political leaders who came to the DePasquale house to consult with his father at election time. Although they sometimes squabbled, Tony DePasquale usually

FIGURE 11.17

ANTHONY E. DE PASQUALE

Tony DePasquale was the eldest of 15 children, 11 boys and four girls. His parents, Santo DePasquale and Assunta Casanova, immigrated from Roccamorice, Abruzzo, to Palo Alto, Pennsylvania, as did Santo's brothers Salvatore and Donato and their families. Tony DePasquale was born in Palo Alto in 1904 and by age 14 was a slate-picker in the coal colliers. Salvatore and Donato DePasquale moved their families, including 12 children between them, to Lackawanna and were followed in 1921 by Santo

Anthony E. DePasquale. Photo source: "St. Anthony's Holy Name Society, First Annual Dance," booklet, 11/30/46

and Assunta and their offspring. Tony soon went to work in the steel plant, where he was a pit foreman by 1925. He married Pauline Ginnetti that same year, and the couple had four children.

Tony DePasquale was constantly active in sports and managed a number of baseball and softball teams, including the Robins, Giudittas, the Stags, First Ward Democrats, Pappy's Grille, Baker Homes, and St. Anthony's, on which his son Jerry was a star pitcher. DePasquale was principal organizer of the Vagabonds Athletic Club, and the group's charter was drawn up in a meeting held at his Pine Street home in 1944. The Vagabonds membership was principally teenage boys from Bethlehem Park but also included several adults. DePasquale became the first president of the Vagabonds and managed the club's baseball team for several years. His dedicated encouragement of youth athletics eventually led to his induction into the Lackawanna Baseball Hall of Fame as well as the Erie County Softball Hall of Fame; he was the first nonplayer to receive the latter honor.

Tony DePasquale's brother Mike and son Jerry were later active in the political life of the city, each holding public office for a number of years.

Sources: Interviews with Jerry DePasquale, June 30, 1996; and Francis DePasquale, December 28, 1977; *Lackawanna Leader*, 8/28/41, 5/18/44, 4/10/75; *Steel City Press*, 3/19/47; N.Y. Census, 1925.

Mike DePasquale served four terms on the Lackawanna City Council, from 1964 to 1973. Photo source: Susan DePasquale

Jerry DePasquale was very active in politics, sports, and Italian societies. He served one term as Third Ward councilman. Photo source: Lake Erie Italian Club

Charles Barone Jr., the son of an immigrant barber, served in many appointed positions, including executive Director of the Municipal Housing Authority. Photo source: Charles Barone Jr.

got along with Tom Joyce, the city's Democratic powerhouse. Jerry DePasquale, with some help from his dad and Joyce, got a job in the Locomotive Shop at Bethlehem Steel in 1952 and that same year became treasurer of the First Ward Men's Democratic Club. He and his cousin Charles Barone became disillusioned with the bossism of the Democratic Party, and joined the Republicans. Jerry DePasquale voted for Eisenhower and helped in the campaigns of several local Republicans. In 1961, he was appointed to fill the vacant office of city clerk, but when the Democrats returned to power six months later, he was ousted from this job. When the new city charter of 1964 reduced the number of Lackawanna wards to three and created two councilman-at-large positions, Jerry DePasquale and Charles Barone encouraged Jerry's uncle Mike to run for one of the citywide seats. Mike DePasquale was well known in local circles, having been a city assessor since 1955, a committeeman, and president of Local No. 2603 of the United Steelworkers of America. Jerry DePasquale and Barone, who had returned to the Democratic party, organized the large extended family of DePasquales in the city for the campaign. Jerry relates the story of a phone call that his uncle Mike received during the campaign: "Tom Joyce had gotten a hold of him and said: 'Mike, why don't you run for [county] supervisor? We'll guarantee you to win. We have got someone else in mind for the council-at-large job.'" Mike DePasquale, at his nephew's urging, rejected Joyce's offer. Running on the Steelworkers' ticket, he defeated Joyce's candidate in the Democratic primary, which was tantamount to victory.[70]

After his victory, Mike DePasquale lobbied for his nephew Jerry to be appointed city clerk. The rest of the city council, including the newly elected Joe Caligiuri, went along, and in 1964 Jerry DePasquale became the first full-time city clerk in Lackawanna, a position he held for 28 years. Mike DePasquale went on to be reelected three times councilman-at-large and for nine of the 12 years was made council president by his colleagues. In three of the elections, he ran as an Independent Democrat after being denied the party's endorsement. In profiling candidate DePasquale in 1971, the *Front Page* noted that, " 'Mike' has the enviable reputation of having never lost a Lackawanna city election. He has been the mainstay in the vote getting ability of the Lackawanna Democratic organization although he has not always had the endorsement of his party. He has assumed an independent stance from time to time which has gained him a following among the undecided voting groups in Lackawanna." DePasquale's long run of election victories ended when his reelection bid in 1975 was unsuccessful.[71]

Charles Barone Jr. served in a variety of political positions beginning in 1972, including 13 years as secretary to the Civil Service Commission, Director of Administration and Finance (from 1985 to 1989), and two years as the city's Public Information Director. Barone also was executive director of the city's Municipal Housing Authority from 1993 to 2000, receiving, along with the other board members, several awards for outstanding service from the U.S. Department of Housing and Urban Development. Jerry DePasquale retired from his city clerk job in 1992. Like his father before him, and many

An Italian finally became chair of the city's Democratic Party in 1972 when Tony Mingarelli assumed the role. Mingarelli, on the left, is shown here with New York Governor Mario Cuomo in 1985, when he directed the governor's reelection campaign in Lackawanna. Photo source: Tony Mingarelli

Louis Violanti Sr. became the city's Republican Party chairman in 1963. Photo source: Louis Violanti Jr.

Nick Canali was the first Italian to become city chair of the Republican Party. Shown here (standing at upper left), he and two other Lackawannans are in the office of Erie County Executive Edward Rath (seated at right), circa 1961. Standing at right is Erie County Comptroller Bud Couhig, and seated at left is George Bigaj of the Lackawanna School Board. Photo source: Nick Canali

Thomas Joyce was the Democratic Party boss in Lackawanna for three decades, starting in the 1930s. Photo source: *Lackawanna High School Yearbook*, 1966.

others involved in the city's political life, DePasquale remained active in community groups, serving as president of the Lake Erie Italian Club from 1992 to 1994. He also served as a Democratic committeeman in the Third Ward and was on the executive board of the Erie County Democratic Committee. He made an unsuccessful bid for mayor in 1995 but was elected Third Ward Councilman in 1997. After losing his bid for reelection, he ran for the school board but was unsuccessful. He was appointed the deputy city clerk in 2004, and in the following year was named to the Erie County Charter Review Commission. Other members of the extended DePasquale family have been involved in politics. Patricia DePasquale-Caligiuri was a city assessor from 1986 to 1993, then held a similar job in the town of Aurora after she and her husband, former councilman Joe Caligiuri, moved from Lackawanna. Bernard DePasquale, Jerry's son, was elected a Third Ward Democratic committeeman in 2004. Jeffrey DePasquale became a Fourth Ward committeeman in 2000, as did Lisa Collarino-DePasquale in 2004.[72]

Party Chairmen

A number of Italians became members of the Lackawanna Liberal party in the mid-1940s, and V. Jimmy D'Alessandro was the city chairman. It took many years, however, before Italians gained leadership of the city Democratic and Republican parties. Poles and other eastern Europeans dominated the leadership ranks of the Republican Party for many years. Nick Canali was the first Italian to become city chairman of the party. Raised on Ingham Avenue, where his immigrant father ran a shoe repair shop, Canali was elected a committeeman in

1954 and became vice chairman of the city GOP five years later. When the Party's city chairman moved up to the Erie County committee in 1960, Canali became the Lackawanna city chairman, then was elected to continue in this position for the 1961-1962 term. Louis Violanti became the city's Republican Party chairman in 1963. He had joined the Republican Party in the early 1950s so he could vote for the ticket of young Canisius College men running for office in the Third Ward. In addition to leading meetings, the party chairman made sure election materials got to campaign workers and represented the city on the Erie County Republican Committee. Violanti said he "acted like a coach" to encourage party regulars to turn out the vote at election time. During this period, there were plentiful city and county jobs that committeemen, in conjunction with city councilmen, were able to distribute. If the Republicans didn't always do well in Lackawanna elections and the patronage jobs that followed, they could look to the county, where they usually fared better on election day. In the 1930s, Patsy Ricci was rewarded for his active work in the Republican Party with an appointment to the sheriff's department. Thirty years later, County Sheriff B. John Tatuska, a Republican, appointed Nick Canali as a deputy sheriff, and Louis Violanti Sr. became a deputy in 1967. A few years later, Violanti ceased his involvement in political circles after becoming "disgusted with politics."[73]

Lackawanna has historically been heavily Democratic, and throughout the years, the boss of the Lackawanna Democratic Party, usually also the party chairman, had been an Irishman. Early in the twentieth century, it was Harry Kelley, followed by Nicholas Eagan, who was party chair until 1932. Born in Ireland, Eagan immigrated to Scranton, Pennsylvania, came to Lackawanna, and had a 27-year tenure as a school-board trustee—a pattern duplicated by at least one of his successors. Tom Hayden became the city Democratic chairman in 1932, and Tom Joyce held the position for several terms in the late 1930s and again from the mid-1940s to 1951. Joseph Mescall, party chair for a period during the 1940s, held informal meetings at the Lackawanna Hotel, which he owned. Joe Moretti, a janitor at the hotel in 1944-45, observed as Republican Party and Democratic Party leaders "gathered at Mescall's round table and discussed who would run for political office and who would win." Sitting at the table with Mescall were Democrats Tom Joyce, Jim Galligan, Jim Burke, and Tom Cusack, and Republicans Walter Ogarek, John Pillion, and Steve Vukelic. Bill Eagan began a decade-long chairmanship in the early 1950s followed by Francis Downing from 1963 to 1971. Tom Joyce remained the political power broker in Lackawanna into the late 1960s. What happened in the Third Ward during the 1950s—when a coalition of young, educated men of diverse ethnic backgrounds successfully challenged the established

FIGURE 11.18
A VARIETY OF POLITICAL PARTIES

During the past century, a number of political parties have existed in Lackawanna, and Italians have had a connection with virtually all of them. In the 1910s, the Progressive and Socialist parties had tickets of candidates for all city positions, and in 1919, Socialist John Gibbons was elected mayor by the city's workers in the midst of that year's Great Steel Strike. When Joe Milano ran for assessor in 1931, he had the endorsements of the Democratic and Socialist parties. Also that year, Joseph Fusco was an activist in the Independent Labor Party, and V. Jimmy D'Alessandro was one of that party's three candidates for an assessor's seat. Two years later, Tony Falcone sought the county supervisor's seat on the Republican and Socialist tickets, and Angelo Grosso was on the Democratic and Socialist tickets for assessor.

The gains made by industrial unions during the 1930s led to the formation of the American Labor Party (ALP). During the 1940s, 12 Italians throughout the city served as ALP committeemen. John Falbo chaired the city's 1941 ALP election campaign, Ed Manzetti was a local representative to the state committee, and Angelo Licata was one of the party's three city trustees. A decade later, Joe Amorosi, who received the greatest number of votes of the three assessors, was endorsed by the Democratic Party and the ALP. A faction of the city ALP lost control of the committee in 1944 and broke from the party, forming the Liberal and Labor Committee. The group, which included a number of Italians, joined the Liberal Party, which elected V. Jimmy D'Alessandro as city chairman and Charles Conti as recording secretary in 1948. Some of the candidates who received the party's endorsement were: Tony DePasquale for First Ward councilman, 1947; Costantino Novelli for assessor, 1951; Mike DePasquale for assessor, 1957; and Bill Delmont for Third Ward councilman, 1955 and 1957. Josephine D'Alessandro was city vice chair of Lackawanna's Liberal Party and Sandra Marinelli the secretary-treasurer during the late 1990s.

In the late twentieth century the Conservative Party had grown, and 16 individuals with Italian surnames were committee persons by 1999. Bill Delmont joined the Conservative Party in the 1970s, was the chairmen of the Erie County branch in the early 1990s and became the Lackawanna chairman in 2001. In that same year Alex Billi was elected as the sergeant-at-arms. In recent elections candidates have garnered endorsements from a number of political parties. Jerry DePasquale carried the Democrat, Conservative, Republican, and Right to Life endorsements in his successful bid for Third Ward councilman in 1997. In the 2003 elections, Ron Spadone was elected council president with the endorsement of the Democratic, Conservative, and Working Families Parties, while Joe Schiavi had the endorsement of these three parties plus the Independence Party in his successful bid for Fourth Ward councilman

Sources: *Lackawanna Journal*, 10/28/15; *Lackawanna News*, 9/17/31, 10/15/31; *Lackawanna Leader*, 4/27/44, 10/30/47, 11/8/51, 8/22/57; *Steel City Press*, 4/21/48; *Front Page*, 6/18/97, 11/12/97, 9/23/98; 6/27/2001, 9/17/2003.

Republican leadership—occurred again a decade later in the Democratic Party. Mark Balen created a strong political organization that included other young men who grew up in the new housing tracts in the eastern part of the city, where the mixture of European ethnics reduced the strong emphasis on ethnic cohesion. Balen recruited men of all ethnic groups, including Ron Spadone and Tony Mingarelli in eastern Lackawanna, Ralph Fiore on Ingham Avenue, and Jerry and Ron Baldelli in Bethlehem Park. Balen's group came to full power when he was elected mayor in 1967, which, he said, "pushed Tom Joyce aside." This change in the political landscape helped Italians, who had a "formidable role and were politically astute," according to Balen. Prior to this time, Italians had held lesser leadership roles in the Democratic Party, such as party treasurer—Tony Amorosi in 1932, Ed DiCenzo during the late

1940s, and Roman Catuzza in 1964. It wasn't until the 1970s that an Italian American assumed the party chairman's seat.[74]

After completing high school and a tour of duty in the Navy, Tony Mingarelli began work at Bethlehem Steel. In 1960, he became involved in politics via Fourth Ward councilman Mark Balen. Three years later, Mingarelli was elected a Democratic committeeman, a position he held until 2003. He was very active in Balen's successful mayoral campaign of 1967, and two years later was appointed a firefighter and was soon Balen's liaison with the Fire Department. In 1972, the 64 Democratic committeemen took five ballots, and Tony Mingarelli, nominated by Ron Spadone, finally emerged as chairman. In his new role, Mingarelli called meetings for endorsing candidates to all elective positions and coordinated the handing out of patronage jobs. He served as chairman from

Joe Caligiuri, at left, was active in the Democratic Party, serving one term as First Ward councilman in 1964–65. He is shown here with two other Bethlehem Park political activists, Josh Bellagamba, seated, and John Christiano, at right. Caligiuri's parents were immigrants from Calabria. Photo source: Aldo Filipetti

1972 to 1984 and again from 1992 to 1994. During much of this time, Balen was a strong influence in Democratic circles, especially in the realm of the city's school system. For Mingarelli and Balen, the decline of the steel plant meant less tax revenue and fewer city and plant jobs to hand out to supporters. The ethnic equation had also changed. Both men observed that the ethnic factor—at least among European Americans, and especially in the eastern section of the city—was not as crucial as it had previously been in either the elections or the doling out of patronage jobs. What did matter was a group's ability to organize and produce votes. The new group of Democrats in power forged a stronger connection to Erie County political leaders. Throughout his tenure as the city Democratic Party chairman, Mingarelli, while not always close to the Democratic mayors, maintained strong ties with Joseph Crangle and James Sorrentino of the Erie County Democratic party. Mingarelli's political connections brought him a series of city and county appointments; he was a bingo inspector, housing inspector, and the chief fire inspector between 1966 and 1980. After retiring from Bethlehem Steel and the Fire Department, he was appointed superintendent of Emery Park in 1988 and served as a commissioner on the Lackawanna Housing Authority from 1992 to 2006. Today, Mingarelli is chair of the city's Independence Party.[75]

The Continuing Italian American Presence on the Council

Mike DePasquale was one of two Italian Americans elected to Lackawanna's city council in 1963. The other was Democrat Joseph Caligiuri, who was a committeeman in Bethlehem Park from 1958 to 1963. Caligiuri steered his own course and was affiliated with a group of independent Democrats, most notably Arc Petricca, who was the other Democratic committeeman from Bethlehem Park. Prior to Caligiuri's election as councilman, Petricca, who had been appointed as assistant corporation council, decided to run for chairman of the City Democratic Party. Caligiuri backed this bid, and he and Petricca lined up support among other committeemen who would elect the chairman. Tom Joyce, Mike Dillon, and Mayor John Ogarek all backed Bill Eagan for reelection and used their power to persuade other committeemen to vote against Petricca. After Eagan's victory, Petricca was fired from his job. Caligiuri then circulated a petition, signed by 300 Bethlehem Park residents, demanding that Petricca be rehired. He presented the petition to Mayor Ogarek, telling him "you'll have 300 voters against you" if he didn't comply. Ogarek agreed to appoint Petricca as acting City Court judge, then to the position of assistant corporation council until 1964. Caligiuri and Petricca rediscovered a lesson learned by earlier politicians: Following an independent course gets one on the wrong side of major party leaders.[76]

In the early 1970s, First Ward councilman Celestino "Chet" Catuzza throws the first bocce ball at the Bethlehem Park courts where the Lackawanna squad played its annual tournament against the Century Club of Niagara Falls. Catuzza, whose parents were born in Giuliano di Roma, was on the city council from 1970 to 1973. Photo source: Chet Catuzza

FIGURE 11.19

Italian Americans Elected as Councilmen in Lackawanna

Name	Party / Residence	Ward*	Years Served	Terms
Joseph Milano	Democrat Ingham Avenue	1st	1934-1935 1936-1937	2
Angelo Grosso	Democrat Bethlehem Park	1st	1941-1943	1
Joseph Amorosi	Democrat Ingham Avenue	1st	1956-1957	1
William Delmont	Republican Milnor Avenue	3rd	1956-1957	1
Aldo Filipetti	Democrat Bethlehem Park	1st	1958-1959 1960-1961	2
Joseph Caligiuri	Democrat Bethlehem Park	1st	1964-1965	1
Michael DePasquale	Democrat Shannon Drive	Councilman- at-Large	1964-1965 1966-1967 1968-1971** 1972-1975	4
Celestino Catuzza	Democrat Bethlehem Park	1st	1970-1973	1
Anthony Caferro	Democrat Bethlehem Park	1st	1978-1981 1982-1985 1986-1989	3
Ronald Spadone	Democrat Willett Road	4th Council President	1992-1995 1996-1999 2000-2003 2004-2007	4
Richard Baldelli	Democrat Bethlehem Park	1st	1994-1997	1
Gerald DePasquale	Democrat Ridgewood Village	3rd	1998-2001	1
Joseph Schiavi	Democrat Bedford Avenue	4th	2004-2007 2008 – present	2

*The First Ward was the area between Lake Erie and the railroad tracks until recently, when it expanded eastward to include the sliver of land between the railroad tracks and Center Street. The boundaries of the Second, Third, and Fourth Wards have changed several times. Originally, the Second Ward was the area extending east from the railroad tracks to South Park Avenue and from the city's northern boundary to Kirby Avenue. The Third Ward was the territory south of Kirby Avenue, in between the railroad tracks and South Park Avenue. The Fourth Ward included everything east of South Park Avenue. In 1964, the Fourth Ward was abolished, and the total area of the city between the railroad tracks and South Park Avenue became the Second Ward, and the Third Ward took in everything east of South Park Avenue. Under this plan, a councilman was elected for each ward, and a council president and councilman-at-large were also elected by all the city's voters. In 1979, the boundaries of the Second Ward remained the same, but the Fourth Ward was resurrected. The area east of South Park Avenue and north of Smokes Creek and Wiesner Road became the Third Ward, and the section of the city south of this line and east of South Park Avenue became the Fourth Ward. Since 1980, each ward has elected a councilman and a citywide vote selects the council president.

**In 1968, terms increased from two to four years.

Sources: City Clerk's office, "City of Lackawanna—Elected Officials," 1906-94; interviews

When Joe Caligiuri ran for First Ward councilman in the fall of 1963, he was not opposed by a Tom Joyce-backed candidate. After winning the election, Caligiuri continued on his independent course, disagreeing with the Democratic administration on several issues. One of these focused on Bethlehem Steel's new Basic Oxygen Furnace (BOF), a high-tech open hearth, located due west of Bethlehem Park, that spewed ore dust and soot into the neighborhood. Caligiuri took the complaints of Bethlehem Park residents to a steel-plant official who responded, "Joe, you're stopping progress." When the steel plant wanted to expand the BOF, Caligiuri pointed out that the scrubbers, or air filters, didn't function well on the existing facility, let alone considering a mill expansion. Caligiuri lobbied to have the scrubbers improved before the BOF could be expanded. Other public officials were not as outspoken on this issue, fearing the wrath of Bethlehem Steel and its political allies in city hall.[77]

By the 1960s, patronage jobs had become scarce within the city, and Joe Caligiuri could line up only a few for constituents. With the assistance of Mike DePasquale, Caligiuri was also able to get several Italian Americans into civil service jobs. Outside the circle of powerful political leaders, he did not have access to the jobs at Bethlehem Steel. When it came time for reelection, Caligiuri felt he had 15 First Ward committeemen standing behind his nomination. But the Democratic leadership, still upset by Caligiuri's nonconformity on issues, used their control over money and patronage jobs during the campaign prior to the primary to convince many committeemen to support another Democrat, "He beat me in the primary by 65 votes," recalls Caligiuri. Caligiuri was later appointed by Mayor Tom Radich as his confidential secretary, then went on to a job with the Lackawanna Recreation Department.[78]

Of the 13 Italian Americans who have served as Lackawanna city councilmen from 1934 to present, eight have represented the First Ward, and six have been from Bethlehem Park. Chet Catuzza was sixth in the line of Italian American councilmen representing the First Ward. His father Fred was very active in politics, and his brother Roman was a Democratic committeeman in Bethlehem Park from 1964 to 1970. Catuzza became a city fireman and in 1957 sought the Democratic endorsement for councilman, but "I withdrew for the sake of party unity and backed Aldo Filipetti." In 1969, he ran for councilman, backed by most Democratic committeemen in the First Ward, including his brother Roman and John Masocco of Bethlehem Park, and ex-councilmen Aldo Filipetti and Joe Caligiuri. On Ingham Avenue, he had the support of former committeeman Joe Bernardi. Republican committeeperson Adele Panzetta offered encouragement and even donated money to Catuzza's campaign, perhaps because he was a fellow Italian

but also because she knew that Republicans rarely won these contests. Chet Catuzza defeated two other Democrats in the primary, then won the general election against Republican Joe Sperduti. Republican strategists may have hoped to splinter Catuzza's Bethlehem Park base by running an Italian candidate from the same neighborhood against him. By the late 1960s, ethnicity, or at least nationality, was less important than in previous years. Catuzza noticed that race was becoming a more important variable, as a block of African American voters was present in the First Ward, and that other voting blocks were shaped by neighborhood and party affiliation as much as by ethnicity. Catuzza took a leave of absence from the Fire Department during his tenure as councilman but continued to work at the steel plant. At one point, Bethlehem Steel wanted the plant's assessment lowered, claiming its property was movable, and attempted to get the New York State legislature to pass a machinery-exemption law. Catuzza was offered a promotion to a foreman's post by Bethlehem with the understanding that he would not contest their plan. "I said 'no,'" recalls Catuzza, "and I insisted that the city fight the plant in court." The city did pursue the case at first, but newly elected officials voted to drop it in 1974. Catuzza had a few political appointments that he gave to neighbors from Bethlehem Park, naming Anthony Caferro, who cochaired his election campaign, as sergeant-at-arms of the city council, and Arc Petricca as legislative consultant.[79]

In 1973, other developments overshadowed Lackawanna politics. The Common Council had in 1968 initiated construction of an addition to Lackawanna City Hall, a job completed in 1970. Charges arose regarding kickbacks, and Republican Mayor Joe Bala began an investigation. In 1973, the city clerk and five councilmen, all Democrats—including Catuzza and another man who were not in office until 1970—were indicted. That year, Catuzza ran for reelection but was defeated in the Democratic primary. He was also defeated running as a Liberal in the general election. "The indictments destroyed my career," Catuzza observed. He spent large sums of money on attorney fees, and endured the humiliation of people telling his family members he was a "crook." Although it was too little too late, in 1975, the indicted parties were exonerated.[80]

Tony Caferro, a Bethlehem Park resident, held the First Ward councilman's office from 1978 until 1989. A third-generation Italian American of Calabrian lineage, Caferro graduated from Lackawanna High School and ran several businesses, including the Park Grille in Bethlehem Park. In the late 1960s, Chet and Roman Catuzza got him involved in politics. After serving as sergeant-at-arms of the city council, Caferro was a bingo inspector for two years. In 1977, he ran for the First Ward council seat, with Mike DePasquale

FIGURE 11.20
ITALIANS IN OTHER CITY POSITIONS

Since World War II, many Italian Americans have secured jobs with the City of Lackawanna. Attorney Arc Petricca was a Democratic committee man in Bethlehem Park and in 1958 was appointed as assistant corporation council. In that year and again in 1991 and 2008 he was named city attorney. He has also been appointed as the city's legislative consultant. Petricca was the first Italian American to be elected municipal judge, holding that position from 1972 to 1977, and at various times he served as acting city judge.

Frederic Marrano was appointed acting city judge in 1985 and city judge three years later. In 1989, he was elected associate city court judge, and since 1995 has been the senior city court judge. Louis Violanti Jr. completed his law degree in 1999, was employed as an assistant district attorney in Erie County, and became a city judge in 2007. Five decades earlier, another Italian served as acting city judge in Lackawanna. Richard Buscaglia, a Buffalo attorney who set up a law practice in the Steel City in 1946, periodically sat in for the city court judge until his death in 1953.

Listed below* are some of the many Italians who have held appointed city positions in Lackawanna since World War II.

Dominic Jennetti	Commissioner of Public Works	1946
Joseph Bellagamba	Secretary to Mayor Szczygiel	1952
George Yoviene	Fire Chief	1956
John Moretti	Secretary to Mayor Ogarek Purchasing Director Director of Administration Finance Director	1958
Nicholas Colello	Director of Development	1964
Anthony Collarino	Director of the Engineering Department	1969
Samuel Violanti	Director of Tariff	1973
Donald Grosso	Personal Secretary to Mayor Kuryak	2000
Ronald Cardinale	Chief Engineer	1976
Bruce Colello	Chief Clerk, Department of Public Works	1980
John Fortini	Recreation Director	1993
Angelo Iafallo	Recreation Director	1994
Joe Carnevale	City Clerk	1996
Reynold Jennetti	Fire Chief	1997
Carol Camillone-Daley	City Clerk	2000
Ralph Galanti III	Fire Chief	2006
Tom Nicometo	Purchasing Manager	2006

*This list represents only a sample of the Italian Americans who have held city positions in Lackawanna; it is not intended as a complete listing.
Source: *Front Page*, 9/29/99, 5/22/2002, interviews.

A meeting of the committee advocating for Arc Petricca to be named city judge, Pony Post Restaurant, 1971. From left are: Chet Catuzza, Ralph Fiore, John Mecca, Al Billi, Aldo Filipetti (standing), Arc Petricca, and Aldo Canestrari. Photo source: Chet Catuzza.

Arcangelo "Arc" Petricca was the first Italian to serve as a city judge (from 1972 to 1978). He also held the posts of assistant city attorney and legislative consultant. Photo source: Arc Petricca

As of 2009, Frederic Marrano, at right, serves as Lackawanna's senior city judge, with 24 years of service as a judge. Louis Violanti Jr., left, became an associate city judge in 2007. Photo source: Louis Violanti Jr.

serving as his political tutor. Caferro visited the members of large Italian Bethlehem Park families who had been active as committeemen as he sought the Italian vote that made up about two-thirds of that neighborhood's registered voters. He called on Italians including Joe Capuani and Bob and Alexander D'Amico, who were active politically on Dona Street and Ingham Avenue. Courting blocks of ethnic voters, Caferro made appearances at the Puerto Rican and Mexican American clubs, went to a Serbian pig roast, attended an African American dance, and courted Polish voters at the Harvest Ball at Dom Polski. He also made contacts with the growing Yemeni population and visited their mosque and the Yemenite Benevolent Association. Caferro won the primary running as an independent Democrat, then received the Republican Party and Conservative Party endorsements and went on to win the general election.

During the 1960s and early 1970s, the city council had First Ward homes assessed at a high level to aid residents of that ward who were moving to new homes in the Third Ward. This was finally corrected in the mid-1980s when Third Ward properties were assessed at a higher rate. In a pattern begun decades earlier, the city had again hired more workers than were needed—in this case, hiring men to wheel the garbage cans from people's backyards to the street for pickup then returning them to the backyard. When Bethlehem Steel complained of their high tax rate, Caferro and other councilmen

George Yoviene began a two-year term as Fire Chief in 1956.
Photo source: Jim Yoviene

Dominic Jennetti was appointed Commissioner of Public Works in 1946.
Photo source: Bridget Ginnetti-Bracci

Don Grosso, has held a variety of political posts, assisted five mayors or mayoral candidates, and was personal secretary to Mayor John Kuryak. Photo source: Don Grosso

Joe Carnevale became the City Clerk in 1996.
Photo source: Joe Carnevale

Reynold Jennetti had a 42-year career in the Fire Department and served as Fire Chief from 1997 to 2004. Photo source: Reynold Jennetti

Tony Caferro, Bethlehem Park native, served three terms as First Ward councilman.
Photo source: Tony Caferro

FIGURE 11.21

THE IMPORTANCE OF
AN INDEPENDENT JOB
FOR POLITICIANS

Ron Spadone's long and successful political career was due in part to one advantage he had over most other Lackawanna elected officials: his livelihood never depended on political jobs; he had a good job at Peninsular Steel. Another city councilman who had an independent job was Tony Caferro, who ran his own business. Most of the city's politicians over the past century—such as committeemen, assessors, and councilmen, have had jobs with the city or the steel plant or both. Given the entanglement of the steel plant and city hall, these jobs were always vulnerable to political influences, as Joe Milano discovered in the 1930s.

Several other Italian American politicians had independent jobs that enhanced their ability to resist political coercion. In the early 1930s, city assessor Tony Falcone, a Republican from Roland Avenue, rallied the other two assessors to stand with him against Bethlehem Steel and its city-hall allies and raise the tax assessment on the plant to a more realistic level. Falcone took part in litigation that increased Bethlehem Steel's assessment from $21 million to $34 million. Falcone's outspoken critique of the steel-plant city-hall alliance was possible because he didn't have to fear for his livelihood. He worked as a yardmaster for the New York Central Railroad in the Seneca yard in Lackawanna, a rare post where the mayor and the management of Bethlehem Steel had little influence.

Jerry Baldelli was a committeeman in Bethlehem Park for two terms during the 1960s. Unlike most committeemen of that time, Baldelli did not work for the city or in the steel plant. During elections, he, along with his brother Ron, canvassed door to door, arranging rides to the polls for people who had difficulty with mobility, and usually got 60-70% of their neighbors to vote. Baldelli was well respected in Bethlehem Park and had a large following, a fact well noted by another resident of the neighborhood, Tony Moretti. A close ally of Democratic Party boss Tom Joyce, Moretti wielded much clout in the steel plant and city hall. Jerry Baldelli demonstrated his independence, backing Ron Spadone's bid for office and writing his campaign platform. Though Spadone was not in the Joyce camp, Moretti was always careful not to alienate Baldelli.

Sources: Interviews with Ron Spadone, December 18, 2005; and Jerry Baldelli, December 18, 2005; *Lackawanna Leader*, 9/11/41.

voted to end the practice of moving the garbage cans. Caferro found that Steel City residents turn out to vote, with some 65% of voters appearing for primaries compared to the Erie County average of 30%. "People in Lackawanna play politics with a passion," he said. "They play hardball. People let you know weekly how they feel—happy or angry." As to ethnic politics, he stated, "Italians don't stick together today like they used to. I caught the tail end of Italians voting for Italian candidates." Tony Caferro was twice reelected to his First Ward councilman's seat, and in 1979 was elected city council president by his peers. His career as a councilman came to an end when George Halsey defeated him in the election of 1989. Caferro was appointed the city's Director of Administration and Finance in 1992 and 1993.[81]

Rich Baldelli was the last in the 50-year succession of Italian American councilmen from Bethlehem Park. A third-generation Italian American who traces his lineage to Marche and Calabria, Baldelli worked as a maintenance man in the Lackawanna schools. He was campaign manager for Tony Caferro, a Democratic committeeman in 1992-93, and was elected First Ward councilman the following year. When Baldelli was sworn in at city hall, an elderly man approached him, offered his congratulations, and said: "I've been in your position before." The man was Joe Milano, who, 60 years earlier, was the first Italian American elected as a Lackawanna councilman.[82]

Ronald Spadone has had the longest political career of any Italian American in the city, and the most successful in terms of elections won. A member of the board of education for 16 years, Spadone then served on the city council for 14 years. He grew up on Milnor Avenue and then Greenwood Street in the Fourth Ward. His father Enrico was an immigrant from Marche, as was his mother, Josephine, who was a child when she emigrated from Italy with her parents. Spadone commenced a four-decade career at the Tonawanda office of Peninsular Steel in 1960, then became involved in politics for a similar length of time. In 1962, he was recruited into the emerging political organization of councilman Mark Balen, for whom he campaigned in subsequent elections. Four years later, Spadone was elected as a Democratic committeeman in the Fourth Ward, a position he has held since then. Like others before him, he learned that political power in multiethnic Lackawanna involved making alliances with people of various ethnic backgrounds. As he pondered a run for the school board, Spadone observed that many people holding high city positions were of Irish or Serbian background, and that the number of school-board members had been reduced from nine to seven in the 1950s. He ran for a school-board seat in 1969 against a well-known and well-financed opponent who had the backing of Tom Joyce. Spadone was supported by the Balen organization

FIGURE 11.22
THE MAYOR'S OFFICE

Lackawanna's highest elective position has eluded Italian American candidates. Since 1924, when Walter Lohr began his first term as mayor, the vast majority of mayors in Lackawanna have been Polish or of other eastern European descent. During the past four decades, a number of Italian candidates have emerged, but none has been able to secure the mayor's seat. In 1957, Joe Milano made his last attempt at elective office, running as an Independent Democrat for mayor. Joe Amorosi, who had earlier lost the Democratic primary for First Ward councilman, also ran for mayor that year. Both men were opponents of John Ogarek in the Democratic primary, which set the scene for splitting the Italian vote. Milano attempted to strike a deal with Amorosi, promising that he would run only in 1957 and asking Amorosi to drop out of the race and wait until 1959 to seek the Democratic mayoral endorsement. But the two men could not come to terms, and Milano assumed that a combination of Irish and Polish politicians helped create the situation that kept Amorosi in the race. An Italian candidate needed to capture the majority of Italian voters as well as many voters from other ethnic groups to win the all-important Democratic primary. Poles, who have constituted the city's largest ethnic group, were heavily Republican, while most Irish, Serbian, Croatian, Hispanic, and black voters were Democrats. Partly as a result of the Italian vote being split between two Italian American candidates, John Ogarek, a Polish American, won the Democratic primary and went on to be elected mayor. During the campaign, Milano had picked up the Liberal Party endorsement and planned to carry out only a token campaign. Reminiscent of a scenario from the 1930s, Milano was asked by Democratic boss Tom Joyce to drop out of the race and make a statement urging his followers to vote for John Ogarek. If he did so, Joyce would see that Milano got any city job he wanted. Milano declined the offer. Following Ogarek's victory in the 1957 election, Joe Milano retired from politics.

In the 1980s, Roman Catuzza and Arc Petricca both ran for the mayor's office. Both men were raised in Bethlehem Park, which had the largest single concentration of Italian American voters. A letter addressed to "Italian Friends & Neighbors" from the "Italian American Committee to Elect Arcangelo Petricca Mayor of Lackawanna" called for ethnic unity: "Remember it's time for all sincere and dedicated Italian-Americans to band together for the good of the entire community." Despite this effort, Petricca, like Catuzza, was unsuccessful in his bid for mayor. Petricca ran against Tom Radich two times. "The first election was close," he recalls, but "in the second I was defeated by 600 votes."

Jerry DePasquale was a candidate for mayor in 1995, launching his campaign at the Lake Erie Italian Club, of which he was then president. Some Italians were skeptical about the chances of a member of their ethnic group running for mayor, several even telling DePasquale that "an Italian can't win." He responded that several Irishmen have been mayors, as have two Croatians, Mark Balen and Tom Radich. DePasquale, who had been out of the public eye since retiring from the City Clerk post three years earlier, worked hard on his campaign but lost the Democratic primary to incumbent Kathleen Staniszewski. After serving on the city school board for six years, Annette Iafallo became the first Italian American woman to run for the mayor's seat. She ran in the 2007 Democratic primary against incumbent Norm Polanski but lost the contest after a spirited campaign. To date, Aldo Filipetti, who temporarily filled in for the mayor, has been the only Italian American to sit at the mayor's desk.

Sources: Interviews with Joe Milano, April 9, 1994; Arc Petricca, July 9, 1996; and Jerry DePasquale, June 30, 1996; *Front Page*, 9/12/2007, 9/26/2007.

in the Third Ward; in the Second Ward by Ben Falbo, who helped mobilize Roland Avenue voters; and by Don Grosso and Ron and Jerry Baldelli, who campaigned for him in Bethlehem Park. Spadone attacked the nepotism that had existed for many years, calling it "a danger that bestows patronage on family relations rather than on merit or qualifications. It makes superiors afraid of subordinates who happen to be related to school board members and it makes subordinates fear that their actions will be reported directly to top school officials by these ' relatives.' " This touched a nerve among voters and Spadone was successful in his first run for elective office. But his initial school-board meeting was a cold introduction to Lackawanna politics. The board's six other members were in the Joyce camp and were upset that Spadone defeated their candidate. During this time, each public board meeting was preceded by a closed "premeeting" at which many of the actual decisions were made. When Ron Spadone entered the room, the six other members walked out, and one actually said, "We don't want you here!"— to which the new member replied, "Two thousand people want me here, this is where I am staying, you're stuck with me for five years." At first, the premeetings were held elsewhere, without Spadone's knowledge, and it was tough going for him

Ron Spadone has been a committeeman, school-board member, and city-council member and president over the past 43 years. His 16 years on the city council represent the longest tenure of any Italian American. Photo source: Ron Spadone

Rich Baldelli was the most recent Bethlehem Park Italian to sit on the city council. His single term lasted from 1994 to 1997. Photo source: Rich Baldelli

Joe Schiavi, in his second term as Fourth Ward councilman, is the only Italian American currently on the city council. Photo source: Joe Schiavi

in his new position. The school superintendent recommended people to be hired, but the board did the actual hiring. When the other six board members learned that two of the 20 night watchmen were supporters of Spadone's, they fired all 20 then rehired all but the two Spadone men. The stances Spadone supported were often outvoted by the other board members one to six or two to five.[83]

Eventually, the newcomer made friends with at least one of the other members, and a few years later, four of the six went to jail after being convicted of corruption. Spadone went on to win reelection for the next 10 years. In 1979, however, the school board was again reduced, this time to five members, and Spadone did not seek reelection. He ran again in 1981 but was unsuccessful, losing by 12 votes. He quickly sprang back in 1982, winning a four-year term. Shifting his focus to the city council in 1987, Spadone was defeated in the Democratic primary in his first bid for a council seat. He won the 1991 election for Fourth Ward councilman, and held this seat until 2003, when he was elected president of the council. Spadone attributes his political success to his door-to-door campaigns in every election and, once in office, always being available for citizens' phone calls. In Lackawanna, Spadone said, where "seven of every 10 families is involved in politics," and, due to past practices when many people had patronage and no-show jobs, "everyone is looking for something." He himself made few promises regarding jobs. Spadone said he "learned the art of compromise," even as he pursued

educational, athletic, and extracurricular programs for Lackawanna's youth. While in the citywide post of council president, Spadone touched base with European ethnic groups, often attending their festivals, and consulted with African American and Puerto Rican leaders as well as those of the growing Yemeni community. His 14-year tenure on the council has been the longest of any Italian American politician.[84]

Joe Schiavi was elected Fourth Ward councilman in 2003 and reelected in 2007. He grew up on Ingham Avenue, the son of immigrants from Lazio, and graduated from Lackawanna High School in 1962. After military service, he worked as a clerk at Bethlehem Steel until he was laid off, then was employed by the Lackawanna School District. Schiavi moved to the Fourth Ward in 1979 and served as a Democratic committeeman from 1982 to 2005. The current challenges that he and other Lackawanna councilmen face are immense. The city is near its taxing limit, and the population is shrinking. The steel plant which brought the city tremendous wealth is a thing of the past. The problem that all Lackawanna politicians have faced since 1983 is the economic disaster caused by the closing of the Bethlehem Steel plant. The situation has grown worse in the ensuing 25 years. The coke division of Bethlehem was shut down in 2001, causing a loss of 340 jobs and leaving only 420 steelworkers at the Galvanizing Mill and Cold Mill division of the Strip Mill. That same year, the South Buffalo Railway was sold to Genesee and Wyoming

Industries, a regional operator. Following the bankruptcy of the Bethlehem Steel Corporation in 2001, its remaining Lackawanna facilities were purchased by a series of international corporations that sought to lower the taxes paid on property in the Steel City, opening a new episode in the plant's century-old tax-assessment battle. The final owner, the ArcelorMittal Corporation, closed the Lackawanna plant in 2009 by shutting down the last facilities, the Galvanizing Mill and the Cold Mill of the Strip Mill.[85]

New York State and Erie County have helped fund the Gateway Port complex located at the north end of the former Bethlehem Steel site, including dredging the ship canal and improving the rail network serving the area. The city of Lackawanna has redeveloped the land along Ridge Road and Hamburg Turnpike, attracting a number of small businesses in the First Ward. But the city struggles to meet its basic budget. During the last four decades, the city has lost almost half its population due mostly to the departure of younger people relocating in search of jobs. The 1960 population of 29,564 dropped to 19,064 in 2000, and the estimated population in 2007 was 17,707. Only the influx of hundreds of Yemeni has prevented an even greater decline. The city and the region are now part of the so-called rust belt, and the huge industrial complexes that once produced thousands of jobs and countless dollars in property taxes are things of the past. The city's colorful political days have passed along with the mighty steel plant that a century ago was called the "eighth wonder of the world."[85]

ITALIAN-AMERICAN COMMITTEE
TO ELECT ARCANGELO PETRICCA MAYOR OF LACKAWANNA

Dear Italian Friends & Neighbors,

ARCANGELO (ARC) PETRICCA, one of our very own, is a candidate for Mayor of Lackawanna.

As you know, Arc is a first generation Italian-American born right here in Lackawanna. His parents, Guiseppe and Lidia Petricca were from Guiliano di Roma about 35 miles south of Rome. His dad, Joe or Peppino as he was affectionately known, immigrated to America in 1910, to work on the Erie Barge Canal, and from there to Lackawanna, and the Bethlehem Steel Company, where he worked in the open hearths for about 50 years.

Arc comes from honest, hard working parents and he has followed in their tradition, working since he was a kid, first on the farms, then for Pliss Brothers Clothiers, then the Bethlehem Steel Company where he worked his way through college and law school. After serving his country overseas for 2 years he returned to Lackawanna and started a law practice. He is respected wherever he goes, as a first class lawyer and he served the community for many years as council attorney and then as our City Court Judge. Arc has come up the hard way, in fact, he has been up and down and back up again the hard way.

Arc lives with his wife, Nancy, and their three children, Cathy, Joe and Lidia at 59 Pellman Place. He is a good person and he deserves our support, not because of his ancestry but because he is immensely qualified to be mayor. He is one of us and we can be proud of him and his decision to run at such a crucial time.

One November 3rd, election day, Arc needs your help. Please give him your vote and ask your family to vote for Arc Petricca on line 9B or 9E. IT IS IMPORTANT TO REMEBER LINE 9B or 9E. You'll be glad you did.

Sincerely,

Anthony Anticola , John Falbo Jimmy D'Alessandro

P.S. Remember it's time for all sincere and dedicated Italian-Americans to band together for the good of the entire community.

Arc Petricca twice ran for mayor in the 1980s. His supporters used this letter to campaign for him in Lackawanna's Italian American community. To date no Italian candidate has been elected mayor of the city.

AFTERWORD

This book has told the story of transitions endured by Italians as they assimilated into the Lackawanna community. It is a history set against the backdrop of a small industrial city that was also home to 91 other ethnic groups, and a nation that was going through a period of great change during the first half of the twentieth century. The focus has been on Italian immigrants—the first generation—and their American-born children—the second generation; these two generations faced the most challenging circumstances while trying to make a life in Lackawanna in the years 1900 to 1945. The immigrants, mostly from small farming villages in southern Italy, had the difficult task of adjusting to city life, and a language, culture, and work settings in a huge steel plant that were very different from their experience in Italy.

The Italians and other southern and eastern Europeans were viewed as inferior by American nativists, and prejudice and discrimination against them were common. Yet the Lackawanna Italians seemed to have escaped the harsh discrimination that their fellow Italians endured in big cities such as Buffalo. This may have come about because the southeastern European immigrant groups constituted the majority of Lackawanna's population and the Irish political leaders could ill afford to alienate so many Catholics and voters in a town were virtually everyone went to the polls on election day. Also, the arrival of blacks and other people of color in the 1920s drew the attention of nativists and bigots away from Italians. Nativists began to focus more on race, the most virulent prejudice in American society, which continues to haunt our social order.

The Steel City Italians were unusual in that they worked in a steel plant during the 1900 era, when few other Italians did so. They were mostly from south central Italy, especially the regions of Lazio and Abruzzo, which differed from many other Italian colonies where the more numerous Siciliani and Napolitani often dominated. Also, the 3,070 Italian immigrants who came to Lackawanna displayed tremendous mobility, most of them remaining only a short period and then moving on. Many of those that did settle in the Steel City had previously lived in other countries and in other locales within the United States. As they adjusted to their new location, it was common for immigrants and their families to move several times within the city before buying a permanent home.

The maturation of the second generation during the late 1920s and 1930s brought the energy and skills of well acculturated young adults into the Italian community. These Italian American men and women both challenged the leadership and lifestyle of their immigrant parents and also worked with them on important issues. Both generations struggled with their identity—the immigrants challenged by the strong provincialism that often divided the Italian colony, and the second generation facing the prejudice of nativists who saw even the American-born Italians as too foreign.

The Great Depression presented a tremendous challenge to both the first and second generations, and the drive to organize a steelworkers union that began in 1936 involved the immigrants and their sons, who along with other white ethnic groups sensed a common cause with all other blue-collar workers. One immediate result of this unity was seen in the 1936 presidential election, 66% of the 1,207,674 steelworkers in 91 American towns voted for Franklin D. Roosevelt, and in Lackawanna the vote was an impressive 80% of the city's 7,955 steelworkers. It was a long road to the ultimate union victory in 1941 at the Lackawanna plant, which was a great moment in American labor history for both white ethnics and steelworkers of color. It led to the defeat of "Little Steel"—Bethlehem, Republic and other companies that were smaller than U.S. Steel, but that collectively made up a large part of the steel industry. The victory at the Lackawanna plant in February 1941 was followed by a cascade of other victories that brought unions to all steel plants. The birth of the United Steelworkers of America ended the arbitrary power of foremen, won better pay and working conditions for workers, and provided opportunities to move up to higher positions in the mills and in the new structure of the union. It was a revolutionary event that removed many types of inequality; it represented a redistribution of wealth and social services, the end of the unlimited use of power by supervisors, and the start of using the grievance process to solve problems. [1]

Pearl Harbor came shortly after the union victory and represented a formidable hurdle and litmus test for Italian Americans, especially the second generation, which proved its loyalty through military service against enemy nations that included Italy from 1941 to 1943. At home their immigrant parents supported the war effort. The war's end brought the end of systematic prejudice against Italians. It also brought the benefits of the GI bill that helped so many Italian Americans buy homes and get a college education. After two generations in America, Italians were finally being accepted into mainstream society.

In the 1960s a Catholic was elected as president and a new immigration law did away with the insulting national-origins and quota-system legislation of the 1920s. Italians, Slavs, and other Catholic ethnic groups, along with Jews, finally were free of the official cloud of distrust that hovered over their heads for years. The white-ethnic movement that began in the late 1960s afforded Italians and other groups from southern and eastern Europe an opportunity to display pride in their ethnic roots and accomplishments, an action they had stifled as part of their assimilation. The general acceptance finally accorded Italian Americans by the nation's elite and their gradual entry into the highest stations of American society in the late twentieth century led to an even more dramatic cultural transition. Italians and the other white ethnics were becoming part of the mainstream's official story. Suddenly, it wasn't only the WASP settlers, Revolutionary War heroes, and founders of the United States who were models of true Americanism, but also the humble immigrants from southern and eastern Europe who had passed through Ellis Island and helped build the country in the past 130 years.

Since 1950, many of the younger members of the second generation and coming-of-age members of the third generation attended college, entered professional careers, or attained skilled positions. The third-generation Italian Americans in Lackawanna were doing well for themselves. Since the demise of the local steel industry over the past 25 years many third-, fourth-, and fifth-generation Italians have joined the exodus from Lackawanna and Buffalo. Once again the economic system of their homeland has forced people with Italian roots to consider migrating in search of stable jobs and income.

Some Historical Themes

The long view of history often adds to our understanding of themes that run throughout our country's story. Although history may not repeat itself in the form of specific events being acted out again, themes often repeat themselves. Rebellion and terrorism, immigration, and the corporate domination of the U. .S. economy are current challenges that Americans must address. These were also issues for previous generations. In eastern Pennsylvania during the 1860s and 1870s Irish American coalminers belonging to the Molly Maguires used violence to combat the brutal policies of the coal companies. Following several unfair trials 20 men were executed, although a number of them probably were not guilty of murder. In 1900, an Italian-American anarchist, Gaetano Bresci, traveled from Paterson,

New Jersey to Italy and assassinated King Umberto I. The next year Leon Czolgosz, a Polish American, came to western New York from Ohio and is thought to have lived for a brief period in the part of West Seneca that became Lackawanna. He shot and mortally wounded President William McKinley in Buffalo, a crime for which he was tried and executed shortly afterward. During the first quarter of the twentieth century, radicals and anarchists from southern and eastern Europe were seen as terrorists and blamed for a number of bombs that were exploded throughout the United States. In 1927, Italian immigrants Nicola Sacco and Bartolomeo Vanzetti were executed in Massachusetts for being anarchists. Seventy five years later, members of Lackawanna's large Yemeni community of Muslims were accused by the U.S. government of being terrorists. These men, known as the "Lackawanna Six," were investigated, and they eventually pleaded guilty to providing material support to the Al-Qaida terrorist group.[2]

Immigration, both legal and illegal, has been a passionate and divisive topic for as long as the United States has been in existence. The arrival of Irish and German Catholics in the 1840s and Chinese and Japanese immigrants several decades later led to violence and, in the case of Asians, the passage of exclusionary immigration laws. In the early 1920s, the infamous national-origins and quota laws significantly reduced the number of immigrants from southern and eastern Europe allowed to enter the United States. Furthermore, nativists were pushing for action to stop the flow of illegal arrivals. To thwart such efforts to keep them out, many immigrants went to Canada and entered the United States at desolate points along the 2,000-mile border. In western New York, it was common for immigrants to make nighttime crossings of Lake Erie or Lake Ontario to secretly enter the United States. In view of the strict immigration laws passed a few years earlier, Congressman James Mead advised his constituents in 1929 that a new federal ruling would allow people who couldn't prove their legal entry into the United States to become citizens. The congressman promised to take up the cases of these individuals with the Immigration Bureau in Washington, DC. The current (as of June 2009) issue about legal versus illegal immigrants from Mexico is another sad repetition of this theme, with businesses and corporations wanting the migrants for their cheap labor, but joining nativists in refusing to welcome them as potential citizens. A century ago Italians were the largest group of immigrants, and the most disadvantaged of the major immigrant groups in terms of social capital—literacy, education, job skills. In recent times it is Mexicans who compose the largest group of immigrants coming into the United States and who are the most disadvantaged. While there are important differences in the experiences of these two groups, there is much in common—

both of these Latin cultural groups have endured significant discrimination and have been the main targets of restrictive immigration laws. Italian Americans and Mexican Americans have much they can learn from each other, and all Americans could benefit from discussing the similarities and differences in the experiences of these and other minority groups.[3]

The robber barons who headed American corporations during the Gilded Age a century ago were much like the powerful corporations of today. The Lackawanna Steel Company's profits at times were huge, while the wages of its workers, who often toiled 12 hours per day, were not. A larger, even more aggressive corporation, Bethlehem Steel, bought out Lackawanna Steel in 1922. During the union-organizing campaign of the late 1930s, workers at the steel plant were outraged to learn of the hefty salaries and huge bonuses earned by the top executives of Bethlehem. Just as Lackawanna Steel fell on hard times and was bought out by Bethlehem in 1922, Bethlehem went bankrupt eight decades later and was purchased by a larger corporation, International Steel. The company was in turn gobbled up by Mittal, which then merged with Arcelor Steel in 2006 to become ArcelorMittal, at present the largest steel company in the world with 326,000 employees in 60 countries. In the past the owner of the steel plant became deeply involved in Lackawanna politics, including such destructive acts as: prohibiting blacks from living in its Bethlehem Park subdivision, allowing its private police to use deadly force in the 1919 strike, setting up a phony union and forcing workers to vote for company-approved representatives, using a system of spies to disrupt and punish pro-union workers, and encouraging the use of force by the Buffalo police in the 1941 strike. Similar tactics are still in use by American corporations, and union membership is at a low point. American workers again must face the daunting task of expanding existing unions and organizing new ones to get fair wages and working conditions from corporations obsessed with the bottom line and quick profits. Like previous owners of Lackawanna's steel plant, ArcelorMittal sought property tax reductions. Finally, in 2009, it closed down the last two mills—the Cold Mill division of the Strip Mill and the Galvanizing Mill.[4]

Most of the structures on the site of Lackawanna's steel plant have been torn down. This strip of land, where the largest steel plant in the world was erected more than 100 years ago, has for the last 20 years looked more like an abandoned airfield, until a series of huge wind turbines were recently installed atop the hills of slag on the shore of Lake Erie.

The Future of Lackawanna's Italian Community

Assimilation, which occurred via the eight steps described in Chapter 4, took a hefty toll on Italian American culture. While many members of the second generation spoke Italian and knew the customs of their immigrant parents, these characteristics are rare among the third and later generations. The payoff for assimilation has been the dramatic reduction in belittling remarks and denied opportunities that were present prior to 1945, before the second generation had proved its patriotism and acceptance of American cultural ways to the nativists' satisfaction. As long as Italian Americans, as well as other white ethnics, didn't get too exuberant about publicly pursuing ethnic issues, they were for the most part spared bigoted responses. In many ways, this was a tremendous relief, and as the second generation formed their own families, many kept their ethnic past and traditions under wraps, as if they were sensitive secrets. This was most apparent with the language spoken. Many third generation Italian-Americans report that their parents never attempted to teach them the Italian language, and spoke Italian only to keep sensitive matters from their children's ears or to communicate with their immigrant parents. In a sense, Italians finally began to feel that they fit in and were full members of the wider community. At the same time, they were proud of their personal accomplishments and those of their ethnic group. Within their homes they celebrated the entertainers, athletes, and other Italian Americans who had achieved fame, and they lamented the media and government's constant fuelling of the myth about Italians and the Mafia. Well aware of the sacrifices they and their parents made to acculturate, the second generation sought a happy life for its children, sharing only pieces of the history of bigotry that they and their parents endured. Outward expression of ethnicity by their children was not often encouraged.

Since the late 1960s, white ethnics have gradually advanced to a new level of respectability and can now speak publicly of their ethnic roots, invoking images of poor immigrants at Ellis Island whose offspring eventually achieved success and acceptance in America. Today, Italian Americans are basically well assimilated and accepted as part of the European American racial group, and even the organized crime stereotype is slowly beginning to fade. The questions now are where do we go from here? And what do we do with the story of the Italian American experience?

I propose that the first thing we do is learn the stories of our individual families and how these fit into the general Italian American experience as well as the story of the United States. Sharing and passing on family stories from one generation to another helps establish a sense of identity and continuity. From there, it's only a matter of steps to writing a family history, or preserving an oral account of it and sharing this with our relatives and friends. We can also advocate that the story of Italian Americans, as well as those of all ethnic groups, be accurately and fairly told especially in textbooks and other official histories. A full history of Lackawanna and its 92 ethnic groups would represent one important step in this direction. An expanded Steel Plant Museum that includes information and artifacts from all the city's ethnic groups is another worthy goal. It is important for us to rediscover our humble roots so that we can both understand where we are now and where we need to go. This is one of the factors that led me to write this history.

We can learn lessons from the sad aspects of our own immigrant group history, such as the importance of acceptance, inclusiveness, and the terrible price exacted by inequality. America's mistakes in labeling and treating certain groups of people as inferior flies in the face of our belief in democracy and fair play, and creates rigid social hierarchies that can devastate members of minority groups. The harsh treatment of immigrant groups including the Irish, German Catholics, Italians, Poles, and other Slavs was unnecessary and unjust. This understanding on the part of white ethnic groups can yield valuable lessons toward a greater understanding of current racial and religious minorities. It is crucial that we European Americans realize that immigrants from Europe usually endured two or three generations of minority status, while Native Americans, blacks, Latinos, and Asians have endured centuries of minority status. Such an endeavor can create the possibility of blending the components of the Quintuple Melting Pot into a single multicultural melting pot that truly welcomes all ethnic groups. A multicultural society is one that respects all peoples and provides equal opportunity to all.

Today's Italian Americans can reclaim aspects of their ethnic heritage by examining the beliefs, institutions, and practices of the first and second generations and choosing values or traditions that are personally meaningful and valuable in view of today's society. One practice that came about from living in poverty in Italy and surviving the Great Depression in Lackawanna was that of recycling everything, leaving nothing to waste. The immigrants and their children maintained vegetable and flower gardens, made wine or liqueur, and canned tomatoes or made conserv' (tomato paste), all of which support current concerns about the environment and the health of the planet. Simply continuing the preparation of Italian foods, or taking cooking classes, can help revive and preserve the regional specialties that many second- and third-generation Italians savored as children. Italian American restaurants serving Italian food can offer authentic regional specialities as well as occasional cooking classes.

Reclaiming Italian traditions that were discontinued by the first and second generation also can be fruitful. The religious *feste* at St. Anthony's Church had ceased by the late 1930s. Over the past two decades, post-World War II immigrants from Molise instituted a small *festa* in honor of St. Ann. While St. Anthony's Church is still functioning, perhaps a more elaborate *festa* could include a number of the Italian saints that used to be honored— San Biagio, San Pio delle Camere, Our Lady of Mount Carmel—along with St. Ann and Our Lady of Guadalupe, the saint honored by Latinos at the now multicultural parish. It is important to remember that Italian culture is considered a Latin culture. The Italian language might be taught, not only to retain that crucial element of Italian culture, but also to help young people find jobs in the global marketplace.

Many aspects of Italian American ethnicity have persisted in the customs of individual families, small groups of neighbors, and relatives hosting annual family picnics. A number of Italians in Lackawanna speak of corresponding and exchanging visits with relatives who live in other states, and some have an interest in genealogy and reconnecting with relatives in this country and abroad. Some Lackawannans have maintained contact with relatives in Italy and taken trips to the hometowns of the immigrants.

A handful of Italian organizations still function in Lackawanna, and several—such as the Lake Erie Italian Club, the Lake Erie Women's Auxiliary, and the New Beginnings Italian Club— have large memberships and impressive lists of activities. A big Italian festival is held annually on Hertel Avenue (on Buffalo's north side), and a smaller one has been established in South Buffalo in recent years. The spring 2009 earthquake in Aquila, Abruzzo, prompted Italians in western New York, many of whom have roots in that region, to collect funds for the rebuilding effort. The Lake Erie Italian Club has sponsored two pasta dinners to benefit the Italian Earthquake Relief Fund. Organizations that can maintain ethnic traditions and also address current needs and interests are better able to attract new members.[5]

In writing this book, I have found Lackawanna's ethnic heritage to be rich, vital, and very active. My research has helped me to learn and savor the story of the Italian community that was the crucible of my own family's experience. I have a much greater understanding of where I came from and take pride and humility in sharing that experience with fellow Italian Americans as well as people of other ethnic groups. Ultimately, the stories of our families and ethnic groups are really one big story with many branches—the universal story of human beings. The common themes and joys and struggles are all there, we just need to face them, embrace them, and talk to one another.

ENDNOTES

ABBREVIATIONS USED IN FOOTNOTES

Directories:

BCD   Buffalo City Directory

BCDL   Buffalo City Directory: Including Lackawanna

BSDH   Buffalo Suburban Directory of Householders

BSESD   Buffalo Southeast Suburban Directory

BSSD   Buffalo South Suburban Directory

ECD   Erie County Directory

LCD   Lackawanna City Directory

LSBD   Lackawanna Street and Business Directory

Newspapers:

A. Buffalo:

BC   Buffalo Courier

BCAJ   Buffalo Commercial Advertiser & Journal

BCE*   Buffalo Courier Express

BDC   Buffalo Daily Courier

BE   Buffalo Express

BEN   Buffalo Evening News

BIT   Buffalo Illustrated Times

BME   Buffalo Morning Express

BN   Buffalo News

BST   Buffalo Sunday Times

BT   Buffalo Times

BUL   Buffalo Union Leader

CE*   Courier Express

CI   Il Corriere Italiano

CUT   Catholic Union Times

IBE   Illustrated Buffalo Express

LF   La Fiaccola

TB   Times of Buffalo

B. Lackawanna:

FP   Front Page

LDJ   Lackawanna Daily Journal

LH   Lackawanna Herald

LJ   Lackawanna Journal

LL   Lackawanna Leader

LN   Lackawanna News

LP   Lackawanna Press

LR   Lackawanna Republic

SCP   Steel City Press

C. Other Newspapers:

AJ   Amalgamated Journal (Amalgamated Association of Iron, Steel, and Tin Workers)

NYT   New York Times

PP   Pioneer Press (St. Paul, MN)

SL   Steel Labor

Archives and Organizations:

BSC   Bethlehem Steel Company

ECC   Erie County Courthouse

ICS   Instituto Centrale di Statistica

INS   Immigration and Naturalization Service

LEIC   Lake Erie Italian Club

LHS   Lackawanna High School

NY   New York State

OSIA   Order Sons of Italy in America

USIC   United States Immigration Commission

WWIDRR World War I Draft Registration Records

3) Other

n.d.   no date is provided on a document

All footnote references to the United States Census and the New York State Census, unless otherwise indicated, regard the enumeration sheets on which the census-takers recorded information about every individual in each family. These sheets are available on microfilm.

INTRODUCTION

1. BE, 10/28/1899; Mark Goldman, *High Hope: The Rise and Decline of Buffalo, New York*, 1983, pp. 133-34.

2. N.Y. Census, 1925; BC, 6/12/1900; U.S. Immigration Commission (USIC), *Immigrants in Industries, Volume 8, Part 2: Iron and Steel Manufacturing, Volume I*, 1911, pp. 736, 741, 744.

3. U.S. Census, 1920, 1930; LJ, 5/10/17; The exact number of ethnic groups represented in the city's population at any one time is difficult to ascertain. A 1937 study claimed that over 40 countries were represented on Gates Avenue alone; see Donald Adams Clarke, "Men On Relief In Lackawanna, N.Y., 1934-35: Social Pathology In A Satellite City," *The University of Buffalo Studies*, Volume XIV, No. 4, August, 1947, p. 75. Fifty-three nationality groups participated in the city's 30th anniversary celebration in 1939; LL, 7/13/39. A book on the life of Father Baker notes that "Lackawanna is a city of almost 60 nationalities;" Floyd Anderson, *The Incredible Story of Father Baker*, 1974, p. 131.

4. U.S. Census, 1960, 2000; Thomas E, Leary and Elizabeth Sholes, *From Fire To Rust*, 1987, p. 127.

5. Roger Daniels, *Not Like Us: Immigrants and Minorities in America, 1890-1924*, 1997, p. 67.

6. USIC, *Immigrants in Industries, Volume 8, Part 2: Iron and Steel Manufacturing, Volume I*, p. 765.

7. Ferdinando Magnani, *La Citta di Buffalo, N.Y. e Paesi Circonvicini e Le Colonie Italiane*, 1908, p. 30

8. U.S. Census, 1930.

9. Clarke, p. 74

CHAPTER 1

1. Each region in Italy has from two to eleven provinces. For the 3058 immigrants who lived in Lackawanna at one time or another, the regions of origin of 1907 (62%) have been identified, and for 1608 (53% of the total) of these the hometowns have also been determined.

2. Interviews with Mario Infante, July 7, 1995; and Concezio "John" Novelli, April 18, 1995; Comune di Pettorano sul Gizio, *Pettorano Sul Gizio e la Riserva Naturale Regionale Monte Genzana e Alto Gizio*, 1998, pp. 17-18; Franc Sturino, *Forging the Chain: Italian Migration to North America, 1880–1930*, 1990, pp. 13-14.

3. Interviews with Mario Infante, July 7, 1995; Alfredo Campanelli, December 26, 1986: and Lelio DeSantis; Christopher Duggan, *A Concise History of Italy*, 1994, p. 18.

4. Interviews with Alberto Andreozzi and Aldo Catalucci, September, 1980, Falvaterra, Lazio.

5. Sturino, pp. 27-28

6. Interviews with Armando Torella, December 23, 1986; and Tom Ventre, September 23, 1994.

7. Interviews with Giustino DeSantis, July 9, 1985; Alberto Andreozzi, September 9, 1980; Iole Schiavi-Murray, October 18, 1996; Adeline Covelli-Andreozzi, November 28, 1970; Duggan, p. 18.

8. Interview with Armando Torella, December 23, 1986.

9. Interviews with Tom Ventre, September 23, 1994; Romolo Petricca, March 27, 1986; Augusta Lampazzi-Anticoli, December 26, 1995; Ennio Guglielmi, April 1, 1996.

10. Interviews with Carmine DelMonaco, December 26, 1994; Adeline Covelli-Andreozzi, December 28, 1981.

11. Interviews with Guy Iannarelli, April 7, 1994; and Joe Violanti, April 5, 1994.

12. Interview with Alfredo Campanelli, December 26, 1986.

13. Interviews with Armando Torella, December 23, 1986; Augusta Lampazzi-Anticoli, December 26, 1995; Adeline Covelli-Andreozzi, December 26, 1981; Tony Grasso. "Grandfather's Vineyard," unpublished, 1982, p. 3.

14. Interview with Iole Schiavi-Murray, October 18, 1996.

15. Interview with Adcline Covclli-Andreozzi, December 28, 1969.

16. Interview with Iole Schiavi-Murray, October 18, 1996; and Adeline Covelli-Andreozzi, December 28, 1969.

17. Interview with Iole Schiavi-Murray, October 18, 1996; and Adeline Covelli-Andreozzi, December 28, 1969.

18. Tony Grasso, "Grandfather's Vineyard," p. 2.

19. Interviews with Augusta Lampazzi-Anticoli, December 26,1995; Ennio Guglielmi, April 1, 1996; Joc Violanti, April 5, 1994. Romolo Petricca, March 27, 1986.

20. Interviews with Armando Torella, December 23, 1986: and Adeline Covelli-Andreozzi, December 26, 1981. Tony Grasso, "The Shepherdess Call," unpublished, 1981, p. 2.

21. Interview with John Novelli, April 18, 1995; Tony Grasso, "Grandfather's Vineyard," p. 3.

22. Adeline Covelli-Andreozzi, December 28, 1969.

23. Interviews with Tom Ventre, September 23, 1994; Guy Iannarelli, April 7, 1994; Vince Piccirilli, April 16, 1979.

24. Tony Grasso, "Grandfather's Vineyard," p. 4 (quote); interviews with Louie Petrucci, December 27, 1984; and Alfredo Camapnelli, December 26, 1986.

25. Interviews with Armando Torella, December 23, 1986; and Adeline Covelli-Andreozzi, November 28, 1970 and December 26, 1981.

26. Interviews with Mario Infante, July 7, 1995; and Michelina Colosimo-Bevilacqua, October 17, 1996 .

27. Interviews with Alfredo Campanelli, December 26, 1986 (quote); and Adeline Covelli-Andreozzi, December 28, 1969 and April 29, 1991.

28. Interview with Vince Piccirilli, April 16, 1979; Tony Grasso. "A Sea of Tears," unpublished, p. 1.

29. Interviews with Mary Maturani-Federici, September 19, 1995; and Lelio DeSantis, April 4, 1996.

30. Interview with Mario Infante, July 7, 1995; Sturino, pp. 10, 13, 24.

31. Interviews with Carmine DelMonaco, December 26, 1994; and Vincenzo "Jimmy" D'Alessandro, April 9, 1985.

32. Interviews with Adeline Covelli-Andreozzi, July 14, 1991; Guy and Delia Iannarelli, November 25, 2008; Gene DeSantis, April 20, 1995; Alfredo Campanelli, December 26, 1986; and Michelina Colosimo-Bevilacqua, October 17, 1996; Sturino, pp. 24—25.

33. Interviews with Ezio Millanti, November 11, 1998; and Louie Petrucci, December 27, 1984.

34. Interviews with Flora Paolini-Olivieri, July 13, 1994; Augusta Lampazzi-Anticoli, December 26, 1995; and Tony Grasso, December 28, 1984.

35. Interviews with Michelina Colosimo-Bevilacqua, October 17, 1996; Gelsomina Caira-Covelli, December 26, 1990; and John Novelli, April 18, 1995 (quote).

36. Interviews with Tom Ventre, September 23, 1994; Alfredo Campanelli, December 26, 1986; Concetta Marinelli-Risio, September 19, 1995; and Carmine DelMonaco, December 26, 1994.

37. Joseph Lopreato, *Italian Americans*, 1970, pp. 58—50; Lydio F. Tomasi, *The Italian American Family*, 1972, p. 30; Leonard Covello, *The Social Background of the Italo-American School Child: A Study of the Southern Italian Family Mores and Their Effect on the School Situation in Italy and America*, 1967, pp. 400-402; Donna R. Gabaccia, *From Sicily to Elizabeth Street: Housing and Social change Among Italian Immigrants, 1880-1930*, 1984, pp. 3-4.

38. Phyllis Williams, *South Italian Folkways In Europe and America: A Handbook For Social Workers, Visiting Nurses, School Teachers, and Physicians*, 1938, p.135.

39. Covello, pp. 132, 137 (1st quote), 138; interview with Josephine Ferrelli, March 29, 1996 (2nd quote).

40. Rudolph Vecoli, "Cult and Occult in Italian American Culture: The Persistence of A Religious Heritage," in Randall M. Miller and Thomas D. Marzik, eds. *Immigrants and Religion in Urban America*, 1977, p. 27 (quote); Lopreato, Italian Americans, p. 140.

41. Interviews with Iole Schiavi-Murray, October 18, 1996; Guy Iannarelli, April 7, 1994; and Adeline Covelli-Andreozzi, November 28, 1970.

42. Interviews with Josephine Ferrelli, March 29, 1996; Adcline Covelli-Andreozzi, August 23, 1970; Alfredo Campanelli, December 26, 1986.

43. Interviews with Augusta Lampazzi-Anticoli, December 26,. 1995; Guy Iannarelli, April 7, 1994.

44. Interviews with Tom Ventre, September 23, 1994; Josephine Ferrelli, March 29, 1996; Adeline Covelli-Andreozzi, August 23, 1970; Williams, p. 139.

45. Covello, pp.122 (1st quote), 123, 126 (2nd quote); interview with Alberto Andreozzi, September 8, 1980.

46. The vada is a small wooden platform with two long poles extending from each end. At least one of two men grasped each of the four poles. It had legs that enabled the bearers to occasionally stop and lower it into a standing position; Phyllis Williams, p.139.

47. Interview with Michelina Colosimo-Bevilacqua, October 17, 1996.

48. Interviews with Augusta Lampazzi-Anticoli, December 26, 1995; Mary Maturani-Federici, September 9, 1995: Joe Violanti, April 5, 1994.

49. Interviews with Iole Schiavi Murray, October 18, 1996; Flora Paolini-Olivieri, July 13, 1994; Tom Ventre, September 23, 1994; Giustino DeSantis, July 9, 1985; Mary Elizabeth Brown, "Women In The Church," in Salvatore J. LaGumina, Frank J. Cavaioli, Salvatore Primeggia, Joseph A. Varacalli, eds., *The Italian American Experience: An Encyclopedia*, 2000, p. 681. Brown describes the Black Madonna as a "woman who was doubly powerful: she was in command of her own sexuality and she was fertile; men admired her for both the passion she aroused and the children she produced." This image had its origins in 20,000 to 10,000 BC, and was later adopted by the Catholic Church, which emphasized Mary as the Mother of God, while "the Italian laity emphasized how Mary's maternity made her a powerful intercessor."

50. Interviews with Mario Infante, July 7, 1995; and Alfredo Campanelli, December 26, 1985.

51. Interview with Augusta Lampazzi-Anticoli, December 26, 1995.

52. Interviews with Guy Iannarelli, April 7, 1994 (quotes); Concetta Marinelli-Risio, September 19, 1995; Adeline Covelli-Andreozzi, December 26, 1981; and Anne Scarsella-Antes, December 26, 1996; Williams, p. 135.

53. Interview with Santino Carnevale, September 22, 1994.

54. Phyllis Williams, pp.141, 142 (quote), 143-144; Vecoli, p. 29.

55. Interviews with Josephine Ferrelli, March 29, 1996; and John Novelli, April 18, 1995. He was a teenager at the time and soon lost interest in the ritual and ceased reciting the prayers.

56. Ministero Di Agricoltura, Industria E Commercio; Direzione Generale della Statistica, *Elenco Delle Societa Di Mutuo Soccorso Esistenti al 1 Gennaio 1895*, 1898, pp. 3-200; and Societa Di Mutuo Soccorso, *Elenco delle Societa Esistenti al 31 Decembre 1912*, 1913, pp. 63-173.

57. John W. Briggs, *An Italian Passage: Immigrants to Three American Cities, 1890-1930*, 1978, pp. 18-21; Sturino, p. 35 (quotes); Ministero Di Agricoltura, Industria E Commercio; Direzione Generale della Statistica, 1898 and 1913; Istituto Centrale di Statistica (ICS), *Popolazione Residente e Presente dei Comuni: Censimenti dal 1861 al 1981*, 1985, pp. 246-247. The 54 organizations in 1912 do not include the 136 groups in the six large cities from which only a few immigrants came to Lackawanna.

58. Interviews with Alfredo Campanelli, December 26, 1986; Sam Violanti, December 29, 1987; Armando Torella, December 23, 1986; Mario Infante, July 7, 1995; Giustino DeSantis, July 9, 1985.

59. Interviews with Ezio Millanti, November 11, 1998; Romolo Petricca, March 27, 1986; and Ennio Guglielmi, April 1, 1996 (quotes); letter from bank president Giuseppe Sperduti to Ferdinando Catuzza, 11/9/26, provided by Chet Catuzza.

60. Briggs, pp. 38, 46 (1st quote); Covello, pp. 248-55, 56 (2nd quote), 274.

61. Interview with Iole Schiavi-Murray, October 18, 1996; Duggan, pp. 226—27.

62. Interviews with Tom Ventre, September 23, 1994 (quote); Alfredo Campanelli, December 26, 1986; and Flora Paolini-Olivieri, July 13, 1994.

63. Tony Grasso, "The Pains of the Alphabet," unpublished, undated, p. 2.

64. Sturino, pp. 36-38; interview with Adeline Covelli-Andreozzi, November 28, 1970.

65. Interview with Adeline Covelli-Andreozzi, November 28, 1970.

66. Interview with John Novelli, April 18, 1995.

67. Interview with Joe Violanti, April 5, 1994.

68. Interview with Tom Ventre, September 23, 1994.

69. Interview with Adeline Covelli-Andreozzi, December 28, 1969. The toilet was a gravity affair into which water was occasionally poured to flush the waste through a pipe to a leach bed. Morra involves two players. Each simultaneously and quickly extends one hand and displays anywhere from one to five fingers. As they do so each men yells the number which he thinks will be the total number of fingers displayed by both. The process is then repeated until one person wins a certain number of rounds.

70. Interview with Ennio Guglielmi, April 1, 1996. Tony Grasso, "Taking Chances," unpublished, 1982, pp., 1-2.

71. Interview with Gene Covelli, July 20, 1991; Tony Grasso, "Taking Chances," pp. 1-2.

72. Duggan, p. 149.

73. Robert F. Forester, *The Italian Emigration of Our Times*, 1919, p. 63; Sturino, p. 42. Interview with Gelsomina Caira-Covelli, December 26, 1990 (quote).

74. Interviews with Mario Infante, July 7, 1995; Concetta Marinelli-Risio, September 19, 1995; and Josephine Ferrelli, March 29, 1996.

75. Interviews with Giustino DeSantis, July 9, 1985; John Novelli, April 18, 1995; and Louie Petrucci, December 27, 1984; Duggan, pp. 169-70, 186-87

76. Alexander DeConde, *Half Bitter, Half Sweet: An Excursion Into Italian-American History*, 1971, pp. 144-145; interviews with Anne Scarsella-Antes, December 26, 1995; and Adeline Covelli-Andreozzi, December 26, 1981.

77. Interviews with Ben Vittorini, July 16, 1992; and Flora Paolini-Olivieri, July 13, 1994.

78. Interviews with Ennio Guglielmi, April 1, 1996; Ezio Millanti, November 11, 1998; and Tom Ventre, September 23, 1994.

79. Interview with Joe Violanti, April 5, 1994.

80. Interviews with Ann Scarsella-Antes, Alfredo Campanelli, December 26, 1986; Ralph Galanti, September 22, 1983; and John Novelli, April 18, 1995

81. Joseph Lopreato, *Peasants No More: Social Class and Social Change in an Underdeveloped Society*, 1967, pp. 29-32; interview with Lucia Caracci-Cullens, March 22, 1989.

82. Interview with Ezio Millanti, November 11, 1998; Duggan, p. 218.

83. Interviews with Ennio Guglielmi, April 1, 1996 (1st & 2nd quotes); and Dewey Montanari, July 15, 1994 (3rd quote).

84. Interview with Ennio Guglielmi, April 1, 1996; Duggan, p. 238.

85. Interviews with Egino DeSantis, April 20, 1995; and Lelio DeSantis, April 4, 1996.

86. Interview with Santino Carnevale, September 22, 1994; Rick Atkinson, *The Day of Battle: The War in Sicily and Italy, 1943-1944*, 2007, pp. 557-558. Perhaps the Moroccan and Algerian soldiers, who were Arabs, committed the crimes against Italians in part as revenge: the Italian military had invaded Libya in 1911 and in the following three decades killed thousands of Arabs in brutal campaigns to put down resistance to Italian rule; see Duggan, pp. 186, 233.

87. Interview with Angelo DeGiulio, December 23, 1994.

88. Lopreato, *Peasants No More*, p. 32.

89. Interview with Augusta Lampazzi-Anticoli, December 26, 1995.

90. Interview with Joe Violanti, April 5, 1994.

91. Interview with Iole Schiavi-Murray, October 18, 1996.

92. Interview with Santino Carnevale, September 22, 1994.

93. Interview with Guy Iannarelli, April 7, 1994.

94. Lopreato, *Peasants No More*, p. 153; Francesco Cerase. "Nostalgia or Disenchantment: Considerations on Return Migration," in Silvano M. Tomasi and Madeline H. Engel, eds. *The Italian Experience in the United States*, 1970, p. 230

95. Interview with Michelina Colosimo-Bevilacqua, October 17, 1996.

96. Interview with Adeline Covelli-Andreozzi, December 26, 1981; Sturino, p. 48.

97. Tony Grasso, "A Sea of Tears," unpublished, undated, pp. 1-4.

CHAPTER 2

1. Tony Grasso, "A Sea of Tears," unpublished, 1989, p. 16. This is one of many stories that Grasso penned, others are cited below; all are unpublished.

2. Donna Gabaccia, *Italy's Many Diasporas*, 2000, p. 3; Gianfausto Rosoli, "The Global Picture of the Italian Disapora to the Americas," in Lydio Tomasi, Piero Gastaldo, and Thomas Row, eds. *The Columbus People: Perspectives in Italian Immigration to the Americas*, 1994, p. 309. Emigration refers to leaving from one's home country to settle in another country; a person departing from his homeland is an emigrant, example: Salvatore emigrated from Italy. Immigration refers to migrating to a different country to settle; a person coming to a new country is an immigrant; example: Rosina immigrated to the United States.

3. Immigration and Naturalization Service (INS), *Statistical Yearbook of the Immigration and Naturalization Program*, 2000, pp.18, 21. German immigrants numbered 7,176,071 and Mexicans 6,135,150; Maldwyn Allen Jones. American Immigration, 1960, p. 179. The Austrian Hungarian empire included part of Poland, Czechoslovakia, and the Balkans.

4. INS, p. 20; Roger Daniels, *Not Like Us: Immigrants and Minorities In America, 1890 - 1924*, 1997, p. 68; Gabaccia, *Italy's Many Diasporas*, p. 3.

5. Instituto Centrale di Statistica (ICS), *Popolazione Residente e Presente dai Comuni: Censimenti dal 1861 al 1981*, Roma, 1985, pp. 228-29, 244-49, 250-51, 254-55, 258-59, 262-63, 270-71, 278-79, 294-95, 300-01. The Italian census was not taken in 1891 and 1941, but a special one was completed in 1936. The 20 towns for which data is available averaged 11% of their residents not present in 1911, and 12% in 1921. San Pio had 21% of residents not present in 1911, and 33% in 1921; for Settefrati the figures were 19% and 30%, respectively. The sixteen towns averaged 11% to 12% of residents not present during the period 1902 to 1921. San Pio delle Camere had 21% of its residents not present in 1911 and 33% in 1921, and in Settefrati it was 19% and 30%, respectively.

6. ICS, pp. 244-47, 250-51.

7. ICS, pp .228-29, 246-47, 250-51, 300-01; interviews with Alberto Andreozzi, September, 1980: and Aldo Catalucci, September, 1980, in Falvaterra, Italy. Among the towns that gained residents, the smallest gain was 8% in Capriglia Irpina, and the largest was in the city of Fano, where the population more than doubled, growing from 24,898 to 52,116. Among those towns in decline, Bagnoli Irpino had the smallest loss of residents, only 1%, while Cantalupo nel Sannio had a 74% drop in population.

8. Data on immigrants and their hometowns in Italy were drawn from a wide variety of primary and secondary sources.

9. A pattern found among the Italians who immigrated to Buffalo; see Virginia Yans-McLaughlin, *Family and Community: Italian Immigrants in Buffalo: 1880-1930*, 1971, p. 35.

10. Interview with Mary Maturani-Federici, September 19, 1995.

11. Interview with Flora Paolini-Oliveri, July 13, 1994.

12. Interview with Alfredo Campanelli, December 26, 1986.

13. Interview with Louie Petrucci, December 27, 1984.

14. Interview with Michelina Colosimo-Bevilacqua, October 17, 1996.

15. Interviews with Flora Paolini-Olivieri, July 13,1994; Ezio Millanti, November 11, 1998; Tony Grasso, December 28, 1984; and Carmen DelMonaco, December 26, 1994.16. Interviews with Evangelisto Ceccarelli, September 9, 1980, Falvaterra, Italy; and Ezio Millanti, November 11, 1998.

17. Interviews with Giovanni Andreozzi (no relation to the author), September 9, 1980; Andrea Ceccarelli, September 9, 1980; and Evangelisto Ceccarelli, September 9, 1980, all in Falvaterra, Italy; and interview with Iole Schiavi-Murray, October 18, 1996; *SS Barbarosa,* passenger list, May 5, 1906: http://ellisisland.org/; Franc Sturino, *Forging the Chain: Italian Migration to North America, 1880-1930*, 1990, p. 96.

18. Grasso, "A Sea of Tears," pp. 12, 17.

19. Grasso, "A Sea of Tears," p. 17.

20. Grasso. "A Sea of Tears," pp. 18-20; Tony Grasso, "Remembrance: A Lonely Boy's Journey To Ellis Island," December, 1988, pp. 2-3.

21. Grasso, "Remembrance . . .," pp. 3-5.

22. Grasso, "Remembrance . . .," pp. 5-7.

23. Grasso, "Remembrance . . .," p. 8.

24. U.S. Census, 1900; LL, 6/13/40.

25. BCD, 1890-1903; interviews with Bruce Tarquino, 8/3/1998; and John Fadale, November 23, 1979 ; CI, 6/6/1903.

26. John and Leatrice MacDonald, "Chain Migration, Ethnic Neighborhood Formation, and Social Networks," *Milbank Memorial Fund Quarterly*, No. 42, 1964, 82 - 97. They defined chain migration as "that movement in which prospective migrants learn of opportunities, are provided with transportation, and have initial accommodation and employment arranged by means of primary social relationships with previous migrants."

27. LL, 6/13/40; Erie County Courthouse (ECC), *Mortgage Grantee Index,* 1898 - 1903, pp. 540-41.

28. Giovanni Banchetti, "Gl'Italiani In Alcuni Distretti Dello Stato Di Nuova York," in *Bollettino dell'Emigrazione*, No. 5, 1902, p. 21; BDC, 6/2/1902; BC, 6/ 22/1902; BE, 11/11/1902.

29. *Scranton City Directory*, 1896, p. 540; interviews with Joe Milano, November 23, 1977 and July 17, 1989; and Mary Sperduto-Cuomo, August 23, 1998. Of the hundreds of Italians living in Dunmore in 1900, apparently few worked at the Lackawanna Iron and Steel Company. Most were "day laborers," as enumerated in the 1900 U. S. Census, while others were coal miners, slate pickers, coal breakers, or street maintenance laborers. The same was true of Scranton; only three Italian men were identified as steel mill laborers. In the nearby town of Old Forge, the majority of Italians were coal miners. The term "day laborer" could have referred to virtually any type of work, as laborers were often hired on a daily basis in many industries. Starting in 1910 the U. S. Census, in addition to asking about occupation, also inquired as to the nature of the work or the setting.

30. Interviews with Joe Milano, November 23, 1977 and July 17, 1989; U. S. Census, 1910.

31. Interview with Angelo Grosso, November 22, 1977.

32. U. S. Immigration Commission, *Immigrants in Industries, Volume 8, Part 2: Iron and Steel Manufacturing, Volume 1*, 1911, p. 33; interviews with Nunze Oddy, April 12, 1982, Margaret Oddy-Guastaferro, July 5, 1996.

33. CI, 6/6/1903; *SS California*, passenger list, April 25, 1903:http://ellis island,org/. Gates Avenue was then called The Avenue.

34. Arrival dates for many immigrant are approximate, due to lack of yearly city or county directories. The average interval between arrival in the U. S. and arrival in Lackawanna was 4.3 years for both men and women, ages ten and over.; 62 % of the men and 63 % of the women came within one to five years of their arrival in the

35. N. Y. Census, 1905, and U. S. Census, 1910.

36. N. Y. Census, 1905-1925; U. S. Census, 1900-1930.

37. Yans-McLaughlin, p. 28; *La Fiaccola*, 1/6/12; Town of West Seneca, *Birth Records, 1903-1905*; N. Y. Census, 1905-1925; U. S. Census, 1910; WWIDRR.

38. Philip A. Bean, "The Role of Community in the Unionization of Italian Immigrants: The Utica Textile Strike of 1919." *Ethnic Forum,* Volume 12, No. 1, 1982, p. 40; Michael LaSorte, "Retsof, New York: A Salt Mine Company Town," in Jerome Krase and Judith N. DeSena, eds., *Italian Americans in A Multicultural Society*, 1994, p. 173. In Lackawanna exactly 64% of the Italian male immigrants arriving between 1911 and 1915 departed within five years.

39. Length of residence in Lackawanna was calculated by recording for each immigrant the known dates he or she resided in the Steel City. Since there are no yearly city directories, a variety of sources were used: interviews, city and Erie County directories, *Buffalo Suburban Directory of Householders*, 1949, lists of registered voters, city and church records, newspaper obituaries and articles, WWIDRR, United States and New York State censuses, naturalization papers, telephone directories, ship passenger lists, City of Lackawanna records, Town of West Seneca records, and minutes of the Lake Erie Italian Club. The resulting data therefore are not always precise, but do afford an estimate on the length of time each immigrant lived in Lackawanna. ECC, *Naturalization Petition,* Matteo Iorio, September 14, 1926. Luigi Scarnecchia, October 6, 1919, Domenico Iacobucci, March 3, 1927; U. S. Census, 1910; interview with Julius Baldassari, August 2, 1998. Males comprised exactly 72% of the immigrants between 1900 and 1930.

40. The rate of same year arrivals for men fell from 14% in 1900-10 to four percent in 1921-30.

41. Interviews with Tony DiMillio, October 17, 1996, and Emilia Cutre, August 24, 1998; ECC, *Naturalization Petition,* Domenico Giansante, May 5, 1922; U. S. Census, 1920, 1930; N. Y. Census, 1925; WW1DRR. For the male immigrants coming to Lackawanna between 1911 and 1915, exactly 24% became permanent residents.

42. Bean, p. 40. The end date of the time period is slightly different - 1919 for Utica and 1920 for Lackawanna—because there is no directory for the Steel City in 1919. The 1920 U. S. census is the most complete listing for Lackawanna residents, and, since it was taken in January 1920, it offers a nearly identical end date as that of the Utica study.

43. Interview with Tony Grasso, December 23, 1987.

44. Bureau of the Census, *U. S. Census, 1930: Population, Volume 3, Part 2*, pp. 300-303; and *U. S. Census, 1940: Population, Part 5*. Of the 150 Italian immigrants who settled in Lackawanna between 1931 and 1940, exactly 27% of them were women.

45. INS, pp. 20-21; ICS, pp. 246-47.

46. Interview with Santino Carnevale, September 22, 1994.

47. Interview with Guy and Delia Iannarelli, April 7, 1994. Domenico Iannarelli had made his first trip to America in 1901 at the age of sixteen. After returning to Italy he married Concetta Tristani and fathered two sons. In 1920 he again left Abruzzo and arrived in Follansbee, West Virginia. Leaving the Pettoranesi colony there, he joined paesani in Lackawanna in 1924. His son Pietro arrived in the Steel City in 1930, and several years later the second son, Rosario, arrived. Domenico travelled back and forth to Abruzzo until the mid-1930s and fathered Gaetano and another child. World War II interfered with any further plans for family unification in either country.

48. Interview with Raffaele Vivolo, December 27, 1996; LL, 11/6/57.

49. Interview with Lelio DeSantis, April 4, 1996.

50. Interview with Carlo Savaglio, July 13, 1995.

51. Interview with Cesare Cardi, April 3, 1997.

52. Interview with Elio Liberta, October 16, 1996 (1st quote); and Gene DeSantis, April 20, 1995 (2nd quote).

53. Interview with Lelio DeSantis, April 4, 1996.

54. Interview with Ezio and Cleo Millanti, November 11, 1998.

55. Interview with Ennio Guglielmi, April 1, 1996.

56. Interview with Carlo Savaglio, July 13, 1995.

57. Interview with Cesare Cardi, April 3, 1997.

58. Bureau of the Census, *U. S. Census, 1930: Population, Volume 2,* pp. 45, 49.

59. Buffalo's Italian population was 18,722 in 1900: Bureau of the Census. *1900 Census, Supplement for New York*, p. 620; interview with Mike Morgan, April 18, 1995.

60. Interviews with Camille Falcone-Schwan, April 5, 1996, and Nick Vertalino, October 19, 1996.

61. Interviews with Elizabeth George-Rosati, September 8, 1984, and Tony Falbo, February 25, 1978; BCD, 1896 - 1908. Italian residents later successfully petitioned to have Canal Street renamed Dante Place in 1909: Michael N. Vogel, Edward J. Patton, Paul F. Redding, *America's Crossroads: Buffalo's Canal Street/Dante Place, The Making of A City,* 1993, p. 257.

62. CI, 5/4,/1907, 6/22/1907, 11/14/08, 8/14/09, 11/6/09.

63. Interview with Joe Violanti, April 5, 1994.

64. Interview with Mary Maturani-Federici, September 19, 1995.

65. Interview with Louie Petrucci, December 27, 1984.

66. Interview with Ralph Galanti, September 22, 1983.

67. For example, a large number of Sicilian immigrants who had worked in the mines of Pittston, Pennsylvania moved to Buffalo's west side where they organized the Pittston Club.

68. Interview with Tony Falbo, February 25, 1978; U. S. Census, 1910.

69. Interview with Francis DePasquale, December 28, 1977.

70. Interview with Mary Yoviene-Clark, December 29, 1983. The Buffalo and Susquehanna Railroad was absorbed into the Baltimore and Ohio Railroad.

71. Interview with Giulio Maturani, December 27, 1994.

72. Interviews with Clyde Capasso, November 8, 1998, and Ralph D'Amore, April 20, 1995; U. S. Census, 1930; N. Y. Census, 1925;

73. Interview with Michelina Colosimo-Bevilacqua, October 17, 1996.

74. Interview with Michelina Colosimo-Bevilacqua, October 17, 1996.

75. Interview with Michelina Colosimo-Bevilacqua, October 17, 1996.

76. Interview with Michelina Colosimo-Bevilacqua, October 17, 1996.

77. Interview with Michelina Colosimo-Bevilacqua, October 17, 1996.

78. Interviews with Michelina Colosimo-Bevilacqua, October 17, 1996, and Joe Caligiuri, April 5, 1994.

79. Interview with Joe Caligiuri, April 5, 1994.

80 Interview with Joe Caligiuri, April 5, 1994.

81. Interview with Joe Caligiuri, April 5, 1994.

82. Interview with Joe Caligiuri, April 5, 1994.

83. Interview with Michelina Colosimo-Bevilacqua, October 17, 1996.

84. Interview with Michelina Colosimo-Bevilacqua, October 17, 1996.

85. Interviews with Leo and Dario "Doc" Baldelli, July 14, 1994, and Ron Baldelli, September 21, 1994.

86. Interviews with Frank Rosati, April 19, 1995, and Thomas Ventre, September 23, 1994. A number of Italians who eventually settled in Lackawanna sailed to North America from France. Departing Europe from Cherbourg, LeHarve, or Verso were: Domenico, Romolo, Vincenzo Sperduti, Giuseppe Schiavi, and Antonio Andreozzi of Lazio; Innocenzo Guerrini of Emilia-Romagna; and Giovanni Sambuchi and Attilio Lorenzetti of Marche. Some of the men perhaps first worked in France and then decided to cross the ocean. Others may have sailed from France at times when Italy was restricting emigration, or was at war and blocked the departure of draft-eligible men from Italian ports.

87. Interview with Tony and Mary Grasso, November 27, 1981.

88. N.Y. Census, 1925; WWIDRR; interviews with Loretta Amorosi-Nicometo, November 29, 1977, Ralph Galanti, September 22, 1983, and Mary Sorci-Leonetti, December 28, 1994. Gennaro Leonetti died tragically, of a bee sting, in Brazil in 1946.

89. Interview with Carmen and Josephine DelMonaco, December 26, 1994.

90. Interview with Carmen and Josephine DelMonaco, December 26, 1994.

91. Interview with Armando Torella, December 23, 1986.

92. Interview with Augusta Lampazzi-Anticoli, December 26,1995.

93. SS. Phoenicia, passenger list, May 3, 1902, Ellis Island records website; SS. Gallia, passenger list, March 28, 1902, Family History Library microfilm.

94. SS. Equita, passenger list, April 13, 1903, Ellis Island records website; U. S. Census, 1910; interview with Lou Colello, September 23, 1983; SS. Conte Rosso, passenger list, July 19, 1923, Ellis Island records website; N. Y. Census, 1925; SS. America, passenger list, July 26, 1922, Ellis Island records website.

95. Interview with Vince Morga, April 7, 1999; for the Ciociari di Detroit group see: Ministero Degli Affari Esteri, Associazioni Italiane Nel Mondo, 1984, p.106. In this chapter, the lists of settlements in the United States for immigrants from specific towns are not necessarily complete as most are based on information only from Lackawanna Italians.

96. Interviews with Guy Iannarelli, April 7, 1994, and Nunze Oddy, April 12, 1982.

97. Interview with Mario Infante, July 7, 1995; family data form completed by Carmen Basile; ECC, Naturalization Petition, Francesco Palante, February 18, 1927.

98. SS. La Gascogne, passenger list, August 6, 1906, Ellis Island records website; Interview with Art and Ed Sambuchi, December 27 -28, 2002; NY Census, 1905; interviews with Duilio "Dewey" Montanari, July 15, 1994, Aldina Manna-Wichrowski, April 22, 1995, Aldo Filipetti, July 11, 1996, and Ron Spadone, July 12, 1994.

99. John Andreozzi, "Italian Farmers in Cumberland," in Rudolph J. Vecoili, editor, Italian Immigrants in Rural and Small Town America, 1987, pp 110-125. Interview with Tony Falbo, February 25, 1978.

100. Interview with Joe Mancuso, July 3, 1996.

101. Interviews with Joe Cosentino, April 18, 1979, July 13, 1994, and July 14, 1995.

102. Interviews with Joe Cosentino, April 18, 1979 and July 13, 1994; and Michael Moretti, November 26, 2008; SS. Brasile, passenger list, May 6, 1907: http://ellisisland,org/.

103. BCD, 1915, 1923-27; interviews with Adeline Covelli-Andreozzi, April 22, 1981 and April 10, 2002, Eugene Covelli, July 20, 1991, and Carlo Savaglio, July 13, 1995.

104. See Jennifer Guglielmo and Salvatore Salerno, editors, Are Italians White? How Race Is Made in America, 2003, p. 9; John Dickie. Darkest Italy: The Nation and Stereotypes of the Mezzogiorno, 1860-1900, 1999, p. 20; and Gabriella Gribaudi, "Images of the South: The Mezzogiorno As Seen By Insiders and Others," in Robert Lumley and Jonathan Morris, editors, The New History of the Italian South, 1997, p. 87. Two authors exclude Lazio from southern Italy (Joseph Lopreato, Italian Americans, 1970, p. 35, and Silvano Tomasi, Piety and Power, 1975, pp. 17-18), and others also exclude Sardinia, Abruzzo, and Molise. One scholar contends that everything south of Rome, including southern Lazio, Abruzzo and Molise, is part of southern Italy; see Donald S. Pitkin, "Land Tenure and Family Organization In An Italian Village," unpublished PhD. dissertation, Harvard University, 1954, p. 24. Phyllis Williams draws a line starting at Giulianova, Abruzzo, on the Adriatic Sea, across the peninsula to Anzio, Lazio on the Tyrrhenean Sea, thus placing most of Abruzzo and most of Lazio's Frosinone and Latina provinces in southern Italy; see Phyllis H. Williams, Southern Italian Folkways In Europe And America, 1938, pp. i, frontispiece. Lastly, one Italian American scholar wrote: "Northern Italy refers to the Italy north of Naples and includes Central Italy;" see Leonard Covello, The Social background of the Italo-American School Child: A Study of the Southern Italian Family Mores and Their Effect on the School Situation in Italy and America, 1967, p. 4. In this book the two southern-most provinces of Lazio, Frosinone and Latina, are considered as part of southern Italy, and since all but a few Laziali towns represented in Lackawanna are in these two provinces, this study will refer to all immigrants from Lazio who settled in Lackawanna as meridianali, or southerners.

105. Pitkin, pp. 166-169; John Andreozzi, "Contadini and Pescatori in Milwaukee: Assimilation and Voluntary Organizations," unpublished masters thesis, University of Wisconsin-Milwaukee, 1974. Italy is often viewed as consisting of three general districts: north, central, and south. In the early 20th century, when Italy had 16 regions, one scholar defined Central Italy as the regions of Emila-Romagna, Tuscany, Umbria, Marche, and Lazio, those regions to the north as northern Italy, and Abruzzo-Molise, Campania, Puglia, Basilicata, Calabria, Sicily, and Sardinia as southern Italy; see Robert F. Foerster, The Italian Emigration Of Our Times, 1919 (1969), p. 38. Since that time the regions of Valle D'Aosta, Trentino-Alto Adige, Friuli-Venezia-Giulia, and Molise have been added, and modern writers have redefined the three districts as follows: Central Italy includes Tuscany, Umbria, Marche, Lazio, Abruzzo, and Molise; the eight regions to north compose northern Italy, and the six regions to the south compose southern Italy; see Gabaccia, Italy's Many Diasporas, pp. 69-70. Even more confusing was the two-way division of Italy used by American immigration officials between 1899 and 1924; it defined southern Italy as including Tuscany, Marche, and Umbria and all other regions to the south. In Milwaukee, unlike Lackawanna, the majority of Italian immigrants were from Sicily in the deep south, who were probably

viewed by that city's Marchegiani as more culturally distant than were the Abruzzesi and Laziali by Lackawanna's Marchegiani, who seemed to have viewed the Laziali and Abruzzesi as fellow central Italians.

106. Ferdinando Magnani, *La Citta di Buffalo*, 1908, p.30. The statistics on regions of origin of Lackawanna Italians are based on current regional boundaries. It is important to note that in the 1920s provinces in Lazio and Puglia were expanded to include towns, such as Pico (Lazio) and Accadia (Puglia), that were previously within Campania. If 1900 era boundaries were used, Lazio would still account for the largest number of immigrants in the Steel City, but Campania's portion would increase and be close to that of second-ranked Abruzzo. Most likely the number of Laziali in Buffalo in 1906 would have jumped considerably if the 1920s boundary changes were used to determine regional origins of the immigrants.

107. For each decade the regional roots of anywhere from 40% to 100% of the arriving immigrants was determined: 1900-10 = 41%; 1911-20 = 59%; 1921-30 = 62%; 1931-40 = 88%; 1941-50 = 75%; 1951-60 = 100%; 1961-99 = 100%; arrival date unknown = 76%.

108. ECC, *Naturalization Petition*, Vincenzo Suffoletta, May 24, 1921; WWIDRR.

109. Interview with Guy and Delia Iannarelli, July 10, 2001.

110. LL, 10/13/38.

111. Interview with Celestino "Chet" Catuzza, September 18, 1994.

112. Interview with Pat Vertalino, July 13, 1994.

CHAPTER 3

1. The United States began keeping statistics on immigrant arrivals in 1820. By 2000, the total number of arrivals from Italy stood at 5,435,830. Gianfausto Rosoli uses Italian statistics to calculate that 5,700,000 Italians immigrated to the United States between 1876 and 1980; adding to this the U. S. statistics from 1820 to 1875, and 1981 to 2000, yields a total of approximately 5,880,000 for the years 1820 to 2000. In this study I will use the rough figure of 5,500,000. U.S. Immigration and Naturalization Service, *2000: Statistical Yearbook of the Immigration and Naturalization Service,* 2002, p. 21; Gianfausto Rosoli. "The Global Picture of the Italian Disapora to the Americas," in Lydio Tomasi, Piero Gastaldo, and Thomas Row, eds. *The Columbus People: Perspectives in Italian Immigration to the Americas,* 1994, p. 309.

2. John Bodnar, *The Transplanted: A History of Immigrants in Urban America,* 1987, p. 217: the exact total for immigrants arriving between 1820 and 1955 is 40,413,120, of which 33,874,574 came from Europe; Roger Daniels, *Not Like Us: Immigrants and Minorities in America,* 1997, pp. viii, ix, 43 (1st quote), 61; Alexander DeConde, *Half Bitter, Half Sweet: An Excursion Into Italian-American History,* 1971, p. 101 (2nd quote), Betty Boyd Caroli, *Italian Repatriation from the United States,* 1900–1914, 1973, pp. 93, 96; Aristide R. Zolberg, *A Nation by Design: Immigration Policy in the Fashioning of America,* 2006, p. 205; Joe R. Feagin, *Racial and Ethnic Relations, Second Edition,* 1984, p. 57

3. The province of Trentino Alto-Adige, which was annexed from Austria by Italy in 1918, is also part of the northern-most area of the country. Edward A. Ross, *The Old World In the New,* 1914, p. 97; Edward A. Ross, "Italians In America," *The Century Magazine,* 1914, p. 441.

4. Seymour Martin Lipset and Earl Rabb, *The Politics of Unreason: Right-Wing Extremism in America,* 1790–1970, 1970, p. 92; Joe R. Feagin, p. 113

5. NYT, 4/16/1876, as quoted in Salvatore J. LaGumina, *WOP! A Documentary History of Anti-Italian Discrimination in the United States, 1973,* p. 31; Feagin, p. 114. Oscar Handlin provides an example of the statistical tricks used by the Commission to justify the bigoted conclusions it drew prior to collecting data. The Commission concluded that the foreign-born, especially Italians, committed more offenses of personal violence than native-born Americans. Looking at the 1229 assaults in New York County in 1907 and 1908, the two highest group totals were 630 (51%) committed by persons born in the U. S., and 342 (28%) by Italian immigrants. But the fact that the native-born had the highest percentage of assaults didn't agree with the Commission's foregone conclusions. Handlin describes what the Commission did to "correct" this problem. It totalled up all the types of crime committed by each group, and "within each group it compared the incidence of each specific type of crime with the total number of crimes in that group. That is, it reckoned up all the crimes charged to Italians and then computed what percentage of that number were homicides, larcenies, and the like. It did the same for every other group by nativity and then compared the resultant percentages for larceny and homicide. When therefore, it said that the foreign-born were more prone than natives to crimes of personal violence, it did not mean that the foreign-born committed more such crimes than the natives either absolutely or relative to their percentage in the total population. It meant only that such crimes accounted for a larger part of the total criminality of the group." So in regard to assaults in New York County, the Commission wrote that Italian immigrants had the highest rate, with a "relative frequency" of 28.9% "of the total", while the native-born had 8.7%, the second lowest of the nine groups studied. So the reader would conclude that Italians committed more assault offenses than the native-born, "whereas the exact opposite was true." This presentation "could only be accurately understood only if one remembered that 'percent of the total' meant per cent of the crimes of this category of the total number of crimes committed by the nativity group." The high position of Italians, for example, was not due to the fact that they perpetrated more assaults than the natives, but to the fact that they were responsible for fewer crimes of other types." See Oscar Handlin, *Race and Nationality in American Life,* 1948 (1957), pp. 125–128.

6. U. S. Immigration Commission (USIC), *Immigrants In Industries, Volume 8, Part 2: Iron and Steel Manufacturing, Volume 1,* 1911, p. 735; David R. Roediger, *Working Toward Whiteness: How America's Immigrants Became White,* 2005, .p.116; Luciano J. Iorizzo and Salvatore Mondello, *Italian-Americans,* 1971, p. 223; Richard Gambino, *Blood of My Blood: The Dilemma of the Italian-Americans,* 1974, pp. 109-10; DeConde, pp. 125, 168; Stefano Luconi, *From Paesani to White Ethnics: The Italian Experience in Philadelphia,* 2001, p. 40.

7. BE, 6/17/1902.

8. BME, 11/11/1902 (1st quote), February 12, 1904 (2nd quote); City of Lackawanna, *Proceedings of the Common Council,* June 13, 1910 (3rd quote). The northern edge of the steel plant and part of the New Village were within the City of Buffalo.

9. CI, 10/12/1907.

10. Bruce Nelson, *Divided We Stand: American Workers and the Struggle For Black Equality,* 2001, p. 145.

11. Luconi, p. 32.

12. Donna Gabaccia, *From Sicily to Elizabeth Street,* 1984, p. 81. Interviews with immigrants in Lackawanna revealed that few families in Italy took in boarders, mostly because the houses were so small; when they did it was usually a sibling of the husband or wife and his/her spouse. Several towns had small row houses to which units were added and a number of more distant relatives lived in this type of communal type setting.

13. DeConde, pp. 144–45; CI, September April 15; interviews with Adeline Covelli-Andreozzi, December 15, 1976 and Armondo Pietrocarlo, April 7, 1994.

14. Lake Erie Italian Club (LEIC), *Processo Verbale,,* May 5, 1917; LDJ, 1/3/16; 6/22/16; 4/16, 4/19, 4/24, 4/25, 4/27, 4/30/18, 9/12/18. The Third Liberty Loan Drive raised a total of $4,176,000,000.

15. John Higham, *Strangers In The Land: Patterns of American Nativism, 1860–1925,* pp. 215-16, 266; DeConde, pp. 156–57; Richard Slotkin, *Lost Battalions: The Great War and the Crisis of American Nationalty,* 2005, pp. 75, 92.

16. Roger Daniels, *Coming To America: A History of Immigration and Ethnicity in American Life,* 1990, pp. 103, 123; Higham, p. 266.

17. Higham, p. 234.

18. Roediger, pp. 148, 171–173; Roger Daniels, *Not Like Us,* p. 104.

19. LDJ, 8/22/18; BCAJ, 9/24/19; CE, 7/28/23; Shawn Lay, *Hooded*

Knights of the Niagara Frontier, 1995, p. 64; interviews with Al Croce, April 8, 1994; and Rose Carestio-Iacobucci-Haggerty, April 2, 1997.

20. LL, 11/20/55; interviews with Nunze Oddy, April 12, 1982; Alfredo Campanelli, December 26, 1986; and Vincenzo "Jimmy" D'Alessandro, April 9, 1985.

21. U. S. Census, 1930. Only about 20% of the city's population in 1930 had roots in the protestant countries of northwest Europe. They comprised 5% of the foreign stock, and of the 18% of the city's population that was third or later generation, with no ethnicity specified, it was guesstimated that 80% of them had roots in northwest European protestant countries.

22. U. S. Census, 1910, 1930; BEN, 1/12/24.

23. BC, 4/6/24.

24. Judith R. Kramer, *The American Minority Community,* 1970, pp. 47, 86; interviews with Gene Covelli, July 22, 1990, July 20, 1991.

25. U. S. Census, 1910, 1920.

26. Luconi, p. 53.

27. LL, 3/30/39.

28. LH, 8/17/33, 9/7/33, 3/15/34, 9/26/35; LN, 8/22/32; LL, 6/18/36, 8/ 20/36, 2/11/37, 1/27/38, 6/23/38, 7/28/38, 2/9/39, 4/30/39, 7/20/39, 5/31/40, 5/22/41, 7/17/41, 10/2/41.

29. Richard Alba & Victor Nee, *Remaking the American Mainstream: Assimilation and Contemporary Immigration,* 2003, p. 41.

30. William Foote Whyte, *The Streetcorner Society: The Social Structure of An Italian Slum,* 1943 (1966), p. 274; John P. Diggins, *Mussolini and Fascism: The View From America,* 1972, pp. 28–33; LR, March 24, 1933.

31. George DeStefano, *An Offer We Can't Refuse: The Mafia In the Mind of America,* 2006, pp. 70–73; John Dickie, *Cosa Nostra: A History of the Sicilian Mafia,* 2004, p. 21.

32. CI, 11/21/35, 12/19/35.

33. CI, 10/19/33, 6/6/35, 5/24/36, 10/1/36; LL, 10/10/40; John Andreozzi, "We Need New Heroes," *Colors,* September/October, 1992, pp. 10–11.

34. LN, 7/23/31; 7/14/32; LH, 8/16/34, 8/30/34; BEN, 9/7/35; LR, 7/15/32.

35. Interviews with Vince Morga, April 7, 1999 & July 20, 2007; Louie Petrucci, December 27, 1984; and Tony DiMillo, October 17, 1996.

36. Rev. John. Botty, "The International Character of Lackawanna," address given at Friendship House, July 12, 1934.

37. John Andreozzi, "Pescatori and Contadini In Milwaukee: Assimilation and Voluntary Organizations," unpublished masters thesis, University of Wisconsin-Milwaukee, 1974, pp. 174–181; John Andreozzi, "List of Italian American Organizations in Buffalo, N. Y.," unpublished paper, 2006.

38. Interviews with Joe Milano, December 27, 1989 and April 9, 1994; and V. Jimmy D'Alessandro, April 9, 1985.

39. Margherita Marchione, "DiMaggio, Joseph Paul," in Salvatore J. LaGumina, Frank J. Cavaioli, Salvatore Primeggia, Joseph A. Varacalli, eds., *The Italian American Experience: An Encyclopedia,* 2000, p. 185.

40. LH, 6/22/33, 1/18/34, 1/17/35, 2/25/37; LN, 10/23/30.

41. LH, 7/13/33, 1/10/35; LN, 10/30/30; LL, 7/9/36; Erie County Courthouse, incorporation papers, Lackawanna Republican Women's Club of the First Ward, Inc., January 24, 1930. By 1932 the name had been changed to the Italian Women's Republican Club of the First Ward.

42. Interviews with Anne Melillo-Corvigno, July 5, 1996; and John Fadale, November 23, 1979.

43. ECD, 1931; like Lincoln School, Franklin School east of the tracks combined elementary and high school classes; interview with Anne Melillo-Corvigno, July 5, 1996.

44. Interview with Adeline Covelli-Andreozzi, April 22, 1981.

45. LDJ, 4/6/21.

46. Interviews with Tom Ventre, September 23, 1994; Marie Ceccarelli-Rosati, July 8, 1996; and Lee Bellagamba-Gordon, August 26, 1998.

47. Interviews with Gene Covelli, July 22, 1990; and John Novelli, April 18, 1995.

48. Interviews with Tom Ventre, September 23, 1994; Lee Bellagamba-Gordon, August 26, 1998. *Cumba,* dialect for *compare,* is a title of respect that used in addressing males involved in godparent relationships, and later came to more broadly indicate respect for any male friend or relative.

49. Interviews with John Novelli, April 18, 1995; Romolo Petricca, March 27, 1996; and Joe Cosentino, July 13, 1994.

50. Interview with Caroline DePaula-Silvaroli, October 13, 1996.

51. LDJ, 4/20/16.

52. Oscar Handlin, *The Uprooted: The Epic Story of the Great Migrations That Made the American People,* 1951, p. 246; interview with Phil Andreozzi, September March 2006

53. Interviews with Mary Yoviene-Clark, December 29, 1983; and Tony Falbo, February 25, 1978.

54. Lackawanna High School (LHS) yearbooks, 1938, 1946; LH, 6/20/35; LL, 6/26/37, 11/26/47; Lackawanna School Board, *Minutes,* May 3, 1934, August 30, 1934, September 29, 1938.

55. ECD, 1931, p. 513; LHS yearbook, 1946; interview with Augusta Anticoli, December 26, 1995.

56. Lackawanna's total population in 1940 was 24,058. Interviews with Gene Covelli, July 22, 1990; Nunze Oddy, April 12, 1982; and Iole Schiavi-Murray, October 18, 1996; LH, 6/27/35; LR, 7/2/32; SCP, 3/5/47.

57. Interviews with Sara Chiac Petition for chia-Kemp, July 12, 1996; and Joe Fox, Jr., March 31, 1996; LN, 6/26/30.

58. LJ, 7/3/13; LDJ, 6/28/18; LH, 5/10/34.

59. Joseph Lopreato, *Italian Americans,* 1970, p.63; Phyllis Williams, *South Italian Folkways In Europe And America,* 1938, pp. 124–25.

60. Lopreato, *Italian Americans,* p.66; Paul J. Campisi, "Ethnic Family Patterns: The Italians Family in the United States," *American Journal of Sociology,* Vol. 53, 1948, p. 444.

61. Lopreato, *Italian Americans,* pp. 64, 66; Perlmann, p. 88; interviews with Gene Covelli, July 22, 1990, July 20, 1991.

62. Jerre Mangione, *Mount Allegro,* 1942 (1972), p. 50.

63. Interviews with Rose Fiore-Pachalczak, July 12, 1996; Yolanda Monaco-Bracci, July 12, 1995; Mike Morgan, April 18, 1995; and Lou Colello, September 23, 1983; LN, January 3, 1929.

64. Interview with Anne Scarscella-Antos, December 26, 1995.

65. Interviews with Sara Chiacchia, July 12, 1996; and Margaret Oddy-Guastaferro, July 5, 1996.

66. Interviews with Rose Fiore-Pachalczak, July 12, 1996; and Dewey Montanari, July 15, 1994.

67. Interviews with Caz DePasquale, December 28, 1977; and Adeline Covelli-Andreozzi, November 28, 1970; Richard D. Alba, *Italian Americans: Into the Twilight of Ethnicity,* 1985, p. 90; Lopreato, *Italian Americans,* p. 57; Frances M. Malpezzi and William M. Clements, *Italian American Folklore,* 1992, pp. 44–45.

68. Lopreato, *Italian Americans,* p. 66; Mangione, p. 221; Handlin, *The Uprooted,* p. 244.

69. Interview with Gene Verel, April 26, 1937; Whyte, p. 273

70. U. S. Census, 1930; Kramer, p. 48..

71. Interview with Iole Schiavi-Murray, October 18, 1996.

72. Kramer, p. 48; interviews with Loretta Amorosi-Nicometo, December 29, 1977; Mary Panzetta-Vertino, August 9, 1977; Gene Verel, September 23, 1994; LN, 8/18/32; 11/3/32, 12/8/32.; LH, 1/11/34.

73. Roediger, pp. 158–59; LL, January 19, 1939. The 158 Italian families owning homes in 1930 represented 48% of the Italian families in Lackawanna.

74. Roediger, pp. 200, 210, 226–27; Christopher, *Crashing the Gates: The De-WASPing of America's Power Elite,* 1989, p. 44; Zolberg, p. 302; Samuel Lubell, *The Future of American Politics,* 1956, p. 82.

75. LH, 12/13/34; LL, 1/6/38. Interviews with Joe Milano, April 9, 1994.

76. Interview with Margaret Oddy-Guastaferro, July 5, 1996; CUT, 1/22/20; LL, 2/6/41.

77. LL, 2/6/41.

78. Interviews with Joe Milano, November 23, 1977; and Phil Andreozzi, April 25, 1903. "Household" refers to any housing unit in which one or more Italians live.

79. LH, 1/30/36; LL, 1/7/37, 1/15/41; LN, 2/18/32; ECD, 1941.

80. U. S. Census, 1930.

81. LJ, 3/15/17; LH, 9/27/34, 10/11/34, 11/22/34; CI, 12/2/37.

82. Charles F. McGovern, *Sold American: Consumption and Citizenship, 1890–1945*, pp. 2–5, 9, 123–24.

83. Bureau of he Census, *U. S. Census, 1940, Housing, Volume II, General Characteristics, Part 4*, p. 335.

84. Interviews with Dorothy Govenettio, June 22, 1997; Dennis Sterlace, March 29, 1997; Caz DePasquale, December 28, 1977; Gene Covelli, July 22, 1990; SCP, 8/4/48.

85. Lubell, p. 71; Vincent A Lapomarda, "Sarazen, Gene," in LaGumina et al., pp. 573–74; Richard Renoff, "Sports," in LaGumina et al., pp. 608-13)

86. "Pop Singers," in LaGumina et al., pp. 489-96; Marion Aste, "Movie Actors and Actresses," in LaGumina et al., pp. 387–89.

87. Lubell, pp. 71, 85.

88. Charity Organization Society of Buffalo, *Fifty Years of Family Social Work,* 1877–1927, p. 89; LL, 10/21/37; interview with Tom Pepper, 1977.

89. LH, 5/11/33; LL, 4/30/42; LN, 12/8/ 1932; Lackawanna Friendship House, "The Chatter Box," May 1942.

90. LN, 3/2/33, 11/17/27 (quote); LH, 6/22/33.

91. Interview with Phil and Adeline Andreozzi, April 8, 1994; Floyd Anderson, *The Incredible Story of Father Baker,* 1974, pp. 110–113.

92. LN, 5/26/32; LH, 1/11/34.

93. Interview with Tom Pepper, 1977; LL, 2/14/46; LN, 12/1/27

94. LL, 8/29/40; Richard W. Steele, "'No Racials': Discrimination Against Ethnics in American Defense Industry, 1940–42," *Labor History,* Vol. 32, No. 1, Winter 1991, p. 72; Christopher Duggan, *A Concise History of Italy,* 1994, pp. 234-35, 237.

95. Interview with Anne Scarsella-Antos, December 26, 1995; LL June 13, 1940.

96. Nancy C. Carnevale, "'No Italian Spoken for the Duration of the War:' Language, Italian-American Identity, and Cultural pluralism in the World War II Years," *Journal of American Ethnic History,* Spring 2003, pp. 7–8; Dan A. D'Amelio, "A Season of Panic: The Internments of World War II," *Italian Americana,* Summer 1999, p. 160.

97. LL, 12/11/41; interview with Armando Torella, December 23, 1986.

98. Richard W. Steele, "'No Racials': Discrimination Against Ethnics In American Defense Industry," *Labor History,* Winter 1991, Vol. 32, No. 1, pp. 69, 73, 85-86, 88; D'Amelio, p. 160.

99. LL, 2/12/42; Peter L. Belmonte, *Italian Americans in World War II,* 2001, p.6, Richard Gambino, p. 292; Humbert Nelli, *From Immigrants To Ethnics, The Italian Americans,* 1983, p. 171; Carnevale, p. 13; interview with John Novelli, April 18, 1995.

100. LL, 4/1/43, 5/6/43, 6/8/44, 1/18/45, 3/15/45, 6/7/45.

101. Albert N. Keim, *The CPS Story: An Illustrated History of Civilian Public Service,* 1990, p. 8; interview with Flora Paolini-Olivieri, July 13, 1994; LL, 10/23/47.

102. LL, 9/ 9/43, 9/16/43.

103. LL, 7/27/44.

104. Carnevale, pp. 10, 12–14 (first 3 quotes); LL, July 6, 1944 (last quote); Nelli, p. 171; Steele, p. 89; Valentine Belfiglio, "Wartime Military and Home front Activities," in LaGumina et al.., p. 672; Jerre Mangione & Ben Morreale, *La Storia: Five Centuries of the Italian American Experience,* 1992, pp. 341–42.

105. Carnevale, pp. 4, 7; Steele, p. 86; Reed Ueda, "Historical Patterns of Immigrant Status and Incorporation in the United States," in Gary Gerstle and John Mollenkopf, editors, *E Pluribus Unum? Contemporary Perspectives on Immigrant Political Incorporation,* 2001, p. 310.

106. Rev. Kenneth D. Miller, D.D., "The Christian Neighborhood House," booklet, 1943, pp. 11–12.

107. LL, 4/10/47, 7/31/47, 8/14/47; SCP, 1/29/47.

108. "A Living Edifice To God: St. Anthony and His Parish," dedication booklet, 1964, p. 12; Roediger, pp. 224, 233; LL, 2/19/48; ECD, 1941, p. 224.

109. Roediger, p. 231.

110. Richard Polenberg, *One Nation Divisible: Class, Race, and Ethnicity in the United States Since 1938,* 1980, p. 55; Virginia Yans-McLaughlin, *Family and Community: Italian Immigrants in Buffalo, 1880–1930,* 1971, p. 83; Rita F. Stein, *Disturbed Youth and Ethnic Family Patterns,* 1971, pp. 249–50;

111. Interview with Rev. Anthony Bilotta, September 24, 1994.

112. Interviews with Frank Chiodo, June 24, 1997; Mike Morgan, April 8, 1995; and Chet Catuzza, September 8, 1994.

113. Interview with Audrey Spagnola-Surgenor, March 29, 1996; BN, March 21, 1991. MIA-POW are the acronyms for Missing In Action—Prisoner of War.

114. Diana Dillaway, *Power Failure: Politics, Patronage, and the Economic Future of Buffalo, New York,* 2006, pp. 80–81; Mark Goldman, *City On The Lake: The Challenge of Change in Buffalo,* New York, 1990, p. 67.

115. Michael Lerner, "Respectable Bigotry," *American Scholar,* August, 1969, pp. 606–17; Peter Maas, The Valachi Papers, 1968;

116. Andrew M. Greeley, *Why Can't They Be Like Us? America's White Ethnic Groups,* 1971, p. 18

117. Zolberg, p. 436; Daniels, *Coming To America,* pp. 332, 341; Vincent N. Parrillo, *Strangers To These Shores: Race and Ethnic Relations in the United States, Fifth Edition,* 1997, p. 180; the 1965 Immigration Act replaced the national origins provision with overall hemispheric caps on visas issued: 170,000 for people in the Eastern hemisphere, and 120,000 for the Western hemisphere. In 1976 a 20,000-per-country annual limit was put into place, and two years later a worldwide ceiling of 290,000 replaced the hemispheric quotas.

118. Alberto Melucci, "The Post-Modern Revival of Ethnicity," in John Hutchinson & Anthony D. Smith, editors, *Ethnicity,* 1996, p. 368.

119. John A. Lent, "Television," in LaGumina et al., p. 625. McClellan's committee was called the Senate Select Committee on Improper Activities in the Labor or Management Field, see DeStefano, p. 43.

120. "Joint Convention Report: National Anti-Defamation Committee and National Deputy," August 20, 1957, p. 1, National OSIA Office collection, OSIA Archives, Immigration History Research Center; Frank A. Salamone, "Italian American Civil Rights League," in LaGumina et al., p. 301.

121. Frank J. Cavioli, "American Committee on Italian Migration," in LaGumina et al., p. 12

122. Luconi, p. 12; Dominic R. Massaro, "National Italian American Coordinating Association (NIACA): The Conference of Presidents of Major Italian American Organizations," in LaGumina et al., p. 400; Alfred Rotondaro, "National Italian American Foundation," in LaGumina et al., pp. 401-02; Rosanne Martorella, "National Organization of Italian American Women," in LaGumina et al., pp. 402-03; John Andreozzi, "Organizations," in LaGumina et al., p. 437; Vincent A. Lapomarda, "Press, Italian American," in LaGumina et al., p. 511; Lent, p. 626; FP, September 4, 2002.

123. Polenberg, p. 246; Public Law 106–451, "The Wartime Violation of Italian American Civil Liberties Act," November 7, 2000.

124. U. S. Census, 1980; Richard D. Alba, *Ethnic Identity: the Transformation of White America,* 1990, p. 13.

125. Richard D. Alba, *Italian Americans: Into the Twilight of Ethnicity,* 1985, p. 149. For individuals with roots in Lackawanna who are third generation and of mixed Italian and non-Italian ancestry, the intermarriage rate has been 77%.

126. Christopher, pp. 96–97; Geno Baroni, Arthur Naperstek, Karen Kollias, "Patterns of Class and Ethnic Discrimination in the Corporate and Philanthropic World," National Center For Urban Ethnic Affairs, 10/23/75.

127. Christopher, pp. 94, 97–98, 101; G. William Domhoff, as quoted in Christopher, p. 97; "Fortune 500, Ranked Within States," *Fortune Magazine,* April 30, 2007, pp. F-38–49.

128. Carlo Ferroni, "Cleveland," in LaGumina et al., p. 119; Frank J. Cavaioli, "Governors," in LaGumina, et al., pp. 270–75; Salvatore J. LaGumina, "Politics," in LaGumina, et al., p. 484; Stefano Luconi, "Rodino, Peter Wallace, Jr.," in LaGumina, et al., p. 555; Margherita Marchione, "Sirica, John Joseph," in LaGumina et al., p. 592.

129. Matthew Frye Jacobson, *Roots Too: White Ethnic Revival in Post-Civil Rights America,* 2006, p. 343; Christopher, p. 98.

130. U. S. Census, 1990.

131. Alba, *Italian Americans,* p. 15; Herbert M. Gans, "Symbolic Ethnicity: The Future of Ethnic Groups and Cultures in America," *Ethnic and Racial Studies,* Vol. 2, No. 1, January 1979, pp. 1–20.

132. FP, 9/25/10991.

133. Alba, *Italian Americans*, p. 159.

CHAPTER 4

1. David A Hollinger, *Postethnic America*, 1995, p. 24; Stefano Luconi, *From Paesani to White Ethnics: The Italian Experience in Philadelphia,* 2001, p. 5

2. Richard Alba & Victor Nee, *Remaking the American Mainstream: Assimilation and Contemporary Immigration*, 2003, p. 11; Martin N. Marger, *Race and Ethnic Relations: American and Global Perspectives*, 1985, p. 31

3. Dvora Yarnow, *Constructing "Race" and "Ethnicity" in America: Category-Making in Public Policy and Administration*, 2003, pp. 36, 57; Richard A. Easterlin, "Economic and Social Characteristics of the Immigrants," in Richard A. Easterlin, David Ward, William S. Bernard, Reed Ueda, *Immigration*, 1982, p. 12; Marger, p. 31; La Vern J. Rippley, "Germans," in Stephan Thernstrom, Ann Orlov, Oscar Handlin, eds, *Harvard Encyclopedia of American Ethnic Groups*, 1980, p. 417; Anglo-Saxon originally designated the descendants of the three Germanic tribal groups that won control of England in the fifth and sixth centuries— the Angles, Saxons, and Jutes; see Stephan Thernstrom, et al., p. 125.

4. Marger, pp. 27, 31

5. Marger, p. 98; Vincent N. Parrillo, *Strangers to these Shores: Race and Ethnic Relations in the United States, Fifth Edition*, 1997, p. 61; for an analysis of four types of multiculturalism, see Douglas Hartmann and Joseph Gertels, "Dealing With Diversity: Mapping Multiculturalism in Sociological Terms," *Sociological Theory*, Vol. 23, June 2005, pp. 218–240.

6. Stephanie Bernardo, *The Ethnic Almanac*, 1981, p. 283; Alba and Nee, pp. 13, 74; Stephen Cornell and Douglas Hartmann, *Ethnicity and Race: Making Identities In A Changing World, 2nd Edition*, 2007, p. 133

7. Richard Alba, *Ethnic Identity: The Transformation of White America*, 1990, p. 312.

8. Alba and Nee, p. 23.

9. Lawrence Fuchs, *The American Kaleidoscope: Race, Ethnicity, and the Civic Culture*, 1990, pp. 22, 23.

10. Marger, 71–73; Milton M. Gordon, *Assimilation In American Life: The Role of Race, Religion, and National Origins*, 1964, p. 32–33; Donald Noel, "The Study of Assimilation," in John Jackson, ed., *Migration*, 1969, p. 221; Alba & Nee, p. 23; Judith R. Kramer, *The American Minority Community*, 1970, p. 49.

11. Gordon, pp. 77–78; Herbert Gans, "Toward A Reconciliation of 'Assimilation' and 'Pluralism': The Interplay of Acculturation and Ethnic Retention," in Charles Hirschman, Philip Kasinitz, and Josh DeWind, eds., *Handbook of International Migration: The American Experience,* 1999, p. 162.

12. Alba & Nee, pp. 38, 48, (quote), 49,66; Kramer, p. 85; Luconi, p. 99; Cornell and Hartmann, p. 228.

13. CI, 7/15/1911; Gordon, pp. 32–33.

14. U. S. Census, 1910, 1920, 1930, N. Y. Census, 1925. In 1930, 72% of the immigrant males and 51% of the females, age 18 or older, were naturalized.

15. Irving L. Child, *Italian or American? The Second Generation in Conflict*, 1943, pp. 71–72. Child used the term "apathetic" instead of accommodation; Lydio Tomasi, *The Italian American Family*, 1972, p. 37; U. S. Census, 1930. In Lackawanna, 63% of the second generation Italian Americans became adults in the 1930s.

16. Joseph Lopreato, *Italian Americans*, 1970, pp. 76; Paul J. Campisi, "Ethnic Family Patterns: The Italians Family in the United States," *American Journal of Sociology*, Vo. 53, 1948, pp. 444–45.

17. James A. Crispino, *The Assimilation of Ethnic Groups: The Italian Case*, 1980, p. 49.

18. Fuchs, also assumes that the American economy has always provided decent living standards and the opportunity for social mobility. In Fuchs' view, it has been the political or civic culture, rather than ethnicity that has been the primary unifying force in America. He exaggerates the extent to which these components were available for past immigrants and is overly optimistic about their availability for both recent non-white immigrants and long term minority groups, such as blacks and Indians. Yet his concept of the civic culture is very helpful in understanding the Italian American experience. pp. 5, 21; Jeremy Hein, "Ethnic Pluralism and the Disunited States of North America and Western Europe," Review Essays, *Sociological Forum*, Vol. 8, No. 3, 1993, pp. 507–16.

19. John Dickie, "Stereotypes of the Italian South, 1860–1900," in Robert Lumley and Jonathan Morris, editors, *The New History of the Italian South*, 1997, pp. 121–2; letter to author from Donna Gabaccia, 1/21/2008. The term Nordic included Anglo-Saxon and Teutonic or Aryan peoples; Stephan Thernstrom, Ann Orlov, and Oscar Handlin, editors, *Harvard Encyclopedia of American Ethnic Groups*, 1980, p. 749

20. Fuchs, pp. 22–23; Luconi, p. 32.

21. Interview with Tony Grasso, December 23, 1987.

22. Interviews with Adeline Covelli-Andreozzi, April 22, 1981; Dora Sambuchi-Grosso, July 18, 1986; and Augusta Lampazzi-Anticoli, December 26, 1995.

23. Cornell and Hartmann, p. 90.

24. Cornell and Hartmann, pp. 18, (quote) 76, 77.

25. Raymond Breton, "Institutional Completeness of Ethnic Communities and the Personal Relations of Immigrants," *American Journal of Sociology*, Vol. LXX, September 1964, pp. 194. Humbert Nelli, *From Immigrants To Ethnics, The Italian Americans*, 1983, p. 173, indicates that in both New York City and Chicago during the years 1910 to 1920, about 50% of adult Italian males belonged to an Italian organization. The 1940 Census does not provide data on second generation Italians, so the total Italian population for that census in not known.

26. Breton, p. 194.

27. BC, 6/7/1902; Marger, p.52.

28. Niles Carpenter, *Nationality, Color, and Economic Opportunity in the City of Buffalo,* 1927, pp. 113, (1st and 2nd quotes) 120, (4th quote) 129, (3rd quote) 130, 139, 193.

29. Feagin, p.116 (quote); Andrew Rolle, *The Immigrant Upraised: Italian Adventurers and Colonists In An Expanding America*, 1968, pp. 177–78; Luciano J. Iorizzo and Salvatore Mondello, *The Italian-Americans*, 1971, p. 223; Richard Gambino, *Blood of My Blood: The Dilemma of the Italian-Americans, Twenty Million Much-Misunderstood Americans*, 1974, p. 110.

30. Bruce Watson, *Sacco and Vanzetti: The Men, The Murders, and the Judgement of Mankind*, 2007, 253 (1st quote), 313; CI, 5/12/27, 8/25/27; Samuel Lubell, *The Future of American Politics*, 1956, pp. 41 (2nd quote), 42.

31. Interviews with Frank Moretti, April 2, 1996 (1st quote), and Frank Scaletta, 4/4/88 (2nd quote); Gordon, pp. 75–78; the concept for ethnic micro-aggressions comes from Derald Wing Sue, et al, "Racial Microaggressions in Everyday Life," *American Psychologist*, May–June 2007, pp. 271–275.

32. City of Lackawanna, *Oaths of Office,* Books 3–5, 1930–42; City of Lackawanna*, Common Counsel Proceedings*, 11/18/12, 11/4/18, 9/30/24, 9/30/25, 11/16/25, 9/15/26, 11/15/26, 10/31/27, 4/16/28.

33. *Statuto e Regolamento: Italian-American Citizens Club of Lackawanna, N. Y.*, n.d.; the three neighborhoods at that time were Ingham Avenue, the Old Village, and Roland Avenue; Papers of Joe Milano: brochure, "Testimonial Banquet In Honor of Hon. Joseph J. Milano," 5/18/35.

34. Erie County, *Official List of Registered Voters*, 1926, 1940, 1945, 1950

35. Interview with Arc Petricca, July 9, 1996; after St. Charles Church was torn down, the OLV Mission Church and School was constructed in 1923 and staffed by priests from Our Lady of Victory Basilica until the late 1930s. In 1949, it was renamed as Queen of All Saints Church and School; see William H. Emerling and John P. Osborne, *The History of Lackawanna*, 1976, p. 22.

36. LL, 10/28/37, 1/27/38, 6/30/38, 12/19/40.

37. Interviews with Frank Chiodo, December 28, 1983; Gene Verel, September 23, 1994; Flora Paolini-Olivieri, July 13, 1994; and Blanche Rice, July 9, 1996.

38. Interview with Rev. Anthony Bilotta, September 24, 1994.

39. ECD, 1941; BSDH, 1949; LCD, 1960; BSESD, 1973, BSSD, 2006.

40. LL, 9/4/58, 2/5/59, 3/7/68, 10/3/68, 12/31/68, 6/11/70, 4/22/76; letter to author from Gregory F. and Gregory M. Paolini, 7/17/2000; interviews with Frank Scaletta, April 4, 1988; and Al and Elaine Ceccarelli, July 5, 1993.

41. See Chapter 8 for more details regarding Italian businesses.

42. LL, 6/20/46, 11/7/46, 12/19/46, 3/13/47; 4/24/47, 2/5/48, 5/6/48, 10/14/48, 12/9/48, 2/17/49, 3/10/49, 4/28/49, 6/2/49, 6/9/49, 7/7/49, 9/14/49, 10/20/49.

43. LJ, 3/15/17; LH, 9/27/34, 10/11/34, 11/22/34.

44. Peter Bondanella, *Hollywood Italians: Dagos, Palookas, Romeos, Wise Guys, and Sopranos*, 2006, pp. 21–34, 38–46.

45. Interviews with Dorothy Goventtio, June 22, 1997; Dennis Sterlace, Match 29, 1997; Caz DePasquale, December 28, 1977; Gene Covelli, July 22, 1990; SCP, 8/4/48.

46. Richard Renoff, "Sports," in Salvatore J. LaGumina, Frank J. Cavaioli, Salvatore Primeggia, and Joseph A. Varacalli, eds., *The Italian American Experience: An Encyclopedia*, 2000, pp. 609, 612–14; Joseph Fioravanti, "Pop Singers," in LaGumina, et al., pp. 489–96.

47. FP, 12/28/77; SCP, 2/4/48, 2/25/48; LL, 9/18/41, 7/20/44; interview with Caz DePasquale, December 28, 1977.

48. LL, 11/14/46, 5/3/51, 11/15/51, 12/10/53.

49. City of Lackawanna, *Births, Book.#3,1911–12*; LCD, 1914–15; interview with Elmer Covelli, December 29, 1992.

50. Kramer, p. 48; interviews with Loretta Amorosi-Nicometo, December 29, 1977; Mary Panzetta-Vertino, August 9, 1977; Gene Verel, September 23, 1994; LN, 8/18/32, 11/3/32, 12/8/32.

51. U. S. Census, 1930; Kramer, p. 48.

52. Interview with Jay Covino-Masters, July 6, 1996.

53. Gordon, p. 77.

54. Gordon, pp. 76–77; Gordon's formulation did not include assimilation into the formal social institutions or structures of society.

55. Alba & Nee, p. 17; Marger, p. 73.

56. Cornell & Hartmann, p. 26.

57. Richard Polenberg, *One Nation Divisible: Class, Race, and Ethnicity in the United States Since 1938*, 1980, pp. 282–83; Alda C. Mui and Suk-Young Kang, "Acculturation Stress and Depression Among Asian Immigrants Elders," *Social Work,* Vol. 51, No. 3, July 2006, p. 141.

58. Fuchs, p. 405; *PP,* 4/13/2007.

59. Yanow, pp. 62, (1st quote) 67; Cornell & Hartmann, (2nd quote) p. 26.

60. John Hutchinson, "Ethnicity and Multiculturalism in Immigrant Societies," in John Hutchinson & Anthony D. Smith, editors, *Ethnicity*, 1996, p. 375.

61. Benjamin B. Ringer & Elinor R. Lawless, *Race— Ethnicity and Society*, 1989, p. 27; Vincent Jeffries and H. Edward Hansford, *Social Stratification: A Multiple Hierarchy Approach*, 1980.

62. Reed Ueda, "Naturalization and Citizenship," in Richard A. Easterlin, David Ward, William S. Bernard, Reed Ueda, *Immigration*, 1982, p. 116.

63. Ueda, pp. 124–25, 129, (1st quote) 130, 131, 136; William S. Bernard, "A History of U. S. Immigration Policy," in Richard A. Easterlin, et al.., p. 94; Ian F. Hancock, "Gypsies," in Thernstrom, et al., pp. 441–42; Aristide R. Zolberg, *A Nation By Design: Immigration Policy in the Fashioning of America*, 2006, pp. 254, (2nd quote) 256.

64. Bernard, pp. 88, 93; Roger Daniels, *Coming To America: A History of Immigration and Ethnicity in American Lif*e, 1990, p. 114.

65. Ringer & Lawless, pp. 151–52, 161, 168.

66. Ringer & Lawless, p. 27 (1st quote); Alba & Nee, p. 54 (2nd quote).

67. U. S. Census, 1930–2000.

68. U.S. Census, 1900, 1910; *Friendship House, Annual Report*, 1939–1941, p. 11.

69. Ethel E. Thompson, *The Day Before Yesterday in Blasdell*, 1951, pp. 19, (1st quote) 20; LJ, 1/7/15, 5/3/17; (2nd quote) LN, 12/22/32; LL, 9/16/43; interviews with Tony DiMillo, June 27, 1997, and Caroline DePaula-Silvaroli, October 13, 1996.

70. U.S. Census, 1940, 1980, 2000; BEN, 3/10/24; David Brody, *Steelworkers In America: The Nonunion Era*, 1960, p. 266; interview with Tony DiMillo, October 17, 1996.

71. U. S. Census, 1930, 1990; interview with Abdul Nashir, August 24, 1998.

72. Interviews with Lucy Pietrocarlo and Concetta Risio, September 9, 1995; Carmella Macaluso-Pawlowski, April 3,1996; and Al Croce, April 8, 1994 (quotes); U.S. Census, 2000.

73. LL, 8/25/38 (1st quote); BME, 1/26/1906 (2nd & 3rd quotes); Lillian S. Williams, *Strangers in the Land of Paradise: The Creation of an African American Community, Buffalo, New York, 1900–1940*, pp. 72, 74, 75, 94; U. S. Census, 1920, 1930; N. Y. Census, 1925. Many blacks lived on Gates Avenue, and Steelawanna, Bethlehem, and Lebanon streets.

74. Interview with Nunze Oddy, April 12, 1982; and Jerry DePasquale, June 30, 1996.

75. Interview with Joe Cosentino, April 18, 1979.

76. U.S. Census, 1930; N.Y. Census, 1925; ECD, 1931; LL, 7/13/39. The property deeds of Bethlehem Park stated: "That at no time shall said premises or any part thereof or any building erected thereon be occupied by Negro or person of Negro extraction," unless the person was a domestic servant living with his or her employer.

77. Friendship House, *Annual Report, 1939–1940*; Catholic Charities Center of Lackawanna, "Social Conditions in City of Lackawanna, New York", April, 1934 (1st quote); *Catholic Citizen* (Milwaukee), 1/12/35; interview with Bobby Pino, December 19, 1905 (2nd quote).

78. N. Y. Census, 1925; U.S. Census, 1930; LL, 7/21/38 (quote).

79. Ira Katznelson,. *When Affirmative Action Was White: An Untold History of Racial Inequality in Twentieth Century America*, 2005, pp. 25-79. David R. Roediger, *Working Toward Whiteness: How America's Immigrants Became White, The Strange Journey from Ellis Island to the Suburbs*, 2005, pp. 227–28; LL, 1/19/39; 3/21/41; David J. Corcoran, "A Study of the Lackawanna Neighborhood Cooperative Committee," masters thesis, University of Buffalo, 1950, p. 41.

80. CE, 9/14/43 (1st quote); 9/20/43 (2nd quote).

81. CE, 9/14/43 (1st quote) , 9/15/43, 9/20/43, 9/24/43; LL, 9/2/43, (2nd quote) 9/16/43, 9/23/43, 9/30/43; Arthur H. Estabrook, Ph.D., "A Roof Over Their Heads," Council of Social Service Agencies, Buffalo, New York, October 15, 1943; interview with John Mecca and Nick Canali, October 13, 1996.

82. LL, 9/20/51.

83. Interview with Aldo Filipetti, July 11, 1996; LL, 12/15/49; 5/3/51; 9/20/51; 9/27/51; 10/3/51.

84. U. S. Census, 1940, 1950, 1960; Corcoran, pp. 40, (1st quote) 41, (2nd quote) 42; Henry Taylor, "The Rape of Lackawanna: The Untold Story of Bethlehem Steel," unpublished paper, May 1972, pp. 75, 92, 94, 99; Henry Taylor, "Race, Nationality, Class and Black Neighborhood Development In Lackawanna, New York, 1900–1970," unpublished and undated paper, (3rd quote) p. 49; Msgr. Julius J. Szabo, "Struggles of A Civic Conscience: A Study of the Lackawanna Experiment In Neighborly Cooperation," unpublished paper, 1960, p. 11. In 1960, 54% of the housing in the Ridge Road area of the First Ward was considered dilapidated.

85. BCE, 10/20/68; BEN, 10/22/68 (1st & 2nd quotes), (3rd quote) 11/19/68; NYT, 12/16/68.

86. LL, 12/5/68; 1/16/79; 12/17/70; 2/25/71; (1st & 2nd quotes) BEN, 12/2/68; BCE, (3rd quote) 1/9/69, 2/19/71; interviews with Bobby Pino, December 19, 2005; and James Singletery, December 20, 2005.

87. BCE, 8/13/68.

88. Interview with Gene Covelli, June 26,1997.

89. LH, 6/22/33; LL, 3/7/68, 2/5/70; CE, 7/31/67, 2/3/70, 2/10/70; BEN, 2/15/68, 2/4/71,.2/22/71, 8/25/71, 4/10/72, 4/9/74.

90. BEN, 11/14/75, 5/10/76 (quote); CE, 2/10/70, 2/11/70; FP, 4/8/76; interview with Ron and Anne Spadone, November 23, 2008. The first black policeman, college-educated William Melvin, had joined the force in 1951, LL, 4/19/51. The University of Buffalo has been known since the 1960s as SUNYAB-State University of New York at Buffalo.

91. BEN, 11/2/71.

92. Kelly L. Patterson, "From A Different Place: The Residential and Occupational Experience of Blacks In A Steel Making Suburb," unpublished MS thesis, SUNYAB, 1995, pp. 43–46; interviews with Giustino DeSantis, July 9, 1985; and Al Croce, April 20, 1995; N. Y. Census, 1925, lists Chiacchia as running a labor agency.

93. Carpenter, p. 139; SL, 2/20/37.

94. *Federal Reporter*, Vol. 446, United States v. Bethlehem Steel Corporation 1971, pp. 652 (1st quote), 654 (2nd and 4th quotes), 655 (3rd quote); BEN, 12/6/68; LL, 12/9/71; interview with Jack Meta, July 17, 1986.

95. Fuchs, pp. 230, 233; Daniels, *Coming To America*, p. 330; Bernard, pp. 98, 100–102; Zolberg, pp. 312, (quote) 316.

96. Bernard, p. 104; Marger, p. 99; Alba and Nee, p. 71; Fuchs, p. 158

97. Lillian Serece Williams, *Strangerrs in the Land of Paradise: The Creation of An African American Community, Buffalo, New York*, 1999, p. 145; Joint Charities & Economic Fund of Buffalo and Erie County, N. Y., "Lackawanna In 1942," 1943, unpublished report, p. 10; interview with Abdul Nashir, August 24, 1998.

98. P. David Finks, *The Radical Vision of Saul Alinsky*, 1984, pp. 85, (2nd and 3rd quotes) 86, 87–88; Szabo, p. 6; LL, (1st quote) 9/10/53, 3/13/57, 3/5/59, 3/12/59, 4/22/63, 6/8/67.

99. LL, 2/29/68, 3/21/68 (quote).

100. Walter Lippmann, "The Underworld As Servant," in Francis A. J. Ianni and Elizabeth Reuss-Ianni, eds., *The Crime Society: Organized Crime and Corruption in America*, 1976, p. 169; Joseph L. Albini, *The American Mafia: Genesis of A Legend*, 1971 (1979), pp. 178–182; Lincoln Steffens, *The Shame of the Cities*, 1904, pp. 47–54. Michael Woodiwiss, *Organized Crime and American Power*, 2001, p. 10. A syndicate is a loose association of criminals who obtain money illegally, usually through the use of intimidation.

101. Daniel Bell, *The End of Ideology: On the Exhaustion of Political Ideas in the Fifties, revised edition* 1960 (1962), pp. 128–29.

102. DeConde, pp. 121–22, 181; George DeStefano, *An Offer We Can't Refuse: The Mafia in the Mind of America*, 2006, pp. 53–54; Richard Gambino, *Vendetta*, 1977, pp. 77,87, 150–51. Gambino's study provides a detailed account of the New Orleans incident.

103. Interview with Capone in 1929, quoted in: Claude Cockburn, *In Time of Trouble*, 1956, as cited in Chuck Stone, *Black Political Power, revised edition,* 1970, p. 155; Mangione & Morreale, pp. 250–260.

104. Jerre Mangione & Ben Morreale, *La Storia: Five Centuries of the Italian American Experience*, 1992, pp. 250–252; Woodiwiss, pp. 149, 210

105. Alan A. Block, *Perspectives on Organizing Crime: Essays in Opposition*, 1991, p. 37; Mark H. Haller, "Organized Crime in Urban Society," *Journal of Social History*, Winter, 1971–72, as quoted in Block, p. 11.

106. Woodiwiss, p. 10.

107. Woodiwiss, pp. 11, 226.

108. Woodiwiss, pp. 3, 6, 10, 151.

109. William Kleinknecht, *The New Ethnic Mobs: The Changing Face of Organized Crime in America*, 1996, pp. 55–59, 85–88, 230–33; Francis J. Ianni, *Black Mafia*, 1974 (1975), p. 313.

110. Interviews with Frank Morinello, December 26, 1983; and Loretta Amorosi-Nicometo, December 29, 1977; CI, 5/16/18.

111. BEN, 2/12/1904 (1st quote); City of Lackawanna, Common Council Proceedings, 8/16, 1909 (2nd quote); interview with Armondo Pietrocarlo, April 7, 1994.

112. Nelli, *The Italians In Chicago*, p. 217; CE, 6/29/38; LN, 9/18/30.

113. Yans-McLaughlin, pp. 126–27; B. F. Ruby, "DiCarlo —'Public Enemy,'" *Town Tidings*, September 1933, pp. 13, 28–29.

114. Ruby, p. 13; *Time Magazine, 8/22/66.*

115. "The Conglomerate of Crime," *Time*, 8/22/1969, p. 22; BEN, 7/20/74; U. S. Senate, *Permanent Subcommittee On Investigations of the Committee On Government Operations, Organized Crime and Illicit Traffic in Narcotics, Part 2,* 1963, pp. 587, 595 (88th Congress, First Session); Joe Griffin with Don DeNovi, *Mob Nemesis: How the FBI Crippled Organized Crime*, 2002, pp. 99–104

116. BEN, 3/22/23; 1/2/24; LDJ, 2/8/21

117. LH, 6/7/34, prohibition ended in 1933, but bootleggers continued to produce alcohol which they could sell more cheaply because no taxes were involved; LDJ, 3/12/21.

118. LDJ, 3/12/21; BEN, 1/12/24; 2/27/29; BT, 8/31/32; LH, 4/12/34; interviews with Nunze Oddy, April 12, 1982; and others.

119. Interview with Armondo Pietrocarlo, April 7, 1994.

120. LL, 12/10/70; BEN, 12/12/68, 12/14/68, 9/27/69, 3/17/72 (quotes); interview with Sam Cardinale, November 12, 1998.

121. U.S. Census 2000: http://factfinder.census.gov/servlet/SAFFIteratedFacts?_event=&geo_id01000US&_geoC...

CHAPTER 5

1. TB, 1/18/1903. Prior to the city of Lackawanna being founded in 1909, this area of West Seneca was known as Limestone Hill, the Steel Plant District, and Lackawanna City.

2. BDC, 6/2/1902.

3. Interviews with Joe Milano, April 20, 1979; and Angelo Grosso, November 22, 1977; U.S. Immigration Commission (USIC), *Volume 8, Immigrants in Industries, Part 2, Iron and Steel Manufacturing, Volume 1,* 1911, p. 743.

4. CI, 6/6/1903; during this time Church Street was named Lackawanna Street.

5. City of Lackawanna, *Tax Book, 1924*; Joint Charities & Community Fund of Buffalo and Erie County, New York, "Lackawanna in 1942," 1943. In 1924, Lackawanna's 4.8 square miles represented 3072 acres; the steel plant, small factories, and railroads occupied 1177 acres, or 38%, of the total. In 1943, the city acquired additional land from West Seneca when the Ridgewood Village was built.

6. World War I Draft Registration Records (WWIDRR); the 490 Lackawanna Italian men who registered for the draft in 1917–18 are more than twice the number of Italian male adults listed in the 1915 census. The exact proportion of newcomers not listed in later censuses is 68%.

7. David Brody, *Steelworkers in America: The Nonunion Era,* 1960, pp. 183–84, 225.

8. LJ, 6/25/14, 7/20/16; LDJ, 1/3/18, 4/28/19; LN, 2/2/28, 6/14/28.

9. Arthur H. Estabrook, "A Roof Over Their Heads," Council of Social Agencies, Buffalo, October 15, 1943, unpublished paper, University of Buffalo Center for Urban Policy Studies. The 24 buildings of the Baker Homes were situated on 17 acres extending east from Steelawanna Avenue to Wilmuth Street, and from Wilson Street south to Holbrook Street. Albright Court had 34 buildings on a site bordered by Hamburg Turnpike on the west, the Dona Street soccer field on the south, and Wilmuth Street on the east. The Ridgewood Village was built on a 57-seven acre plot at the southeast corner of Ridge and Abbott Roads and included 116 buildings.

10. The number of Italians living outside the four ethnic enclaves gradually increased from fourteen in 1905 to 69 in 1920, and reached 210 in 1930, but this was only 11% of the 1930 Italian population of the city.

11. LL, 3/15/51; 2/9/56; Henry Taylor, "The Rape of Lackawanna: The Untold Story of Bethlehem Steel," unpublished paper, University of Buffalo Center for Urban Policy Studies, May 1972, p. 99. The Lincoln Avenue homes were moved to side streets off Ingham Avenue.

12. Interview with Joe Milano, April 20, 1979; Erie County Courthouse (ECC), *Declaration of Intent*, Gaetano Milano: March 7, 1904. The street numbers were changed in 1938 and it is the numbers used since then that are listed here.

13. Interview with John Fadale, November 23, 1979.

14. Interview with Louis Colello, April 2, 1997; New Century Atlas-Erie County, 1909; N. Y. Census, 1905, 1915; U. S. Census, 1910.

15. Interview with Caroline DePaula-Silveroli, October 13, 1996: U. S. Census, 1920; N. Y. Census, 1925.

16. City of Lackawanna, *Common Council Proceedings*, April 17 and May 8, 1911; interviews with Nunze Oddy, April 4, 1982; and Joe Cosentino, April 18, 1979.

17. City of Lackawanna, *Common Council Proceedings*, May 15, 1911; interview with Santino Carnevale, September 22, 1994; interviews with Giustina "Jay" Covino-Masters, July 6, 1996; and Al Croce, April 8, 1994.

18. U. S. Census, 1910, 1920, 1930; N. Y. Census, 1905, 1915, 1925; City of Lackawanna, *Building Permits*, volumes for 1910–1925, 1929–1930.

19. Interview with Nunze Oddy, April 12, 1982; U. S. Census, 1920, 1930; N. Y. Census, 1925; City of Lackawanna, *Building Permits*, volumes for 1910–1925, 1929–1930.

20. U. S. Census, 1930; interview with Tony Grasso, December 28, 1981.

21. Interviews with Jay Covino-Masters, July 6, 1996; and Nick Canali, December 26, 1996.

22. CI, 12/2/22; interview with Yolanda Monaco-Bracci, July 9, 1996.

23. Interviews with Charles Orlando, October 16, 1996; and Yolanda Monaco-Bracci, July 9, 1996;

24. Interviews with Audrey Spagnolo-Surgernor, March 29, 1996; Rose Fiore-Pacholczak, July 12, 1996; and Yolanda Monaco-Bracci, July 9, 1996.

25. Interviews with Mike Morgan, April 18, 1995; Tony DiMillo, October, 17 1996; and Audrey Spagnolo-Surgernor, March 29, 1996.

26. CI, 4/25/1908; interview with Tony DiMillo, October 17, 1996.

27. Interviews with Tony DiMillo, October 17, 1996; and Gerald DePasquale, June 30, 1996.

28. Interviews with Angela Morgan, December 26, 1995; Nick Canali, December 26, 1996; and Theresa DeSantis-DiBlasi, July 1, 1996.

29. Interview with Helen Hrbaczik-Dankovich, October 14, 1996.

30. Interviews with Jay Covino-Masters, July 6, 1996; Audrey Spagnolo-Surgenor, March 29, 1996; Tony Grasso, December 27, 1982; and Clyde Capasso, November, 1998.

31. Interview with Yolanda Monaco-Bracci , July 9, 1996; and Nunze Oddy, April 12, 1982;.

32. Interviews with Yolanda Mattucci-Nigro and Tina Mattucci-Ginnetti, September 20, 1994; Nunze Oddy, April 12, 1982; Adeline Covelli-Andreozzi, July 20, 1996; and Theresa DeSantis-DiBiasi, July 1, 1996.

33. LL, June 8, 1950.

34. BE, 6/12/1902; LL, 7/13/39.

35. Fitch, pp. 932–33; Steel Plant Museum, platt map of the Smokes Creek Village (Old Village).

36. Interviews with Ralph D'Amore, April 20, 1995; and Adeline Covelli-Andreozzi, April 22, 1981.

37. U. S. Senate, *Labor Conditions in the Iron and Steel Industry, Volume III, Working Conditions and Relations of Employers and Employees,* 1913, p. 437. Lackawanna is designated as "Community E, Great Lakes District" in this report.

38. The Old Village held the largest number of Italian residents in four of the five censuses taken between 1905 and 1925; WWIDRR, 1917–1918.

39. Interview with Ralph D'Amore, April 20, 1995; U. S. Census, 1910, 1920.

40. Interview with Joe Cosentino, July 13, 1994.

41. Interviews with Al Croce, April 8, 1994; and Sara Chiacchia-Kempf,

July 12, 1996; LDJ, 2/9,/16, 12/16/21.

42. Interview with Adeline Covelli-Andreozzi, April 22, 1981.

43. Interviews with Gene Covelli, July 20,1991; and Mary Core-Brasch, April 20, 1995.

44. Interview with Joe Violanti, April 5, 1994.

45. Interviews with Ralph D'Amore, April 20, 1995; Adeline Covelli-Andreozzi, April 22, 1981; and Al Croce, April 20, 1995.

46. Interview with Gene Covelli, July 20, 1991.

47. Interviews with Joe Milano, December 28, 1988; and Al Croce, April 20, 1995.

48. Interview with Ralph D'Amore, April 20, 1995.

49. Interviews with Armondo Pietrocarlo, March 24, 1986; Mary Core-Brasch, April 20, 1995; Jay Covino-Masters, July 6, 1996; and Margaret Monaco-Sperduto, April 4, 1994.

50. Tony Grasso, untitled autobiographical essay, unpublished, n.d.

51. Tony Grasso, untitled autobiographical essay, unpublished, n.d.

52. Tony Grasso, untitled autobiographical essay, unpublished, n.d.; Tony Grasso, "Summer Evenings in the Old Village," unpublished story, 1988; interview with Josephine Marrano-Fistola, July 2, 2006.

53. Tony Grasso, "The Hurdy-gurdy Player and His Monkey," unpublished story, n.d., "The Knife and Scissors Sharpener," unpublished story, 1988.

54. Tony Grasso, "Giammarone," unpublished story, 1988.

55. Tony Grasso, "A Card In the Window," unpublished story, 1988.

56. Tony Grasso, "A Card In the Window." The word huckster, while taken by some to be a demeaning term, was used in a neutral way to connote a street peddler by Grasso and other Lackawannans interviewed.

57. Interviews with Al Croce, April 8, 1994 , April 20, 1995; Mary Core-Brasch, April 20. 1995; and Adeline Covelli-Andreozzi, April 22, 1981. Curtis was an immigrant from Greece.

58. CE, 2/23/30.

59. LN, 7/7/30; Erie County, *Official List of Registered Voters,* 1931–1935. Given Lackawanna's colorful political history, some of these listings may have been fictitious ones used in the same vein as names taken from the gravestones in Holy Cross Cemetery.

60. John Andreozzi, "Contadini and Pescatori in Milwaukee: Assimilation and Voluntary Organizations," 1974, unpublished masters thesis in sociology, University of Wisconsin-Milwaukee; Herbert Gans, *The Urban Villagers: Group and Class in the Life of Italian-Americans,* 1965.

61. Interview with Sara Chiacchia-Kempf, July 12, 1996.

62. City of Lackawanna, *Building Permits*, July 12, 1910-November 24, 1925; Eugene J. Covelli, "Bethlehem Park: 1925–39, Reunion and Celebration," 1993, p. 9.

63. LN, 11/12/31; LR, 6/10/32; LL, 11/21/57; Covelli, p. 49.

64. N. Y. Census, 1925; this was the last census taken by the state. ECD, 1931, 1941; interview with Paul Zaccarine, December 13, 1998; LCD, 1960; "Lackawanna Plant—Bethlehem Park Development," 1958, provided by Lil Bracci. There were 96 Italian households in Bethlehem Park in 1941.

65. "Lackawanna Plant—Bethlehem Park Development," 1958; Italians owned 81% of the homes on Elm Street, 72% of the homes on Jackson Avenue, and 63% of the dwellings on Madison Avenue in 1958. U. S. Census, 1930; interview with Armando Torella, December 23, 1986.

66. Interview with Augusta Anticoli, December 26, 1995; ECD, 1941; LL, 4/1/37, 11/7/40.

67. Interviews with Marie Ceccarelli-Rosati, July 8, 1996; Aldo Filipetti, July 11, 1996; Chet Catuzza, September 18, 1994.

68. Interviews with Phil Andreozzi, April 10, 1988; Emilia Cardoni-Cutre, August 24, 1998; and Adeline Covelli-Andreozzi, December 25, 1990.

69. Interviews with Joe Ceccarelli, July 14, 2001; and Chet Catuzza, September 18, 1994.

70. Interviews with Chet Catuzza, September 18, 1994; and Dewey Montanari, July 15, 1994.

71. Interview with Aldo Filipetti, July 11, 1996; LL, 11/14/40.

72. Interview with Adeline Covelli-Andreozzi, April 22, 1981.

73. Interviews with Phil Andreozzi, July 4, 1996; and Don Grosso, November 22, 2008.

74. Interview with Don Grosso, September 4, 2002

75. Interviews with Phil Andreozzi, July 4, 1996; Don Grosso, September 4, 2002; and Dewey Montanari, July 15, 1994; newspaper clipping, 1/73.

76. Interview with Frank Moretti, April 2, 1996.

77. Interview with Phil Andreozzi, July, 25,1978.

78. Interview with Phil and Adeline Andreozzi; LL, 10/13/55.

79. Interviews with Frank Saccomanno, April 2, 1996; Phil Andreozzi, September 10, 1994; and Aldina Manna-Wichrowski, December 25, 1995.

80. Interviews with Aldina Manna-Wichrowski, December 21, 1999; Gene Amadori, July 12, 1994; Audrey Spagnolo-Surgenor, March 29, 1996; and Josie Andreozzi, December 25, 1990..

81. Interviews with Julius Baldassari, August 29, 1998; and Aldina Manna-Wichrowski, December 21, 1999; LH, 10/24/35.

82. CE, 3/2/55; interview with Frank Moretti, April 2, 1996.

83. ECC, *Mortgage Grantees Index, 1898–1903*; N.Y. Census, 1905.

84. Interview with Frank Chiodo, December 29, 1983

85. Interviews with Ang Pitillo, July 6, 1995; and Tony Falbo, February 25, 1978; LDJ, 1/9/16.

86. Interviews with Mary Cardinale-Mastrobattista and Margaret Cardinale-Battista, April 5, 1996; Frank Sanak, December 23, 1995; Tony Falbo, February 25, 1978; and Frank Chiodo, December 28, 1983.

87. Interviews with Mary Cardinale-Mastrobattista and Margaret Cardinale-Battista, April 5, 1996; Dominick Selvaggio, March 31, 1997; John Falbo, July 12, 1994; and Tony Falbo, February 25, 1978.

88. Interview with Tony Falbo, February 25, 1978.

89. Interviews with Tony Falbo, February 25, 1978; Frank Chiodo, December 28, 1983; Ang Pitillo, April 15, 1994; and Pat Vertalino, July 13, 1994.

90. Interviews with Nick Vertalino, October 15, 1996; Ang Pitillo, April 15, 1994; and Frank Chiodo, December 28, 1983 and June 24, 1997.

91. Interview with Frank Chiodo, December 28, 1983.

92. Interviews with Ang Pitillo, April 3, 1996.

93. Interviews with Frank Morinello, July 7, 1996; Frank Chiodo, September 20, 1994; and Ang Pitillo, April 3, 1996.

94. Interview with Frank Sanak, December 23, 1995.

95. Interview with Ang Pitillo, April 3, 1996.

96. Interview with Ang Pitillo, April 3, 1996.

97. Dominic Selvaggio, March 31, 1997; Frank Chiodo, June 24, 1997; and Sam Cardinale, September 15, 1997.

98. U. S. Census, 1900; N. Y. Census, 1915, 1925; ECD, 1931, 1938, 1941; interview with Frank Chiodo, September 20, 1994.

99. Interview with Dorothy Govenettio, June 22, 1997; U. S. Census, 1920, N. Y. Census, 1915, 1925; ECD, 1931, 1938, 1941.

100. Interview with Anne Scarsella-Antes, December 26, 1995.

101. Interview with Carmella Macaluso-Pawlowski, February, 19, 1995.

102. U. S. Census, 1910; WWIDRR, 1917–1918; ECD, 1936.

103. Interview with Aldina Manna-Wichrowski, December 21, 1999.

104. Interviews with Tony Grasso, December 26,1994; Giulio Maturani, December 27, 1994; and Phil Andreozzi, July 17, 1990.

105. Interviews with Tom Pepper, 1977; and Phil Andreozzi, July 4, 1996.

106. Interview with Phil Andreozzi, July 4, 1996; and Phil and Adeline Andreozzi, July 8, 1994.

107. Interviews with Tony DiMillo, October 17, 1996; and John Fadale, November 23, 1979; City of Lackawanna, *Death Register, Book No. 9, 1916–1918.*

108. BME, 1/4/1903, 2/12/1904; USIC, I*mmigrants in Industries, Part 2, Iron and Steel Manufacturing*, p. 779; City of Lackawanna, "Annual Report of the Health Department," in *Common Council Proceedings*, February 5, 1912, p. 178, and *Death Register, Book No. 10, 1918–20*; interviews with Mary Pacillo-Grasso, July 16, 1992; and Sara Chiacchia-Kempf, July 12, 1996; LDJ, 1/10/22.

109. City of Lackawanna, *Death Register,* Books No. 2-9; St. Anthony Church records; Buffalo Tuberculosis Association, report to Lackawanna Health Department, August 15, 1934, interview with Audrey Spagnolo-Surgenor, March 29, 1996.

110. Interview with Angelo Grosso, July 18, 1986.

111. Interview with John Fadale, November 23, 1979; LJ, 6/28/17; City of Lackawanna, *Death Register, Book No. 10, 1918–1921*; LH, 8/15/41.

112. CI, 12/13/17; LL, 12/28/50.

113. Interviews with Santino Carnevale, September 22, 1994; and Caroline DePaula-Silvaroli, October 13, 1996.

114. Interview with Caroline DePaula-Silvaroli, October 13, 1996.

115. Virginia Yans McLaughlin, *Family and Community: Italian Immigrants in Buffalo, 1880–1930*, 1971, pp. 52–53.

116. Interview with Phil Andreozzi, July 21, 1990.

117. Interviews with Iole Schiavi-Murray, March 31, 1997; Jay Covino-Masters, July 6, 1996. There were also a few non-Italian men who boarded with Italian families.

118. Interviews.

119. Interview with Tony Falbo, February 25, 1978.

120. Bureau of the Census, *U.S. Census, 1930, Population-Composition and Characteristics*, Table 12, p. 21. Of the 23,998 city inhabitants in 1930, 11,428, or 48%, were 19 years old or younger.

121. U. S. Census, 1930; Italian property owners were identified in the City of Lackawanna, *Tax Book* for each even numbered year from 1910 to 1926, and for 1929; the 1929 figures does not include large holdings of Natale Pacifico who owned over eight acres on Abbott Road, and John Verel and Josephine Yoviene who had been developing and selling lots on eight acres along South Park Avenue since 1922. Some of the property holders, such as Pacifico and business woman Gertrude Ricigliano, were Buffalo residents.

122. Interview with Aldo Filipetti, July 11, 1996. Tony Grasso—untitled "reflections and observations," unpublished essay, n.d.

123. Interviews with Joe Milano, October 16, 1996; Nick Canali, October 13, 1996; Mary Core-Brasch, April 20, 1995; Lou Colello, April 21, 1995; Aldo Filipetti, July 11, 1996; Phil Andreozzi, January 30, 2004; and Joe Caligiuri, April 5, 1994.

124. Interviews with Armondo Pietrocarlo, March 24, 1986; and Dewey Montanari, July 15, 1994.

125. Interviews with Aldo Filipetti, July 11, 1996; Anne Scarsello-Antes, December 26, 1995; Frank Chiodo, June 24, 1997; Caroline DePaula-Silveroli, October 13, 1996; and Yolanda Mattucci-Nigro and Tina Mattucci Ginnetti, September 20, 1994; this was Mattucci's address prior to the street number changes instituted in 1938.

126. Interviews with Frank Sanak, December 23, 1995; Ang Pitillo, April 15, 1994; LR, 10/28/32.

127. Interviews with Anne Scarsella-Antes, December 26, 1995; Aldo Filipetti, July 11, 1996; Nick Canali, October 13, 1996; Rose Fiore-Pacholczak, July 12, 1996; Caroline DePaula-Silveroli, October 13, 1996; Tony DiMillo, October 17, 1996; Anne Melillo-Corvigno, April 17, 1998; Yolanda Monaco-Bracci, July 9, 1996; and Clyde Capasso, February 28, 2009. The city used rubble, bricks, and slag to fill in the swamp. Monaco, Gemmati, and Melillo later bought their garden lots from the city, as did other Italians on nearby streets.

128. Map of Lackawanna Steel garden plots, Steel Plant Museum; interview with Joe Milano, October 16, 1996,

129. Interview with Margaret Oddy-Guastaferro, July 5, 1996.

130. Interview with Marie Ceccarelli-Rosati, July 8, 1996.

131. Interviews with Charley Orlando, October 16, 1996; Mary Novelli-Barone, April 1, 1997; Frank Sanak, December 23, 1995; Joe Nasso, December 28, 1994; and Ang Pitillo, June 26, 1997; Tony Grasso, untitled autobiographical essay, unpublished, n.d.

132. Interviews with Ang Pitillo, June 26, 1997; Frank Chiodo, June 24, 1997; Anne Fox-Skrzynski, April 13, 1998, and July 11, 2006.

133. Interview with Dan Radwanski, April 23, 2003.

134. Interviews with Phil Andreozzi, July 17, 1990, September 2, 2002; Rose Fiore-Pacholczak, July 12, 1996; and Gene Covelli, July 17, 1990.

135. Interviews with Joe Caligiuri, April 5, 1994; Julius Baldassari, August 29, 1998; Dick Ross, June 29, 1997; Domenico Cellini, April 14, 1998.

136. Interviews with Sara Chiacchia-Kempf, July 12, 1996; Anne Scarsella-Antes, December 26, 1995; Lou Colello, April 21, 1995; and Aldo Filipetti, July 11, 1996.

137. Interviews with Phil Andreozzi, December 3, 1989; Anne Scarsella-Antes, December 26, 1995; Angela Morgan, December 26, 1995; Caroline DePaula-Silveroli, October 13, 1996.

138. Interviews with Yolanda Monaco-Bracci, July 9, 1996; and Joe Milano, October 16, 1996; Albert Covino, unpublished, untitled memoir, n. d.

139. Interviews with Pat Giordano, July 3, 1996; Augusta Anticoli, December 26, 1995; and Pat Bonitatibus, July 6, 1995.

140. Interviews with Josie Andreozzi, March 30, 1986; Phil Andreozzi, October 13, 1991; Gene Covelli, July 17, 1990; Lou Colello, April 2, 1997; and Pat Giordano, July 3, 1996.

141. Interviews with Augusta Anticoli, December 26, 1995; Rose Anticoli-Wagner, July 19, 2002; Aldo Filipetti, July 11, 1996; Albert Covino, untitled, unpublished memoir, no date.

142. Interviews with Caroline DePaula-Silveroli, October 13, 1996; Phil Andreozzi, October 14, 1993; Phil and Adeline Andreozzi, April 4, 1994; Larry Covelli, July 14, 1992. Pat Bonitatibus, July 6, 1995; Aldo Filipetti, July 11, 1996; and Anne Scarsella-Antes, December 26, 1995.

143. Interviews with Josie Andreozzi, March 30, 1986; and Phil Andreozzi, October 14, 1993.

144. Dora Sambuchi-Grosso, July 18, 1986; Charles Barone, April 6, 1994; Armondo Pietrocarlo, March 24, 1986; Chet Catuzza, September 8, 1994; Josephine Ferrelli, April 2, 1996; Anne Scarsella-Antes, December 26, 1995; Mary Cardinale-Mastrobattista and Margaret Cardinale-Battista, April 5, 1996; Audrey Spagnolo-Surgenor, March 29, 1996; Joe Caligiuri, April 5, 1994; and Augusta Anticoli, December 26, 1995.

145. Interviews with Anne Scarsella-Antes, December 26, 1995; Mary Cardinale-Mastrobattista and Margaret Cardinale-Battista, April 5, 1996; Rose Anticoli-Wagner, July 19, 2002; Augusta Lampazzi-Anticoli, December 26, 1995; Josephine Ferrelli, April 2, 1996; and Pat Bonitatibus, July 6, 1995.

146. Interviews with Anne Scarsella-Antes, December 26, 1995; Dora Sambuchi-Grosso, July 18, 1986; Josephine Ferrelli, April 2, 1996; and Adeline Covelli-Andreozzi, December 27, 1994.

CHAPTER 6

1. Interview with Rev. Secondo Casarotto, pastor of St. Anthony's Church in Buffalo, 7/2/96; *Storia della Parrocchia Italiana di Sant'Antonio in Buffalo, N.Y.*, Golden Jubilee booklet, 1941, p. 6.

2. Interviews with Nunze Oddy, 4/12/82; and Jay Covino-Masters, 7/6/96; William H. Emerling and John P. Osborne, *The History of Lackawanna*, 1976, p. 16.

3. News clipping, 1913, provided by Art Sambuchi; St. Charles church, *Baptism Register #1*, 1903-14, *Baptism Register #2*, 1914-17, *Marriage Register*, 1903-30. CI, 11/6/1909; St. Agatha's Church, "Historical Sketch, St. Agatha's/All Souls Parish," 1943, unpublished; *Baptism and Death Register, 1909-14*.

4. *A Living Edifice to God: St. Anthony and His Parish, Past, Present, Future*, dedication booklet, 1964; Tony Grasso, "A Magnet, Our Church," unpublished story, no date; interviews with Joe Milano, July 12, 1996; Angelo Grosso, November 22, 1977; and Nunze Oddy, April 12, 1982. The building housing the mission was later demolished and replaced by a structure that had a storefront, with the street number of 250 Ingham Avenue.

5. *A Living Edifice to God*, 1964; interviews with Elizabeth Rosati, September 8, 1984; and Joe Milano, July 12, 1996; CUT, 6/21/17; *Buffalo Telephone Directory*, 10, 1917, p. 298; *Official Catholic Directory, 1918*, p. 281.

6. A Living Edifice to God, 1964; interviews with Joe Milano, April 12, 1996; and Nunze Oddy, April 12, 1982.

7. Interviews with Joe Milano, July 12, 1996; Tony DiMillo, October 17, 1996; and Nunze Oddy, April 12, 1982. Archives of the Buffalo Diocese,

St. Anthony's Church folder, "History of the Parish," by Rev. Vifredo, 6/28/46; Tony Grasso, "A Magnet, Our Church;" City of Lackawanna Engineer's Office, *Building Permits, Volume 1, 1910-1925*.

8. CUT, 12/27/17; LL, 11/23/55; *A Living Edifice to God*, 1964. Rev. Secondo Casarotti reports that in 1891, Basilicati and Siciliani, the two largest regional groups in Buffalo, each wanted the city's first Italian church named after a regional patron saint. They finally compromised and accepted the name of a saint popular throughout the world, St. Anthony. Many other Italian American parishes were also named after this saint, including those in the western New York towns of Rochester, Batavia, and Fredonia. Interview with Nunze Oddy, April 12, 1982.

9. Interviews with Joe Milano, July 12, 1996; and Nunze Oddy, April 12, 1982; *Official Catholic Directory, 1919*, pp. 286, 960; *Assumption of the Blessed Virgin Mary Roman Catholic Church, 1918-1968*, Golden Jubilee Booklet, 1968, pp. 9-10.

10. Interviews with Joe Milano, November 23, 1977 and October 16, 1996; *Official Catholic Directory, 1916*, p. 975, 1917, p. 942, 1918, p. 958, 1919, p. 970. St. Anthony's, *Baptism Register # 1-A, 1918-1928, Marriage Register, 1918-1936, Death Register, 1918-94*6. Archives of the Buffalo Diocese, St. Anthony's Church folder, "History of the Parish," by Rev. Vifredo, 6/28/46.

11. Silvano Tomasi, *Piety and Power: The Role of Italian Parishes in the New York Metropolitan Area, 1880-1930*, 1975, p.180; Tony Grasso, "A Magnet, Our Church;" FP, 5/27/92.

12. Tomasi, pp. 47, 67, 143.

13. Tomasi, p. 128; Rudolph Vecoli, "Cult and Occult in Italian-American Culture: The Persistence of a Religious Heritage," in Randal Miller, Thomas Marzik, editors, *Immigrants and Religion in Urban America*, 1977, p. 25.

14. Interviews with Joe Milano, July 12, 1996; and Caz DePasquale, December 28, 1977.

15. Archives of the Buffalo Diocese, St. Anthony's Church folder, letter from Rev. Vifredo to Rev. Murphy, Vice Chancellor, 8/8/21.

16. Interviews with Caz DePasquale, December 28, 1977; and Rev. Anthony Bilotta, September 24, 1994.

17. Interview with Joe Milano, July 12, 1996; LN, 3/19/31..

18. Tomasi, p. 126; Christopher Duggan, *A Concise History of Italy*, 1994, pp. 3, 132-33, 137-41, 226.

19. Vecoli, p. 27; interview with Al Croce, April 8, 1994.

20. Interview with Flora Paolini-Olivieri, July 13, 1994.

21. Interviews with Romolo Petricca, March 27, 1986; Anne Scarsella-Antes, December 26, 1995; and Nunze Oddy, April 12, !982.

22. Interviews with Joe Milano, July 12, 1996; and Nunze Oddy, April 12, 1982.

23. Interviews with Joe Milano, July 12, 1996; and Ralph Galanti, September 22, 1983; Tony Grasso, "A Magnet, Our Church."

24. Interview with Caz DePasquale, December 28, 1977; Tony Grasso, "A Magnet, Our Church."

25. Interviews with John Fadale, November 23, 1979; and Dick Fadale, April 24, 2000.

26. Interview with Caz DePasquale, December 28, 1977.

27. Interview with Caz DePasquale, December 28, 1977; Augusta Anticoli, December 26, 1995; Tina Mattucci-Ginnetti and Yolanda Mattucci-Nigro, September 20, 1994; and Lucy Risio-Pietrocarlo and Concetta Risio, September 19, 1995.

28. Interviews with Caz DePasquale, December 28, 1977; and Charles Barone, April 6, 1994.

29. Interviews with Al Croce, April 8, 1994; Caroline DePaula-Silvaroli, October 13, 1996; Yolanda Monaco-Bracci, July 9, 1996; and Joe Milano, October 16, 1996.

30. Perhaps the poverty of the parish led Rev. Vifredo and his sister Maria to take in an occasional renter at the rectory, as Jennie Caffo, a factory accountant, was listed as a lodger in 1925, N.Y. Census, 1925; LN, 11/24/32; LH, 6/28/34; LL, 9/3/36; interviews with Yolanda Sperduti-Tobias, April 20, 1995; Rose Turchiarelli-Shawat, December 28, 1977; and Arc Petricca, July 9, 1996.

31. Lake Erie Italian Club, *Treasurer's Log of Expenses, 1918-1932*, p. 58, and *Processi Verbale, 1936-1940*, p. 1; LN, 6/9/27, 11/21/29.

32. LN, 7/14/32; LL, 9/3/36, 3/18/37, 1/19/39; *A Living Edifice to God*, 1964.

33. Interviews with Yolanda Monaco-Bracci, July 12, 1995; Ann Melillo-Corvigno, July 5, 1996; Anne Scarsella-Antes, December 26, 1995; Carmella Macaluso-Pawlowski, April, 3, 1996;

34. Interviews with Caz DePasquale, December 28, 1977; Tony DiMillo, October 17, 1996; Charles Barone, April, 6, 1994; and Tony Andreozzi Jr., July 18, 1991 and July 14, 2001; U.S. Census, 1930; LN, 12/22/32; LH, 6/28/34, 1/7/35.

35. Interviews with Anne Hurley, December 26, 1995; and Caz DePasquale, December 28, 1977; LN, 3/2/33. St. Anthony's, *Baptism Register #1-A, 1918-1928, Marriage Register, 1918-1936, Death Register, 1918-1946*. There were 23 marriages between 1919 and 1939, 26 baptisms between 1920 and 1925, and 56 funeral masses from 1921 to 1946 that involved Spanish and Latino individuals

36. Interviews with Charles Nigro, April 7, 1999; Tina Mattucci-Ginnetti and Yolanda Mattucci-Nigro, July 20, 1994; and Rev. Secondo Casarotto, July 2, 1996.

37. LDJ, 6/13/19; LN, 6/9/27; interview with Joe Milano, July 12, 1996.

38. Interview with Adeline Covelli-Andreozzi, December 27, 1991; Ann Melillo-Corvigno, July 5, 1996; and Caz DePasquale, December 28, 1977; CI, 8/8/18, 8/28/20.

39. Interview with Ann Melillo-Corvigno, July 5, 1996; LN, 7/23/31; LH, 7/13/33.

40. Tony Grasso, "A Magnet, Our Church;" LH, 9/7/33.

41. Tony Grasso, "A Magnet, Our Church."

42. Interview with Joe Milano, July 12, 1996; LL, 7/9/36; LN, 8/30/28.

43. LL, 5/25/39; interview with Augusta Anticoli, December 26, 1995; scrapbook of Loretta Amorosi-Nicometo, unlabeled newspaper clipping. Father Bakers Boys refers to youth who resided in the St. John Protectory or the St. Joseph Orphanage, two of the many institutions of Our Lady of Victory that Monsignor Baker led.

44. Interviews with Tony Grasso, December 28, 1988; Nunze Oddy, April 12, 1982; and Joe Milano, July 12, 1996.

45. Interviews with Tony Grasso, December 28, 1988; Joe Milano, July 12, 1996; and Yolanda Sperduti-Tobias, April 20, 1995; and Lil Colafranceshi-Bracci, November 23, 2008.

46. Interviews with Aldo Filipetti, July 11, 1996; and Millie Sambrotto, July 12, 1994.

47. William H. Emerling and John P. Osborne, *The History of Lackawanna*, p. 16; Ethel E. Thompson, *The Day Before Yesterday In Blasdell*, 1951, p. 47; James Jan Kaminski, "History of Saint Barbara's Roman Catholic Church, Lackawanna, New York," unpublished term paper, 1977, p. 5. St. Patrick's church was torn down in 1921 and the new Our Lady of Victory Basilica built at the site, LR, 4/7/33.

48. Interview with Frank Chiodo, December 28, 1983.

49. LL, 10/21/37; CI, 10/28/37; LH, 7/14/41.

50. U.S. Census, 1920, 1930; N.Y. Census, 1925; interview with Gene Verel, September 23, 1994.

51. Elizabeth Mathias and Angelamaria Varesano, "The Dynamics of Religious Reactivation: A Study of a Charismatic Missionary to Southern Italians in the United States," *Ethnicity*, Vol. 5, 1978, pp. 301- 311; CI, 5/14/25, Secondo Casarotto, "Italian Protestants and the Catholic Church in Buffalo, NY," in Frank J. Cavioli, Angela Danzi, Salvatore J. LaGumina, editors., *Italian Americans and Their Public and Private Life*, 1993, p. 83

52. Interviews with Tony Grasso, December 30, 1992; Frank Chiodo, September 20, 1994; Casarotto, p.87.

53. Interviews with Millie Pitillo-Savarise, April 15, 1994; Frank Chiodo, September 20, 1994; Dolores DeMaria-Antecki, July 7, 1995.

54. Interviews with Tony Grasso, December 30, 1992; and Rev. Anthony Bilotta, September 24, 1994.

55. Interviews with Flora Paolini-Olivieri, July 13, 1994; Frank Chiodo, September 20, 1994; Dolores DeMaria-Antecki, July 7, 1995.

56. U.S. Census, 1920; *Genesee Conference of Methodist Episcopal Church, Official Minutes, 1919*, p. 29; 1921, p. 207; Anna Maria Martellone, *Una Little Italy Nell'Atene D'America: La Communita Italiana Di Boston dal 1880-1920*, 1973, pp. 458-461; interviews with Edith Blattenburger, October 14, 1996; and Rev. Fred Weber, October 14, 1996.

57. Interview with V. Jimmy D'Alessandro, April 9, 1985; BE, 5/24/1908.

58. Interviews with Flora Paolini-Olivieri, July 13, 1994; and John Andrisani, December 28, 1994; taped interview of Angelo Iafallo by Dan Kij, April 6, 1995.

59. Leonard Covello, *The Social Background of the Italo-American School Child: A Study of the Southern Italian Family More and Their Effect on the School Situation in Italy and America*, 1967, p. 139; interviews with Nick Canali, October 13, 1996; and Arc Petricca, July 9, 1996.

60. Interviews with Yolanda Monaco-Bracci, July 9, 1996; Adeline Covelli-Andreozzi, July 7, 1996; Aldo Filipetti, July 11, 1996; and Iole Schiavi-Murray, October 18, 1996 .

61. Interview with Adeline Covelli-Andreozzi, December 27, 1994.

62. Interview with Rev. Anthony Bilotta, September 24, 1994.

63. *A Living Edifice to God*, 1964; *Society of Our Lady of Mt. Carmel*, bylaws book.

64. Interview with Millie Sambrotto, July 12, 1994.

65. LN, 7/14/32, 9/15/32, 12/22/32; LH, 1/18/34, 1/25/37; interviews with Augusta Anticoli, December 26, 1995; Yolanda Sperduti-Tobias, April 20, 1995; and Joe Milano, November 23, 1977; A Living Edifice to God, 1964.

66. LL, 11/4/37, 8/24/39, 1/30/41.

67. LH, 2/25/37, 5/13/39; LL, 6/30/38, 12/19/40.

68. LH, 4/26/34; LL, 12/22/38, 12/15/45.

69. LL, 12/31/46, 1/30/47, 4/20/50; SCP, 1/28/48.

70. SCP, 4/16/47, 4/7/48; LL, 11/28/46, 3/30/50; LL, 3/17/55.

71. LL, 10/17/46; SCP, 3/18/47; LN, 11/8/28.

72. LL, 4/22/48, 6/10/48, 6/16/49; SCP, 5/14/47, 6/9/48.

73. SCP, 10/8/47; LL, 1/23/47, 12/9/48.

74. Interviews with Mary Sperduto-Cuomo, August 23, 1998 (quotes); and other interviews.

75. *A Living Edifice to God*, 1964; Archives of the Buffalo Diocese, St. Anthony's Church folder, parish report and history form, 6/28/46; Vecoli, p. 36; Tony Grasso, "A Magnet, Our Church." Interviews with Armondo Pietrocarlo, March 24, 1986; and Gerald DePasquale, June 30, 1996.

76. Interview with Loretta Amorosi-Nicometo, July 13, 1994; Catholic Magnificat, 10/7/68; St. Anthony's, "Dedication Booklet, St. Anthony's New Hall," 11/20/54; *Official Catholic Directory*, 1958-1973.

77. SCP, 4/7/50; LL, 1/27/55, 2/10/55, 2/24/55, 3/3/55, 11/17/55, 11/23/55, 11/13/58.

78. Interview with Rev. Anthony Bilotta, September 24, 1994; LL, 2/24/55; 11/17/55; 4/24/58.

79. Interview with Rev. Anthony Bilotta, September 24, 1994.

80. Interview with Rev. Anthony Bilotta, September 24, 1994; A Living Edifice to God, 1964; papers of Jo Andreozzi, St. Anthony's weekly bulletin, May 19, and June 9, 1963, window placard.

81. Interview with Rev. Anthony Bilotta, September 24, 1994.

82. Interview with Rev. Anthony Bilotta, September 24, 1994; Harold J. Abramson, *Ethnic Diversity in Catholic America*, 1973, pp. 107-110; Joseph Lopreato, "Religion and the Immigrant Experience," in Joseph A. Ryan, ed., *White Ethnics: Life in Working-Class America*, 1973, p. 64.

83. Interview with Rev. Anthony Bilotta, September 24, 1994.

84. Interview with Rev. Anthony Bilotta, September 24, 1994.

85. Interviews with Rev. Anthony Bilotta, September 24, 1994; and Guy Iannarelli, July 20, 2007; Tony Grasso, "A Magnet, Our Church," unpublished story, n.d.

86. FP, 1/14/98, 4/22/98; interview with Guy Iannarelli, November 7, 2007.

87. LH, 1/18/34, 12/12/35. Many Spanish and Latino families attended Assumption Hungarian Church by 1961, when Spanish-speaking priests

were present, and soon after the Sisters of Social Service joined in the effort. The priests apparently also reached out to Latinos at Queen of All Saints. By 1971, the Spanish Allied Societies of Assumption Church was sponsoring a dance with Latin American food to honor Our Lady of Guadalupe and Pan-American Day; LL, 12/9/71; interview with Lupe Sanchez, July 11, 2001; *Official Catholic Directory*, 1961-1976. The 19 non-Italian men active in St. Anthony's organizations were George Hund, Chester Kozlowski, Eugene Otremba, Stanley Lukasik, Henry Skowronski, Michael Egana, Peter Stoycoff, Casimier Michaels, George Hassett, Stanley Georgeski, Joe Spiker, Stanley Amrozowicz, John Rusczyck, Rudy Rusczyck, Vincent Madar, Walter Kurnik, Joseph Zawacki, Duke La Mere, and Leon Moskal; SCP, 10/8/47, 4/7/48; LL, 2/24/55, 11/17/55, 11/15/56, 12/20/56, 3/19/59, 12/17/64; *A Living Edifice to God,* 1964.

88. FP, 2/4/98, BN, 2/7/98.

89. Interviews with Luz Rivera, July 12, 2001, June 7, 2005; FP, 2/7/98, 3/11/98, 12/6/2000, 2/9/2005.

90. Interviews with Rev. David Glassmire, June 8, 2005; Rose Anticoli-Wagner, November 1, 2008; and Don Grosso, November 1, 2008.

CHAPTER 7

1. U.S. Immigration Commission (USIC), *Immigrants in Industries, Volume 8, Part 2, Iron and Steel Manufacturing, Volume 1,* 1911, p. 735.

2. Untitled manuscript, January 14, 1919, updated December 9, 1926 and April 25, 1927, vertical file, Lackawanna Public Library; BIT, 1/18/1903; BC, 4/8/1900; BCAJ, 2/6/1902.

3. Milton Rogovin and Michael Frisch, *Portraits In Steel*, 1993, p. 9.

4. LDJ, 1/3/1918; Mark Goldman, *High Hopes: the Rise and Decline of Buffalo, New York,* 1983, p. 137;

5. USIC, *Immigrants in Industries, Volume 8, Part 2, Iron and Steel Manufacturing, Volume 1,* pp. 741, 743; U.S. Census, 1900; N.Y. Census, 1905; Goldman, p. 141; LDJ, 4/28/1919.

6. New York State Department of Labor, *Industrial Directory of New York State, 1912,* p. 84; USIC, *Immigrants in Industries, Volume 8, Part 2, Iron and Steel Manufacturing, Volume 1,* pp. 734, 736, 763; U.S. Senate, *Report On Conditions of Employment in the Iron and Steel Industry, Volume II: Wages and Hours of Labor, 1912,* pp. 958–59. Among the other factories in Lackawanna, there were 70 employees at Buffalo Brake Beam, 10 at Trimble, Mudge and Company, 202 at the repair shop of the Lake Shore and Michigan Southern Railroad (which later was absorbed by the New York Central), and 39 at the South Buffalo Railway roundhouse.

7. USIC, *Immigrants in Industries, Volume 8, Part 2, Iron and Steel Manufacturing, Volume 1,* p. 748, USIC, *Abstracts of the Reports, Volume 1,* p. 33; U.S. Senate, *Report On Conditions of Employment in the Iron and Steel Industry, Volume III, Working Conditions and the Relations of Employers and Employees,* 1913, pp. 83; John A. Fitch, *The Steel Workers,* 1911, pp. 349–353. According to Fitch, at the Carnegie plants in Allegheny County in 1907, Slovaks, Poles, Magyars, and Croatians made up 47% of the workforce; native-born Americans represented 26%, and Italians only 4%. Almost 40% of the Italians were from northern Italy; 8% of Italians held skilled or semi-skilled jobs, higher than the percentage of their ethnic fellows in Lackawanna. Northern Italians were also present in Lackawanna in the 1907–1910 period, but then left. Perhaps the northerners had more experience in industrial work, as this was more common in the northern regions of Italy, and workers there were geographically closer and could more easily migrate to industrial centers in Germany or France One study, however, found that Italian iron and steel workers in several areas of Germany were usually from central or southern Italy; see Robert Foerster, *The Italian Emigration of Our Times,* 1919, pp. 157–58.

8. The military draft sought only men, so the 1917–18 draft records do not include females. The occupational categories are based on a format developed in a study of Buffalo's Italians: Virginia Yans McLaughlin, "Like the Fingers of the Hand: The Family and Community Life of First Generation Italian-Americans in Buffalo, New York, 1880–1930," unpublished doctoral dissertation, State University of New York at Buffalo, 1971, pp. 26–27.

9. Colin J. Davis, *Power At Odds: The 1922 National Railroad Shopman's Strike,* 1997, p. 11; memo "Employees transferred from General Lackawanna Payroll to S. B. Ry. Co., Dec. 1, 1922," South Buffalo Railway (SBR) office.

10. N.Y. Census, 1925. The 112 Yard workers represented 41% of the total, and their number included 33 construction workers and 14 locomotive steam crane operators. The 1930 U.S. Census did not provide as much information on which steel plant department employed each individual.

11. The workforce refers to those people laboring outside of the home. LCD, 1914–1915. There were also 13 Italian women listed.

12. One sociologist would include youngsters who migrated from Italy by age ten or earlier as members of the second generation; current researchers have dubbed this group the "1.5" generation. Joseph Lopreato, *Italian Americans,* 1970, p. 74; Ruben G. Rumbaut, "Assimilation and Its Discontents: Between Rhetoric and Reality," *International Migration Review,* Volume 31, Number 4, Winter 1997, p. 936.

13. Interviews with Joe Milano, April 8, 1988; Brownie Leo, July 8, 1993; and Dan and Claude Thomas, July 12, 1994.

14. Interviews with Ralph D'Amore, April 20, 1995; and Nunze Oddy, April 12, 1982, like Milano and Leo, he too claimed he was older, he was actually fourteen when he stated he was fifteen.

15. U. S. Census, 1910; interviews with Armondo Pietrocarlo, March 24, 1986; and Pat Vertalino; July 13, 1994. Both Pietrocarlo and Vertalino fibbed about their ages. Later in his life, Pietrocarlo changed the spelling of his first name from Armando to Armondo.

16. ECD, 1941, lists 414 Italian adults in Lackawanna: 396 males and 18 females. The ECD, 1931, includes 298 Italian men and 13 Italian women working outside of the home. At least 80% of the men held jobs in the steel mills and on the railroads. The remainder of the men, and all the women, had non-industrial occupations; 51 men and two women ran their own businesses. The ECD, 1938, completely omits the residents of the First Ward, but include 106 Italian American males living east of the railroad tracks: 53 of them worked in the steel industry, 16 on the railroads, seven worked for the city, and 13 ran small businesses. Interview with Tony Andreozzi, Jr., July 18, 1991.

17. Interviews with Mary Core-Brasch, April 20, 1995; Sara Chiacchia-Kempf, July 12, 1996; Phil Andreozzi, April 7, 1994; Alex Coviello, April 7, 1994; Jo Andreozzi, July 20, 1990; Anne Melillo-Corvigno, July 5, 1996; and Iole Schiavi-Murray, March 31, 1990.

18. LCD, 1960; BSDH, 1949 also included three female heads of household. The adult children with occupations unspecified represent 39% of the Italians listed. It was assumed that many of the 100 industrial jobs, all but two of which are noted as "steelworker", are unskilled positions. The generational status of 84% of the 331 household heads was ascertained. Of the 29 females, 22 are first generation and seven second generation. For the males, 130 are first generation, 124 second generation, and the generation status of 48 are unknown.

19. Thomas E. Leary and Elizabeth C. Sholes, *From Fire To Rust,* 1987, pp. 127.

20. Bethlehem Steel Company (BSC), "A Visit to the Lackawanna Plant of Bethlehem Steel Company," Booklet 104, 1939, pp. 7–10.

21. BSC, "A Visit to the Lackawanna Plant . . .," pp. 5–7, 28–29; Leary and Scholes, pp. 59, 61, 63, 65.

22. David Brody, *Steelworkers In America: The Nonunion Era,* 1960, p. 10; Leary & Scholes, p. 76; *Bethlehem Review,* No. 70, Autumn, 1956, p. 22.

23. Leary and Scholes, p. 127.

24. ECC, *Naturalization Petition,* Gerald Omicioli, April 20, 1925; U. S. Census, 1910; interviews with Adeline Covelli-Andreozzi, December 26, 1990; and Phil Andreozzi, August 15, 1999; N. Y. Census, 1925.

25. Leary and Scholes, pp. 63, 69, 79, 81; U.S. Census, 1910; interview with Al Croce, April 8, 1994.

26. Interviews with Alfredo Campanelli, December 26, 1986; Dewey Montanari, July 15, 1994; Art Sambuchi, July 24, 1987; and Norman Sambuchi, July 13, 1995; letter from Gregory Paolini, 2000; BSC, "A Visit to the Lackawanna Plant," p. 12, gives capacities of the open hearths in 1939: No. 1 Open Hearth: 14 furnaces, each of 100 tons capacity; one hot-metal mixer with 600 tons capacity; No. 2 Open Hearth: 10 furnaces, each of 110 tons capacity; two hot-metal mixers

613

of 300 tons capacity, and one of 250 tons capacity; and No. 3 Open Hearth: six furnaces of 150 tons capacity; one hot-metal mixer of 1200 tons capacity, and a second of 450 tons capacity.

27. N.Y. Census, 1925; interview with Dewey Montanari, July 15, 1994.

28. N.Y. Census, 1915, 1925; ECD, 1931; interviews with Louis Patrucci, April 19, 1995, and Gene Giannoni, November 2, 1987.

29. Interviews with Joe Violanti, April 5, 1994; Romolo Petricca, March 27, 1986; and Phil Andreozzi, July 20, 2002. Electric-powered overhead cranes were located in mills and in outdoor areas. These huge cranes ran back and forth on large, stationary beams that were part of the structure of the mill. Those outside ran on stationary beams resting on top of a series of vertical supports. The smaller cranes were capable of lifting 10 to 50 tons, and some of the large open hearth cranes could lift 300 or 450 tons. In addition to the three highlines serving the three open hearth shops, a fourth highline trestle ran along side the blast furnaces, where hopper cars dumped coke that was then loaded into skip cars and carried to the top of each furnace.

30. U.S. Census, 1910, 1920, 1930; N.Y. Census, 1905, 1915, 1925; WWIDRR, 1917–18; ECD, 1931

31. U.S. Census, 1910, 1920; N.Y. Census, 1925; WWIDRR, 1917–18; ECD, 1931; BSC, "Lackawanna Plant Telephone Directory," 12/15/48.

32. U.S. Census, 1910, 1920; N.Y. Census, 1925; WWIDRR, 1917–18; interviews with Tony Grasso, December 23, 1987; Joe Cosentino, July 14, 1995; and Phil Andreozzi, April 17, 1995.

33. U.S. Census, 1910, 1930; N.Y. Census, 1905, 1925; WWIDRR, 1917–18; ECD, 1931; Leary and Scholes, p. 27; interviews with Tony Grasso, December 23, 1987; V. Jimmy D'Alessandro, April 9, 1985; and John Andrisani, December 28, 1994.

34. Interview with Phil Andreozzi, June 30, 1987.

35. Interview with Carl Covino, April 17, 1995. To get a job, Covino had changed his birth certificate to indicate he was a year older.

36. Interview with Frank Rosati, April 19, 1995.

37. Interview with Frank Rosati, April 19, 1995. Rosati explained the Bar Mill hierarchy at the time he worked there: under the superintendent was (1) the Roller, who directs the three pulpit operators, then (2) the assistant roller, (3) the mill adjuster, and (4) the finishing pulpit operator. The heater, who directs a separate function under the roller's supervision, earns as much or more than the assistant roller.

38. Leary and Scholes, p. 71.

39. Interviews with Al Croce, April 20, 1995; and Carl Covino, April 17, 1995.

40. Interviews with Ang Pitillo and John and Millie Savarese, April 15, 1994; Ben Vittorini, July 16, 1992; Anthony Pavone, Jr., March 29, 1996; Jack Meta, July 17, 1986; and Josephine Suffoletta-Del Monaco, December 26, 1994.

41. Interviews with V. Jimmy D'Alessandro, April 9, 1985; Phil Andreozzi, April 17, 1995; John Falbo, July 12, 1994; BSC, "Lackawanna Plant, Telephone Directory," 12/15/48. Nick Sperduto had been on a three-year leave of absence to serve as secretary to the Lackawanna Board of Assessors.

42. U.S. Census, 1920; N.Y. Census, 1925; interview with Art Sambuchi, December 27, 2002; document, "Seniority Unit Length of Continuous Service: Structural Shipping," 5/1/60, provided by Art Sambuchi.

43. N.Y. Census, 1925; interviews with Armando Torella, December 23, 1986; and Mary Leonetti, December 28, 1994. Gantry cranes, which were located outdoors, had a horizontal beam supported by two vertical supports, each with flanged railroad wheels at the base. The whole structure, which resembled an inverted "u," moved along rails on the ground.

44. U.S. Census, 1920, 1930; N.Y. Census, 1915, 1925; interviews with Nunze Oddy, April 12, 1982; V. Jimmy D'Alessandro, April 9, 1985; Ralph D'Amore, April 20, 1995; and Mary Leonetti, December 28, 1994; N. Y. Census, 1925. The roll turner and roll burner repair and balance the rolls, or large cylinders, used in the process of rolling steel.

45. Interviews with Mary Core-Brasch, April 20, 1995; Alex Filipetti, July 11, 1996; Dewey Montanari, July 15, 1994; and Leo and Doc Baldelli, July 14, 1994.

46. U.S. Census, 1910, 1920, 1930; N.Y. Census, 1925.

47. WWIDRR, 1917–18; "Lackawanna Plant History," January 14, 1919, updated December 9, 1926, April 25, 1927, and March 30, 1958, vertical file, Lackawanna Public Library.

48. City of Lackawanna, *Oaths of Office, Book #2, 1920–29, Book #3, 1930–37, Book #4, 1937–40*; interviews with Al Croce, April 20, 1995; and Pat Bonitatibus, July 6, 1995.

49. U.S. Census, 1920, 1930; N.Y. Census, 1925; CI, 4/30/1904, 2/15/13; LJ, 7/30/14. Electric welding involved tasks such as joining two pieces of steel.

50. N.Y. Census, 1925; interview with John Barbati, July 9, 1995; letter from Charles Hinman to author, September 9, 1986, in which he noted that 22 of the 42 foremen were Italian, and he provided these statistics on the ethnic composition of the Yard workforce: Italians-47%, Black-30%, Irish-7%, Polish-5%, German-5%, English and other-6%. Regions of origin in Italy were ascertained for 76 of the 109 men; other regions are Campania-9%, Marche-9%, and Molise-5%.

51. N.Y. Census, 1925; naturalization papers; interviews with Armondo Pietrocarlo, March 24, 1986; and Giulio Maturani, December 27, 1994. In 1930 there was only one Italian steam crane operator; no doubt the work slowdown of the depression idled a number of the railroad steam cranes.

52. Interviews with Joe Violanti, April 15, 1994; and Phil Andreozzi, April 15, 1995; U. S. Census, 1930. Cobble is a ribbon of metal that splits off the bloom, billet, or slab when it hits the guide on the edge of a roll stand. The splinter is often caused by air pockets in the steel. In the high speed rolling process a strand of cobble up to 300 or 400 feet long shot up into the air or off to the side, curling up like a pretzel and endangering workmen. A series of electric plug-ins along the sidings provided power for the magnet on the railroad steam crane. The diesel railroad cranes that later came into use generated their own electricity. The bales produced by the baler were rectangles that were 30" high and wide, and 36" to 48" long.

53. N.Y. Census, 1925; ECC, *Naturalization Petition,* Luigi Scarnecchia, October 6, 1919; interview with Phil Andreozzi; April 15, 1995. The High Drop was also known as the Drop, the Ladle Drop and the Breaking Drop. The non-metallic debris were dumped near the Strip Mill and Bar Mill, or along the lake.

54. Interviews with Armando Torella, December 23, 1986; Brownie Leo, July 8, 1993; Alfredo Campanelli, December 26, 1986; Millie Sambrotto, July 12, 1994; Ralph Galanti, September 22, 1983; and Tony Grasso, December 23, 1987; N.Y. Census, 1925.

55. Interview with Mario Infante, July 7, 1995. Coke breeze was produced as the coke was cooled with water, dumped into pits, and carried by conveyor belts.

56. "Lackawanna Plant History," January 14, 1919, with updates; interviews with Angelo Grosso, July 18, 1986; and Joe Streamer, September 18, 1995.

57. Interview with John Barbati, July 9, 1995.

58. ECD, 1941, p. 212; BSC, "Statistical Data, Lackawanna Plant," May 1969, pp. 8–9; interviews with John Barbati, July 9, 1995; and Mike Morgan, April 18, 1995. The Garage moved its headquarters to the plant's Fire Department, at #1 Gate. When this structure burned down in 1950 a new facility was built further north, along the Union Ship Canal. With the construction of the new Bethlehem office building in Woodlawn in 1958, the limousine service was relocated to the new structure's underground garage. Three or four black Ford sedans and a limousine where maintained there by a chauffeur and a man who washed the cars. This had previously been down at the Garage Department's north building.

59. Edward T. Dunn, *A History of Railroads in Western New York, 2nd edition,* 2000, p. 166. South Buffalo Railway seniority lists: Maintenance of Way (Track Department): 1941, 1942, January 1, 1946, January 1, 1951, July 1, 1957, January 1, 1961, January 1, 1966, January 1, 1971, January 1, 1976, January 1, 1981, January 1, 1985, January 1, 1986; Switchmen (trainmen): January 1, 1930, January 1, 1940, January 1, 1941, July 1, 1946, July 1, 1951, July 1, 1956, January 1, 1961, January 1, 1966, July 1, 1971, January 1, 1976; Engineers and Firemen: December 8, 1930, June 4, 1932, August 1, 1934, January 1, 1939, January 1, 1940, July 1, 1946, July 1, 1951, July 1, 1956, July 1, 1961, July 1, 1966, July 1,

1971, July 1, 1976, January 1, 1981, January 1, 1986; Car Department:
July 1, 1946, January 1, 1951, January 1, 1956, January 1, 1961, January
1, 1966, January 1, 1971, January 1, 1976, January 1, 1981, January 1,
1986; Yard Clerks: October 7, 1942, January 1, 1946, January 1, 1951,
July 1, 1956, July 1, 1961, January 1, 1966, January 1, 1971, January 1,
1981, January 1, 1986; Roundhouse: January 1, 1946, January 1, 1951,
January 1, 1956, January 1, 1961, January 1, 1966, January 1, 1971,
January 1, 1976, January 1, 1981, January 1, 1986.

60. U.S. Census, 1920; N.Y. Census, 1925; WWIDRC, 1917–18; interviews with
Frank Chiodo, December 28, 1983; and Tony Falbo, February 25, 1978.

61. Interviews with Frank Scaletta, April 4, 1988; and Mary Mesi-Peters,
July 19, 1986.

62. U.S. Census, 1920; N.Y. Census, 1925; WWIDRR, 1917–18; interviews
with Phil Andreozzi, 1980s; Lou Colello, September 23, 1983; and Mike
Militello, August 11, 1977.

63. Phil Andreozzi, "The South Buffalo Railway and the Bethlehem Steel
Plant: Memories," audio tape, November 11, 1981; N.Y. Census, 1925;
interviews with Lou Colello, September 23, 1983; and Phil Andreozzi,
1980s.

64. U.S. Census, 1920; N.Y. Census, 1925; BSC, "A Visit to the Lackawanna
Plant...," 1939, p. 28.

65. U.S. Senate, *Report On Conditions of Employment in the Iron and Steel
Industry, Volume III, Working Conditions and the Relations of Employers
and Employees*, pp. 22, 206, 214; U.S. Census, 1910.

66. Goldman, p. 141; David Brody, *Steelworkers in America: The Nonunion
Era*, 1960, pp. 269–70; William Hogan, *Economic History of the Iron
and Steel Industry*, 1971, p. 927; Vernon M. Briggs, Jr., *Immigration and
American Unionism*, 2001, pp. 82-83.

67. LJ, 1/29/1914; Goldman, 1983, p. 141; John Fitch, *The Steel Workers*,
1910, pp. 226–227.

68. Dick Roberts, *American Railroads: The Case for Nationalization*, 1980,
p. 34; Robert Ziegler and Gilbert Gall, *American Workers, American
Unions, Third Edition*, 2002, p.13; U.S. Senate, *Report On Conditions
of Employment in the Iron and Steel Industry, Volume IV, Accidents and
Accident Prevention*, 1913, pp. 38, 43, 87, 89, 99–100; Commission on
Employers' Liability, *Report to the Legislature of the State of New York*,
March 19, 1910, pp. 88, 95–96; U.S. Senate, *Report On Conditions of
Employment in the Iron and Steel Industry, Volume 4, Accidents and
Accident Prevention*, 1913, pp. 43, 87, 98–100; CI, 7/5, 11/1, 11/8/1902,
1/3/1903; BE, 3/26/1906; letter from F. G. Slagel to H. Shumway Lee,
"Hours and Conditions of Labor, Lackawanna Plant," March 28, 1912,
Buffalo and Erie County Historical Society, Mss. A 64–142, Box 29.

69. Interview with Frank Scaletta, April 4, 1988; LL, 1/24/1952.

70. Interview with Joe Violanti, July 11, 1995.

71. Interviews with Joe Violanti, July 11, 1995; and Carl Covino, April 17, 1995.

72. Interviews with Iole Schiavi-Murray, October 18, 1996; Phil Andreozzi,
June 10, 1995; and Ron Baldelli, September 21, 1994.

73. U.S. Census, 1910, 1920, 1930; N.Y. Census, 1915, 1925; WWIDRR,
1917–18; clipping from unidentified Buffalo newspaper, 8/1913,
provided by Art Sambuchi; interviews with Angelo Grosso, November
22, 1977; and Nunze Oddy, April 12,1982.

74. Interviews with Angelo Grosso, July 18, 1986; Nunze Oddy, April 12,
1982; and Joe Cosentino, July 14, 1995.

75. Interviews with Angelo Grosso, July 18, 1986; and Louie Petrucci,
December 27, 1984.

76. Interviews with Mike Morgan, April 18, 1995; and Joe Streamer,
September 18, 1995; N.Y. Census, 1915.

77. U.S. Census, 1930; interview with Giustino DeSantis, July 9, 1985. The
regional backgrounds of the other Italian Track Department foremen
were: two Molisani, two Calabresi, and one Siciliano. The Garage was
known as the Automotive Division in 1960s.

78. N.Y. Census, 1925; ECD, 1941; interview with Tony Falbo, February 25, 1978.

79. Interviews with Louis Patrucci, April 19, 1995; and Ron Baldelli,
September 21, 1994. A turn foreman supervised all workers, including
other foremen, on a specific shift or "turn."

80. BSC, "Lackawanna Plant, Telephone Directory," 1974; LL, 9/4/1958;
interview with Albert Ceccarelli, July 5, 1993.

81. LL, 9/4/58, 10/3/68; interview with Leo and Doc Baldelli, July 14, 1994.

82. N.Y. Census, 1915; letter from Gregory M. Paolini, 7/17/2000; LL,
2/5/59, 12/31/68.

83. Interviews with Tony Grasso, December 23, 1987; and Alex Filipetti,
July 5, 1995.

84. New York State Department of Labor, *First Annual Industrial Directory
of New York State*, 1912, p. 84.

85. Interviews with Joe Milano, April 9, 1988; Phil Andreozzi, April 16, 1995;
BSC, employee roster, Specialty Products, 1934. The unusual process
for producing the H-beam at Kalman involved punching triangular holes
at regular intervals into a heated beam, and then stretching the beam by
pulling it from both ends. It then took its final shape, resembling two flat
bars connected by a series of X - shaped braces. Seneca Steel, Buf Tank

86. In 1910, the Rogers-Brown Company acquired and expanded the plant.
In 1920 the facility was leased to the M. A. Hanna Company, and in
1927 acquired by the Buffalo Union Furnace Company; interview with
Santino Carnevale, September 22, 1994; CI, 5/18/1907.

87. N.Y. Census, 1925; WWIDRR, 1917–18; ECC, *Naturalization Petition*
of Francesco Marsillo, February 4, 1927.

88. Dunn, p. 218; DJ, 1/3/18; U.S. Census, 1910, 1920, 1930; N.Y. Census,
1905, 1915, 1925; WWIDRR, 1917–18; naturalization papers; interviews
with Dan and Claude Thomas, July 12, 1994; and Tony Falbo, February
25, 1978.

89. Interview with Mary Yoviene-Clarke, December 29, 1983; City of
Lackawanna, *Births and Deaths, Book 5, 1912–1913*.

90. U.S. Census, 1910, 1920; N.Y. Census, 1925; WWIDRR, 1917–18; FP,
6/24/59.

CHAPTER 8

1. LDJ, 4/2/19.

2. U.S. Senate, *Report On Conditions of Employment in the Iron and Steel
Industry, Volume III, Working Conditions and the Relations of* Employers
and Employees, 1913, p. 31.

3. U.S. Immigration Commission (USIC), *Volume 8: Immigrants In
Industries, Part 2: Iron and Steel Manufacturers, Volume 1*, 1911, p.
765; U.S. Senate, *Report On Conditions of Employment in the Iron and
Steel Industry, Volume III*, p. 88.

4. David Montgomery, *Workers' Control In America*, 1979, p. 97.

5. John Hinshaw, *Steel and Steelworkers: Race and Class in Twentieth-
Century Pittsburgh*, 2002, pp. 3, 5; Montgomery, pp. 4–5.

6. BT, 8/24/1900; BC, 5/11/1902; BDC, 8/24/1902; BE, 8/12, 10/9, 11 &
14/1902; Buffalo and Erie County Public Library (BECPL), *Lackawanna
Scrapbook*, clippings, pp. 108, 126.

7. BE, 6/17/1902; BC, 6/17/1902; CI, 6/21/1902.

8. CI, 12/21/1907; 1/4/1908; 3/21/1908; 4/11/1908.

9. BME, 3/2/1909; AJ, 7/1/1909, 5/19/10, 10/12/11, 2/8/12, 8/13/14,
5/27/15, 7/29/15; Mark Goldman, *High Hope and Decline of Buffalo,
New York*, 1983, p. 203.

10. AJ, 7/18/11.

11. David Brody, *Steelworkers in America: The Nonunion Era*, 1960, pp.
170–71, 197. *The Survey*, "Seven-Day Labor Because of Prosperity,"
10/14/16, p. 38; "The Hours of Work and the Efficiency of Labor,"
11/11/16, pp. 37–38; John Fitch, "Old Age by Forty," American
Magazine, 71, March 1911, pp. 655-662.

12. Brody, *Steelworkers in Americ*a, pp. 197, 203–03, 208–09, 212. *The
Survey*, "Seven-Day Labor Because of Prosperity," 10/14/16, p. 38;
"The Hours of Work and the Efficiency of Labor," 11/11/16, pp. 37–38.

13. Brody, *Steelworkers in America*, pp. 198, 229; Robert K. Murray, *Red
Scare: A Study in National Hysteria, 1919–1920*, 1955, p. 137; "Annual
Report of the Lackawanna Steel Company," 1922, Library of Congress.

14. John D. Hicks, *Rehearsal for Disaster: The Boom and Collapse of
1919–1920*, 1961, pp. 40–44.

15. LDJ, 2/15, 2/19, & 4/21/19.

615

16. LDJ, 2/20, 2/21, 2/24, 3/3, & 3/10/19.

17. LDJ, 3/15, 3/26, & 7/31/19; AJ, 9/25, 10/2, & 10/23/19; Goldman, p. 204. Street numbers changed in the 1930s; the original address for the union office in 1919 was 412 Ingham.

18. LDJ, 7/31, 8/2, 8/6, 8/11, 8/18, 8/19, 8/21, 8/23, 8/25, 9/5/19.

19. BCE, 9/20/19; BCAJ, 9/20/19; BST, 9/21/19 (1st quote); BE, 9/22/19 (2nd quote); BIE, 9/21/19; LDJ, 9/29 & 10/10/19; Brody, *Steelworkers in America*, p. 241. The Hindoos mentioned most likely refer to Asian Indians.

20. BET, 9/22 & 9/29/19; BE, 10/1/19; BDC, 10/10/19; BCAJ, 9/24/19. By early 1919, the South Buffalo Railway's 150 switchmen were members of the Switchmen's International Union, and, those who were temporarily laid off had to report back to work on September 29, 1919 because their union did have a contract with Lackawanna Steel. Apparently the switchmen's union activity ceased after the defeat of the Great Steel Strike, but did re-emerge in 1926, and by the late 1930s the men were under the umbrella of the Brotherhood of Railroad Trainmen. The engineers and firemen on the SBR engines apparently belonged to the Brotherhood of Locomotive Firemen and Enginemen since at least 1905.

21. Interviews with Tony Grasso, November 27, 1981; and Joe Milano, April 9, 1988.

22. BCAJ, 9/24/19; LDJ, 9/19, 9/26, 9/29, 10/2 & 10/3/19; BE, 9/26 & 10/1/19; BDC, 10/9 & 10/10/19; LDJ, 11/4/19.

23. CAJ, 9/25/19; Floyd Anderson, *The Incredible Story of Father Baker*, 1974, p. 95; LDJ, 10/27 & 11/1/19.

24. LDJ, 10/6/19; David Brody, *Labor In Crisis: The Steel Strike of 1919*, 1965, p. 152.

25. LDJ, 10/6/19; BET, 9/30/19; AJ, 10/30, 11/6, & 12/18/19; William Z. Foster, *The Great Steel Strike and Its Lessons*, 1922, p. 191; David Brody, *Labor In Crisis: The Steel Strike of 1919*, 1965, p. 152; FBI, "Field Agent Reports," Microfilm Reel 187, 11/22/19.

26. BIE, 11/20/19; LDJ, 10/21, 10/27, 11/17, & 11/21/19; FBI, Microfilm Reel 187, 11/26/19.

27. AJ, 2/26, 4/22, & 5/13/20; Foster, pp. 183, 223; David Brody, *Steelworkers in America*, p. 262; FBI, Microfilm Reel 187, 1/15/20.

28. Interviews with Joe Milano, April 9, 1988; and Joe Cosentino; July 14, 1994; Papers of David Saposs, Wisconsin State Historical Society, microfilm reel #1, p. 66.

29. BET, 10/23/19; AJ, 9/25 & 10/2/19; LDJ, 12/3, 12/8, & 12/22/19.

30. Interviews with Joe Milano, April 9, 1988; Tony Grasso, November 27, 1981; and Nunze Oddy, April 12, 1982.

31. Interviews with Al Croce, April 8, 1994 and April 20, 1995; Tony and Mary Grasso, July 16, 1992; and Adeline Covelli-Andreozzi, 1990; BDC, 9/29/19

32. Interviews with Joe Cosentino, July 14, 1995; and Joe Milano, April 9, 1988; LDJ, 12/15/19 (two quotes); FBI, Microfilm Reel 187, 12/26/19.

33. Interviews with Joe Milano, July 17, 1989; Nunze Oddy, April 12, 1982; and Al Croce, April 20, 1995.

34. Interviews with Ralph D'Amore, April 20, 1995; and Joe Cosentino, July 3, 1994.

35. Interviews with Frank Chiodo, December 28, 1983; and Ralph D'Amore, April 20, 1995; Interchurch World Movement, *Report on the Steel Strike of 1919*, 1920, p. 239.

36. AJ, 5/27/1920; Colin J. Davis, *Power At Odds: The 1922 Railroad Shopmen's Strike*, 1997, pp. 170–171; Gerda W. Ray, "'We Can Stay Until Hell Freezes Over': Strike Control and the State Police in New York, 1919–1923," *Labor History*, Volume 37, No. 3; p. 424; Interchurch World Movement, 1920, p. 226.

37. LDJ, 1/31 & 8/24/22; E. Emmet Murray, *The Lexicon of Labor*, 1998, p. 15; David Brody, *Steelworkers in America*, 1960, p. 273–75

38. E. Emmet Murray, p. 44 (quote); Montgomery, p. 44; interview with Joe Milano, December 28, 1988. BSC, "Annual Conference Program: Employees' Representatives and Company's Representatives," 1926, pp. 3, 20–21; *Iron Age*, 6/13/23, pp. 1693–94; *Labor Age*, September 1926, p. 15–17, and November 1926, p. 15. The Bethlehem Steel ERP was created in 1918 following a ruling of the War Labor Board that ordered the corporation's South Bethlehem, Pennsylvania plant to cease interfering with union organizing and to institute shop committees. But Bethlehem complained that the War Board committee system set up at the plant was inefficient and "was practically manipulated in the interests of a small organized minority"—that is, union men. The corporation then decided to co-opt any union activity by forming its own company-controlled union; *Iron Age*, 6/14/1923, p. 1690.

39. *Labor Age*, September 1926, pp. 16–17 (1st quote); James McDonnell, "The Rise of the CIO in Buffalo, New York, 1936–1942," doctoral dissertation, University of Wisconsin, 1970, p. 68 (2nd quote); BSC, "Annual Conference Program: Employees' Representatives and Company's Representatives," 1926, pp 16, 18; *Iron Age*, 6/14/23, p. 1694 (1st quote). Interviews with Joe Milano, December 28, 1988; and Frank Scaletta, April 4, 1988.

40. *Labor Age*, November 1926, p. 17 (quote); *Iron Age*, 12/20/23, p. 1669, and 5/26/27, p. 1576; interview with Frank Scaletta, April 4, 1988.

41. *Iron Age*, 2/14/1924, p. 522; 12/3/1925, p. 1527; and 2/7/1929, p. 451; *Labor Age*, November 1926, p. 17.

42. *Labor Age*, September 1926, p. 17 (quote). The monthly payments and benefits were determined by a three-fold classification of employees by annual income, as follows: I: under $1500: payment: $1; death benefit: $500; sick benefit: $10/ week; II: $1500 to $2500: payment: $1.50; death benefit: $1000; sick benefit: $11/week; III: over $2500: payment: $2.50; death benefit: $1500; sick benefit: $12/week. *Iron Age*, 2/21/29, p. 569.

43. *Labor Age*, October 1926, p. 4 (quote); Students of 1924-25 Industrial Research Class, *A Study of Steel*, Bryant & Stratton College, p. 104

44. Papers of David Saposs, Wisconsin State Historical Society, microfilm reel #1, p. 141; BT, 1/31/33; Horace B. Davis, Labor and Steel, 1933, pp. 68–69; *Wall Street Journal*, 2/2/33; BT, 1/30/33; LN, 1/3/29; interview with Tony DiMillo, October 17,1996 (quote).

45. LL, 10/22/36; *Steel Struggle*, September 1931, mimeographed newsletter, Papers of Joe Milano (all quotes).

46. LH, 11/2/33; BEN, 10/27/33 (quote), 5/24, 5/28, & 5/29/34; Max Gordon, "The Communists and the Drive to Organize Steel, 1936," *Labor History*, Volume 23, Spring 1982, p. 258; Hinshaw, 2002, pp. 48–52; McDonnell, pp. 67–68.

47. E. Emmet Murray, p. 125.

48. U.S. Senate, *Report On Conditions of Employment in the Iron and Steel Industry, Volume III*, p. 88; LL, 7/7/38; *A Study of Steel, p. 104*; interview with Tony DiMillo, October 17, 1996.

49. Horace B. Davis, *Labor and Steel*, 1933, pp. 28–31; Thomas Gobel, "Becoming American: Ethnic Workers and the Rise of the CIO," *Labor History*, Volume 29, No. 2, pp. 174–76; LL, 11//5/36.

50. Gobel, pp. 188–89, 194–95.

51. Gobel, p. 197.

52. Gobel, p. 195

53. LL, 7/2/36 (quotes), 10/15/& 10/22/36; SL, 8/20 & 10/20/36.

54. BEN, 10/15/36; SL, 8/20 (3rd quote) & 10/20/36, 2/20/37 (1st & 2nd quotes); Goldman, p. 229.

55. McDonnell, pp. 65, 159; BEN, 10/9/39.

56. SL, 2/20/37 (1st quote); McDonnell, p. 59 (2nd quote); LL, 1/14/37, 3/4 & 25/37, 8/11/38; LH, 7/15 & 29/37.

57. Interview with Joe Milano, December 27, 1989; Buffalo and Erie County Historical Society, United Steel Workers Collection, SWOC Lodge No. 1024, *Ledger Book*, 1937.

58. Hinshaw, 59; McDonald, pp. 74–83; American Social History Project, *Who Built America? Working People and the Nation's Economy, Politics, Culture, and Society, Volume 2, From the Gilded Age To The Present*, 1992, pp. 416–18.

59. BCE, 12/17/37; LL, 12/9, & 12/16/37; interview with Joe Milano, December 27, 1989.

60. Interview with Jack Meta, January 17, 1986.

61. Interview with Jack Meta, January 17, 1986.

62. Interviews with John McCann, July 15, 1986; and Joe Fiorella, July 14, 1986. Most of the Italians mentioned were not from Lackawanna, but Fiorella and Loiacano soon moved to the city.

63. Interview with Joe Fiorella, July 14, 1986. Vacation time was allowed only for clerks and foremen.

64. McDonnell, pp. 136–38; SL, 11/19/37, 9/23/38, 1/27/39; William T. Hogan, *Economic History of the Iron and Steel Industry in the United States*, 1971, p. 1182.

65. Mark McColloch, "Consolidating Industrial Citizenship: The USWA at War and Peace, 1939–46," in Paul F. Clark, et. al., editors, *Forging A Union of Steel: Philip Murray, SWOC, and the United Steelworkers*, 1987, p. 47; Vincent D. Sweeney, *The United Steelworkers of America: Twenty Years Later, 1936–1956*, 1956, pp. 49–50; BUL, 4/11, 8/22, & 10/3/40; interview with Gene Covelli, April 29, 1988.

66. LL, 11/7 & 11/14/40, 7/8/43, 3/29/45; SL, 12/27/40. The Spring Perch agreement gave one week of vacation to employees with one year of seniority, and two weeks to those with over five years' seniority.

67. McDonnell, pp. 161–62; BUL, 12/12/40; LL, 11/14/40, 1/19/41.

68. LL, 2/13/41 (1st quote), 2/20/41; McDonnell, pp. 162–63 (2nd quote); SL, 2/28/41; 3/20/41 (3rd quote); BUL, 2/13/41, 2/20/41, 2/27/41, 3/6/41; photos of picketers at Three Gate in Collection of Frank Chiodo***; interview with Joe Cosentino, July 13, 1994.

69. SL, 3/20/41 (1st quote); McDonnell, pp. 165–68 (2nd quote).

70. McDonnell, pp. 168–72; SL, 5/23/41.

71. SL, 3/20/41.

72. SL, 5/23/41; LL, 5/8/41 (quotes) & 9/11/41.

73. LL, 5/1, 5/8, & 5/14/41; BUL, 2/5/42; SL, 4/18, 6/25, & 9/25/41.

74. Interviews with Art Sambuchi, July 14, 1986; and John McCann, July 15, 1986; John McCann provided officer, steward, and delegate lists for Lackawanna locals, 1956–1958.

75. BECHS, United Steelworkers Collection, Box A, South Buffalo Railway folder; SL, 3/31/44.

76. Interviews with Steve Lanza, March 25, 1986; Tony Zuppa, November 22, 2004; and Phil Andreozzi, April 9, 1988; LDJ, 2/24/19, BCA&J, 9/24/19; BET, 9/29/19; *Labor Age*, September 1926, p. 17; Dick Roberts, *American Railroads: The Case For Nationalization*, 1980, p. 39. The SBR locomotive engineers and firemen were unionized in 1905, when Frank Columbus became an engineer and joined the Brotherhood of Locomotive Firemen and Enginemen.

77. Robert H. Zieger and Gilbert J. Gall, *American Workers, American Unions, third edition*, 2002, pp. 106, 108, 110, 127, 132–33, 144; LL, 4/29/43.

78. Montgomery, p. 166; Hinshaw, pp. 83–85.

79. Ziegler and Gall, 146–48; Clark, p. 97; Hinshaw, pp. 83–84. American business in general had led a strong counterattack against unions that culminated in Congress passing the Taft-Hartley Act of 1947, which amended the Wagner Act of 1935 by imposing limitations on unions, refocusing the National Labor Relations Board, limiting the right to strike, and requiring union officers to sign anti-communist pledges; see Ziegler and Gall, p. 152.

80. LP, 7/8/49 (quote), 10/7/49; 3/24/50, 6/30/50, 9/8/50, 10/27/50; LL, 7/14/49, 9/15/49, 3/23/50, 5/4/50, 9/7/50, 11/2/50; 3/12/53, 8/20/53, 9/17/53; Ziegler and Gall, p. 196.

81. Ziegler and Gall, p. 201; Hinshaw, pp. 123, 182; Montgomery, pp. 166–67; Paul A. Tiffany, *The Decline of American Steel: How Management, Labor, and Government Went Wrong*, 1988, pp. 160, 177, 181.

82. Interviews with Art Sambuchi, December 27, 2002 and June 7, 2004.

CHAPTER 9

1. Interviews with Bruce Tarquinio, March 31, 1996, June 6, 1996; BCD, 1890 p. 910; 1891, p. 989; 1894, 1248; 1895, p. 1265; CI, 2/21/1903, 6/6/1903

2. Town of West Seneca, *Birth Records, 1903–05*; U.S. Census, 1910; BEN, 12/17/37.

3. U.S. Census, 1910, 1920, 1930; N.Y. Census, 1905, 1915, 1925.

4. U.S. Census, 1910, 1920, 1930; N.Y. Census, 1905, 1915, 1925; ECD, 1941.

5. Interviews.

6. U. S. Census, 1900; Humbert Nelli, *From Immigrants To Ethnics,* 1983, pp. 63–64; interviews with Frank Morinello, Jr., December 26, 1983, and December 26, 1995.

7. Interview with Patricia Fadale-Pellegrino, July 8, 1996; Michael LaSorte, "The Immigrant Grocer," in Salvatore J. LaGumina, Frank J. Cavaioli, Salvatore Primeggia, Joseph A. Varacalli, Eds., *The Italian American Experience: An Encyclopedia*, 2000, pp. 420–22; BCD, 1931.

8. The category of grocery stores also included meat markets. BCD, 1903, p. 535; NY Census, 1905; ECD, 1931; interview with John Fadale, 11/23/79.

9. Interviews with Tony Grasso, December 28, 1989; Joe Milano, July 17, 1989; Nunze Oddy, April 12, 1982; Joe Cosentino, July 13, 1994; Aldina Manna-Wichrowski, December 28, 1995; Frank Saccomanno, April 2, 1996; Frank Moretti, April 2, 1996; John Palumbo, September 22, 1995; LSBD; 1938; LL, 4/17/47.

10. Interviews with Angelo Pitillo, July 6, 1995; and Frank Chiodo, July 7, 1996.

11. Interviews with Anne Melillo-Corvigno, July 5, 1996; Millie Covelli-Marinelli, July 10, 1994; Loretta Amorosi-Nicometo, July 13, 1994; Audrey Spagnolo-Surgeoner, March 29, 1996; Yolanda Mattucci-Nigro and Tina Mattucci-Ginnetti, September 20, 1994; and Pat Tronconi, July 5,1995.

12. Interviews with Tony Ziccarelli, July 11, 1995; LJ, 8/15/22.

13. Interview with Tony and Mary Grasso, September 21, 1994.

14. LSBD, 1938 ; interview with Phil Andreozzi, October 15, 1996; LCD, 1960.

15. Interviews with Anne Melillo-Corvigno, July 5, 1996; Bridget Ginnetti-Bracci, July 10, 1995; Patricia Fadale-Pellegrino, July 8, 1996; Frank Saccomanno, April 2, 1996.

16. CI, 6/6/1903; LSBD, 1938; interviews with Blanche Rice, July 9, 1996; and Margaret Monaco-Sperduto, July 4, 1994

17. ECD, 1941; interviews with Angelo Pitillo, April 15, 1994; Dewey Montanari, July 15, 1944; Gene Amadori, July 12, 1994; Ilio DiPaolo, December 29, 1994, Donna Gabaccia, *We Are What We Eat: Ethnic Food and the Making of America,* 1998, p. 218.

18. Interview with V. Jimmy D'Alessandro, April 9, 1985.

19. Interviews with John Masocco, July 5, 1996; Augusta Lampazzi-Anticoli, December 26, 1995; and Carlo Savaglio, July 13, 1995.

20. U.S. Census, 1900, 1910; LCD, 1914–15; John Daniels, "Lackawanna's Opportunity," *The Survey*, October 7, 1911, p. 925.

21. U.S. Census, 1910; N.Y. Census, 1905; City of Lackawanna, *Births, Book #3, 1911–12*; interviews with Nunze Oddy, 4/12/82; and Rose Turchiarelli-Shawat, 12/28/77.

22. U.S. Census, 1910; N.Y. Census, 1905, 1915; interviews with Loretta Amorosi-Nicometo, December 29, 1977; Dan and Claude Thomas, July 12, 1994; Yolanda Mattucci-Nigro and Tina Mattucci-Ginnetti, September 20, 1994; Ron Rothbart, "The Ethnic Saloon As A Form of Immigrants Enterprise," *International Migration Review*, Vol. xxvii, No. 2, 1993, pp. 332–58.

23. Interviews with Dorothy Govenettio, June 22, 1997; and Audrey Spagnolo-Surgeoner, March 29, 1996. The saloons which were expanded into restaurants are listed under restaurants, not saloons, in the compilations. The street number of 242 Ingham Avenue is an educated guess, as street numbers were changed several times before the final numbering system was put in place in 1938. Originally this building was numbered as 616 Ingham Avenue.

24. ECD, 1941; U.S. Census, 1910: N.Y. Census 1915; LCD, 1914–15; LL, 3/19/70; interview with John Tiberio, July 2, 1996; barbers 1900, US and NYC???

25. LCD, 1962; LL, 10/7/43; interview with Audrey Spagnolo-Surgeoner, March 2, 1996.

26. U.S. Census, 1910, 1920; N.Y. Census, 1915; ECD, 1931; West Seneca Town Hall, Births, 1907–08.

27. N.Y. Census, 1925; interviews with Carmella Macaluso-Pawlowski, February 19, 1995; Frank Chiodo, July 7, 1996; Buffalo Telephone Directory, 1928.

28. Interviews with Gene Amadori, July 12, 1994; Carmen DelMonaco, December 26, 1994; Joe Streamer, September 18, 1995; and John Barbati, July 9, 1995; ECC, *Assumed Business Names, I–M, 1939–1948, certificate #8533*; ECD, 1941.

29. U.S. Census, 1930; N.Y. Census, 1925; interviews with James Yoviene, September 17, 1997; and John Tiberio, July 2, 1996.

30. U.S. Census, 1910; interviews with Sal Mesi, July 21, 1994, December 28, 1995; Al D'Alessandro, July 10, 1995; and Carlo Savaglio, July 7, 1995.

31. U.S. Census, 1910; N.Y. Census, 1915, 1925; copies of Mattioli's diary books, 1926–28, 1930, 1935–37, 1939, and 1941, provided by Art Sambuchi and Tom Leary.

32. BCD, 1918; interviews with Frank Chiodo, December 28, 1983; and Anne Fox-Skraynski, March 31, 1996.

33. N.Y. Census, 1925; ECD, 1931; LL, 6/10/48; interview with Frank Chiodo, September 20, 1994.

34. ECC, *Assumed Business Names, I–M, 1900–1933*, certificate # 17732. Among the 42 non-Italian partners included people with Irish, Polish, German, Ukrainian, Croatian, Macedonian, and Spanish surnames.

35. ECD, 1931; interview with Anne Scarsella-Antes, December 26, 1995.

36. Neighborhoods that were completely inhabited by one ethnic group were fairly rare in American cities; usually one ethnic group was numerically dominant, but other ethnic groups were also present. See Humbert Nelli, *From Immigrants To Ethnics*, 1983, p. 61.

37. Interviews with Carlo Savaglio, July 13, 1995; Al D'Alessandro, July 10, 1995; and Lou Colello, April 21, 1995.

38. Interviews with Patsy Giordano, July 5, 1995; Mike Giordano, July 5, 1995; Nick Vertalino, October 15, 1996; LCD, 1960.

39. Interviews with Rose Turchiarelli-Shawat, December 28, 1977; John Fadale, November 23, 1979; Frank Morinello Jr., December 26, 1983; Loretta Amorosi-Nicometo, December 29, 1977; Aldo Filipetti, July 11, 1996; Louis Colello, April 21, 1995; Tony Falbo, February 25, 1978; and Angelo Pitillo, April 3, 1996.

40. Interviews with Yolanda Mattucci-Nigro and Tina Mattucci-Ginnetti, September 20, 1994; and Mike Morgan, April 18, 1995.

41. City of Lackawanna, *Tax Assessment Book*, 1910–1930; interview with Frank Morinello Jr., December 26, 1995.

42. LCD, 1960, 1962; LL, 12/11/52; LP, 6/2/50; BSSD, 1973; interviews with Egino DeSantis, April 20, 1995; Cesare Cardi, April 3, 1997; and Rose Provinzano, March 31, 1997; letter to author from Chris DeSantis-Coviello, July, 2000.

43. LL, 12/11/52; Bureau of the Census, *Census of Business Retail Distribution*, 1954, pp. 32–6, 32–7.

44. LH, 1/30/36; City of Lackawanna, *Common Council Proceedings*, 1918, 1919; interviews with Phil Andreozzi, September 10, 1994; Al D'Alessandro, July 10, 1995; and Gene Amadori, July 12, 1994.

45. LDJ, 4/2/21, U.S. Census, 1920; N.Y. Census, 1925; Lackawanna School Board, *Minutes*, 6/7/17, 2/7/18; interviews with Mary Clark-Yoviene, December 29, 1983; John Fadale, November 23, 1979. Rev. Musso became a methodist in Italy, and immigrated to the United States in 1902 when he was transferred to an Italian Methodist church in Boston. In 1910 he was sent to a Methodist Italian mission in Pittsburgh. After a three year stay in Lackawanna, 1918–1921, he went to a post in central New York State. Anna Maria Martellone, *Una Little Italy Nell'Atene D'America: La Communita Italiana Di Boston dal 1880–1920*, 1973, pp.458–61; Committee on Archives and History, Western New York Conference of the United Methodist Church, Genesee Conference of the Methodist Episcopal Church, *Official Minutes, 1919,* p. 29, 1921, p. 207.

46. SCP, 2/5/47; interviews with Joe Milano, December 27, 1989; and Al Croce, April 20, 1995.

47. N.Y. Census, 1925; U.S. Census, 1930; LL, 12/24/40, 10/14/43, 6/7/45; LH, 10/2/41; interviews with Rose Fiore-Pacholczak, July 12, 1996; Ralph Galanti Jr., April 22, 1995; Josephine Marrano-Fistola, July 2, 2006; and Anna Morgan, March 29, 1996.

48. *Lackawanna High School Yearbook*, 1939, p. 5; ECD, 1941; U.S. Census, 1930; interviews with Nick Milano, June 24, 1997; Joe Milano, December 27, 1989; and Bruce Tarquino, March 31, 1996;

49. Interviews with Angelo D'Alessandro, April 17, 1994; Joe Saccomanno, October 14, 1996; and Phil Andreozzi, July 13, 1990; letter to author from John D'Alessandro, May 27, 2007; ECD, 1941; LL, 9/1/55, 12/27/56, 9/12/68; FP, 6/28/2000.

50. Interviews with Arcangelo Petricca, July 9, 1996; LL, 6/26/41, 2/19/53.

51. Interview with Neil and Adeline Marrano, April 27, 2000; LL, 10/11/55; 2/6/58. 10/28/71.

52. LN, 10/23/30; LR, 1/1/32; LL, 10/22/42, 3/1/55; interviews with Florence DaLuiso, July 14, 1994; Mike Morgan, April 18, 1995; Jim Yoviene, September 17, 1997; Paul and Ron Yoviene, April 4, 1996; Linda Cipriano, November 23, 2008; and Anne Ginnetti-Spadone, October 26, 2008.

53. Interviews with Gene Covelli, July 22, 1990; Tony and Marge Ziccarelli, July 11, 1995; Mary Core-Brasch, April 20, 1995, July 12, 1995.

54. Interviews with Tony Grasso, September 20, 1995; Mary Core-Brasch, April 20, 1995, July 12, 1995.

55. Interview with Tony and Marge Ziccarelli, July 11, 1995.

56. Interviews with Nunze Oddy, April 12, 1982; Tony and Marge Ziccarelli, July 11, 1995.

57. BDC, 8/21/21; interviews with Lou Colello, April 21, 1995; and Phil Andreozzi, December, 1992.

58. Interview with Phil Andreozzi, December, 1992.

59. Interview with Nunze Oddy, April 12, 1982; and Ralph D'Amore, April 20,1995.

60. Robert J. Norrell, "Steelworkers and Storekeepers: Social Mobility Among Italian Immigrants in Birmingham," in Rocco Caporale, The Italian Americans Through The Generations, 1986, pp.98–111.

CHAPTER 10

1. Tony Grasso, "Bridging the Bitter Years," unpublished story, October 1984, pp. 7–9.

2. Edwin Fenton, *Immigrants And Unions, A Case Study: Italians and American Labor, 1870–1920*, 1975, p. 39; Alexander deConde, *Half Bitter, Half Sweet: An Excursion Into Italian-American History*, 1971, p. 351. The author has to date gathered a list of over 8,000 Italian groups founded in the United States since the 1820s, and estimates that this represents only one-third to one-half of the total number.

3. U.S. Census, 1910.

4. Erie County Courthouse (ECC), *Incorporation Papers*, Lake Erie Cooperative Society of Lackawanna, N.Y., 9/29/10; the regional backgrounds of four of the founders are not known.

5. Interviews with Joe Milano, 7/12/96; Al Croce, 4/18/94; Ralph D'Amore, 4/20/95; LN, 11/21/29; LJ, 5/3/17.

6. LH, 9/7/33; LL, 5/5/38, 2/16/39;

7. Lake Erie Italian Club (LEIC), *Processo Verbale*, 12/3/18; 1/9/19; 3/4/25; *Bylaws of Lake Erie Cooperative Society of Mutual Aid*, circa 1944, pp. 7–8.

8. *Constitution and By-Laws of the Lake Erie Ladies Auxiliary Society*, 1945, p. 5; ECC, *Incorporation Papers*, Circolo D'Annunzio Dopolavoro, 7/19/38; *Bylaws booklet, Roland Italian American Lodge*, n. d.; "Statute and Regulations," Roman Independent Club, circa 1936, p. 3; *Society of Our Lady of Mt. Carmel*, circa 1938, pp. 2–3; ECC, *Incorporation Papers,* Galanti Athletic Association, 1/24/39; interview with Tony Grasso, April 6, 1994.

9. LH, 4/6/39; LL, 11/14/40; *Society of Our Lady of Mt. Carmel,* circa 1938, p. 2; LEIC, *Processo Verbale,* 12/13/18.

10. Interview with Tony Grasso, November 27, 1981; LH, 2/16/39. Exactly 80% of those organizations formed in the years 1942 to 1949 had second generation memberships.

11. LH, 2/25/37; LL, 1/27/38, 6/30/38, 12/19/40, 10/17/46, 1/30/47, 9/29/49.

12. LL, 7/9/42.

13. LL, 1/27/38, 5/5/38, 7/27/39, 8/31/39; interview with Leo and Doc Baldelli, July 14, 1994.

14. Interviews with Nunze Oddy, 4/12/82; Sara Chiacchia-Kempf, 7/12/96; CI, 1/24/18, 3/8/28, 1/29/31, 12/29/32.

15. CI, 9/20/17; 1/3/18, 1/25/19, , 8/26/37, 9/23/37, 1/20/38.

16. LEIC, *Processo Verbale,* 1/9/36, 4/2/41; LH, 12/14/33; CI, 11/21/35, 11/28/35, 12/19/35; Dominic Candeloro, *Chicago's Italians: Immigrants, Ethnics, Americans,* 2003, p.135; John Diggins, *Mussolini and Fascism: The View From America,* 1972, pp. 58–73.

17. LL,10/13/38, 11/3/38, 2/16/39; interview with Ralph Galanti, 9/22/83;.

18. LR, 4/14/33; LL, 6/30/38, 10/13/38, 10/27/38, 3/30/39.

19. LN, 11/21/29; SCP, 3/3/48; LL, 6/22/44; 6/22/50.

20. *Statuto e Regolamento: Italian-American Citizens Club of Lackawanna, N. Y.,* n. d., p. 14; LCCP, 4/1/40; interview with Joe Milano, 11/23/77; LN, 7/17/30, 10/30/30.

21. ECC, *Incorporation Papers,* Lackawanna Republican Women's Club of the First Ward, 1/24/30; LR, 3/18/32; LH, 1/10/35, 10/5/39; LL, 10/21/37, 8/3/39, 2/1/40, 1/16/41, 10/1/42.

22. LL, 6/30/38, 2/16/39, 1/16/41.

23. LEIC, *Processo Verbale,* 1/7/42; 4/11/43; 9/1/43, 3/17/44; LL, 3/12/42, 4/29/43, 2/17/44.

24. Peter L. Belmonte, *Italian Americans in World War II, 2001,* p. 6; Bob Curran, "Commentary," BN, 4/13/95; LEIC, meeting minutes, 5/21/43, 9/1/43; LL, 4/29/43, 5/4/44; 3/29/45; interview with Frank Chiodo, July 7, 1996.

25. Interviews with Lou Colello, March 27, 1986; and Tony Grasso, December 26, 1989 & April 18, 1995.

26. LL, 8/31/44. The ladies auxiliary of Circolo D'Annunzio Dopolavoro apparently never got off the ground.

27. LL, 10/17/46, 1/23/47, 6/10/48, 4/20/50, 11/17/53, 5/13/54, 12/8/55; SCP, 5/14/47.

28. U.S. Census, 1930; the two following censuses listed only foreign-born Italians in Lackawanna: 775 in 1940, and 648 in 1950, as compared to 752 in 1930. In 1960, Italian foreign stock in the city was 2.085, 637 of them foreign-born; interview with Yolanda Sperduti-Tobias, 4/20/95.

29. LL, 1/29/48.

30. Humbert Nelli, *The Italians in Chicago: 1880–1930,* 1970, p. 173; Caroline Ware, *Greenwich Village: 1920–1930,* 1965, p. 157. The 1098 individual men and women were not all involved in Lackawanna's Italian organizations at one specific point in time, but each was in at least one society at some point time during the 20 year period. Many other factors effected the number of Italians living in Lackawanna and joining the city's Italian organizations between 1930 and 1949. Immigrant and second-generation men moved to the city in search of jobs during the Depression and World War II. A number of the American-born men moved to Lackawanna from Buffalo when they married Italian American females who resided in the city. Several Italian men from South Buffalo and Blasdell were members of Italian groups, especially the Lake Erie Italian Club. A small number of new immigrants arrived in the city just after the war and joined Italian societies prior to 1950. On the other hand, some Italian men born in the Steel City moved to other areas when they married, and married couples were moving out of Lackawanna during this period, and not all kept their organizational ties with the city, even if they did live nearby.

31. LL, 8/24/39; in the late twentieth century Larry Colello held the presidency of the Lake Erie Italian Club for fourteen one-year terms and Sam Angrisano for nine terms, but these were not consecutive years.

32. Interview with Frank Chiodo, September 20, 1994; Lackawanna School Board, minutes, 8/7/34; LR, 2/3/33; LH, 12/28/33; LL, 4/7/55; see Chapters 8 and 11 for information on union officials and politicians. In Buffalo, Angelo Taibi was president of the Racalmuto Society from its founding in 1912 to 1950, CI, 12/12/40, 5/7/43, 12/28/50.

33. Interviews with Nunze Oddy, April 12, 1982; Tony Grasso, September 21, 1983; Angelo Grosso, November 12, 1977; Chet Catuzza, September 18, 1994; and Frank Morinello, July 7, 1996; LDJ, 6/10/16; LL, 4/10/47, 11/24/54, 12/16/54, 12/11/58; FP, 10/18/95.

34. In addition to Roman Catholic parishes, there were three Eastern Orthodox churches—Saints Peter and Paul Russian Orthodox, St. Stephan Serbian, and Holy Ghost Ukrainian Greek (which later became Our Lady of Perpetual Help), and also Holy Trinity Polish National Catholic Church; Will Herberg, *Protestant, Catholic, Jew,* 1960; LN, 2/11/31; LL, 3/18/37, 10/3/40, 10/31/46, 12/31/46; interview with Charles Barone, April 6, 1994.

35. LN, 1/12/33; LH, 5/18/33; LL, 3/5/53.

36. LL, 1/18/40, 2/1/40; 1/16/41.

37. Interviews with Ben Falbo, December 17, 2005; and Ron Baldelli, September 21, 1994; LL, 5/13/54; 5/20/54; 9/23/54; 9/22/55; 4/3/58; 6/5/58.

38. LL, 10/27/38, 11/27/41, 2/5/53, 2/19/53; ECC, *Incorporation Papers,* Park Athletic and Social Club, Inc. of Lackawanna, 8/28/33; interviews with Al Croce, April 8, 1994; and Leo and Doc Baldelli, July 14, 1994.

39. Interview with Dora Sambuchi-Grosso, July 18, 1986; LL, 1/27/38; 4/13/50; SCP, 12/10/47.

40. LEIC, *Processo Verbale,* 9/3/18, 8/24/19; LL, 7/20/39, 7/25/40, 7/17/41, 7/19/45; LH, 8/17/33, 6/13/36, 7/16/36, 7/20/39, 7/27/39; LN, 8/30/28; SCP, 6/2/48.

41. LH, 7/27/39; LL, 7/28/38; 5/31/40; 5/22/41; 5/28/42, 6/11/42; 5/4/44, 5/18/44, 6/8/44, 5/3/45, 4/4/46, 5/19/49, 5/24/51.

42. LEIC, *Processo Verbale,* 3/12/42, 3/3/43, 4/11/43; LL, 2/10/42; 5/22/52.

43. SCP, 1/29/47, 4/2/47, 7/2/47, 11/19/47; LL, 7/31/47, 10/23/47, 1/15/48, 1/29/48, 3/18/48, 4/29/48, 11/14/48, 12/6/48, 10/6/49, 12/22/49, 8/10/50, 12/21/50, 12/28/50, 2/1/51, 3/15/51, 3/13/52, 8/11/55, 2/9/56, 4/12/56, 11/29/56, 1/31/57, 8/15/57; interview with Clyde Capasso, August 9, 2008.

44. LH, 2/28/35; LL, 9/4/47, 4/7/55.

45. Of the eighteen organizations with mixed ethnic memberships, fifteen were made up of second-generation individuals, the remaining three had a combination of first- and second-generation participants. Interview with Gene Covelli, 7/9/96; LL, 9/1/38, 10/27/38, 12/1/38, 8/17/39;1/4/40;8/29/40, 11/13/41.

46. LL, 7/27/39, 8/31/39.

47. Interviews with Gene DeSantis, December 29, 1994, April 20, 1995, November 25, 2008; Mary Panzetta-Vertino, April 21, 1995; LL, 6/5/58, 7/17/58, 7/31/58, 9/11/58, 10/9/58.

48. Interviews with Guy and Delia Iannarelli, July 6, 1995, July 10, 2001, February 25, 2006, December 27, 2007; and Ida Liberta, July 9, 2001; FP, 2/5/86.

49. Interviews with Mary Leonetti, December 20, 2005; Rose Anticoli-Wagner, December 17, 2005; Guy and Delia Iannarelli, April 7, 1994, December 27, 2001, June 4 & December 20, 2005, February 25, 2006; Linda Perry, November 19 & 25, 2006; and Lou Colello, September 23, 1983; FP, 11/24/2004, 4/27/2005.

50. Interviews with Rose Anticoli-Wagner, December 17, 2005; Tony Grasso, n. d.; and Joe Milano, October 16, 1996; Joe Milano, memo regarding Milano Athletic Club, n. d.

51. Interviews with Ben Falbo, December 17, 2005; Don Grosso, December 17, 2005 & November 11, 2008, Chico Galanti, December 17, 2005; Leo and Doc Baldelli, July 19, 1994; Ron Baldelli, September 21, 1994; Jerry Baldelli, December 18, 2005.

52. Interviews with Nick Liberta, December 21, 2005; Gene DeSantis, December 17, 2005; and Guy Iannarelli, December 27, 2007, November 11, 2008; FP, 7/9/2008, 8/6/2008.

53. Group interview with Vince Morga, Paul Fino, Guy Iannarelli, Rich Angrisano, Pete Marrocco, Matteo Sassarelli, Joe Pallante, and Tony Monaco, November 22, 2006; interview with Ernie Leonetti, December 17, 2005.

54. Interviews with Gene DeSantis, July 9, 2001; Vince Morga, November 22, 2006; and Pete Marrocco, November 22, 2006.

CHAPTER 11

1. Interviews with Chet Catuzza, September 8, 1994; and Joe Milano, April 10, 1994; FP, 2/28/2001.

2. BCA&J, 4/24/1899; BDC, 7/2/1902 (1st quote); BME, 1/4/1903; BE, 1/18/1903 (2nd quote), 1/20/1904, 1/24/1904 (3rd quote).

3. BME, 2/12/1904; William Scheuerman, "The Politics of Protest: The Great Steel Strike of 1919–20 in Lackawanna, New York," *International Review of Social History*, Vol. 31, 1986, pp. 123–24 (quote).

4. BME, 2/12/1904 (quote), 9/4/1908; Scheuerman, p. 125.

5. BEN, 12/15/22; Joint Charities & Economic Fund of Buffalo and Erie County, N. Y., "Lackawanna In 1942," 1943, unpublished report, pp. 5, 18; 43% of the 1941 voters resided in the First Ward.; LL, 11/5/53.

6. BME, 2/12/1904; LJ, 1/25/17; U.S. Census, 1940.

7. LL, 11/27/41 (1st quote), 8/9/48 (2nd quote).

8. Interviews with Joe Milano, 7/17/89; and Armondo Pietrocarlo, April 7, 1994.

9. LJ, 6/19/13; William Emerling and John Osborne, *The History of Lackawanna*, 1976, p. 25.

10. LJ, 3/1/17 (1st quote), 3/15/17; LDJ, 1/3/18, 3/1/19 (2nd quote); BEN, 10/3/22.

11. LJ, 7/20/16 (2nd and 3rd quotes), 1/4/17 (4th quote); LDJ, 4/7/16, 4/21/16; 2/6/19 (5th quote), 2/15/19, 2/18/19, 3/1/19, 3/24/19, 9/3/19 (1st quote).

12. LDJ, 8/13/19 (2nd quote), 8/27/19 1st & 3rd quotes); interview with Joe Milano, 12/27/89.

13. City of Lackawanna, *Common Council Proceedings*: 3/21/10; 12/29/10, 5/15/11, 11/18/12, 2/5/17, 11/7/17, 11/4/18, 11/18/18, 12/1/19, 2/1/21, 6/22/21, 1/31/24, 4/30/25, 8/17/25, 10/31/25, 2/1/26, 6/30/26, 10/31/27.

14. LCCP, 12/3/17; interviews with Chet Catuzza, September 8, 1994; Mary Panzetta-Vertino, August 9, 1977; and John Christiano, November 11, 1923/2004. LL, 3/9/44, 12/27/51, 3/10/66; FP, 4/9/70; ECC, *Naturalization Petition*, Ferdinand Catuzza, 6/4/19, and Antonio Turchiarelli, 2/4/14. Erie County, *Official List of Registered Voters*, 1931, 1940, 1950.

15. Interview with Joe Milano, November 11, 1977; BEN, 1/25/35, clipping from scrapbook of Loretta Amorosi-Nicometo.

16. LCCP: 9/30/24, 11/16/25, 9/15/26, 10/15/26, 11/15/26, 4/16/28.

17. U.S. Census, 1920, 1930; N.Y. Census, 1915, 1925; WWIDRC; 1917, LCCP, 9/15/19; City of Lackawanna, *DPW Time Book, 1931–34*.

18. LR, 7/29/32, LL, 1/6/38, 6/24/43; LH, 12/21/33, 1/2/36. Interview with Joe Milano, November 23, 1977.

19. LH, 5/18/33, 12/7/33, 1/10/35, 1/16/36, 7/2/36.

20. Interviews with Al Croce, April 8, 1994; Joe Milano, November 23, 1977; Loretta Amorosi-Nicometo, December 29, 1977

21. Interviews with Joe Milano, September 21, 1994; Angelo Grosso, July 18, 1986; and Loretta Amorosi-Nicometo, December 29, 1977, July 13, 1994.

22. Interview with Loretta Amorosi-Nicometo, July 13, 1994.

23. Interview with Mary Panzetta-Vertino, August 9, 1977; ECD, 1931; CI, 4/15/43; BEN, 4/9/43.

24. Interview with Mary Panzetta-Vertino, August 9, 1977; LH, 12/16/37.

25. Interview with Nick Canali, December 26, 1996.

26. Interview with Tony Grasso, December 26, 1994; undated clipping of FP Adele Panzetta obituary.

27. Interview with Mary Panzetta-Vertino, August 9, 1977.

28. Interview with Chet Catuzza, September 8, 1994; LL, 4/9/70.

29. Interview with Chet Catuzza, September 8, 1994.

30. LN, 8/2/28, 11/7/29; a study of Philadelphia found that Italian American politicians fostered a similar sense of Italianness to transcend regional loyalties; see Stefano Luconi, *From Paesani to White Ethnics: The Italian Experience in Philadelphia*, 2001, p. 33.

31. Interview with Angelo Grosso, July 18, 1986.

32. Interview with Joe Milano, July 20, 1990; BCE, 5/8/41.

33. Interviews with Joe Milano, April 9, 1988, July 17, 1989; CI, 11/24/27. Highland Acres is a section in the Town of Hamburg along South Park Avenue, just south of Blasdell.

34. Interview with Joe Milano, April 9, 1994.

35. Interview with Joe Milano, April 9, 1994.

36. Interviews with Joe Milano, April 9, 1994, October 16, 1996.

37. Interviews with Joe Milano, April 9, 1994, July 19, 1994.

38. Interviews with Joe Milano, April 9, 1994, July 19, 1994.

39. Interview with Joe Milano, April 9, 1994; LH, 3/28/35.

40. Interview with Joe Milano, December 27, 1989; BCE, 4/6/34.

41. Interviews with Joe Milano, April 9, 1994, April 22, 1995.

42. Interviews with Joe Milano, November 23, 1977, December 27, 1989.

43. Interviews with Joe Milano, April 10, 1995, July 11, 1995.

44. BN, 8/3/89 (1st quote), 12/11/89 (2nd quote); LL, 4/20/44; 9/12/46; 4/15/48.

45. Interview with Joe Milano, December 27, 1989.

46. Interview with Joe Milano, July 14, 1994; Papers of Joe Milano, unlabeled newspaper clipping, 1939.

47. U.S. Census, 1910; N.Y. Census, 1925; LH, 10/12/33.

48. BCE, 4/6/34 (quotes); LCCP, 10/5/25; 9/11/41; interview with Ang Pitillo, April 15, 1994.

49. Interview with Angelo Grosso, November 22, 1977.

50. "Testimonial Roast: Ralph J. Galanti, Sr.," program booklet, 11/24/84 (quote); LH, 9/26/41; interview with Ralph Galanti, September 22, 1983.

51. Tabulated from: Erie County, *Official List of Registered Voters*, 1926, 1930, 1935, 1940, 1945, 1950. The exact percentage of second generation Italian American voters in 1930 is 58%.

52. Interview with Joe Milano, December 27, 1989 (quote); BCE, 6/28/38.

53. LH, 7/15/37, 7/6/39 (quotes); LL, 6/30/38; interview with Tom Pepper, 1977.

54. BN, 8/3/89 (quote); interviews with Joe Moretti, April 8, 1994; Frank Moretti, April 2, 1996; and Joe Milano, October 16, 1996.

55. LL, 5/29/52 (1st quote), 4/16/53, 5/7/53, 5/1/58 (2nd quote).

56. LL, 3/5/59, 10/13/60, 4/13/61; FP, 4/19/95, 5/23/01, 5/29/2002, 5/26/2004, 7/14/2004, 7/13/2005, 7/19/2006; interviews with Ron Spadone, July 12, 1994; Annette Iafallo, June 7, 2005 (quote); and Chico Galanti, April 22, 1995.

57. LN, 11/14/29.

58. LL, 9/10/53, 7/28/55, 2/9/56; interview with Ang Pitillo, April 15, 1994.

59. Interview with Aldo Filipetti, July 11, 1996.

60. Interview with Aldo Filipetti, July 11, 1996.

61. Interview with Aldo Filipetti, July 11, 1996.

62. Interview with Aldo Filipetti, July 11, 1996.

63. Interview with Aldo Filipetti, July 11, 1996.

64. Interview with Aldo Filipetti, July 11, 1996.

65. Interviews with Ang Pitillo, July 11, 1994, July 6, 1995.

66. Interviews with Ang Pitillo, July 11, 1994; and Bill Delmont, June 10, 2005 (quotes); LL, 7/2/36. The Third Ward up until 1964 was the area south of Kirby Avenue, between the railroad tracks and South Park Avenue.

67. Interview with Frank Chiodo, June 24, 1997; LL, 8/20/53, BN, 12/23/2000; FP, 12/27/2000.

68. LL, 2/29/40; interviews with Don Grosso, September 4, 2002 and November 1, 2008; and Charles Orlando, October 16, 1996. Gioacchino Orlando moved to the Fourth Ward in 1953 and was elected a committeeman there.

69. Interview with Jerry DePasquale, June 30, 1996; LL, 8/28/41, 4/10/75.

70. Interview with Jerry DePasquale, June 30, 1996 (quote); LL, 5/25/67, 12/7/67; BN, 8/20/95.

71. Interview with Jerry DePasquale, June 30, 1996; letter from Jerry DePasquale, 6/18/05; unlabeled news clipping, FP, 1971, provided by Susan DePasquale-Brehm (quote).

72. Interviews with Jerry DePasquale, June 30, 1996; Charles Barone, April 6, 1994; and Joe Caligiuri, April 5, 1994; correspondence from Jerry DePasquale, June 30, 1996; FP, 2/1/84, 5/13/98, 11/4/98, 11/3/99, 5/8/2002, 9/22/2004, 5/26/2004, and 11/2/2005.

73. Interviews with Nick Canali, December 26, 1996; and Louis Violanti, June 6, 2005 (quotes); SCP, 1/29/47, 4/21/48; LL, 6/25/64.

74. LR, 4/15/32, 1/15/32; LH, 1/7/37; LL, 9/12/46, 6/14/51, 6/25/64; interviews with Joe Moretti, April 8, 1994 (1st quote); Don Grosso, June 9, 2005; and Mark Balen, June 6, 2005 (2nd & 3rd quotes).

75. Interviews with Tony Mingarelli, July 11, 1994, November 23, 2008; BN, 4/15/85.

76. Interview with Joe Caligiuri, April 5, 1994.

77. Interview with Joe Caligiuri, April 5, 1994.

78. Interview with Joe Caligiuri, April 5, 1994.

79. Interview with Chet Catuzza, September 8, 1994.

80. Interview with Chet Catuzza, September 8, 1994.

81. Interview with Tony Caferro, July 6, 1996.

82. Interview with Richard Baldelli, July 14, 1994.

83. LL, 4/10/69; interviews with Ron Spadone, July 12, 1994, June 6, 2005, December 18, 2005 (quotes).

84. Interviews with Ron Spadone, July 12, 1994, June 6, 2005, December 18, 2005.

85. FP, 8/1/2001, 5/7/2003, 6/7/2006, 5/16/2007; PP, 2/19/2009; Stephan M. Koenig, *South Buffalo Railway: Bethlehem Steel Company Railroad Operations in Lackawanna, New York*, 2004, p.7.

86. Interview with Ron Spadone, December 18, 2005; FP, 4/12/2000, 10/13/2004; U.S. Census Bureau, American Factfinder, http:// factfinder.census.gov/servlet/SAFFPopulation?_event=Search&_ name=Lackawanna.

AFTERWORD

1. SL, 11/20/36.

2. Alexander DeConde, *Half Bitter, Half Sweet: An Excursion Into Italian -American History,* 1971, p. 165; Mark Goldman, *High Hopes: The Rise and Decline of Buffalo, New York*, 1983, pp. 9-12, 15-17; PP, 5/20/2003; FP, 10/15/2003; John B. Duff, *The Irish in the United States*, 1971, pp. 36,37; Wayne G. Broehl, Jr., *The Molly Maguires*, 1983, pp. 337-344.

3. LN, 11/7/29; Joel Perlmann, *Italians Then, Mexicans Now: Immigrant Origins and Second Generation Progress, 1890 to 2000*, 2005, pp. 44-45.

4. FP, 8/1/2001, 5/7/2003, 6/7/2006, 5/16/2007; PP, 2/19/2009; Stephan M. Koenig, *South Buffalo Railway: Bethlehem Steel Company Railroad Operations in Lackawanna, New York*, 2004, p.7; Wikipedia, http:// enwikipedia.org/wiki/ArcelorMittal.

5. LEIC, Newsletter, May 2009, August 2009.

BIBLIOGRAPHY

General: Books, Articles

Abramson, Harold J. *Ethnic Diversity in Catholic America*, 1973.

Alba, Richard D. *Ethnic Identity: the Transformation of White America*, 1990.

Alba, Richard D. *Italian Americans: Into the Twilight of Ethnicity*, 1985.

Alba, Richard D., and Victor Nee. *Remaking the American Mainstream: Assimilation and Contemporary Immigration*, 2003.

Albini, Joseph L. *The American Mafia: Genesis of A Legend*, 1971 (1979).

American Social History Project. *Who Built America? Working People and the Nation's Economy, Politics, Culture, and Society, Volume 2, From the Gilded Age To The Present*, 1992.

Anderson, Floyd. *The Incredible Story of Father Baker*, 1974.

Andreozzi, John. "Contadini and Pescatori in Milwaukee: Assimilation and Voluntary Organizations," unpublished masters thesis, University of Wisconsin-Milwaukee, 1974.

Andreozzi, John. "Italian Farmers in Cumberland," in Rudolph J. Vecoli, editor, *Italian Immigrants in Rural and Small Town America*, 1987.

Andreozzi, John. "Organizations," in LaGumina, et al., 2000.

Andreozzi, John. "We Need New Heroes," *Colors,* September/October, 1992.

Atkinson, Rick. *The Day of Battle: The War in Sicily and Italy, 1943-1944*, 2007.

Baroni, Geno, Arthur Naperstek, Karen Kollias, "Patterns of Class and Ethnic Discrimination in the Corporate and Philanthropic World," National Center For Urban Ethnic Affairs, 10/23/75.

Bean, Philip A. "The Role of Community in the Unionization of Italian Immigrants: The Utica Textile Strike of 1919." *Ethnic Forum,* Volume 12, No. 1, 1982.

Belfiglio, Valentine. "Wartime Military and Home front Activities," in LaGumina, et al., 2000.

Bell, Daniel. *The End of Ideology: On the Exhaustion of Political Ideas in the Fifties, revised edition* 1960 (1962).

Belmonte, Peter L. *Italian Americans in World War II*, 2001.

Bernard, William S. "A History of U. S. Immigration Policy," in Richard A. Easterlin, et al.

Bernardo, Stephanie. *The Ethnic Almanac*, 1981.

Block, Alan A. *Perspectives on Organizing Crime: Essays in Opposition*, 1991.

Bodnar, John. *The Transplanted: A History of Immigrants in Urban America*, 1987.

Bondanella, Peter. *Hollywood Italians: Dagos, Palookas, Romeos, Wise Guys, and Sopranos*, 2006.

Breton, Raymond. "Institutional Completeness of Ethnic Communities and the Personal Relations of Immigrants," *American Journal of Sociology*, Vol. LXX, September 1964.

Briggs, John W. *An Italian Passage: Immigrants to Three American Cities, 1890-1930*, 1978.

Briggs, Vernon M. Jr., *Immigration and American Unionism*, 2001.

Brody, David. *Labor In Crisis: The Steel Strike of 1919,* 1965.

Brody, David *Steelworkers In America: The Nonunion Era*, 1960.

Brown, Mary Elizabeth. "Women In The Church," in LaGumina, et al., 2000.

Broehl, Wayne G. Jr., *The Molly Maguires*, 1983

Campisi, Paul J. "Ethnic Family Patterns: The Italians Family in the United States," *American Journal of Sociology,* Vol. 53, 1948.

Carnevale, Nancy C. "'No Italian Spoken for the Duration of the War:' Language, Italian-American Identity, and Cultural pluralism in the World War II Years," *Journal of American Ethnic History,* Spring 2003.

Caroli, Betty Boyd. *Italian Repatriation from the United States, 1900–1914*, 1973.

Carpenter, Niles. *Nationality, Color, and Economic Opportunity in the City of Buffalo,* 1927.

Cavaioli, Frank J. "American Committee on Italian Migration," in LaGumina, et al., 2000.

Cavaioli, Frank J. "Governors," in LaGumina, et al., 2000.

Cerase, Francesco. "Nostalgia or Disenchantment: Considerations on Return Migration," in Silvano M. Tomasi and Madeline H. Engel, eds. *The Italian Experience in the United States*, 1970.

Child, Irving L. *Italian or American? The Second Generation in Conflict*, 1943.

Christopher, Robert C. *Crashing the Gates: The De-WASPing of America's Power Elite*, 1989.

Cockburn, Claude. *In Time of Trouble*, 1956, as cited in Chuck Stone, *Black Political Power, revised edition*, 1970.

Cornell, Stephen and Douglas Hartmann. *Ethnicity and Race: Making Identities In A Changing World, 2nd Edition*, 2007.

Covello, Leonard. *The Social Background of the Italo-American School Child: A Study of the Southern Italian Family Mores and Their Effect on the School Situation in Italy and America*, 1967.

Crispino, James A. *The Assimilation of Ethnic Groups: The Italian Case*, 1980.

D'Amelio, Dan A. "A Season of Panic: The Internments of World War II," *Italian Americana*, Summer 1999.

Daniels, Roger. *Coming To America: A History of Immigration and Ethnicity in American Life*, 1990.

Daniels, Roger. *Not Like Us: Immigrants and Minorities in America, 1890-1924*, 1997.

Davis, Colin J. *Power At Odds: The 1922 National Railroad Shopman's Strike*, 1997.

Davis, Horace B. *Labor and Steel*, 1933.

DeConde, Alexander. *Half Bitter, Half Sweet: An Excursion Into Italian-American History*, 1971.

DeStefano, George. *An Offer We Can't Refuse: The Mafia In the Mind of America*, 2006.

Dickie, John. *Cosa Nostra: A History of the Sicilian Mafia*, 2004.

Dickie, John. *Darkest Italy: The Nation and Stereotypes of the Mezzogiorno, 1860-1900*, 1999.

Dickie, John. "Stereotypes of the Italian South, 1860–1900," in Robert Lumley and Jonathan Morris, editors, *The New History of the Italian South*, 1997.

Diggins, John P. *Mussolini and Fascism: The View From America*, 1972.

Dillaway, Diana. *Power Failure: Politics, Patronage, and the Economic Future of Buffalo, New York*, 2006.

Duff John B. *The Irish in the United States*, 1971.

Duggan, Christopher. *A Concise History of Italy*, 1994.

Dunn, Edward T. *A History of Railroads in Western New York, 2nd edition*, 2000.

Easterlin, Richard A. "Economic and Social Characteristics of the Immigrants," in Richard A. Easterlin, David Ward, William S. Bernard, Reed Ueda, *Immigration*, 1982.

Feagin, Joe R. *Racial and Ethnic Relations, Second Edition*, 1984.

Federal Reporter, Vol. 446, United States v. Bethlehem Steel Corporation 1971.

Fenton, Edwin. *Immigrants And Unions, A Case Study: Italians and American Labor, 1870–1920*, 1975.

Ferroni, Carlo. "Cleveland," in LaGumina, et al., 2000.

Finks, P. David. *The Radical Vision of Saul Alinsky*, 1984.

Fioravanti, Joseph. "Pop Singers," in LaGumina, et al.

Fitch, John A. "Old Age by Forty," *American Magazine*, 71, March 1911.

Fitch, John A. *The Steel Workers*, 1911.

Forester, Robert F. *The Italian Emigration of Our Times*, 1919.

Foster, William Z. *The Great Steel Strike and Its Lessons*, 1922.

"Fortune 500, Ranked Within States," *Fortune Magazine*, April 30, 2007.

Fuchs, Lawrence. *The American Kaleidoscope: Race, Ethnicity, and the Civic Culture*, 1990.

Gabaccia, Donna R. *From Sicily to Elizabeth Street: Housing and Social change Among Italian Immigrants, 1880-1930*, 1984.

Gabaccia, Donna R. *Italy's Many Diasporas*, 2000.

Gabaccia, Donna R. *We Are What We Eat: Ethnic Food and the Making of America*, 1998.

Gambino, Richard. *Blood of My Blood: The Dilemma of the Italian-Americans*, 1974.

Gambino, Richard. *Vendetta*, 1977.

Gans, Herbert M. "Symbolic Ethnicity: The Future of Ethnic Groups and Cultures in America," *Ethnic and Racial Studies*, Vol. 2, No. 1, January 1979.

Gans, Herbert M. *The Urban Villagers: Group and Class in the Life of Italian-Americans*, 1965.

Gans, Herbert M. "Toward A Reconciliation of 'Assimilation' and 'Pluralism': The Interplay of Acculturation and Ethnic Retention," in Charles Hirschman, Philip Kasinitz, and Josh DeWind, eds., *Handbook of International Migration: The American Experience*, 1999.

Gobel, Thomas. "Becoming American: Ethnic Workers and the Rise of the CIO," *Labor History,* Volume 29, No. 2, 11/5/36.

Goldman, Mark. *City On The Lake: The Challenge of Change in Buffalo,* New York, 1990.

Goldman, Mark. *High Hope: The Rise and Decline of Buffalo, New York,* 1983.

Gordon, Max. "The Communists and the Drive to Organize Steel, 1936," *Labor History,* Volume 23, Spring 1982.

Gordon, Milton M. *Assimilation In American Life: The Role of Race, Religion, and National Origins,* 1964.

Greeley, Andrew M. *Why Can't They Be Like Us? America's White Ethnic Groups,* 1971.

Gribaudi, Gabriella. "Images of the South: The Mezzogiorno As Seen By Insiders and Others," in Robert Lumley and Jonathan Morris, editors, *The New History of the Italian South,* 1997.

Griffin, Joe, with Don DeNovi. *Mob Nemesis: How the FBI Crippled Organized Crime,* 2002.

Guglielmo, Jennifer and Salvatore Salerno, editors, *Are Italians White? How Race Is Made in America,* 2003.

Haller, Mark H. "Organized Crime in Urban Society," *Journal of Social History,* Winter, 1971–72.

Hancock, Ian F. "Gypsies," in Thernstrom, et al., 1980.

Handlin, Oscar. *Race and Nationality in American Life,* 1948 (1957).

Handlin, Oscar. *The Uprooted: The Epic Story of the Great Migrations That Made the American People,* 1951.

Hartmann, Douglas and Joseph Gertels. "Dealing With Diversity: Mapping Multiculturalism in Sociological Terms," *Sociological Theory,* Vol. 23, June 2005.

Hein, Jeremy. "Ethnic Pluralism and the Disunited States of North America and Western Europe," Review Essays, *Sociological Forum,* Vol. 8, No. 3, 1993.

Hicks, John D. *Rehearsal for Disaster: The Boom and Collapse of 1919–1920,* 1961.

Higham, John. *Strangers In The Land: Patterns of American Nativism, 1860–1925.*

Hinshaw, John. *Steel and Steelworkers: Race and Class in Twentieth-Century Pittsburgh,* 2002.

Hogan, William T. *Economic History of the Iron and Steel Industry in the United States,* 1971.

Hollinger, David A. *Postethnic America,* 1995.

Hutchinson, John. "Ethnicity and Multiculturalism in Immigrant Societies," in John Hutchinson & Anthony D. Smith, editors, *Ethnicity,* 1996.

Ianni, Francis J. *Black Mafia,* 1974.

Iorizzo, Luciano J. and Salvatore Mondello, *Italian-Americans,* 1971.

Interchurch World Movement. *Report on the Steel Strike of 1919,* 1920.

Jacobson, Matthew Frye. *Roots Too: White Ethnic Revival in Post-Civil Rights America,* 2006.

Jeffries, Vincent and H. Edward Hansford. *Social Stratification: A Multiple Hierarchy Approach,* 1980.

Katznelson, Ira. *When Affirmative Action Was White: An Untold History of Racial Inequality in Twentieth Century America,* 2005.

Keim, Albert N. *The CPS Story: An Illustrated History of Civilian Public Service,* 1990.

Kleinknecht, William. *The New Ethnic Mobs: The Changing Face of Organized Crime in America,* 1996.

Kramer, Judith R. *The American Minority Community,* 1970.

LaGumina, Salvatore J. "Politics," in LaGumina, et al., 2000.

LaGumina, Salvatore J., Frank J. Cavaioli, Salvatore Primeggia, Joseph A. Varacalli, eds., *The Italian American Experience: An Encyclopedia,* 2000.

LaGumina, Salvatore J. *WOP! A Documentary History of Anti-Italian Discrimination in the United States,* 1973.

Lapomarda, Vincent A. "Press, Italian American," in LaGumina, et al., 2000.

LaSorte, Michael. "The Immigrant Grocer," in Salvatore J. LaGumina, Frank J. Cavaioli, Salvatore Primeggia, Joseph A. Varacalli, Eds., *The Italian American Experience: An Encyclopedia,* 2000.

LaSorte, Michael. "Retsof, New York: A Salt Mine Company Town," in Jerome Krase and Judith N. DeSena, eds., *Italian Americans in A Multicultural Society,* 1994.

Lay, Shawn. *Hooded Knights of the Niagara Frontier,* 1995.

Lerner, Michael. "Respectable Bigotry," *American Scholar,* August, 1969.

Lippmann, Walter. "The Underworld As Servant," in Francis A. J. Ianni and Elizabeth Reuss-Ianni, eds., *The Crime Society: Organized Crime and Corruption in America,* 1976.

Lipset, Seymour Martin and Earl Rabb, *The Politics of Unreason: Right-Wing Extremism in America, 1790–1970,* 1970.

Lopreato, Joseph. *Italian Americans*, 1970.

Lopreato, Joseph. *Peasants No More: Social Class and Social Change in an Underdeveloped Society,* 1967.

Lopreato, Joseph. "Religion and the Immigrant Experience," in Joseph A. Ryan, ed., *White Ethnics: Life in Working-Class America,* 1973.

Lubell, Samuel. *The Future of American Politics*, 1956.

Luconi, Stefano. *From Paesani to White Ethnics: The Italian Experience in Philadelphia,* 2001.

Luconi, Stefano. "Rodino, Peter Wallace, Jr.," in LaGumina, et al.

Maas, Peter. *The Valachi Papers,* 1968.

MacDonald, John and Leatrice. "Chain Migration, Ethnic Neighborhood Formation, and Social Networks," *Milbank Memorial Fund Quarterly*, No. 42, 1964.

Malpezzi, Frances M., and William M. Clements, *Italian American Folklore,* 1992.

Mangione, Jerre. *Mount Allegro*, 1942 (1972).

Mangione, Jerre, and Ben Morreale. *La Storia: Five Centuries of the Italian American Experience*, 1992.

Marchione, Margherita. "DiMaggio, Joseph Paul," in LaGumina, et al., 2000.

Marchione, Margherita. "Sirica, John Joseph," in LaGumina, et al., 2000.

Marger, Martin N. *Race and Ethnic Relations: American and Global Perspectives*, 1985.

Martorella, Rosanne. "National Organization of Italian American Women," in LaGumina, et al., 2000.

Mathias, Elizabeth, and Angelamaria Varesano. "The Dynamics of Religious Reactivation: A Study of a Charismatic Missionary to Southern Italians in the United States," *Ethnicity*, Vol. 5, 1978

Massaro, Dominic R. "National Italian American Coordinating Association (NIACA): The Conference of Presidents of Major Italian American Organizations," in LaGumina, et al., 2000.

McColloch, Mark. "Consolidating Industrial Citizenship: The USWA at War and Peace, 1939–46," in Paul F. Clark, et. al., editors, *Forging A Union of Steel: Philip Murray, SWOC, and the United Steelworkers*, 1987.

McGovern, Charles F. *Sold American: Consumption and Citizenship,* 1890–1945.

Melucci, Alberto. "The Post-Modern Revival of Ethnicity," in John Hutchinson & Anthony D. Smith, editors, *Ethnicity,* 1996.

Miller, D.D., Rev. Kenneth D. "The Christian Neighborhood House," booklet, 1943.

Montgomery, David. *Workers' Control In America*, 1979.

Mui, Alda C., and Suk-Young Kang, "Acculturation Stress and Depression Among Asian Immigrants Elders," *Social Work,* Vol. 51, No. 3, July 2006.

Murray, E. Emmet. *The Lexicon of Labor*, 1998.

Murray, Robert K. *Red Scare: A Study in National Hysteria, 1919–1920*, 1955.

Nelli, Humbert. *From Immigrants To Ethnics, The Italian Americans,* 1983.

Nelli, Humbert. *The Italians in Chicago: 1880–1930,* 1970.

Nelson, Bruce. *Divided We Stand: American Workers and the Struggle For Black Equality,* 2001.

Noel, Donald. "The Study of Assimilation," in John Jackson, ed., *Migration,* 1969.

Norrell, Robert J. "Steelworkers and Storekeepers: Social Mobility Among Italian Immigrants in Birmingham," in Rocco Caporale, *The Italian Americans Through The Generations*, 1986.

Order Sons of Italy in America (OSIA) Office, National. "Joint Convention Report: National Anti-Defamation Committee and National Deputy," August 20, 1957, National OSIA Office collection, OSIA Archives, Immigration History Research Center.

Parrillo, Vincent N. *Strangers to these Shores: Race and Ethnic Relations in the United States, Fifth Edition*, 1997.

Perlmann, Joel. I*talians Then, Mexicans Now: Immigrant Origins and Second Generation Progress, 1890 to 2000,* 2005.

Polenberg, Richard. *One Nation Divisible: Class, Race, and Ethnicity in the United States Since 1938,* 1980.

Pitkin, Donald S. "Land Tenure and Family Organization In An Italian Village," unpublished PhD. dissertation, Harvard University, 1954.

Ray, Gerda W. "'We Can Stay Until Hell Freezes Over': Strike Control and the State Police in New York, 1919–1923," *Labor History*, Volume 37, No. 3.

Ringer, Benjamin B. & Elinor R. Lawless. *Race—Ethnicity and Society*, 1989.

Rippley, La Vern J. "Germans," in Stephan Thernstrom, et al., 1980.

Renoff, Richard. "Sports," in LaGumina, et al., 2000.

Roberts, Dick. *American Railroads: The Case for Nationalization*, 1980.

Roediger, David R. *Working Toward Whiteness: How America's Immigrants Became White, The Strange Journey from Ellis Island to the Suburbs*, 2005.

Rogovin, Milton and Michael Frisch. *Portraits In Steel*, 1993.

Rolle, Andrew. *The Immigrant Upraised: Italian Adventurers and Colonists In An Expanding America*, 1968.

Rosoli, Gianfausto. "The Global Picture of the Italian Disapora to the Americas," in Lydio Tomasi, Piero Gastaldo, and Thomas Row, eds. *The Columbus People: Perspectives in Italian Immigration to the Americas*, 1994.

Ross, Edward A. "Italians In America," *The Century Magazine,* 1914.

Ross, Edward A. *The Old World In the New,* 1914.

Rothbart, Ron. "The Ethnic Saloon As A Form of Immigrants Enterprise," *International Migration Review*, Vol. xxvii, No. 2, 1993.

Rotondaro, Alfred. "National Italian American Foundation," in LaGumina, et al., 2000.

Rumbaut, Ruben G. "Assimilation and Its Discontents: Between Rhetoric and Reality," *International Migration Review*, Volume 31, Number 4, Winter 1997.

Salamone, Frank A. "Italian American Civil Rights League," in LaGumina, et al., 2000.

Scranton City Directory, 1896.

Slotkin, Richard. *Lost Battalions: The Great War and the Crisis of American Nationalty,* 2005

Steele, Richard W. "'No Racials': Discrimination Against Ethnics In American Defense Industry," *Labor History,* Winter 1991, Vol. 32, No. 1.

Stein, Rita F. *Disturbed Youth and Ethnic Family Patterns,* 1971.

Steffens, Lincoln. *The Shame of the Cities,* 1904.

Sturino, Franc. *Forging the Chain: Italian Migration to North America, 1880-1930*, 1990.

Sweeney, Vincent D. *The United Steelworkers of America: Twenty Years Later, 1936–1956,* 1956.

Thernstrom, Stephan, Ann Orlov, and Oscar Handlin, editors, *Harvard Encyclopedia of American Ethnic Groups*, 1980.

Thompson, Ethel E. *The Day Before Yesterday in Blasdell*, 1951.

Tiffany, Paul A. *The Decline of American Steel: How Management, Labor, and Government Went Wrong*, 1988.

Tomasi, Lydio F. *The Italian American Family*, 1972.

Tomasi, Silvano. *Piety and Power: The Role of Italian Parishes in the New York Metropolitan Area, 1880-1930*, 1975.

Ueda, Reed. "Historical Patterns of Immigrant Status and Incorporation in the United States," in Gary Gerstle and John Mollenkopf, editors, *E Pluribus Unum? Contemporary Perspectives on Immigrant Political Incorporation,* 2001.

Ueda, Reed. "Naturalization and Citizenship," in Richard A. Easterlin, David Ward, William S. Bernard, Reed Ueda, *Immigration,* 1982.

Vecoli, Rudolph. "Cult and Occult in Italian American Culture: The Persistence of A Religious Heritage," in Randall M. Miller and Thomas D. Marzik, eds. *Immigrants and Religion in Urban America*, 1977.

Watson, Bruce. *Sacco and Vanzetti: The Men, The Murders, and the Judgement of Mankind*, 2007.

Ware, Caroline. *Greenwich Village: 1920–1930*, 1965.

Whyte, William Foote. *The Streetcorner Society: The Social Structure of An Italian Slum,* 1943 (1966).

Williams, Lillian Serece. *Strangers in the Land of Paradise: The Creation of An African American Community, Buffalo, New York*, 1999.

Williams, Phyllis H. *South Italian Folkways In Europe and America: A Handbook For Social Workers, Visiting Nurses, School Teachers, and Physicians,* 1938.

Woodiwiss, Michael. *Organized Crime and American Power,* 2001.

Yarnow, Dvora. *Constructing "Race" and "Ethnicity" in America: Category-Making in Public Policy and Administration*, 2003.

Ziegler, Robert, and Gilbert Gall. *American Workers, American Unions, Third Edition*, 2002

Zolberg, Aristide R. *A Nation by Design: Immigration Policy in the Fashioning of America,* 2006.

Materials Regarding Lackawanna and the Buffalo Area:

Andreozzi, John. "Italians in a Mill Town: Lackawanna, N. Y.," in Richard N. Juliani, Philip V. Cannistraro, editors, *Italian Americans: The Search for a Usable Past*, 1989.

Andreozzi, John. "List of Italian American Organizations in Buffalo, N. Y.," unpublished paper, 2006.

Bethlehem Steel Company (BSC). "A Visit to the Lackawanna Plant of Bethlehem Steel Company," Booklet 104, 1939.

BSC. "Annual Conference Program: Employees' Representatives and Company's Representatives," 1926.

BSC. "Lackawanna Plant, Telephone Directory," 12/15/48.

BSC. "Statistical Data, Lackawanna Plant," May 1969.

Buffalo and Erie County Public Library. *Lackawanna Scrapbook.*

Buffalo and Erie County Historical Society, United Steel Workers Collection, 1937.

Buffalo Tuberculosis Association, report to Lackawanna Health Department, August 15, 1934.

Charity Organization Society of Buffalo. *Fifty Years of Family Social Work,* 1877–1927.

Clarke, Donald Adams. "Men On Relief In Lackawanna, N.Y., 1934-35: Social Pathology In A Satellite City," *The University of Buffalo Studies*, Volume XIV, No. 4, August, 1947.

Corcoran, David J. "A Study of the Lackawanna Neighborhood Cooperative Committee," masters thesis, University of Buffalo, 1950.

Emerling, William H., and John P. Osborne. *The History of Lackawanna,* 1976.

Estabrook, Arthur H., Ph.D. "A Roof Over Their Heads," Council of Social Service Agencies, Buffalo, New York, October 15, 1943.

Friendship House, Annual Report, 1939–1941.

Grasso, Tony. "A Card In the Window," unpublished story, 1988.

Grasso, Tony. "A Magnet, Our Church," unpublished story, n.d.

Grasso, Tony. "A Sea of Tears," unpublished.

Grasso, Tony. "Bridging the Bitter Years," unpublished story, October 1984.

Grasso, Tony. "Giammarone," unpublished story, 1988.

Grasso, Tony. "Grandfather's Vineyard," unpublished, 1982.

Grasso, Tony. "Remembrance: A Lonely Boy's Journey To Ellis Island," December, 1988.

Grasso, Tony. "Summer Evenings in the Old Village," unpublished story, 1988.

Grasso, Tony. "Taking Chances," unpublished, 1982.

Grasso, Tony. "The Hurdy-gurdy Player and His Monkey," unpublished story, n.d.

Grasso, Tony. "The Knife and Scissors Sharpener," unpublished story, 1988.

Grasso, Tony. "The Shepherdess Call," unpublished, 1981.

Grasso, Tony. "The Pains of the Alphabet," unpublished, undated.

Grasso, Tony. Untitled autobiographical essay, unpublished, n.d.

Grasso, Tony. Untitled "reflections and observations," unpublished essay, n.d.

Joint Charities & Economic Fund of Buffalo and Erie County, N. Y., "Lackawanna In 1942," 1943, unpublished report.

Koenig, Stephan M. *South Buffalo Railway: Bethlehem Steel Company Railroad Operations in Lackawanna, New York,* 2004.

Leary, Thomas E., and Elizabeth Sholes, *From Fire To Rust*, 1987.

Patterson, Kelly L. "From A Different Place: The Residential and Occupational Experience of Blacks In A Steel Making Suburb," unpublished MS thesis, SUNYAB, 1995.

Ruby, B. F. "DiCarlo —'Public Enemy,'" *Town Tidings*, September 1933.

Scheuerman, William. "The Politics of Protest: The Great Steel Strike of 1919–20 in Lackawanna, New York," *International Review of Social History*, Vol. 31, 1986.

Szabo, Msgr. Julius J. "Struggles of A Civic Conscience: A Study of the Lackawanna Experiment In Neighborly Cooperation," unpublished paper, 1960.

Taylor, Henry. "Race, Nationality, Class and Black Neighborhood Development In Lackawanna, New York, 1900–1970," unpublished and undated paper.

Taylor, Henry. "The Rape of Lackawanna: The Untold Story of Bethlehem Steel," unpublished paper, May 1972.

Vogel, Michael N., Edward J. Patton, and Paul F. Redding, *America's Crossroads: Buffalo's Canal Street/Dante Place, The Making of A City,* 1993.

Yans McLaughlin, Virginia. *Family and Community: Italian Immigrants in Buffalo, 1880–1930,* 1971.

Yans McLaughlin, Virginia. "Like the Fingers of the Hand: The Family and Community Life of First Generation Italian-Americans in Buffalo, New York, 1880–1930," unpublished doctoral dissertation, State University of New York at Buffalo, 1971.

Church:

A Living Edifice to God: St. Anthony and His Parish, Past, Present, Future, dedication booklet, 1964.

Archives of the Buffalo Diocese, St. Anthony's Church folder, "History of the Parish," by Rev. Vifredo, 6/28/46.

Assumption of the Blessed Virgin Mary Roman Catholic Church, 1918-1968, Golden Jubilee Booklet, 1968.

Casarotto, Secondo. "Italian Protestants and the Catholic Church in Buffalo, NY," in Frank J. Cavioli, Angela Danzi, Salvatore J. LaGumina, editors., *Italian Americans and Their Public and Private Life*, 1993.

Catholic Charities Center of Lackawanna. "Social Conditions in City of Lackawanna, New York," April, 1934.

Kaminski, James Jan. "History of Saint Barbara's Roman Catholic Church, Lackawanna, New York," unpublished term paper, 1977.

Official Catholic Directory

St. Agatha's Church. "Historical Sketch, St. Agatha's/All Souls Parish," 1943.

Storia della Parrocchia Italiana di Sant'Antonio in Buffalo, N.Y., Golden Jubilee booklet, 1941.

Records at local parishes:

St. Anthony

St. Charles

Our Mother of Good Counsel

St. Agatha

Our Lady of Victory

Italian Sources:

Banchetti, Giovanni. "Gl'Italiani In Alcuni Distretti Dello Stato Di Nuova York," in *Bollettino dell'Emigrazione*, No. 5, 1902.

Comune di Pettorano sul Gizio, *Pettorano Sul Gizio e la Riserva Naturale Regionale Monte Genzana e Alto Gizio*, 1998.

Instituto Centrale di Statistica (ICS), *Popolazione Residente e Presente dai Comuni: Censimenti dal 1861 al 1981*, Roma, 1985.

Magnani, Ferdinando. *La Citta di Buffalo, N.Y. e Paesi Circonvicini e Le Colonie Italiane*, 1908.

Martellone, Anna Maria. *Una Little Italy Nell'Atene D'America: La Communita Italiana Di Boston dal 1880-1920*, 1973.

Ministero Degli Affari Esteri, *Associazioni Italiane Nel Mondo*, 1984.

Ministero Di Agricoltura, Industria E Commercio; Direzione Generale della Statistica. *Elenco Delle Societa Di Mutuo Soccorso Esistenti al 1 Gennaio 1895*, 1898.

Ministero Di Agricoltura, Industria E Commercio; Direzione Generale della Statistica. *Societa Di Mutuo Soccorso, Elenco Delle Societa Esistenti al 31 Decembre 1912*, 1913.

Government Sources
United States:

Bureau of the Census. *Census of Business Retail Distribution*, 1954.

Bureau of the Census. *U. S. Census, 1930: Population, Volume 2*.

Bureau of the Census. *U.S. Census, 1930, Population-Composition and Characteristics*.

Bureau of the Census. *U. S. Census, 1940, Housing, Volume II, General Characteristics, Part 4*.

FBI. "Field Agent Reports," Microfilm Reel 187, 11/22/19.

Immigration and Naturalization Service (INS), *Statistical Yearbook of the Immigration and Naturalization Program*, 2000.

"The Wartime Violation of Italian American Civil Liberties Act," *Public Law* 106–451, November 7, 2000.

U. S. Immigration Commission (USIC), *Immigrants In Industries, Volume 8, Part 2: Iron and Steel Manufacturing, Volume 1*, 1911.

U. S. Immigration and Naturalization Service, *2000: Statistical Yearbook of the Immigration and Naturalization Service*, 2002.

U. S. Senate. *Permanent Subcommittee On Investigations of the Committee On Government Operations, Organized Crime and Illicit Traffic in Narcotics, Part 2*, 1963.

U.S. Senate. *Report On Conditions of Employment in the Iron and Steel Industry, Volume II: Wages and Hours of Labor, 1912*.

U. S. Senate. *Report On Conditions of Employment in the Iron and Steel Industry, Volume III, Working Conditions and the Relations of Employers and Employees*, 1913.

U. S. Senate. *Report On Conditions of Employment in the Iron and Steel Industry, Volume IV, Accidents and Accident Prevention*, 1913

USIC, *Immigrants in Industries, Volume 8, Part 2: Iron and Steel Manufacturing, Volume I*.

New York State:

Commission on Employers' Liability. *Report to the Legislature of the State of New York*, March 19, 1910.

New York State Department of Labor. *Industrial Directory of New York State, 1912*.

Erie County Courthouse:

Declaration of Intent (first papers)

Naturalization Petition (second papers)

Mortgage Grantees Index

Mortgage Grantors Index

City of Lackawanna:

Common Council Proceedings

Building Permits

Oaths of Office

Tax Books

Useful Sources:

Buffalo & Erie County Public Library, Lafayette Square
(BECPL); Buffalo & Erie County Historical Society (BECHS)
Directories:
Buffalo City Directory
Buffalo City Directory: Including Lackawanna
Buffalo Suburban Directory of Householders, 1949
Buffalo Southeast Suburban Directory
Buffalo South Suburban Directory
Erie County Directory, 1931, 1941 (Lackawanna Library)
Lackawanna City Directory, 1960, 1962 (Lackawanna Library)
       1914-15 (Library of Congress, Washington D.C.)
Lackawanna Street and Business Directory, 1938 (Lackawanna
       Library)
Newspapers:
A. Buffalo: (BECPL)
Buffalo Courier
Buffalo Commercial Advertiser & Journal
Buffalo Courier Express
Buffalo Daily Courier

Buffalo Express
Buffalo Evening News
Buffalo Illustrated Times
Buffalo Morning Express
Buffalo News
Buffalo Sunday Times
Buffalo Times
Buffalo Union Leader
Courier Express
Catholic Union Times
Illustrated Buffalo Express
Times of Buffalo
B. Lackawanna: (Lackawanna Library)
Front Page
Lackawanna Daily Journal
Lackawanna Herald
Lackawanna Journal
Lackawanna Leader
Lackawanna News
Lackawanna Press
Lackawanna Republic
Steel City Press
C. Other Newspapers:
Amalgamated Journal (Amalgamated Association of Iron,
Steel, and Tin Workers)
Steel Labor
Il Corriere Italiano (BECHS)
La Fiaccola (Immigration History Research Center, St. Paul. MN)
Other:
World War I Draft Registration Records
Manuscript Census Records - enumeration sheets listing all
       individuals (BECPL):
       New York State Census, 1892, 1905, 1915, 1925.
       United States Census, 1900, 1910, 1920, 1930.

NAME INDEX

Bracci, Kenneth, *326*
Bracco, Rosario, *383*
Brasch, Al, *136*
Brasch, Albert, *136*
Brasch, Anthony, *136*
Brasch, Mary Core, 243, 345, 474, *501*
Brockto, Mary Fadale, *234*
Brooks, Jeanette Andreozzi, *159*
Bruce, Julian, 418
Bulone, Domenico, 393
Burns, Jim, *187*
Burns, Rose Schole, *187*
Burns, Timothy, 374, *375*, 409, 562, 564, 565, 567
Buscaglia, Richard "Dick," *373*, 468, 587
Butera, Cathy, *529*
Butera, Florence Giordano, *533*
Butera, James, *529*, *531*
Butera, Joey, *531*
Butera, Salvatore "Sam," 439, *530, 533*

C

Caferro, Anthony "Tony," *585*, 586, 589-590, *589*, 590
Caferro, Francesco, *111*
Caferro, Molly, *281*
Caira, Albert, 96, 348
Caira, Gelsomina, 33
Caira, Leopoldo, 96-97
Caito, Ignazio, 382
Caito, Mike, 382-383, 388
Caitrone, Concetta, *446*
Cala, Vince, *540*
Calabrese, Angelo, 404
Calderon, Joe, *542*
Caligiuri family, 294
Caligiuri, Domenico, 87
Caligiuri, Filippo, 89
Caligiuri, Giuseppina, 89
Caligiuri, Joseph "Joe," 88, 577, 582, 584, *584, 585*, 586
Caligiuri, Louis, 89
Caligiuri, Luigi, 87-89, 283-284, 288
Caligiuri, Patricia DePasquale, 582

Caligiuri, Rosina, 87-89, 294
Calzone, Antoinette (Sister Mary Goretti), 324
Calzone, Maria, *271*
Calzone, Salvatore, *271*
Camarotta, Louis, 386
Cambria, Louis, *495*
Camillone-Daley, Carol, *587*
Camilloni, Tina DiTommaso, *521*
Cammillieri, John, 213
Campanelli, Alfredo "Alfred," 14, 19, 21, 30-31, 35, 58, 114, *280*, 349, *359*, 373, *481*
Campanelli, Antonio, 447
Campanelli, Berta Ambrosini, 58
Campanelli, Ermina, 14
Campanelli, Francis, 130
Campanelli, Mario, 467
Campanelli, Vincenzo, 14
Campbell, L.J., 377
Campoli, Camillo, 515
Campoli, Felice, 96
Campoli, Giuseppe, 96
Campoli, Nicola, 12, 96
Campoli, Rocco, 12, 120
Canali, Domenico, 283
Canali, Francesco, 290
Canali, Laura, *320*
Canali, Nick, 223, 225, 319, 557, *581*, 582
Canestrari, Aldo, *149, 527, 530, 531*, 537, *588*
Canestrari, Carmela, 123-124, 308, 554
Canestrari, Nora, *529*
Canestrari, Stefano "Stephen" "Steve," *112*, 308, 321, *383, 437, 442*, 554
Capasso, Anna, 87
Capasso, Camillo, 87, 285
Capasso, Clyde, 228, *232, 530, 538*
Capasso, Rose, *230*
Capodagli, Agosto, 357, 359
Capodagli, Armando "Armand," *427, 428*, 512
Capodagli, Augusto, *112*
Capodagli, Dominic, *481*

Capodagli, Gina, 346, *509*
Capodagli-Hund, Olivia, *321, 509*
Capozzi, Antonetta, *225*
Capozzi, Joe, *225*
Capponi, Carl, *378*
Capriotti, Brondo, 147, 458
Capriotto, Carmen, 458
Capriotto, Rosa Orefice, 455, 458, 514
Capriotto, Serafino "John," 455, 458
Capuani, Carlo, 368
Capuani, Joe, 187, 589
Caracci-Cullens, Lucia, 473, *473*
Cardamone, Joe, *510*
Cardamone, Mario, *282*
Cardamone, Tony, *510*
Cardero, Carmella, *525*
Cardi, Cesare, 77-78, 282, 461, *525, 571*
Cardi, Elide, 78
Cardinale family, 294
Cardinale, Ercolino, *52*
Cardinale, Giuseppe "Josie," *76*, 213, 265, *287, 378*, 389
Cardinale, Luisa, *52*, 265
Cardinale, Margaret, *52*, 265
Cardinale, Mary, *52*, 265
Cardinale, Ronald, *587*
Cardinale, Sam, *37, 52*, 187, 213, 269, *270*, 445, *510*
Cardoni, Alessandro, *288*
Cardoni, Clementine Miniri, *257, 451*
Cardoni, Emilia, *235*
Carducci, Domenico, 259
Carducci, Maria, *541*
Carestio, Antonio, *147, 277*, 361
Carestio, Assunta, *278*
Carestio, Bradley "Brad," *185*, 186-187, *502*, 503, 511, 513
Carestio, Mary, *278*
Carestio, Quintina, *278*
Carestio, Ralph, *147, 185*, 186, *427*, 512, *521*, 573
Carestio, Sally, *278*
Carfagna, Ermina, 72

Carlini, Angelo, *113*, 298, *307*, 317, 435, 536
Carlini, Antonio, *479*
Carlini, Arcangelo, 124, *231*
Carlini, Vittoria, *113-114*, 317, *479*
Carmillone, Antonio, 273
Carnevale, Anita, *519*
Carnevale, Antonino, 43
Carnevale, Antonio, 27, 43, 392
Carnevale, Antonio, 72-73, 215
Carnevale, Antonio, 92
Carnevale, Ausilia Ruscetta, 43
Carnevale, Dan, *519*
Carnevale, Ena, 43, 76-77
Carnevale, Joe, 512, 521, *525*, 537, *587, 589*
Carnevale, Pietro, 75
Carnevale, Santino, 38, 43, 76-77
Carnevale, Vincenzo, 358
Carpentieri, Aniello, 275
Carroccia, Evelyn, *266,* 268
Carroccia, Frank, *538*
Carroccia, Giovanni "John," *266,* 268, 286
Carroccia, Mary, *266,* 268
Carroccia, Rosanne, *529*
Carroccia, Russell, *529, 531*
Carsiggi, Gaetano, 110
Carter, Peter, 205
Casanova-DePasquale, Assunta, 80, 86, 225, 309, 324, 579
Casarotto, Rev. Secondo, 315, 473
Casazza, Tony, 369
Casciano, Vito, 274
Case, Rosalind Andreozzi, *159*
Caselli, Rico, *112, 481*
Casilio, Clementina, 57
Castiglia, Sam, 386
Castillo, Catalina, *334*
Castro, Louise, 310
Castro, Porfirio, 310
Catalucci, Stefano, *159*
Catuzza, Amedeo "Mike," 317, 363, 558
Catuzza, Biagio, 79, *229*

Catuzza, Celestino "Chet," 158, 252-253, 292, 325, 514, 558, *584, 585,* 586, *588*
Catuzza, Ferdinando "Ferdinand" "Fred," 101, 123, 136, 253, *262,* 325, 358, 367, *481,* 494, 496, 502, 511, 512, 514, 550, *550,* 551, *551, 552,* 554, 555, 558, 559, 564, 565, 577, 586
Catuzza, Fred Jr., 513, 514
Catuzza, Gertudda, 558
Catuzza, Giulia, 317
Catuzza, Lawrence, 574
Catuzza, Roman, 558, 583, 586, 591
Catuzza, Rosa DeSantis, 253, 558
Caz, Jimmy, 187 (*See also* DePasquale, Francis "Caz")
Ceccarelli, Albert "Al," 309, *427,* 512
Ceccarelli, Andrea, 59, 61
Ceccarelli, Arduino, 285, 287, 290, 368
Ceccarelli, Dolly, *146, 320*
Ceccarelli, Evangelisto, 59
Ceccarelli, Filomena, *261*
Ceccarelli, Joe, 253
Ceccarelli, John, *146,* 261
Ceccarelli, Sosio "S. John," "John," 124, *159,* 183, *183,* 390
Ceccarelli-Rosati, Marie, 125, 252
Cellini, Anthony, *230*
Cellini, Domenico "Dominic", *18,* 67, 288, *293*
Cellini, Joseph "Joe," 512, *575,* 577
Cellini, Maria, 18, *293*
Cellini-Schiavi, Nazzarena, 15-16, *18,* 43, 59, *62,* 64, 69, 136, *226, 235,* 278, *293*
Celotto, Elvia, *334*
Cennamo, Angelina "Angeline" Pinto, *276, 452*
Cennamo, Thomas, 270, 452, *452*
Ceroni, Joe, *378*
Cervolia, Tom, *427*

Cervoni, Arcangelo, *74, 230,* 367, 537
Cervoni, Dewey, 367
Cervoni, Michelina, *230*
Chatak, Smoile "Smiley," 419
Chentfant, Carl, *551,* 559
Cheroti, James, 455
Chiacchia, Donato "Dan," 124, 129, 205, 318, 358, 455, 458, *460,* 493, 495, 497, 550, 551, *553, 571*
Chiacchia, Emedio, 458, *551, 553, 571,* 578
Chiacchia, Lucia Fiorella, 129, 132, 288, 318, 493
Chiacchia-Kempf, Sara, 115, 129, 132, 242, 249, 275, 318, 345
Chini, Marino, *540*
Chiodo family, 578
Chiodo, Angeline, *268*
Chiodo, Anthony "Tony," *144, 268*
Chiodo, Carmen, *268*
Chiodo, Claudia Kuclich, *517*
Chiodo, Frank, *138,* 153, 265, 268, *268,* 286, 314, 315, 317, 318, *438, 441, 462, 495, 510,* 511-512, 513, 515, *551,* 578
Chiodo, Maria "Mary," Pinto, 101, *265,* 268, 286, *517*
Chiodo, Michael, *462*
Chiodo, Natale, 124, 265, *265,* 268-270, 279, 283, 286, 377, 391, 407, 511
Chiodo, Sam, *265, 268, 462*
Chiodo-Falbo, Rosamaria, 80, *273,* 318
Christ, Larry, 207
Christ, Louis, 453
Christiano, Daniel, 550
Christiano, Dorothy Kresconko, *509*
Christiano, Joe, 515
Christiano, John, 128, *321*
Christiano, Justino, *427*
Christiano, Lulu Mae, *509*
Christiano, Mary, *509*

Christiano, Nick, *498*

Christiano, Theresa, *509*

Christiano, Vito, 550

Christiano-Hughes, Frances, *509*

Ciccarelli, Louis, *445*

Ciccarelli, Pasquale, 74

Ciccarelli, Teresa, 74

Ciletti, Carlo, 12

Ciletti, Edoardo, 12

Ciletti, Michele, 12

Ciletti, Publeo, 12

Cino, Joe, *538*

Ciolino, Rev. Thomas, 300, 302, 319, 322, 323, 324, *324,* 325, *326,* 326, 327, *333,* 504, *519*

Cipriani, Alvira, *501*

Cipriani, Dan, *501*

Cipriani, Frank, 203

Cipriani, Mario, 147

Cipriano, Linda, 469

Cipriano, Margaret, *509*

Cirello, Ralph, *138, 438, 441*

Cisela, John, *138*

Clark, Bob, 463

Clark, Maria "Mary" Yoviene (Iovieno), 86, 108, 123, 128, 136, 265, 268, 457, *459,* 463, 464, 465, 469

Clarone, Iano, *540*

Claroni, Amy, *531*

Claroni, Arcangelo, *501*

Claroni, Dina, *531*

Clemente, Rev. Antonio, 297, 298-299, 300, 301, 306, *333,* 464

Cocina, Jesus, 136

Cocina-Marrano, Evelyn, *519*

Colafranceschi, Achille, 79

Colafranceschi, Al, *522, 523*

Colafranceschi, Arcangelo, 59, 92

Colafranceschi, Biagio, 79

Colafranceschi, Giuseppe, 92

Cole, John, 357

Colella, Antonio, 92

Colello, Angleo "Bing," *459,* 514, 515, *530*

Colello, Antonio "Tony," *112,* 131, *227,* 382, 383, *446, 459,* 489, *498,* 514, 555, 559, 564, 565, *571*

Colello, Bruce, *459, 587*

Colello, Dominic, *378*

Colello, Erasmo, 92, *498,* 537

Colello, Eugenio, 43, 73

Colello, Gaetano, 73

Colello, Giuseppina, 43

Colello, Larry, *331, 524,* 537

Colello, Louis "Lou," 288, 458, *459,* 475, 503, *530,* 537, 573-574

Colello, Maria Civita Grosso, *227*

Colello, Maria Civita, 43

Colello, Maria, 38, 43

Colello, Nicholas, 207, *459, 587*

Colello, Richard, *459*

Collana, Tom, 521

Collareno, Earl, 259

Collarino, Nunzio, *383*

Collarino, Orlando, *502*

Collarino, Tony, 391, *587* (*See also* Gallarney, Tony)

Collarino-DePasquale, Lisa, 582

Cologgi, Francesco, 554

Cologgi, Julia *321*

Colosimo, Antoinette, *254*

Colosimo, Carmine, 44, 58, 67, 89, *254,* 576

Colosimo, Domenico, *254*

Colosimo, Dominic, 89

Colosimo, Jim, 89, *254*

Colosimo, Maria, 44, 58, 87-89, *254*

Colosimo-Bevilacqua, Michelina "Madge," 21, 25, 44, 58, 67, 87-89

Columbus, Frank, 382, 409, *410,* 411, *411*

Conte, Alfred, 452

Conte, Luigi, *383*

Conte, Sabato, 75

Conte, Samuel D., 128, 321, 465, 469, 491, 513, 514

Conti, Antonio, 90

Conti, Caterina, 441, *446*

Conti, Charles "Charley," *530,* 583

Conti, Daniel, 551

Conti, Giuseppe, 377

Conti, James, *502*

Conti, Luigi, 389, 441, *446*

Conti, Rose Olivieri, *509*

Conti, Sam, *261*

Coppola, Rev. Paul, 332, *333*

Corbo, Joseph, 272, 451

Corbo, Louis, 514

Core, Anna, 242, *236,* 474

Core, Antonio, 242, 283, 406

Core, John, 368, *501, 502*

Core, Louis, 368

Core-Brasch, Mary, 243, 345, 474, *501*

Corotici, Antonio, 386

Corsaro, Jim, 390

Corsi, Bridget, 514

Corsi, Luigi "Louis," 367, *498,* 511, *530, 551, 552, 571*

Corsi, Salvatore, *427*

Cortello, Antonio, *447*

Corvigno, Alberto, 37

Corvigno, Anne Melillo, 37, 124-125, *182,* 311, 346, *431,* 511, *517, 533*

Corvigno, Carmine "Carmen," 37, *237, 533*

Corvigno, Luisella, 37

Corvodi, Peter, *383*

Cosentino, Alessandro "Alex," 96, 406, 358

Cosentino, Ferdinando, 95-96, 373

Cosentino, Giuseppe "Joe," 96, 115-116, 123, *170,* 126, 363, 405, 420, *493,* 494, *498,* 511, 514, 555, 562, 565, *568*

Costantino, Anthony, 419

Costanzi, Angelo, 108, 110, *112,* 463, 514

Costanzi, Elisabetta "Elizabeth," 110, 279, 514

Costanzi, Marco, 279, 453, 497, 494

Costanzo, John, 465

Costanzo, Louis, 94

Costanzo, Luigi, *427*

Costanzo, Mary Mancuso, 94
Costello, Helen Fadale, *234, 459*
Costello, Marie, *517*
Covelli, Adelina "Adeline," 19, 23, 32, *43,* 65-66, 174, 242-243, *247,* 257, 318, 319
Covelli, Carol Pastore, 186
Covelli, Elmer, 134
Covelli, Filiberto, 15, 34, *43,* 44, 59, 65-66, 96, 107, 188, 242, 248, 286-287, 368
Covelli, Fiore, 96, 286
Covelli, Florindo Eugenio "Gene," *43,* 65-66, 67, 96, 125, 141, 242, *247,* 419, 474
Covelli, Gelsomina, 44, 65-66, 248, 292, 294
Covelli, Gilda, *43,* 65-66, *247*
Covelli, Larry, 186, *186,* 187, 292
Covelli, Leo, 242, 290
Covelli, Leopoldo, 23-24, 32, *43,* 44, 186
Covelli, Raffaela, 19
Covelli, Rosina, 15-16, *43,* 44, 77
Covelli, Sanumele, 14
Covelli, Teresina, 44
Covelli, Umele, 20
Coviello, Alex, *538*
Coviello, Carmela, 346
Coviello, Chris, *526, 528, 541*
Coviello, Christina DeSantis, 461
Coviello, Lorenzo, 363
Covino family, 291
Covino, Albert "Al," 278, 279, 291-292, 357
Covino, Aniello, 189, *235,* 279, 290, 297, 359, 386, 389, *447*
Covino, Carl, 278, 359-360, 361, *502, 519*
Covino, Carmella, 279, 297
Covino, Cosmo, 515
Covino, Donato, *235*
Covino, Giustina, 297
Covino, Ilario, *235*
Covino, Sally, *519*
Covino-Kurnik, Mary, *320*

Covino-Masters, Giustina "Jay," 189, 223, 244, 278
Cozzo, Mario, 436
Crappo, Bill, *542*
Crescenza, Santo, 393
Cribari, Professor, 32
Cristiano, Daniele, *447*
Croce, Al, 113, 199, 242-244, *244,* 248, 308, 361, 369, 388, 392, 406, 407, 516, 554
Croce, Angelo (Tony George), 74, 115, *224,* 133, 349, 388, 406, 489, *530*
Croce, Mary, 244
Croce, Virginia, 242, *244,* 308
Croce, Vito, *244*
Cswaykus, Carolyn, *501*
Cswaykus, John, *501, 502*
Cullens, Lucia Caracci, 473, *473*
Culver, Yolanda Mazzucchi, 522
Cuomo, Dorothy, *233*
Cuomo, Florence Milano, *233*
Cuomo, Frank, *233, 530*
Cuomo, Neal, *233*
Cuozzo, Frances, 464
Curtin, Charles, 113, 555
Cuzzarella, Maria Antonia, *254*

D

D'Alessandro, Addolorata, 37
D'Alessandro, Alberto "Al," 37, *523*
D'Alessandro, Angelo, 467, *467*
D'Alessandro, Ann, *501*
D'Alessandro, Arnold, *501*
D'Alessandro, Carmellina, 37
D'Alessandro, Carmine, 37, *523*
D'Alessandro, Christopher, 370
D'Alessandro, Cristoforo, 365
D'Alessandro, Frances, 328
D'Alessandro, Giovanni, 40, 370
D'Alessandro, Innocenzo, 20
D'Alessandro, John, 467, *467*
D'Alessandro, Josephine, *128,* 583
D'Alessandro, Luisa, 73
D'Alessandro, Marion, *501*
D'Alessandro, Nunzia, 37, 455
D'Alessandro, Orlando, 37, *192*

D'Alessandro, Vincenzo "Jimmy," "V. Jimmy," 37, 114, 123, 328, 359, 364, 367, 443, 511, 551, *571,* 581, 583, 593
D'Alessio, Cristoforo, 20
D'Alessio, Giovanna, 20
D'Alfonso, Rev. Raffaele, 110, 300, 301, 306, *333,* 464
D'Amato, Angelo, 91
D'Amico, Alexander, 589
D'Amico, Bob, 455, 589
D'Amico, Peter, 224
D'Amore, Cesidio, 87, 240, 348, 389
D'Amore, Ralph, 240, 243-244, 343, 367, 407
D'Amore, Rosina Ginnetti, 87, 240
Daggart, Fred A., *375*
Daley, Carol Camillone, *587*
DaLuiso, Florence Simini, 467, 468-469
DaLuiso, Gustave, 465, 467, 468, 513, 515
Danch, Margaret, *509*
Daniels, Kid, 199, 228
Dankovich, Helen Hrabocsak, 225-226
Davis, George W., 343
Dean, Edward, *334*
DeAngelis, Francesco "Arcadio," 90, 278
DeAngelis, Sosio, 59
DeBello, Pasquale, 106
DeCarolis, Anna, 67, 223
DeCarolis, Giovanni, 223
DeCarolis, Marius, 424, 427, *429,* 512
DeGiuli, Angelo, 38, 42, *528*
DeGiuli, Teresa, *528, 541*
DeLallo, Betty, 554
DeLallo, Paul, 382, 383
DelBello, Michele, *113*
DelBello, Nick, 269, 455, 462, *501,* 511, *519,* 522, *523, 530*
Delgado, Aqria, *334*
Delgatto, Rosa, 312, *256,* 509

DiCarlo, Giuseppe, 211
DiCarlo, Joseph, 211, *212,* 213
DiCarlo, Sam, 211
DiCenzo, Domenico, 136, 373
DiCenzo, Edwin "Ed," 202,
    501, 514, *551, 552, 571,*
    575, 583
DiCenzo, Vincenzo, 110, 275
DiCenzo-Myzel, Frances, *501*
DiCenzo-Rosati, Mary, 90, *501*
DiCioccio, Ron, *538*
DiCorpo, Frank, 90, 272
DiCristofero, Gemma, *529*
Difonzo, John, *383*
DiGiuseppi, Samuel, 455
DiLallo, Paul, 382, 383
DiManno, Benedetto, 367
DiMasi, Anthony "Tony," *227,*
    553, 571
DiMasi, Ermete, *437,* 445
DiMiceli, Salvatore, *383*
DiMillo, Antonio "Tony," 67,
    75, 80, 120, 299, 309, *352,* 413
DiMillo, Ida, *234*
DiMillo, Inez, *234*
DiMillo, Maria, 75, 198, 225
DiMillo, Tony, 198, 224-225,
    230, 274
DiMillo, Yolanda, *234*
DiPaolo family, 94
DiPaolo, Dennis, 443
DiPaolo, Ilio, 41, 94, *94,* 442-
    443, *524*
DiPasquale, Ned, *535*
DiPronio, Anthony, 370, *498*
DiPronio, Felice, 370
DiPronio, Gaetano, 368
Diranio, Antonio, 367
DiRe, Tony, *232,* 281
DiRosa, Louis, *427*
DiStefano, Joe, *535*
DiStefano, Joe Jr., *542*
Ditillio, Alfonso, 90-91
Ditillio, Irene, 91
DiTommaso, Mafalda, 153
DiTommaso, Nick (*See*
    Thomas, Nick)

DiTommaso, Robert, 153
DiTommaso, Salvatore, 73, 90,
    135, 286, 316, 389, 493
DiTommaso, Saverio, 368
DiTommaso, Teresa, 73, 90, 135
DiTommaso-Camilloni, Tina, *521*
DiVito, Dan, *550*
Dolce, Phillip, 453
Doty, John, *383*
Downing, Dorothy, *183*
Downing-Yoviene, Helen, *191,* 455
Doyle, Charles, 418
Drilling, Rev. Peter, 332, 333,
    333, 334
Drozdowski, Edward, *545*

E
Eagan, Bob "Bobby," *270, 445, 510*
Eagan, Nicholas, 582
Eagan, William "Bill," *138,*
    150, *510,* 547, *575,* 576-
    577, 582, 584, 587
Ellis, Charles, 403-404, 547-
    549, 570
Eposito, Frances, 252-253
Evans, John, *510*
Evans, Mary Leo, *517*
Evans, Ralph "Murphy," *495*
Evans, Randy, *540*

F
Fabi-DeSantis, Faustina, 77
Fadale, Calogero "Charles,"
    63, 123, 221, 279-281, 299,
    307, *307,* 309, 431, *432,*
    435, *437,* 439, 441, *442,*
    459, 461, 462, *459,* 466, 549
Fadale, Cosmer, 281, *459,* 550
Fadale, Delores, *459*
Fadale, Dick, 186-187, *459*
Fadale, James, *459*
Fadale, Joe, 121
Fadale, John D., 108, 120, 123-
    124, 130, 136, 187, 245,
    274-275, 307, 435, *442,*
    459, 464, 466, 468, 469,
    488, 493, 515, 549, 550,
    551, *551,* 560, *571*
Fadale, Lois, *459*

Fadale, Louis, 439, *459*
Fadale, Lucia, *113, 479*
Fadale, Nick, 466
Fadale, Nina Mayne, 466
Fadale, Serafina "Sara," 63,
    234, 221, 307, *432,* 435,
    437, 439, *459*
Fadale-Brockto, Mary, *234*
Fadale-Costello, Helen, *234, 459*
Fadale-Ippolito, Josephine, 115,
    234, 441, *459,* 465
Fadale-Killingbeck, Lucy, *234*
Fadale-Pellegrino, Patricia
    "Pat," 115, *234,* 441, 466
Falbo family, 516, 578
Falbo, Ben, *540,* 591
Falbo, Bruno, 80, 101, 265,
    273, 282, 393, 394
Falbo, Carmela, *273*
Falbo, Jerry, *273*
Falbo, John, 265, 364, 583, 593
Falbo, Micolina, *273*
Falbo, Rosamaria Chiodo, 80,
    273, 318
Falbo, Tony, *150,* 265, 377, 390,
    427, 429, 438, 495, 510, 512
Falcone, Anna, 514
Falcone, Anthony "Tony," 123,
    136, 270, 387, 395, 514,
    551, *551,* 554, 559, 561,
    566-568, *571,* 577, 583, 590
Falcone, Camile, 280
Falcone, Carmela, 78, 318, 436
Falcone, Francesco, 78, 318, 436
Falcone, Michael "Mike," 110,
    280, 377, 390
Falcone, Nicola "Nicholas"
    "Nick," 110, *112,* 221, 276, *567*
Falconio, Antonio, *442*
Fanone, Angelo, 325, *325*
Fanone, Filippo "Phil," *22, 25,*
    474, 522, 535, 538
Fanone, Giovanna Viglietta, *22,*
    232, 325 *325, 475*
Fanone, Iolanda, *22*
Fanone, Maria, *25, 192, 287,*
    292, 325, *325, 474*

Fanone, Mario, *22, 25, 192,* 282, *282, 287,* 325, *325, 474*

Faraci, John, *520*

Faraci, Philip, 455

Faranti, Joseph, 357

Faso, Carl, 465

Federici, Alberto "Albert" "Al," 79, 124, *378,* 390

Federici, Maria Maturani, 79

Felici family, 12

Felici, Giovanni Battista, 299, *307*

Ferrelli, Aldo, *67*

Ferrelli, Cesidio "Jesse," 34, *67, 256*

Ferrelli, Giuseppina "Josephine," 23-24, *67,* 69, 293, 294

Ferrelli, Vincenzo, *32,* 69

Filighera, Michele "Mike," 110, *112,* 368

Filipetti family, 449

Filipetti, Aldo, *129,* 252, 255, 314, 319, 465, 522, *522, 523, 545,* 574, *574,* 575-577, *575, 585,* 586, 587, *588,* 591

Filipetti, Alex, *144, 256, 280,* 368, 391

Filipetti, Luigi, 281, *481*

Filipetti, Paolo "Paul," 93, *112, 254,* 255, *257, 280,* 281, 283, 288, 290-291, 368, *481,* 574

Filipetti, Rose Colosimo, *254*

Filipetti, Silvio, *144, 254,* 513, 515

Filipetti-Pascucci, Adele, *254,* 285, 288, 291, 314, 574

Fini, Gino, 476, *522, 523*

Finley, H.R., *383*

Fino, Paul, 537

Fiore, Angelo, 368

Fiore, Caroline, 465, 514, 515

Fiore, Frank, 183, 207, 514, 573, 574

Fiore, Giulia Violanti, 14, *232, 475*

Fiore, Joseph, 324

Fiore, Mamie, 464

Fiore, Pietro "Peter," 123, 132, 288, *378,* 389

Fiore, Ralph, 322, *331,* 512, *530,* 537, *571,* 577, 583, *588*

Fiore, Rose, 131, *189,* 224, 288, 464, *469*

Fiore, Tommy, *149*

Fiorella, Joe, 417-418, *427*

Fiorella, Rosabella, 132, *276,* 318

Fiorella-Chiacchia, Lucia, 129, 132, 288, 318, 493

Fischione, Remo, *525*

Fistola family, 245

Fistola, Anna, 318, *320*

Fistola, Carmela, 318

Fistola, Cesidio, 533

Fistola, Charles, *331,* 512, 512, *530,* 537

Fistola, Josephine Marrano, 464, *469, 519*

Fistola, Lou, *519, 520*

Fistola, Mary Panzetta, *331*

Fistola, Sabatino "Sebastian," *320,* 368, 464, *464,* 515, 551, 562

Florino, Christine Ricci, *509*

Florino, Joseph "Joe," 358, 367

Fortini, John, *587*

Fox, Anne, *276, 286*

Fox, George, 383

Fox, Irene, *452*

Fox, Joe, 110, 129, 264, 286, 314, 395, *440,* 441, *452* (*See also* Volpe, Giuseppe)

Fox, Joe, Jr., 129-130

Fox, June, *276*

Fox, Susan "Sue" Pinto, 129, 286, 314, *440,* 441

Fraschetti, Umberto, 59

Fresco-Amorosi, Pasqualina "Lena," 91, 123, 136, 437, 554, 555, 557, 575

Frisolone, Vito, 110

Fuoco, Tom, 89

Fusco, Joseph "Joe," 551, 560, 583

Fusco, Thomas, 445, 447

Fusco-Rogers, Mary, 110, 212, 280, 402, 440, *442, 446,* 457

G

Gabrielle, Arcangelo, 79

Gabrielle, Cleo, 78

Gabrielli, Giuseppe, 373

Gabrielli, Ottavio, 110

Gaglia, Mike, 226

Gaglia, Rose, 226

Galanti family, 394, 476

Galanti, Diane, 472

Galanti, Eugenio "Eugene," 80, 248, 281, 348, 373, *437, 442,* 445, 463, 476, 490, *491, 501, 520,* 535, 569

Galanti, Filomena Paolozzi, 80, 91, *501,* 569

Galanti, Grace Marrano, *256, 501, 519*

Galanti, Jo, *501*

Galanti, John, 325, *326,* 326, 327, 512

Galanti, Ralph "Chico" Jr., 184, 472, *472,* 511, 514, 522, 569, 574

Galanti, Ralph III, 472, *587*

Galanti, Ralph Sr., 136, 184, 213, 368, *519, 520,* 551, *563,* 569, 570

Galfo, Guido, 515

Gallarney, Tony, 363, 391 (*See also* Collarino, Tony)

Gallo, Guglielmo, *447*

Galluch, Dominic "Dom," 417, *427*

Gangarosa, Joe, *535*

Gardina, Jack, *427,* 512

Gargano, Antonio, 393

Gatto, Michele, 221

Gemmiti, Rev. Dante, *29*

Gemmiti, Vincenzo, *22*

Gennari, _?_, *438*

Gennetti, Dominic, *373*

George (Giorgio), Angelamaria, 79, 443, 464

George (Giorgio), Antonio, 79, 431, 443

George (Giorgio), Frank, 443

George family (*See also* Giorgio as a surname)

Manzetti, Ed, *246, 502*, 583
Manzetti, Emilio, 90
Manzetti, Filomena, 90
Manzetti, Maria, *317*
Manzetti, Nicola, *317*
Manzo, Rev. Louis, 324
Marchese, Jenelle, *529*
Marchese, Rose, 204, 521, *531*
Marchetti, Antonio "Pipp'
   Antonio," 245
Marchetti, Carmela, 245, 312
Marchi, Constantino, 451
Marchinda, John, *538*
Marchio, Saveria, 88-89
Marchio, Tomasso, 88-89
Marco, Domenico, 368
Marcocci, Antonio, 96
Mariani, Bill, 574
Mariani, Bruno, 389
Mariano, John, *535*
Marinaccio, Rose, *517*
Marinaccio, Samuel "Sam,"
   437, 514
Marinelli, Annaregina, 475
Marinelli, Cecile, 464
Marinelli, Concetta "Connie,"
   21, 34, *88, 128*
Marinelli, Domenico A. "Tony,"
   301, 357-358, 371, *447*
Marinelli, Domenico
   "Dominick," 90, 297, 488
Marinelli, Ed, *230*
Marinelli, Frank, 120, *501, 551*
Marinelli, Giovanni, 475
Marinelli, John, 322
Marinelli, Louis, *502*
Marinelli, Margaret Ginnetti,
   297, 474
Marinelli, Margherita
   "Margaret," *235*
Marinelli, Maria "Marietta," *307*
Marinelli, Marietta Risio, 299, 301
Marinelli, Ralph, 458, *501, 510,*
   518, 519, 520
Marinelli, Rocco, 90, 367
Marinelli, Sandra, 469-470, 583
Marinelli-Staniszewski, Connie,

501, 521
Mariotti, Domenico Antonio,
   297, 367
Mariotti, Maria, 297
Mariotti, Pietro, 297
Mariotti, Valentino, 383
Marks, Mary, *334*
Marmineo, Lawrence, 110
Marosi, Gabrielle, 369
Marracino, Angelo, 90, 281
Marrano, Adeline, *519*
Marrano, Ermelindo, 223
Marrano, Evelyn Cocina, *519*
Marrano, Federico, *110*
Marrano, Frederic, 587, *588*
Marrano, Louis, 468, *469*
Marrano, Maria, *110,* 249-250
Marrano, Neil, *147, 519*
Marrano, Ralph, *519*
Marrano, Virginia, 305, 464
Marrano-Fistola, Josephine,
   464, *469, 519*
Marrano-Galanti, Grace, *256,*
   501, 519
Marrocco, Anita, *526, 528, 541*
Marrocco, Pete, *538, 539, 539*
Marrocco, Steven, *539*
Marsillo, _?_, *378*
Marsillo, John, 389
Marsillo Mary Carmella, *528*
Martin, Ginny, *509*
Martin, Mary, 465
Martini, William, 212
Martino, Giovanni, 72, 215
Martino, Joseph, 156
Mary Agnes, Sister, *327*
Mary Cross, Sister, *327*
Masella, Clara, *528*
Masella, Tony, *535*
Masella-Perry, Linda, *526*
Masocco, Dominic, *261*, 444
Masocco, Gaetano, 79, 444-445
Masocco, John, *261*, 444, 586
Masocco, Maria, 79
Masocco, Natale, 58

Masters, Giustina "Jay,"
   Covino, 189, 223, 244, 278
Mastrangelo, Art, *427*
Mastrangelo, Ed, 416
Mastrobattista, Peter, 395
Mateja, Kathleen, *334*
Matre, Nicholas, 212
Matre, Rose, 212
Mattioli, Domenico, 368
Mattioli, Isadore, 455*, 481*
Mattioli, Liso, *257*, 522
Mattone, Domenico, 108, 110
Mattone, Sosio, 110
Mattucci, Anna Milano, *233*
Mattucci, Joe, *233*
Mattucci, John, *233*
Mattucci, Nicola "Nicholas,"
   188, 440, *446*, 450, 470,
   490, 513, 514
Mattucci, Serafino, 108, *113,*
   123, 228, *228,* 281, *281,*
   283, 298, 299, 304, *307,*
   309, 310-311, *324,* 327,
   437, *437, 442, 445, 446,*
   447, 448-449, 455, 457,
   460, 458, 462, 480, *480,*
   489, 490, 491, 493, *530,*
   533, 536
Mattucci, Viola, *233*
Mattucci, Virginia, *113-114,*
   437, 460
Mattucci, Yolanda, 309
Maturani, Biagio, 55-56, 67, 79
Maturani, Edimondi, 64
Maturani, Giulio, 25, 87, 289,
   371
Maturani, Giuseppina DeSantis,
   55-56, 64, 68, 79
Maturani, Luigi, 19, 87
Maturani, Maria, 56, 64, 67
Maturani, Pasquale "Patsy," 64, 67
Maturani, Rosa, 19
Maturani, Vincenzina, 35
Mauriello, Antonio "Tony," 63,
   73, 123, 216, 431, 435, 440,
   442, 445, *446,* 460, 549,
   550, 555

Nasso, Mike, *510*
Nasso, Molly, 286, 317, 578
Navarra, Carmen, 187
Nelles, Lorne, 419-420
Nicometo, Charles, 537
Nicometo, Loretta Amorosi, 325, 555, 557
Nicometo, Tom, *587*
Nicometo, Tommy, *531*
Nicometo, Tony, *531, 535*
Nigro, Alex "Al," 201, *237*, 419, 453, *459*, 512, *530*, 554, *571*
Nigro, Antonetta, *58*
Nigro, Celestino, *34*, 73, 443, 445, *459*, 537
Nigro, Charles "Charley," 147, *280*, 367, 453, *459*, 512, 535
Nigro, Kenneth "Ken," *280*, 453, *459*
Nigro, Luigi, 73
Nigro, Michele, 73
Nigro, Patricia, 147
Nigro, Rose Mary, 147
Nigro, Shirley, *521*
Nigro-Katra, Lorraine, *521*
Nigro-Vertalino, Jennie, 123, 458, *459*
Notto, Mary Ann, *541*
Novelli, Concezio "John," 16, 21, 28, 33, 35, 65, 69, 125-126, 147, *335, 468*
Novelli, Costantino, 34, 180, 285-286, 489, 491, *498*, 511, 512, 535, 537, *551, 571*, 583
Novelli, David, 467*, 468*
Novelli, Vincenza, 285, *509*
Nowak, Frank, *540*
Nowak, John, *334*
Nowak, Migdalia, *334*

O
Oddi family (*See also* Oddy as a surname)
Oddi, Annie, *71*
Oddi, Benigno, *71*, 72-73, 123, 132, 138, 285, 470

Oddi, Don, 285
Oddi, Enrichetta Monaco, 72, 123, 215-216, 225, 228, *235*, 279, 297, 298, 435-436, *437, 442*, 447, *447*
Oddi, Ermina Carfagna, 72
Oddi, Giselda Monaco, *71*, 72, 132, 285
Oddi, Margaret, 285
Oddi, Pietro, 72-73, 123, 215-216, 279, 297, 298, *307*, 387-388, 447, *447*, 492-493, 512
Oddi, Raffaele, 72-73
Oddy family (*See also* Oddi as a surname)
Oddy, Giacomo (Oddi), "James," "Jim," *72*, 132, 139, 184, 245, 322, 464, 469, 470, 512
Oddy, Nunzio (Oddi) "Nunze," 113-114, 129, 199, 221, 223, *227*, 228, 279, 282, 297, 299, 306, *307*, 343, 367, 406, 407, 441, 475, 476, *530*, 543
Ogarek, Mayor John, 522, *530*, *545, 575*, 577, 582, 584, 587, *587*, 591
Olivieri, Alfred, 355
Olivieri, Dave, *542*
Olivieri, Flora Paolini, 25, 31, 57, 316, *533*
Olivieri, Gene Jr., *542*
Olivieri, Giovanni, 90
Olivieri, Louis, 124
Olivieri, Maria, 90, 318
Olivieri, Pasquale "Patsy," 57, 358-359, *533*
Olivieri, Tessa, *542*
Olivieri-Conti, Rose, *509*
Omicioli, Jerry, 348
Orefice, Angelo, *447*
Orefice-Capriotto, Rosa, 455, 458, 514
Orlando, Charley, 224
Orlando, Gioacchino, *168*, 281, *551*, 557, 578
Orlando, Joseph, 393

Orlando, Mary, 187
Orlando, Michele "Michael," 393, *438*
Orlando, Nunzia, 285
Orsini, Julius, 344
Orzulak, Rev. Henry, *540*
Ottariona, Giuseppe, 73

P
Pacholczak, John, *189*
Pacifico, Louie "Lou," *535, 538*
Pacillo family, 441
Pacillo, Ann, 158, 247
Pacillo, Antonio "Anthony," 90-91, *254*, 304, 309, 363, 406, 439, *442*
Pacillo, Caterina, *254*, 299, *307*, 309, 439
Pacillo, Edmund "Ed," 123, *148*, , 309, 502, 512, 513, *530, 531*, 537
Pacillo, Gerald "Jerry," 124, 299, *307*, 309
Pacillo, Joseph "Joe," 123, *307*, 309, 321, 367, 489, 511, 513
Pacillo, Josephine, 314
Pacillo, Mark*, 331*
Pacillo, Mary, *254*, 275
Pacillo, Mike, 358, *383, 427*, 512
Pacillo, Nicole, *531*
Pacillo, Vito, 314, 368, 439
Pagliei, Antonio, 73
Pagona, James, 158
Palante, Marie, *529*
Palante, Raffaele, 93
Palermo, Angelo "Buffalo Bill," 211
Pallante, Ralph, *538*
Palmeri, Michelina, *528*
Palmisano-Green, Aurora, 246, 464, 515
Palumbo, Antonio, 394
Palumbo, Fred, *532, 535, 538*
Palumbo, John, 322, 394
Palumbo, Simon, 514
Palumbo, Tony, 124
Panczykowski, John, *501*
Pandozzi, Silvio, 110
Panniccia, Angelo, 96

Thomas, Clara, 562
Thomas, Daniel "Dan," 343, *492*, 513, 554
Thomas, Oliver, 393
Thomas, Salvatore, *447*, 448
Tiberio, John, 451, *451, 528*
Tiberio, Maria, *529*
Tibollo, Maria Giuseppa, *225, 226, 232*
Tibollo, Michele, 110, 488, 493
Tibollo, Pasquale "Shorty," *225, 226, 235*, 282, *437*, 443, 493
Tobias, Frank, *261*
Tobias, Mike, *501*
Tobias, Yolanda Sperduti, 321, *326*, 505
Tomaka, Mayor Paul, *499*, 550, 551, 554, 561, 562, 564-565, *564*, 568
Tomilo, Tom, *516*
Tomjanovich, Walter, *545*
Tonucci, Albert, *280*
Tonucci, Alfredo, *359*
Tonucci, Ann Marie, *185*
Tonucci, Gino, 262, *359, 481*
Tonucci, Nelson, *185*
Tonucci, Terso, *481*
Toomey, Mayor John, 402, 403, 549
Topinko, Carol, *233*
Topinko, Dick, *233*
Topinko, Virginia Milano, *233, 501*
Topinko, Walter, *233, 248, 501, 520*
Topinko, Walter, Jr., *233*
Torella, Antonio, 14-15, 16, 69, 91, 373
Torella, Armando, 13, 30, 69, 91, 146, 259, 367
Torella, Giulia, 14-15
Tornatore, Antonio, *113*
Tornatore, Michele, *479*
Torres, Angel, *540*
Torres, Daniel, *334*
Tortis, Franco, 35
Tracy, John, 466
Tripoli, Domenico, 311, 381, 551
Tripoli, Rosina, 311, 318

Tristani, Cesidio, *14*
Tristani, Domenico, *59,* 92
Tristani, Gaetano, *59,* 92
Tristani, Maria, *14*
Tristani, Raffaela, *14*
Tronolone, Rev. Paschal, 145
Trotta, Mary, *509*
Tucci, Cesare, *437*
Tulio, Antonio, *427*
Turchiarelli, Antonio "Tony," 108, 123, 188, *224*, 276, 304, 309, *437, 442*, 447, *447*, 448-449, 460, 462, *464*, 493, 512, 514, 536, 550, *550*, 551, *551*, 555, 557, 559
Turchiarelli, Jenny, 309, 447
Turkovich, Josephine, *509*
Turkovich-Juran, Katie, *509*

U

Ungaro, Betty, 332
Ungaro, Dominic, *231*
Urbanczyk, Tony, *378*

V

Valentine, Frances, 451
Valentine, George, *150, 268*
Valentine, Grace, 101
Valentine, James, 363
Valetta-Schiavi, Gladys, *509*
Vallone, Angelantonio, 92
Vaughn, Kathy, *541*
Ventre family, 17, 25
Ventre, Antonio "Tony," 31, 35, 64, 126
Ventre, Ausilio, 64
Ventre, Domenico, 13, 21, 96
Ventre, Elisabetta, 13, 21, 64
Ventre, Filippo, 13
Ventre, Mirella, *541*
Ventre, Tomasso "Tom," 17, 24-25, 31, 33, 35, 64, 125-126, 280
Ventura, Joe, *427*
Venturi, Louis, *501*
Verel, Al, 364
Verel, Alphonse, 513, 516
Verel, Gene, 513

Verel, John, 124, 135, 182, 188, 219, 265, 279, 314, 317, 394, *442*, 449, 453, 454, *454*, 456, 461, 463, 470, 512 (*See also* Verrilli, Giovanni)
Verel, John, 551
Verel, John, Jr., 137
Verel, Mellie, 441
Verel, Nicolina Yoviene, 135, 317, 454
Verel, Philip "Phil," 124, 363, 395, *438*, 454 (*See also* Verrilli, Filippo)
Verel, Rocco, 513
Verel, Virginia, 451
Verrastro, Leonard, *427*
Verrilli, Filippo, 454 (*See also* Verel, Philip)
Verrilli, Giovanni, 454 (*See also* Verel, John)
Vertalino family, 516, 578
Vertalino, Ben, *510*
Vertalino, Biagio, 78-79, 264-265, 268, *269*
Vertalino, Florence, 514
Vertalino, Fonsina, 78-79, 264, 268, *269*
Vertalino, Frank, *510, 511*
Vertalino, Jennie Nigro, 123, 458, *459*
Vertalino, Jim, *516*
Vertalino, Joseph, "Joe," 147 *397*, 420, *421*
Vertalino, Nick, 79, *269*, 458
Vertalino, Patrick "Pat," 101, *150*, 344, *511*, 514, *516, 551, 552*
Vertino, Mary Panzetta, *230, 521*, 556, 561
Vicaretti, Dominic, *538, 542*
Vifredo, Maria, 302
Vifredo, Rev. Joseph Benoit Louis, 116-117, 289, *297*, 299, 300, 301, 302, 304, *305*, 307, 309, 312, 314, 319, 321, 323, 324, 333, *333*, 368, 464, 494

SUBJECT INDEX

Italicized page numbers indicate mentions in photos and lists; n indicates footnote

during Great Depression, 143–144
meeting basic needs, 488
non-Italian, 143
relief for Italy, 145, 148

N

name changes, 78, 79, 133–135, 147
National Italian American Foundation, 155
National Labor Relations Act (1935), 413
National Organization of Italian American
    Women, 155
National Organizing Committee for Iron and Steel
    Workers, 400
nationality group, defined, 162
Native Americans, 195–199
nativists
    African Americans, 199
    after World War I, 108–109
    Anglo-conformity and, 164
    assimilation expectations of, 164, 166
    blacks and Latinos, 177
    focus shift to blacks and Mexicans, 111
    history of, 3, 103–105
    immigrants' increased pride in Italy and, 170
    immigration restrictions, 111
    Ku Klux Klan, 111, 113
    Yankee-American Action Organization, 142
naturalization. (*See also* citizenship)
Nee, Victor, 166
neighborhoods, Italian. (*See also specific areas*)
    decline of, 157, 461
    early residents, 105, 219, 608n10
    map of, 84
    post World War I housing shortages, 219, 221
    relationships in, 172, 223, 225–226, 228
    segregation and, 111, 219
nepotism in politics, 570–571, 591
New Beginnings Italian Group, 527, *541*
New Village, 67, 106, *107*
New York State Italian communities, 79, *83, 86*
newspapers. (*See also specific titles*)
    articles by Italian Americans, 140, 184
    assimilation and, 182
    denigration by, 106, *108,* 109, 177
    improved treatment by, 140
Nordic superiority, 105
nursing, 464–465

O

occupations of Italians in the U.S. (*See also
        specific jobs*)
    1900-1905, 337–340, 601n29
    1905-1930, 340–342
    1931-1983, 344–347
    1960, 349
odd jobs, 475, 476
Old Village
    African Americans in, 199
    boarding houses, 239
    businesses, *239,* 240, 242, 248
    Clubhouse, 242
    conditions in, 67, 69, 242–243
    early residents, 63, 73, 80, 216, 239
    immigrants' reactions, 242
    map, *84,* 237
    1919-1930, 240
    personal relationships in, 243, 245
    population (1905-1930), 235, 242, 609n38
    razed, 248–249
    recreation/pastimes, 242, 243–245247, *244*
    row houses, 237–238, *238,* 240, *241, 243*
    schools, *246*
    Smokes Creek and, 243–244
    street peddlers, 246–248
Old Village Annex School, 124, 132, *246*
Old Village Clubhouse, 242
1.5 generation, 124, 162
Order Sons of Italy in America (OSIA), 121, 155
organizations. (*See also* civic organizations;
        mutual-aid societies; *specific organizations*)
    assimilation process and, 119, 176, 181,
        606n25
    based on hometowns and regions, 122
    becoming inactive, 503
    bilingual meetings, 489, 491
    business, 514
    characteristics and functions of, 484–486
    characteristics of 1930s', 122
    charity, 515
    college, 515
    development of, 479–486
    disbanded, 527, 532
    early, 170
    fascist, 30, 35
    feste sponsorship, 30

United States Steel, 398, 400
United Steelworkers of America (USWA)
    advancement of workers, 424
    benefits realized, 385
    and downsizing of steel industry, 426, 428
    ethnic composition of members, 423–424
    formation of, 150
    Italian officers in Lackawanna, 427, *428*
    originally Steelworkers Organizing Committee
        (SWOC), 423
    racial discrimination alleged, 206
    recognized by Bethlehem Steel, 398
    strikes, 1946-1959, 425–426
    wealth redistribution, 424–425
    women's auxiliaries, 416

V

vacation time, 617nn63, 66
vada, 599n46
Vagabond Athletic and Social Club, 504, 532
Vanzetti, Bartolomeo, 111, 178
Vecoli, Rudolph, 23
vice crimes, 212–213, 359, 547, 565
violence
    against African Americans, 205
    against Italian Americans, 205
    against new immigrants, 105–106
    1907 Labor Union of Buffalo march, 109
    among residents of Little Italy, 275–276, 603n5
vocational education, 33
voluntary pluralism, 169
von Hoffman, Nicholas, 207
voting in Italy, 568
voting in the U.S., 566, 568, 570

W

wages and hours
    cuts due to economic depression, 399
    "the man-killing system," 399, 400
    1905-1947, 424
    early 1900s, 339
    vacation and overtime pay, 423
Wagner Act (1935), 137, 344, 418, 617n79
War Labor Board, 400
wars prior to World War I, 34
Washington Elementary School, 124, *127,* 128
wealth redistribution in U.S., 424–425
Weber, John Baptiste, 104
weighers (steelworkers), 358

welfare, 143–144, 273
West Seneca, New York, 63, 70. (*See also*
        Limestone Hill district)
western New York, 71, 73, *82*
"Where Do You Work - A John?", 141
White Anglo-Saxon Protestants (WASPs), 303
"white ethnics," 153–157, 159, 165, 191–194
Whyte, William Foote, 135
Wickwire, 391
Williams, Phyllis, 25, 27–28
Wilson, Woodrow, 104
winemaking, 283–285
witches, 28
women in Italy. (*See also* family reunification)
    Black Madonna and, 25, 599n49
    chestnut gathering, 18–19
    chores, 16
    family dynamics, 22
    lives with husbands in U.S., 42–44
    north/south differences in Italy, 97–98
    religious participation, 23
    during World War II, 38
women in politics, 557, 578
women in the U.S.
    in armed forces during World War II, 147
    business owners, 158, 184
    changing role of, 171
    defense plant jobs during World War II, 147
    education of, 130
    honor of, 175
    increase in education, 130
    increase in independence, 130
    marriage and, 136, 152, 189
    migration pattern of, 75, 76
    as organizational leaders, 123, 137
    organizations, 155
    percentage of immigrant in Lackawanna, 218,
        601n44
    in politics, 123, 156
    politics and, 180–181
    in sports, 186
women in the workforce
    beauty shops, 451–452
    business management, 341, 432
    farm labor, 474–475
    1914-1915, 613n11
    nursing, 464–465